THE
MILITARY
BALANCE
2011

published by

Routledge
Taylor & Francis Group

for

The International Institute for Strategic Studies

Arundel House | 13–15 Arundel Street | Temple Place | London | WC2R 3DX | UK

THE **MILITARY BALANCE** 2011

The International Institute for Strategic Studies
ARUNDEL HOUSE | 13–15 ARUNDEL STREET | TEMPLE PLACE | LONDON | WC2R 3DX | UK

DIRECTOR-GENERAL AND CHIEF EXECUTIVE **Dr John Chipman**
DIRECTOR FOR DEFENCE AND MILITARY ANALYSIS **Dr Tim Huxley**
EDITOR **James Hackett**

DEFENCE AND MILITARY ANALYSIS
LAND WARFARE **Brigadier (Retd.) Benjamin Barry**
MILITARY AEROSPACE **Douglas Barrie**
NAVAL FORCES AND MARITIME SECURITY **Christian Le Miére**
CONFLICT **Virginia Comolli and Hanna Ucko Neill**

EDITORIAL **Dr Ayse Abdullah, Jessica Delaney, Sarah Johnstone, Janis Lee,
Dr Jeffrey Mazo, Carolyn West**
DESIGN, PRODUCTION AND INFORMATION GRAPHICS **John Buck**
CARTOGRAPHER **Steven Bernard**

RESEARCH ASSISTANTS **Henry Boyd, Charlotte Laycock, Gary Li, Veronica Prates,
Giri Rajendran, Raffael Sturm, George Towers, Henry White**

This publication has been prepared by the Director-General and Chief Executive of the Institute and his Staff, who accept full responsibility for its contents. The views expressed herein do not, and indeed cannot, represent a consensus of views among the worldwide membership of the Institute as a whole.

FIRST PUBLISHED March 2011

ISBN 978-1-85743-606-8
ISSN 0459-7222

The *Military Balance* (ISSN 0459-7222) is published annually by Routledge Journals, an imprint of Taylor & Francis, 4 Park Square, Milton Park, Abingdon, Oxfordshire OX14 4RN, UK. The 2011 annual subscription rate is: UK£126 (individual rate), UK£268 (institution rate) UK£241 (online only); overseas US$210 (individual rate), US$468 (institution rate), US$422 (online only).

A subscription to the institution print edition, ISSN 0459-7222, includes free access for any number of concurrent users across a local area network to the online edition, ISSN 1479-9022.

Dollar rates apply to subscribers in all countries except the UK and the Republic of Ireland where the pound sterling price applies. All subscriptions are payable in advance and all rates include postage.

Journals are sent by air to the USA, Canada, Mexico, India, Japan and Australasia. Subscriptions are entered on an annual basis, i.e. January to December. Payment may be made by sterling cheque, dollar cheque, international money order, National Giro, or credit card (Amex, Visa, Mastercard).

Please send subscription orders to: USA/Canada: Taylor & Francis Inc., Journals Department, 325 Chestnut Street, 8th Floor, Philadelphia, PA 19106, USA. UK/Europe/Rest of World: Routledge Journals, T&F Customer Services, T&F Informa UK Ltd., Sheepen Place, Colchester, Essex, CO3 3LP, UK.

The print edition of this journal is printed on ANSI conforming acid-free paper by Bell & Bain, Glasgow, UK.

CONTENTS

Index of TABLES

Index of FIGURES

Index of MAPS

The Military Balance 2011
Editor's Foreword

The Military Balance 2011 is a comprehensive and independent assessment of the military capabilities and defence economics of 170 territories. It is also a reference work on developments in global military and security affairs.

Operations in Afghanistan remain of central importance to the military and political establishments of NATO members and other troop-contributing countries, as well as those of regional states. As an essay (pp. 9–19) notes, for NATO and the Afghan government the campaign is a race against the clock to improve security; expand the Afghan National Security Forces' (ANSF) capabilities; develop the capacity of the Afghan state; reduce corruption; and persuade 'reconcilable' Taliban to lay down their arms. All of this must be done in time to meet the objective of NATO and Afghan President Hamid Karzai that the ANSF should take responsibility for security operations in all provinces by the end of 2014.

The conflict in Afghanistan has other implications for troop-contributing countries, particularly those affected by the global economic crisis. The nature of the military operations pursued there, with a heavy focus on counter-insurgency, is leading many militaries to reconsider future force structures and procurement strategies. Some countries may feel that the financial and human cost of participation in the conflict – at least in combat operations – outweigh the benefits to be derived from such participation, leading to a desire to reduce troop levels. This is particularly the case where purse-strings are being tightened as part of efforts to reduce budget deficits following the 2008–09 financial crisis – although not all countries are cutting spending.

Defence planning remains a matter of balancing risk against political priority as well as available and projected funding. It is normal for these judgements to be based, ostensibly at least, on assessments of the likely strategic situation decades ahead. This is perfectly understandable, but it means that nations must retain enough military flexibility and mass to adjust forces should the international environment develop in a way that planners had not foreseen, or had placed in the 'unlikely' file. Some militaries are trying to anticipate such possibilities by developing modular land formations and increasing the acquisition of multi-role air and sea platforms. Some states are also choosing to pursue collaborative planning and procurement activities with allies in a bid to generate economies of scale. But this is not the case for all nations, especially those whose strategic priorities focus on more traditional state-based threats.

The work of force planners is complicated by the range of potential tasks that they now feel obliged to consider, which include conventional state-on-state conflict, combating asymmetric threats, counter-insurgency, cyber warfare, humanitarian operations and partner training activities. This increasingly complex environment was indicated in the criticism levelled at the US Quadrennial Defense Review (QDR), both at the time it was published in February 2010 and afterwards by the QDR Independent Panel (also mandated by Congress). The QDR, the panel said, did not provide the 'kind of long-term planning document that Congress envisioned when it enacted the QDR requirement'. The panel recommended a sweeping overhaul of the Cold War-era defence framework that was designed to address the Soviet Union. While the panel's conclusions may in part reflect changing US strategic priorities as China continues to emerge as a potential strategic competitor, the range and complexity of the security and military challenges faced by the administration may have complicated the presentation of a clear set of messages in the QDR.

The range of potential new tasks preoccupying military planners is daunting. For some states facing financial cutbacks, but with an actual or perceived global role, boosting the capacity of partner nations to improve burden sharing may be one way of ensuring continued influence: this was one conclusion of the British Strategic Defence and Security Review (SDSR) in 2010. Assisting the civil power at home or in other countries in responding to humanitarian emergencies is a task for which some segments of military forces are suited in terms of their equipment and training. But are these tasks for which militaries facing budget cuts should retain a planning focus or particular capabilities?

The military dimension of cyberspace has been much discussed over the past year (see the essay pp. 27–32). In response to rising concerns over the vulnerability of national information and communication technology systems, many militaries are developing capabilities for assessing, countering and, presumably, prosecuting operations in cyberspace. But this again is a grey area: the boundaries between civil and military cyberspace are unclear, as is the role that the military should have in this realm. In a developing area with potential national security implications, it is perhaps unsurprising that militaries will seek to explore a potential role.

In its new Strategic Concept agreed in November 2010, NATO recognised cyberspace as an area that the Alliance should address. NATO Secretary-General Anders Fogh Rasmussen suggested that NATO could develop its own cyber-defence capacity 'including a deployable capability to support Allies under cyber attack'. Pressed on this point in

October 2010, Rasmussen refused to rule out cyber attacks as an Article V issue (where an armed attack against one or more members in Europe or North America 'shall be considered an attack against them all'). Instead, he argued, each situation had to be assessed by Allies on a case-by-case basis. But mention of such issues, together with the need to balance the divergent perspectives of NATO member states, opened the Strategic Concept up to the criticism that – like the QDR – it was unfocused and vague.

As militaries address an ever-expanding range of potential tasks, it is perhaps to be expected that they face criticism for losing focus on previously core roles. If armed forces are unsure of the range of potential contingencies they will face in future, the same is true of the policymakers who oversee them. There remains a tendency to try to direct forces, even if these are reducing in size, to carry out an increasingly wide range of tasks. But it is likely that, for some nations, current force reductions and financial considerations will eventually necessitate hard decisions about levels of ambition and strategic priorities. Thus, the currently diffuse defence debate in many countries, while perhaps reflecting contemporary strategic complexity, merely postpones the need for such decisions. Many militaries are being asked to do more with less money, and with less focused strategic guidance.

Developments in *The Military Balance*

The complexity of global defence debates has over the years been reflected in the content of *The Military Balance*. From the first edition in 1959, an 11-page pamphlet entitled *The Soviet Union and the NATO Powers: The Military Balance*, the book has increasingly enumerated military inventories around the world. It has also displayed a growing appreciation of military developments outside Europe and North America as significant in their own right and not simply in relation to the Western defence debate. The way the data has been presented has also changed, and this edition heralds a period of further change to both the way the IISS presents its defence data, and the range of data presented.

The newly constituted Defence and Military Analysis Programme at the IISS has implemented several changes to this year's *Military Balance*. One of the key benefits of the book has always been the ability it gives its users to generate comparisons between the military capabilities and defence economics of different nations. This remains a central objective in the Institute's presentation of data within the book. *The Military Balance* has long contained a reference segment at the back of the book, where presentation of comparative information on military deployments and manpower, and defence economics, for example, has resided.

To this we have now added a new segment at the start of the book. These tabular and graphical features seek to highlight key defence issues that are pertinent in light of current defence issues, as well as particularly relevant thematic issues, inventory developments or comparisons between nations, and defence economic developments, that may not have been analysed, presented or extrapolated in similar formats elsewhere. This year's essays comprise detailed analyses of the war in Afghanistan, developments in unmanned aerial vehicles, and the military dimension of cyberspace. In terms of regional data coverage, the section on Europe now combines NATO and non-NATO Europe, while Asia combines the previous South and Central Asia and East Asia and Australasia sections, in order to better reflect the military and economic ties across these continents.

Meanwhile, there has been a change in understanding of the factors constituting military capability. *The Military Balance* has traditionally focused on key combat capabilities and equipment inventories. However, quantitative indicators are of limited utility as indicators of military capability, and we are consequently including more qualitative judgements. *The Military Balance* has historically applied caveats to equipment holdings such as 'serviceability in doubt', 'combat capable' and 'in store'. This year we have adopted and added a new defintion for equipment judged obsolescent, namely equipment whose basic design is 40 or more years old and which has not been significantly upgraded (factors which may limit its usefulness in conflict). So far this definition has only been applied to guided weapons, but it is intended to extend its usage, where relevant, across all military branches in the future.

The 2011 edition also sees some equipment change category in the air and naval inventories. In the air fleets, UAVs are now broken down by weight, and transport fleets by role, allowing the reader to determine more easily the particular capabilities available to nations using such equipment. For naval forces, a classification system has been developed based on full-load displacement rather than role. This will allow for easier and more useful international comparisons of navies according to the tonnage of vessels. (More detailed information can be found in the Explanatory Notes beginning on p. 483.) For *The Military Balance* 2012, the IISS will engage in a thorough reassessment of the presentation of ground forces information.

Looking towards the structure of future editions of *The Military Balance*, it is planned to develop and expand these qualitative judgements as well as graphical and tabular features, and to include further innovative means of assessing and displaying defence data. We will of course retain the core inventory assessments that have proven of such value to defence analysts and policymakers since the first *Military Balance* appeared. Indeed, there are arguments for expanding the range of inventory information presented. The equipment categories traditionally counted remain of critical importance in assessing defence capability, but consideration is being given to adding other categories of information such as selected logistic assets. How effective are armies, for instance, if they cannot effectively deploy and sustain their personnel or equipment, or force entry, overcoming opposition forces, difficult terrain and logistical problems?

However, adding further content may mean that the place of existing information has to be questioned. Feedback from readers has always been welcomed. Please address such communications to the editor, at dmap@iiss.org.

The Military Balance 2011
Preface

The Military Balance is updated each year to provide an accurate assessment of the military forces and defence economics of 170 countries. Each edition contributes to the provision of a unique compilation of data and information, enabling the reader to discern long-term trends through a study of previous editions dating back to 1959. The data in the current edition are according to IISS assessments as at November 2010. Inclusion of a territory, country or state in The Military Balance does not imply legal recognition or indicate support for any government.

GENERAL ARRANGEMENT AND CONTENTS

The Editor's Foreword contains a general comment on defence matters and a summary of the book.

The Military Balance comprises the regional trends, military capabilities and defence-economics data for countries grouped by region. There are also three essays at the front of the book on the war in Afghanistan, unmanned aerial vehicles, and the military aspects of cyber security. Another essay on the modernisation of the Chinese defence industry is found in the Asia chapter. Throughout, readers will find maps showing selected deployments in Afghanistan; NATO's membership, cooperation and partnership programmes; new Russian military districts; Chinese military regions and major formations; how Brazil's national defence strategy is affecting its army and navy; and piracy off the coast of Somalia.

There are also tables depicting aspects of defence activity, including salient comparative analyses, selected major training exercises, non-UN and UN multinational deployments, international defence expenditure, and the international arms trade.

The Chart of Conflict inserted loose into The Military Balance is updated to show data on recent and current armed conflicts up to 1 November 2010.

USING THE MILITARY BALANCE

In order to interpret the data in the country entries correctly, it is essential to read the Explanatory Notes beginning on page 483.

The large quantity of data in The Military Balance has been compressed into a portable volume by the extensive employment of abbreviations. An essential tool is therefore the alphabetical index of abbreviations for data sections, which starts on page 491.

ATTRIBUTION AND ACKNOWLEDGEMENTS

The International Institute for Strategic Studies owes no allegiance to any government, group of governments, or any political or other organisation. Its assessments are its own, based on the material available to it from a wide variety of sources. The cooperation of governments of all listed countries has been sought and, in many cases, received. However, some data in The Military Balance are estimates.

Care is taken to ensure that these data are as accurate and free from bias as possible. The Institute owes a considerable debt to a number of its own members, consultants and all those who help compile and check material. The Director-General and Chief Executive and staff of the Institute assume full responsibility for the data and judgements in this book. Comments and suggestions on the data and textual material contained within the book, as well as on the style and presentation of data, are welcomed and should be communicated to the Editor of The Military Balance at: IISS, 13–15 Arundel Street, London WC2R 3DX, UK, email: dmap@iiss.org. Copyright on all information in The Military Balance belongs strictly to the IISS. Application to reproduce limited amounts of data may be made to the publisher: Taylor & Francis, 4 Park Square, Milton Park, Abingdon, Oxon, OX14 4RN. Email: permissionrequest@tandf.co.uk. Unauthorised use of Military Balance data will be subject to legal action.

Chapter One
The war in Afghanistan

Afghan, US and NATO-led forces conducting operations in Afghanistan are continuing to face a complex, adaptable, resilient and inventive set of adversaries. International Security Assistance Force (ISAF) and Afghan troops are employed as part of a comprehensive counter-insurgency (COIN) strategy, where reinforcing troops, principally from the US, have been used to contest Taliban control of key population centres, especially in southern Afghanistan. This has resulted in expanded security, particularly in the southern provinces of Kandahar and Helmand, but progress remains slow.

For NATO and the Afghan government, the campaign is a race against the clock: to improve security, grow the Afghan forces, develop the capacity of the Afghan state, reduce corruption and persuade 'reconcilable' Taliban to lay down their arms, all in time to meet the objective of Afghan President Hamid Karzai that Afghan National Security Forces (ANSF) should have the lead in conducting security operations in all provinces by the end of 2014. This timetable is known to Afghans of all persuasions: the Taliban, for their part, intend to frustrate these objectives, exploiting many Afghans' belief that insufficient enduring improvement in security and governance will be made before NATO leaves.

The conflict constitutes a test for the Alliance that, while not existential, was certainly central to the debates leading up to the November 2010 Lisbon Summit, where NATO announced its much-anticipated Strategic Concept. While the precise outcome of this debate is discussed elsewhere in this volume (p. 74), the 20 November 'Declaration by the Heads of State and Government of the Nations contributing to the UN-mandated, NATO-led International Security Assistance Force in Afghanistan' said that 'based on the progress we have made, ISAF and the Government of Afghanistan are entering a new phase of our joint effort'. The declaration noted the emerging timelines on transitioning to Afghan security responsibility, as well as the development of a longer-term approach that 'demonstrates that the Alliance's commitment to Afghanistan will endure beyond ISAF's current mission and is intended to be consistent with broader international efforts under UN leadership'.

NATO strategy

The majority of US and foreign forces in Afghanistan are part of ISAF. NATO describes its role in Afghanistan as assisting the Afghan government and that 'ISAF, in partnership with the Afghan Government and the international community, conducts comprehensive, population-centric counter-insurgency operations, and supports development of legitimate governance, Afghan National Security Forces, and socio-economic institutions in order to neutralize the enemy, safeguard the people, enable establishment of acceptable governance, and provide a secure and stable environment'.

ISAF, led by the US since early 2007, now consists of around 131,000 troops from 20 NATO and 28 non-NATO nations. Ninety thousand troops are from the US (with another 16,000 employed on US national operations, but under the command of COMISAF), 9,500 from the UK, and these are substantial (greater than 1,000 servicemen) contingents from Poland, Romania, Spain, Germany, France, Italy, Canada and Turkey. Apart from Turkey, the only Muslim nations represented in ISAF are Malaysia and the UAE, which all have small contingents.

Shortly after his election, US President Barack Obama announced an integrated civil–military US strategy for Afghanistan and Pakistan. He then announced, in June 2009, the deployment of an additional 17,000 US troops, and in December endorsed ISAF's counter-insurgency strategy that had been developed by the then-commander of ISAF, US General Stanley McChrystal. This was accompanied by the announcement of a reinforcement of 30,000 more US troops, with Obama stating that after 18 months (that is, in mid-2011) 'our troops will begin to come home'. Obama's comment has set the agenda. There remain substantial public and political doubts about the mission in many NATO countries, and the Netherlands and Canada have already committed to withdraw their troops from combat roles. Both will retain contingents contributing to the training of the

ANSF and Canada has substantially increased the number of troops allocated to this role. At the Lisbon Summit, NATO declared its support for Karzai's broader 2014 objective, as well as its intention to begin transferring lead responsibility for security in some provinces and districts to Afghan forces early in 2011. Both US Defense Secretary Robert Gates and UK Prime Minister David Cameron have made it clear that they see US and UK forces moving from a combat to a training, mentoring and supporting role by 2015. It is likely that the majority of troop-contributing nations will take their cue from the US.

Since November 2008 General David Petraeus – firstly as the commander of US Central Command (CENTCOM), and then in succession to General McChrystal as the commander of ISAF – has sought to create a more appropriate strategic framework for the campaign, which he has described as getting 'the inputs right'. Applying lessons learned in Iraq, this has led to the establishment of an improved civil–military machinery for coordinating operations with the Afghan government at all levels, from Kabul to province and district. It has also included activating an additional division-level regional command headquarters (see map). Currently based on a US Marine Corps HQ, Regional Command Southwest covers Helmand and Nimruz provinces and includes 20,000 US Marines, 10,000 British troops and smaller contingents from Denmark and Estonia: NATO-led forces in the area have increased tenfold since 2006.

The other main strands of NATO operational design are to clear the main Taliban-controlled populated areas of insurgents, as well as conduct targeted raids to capture or kill Taliban leaders, develop the ANSF, support Afghan efforts for the reintegration of 'reconcilable' Taliban and support the development of Afghan governance. While foreign governments continue to contribute substantial aid as well as civilian development experts, these donors have made no secret of their impatience with the corruption and inefficiency displayed by the Afghan government, not least the extensive voting irregularities in recent elections.

Expanding the ANSF

A keystone of NATO strategy is to develop the capacity of the Afghan National Security Forces, to prepare them for the transfer of security responsibility by the end of 2014. Increased ISAF and US troop deployments have allowed greater support for ANSF training and capability development.

The greatest effort has been to build the capacity of the Afghan National Army (ANA). The NATO Training Mission Afghanistan (NTM-A) was established in November 2009 and numbers of ISAF trainers were considerably increased. The mission is commanded by a US general, who also leads US forces training the ANA. This latter force reached a strength of 134,000 in August 2010, two months ahead of schedule, and is assessed as likely to reach its target strength of 171,600 by October 2011. The ANA's effectiveness as well as numerical strength has increased. For example the third phase of *Operation Moshtarak* around Kandahar in autumn 2010 saw an ANA Corps HQ take the lead in a substantial 'clear, hold, build operation', while the stronger ANA units and formations have proved themselves capable of taking the lead in operations against the Taliban. Overall performance across the force, though, remains variable.

The Army is a genuinely national institution, its composition reflecting the ethnic mix of Afghanistan as a whole. But this means that most of the Afghan soldiers in the south – including Pashtuns – are not from that region. An initiative to allow southern Pashtuns to serve in the south seeks to address this, while there has been growth in novel initiatives designed to maintain force strength. For example, because some Afghan soldiers were going absent without leave to visit their families, ISAF established a 'chartered air service' to help soldiers wishing to go on leave, and then return to their units.

By 2009, it was clear that the Afghan National Police (ANP) was almost as much a part of the security problem as of the solution, with low-level corruption and predatory extortion at checkpoints a particular concern for both the Afghan people and ISAF. In part this reflected the fact that, before 2009, police recruits had no formal training. National training efforts are now supported by NTM-A and local NATO initiatives such as the British-led Helmand Police Training Centre. Meanwhile, the Afghan Civil Order Police (ANCOP) – a paramilitary force – is often judged as relatively trustworthy and effective. For example it has accompanied ISAF special-forces raids, liaising with civilians as the 'Afghan face'. NATO is putting considerable effort into mentoring and developing the ANCOP, especially as its attrition rates have been high.

Shortly after his arrival in 2009 General McChrystal placed increased emphasis on building the capability of the ANSF. This has been continued by General Petraeus. Both ANA and ANP units are supported

The Taliban and Related Jihadist Groups

The Afghan Taliban are not a unitary insurgent force, more a common branding of groups with shared objectives: expulsion of ISAF forces; the overthrow of the current Afghan government; and, for some groups, imposition of a Salafist Islamic regime. The Pentagon's November 2010 'Report on Progress Toward Security and Stability in Afghanistan' to the US Congress stated that 'the Taliban is not a popular movement, but it exploits a population frustrated by weak governance. The Taliban's strength lies in the Afghan population's perception that Coalition forces will soon leave, giving credence to the belief that a Taliban victory is inevitable.'

The Taliban seek to influence the Afghan people by attacking Afghan and ISAF security forces, creating a gap in local security that they can fill. By assassination and intimidation, they seek to neutralise both government institutions and traditional local tribal and religious leadership, in order to impose their own local governance in areas they control or as 'shadow' administration in contested areas. Their campaign of assassinating Afghan officials was increased in 2010, with some success in targeting mid-level officials. Attacks on ISAF forces, meanwhile, seek to kill troops as well as to provoke over-reaction. Resulting civilian casualties, coupled with foreign media coverage of ISAF losses, will, they hope, force troop-contributing states to withdraw their forces.

The Taliban insurgency is almost exclusively based amongst ethnic Pashtuns. The majority of Afghan Pashtuns are based in the southwest, south and east of the country. This is where the insurgency is strongest. There are pockets of Pashtuns and limited Taliban activity in Kabul and northern and western Afghanistan.

Although there are full-time members of the Taliban, many 'foot soldiers' are young men who take up arms on a part-time basis. Very few fight for ideological reasons; the majority are motivated by local grievances, including the desire to avenge friends and family members killed in the fighting. But there are further complications: at the tactical level it can be very difficult to distinguish between Taliban groupings and the militias of local drug barons. Afghanistan's complex tribal system has made it difficult for ISAF forces to understand the difference between such groups. The Taliban's offer to the Afghan people is simple – security and dispute resolution based on the Taliban's interpretation of Islamic law. The Taliban exploit grievances between tribes, particularly over land disputes.

There are three major Taliban groups. The Quetta Shura Taliban are led by Mullah Omar, based in Quetta, Pakistan. The Shura is the former governing body of Afghanistan and is the most active and widespread insurgent movement. Their operations have spread from their main operating area of southern Afghanistan to Pashtun areas in the west and north of the country. The Haqqani Network is responsible for many attacks in the east and in Kabul, and has sought to counter the Indian presence in Afghanistan. Its leadership and infrastructure are based in North Waziristan, Pakistan. The other major Taliban group, Hizb-i-Islami Gulbuddin, also based in Pakistan, is somewhat less capable than the others. In all these groups foreign fighters play a role, especially as the principal source of suicide bombers, but this is not decisive. Al-Qaeda provides support and funding from safe havens in Pakistan.

External linkages and support

Many Pakistani extremist groups are now increasingly focusing their efforts either on operations inside Afghanistan or against the Pakistani state, both in the Federally Administered Tribal Areas or the settled areas, including Peshawar, Rawalpindi and Islamabad. This shift is part of a complex series of moves in anticipation of an endgame in Afghanistan, which is widely expected at some point to involve a negotiation between the Afghan government and the main insurgent groups. Pakistan has sought to insert itself into any such negotiation by manipulating its relationships with the Taliban groups described above as well as Lashkar-e-Tayiba (LeT), the Pakistan-based group behind the 2008 Mumbai attacks. According to Major-General Michael Flynn, the senior US military intelligence officer in Afghanistan, LeT operatives are coming to Afghanistan in increasing numbers to gain combat experience and are active in eight Afghan provinces. Much of the focus of these groups, in particular the Haqqani Network, has been on countering an Indian presence in Afghanistan which represents a constant source of strategic concern for Pakistan. Indeed, Pakistani politicians have begun to talk about the resolution of the Afghan conflict as more important than Kashmir in terms of defining their country's relations with India.

Pakistan's ultimate aim is a reasonably stable Afghanistan not inimical to Pakistan and in which Indian influence is limited to a point where it presents no strategic threat. Pakistani political leaders appear to have modified their position to a point where they talk publicly of not wishing to 'repeat the mistakes of the 1990s' – a reference to Pakistan's role in enabling the Taliban to assume power in 1996. Pakistani Chief of Army Staff General Ashfaq Kayani has been increasingly open in discussing with US counterparts Pakistan's interests and ability to help achieve a negotiated settlement. At the same time, Pakistan has shown itself ready to act forcefully to ensure a seat at the negotiating table for itself, as demonstrated by its arrests of a number of high-ranking members of the Quetta Shura – including Taliban military commander Mullah Abdul Ghani Baradar – who were suspected of pursuing negotiations with the Afghan government independently of Pakistan.

Referring to it as a 'national interest', Pakistan has also been more ready to acknowledge the nature of its relationship with the Haqqani Network, an organisation with close links to al-Qaeda that has been at the forefront of attacks against both the NATO-led International Security Assistance Force (ISAF) and Indian interests in Afghanistan. Pakistan's increasingly thinly disguised support for the Haqqani Network represents a source of increasing frustration to ISAF commanders, who have determined until now that hot-pursuit operations inside Pakistani territory would prove counterproductive. The nearest ISAF has come to such operations was in September 2010 when US forces killed two Pakistani border guards who were providing covering fire for Haqqani fighters escaping back from

Afghanistan into Pakistan. This incident led Pakistan temporarily to close the Torkham Gate border crossing in Khyber Agency through which 1,000 trucks, carrying 25% of ISAF non-lethal supplies, cross each day into Afghanistan, and served as a reminder of ISAF's dependence on Pakistan's goodwill.

Lashkar al-Zil: alliance of jihadist groups

Meanwhile, links between a variety of jihadist groups spanning both sides of the Afghanistan–Pakistan border appear to have grown closer. In 2009, ISAF sources in Afghanistan began to talk of the emergence of a new umbrella group, known as Lashkar al-Zil – 'Shadow Army' – comprising al-Qaeda, the Afghan Taliban, the Haqqani Network and the Tehrik-e-Taliban Pakistan (TTP), which has been waging war against the Pakistani state in Pakistan's tribal areas and Swat. The commander of Lashkar al-Zil is reported to be Ilyas Kashmiri, a senior commander in the Pakistani jihadist group Harkat-ul-Jihad-al-Islami (HUJI), who is also thought to have replaced Mustafa Abu al-Yazid, killed in a CIA drone strike in May 2010, as al-Qaeda's military chief in Afghanistan and Pakistan. Kashmiri has also been identified as the driving force behind a number of recent al-Qaeda plots aimed at Western Europe.

Characterised as a replacement for al-Qaeda's Afghan-based guerrillas known as 'Brigade 055', it is far from clear how structured this new entity is. But ISAF commanders have cited evidence of increasing collaboration between jihadist groups which until recently had pursued their own agendas. Meanwhile, senior US officials have claimed that al-Qaeda's presence in Afghanistan is now limited to as few as 100 fighters. Its leadership in Pakistan's tribal areas has been subject to a ferocious campaign of attrition by means of CIA drone strikes. Lashkar al-Zil may, therefore, enable al-Qaeda to have a greater impact in Afghanistan than the small numbers quoted might suggest. But it is clear that an exclusive focus on al-Qaeda as an organisation may be increasingly meaningless as other related groups take up the al-Qaeda baton.

Al-Qaeda's leadership recently received a shot in the arm when an undetermined number of its senior figures, as well as members of the family of Osama bin Laden, were released after being detained in Iran since 2002. According to the Kuwaiti newspaper *Al-Watan*, their release was brokered by Sirajuddin Haqqani, de facto leader of the Haqqani Network, as part of negotiations that included the release of Heshmetollah Attarzadeh, an Iranian diplomat kidnapped in Peshawar in late 2008. The same report suggested that Haqqani secured a supply of anti-aircraft weapons as part of the deal.

In addition to holding a number of al-Qaeda leaders under house arrest, Iran has for some time been supplying training, weapons and money to the Afghan Taliban as a relatively low-risk way of sustaining pressure on the US. The release of senior and experienced al-Qaeda leaders suggests that Iran may have decided the moment has come to up the ante. Although experience suggests that any of the al-Qaeda leaders who make their way from Iran to Afghanistan or Pakistan will be targeted by CIA drone strikes, the return to battle of some experienced fighters and leaders is bound to have an impact, at least in the short term.

Continuing violence in Pakistan

Within Pakistan itself, levels of jihadist violence remained high throughout 2010, though the total number of fatalities, at 7,199, was markedly lower than the 2009 figure of 11,704, possibly reflecting the slowdown in military operations in Pakistan's tribal areas. Following the operations in 2009 to clear the TTP out of Swat and South Waziristan, the Pakistani Army now has a presence in six of the seven tribal agencies, with the majority of insurgents now bottled up in North Waziristan, which was the target of 104 of the 118 drone strikes launched by the CIA in 2010.

According to US Defense Secretary Robert Gates, the Pakistani Army has transferred the equivalent of six divisions from the border with India, representing a significant departure from its previous preoccupations. It has so far resisted US pressure to move against militant groups in North Waziristan, citing the need to consolidate existing gains in the other tribal agencies and to allow its forces to rest and recuperate – a genuine necessity given the high level of casualties suffered during the 2009 operations.

Meanwhile, within the settled areas, Pakistan has continued to see high levels of jihadist violence both against its security forces and other government targets, and against minority Shia and Ahmadiyah communities. Much of this violence has been perpetrated by groups such as Lashkar-e-Jhangvi, Jaish-e-Mohammed, HUJI and Harkat-ul-Mujahedin which, together with LeT, are collectively known as the 'Punjab Taliban', a term which reflects their growing alignment with the TTP and Afghan Taliban. That such groups pose a serious threat to the Pakistani state is no longer in doubt and reflects the degree to which jihadism in Pakistan has become a double-edged sword. The growing culture of radicalisation within Pakistan was exemplified by the assassination on 4 January 2011 of Punjab governor Salman Taseer by a member of his security detail. The assassin, who was allegedly under investigation for his extremist links, was motivated by a desire to punish Taseer for seeking amendments to Pakistan's harsh blasphemy laws. It is unclear whether he was linked to any specific group. The high level of public support for Taseer's murder, including among Pakistan's Islamic clergy, is indicative of the degree to which radical views have entered Pakistan's mainstream.

Green shoots?

Intelligence cooperation between South Asian states has seen some cautious improvements over the past two years, notably between Pakistan and Afghanistan where intelligence relationships, though still suffering from high levels of mistrust, are starting to become institutionalised. In the long term the relationship between India and Pakistan remains the key determinant of regional stability. And for as long as the two states remain locked in an intelligence war, with India supporting Baluch separatist groups, and the TTP and Pakistan continuing to see jihadism as an asymmetric tool against India, a significant drop in violent extremism seems a remote prospect.

by integrated NATO mentoring and liaison teams. Termed Operational Mentoring and Liaison Teams (OMLTs), these not only assist ANA commanders with operational planning, but also help the ANA to obtain NATO support, including artillery, helicopters and air strikes. OMLTs have succeeded in this role since 2006, being typically deployed at every level of ANA command from corps to company. There has also been a significant increase in similar teams working with the Afghan police. Over 300 'POMLTs' have been fielded, 90% of them provided by US military police battalions specially trained for the role, using similar techniques to those applied in Iraq from 2008. ANP strength stands at 109,000 as of January 2011, with NATO confident that its target of 134,000 can be reached by late 2011.

Similar efforts are in progress with the Afghan Border Police, the Counter-Narcotics Police and the Afghan Air Force. The Air Force's emerging capabilities were demonstrated when it deployed four helicopters to assist with Pakistan's flood-relief effort. Although little publicised, much UK and US effort has also been applied to the Afghan security service, the National Directorate for Security (NDS), helping the NDS contribute to counter-Taliban intelligence efforts. Meanwhile, efforts are being applied to the human-intelligence capabilities of the ANA and ANP in southern Afghanistan, where the US Marine Corps (USMC) has engaged a private military company to field mentors to Afghan intelligence staff.

But despite the undoubted results accruing from the major US–ISAF effort to generate and sustain the ANSF, there are still some serious signs of weakness in the Afghan forces. Not only have there been incidents of individual soldiers and police turning their weapons on their ISAF mentors, it is also clear that considerable low-level corruption remains. High levels of illiteracy – and difficulties in identifying and developing sufficient commanders and leaders – may be a brake on achieving the necessary quality in the ANSF. And, notwithstanding the chartered airlift initiative, the lack of an institutionalised system to rotate Afghan soldiers and units in and out of the combat zone means that many personnel fighting in the south are becoming battle weary.

The military campaign and security

ISAF has sought to execute a comprehensive COIN strategy that protects the Afghan people from the Taliban, in conjunction with reconstruction, development and increasing the influence of the Afghan government. The two US surges noted above brought ISAF strength to 130,000 and, during 2010, ISAF has sought to take advantage of this cumulative increase to achieve a significant improvement in security.

Southern Afghanistan is the heartland of the Pashtun and since 2006 it has seen the majority of Taliban activity. Since early 2010 this region has been the focus of ISAF's main effort and the majority of the additional US reinforcements have been employed there. In 2006 there were two NATO brigades in the south; now there are 13. There has been a corresponding increase in helicopters, intelligence and surveillance assets and special forces. Two regional command headquarters based on a US divisional HQ and a US Marine Expeditionary Force HQ now command ISAF activity in southern Afghanistan, the increase in NATO forces having required the formation of HQ Regional Command Southwest to command USMC, UK, Georgian, Danish and Estonian troops in Helmand and Nimruz provinces.

Between 2002 and 2009 ISAF and US forces were often able to clear Taliban from areas they controlled. But the low numbers of Western forces meant that many of these areas were subsequently abandoned to the Taliban, with dire consequences for any remaining Afghan government officials and civilians who had cooperated with the international forces. By 2009 this was recognised as a counterproductive approach and ISAF sought to clear only areas that it could hold. The recent reinforcements and increase in strength of ANSF have thus provided a strategic opportunity.

Since February 2010 ISAF's main effort has been *Operation Moshtarak* in southern Afghanistan. Exploiting the majority of reinforcing US forces as well as significant reinforcement by ANSF (ANA troop levels in Helmand have risen from one brigade to three), it has sought to extend security and Afghan government control over the majority of the populated areas in Helmand and Kandahar provinces. The operation was approved by President Karzai and ISAF, and the ANSF used a deliberate programme of media announcements and consultation with Afghan officials and local elders to signal their intentions in advance.

Both McChrystal and Petraeus have sought to reduce collateral damage and civilian casualties, particularly by imposing greater restrictions on the use of heavy weapons, artillery and air strikes. This application of a tested COIN principle, initially termed 'courageous restraint', has reduced civilian casualties, though at increased risk to ISAF troops

Operation Moshtarak

The first phase of *Operation Moshtarak* was launched in Nad-e Ali and Marjah, central Helmand province, in February 2010 by US Marine Corps and British forces, both accompanied by the ANA. Night helicopter assaults enabled complete tactical surprise. The next phase of the operation was to extend Afghan government influence in the cleared areas. In the case of the British sector, around Nad-e Ali, the subsequent stabilisation operation, and the restoration of Afghan governance, has been assessed as relatively successful. It has proved to be more difficult to improve security and governance in Marjah. This results in part from the difficulty of controlling civilian and insurgent movement over a complex topography of fields and canals. It is also a consequence of the complete disbandment of the Marjah ANP, as a result of their being considered too corrupt to be employed, with a consequent reduction in 'local knowledge'. Marjah has been far from the 'bleeding ulcer' described by General McChrystal in an off-guard moment, but the Taliban's stubbornness there has indicated that, in 'clear, hold and build' operations, the hold phase can be much more difficult than the clear. ISAF may also have underestimated the amount of time and force levels necessary to stabilise Marjah over the months following the start of the operation.

The third and final phase of *Moshtarak* has been named *Operation Hamkiri*. It seeks to reduce Taliban influence and extend that of the Afghan government by clearing and then holding Kandahar City and its environs, especially the districts of Panjawi, Zhari and Arghandab. By dedicating a high-technology US Stryker brigade exclusively to securing the major roads in southern Afghanistan, ISAF has sought to achieve freedom of movement to reduce a significant limitation to economic development. *Moshtarak* has resulted in a slow growth in security in central Helmand and in and around Kandahar. This is a result of patient tactical execution of the 'clear, hold, build' COIN approach by a sufficient density of ISAF and ANSF troops, and better coordination of military security with the reconstruction and development agendas. ISAF is not attempting to contest all of the country: in the south, for example, it seeks to secure central Helmand, Kandahar and the main roads, covering about two million of the three million-strong population of Helmand and Kandahar provinces.

ISAF has also sought to use *Moshtarak* as a vehicle for developing the capability and confidence of the ANA. Early indications are that this has succeeded. For example, recent phases of the operation have been initiated with set-piece orders by Afghan, not NATO, commanders, indicating the developing ability of the ANA to plan complex missions and deliver mission orders that can then be fed down through the chain of command.

on the ground. Compared with the same period in 2009, figures for the second quarter of 2010 suggest that civilian fatalities inflicted by ISAF and the ANSF were cut from over 60 per quarter to 40 per quarter, during a period when ISAF operations had considerably expanded in scope. In the same period civilian fatalities caused by the Taliban had increased from over 220 per quarter to 323 per quarter. But US servicemen have expressed concern that this 'courageous restraint' was increasing the risk to them. In response, Petraeus redrafted the rules, quietly dropping the term and replacing it with 'disciplined use of force' and embarked on a programme of explanation and education within ISAF.

Evidence from historic counter-insurgency campaigns not only demonstrates the value of an expanded and decentralised intelligence network, but also shows that this takes time to develop to full effectiveness. The same applies to human-intelligence operations. Both intelligence and operations at all levels are starting to benefit from a significant improvement in ISAF's understanding of the conflict. This has resulted from an increasing familiarity with the environment, as well as improved training. Both the US and UK, for example, are able to focus on preparing their forces for Afghanistan with far fewer competing pressures from the Iraq campaign. And there is greater 'campaign continuity', with commanders, staff and troops now returning to Afghanistan on second, third or fourth tours.

Many of the criticisms made publicly about the US intelligence effort in Afghanistan during this period by US Major-General Michael Flynn, ISAF's chief of intelligence, are being addressed. And ISAF is beginning to see the benefit of patient development of its own as well as Afghan intelligence resources, and the significant reinforcement of the Afghan theatre by UK and US reconnaissance and surveillance assets redeployed from Iraq. As demonstrated during the surge in Iraq, where ISAF and Afghan forces are present in sufficient strength, over time, to provide an enduring improvement in security, the local population is more likely to provide intelligence. An example is Kandahar City, where in autumn 2010 approximately 80% of all Taliban improvised explosive devices (IEDs) were reported to ISAF or the ANSF by locals.

Troops deploying to ISAF are increasingly well trained and relevant lessons from Iraq and other COIN campaigns are being applied at the tactical level. The principal source of NATO casualties has been the Taliban's use of large numbers of comparatively simple IEDs, a weapon that was heavily used against Coalition forces in Iraq. NATO forces have devoted considerable tactical effort and technical resources to countering this threat, including the deployment of tanks and heavy armoured engineer vehicles using mine ploughs, rollers and explosive hoses to break through high-density IED belts. The UK has fielded a battalion-sized Counter-IED Task Force, equipped with a variety of specialist equipment, armoured vehicles and micro-unmanned aerial vehicles. But with the density of IEDs laid by the Taliban in southern Afghanistan often approaching that of a high-density conventional minefield, there are physical limits to the degree of protection that can be achieved – particularly if troops are to continue efforts to interact with the local population by patrolling. ISAF maintains that these defensive measures have to be complemented by attacks on Taliban networks.

Attacking Taliban leadership and networks

ISAF and Afghan government efforts to reduce the supply of ammonium nitrate and potassium chloride, key ingredients of Taliban home-made explosives, have only been partially successful, but there is evidence that a concerted ISAF effort to attack the Taliban command and logistic networks has eroded Taliban capability in southern and eastern Afghanistan.

These operations have mainly been conducted by special forces, using similar approaches to those seen in Iraq, including the use of multiple sources to generate an accurate intelligence picture, followed by strikes on key Taliban fighters by aircraft, UAVs or attack helicopters, followed by rapid exploitation of captured personnel and material to gather further intelligence. Afghan special forces, attack helicopters and the use of precision bombs and rockets have also played a part. The employment of additional US and other ISAF special forces, coupled with improved intelligence, has resulted in a tripling in the number of raids mounted in 2010, with ISAF claiming to have killed over 1,200 Taliban in such raids during the year, including over 300 individuals assessed as Taliban leaders.

Meanwhile, an increase in special-forces attacks in part compensates for the reduction, across the border, in Pakistani Army activity against the Taliban. Pakistani forces are still recovering from the Swat and South Waziristan campaigns in 2009–10, during which they sustained significant losses. They are reported to be having trouble maintaining security in South Waziristan and their extensive contribution to flood-relief operations in 2010 has also reduced operations against the Taliban. Meanwhile, there are persistent allegations that Pakistan's Inter-Services Intelligence is not only unwilling to tackle Afghan Taliban and other extremists based in North Waziristan, but is also rendering active support to the Haqqani Network (see box, p. 11).

Development, governance and politics

Reconstruction and development in Afghanistan has been hindered by the damage to infrastructure and human capital resulting from three decades of conflict. At the national level there has been considerable progress since 2001, including significant improvements in education and literacy, and the establishment of a rudimentary health-care system. There have also been advances in modern communications: the developing mobile-phone network, for instance, has millions of subscribers.

Development has been most successful and most noticeable in the main population centres, especially Kabul and its environs. Afghan forces control security in the capital in all but one district. Herat City and Mazar-e Sharif are also thriving: given their relative security, the economy in these areas has greatly improved and GDP has more than tripled nationwide since 2001, from $4 billion to more than $13bn. But in the areas that are controlled or contested by the Taliban, local farmers and businesses have not benefitted from this economic regeneration as both they, and opium growers, are taxed by the Taliban. This means that, in order to realise local benefits from evicting the Taliban, ISAF operations to clear these areas of insurgents have to be accompanied by improved governance, reconstruction and development, though in some areas the effectiveness of these efforts is limited by the highly variable standard of provincial and district governors.

During 2010, ISAF-contributing nations have increased the numbers of civilians deployed to Afghanistan so as to increase the international development and reconstruction effort, with the number of US civilians, for example, increasing threefold to over 1,100. Equally important, NATO has sought to better coordinate ISAF's military operations with the multitude of Afghan and international civilian governmental and non-governmental organisations. This received extra impetus in January 2010 when UK Ambassador Mark Sedwill was appointed as ISAF's new senior civilian representative. Sedwill is responsible for coordinating the delivery of ISAF 'civil effect', including political, governance and economic initiatives, as well as improving engagement with neighbouring states. ISAF considers that this has improved coordination, and there is deeper engagement with the Afghan National Security Council.

International efforts to improve Afghan governance continue, with considerable civilian reconstruction and development being conducted at the local level by Provincial Reconstruction Teams. This is complemented by a large variety of similar efforts at the national level. While Karzai has at times made outspoken public comments critical of ISAF operations, it is unclear if these are a calculated effort to distance himself from unpopular actions by ISAF, including civilian casualties, or a reaction to the intense pressure that he is under. There have also been allegations in the media that Karzai's attitude has been influenced by medication. These comments have done little for ISAF nations' political confidence in Karzai, already dented by widely circulated media stories relating to the dubious business ties of the wider Karzai family, the failure to confront organised-crime and drug-trafficking organisations and their protection networks, and the lack of reform in national government institutions. Continued failure to address these problems could erode the fragile confidence of troop-contributing governments. Of key significance to the Afghan government are the so-called 'night raids': arrest operations conducted by ISAF special forces, which many Afghans are coming to regard as an unacceptable infringement of their sovereignty.

This friction between ISAF and Karzai may conceal an underlying political fragility within Karzai's administration. But it also indicates that a perception of widespread corruption and criminalised patronage networks, many of which are connected to and reflect the existing political settlement in Afghanistan, could pose a potentially fatal threat to the viability of the Afghan state. At the local level, widespread sentiments of abuse of power and injustice fuel the insurgency. A September 2010 nationwide poll for ISAF indicated that over 80% of Afghans believed corruption affected their daily lives. All of these factors could also, by increasing the gap between Afghan authorities and the population, contaminate or erode the local political progress necessary to realise the benefits of successful security operations.

An example of this at the tactical level is Helmand province, where Governor Gulab Mangal has, in the view of many ISAF officers and US commentators proven himself to be one of the more effective provincial governors. Not only has he gained and sustained the confidence of UK and US forces, his personal leadership has been a major factor in the significant progress achieved in Helmand since mid-2009. But President Karzai has displayed greater personal support for Sher Mohammed Akhundzada, the senator for northern Helmand and one of Mangal's predecessors, allegedly with previous links to the narcotics trade, who acts as a rival power broker with a personal network in northern Helmand that competes with the legitimate local governance. And even in the relatively secure areas of Helmand, the Afghan governance and justice systems are unable to resolve the many disputes that exist over land ownership. Such low-level disputes are endemic, but the Taliban appear to be much more effective at resolving such disputes, further undermining Afghan governance.

ISAF has responded by recently establishing a multinational interagency task force (Combined Joint Interagency Task Force – Shafafiyat ['Transparency']) to better understand corruption in Afghanistan and plan and coordinate future US and ISAF anti-corruption efforts. It is not yet clear what initiatives will result from this work. ISAF had already come to the view that the letting of contracts by NATO and other international organisations had not only contributed to corruption, but had also helped fund warlords, drug barons and private militias. This has required more rigour and formal assessment of the impact of contracts on the campaign. ISAF has recently suspended operations by a major US contractor as a result of allegations of non-payment of Afghan subcontractors.

Reconciliation and reintegration

Both the Afghan government and ISAF have repeatedly declared a willingness to allow Taliban fighters who lay down their arms to reintegrate into Afghan society. In June 2010 a National Consultative Peace Jirga gave Karzai a mandate to pursue peace and end the conflict. Indeed, there is now an Afghanistan Peace and Reintegration Programme steered by a national-level High Peace Council. This has been replicated in a few provinces and districts, but not across the whole country. Afghanistan is taking the lead in reconstruction efforts, with NATO providing financial and technical support.

If durable reconciliation is to be achieved across the country, it needs not only effective negotiation and mechanisms to enable coherent delivery of the policy, but also a way of gainfully employing any Taliban deemed to be 'reconciled'. This requires credible capabilities to re-train and then provide employment, which in themselves will depend on the local security and economic situation. A large sum of international money has been allocated to support the Afghanistan Peace and Reintegration Programme, but this remains largely unspent.

Considerable effort has been expended in reconciliation initiatives since the beginning of 2010. Karzai has authorised negotiations with the Quetta Shura Taliban and the Haqqani Network, although many analysts consider the latter group's links to al-Qaeda make them the least amenable of all to compromise. There are further reports that Gulbuddin Hekmatyar's Hizb-i-Islami grouping – one of the less capable Taliban groups – is moving towards reconciliation with the Karzai government. By November 2010, some media statements from Quetta Shura figures conceded that their fighters were 'very tired' and a total of 250 Taliban insurgents appeared to have ceased fire and reconciled. In early 2011 there were also reports of villagers in Helmand's Sangin and Marjah areas rejecting the Taliban. But a major switching of sides by a significant insurgent group, similar to that of the Anbar Awakening in western Iraq in 2006, has eluded ISAF and the Afghan government. The practical difficulties were illustrated by November 2010 media reports that an enterprising Afghan had duped British intelligence and the Afghan government into believing he was a senior Taliban commander.

A linked initiative has been Village Stability Operations, an effort to generate and sustain anti-Taliban self-defence forces in villages that have opted to resist the Taliban in areas with limited ISAF and ANSF presence. The initiative relies on US and Afghan special forces living in these communities. It has exploited successful revolts against the Taliban by some villages and has been combined with reconstruction and development. As of January 2011 eight Afghan teams were deployed, and there were plans to increase the number ninefold over the year. The programme has seen some success, but it has proved difficult to counter Taliban intimidation.

ISAF thinking has been that this programme will in the future become part of the Afghan Local Police initiative. This is a community-recruited and community-based force that answers to a representative shura and the district police chief. Some contingents have already been formed in southern Afghanistan. Thus far, these have been raised by US special forces working in areas where they are the only NATO presence. The programme seeks to avoid a situation arising in which such developing police forces may become militias of a local warlord or drug baron. There are considerable expectations for this initiative, but it is too early to forecast its overall success, and it is not yet clear how these detachments would in time be integrated into a unified national police force.

Security transition
At the Kabul International Conference, held in July 2010 to 'deliberate and endorse an Afghan Government-led plan for improved development, governance, and stability', the Afghan government and NATO endorsed *Intequal*, a plan for transition which would allow Afghans gradually to take full responsibility for security, governance and development. It was agreed that transition would be a process based on the conditions on the ground rather than being driven by set timelines. ISAF and the international civilian effort, including Provincial Reconstruction Teams, would gradually change roles, from supporting to mentoring, then enabling and finally sustaining, as ANSF and Afghan government capabilities develop.

A combined Afghan–NATO assessment process for *Intequal* has been agreed, but the experience of Iraq suggests that ISAF and the Afghan government might have to resist political pressure from troop-contributing nations' governments anxious to declare success as early as possible, in order to withdraw their forces. ISAF expects that Kabul province will be the first to transition to full Afghan security control, with the hope that this will act as a model for the rest of the country. As ISAF forces reduce in some areas, some of this 'transition dividend' is expected to be redeployed in other areas. This is a possible area of contention between ISAF commanders (who will be keen to use forces released in this way to expand secure areas) and governments of troop-contributing nations (who will likely be equally keen to bring troops home).

Assessment
Only after mid-2009 did the Afghan campaign begin to receive the resources and political capital needed to counter the Taliban by executing a comprehensive COIN strategy, a point now conceded by many ISAF officers and officials from the troop-contributing nations. Indeed, it was only towards the end of 2010 that ISAF troop levels became adequate to contest

Taliban-controlled areas in the south. US troop numbers have peaked and, even if Obama's declared date for US force reductions slips, these numbers will start to reduce. ISAF's plan is that the growing ANSF will fill the resulting gap.

The progress of a complex and non-linear military campaign is often difficult to assess while the conflict is being fought. Like many counter-insurgencies, Afghanistan is a multifaceted contest between insurgents and governments. Afghan and ISAF efforts to secure the majority of the Afghan population must reduce Taliban capability and influence sufficiently to allow ANSF capacity to reach a level where government forces can take the lead in ensuring security by the end of 2014. This would be assisted by a reduction of Taliban capability in Pakistan by that country's security forces. But military efforts to improve security will, on their own, be insufficient to neutralise the insurgency. Just as important are Afghan and ISAF initiatives to build credible local development, reconstruction and governance that would constitute a better 'offer' to the Afghan people at the local level than that made by the Taliban.

A total of 711 NATO troops were killed in 2010, the highest annual total since 2001. This reflects the increased troop numbers and ISAF efforts to contest Taliban-controlled territory. The Netherlands has withdrawn its combat troops. Canada will shortly do the same, although both countries will contribute personnel to the NATO Training Mission. Overall, the war is becoming increasingly hard to explain to sceptical publics in NATO nations. It is not yet clear that sufficient progress will have been made by June 2011 for any significant handovers of districts or provinces from NATO to the ANSF. According to US, NATO and media reports, many Afghans believe that once ISAF reduces its strength after 2014, a Taliban victory is inevitable. This allows the Taliban to play a waiting game.

To prevail, however, the Taliban have to retain sufficient leadership capacity by surviving in Pakistan and Afghanistan. They also have to retain sufficient military and political capability to sustain assassination and intimidation efforts inside the areas controlled by ISAF and Afghan forces, and to inflict casualties among ISAF troops sufficient to influence member-states to withdraw contingents. The Taliban have to make their 'offer' of security and Islamic justice, not only to the Afghan people but also to their own commanders and troops inside Afghanistan, sufficiently strong that it neutralises Afghan-led efforts to undermine them, both by raising local police and by reconciling Taliban. And the smaller the improvement in Afghan governance, especially at the local level, the easier it will be for the Taliban to prevail.

NATO and ISAF strategy hinges on transition and reconciliation. Both could be placed in jeopardy not only by the regenerative capacity of the Taliban but also by the weakness of the Afghan government. To consolidate political gains in the wake of improved security, Afghan government leaders, especially President Karzai, must see it as in their interests to undertake political reform so that corruption and criminality no longer pose a threat to the legitimacy and viability of the Afghan state. This is rendered more difficult by the current balance of power within the state, which may reflect a short-term effort to maximise the spoils of power. Various groups, many of which are organised around power brokers and warlords, appear to be motivated primarily by a desire to consolidate their position in advance of a post-ISAF Afghanistan. This further complicates attempts to craft a political settlement capable of providing long-term security and stability.

Map 1 **Afghanistan**

Information as of mid-December 2010. Units below battalion level are not shown. The military symbols of ISAF units show their normal role, but in the majority of cases these units are operating in a specific task organisation for their mission and have been allocated theatre-specific equipment such as heavy APCs and protected patrol vehicles, and counter-IED equipment.

Estimated troop contributions of NATO–ISAF nations

Albania	258	Canada (CAN)	2,913	Georgia	924	Latvia	190	Norway (NOR)	352	Sweden (SWE)	491
Armenia	40	Croatia	311	Germany (GER)	4,877	Lithuania (LTU)	179	Poland (POL)	2,488	Turkey (TUR)	1,815
Australia (AUS)	1,550	Czech Republic (CZE)	472	Greece	134	Luxembourg	9	Portugal	95	Ukraine	17
Austria	3	Denmark (DNK)	750	Hungary (HUN)	522	Malaysia	30	Romania	1,664	United Arab Emirates	35
Azerbaijan	94	Estonia (EST)	139	Iceland	4 (civilians)	Mongolia	49	Singapore	38	UK	9,500
Belgium	519	Finland	165	Ireland	7	Montenegro	31	Slovakia	293	US	90,000
Bosnia-Herzegovina	45	France (FRA)	3,850	Italy (ITA)	3,770	Netherlands (NLD)	190	Slovenia	80	US (OEF-A)	ε7,000
Bulgaria	589	FYR Macedonia	163	Rep. of Korea (ROK)	246	New Zealand (NZL)	234	Spain (ESP)	1,505	**Total (rounded)**	**138,730**

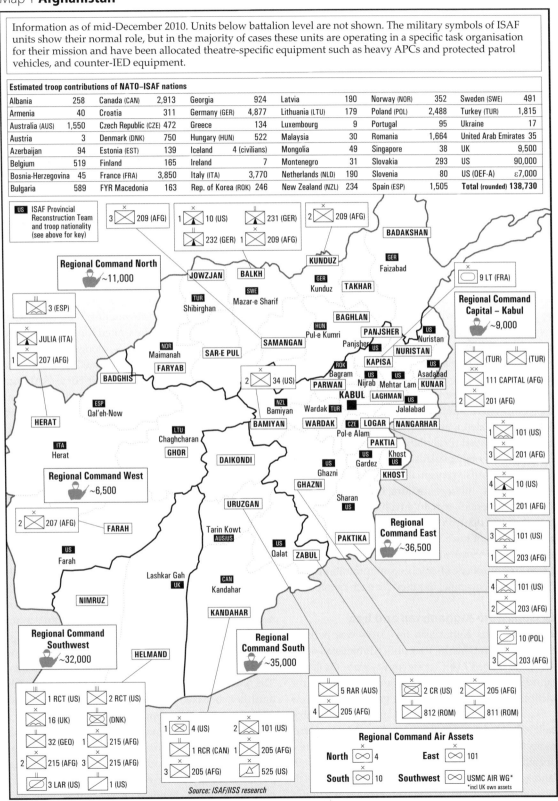

Source: ISAF/IISS research

Unmanned aerial vehicles: emerging lessons and technologies

The role of unmanned aerial vehicles (UAVs) in continuing combat operations in Afghanistan is increasingly the subject of public debate, with weaponised UAVs becoming almost integral to the prosecution of many military operations by the United States. But the first missile test firing from a US MQ-1 *Predator* UAV took place only ten years ago. These aircraft were initially developed with a view to carrying payloads designed to increase situational awareness and enhancing the timeliness and persistence of intelligence, surveillance and reconnaissance (ISR) assets available to commanders. But they are increasingly seen as part of a suite of platforms able to deliver weapons within the area of operations.

However, if the utility and effectiveness of UAVs used in Afghanistan is generally accepted, their employment has raised a range of issues – operational, procedural, force structure, technical, legal and ethical – that require increased attention. Indicating the comparative immaturity of the sector, even the lexicon associated with these systems remains uncertain. The preferred vocabulary in some military circles is now the remotely piloted air system, rather than the UAV. This reflects a concern that the wider public may – or already is – underestimating the extent to which military personnel remain involved in unmanned activity, particularly in those circumstances involving the use of lethal force. In fact, unmanned operations are, perhaps surprisingly, still heavily 'manned', given the numbers of pilots, communications and maintenance personnel required for each mission.

Lessons from Afghanistan and Iraq

While previous enthusiasm for UAVs was perhaps episodic, operations in Iraq and Afghanistan have served to embed UAV technology – from the hand-launched system used by an infantry section, to the tactical and medium- and long-endurance systems – as a permanent element of air and ground combat capability. Deployed as an ISR platform, the UAV has more than proved its worth in counter-insurgency operations, for example providing persistent surveillance to build up a picture of daily life on a regional or even an individual basis, and has emerged as a useful tool in countering the utilisation of improvised explosive devices (IEDs). Contributions in this area can be direct, such as in carrying out change-detection flights over convoy routes or in stemming the flow of materials required for the production of IEDs. In addition, the ability of some unmanned air systems to deliver guided weapons such as the AGM-114 *Hellfire*, or the GBU-12 *Paveway* II laser-guided bomb and the dual-mode GBU-49 Enhanced *Paveway* II GPS and laser-guided bomb, means that military forces are increasingly considering these unmanned systems as integral to future force structures.

Besides the US, many other NATO nations involved in Afghanistan are building their UAV experience and aspirations. The United Kingdom operates *Predator* and MQ-9 *Reaper* UAVs alongside the US Air Force (USAF) – with pilots co-located at Creech Air Force Base in Nevada. The Royal Air Force (RAF) has so far ordered around ten *Reaper* airframes – but at least two of these have been destroyed. As of the end of the third quarter of 2010, the RAF had recorded 13,000 flight hours with the MQ-9 since bringing it into service in October 2007. London is also leasing UAV capability, using the *Hermes* 450, the air vehicle that will be at the heart of the UK's *Watchkeeper* system when it enters service. The leasing approach has also been adopted by Australia, Canada and Germany, all of which are using the Israeli-manufactured *Heron* UAV for operations in Afghanistan.

By the end of 2011 the USAF's ability to launch *Predator* and *Reaper* combat air patrols (CAP) will have grown tenfold. Having fielded five CAPs in 2004, the target for the end of fiscal year 2011 is 50, with a surge capacity of 65 by the end of FY2013. Presently, a single CAP – based on four *Predators* or *Reapers* – requires 168 personnel, including ten pilots. The 50 CAP target currently requires 500 pilots – with a further 70 tasked with transiting the aircraft to and from the area of operations.

To reduce the demand on aircrew numbers, along with the cost of operations, the USAF is aiming to use multi-aircraft control technologies by 2012, enabling one pilot to operate several UAVs, thus halving the number of pilots required. Beyond this, it is also considering increasing the level of autonomy on 50% of CAPs, which would further reduce the demand for pilots. Meanwhile, the role and number of aircrew in UAV operations is under scrutiny. Land forces have so far mainly been employing small UAVs and these can be operated by personnel who have not been trained as pilots. In the case of medium-sized UAVs, the US and UK already have trials under way examining the use of personnel other than pilots to fly them. The issue of service ownership of UAVs remains an area of contention, particularly between armies and air forces.

The utility of the UAV in Afghanistan is also serving to underscore the need for ever-greater integration of ISR data within an overall collection, analysis and dissemination framework, providing appropriate and timely exploitation.

Though war on the ground in Afghanistan is complex and challenging, the air domain remains relatively benign; in terms of classical air doctrine coalition forces have dominance, allowing relatively unconstrained use of airspace. Small-arms fire and rocket-propelled grenades are a concern at a low level, particularly for helicopter operations, and there has been sporadic use of man-portable air-defence systems. Overall, attrition rates are a fraction of the losses suffered by Soviet forces during the 1980s, though non-combat attrition rates for UAVs are far higher than for manned aircraft. The relatively permissive air environment in current areas of operation does raise the question of how well many of the present generation of UAVs would fare in a higher-threat environment, and how current concepts of operation would need to be revised to cope with advanced air-defence systems. Anti-aircraft artillery such as the Russian 2S6 *Tunguska* (SA-19 *Grison*) and *Panstyr* S-1 (SA-22 *Greyhound*) would provide a credible threat to low-level UAV operations.

Another challenge relates to communications security. Incidents such as the intercept of a UAV data downlink in Iraq in late 2008 highlight the vulnerability of unencrypted data streams. Irrespective of the cost of encryption, operating nations are increasingly interested in improving the security of space-based communications and two-way line-of-sight data links, especially for more sensitive platforms working in high-threat environments.

Beyond *Predator* and *Reaper*
While Afghanistan may be the focus of operational attention for Washington and its allies, they are also seeking to determine future requirements.

The USAF is looking to a successor for the *Reaper* in the form of the MQ-X, while France, Germany, Italy and the UK are considering the acquisition of similar systems. The MQ-X is envisaged as a family of medium-class UAVs capable of carrying modular payloads designed to meet a broader range of mission tasks than those undertaken by the MQ-9 *Reaper*. Given the likely size of the requirement – in excess of 250 air platforms – it is attracting considerable industry attention. Boeing, Raytheon, Lockheed Martin and Northrop Grumman have all produced notional designs for the MQ-X programme. General Atomics, meanwhile, has offered its *Avenger* (*Predator* C) as a candidate.

The UK's *Scavenger* project broadly fills a similar requirement to the MQ-X. Whichever platform – or possibly platforms – emerges to meet the *Scavenger* requirement is also likely to replace the *Reaper* in the British inventory.

Scavenger is a core element of the RAF's Combat ISTAR (intelligence, surveillance, target acquisition and reconnaissance) concept. The programme emerged from the UK's Strategic Defence and Security Review (SDSR), released in October 2010, with an enhanced status. In common with many Western militaries, the problems facing the British military that the SDSR sought to confront were a result of the financial crisis that began in 2008. Faced with significant budgetary pressures, the RAF axed two manned ISR-capable aircraft, the *Nimrod* MRA4 for maritime patrol and the *Sentinel* R1 for radar ground surveillance. The latter will be withdrawn following the end of the air force commitment in Afghanistan. Mission requirements remain unchanged, however, and there are aspirations to transition elements of these into the realm of the unmanned system. In the US, there are also signs of renewed interest in using long-endurance platforms as part of a missile-defence system. These were originally considered in the 1990s.

Unmanned combat platforms
Defence establishments and the defence industry, meanwhile, continue to develop unmanned combat aerial vehicle (UCAV) concepts. Afghanistan has provided Washington with an environment in which to test the Lockheed Martin RQ-170 *Sentinel*. The low-observable flying-wing design is the result of a classified R&D programme, but the exact nature of the deployment in Kandahar remained uncertain at time of writing.

The blended-wing body planform is being adopted for low-observable high-end unmanned platforms to address issues of survival in contested – or non-permissive – airspace. US UCAV demonstrator projects, and European efforts such as the multi-national *Neuron*, the British *Taranis* and the Russian *Skat*, have all been driven by a desire to optimise survivability by minimising radar and infrared signatures, which also drives the embedded engine and internal weapons bay configuration seen on flying wings.

Technology challenges

Such designs, however, bring with them considerable challenges, not least in terms of stability and the associated control systems required to maintain this. In addition to maintaining control of a blended wing-body configuration, integration of the propulsion system also poses particular demands. The current design preference is for top-mounted intakes – obscured from ground-based radar – coupled with shaped ducts to keep the engine face from direct exposure to radio-frequency energy, and infrared signature-reduction techniques for the jet plume.

Alongside the US MQ-X medium UAV requirement, the USAF is also pursuing MQ-L – a larger air vehicle – to meet a variety of support and combat roles. These include air-to-air refuelling, ISR and global strike. A 'Special Unmanned Aerial System' development track is also foreseen that will include a low-observable – or even extremely low-observable – platform. R&D work in this area is near certain to remain highly classified.

The US Navy's Unmanned Combat Air System Demonstration Program (UCAS-D) was due to be flown around the end of 2010 – representing a delay of six months. The UCAS-D project uses the Northrop Grumman X-47B air vehicle and is aimed at exploring the requirement to operate a low-observable unmanned system from an aircraft carrier. The project will culminate in carrier trials in FY2013, with the results feeding into the navy's programme to develop an unmanned carrier-launched airborne surveillance and strike system. The present ambition within the navy is to be able to field an experimental force of four to six air vehicles around 2018, or earlier if the pace of development allows.

Given the technology demands, programme slippage is far from unusual. Along with the UCAS-D, the UK's *Taranis* and the European *Neuron* have also seen test schedules amended as development issues have arisen. A *Taranis* demonstrator was to have started flight testing during 2010 – this will not now occur until 2011. One of the areas that took longer to resolve than initially anticipated was the integration of the propulsion system – including the low-observable intake and duct configuration.

A mock-up of Russia's *Skat* was displayed to a limited audience in 2007. The current status of the programme remains unclear, though the Russian air force remains interested in UCAV technology. Sukhoi has also shown concepts for comparatively large ISR UAVs, though again the status of any work in this area remains unclear.

China and India are also at varying stages of developing national requirements, with the latter looking to its autonomous unmanned research aircraft (AURA) project to provide a technology base. The two states also have an interest in medium- and high-altitude long-endurance (MALE/HALE) ISR platforms. China has the BZK-005 and BZK-009 development projects, while India is working on the *Rustom*-H MALE UAV. The Indian Navy also issued a request for information on a 25-hour-plus HALE system in October 2010.

Earlier in 2010, South Korea released a request for proposals for a low-observable UCAV demonstrator. Australia and Japan also have an interest in multi-mission HALE platforms. Australian interest in the Northrop Grumman *Global Hawk*, however, did not extend to taking up an early option in the US Broad Area Maritime Surveillance programme.

Israel, an early adopter of UAV technology, continues to develop systems across nearly all platform classes. In 2010, the Israeli Air Force formally brought the *Heron* TP, known as *Eitan* domestically and manufactured by Israel Aircraft Industries (IAI), into service. The *Heron* TP has a maximum take-off weight of around five tonnes, offers an endurance of 24 hours and has a mission radius of 1,000 kilometres. It can carry a variety of sensors, including electro-optical, radar, and electronic intelligence payloads. Given its ongoing interest in UAV technology, Israel is also likely exploring requirements for low-observable unmanned platforms, though no formal programme has been publicly acknowledged. Israeli weapons manufacturers, however, have shown interest in the development of classes of small weapons suitable for UAVs and UCAVs. Israeli UAV systems have been used by several nations involved in Afghanistan, while in mid-October 2010 IAI agreed a deal with Russian company Oboronprom to sell 'UAV assembly elements and services'.

Airspace access

Beyond current conflict zones, military UAV operations are generally limited to 'restricted' airspace in the US and Europe because of civil-certification concerns. This has implications for military UAV training, and also for non-combat operational roles that could require unmanned systems to be flown over national territory (this applies both within states, due to their own civil aviation law, as well as internationally), though waivers and experimental category exceptions can be applied for the occasional operation of a UAV in non-military airspace.

In the US, the Federal Aviation Administration (FAA) is working on how to integrate UAVs into the national air-space system. The FAA's Unmanned Aircraft Program Office has been set up to consider this issue, while Washington has asked the Radio Technical Commission for Aeronautics (RTCA) to examine two key questions – how will communication, command and control be addressed, and how will the UAVs meet the 'sense and avoid' requirement with regard to other aircraft. The RTCA work is due to be completed by 2015.

Similar efforts are under way in Europe. The UK's Autonomous Systems Technology Related Airborne Evaluation and Assessment (ASTRAEA) programme is now in its second phase, following a year-long hiatus resulting from a failure to secure government funding. 'Sense and avoid' is being addressed within one of ASTRAEA's two main work strands, that of separation and assurance control. 'Sense and avoid' is a key issue for military, as well as civil, airspace regulators: the proliferation of UAVs operating at differing flight levels has led to a substantial increase in the risk of collision, particularly over air bases with busy operational schedules, and there have been cases of near misses between UAVs and other military, as well as non-military, air traffic.

Rules of engagement

It is not only in the aerospace arena where the use of UAVs raises regulatory issues. The increasing use of UAVs – particularly in the combat role – and the move toward UCAVs requires consideration in light of the laws of armed conflict. In March 2010, in a keynote address to the American Society of International Law, State Department legal adviser Harold Koh stated that there was 'no prohibition under the laws of war on the use of technologically advanced systems in armed conflict … so long as they are employed in conformity with applicable laws of war'.

This area has become the focus of attention partly as a result of the use of UAVs to strike at al-Qaeda and related groups outside the conflict zones of Iraq and Afghanistan. In the medium to long term, the legal implications for the emergence of UCAVs will also need to be considered. But while these legal and ethical concerns will be of relevance to the employment of UAVs and UCAVs in the future – particularly in actions outside conflict zones – the rapid growth of the sector in general will continue nonetheless.

Research organisations such as Teal Group and *Aerospace and Defence News* estimate that the value of the global UAV market will grow to $70–80 billion over the coming decade. According to Teal, the Pentagon will account for 58% of UAV procurement expenditure, while its research, development, test and evaluation spending will amount to three-quarters of the global spend. Deployed by land, naval and air forces, UAVs are seen as an integral part of future force structures, and as key means to deliver effect through their employment as ISR assets or as weapons platforms. One crucial area that remains open to debate is the extent to which – particularly in the air-combat arena – unmanned systems are used as a complement to crewed aircraft fleets, or as a replacement for them.

Table 1 **Selected UAV holdings 2011**

Country	Name	Type	Size	Number	Service
North America					
Canada	*Heron*	ISR	Heavy	5	Air Force
USA	*I-Gnat*	ISR	Heavy	3	Army
USA	RQ-5 *Hunter*	ISR	Heavy	20	Army
USA	*Sky Warrior*	ISR	Heavy	4	Army
USA	*Warrior*	ISR	Heavy	15	Army
USA	RQ-7A *Shadow*	ISR	Medium	236	Army
USA	MQ-8B *Fire Scout*	ISR	Heavy	5	Navy
USA	RQ-4A *Global Hawk*	ISR	Heavy	2	Navy
USA	RQ-2B *Pioneer*	ISR	Medium	35	Navy
USA	RQ-7B *Shadow*	ISR	Medium	32	Marines
USA	MQ-1B *Predator*	CISR	Heavy	130	Air Force
USA	MQ-9 *Reaper*	CISR	Heavy	47	Air Force
USA	RQ-4A *Global Hawk*	ISR	Heavy	7	Air Force
USA	RQ-4B *Global Hawk*	ISR	Heavy	3	Air Force
USA	RQ-170 *Sentinel*	ISR	Heavy	1	Air Force
USA	MQ-1 *Predator*	CISR	Heavy	8	Air National Guard
USA	MQ-9 *Reaper*	CISR	Heavy	1	Air National Guard
Europe					
Azerbaijan	*Aerostar*	ISR	Medium	3	Army
Azerbaijan	*Aerostar*	ISR	Medium	4	Air Force
Belgium	RQ-5A *Hunter*	ISR	Heavy	13	Air Force
Finland	ADS-95 *Ranger*	ISR	Medium	6	Army
France	*Sperwer*	ISR	Medium	20	Army
France	*Harfang*	ISR	Heavy	3	Air Force
Germany	KZO	ISR	Medium	6	Army
Germany	*Luna*	ISR	Medium	6	Army
Germany	*Heron*	ISR	Heavy	3	Air Force
Greece	*Sperwer*	ISR	Medium	2	Army
Italy	RQ-1B *Predator*	ISR	Heavy	6	Air Force
Netherlands	*Sperwer*	ISR	Medium	14	Army
Spain	*Searcher* MkIIJ	ISR	Medium	4	Army
Sweden	*Sperwer*	ISR	Medium	3	Army
Switzerland	ADS-95 *Ranger*	ISR	Medium	4	Air Force
Turkey	*Falcon* 600	ISR	Heavy	n.k.	Army
Turkey	*Firebee*	ISR	Heavy	n.k.	Army
Turkey	CL-89	ISR	Medium	n.k.	Army
Turkey	*Gnat*	ISR	Medium	196	Army
Turkey	*Heron*	ISR	Heavy	10	Air Force
Turkey	*Gnat* 750	ISR	Medium	18	Air Force

Table 1 **Selected UAV holdings 2011**

Country	Name	Type	Size	Number	Service
UK	*Hermes* 450	ISR	Medium	n.k.	Army
UK	*Watchkeeper*	ISR	Medium	n.k.	Army
UK	MQ-9 *Reaper*	CISR	Medium	5	Air Force
Asia					
Australia	*Heron*	ISR	Heavy	8	Army
China	BZK-005	ISR	Heavy	n.k.	Army
China	WZ-5	ISR	Heavy	n.k.	Army
China	ASN-105	ISR	Medium	n.k.	Army
China	ASN-206	ISR	Medium	n.k.	Army
China	CH-1 *Chang Hong*	ISR	Heavy	n.k.	Air Force
China	*Chang Kong*-1	ISR	Heavy	n.k.	Air Force
China	*Firebee*	ISR	Heavy	n.k.	Air Force
India	*Nishant*	ISR	Medium	14	Army
India	*Searcher* MkI/II	ISR	Medium	12	Army
India	*Heron*	ISR	Heavy	4	Navy
India	*Searcher* MkII	ISR	Medium	8	Navy
India	*Searcher* MkII	ISR	Medium	n.k.	Air Force
South Korea	*Night Intruder*	ISR	Medium	n.k.	Air Force
South Korea	*Searcher*	ISR	Medium	3	Air Force
Malaysia	*Eagle* ARV	ISR	Heavy	3	Air Force
Malaysia	*Aludra*	ISR	Medium	n.k.	Air Force
Philippines	*Blue Horizon* II	ISR	Medium	2	Air Force
Singapore	*Hermes* 450	ISR	Heavy	n.k.	Air Force
Singapore	*Searcher* MkII	ISR	Medium	40	Air Force
Sri Lanka	*Seeker*	ISR	Medium	1	Army
Sri Lanka	*Blue Horizon* II	ISR	Medium	n.k.	Air Force
Sri Lanka	*Searcher* MkII	ISR	Medium	2	Air Force
Thailand	*Searcher*	ISR	Medium	n.k.	Army
Middle East and North Africa					
Egypt	R4E-50 *Skyeye*	ISR	Heavy	20	Air Force
Egypt	Teledyne-Ryan 324 *Scarab*	ISR	Heavy	29	Air Force
Iran	*Mohajer* IV	ISR	Medium	n.k.	Army
Israel	*Hermes* 450	ISR	Heavy	n.k.	Air Force
Israel	*Heron*	ISR	Heavy	n.k.	Air Force
Israel	*Heron* II	ISR	Heavy	4	Air Force
Israel	RQ-5A *Hunter*	ISR	Heavy	n.k.	Air Force
Israel	*Searcher* MkII	ISR	Medium	22	Air Force
Jordan	*Seeker* SB7L	ISR	Heavy	6	Air Force
Lebanon	*Mohajer* IV	ISR	Medium	8	Army
Morocco	R4E-50 *Skyeye*	ISR	Heavy	n.k.	Army

Table 1 **Selected UAV holdings 2011**

Country	Name	Type	Size	Number	Service
Latin America and Caribbean					
Brazil	*Heron*	ISR	Heavy	3	Public Security Forces
Ecuador	*Heron*	ISR	Heavy	2	Navy
Ecuador	*Searcher* MkII	ISR	Medium	4	Navy
Mexico	*Hermes* 450	ISR	Heavy	2	Air Force
Sub-Saharan Africa					
South Africa	*Seeker* II	ISR	Medium	n.k.	Air Force

Cyberspace: assessing the military dimension

In recent years much comment and analysis has been devoted to questions surrounding the potential or actual military uses of cyberspace, particularly following the attacks, allegedly originating in Russia, on Estonian computer systems in 2007 and on Georgian government websites in 2008, and the much-publicised 2010 Stuxnet worm that reportedly attacked (among other locations) the computer-management systems for centrifuges at Iran's Natanz uranium-isotope enrichment plant.

Cyberspace can be used for a range of tasks, including gathering sensitive information, infiltrating and exploiting networked systems of potential or actual adversaries, and delivering (or assisting in delivering) effect that may have implications for military forces, either in terms of the impact on them or in terms of tasks that they may be called on to undertake in response. It is important that *The Military Balance* begin to include assessments of the military components of cyber power, but the problem lies in defining what to assess.

Many states are creating organisations tasked with tracking, assessing, countering and prosecuting designated tasks in cyberspace. Administrative and operational responsibility can range from defence ministries to other government departments, including interior ministries and intelligence agencies, while private organisations can also be contracted. By no means all groups active in this area are sponsored by states or affiliated to them, but an incident which is technically sophisticated and apparently underwritten with substantial financial and organisational resources may raise suspicions of state involvement. Many perpetrators of cyber attacks appear to be civilians with motivations ranging from criminal to nationalistic; however, governments may coerce or otherwise motivate such unofficial actors.

The involvement of hostile civilian actors means it can be difficult to hold states responsible for cyber incidents. This difficulty of attribution also arises because computers at the apparent point of origin of an attack may have been hijacked or harnessed by a third party. It can thus be hard for a state to find the source of a cyber attack and to decide on an appropriate response.

The organisations created by states to operate in cyberspace thus have several purposes. They can be charged with general information-gathering and prosecuting defensive and offensive operations in cyberspace, sometimes against ostensibly friendly states as well as adversaries (if, for example, there is an information requirement for sensitive defence or commercial data). With military forces increasingly networked, they are also increasingly vulnerable to cyber attacks. Moreover, the greater a nation's dependence on network-enabled systems, the more a potential or actual adversary may resort to cyber activities to circumvent or exploit asymmetries in traditional military capabilities. This dependence on networks reaches beyond the defence realm, creating wider potential vulnerabilities: public utilities, banking and financial services, and commercial supply chains are all highly connected and could be attacked. Further, as Iain Lobban, director of the UK's Government Communications Headquarters, pointed out at the IISS on 12 October 2010, by 'getting cyber right enables the UK's continuing economic prosperity'. A knowledge economy needs to protect its intellectual property and 'maintain the integrity of its financial and commercial services'. Lobban's comments in the UK context hold true for other developed economies: addressing cyber threats in a comprehensive manner can give businesses the confidence to base in a location, knowing they can use modern IT infrastructure and reduce risk. (See http://*www.iiss.org/recent-key-addresses/iain-lobban-address.*)

The creation of organisations tasked with tracking, assessing, countering and prosecuting designated tasks in cyberspace can also result from national drives to better organise domestic cyber capacities and responsibilities. Many governments are only now – some 15 years after widespread public use of the Internet began – engaged in moves to 'reverse-engineer' some form of coherence in this regard. In some states this is being carried out alongside drives to improve information assurance, to reduce through improved protection the chances of any attack being successful. Organisational developments can be of value in developing international collaboration involving elements such as reporting mechanisms, and procedures and expertise that may be activated in case of attack.

The multiplicity of organisations and their varying reporting lines raises important questions: when is a cyber incident military or civil, who decides this, and is this realm the concern of law-enforcement, intelligence or military organisations? Incidents where armed forces are targeted seem intuitively to be a military responsibility, but would a military counter-attack be merited, at whom would this be directed, and what level or type of response would be proportionate? If there are military responses in cyberspace, directed against targets in cyberspace assessed as 'military', would it be possible (given the interconnected nature of cyberspace) for any response to avoid collateral damage, and would a response that cannot be precisely targeted be legitimate in national and international law? There is a further complication and risk in that states may perceive an attack directed through cyberspace with very serious intended or unintended consequences as meriting a kinetic response, particularly as states maintain differing interpretations of what is vital to national security. The IISS examines questions such as these, as well as some of the broader conceptual issues relating to cyberspace, in its forthcoming Adelphi Book *Power in Cyberspace in Theory and Practice*.

Despite these uncertainties, *The Military Balance* intends to begin assessing national and multinational cyber capacities, both civil and military, even if these are difficult to detail in the traditionally quantitative way that we have addressed military inventories. A useful starting point is detailing organisational developments as a way of indicating the resources nations are mobilising in response to cyber threats. Groupings such as national Computer Emergency Response Teams (CERT) will be excluded where they cannot be assessed as reporting to defence organisations, though of course such groupings may list defence organisations among their key constituencies. The following preliminary assessment is necessarily selective; the absence of countries or organisations does not necessarily mean that they do not have relevant capacities.

NATO

NATO approved a cyber-defence policy in January 2008, which was endorsed by heads of state the following April at its Bucharest summit. NATO organisations dedicated to cyber security include the NATO Cyber Defence Management Authority, based in Brussels, which has responsibility for coordinating Alliance-wide cyber defence. Its management board is composed of political, military, operational and technical personnel in NATO states with responsibility for cyber defence. In 2008, the Cooperative Cyber Defence Centre of Excellence was established in Tallinn, Estonia. This centre, one of a number of NATO centres of excellence, 'conducts research and training on cyber warfare' and other tasks including improving cyber defence interoperability 'within the NATO network enabled capability environment'.

NATO maintains information-assurance groupings such as the NATO Information Assurance Technical Centre (NIATC) which can help improve system protection and best practice in member states. NATO's Computer Incident Response Capability – Technical Centre, maintained by the NIATC, provides 'operational CSIRT [Computer Security Incident Response Team] support to the NATO CIS community'. NATO Secretary-General Anders Fogh Rasmussen said in October 2010 that NATO needed to defend itself 'across the spectrum' and that meant 'taking on cyber defence'. He said that 'we … need to be able to support allies who come under attack, with a deployable capability. But … NATO should also help Allies share experiences and set common approaches to cyber-defence.'

Australia

The Cyber Security Operations Centre (CSOC), established in January 2010, is a Defence Signals Directorate (DSD) capability serving government agencies. Analysts are drawn from the DSD, the Defence Intelligence Organisation and the Australian Defence Force, as well as from the Defence Science and Technology Organisation, the Australian Security Intelligence Organisation and the Australian Federal Police. CSOC is tasked with providing an understanding of cyber threats to Australian interests, as well as coordinating operational responses to cyber events of national importance across government and critical infrastructure. (For the private sector, CSOC is complemented by the CERT Australia initiative, under the Attorney General's Office.) Australia published a Cyber Security Strategy in 2009, while the issue featured heavily in the 2009 Defence White Paper.

Canada

Canada published its Cyber Security Strategy in October 2010. This detailed several bodies working on cyber security to protect Canadian infrastructure. The White Paper said that the Communications Security Establishment Canada will enhance its 'capacity to detect and discover threats, provide foreign intelligence and cyber security services, and respond to cyber threats and attacks against Government networks and [IT] systems'. The Canadian Security Intelligence Service and Royal Canadian Mounted Police will investigate incidents according to their relevant mandates, the Department of Foreign Affairs will develop 'a cyber security foreign policy that will help strengthen coherence in the Government's engagement abroad on cyber security'. Meanwhile, 'the Department of National Defence and the Canadian Forces will strengthen their capacity to defend their own networks, will work with other Government departments to identify threats and possible responses, and will continue to exchange information about cyber best practices with allied militaries'. The Canadian Forces Network Operation Centre, meanwhile, is the 'national operational Cyber Defence unit' permanently assigned tasks to support Canadian Forces operations under Canadian Expeditionary Force Command and Canada Command.

China

In July 2010, colours were presented by General Cheng Bingde, head of the PLA General Staff Department, to a new 'Information Safeguards Base'. The base is tasked with addressing cyber threats and safeguarding China's information security and information infrastructure. Some PLA sources claim that the base is not an offensive cyber capability but rather is intended to bolster resilience. It is possible that the new base will come under the command of the Fourth Department of the PLA, responsible for electronic warfare. It appears to be an army-level unit, with some credence lent to this judgement by the high-ranking officers present at the ceremony: four deputy chiefs of staff and two assistant chiefs of staff attended.

The PLA has devoted much attention to information warfare over the past decade, both in terms of battlefield electronic warfare (EW) and wider cyber-warfare capabilities. The main doctrine is the 'Integrated Network Electronic Warfare' document, which guides PLA computer-network operations and calls for the combination of network warfare and EW tools at the start of a conflict in order to paralyse (or at least degrade) an opponent's C4ISR (command, control, communications, computers, intelligence,

surveilllance and reconnaissance) capabilities. China's cyber assets fall under the command of two main departments of the General Staff Department. Computer network attacks and EW would in theory come under the Fourth Department (Electronic Countermeasures), and computer-network defence and intelligence-gathering comes under the Third Department (Signals Intelligence). The Third Department is supported by a variety of 'militia units' comprising both military cyber-warfare personnel and civilian hackers

France

The French Network and Information Security Agency (Agence Nationale de la Sécurité des Systèmes d'Information) was established in 2009 to conduct surveillance on sensitive French government networks and respond to cyber attacks. It also advises government departments and commercial network operators on best practices, and provides information about information-security threats and how to avoid them. This organisation comes under the authority of the prime minister and is attached to the office of the secretary-general for national security and defence. The 2008 French Defence White Paper placed substantial emphasis on cyber threats, calling for new programmes in offensive and defensive cyber-war capabilities. The White Paper noted that part of the offensive capability 'will come under the Joint Staff and the other part … developed within specialised services'.

Germany

Germany established a Department of Information and Computer Network Operations during 2009 under the guidance of the then-chief of the Bundeswehr's Strategic Reconnaissance Command, which already controlled 'fixed and mobile signal intelligence, electronic warfare and satellite intelligence forces and institutions'. Reports stated that the group's mandate could include testing means of cyber infiltration and exploitation, while the German government is examining legal regulations which would give the unit more powers than it currently has; these are limited by civilian regulations. The corresponding civilian agency is the Federal Office for Information Security in Bonn.

India

New Delhi has formulated a Crisis Management Plan for countering cyber attacks and cyber terrorism 'for implementation by all Ministries/Departments of Central Government'. National agencies include the Computer and Emergency Response Team (CERT-In), which has authorised designated individuals to carry out penetration tests against infrastructure. Meanwhile, the Defence Information Assurance and Research Agency, which is mandated to deal with cyber-security-related issues of the armed services and Defence Ministry, has close ties with CERT-In and the National Training Research organisation. All services have their own cyber-security policies, and respective headquarters maintain information-security policies, with associated network audits becoming more routine. These are often conducted by the National Informatics Centre as well as the services themselves; meanwhile, the services maintain their own CERT teams. The Indian Army in 2005 raised the Army Cyber Security Establishment and in April 2010 set up the Cyber Security Laboratory at the Military College of Telecommunications Engineering in Mhow (under the Corps of Signals). The importance of the issue for the Indian security establishment was highlighted by Defence Minister A.K. Antony in a speech to the National Defence College in October 2010: 'The next generation of threats will undoubtedly emerge out of cyber security. We need to make our cyber systems as secure and as non-porous as possible.'

Italy

A CERT-Defence team has been established within the defence staff. Its purpose is to provide institutional support for defence-ministry users in the defence of computer networks. The unit devotes much attention to discovering vulnerabilities in operating systems and applications. Groups within the Defence Innovation Centre and the Division for Information Security of the Defence Staff, as well as the Technical Investigations Division of the Carabinieri, are also monitoring cyber-security issues. Following an October 2010 meeting between the Italian National Agency for New Technologies, Energy and Sustainable Economic Development, and the Italian Association of Critical Infrastructure Experts, a recommendation was made to establish a laboratory to test and analyse scenarios involving cyber attacks.

Japan

The National Information Security Center was established in 2005. It reports to the Cabinet Secretariat and has dual responsibility for national-security and emergency-response systems, including physical security and cyber security. The Government Security Operation Coordination team (GSOC), which became fully operational in 2008, conducts 24-hour monitoring of government-agency information systems. According to the government's 'Secure Japan 2009' document, all government agencies should assist GSOC in improving its capability to analyse cyber attacks. The Ministry of Defense was to be involved in investigating the latest technological trends in cyber attacks. In order to analyse attacks on MOD information systems, as well as response capabilities, government agencies were to 'study the basics of illegal access monitoring and analysis technology, cyber attack analysis technology, and active defense technology'. Further, the 'Information Security 2010' document stated that 'at the end of FY2010, a cyber planning and coordination officer (provisional title) will be stationed in the Joint Staff Office of the Ministry of Defense to enhance … preparedness against cyber attacks'.

North Korea

Since the 1970s the North Korean military (the Korean People's Army, KPA) has maintained a modest EW capability. As a result of strategic reviews following *Operation Desert Storm*, the KPA established an information warfare (IW) capability under the concept of 'electronic intelligence warfare' (EIW). The KPA describes this as a new type of warfare, the essence of which is the disruption or destruction of the opponent's computer networks, thus paralysing the enemy's military command-and-control system. Although this appears to be analogous to IW, the KPA's understanding is believed to include elements of reconnaissance, cryptanalysis, intelligence collection, electronic warfare and disinformation operations, as well as the use of the Internet to cause disruption within an enemy's social and economic environments. Complementing these EIW developments, the KPA expanded its EW capabilities with the introduction of more modern ELINT equipment, jammers and radars. As a counter to South Korean and US EW capabilities the KPA has reportedly fielded a fibre-optic based command-and-control system.

South Korea

South Korea established a Cyber Warfare Command Centre in early 2010, with over 200 personnel, in the wake of a substantial distributed denial-of-service attack in 2009. The new centre responds to the attention given to cyber and information security by the National Intelligence Service and the Defense Security Command. South Korea published an Internet White Paper in 2009, which noted the creation of the Korea Internet and Security Agency, combining the former Korea Internet Security Agency, Korea IT International Cooperation Agency and the Korea Information Security Agency, which works to promote internet use, enhance and monitor network security, and develop international cooperation on matters of cyber security.

Russia

Russia does not yet have a 'Cyber Command' as such, but it has developed capacity in this area and has incorporated the cyber domain into existing doctrines of information warfare. Russia has also been engaged over the past decade in discussions with the US in efforts to incorporate the cyber domain into the arms-control agenda with a particular focus on 'information integrity', or policing the content of the Internet, something the US has resisted. Russian-based organised-crime groups such as the Russian Business Network (RBN), BadB and SpamIt.com have accounted for

a high proportion of all Internet-based organised crime and have until recently been able to operate with minimal state interference, as have nationalist groups such as Nashi. There is strong circumstantial evidence that such groups, notably RBN and Nashi, were involved in cyber attacks against the Estonian and Georgian governments in 2007 and 2008 respectively; in the latter case, cyber attacks on Georgian government websites were closely coordinated with Russian military deployments.

Until 2003, activities within the cyber domain were the responsibility of the Russian signals-intelligence agency, FAPSI. In 2003, this agency was abolished and its responsibilities divided between the Defence Ministry and the internal security service (FSB), with the latter having responsibility for investigating cyber crime. Moscow State University's Institute for Information Security Issues conducts research on technical issues including cryptography and counts the General Staff and the FSB among its clients.

Singapore

The Singapore Ministry of Defence has long identified the potential damage that could be caused by

Problems of definition

An immediate difficulty for discussions of cyberspace, cyber warfare and cyber security is that there are no widely accepted definitions of these terms. Cyberspace, for instance, has emerged as a theatre of operations for military and civilian users before the nature of that space has been clearly defined. This makes it difficult to apportion responsibilities in cyberspace and discuss, for example, what could constitute norms of behaviour. One possible definition of cyberspace is, broadly, a digital domain enabled by the networking of computers, with fluctuating parameters due to the human influence in continually re-moulding networks and systems and in changes in how they are used. The domain also evolves in response to the technical requirements of the information sets it carries.

The difficulty of assigning boundaries in cyberspace – defining what it is, drawing lines dividing military and civil assets, and differentiating targets and responsibilities – has led governments to reflect on where, in bureaucratic terms, cyberspace, cyber warfare, cyber security and so on belong. A further problem in considering cyberspace or cyber warfare concerns terminology. One complication stems from the concept of 'electronic warfare' (EW). This usually refers to forces and activities concerned with exploitation of the electromagnetic spectrum to protect, enhance, penetrate or

degrade secure emissions that contribute to mission success. Due to the uncertainty about the definition and the nature of cyberspace, and developing ownership issues within governments and militaries – and also because 'cyber' has been associated, in a simplistic bout of word association, with the word 'electronic' – there has been a risk of conflating 'cyber warfare' with 'electronic warfare', particularly through early assignment of ownership in militaries with existing EW structures. Bureaucracies can find it easier to conceive of, or organise thoughts about, cyber warfare on the basis of assumed similarity with existing constructs rather than to create new ones.

Some states may likewise view cyber activity as properly categorised within existing structures or doctrines for the assessment of, countering or prosecution of 'information-warfare' activities. While some states may not have units or organisations assigned to 'cyber', they may assign cyber-security responsibilities under the terms 'information security' or 'information assurance' – the latter increasingly used in the context of active-defence measures. But for nations where cyber warfare is not historically analogous with information warfare, cyber warfare and associated activities in cyberspace may be best viewed as, to borrow from the title of a 2001 US Department of Defense paper referenced by the IISS *Adelphi* authors, akin to 'information-age warfare'.

cyber attacks, with this concern perhaps more acute following its adoption of the Integrated-Knowledge-based Command-and-Control doctrine, designed to aid the transition of Singapore's armed forces to a 'third generation' force. Meanwhile, Singapore established the Singapore Infocomm Technology Security Authority on 1 October 2009, as a division within the Internal Security Department of the Ministry of Home Affairs. Its main responsibilities will be dealing with cyber terrorism and cyber espionage, as well as operational IT security development.

United States

The US Department of Defense (DoD) has invested substantial resources in organisations concerned with cyberspace, and it is reported to be working on refining a draft cyber strategy. Meanwhile, October 2010 saw DoD announce a strategy to work with the Department of Homeland Security on cyber security, reflecting the difficulty in assigning boundaries in cyberspace, and in a bid to promote an active, layered defence. DoD also announced that the Defence Advanced Projects Agency was working on a 'cyber range' where advanced systems and concepts could be tested before field deployment.

Each arm of the US military is developing capacity in this area. US Army Cyber Command (ARCYBER) is mandated to 'plan, coordinate, integrate, synchronize, direct, and conduct network operations and defense of all Army networks'. Meanwhile, 'when directed, ARCYBER will conduct cyberspace operations in support of full spectrum operations to ensure U.S. and allied freedom of action in cyberspace, and to deny the same to adversaries'. The 24th Air Force, fully operational in October 2010, has among its tasks providing 'combatant commanders with trained and ready cyber forces to plan and conduct cyberspace operations'; the air force in October 2010 issued a doctrine entitled 'Cyberspace Operations' and now includes cyber security as part of recruits' basic-training curriculum. The navy, meanwhile, established Fleet Cyber Command (the US 10th Fleet) 'to deliver integrated cyber, information operations cryptologic and space capabilities; and to deliver global Navy cyber network common cyber operational requirement'.

These service groups are commanded by US Cyber Command (itself under US Strategic Command), which achieved initial operating capability in May 2010. As well as centralising command of cyberspace operations and enhancing resilience, USCYBERCOM will 'direct the operations and defense of specified Department of Defense information networks and; prepare to, and when directed, conduct full-spectrum military cyberspace operations in order to enable actions in all domains, ensure US/Allied freedom of action in cyberspace and deny the same to our adversaries'.

UK

The Office of Cyber Security and Information Assurance (OCSIA) supports the UK security minister and the National Security Council in 'determining priorities in relation to securing cyberspace'. OCSIA provides 'strategic direction and coordinates action relating to enhancing cyber security and information assurance' and works with the Cyber Security Operations Centre (CSOC) and government ministries and agencies to implement cyber-security programmes. Initially called simply the 'Office of Cyber Security' (established in 2009 following the National Cyber Security Strategy), the addition of 'information assurance' in 2010 serves to underscore the importance placed by London on protection of information – and thus reducing vulnerabilities – in cyberspace. CSOC, meanwhile, is hosted by the Government Communications Headquarters and was also established in 2009. CSOC is engaged in monitoring cyberspace, coordinating incident response, research into attacks on UK networks and cyber-security exercises.

The UK's October 2010 Strategic Defence and Security Review said that the country would 'establish a transformative national programme to protect ourselves in cyber space'. This 'National Cyber Security Programme' will be supported by £650m – with programme management by OSCIA – and will lead to a new Cyber Security Strategy in 2011. It will also see the foundation of a UK Defence Cyber Operations Group, which will provide experts 'to support our own and allied cyber operations to secure our vital networks and to guide the development of new cyber capabilities'.

Chapter Two

Comparative major defence statistics

Key nations' defence budgets 2008–11
(as a percentage of GDP, US$bn)

US

| 696.3 (4.9) | Defence budget
Defence as % of GDP | 693.6 (4.9) | Defence budget
Defence as % of GDP | 692.8 (4.7) |

2008–09 GDP 14,264 | 2009–10 GDP 14,119 | 2010–11 GDP 14,624

China

| 60.1 (1.4) | Defence budget
Defence as % of GDP | 70.4 (1.4) | Defence budget
Defence as % of GDP | 76.4 (1.3) |

2008–09 GDP 4,422 | 2009–10 GDP 4,984 | 2010–11 GDP 5,733

UK

| 71.4 (2.7) | Defence budget
Defence as % of GDP | 60.5 (2.8) | Defence budget
Defence as % of GDP | 56.5 (2.5) |

2008–09 GDP 2,670 | 2009–10 GDP 2,179 | 2010–11 GDP 2,255

Japan

| 46 (0.9) | Defence budget
Defence as % of GDP | 50.3 (1.0) | Defence budget
Defence as % of GDP | 52.8 (1.0) |

2008–09 GDP 4,926 | 2009–10 GDP 5,075 | 2010–11 GDP 5,387

France

| 44.6 (1.6) | Defence budget
Defence as % of GDP | 46.0 (1.7) | Defence budget
Defence as % of GDP | 42.6 (1.6) |

2008–09 GDP 2,863 | 2009–10 GDP 2,656 | 2010–11 GDP 2,587

Germany

| 43.3 (1.2) | Defence budget
Defence as % of GDP | 43.5 (1.3) | Defence budget
Defence as % of GDP | 41.2 (1.2) |

2008–09 GDP 3,659 | 2009–10 GDP 3,339 | 2010–11 GDP 3,346

Saudi Arabia

| 38.2 (8.1) | Defence budget
Defence as % of GDP | 41.3 (11.0) | Defence budget
Defence as % of GDP | 45.2 (10.4) |

2008–09 GDP 469 | 2009–10 GDP 376 | 2010–11 GDP 434

Russia

| 40.5 (2.4) | Defence budget
Defence as % of GDP | 38.3 (3.1) | Defence budget
Defence as % of GDP | 41.4 (2.8) |

2008–09 GDP 1,680 | 2009–10 GDP 1,236 | 2010–11 GDP 1,488

India

| 28.4 (2.3) | Defence budget
Defence as % of GDP | 34.4 (2.8) | Defence budget
Defence as % of GDP | 38.4 (2.5) |

2008–09 GDP 1,223 | 2009–10 GDP 1,231 | 2010–11 GDP 1,545

Brazil

| 23.3 (1.5) | Defence budget
Defence as % of GDP | 28.0 (1.8) | Defence budget
Defence as % of GDP | 34.7 (1.7) |

2008–09 GDP 1,579 | 2009–10 GDP 1,592 | 2010–11 GDP 2,039

Aggregate combat power

Economic

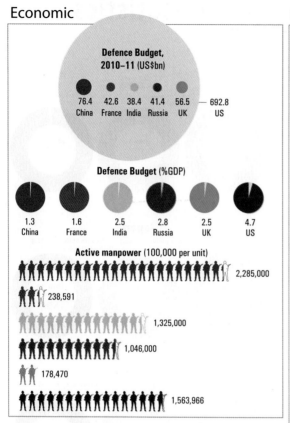

Defence Budget, 2010–11 (US$bn)

76.4 China	42.6 France	38.4 India	41.4 Russia	56.5 UK	692.8 US

Defence Budget (%GDP)

1.3 China	1.6 France	2.5 India	2.8 Russia	2.5 UK	4.7 US

Active manpower (100,000 per unit)

- 2,285,000
- 238,591
- 1,325,000
- 1,046,000
- 178,470
- 1,563,966

Strategic

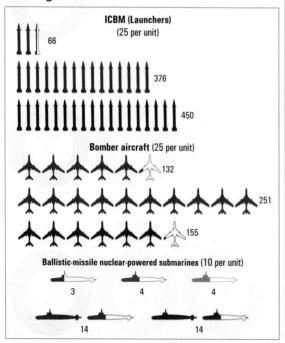

ICBM (Launchers) (25 per unit)

- 66
- 376
- 450

Bomber aircraft (25 per unit)

- 132
- 251
- 155

Ballistic-missile nuclear-powered submarines (10 per unit)

- 3
- 4
- 4
- 14
- 14

Manoeuvre

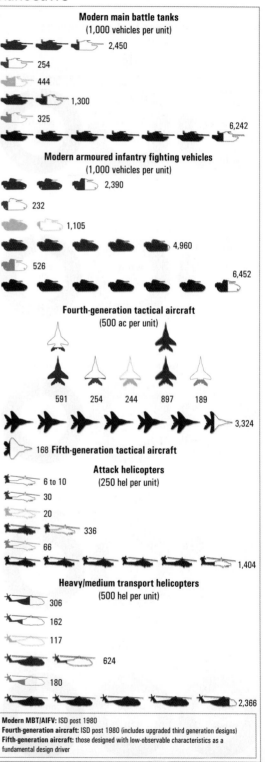

Modern main battle tanks (1,000 vehicles per unit)

- 2,450
- 254
- 444
- 1,300
- 325
- 6,242

Modern armoured infantry fighting vehicles (1,000 vehicles per unit)

- 2,390
- 232
- 1,105
- 4,960
- 526
- 6,452

Fourth-generation tactical aircraft (500 ac per unit)

- 591
- 254
- 244
- 897
- 189
- 3,324

168 **Fifth-generation tactical aircraft**

Attack helicopters (250 hel per unit)

- 6 to 10
- 30
- 20
- 336
- 66
- 1,404

Heavy/medium transport helicopters (500 hel per unit)

- 306
- 162
- 117
- 624
- 180
- 2,366

Modern MBT/AIFV: ISD post 1980
Fourth-generation aircraft: ISD post 1980 (includes upgraded third generation designs)
Fifth-generation aircraft: those designed with low-observable characteristics as a fundamental design driver

Projection

China   France   India   Russia   UK   US

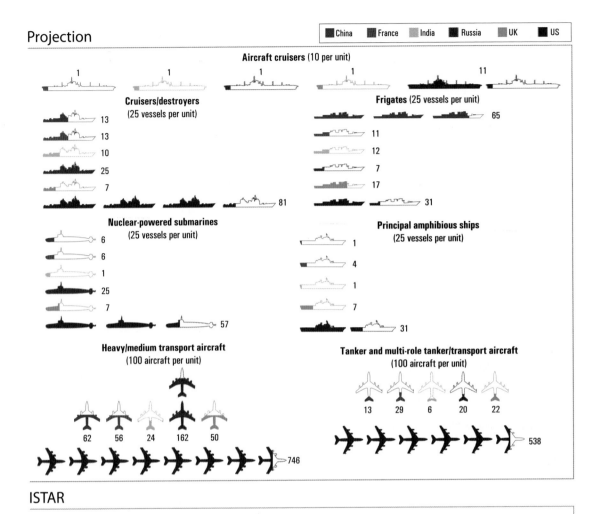

Aircraft cruisers (10 per unit)

Cruisers/destroyers (25 vessels per unit)

Frigates (25 vessels per unit)

Nuclear-powered submarines (25 vessels per unit)

Principal amphibious ships (25 vessels per unit)

Heavy/medium transport aircraft (100 aircraft per unit)

Tanker and multi-role tanker/transport aircraft (100 aircraft per unit)

ISTAR

Airborne early-warning and control aircraft (100 aircraft per unit)

Heavy unmanned aerial vehicles (50 aircraft per unit)

Imagery satellites (5 per unit)

Electronic-/signals-intelligence satellites (5 per unit)

Navigational satellites (5 per unit)

Middle East air power

Air power in the Gulf region came increasingly into focus in 2010 as concern over Iran's nuclear programme continued to mount. The US Central Command, which takes the lead on Gulf security for Washington, in January 2011 held its first 'Regional Combating Weapons of Mass Destruction' symposium. Attendees included officials from Saudi Arabia, the United Arab Emirates and Qatar. The US has substantial air assets based in theatre, as well as the air element of the US Navy's 5th Fleet.

Israel also retains the option of a direct strike should broader diplomatic efforts fail to provide guarantees that Iran's aim in future will be limited to nuclear-power generation. Any effort directly to curtail Iran's nuclear programme by targeting related sites would almost certainly involve a significant element of air power. This raises questions over Tehran's ability to directly, and indirectly respond to any air strikes against its nuclear facilities. This graphic shows selected elements of the relative air power of the states in the region along with key air-to-surface and surface-to-air weapons systems.

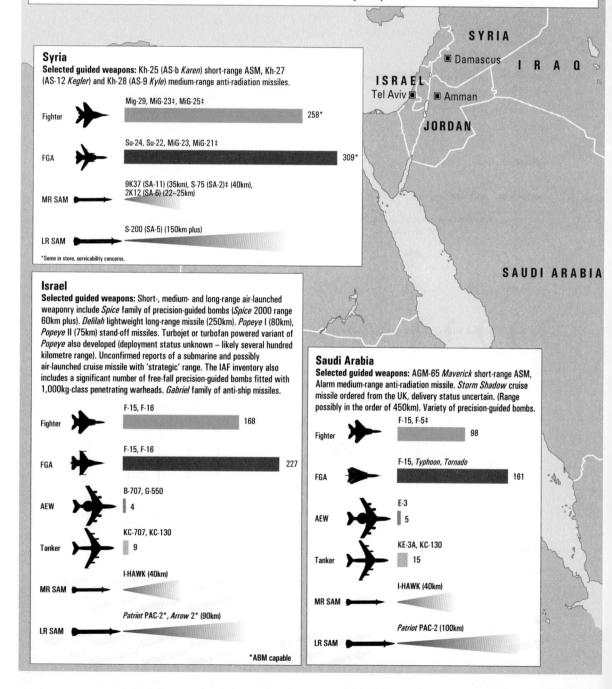

Syria
Selected guided weapons: Kh-25 (AS-b *Karen*) short-range ASM, Kh-27 (AS-12 *Kegler*) and Kh-28 (AS-9 *Kyle*) medium-range anti-radiation missiles.

Fighter — Mig-29, MiG-23‡, MiG-25‡ — 258*

FGA — Su-24, Su-22, MiG-23, MiG-21‡ — 309*

MR SAM — 9K37 (SA-11) (35km), S-75 (SA-2)‡ (40km), 2K12 (SA-6) (22–25km)

LR SAM — S-200 (SA-5) (150km plus)

*Some in store, servicability concerns.

Israel
Selected guided weapons: Short-, medium- and long-range air-launched weaponry include *Spice* family of precision-guided bombs (*Spice* 2000 range 60km plus). *Delilah* lightweight long-range missile (250km). *Popeye* I (80km), *Popeye* II (75km) stand-off missiles. Turbojet or turbofan powered variant of *Popeye* also developed (deployment status unknown – likely several hundred kilometre range). Unconfirmed reports of a submarine and possibly air-launched cruise missile with 'strategic' range. The IAF inventory also includes a significant number of free-fall precision-guided bombs fitted with 1,000kg-class penetrating warheads. *Gabriel* family of anti-ship missiles.

Fighter — F-15, F-16 — 168

FGA — F-15, F-16 — 227

AEW — B-707, G-550 — 4

Tanker — KC-707, KC-130 — 9

MR SAM — I-HAWK (40km)

LR SAM — *Patriot* PAC-2*, *Arrow* 2* (90km)

*ABM capable

Saudi Arabia
Selected guided weapons: AGM-65 *Maverick* short-range ASM, Alarm medium-range anti-radiation missile. *Storm Shadow* cruise missile ordered from the UK, delivery status uncertain. (Range possibly in the order of 450km). Variety of precision-guided bombs.

Fighter — F-15, F-5‡ — 98

FGA — F-15, *Typhoon*, *Tornado* — 161

AEW — E-3 — 5

Tanker — KE-3A, KC-130 — 15

MR SAM — I-HAWK (40km)

LR SAM — *Patriot* PAC-2 (100km)

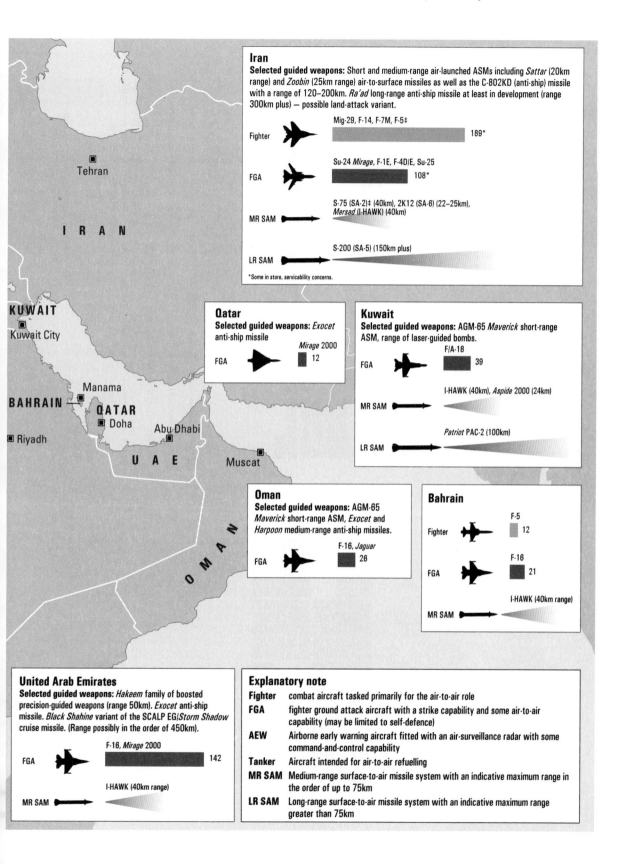

Iran
Selected guided weapons: Short and medium-range air-launched ASMs including *Sattar* (20km range) and *Zoobin* (25km range) air-to-surface missiles as well as the C-802KD (anti-ship) missile with a range of 120–200km. *Ra'ad* long-range anti-ship missile at least in development (range 300km plus) — possible land-attack variant.

Fighter — Mig-29, F-14, F-7M, F-5‡ — 189*

FGA — Su-24 *Mirage*, F-1E, F-4D/E, Su-25 — 108*

MR SAM — S-75 (SA-2)‡ (40km), 2K12 (SA-6) (22–25km), *Mersad* (I-HAWK) (40km)

LR SAM — S-200 (SA-5) (150km plus)

Some in store, serviceability concerns.

Qatar
Selected guided weapons: *Exocet* anti-ship missile

FGA — *Mirage* 2000 — 12

Kuwait
Selected guided weapons: AGM-65 *Maverick* short-range ASM, range of laser-guided bombs.

FGA — F/A-18 — 39

MR SAM — I-HAWK (40km), *Aspide* 2000 (24km)

LR SAM — *Patriot* PAC-2 (100km)

Oman
Selected guided weapons: AGM-65 *Maverick* short-range ASM, *Exocet* and *Harpoon* medium-range anti-ship missiles.

FGA — F-16, *Jaguar* — 26

Bahrain

Fighter — F-5 — 12

FGA — F-16 — 21

MR SAM — I-HAWK (40km range)

United Arab Emirates
Selected guided weapons: *Hakeem* family of boosted precision-guided weapons (range 50km). *Exocet* anti-ship missile. *Black Shahine* variant of the SCALP EG/*Storm Shadow* cruise missile. (Range possibly in the order of 450km).

FGA — F-16, *Mirage* 2000 — 142

MR SAM — I-HAWK (40km range)

Explanatory note

Fighter	combat aircraft tasked primarily for the air-to-air role
FGA	fighter ground attack aircraft with a strike capability and some air-to-air capability (may be limited to self-defence)
AEW	Airborne early warning aircraft fitted with an air-surveillance radar with some command-and-control capability
Tanker	Aircraft intended for air-to-air refuelling
MR SAM	Medium-range surface-to-air missile system with an indicative maximum range in the order of up to 75km
LR SAM	Long-range surface-to-air missile system with an indicative maximum range greater than 75km

Map labels: Tehran, I R A N, KUWAIT, Kuwait City, Manama, BAHRAIN, QATAR, Doha, Abu Dhabi, Riyadh, U A E, Muscat, O M A N

NATO airlift 2011

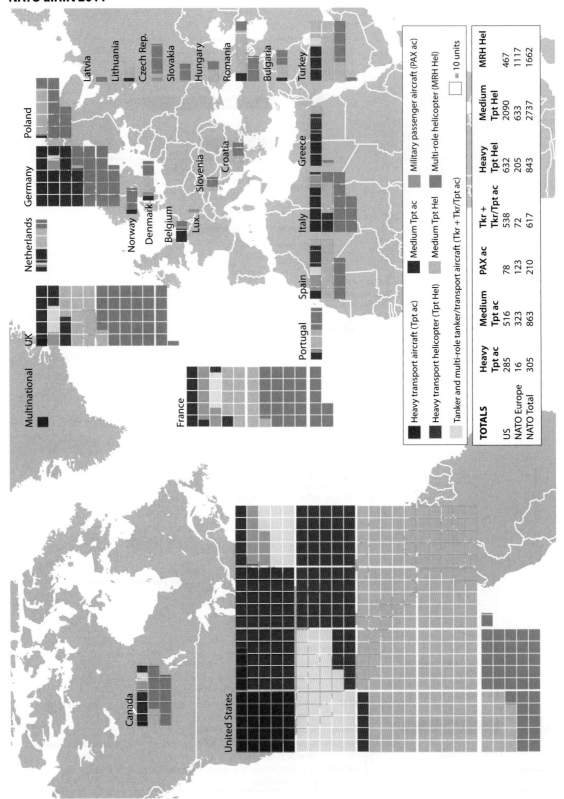

TOTALS	Heavy Tpt ac	Medium Tpt ac	PAX ac	Tkr + Tkr/Tpt ac	Heavy Tpt Hel	Medium Tpt Hel	MRH Hel
US	285	516	78	538	632	2090	467
NATO Europe	16	323	123	72	205	633	1117
NATO Total	305	863	210	617	843	2737	1662

Legend:
- Heavy transport aircraft (Tpt ac)
- Medium Tpt ac
- Military passenger aircraft (PAX ac)
- Heavy transport helicopter (Tpt Hel)
- Medium Tpt Hel
- Multi-role helicopter (MRH Hel)
- Tanker and multi-role tanker/transport aircraft (Tkr + Tkr/Tpt ac)
- ☐ = 10 units

Key global tactical aviation assets 1990–2010

Fighter, fighter-ground-attack and attack-aircraft holdings

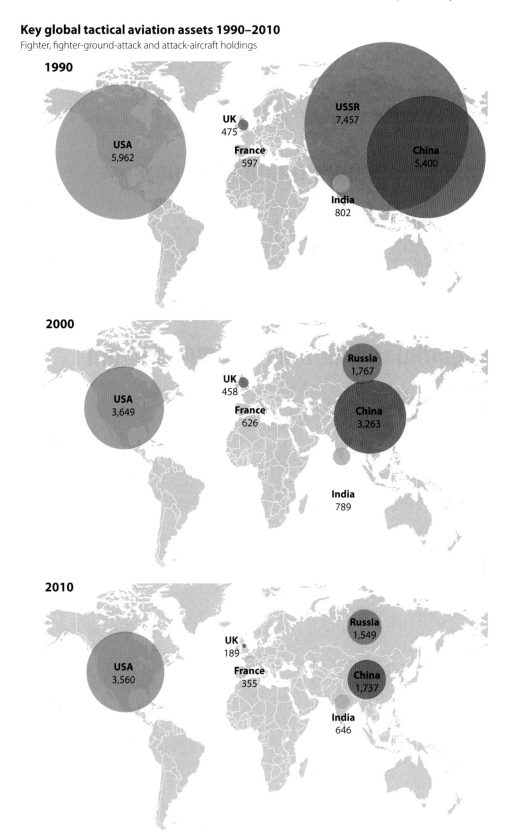

1990

UK
475

USA
5,962

France
597

USSR
7,457

China
5,400

India
802

2000

UK
458

USA
3,649

France
626

Russia
1,767

China
3,263

India
789

2010

UK
189

USA
3,560

France
355

Russia
1,549

China
1,737

India
646

East Asia: selected maritime assets

Nuclear powered submarines* ■ Submarines ■ Coastal/inshore submarines ■ Aircraft carriers ■ Cruisers ■ Destroyers ■ Frigates

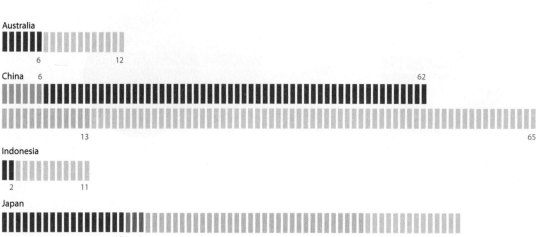

Australia
6   12

China   6   62
                                                                13   65

Indonesia
2   11

Japan
18 1   2   30   16

North Korea
22   48   3

South Korea
12   11 1   6   12

Malaysia
2   8

Philippines
1

Russia (Pacific Fleet)
18 1   7

Singapore
5   6

Taiwan (ROC)
4   4   22

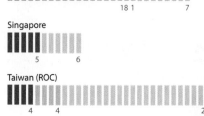

Thailand
1   10

USA (7th fleet)†
3 1 2   7

Vietnam
2

*not incl ballistic missile submarines

†Forward deployed forces only

Chapter Three
North America

THE UNITED STATES

In 2010 the administration of President Barack Obama placed its stamp on US national security policy. The publication of the National Security Strategy and the Quadrennial Defense Review showed both marked shifts away from the policies of the administration of President George W. Bush as well as continuity. The continued service of Dr Robert Gates as secretary of defense – the first time in US history that a secretary of defense has stayed on after a change in presidents – provided stability in the transition between the two administrations as well as a firm and respected hand on the helm at the Department of Defense (DoD). Gates has served as defense secretary since December 2006, and during his tenure has overseen the significant reduction of US forces in Iraq and a change in their status from combatants to advisers to the Iraqi security forces. The reductions in Iraq were in keeping with the Status of Forces Agreement (SOFA) negotiated by the Bush administration and Obama's campaign pledge to end the war in Iraq (see p. 293). Simultaneously, Gates has supported Obama's shift in US strategy in Afghanistan and a significant troop build-up there (see p. 9).

At the September 2010 change-of-command ceremony in Baghdad between General Raymond T. Odierno and General Lloyd J. Austin, US Vice President Joe Biden stated that the United States had ended its combat mission in Iraq and that 'Iraqi troops are taking lead responsibility for their country's security'. The war in Iraq had by that point exacted a heavy price: 4,427 American service members killed and some 34,268 wounded. In August 2010 – the same month in which Gates announced his intention to leave his post in 2011 – US troop numbers, which at their peak had reached 176,000, had fallen to 49,775. American commanders in Iraq expect that troop numbers will continue to be reduced to at least the low hundreds as the final SOFA deadline of 31 December 2011 approaches. The time-constrained goal of the new Iraq Training and Advisory Mission is to train and mentor the Iraqi security forces in the hope that they can reach what the US government has termed the 'minimum essential capability' standards needed to replace all US forces by the end of 2011 (see p. 294). Meanwhile, in March 2010, inconclusive national elections created uncertainty as Prime Minister Nuri al-Maliki and his chief rival Ayad Allawi maneuvered to garner sufficient support to form a government, though an accommodation seemed to have been reached by November 2010. Efforts to shape the government, particularly by Iran, complicated the effort.

Afghanistan has become the Obama administration's principal military effort, as the president promised when he ran for office. In September 2009, General Stanley McChrystal, then commander of the International Security Assistance Force (ISAF), submitted a new strategy for Afghanistan consisting of three options, all of which entailed substantial troop increases. The first was to send 10–11,000 American troops to train local security forces; the second was to launch a 40,000-strong deployment to conduct population-centric counter-insurgency (COIN); and the third was to deploy 85,000 troops to conduct a robust COIN effort. McChrystal recommended the second course, noting that such a deployment would consist of four combat brigades with enablers. The principal alternative to McChrystal's COIN strategy came from Vice President Biden, who recommended 'counterterrorism plus', relying heavily on special-operations forces and precision strike to kill or capture terrorists and thus keep al-Qaeda and associated groupings out of Afghanistan, rather than the substantial forces and resources associated with COIN and nation building. Obama chose the COIN approach, but with limits. In a 1 December 2009 speech, he said that he had 'determined that it is in our vital national interest to send an additional 30,000 US troops to Afghanistan. After 18 months, our troops will begin to come home. These are the resources that we need to seize the initiative, while building the Afghan capacity that can allow for a responsible transition of our forces out of Afghanistan.' In a document leaked to author Bob Woodward and quoted in his book *Obama's Wars*, the administration acknowledged that 'this approach is not fully resourced counterinsurgency or nation building, but a narrower approach tied more tightly to the core goal of disrupting, dismantling and eventually defeating al-Qaeda and preventing al-Qaeda's return to safe haven in Afghanistan or Pakistan'.

The new strategy, and the US political–military dynamic, were buffeted in June 2010 when *Rolling Stone* magazine published an interview with General McChrystal that contained highly unflattering remarks about the administration, made mainly by McChrystal's staff. In the aftermath of the interview, McChrystal was summoned back to Washington and relieved of his post as ISAF commander; he subsequently retired from the US Army. President Obama turned to General David A. Petraeus, then commander of US Central Command (USCENTCOM) – and McChrystal's boss – to replace him. Petraeus was perhaps the obvious candidate to succeed McChrystal, given his previous experience in Iraq. In his new post, Petraeus seems to have largely adopted the strategy pursued by McChrystal, while the July 2011 drawdown date (which many analysts had assessed as dependent on conditions on the ground) has been qualified by the common NATO commitment to transition to Afghan security control by the end of 2014, articulated at the Lisbon Summit (see p. 74). The Afghanistan–Pakistan Security Review, published in December, was clear about the overall goal of the mission: 'It's not to defeat every last threat to the security of Afghanistan, because, ultimately, it is Afghans who must secure their country. And it's not nation-building, because it is Afghans who must build their nation. Rather, we are focused on disrupting, dismantling and defeating al Qaeda in Afghanistan and Pakistan, and preventing its capacity to threaten America and our allies in the future.' The transition to Afghan security control, meanwhile, 'will begin in 2011 and conclude in 2014'. It is unclear, however, how the United States will reconcile the need to strengthen Afghan institutions so that they are prepared to assume the lead in security, rule of law, and other areas with Washington's explicit rejection of state building. The effort to improve state capacity and governmental functioning in Afghanistan has been hindered by a fragmented international effort and the corrosive effects of systematised administrative corruption.

Defence policy and strategy

In 2010 the administration published a number of policy documents outlining its national security philosophy: the Quadrennial Defense Review; the National Security Strategy; the Nuclear Posture Review; the Ballistic Missile Defense Review; and the Space Policy Review. Individually and collectively, these documents reflect a philosophical shift towards a more measured view of the use of military force from that held by the Bush administration. The Obama administration has indicated that it views the use of military force as a last resort, rather than as a means by which the government can take pre-emptive action. Unlike the 2006 National Security Strategy, which noted that, 'if necessary, under long-standing principles of self defense, we do not rule out the use of force before attacks occur', its 2010 successor, in a segment headed 'Use of Force', asserted that 'while the use of force is sometimes necessary, we will exhaust other options before war whenever we can, and carefully weigh the costs and risks of action against the costs and risks of inaction'. (The document goes on to say that 'the United States must reserve the right to act unilaterally if necessary to defend our nation and our interests, yet we will also seek to adhere to standards that govern the use of force'.) The new policy positions outlined in this and the other documents were generally well received, though critics asserted they lacked a longer-term focus, and in some cases a clear set of 'messages'; it may be that the range and complexity of the security and military challenges faced by the administration preclude this.

The Quadrennial Defense Review (QDR), published in February 2010, was, in the words of Secretary Gates, 'a truly wartime QDR'. For the first time, it places the current conflicts at the top of our budgeting, policy, and program priorities.' The QDR's two principal objectives were, firstly, to 'further rebalance the capabilities of America's Armed Forces to prevail in today's wars, while building the capabilities needed to deal with future threats'; and secondly, to reform the department's institutions and processes to meet warfighters' urgent requirements and to fix the weapons-acquisition process so that the armed forces received 'weapons that are usable, affordable, and truly needed'. This latter statement is more than an aspiration; it reflects Gates's track record of challenging, restructuring and even cancelling acquisition programmes (see *The Military Balance 2010*, pp. 15–16).

The QDR identifies four overriding priorities for the US defence and security establishment: to prevail in today's wars; to prevent and deter conflict; to prepare to defeat adversaries and succeed in a wide range of contingencies; and to preserve and enhance the all-volunteer force. Again, the heaviest emphasis was on the near term, perhaps best seen in the statement that ongoing operations in Iraq, Afghanistan

Table 2. 2010 QDR: Main Elements of the US Force Structure

Army	Navy	Marine Corps	Air Force	Special Operations
• 4 corps headquarters • 18 division headquarters: 73 total brigade combat teams (45 Active Component and 28 Reserve Component), consisting of 40 infantry brigade combat teams; 8 *Stryker* brigade combat teams; 25 heavy brigade combat teams • 21 combat aviation brigades (13 AC and 8 RC) • 15 *Patriot* battalions; 7 Terminal High Altitude Area Defense batteries	• 10–11 aircraft carriers and 10 carrier air wings • 84–88 large surface combatants, including 21–32 ballistic-missile defence-capable combatants and *Aegis* Ashore • 14–28 small surface combatants (+14 mine counter-measure ships) • 29–31 amphibious warfare ships • 53–55 attack submarines and 4 guided-missile submarines • 126–171 land-based intelligence, surveillance, reconnaissance and electronic warfare aircraft (manned and unmanned) • 3 maritime prepositioning squadrons • 30–33 combat logistics force ships (+1 Mobile Landing Platform) • 17–25 command and support vessels • 51 roll-on/roll-off strategic sealift vessels	• 3 Marine expeditionary forces • 4 Marine divisions (3 AC and 1 RC) consisting of 11 infantry regiments and 4 artillery regiments • 4 Marine aircraft wings (6 fixed-wing groups, 7 rotary-wing groups, 4 control groups, 4 support groups) • 4 Marine logistics groups (9 combat logistics regiments) • 7 Marine expeditionary unit command elements	• 8 intelligence, surveillance, reconnaissance wing-equivalents (with up to 380 primary mission aircraft) • 30–32 airlift and aerial refuelling wing-equivalents (with 33 primary mission aircraft per wing-equivalent) • 10–11 theatre strike wing-equivalents (with 72 primary mission aircraft per wing-equivalent) • 5 long-range strike (bomber) wings (with up to 96 primary mission aircraft) • 6 air superiority wing-equivalents (with 72 primary mission aircraft per wing-equivalent) • 3 command and control wings and 5 fully operational air and space operations centres (with a total of 27 primary mission aircraft) • 10 space and cyberspace wings	• Approximately 660 special-operations teams (includes Army Special Forces Operational Detachment-Alpha (ODA) teams; Navy Sea, Air, and Land (SEAL) platoons, Marine special-operations teams; Air Force special-tactics teams; and operational aviation detachments (OADs)) • 3 Ranger battalions • 165 tilt-rotor/fixed-wing mobility and fire support primary mission aircraft

and elsewhere to defeat al-Qaeda and its allies 'will substantially determine the size and shape of major elements of U.S. military forces for years to come'. The inclusion of the 'all-volunteer force' as a priority reflects the understanding that nine years of continuous fighting have exacted a heavy toll on US service personnel and their families (see *The Military Balance 2009*, p. 17; and *The Military Balance 2010*, p. 15).

In terms of meeting defence needs beyond those of current contingencies, the QDR is more vague, although it does briefly note increased focus and investments in defending the US and supporting civil authorities, a new Air–Sea Battle concept, long-range strike, space and cyberspace capabilities, and countering anti-access capabilities. The document also implies that the DoD will rely on allies, partners and the wider US government more heavily to meet future demands. Clearly, the looming reductions in defence spending by key NATO allies (few of whom meet the current goal of spending 2% of GDP on defence), and the accompanying decrease in military capacity and capability, will affect how much the United States can rely on allies and partners as a hedge against future

challenges. To meet the demands of its strategy across the FY2011–15 Future Years Defense Program (FYDP), the DoD identified the following force-structure requirements, with the important caveat that the demands of ongoing operations on various parts of the force were a key factor in this structure and that 'the appropriate size and mix of forces' would be revisited as demand evolves.

The military sections of the May 2010 National Security Strategy (NSS) echoed the tone of the QDR, though in general terms. Key segments of the broader 'security' section in the document stressed the need to strengthen security and resilience at home; disrupt, dismantle and defeat al-Qaeda and violent extremist affiliates in Afghanistan, Pakistan and around the world; reverse the spread of nuclear and biological weapons and secure nuclear materials; advance peace and prosperity in the greater Middle East; invest in the capacity of strong and capable partners; and secure cyberspace. Importantly, the NSS, while reserving the right of the United States to use military force unilaterally to defend itself and its interests, said that it would do so only after all other options

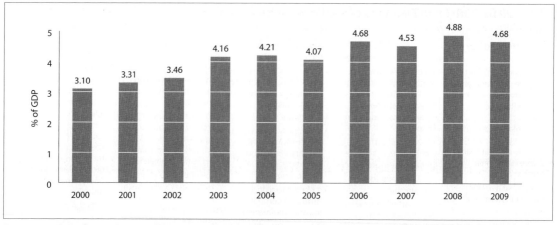

Figure 1 **US Defence Expenditure (Budget Authority)** as % of GDP

were exhausted, and that it would 'seek broad international support, working with such institutions as NATO and the U.N. Security Council'.

In the aftermath of the QDR, a congressionally chartered, bipartisan QDR Independent Panel, chaired by former Defense Secretary William Perry and former National Security Advisor Stephen Hadley, reviewed the DoD document to assess its assumptions, strategy, findings and risks, and to provide possible alternative force structures, along with the resulting resource implications. The key finding in their August 2010 report was that, while the QDR was

Table 3 **DoD's War Budget Authority by Title FY2009 (US$bn)**

Regular Titles	2009
Military Operations	18.7
Operations & Maintenance	82.2
Defence Health	1.8
Other Defence Programmes	0.3
Procurement	32.0
R,D,T & E	1.3
Working Capital Funds	0.4
Military Construction	0.9
Subtotal: Regular Titles	**138.0**
Special Funds	
Iraqi Freedom Fund	0
Afghan Sec Forces Training Fund	5.6
Iraq Sec Forces Training Fund	1.0
Joint IED Defeat Fund	3.1
Strategic Reserve Readiness Fund	0
Pakistan Counterinsurgency Fund	0
Subtotal: Special Funds	**10.1**
DoD Total	**148.2**

valuable for 'responding to the threats America now faces and winning the wars in which America is now engaged', it did not provide the 'kind of long term planning document that Congress envisioned when it enacted the QDR requirement'. Panel members themselves identified five long-term 'gravest potential threats' to US interests, namely radical Islamist extremism and the threat of terrorism; the rise of new global powers in Asia; continued struggle for power in the Persian Gulf and the greater Middle East; an accelerating global competition for resources; and persistent problems from failed and failing states. In the view of the panel, the US was not prepared for these challenges. It recommended a sweeping overhaul of the 1940s-era defence framework designed to address the Soviet Union; reforming the National Security Strategic Planning Process; and increasing US military and 'soft power' capabilities. The panel also warned that 'the aging of the inventories and equipment used by the services, the decline in the size of the Navy, escalating personnel entitlements, increased overhead and procurement costs, and the growing stress on the force means that a train wreck is coming in the areas of personnel, acquisition, and force structure'.

In April 2010 the DoD published the Nuclear Posture Review (NPR). While expressing the administration's long-term goal of a world free of nuclear weapons, the document also realistically acknowledged that this may not occur in the foreseeable future. Still, it noted the president's 'determination to take concrete steps toward that goal, including by reducing the number of nuclear weapons and their role in U.S. national security strategy'. It also contained the president's pledge that, 'as long as nuclear weapons exist, the

Table 4 **Budget Authority for Iraq, Afghanistan, and Other Global War on Terror Operations FY2001–FY2011 (US$bn)**

Operation and Source of Funding	FY01 & FY02	FY03	FY04	FY05	FY06	FY07	FY08	FY09	FY10	FY11 Pending Request	Cumulative Total FY01–FY11 incl Request
Iraq											
Dept of Defense	0	50.0	56.4	83.4	98.1	127.2	138.5	92.0	61.1	45.8	705.5
Foreign Aid & Diplomatic Operations	0	3.0	19.5	2.0	3.2	3.2	2.7	2.2	3.3	3.9	43.0
VA Medical	0	0	0	0.2	0.4	0.9	0.9	1.2	1.5	1.4	6.5
Total Iraq	0.0	53.0	75.9	85.5	101.6	131.2	142.1	95.5	65.9	51.1	748.2
Afghanistan											
Dept of Defense	20.0	14.0	12.4	17.2	17.9	37.2	40.6	56.1	99.5	113.5	428.4
Foreign Aid & Diplomatic Operations	0.8	0.7	2.2	2.8	1.1	1.9	2.7	3.1	4.9	4.6	24.9
VA Medical	0	0	0	0	0	0.1	0.1	0.2	0.5	1.2	2.1
Total Afghanistan	20.8	14.7	14.5	20.0	19.0	39.2	43.5	59.5	104.9	119.4	455.4
Enhanced Security											
Dept of Defense	13.0	8.0	3.7	2.1	0.8	0.5	0.1	0.1	0.1	0.1	28.6
Total Enhanced Security	13.0	8.0	3.7	2.1	0.8	0.5	0.1	0.1	0.1	0.1	28.6
DOD Unallocated	0	5.5	0	0	0	0	0	0	0	0	5.5
Total All Missions	33.8	81.2	94.1	107.6	121.4	170.9	185.7	155.1	171.0	170.7	1,291.5

United States will maintain a safe, secure, and effective arsenal, both to deter potential adversaries and to assure U.S. allies and other security partners that they can count on America's security commitments'.

The administration also took concrete steps to begin reducing US and Russian nuclear weapons. On 5 December 2009, the Strategic Arms Reduction Treaty I (START I), signed on 31 July 1991 and in effect since 5 December 1994, expired. Following months of negotiations, Obama and Russian President Dmitry Medvedev signed a successor treaty on 8 April 2010, known as New START. The new treaty places a 1,550 limit on accountable strategic warheads, with separate sub-limits on launchers. The new treaty cleared the Senate Foreign Relations Committee with a bipartisan vote of 14–4, and was approved by the Senate on 22 December on a vote of 71–26, six votes more than the two-thirds required for ratification. Thirteen Republican senators voted in favour, although several key Republican senators opposed the treaty, believing that it endangers the US by not taking sufficient steps to modernise the US nuclear arsenal.

The February 2010 Ballistic Missile Defense Review report, while recognising the growing threat to the United States and its deployed forces, sought to present a slightly different approach to missile defence than that of the Bush administration. Importantly, it called for new capabilities to be thoroughly tested before being fielded and to be fiscally sustainable, and advocated partnering with other nations. The June 2010 National Space Policy report also called for international cooperation in space. Nevertheless, it expressed Washington's commitment to using space for defence purposes by calling for investment in space situational-awareness capabilities and launch-vehicle technologies, and for the development of 'capabilities, plans, and options to deter, defend against, and, if necessary, defeat efforts to interfere with or attack US or allied space systems'.

In the realms of future military readiness and capabilities, the central question facing the US military services, as they gain some breathing space with the drawdown in Iraq, concerns what contingencies they should prepare for. Traditionally, the US has reduced its forces (particularly its ground forces) at the conclusion of a major military intervention. This was the case after the Second World War, the Korean War, Vietnam and the Cold War. What seems somewhat different in the aftermath of the Iraq withdrawal is the assumption that the United States still faces an 'era of persistent conflict'. Thus, US military capacity must remain sufficient to meet the threats posed to a nation that is no longer isolated from the rest of the world when it brings its troops home. The lesson of 9/11 is that the homeland is vulnerable to attack, and that the US must be prepared to address threats to

Table 5 **US National Defense Budget Authority FY2008–FY2011**

(US$million)	2008	2009	2010 Base + Bridge	Remaining Supplemental Request	Total	2011 Request Base	Overseas Contingency Operations	Total
Military Personnel	139,033	149,290	154,492	1,896	156,388	143,524	15,276	158,600
Operations & Maintenance	256,223	271,564	272,827	24,494	297,321	200,875	117,071	317,946
Procurement	165,006	135,438	129,650	4,843	134,493	112,873	24,612	137,485
R,D,T & E	79,567	80,005	80,366	277	80,643	76,131	635	76,766
Military Construction	22,064	26,815	22,420	521	22,941	16,924	1,257	18,181
Family Housing	2,846	3,848	2,259	8	2,267	1,823	-	1,823
Other	9,976	554	1,916	975	2891	785	485	1,270
Total Department of Defense	**674,715**	**667,514**	**663,930**	**33,014**	**696,944**	**552,935**	**159,336**	**712,271**
Department of Energy (defence-related)	16,636	22,991			17,765			18,835
Other (defence-related)	4,917	7,258			7,429			7,617
Total National Defense	**696,268**	**697,763**			**722,138**			**738,723**

its security offshore. The US government must determine which capabilities and force structure will be needed in the future once the major ground-force engagements in Iraq and Afghanistan end.

The US Army went some way towards answering the readiness question with the publication of US Army Training and Doctrine Command (TRADOC) Pamphlet 525-3-0, *The Army Capstone Concept Operational Adaptability – Operating Under Conditions of Uncertainty and Complexity in an Era of Persistent Conflict*. This document calls for Army forces that are 'capable of developing the situation in close contact with the enemy and civilian populations'. This is a major shift away from early concepts that relied on exquisite situational awareness provided by information technologies. In short, the Army is stepping back from the promises of the Revolution in Military Affairs (RMA) and returning to a Clausewitzian view that recognises the importance of uncertainty and friction in war – and the human element. (This is not to say that the 'transformational' military technologies discussed in the context of the RMA are now seen as necessarily secondary; rather, as noted in *The Military Balance 2010* (p. 5), such technologies are seen as a key component of, rather than a framework for, the application of military force.) The Army continues to adapt its training and education programmes in keeping with the demands of the war in Afghanistan and its Capstone Concept and associated documents, emphasising knowledge of the culture and history of the countries in which it operates; it has also added negotiation as a key leadership skill. The Army is increasingly focused on how best to ensure that mili-

tary operations contribute to achieving political goals, and on ways of operating as part of multinational and civil–military teams in conflicts involving overlapping problems such as state weakness, organised crime, insurgency, narco-trafficking and criminality.

The major issue facing the US Marine Corps is the viability of its traditional mission of amphibious assault. General James T. Conway, former commandant of the Marine Corps, wrote in the *Marine Corps Vision & Strategy 2025* that the Corps must focus on ways it can fulfil its 'unique role' and extend its 'legacy as the world's premier expeditionary fighting force' after what Conway termed 'sustained operations ashore'. A central element of this vision was the Expeditionary Fighting Vehicle (EFV) programme. However, this programme was cancelled by Defense Secretary Gates on 6 January 2011 as part of a spending and reform package. The capability requirement is now to be met with a more affordable vehicle. Gates said that the EFV decision 'did not call into question the Marine's amphibious assault mission', but debate continues over the Corps' roles, and this will likely shape the future US Marine Corps, perhaps both structurally and doctrinally.

Meanwhile, the US Navy views the withdrawals from Iraq and, eventually, Afghanistan as possibly increasing its importance to US national security. These views were voiced by Admiral Gary Roughead, chief of naval operations, at an October 2010 University of Chicago-sponsored conference on terrorism and strategy. The admiral was quite explicit about his view of the future, and of the US Navy's predominant role in that future:

it is quite likely to be an era where we can expect two broad developmental trends to take place. That sovereignty concerns, either where we are operating or where we are operating from, will limit or outright preclude the involvement of extensive land-based forces in the future, making offshore options for deterrence at sea and power projection from the sea all the more essential. And that this will be accompanied by a corresponding reawakening to the naval dimension of American power and influence, capable of assuring the mechanisms of global prosperity in peace and countering anti-access or area denial in times of conflict.

Admiral Roughead's views are not that far removed from what has historically happened in the aftermath of protracted US overseas engagements: the ground forces come home and the Navy and the Air Force assume a leading role in deterrence and offshore presence.

The US Air Force has, unlike the Navy, yet to publicly articulate its position, but its embrace of concepts like Air–Sea Battle suggest that it too is preparing for a future beyond the wars in Iraq and Afghanistan. Its partnership with the Navy, although still in its infancy, may be one of the more noteworthy developments of the past year, and could well signal the emergence of a new set of joint relationships among the military services. According to the Chief of the US Air Force, General Norton Schwartz, speaking at the US National Press Club in October 2010, the Air–Sea Battle concept will focus on three areas of joint cooperation: the institutional, 'with dedicated organizational constructs that normalize Navy and Air Force collaboration'; the conceptual, 'with institutional agreement on how Navy and Air Force systems will integrate and operate together'; and the material, 'with interoperability among current systems and integrated acquisition strategies for future Joint capabilities'.

All of the military services have been active in developing an array of cyber capabilities. The establishment of a new US Cyber Command, which is subordinate to US Strategic Command, will help give focus and coherence to the separate service efforts. Attention will be given to offensive and defensive capabilities. Thorny concepts, like cyber deterrence, are far from maturity (see p. 26).

A defence budget under pressure

Despite the flurry of new policy documents over the past year, there is no question that US defence spending is coming under greater pressure. US

Aviation programmes

At the end of 2010 the Pentagon was grappling with a raft of issues on the tri-service F-35 Joint Strike Fighter, culminating in Defense Secretary Gates's 6 January 2011 announcement that the F-35B Advanced Short Take-off/ Vertical Landing (ASTOVL) variant was being put on 'probation'. In two years a decision will be taken as to whether and how to go ahead with this version of the F-35. The Pentagon carried out a Technical Baseline Review of the F-35 in 2010.

Despite the problems, the DoD placed a US$3.49bn contract with Lockheed Martin in November 2010 for LRIP 4 (low-rate initial production lot 4) aircraft covering the production of 31 aircraft. The order is split mainly between the Air Force's F-35A and the US Marine Corps' F-35B, with a small number of the Navy's F-35C making up the remainder. LRIP 4 also includes one F-35B for the UK, though London has decided to drop the B model in favour of the F-35C. The British decision to shift from the B to the C model reportedly caused consternation among the US Marines, reflecting concern over the vulnerability of the ASTOVL variant.

The F-35 schedule slip means that the US Navy will purchase at least another 41 F/A-18E/F aircraft. The Navy is trying to minimise the overall drop in its combat-aircraft fleet in light of the ongoing retirement of F/A-18C/D aircraft and its transition to the F-35C. (In September 2010, the Navy secured a 124-aircraft, multi-year deal for 66 F/A-18 E/F and 58 EA-18G *Growler* aircraft.) The US Marine Corps also faces a similar issue in managing the size of its fighter fleet, a concern now compounded by the doubts surrounding the F-35B.

The Air Force, meanwhile, is now on the third iteration of an effort to procure a successor to the KC-135 for its KC-X programme. Rival offers from EADS (the KC-45 variant of the Airbus A330) and Boeing's 767-based bid are now with the Pentagon. The two offers were submitted in July 2010, with a decision due in early 2011. The Army is also beginning to look at a replacement for its fleet of *Kiowa Warrior* helicopters, with an analysis of alternatives for its Armed Aerial Scout project due to be concluded early in the second quarter of 2011.

Table 6 **Major US Research & Development FY2009–FY2011**

Classification	Designation	Estimate FY2009 Value ($m)	Estimate FY2010* Value ($m)	Request FY2011 Value ($m)
Joint				
UAV	Global Hawk	743	783	780
tpt	C-130	206	231	42
JTRS	Joint Tactical Radio System	843	876	689
JTRS	Missile Defense	9372	8186	8,462
	Joint Air to Ground Missile	118	127	231
	Small Diameter Bomb	145	197	197
Army				
	Warfighter Information Network	393	180	191
hel	AH-64 Apache	197	151	93
APC	Stryker	80	90	136
Navy				
EW	EA-18G Growler	55	55	22
FGA	F-35 JSF	1744	1741	1,376
hel	V-22	68	89	46
MPA	P-8A Poseidon	1129	1162	929
CVN	Carrier Replacement	147	173	94
LCS	Littoral Combat Ship	368	360	226
SSN	Virginia	190	154	155
AEW	E-2 Hawkeye	482	364	171
SAM	Standard	237	182	96
Air Force				
bbr	B-2	364	415	260
tpt	C-17	162	162	177
tpt	C-5	127	95	59
FGA	F-22	605	569	576
FGA	F-15	198	311	222
FGA	F-16	127	141	129
FGA	F-35 JSF	1734	1858	884
tkr	KC-X	23	439	863
sat	SBIRS	542	512	530

*data refer to budget request rather than final appropriation

defence spending nearly doubled over the last decade (in constant dollars), but much like the American economy as a whole, most of the growth was allocated to consumption (in support of ongoing wars) rather than investment. Defense Secretary Gates initiated a series of cost-saving initiatives in 2010 in the hope of freeing up funding for badly needed modernisation and investment. His goal was to identify some US$100 billion worth of savings over the next five years by targeting some of the inevitable bloat, including growth in general officer ranks, that has crept into the system. He also targeted what many perceived to be an underperforming organisation by calling for the elimination of Joint Forces Command (JFCOM), one of ten combatant commands. JFCOM has been criticised for having many disconnected elements, and eliminating it would reduce the need for one four-star general-officer position, one three-star position, and several two- and one-star positions. Ironically, Gates's search for efficiencies excluded specific examination of the ongoing wars, which is perhaps where the greatest savings could be found.

Gates also moved to begin to address rapidly increasing personnel costs, which are consuming an ever greater portion of the defence budget. Health costs alone will exceed US$50bn in FY2011, which is nearing 10% of the base DoD budget. Announcing the outcome of the savings efforts on 6 January 2011, Gates identified proposals from the Air Force, Army and Navy which included personnel cuts and staff changes. He has also said that the FY2012 budget will include proposals for military health-care reform.

Despite Gates's impressive earlier successes in curtailing or cutting programmes deemed to be lingering Cold War legacies – perhaps most notably his early termination of the Air Force F-22 fighter programme – early returns on his latest cost-cutting efforts may be more mixed. Congress has seemed much less willing to support Gates on ending the C-17 inter-theatre airlift programme and the second engine for the F-35 Joint Strike Fighter. (The US generally maintains a two-engine programme for its fighter aircraft to ensure competition between engine manufacturers, and to provide an alternative power source should one engine encounter problems.) It remains reluctant to support defence cuts tied to civilian jobs, particularly while unemployment is at almost 10%. While it is not yet clear how a new Congress may act, the threat of a presidential veto may not be enough to deliver Gates a victory.

Whether or not Gates succeeds with his latest savings efforts, he must be aware that US defence spending will soon be under real long-term pressure. With troop commitments down in Iraq to just under 50,000 and likely to decrease more, and with coming pressure to decrease commitments in Afghanistan, the administration will be expected to cut, not simply cap, defence spending. Recent reports from two separate US deficit-reduction commissions clearly point

Table 7 **US National Defense Budget Function[1] and Other Selected Budgets[2] 1992, 2001–11**

(US$bn)	National Defense Budget Function		Department of Defense		Atomic Energy Defense Activities	Department of Homeland Security	Veterans Administration	Total Federal Government Outlays	Total Federal Budget Surplus/ Deficit
FY	BA	Outlay	BA	Outlay	BA	BA (Gross)	BA		
1992	295.1	298.3	282.1	286.9	10.6	n.a.	33.9	1,381	-290
2001	335.5	305.5	319.4	290.9	13.0	16.4	47.6	1,863	128
2002	362.1	348.5	344.9	331.9	14.9	30.5	52.1	2,011	-157
2003	456.2	404.9	437.9	387.3	16.4	30.8	59.1	2,160	-377
2004	490.6	455.9	471.0	436.5	16.8	31.6	60.5	2,293	-412
2005	505.7	495.3	483.9	474.1	17.9	100.7	69.2	2,472	-318
2006	617.1	521.8	593.7	499.3	17.4	32.4	71.0	2,655	-248
2007	625.8	551.2	602.9	528.6	17.2	39.7	79.5	2,728	-160
2008	696.3	616.1	674.7	594.6	16.6	50.6	88.3	2,982	-458
2009	697.8	661	667.5	631.9	22.9	45.3	96.9	3,517	-1,412
2010 est.	722.1	719.2	696.9	688.4	17.7	41.4	125	3,720	-1,555
2011 est.	738.7	749.7	712.1	717	18.8	45.9	122	3,833	-1,266

Notes

FY = Fiscal Year (1 October–30 September)
[1] The National Defense Budget Function subsumes funding for the DoD, the Department of Energy Atomic Energy Defense Activities and some smaller support agencies (including Federal Emergency Management and Selective Service System). It does not include funding for International Security Assistance (under International Affairs), the Veterans Administration, the US Coast Guard (Department of Homeland Security), nor for the National Aeronautics and Space Administration (NASA). Funding for civil projects administered by the DoD is excluded from the figures cited here.
[2] Early in each calendar year, the US government presents its defence budget to Congress for the next fiscal year, which begins on 1 October. The government also presents its Future Years' Defense Program (FYDP), which covers the next fiscal year plus the following five. Until approved by Congress, the Budget is called the Budget Request; after approval, it becomes the Budget Authority.

to defence as a target for cuts. The coming cuts may not be as deep as previous post-war drawdowns; cuts following the wars in Korea and Vietnam and the end of the Cold War amounted to 30–40% of total spending. Some of the savings will come naturally by eliminating the routine supplemental appropriations that have underwritten the day-to-day costs of the wars. This has accounted for approximately 20% of total defence spending over the past decade, or more than US$1 trillion. But this alone will not begin to generate the kind of savings the White House and Congress will likely seek. The current effort to save US$100bn over five years is sure to appear meagre as government expenditure comes under increasing pressure, regardless of which political party is in power. The pressure will intensify as interest rates climb, adding greatly to the burdens of national debt. At current levels of debt, every percentage point of interest will add more than $140bn a year to the US government's debt-service bill.

Four services in need of investment

This pressure on spending comes at an unfortunate time for the US military. Despite unprecedented levels of expenditure, each of the services is in need of modernisation and investment. The Navy and Air Force, which were to have benefited from substantial investment this past decade, found themselves instead supporting ground operations in Iraq and Afghanistan. Both services are managing ageing fleets (ships and aircraft), and both have had to adjust their expectations regarding funds available for investment. As ships and aircraft age, the cost of maintaining them grows, which in turn places even greater pressure on investment accounts. Shipbuilding and aircraft construction are at historically low levels. The Air Force and Navy, along with the Marine Corps, have waited more than a decade for the F-35. Few insiders now believe the three services will ever procure the numbers that are currently projected. Meanwhile, Gates's decision to put the F-35B on probation, continuing development problems with this variant, and the UK's decision to withdraw from the F-35B programme and to procure a single variant, the F-35C, instead, leaves the Advanced Short Take-off/Vertical Landing (ASTOVL) portion of the programme in real jeopardy. Surface combatants, submarines, long-range bombers, refuelling aircraft and space communications and surveillance assets are all in the queue for future investment, to say nothing of assets such as unmanned aerial vehicles, which are so important to the current wars. The Air Force is poised to move

Table 8 **US Agency for International Development: International Affairs Budget**

Budget Authority in US$m	FY2009 Actual	FY2010 Estimate	FY2011 Request
Economic Assistance for Europe, Eurasia and Central Asia	922	741	716
Economic Support Fund	7,116	8,164	7,811
Foreign Military Financing	6,321	4,255	5,473
Global Health and Child Survival	7,339	7,779	8,513
International Disaster Assistance	820	845	860
International Military Education and Training	93	108	110
International Narcotics Control and Law Enforcement	1,876	2,356	2136
Migration and Refugee Assistance	1,614	1,693	1,605
Non-proliferation, Anti-Terrorism, De-mining	631	754	757
Pakistan Counterinsurgency Capability Fund	700	–	1,200
Peacekeeping Operations	530	331	285
Total International Affairs (excluding supplementals)	**52,631**	**55,028**	**58,492**

ahead with its aircraft-refuelling programme, known as the KC-X, by early next year. It would also like to begin work on a next-generation bomber, though funding for this remains in doubt.

While the Navy has made reasonable progress with its tactical aviation programme, it has sought to generate internal and external support for ship-building. In the near term, Navy shipbuilding is weighted disproportionately toward small combat-ants, though its long-term plan is to have a mixed large and small fleet. Analysts at the Congressional Research Service and Congressional Budget Office note that funding for Navy shipbuilding is probably not sufficient to sustain a 313-ship combatant force over the longer term. The Army and Marine Corps have benefited from substantial investment during the course of the wars in Iraq and Afghanistan, but not necessarily the investment they see as essential to prepare themselves for the coming decade. While much current ground equipment is relatively new, it is not modern in the way that Army and Marine Corps leaders had hoped. Programmes like the future combat system (FCS) and expeditionary fighting vehicle were to be the mainstays of future ground operations, yet the Army FCS vehicle programme was terminated and the ground combat vehicle (GCV) programme is yet to be fully defined (it is clearly less ambitious than FCS). The Marine Corps proved unsuccessful in its fight for the expeditionary fighting vehicle (EFV)

programme; many in the Pentagon questioned the viability of the concept (slow-moving ship-to-shore vehicles) in the face of enemy precision weapons. The cancellation of the EFV and growing doubt over the F-35B could see the Marine Corps lose two of the three pillars it had defined for its future force, the third being the V-22 tilt-rotor aircraft. Indeed, it now looks increasingly likely that the Army and Marine Corps will need to be content with the modernisation efforts that took place during the course of the wars, such as the integration into force structures of differing types of protected vehicles and greater numbers of unmanned systems, to name but two.

Given real pressures to cut defence spending, rapidly escalating personnel costs, and a long-overdue need to invest in new materiel, the DoD will almost certainly be unable to both modernise and maintain current manpower levels. Army and Marine Corps chiefs have already signalled their unease at taking any manpower reductions, motivated by the goal of bringing more normalcy to troop rotations, and Navy and Air Force chiefs have pointed out that their personnel numbers have already been cut and that additional cuts are not welcome, certainly not until the ground forces return to something more like pre-war strengths. But as commitments in Iraq and Afghanistan draw down, pressure on troop strength will be inevitable. Unless personnel costs can be brought under control, some analysts assert that US ground forces will see troop levels that more closely approximate the Clinton years rather than the Bush or early Obama years. Short of a national emergency, this supply of troops will dictate the size of commit-ments abroad, including advisory and counter-terrorism missions.

Basic missions in need of review

All of this is sure to lead to discussions, and probably disagreements, among the four services over basic missions. Debates are under way over the degree to which the Army and Marine Corps will be asked, when they return to a more normal posture, to focus more on training and advising foreign forces than on direct combat roles. President Obama seemed to affirm this when, speaking at the UN, he stated that 'from South Asia to the Horn of Africa, we are moving toward a more targeted approach – one that strengthens our partners and dismantles terrorist networks without deploying large American armies'. Gates has also been consistent in urging this theme and his succes-sors are likely to do so as well. The counter-insurgency emphasis that currently dominates ground-force training and deployments, and which has required large numbers of US troops in Iraq and Afghanistan, could change to smaller deployments to more areas of the world, with an emphasis on training, advising and assisting foreign partners. Moreover, as political leaders look for Plan B or even Plan C in Afghanistan, the outcome might lead to even greater reliance on air and special-operations forces.

At the same time, US ground forces will be challenged to redefine their roles in future large-scale combat missions. The experiences in Iraq and Afghanistan have led to increased appreciation of the challenges in undertaking overseas military operations and have further complicated defence planning assumptions and procurement decisions. Nevertheless, US ground forces must maintain expeditionary capabilities and structures sufficient to deter potential adversaries from threatening allies and security partners, much as they did in Operations *Desert Shield* and *Desert Storm*. Operations in both Afghanistan and Iraq have highlighted the limitations of working through indigenous forces (along with the possibilities). It is clear that ground forces will still play important roles in defending the territory of key partners. They may even be called upon to secure or destroy nuclear weapons should states such as North Korea collapse, or to support special forces in recovering nuclear weapons should they fall into terrorist hands. Because many of the unconventional forces faced by the US Army in recent years have possessed capabilities previously seen only in the fielded forces of nation states, the Army has made a compelling argument that it must maintain its more traditional combined-arms capability. While the Army will continue to be structured around brigade combat team (BCT) formations, its emerging doctrinal literature indicates a continuing move towards operational and institutional adaptability (in the face of adaptable adversaries) and joint-force operations in an increasingly broad range of contingencies. The complex future operating environment is acknowledged by the Army in its August 2010 *Army Operating Concept*: 'to succeed in the future operational environment, Army forces must be able to conduct full-spectrum operations, rapidly transition between types of operations, and conduct operations decentralized [*sic*] consistent with the concept of mission command'. Ground forces will also play more important roles in protecting US territory and supporting civil authorities in the event of a catastrophic attack on the US homeland.

The Navy and Air Force see their futures linked to Asia. While political leaders hope that the economic and political rise of emerging powers such as China and India will be smooth, it is logical to prepare for the possibility of friction and tension. China watchers point to the country's growing array of military capabilities, and US Navy and Air Force leaders, working jointly with US Pacific Command, have quietly been working on ways to maintain US power and influence in the Asia-Pacific. Emerging concepts, such as Air–Sea Battle, have brought the Navy and Air Force into closer cooperation, and recent disputes in the South China Sea, and greater assertiveness by China over access to coastal waters and surrounding seas, have added further urgency to this type of cooperation. It is unclear, however, whether the two services can work fast enough to develop concepts and field needed capabilities to arrest shifts to China's advantage in several important areas. Concerns over aircraft-carrier and air-base survivability, among others, have begun to raise doubts about the long-term viability of US commitments among key partners in Asia. Furthermore, some US allies are concerned by the regional perception of damage to US military prestige arising from operations in Afghanistan. At the same time, should uncertainty over China's intentions and actions continue along with the rapid growth in its military capabilities, it is practically inevitable that political and, more particularly, military linkages between the US and its Asia-Pacific allies and partners will tighten. For the United States, the ability to project credible military power from a distance will be a crucial element in this equation. Such a capability will be necessary to contend with other problems, such as the possible emergence of a nuclear-capable Iran. The inevitable sorting of missions among the US military services will not come without tensions. Debates over budgets will only serve to mask the real debate about how the US will organise its military capabilities to meet the demands of the coming decade.

CANADA

On 16 November 2010, it was announced that Canada would withdraw combat forces from Afghanistan in 2011. Given that this announcement had been expected (see *The Military Balance 2010*, p. 21), its main outcome was to define the nature and focus of Canada's remaining presence. After 2011, Canadian forces will continue to be deployed in Afghanistan until March 2014, though in a non-combat role as part of the NATO Training Mission – Afghanistan. It was announced that the Canadian contingent would consist of up to 950 military trainers and support personnel, along with up to 45 police advisers. The security-assistance element of this role will be complemented by a foreign-affairs and development agenda, including programmes to develop health and education, diplomatic initiatives to assist dialogue and cooperation among regional states, and humanitarian assistance. Until 2011, Canada will remain the lead nation in the Kandahar Provincial Reconstruction Team, with around 3,000 personnel deployed in the south, as well as in Kabul. At time of writing, six Operational Mentor and Liaison Teams and four Police Operational Mentor and Liaison Teams served to fulfil the current mentoring role. When the Canadians draw down their combat capability (which as of late 2010 included a LAV-3 battalion and a rotary-wing and fixed-wing contingent), a US brigade HQ will take over Kandahar City. However, drawing conclusions simply by reading the numbers can be misleading: although the Canadian battlegroup will leave, the 950 personnel then to be deployed will actually constitute an increase in the specific training capability in relation to those currently in the south.

Despite the new role now envisaged for Canada's contribution in Afghanistan, and the planned slow-down in defence-budget growth outlined in the 2010 defence budget, Ottawa has shown no sign that it plans to dramatically change the priorities outlined in the 2008 *Canada First* defence strategy. Indeed, 2010 saw a further raft of announced investments in infrastructure at Greenwood, Bagotville, Cold Lake and Comox, among other locations. Canadian investment in the high north continued in 2010, with the latest *Operation Nanook* (see *The Military Balance 2010*, p. 21) leading to the first deployment of the Maritime Component Command, along with 1,000 personnel, in the Arctic, as well as the first C-17 deployment to Resolute Bay.

In September, Bagotville and Cold Lake were announced as the preferred base locations for Canada's future F-35 *Lightning* aircraft. In July, Ottawa announced that it intended to acquire 65 F-35s and associated weapons and material, at a cost of approximately CDN$9m (US$9m), with delivery expected to start in 2016. Twenty-four of these aircraft will be based at Bagotville; 24 at Cold Lake; and 17 will be used for training at an as yet undecided location. June 2010, meanwhile, saw the delivery of Canada's

first C-130J transport aircraft. (Canada had hitherto operated –E and –H models.) The improvements to the Canadian *Hercules* fleet, such as reduced aircrew due to the glass cockpit, and the greater range and fuel economy stemming from increased altitude and improved power plants, led to shorter landing and take-off requirements and, according to the Canadian Department of National Defence, a 50% reduction in climb-time compared to the older models. The 2007 contract was valued at US$1.4bn, and deliveries of the rest of the fleet will continue from 2010.

Canada also re-established the 1st Canadian Division in October 2010. This is intended to give Canada the capability to deploy command and control functions to joint forces 'during domestic and complex missions'. The division has three high-readiness tasks: humanitarian operations; non-combatant evacuation operations; and full-spectrum operations. The HQ includes electronic-warfare, engineer, air-defence and counter-IED capabilities.

The June announcement of the National Shipbuilding Procurement Strategy highlighted Ottawa's concern over a perceived erosion in Canada's shipbuilding capacity, which the Department of National Defence said could 'severely hinder Canada's ability to build complex ships cost-effectively, resulting in delays to federal fleet renewal'. Two shipyards are to be selected, by competition, with one to build combat vessels such as the planned Canadian Surface Combatant (to replace capabilities currently seen on the *Iroquois* and *Halifax* classes) and Arctic/Offshore Patrol Vessels, and the other to build non-combat vessels, such as the Joint Support Ship. The latter, which had been cancelled in 2008, remained an aspiration of the government, particularly in light of the *Canada First* strategy, and a process that will lead to the production of a ship design by 2012 was initiated in July. In October, the refit and modernisation programme for HMCS *Halifax* began; this initiates an upgrade programme for the 12 *Halifax*-class vessels whereby they will be fitted with a new command and control system, new radar, a new electronic-warfare system and improved communications and missiles. Meanwhile, Canada withdrew its contingent from Bosnia-Herzegovina in March 2010, ending a 19-year series of deployments of which the last, *Operation Bronze*, began in 2004. Canada retains a military presence in the Balkans with *Operation Kobold*, its contribution to the NATO mission supporting the Kosovo Security Force.

Canada CAN

Canadian Dollar $		2009	2010	2011
GDP	C$$	1.53tr	1.62tr	
	US$	1.34tr	1.57tr	
per capita	US$	39,783	46,331	
Growth	%	-2.5	3.4	
Inflation	%	0.3	1.6	
Def exp	C$$	22.3bn		
	US$	19.6bn		
Def bdgt	C$$	21bn	20.6bn	18.9bn
	US$	18.5bn	19.9bn	
US$1= C$$		1.14	1.03	

Population	33,889,747

Age	0 – 14	15 – 19	20 – 24	25 – 29	30 – 64	65 plus
Male	8.0%	3.3%	3.5%	3.5%	24.4%	7.0%
Female	7.6%	3.2%	3.3%	3.3%	24.1%	8.9%

Capabilities

ACTIVE 65,722 (Army 34,775 Navy 11,025 Air 19,922)

CIVILIAN 4,554 (Coast Guard 4,554)

RESERVE 33,967 (Army 23,153 (Rangers 4,303), Navy 4,167, Air 2,344)

Canadian Forces operations are organised with four joint operational commands. Canada Command (CANADACOM) is responsible for all domestic and continental operations through six regional sub-commands. Canadian Expeditionary Force Command (CEFCOM) is responsible for all international operations. Canadian Special Operations Forces Command (CANSOFCOM) is responsible for generating all Special Forces operations and has forces permanently assigned to it. Canadian Operational Support Command (CANOSCOM) has responsibility for generation and employment of the operational-level support to CANADACOM and CEFCOM (and if required CANSOFCOM) for logistics, movements, general engineering, health services, communications, human resource management and military police support either through its permanently assigned forces or through augmented force generation. CANADACOM and CEFCOM normally have no permanently assigned forces allocated for operations but receive them from force generation commands; Maritime Command (MARCOM), Land Force Command (LFC) and Air Command (AIRCOM). Each of these commands have forces normally assigned to them for force generation by the Chief of Defence Staff (CDS) who has full command. Canadian Forces are expanding and the expected strength will be increasing to 70,000 Regular Force members and 30,000 Reserve Force members (less Rangers).

ORGANISATIONS BY SERVICE

Army (Land Forces) 34,775

FORCES BY ROLE

1 Task Force HQ

Comd	1 TF HQ; 3 bde gp HQ and sig sqn to form national cadre of a multi-national TF HQ or a Land Component Command (LCC) of a joint operation
Mech Inf	1 (Canadian Mechanised) bde gp (1st CMBG) with 1 armd regt, (two *Leopard* 1C2 sqns and 1 armd recce sqn), 2 mech inf bn, 1 lt inf bn, 1 arty regt, 1 cbt engr regt; 2 bde gp (2nd CMBG and 5th CMBG) each with 1 armd recce regt, 2 mech inf bn, 1 lt inf bn, 1 arty regt, 1 cbt engr regt
AD	1 indep regt
Spt/Engr	1 indep regt
Cbt Spt	3 MP pl, 3 MI coy
Logistic	3 svc bn
Med	3 fd amb bn

EQUIPMENT BY TYPE

MBT 121: 20 *Leopard* 2 A6M on lease; 61 *Leopard* 1C2; 40 *Leopard* 2 A4

RECCE 201 LAV-25 *Coyote*

APC 1,220

  APC (T) 332: 64 Bv-206; 235 M-113; 33 M-577

  APC (W) 888: 635 LAV-III *Kodiak* (incl 33 RWS); 175 MILLAV *Bison* (incl 10 EW, 32 amb, 32 repair, 64 recovery); 68 RG-31 *Nyala*; 5 *Cougar*; 5 *Buffalo*

ARTY 295

  TOWED 171 **105mm** 153: 27 C2 (M-101); 98 C3 (M-101); 28 LG1 MK II; **155mm** 18 M-777

  MOR 81mm 100

    SP 81mm 24 *Bison*

AT

  MSL 493

    SP 33 LAV-TOW

    MANPATS 460: 425 *Eryx*; 35 TOW-2A/ITAS

  RCL 84mm 1,075 *Carl Gustav*; M2/M3

  RL 66mm M-72 *LAW*

UAV • ISR • Light *Skylark*

AD

  SAM • SP 33 ADATS

    MANPAD *Starburst*

Land Reserve Organisations 23,153

Canadian Rangers 4,303 Reservists

The Canadian Rangers are a Reserve sub-component of the Canadian Forces, which provide a limited military presence in Canada's northern, coastal and isolated areas. They have sovereignty, public safety and surveillance roles.

Ranger   5 (patrol) gp (165 patrols)

Army Reserves

Most units have only coy sized establishments.

Comd	10 bde gp HQ
Armd Recce	18 regt
Inf	51 regt
Fd Arty	14 regt, 2 indep bty

Signals	6 regt, 16 indep sqn, 1 EW sqn
Engr	7 regt, 3 indep sqn
Cbt Engr	1 regt
MP	4 coy
Log	10 bn
Medical	14 coy, 4 dets
MI	4 coy

Navy (Maritime Command) 11,025

EQUIPMENT BY TYPE
SUBMARINES SSK 4

4 *Victoria* (ex-UK *Upholder*) each with 6 single 533mm TT each with Mk48 *Sea Arrow* HWT (2 currently operational)

PRINCIPAL SURFACE COMBATANTS 15

DESTROYERS • DDHM 3 mod *Iroquois* each with 1 Mk 41 VLS with SM-2MR SAM, 2 triple 324mm ASTT (6 eff.) each with Mk46 LWT, 1 76mm gun, (capacity 2 SH-3 (CH-124) *Sea King* ASW hel)

FRIGATES • FFGHM 12 *Halifax* each with 2 quad lnchr (8 eff.) each with RGM-84 Block II *Harpoon* AShM, 2 octuple Mk48 lnchr (16 eff.) each with RIM-7P *Sea Sparrow* SAM/RIM-162 ESSM SAM, 2 twin 324mm ASTT (4 eff.) with Mk46 LWT, (capacity 1 SH-3 (CH-124) *Sea King* ASW hel)

MINE WARFARE • MINE COUNTERMEASURES • MCO 12 *Kingston*

LOGISTICS AND SUPPORT 18

AOR 2 *Protecteur* each with 3 SH-3 (CH-124) *Sea King* ASW hel

AGOR 1

YDT 8 (2 MCM spt; 6 diving tender/spt)

TRG 9: **AXL** 8 *Orca;* **AXS** 1

FACILITIES

Bases Located at Esquimalt (Pacific), Halifax (Atlantic), Ottawa (National HQ), Quebec City (Naval Reserve HQ). Commanders for MARPAC and MARLANT, directly or through their respective at-sea fleet commander, act as the MCC for the operational commands of CANADACOM and/or CEFCOM.

Reserves 4,167 reservists

HQ	1 HQ located at Quebec
Navy	24 div (tasks: crew 10 of the 12 MCDV; harbour defence; naval control of shipping)

Air Force (Air Command) 19,922 (plus 2,344 Primary Reservists integrated within total Air Force structure)

FORCES BY ROLE

1 CAN Air Division, HQ Winnipeg, is responsible for all CF air op readiness, combat air-spt, air tpt, SAR, MR and trg. This HQ is the ACC HQ for CANADACOM and CEFCOM. 1 CAN Air Div wgs directly support land forces (tac avn and UAV), maritime forces (maritime hel and long range MP), and Special Forces (hel) with OPCOM status. Other wgs undertake directly related air roles (AD, AT, SAR, trg) while remaining under direct 1 CAN Air Div control.

2 CAN Air Div is responsible for Air Force doctrine, initial training and education.

13 Wgs: 1 Wg (Kingston); 3 Wg (Bagotville); 4 Wg (Cold Lake); 5 Wg (Goose Bay); 8 Wg (Trenton); 9 Wg (Gander); 12 Wg (Shearwater); 14 Wg (Greenwood); 15 Wg (Moose Jaw); 16 Wg (Borden); 17 Wg (Winnipeg); 19 Wg (Comox); 22 Wg (North Bay). In addition, an Air Expeditionary Wg (AEW) at Bagotville (up to 550 personnel) will train and deploy together, and will comprise a cmd element, an ops support flt and a mission support flt.

FORCES BY ROLE

Strategic Surveillance	1 (NORAD Regional) HQ located at Winnipeg; 1 Sector HQ at North Bay with 11 North Warning System Long Range; 36 North Warning System Short Range; 4 Coastal; 2 Transportable (total of 53 Radar stn)
FGA	3 sqn with F/A-18A/B *Hornet* (CF-18AM/CF-18BM*)* (1 sqn at Bagotville and 2 sqns at Cold Lake)
ASW	3 sqn (2 sqn at Shearwater, 1 sqn at Victoria) with SH-3 *Sea King* (CH-124)
MP	3 sqn (2 sqn at Greenwood, 1 sqn at Comox) with P-3 *Orion* (CP-140 *Aurora*)
SAR/Tpt	4 sqn with AW-101 *Merlin* (CH-149 *Cormorant*); C-130E/H/J (CC-130); 1 sqn with DHC-5 (CC-115) *Buffalo;*
Tkr/Tpt	1 sqn with KC-130H; 1 sqn with A310/310 MRTT (CC-150/CC-150T)
Tpt	1 tpt sqn with C-17 (CC-177); 1 (utl) sqn with DHC-6 (CC-138) *Twin Otter;* 1 sqn with CL-600 (CC-144B)
Trg	1 nav trg school in Winnipeg with *Dash*-8 (CT-142); 1 SAR trg school in Comox (see also NATO Flt Trg Canada)
Tpt Hel	5 sqn (Edmonton, Borden, Valcartier, St Hubert, Gagetown) with Bell 412 (CH-146 *Griffon);* 3 (cbt spt) sqns (Cold Lake, Bagotville & Goose Bay) with Bell 412 (CH-146 *Griffon);* 1 (Spec Ops) sqn with Bell 412 (CH-146 *Griffon*) (OPCON Canadian Special Operations Command)
ISR UAV	1 unit with *Heron* (CU-170)

EQUIPMENT BY TYPE

AIRCRAFT 95 combat capable

FGA 77: 59 F/A-18A (CF-18AM) *Hornet;* 18 F/A-18B (CF-18BM) *Hornet*

ASW 18 P-3 *Orion* (CP-140 *Aurora*)

TKR/TPT 7: 2 A-310 MRTT(CC-150T); 5 KC-130H

TPT 47: **Heavy** 4 C-17 (CC-177) *Globemaster;* **Medium** 24 C-130E/H (CC-130) *Hercules* (16–E, 8–H, of which 3 grounded) **Light** 10: 6 DHC-5 (CC-115) *Buffalo;* 4 DHC-6 (CC-138) *Twin Otter* **PAX** 9: 3 A310 (CC-150 *Polaris*); 6 CL-600 (CC-144B)

TRG 4 DHC-8 (CT-142) *Nav Trainer*

HELICOPTERS
ASW 28 SH-3 (CH-124) *Sea King*
MRH 78 Bell 412 (CH-146 *Griffon*) (incl 10 spec ops)
TPT 20 **Heavy** 6 CH-47D (CH-147D) *Chinook* **Medium** 14
AW-101 *Merlin* (CH-149 *Cormorant*)
UAV • ISR • Heavy 5 *Heron* (CU-170) (leased for 3 yrs)
RADARS 53
AD RADAR • NORTH WARNING SYSTEM 47: 11
Long Range; 36 Short Range
STRATEGIC 6: 4 Coastal; 2 Transportable
MSL
ASM AGM-65 *Maverick*
AAM • IR AAM AIM-9L *Sidewinder* **SARH AAM** AIM-7M *Sparrow* **ARH AAM** AIM-120C AMRAAM
BOMBS
Conventional: Mk 82; Mk 83; Mk 84
Laser-Guided: GBU-10/GBU-12/GBU-16 *Paveway II*;
GBU-24 *Paveway III*

NATO Flight Training Canada
AIRCRAFT
TRG 45: 26 T-6A *Texan II* (CT-156 *Harvard II*); 19 *Hawk*
115 (CT-155) (advanced wpns/tactics trg)

FACILITIES
Trg	1 pilot trg school in Moose Jaw with *Hawk* 115 (CT-155), T-6A *Texan II* (CT-156 *Harvard II*); 1 pilot trg school in Cold Lake with *Hawk* 115 (CT-155)

Contracted Flying Services – Southport
AIRCRAFT
TRG 34: 11 Grob G120A; 7 *King Air* C90B; 7 *Jet Ranger*
(CH-139); 9 Bell 412 (CH-146*)*
TPT • Light 7 Beech C90B *King Air*
TRG 11 G-120A
HELICOPTERS
MRH 9 Bell 412 (CH-146)
TPT • Light 7 Bell 206; *Jet Ranger* (CH-139)

FACILITIES
Trg	1 pilot trg school in Southport with Grob 120A, *Jet Ranger/Griffon* and *King Air*

Canadian Special Operations Forces Command 1,500
FORCES BY ROLE
Comd	1 HQ
SF	1 regt (Canadian Special Operations Regiment) located at CFB Petawawa
Counter-Terrorist	1 bn (JTF2) located at Dwyer Hill (CT, Surv, security advice and CP)
Special Ops Avn	1 sqn, with Bell 412 (CH-146 *Griffon*) located at CFB Petawawa
CBRN	Canadian Joint Incidence Response Unit (CJIRU) located at CFB Trenton

EQUIPMENT BY TYPE
RECCE 4 LAV *Bison* (NBC)
HEL • MRH Bell 412 (CH-146 *Griffon*)

Canadian Operational Support Command 2,000
Comd	1 HQ
Engr	1 engr support coy
Sigs	CAN Forces Joint Sig Regt (strategic and op signals and info management)
MP	1 (close protection) coy
Log	3 CAN support units; 4 Cdn movement units; 1 postal coy (1 supply, 1 postal, 1 movement unit); 1 CAN Material Support Gp (2x supply depots, 3 ammo depots)
Medical	1 (1 CAN Forces Field Hospital) bn

Canadian Coast Guard 4,554 (civilian)
Incl Department of Fisheries and Oceans; all platforms are designated as non-combatant.
PATROL AND COASTAL COMBATANTS 73
PSO 2: 1 *Leonard J Cowley*; 1 *Sir Wilfred Grenfell*
PCO 7: 2 *Cape Roger*; 1 *Dumit*; 1 *Eckaloo*; 1 *Gordon Reid*; 1 *Nahidik*; 1 *Tanu*;
PCC 4: 1 *Arrrow Post*; 1 *Harp*; 2 *Louisbourg*;
PB 60: 4 *Cove Island*; 4 *Point Henry*; 3 *Post*; 1 *Quebecois*; 1 *Tembah*; 1 *Vakta*; 5 Type 100; 10 Type 300-A; 31 Type-300B
AMPHIBIOUS • LANDING CRAFT • UCAC 4
LOGISTICS AND SUPPORT 35
AG 5
AGB 13 (2 hvy; 4 med; 7 lt)
AGOR 10 (coastal and offshore fishery vessels)
AGOS 7
HELICOPTERS • TPT 22 **Medium** 1 S-61 **Light** 21: 3 Bell 206L *Long Ranger*; 4 Bell 212; 14 Bo-105

DEPLOYMENT

AFGHANISTAN
NATO • ISAF • *Operation Athena/Archer* 2,922; **Army:** 1 bde HQ, 1 inf BG with (1 lt inf bn HQ; 3 lt inf coy; 1 armd sqn; 1 armd recce sqn; 1 arty bty; 1 UAV flt; 1 cbt engr sqn); 1 MP coy; 20 *Leopard C2* MBT; some LAV III *Kodiak*; some LAV-25 *Coyote*; 6 M-777; 6 CH-47 *Chinook* (CH-147); 8 Bell 412 (CH-146 *Griffon*); *Heron* (CU-170)

BOSNIA-HERZEGOVINA
OSCE • Bosnia and Herzegovina 2

CYPRUS
UN • UNFICYP (*Operation Snowgoose*) 1

DEMOCRATIC REPUBLIC OF THE CONGO
UN • MONUSCO (*Operation Crocodile*) 10 obs

EGYPT
MFO (*Operation Calumet*) 28

GERMANY
NATO (ACO) 287

HAITI
UN • MINUSTAH (*Operation Hamlet*) 8

MIDDLE EAST
UN • UNTSO (*Operation Jade*) 8 obs

SERBIA

NATO • KFOR • *Joint Enterprise* (*Operation Kobold*) 5
OSCE • Serbia 1
OSCE • Kosovo 4

SIERRA LEONE

IMATT (*Operation Sculpture*) 8

SUDAN

UN • UNAMID 5
UN • UNMIS (*Operation Safari*) 7; 20 obs

SYRIA/ISRAEL

UN • UNDOF (*Operation Gladius*) 2

UNITED STATES

US CENTCOM (*Operation Foundation*) 3
US NORTHCOM/NORAD/NATO (ACT) 303

FOREIGN FORCES

United States 133

United States US

United States Dollar $		2009	2010	2011
GDP	US$	14.1tr	14.6tr	
per capita	US$	45,989	46,040	
Growth	%	-2.4	3.3	
Inflation	%	-0.4	1.4	
National Def Budget BA	US$	697.8bn	722.1bn	
Outlay	US$	690.3bn	712.8bn	
Request BA	US$			738.7bn
Population	317,641,087			

Age	0 – 14	15 – 19	20 – 24	25 – 29	30 – 64	65 plus
Male	10.3%	3.5%	3.6%	3.5%	22.7%	5.7%
Female	9.8%	3.4%	3.5%	3.4%	23.3%	7.5%

Capabilities

ACTIVE 1,563,996 (Army 639,063 Navy 336,289 Air 340,990 US Marine Corps 204,056 US Coast Guard 43,598)

CIVILIAN 11,035 (US Special Operations Command 3,376 US Coast Guard 7,659)

RESERVE 871,240 (Army 483,393 Navy 102,998 Air 170,695 Marine Corps Reserve 106,670 US Coast Guard 7,484)

ORGANISATIONS BY SERVICE

US Strategic Command

HQ at Offutt AFB (NE). Five missions: US nuclear deterrent; missile defence; global strike; info ops; ISR

US Navy

SUBMARINES • STRATEGIC • SSBN 14 *Ohio* (mod) SSBN 730 each with up to 24 UGM-133A *Trident* D-5 strategic SLBM

US Air Force • Global Strike Command

Msl   9 sqn at 3 AFB with 450 LGM-30G *Minuteman III* (capacity 1-3 MIRV Mk12/ Mk12A per missile)

Bbr   6 sqn (incl 1 AFRC) at 2 AFB with 71 B-52H *Stratofortress* each with up to 20 AGM-86B nuclear ALCM and/or AGM-129A nuclear ALCM; 2 sqn at 1 AFB with 19 B-2A *Spirit* each with up to 16 free-fall bombs (or up to 80 when fitted with Small Diameter Bombs); 4 B-52 test hvy bbr; 1 B-2 test hvy bbr

Strategic Recce/Intelligence Collection (Satellites)

SPACE BASED SYSTEMS
  SATELLITES 60
    IMAGERY 5: 3 *Improved Crystal* (visible and infra-red imagery, resolution 6 inches); 2 *Lacrosse* (*Onyx* radar imaging satellite)
    ELINT/SIGINT 17: 3 *Mentor* (advanced *Orion*); 1 Advanced *Mentor*; 3 *Trumpet*; 2 *Mercury*; 8 SBWASS (Space Based Wide Area Surveillance System); Naval Ocean Surveillance System
    ELECTRONIC OCEAN RECCE SATELLITE 6 DMSP-5
    SATELLITE TIMING AND RANGING 32: 12 NAVSTAR Block I/II/IIA; 20 NAVSTAR Block IIR (components of Global Positioning System (GPS))
  SENSORS • NUCLEAR DETONATION DETEC-TION 24: (detects and evaluates nuclear detonations. Sensors deployed in NAVSTAR satellites)

Strategic Defenses – Early Warning

North American Aerospace Defense Command (NORAD), a combined US–CAN org.
SPACE BASED SYSTEMS • SATELLITES 4 Defense Support Programme *DSP* (Infra-red surveillance and warning system. Detects missile launches, nuclear detonations, ac in afterburn, spacecraft and terrestrial infra-red events. Approved constellation: 3 operational satellites; 1 operational on-orbit spare)
  NORTH WARNING SYSTEM 15 North Warning System Long Range (range 200nm); 40 North Warning System Short Range (range 80nm)
  OVER-THE-HORIZON-BACKSCATTER RADAR (OTH-B) 2: 1 AN/FPS-118 *OTH-B* (500–3,000nm) located at Mountain Home AFB (ID); 1 non-operational located at Maine (ME)
  STRATEGIC 2 Ballistic Missile Early Warning System *BMEWS* located at Thule, GL and Fylingdales Moor, UK; 1 (primary mission to track ICBM and SLBM; also used to track satellites) located at Clear (AK)
  SPACETRACK SYSTEM 11: 8 Spacetrack Radar located at Incirlik (TUR), Eglin (FL), Cavalier AFS (ND), Clear (AK), Thule (GL), Fylingdales Moor (UK), Beale AFB (CA), Cape Cod (MA); 3 Spacetrack Optical

Trackers located at Socorro (NM), Maui (HI), Diego Garcia (BIOT)

USN SPACE SURVEILLANCE SYSTEM *NAV SPASUR* 3 strategic transmitting stations; 6 strategic receiving sites in southeast US

PERIMETER ACQUISITION RADAR ATTACK CHARACTERISATION SYSTEM *PARCS* 1 at Cavalier AFS, (ND)

PAVE PAWS 3 at Beale AFB (CA), Cape Cod AFS (MA), Clear AFS (AK); 1 (phased array radar 5,500km range) located at Otis AFB (MA)

DETECTION AND TRACKING RADARS Kwajalein Atoll, Ascension Island, Antigua, Kaena Point (HI), MIT Lincoln Laboratory (MA)

GROUND BASED ELECTRO OPTICAL DEEP SPACE SURVEILLANCE SYSTEM *GEODSS* Socorro (NM), Maui (HI), Diego Garcia (BIOT)

STRATEGIC DEFENCES – MISSILE DEFENCES

SEA-BASED: *Aegis* engagement cruisers and destroyers
LAND-BASED: 21 ground-based interceptors at Fort Greeley, (AK); 3 ground-based interceptors at Vandenburg, (CA).

US Army 566,065; 46,878 active ARNG; 26,120 active AR (total 639,063)

FORCES BY ROLE

Comd	6 army HQ; 3 corps HQ; 10 div HQ
Armd	16 HBCT (each: 2 (combined arms) armd/ armd inf bn, 1 armd recce sqn, 1 SP arty bn, 1 BSTB, 1 BSB)
Armd Cav	1 (3rd) regt with (3 cav sqn (each: 3 cav tps, 1 tk coy, 1 arty bty), 1 air cav sqn with (3 atk tps, 1 lift coy), 1 chemical coy, 1 engr coy, 1 int coy); 1(11th) regt (OPFOR)
Armd Inf	2 (170th & 172nd) bde (each: 1 armd bn, 2 armd inf bn, 1 armd recce tp, 1 SP arty bty, 1 cbt engr bn, 1 BSB)
Mech Inf	6 SBCT (each: 1 HQ coy, 3 mech inf bn, 1 fd arty bn, 1 recce sqn, 1 AT coy, 1 engr coy, 1 sigs coy, 1 int coy, 1 BSB)
Lt Inf	10 IBCT (each: 2 inf bn, 1 recce sqn, 1 fd arty bn, 1 BSB, 1 BSTB)
Air Aslt	4 BCT (each: 2 air aslt bn, 1 RSTA bn, 1 arty bn, 1 BSB, 1 BSTB (1 int coy, 1 engr coy, 1 sigs coy))
AB	6 BCT (each: 2 para bn, 1 recce bn, 1 arty bn, 1 BSB, 1 BSTB (1 int coy, 1 engr coy, 1 sigs coy))
Arty	6 (Fires) bde (each: HQ coy, 1 MRL bn, 1 UAV coy, 1 TA coy, 1 BSB bn)
AD	5 bde with MIM-104 *Patriot*
Engr	5 bde
ISTAR	3 BfSB (each: 1 recce and surv sqn, 1 BSTB bn, 1 int bn)
Sigs	7 bde
MP	4 bde
Int	5 bde; 1 regt; 2 gp

Cbt Spt	3 (Manoeuvre enhancement) bde (each: 1 spt bn, 1 sigs coy)
Spt	13 (Sustainment) bde (each: 1 BSTB, 2 Cbt Spt bn, 1 Sigs coy)
CBRN	1 (CBRNE) comd with (1 chemical bde with (2 chemical bn), 1 asymmetric warfare regt)
EOD	2 EOD gp (each: 2 EOD bn)
Avn	12 (Cbt Avn) bde (4 hvy, 6 med, 2 lt) (each: 1 aslt hel bn, 2 atk hel bn, 1 avn spt bn, 1 gen spt avn bn); 1 (theatre avn) bde

Reserve Organisations

Army National Guard 358,391 reservists (incl 46,878 active)

Normally dual funded by DoD and states. For civil emergency responses can be mobilised by state governor. Federal government can mobilise for major pan-sate emergencies and for overseas operations. Currently capable of manning 8 divs after mobilisation. Under the army's transformation process, the ARNG will assume an end-state structure consisting of 28 BCT (7 HBCT, 1 SBCT, 20 IBCT)

FORCES BY ROLE

Comd	8 div HQ
Armd	7 HBCT, 3 (combined arms) bn
Recce	3 RSTA sqn
Mech Inf	1 SBCT (equipping)
Lt Inf	20 IBCT; 11 indep bn
Arty	7 (Fires) bde
AD	2 bde with MIM-104 *Patriot*; FIM-92A *Avenger*
Engr	4 bde
ISTAR	5 BfSB (each: 1 recce/surv sqn, 1 BSTB, 1 int bn)
Sigs	2 bde
MP	3 bde
Int	1 bde
Cbt Spt	10 (Manoeuvre enhancement) bde (transforming)
Spt	9 spt bde, 17 regional spt gps
CBRN	1 chemical bde; 32 WMD-CST (Weapons of Mass Destruction–Civil Support Team) unit
EOD	1 EOD regt
Avn	2 (hvy cbt avn) bde; 6 (air expeditionary) bde (each: 1 aslt hel bn, 1 atk hel bn, 1 gen spt avn bn, 1 avn spt bn, 1 spt/sy hel bn (each: 3 spt/sy coy – to become 4)); 4 (theatre avn) bde

Army Reserve 198,000 reservists (incl 26,120 active)

Reserve under full command of US Army. Does not have state emergency liability of Army National Guard.

FORCES BY ROLE

Inf	5 div (exercise); 7 div (trg)
Engr	4 bde
Sigs	1 bde

Spt	8 spt bde, 2 cbt spt bde
Regional Spt	13 comd gps
Avn	1 theatre avn bde with (air aslt hel, atk hel and gen spt avn bns)

Army Standby Reserve 700 reservists
Trained individuals for mobilisation

EQUIPMENT BY TYPE
MBT 5,795 M1-A1/M1-A2 *Abrams*
RECCE 335: 239 M-1200 *Armored Knight*; 96 Tpz-1 *Fuchs*
AIFV 6,452 M-2 *Bradley*/M-3 *Bradley*
APC 19,881
    APC (T) 3,943 M-113A2/M-113A3
    APC (W) 15,938: 12,000 MRAP (all models); 950 M-ACV; 2,988 *Stryker*
ARTY 6,445+
    SP 155mm 1,594 M-109A1/M-109A2/M-109A6
    TOWED 1,771: **105mm** 850: 434 M-102; 416 M-119; **155mm** 921: 656 M-198; 265 M-777
    MRL 227mm 1,014: 184+ HIMARS; 830 M270/M270A1 MLRS (all ATACMS-capable)
    MOR 2,066: **81mm** 990 M-252; **120mm** 1,076 M-120/M-121
AT
    MSL
        SP 2,005: 1,379 HMMWV TOW; 626 M-901
        MANPATS *Javelin*
    RL 84mm M136 (AT-4)
AMPHIBIOUS 124
    LCU 45: 11 LCU-1600 (capacity either 2 M1-A1 *Abrams* MBT or 350 troops); 34 LCU-2000
    LC 79: 6 *Frank Besson* (capacity 32 *Abrams* MBT); 73 LCM-8 (capacity either 1 MBT or 200 troops)
AIRCRAFT
    ISR 51: 2 O-2 *Skymaster*; 37 RC-12D/H/K *Guardrail*; 12 RC-12P/Q *Guardrail*
    ELINT 9: 3 *Dash-7* ARL-M (COMINT/ELINT); 3 *Dash-7* ARL-1 (IMINT); 3 *Dash-7* ARL-C (COMINT)
    TPT 196 **Light** 194: 113 Beech A200 *King Air* (C-12 *Huron*); 28 Cessna 560 *Citation* (UC-35); 11 SA-227 *Metro* (C-26); 42 Short 330 *Sherpa* (C-23A/B) **PAX** 2 Gulfstream (C-20)
HELICOPTERS
    ATK 1,239: 697 AH-64A *Apache*; 542 AH-64D *Apache*
    MRH 344: 6 AH-6/MH-6 *Little Bird*; 338 OH-58D *Kiowa Warrior*
    ISR 247 OH-58A/C *Kiowa*
    SAR 15 HH-60L *Black Hawk*
    TPT 2,270 **Heavy** 372: 309 CH-47D *Chinook*, 63 CH-47F *Chinook* **Medium** 1,740: 951 UH-60A *Black Hawk*; 681 UH-60L *Black Hawk*; 108 UH-60M *Black Hawk*; **Light** 158: 58 EC-145 (UH-72A *Lakota*); 100 UH-1H/V *Iroquois*
    TRG 154 TH-67 *Creek*
UAV • ISR 278
    Heavy 42: 3 *I-Gnat*; 20 RQ-5A *Hunter*; 4 *Sky Warrior*; 15 *Warrior*;
    Medium 236 RQ-7A *Shadow*
AD• SAM 1,281+
    SP 798: 703 FIM-92A *Avenger* (veh-mounted *Stinger*); 95 M-6 *Linebacker* (4 *Stinger* plus 25mm gun)
    TOWED 483 MIM-104 *Patriot*
    MANPAD FIM-92A *Stinger*

RADAR • LAND 251: 98 AN/TPQ-36 *Firefinder* (arty); 56 AN/TPQ-37 *Firefinder* (arty); 60 AN/TRQ-32 *Teammate* (COMINT); 32 AN/TSQ-138 *Trailblazer* (COMINT); 5 AN/TSQ-138A *Trailblazer*

US Navy 330,065; 6,229 active reservists (total 336,289)

Comprises 2 Fleet Areas, Atlantic and Pacific. All combatants divided into 6 Fleets: 2nd – Atlantic, 3rd – Pacific, 4th – Caribbean, Central and South America, 5th – Indian Ocean, Persian Gulf, Red Sea, 6th – Mediterranean, 7th – W. Pacific; plus Military Sealift Command (MSC); Naval Reserve Force (NRF); for Naval Special Warfare Command, see US Special Operations Command element.

EQUIPMENT BY TYPE
SUBMARINES 71
    STRATEGIC • SSBN 14 *Ohio* (mod) SSBN 730 opcon US STRATCOM each with up to 24 UGM-133A *Trident* D-5 strategic SLBM
    TACTICAL 57
        SSGN 4 *Ohio* (mod), with total of 154 *Tomahawk* LACM
        SSN 53:
            20 *Los Angeles* each with 4 single 533mm TT each with Mk48 *Sea Arrow* HWT/UGM-84 *Harpoon* AShM
            23 *Los Angeles* imp, each with up to 12 *Tomahawk* LACM, 4 single 533mm TT each with Mk48 *Sea Arrow* HWT/UGM-84 *Harpoon* AShM
            3 *Seawolf* each with 8 single 660mm TT each with up to 45 *Tomahawk (TLAM)* LACM/UGM-84C *Harpoon* AShM, Mk48 *Sea Arrow* HWT
            7 *Virginia* with SLCM *Tomahawk*, 4 single 533mm TT each with Mk48 ADCAP mod 6 HWT, 1 12 cell vertical launch system (12 eff.) (additional vessels in build)
PRINCIPAL SURFACE COMBATANTS 114
    AIRCRAFT CARRIERS 11
        CVN 11:
            1 *Enterprise* with 3 octuple Mk29 GMLS (24 eff.) each with RIM-7M/P *Sea Sparrow* SAM, 2 Mk49 GMLS each with RIM-116 RAM SAM (typical capacity 55 F/A-18 *Hornet* FGA ac; 4 EA-6B *Prowler* EW ac; 4 E-2C *Hawkeye* AEW ac; 4 SH-60F *Seahawk* ASW hel; 2 HH-60H *Seahawk* SAR hel)
            10 *Nimitz* each with 2–3 octuple Mk29 lnchr (16-24 eff.) each with RIM-7M/P *Sea Sparrow* SAM, 2 Mk49 GMLS each with RIM-116 RAM SAM (typical capacity 55 F/A-18 *Hornet* FGA ac; 4 EA-6B *Prowler* EW ac; 4 E-2C *Hawkeye* AEW ac; 4 SH-60F *Seahawk* ASW hel; 2 HH-60H *Seahawk* SAR hel)
    CRUISERS • CGHM • 22 *Ticonderoga* Aegis Baseline 2/3/4 (CG-52-CG-74) each with *Aegis* C2, 2 quad lnchr (8 eff.) each with RGM-84 *Harpoon* AShM, 2 61 cell Mk41 VLS (122 eff.) each with SM-2ER SAM/*Tomahawk (TLAM)* LACM, 2 127mm gun (capacity 2 SH-60B *Seahawk* ASW hel), (Extensive upgrade programme scheduled from 2006–2020, to include sensors and fire control systems, major weapons upgrade to include Evolved *Sea Sparrow* (ESSM), SM-3/SM-2 capability and 2 Mk45 Mod 2 127mm gun)

DESTROYERS 59

DDGHM 31 *Arleigh Burke* Flight IIA each with *Aegis* C2, 2 quad lnchr (8 eff.) each with RGM-84 *Harpoon* AShM, 1 32 cell Mk41 VLS (32 eff.) with ASROC ASsW/SM-2ER SAM/*Tomahawk* (TLAM) LACM, 1 64 cell Mk41 VLS (64 eff.) with ASROC ASsW/SM-2 ER SAM/*Tomahawk* (TLAM) LACM, 2 triple 324mm ASTT (6 eff.) each with Mk46 LWT, 1 127mm gun, (capacity 2 SH-60B *Seahawk* ASW hel), (additional ships in build)

DDGM 28 *Arleigh Burke* Flight I/II each with *Aegis* C2, 2 quad lnchr (8 eff.) each with RGM-84 *Harpoon* AShM, 1 32 cell Mk41 VLS (32 eff.) with ASROC ASW/SM-2ER SAM/*Tomahawk* (TLAM) LACM, 1 64 cell Mk 41 VLS (64 eff.) with ASROC ASsW/SM-2 ER SAM/*Tomahawk* (TLAM) LACM, 2 Mk49 RAM each with RIM-116 RAM SAM, 2 triple 324mm ASTT (6 eff.) each with Mk46 LWT, 1 127mm gun, 1 hel landing platform

FRIGATES 22

FFHM 2:

1 *Freedom* with RIM-116 RAM, Mk15 *Phalanx* CIWS, (capacity 2 MH-60R/S *Seahawk* hel or 1 MH-60 with 3 MQ-8 *Firescout* UAV)

1 *Independence* with RIM-116 RAM, Mk15 *Phalanx* CIWS, (capacity 1 MH-60R/S *Seahawk* hel and 3 MQ-8 *Firescout* UAV)

FFH 20 *Oliver Hazard Perry* each with 2 triple 324mm ASTT (6 eff.) with 24 Mk 46 LWT, 1 76mm gun, (capacity 2 SH-60B *Seahawk* ASW hel)

PATROL AND COASTAL COMBATANTS 28

PCF (8 *Cyclone* currently non-operational)

PBF 12

PBR 16

MINE WARFARE • MINE COUNTERMEASURES 9

MCO 9 *Avenger* (MCM-1) each with 1 SLQ-48 MCM system, 1 SQQ-32(V)3 Sonar (mine hunting)

COMMAND SHIPS • LCC 2:

2 *Blue Ridge* (capacity 3 LCPL; 2 LCVP; 700 troops; 1 med utl hel)

AMPHIBIOUS

PRINCIPAL AMPHIBIOUS SHIPS 31

LHD 8:

8 *Wasp* each with 2 octuple Mk29 GMLS (16 eff.) each with RIM-7M/RIM-7P *Sea Sparrow* SAM, 2 Mk49 GMLS with RIM-116 RAM SAM (capacity: 5 AV-8B *Harrier II* FGA; 42 CH-46E *Sea Knight* hel; 6 SH-60B *Seahawk* hel; 3 LCAC(L); 60 tanks; 1,890 troops)

LHA 2:

2 *Tarawa* each with 2 Mk49 GMLS each with RIM-116 RAM SAM (capacity 6 AV-8B *Harrier II* FGA ac; 12 CH-46E *Sea Knight* hel; 9 CH-53 *Sea Stallion* hel; 4 LCU; 100 tanks; 1,900 troops)

LPD 9:

4 *Austin* (capacity 6 CH-46E *Sea Knight* hel; 2 LCAC(L)/LCU; 40 tanks; 788 troops)

5 *San Antonio* (capacity 1 CH-53E *Sea Stallion* hel or 2 CH-46 *Sea Knight* or 1 MV-22 *Osprey*; 2 LCAC(L); 14 AAAV; 720 troops) (5 additional vessels in build)

LSD 12:

4 *Harpers Ferry* each with 1–2 Mk 49 GMLS each with RIM-116 RAM SAM, 1 hel landing platform (capacity 2 LCAC(L); 40 tanks; 500 troops)

8 *Whidbey Island* each with 2 Mk49 GMLS each with RIM-116 RAM SAM, 1 hel landing platform (capacity 4 LCAC(L); 40 tanks; 500 troops)

AMPHIBIOUS CRAFT 269+

LCU 34 LCU-1600 (capacity either 2 M1-A1 *Abrams* MBT or 350 troops)

LCVP 8

LCPL 75

LCM 72

LCAC 80 LCAC(L) (capacity either 1 MBT or 60 troops; (undergoing upgrade programme))

SF 6 DDS opcon USSOCOM

FACILITIES

Bases	1 opcon EUCOM located at Naples, ITA, 1 opcon EUCOM located at Soudha Bay, GRC, 1 opcon US Pacific Fleet located at Yokosuka, JPN, 1 opcon EUCOM located at Rota, ESP, 1 opcon US Pacific Fleet located at Sasebo, JPN
Naval air bases	1 opcon US Pacific Fleet (plus naval comms facility) located at Andersen AFB, 1 opcon US Pacific Fleet located at Diego Garcia (BIOT)
SEWS	1 opcon US Pacific Fleet located at Pine Gap, AUS
Comms facility	1 opcon US Pacific Fleet located at NW Cape, AUS
SIGINT stn	1 opcon US Pacific Fleet located at Pine Gap, AUS
Support facility	1 opcon EUCOM located at Ankara, TUR, 1 opcon EUCOM located at Izmir, TUR, 1 opcon US Pacific Fleet located at Diego Garcia, (BIOT), 1 opcon US Pacific Fleet located at Singapore, SGP

Combat Logistics Force
LOGISTICS AND SUPPORT

AOE 5: 4 *Sacramento* (capacity 2 CH-46E *Sea Knight* spt hel); 1 *Supply* (capacity 3 CH-46E *Sea Knight* spt hel)

Navy Reserve Surface Forces
PRINCIPAL SURFACE COMBATANTS

FFG 9 *Oliver Hazard Perry* in reserve each with 2 triple 324mm ASTT (6 eff.) with 24 Mk 46 LWT, 36 SM-1 MR SAM, 1 76mm gun, (capacity 2 SH-60B *Seahawk* ASW hel)

MINE WARFARE • MINE COUNTERMEASURES 15:

MCO 5 *Avenger* in reserve each with 1 SLQ-48 MCM system, 1 SQQ-32(V)3 Sonar (mine hunting)

MHC 10 *Osprey* in reserve each with 1 SLQ-48 MCM system, 1 SQQ-32(V)2 Sonar (mine hunting)

INSHORE UNDERSEA WARFARE 45 HDS/IBU/MIUW

Naval Reserve Forces 109,222 (incl 6,224 active)

Selected Reserve 66,455

Individual Ready Reserve 42,767

Naval Inactive Fleet

Under a minimum of 60–90 days notice for reactivation and still on naval vessel register

PRINCIPAL SURFACE COMBATANTS 2
  AIRCRAFT CARRIERS 1 CV
  FRIGATES 1 FFG
AMPHIBIOUS 9
  1 LHA 5 LKA
  3 LPD
LOGISTICS AND SUPPORT 2: 1 AGS 1 ATF

Military Sealift Command (MSC)

Naval Fleet Auxiliary Force
LOGISTICS AND SUPPORT 42
  AEH 3 *Kilauea*
  ARS 4 *Safeguard*
  AH 2 *Mercy*, with 1 hel landing platform
  ATF 4 *Powhatan*
  AO 15 *Henry J. Kaiser*
  AOE 4 *Supply* class
  AKEH 10 *Lewis* and *Clark* (2 additional vessels in build)

Maritime Prepositioning Program
LOGISTICS AND SUPPORT 32
  AOT 1 *Champion*
  AG 1
  AK 8: 1 (break bulk); 7
  AKR 13: 5; 8 *Watson*
  AKRH 5
  AVB 2
  TPT 2 HSV

Strategic Sealift Force
(At a minimum of 4 days readiness)
LOGISTICS AND SUPPORT 17:
  AGMS 1
  AOT 3 (of which 2 are long-term chartered)
  AK 3
  AKR 10

Special Mission Ships
LOGISTICS AND SUPPORT 18:
  AS 2 *Emory S Land*
  AGM 3 (additional vessel awaiting commissioning)
  ARC 1 *Zeus*
  AGOS 5: 1 *Impeccable*; 4 *Victorious*
  AGS 6 *Pathfinder*
  LCC 1 *Mount Whitney*

US Maritime Administration Support • National Defense Reserve Fleet
LOGISTICS AND SUPPORT 32:
  ACS 3 *Keystone State*
  AFS 1
  AGM 1
  AGOS 3
  AGS 3
  AK 16: 13 T-AK (breakbulk); 3 T-AK (heavy lift)
  AKR 2
  AO 1

  AP 1
  APB 1

Ready Reserve Force
Ships at readiness up to a maximum of 30 days
LOGISTICS AND SUPPORT 49:
  ACS 6 *Keystone State*
  AK 7: 3 T-AK (breakbulk); 4 T-AK (heavy lift)
  AKR 35: 27 *Ro Ro*; 8 *Algol*
  AOT 1

Augmentation Force • Active
Cargo handling   1 bn

Reserve
Cargo handling   12 bn

Naval Aviation 98,588

Operates from 11 carriers, 11 air wings (10 active 1 reserve). Average air wing comprises 7 sqns: 4 each with 12 F/A-18 (2 with F/A-18C, 1 with F/A-18E, 1 with F/A-18F), 1 with 6 SH-60, 1 with 4 EA-6B, 1 with 4 E-2C. (Numbers exclude Fleet Replacement Squadrons.)

FORCES BY ROLE

FGA	1 sqn with F/A-18A+ *Hornet*; 13 sqn with F/A-18C *Hornet*; 11 sqn with F/A-18E *Super Hornet*; 10 sqn with F/A-18F *Super Hornet*
ASW	7 sqn with HH-60H *Seahawk*; SH-60F *Seahawk*; 3 sqn with MH-60R *Seahawk*; 9 sqn with SH-60B *Seahawk*
ELINT	2 sqn with EP-3E *Aries II*
ELINT/ECM	10 sqn with EA-6B *Prowler*; 3 sqn with EA-18G *Growler*
MP	12 (land-based) sqn with P-3C *Orion*
AEW&C	10 sqn with E-2C *Hawkeye*
C&C	2 sqn with E-6B *Mercury*
MCM	2 sqn with MH-53E *Sea Dragon*
Spt	9 sqn with MH-60S *Knight Hawk*
Tpt	2 sqn with C-2A *Greyhound*
Trg	1 (aggressor) sqn with F/A-18C/D *Hornet*/F/A-18E/F *Super Hornet*; 1 (aggressor) sqn with F/A-18B/C/D *Hornet*; 1 sqn with F/A-18E/F *Super Hornet*; 3 sqn with T-6A/B *Texan II*/T-39D/G/N *Sabreliner*; 5 sqn T-34C *Turbo Mentor*; 2 sqn with T-44A *Pegasus*; 4 sqn with T-45A/C *Goshawk*; 2 sqn with TH-57B/C *Sea Ranger*

EQUIPMENT BY TYPE
AIRCRAFT 947 combat capable
  FGA 800: 33 F/A-18A *Hornet*; 24 F/A-18B *Hornet*; 268 F/A-18C *Hornet*; 41 F/A-18D *Hornet*; 195 F/A-18E *Super Hornet*; 239 F/A-18F *Super Hornet*
  ASW 147 P-3C *Orion*
  EW 133: 92 EA-6B *Prowler*; 41 EA-18G *Growler*
  ELINT 11 EP-3E *Aries II*
  ISR 4: 2 RC-12F *Huron*; 2 RC-12M *Huron*
  AEW&C 66 E-2C *Hawkeye*
  C&C 16 E-6B *Mercury*

North America

TPT 92: **Medium** 3: 2 LC-130F *Hercules*; 1 LC-130R *Hercules*; **Light** 80: 4 Beech A200 *King Air* (C-12C *Huron)*; 21 Beech A200 *King Air* (UC-12B *Huron)*; 35 C-2A *Greyhound*; 1 Cessna 560 *Citation Encore* (UC-35D); 1 *Sabreliner* (CT-39G); 2 DHC-2 *Beaver* (U-6A); 7 SA-227-BC *Metro III* (C-26D); 4 UP-3A *Orion*; 5 VP-3A *Orion* **PAX** 9: 1 Gulfstream III (C-20A); 2 Gulfstream III (C-20D); 5 Gulfstream IV (C-20G); 1 Gulfstream V (C-37);

TRG 648: 47 T-6A *Texan II*; 2 T-6B *Texan II*; 270 T-34C *Turbo Mentor*; 9 T-38 *Talon*; 1 T-39D *Sabreliner*; 8 T-39G *Sabreliner*; 15 T-39N *Sabreliner*; 55 T-44A *Pegasus*; 74 T-45A *Goshawk*; 144 T-45C *Goshawk*; 21 TC-12B *Huron*; 2 TE-2C *Hawkeye*

TRIALS AND TEST 50: 5 EA-18G *Growler*; 1 NF/A-18A *Hornet*; 2 NF/A-18C *Hornet*; 3 NF/A-18D *Hornet*; 1 NP-3C *Orion*; 11 NP-3D *Orion*; 1 NT-34C *Mentor*; 1 NU-1B *Otter*; 2 QF-4N *Phantom II*; 16 QF-4S *Phantom* II; 2 X-26A; 1 X-31A; 1 YF-4J *Phantom II* (prototype, FGA); 1 YSH-60 *Seahawk* (prototype); 1 YSH-60B *Seahawk*; 1 YSH-60F *Seahawk*

HELICOPTERS

MRH 123 MH-60S *Knight Hawk* (Multi Mission Support)

ASW 255: 35 MH-60R *Strike Hawk*; 148 SH-60B *Seahawk*; 72 SH-60F *Seahawk*

MCM 28 MH-53E *Sea Dragon*

ISR 3 OH-58A *Kiowa*

SAR 63: 23 HH-1N *Iroquois*; 4 HH-46D *Sea Knight*; 36 HH-60H *Seahawk*

TPT 37 **Heavy** 18: 9 CH-53D *Sea Stallion*; 9 CH-53E *Sea Stallion* **Medium** 14: 9 UH-46D *Sea Knight*; 3 UH-60L *Black Hawk*; 2 VH-3A *Sea King* (VIP) **Light** 5: 1 UH-1N *Iroquois*; 4 UH-1Y *Iroquois*;

TRG 132: 44 TH-57B *Sea Ranger*; 82 TH-57C *Sea Ranger*; 6 TH-6B

TEST 3 N-SH-60B *Seahawk*

UAV 42:

Heavy 7: 5 MQ-8B *Fire Scout* (under evaluation and trials); 2 RQ-4A *Global Hawk* (under evaluation and trials)

Medium 35 RQ-2B *Pioneer*

MSL

AAM • IR AAM AIM-9 *Sidewinder*, **IIR AAM** AIM-9X *Sidewinder* II, **SARH AAM** AIM-7 *Sparrow*, **ARH AAM** AIM-120 AMRAAM

ASM AGM-65A/F *Maverick*; AGM-84D *Harpoon* AShM; AGM-84E SLAM/SLAM-ER LACM; AGM-114B/K/M *Hellfire*; AGM-119A *Penguin* 3 AShM; AGM-154A JSOW; AGM-88 HARM ARM

BOMBS

Conventional: BLU-117/Mk 84 (2,000lb); BLU-110/Mk 83 (1,000lb); BLU-111/Mk 82 (500lb); Mk 46; Mk 50; Mk 54

Laser-Guided: *Paveway* II; *Paveway* III (fits on Mk 82, Mk 83 or Mk 84)

INS/GPS guided: JDAM (GBU-31/32/38); Enhanced *Paveway* II

Naval Aviation Reserve

FORCES BY ROLE

FGA	1 sqn with F/A-18A+ *Hornet*
ASW	1 sqn with HH-60H *Seahawk*; 1 sqn with SH-60B
MR	2 sqn with P-3C *Orion*
AEW	1 sqn with E-2C *Hawkeye*
Spt	1 sqn with MH-60S *Knight Hawk*
ECM	1 sqn with EA-6B *Prowler*
Log spt	1 wg (3 log spt sqn with C-40A *Clipper*, 3 log spt sqn with C-20 A/D/G Gulfstream; C-37A/C-37B Gulfstream, 5 tactical tpt sqn with C-130T *Hercules*, 4 log spt sqn with C-9B *Skytrain II/DC-9 Skytrain*)
Trg	2 (aggressor) sqn with F-5F/N *Tiger II*; 1 (aggressor) sqn with F/A-18C *Hornet*

EQUIPMENT BY TYPE

AIRCRAFT 68 combat capable

FTR 32: 2 F-5F *Tiger II*; 30 F-5N *Tiger II*

FGA 24: 12 F/A-18A+ *Hornet*; 12 F/A-18C *Hornet*

ASW 12 P-3C *Orion*

EW 4 EA-6B *Prowler*

AEW&C 6 E-2C *Hawkeye*

TPT 59: **Medium** 19 C-130T *Hercules*; **Light** 5 Beech A200C *King Air* (UC-12B *Huron*); **PAX** 35: 9 B-737-700 (C-40A *Clipper*); 15 DC-9 *Skytrain II* (C-9B); 7 Gulfstream *III/IV* (C-20A/D/G); 1 Gulfstream *V* (C-37A); 3 Gulfstream *G550* (C-37B);

HELICOPTERS

ASW 11: 6 SH-60B *Seahawk*; 5 MH-60S *Knight Hawk*

MCM 8 MH-53E *Sea Stallion*

SAR 17 HH-60H *Rescue Hawk*

US Marine Corps 204,056 (incl 2,930 active reservists)

3 Marine Expeditionary Force (MEF), 3 Marine Expeditionary Brigade (MEB), 7 Marine Expeditionary Units (MEU) drawn from 3 div. An MEU usually consists of a battalion landing team (1 inf bn, 1 arty bty, 1 lt armd recce coy, 1 armd pl, 1 amph aslt pl, 1 cbt engr pl, 1 recce pl), an aviation combat element (1 medium lift sqn with attached atk hel, FGA ac and AD assets) and a composite log bn, with a combined total of about 2,200 men. Composition varies with mission requirements.

FORCES BY ROLE

Marine	1 div (1st) with (3 inf regt (each: 4 inf bn), 1 arty regt (4 arty bn), 1 armd bn, 2 (LAV-25) lt armd recce bn, 1 recce bn, 1 amph aslt bn, 1 cbt engr bn); 1 div (2nd) with (3 inf regt (each: 4 inf bn) 1 arty regt (4 arty bn), 1 armd bn, 1 lt armd recce bn, 1 recce bn, 1 amph aslt bn, 1 cbt engr bn,); 1 div (3rd) with (1 inf regt (3 inf bn), 1 arty regt (2 arty bn), 1 recce bn, 1 cbt spt bn (1 lt armd recce coy, 1 amph aslt coy, 1 cbt engr coy))
Spec Ops	3 MEF recce coy
Log	3 gp

EQUIPMENT BY TYPE

MBT 447 M1-A1 *Abrams*
RECCE 252 LAV-25 *Coyote* (25mm gun, plus 189 variants)
AAV 1,311 AAV-7A1 (all roles)
APC (W) 2,225 MRAP
ARTY 1,926
    TOWED 1,301: **105mm**: 331 M-101A1; **155mm** 970: 595 M-198; 375 M-777(to replace M-198)
    MRL 227mm 40 HIMARS
    MOR 81mm 585: 50 LAV-M; 535 M-252
AT
    MSL 2,299
      SP 95 LAV-TOW
      MANPATS 2,204: 1,121 *Predator*; 1,083 TOW
    RL 2,764: **83mm** 1,650 SMAW; **84mm** 1,114 AT-4
AD • SAM • MANPAD FIM-92A *Stinger*
UAV • Light 100 BQM-147 *Exdrone*
RADAR • LAND 23 AN/TPQ-36 *Firefinder* (arty)

Marine Corps Aviation 34,700

3 active Marine Aircraft Wings (MAW) and 1 MCR MAW
Flying hours   365 hrs/year on tpt ac; 248 hrs/year on ac; 277 hrs/year on hel

FORCES BY ROLE

Ftr	2 sqn with F/A-18A/A+ *Hornet*; 5 sqn with F/A-18C *Hornet*; 5 sqn (All Weather) with F/A-18D *Hornet*
FGA	7 sqn with AV-8B *Harrier II*
ECM	4 sqn with total of EA-6B *Prowler*
CSAR/Tpt	1 sqn with Beech A200/B2000 *King Air* (UC-12B/F *Huron*); Cessna 560 *Citation Ultra/ Encore* (UC-35C/D); DC-9 *Skytrain* (C-9B *Nightingale*); Gulfstream *IV* (C-20G); HH-1N *Iroquois*, HH-46E *Sea Knight*
Tkr	3 sqn with KC-130J *Hercules*
Trg	1 sqn with AH-1W *Cobra*, HH-1N *Iroquois*, UH-1N *Iroquois*, UH-1Y *Venom*; 1 sqn with AV-8B *Harrier II*, TAV-8B *Harrier*; 1 sqn with CH-46E *Sea Knight*; 1 sqn with CH-53E *Sea Stallion*; 1 sqn with F/A-18B/C/D *Hornet*; 1 sqn with MV-22A *Osprey*
Test	1 sqn with V-22 *Osprey*
Atk Hel	5 sqn with AH-1W *Cobra*, UH-1N *Iroquois*; 3 sqn with AH-1W *Cobra*, UH-1Y *Venom*
Tpt Hel	8 sqn with CH-46E *Sea Knight* (2 converting to MV-22); 1 (VIP) sqn with CH-46E *Sea Knight*; CH-53E *Sea Stallion*; VH-3D *Sea King*; VH-60N *Presidential Hawk*; 3 sqn with CH-53D *Sea Stallion*; 7 sqn with CH-53E *Sea Stallion*; 6 sqn with MV-22B *Osprey*
ISR UAV	3 sqn with RQ-7B *Shadow*
AD	2 bn with FIM-92A *Avenger*; FIM-92A *Stinger* (can provide additional heavy calibre support weapons)

EQUIPMENT BY TYPE

AC 370 combat capable
  FGA 370
    43 F/A-18A/F/A-18 A+ *Hornet*; 2 F/A-18B *Hornet*;
    83 F/A-18C *Hornet*; 94 F/A-18D *Hornet*; 131 AV-8B *Harrier II*; 17 TAV-8B *Harrier*
  EW 29 EA-6B *Prowler*
  TKR 36 KC-130J *Hercules*
  TPT 19 **Light** 16: 9 Beech A200/B200 *King Air* (UC-12B/F *Huron*); 7 Cessna 560 *Citation Ultra/Encore* (UC-35C/D)
  PAX 3: 2 DC-9 *Skytrain* (C-9B *Nightingale*); 1 Gulfstream *IV* (C-20G);
  TRG 3 T-34C *Turbo Mentor*
TILTROTOR 86+
  20 MV-22A *Osprey*; 62+ MV-22B *Osprey* (360 on order, deliveries continuing); 4 V-22 *Osprey*
HELICOPTERS
  ATK 147: 139 AH-1W *Cobra*; 8 AH-1Z *Viper*
  SAR 9: 5 HH-1N *Iroquois*; 4 HH-46E *Sea Knight*
  TPT 436 **Heavy** 180: 35 CH-53D *Sea Stallion*; 145 CH-53E *Sea Stallion*; **Medium** 155: 136 CH-46E *Sea Knight*; 8 VH-60N *Presidential Hawk* (VIP tpt); 11 VH-3D *Sea King* (VIP tpt); **Light** 101: 76 UH-1N *Iroquois*; 25 UH-1Y *Iroquois*
UAV • ISR • Medium 32 RQ-7B *Shadow*
AD
  SAM • SP some FIM-92A *Avenger*
    MANPAD some FIM-92A *Stinger*
MSL
  AAM • IR AAM AIM-9M *Sidewinder*; **IIR AAM** AIM-9X; **SARH AAM** AIM-7 *Sparrow*; **ARH AAM** AIM-120 AMRAAM
  ASM AGM-65F IR *Maverick*/AGM-65E *Maverick*; AGM-84 *Harpoon* AShM; AGM-114 *Hellfire*; ARM AGM-88 HARM
BOMBS
  Conventional: CBU-59; CBU-99; MK-82 (500lb), MK-83 (1,000lb)
  Laser-Guided: GBU 10/12/16 *Paveway* II (fits on Mk82, Mk 83 or Mk 84)
  INS/GPS Guided: JDAM

Reserve Organisations

Marine Corps Reserve 109,600 (incl 2,930 active)

FORCES BY ROLE

Marine	1 div (4th) with (3 inf regt (each: 3 inf bn), 1 arty regt (4 arty bn), 1 (LAV-25) lt armd recce bn, 1 recce bn, 1 amph aslt bn, 1 cbt engr bn)
Spec Ops	2 MEF recce coy
Log	1 gp

Marine Corps Aviation Reserve 11,592 reservists

FORCES BY ROLE

Ftr	1 sqn with F/A-18A/A+ *Hornet*
Tkr	2 sqn with KC-130T *Hercules*
Atk hel	1 sqn with AH-1W *Cobra*; UH-1N *Iroquois*
Spt hel	2 sqn with CH-46E *Sea Knight*; 1 det with CH-53E *Sea Stallion*
Trg	1 sqn with F-5F/N *Tiger II*

EQUIPMENT BY TYPE

AIRCRAFT 27 combat capable

FTR 12: 1 F-5F *Tiger II*; 11 F-5N *Tiger II*
FGA 15 F/A-18A/A+ *Hornet*
TKR 28 KC-130T *Hercules*
TPT • Light 7 2 Beech A200 *King Air* (UC-12B *Huron*); 5 Cessna 560 *Citation Ultra/Encore* (UC-35C/D)
HELICOPTERS
 ATK 18 AH-1W *Cobra*
 TPT 41 **Heavy** 6 CH-53E *Sea Stallion* **Medium** 26 CH-46E *Sea Knight* **Light** 9 UH-1N *Iroquois*

Marine Stand-by Reserve 700 reservists
Trained individuals available for mobilisation

US Coast Guard 43,598 (military); 7,659 (civilian)

Two Area Commands: Pacific (Alameda, California) and Atlantic (Portsmouth, Virginia), supervising 9 districts (4 Pacific, 5 Atlantic). 2 (1 Atlantic, 1 Pacific) Maintenance and Logistics Command Atlantic (MLCA).
PATROL AND COASTAL COMBATANTS 160
 PSOH 28: 1 *Alex Haley*; 13 *Famous*; 12 *Hamilton*; 2 *Legend*
 PSO 1 *Diver*
 PCO 14 *Reliance*,
 PFC 3 *Cyclone*
 PCC 41 *Island*
 PBI 73 *Marine Protector*
LOGISTICS AND SUPPORT 92
 ABU 16 *Juniper*
 AGB 4: 1 *Mackinaw*; 1 *Healy*; 2 *Polar Icebreaker*
 Trg 2
 WLI 5
 WLIC 13
 WLM 14 *Keeper*
 WLR 18
 WTGB 9 *Bay Class*
 YTM 11

US Coast Guard Aviation
AIRCRAFT
 MP 26: 9 HU-25A *Guardian* (Additional 16 in reserve); 3 HU-25B (Additional 4 in store); 8 HU-25C (Additional 9 in store); 6 HU-25D
 SAR 27: 21 HC-130H *Hercules* (Additional 5 in store); 6 HC-130J *Hercules*
 TPT 13 **Light** 11 CN-235-200 (HC-144A) PAX 2; 1 CL-604 (C-143-A); 1 Gulfstream V (C-37A)
HELICOPTERS
 SAR 125: 35 HH-60J *Jayhawk* (Additional 7 in store); 90 AS-366G1 (HH-65C) *Dauphin II* (Additional 12 in store)
 TPT • Light 8 MH-68A (A-109E) *Power*
 UAV 3 (trials)

US Air Force (USAF) 337,505; 2,516 active ANG; 969 active AFR (total 340,990)

Flying hours ftr 189, bbr 260, tkr 308, airlift 343
 Almost the entire USAF (plus active force ANG and AFR) is divided into 10 Aerospace Expeditionary Forces (AEF), each on call for 120 days every 20 months. At least 2 of the 10 AEFs are on call at any one time, each with 10,000–15,000 personnel, 90 multi-role ftr and bbr ac, 31

intra-theatre refuelling aircraft and 13 aircraft for ISR and EW missions.

Global Strike Command (GSC)
GSC (HQ at Barksdale AFB, LA) combines all USAF strategic nuclear forces under a single commander, and will provide combatant commanders with the forces to conduct strategic nuclear deterrence and global strike operations through ICBM, B-2 *Spirit* and B-52 *Stratofortress* operations. 2 active air forces (8th & 20th); 6 wg
FORCES BY ROLE

Msl	9 sqn with LCM-30 *Minuteman III* ICBM
Bbr	5 sqn with B-52 *Stratofortress*; 2 sqn with B-2A *Spirit*

Air Combat Command (ACC)
ACC (Langley AFB, VA.), is the primary US provider of air combat forces. ACC operates ftr, bbr, recce, battle-management, and electronic-combat aircraft, provides C3I systems and conducts global information operations. ACC numbered air forces provide the air component to CENTCOM, SOUTHCOM and NORTHCOM. 2 active air forces (9th & 12th); 15 wg
FORCES BY ROLE

Bbr	4 sqn with B-1B *Lancer*
Ftr	4 sqn with F-22A *Raptor*
FGA	4 sqn with F-15E *Strike Eagle*; 5 sqn with F-16C/D *Fighting Falcon*
Atk	5 sqn with A-10C *Thunderbolt II*/OA-10A *Thunderbolt II*
EW	1 sqn with EA-6B *Prowler* (personnel only – USN aircraft); 2 sqn with EC-130H *Compass Call Solo*
ISR	5 sqn with OC-135/RC-135/WC-135; 2 sqn with U-2S/TU-2S
AEW&C	5 sqn with E-3B/C *Sentry*
C&C	1 sqn with E-4B
CSAR	3 sqn with HC-130N/P *Hercules*/HH-60G *Pave Hawk*
Trg	2 sqn with F-15E *Strike Eagle*; 1 sqn with MQ-1 *Predator*; 1 sqn with MQ-9 *Reaper*
CISR UAV	3 sqn with MQ-1 *Predator*; 1 sqn with MQ-1 *Predator*/MQ-9 *Reaper*; 1 sqn with MQ-1 *Predator*/RQ-170 *Sentinel*; 3 sqn with MQ-9 *Reaper*
ISR UAV	1 sqn with RQ-4A *Global Hawk*

Pacific Air Forces (PACAF)
Provides the air component of PACOM, and commands air units based in Alaska, Hawaii, Japan and South Korea. 4 active air forces (5th, 7th, 11th & 13th); 8 wg
FORCES BY ROLE

Ftr	2 sqn with F-15C/D *Eagle*; 2 sqn with F-22A *Raptor*
FGA	5 sqn with F-16C/D *Fighting Falcon*;

Atk	1 sqn with A-10C *Thunderbolt II*/OA-10A *Thunderbolt II*
AEW&C	2 sqn with E-3B/C *Sentry*;
CSAR	1 sqn with HH-60G *Pave Hawk*
Tkr	1 sqn with KC-135R
Tpt	1 sqn with B-737-200 (C-40B); Gulfstream V (C-37); 2 sqn with C-17 *Globemaster*; 1 sqn with C-130H *Hercules*; 1 sqn with *Learjet* 35A (C-21); UH-1N *Huey*
Trg	1 (aggressor) sqn with F-16 *Fighting Falcon*

United States Air Forces Europe (USAFE)

Provides the air component to both EUCOM and AFRICOM. 2 active air forces (3rd & 17th); 5 wg

FORCES BY ROLE

Ftr	1 sqn with F-15C/D *Eagle*
FGA	2 sqn with F-15E *Strike Eagle*; 3 sqn with F-16C/D *Fighting Falcon*
Atk	1 sqn with A-10C *Thunderbolt II*/OA-10A *Thunderbolt II*
CSAR	1 sqn with HH-60G *Pave Hawk*
Tkr	1 sqn with KC-135R *Stratotanker*
Tpt	1 sqn with C-130J *Hercules*; 2 sqn with Gulfstream III/IV (C-20); Gulfstream V (C-37); *Learjet* 35A (C-21)

Air Mobility Command (AMC)

Provides strategic and tactical airlift, air-to-air refuelling and aero medical evacuation. 1 active air force (18th); 13 wg and 1 gp

FORCES BY ROLE

Tkr	4 sqn with KC-10A *Extender DC-10*; 8 sqn with KC-135 *Stratotanker* (+3 sqn with personnel only)
Tpt	1 (VIP) wg with B-737-200 (C-40B); B-757-200 (C-32A); Gulfstream III/IV (C-20); VC-25 *Air Force One*; 2 sqn with C-5 *Galaxy*; 11 sqn with C-17 *Globemaster* III; 7 sqn with C-130E/H/J *Hercules*; 1 sqn with Gulfstream V (C-37A); 4 sqn with *Learjet* 35A (C-21)

Air Education and Training Command

2 active air forces (2nd and 19th), 10 active air wgs

FORCES BY ROLE

Trg	1 sqn with C-5 *Galaxy*; 1 sqn with C-17 *Globemaster*; 1 sqn with C-21 *Learjet*; 3 sqn with C-130E/J *Hercules*; 7 sqn with F-16 *Fighting Falcon*; 1 sqn with F-22A *Raptor*; 1 sqn with F-35 *Lightning II*; 2 sqn with KC-KC-135 *Stratotanker*; 24 (flying trg) sqns with T-1 *Jayhawk*; T-6 *Texan II*; T-38 *Talon*; T-43

EQUIPMENT BY TYPE
AIRCRAFT 1,808 combat capable
  BBR 146: 64 B-1B *Lancer* (2 more in test); 19 B-2A *Spirit* (1 more in test); 63 B-52H *Stratofortress* (4 more in test; 18 in store)

FTR 468: 301 F-15C/D *Eagle*; 167 F-22A *Raptor*
FGA 978: 223 F-15E *Strike Eagle*; 755 F-16C/D *Fighting Falcon*
ATK 216: 146 A-10C *Thunderbolt* II; 70 OA-10A *Thunderbolt* II
EW 14 EC-130H *Compass Call*
ISR 96: 37 Beech 350ER *King Air* (MC-12W *Liberty*); 2 E-9A; 2 OC-135B *Open Skies*; 5 TU-2S; 28 U-2S; 2 WC-135 *Constant Phoenix*
ELINT 19: 17 RC-135V/W *Rivet Joint*; 2 RC-135U *Combat Sent*
AEW&C 32 E-3B/C *Sentry* (1 more in test)
C&C 4 E-4B
TKR 176 KC-135A/E/R/T *Stratotanker*
TKR/TPT 59 KC-10A *Extender*
CSAR 13 HC-130P/N *King*
TPT 398 **Heavy** 194: 31 C-5B *Galaxy*; 2 C-5C *Galaxy*; 3 C-5M *Galaxy*; 158 C-17A *Globemaster* III **Medium** 145 C-130E/H/J *Hercules*; **Light** 35 *Learjet* 35A (C-21) **PAX** 24: 2 B-737-700 (C-40B); 4 B-757-200 (C-32A); 5 Gulfstream III (C-20B); 2 Gulfstream IV (C-20H); 9 Gulfstream V (C-37A); 2 VC-25A *Air Force One*
TRG 1,130: 179 T-1A *Jayhawk*; 405 T-6A *Texan* II; 546 T-38A *Talon*
HELICOPTERS
  CSAR 70 HH-60G *Pave Hawk*
  TPT • Light 62 UH-1N *Huey*
UAV 188:
  Cbt ISR • Heavy 177: 130 MQ-1B *Predator*; 47 MQ-9 *Reaper*
  ISR • Heavy 11: 7 RQ-4A *Global Hawk*; 3 RQ-4B *Global Hawk*; 1 RQ-170 *Sentinel*
MSL
  AAM • IR AAM AIM-9 *Sidewinder* **IIR AAM** AIM-9X *Sidewinder* II **SARH AAM** AIM-7M *Sparrow* **ARH AAM** AIM-120A/B/C AMRAAM
  ASM: 1,142 AGM-86B (ALCM) LACM (strategic); 239 AGM-86C (CALCM) LACM (tactical); 50 AGM-86D LACM (penetrator) 460 AGM-129A (ACM) LACM (strategic); AGM-130A; JASSM (IOC 2011); AGM-65A *Maverick*/AGM-65B *Maverick*/AGM-65D *Maverick*/AGM-65G *Maverick*; AGM-88A HARM/AGM-88B HARM ARM
BOMBS
  Conventional: BLU-109/Mk 84 (2,000lb); BLU-110/Mk 83 (1,000lb); BLU-111/Mk 82 (500lb)
  Laser-guided: *Paveway* II, *Paveway* III (fits on Mk82, Mk83 or Mk84)
  INS/GPS guided: JDAM (GBU 31/32/38); GBU-15 (with BLU-109 penetrating warhead or Mk 84); GBU-39B Small Diameter Bomb (250lb); Enhanced *Paveway* III

Reserve Organisations

Air National Guard 106,680 reservists (incl 2,516 active)

FORCES BY ROLE

Bbr	1 sqn with B-2A *Spirit* (personnel only)

Ftr	1 sqn with F-15A/B *Eagle*; 5 sqn with F-15 C/D *Eagle*; 1 sqn with F-22A *Raptor* (personnel only)
FGA	17 sqn with F-16C/D *Fighting Falcon*
Atk	5 sqn with A-10 *Thunderbolt* II/OA-10 *Thunderbolt* II
ISR	3 sqn with E-8C J-STARS (mixed active force and ANG personnel)
CSAR	6 sqn with HC-130 *Hercules*/MC-130P *Combat Shadow*; HH-60G *Pavehawk*
Tkr	20 sqn with KC-135R *Stratotanker* (+2 sqn with personnel only)
Tpt	1 sqn with B-737-700 (C-40C); 3 sqn with C-5A *Galaxy*; 2 sqn with C-17 *Globemaster* (+1 sqn with personnel only); 1 sqn with C-27J *Spartan*; 17 sqn with C-130E/H/J *Hercules*; 1 sqn with C-130H/LC-130H *Hercules*; 3 sqn with *Learjet 35A* (C-21)
Trg	1 sqn with C-130 *Hercules*; 1 sqn with F-15 *Eagle*; 4 sqn with F-16 *Fighting Falcon*
Cbt ISR UAV	2 sqn with MQ-1 *Predator* (+ 1 sqn personnel only); 1 sqn with MQ-9 *Reaper* (personnel only)

EQUIPMENT BY TYPE
AIRCRAFT 522 combat capable
FTR 108 F-15C/D *Eagle*
FGA 318 F-16C/D *Fighting Falcon*
ATK 96: 78 A-10C *Thunderbolt* II; 18 OA-10A *Thunderbolt* II;
ISR 17 E-8C J-STARS
ELINT 11 RC-26B *Metroliner*
CSAR 13 HC-130P/N *King*
TKR 175 KC-135R/T *Stratotanker*
TPT 250 **Heavy** 41: 33 C-5A *Galaxy*; 8 C-17A *Globemaster III* **Medium** 186: 5 C-27J *Spartan*; 181 C-130E/H/J *Hercules*/LC-130H *Hercules* **Light** 21 *Learjet* 35A (C-21) **PAX** 2 B-737-700 (C-40C)
HELICOPTERS • CSAR 18 HH-60G *Pave Hawk*
UAV • Cbt ISR • Heavy 9: 8 MQ-1 *Predator*; 1 MQ-9 *Reaper*

Air Force Reserve Command 67,500 reservists (incl 969 active)

FORCES BY ROLE

Bbr	1 sqn with B-52H *Stratofortress*
Ftr	2 sqn with F-22A *Raptor* (personnel only);
FGA	2 sqn with F-16C/D *Fighting Falcon* (+3 sqn personnel only)
Atk	4 sqn with A-10 *Thunderbolt* II/OA-10 *Thunderbolt* II
ISR	1 (Weather Recce) sqn with WC-130H/J *Hercules*
AEW&C	1 sqn with E-3 *Sentry* (personnel only)
CSAR	3 sqn with HC-130P/N *Hercules*; HH-60G *Pavehawk*
Tkr	4 sqn with KC-10A *Extender* (personnel only); 6 sqn with KC-135R *Stratotanker* (+2 sqn personnel only)

Tpt	3 sqn with C-5A/B *Galaxy* (+2 sqn personnel only); 1 (VIP) sqn with C-9C *Nightingale*; C-40B/C; 1 sqn with C-17 *Globemaster* (+8 sqn personnel only); 10 sqn with C-130E/H/J *Hercules*; 1 (Aerial Spray) sqn with C-130H *Hercules*
Trg	1 sqn with A-10 *Thunderbolt* II; F-15 *Eagle*; F-16 *Fighting Falcon* 1 sqn with B-52H *Stratofortress*; 1 sqn with C-5A *Galaxy*; 1 sqn with F-16 *Fighting Falcon*
C/ISR UAV	1 sqn with MQ-1 *Predator*/MQ-9 *Reaper* (personnel only)
ISR UAV	1 sqn with RQ-4A *Global Hawk* (personnel only)

EQUIPMENT BY TYPE
AIRCRAFT 130 combat capable
BBR 9 B-52H *Stratofortress*
FGA 69 F-16C/D *Fighting Falcon*
ATK 52: 46 A-10A *Thunderbolt* II; 6 OA-10A *Thunderbolt* II
ISR 10 WC-130J *Hercules* (Weather Recce)
CSAR 10 HC-130P/N *King*
TKR 64 KC-135 A/E/R/T *Stratotanker*
TPT 155 **Heavy** 50: 26 C-5A *Galaxy*; 16 C-5B *Galaxy*; 8 C-17A *Globemaster III* **Medium** 102 C-130E/H/J *Hercules* **PAX** 3 B-737-700 (C-40C); 3 DC-9 (C-9C *Nightingale*)
HELICOPTERS • CSAR 23 HH-60G *Pave Hawk*

Civil Reserve Air Fleet
Commercial ac numbers fluctuate
AIRCRAFT • TPT 37 carriers and 1,376 aircraft enrolled, including 1,273 aircraft in the international segment (990 long-range and 283 short-range), plus 37 national, 50 aeromedical evacuation segments and 4 aircraft in the Alaskan segment.

Air Force Stand-by-Reserve 16,858 reservists
Trained individuals for mobilisation

US Special Operations Command 31,496; 3,376 (civilian); 11,247 reservists (SOF) (total 46,119)
Commands all active, reserve, and National Guard Special Operations Forces (SOF) of all services based in CONUS
FORCES BY ROLE
Combined Service   1 HQ located at MacDill AFB (FL)

Joint Special Operations Command
Reported to comprise elite US SF including Special Forces Operations Detachment Delta ('Delta Force'), SEAL Team 6 and integral USAF support.

US Army Special Operations Command
FORCES BY ROLE

SF	5 gp (each: 3 SF bn)
Ranger	1 regt (3-4 Ranger bn)
Sigs	1 bn
Spt	1 sustainment bde

Avn	1 regt (160 SOAR) with (4 avn bn)
Psyops	1 gp (5 psyops bn)
Civil Affairs	1 bn (5 civil affairs coy)

EQUIPMENT BY TYPE
HELICOPTERS
TPT 116 **Heavy** 56: 6 MH-47E *Chinook*; 50 MH-47G *Chinook* **Medium** 60 MH-60K *Black Hawk*/MH-60L *Pave Hawk*
UAV 57
ISR • **Light** 29: 15 XPV-1 *Tern*; 14 XPV-2 *Mako*;
TPT • **Heavy** 28 CQ-10 *Snowgoose*

Reserve Organisations

Army National Guard
FORCES BY ROLE
SF   2 gp (total: 3 SF bn)

Army Reserve
FORCES BY ROLE
Psyops   2 gp
Civil Affairs   12 (4 comd, 8 bde) HQ; 36 (coys) bn

US Navy Special Warfare Command 5,400

Naval Special Warfare Command (NSWC) is organised around eight SEAL Teams and two SEAL Delivery Vehicle (SDV) Teams. These components deploy SEAL Teams, SEAL Delivery Vehicle Teams, and Special Boat Teams worldwide to meet the training, exercise, contingency and wartime requirements of theatre commanders. Operationally up to two of the eight SEAL Teams are deployed at any given time.

FORCES BY ROLE
NSWC   1 comd; 8 SEAL team (48 pl);

2 SDV team

EQUIPMENT BY TYPE
SF 6 DDS

Naval Reserve Force

Delivery veh	1 det
Naval Special Warfare	6 (Gp) det; 3 det; 1 det
Special Boat	2 unit; 2 sqn
HQ	1 (CINCSOC) det
SEAL	8 det

FACILITIES
Navy Special Warfare Command (NSWC), Coronado CA

US Marine Special Operations Command (MARSOC)

Marine Special Operations Command (MARSOC) is a component of USSOCOM and consists of four subordinate units: the 1st and 2nd Marine Special Operations Battalions (MSOB); the Marine Special Operations Advisory Group; and the Marine Special Operations Support Group. MARSOC Headquarters, the 2nd Marine Special Operations Battalion, the Marine Special Operations School, and the Marine Special Operations Support Group are stationed at Camp Lejeune, NC. The 1st Marine Special Operations Battalion is stationed at Camp Pendleton, CA. In the months after the activation of MARSOC, the structure and personnel of both 1st and 2nd Force Reconnaissance Company transferred to MARSOC to form 1st and 2nd Marine Special Operations Battalions. In Apr 2009, MSOAG was re-designated as the Marine Special Operations Regiment with the 1st, 2nd, and 3rd MSOBs as subordinate units. The newly designated 3rd MSOB incorporated the structure and personnel from MSOAG's former companies.

Air Force Special Operations Command (AFSOC)

FORCES BY ROLE

Atk	2 sqn with AC-130H/U *Spectre*
Tpt	1 sqn with An-26; C-130E *Hercules*; Mi-8 *Hip*; UH-1N *Iroqouis*; 1 sqn with C-130 *Hercules*/MC-130P *Combat Shadow*; 2 sqn with CV-22A *Osprey* (+2 sqn personnel only); 3 sqn with MC-130H *Combat Talon*; 1 sqn with MC-130P *Combat Shadow*; 1 sqn with MC-130W *Combat Spear*; 2 sqn with PC-12 (U-28A)
Trg	1 sqn with CV-22A *Osprey*; 1 sqn with HC-130/MC-130H *Combat Talon II*; MC-130P *Combat Shadow*; 1 sqn with UH-1H *Iroquois*; 1 sqn with HH-60G *Pave Hawk*; UH-1N *Huey*
ISR UAV	1 sqn with MQ-1B *Predator*

EQUIPMENT BY TYPE
AIRCRAFT 25 combat capable
ATK 25: 8 AC130H *Spectre*; 17 AC130U *Spectre*;
CSAR Some HC-130P/N *King*
TPT 55+ **Medium** 55+: Some C-130 *Hercules*; 20 MC-130H *Combat Talon* II; 23 MC-130P *Combat Shadow*; 12 MC-130W *Combat Spear* **Light** Some An-26 *Curl*; Some PC-12 (U-28A)
TILT-ROTOR 9 CV-22A *Osprey* (3 more in test)
HELICOPTERS
CSAR Some HH-60G *Pave Hawk*
TPT • **Medium** Some Mi-8 *Hip* **Light** Some UH-1N *Huey*
UAV • **CISR** • **Heavy** Some MQ-1 *Predator*

Reserve Organisations

Air National Guard
FORCES BY ROLE
EW   1 sqn with EC-130J/SJ *Commando Solo*

EQUIPMENT BY TYPE
AIRCRAFT
EW 7: 3 EC-130J *Commando Solo*; 4 EC-130SJ *Commando Solo*
TPT • **Medium** 4 MC-130P *Combat Shadow*

Air Force Reserve
FORCES BY ROLE

Tpt   2 sqn with MC-130E *Combat Talon*; 1 sqn with MC-130P *Combat Shadow* (personnel only)

EQUIPMENT BY TYPE
AIRCRAFT
TPT • Medium 10 MC-130E *Combat Talon I*

DEPLOYMENT

AFGHANISTAN
NATO • ISAF 90,000; 1 corps HQ; 1 div HQ; 1 armd HBCT; 1 mech inf SBCT; 1 lt inf IBCT; 4 Air Aslt IBCT; 1 AB IBCT; 1 BfSB; 3 cbt avn bde; 1 ARNG IBCT; 1 USMC MEF HQ with (2 RCT)
US Central Command • *Operation Enduring Freedom – Afghanistan* ε7,000
  EQUIPMENT BY TYPE (ISAF and OEF-A)
  AH-64 *Apache*, OH-58 *Kiowa*, CH-47 *Chinook*, UH-60 *Black Hawk*, M1-A1 *Abrams*; M119, M198, *Stryker*, 3,200 MRAP, M-ATV, F-15E *Strike Eagle*, A-10 *Thunderbolt II*, EC-130H *Compass Call*, C-130 *Hercules*, HH-60 *Pave Hawk*, MV-22B Osprey, AV-8B *Harrier*, KC-130J *Hercules*, AH-IW *Cobra*, CH-53 *Sea Stallion*, UH-IN *Iroquois*, RQ-7B *Shadow*, MQ-1 *Predator*, MQ-9 *Reaper*

ANTIGUA AND BARBUDA
US Strategic Command • 1 detection and tracking radar at Antigua Air Station

ARABIAN SEA
US Central Command • Navy • 5th Fleet • (5th Fleet's operating forces are rotationally deployed to the region from 2nd and/or 3rd Fleet.);
  EQUIPMENT BY TYPE
  2 CVN; 2 CGHM; 5 DDGHM; 1 DDGM; 1 LHD; 1 LHA; 1 LPD; 1 LSD; 2 AOE
Combined Maritime Forces • TF 53: 1 AE; 2 AKE; 1 AOH; 3 AO
Combined Maritime Forces • CTF-151: 1 CGHM; 1 DDGHM; 1 FFH; 1 LPD; 1 LSD

ARUBA
US Southern Command • 1 Forward Operating Location at Aruba

ASCENSION ISLAND
US Strategic Command • 1 detection and tracking radar at Ascension Auxiliary Air Field

ATLANTIC OCEAN
US Northern Command • US Navy • 2nd Fleet
  EQUIPMENT BY TYPE
  6 SSBN; 2 SSGN; 21 SSN; 4 CVN; 9 CGHM; 8 DDGHM; 13 DDGM; 15 FFH; 3 LHD; 1 LHA; 3 LPD; 5 LSD

AUSTRALIA
US Pacific Command • 129; 1 SEWS at Pine Gap; 1 comms facility at Pine Gap; 1 SIGINT stn at Pine Gap

BAHRAIN
US Central Command • 1,339; 1 HQ (5th Fleet)

BELGIUM
US European Command • 1,261

BOSNIA-HERZEGOVINA
OSCE • Bosnia and Herzegovina 9

BRITISH INDIAN OCEAN TERRITORY
US Strategic Command • 261; 1 Spacetrack Optical Tracker at Diego Garcia; 1 ground based electro optical deep space surveillance system (*GEODSS*) at Diego Garcia
US Pacific Command • 1 MPS sqn (MPS-2 with equipment for one MEB) at Diego Garcia with 5 logistics and support ships; 1 naval air base at Diego Garcia, 1 support facility at Diego Garcia

CANADA
US Northern Command • 133

CENTRAL AFRICAN REPUBLIC/CHAD
UN • MINURCAT 2

COLOMBIA
US Southern Command • 65

CUBA
US Southern Command • 886 at Guantánamo Bay

DJIBOUTI
US Africa Command • 1,285; 1 naval air base at Djibouti

DEMOCRATIC REPUBLIC OF THE CONGO
UN • MONUSCO 2

EGYPT
MFO 688; 1 inf bn; 1 spt bn

EL SALVADOR
US Southern Command • 1 Forward Operating Location (Military, DEA, USCG and Customs personnel)

GERMANY
US Africa Command • 1 HQ at Stuttgart; 1 USAF HQ (17th Air Force) at Ramstein AB
US European Command • 53,130; 1 Combined Service HQ (EUCOM) at Stuttgart–Vaihingen
  US Army 37,828 (reducing)
    FORCES BY ROLE
    1 HQ (US Army Europe (USAREUR)) at Heidelberg; 2 armd inf bde; (1 mech inf SBCT currently deployed to AFG); 1 (hvy) cbt avn bde; 1 engr bde; 1 spt bde; 1 int bde; 2 sigs bde; 1 (APS) armd HBCT eqpt set (transforming)
    EQUIPMENT BY TYPE
    M-1 *Abrams*; M-2/M-3 *Bradley*; *Stryker*, M109; MLRS; AH-64 *Apache*; CH-47 *Chinook* UH-60 *Black Hawk*
  US Navy 225
  USAF 14,708
    FORCES BY ROLE
    1 HQ (US Air Force Europe (USAFE)) at Ramstein AB; 1 HQ (3rd Air Force) at Ramstein AB; 1 ftr wg at Spangdahlem AB with (1 ftr sqn with 24 F-16C *Fighting Falcon*; 1 atk sqn with 12 A-10 *Thunderbolt II*; 6 OA-10A *Thunderbolt II*); 1 tpt wg at Ramstein AB with 16 C-130E *Hercules*; 2 C-20 Gulfstream; 9 C-21 *Learjet*; 1 CT-43 Boeing 737
  USMC 369

GREECE

US European Command • 346; 1 naval base at Makri; 1 naval base at Soudha Bay; 1 air base at Iraklion

GREENLAND (DNK)

US Strategic Command • 133; 1 ballistic missile early warning system (BMEWS) at Thule; 1 Spacetrack Radar at Thule

GUAM

US Pacific Command • 2,982; 1 air base; 1 naval base

EQUIPMENT BY TYPE

3 SSN; 1 MPS sqn (MPS-3 with equipment for one MEB) with 4 Logistics and Support vessels

GULF OF ADEN & SOMALI BASIN

NATO • *Operation Ocean Shield* 1 DDGM; 1 FFH

HAITI

UN • MINUSTAH 9

HONDURAS

US Southern Command • 397; 1 avn bn with CH-47 *Chinook*; UH-60 *Black Hawk*

IRAQ

NATO • NTM-I 12
UN • UNAMI 4 obs
US Central Command • *Operation New Dawn* 49,775

FORCES BY ROLE

1 corps HQ; 3 div HQ; 3 armd HBCT (AAB); 1 armd HBCT HQ (AAB); 1 armd cav regt (AAB); 1 mech inf SBCT (AAB); 1 lt inf IBCT (AAB); 1 ARNG lt inf IBCT (LoC duties); 2 cbt avn bde

EQUIPMENT BY TYPE

M1 *Abrams*, M2 *Bradley*, M3 *Bradley*, *Stryker*, M109, M198, 9,341 MRAP, AH-64 *Apache*, OH-58 *Kiowa*, UH-60 *Black Hawk*, CH-47 *Chinook*, F-16D *Fighting Falcon*; A-10 *Thunderbolt II*; C-130 *Hercules*; C-17 *Globemaster III*; HH-60G *Pave Hawk*; RQ-1B *Predator*

ISRAEL

US European Command • 1 AN/TPY-2 X-band radar at Nevatim

ITALY

US European Command • 9,665
US Army 3,321; (1 AB IBCT currently deployed to AFG)
US Navy 2,155; 1 HQ (US Navy Europe (USNAVEUR)) at Naples; 1 HQ (6th Fleet) at Gaeta; 1 MP sqn with 9 P-3C *Orion* at Sigonella
USAF 4,131; 1 ftr wg with (2 ftr sqn with 21 F-16C/D *Fighting Falcon*) at Aviano
USMC 58

JAPAN

US Pacific Command • 35,598
US Army 2,677; 1 HQ (9th Theater Army Area Command) at Zama
US Navy 3,539; 1 HQ (7th Fleet) at Yokosuka; 1 base at Sasebo; 1 base at Yokosuka

EQUIPMENT BY TYPE

1 CVN; 2 CGHM; 3 DDGHM; 4 DDGM; 1 LCC; 4 MCO; 1 LHD; 1 LPD; 2 LSD
USAF 12,380

FORCES BY ROLE

1 HQ (5th Air Force) at Okinawa – Kadena AB; 1 ftr wg at Okinawa – Kadena AB with (2 ftr sqn with 18 F-16 *Fighting Falcon* at Misawa AB); 1 ftr wg at Okinawa – Kadena AB with (1 AEW&C sqn with 2 E-3B *Sentry*, 1 CSAR sqn with 8 HH-60G *Pave Hawk*, 2 ftr sqn with 24 F-15C/D *Eagle*); 1 tpt wg at Yokota AB with 10 C-130H *Hercules*; 2 C-12J; 1 Special Ops gp at Okinawa – Kadena AB
USMC 17,002

FORCES BY ROLE

1 Marine div (3rd); 1 ftr sqn with 12 F/A-18D *Hornet*; 1 tkr sqn with 12 KC-130J *Hercules*; 2 tpt hel sqn with 12 CH-46E *Sea Knight*; 1 tpt hel sqn with 12 MV-22B *Osprey*; 3 tpt hel sqn with 10 CH-53E *Sea Stallion*

KOREA, REPUBLIC OF

US Pacific Command • 25,374
US Army 17,130

FORCES BY ROLE

1 HQ (8th Army) at Seoul; 1 div HQ (2nd Inf) located at Tongduchon, 1 armd HBCT, 1 (hvy) cbt avn bde, 1 arty (fires) bde; 1 AD bde

EQUIPMENT BY TYPE

M-1 *Abrams*; M-2/M-3 *Bradley*; M-109; AH-64 *Apache* CH-47 *Chinook*; UH-60 *Black Hawk*; MLRS; MIM-104 *Patriot*/FIM-92A *Avenger*; 1 (APS) HBCT set
US Navy 254
USAF 7,857

FORCES BY ROLE

1 (AF) HQ (7th Air Force) at Osan AB; 1 ftr wg at Osan AB with (1 ftr sqn with 20 F-16C *Fighting Falcon*/F-16D *Fighting Falcon*, 1 ftr sqn with 12 A-10 *Thunderbolt II*, 12 OA-10 *Thunderbolt II*); 1 ftr wg at Kunsan AB with (1 ftr sqn with total of 20 F-16C *Fighting Falcon*/F-16D *Fighting Falcon*); 1 Special Ops sqn
USMC 133

KUWAIT

US Central Command • Troops deployed as part of *Operation New Dawn*; 2 AD bty with 16 PAC-3 *Patriot*; elm 1 (APS) HBCT set (Empty – equipment in use)

LIBERIA

UN • UNMIL 5; 4 obs

LITHUANIA

NATO • Baltic Air Policing 4 F-15C *Eagle*

MARSHALL ISLANDS

US Strategic Command • 1 detection and tracking radar at Kwajalein Atoll

MEDITERRANEAN SEA

US European Command • US Navy • 6th Fleet

EQUIPMENT BY TYPE

1 LCC

MIDDLE EAST

UN • UNTSO 2 obs

MOLDOVA

OSCE • Moldova 2

NETHERLANDS
US European Command • 477

NORWAY
US European Command • 1 (APS) SP 155mm arty bn set

PACIFIC OCEAN
US Pacific Command • US Navy • 3rd Fleet
EQUIPMENT BY TYPE
8 SSBN; 2 SSGN; 29 SSN; 4 CVN; 8 CGHM; 12 DDGHM; 9 DDGM; 12 FFH; 2 LCS; 6 MCO; 3 LHD; 3 LPD; 3 LSD

PERSIAN GULF
Combined Maritime Forces • CTF-152: 4 MCO

PHILIPPINES
US Pacific Command • 117

PORTUGAL
US European Command • 705; 1 spt facility at Lajes

QATAR
US Central Command • 531; elm 1 (APS) HBCT set (Empty – equipment in use)

SAUDI ARABIA
US Central Command • 258

SERBIA
NATO • KFOR • *Joint Enterprise* 810; 1 ARNG cbt spt bde
OSCE • Serbia 5
OSCE • Kosovo 18

SEYCHELLES
US Africa Command • some MQ-9 *Reaper* UAV

SIERRA LEONE
IMATT 3

SINGAPORE
US Pacific Command • 122; 1 log spt sqn; 1 spt facility

SPAIN
US European Command • 1,256; 1 air base at Morón; 1 naval base at Rota

THAILAND
US Pacific Command • 122

TURKEY
US European Command • 1,560; 1 air base at Incirlik; 1 support facility at Ankara; 1 support facility at Izmir
US Strategic Command • 1 Spacetrack Radar at Incirlik

UNITED ARAB EMIRATES
US Central Command • 2 bty with MIM-104 *Patriot*

UNITED KINGDOM
US European Command • 9,221
FORCES BY ROLE
1 ftr wg at RAF Lakenheath with (1 ftr sqn with 24 F-15C *Eagle*/F-15D *Eagle*, 2 ftr sqn with 24 F-15E *Strike Eagle*); 1 tkr wg at RAF Mildenhall with 15 KC-135 *Stratotanker*; 1 Spec Ops gp at RAF Mildenhall with 5 MC-130H *Combat Talon II*; 5 MC-130P *Combat Shadow*; 1 C-130E *Hercules*
US Strategic Command • 1 ballistic missile early warning system (BMEWS) and 1 Spacetrack Radar at Fylingdales Moor

FOREIGN FORCES

Canada 3 USCENTCOM; 303 NORTHCOM (NORAD)
Germany Air Force: trg units at Goodyear AFB (AZ)/Sheppard AFB (TX) with 40 T-38 *Talon* trg ac; 69 T-6A *Texan* II; 1 trg sqn Holloman AFB (NM) with 24 *Tornado* IDS; NAS Pensacola (FL); Fort Rucker (AL) • Missile trg located at Fort Bliss (TX)
United Kingdom Army, Navy, Air Force ε540

Table 9 **Selected US Arms Orders**

Classification	Designation	FY2009 Units	FY2009 Value ($m)	Estimate FY2010 Units	Estimate FY2010 Value ($m)	Request FY2011 Units	Request FY2011 Value ($m)
JOINT							
UAV	RQ-4A *Global Hawk*	5	710	4	666	4	740
UAV	MQ-1 *Predator*	38	224	24	480	29	506
UAV	RQ-7 *Shadow*			4	51		
UAV	MQ-9 *Reaper*	24	444	24	488	48	1,080
Tpt	C-27J (Joint Cargo Aircraft)	7	262	8	318	8	351
Trg	T-6 *Texan II*	43	310	37	271	38	266
	Missile Defence	n/a	717	n/a	986	n/a	1,433
AIR FORCE							
FGA	F-35A *Lightning II*	7	1,661	10	2,355	23	4,191
Ftr	F-22A *Raptor*	24	3,636		78		158
FGA	F-16 Upgrades		373		223		167
Bbr	B-2 Upgrades		347		267		63
Tpt	C-17A *Globemaster*	8	2,488	10	2,580		14
Tpt	C-130J *Hercules*	0	61	4	459	8	511
Tpt/SAR	HC/MC-130 (recap)	13	1,042	2	511		
Tpt	C-5 Upgrades		552		726		981
Tilt rotor	CV-22 *Osprey*	6	422	5	450	5	407
AAM	AIM-120 AMRAAM	133	203	170	273	246	355
ASM	JASSM	100	140	0	53	171	216
ASM	AGM-114 *Hellfire* (for MQ-1)	1,263	113	1,008	87	891	86
Sat	SBIR	2	1,833	1	465	1	971
Sat	GPS		128		53		
Launcher	EELV	2	1,334	3	1,099	3	1,154
ARMY							
Hel	Light Utility Helicopter	44	276	54	325	50	305
Hel	UH-60 *Blackhawk*	66	1,111	81	1,391	74	1,392
Hel	AH-64D *Apache*			8	219	16	494
Hel	CH-47 *Chinook*	28	696	37	1,001	42	1,230
MRL	HIMARS	57	228	46	208	44	212
MANPAT	*Javelin*	1,320	368	1,265	259	715	164
MBT	*Abrams* modifications		737		183		231
MBT	*Abrams* upgrade	111	581	22	185	21	183
APC (W)	*Stryker*	352	1,499	93	513	83	300
Veh	HMMWV	9,202	1,511	8,120	1,344		
Veh	FHTV	30,137	1,975	20,645	1,414	12,227	738
Veh	FMTV	2,716	631	5,181	1,360	5,992	1,435
Veh	M1117 ASV	328	319	150	149	150	167
NAVY and MARINES							
FGA	F/A-18 E/F *Super Hornet*	23	1,855	18	1,551	22	1,787
FGA	F-35B *Lightning II*					13	2,576
FGA	F-35C *Lightning II*	7	1,693	20	4,464	7	1,887
EW	EA-18G *Growler*	22	1,614	22	1,627	12	1,084
Tilt-rotor	MV-22 *Osprey*	30	2,214	30	2,293	30	2,203

North America

Table 9 **Selected US Arms Orders**

Classification	Designation	FY2009 Units	FY2009 Value ($m)	Estimate FY2010 Units	Estimate FY2010 Value ($m)	Request FY2011 Units	Request FY2011 Value ($m)
Hel	UH-1Y	15	374	18	424	18	410
Hel	AH-1Z *Venom*	9	260	9	273	13	417
Hel	MH-60R	30	1,171	24	932	24	1,060
Hel	MH-60S	20	594	18	472	18	549
AEW&C	E-2D *Hawkeye*	2	414	3	742	4	938
Tkr	KC-130J	2	150				
MP	P-8 *Poseiden*	0	110	6	1,797	7	1,991
UAV	MQ-8 *Fire Scout*	3	50	5	90	3	47
SLBM	*Trident* modifications	24	1,085	24	1,052	24	1,107
LACM	*Tomahawk*	207	280	196	277	196	300
SAM	*Standard*	69	221	45	189	67	296
CVN	*Gerald R. Ford*-class		4,476		1,220		2,640
CVN	Refueling/overhaul	1	613		1,770		1,664
SSN	*Virginia*-class	1	3,573	1	3,957	2	5,133
CG	DDG 1000	1	1,504		1,379		186
DGG	*Arleigh Burke*-class		199	1	2,484	2	2,970
FFG	Littoral Combat Ship	2	1,017	2	1,077	2	1,509
LPD	LDP-17	1	963		969		

Table 10 **Selected Arms Procurements and Deliveries, Canada**

Designation	Type	Quantity	Contract Value	Supplier Country	Prime Contractor	Order Date	First Delivery Due	Notes
LAV III	APC (W) Upgrade	550	CAN$1bn (US$859.7m)	CAN	General Dynamics (GDLS)	2009	2012	Focus on weapons and mobility systems. Part of FLCV upgrade and procurement project worth CAN$5bn
M777 *Howitzer*	Towed 155mm arty	25	n.k.	US	BAE	2009	2009	Acquired from US through Foreign Military Sales Programme. Total contract with BAE (63) worth US$118m. 2 delivered June 2009 - remainder by 2011
Halifax class	FFGHM Upgrade	12	CAN$3.1bn (US$2.9bn)	CAN	Halifax and Victoria Shipyards	2007	2010	SLEP: *Halifax*-class HCM/FELEX project. To be fitted with *Sea Giraffe* 150 HC surv radar. Final delivery due 2017
150 HC 2D *Sea Giraffe*	Naval Radar	12	US$23m	CAN	Saab	2009	2010	For *Halifax* class FFGHM. Part of Frigate Equipment Life Extension Combat Systems Integration programme
F-35 *Lightning II*	FGA ac	65	CAN$9bn (US$8.5bn)	US	Lockheed Martin	2010	2016	To replace F/A-18 *Hornet* fleet
CP-140 (P-3) *Aurora*	ASW ac Upgrade	10	US$156m	US	Lockheed Martin	2008	n.k.	SLEP: To extend service life by 15,000 flight hours over 20 to 25 years
C-130J *Super Hercules*	Tpt ac	17	US$1.4bn	US	Lockheed Martin	2007	2010	To replace current CC130 E. First delivered June 2010. Final delivery due 2013
CH-148 *Cyclone*	Tpt Hel	28	US$5bn	US	Sikorsky	2004	2010	(H-92 *Superhawk*). Incl US$1.8bn 20-year parts/training package. Deliveries delayed. Final fully capable hel due 2012
CH-47F *Chinook*	Tpt Hel	15	US$1.15bn	US	Boeing	2009	2013	For Army use in AFG

Chapter Four
Europe

NATO

NATO's new Strategic Concept was adopted at the Lisbon Summit meeting on 19–20 November 2010. The document provides overall political guidance to the Alliance and expresses the organisation's purpose and core functions in the context of the international security environment. It thus provides overall guidance for NATO's development. NATO has expanded to 28 member states and has taken on new operational challenges beyond its borders, including, of course, in Afghanistan. But security challenges have become more diffuse, transnational and complex since the last strategic concept was written in 1999, while both the Alliance and the international environment have changed considerably. These factors made the revision necessary.

The road to Lisbon
Member states set out a three-stage process for the task. To assist with the 'reflection' and 'consultation' phases, NATO appointed a 12-member Group of Experts (GoE), which began work in September 2009 under the chairmanship of former US Secretary of State Madeleine Albright. The group reported in May 2010 and, while the document was not as visionary as some commentators had hoped, it incorporated important messages. Even the title, 'Assured Security; Dynamic Engagement', reflected the need to balance different perceptions of NATO's purpose with regard to homeland defence and expeditionary commitments. The group testified to a central problem: 'Although NATO is busier than it has ever been, its value is less obvious to many than in the past.' Reassurance was to be achieved through the rather predictable means of contingency planning, exercises and readiness. As far as operations beyond NATO territory were concerned, the report underlined that NATO remained a regional organisation, but one that needed guidelines about when and where to act in a broader setting. An important message concerned the role of partnerships with other countries and organisations, because NATO will be unlikely to operate alone in the future. Related to this was an effort to improve NATO's ability to contribute to the comprehensive approach, which could see the Alliance providing a military component to a broader solution or acting to bring different instruments together. Furthermore, the GoE pointed to the need to fully exploit the potential benefits of Article IV, which allows for political consultations on security problems among members. Making more thorough use of this provision could enable NATO members to prepare the ground for action before a problem becomes a full-blown crisis or threat.

While the GoE's deliberations were intended to be free from undue influence, NATO governments did supply policy papers and the group was supported by several circles of advisers from both within and outside NATO. During the reflection phase, which ended in February 2010, NATO brought together groups of stakeholders, including external experts, in seminars to encourage debate on specific aspects of the strategic concept. During the subsequent consultation phase, members of the GoE visited the capitals of NATO members and other countries. In May 2010 the group provided NATO Secretary-General Anders Fogh Rasmussen with a policy paper outlining recommendations for the content of the concept document. Based on this input and Allied reactions to it, the secretary-general wrote his own paper – submitted to member governments at the end of September 2010 – to canvass their views and solicit guidance.

Drafting of and negotiation on the new strategic concept did not, therefore, really begin until late summer 2010. The long build-up was billed as an exercise in transparency, but was also clearly driven by the need to reconcile divergent views into a coherent picture with higher levels of consensus than were visible. It contrasted with the last phase of the process, which was tightly controlled by the secretary-general. Giving member-state governments only two weeks to digest his draft before it was discussed at a NATO ministerial meeting in October, Rasmussen ran the risk of running into resistance from Alliance members at the last minute.

When he outlined his thinking on the new concept publicly in early October, it became clear that he envisaged a document that would try to balance many divergent perspectives. While necessary to integrate

The new Strategic Concept

The final document, called *Active Engagement, Modern Defence*, provides little in terms of technical detail but builds a consensual statement of how NATO seeks to position itself for the coming decade. Secretary-General Anders Fogh Rasmussen successfully navigated many of the pitfalls presented by different member-government positions. Nevertheless, it is clear that implementation of the guidelines agreed at Lisbon will be the proof, or otherwise, of NATO's successful adaptation to modern demands. The strategic concept comprises a number of core messages:

- NATO will focus on three core tasks: collective defence, crisis management (before, during and after conflict) and cooperative security.
- NATO is at its core a political alliance. Thus, 'any security issue of interest to any Ally can be brought to the NATO table, to share information, exchange views and, where appropriate, forge common approaches'.
- NATO faces a diffuse security environment which combines a variety of threats and challenges, including the proliferation of ballistic missiles, the proliferation of WMD, terrorism, international instability and conflict, cyber attacks, the security of lines of communication, technological trends, and environmental and resource constraints.
- NATO's deterrence posture will continue to foresee a clear role for nuclear weapons: 'As long as nuclear weapons exist, NATO will remain a nuclear alliance.'
- NATO will develop an alliance-wide ballistic-missile defence system to protect allied populations and territories.
- NATO will adopt limited roles in the prevention of, detection of, defence against and recovery from cyber attacks and will also seek to develop its capacity to protect critical energy infrastructure and transit areas/lines.
- Struggling to operationalise the comprehensive approach, NATO will equip itself with an 'appropriate but modest civilian crisis management capability to interface more effectively with civilian partners'.
- NATO is open to cooperation with third countries on issues of mutual concern and promises third countries that contribute to its operations 'a structural role in shaping strategy and decisions' within the context of those operations.
- In an overture to Russia, the strategic concept unequivocally states 'NATO poses no threat to Russia. On the contrary: we want to see a true strategic partnership between NATO and Russia, and we will act accordingly, with the expectation of reciprocity from Russia.'

At the summit, NATO leaders also emphasised that they plan to begin handing over responsibility for security in Afghanistan to local authorities from 2011 with a view to complete this transition by 2014. Secretary-General Rasmussen and Afghan President Hamid Karzai, however, also struck a long-term agreement to demonstrate that NATO allies will remain committed to Afghanistan even beyond that timeline.

An invigorated NATO–Russia relationship was one of the headline-grabbing events of the summit. In the framework of the NATO–Russia Council it was decided that NATO–Russia cooperation on ballistic-missile defence should begin with a joint threat assessment before any technical steps can be taken. Furthermore, Russia further expanded the transit agreement with NATO, allowing allies to transport a greater number of non-lethal goods through Russian territory towards Afghanistan and, crucially, also use this northern supply route to transport items back out of Afghanistan. Aside from missile defence, the issues of counter-terrorism, counter-narcotics and counter-piracy were identified as ripe for practical cooperation and consultation between the Alliance and Russia.

the partly conflicting views of NATO governments, this will open the strategic concept to criticism that it is unfocused and vague. As the secretary-general explained, NATO needed to confirm its core task of collective defence; underline the need for strong military capabilities, which would require continued investment in deployable, flexible and sustainable forces; and reiterate the importance of political consultations within the Alliance. However, in a speech to the German Marshall Fund in Brussels he explained that 'there are fewer military threats to [NATO] territory, but more challenges to our security, from every direction, including cyberspace'. On the latter point, Rasmussen suggested NATO would need to develop its cyber-defence capacity – including a deployable capability to support Allies under cyber attack. Many Allies felt that cyber threats would not fall under the Alliance's collective defence obligations embodied in Article V, because it was difficult to see how useful NATO's military capabilities would be in such a case, especially as the perpetrator of such an attack might not be readily identifiable. When pressed on this

Map 2 NATO's Members, Cooperation and Partnership Programmes

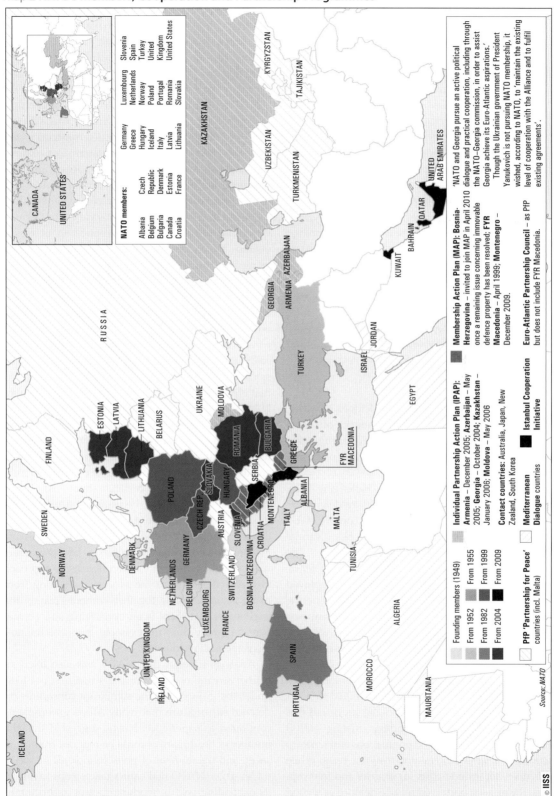

NATO members:

Albania	Czech	Germany	Luxembourg	Slovenia
Belgium	Republic	Greece	Netherlands	Spain
Bulgaria	Denmark	Hungary	Norway	Turkey
Canada	Estonia	Iceland	Poland	United
Croatia	France	Italy	Portugal	Kingdom
		Latvia	Romania	United States
		Lithuania	Slovakia	

Individual Partnership Action Plan (IPAP): Armenia – December 2005; Azerbaijan – May 2005; Georgia – October 2004; Kazakhstan – January 2006; Moldova – May 2006
Contact countries: Australia, Japan, New Zealand, South Korea

Founding members (1949)
From 1952
From 1982
From 2004

From 1955
From 1999
From 2009

PfP 'Partnership for Peace' countries (incl. Malta)

Membership Action Plan (MAP): Bosnia-Herzegovina – invited to join MAP in April 2010 once a remaining issue concerning immovable defence property has been resolved; **FYR Macedonia** – April 1999; **Montenegro** – December 2009.

Euro-Atlantic Partnership Council – as PfP but does not include FYR Macedonia.

Istanbul Cooperation Initiative

Mediterranean Dialogue countries

'NATO and Georgia pursue an active political dialogue and practical cooperation, including through the NATO–Georgia commission, in order to assist Georgia achieve its Euro-Atlantic aspirations.'
Though the Ukrainian government of President Yanukovich is not pursuing NATO membership, it wished, according to NATO, to 'maintain the existing level of cooperation with the Alliance and to fulfil existing agreements'.

Source: NATO

© IISS

Europe

Across Europe

- Deliveries of Eurofighter *Typhoon* continue to European partners from the tranche-2 production run, with numbers delivered to the Royal Saudi Air Force increasing.
- The NH Helicopter Industries NH-90 helicopter has seen deliveries increase slowly. Finland now operates the type, while Germany, for instance, continues its training flights.
- The UK is to purchase three *Rivet Joint* signals-intelligence aircraft to replace the *Nimrod* R1. There will be a gap, however, between the retirement of *Nimrod* and the arrival of *Rivet Joint*.
- Sweden abolished conscription, while Germany moved to reduce the term conscripts must serve to six months, effective from January 2011, with conscription to be effectively 'discontinued' after mid-2011.
- The first FREMM frigate was launched in France. Vessels are being built for the French, Italian, Greek and Moroccan navies.
- Test flying of the A400M continues, with partner nations and industry moving forward in November 2010 on details of the broad agreement reached in March.

point during a press conference in October, however, Rasmussen refused to rule cyber attacks out, as a matter of principle, as an Article V issue, arguing that each situation had to be assessed by Allies on a case-by-case basis.

Missile defence was another challenging area, given its perceived linkages to nuclear deterrence. This, in turn, had to be seen in the context of US President Barack Obama's push for nuclear disarmament, encapsulated in the concept of 'global zero'. The secretary-general argued that NATO missile defence, which had previously been limited to deployed troops, was not a substitute for nuclear deterrence, but rather a complementary capability. Rasmussen maintained, in a 12 October article in the *New York Times*, that 'we need to protect our populations and territories from the threat posed by the proliferation of missiles. NATO can do it, and at an affordable cost.' Insisting that NATO would be able to field systems with proven technical capabilities, he suggested that the additional cost of expanding existing NATO missile plans to cover Allied populations and territory would be around €200 million over ten years. While this does not include costs for sensors and interceptors, Rasmussen portrayed missile defence as a good

return on investment, providing a new capability, underlining the principles of solidarity and burden-sharing within the Alliance, and offering an opportunity for practical cooperation with Russia.

But the question of nuclear deterrence put Germany and France, among others, at loggerheads. Germany had argued that the strategic concept should de-emphasise nuclear deterrence and affirm the global zero idea, whereas France was strongly in favour of confirming nuclear deterrence as a core principle. While some commentators in Germany suggested a NATO ballistic-missile-defence capability that included populations and territory should lead to a reduced role for nuclear deterrence, other Allies, including the US, did not hold this view. The German government had initially been sceptical about missile defence, but endorsed the idea after the US suggested using its national system (still under development) as the backbone of a NATO capability rather than pursuing bilateral agreements with individual Allies, and after a consensus emerged to explore cooperation with Russia.

On the question of partnerships, Rasmussen called for NATO to become a hub for security discussions on issues of mutual concern and indicated that NATO would need to define ways in which non-NATO states that contributed to operations would be able to shape operations in which they were involved. He underlined that NATO, in its efforts to operationalise the comprehensive approach (broadly speaking, an attempt to bring a wide range of civilian and military instruments to bear on crisis situations), should stress that it would not necessarily be in the lead in such endeavours: the Alliance does not have the capacity to play a leading role on civilian reconstruction and development. Hence, NATO and its partners will need to implement the comprehensive approach in a way that stresses the synergies resulting from many actors working together without creating the impression that there is an underlying and permanent hierarchy that, for example, puts the military instrument above others.

Analysts thought that NATO was also likely to further streamline its command structures, not least under the influence of the significant constraints on defence expenditure that many Allied governments continued to experience. It was suggested that the number of headquarters could be reduced from 11 to seven and the number of posts from some 12,500 to under 9,000. NATO had earlier taken steps to rein in its expanding web of working groups and committees, though these measures were of limited success; in some cases, for example, when groups were merged, they continued to meet in separate incarnations. Thus, while structures were eliminated on paper, true streamlining had yet to occur.

Renewed interest in capability pooling and sharing

During 2010, defence establishments throughout Europe tried to come to terms with the implications of the budgetary constraints imposed by the financial and economic crisis of 2009. In October, Rasmussen implored Alliance governments to coordinate their approach to defence cuts and think seriously about pooling capabilities and enhancing role specialisation, enabling one country to give up certain capabilities in the knowledge that another would provide it. Rasmussen insisted that 'there is a point where you are no longer cutting fat; you're cutting into muscle, and then into bone … Cuts can go too far. We have to avoid cutting so deep that we won't, in future, be able to defend the security on which our economic prosperity rests.'

Meanwhile, at an informal meeting of EU defence ministers on 23–24 September, the EU's High Representative for Foreign Affairs and Security Policy, Baroness Catherine Ashton, argued that EU member governments should cooperate more in order to deliver defence capability and focus 'spending on our agreed priorities. We need to explore ways of pooling and sharing. Our existing resources need to better fit our needs.' The theme of closer cooperation, including ways in which member states might be able to share and pool capability and possibly even engage in role and task sharing (see *The Military Balance 2010*, pp. 107–8), was taken up by defence ministers. German Defence Minister Karl-Theodor zu Guttenberg suggested member states should evaluate three core questions. Which capabilities would have to remain outside of pooling and sharing arrangements for national security reasons? For which capability areas could member states envision pooling arrangements? And, finally, where would member governments be willing to consider task and role sharing with other EU partners?

This tiered approach acknowledges that there will be capabilities that are likely to remain purely national, because governments consider them essential for sovereignty and autonomy. Likewise, it takes into account the fact that pooling might be easier because the governments involved would retain autonomy

in decision-making, whereas role and task specialisation would entail a stronger political commitment and would probably necessitate mutually binding guarantees that governments – due to parliamentary control over the decision to deploy forces abroad, for example – might be unwilling or unable to give. For example, if a government were to rely on an EU partner for a certain capability, there would need to be an arrangement in place to ensure that the capability was actually available when needed. Distinguishing between sovereign capabilities, capabilities that could be pooled and capabilities where role and task specialisation might be appropriate should make it easier to move from expressions of political intent to concrete measures and implementation.

The European Defence Agency (EDA) added to the debate on capability sharing, suggesting that counter-improvised explosive device (C-IED), logistics, training and medical were capabilities suitable for pooling. It was also suggested that the European Air Transport Command could serve as a model for a multinational European helicopter force. The EDA's Helicopter Training Programme (HTP) had, after its 2009 pilot phase, trained some 360 air crews by October 2010 through live exercises and theoretical modules. Its *AZOR 2010* exercise in Spain, involving more than 40 helicopters and some 700 participants, was billed as the biggest live helicopter exercise since the end of the Cold War. Within the framework of the EDA, France is leading a C-IED project with the aim of developing and fielding a laboratory to conduct forensic analysis following an IED blast. Another example of the multinational projects already under way within the EDA is Sweden's initiative seeking to develop sense-and-avoid technology for UAVs, to enable their integration into civilian airspace. (see Unmanned aerial vehicles, p. 20).

Through the so-called Joint Investment Programmes (JIPs), the EDA is trying to break the time-honoured principle of *juste retour*, meaning that industrial workloads are allocated to national defence industries according to the size of the product to be bought by customer governments. This has plagued many multinational development programmes in the past. In JIPs a shared pool of money is awarded competitively to a multinational consortium, with the results of development work available to all contributors. Hence, an investment by a smaller member state might still produce substantial return. A JIP in the area of force protection has already produced results in sniper detection and body armour. In the

Table 11 **EU Battlegroups 2010–14**

Year	Period	Battlegroup	Lead Nation	Contributing nations
2010	Jul–Dec	1	Italy	Romania & Turkey
		2	Spain	France & Portugal
2011	Jan–Jun	1	Netherlands	Austria, Finland, Germany & Lithuania
		2	Sweden	Estonia, Finland, Ireland & Norway
	Jul–Dec	1	Greece	Bulgaria, Cyprus & Romania
		2	Portugal	France, Italy & Spain
2012	Jan–Jun	1	France	Belgium & Luxembourg
		2	Vacant	n/a
	Jul–Dec	1	Italy	Hungary & Slovenia
		2	Germany	Austria, Croatia, Czech Rep. & FYR Macedonia
2013	Jan–Jun	1	Poland	France & Germany
		2	Vacant	n/a
	Jul–Dec	1	UK	Sweden
		2	Vacant	n/a
2014	Jan–Jun	1	Greece	Bulgaria, Cyprus & Romania
		2	Vacant	n/a

Since 2005, the EU has had rapid-response battlegroups on standby for operations under the EU flag. Though never deployed, EU states have invested in capabilities and battlegroup rotations continue to be allocated.

areas of future air systems and ammunition, the EDA is trying to be more forward-looking by identifying those industrial capabilities that would need to be preserved and developed to maintain operational sovereignty. For example, the EDA has signed a contract with a consortium led by Saab to help define capability requirements with a 2035 timeframe to ensure that Europe puts itself in a position to be able to manufacture key equipment in the future.

According to its deputy chief executive for strategy, Carlo Magrassi, the EDA will continue to press member states for harmonised defence requirements, combined R&D investment, the promotion of effective cooperative armaments programmes and increased market competition in defence procurement. These are all issues of substantial importance in times of contraction in defence budgets, because of their potential to lead to efficiency savings and economies of scale. Magrassi nonetheless warned in a speech on 5 October in Brussels that EU 'Member States might fall back in their traditional behaviour of finding purely national solutions, perhaps driven by protecting national industrial interests'. Such a situation would then lead to less interoperability and possibly even more duplication but, on the European level overall, less capability.

Reducing defence expenditure

While overtly protectionist tendencies did not surface in 2010, the desire of many European states to quickly reduce defence expenditure to help control ballooning budget deficits might have a similar result. Most governments make decisions with little or no information about the situation in and decisions of other European countries. One of the few exceptions has been the Franco-German coordination group, intended to ensure that national decisions do not undermine bilateral projects between the two countries. Overall, however, opportunities for cooperation are generally wasted, notwithstanding the developing UK–French collaboration noted below. The risk is that, without coordination, governments will find themselves in a position where they are looking for partners to fill the capability gaps created by national cuts without any forethought as to what the overall balance and spread of capabilities across Europe should look like. It is highly unlikely that such an uncoordinated approach will produce complementarity.

The UK–French Defence and Security Co-operation Treaty, signed during a summit between the British prime minister and French president on 2 November, was clearly designed to create economies through greater coordination. With both nations facing financial pressure on defence budgets, collaboration in certain key areas had been expected on both sides of the English Channel, and followed commitments made in the UK's October 2010 Strategic Defence and Security Review. As part of the treaty, the two nations are to 'develop a Combined Joint Expeditionary Force suitable for a wide range of scenarios, up to and

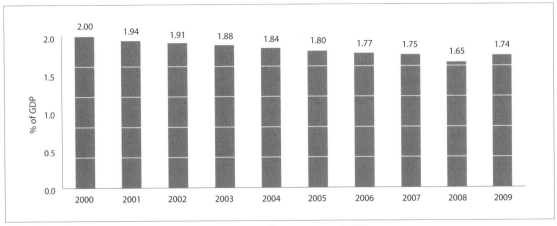

Figure 2 **NATO Europe Regional Defence Expenditure** as % of GDP

including high intensity operations'. In the maritime environment, the two countries 'will aim to have, by the early 2020s, the ability to deploy a UK–French integrated carrier strike group incorporating assets owned by both countries'. Other key issues concerned the extension of 'bilateral co-operation on the acquisition of equipment and technologies, for example in unmanned aerial systems, complex weapons, submarine technologies, satellite communications and research and technology', and 'aligning wherever possible our logistics arrangements – including providing spares and support to the new A400M transport aircraft'. A deal covering computer-modelling support infrastructure for the two states' nuclear weapons was signed separately. However, an agreement between these two nations does not necessarily presage a raft of similar agreements between or among European states.

The UK and France were, paradoxically, the most likely of bedfellows in this regard. Striking similar agreements among broader groups of states, particularly agreements regarding the potential use of force by joint forces, requires a high degree of political and military consensus as well as some similarity in strategic vision, and even then will be subject to voluminous legal commentary, advice and caveats. That such convergence exists more widely in Europe is open to doubt and, as noted above, opportunities for collaboration are generally wasted. Measures either already introduced or under discussion in many European countries are focused on an overall reduction of active forces, reduced or delayed procurements, a lower level of ambition regarding participation in international crisis-management missions, and efficiency savings achieved through a variety of organisational

strategies. Thus far, there is no unified pattern across Europe because the depth and scope of the budgetary crisis differs from country to country, and is, moreover, filtered through specific national lenses such as threat perceptions, operational burdens and defence-reform processes already underway.

Many governments have found it difficult in the past to make inroads into personnel costs, suggesting the axe would fall first on procurement programmes and on research and development. Spanish Secretary of State for Defence Constantino Mendéz Martínez said, after cuts were announced to Spain's defence budget, that the armed forces would find it difficult to invest in new systems while maintaining existing force structures. 'Industry has to be aware that a cycle of modernisation is over and it will be a long time before investments of a similar scale are considered again', he said. However, major European multinational projects already under way with Spanish involvement, such as the A400M and the NH90 and *Tiger* helicopters, seemed exempt from this. In Austria, already among the European states which spend least on defence in relation to GDP, Defence Minister Norbert Darabos said cuts were 'reasonable in economically difficult times' and that 'some acquisitions will have to wait'. Austrian Chief of the General Staff Edmund Entacher responded that this would pose a structural challenge for the armed forces because available resources would not permit them to participate in territorial defence and international crisis-management missions at the same time.

In Italy, the Finance Ministry has demanded across-the-board cuts of 10% for all ministries. While the Ministry of Defence had yet to announce detailed plans at the time of writing, press reports suggested that a number of procurement decisions with a total value of around €5 billion would be delayed, that the number of Eurofighters might be reduced, and that the future of procurement projects such as the FREMM frigates and Joint Strike Fighter is unclear.

Many countries will see their capabilities affected. Lithuania, which cut defence spending by 9% in 2009, announced a moratorium on procurement. Estonia likewise postponed procurement decisions, including on basic items such as trucks and ammunition. Slovenia and Slovakia will cut at least 10% from defence budgets. Poland, which reduced its 2009 budget by 9%, announced that its contributions to operations in Lebanon, Syria and Chad/Central African Republic would have to end because of financial constraints. It also withdrew from NATO's Allied Ground Surveillance project and suggested it would try to renegotiate contracts with industry in an attempt to lower costs. The Netherlands was locked in a debate about a large number of possible scenarios for defence cuts, some of which would jeopardise its future ability to participate in demanding missions such as the NATO-led ISAF in Afghanistan. France, while clearly affected by the financial and economic crisis, tried to safeguard research and development. While a decision was taken in July to cut €3.5bn from defence expenditure over three years, Paris will try to achieve this mostly through efficiency savings and delaying decisions on procurements and capability upgrades in areas such as air-to-air refuelling and satellite-based reconnaissance.

One of the few countries able to buck the trend was Norway, which announced a 4% rise in the defence budget for 2010 and a focus on new equipment. A different picture can still be seen in Sweden, where the defence budget remains largely unaffected by the economic crisis but continues to fall as part of previously agreed defence reforms.

The UK's Strategic Defence and Security Review

The UK's Strategic Defence and Security Review (SDSR) heralded near-term cuts across all three services, as detailed in a number of *IISS Strategic Comments* in 2010. Defence spending is being reduced by 7.5–8% in real terms, with personnel numbers and procurement programmes both affected. The government decided to retain long-term programmes including the Royal Navy's new *Queen Elizabeth*-class aircraft carriers and *Astute*-class nuclear submarines,

and the purchase of a significant number of F-35 Joint Strike Fighters from the United States. It also ring-fenced the nuclear deterrent, though it deferred until 2016 a decision to modernise it with new submarine platforms. One of two future aircraft carriers will be placed into extended readiness (effectively moth-balled) following its completion, while London has also shifted from the F-35B (ASTOVL) to the F-35C (carrier) variant of the US Joint Strike Fighter, and the number purchased will be reduced. These choices reduced the funds available for other elements of military capability.

The army will lose 40% of its main battle tanks, with a 35% cut in heavy artillery. The army's personnel strength will be reduced by 7,000 to roughly 95,000 by 2015, and the number of deployable brigades will be cut by one, to five. The SDSR will likely formalise some of the temporary adaptations made for Afghanistan, such as the redeployment of some Royal Artillery personnel from their current ground-based air-defence role, manning the *Starstreak* missile, to units fielding UAVs. Meanwhile, the huge demand for battlefield information may bring an expansion of company-sized brigade signal squadrons into full-size regiments. The army is likely to take into its core capability many, but not necessarily all, of the equipment it acquired specifically for Afghanistan under Urgent Operational Requirement procedures. This could include the guided multiple-launch rocket system and the *Jackal* patrol vehicle.

While the army will seek to retain its two existing divisional headquarters, as well as its leadership of NATO's Allied Rapid Reaction Corps, it is likely to be under pressure to reduce or eliminate its 20,000-strong bases in Germany. These troops could possibly be accommodated at Royal Air Force bases freed up by expected reductions in fast-jet numbers, though it is not clear that these would be adequate. The government will want to avoid the cost of providing new UK housing.

Much debate has centred on the future of the 27,000-strong reserve force, the Territorial Army. Reservists have been heavily used in Iraq and Afghanistan – both general soldiers and those with a specialist skill, such as medics. While the government will be tempted to slim down the reserves, a counter-argument would be that if the regular army were to face a large reduction in a few years' time, it would be important to maintain the reserves' strength. The indications so far have been that the Territorial Army could be restructured away from formed combat units and instead seek to

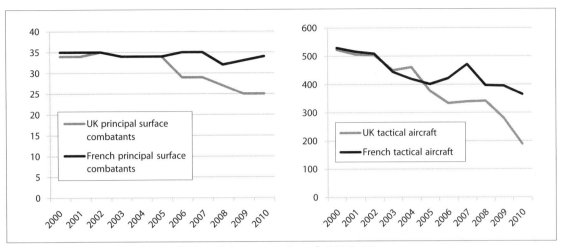

Figure 3 **UK–France Warship and Aircraft Inventory Trends 2000–10**

provide individuals with particular skills, as well as civilian specialists.

The navy's existing flagship light aircraft carrier, HMS *Ark Royal*, has been immediately decommissioned, and amphibious capability will be reduced with the decommissioning of a landing ship and the mothballing of a larger landing platform dock. A further light carrier will be placed in reserve; one will remain in operation as a helicopter platform. In addition, four Type-22 frigates will be decommissioned early in 2011, reducing the total number of escorts (destroyers and frigates) to 19.

It was decided to withdraw the *Harrier* from service, while the *Nimrod* MRA4 maritime anti-submarine warfare aircraft programme has been cancelled. It was announced that the VC-10 and three variants of *Tristar* will be withdrawn from 2013, with a view to the eventual fielding of the A-330 MRTT. Further, the *Sentinel* surveillance aircraft will be withdrawn once it is 'no longer required to support operations in Afghanistan'; the eventual withdrawal date will to some degree depend on how long it is deemed necessary to support whatever forces the UK maintains in Afghanistan, even after 2015 (the date by which London wishes to withdraw most of the British contingent). The fleet of *Tornado* GR4 strike aircraft will be reduced from eight to five squadrons. Unmanned aircraft, requirements for which are being examined in part under the *Scavenger* programme, are expected to play a significant role in the future air force. The emergence of an Anglo-French programme would provide new reconnaissance platforms able to operate at long range over land and sea. In the longer term, a combat-type unmanned aircraft could be in

service by 2030 or 2035. But these unmanned systems remain only at the early stages of development.

The SDSR is intended to begin to shape the UK's armed forces for the coming decade – the so-called Future Force 2020. This is intended to provide as broad a range of capabilities in the medium term as can be afforded, if in the nearer term there are elements of incoherence with regard to some of the capability cuts. But beyond Afghanistan, the SDSR provides a rationale for reducing Britain's capacity for expeditionary operations. 'We will be more selective in our use of the Armed Forces', it says, 'deploying them decisively … but only where key UK national interests are at stake; where we have a clear strategic aim; where the likely political, economic and human costs are in proportion to the likely benefits; where we have a viable exit strategy; and where justifiable under international law'. The review sees greater future emphasis on preventing security problems from escalating into conflict, and provides for an intervention force of up to 30,000 personnel, only two-thirds the size of UK forces deployed to Iraq in 2003. The resultant contraction in military capacity will reduce the nation's ability to project military power and influence internationally. The government had promised a far-reaching, even radical, reassessment of security challenges and how they might best be met, and there were indeed some important new elements, including a major emphasis on the role of the intelligence services in protecting national security. There was stress on the dangers posed by cyber threats, with £650m allocated to tackling this challenge. The SDSR also protected the UK's overseas aid spending, while directing that more be spent on conflict prevention and stabilisation. However, the SDSR was essentially a budget-cutting exercise which degenerated into inter-service rivalry as each of the three military branches lobbied the prime minister and the Treasury in support of what they claimed were vital capacities.

Germany reforms its defence structures

For Germany, budgetary pressure ushered in the most dramatic and radical defence reform effort since East Germany's armed forces were integrated into the Bundeswehr following reunification in 1990. The government mandated a commission to review the organisational structures of and processes in the Bundeswehr to identify ways to increase efficiency. With defence minister zu Guttenberg asserting that 'in part we still have structures that breathe the spirit of 20, 25, 30 years ago', the goal was to get more out of personnel, structures and resources without radical downsizing. The commission was chaired by Frank-Jürgen Wiese, head of the Bundesagentur für Arbeit (the Federal Labour Agency), which provides services to the unemployed and has seen substantial reform. The sole military representative on the commission of six was General Karl-Heinz Lather, a former chief of staff at the Supreme Headquarters Allied Powers Europe (SHAPE). The commission was to streamline administrative processes and review acquisition processes to avoid delays and cost overruns. Set up in April 2010, it reported at the end of October, but was partly overtaken by events.

In spring 2010, the Finance Ministry called for defence expenditure cuts. Following this, the cabinet decided in June that some €8.3bn (US$11.0bn) should be cut between 2011 and 2014, almost half of which was to come from personnel expenditure. The Ministry of Defence was tasked to show the implications of cutting 40,000 active forces for German defence policy, operations, procurement, force posture, conscription and Germany's ability to fulfil its alliance obligations. This report was published in September 2010 by Chief of Defence General Volker Wieker.

As the ministry conducted an internal analysis of shortfalls, Wieker suggested that planning for the period 2011–13 was problematic because current financial resources were aligned neither with Bundeswehr tasks nor with the equipment and force structures that would be required to carry out what was being demanded of it. He suggested that the resource crunch meant the Bundeswehr would

have to accept at least temporary capability gaps, for example by phasing systems out earlier than planned and delaying replacements. (The German navy had retired six out of its ten submarines in 2010, five years earlier than planned to reduce costs.) Meanwhile, a ministry task force reviewing procurement projects reported on 25 June, identifying possible cuts totalling approximately €9.4bn (US$12.44bn). Defence Minister zu Guttenberg explained it was 'self-evident that there will be a stop of one or the other armaments programmes' and that bases below a certain number of personnel would have to be cut was well. Projects thought to be affected included the A400M transport aircraft, where orders might be reduced from 60 to 53; the *Tiger* attack helicopter, where orders might be halved to 40; MEADS missile defence, which might see a reduction of system orders from 12 to 8; and the *Talarion* drone, which was still at an early stage of development and might be cancelled altogether. The government agreed to make 37 of Germany's tranche-3b Eurofighter *Typhoons* available for export.

But the key purpose of the Wieker report was to analyse whether different force structures would help make the Bundeswehr a more effective, more flexible and more deployable force. Part of the problem was that the restructuring of the armed forces into force categories with different levels of capability, a mainstay of a 2006 Defence White Paper, had not yielded the envisioned increases in force-projection capacity. By early 2010, the Bundeswehr still seemed to be limited to sustaining a maximum deployment of 7,000 troops abroad (10,000 for a short period without rotation). The army reportedly argued in internal discussions that, at current resource levels, the 2006 level of ambition was not sustainable as far as the scope of operations and the concurrency of operations was concerned. The division of the military into categories, initially thought to offer an opportunity to modernise the force at affordable costs, turned into an obstacle, because the army did not have enough capabilities to slot into the different force categories at the required levels. For example, the air force still had to deal with limited transport capabilities caused by the delay of major programmes such as the A400M and the NH90 helicopter. Germany often had to rely on commercial solutions or allies for its transport needs. Against this backdrop, Wieker argued that crisis response and stabilisation were part of a continuum, not separate phases, and it was therefore not possible to maintain separate force categories. The level of ambition for the Bundeswehr after the new reform

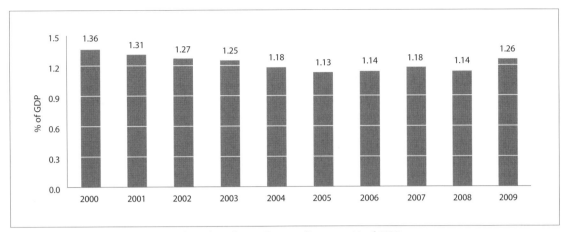

Figure 4 **Non-NATO Europe Regional Defence Expenditure** as % of GDP

effort, Wieker suggested, should be a sustainable deployment of 10,000 troops across several simultaneous operations.

A core assumption of the report, and one that had been publicly supported by zu Guttenberg before the report was published, was that savings targets could only be met with reduced numbers of personnel, both military and civilian. To explore different scenarios, Wieker presented five options and (again very closely aligned with the preferences of zu Guttenberg) recommended a posture that would feature 156,000 professional soldiers augmented by 7,500 voluntary conscripts, for a total of 163,500. This number was seen in the Ministry of Defence as the absolute minimum Germany needed to fulfil its national and alliance obligations, and it was estimated that the transition from the September 2010 total of 251,000 (including around 50,000 conscripts) would take approximately six years.

The coalition agreement between the Christian Democratic Union/Christian Social Union (CDU/CSU) and the Free Democratic Party (FDP) in 2009 had confirmed that the government 'remain[s] firmly committed to the principle of general military service obligation', while also announcing that its duration would be cut to six months from January 2011. Arguably, holding on to conscription but shortening its duration made it even harder to justify. Six months is too short a period to have conscripts

do anything other than basic training; yet the some 50,000 conscripts would continue to tie up considerable resources in terms of infrastructure and training provided by professional soldiers. Zu Guttenberg argued that the budget crunch demanded structural reform of the armed forces and that in this context the continuation of conscription had to be debated anew. He then used his political mandate to outline future force postures to suggest structures that did not feature conscription and let it be known that he favoured such an approach.

The combination of radical cuts to active-service personnel with the spectre of abandoning what many politicians thought was a mainstay of the German armed forces sparked a short but heated debate from which zu Guttenberg's ideas emerged largely intact. While his reform plans still had to clear a number of domestic political hurdles, including party conferences, a coalition committee session and cabinet deliberations (all to be achieved by early 2011), by October 2010 it looked as if a compromise was within reach that would see armed forces' total strength fall to somewhere around 180,000, with approximately 15,000 voluntary conscripts. Decisions were prepared to call up the last batch of conscripts in January 2011, and then discontinue, while not formally abandoning, conscription from July 2011. Effectively this will spell the end of conscription in Germany for the forseeable future.

Albania ALB

Albanian Lek		2009	2010	2011
GDP	lek	1.16tr	1.22tr	
	US$	12.2bn	11.8bn	
per capita	US$	3,863	3,716	
Growth	%	2.2	3.0	
Inflation	%	2.2	3.4	
Def exp	lek	23.5bn		
	US$	248m		
Def bdgt	lek	23.6bn	20.3bn	21.3bn
	US$	249m	195m	
FMA (US)	US$	2.1m	3.0m	5.0m
US$1=lek		94.87	103.93	

Population   3,169,087

Age	0 – 14	15 – 19	20 – 24	25 – 29	30 – 64	65 plus
Male	11.3%	5.2%	4.9%	4.0%	19.2%	4.9%
Female	10.1%	4.9%	5.0%	4.2%	20.8%	5.5%

Capabilities

ACTIVE 14,245 (Joint Force Comd 8,150, Support Command 4,300, TRADOC 1,000, MoD and General Staff 795) Paramilitary 500

Terms of service conscription 12 months

The Albanian Armed Forces (AAF) is a joint, primarily land-oriented force centred on light infantry capabilities supported by naval and air units.

ORGANISATIONS BY SERVICE

Joint Forces Command (JFC) 8,150

Consists of a Land Element (comprising a Rapid Reaction Bde, Cdo Regt, Area Spt Bde, Log Bn and Comms Bn), an Air Bde and Naval Bde. JFC units are intended to conduct and support international peace support and humanitarian operations and other crisis management tasks.

Land Element

FORCES BY ROLE

Lt Inf	1 (Rapid Reaction) bde
Cdo	1 regt
Arty	1 bn
Spt	1 bde
Sigs	1 bn
Logistics	1 bn

EQUIPMENT BY TYPE
MBT 3
APC (T) 6 Type 5310
ARTY
  TOWED 18 **152 mm**
  MOR 81: **82mm** 81
AD • GUNS 42 **37mm** M-1939/S 60

Navy Element

The Albanian Navy Brigade, under the command of JFC, is organised into two naval flotillas with additional hydrographic, logistics, auxiliary and training support services.

EQUIPMENT BY TYPE
PATROL AND COASTAL COMBATANTS • PB 3: 2 *Po-2*† (FSU *Project 501*); 1 *Shanghai* II† (PRC)
MINE WARFARE • MINE COUNTERMEASURES • MSO 1 T-43† (FSU *Project 254*)
LOGISTICS AND SUPPORT • ARL 1
FACILITIES
Base   1 located at Durrës (HQ and 1 Flotilla), 1 (and 1 Flotilla) located at Vlorë

Coast Guard

FORCES BY ROLE
The Albanian Coast Guard (Roja Bregdetare) is under the command of the Navy Brigade's Coastal Defence Command.

EQUIPMENT BY TYPE
PATROL AND COASTAL COMBATANTS 29
  PBF 8 V-4000
  PB 8: 3 *Iluria* (Damen Stan 4207; 1 additional vessel in build); 3 Mk3 *Sea Spectre*; 2 (other)
  PBR 13: 4 Type 227; 1 Type 246; 1 Type 303; 7 Type 2010

Air Element

Flying hours at least 10–15 hrs/year.
EQUIPMENT BY TYPE
HELICOPTERS
  TPT • **Light** 16: 1 AW-109; 3 Bell 205 (AB-205); 7 Bell 206C (AB-206C); 5 Bo-105
FACILITIES
Air base   1 located at Rinas (and Air Surveillance Operation Centre), 2 (reserve) located at Gjadër and Kucova, 1 (helicopter base) located at Farka, 1 (air defence bn) located at Marikaj, 1 (maintenance centre) located at Kucove

Support Command (SC) 4,300

Consists of the Logistics Brigade, GS Support Regiment, Infrastructure Regiment, Personnel and Recruiting Centre, Military Hospital, Systems Development Centre and Military Police Battalion.

FORCES BY ROLE

Med	1 hosp
Security	1 MP bn
Logistics	1 bde (1 GS Spt Regt (tpt, EOD,maint)

Training and Doctrine Command (TRADOC) 1,000

Consists of the Defense Academy, Military University, NCO Academy, Basic Training Brigade, the consolidated Troops School, Centre for Defense Analysis and Training Support Centre.

Paramilitary ε500

DEPLOYMENT

Legal provisions for foreign deployment:
Constitution: Codified constitution (1998)
Decision on deployment of troops abroad: By the parliament upon proposal by the president (Art.171 II)

AFGHANISTAN

NATO • ISAF 250; 1 inf coy

BOSNIA-HERZEGOVINA

EU • EUFOR • *Operation Althea* 13

SERBIA

NATO • KFOR 3

FOREIGN FORCES

Italy 27 (Delegazione Italiana Esperti)

Armenia ARM

Armenian Dram d		2009	2010	2011
GDP	d	3.10tr	3.47tr	
	US$	8.59bn	9.23bn	
per capita	US$	2,787	2,987	
Growth	%	-14.4	1.2	
Inflation	%	3.4	7.8	
Def exp	d	145bn		
	US$	401m		
Def bdgt	d	145bn	163bn	131bn
	US$	401m	434m	
FMA (US)	US$	3.0m	3.0m	3.5m
US$1=d		361.06	375.84	

Population   3,090,379

Age	0 – 14	15 – 19	20 – 24	25 – 29	30 – 64	65 plus
Male	9.4%	4.5%	5.3%	4.8%	19.3%	3.8%
Female	8.2%	4.2%	5.2%	4.8%	24.2%	6.2%

Capabilities

ACTIVE 48,570 (Army 45,393, Air/AD Aviation Forces (Joint) 1,146, other Air Defence Forces 2,031) **Paramilitary 7,163**

Terms of service conscription 24 months.

RESERVES some mob reported, possibly 210,000 with military service within 15 years.

ORGANISATIONS BY SERVICE

Army 19,542; 25,851 conscripts (total 45,393)

FORCES BY ROLE

MR	1 (1st) corps HQ with (2 MR regt; 1 tk bn; 1 recce bn; 1 maint bn); 1 (2nd) corps HQ with (2 MR regt 1 lt inf regt; 1 tk bn; 1 recce bn, 1 arty bn); 1 (3rd) corps HQ with (4 MR regt; 1 lt inf regt; 1 tk bn; 1 recce bn; 1 arty bn; 1 MRL bn; 1 sigs bn; 1 maint bn); 1 (4th) corps HQ with (4 MR regt; 1 SP arty bn; 1 sigs bn); 1 (5th) corps HQ (with 2 fortified areas) with (1 MR regt, 1 lt inf regt); 1 indep bde (trg)
SF	1 regt
Arty	1 bde
AT	1 regt
AD	1 SAM bde; 2 regt; 1 (Radiotech) regt
Engr	1 regt (with demining centre)

EQUIPMENT BY TYPE

MBT 110: 8 T-54/T-55; 102 T-72
AIFV 104: 80 BMP-1; 7 BMP-1K; 5 BMP-2; 12 BRM-1K
APC (W) 136: 11 BTR-60; 100 look-a-like; 21 BTR-70; 4 BTR-80
ARTY 239
  SP 38: **122mm** 10 2S1 *Carnation* **152mm** 28 2S3
  TOWED 131: **122mm** 69 D-30 **152mm** 62: 26 2A36; 2 D-1; 34 D-20
  MRL 51: **122mm** 47 BM-21 **273mm** 4 WM-80
  MOR 120mm 19 M-120
AT • **MSL** 22
  SP 13 9P149 MT-LB *Spiral*
  MANPATS 9 AT-5 9K113 *Spandrel*
AD
  SAM
    SP 2K11 *Krug* (SA-4 *Ganef*); 2K12 *Kub* (SA-6 *Gainful*)
    TOWED S-75 *Dvina* (SA-2 *Guideline*); S-125 *Pechora* (SA-3 *Goa*)
  GUNS
    SP ZSU-23-4
    TOWED 23mm ZU-23-2
RADAR • **LAND** 6 SNAR-10

Air and Air Defence Aviation Forces 1,146

1 Air & AD Joint Command

FORCES BY ROLE

Avn	1 sqn

EQUIPMENT BY TYPE

AIRCRAFT 16 combat capable
  FTR 1 MiG-25 *Foxbat*
  ATK 15 Su-25 *Frogfoot*
  TPT • **Heavy** 2 Il-76 *Candid*
  TRG 4 L-39 *Albatros*
HELICOPTERS
  ATK 8 Mi-24P *Hind*
  ISR 4: 2 Mi-24K *Hind*; 2 Mi-24R *Hind* (cbt spt)
  MRH 10 Mi-17 *Hip H* (cbt spt)
  C&C 2 Mi-9 *Hip G* (cbt spt)
  TPT • **Light** 9 PZL Mi-2 *Hoplite*
FACILITIES
Air base   2

Paramilitary 7,163

Ministry of Internal Affairs

FORCES BY ROLE

Paramilitary 4 bn

EQUIPMENT BY TYPE

AIFV 55: 5 BMD-1; 44 BMP-1; 1 BMP-1K; 5 BRM-1K
APC (W) 24 BTR-60/BTR-70/BTR-152

Border Troops

Ministry of National Security

EQUIPMENT BY TYPE

AIFV 43: 5 BMD-1; 35 BMP-1; 3 BRM-1K
APC (W) 23: 5 BTR-60; 18 BTR-70

DEPLOYMENT

Legal provisions for foreign deployment:
Constitution: Codified constitution (1995, amended 2005)
Specific legislation: 'Law on Defence of the Republic of
Armenia'
Decision on deployment of troops abroad: by the president, in accordance with 'Law on Defence of the Republic
of Armenia' (Article 5 (2) (1). Also, under Art.55 (13) of
constitution, president can call for use of armed forces
(and National Assembly shall be convened). (Also Art.81
(3) of constitution.)

AFGHANISTAN

NATO • ISAF 40

BOSNIA-HERZEGOVINA

OSCE • Bosnia and Herzegovina 1

SERBIA

NATO • KFOR 35
OSCE • Kosovo 1

FOREIGN FORCES

Deployment in Armenia and Azerbaijan unless stated
Bulgaria OSCE 1
Hungary OSCE 2
Kazakhstan OSCE 1
Poland OSCE 1
United Kingdom OSCE 1
Russia 3,214 (Gyumri, Armenia): 1 MR bde; 74 MBT; 201
ACV; 84 arty; (8 mor; 8 MRL 68 SP/towed)
Military Air Forces (Yerevan, Armenia): 1 ftr sqn with 18
MiG-29 *Fulcrum*; 2 SAM bty with S-300V; 1 SAM bty with
SA-6

Austria AUT

Euro €		2009	2010	2011
GDP	€	274bn	284bn	
	US$	382bn	375bn	
per capita	US$	45,677	44,736	
Growth	%	-3.5	1.1	
Inflation	%	0.4	1.4	
Def exp	€	2.01bn		
	US$	2.8bn		
Def budget	€	2.11bn	2.12bn	
	US$	2.94bn	2.81bn	
US$1=€		0.72	0.76	

Population　8,387,491

Age	0 – 14	15 – 19	20 – 24	25 – 29	30 – 64	65 plus
Male	7.2%	3.0%	3.1%	3.1%	24.8%	7.6%
Female	6.9%	2.9%	3.0%	3.1%	24.8%	10.6%

Capabilities

ACTIVE 25,900 (Army 12,800; Air 2,900; Spt 10,200)

CIVILIAN 9,400 (Joint 9,400)

RESERVE 195,000 (Joint structured 35,000; Joint
unstructured 160,000)

Terms of service 6 months recruit trg, 30 days reservist
refresher trg for volunteers; 90–120 days additional for
officers, NCOs and specialists. Authorised maximum
wartime strength is 55,000; Some 66,000 reservists a year
undergo refresher trg in tranches.

ORGANISATIONS BY SERVICE

Joint Command – Land Forces 12,800

Joint Forces Command is located in Graz and Salzburg.

FORCES BY ROLE

Mech Inf　2 bde (3rd) with (1 armd bn; 1 recce/SP arty
bn; 1 mech inf bn; 1 inf bn; 1 cbt engr bn; 1
spt bn); 1 bde (4th) with (1 armd bn; 1 recce/
SP arty bn, 1 mech inf bn; 1 inf bn; 1 spt bn)

Inf　1 bde (6th) with (3 inf bn, 1 cbt engr bn; 1 spt
bn); 1 bde (7th) with (1 recce/arty bn; 3 inf
bn; 1 cbt engr bn; 1 spt bn)

EQUIPMENT BY TYPE

MBT 114 *Leopard* 2A4
LT TK 32 SK-105 *Kuerassier*; (87 more in store)
AIFV 112 *Ulan*
APC 282
　APC (T) 176 4K4E *Saurer*/4K4F *Saurer* (incl look-a-likes);
　(148 more in store)
　APC (W) 106: 35 *Dingo II* (incl variants); 71 *Pandur*
ARTY 352
　SP • 155mm 152 M-109A2/A3/A5ÖE
　MOR • 120mm 200 M-43

Joint Command - Air Force 2,900

The Air Force is part of Joint Forces Comd and consists of 2 bde; Air Support Comd and Airspace Surveillance Comd

Flying hours 120 hrs/year on hel/tpt ac; 110 hrs/year on ftr

FORCES BY ROLE

Ftr	1 wg with (2 ftr sqn with *Typhoon*; 1 trg sqn with Saab 105Öe*)
ISR	1 sqn with PC-6B *Turbo Porter*
Tpt	1 sqn with C-130K *Hercules*
Trg	Trg units with PC-7 *Turbo Trainer*
Tpt Hel	1 wg with (2 sqn with SA-319 *Alouette* III); 2 sqn with Bell 212 (AB-212); 1 hel sqn with OH-58B *Kiowa*; 1 hel sqn with S-70A *Black Hawk*
AD	2 bn
Radar	1 bn

EQUIPMENT BY TYPE

AIRCRAFT 37 combat capable
  FTR 15 Eurofighter *Typhoon* Tranche 1
  TPT 11 **Medium** 3 C-130K *Hercules* **Light** 8 PC-6B *Turbo Porter*
  TRG 34: 12 PC-7 *Turbo Trainer*; 22 Saab 105Öe*
HELICOPTERS
  MRH 24 SA-319 *Alouette III*
  ISR 11 OH-58B *Kiowa*
  TPT 32 **Medium** 9 S-70A *Black Hawk*; **Light** 23 Bell 212 (AB-212)
AD
  SAM 36 *Mistral*
  GUNS • 35mm 53 Z-FIAK system
MSL • AAM
  IR AAM AIM-9P3 *Sidewinder* **IIR AAM** IRIS-T

Joint Command – Special Operations Forces

FORCES BY ROLE

SF	Some gp

Support 10,200

Support forces comprise Joint Services Support Command and several agencies, academies and schools. The agencies include intelligence, security, defence technology, medical and personnel whilst the academies and schools comprise training elements and schools including The National Defence and NCO Academies.

DEPLOYMENT

Legal provisions for foreign deployment:
Constitution: incl 'Federal Constitutional Law' (1/1930)
Specific legislation: 'Bundesverfassungsgesetz über Kooperation und Solidarität bei der Entsendung von Einheiten und Einzelpersonen in das Ausland' (KSE-BVG, 1997)
Decision on deployment of troops abroad: By government on authorisation of the National Council's Main Committee; simplified procedure for humanitarian and rescue tasks (Art. 23f IV of the 'Federal Constitutional Law'; § 2 of the KSE-BVG)

AFGHANISTAN
NATO • ISAF 3

BOSNIA-HERZEGOVINA
EU • EUFOR • *Operation Althea* 304; 1 inf bn HQ; 1 inf coy; 1 recce pl
OSCE • Bosnia and Herzegovina 1

CYPRUS
UN • UNFICYP 4

MIDDLE EAST
UN • UNTSO 7 obs

NEPAL
UN • UNMIN 2 obs

SERBIA
NATO • KFOR 437; 1 inf coy, elm 1 MP coy, elm 1 hel gp
OSCE • Serbia 1
OSCE • Kosovo 13

SYRIA/ISRAEL
UN • UNDOF 378; elm 1 inf bn

WESTERN SAHARA
UN • MINURSO 2 obs

Azerbaijan AZE

Azerbaijani Manat m		2009	2010	2011
GDP	m	34.6bn	41.9bn	
	US$	43.0bn	52.2bn	
per capita	US$	4,899	5,846	
Growth	%	9.3	2.3	
Inflation	%	0.5	5.5	
Def exp	m	1.21bn		
	US$	1.5bn		
Def bdgt	m	1.21bn	1.27bn	2.5bn
	US$	1.5bn	1.59bn	
FMA (US)	US$	3.0m	3.0m	3.5m
US$1=m		0.80	0.80	

Population   8,933,928

Age	0 – 14	15 – 19	20 – 24	25 – 29	30 – 64	65 plus
Male	12.3%	5.1%	5.2%	4.5%	19.8%	2.3%
Female	10.9%	4.8%	5.0%	4.3%	21.7%	4.1%

Capabilities

ACTIVE 66,940 (Army 56,840 Navy 2,200 Air 7,900)
Paramilitary 15,000
Terms of service 17 months, but can be extended for ground forces.

RESERVE 300,000

Reserves some mobilisation reported, 300,000 with military service within 15 years

ORGANISATIONS BY SERVICE

Army 56,840

5 Army Corps HQ

FORCES BY ROLE

MR	23 bde
Arty	1 bde; 1 (trg) bde
MRL	1 bde
AT	1 bde
Engr	1 bde
Sy	1 bde
Sigs	1 bde
Log	1 bde

EQUIPMENT BY TYPE

MBT 339: 95 T-55; 244 T-72

AIFV 111: 20 BMD-1; 43 BMP-1; 33 BMP-2; 15 BRM-1

APC 357

    APC (T) 336 MT-LB

    APC (W) 21: 10 BTR-60; 4 BTR-70; 7 BTR-80A

ARTY 425

    SP 122mm 28 2S1 *Carnation*

    TOWED 210: **122mm** 129 D-30; **130mm** 36 M-46; **152mm** 42: 18 2A36; 24 D-20; **203mm** 3 2S7

    GUN/MOR 120mm 18 2S9 *NONA*

    MRL 62: **300mm** 12 9A52 *Smerch*; **122mm** 43 BM-21

    MOR 120mm 107 PM-38

AT • MSL • MANPATS 9K11 *Malyutka* (AT-3 *Sagger*); 9K111 *Fagot* (AT-4 *Spigot*); 9K113 *Konkurs* (AT-5 *Spandrel*)/9K115 *Metis* (AT-7 *Saxhorn*)

AD • SAM • SP 9K35 *Strela-10* (SA-13 *Gopher*); *Krug* (SA-4 *Ganef*): 9K33 *Osa* (SA-8 *Gecko*)

MSL • SSM ε4 SS-21 *Scarab (Tochka)*

RADAR • LAND SNAR-1 *Long Trough*/SNAR-2/-6 *Pork Trough* (arty); *Small Fred*/*Small Yawn*/SNAR-10 *Big Fred* (veh, arty); GS-13 *Long Eye* (veh)

UAV • ISR • Medium 3 *Aerostar*

Navy 2,200

EQUIPMENT BY TYPE

PATROL AND COASTAL COMBATANTS 8

    FS 1 *Petya II* with 2 RBU 6000 *Smerch 2* (24 eff.), 2 twin (4 eff.) 76mm gun

    PSO 1 *Luga* (*Woodnik 2* Class) (FSU Project 888; additional trg role)

    PCC 3: 2 *Petrushka* (FSU *UK-3*; additional trg role); 1 *Shelon* (FSU *Project 1388M*)

    PB 3: 1 *Bryza* (FSU *Project 722*); 1 *Turk* (TUR AB 25); 1 *Poluchat* (FSU Project 368)

MINE WARFARE • MINE COUNTERMEASURES 4

    MHC 2 *Yevgenya* (FSU *Project 1258*); 2 *Yakhont* (FSU *Sonya*)

AMPHIBIOUS 4

    LSM 3: 1 *Polnochny A* (FSU *Project 770*) (capacity 6 MBT; 180 troops); 2 *Polynochny B* (FSU *Project 771*) (capacity 6 MBT; 180 troops)

    LCU 1 *Vydra*† (FSU) (capacity either 3 AMX-30 MBT or 200 troops)

LOGISTICS AND SUPPORT

    ARS 1 *Iva* (FSU *Vikhr*); **AGS** 1 (FSU Project 10470)

FACILITIES

Base   Located at Baku

Air Force and Air Defence 7,900

FORCES BY ROLE

Ftr	1 sqn with MiG-29
FGA	1 regt with MiG-21 *Fishbed*; Su-17 *Fitter*; Su-24 *Fencer*; Su-25 *Frogfoot*; Su-25UB *Frogfoot B*
Tpt	1 sqn with An-12 *Cub*; Yak-40 *Codling*
Atk Hel/Tpt Hel	1 regt with Mi-8 *Hip*; Mi-24 *Hind*; PZL Mi-2 *Hoplite*

EQUIPMENT BY TYPE

AIRCRAFT 41 combat capable

    FTR 14 MiG-29

    FGA 14: 4 MiG-21 *Fishbed* (+1 in store); 4 Su-17 *Fitter*; 1 Su-17U *Fitter*; 5 Su-24 *Fencer*†

    ATK 13: 10 Su-25 *Frogfoot*; 3 Su-25UB *Frogfoot B*

    TPT 4: **Medium** 1 An-12 *Cub* **Light** 3 Yak-40 *Codling*

    TRG 40: 28 L-29 *Delfin*; 12 L-39 *Albatros*

HELICOPTERS

    ATK 15 Mi-24 *Hind*

    TPT 20 **Medium** 13 Mi-8 *Hip*; **Light** 7 PZL Mi-2 *Hoplite*

UAV • ISR • Medium 4 *Aerostar*

AD • SAM S-75 *Dvina* (SA-2 *Guideline*); S-125 *Neva* (SA-3 *Goa*)/S-200 *Vega* (SA-5 *Gammon*) static

    AAM • IR AAM R-60 (AA-8 *Aphid*); R-73 (AA-11 *Archer*)

    IR/SARH AAM R-27 (AA-10 *Alamo*)

Paramilitary ε15,000

Border Guard ε5,000

Ministry of Internal Affairs

AIFV 168 BMP-1/BMP-2

APC (W) 19 BTR-60/BTR-70/BTR-80

Coast Guard

The Coast Guard was established in 2005 as part of the State Border Service.

EQUIPMENT BY TYPE

PATROL AND COASTAL COMBATANTS 8

    PBF 6: 1 *Osa II* (FSU Project 205); 2 Silver Ships 48ft; 3 *Stenka*

    PB 2: 1 *Point* (US); 1 *Grif* (FSU *Zhuk*)

Militia 10,000+

Ministry of Internal Affairs

APC (W) 7 BTR-60/BTR-70/BTR-80

DEPLOYMENT

Legal provisions for foreign deployment:

Constitution: Codified constitution (1995)

Decision on deployment of troops abroad: By parliament upon proposal by president (Art. 109, No. 28)

AFGHANISTAN

NATO • ISAF 90

Europe

SERBIA
OSCE • Kosovo 2

FOREIGN FORCES

OSCE numbers represents total deployment in Armenia and Azerbaijan unless stated

Bulgaria OSCE 1
Hungary OSCE 2
Kazakhstan OSCE 1
Poland OSCE 1
United Kingdom OSCE 1

Belarus BLR

Belarusian Ruble r		2009	2010	2011
GDP	r	136tr	157tr	
	US$	49.0bn	53.8bn	
per capita	US$	5,071	5,608	
Growth	%	0.2	2.4	
Inflation	%	13.0	7.3	
Def exp	r	2.50tr		
	US$	896m		
Def bdgt	r	1.71tr	2.10tr	
	US$	612m	716m	
US$1=r		2,792	2,938	

Population   9,587,940

Age	0 – 14	15 – 19	20 – 24	25 – 29	30 – 64	65 plus
Male	7.3%	3.0%	4.0%	4.3%	23.4%	4.5%
Female	6.9%	2.9%	3.9%	4.2%	26.0%	9.6%

Capabilities

ACTIVE 72,940 (Army 29,600 Air 18,170 Joint 25,170) **Paramilitary 110,000**
Terms of service 9–12 months

RESERVE 289,500 (Joint 289,500 with mil service within last 5 years)

ORGANISATIONS BY SERVICE

Joint 25,170 (Centrally controlled units and MoD staff)

Army 29,600
FORCES BY ROLE

MoD Comd Tps
SF	1 bde
SSM	2 bde
Sigs	2 bde

Ground Forces
Armd Inf	1 (mobile) bde
Mech Inf	1 (mobile) bde
Arty	1 gp
MRL	1 bde
Cbt Engr	1 bde
Engr Bridging	1 bde
NBC	1 regt

North Western Op Comd
Mech	3 bde
Arty	1 bde
MRL	1 regt
AD	1 bde
Engr	1 regt

Western Op Comd
Mech	3 bde
Arty	1 bde
MRL	1 regt
AD	1 bde
Engr	1 regt

EQUIPMENT BY TYPE
MBT 515: 446 T-72; 69 T-80
AIFV 1,078: 4 BMD-1; 97 BMP-1; 841 BMP-2; 136 BRM-1
APC 280
　APC (T) 88: 22 BTR-D; 66 MT-LB
　APC (W) 192: 39 BTR-70; 153 BTR-80
ARTY 1,003
　SP 432: **122mm** 198 2S1 *Carnation*; **152mm** 236: 108 2S3; 116 2S5; 12 2S19 *Farm*
　TOWED 228: **122mm** 48 D-30; **152mm** 180: 48 2A36; 132 2A65
　GUN/MOR 120mm 48 2S9 *NONA*
　MRL 234: **122mm** 126 BM-21; **220mm** 72 9P140 *Uragan*; **300mm** 36 9A52 *Smerch*
　MOR 120mm 61 2S12
AT • MSL
　SP 236: 126 9P148 *Konkurs*; 110 9P149 *Shturm*
　MANPATS 9K111 *Fagot* (AT-4 *Spigot*); 9K113 *Konkurs* (AT-5 *Spandrel*); 9K114 *Shturm* (AT-6 *Spiral*); 9K115 *Metis* (AT-7 *Saxhorn*)
AD • SAM • SP 350 9K37 *Buk* (SA-11 *Gadfly*); S-300V(SA-12A *Gladiator*/SA-12B *Giant*); 9K35 *Strela*-10 (SA-13 *Gopher*); 9K33 *Osa* (SA-8 *Gecko*) (700–2,100 eff.)
RADAR • LAND GS-13 *Long Eye*/SNAR-1 *Long Trough*/SNAR-2/-6 *Pork Trough* (arty); some *Small Fred*/*Small Yawn*/SNAR-10 *Big Fred* (veh, arty)
MSL • TACTICAL • SSM 96: 36 FROG/SS-21 *Scarab* (*Tochka*); 60 *Scud*

Air Force and Air Defence Forces 18,170

Flying hours 15 hrs/year

FORCES BY ROLE

Ftr	2 bases with MiG-29S *Fulcrum C*/MiG-29UB *Fulcrum*; Su-27P *Flanker-B*/Su-27UB *Flanker C*
FGA/ISR	4 sqn with Su-24MK *Fencer D*/Su-24MR *Fencer-E*; Su-25 *Frogfoot*/Su-25UB *Frogfoot B*

Tpt	1 base with An-12 *Cub*; An-24 *Coke*; 6 An-26 *Curl*; IL-76 *Candid*; Tu-134 *Crusty*
Trg	Some sqn with L-39 *Albatros*
Atk hel	Some sqn with Mi-24 *Hind*
Tpt hel	Some (cbt spt) sqn with Mi-24K *Hind G2*; Mi-6 *Hook*; Mi-24R *Hind G1*; Mi-8 *Hip*; Mi-26 *Halo*

EQUIPMENT BY TYPE

AIRCRAFT 133 combat capable
  FTR 40 MiG-29S *Fulcrum C*/MiG-29UB *Fulcrum*
  FGA 21 Su-27P *Flanker-B*/Su-27UB *Flanker C*
  FGA/ISR 34 Su-24MK *Fencer D* (FGA)/Su-24MR *Fencer-E* (ISR)
  ATK 38 Su-25K *Frogfoot* FGA/Su-25UBK *Frogfoot B*
  TPT 15 **Heavy** 4 Il-76 *Candid* (+12 civ Il-76 available for mil use) **Medium** 3 An-12 *Cub*; **Light** 8: 1 An-24 *Coke*; 6 An-26 *Curl*; 1 Tu-134 *Crusty*
  TRG Some L-39 *Albatros*
HELICOPTERS
  ATK 50 Mi-24 *Hind*
  ISR 20: 8 Mi-24K *Hind G2*; 12 Mi-24R *Hind G1*
  TPT 168: **Heavy** 43: 29 Mi-6 *Hook*; 14 Mi-26 *Halo* **Medium** 125 Mi-8 *Hip*
MSL
  ASM Kh-25 (AS-10 *Karen*); Kh-29 (AS-14 *Kedge*)
  ARM Kh-58 (AS-11 *Kilter*)
  AAM • IR AAM: R-60 (AA-8 *Aphid*); R-73 (AA-11 *Archer*) **SARH AAM** R-24R (AA-7 *Apex D*); R-27R (AA-10 *Alamo A*)

Air Defence
AD data from Uzal Baranovichi EW radar
FORCES BY ROLE
AD   1 bde with (2 bn)
EQUIPMENT BY TYPE
AD • SAM S-300PS (SA-10 *Grumble*); S-125 *Pechora* (SA-3 *Goa*); S-200 (SA-5 *Gammon*) (being withdrawn)

Paramilitary 110,000

Border Guards 12,000
Ministry of Interior

Militia 87,000
Ministry of Interior

Ministry of Interior Troops 11,000

DEPLOYMENT

BOSNIA-HERZEGOVINA
OSCE • Bosnia and Herzegovina 1

SERBIA
OSCE • Kosovo 2

FOREIGN FORCES
Russia: Military Air Forces: 4 SAM units with S-300 (SA-10 *Grumble* (quad))

Belgium BEL

Euro €		2009	2010	2011
GDP	€	321bn	321.6bn	
	US$	447bn	426bn	
per capita	US$	41,440	39,790	
Growth	%	-3.2	1.8	
Inflation	%	-0.3	2.0	
Def exp[a]	€	4.04bn		
	US$	5.62bn		
Def bdgt	€	2.85bn	2.75bn	2.76bn
	US$	3.97bn	3.64bn	
US$1=€		0.72	0.76	

[a] including military pensions

Population   10,697,588

Age	0–14	15–19	20–24	25–29	30–64	65 plus
Male	8.1%	3.0%	3.1%	3.1%	24.2%	7.5%
Female	7.8%	2.9%	3.0%	2.9%	24.0%	10.5%

Capabilities

ACTIVE 37,882 (Army 13,601 Navy 1,590 Air 6,814 Medical Service 1,888 Joint Service 13,989)

RESERVE 1,600

ORGANISATIONS BY SERVICE

Land Component 13,601
FORCES BY ROLE

Comd	2 bde HQ (1st and 7th)
Mech	4 bn
SF	1 gp
Cdo	1 bn
AB	2 para bn
Arty	2 unit
AD	1 2 SAM bty with *Mistral*
Engr	2 bn
Log	3 bn
Info Ops	1 ISTAR gp
Sigs	5 CIS gp
EOD	1 unit
MP	1 coy (1 pl dedicated to EUROCORPS)

EQUIPMENT BY TYPE
MBT 40 *Leopard* 1A5
AIFV 37: 12 *Piranha III-C* DF30; 9 *Piranha III-C* DF90; 16 AIFV-B-C25 (25mm)
APC 340
  APC (T) 70 AIFV-B
  APC (W) 270: 213 *Dingo*; 57 *Piranha III -C*
ARTY 46
  TOWED 105mm 8 LG1 MK II
  MOR 38: **81mm** 6; **120mm** 32
AD • SAM 18 *Mistral*

Reserves 1,600

Territorial Support Units

FORCES BY ROLE

Army   11 unit

FACILITIES

Trg Centre 4; 1 (para); 1 (cdo)

Naval Component 1,590

EQUIPMENT BY TYPE
PRINCIPAL SURFACE COMBATANTS 2
  FRIGATES • FFGHM 2 *Karel Doorman* each with 2 quad lnchr (8 eff.) each with *Harpoon* AShM, 1 16 cell Mk 48 VLS with RIM-7P *Sea Sparrow* SAM, 4 single 324mm Mk 32 MOD 9 ASTT with Mk 46 MOD 5 HWT, 1 76mm gun, (capacity 1 med hel)
PATROL AND COASTAL COMBATANTS • PBR 1 *Liberation* (in reserve)
MINE WARFARE • MINE COUNTERMEASURES • MHC 5 *Flower* (*Tripartite*)
LOGISTICS AND SUPPORT 9:
  AG 1 *Stern*
  AGFH 1 *Godetia* (log spt/comd)
  AGOR 1 *Belgica*
  AXS 1 *Zenobe Gramme*
  YTL 3 *Wesp*
  YTM 2

FACILITIES

Base   Located at Zeebrugge

Naval Aviation
  HELICOPTERS • MRH 3 SA-316B *Alouette III* (part of the Air Component); (eight NH-90 on order with a further two optional; delivery expected from mid-2011)

Air Component 6,814

Flying hours 165 hrs/yr on cbt ac. 500 hrs/yr on tpt ac. 300 hrs/yr on heli; 200 hrs/yr for trg purposes

FORCES BY ROLE

Ftr/FGA/ISR	2 (tac) wg with (4 Ftr/FGA sqn with F-16AM/BM *Fighting Falcon*; 1 Ftr/FGA/Trg unit with F-16AM/BM *Fighting Falcon*)
SAR	1 unit with *Sea King* Mk48
Tpt	1 wg with A-330; C-130H *Hercules*; ERJ-135 LR; ERJ-145 LR; *Falcon* 20 (VIP); *Falcon* 900B
Trg	1 wg with (1 sqn with SF-260D/SF-260M; 1 BEL/FRA unit with *Alpha Jet**)
Tpt Hel	1 wg with AW-109 (ISR); SA-318 *Alouette II*
ISR UAV	1 sqn with B-*Hunter*

EQUIPMENT BY TYPE
AIRCRAFT 88 combat capable
  FTR 60 F-16AM/BM *Fighting Falcon*
  TPT 19 **Medium** 11 C-130H *Hercules* **Light** 4: 2 ERJ-135 LR; 2 ERJ-145 LR; **PAX** 4: 1 A-330; 2 *Falcon* 20 (VIP); 1 *Falcon* 900B
  TRG 60: 28 *Alpha Jet*; 32 SF-260D/M

HELICOPTERS
  MRH 3 SA-318 *Alouette II*
  SAR 4 *Sea King* Mk48
  TPT • Light 27 AW-109 (ISR)
UAV • ISR • Heavy 13 RQ-5A *Hunter* (B-*Hunter*)
MSL
  AAM • IR AAM AIM-9M/N *Sidewinder* **ARH AAM** AIM-120B AMRAAM
BOMBS
  Conventional: Mk 84, Mk 82
  INS/GPS guided: GBU-31 JDAM
  Laser-Guided: GBU-10/GBU-12 *Paveway* II; GBU-24 *Paveway* III
PODS Infra-red/TV: 6 LANTIRN, 7 *Sniper*

FACILITIES

Air bases	Located at Coxijde, Kleine-Brogel, Florennes, Beauvechain, Melsbroek

DEPLOYMENT

Legal provisions for foreign deployment:
Constitution: Codified constitution (1831)
Specific legislation: 'Loi relatif à la mise en oeuvre des forces armées, à la mise en condition, ainsi qu'aux périodes et positions dans lesquelles le militaire peut se trouver' (1994)
Decision on deployment of troops abroad: By the monarch, the government and the minister of defence (1994 law, Art. 3, § 1)

AFGHANISTAN

NATO • ISAF 491; 6 F-16 *Fighting Falcon*

BOSNIA- HERZEGOVINA

OSCE • Bosnia and Herzegovina 1

DEMOCRATIC REPUBLIC OF THE CONGO

UN • MONUSCO 22; 7 obs; 1 avn flt with 1 C-130

FRANCE

NATO • Air Component 28 *Alpha Jet* located at Cazeaux/Tours

GULF OF ADEN & INDIAN OCEAN

EU • *Operation Atalanta* 1 FFGHM

LEBANON

UN • UNIFIL 160; 1 engr coy

MIDDLE EAST

UN • UNTSO 2 obs

NORTH SEA

NATO • SNMCMG 1: 1 MHC

SERBIA

OSCE • Kosovo 1

SUDAN

UN • UNMIS 4 obs

UGANDA

EU • EUTM 5

FOREIGN FORCES

NATO HQ, Brussels; HQ SHAPE, Mons
United States US European Command: 1,261

Bosnia–Herzegovina BIH

Convertible Mark		2009	2010	2011
GDP	mark	24.0bn	24.2bn	
	US$	17.1bn	16.4bn	
per capita	US$	4,536	4,362	
Growth	%	-3.4	0.8	
Inflation	%	-0.4	2.4	
Def exp	mark	341m		
	US$	243m		
Def bdgt	mark	354m	335m	353m
	US$	252m	227m	
FMA (US)	US$	3.6m	4.0m	6.44m
US$1=mark		1.40	1.48	

Population   3,759,633

Age	0 – 14	15 – 19	20 – 24	25 – 29	30 – 64	65 plus
Male	7.2%	3.0%	3.7%	3.5%	25.5%	6.1%
Female	6.8%	2.8%	3.5%	3.5%	25.4%	8.9%

Capabilities

ACTIVE 10,577 (Joint 500 Army 9,205, AF/AD 872)

Bosnia-Herzegovina established a single State level army in a major reform process from 2003–2006. The State Forces now consist of three mixed infantry brigades, one tactical support brigade, an air-force/air-defence brigade and a minor reserve component (about 50% of the standing forces) consisting of former professional soldiers.

ORGANISATIONS BY SERVICE

Joint 500 (Joint Staff 252; Joint Operational Command 148; Support Command 100)

Army 9,205

FORCES BY ROLE
1 Ops Comd; 1 Cbt Spt Comd; 1 Trg Comd; 1 Log Comd

Inf	3 bde
Cbt Spt	1 bde
Log	5 bn

EQUIPMENT BY TYPE
MBT 334: 50 AMX-30; 45 M-60A1/A3; 71 M-84; 6 T-34; 162 T-54/T-55
RECCE 3: 1 BDRM-1; 2 BDRM-2
AIFV 137: 25 AMX-10P; 112 BVP M-80
APC 127
  APC (T) 98: 18 M-60P; 80 M-113A2
  APC (W) 29: 4 BOV-M; 21 BOV-VP; 4 BTR-60

ARTY 1,521
  SP 122mm 24 2S1 *Carnation*
  TOWED 730: **105mm** 161: 36 L-118 Light Gun; 101 M-56; 24 M-101/M-101A1; **122mm** 268 D-30 **130mm** 74: 61 M-46; 13 M-82 **152mm** 30: 13 D-20; 17 M-84 **155mm** 197: 3 M-59; 194 M-114/M-114A2
  MRL 153: **107mm** 28 VLR Type-63; **122mm** 43: 37 APRA 40; 5 BM-21; 1 *Kacusa*; **128mm** 77: 21 M-63; 21 M-77; 35 M-91; **262mm** 5 M-87
  MOR 614: **82mm** 81 MB M-69; **120mm** 538: 23 2B11 (UK-2); 11 HADID; 7 KROM; 1 M-38; 1 M-43; 460 M-74/M-75; 30 UBM-52
AT
  MSL
    SP 60: 8 9P122 *Malyutka*; 9 9P133 *Malyutka*; 32 BOV-1; 11 M-92
    MANPATS 641: 508 9K11 *Malyutka* (AT-3 *Sagger*); 76 9K111 *Fagot* (AT-4 *Spigot*); 1 9K115 *Metis* (AT-7 *Saxhorn*); 51 HJ-8; 5 *Milan*
  RL 90mm 1 M20A1B1 *Super Bazooka*
  GUNS 175:
    SP • 82mm 20 M-60PB
    TOWED • 100mm 155 MT-12/T-12
AD • SAM
    SP 27: 1 *Strela*-10M3 (SA-13 *Gopher*); 20 *Kub* (SA-6 *Gainful*); 6 *Strela*-1 (SA-9 *Gaskin*)
    MANPAD SA-14 *Gremlin*; SA-16 *Gimlet*
  GUNS 764
    SP 169: **20mm** 9 BOV-3 SPAAG; **30mm** 154: 38 M53; 116 M-53-59; **57mm** 6 ZSU 57/2
    TOWED 595: **20mm** 468: 32 M-55A2, 4 M38, 1 M55 A2B1, 293 M55 A3/A4, 138 M75 **23mm** 38: 29 ZU-23, 9 GSh -23 **30mm** 33 M-53 **37mm** 7 Type 55 **40mm** 49: 31 L60, 16 L70, 2 M-12

Air Wing 872

FORCES BY ROLE

Avn	1 avn regt

EQUIPMENT BY TYPE
AIRCRAFT 19 combat capable
  FGA 7 J-22 *Orao*
  ATK 9: 6 J-1 (J-21) *Jastreb*; 3 TJ-1(NJ-21) *Jastreb*
  ISR 2 RJ-1 (IJ-21) *Jastreb**
  TRG 1 G-4 *Super Galeb* (N-62)*
HELICOPTERS
  MRH 18: 4 Mi-8MTV *Hip*; 1 Mi-17 *Hip H*; 1 SA-341H *Gazelle* (HN-42); 7 SA-341H/SA-342L *Gazelle* (HN-42M/HN-45M); 5 SA-342L *Gazelle* (H-45)
  TPT 26 **Medium** 11 Mi-8 *Hip* **Light** 15 Bell 205 (UH-1H *Iroquois*)
  TRG 1 Mi-34 *Hermit*

DEPLOYMENT

Legal provisions for foreign deployment:
Constitution: Codified constitution within Dayton Peace Agreement (1995)
Specific legislation: 'Defence Law of Bosnia and Herzegovina (2003)

Decision on deployment of troops abroad: By the members of the Presidency (2003 'Defence Law' Art. 9, 13)

AFGHANISTAN
NATO • ISAF 45

DEMOCRATIC REPUBLIC OF THE CONGO
UN • MONUSCO 5 obs

SERBIA
OSCE • Serbia 1
OSCE • Kosovo 8

FOREIGN FORCES

Part of EUFOR – *Operation Althea* unless otherwise stated.
Albania 13
Armenia OSCE 1
Austria 304; 1 inf bn HQ; 1 inf coy; 1 recce pl; 3 SA-316 *Allouette III* • OSCE 1
Belarus OSCE 1
Belgium OSCE 1
Bulgaria 120
Canada OSCE 2
Chile 21
Croatia OSCE 1
Czech Republic 2 • OSCE 1
Estonia 2
Finland 4 • OSCE 1
France 4 • OSCE 3
Germany 111 • OSCE 4
Greece 49 • OSCE 4
Hungary 166; 1 inf coy • OSCE 2
Ireland 43 • OSCE 3
Italy 193 • OSCE 5
Kyrgyzstan OSCE 1
Lithuania 1
Luxembourg 1
Macedonia, Former Yugoslav Republic of 12
Netherlands 75 • OSCE 2
Norway OSCE 1
Poland 184; 1 inf coy
Portugal 51 • OSCE 2
Romania 64 • OSCE 3
Russia OSCE 3
Slovakia 40 • OSCE 3
Slovenia 29 • OSCE 1
Spain OSCE 3
Sweden 1 • OSCE 2
Switzerland 20
Tajikistan OSCE 1
Turkey 280; 1 inf coy • OSCE 2
Ukraine OSCE 1
United Kingdom 4 • OSCE 2
United States OSCE 9

Bulgaria BLG

Bulgarian Lev L		2009	2010	2011
GDP	L	66.3bn	69.0bn	
	US$	47.2bn	46.7bn	
per capita	US$	6,225	6,227	
Growth	%	-5.0	0.5	
Inflation	%	2.8	2.2	
Def exp	L	1.27bn		
	US$	905m		
Def bdgt	L	1.46bn	900m	1.02bn
	US$	1.04bn	609m	
FMA (US)	US$	7.4m	9.0m	13.2m
US$1=L		1.40	1.48	

Population   7,497,282

Age	0–14	15–19	20–24	25–29	30–64	65 plus
Male	7.1%	2.6%	3.3%	3.6%	23.9%	7.4%
Female	6.8%	2.4%	3.2%	3.4%	25.5%	10.8%

Capabilities

ACTIVE 31,315 (Army 16,304 Navy 3,471 Air 6,706 Central Staff 4,834) Paramilitary 34,000

RESERVE 303,000 (Army 250,500 Navy 7,500 Air 45,000)

ORGANISATIONS BY SERVICE

Army 16,304
Forces are being reduced in number.

FORCES BY ROLE

Armd Recce	1 regt
Mech Inf	2 bde
Lt Inf	1 bde
SF	1 bde
Arty	1 regt
Engr	1 regt
NBC	1 regt

EQUIPMENT BY TYPE
MBT 301 T-72
AIFV 160: 80 BMP-1; 80 BMP-2/3
APC 1,084
    APC (T) 1,002: 315 MT-LB; 687 look-a-likes
    APC (W) 82 BTR-60
ARTY 738
    SP • 122mm 247 2S1 *Carnation*
    TOWED 152: **122mm** 20 (M-30) M-1938; **152mm** 132 D-20
    MRL 122mm 124 BM-21
    MOR 120mm 215 2S11 SP *Tundzha*
AT
    MSL
        SP 24 9P148 *Konkurs*

MANPATS 236 9K111 *Fagot* (AT-4 *Spigot*)/9K113 *Konkurs* (AT-5 *Spandrel*); (200 9K11 *Malyutka* (AT-3 *Sagger*) in store)
GUNS 126: **100mm** 126 MT-12; **85mm** (150 D-44 in store)

AD
SAM • SP 24 9K33 *Osa* (SA-8 *Gecko*)
MANPAD 9K32 *Strela* (SA-7 *Grail*)
GUNS 400 **100mm** KS-19 towed/**57mm** S-60 towed/**23mm** ZSU-23-4 SP/ZU-23 towed
RADARS • LAND GS-13 *Long Eye* (veh); SNAR-1 *Long Trough* (arty); SNAR-10 *Big Fred* (veh, arty); SNAR-2/-6 *Pork Trough* (arty); *Small Fred/Small Yawn* (veh, arty)

Army Reserve 250,500 reservists

FORCES BY ROLE
Army   4 bde

Navy 3,471

EQUIPMENT BY TYPE
SUBMARINES • TACTICAL
SSK 1 *Slava*† (FSU *Romeo*) (in reserve) with 8 single 533mm TT with 14 SAET-60 HWT
PRINCIPAL SURFACE COMBATANTS 4
FRIGATES 4
FFGM 3 *Drazki* (BEL *Wielingen*) each with 2 twin lnchr (4 eff.) each with MM-38 *Exocet* AShM, 1 octuple Mk29 GMLS with RIM-7P *Sea Sparrow* SAM, 2 single 533mm ASTT each with L5 HWT, 1 sextuple 375mm MLE 54 *Creusot-Loire* A/S mor (6 eff.), 1 100mm gun
FFM 1 *Smeli* (FSU *Koni*) with 1 twin lnchr (2 eff.) with 2 *Osa-M* (SA-N-4 *Gecko*) SAM, 2 RBU 6000 *Smerch 2* (24 eff.), 2 twin 76mm gun (4 eff.)
PATROL AND COASTAL COMBATANTS 6
PCFGM 1 *Mulnaya* (FSU *Tarantul* II) with 2 twin lnchr (4 eff.) each with 4P-15M *Termit-M* (SS-N-2C *Styx*) AShM, 2 quad lnchr (8 eff.) each with 8 *Strela-2* (SA-N-5 *Grail*) SAM, 1 76mm gun
PCM 2 *Reshitelni* (FSU *Pauk I*) each with 1 *Strela-2* (SA-N-5 *Grail*) SAM, 4 single 406mm TT, 2 RBU 1200 (10 eff.), 1 76mm gun
PBFG 3 *Osa* I/II (FSU)† each with 4 P-15/P-15U *Termit* (SS-N-2A/B *Styx*) AShM
MINE COUNTERMEASURES 9
MHC 1 (*Tripartite - BEL Flower*)
MSC 5: 3 *Briz* (FSU *Sonya*); 2 *Iscar* (FSU *Vanya*)
MSI 3: 3 *Olya*, less than 100 tonnes (FSU)
AMPHIBIOUS 2
LSM 1 *Polnochny* A (FSU) (capacity 6 MBT; 180 troops)
LCU 1 *Vydra*
LOGISTICS AND SUPPORT 17: 1 **AORL**; 2 **AOL**; 1 **ARS**; 2 **APT**; 2 **AT**; 2 **YTR**; 1 **AX**; 3 **AGS**; 1 **ADG**; 2 **ADT**

FACILITIES
Bases   Located at Burgas (Atiya), Varna

Naval Aviation
HELICOPTERS
ASW 6 Mi-14 *Haze* (3 operational; to be replaced by 6 AS-565MB *Panther*)

Air Force 6,706

Flying hours   30 to 40 hrs/yr

FORCES BY ROLE
1 AD comd, 1 Tac Avn comd

Ftr/ISR	1 sqn with MiG-21bis/UM *Fishbed*; 1 sqn with MiG-29A/UB *Fulcrum*
FGA	2 sqn with Su-25/UB *Frogfoot*
Tpt	1 sqn with An-2 *Colt*; An-26 *Curl*; C-27J *Spartan*; L-410 UVP; PC-12M; Tu-134B *Crusty*
Atk Hel/ Tpt Hel	2 sqn with AS 532AL *Cougar*; Bell 206 *Jet Ranger*; Mi-17 *Hip H*; Mi-24D/V *Hind D/E*

EQUIPMENT BY TYPE
AIRCRAFT 62 combat capable
FTR 20 MiG-29A/UB *Fulcrum*
FGA 18 MiG-21bis/UM *Fishbed*
ATK 24 Su-25K/UBK *Frogfoot* (5 upgraded to NATO standard)
ISR 1 An-30 *Clank*
TPT 16 **Medium** 3 C-27J *Spartan*; **Light** 13: 1 An-2 *Colt*; 3 An-26 *Curl*; 7 L-410UVP/L-410UVP-E; 1 PC-12M; 1 Tu-134B *Crusty*
TRG 12: 6 L-39ZA *Albatros*; 6 PC-9M (basic)
HELICOPTERS
ATK 18 Mi-24D/V *Hind D/E* (12 being upgraded to NATO standard)
MRH 12 Mi-17 *Hip H* (6 to be upgraded to NATO standard)
TPT 17 **Medium** 11 AS 532AL *Cougar* **Light** 6 Bell 206 *Jet Ranger*
EW UAV • *Yastreb-2S*
AD
SAM S-300 (SA-10 *Grumble*) (quad) S-75 *Dvina* (SA-2 *Guideline* towed); S-125 *Pechora* (SA-3 *Goa*); S-200 (SA-5 *Gammon*)
MSL
AAM IR AAM R-3 (AA-2 *Atoll*)‡ R-73 (AA-11 *Archer*)
SARH AAM R-27R (AA-10 *Alamo A*)
ASM Kh-29 (AS-14 *Kedge*); Kh-23 (AS-7 *Kerry*)‡; Kh-25 (AS-10 *Karen*)

FACILITIES
Air base	1 located at Graf Ignatievo (3rd Fighter), 1 located at Bezmer (22nd Attack); 1 located in Sofia (16th Transport); 1 located at Krumovo (24th Helicopter)
Trg Centre	1 located at Dolpa Milropolia (12th Training Air Base) with L-39ZA *Albatros* trg ac (adv trg); PC-9M (basic trg)

Paramilitary 34,000

Border Guards 12,000
Ministry of Interior
FORCES BY ROLE
Paramilitary 12 regt

EQUIPMENT BY TYPE
PATROL AND COASTAL COMBATANTS 20
PB 20: 9 *Grif* (FSU *Zhuk*); 3 *Nesebar* (FSU *Neustadt*); 8 (other)

Railway and Construction Troops 18,000

Security Police 4,000

DEPLOYMENT

Legal provisions for foreign deployment:
Constitution: Codified constitution (1991)
Decision on deployment of troops abroad: By the president upon request from the Council of Ministers and upon approval by the National Assembly (Art. 84 XI)

AFGHANISTAN
NATO • ISAF 516; 1 mech inf coy

ARMENIA/AZERBAIJAN
OSCE • Minsk Conference 1

BOSNIA-HERZEGOVINA
EU • EUFOR • *Operation Althea* 120

IRAQ
NATO • NTM-I 2

LIBERIA
UN • UNMIL 2 obs

MOLDOVA
OSCE • Moldova 1

SERBIA
NATO • KFOR 3

Croatia CRO

Croatian Kuna k		2009	2010	2011
GDP	k	333bn	334bn	
	US$	63.2bn	60.9bn	
per capita	US$	14,270	13,811	
Growth	%	-5.8	0.5	
Inflation	%	2.4	1.9	
Def exp	k	5.34bn		
	US$	1.01bn		
Def bdgt	k	5.12bn	4.74bn	4.96bn
	US$	972m	863m	
FMA (US)	US$	1.0m	2.5m	5.0m
US$1=k		5.27	5.49	

Population	4,409,659

Age	0 – 14	15 – 19	20 – 24	25 – 29	30 – 64	65 plus
Male	7.7%	3.1%	3.1%	3.5%	24.1%	6.6%
Female	7.3%	3.0%	3.0%	3.4%	24.8%	10.2%

Capabilities

ACTIVE 18,600 (Army 11,390 Navy 1,850 Air 3,500 Joint 1,860) Paramilitary 3,000
The armed forces of Croatia are subject to arms limitations established under the Dayton Peace Accord. An agreement signed by BIH, its two entities, CRO and FRY on 14 June 1996, established ceilings for holdings of the armed forces of the parties.

RESERVE 21,000 (Army 18,500 Navy 250 Air 2,250)

ORGANISATIONS BY SERVICE

Joint 1,860 (General Staff)

Army 11,390
FORCES BY ROLE
Armd	1 bde
Inf	1 bde
Gd	3 regt (org varies)
SF	1 bn
MRL	1 regt
AT	1 regt
AD	1 ADA regt
Engr	1 regt
MP	1 regt

EQUIPMENT BY TYPE
MBT 261: 72 M-84; 3 T-72M; 186 T55; 30 decommissioning
AIFV 103: 103 M80; 1 decommissioning
APC 38
  APC (T) 16 BTR-50
  APC (W) 22: 9 BOV-VP; 13 LOV OP
ARTY 1,436
  SP 122mm 8 2S1 *Carnation*
  TOWED 416: **105mm** 165: 89 M-2A1; 29 decommissioning; 47 M-56H1 decommissioning; **122mm** 95: 53 D-30; 42 *M-1938* decommissioning; **130mm** 78: 44 M-46; 34 M-46H1 **152mm** 41: 20 D-20; 18 M-84; 3 M 84H; **155mm** 18 M-1H1; **203mm** 19 M-2
  MRL 42
    SP 42: **122mm** 39: 1 SVLR M 96 *Typhoon*, 7 M91*Vulkan* 31 BM-21 *Grad*; **128mm** 2 LOV RAK M91 R24; **262mm** 1 M-87 *Orkan*
  MOR 790: **82mm** 475: 339 LMB M96; 136 decommissioning; **120mm** 315: 310M-75; 5 UBM 52
AT
  MSL 603+
    SP 43 POLO BOV 83
    MANPATS 560+: 418 AT-3 9K11 *Malyjutka (Sagger)*; 81 AT-4 9K111 Fagot *(Spigot)*; 23 AT-7 9K115 *Metis (Saxhorn)*; 38 9K113 *Konkurs* M1; *Milan* (reported)
  RL 73mm RPG-22 *Net*/RPG-7 *Knout*; **90mm** M-79
  GUNS 100mm 133 T-12
AD
  MANPADS 619: 539 9K32M *Strela* 2M (SA-7 *Grail*); 80 9K38 *Igla* (SA-18 *Grouse*)
  GUNS 463
    SP 62: **20mm** 45: 44 BOV-3 SP; 1 decommissioning; **30mm** 17 BOV-3
    TOWED 401: **20mm** 390: 177 M55; 213 decommissioning; **40mm** 11

Navy 1,600; 250 conscript (total 1,850)
Navy Central Command HQ at Split. Two naval districts, NAVSOUTH and NAVNORTH

EQUIPMENT BY TYPE
SUBMARINES • SDV 3: 1 *R-1*; 2 *R-2 Mala*
PATROL AND COASTAL COMBATANTS 6
PCGF 1 *Koncar* with 2 twin lnchr (4 eff.) with RBS-15B AShM
PCGM 2 *Helsinki* each with 4 twin lnchr (8 eff.) with RBS-15M AShM, 2 sextuple *Sadral* lnchr (12 eff.) each with *Mistral* SAM
PCG 2 *Kralj* each with 2–4 twin lnchr (4-8 eff.) each with RBS-15B AShM
PBR 1 *OB 93*
MINE WARFARE • MINE COUNTERMEASURES • MHI 1 *Korcula*
AMPHIBIOUS 6
LCT 2 *Cetina*
LCVP 4 *Type 21*
LOGISTICS AND SUPPORT 11:
AXS 1 *Kraljica Mora*; **YTM** 2; **YDT** 2; **YFU** 4; **AKL** 2;

FACILITIES
Bases   Located at Split, Pula, Sibenik, Dubrovnik, Ploče
Minor Bases Located at Lastovo, Vis

Coastal Defence
FORCES BY ROLE
AShM   3 bty with RBS-15K
Arty   21+ bty

EQUIPMENT BY TYPE
MSL • TACTICAL • AShM RBS-15K

Marines
Inf 2 indep coy

Coast Guard
FORCES BY ROLE
The Croatian Coast Guard is a command under the navy. It retains two divisions, headquartered in Split (1st div) and Pula (2nd div).
EQUIPMENT BY TYPE
PATROL AND COASTAL COMBATANTS • PB 4 *Mirna*
LOGISTICS AND SUPPORT • AX 2

Air Force and Air Defence 3,500
Flying hours   50 hrs/year
FORCES BY ROLE
Ftr/FGA   2 (mixed) sqn with MiG-21bis/MiG-21UMD *Fishbed*
Tpt   1 sqn
Tpt Hel   2 sqn
Trg   1 sqn; 1 (hel) sqn
EQUIPMENT BY TYPE
AIRCRAFT 10 combat capable
FGA 10: 6 MiG-21bis *Fishbed*; 4 MiG-21UMD *Fishbed*
TPT • Light 2 An-32 *Cline*

TRG 24: 20 PC-9M; 4 Utva-75 (basic trg; being replaced by 5 Z-242L)
HELICOPTERS
MRH 11 Mi-8MTV *Hip H*
TPT 21 **Medium** 13: 3 Mi-8T *Hip C*; 10 Mi-171Sh **Light** 8 Bell 206B *Jet Ranger II*
AD
SAM
  SP S-300 (SA-10 *Grumble* (quad)); 9K31 *Strela*-1 (SA-9 *Gaskin*)
  MANPAD *Strela*-3 (SA-14 *Gremlin*); 9K310 *Igla*-1 (SA-16 *Gimlet*)
RADAR 8: 5 FPS-117; 3 S-600
MSL • AAM IR AAM R-3S (AA-2 *Atoll*)‡; R-60 (AA-8 *Aphid*)
FACILITIES
Bases   Located at Zagreb-Pleso, Pula, Zadar-Zermunik, Split-Divulje

Paramilitary 3,000
Police 3,000 armed

DEPLOYMENT
Legal provisions for foreign deployment:
Constitution: Codified constitution (2004)
Decision on deployment of troops abroad: By the parliament (Art. 7 II); simplified procedure for humanitarian aid and military exercises

AFGHANISTAN
NATO • ISAF 300

BOSNIA-HERZEGOVINA
OSCE • Bosnia and Herzegovina 1

CYPRUS
UN • UNFICYP 2

INDIA/PAKISTAN
UN • UNMOGIP 9 obs

LEBANON
UN • UNIFIL 1

LIBERIA
UN • UNMIL 2

SERBIA
NATO • KFOR 20
OSCE • Serbia 1
OSCE • Kosovo 8

SUDAN
UN • UNMIS 4

SYRIA/ISRAEL
UN • UNDOF 94; 1 inf coy

WESTERN SAHARA
UN • MINURSO 7 obs

Cyprus CYP

Euro €		2009	2010	2011
GDP	€	16.9bn	17.4bn	
	US$	23.6bn	23.0bn	
per capita	US$	27,098	26,178	
Growth	%	-0.5	2.7	
Inflation	%	0.4	2.2	
Def exp	€	339m		
	US$	472m		
Def bdgt	€	378m	376m	
	US$	526m	498m	
US$1=€		0.72	0.76	

Population   879,723

Age	0 – 14	15 – 19	20 – 24	25 – 29	30 – 64	65 plus
Male	8.3%	4.1%	4.8%	5.1%	24.2%	4.5%
Female	7.9%	3.6%	3.9%	4.2%	23.6%	5.9%

Capabilities

ACTIVE 10,000 (National Guard 10,000)
Paramilitary 750
Terms of service conscription, 24 months, then reserve to age 50 (officers 60)

RESERVE 50,000 (National Guard 50,000)

ORGANISATIONS BY SERVICE

National Guard 900 regular; 9,100 conscript (total 10,000)

FORCES BY ROLE

Armd	1 lt bde with (3 armd bn)
Mech Inf	2 (1st & 2nd) div (each: 3 inf bn)
SF	1 comd (regt) with (1 SF bn)
Lt Inf	1 (4th) bde with (2 inf regt)
Arty	1 comd with (8 arty bn)
Spt	1 (3rd) bde

EQUIPMENT BY TYPE
MBT 147: 41 T-80U; 54 AMX-30G; 52 AMX-30 B2
RECCE 139: 15 EE-3 *Jararaca*; 124 EE-9 *Cascavel*
AIFV 43 BMP-3
APC 294
  APC (T) 168: 168 *Leonidas*
  APC (W) 126 VAB (incl variants)
ARTY 526+
  SP 155mm 24: 12 Mk F3; 12 *Zuzana*
  TOWED 104: **100mm** 20 M-1944; **105mm** 72 M-56; **155mm** 12 TR-F-1
  MRL 22: **122mm** 4 BM-21; **128mm** 18 M-63 *Plamen*
  MOR 376+: **81mm** 240+: 70+ M-1/M-29 in store; 170 E-44; **107mm** 20 M-2/M-30; **120mm** 116 RT61
AT
  MSL • MANPATS 115: 70 HOT; 45 *Milan*
  RCL 153: **106mm** 144 M-40A1; **90mm** 9 EM-67

RL 1,850+: **66mm** M-72 *LAW*; **73mm** 850 RPG-7 *Knout*; **112mm** 1,000 APILAS
AD
  SAM 48
    SP 6 *Tor* (SA-15 *Gauntlet*); *Mistral*
    STATIC 12 *Aspide*
    MANPAD 30 *Mistral*
  GUNS • TOWED 60: **20mm** 36 M-55; **35mm** 24 GDF-003 (with *Skyguard*)

Maritime Wing
FORCES BY ROLE
AShM   1 (coastal defence) bty with MM-40 *Exocet* AShM

EQUIPMENT BY TYPE
PATROL AND COASTAL COMBATANTS 6
  PBF 4: 2 *Rodman* 55; 2 *Vittoria*
  PB 2: 1 *Esterel*; 1 *Kyrenia* (GRC *Dilos*)
MSL • AShM 24 MM-40 *Exocet*

Air Wing
AIRCRAFT
  TPT • Light 1 BN-2B *Islander*
  TRG 1 PC-9
HELICOPTERS
  ATK 11 Mi-35P *Hind*
  MRH 4 SA-342 *Gazelle* (with HOT for anti-armour role)
  TPT • Light 2 Bell 206C L-3 *Long Ranger*

Paramilitary 750+

Armed Police 500+
FORCES BY ROLE
Mech   1 (rapid-reaction) unit

EQUIPMENT BY TYPE
APC (W) 2 VAB VTT
HELICOPTERS • MRH 2 Bell 412 SP

Maritime Police 250
PATROL AND COASTAL COMBATANTS 10
  PBF 5: 2 *Poseidon*; 1 *Shaldag*; 2 *Vittoria*
  PB 5 *SAB-12*

DEPLOYMENT

Legal provisions for foreign deployment:
Constitution: Codified constitution (1960)
Decision on deployment of troops abroad: By parliament, but president has the right of final veto (Art. 50)

LEBANON
UN • UNIFIL 2

FOREIGN FORCES

Argentina UNFICYP 267; 2 inf coy; 1 avn pl
Austria UNFICYP 4
Brazil UNFICYP 1
Canada UNFICYP 1
Chile UNFICYP 15
Croatia UNFICYP 2
Greece Army: 950; ε200 (officers/NCO seconded to Greek-Cypriot National Guard)

Hungary UNFICYP 84; 1 inf pl
Paraguay UNFICYP 14
Peru UNFICYP 2
Slovakia UNFICYP 198; elm 1 inf coy; 1 engr pl
United Kingdom Army 1,678; 2 inf bn; 1 hel flt; **Navy** 42;
Air Force 1,071; 1 hel sqn with 4 Bell 412 *Twin Huey* •
UNFICYP 271: 1 inf coy

TERRITORY WHERE THE GOVERNMENT DOES NOT EXERCISE EFFECTIVE CONTROL

Data presented here represent the de facto situation on the northern half of the island. This does not imply international recognition as a sovereign state.

Capabilities

ACTIVE 5,000 (Army 5,000) **Paramilitary 150**
Terms of service conscription, 24 months, then reserve to age 50.

RESERVE 26,000 (first line 11,000 second line 10,000 third line 5,000)

ORGANISATIONS BY SERVICE

Army ε5,000
FORCES BY ROLE
Inf   7 bn

EQUIPMENT BY TYPE
ARTY
  MOR • **120mm** 73
AT
  MSL • **MANPATS** 6 *Milan*
  RCL • **106mm** 36

Paramilitary

Armed Police ε150
SF   1 (Police) unit

Coast Guard
PATROL AND COASTAL COMBATANTS 6
  PCC 5: 2 SG45/SG46; 1 *Rauf Denktash*; 2 US Mk 5
  PB 1

FOREIGN FORCES

TURKEY
Army ε36,000
  1 army corps HQ, some air det, 1 armd bde, 1 indep mech inf bde, 2 inf div, 1 cdo regt, 1 arty bde, 1 avn comd
EQUIPMENT BY TYPE
  MBT 449: 8 M-48A2 (trg); 441 M-48A5T1/2
  APC (T) 627: 361 AAPC (T) (incl variants); 266 M-113 (T) (incl variants)
  ARTY
    SP **155mm** 90 M-44T
    TOWED 102; **105mm** 72 M-101A1; **155mm** 18 M-114A2; **203mm** 12 M-115

  MRL 122mm 6 T-122
  MOR 450: 81mm 175; **107mm** 148 M-30; **120mm** 127 HY-12
AT
  MSL • **MANPATS** 114: 66 *Milan*; 48 TOW
  RCL 106mm 192 M-40A1; **90mm** M-67
  RL 66mm M-72 *LAW*
AD • **GUNS**
  TOWED 20mm Rh 202; **35mm** 16 GDF-003; **40mm** 48 M-1
  AIRCRAFT • **TPT** • **Light** 3 Cessna 185 (U-17)
  HELICOPTER • **TPT** 4 **Medium** 1 AS-532UL *Cougar* **Light** 3 Bell 205 (UH-1H *Iroquois*)
  PATROL AND COASTAL COMBATANTS 1 PB

Czech Republic CZE

Czech Koruna Kc		2009	2010	2011
GDP	Kc	3.63tr	3.77tr	
	US$	192bn	197bn	
per capita	US$	18,260	18,919	
Growth	%	-4.2	1.9	
Inflation	%	1.0	1.8	
Def exp	Kc	59.2bn		
	US$	3.13bn		
Def bdgt	Kc	56bn	48.9bn	43.9bn
	US$	2.96bn	2.55bn	
FMA (US)	US$	3.0m	6.0m	7.0m
US$1=Kc		18.94	19.17	

Population   10,410,786

Age	0–14	15–19	20–24	25–29	30–64	65 plus
Male	6.9%	2.8%	3.2%	3.4%	25.9%	6.5%
Female	6.5%	2.7%	3.1%	3.3%	25.8%	9.8%

Capabilities

ACTIVE 23,441 (Army 7,026, Air 4,567, Other 11,848) **Paramilitary 3,100**

CIVILIAN 7,888 (Army 803, Air 693, Other 7,360)
The armed forces are being reorganised with full operational capability planned for 2010–12. The military forces are Joint Forces, composed of Army, Air Force and Joint Forces Support Units.

ORGANISATIONS BY SERVICE

Army 7,026; 803 civilian
FORCES BY ROLE
Rapid   1 bde (4th) with (2 mech bn; 1 mot inf bn; 1
Reaction   AB bn)

Recce   1 bn

Mech   1 bde (7th) with (1 armd bn, 2 mech inf bn, 1 mot inf bn)

SF   1 gp

Arty   1 bde (13th) with (2 arty bn)

EQUIPMENT BY TYPE
MBT 169: 139 T-72; 30 T-72M4CZ
AIFV 435: 166 BMP-1; 181 BMP-2; 64 BPzV; 24 *Pandur* II (48 more on order)
APC 78:
  APC **(T)** 29 OT-90
  APC **(W)** 49: 28 OT-64; 21 *Dingo* 2
LAV 42 LMV *Panther*
ARTY 257
  SP 152mm 55 M-77 *Dana* (7 trg); (50 more in store)
  MRL 122mm 59: 19 RM-70 (3 trg); (40 more in store)
  MOR 120mm 90: 40 M-1982; 8 SPM-85; (42 more in store)
AT• MSL 671
  SP 496: 3 9P133 *Malyutka*; 21 9P148 *Konkurs*; 472 9S428
  MANPATS 175 9K111 *Fagot* (AT-4 *Spigot*)
RADAR • LAND 3 ARTHUR

Active Reserve
FORCES BY ROLE
Territorial Def   14 comd
Inf   14 coy (1 per territorial comd) (each: 1 logistic pl, 3 inf pl, 1 cbt spt pl)
Armd   1 coy

Air Force 4,567; 693 civilian
Integrated with Joint Forces. Principal task is to secure Czech airspace. This mission is fulfilled within NATO Integrated Extended Air Defence System (NATINADS) and, if necessary, by means of the Czech national reinforced air defence system. The Air Force also provides CAS for the Army SAR, and performs a tpt role.

Flying hours   100hrs/yr cbt ac 150 for tpt ac

FORCES BY ROLE
FGA   1 sqn with JAS 39C/JAS 39D *Gripen*; 1 sqn with L-39ZA*; 1 sqn with L-159 ALCA/L-159T
Tpt   2 sqn with A319CJ; An-26 *Curl*; CL-601 *Challenger*; L-410 *Turbolet*; Yak-40 *Codling*: C-295M
Atk Hel 1 sqn with Mi-24/Mi-35 *Hind*
Tpt Hel 1 sqn with Mi-17 *Hip H*; Mi-171Sh; 1 sqn with Mi-8 *Hip*; Mi-17 *Hip H*; PZL W-3A *Sokol*
AD   1 SAM bde (25th)
ISR UAV Some units with *Sojka* 3

EQUIPMENT BY TYPE
AIRCRAFT 48 combat capable
  FGA 14: 12 *Gripen* C (JAS 39C); 2 *Gripen* D (JAS 39D)
  ATK 24: 20 L-159 ALCA; 4 L-159T
  TPT 18 **Light** 15: 3 An-26 *Curl*; 2 C-295M; 8 L-410 *Turbolet*; 2 Yak-40 *Codling* **PAX** 3: 2 A319CJ; 1 CL-601 *Challenger*
  TRG 27: 1 EW-97 *Eurostar*; 8 L-39C *Albatros*; 10 L-39ZA*; 8 Z-142C;
HELICOPTERS
  ATK 24: 6 Mi-24 *Hind D*; 18 Mi-35 *Hind E*;
  MRH/TPT 24 Mi-17 Hip-H (MRH)/Mi-171Sh (med tpt)
  TPT 14 **Medium** 4 Mi-8 Hip **Light** 10 PZL W3A *Sokol*
UAV • ISR • Light 2 *Sojka* 3 systems

AD
  SAM 9K35 *Strela*-10 (SA-13 *Gopher*); 2K12 *Kub* (SA-6 *Gainful*); RBS-70; 9K32 *Strela*-2 (SA-7 *Grail*) (available for trg RBS-70 gunners)
MSL
  AAM IR AAM AIM-9M *Sidewinder*; **ARH AAM** AIM-120 AMRAAM
BOMBS
  Conventional: GBU Mk 82; Mk 84
  Laser-guided: GBU *Paveway*
FACILITIES
Air base   1 located at Cáslav (21st Tac Air Base), 1 located at Námest nad Oslavou (22nd Air Base), 1 located at Prerov (23rd Helicopter Base); 1 located at Praha-Kbely (24th Air Transport Base)
Trg centre   1 Air Trg Centre located at Pardubice

Joint Forces Support Units
FORCES BY ROLE
CBRN   1 bde with (2 bn)
Engr   1 bde with (3 bn, 2 (rescue) coy)
CIMIC/Psyops 1 coy with (1 CIMIC pl; 1 Psyops pl)
Logistics   1 bde (14th) with (1 spt bn; 1 supply bn)

FACILITIES
CRBN   1 warning centre
CIMIC/Psyops 1 centre
EW   1 centre

Other Forces
FORCES BY ROLE
Sy   1 (Presidential Gd) bde with (2 bn (each: 3 coy); 1 (Presidential) coy
MP   1 (central) comd; 3 (regional) comd; 1 (protection service) comd
Int 1 gp

Paramilitary 3,100

Border Guards 3,000

Internal Security Forces 100

DEPLOYMENT
Legal provisions for foreign deployment:
Constitution: Codified constitution (1992)
Decision on deployment of troops abroad: By the parliament (Art. 39, 43) or by the government (Art. 43)

AFGHANISTAN
NATO • ISAF 468

BOSNIA-HERZEGOVINA
EU • EUFOR • *Operation Althea* 2
OSCE • Bosnia and Herzegovina 1

DEMOCRATIC REPUBLIC OF THE CONGO
UN • MONUSCO 3 obs

EGYPT
MFO 3

SERBIA
NATO • KFOR 103; elm 1 engr bn
UN • UNMIK 1 obs

Denmark DNK

Danish Krone kr		2009	2010	2011
GDP	kr	1.66tr	1.74tr	
	US$	311bn	309bn	
per capita	US$	56,232	56,355	
Growth	%	-4.9	1.1	
Inflation	%	1.3	2.1	
Def exp	kr	23.2bn		
	US$	4.34bn		
Def bdgt	kr	22bn	20.6bn	20.2bn
	US$	4.11bn	3.66bn	
US$1=kr		5.35	5.63	

Population	5,481,283					
Age	0–14	15–19	20–24	25–29	30–64	65 plus
Male	9.0%	3.4%	3.1%	2.7%	23.6%	7.6%
Female	8.6%	3.2%	3.0%	2.7%	23.6%	9.5%

Capabilities

ACTIVE 18,707 (Army 9,925 Navy 2,959 Air 3,358
Joint 2,465)
Terms of service 4–12 months

CIVILIAN 649 (Army 219 Navy 306 Air Force 118)

RESERVES 53,507 (Army 40,800 Navy 4,500 Air
Force 5,307 Service Corps 2,900)

ORGANISATIONS BY SERVICE

Army 8,155; 1,770 conscript (total 9,925) 219
civilian

FORCES BY ROLE

Recce   1 bn
Mech Inf   1 div (1 mech inf bde with (1 tk bn, 2 mech
             inf bn, 1 SP arty bn, 1 engr coy, 1 MP coy); 1
             (trg) bde (lower readiness; can, if necessary,
             be transformed to mech inf bde))
SF   1 unit
Engr   1 bn

EQUIPMENT BY TYPE
MBT 117: 64 *Leopard* 2 A4/2A5; 53 *Leopard* 1A5 (46 more in
store awaiting disposal)
RECCE 117: 32 *Eagle 1* (MOWAG); 85 *Eagle IV*
AIFV: 45 CV9030 Mk II
APC 403
   APC (T) 290 M-113 (incl variants); (80 more in store
   awaiting disposal)

APC (W) 113 *Piranha* III (incl variants)
ARTY 57
   SP 155mm 24 M-109
   MRL 227mm (12 MLRS in store awaiting disposal)
   MOR • SP 81mm 33 M-125A2
AT
   MSL • SP (21 TOW on M113 in store awaiting disposal)
   MANPATS 20 TOW
   RCL 84mm 349 *Carl Gustav*
   RL 84mm 4,200 AT-4
AD • SAM • MANPAD FIM-92A *Stinger*
RADAR • LAND ARTHUR

Navy 2,806; 153 conscript (total 2,959) 306
civilian

EQUIPMENT BY TYPE
PRINCIPAL SURFACE COMBATANTS 4
   DESTROYERS • DDGHM (1 *Ivar Huitfeldt* (launched
   Nov 2010; expected ISD 2011; weapons systems not yet
   installed; 2 additional vessels expected ISD 2012–13)
   FRIGATES • FFH 4 *Thetis* each with 2 twin lnchr (4 eff.)
   each with *Stinger* SAM, 1 76mm gun, (capacity: 1 *Super
   Lynx* Mk90B)
PATROL AND COASTAL COMBATANTS 11
   PSO 2 *Knud Rasmussen* each with 1 hel landing platform
   PCM 2 *Flyvefisken* each with 1 Mk 48 *Sea Sparrow* VLS
   with *Sea Sparrow* SAM, 2 single 533mm TT, 1 76mm gun
   PCC 7: 1 *Agdlek*; 6 *Diana*
MINE WARFARE • MINE COUNTERMEASURES 8
   MCI 4 MSF MK-I
   MHD 2 *Sav*
   MSD 2 *Holm*
LOGISTICS AND SUPPORT 21:
   AG 2 *Absalon* (flexible-support-ships) each with 2 octuple
   VLS with 16 RGM-84 Block 2 *Harpoon* 2 AShM, 4 twin (4
   eff.) with *Stinger* SAM, 3 12 cell Mk 56 VLS with 36 RIM-
   162B *Sea Sparrow* naval SAM, 1 127mm gun (capacity 2
   LCP, 7 MBT or 40 vehicles; 130 troops)
   AGSC 2 *Holm*
   AGS 4 *Ska 11*
   AGE 1 *Dana*
   AXL 2 *Holm*
   AXS 2 *Svanen*
   AE 1 *Sleipner*
   AGB 3: 1 *Thorbjørn*; 2 *Danbjørn*
   ABU 2 (primarily used for MARPOL duties)
   AKL 2 *Seatruck*
FACILITIES
Bases   Located at Korsør and Frederikshavn
Naval air bases Located at Karup, Jutland

Naval Aviation
HELICOPTERS • ASW 8 *Super Lynx* Mk90B

Air Force 3,258; 100 conscript (total 3,358) 118
civilian

Three air bases

Flying hours   165 hrs/yr

Tactical Air Comd

FORCES BY ROLE

Ftr/FGA   2 sqn with F-16AM/BM *Fighting Falcon*

SAR /Tpt   AW-101 *Merlin*; 1 sqn with AS-550 *Fennec*
Hel   (ISR)

Tpt   1 sqn with C-130J-30 *Hercules*; CL-604
           Challenger (MP/VIP)

Trg   1 unit with MFI-17 *Supporter* (T-17)

EQUIPMENT BY TYPE

AIRCRAFT 48 combat capable
  FTR 48 F-16AM/BM *Fighting Falcon*
  TPT 7 **Medium** 4 C-130J-30 *Hercules* **PAX** 3 CL-604
  Challenger (MP/VIP)
  TRG 28 MFI-17 *Supporter* (T-17)
HELICOPTERS
  MRH 12 AS-550 *Fennec* (ISR)
  SAR/TPT • **Medium** 14 AW-101 *Merlin*
MSL
  AAM • **IR AAM** AIM-9L **IIR AAM** AIM-9X **ARH**
  AAM AIM-120 AMRAAM
  ASM AGM-65 *Maverick*
BOMBS
  INS/GPS-guided: GBU-31 JDAM; EGBU-12/GBU-24
  Paveway LGB
FACILITIES
3 air stations; 1 flying school

Control and Air Defence Group

1 Control and Reporting Centre, 1 Mobile Control and Reporting Centre. 4 Radar sites. No SAM.

Reserves

Home Guard (Army) 40,800 reservists (to age 50)
Army   5 (local def) region (each: up to 2 mot inf
           bn); 2 regt cbt gp (each: 1 arty bn, 3 mot inf
           bn)

Home Guard (Navy) 4,500 reservists (to age 50)
organised into 30 Home Guard units
EQUIPMENT BY TYPE
PATROL AND COASTAL COMBATANTS 30
  PB 30: 18 MHV800; 12 MHV900

Home Guard (Air Force) 5,307 reservists (to age 50)

Home Guard (Service Corps) 2,900 reservists

DEPLOYMENT

Legal provisions for foreign deployment:
Constitution: Codified constitution (1849)
Decision on deployment of troops abroad: On approval by the parliament (Art. 19 II)

AFGHANISTAN
NATO • ISAF 750; 1 mech BG with (2 mech inf coy; 1 tk pl); 1 fd hospital; 4 *Leopard* 2A5; 13 CV9030 MkII; 23 M113
UN • UNAMA 1 obs

DEMOCRATIC REPUBLIC OF THE CONGO
UN • MONUSCO 2 obs

GULF OF ADEN & SOMALI BASIN
NATO • *Operation Ocean Shield* 1 AG

IRAQ
Army 23 (sy forces)
NATO • NTM-I 6
UN • UNAMI 2 obs

LEBNANON
UN • UNIFIL 142; 1 log bn

LIBERIA
UN • UNMIL 3; 2 obs

MIDDLE EAST
UN • UNTSO 10 obs

SERBIA
NATO • KFOR 152
UN • UNMIK 1 obs

SUDAN
UN • UNMIS 4; 5 obs

Estonia EST

Estonian Kroon kn		2009	2010	2011
GDP	kn	217bn	220bn	
	US$	19.3bn	18.7bn	
per capita	US$	14,410	13,930	
Growth	%	-14.1	2.4	
Inflation	%	-0.1	2.5	
Def exp	kn	4bn		
	US$	356m		
Def bdgt	kn	4bn	3.9bn	4.3bn
	US$	356m	330m	
FMA (US)	US$	1.5m	2.5m	3.0m
US$1=kn		11.23	11.82	

Population   1,339,459

Ethnic groups: Russian 26%; Ukrainian 2%; Belarussian 1%

Age	0–14	15–19	20–24	25–29	30–64	65 plus
Male	7.8%	2.8%	4.0%	3.7%	21.5%	5.8%
Female	7.3%	2.7%	3.8%	3.8%	24.9%	11.9%

Capabilities

ACTIVE 5,450 (Army 4,800 Navy 400 Air 250)
Defence League 12,000

RESERVE 30,000 (Joint 30,000)

Terms of service 8 months, officers and some specialists 11 months.

ORGANISATIONS BY SERVICE

Army 2,800; 2,000 conscript (total 4,800)

FORCES BY ROLE

4 Def region. All units except Scouts bn are reserve based

Recce   1 bn

Inf   1 (1st) bde with (2 inf bn (Kalev & Scouts), 1 CSS bn); 3 indep bn (Kuperjanov, Viru & Guards)

Arty   1 bn

AD   1 bn

Engr   1 bn

Log   1 bn

Defence League 12,000

15 Districts

EQUIPMENT BY TYPE

APC (W) 88: 7 *Mamba*; 60 XA-180 *Sisu*; 21 BTR-80

ARTY 334

  TOWED 104: **105mm** 38 H 61-37; **122mm** 42 D-30 (H 63); **155mm** 24 FH-70

  MOR 230: **81mm** 51: 41 B455; 10 NM 95; **120mm** 179: 14 2B11; 165 41D

AT

  MSL • MANPAT *Milan, Mapats*

  RCL 160 **106mm**: 30 M-40A1; **90mm** 130 PV-1110

AD • SAM • MANPAD *Mistral*

FACILITIES

Centre   1 (peace ops)

Navy 400 (inclusive of two platoon size conscript units)

EQUIPMENT BY TYPE

PATROL AND COASTAL COMBATANTS • PB 1 (FIN *Rihtiniemi*)

MINE WARFARE • MINE COUNTERMEASURES 4

  MCD 1 *Tasuja* (DNK *Lindormen*)

  MHC 3 *Admiral Cowan* (UK *Sandown*)

LOGISTICS AND SUPPORT • AGF 1 *Admiral Pitka* with 1 76mm gun

FACILITIES

Base   Located at Tallinn (Miinisadam)

Air Force 250

Flying hours   120 hrs/year

FORCES BY ROLE

Tpt   1 sqn with An-2 *Colt*

Tpt Hel   1 sqn with R-44 *Raven II*

EQUIPMENT BY TYPE

AIRCRAFT • TPT • Light 2 An-2 *Colt*

HELICOPTERS • TPT • Light 4 R-44 *Raven II*

FACILITIES

1 air base

Paramilitary

Border Guard

The Estonian Border Guard is subordinate to the Ministry of the Interior. Air support is provided by the Estonian Border Guard Aviation Corps.

EQUIPMENT BY TYPE

PATROL AND COASTAL COMBATANTS 20

  PB 9: 1 *Maru* (FIN *Viima*); 8 (other)

  PBR 11

AMPHIBIOUS • LANDING CRAFT • LCU 2

LOGISTICS & SUPPORT • AGF 1 *Balsam*

AIRCRAFT • TPT • Light 2 L-410

HELICOPTERS • TPT • 3 AW139

DEPLOYMENT

Legal provisions for foreign deployment:

Constitution: Codified constitution (1992)

Decision on deployment of troops abroad: By parliament (Art. 128). Also, International Military Cooperation Act stipulates conditions for deployment abroad; parliament decides deployment, unless otherwise provided for by international agreement.

AFGHANISTAN

NATO • ISAF 136; 1 mech inf coy with 14 XA-180 *Sisu*; 1 mor det with 3 81mm

BOSNIA-HERZEGOVINA

EU • EUFOR • *Operation Althea* 2

IRAQ

NATO • NTM-I 2

MIDDLE EAST

UN • UNTSO 1 obs

MOLDOVA

OSCE • Moldova 2

NORTH SEA

NATO • SNMCMG 1: 1 MHC

SERBIA

NATO • KFOR 1

Finland FIN

Euro €		2009	2010	2011
GDP	€	171bn	177bn	
	US$	239bn	235bn	
per capita	US$	44,696	43,926	
Growth	%	-7.8	1.5	
Inflation	%	1.6	1.4	
Def exp	€	2.79bn		
	US$	3.89bn		
Def bdgt	€	2.82bn	2.71bn	2.86bn
	US$	3.93bn	3.59bn	
US$1=€		0.72	0.76	

Population   5,345,826

Age	0 – 14	15 – 19	20 – 24	25 – 29	30 – 64	65 plus
Male	8.2%	3.2%	3.1%	3.2%	23.9%	7.3%
Female	7.9%	3.1%	3.0%	3.0%	23.6%	10.5%

Capabilities

ACTIVE 22,250 (Army 16,000 Navy 3,500 Air 2,750)
Paramilitary 2,800

General Conscription terms of Service 6-9-12 months
(12 months for officers NCOs and soldiers with special
duties. 25,000 reservists a year do refresher training: total
obligation 40 days (75 for NCOs, 100 for officers) between
conscript service and age 50 (NCOs and officers to age 60).
Reserve total reducing to 340,000.

CIVILIAN 4,600 (Army 3,000 Navy 500 Air 1,100)

RESERVE 350,000 (Army 280,000 Navy 32,000 Air
38,000) Paramilitary 11,500

ORGANISATIONS BY SERVICE

Army 5,000; 11,000 conscript (total 16,000); civilian 3,000

FORCES BY ROLE
Recent reorganisation has involved the replacement of
the previous commands with seven military provinces.
Finland's army maintains a mobilisation strength of about
300,000. In support of this requirement two cycles, each for
about 15,000 conscripts and 17,000 reservists, take place
each year. After conscript training, reservist commitment
is to the age of 60. Reservists are usually assigned to
units within their local geographical area. All service
appointments or deployments outside Finnish borders
are voluntary for all members of the armed services. All
brigades are reserve based.

Reserve Organisations

60,000 in manoeuvre forces and 220,000 in
territorial forces

FORCES BY ROLE

Armd	2 BG (regt)
Mech	2 (Karelia & Pori Jaeger) bde
Lt Inf	3 (Jaeger) bde; 6 bde
SF	1 bn
AD	Some units
Engr	7 regt
Log	Some units
Hel	1 bn

EQUIPMENT BY TYPE
MBT 100 *Leopard* 2A4
RECCE 10 BMP-1TJ
AIFV 194: 92 BMP-2; 102 CV90
APC 613
  APC (T) 142: 40 MT-LBU; 102 MT-LBV
  APC (W) 471: 260 XA-180/185 *Sisu*; 101 XA-202 *Sisu*; 48
  XA-203 *Sisu*; 62 AMV (XA-360)
ARTY 678
  SP 122mm 36 2S1 *Carnation* (PsH 74)
  TOWED 354: **122mm** 234 D-30 (H 63); **130mm** 36 K 54;
  155mm 54 K 83/K 98

MRL 227mm 22 M270 MLRS
MOR 120mm 265: 261 KRH 92; 4 XA-361 AMOS
AT • MSL 100 *Spike*; TOW 2
HELICOPTERS
  MRH 7 Hughes 500 D/E
  TPT • Medium 10: 2 Mi-8 *Hip*; 8 NH-90 TTH
UAV • ISR • Medium 6 ADS-95 *Ranger*
AD • SAM
  SP 36 +: 16 ASRAD (ITO 05); 20 *Crotale* NG (ITO 90);
  9K37 Buk (ITO 96)
  MANPAD: 86 RBS 70 (ITO 05/05M)
  GUNS 23mm; 30mm; 35mm; 57mm

Navy 1,600; 1,900 conscript (total 3,500); civilian 500

FORCES BY ROLE
Naval Command HQ located at Turku; with two
subordinate Naval Commands (Gulf of Finland and
Archipelago Sea); 1 Naval bde; 3 Spt elm (Naval Materiel
Cmd, Naval Academy, Naval Research Institute)

EQUIPMENT BY TYPE
PATROL AND COASTAL COMBATANTS 10
  PBG 4 *Rauma* each with 6 RBS-15SF3 (15SF) AShM, 1
  sextuple *Sadral* lnchr with *Mistral* SAM
  PCG 4 *Hamina* each with 4 RBS-15 (15SF) AShM, 1
  octuple VLS with *Umkhonto* SAM
  PCC 2 *Kiisla*
MINE WARFARE 18
  MINE COUNTERMEASURES 12
    MHSO 1 *Katanpää*
    MSI 11: 7 *Kiiski*; 4 *Kuha*
  MINELAYERS • ML 6:
    2 *Hameenmaa* each with 1 octuple VLS with *Umkhonto*
    SAM, 2 RBU 1200 (10 eff.), up to 100–120 mine
    3 *Pansio* each with 50 mine
    1 *Pohjanmaa* with up to 100–150 mine
AMPHIBIOUS • LANDING CRAFT 43
  LCU 7: 2 *Kala*; 3 *Kampela*; 2 *Lohi*
  LCP 36
LOGISTICS AND SUPPORT 29:
  AGOR 1 *Aranda* (Ministry of Trade Control)
  AKSL 15: 6 *Hauki*; 4 *Hila*; 5 *Valas*
  AGB 7 (Board of Navigation control)
  AGS 1 *Prisma* (Maritime Administration)
  AX 5: 3 *Fabian Wrede*; 2 *Lokki*

FACILITIES
Bases   Located at Upinniemi (Helsinki) and Turku

Coastal Defence
ARTY •COASTAL 118: **130mm** 102: 30 K-53tk (static);
72 K-54 RT **100mm** 16 (TK) tank turrets
MSL • TACTICAL • 4 RBS-15K AShM

Air Force 2,000; 750 conscript (total 2,750); civilian 1,100

3 Air Comds: Satakunta (West), Karelia (East), Lapland
(North). Each Air Comd assigned to one of the 3 AD areas
into which SF is divided. 3 ftr wg, one in each AD area.

Flying hours 90–140 hrs/year

FORCES BY ROLE

FGA   3 wg with F/A-18C/D *Hornet*

ISR   1 (survey) sqn with *Learjet* 35A

Tpt   1 sqn with C-295M; 4 (liason) sqn with L-90 *Redigo*; PA-31-350 *Piper Chieftain*; PC-12NG

Trg   1 sqn with *Hawk* Mk50; *Hawk* Mk51A*; *Hawk* Mk66* (air defence and ground attack trg); 1 unit with L-70 *Vinka*

EQUIPMENT BY TYPE

AIRCRAFT 121 combat capable

FGA 62: 55 F/A-18C *Hornet*; 7 F/A-18D *Hornet*

ASW 1 F-27 *Maritime Enforcer* (ESM/ELINT)

TPT • Light 9: 2 C-295M; 3 *Learjet* 35A (survey; ECM trg; tgt-tow); 4 PA-31-350 *Piper Chieftain*

TRG 99: 40 *Hawk* Mk50/Mk51A*; 18 *Hawk* Mk66*; 7 L-90 *Redigo*; 28 L-70 *Vinka*; 6 PC-12NG

MSL • AAM • IR AAM AIM-9 *Sidewinder* **ARH AAM** AIM-120 *AMRAAM*

Paramilitary

Border Guard 2,800

Ministry of Interior. 4 Border Guard Districts and 2 Coast Guard Districts

FORCES BY ROLE

Land   4 Border Guard Districts

Coast Guard   6 (offshore patrol) sqn

Air   1 (patrol) sqn with 2 Do-228 (maritime surv); 3 AS-332 *Super Puma*; 3 Bell 206L (AB-206L) *Long Ranger*; 4 Bell 412 (AB-412) *Twin Huey*; 1 Bell 412EP (AB-412EP) *Twin Huey*

EQUIPMENT BY TYPE

PATROL AND COASTAL COMBATANTS 66

  PCC 3

  PBO 3

  PB 60

AMPHIBIOUS • LANDING CRAFT • LCAC 7

AIRCRAFT • TPT • Light 2 Do-228

HELICOPTERS

  MRH 5: 4 Bell 412 (AB-412) *Twin Huey*; 1 Bell 412EP (AB-412EP) *Twin Huey*

  TPT 7 **Medium** 3 AS-332 *Super Puma* **Light** 4 1 AW-119KE *Koala*; 3 Bell 206L *Long Ranger* (AB-206L)

Reserve 11,500 reservists on mobilisation

DEPLOYMENT

Legal provisions for foreign deployment:
Constitution: Codified constitution (2000)
Specific legislation: 'Act on Peace Support Operations' (2000)
Decision on deployment of troops abroad: By president upon proposal by government (Art. 129 of constitution) and after formal consultation of parliamentary Foreign Affairs Committee ('Act on Peace Support Operations', Ch. 1, Section 2)

AFGHANISTAN
NATO • ISAF 150

BOSNIA-HERZEGOVINA
EU • EUFOR • *Operation Althea* 4
OSCE • Bosnia and Herzegovina 1

INDIA/PAKISTAN
UN • UNMOGIP 5 obs

LIBERIA
UN • UNMIL 2

MIDDLE EAST
UN • UNTSO 14 obs

MOLDOVA
OSCE • Moldova 1

SERBIA
NATO • KFOR 196 (reducing to 20 by end 2010)

SUDAN
UN • UNMIS 1; 1 obs

UGANDA
EU • EUTM 4

France FRA

Euro €		2009	2010	2011
GDP	€	1.91tr	1.95tr	
	US$	2.66tr	2.59tr	
per capita	US$	42,420	41,297	
Growth	%	-2.6	1.1	
Inflation	%	0.1	1.7	
Def exp[a]	€	39.1bn		
	US$	54.4bn		
Def bdgt[b]	€	33bn	32.2bn	
	US$	46bn	42.6bn	
US$1=€		0.72	0.76	

[a] Including military pensions

[b] As defined by mission defence parameters in France's 'Loi de Finance'

Population	62,636,580

Age	0–14	15–19	20–24	25–29	30–64	65 plus
Male	9.5%	3.1%	3.2%	3.2%	22.9%	7.0%
Female	9.0%	2.9%	3.0%	3.1%	23.3%	9.7%

Capabilities

ACTIVE 238,591 (Army 130,600 Navy 40,353 Air 52,669, Other Staffs 14,969) **Paramilitary 103,376**

CIVILIAN 70,976 (Army 20,600, Navy 7,091, Air 7,517, Other Staffs 35,768) **Paramilitary 1,925**

RESERVE 33,686 (Army 18,500, Navy 6,012, Air 5,186, Other Staffs 3,988) **Paramilitary 40,000**

ORGANISATIONS BY SERVICE

Strategic Nuclear Forces

Navy 2,200
SUBMARINES • STRATEGIC • SSBN 4
3 *Le Triomphant* S 616 each with 16 M-45 SLBM each with 6 TN-75 nuclear warheads, 4 single 533mm TT each with F17 Mod 2 HWT/SM-39 *Exocet* AShM
1 *Le Triomphant* with 16 M-51 SLBM each with 6 TN-75 nuclear warheads, 4 single 533mm TT each with F17 Mod 2 HWT/SM-39 *Exocet* AShM
AIRCRAFT • FGA 18 *Rafale* M F3 with ASMP-A msl

Air Force 1,800

Air Strategic Forces Command

Strike	3 sqn with *Rafale/Mirage* 2000N with ASMP/ASMP-A msl
Tkr	1 sqn with C-135FR; KC-135 *Stratotanker*

EQUIPMENT BY TYPE
AIRCRAFT 56 combat capable
FGA 56: 40 *Mirage* 2000N; 16 *Rafale* B F3
TKR/TPT 11 C-135FR
TKR 3 KC-135 *Stratotanker*

Paramilitary

Gendarmerie 41

Army 130,600; 20,600 (civilian)
FORCES BY ROLE
regt normally bn size

Comd	2 (task force) HQ; 1 (land) comd HQ; 5 region HQ
Armd	2 bde each: (2 armd regt; 2 armd inf regt; 1 SP arty regt; 1 engr regt); 1 (FRA/GER) bde with (1 armd cav regt; 1 mech inf regt)
Lt Armd	2 bde (each: 1 armd cav regt; 2 mech inf regt; 1 SP arty regt; 1 engr regt)
Mech Inf	2 bde (each: 1 armd cav regt; 1 armd inf regt; 1 mech inf regt; 1 SP arty regt; 1 engr regt)
Mtn Inf	1 bde with (1 armd cav regt; 3 mech inf regt; 1 arty regt; 1 engr regt)
AB	1 bde with (1 armd cav regt; 4 para regt; 1 arty regt; 1 engr regt; 1 spt regt)
ISR	1 bde with (1 recce regt; 1 UAV regt; 2 EW regt; 1 int bn)
AD	1 regt
Sigs	1 bde with (5 sigs regt)
CBRN	1 regt
Avn	3 regt

Foreign Legion 7,300

Armd Cav	1 regt (incl in lt armd bde above)
Mech Inf	1 regt (incl in lt armd bde above); 1 combined arms BG (Djibouti)
Lt inf	1 regt (French Guyana); 1 bn (Mayotte)
Para	1 regt (incl in AB bde above)
Engr	2 regt
Spt	1 regt
Trg	1 Inf regt

Marines 12,800

Armd Cav	2 regt (included in lt armd bde above)
Armd Inf	1 regt (included in lt armd bde above)
Mech Inf	3 regt (included in armd bde above); 2 (combined arms) regt (Djibouti & New Caledonia); 2 bn (Gabon & Senegal)
Lt Inf	1 regt (French West Indies); 1 regt (French Guyana); 1 regt (Polynesia); 1 bn (French West Indies)
Para	2 regt (included in AB bde above); 1 regt (Réunion)
Arty	2 SP regt (included in armd & lt armd bde above); 1 regt (included in lt armd bde above)
SF	1 regt (included in Special Operations Forces below)
SMA	4 regt (French Guiana, French West Indies & Indian Ocean); 5 coy (French Polynesia & New Caledonia)

Special Operation Forces 2,200
FORCES BY ROLE

HQ	1 comd
Para	2 regt
Avn	1 regt

FACILITIES

Trg Centre	3

Reserves 18,500
Reservists form:
79 UIR (Reserve Intervention Units) of about 75 to 152 troops, for 'Proterre' (combined land projection forces) bn
23 USR (Reserve Specialised Units), of about 160 troops, in specialised regt.
EQUIPMENT BY TYPE
MBT 254 *Leclerc*
RECCE 2,010: 256 AMX-10RC; 160 ERC-90F4 *Sagaie*; 1,594 VBL M-ll
AIFV 563: 232 VBCI; 331 AMX-10P/PC
APC (W) 3,586: 3,500 VAB; 60 VAB BOA; 26 VAB NBC
LFV 506 PVP
ARTY 375
SP 155mm 114: 37 AU-F-1; 77 CAESAR
TOWED 155mm 43 TR-F-1
MRL 227mm 26 MLRS
MOR 120mm 192 RT-F1
AT • MSL
SP 325: 30 VAB HOT; 110 VAB *Milan*; 185 VAB *Eryx*
MANPATS 550 *Milan*
RL 84mm AT-4
AIRCRAFT • TPT • Light 13: 5 PC-6B *Turbo-Porter*; 8 TBM-700

HELICOPTERS
ATK 30 AS-665 *Tiger*
MRH 173 SA-342M *Gazelle* (all variants)
TPT 124 **Heavy** 8 EC 725AP *Caracal* (CSAR) **Medium** 116: 23 AS-532UL *Cougar*; 93 SA-330 *Puma*
UAV • ISR • Medium 20 SDTI (*Sperwer*)
AD • SAM 897
TOWED 15 MIM-23B (*I-Hawk*)
MANPAD 882 *Mistral*
RADAR • LAND 66: 10 *Cobra*; 56 RASIT/RATAC

Navy 40,353 (incl 2,200 opcon Strategic Nuclear Forces); 7,091(civilian)
HRF (N) HQ at Toulon; Atlantic HQ at Brest; Indian Ocean HQ at Toulon; Mediterranean HQ at Toulon; North S ea/Channel HQ at Cherbourg; Pacific HQ at Papeete

EQUIPMENT BY TYPE
SUBMARINES 9
STRATEGIC • SSBN 4:
3 *Le Triomphant* opcon Strategic Nuclear Forces each with 16 M-45 SLBM with 6 TN-75 nuclear warheads, 4 single 533mm TT each with F17 Mod 2 HWT/SM-39 *Exocet* AShM
1 *Le Triomphant* opcon Strategic Nuclear Forces with 16 M-51 SLBM with 6 TN-75 nuclear warheads, 4 single 533mm TT each with F17 Mod 2 HWT/SM-39 *Exocet* AShM
TACTICAL • SSN 6:
6 *Rubis* each with 4 single 533mm TT with F-17 HWT/SM-39 *Exocet* AShM
PRINCIPAL SURFACE COMBATANTS 25
AIRCRAFT CARRIERS 1:
CVN 1 *Charles de Gaulle* with 4 octuple VLS (32 eff.) each with *Aster* 15 SAM, 2 sextuple *Sadral* lnchr 912 eff.) each with *Mistral* SAM (capacity: 35-40 *Super Etendard*/*Rafale* M/E-2C *Hawkeye*/SA-360 *Dauphin*)
DESTROYERS • DDGHM 13:
2 *Cassard* each, with 2 quad lnchr (8 eff.) each with MM-40 *Exocet* AShM, 1 Mk 13 GMLS with SM-1MR SAM, 2 single 533mm ASTT each with L5 HWT, 1 100mm gun, (capacity: 1 AS-565SA *Panther* ASW hel)
2 *Forbin* each with 2 quad lnchr (8 eff.) each with MM-40 *Exocet* AShM, 1 48-cell VLS with *Aster* 15/*Aster* 30 SAM, 2 sextuple *Sadral* lnchr (12 EFF.) each with *Mistral* SAM, 2 twin 324mm ASTT (4 eff.) each with MU-90, 2 76mm gun, (capacity: 1 NH90 TTH hel)
2 *Georges Leygues* each with 2 twin lnchr (4 eff.) each with MM-40 *Exocet* AShM, 1 octuple lnchr with *Crotale* SAM, 2 single 533mm ASTT each with L5 HWT, 1 100mm gun, (capacity: 2 *Lynx* hel)
2 *Georges Leygues* each with 2 quad lnchr (8 eff.) each with MM-40 *Exocet* AShM, 1 octuple lnchr with *Crotale* SAM, 2 single 533mm ASTT each with L5 HWT, 1 100mm gun, (capacity: 2 *Lynx* hel)
3 *Georges Leygues* (mod) each with 2 quad lcnhr (8 eff.) each with MM-40 *Exocet* AShM, 1 octuple lnchr with *Crotale* SAM, 2 single 533mm ASTT each with L5 HWT, 1 100mm gun, (capacity: 2 *Lynx* hel)
2 *Tourville* each with 6 single lnchr each with MM-38 *Exocet* AShM, 1 octuple lnchr with *Crotale* SAM,

2 single 533mm ASTT with L5 HWT, 2 100mm gun, (capacity: 2 *Lynx* hel)
FRIGATES • FFGHM 11:
6 *Floreal* each with 2 single lnchr each with MM-38 *Exocet* AShM, 1 twin *Simbad* lnchr with *Mistral* SAM, 1 100mm gun, (capacity: 1 AS-565SA *Panther*)
5 *La Fayette* each with 2 quad lnchr (8 eff.) each with MM-40 *Exocet* AShM, 1 octuple lnchr with *Crotale* SAM, (space for fitting 2 x 8 cell VLS launchers for *Aster* 15/30), 1 100mm gun, (capacity 1 AS-565SA *Panther*/SA-321 *Super Frelon*)
PATROL AND COASTAL COMBATANTS 24
FSG 9 *D'Estienne d'Orves* each with 4 MM-40 *Exocet* AShM, 4 single ASTT, 1 100mm gun
PCC 15: 7 *L'Audacieuse* (all deployed in the Pacific or Caribbean); 8 *Léopard* (trg role)
MINE WARFARE • MINE COUNTERMEASURES 18
MCS 7: 3 *Antares* (used as route survey vessels); 4 *Vulcain* (used as mine diving tenders)
MHO 11 *Éridan*
AMPHIBIOUS
PRINCIPAL AMPHIBIOUS SHIPS 4
LHD 2 *Mistral* (capacity mixed air group of up to 16 NH-90/SA-330 *Puma*/AS-532 *Cougar*/AS-665 *Tiger* hel; 2 LCAC or 4 LCM; 60 AVs; 450 troops) (one more launched 2010; expected ISD 2012)
LPD 2 *Foudre* (capacity 4 AS-532 *Cougar*; either 2 LCT or 10 LCM; 22 tanks; 470 troops)
LANDING SHIPS • LST 3 *Batral* (capacity 12 trucks; 140 troops)
LANDING CRAFT 19:
LCT 4: 2 *Edic 700*; 2 CDIC (4 EDA-R in build; expected ISD 2011/12)
LCM 15 CTMS
LOGISTICS AND SUPPORT 107:
AORH 4 *Durance* (capacity: 1 SA-319 *Alouette III*/AS-365 *Dauphin*/*Lynx*)
AF 3
AG 3 *Chamois*
AGE 1 *Corraline*
AGI 1 *Dupuy de Lome*
AGOR 1
AGM 1 *Monge*
AGS 3 *Lapérouse*
ATA 2
AXL 3: 2 *Glycine*; 1 other
AXS 4: 2 *La Belle Poule*; 2 other
YAG 2 *Phaéton* (towed array tenders)
YD 5
YDT 11: 1 *Alize*; 1 *Le Malin*; 9 VIP 21
YFRT 2
YGS 7 VH8
YTB 3 *Bélier*
YTL 30: 4 PSS 10; 26 P4
YTM 21: 3 *Maïto*; 16 *Fréhel*; 2 *Esterel*

FACILITIES

Bases   1 HQ located at Toulon, 1 HQ located at Brest, 1 located at Cherbourg, 1 located at Lorient, 1 (HQ) located at Papeete (Tahiti), 1 located at Dzaoudzi (Mayotte), 1 HQ located at Port-des-Galets (La Réunion), 1 located at Fort de France (Martinique), 1 located at Nouméa (New Caledonia), 1 located at Cayenne

Naval air bases   Located at Nîmes-Garons, Landivisiau, Lann-Bihoue, Hyères, Lanvéoc, Tontouta (New Caledonia)

Naval Aviation 6,500

| Flying hours | 180 to 220 hrs/yr on *Super Etendard* strike/FGA ac |

FORCES BY ROLE

Strike/FGA	1 sqn with *Rafale* M F3
FGA	2 sqn with *Super Etendard Modernisé*
ASuW	1 sqn with AS-565SA *Panther*
ASW	1 sqn with *Lynx* Mk4
MP	2 sqn with *Atlantique* 2
AEW&C	1 sqn with E-2C *Hawkeye*
SAR	1 sqn with AS-365F *Dauphin* 2; 1 sqn with EC-225
Trg	1 sqn with SA-316B *Alouette*; SA-319B *Alouette III*; 1 unit with *Falcon* 10 M; 1 unit with CAP 10; EMB 121 *Xingu*; MS-880 *Rallye*

EQUIPMENT BY TYPE

AIRCRAFT 86 combat capable
   FGA 52: 18 *Rafale M* F3; 34 *Super Etendard Modernisé*; (10 *Rafale M F1* in store)
   ASW 25 *Atlantique* 2
   AEW&C 3 E-2C *Hawkeye*
   TPT 17 **Light** 11 EMB-121 *Xingu* **PAX** 6 *Falcon* 10 MER
   TRG 16: 7 CAP 10; 9 MS-880 *Rallye**
HELICOPTERS
   ASW 25 *Lynx* Mk4
   MRH 52: 9 AS-365F *Dauphin* 2; 16 AS-565SA *Panther*; 25 SA-319B *Alouette III*
   TPT • Medium 2 EC-225 *Super Puma*
MSL
   AAM • IR AAM R-550 *Magic* 2 **IIR AAM** *Mica* IR **ARH AAM** *Mica* RF
   AShM AM-39 *Exocet*
   ASM ASMP-A; AS-30 *Laser*; AASM

Marines 2,500

Commando Units

FORCES BY ROLE

Recce	1 gp
Aslt	3 gp
Atk Swimmer	1 gp
Raiding	1 gp
Spt	1 gp

Fusiliers-Marin 1,600

FORCES BY ROLE

Force Protection   9 units - 14 (Naval Base) gp

Public Service Force

Naval personnel performing general coast guard, fishery protection, SAR, anti-pollution and traffic surveillance duties. Command exercised through Maritime Prefectures (Premar): Manche (Cherbourg), Atlantique (Brest), Méditerranée (Toulon)

FORCES BY ROLE

MP   1 sqn with Falcon 50M; Falcon 200 *Gardian*

EQUIPMENT BY TYPE

PATROL AND COASTAL COMBATANTS 6
   PSO 1 *Albatros*
   PCO 1 *Arago*
   PCC 4: 3 *Flamant*; 1 *Grèbe*
AIRCRAFT • MP 9: 4 *Falcon* 50M; 5 Falcon 200 *Gardian*
HELICOPTERS • MRH 4 AS-365 *Dauphin* 2

Reserves 6,012 reservists

Air Force 52,669; 7,517 (civilian)

Flying hours   180 hrs/year

Combat Brigade

FORCES BY ROLE

Ftr	1 sqn with *Mirage* 2000-5; 2 sqn with *Mirage* 2000B; *Mirage* 2000C
FGA	3 sqn with *Mirage* 2000D; 1 (composite) sqn with *Mirage* 2000-C/*Mirage* 2000-D (Djibouti); 2 sqn with *Rafale* B F3/C F3
ISR	2 sqn with F-1CR *Mirage**
EW	1 flt with C-160G *Gabriel* (ESM)
OCU	1 sqn equipped with *Mirage* 2000B; 1 sqn with *Mirage* Fl-B; 1 sqn with *Rafale*
Trg	1 sqn with *Alphajet*
ISR UAV	1 sqn with *Harfang*

EQUIPMENT BY TYPE

AIRCRAFT 328 combat capable
   FTR 73: 22 *Mirage* 2000-5; 12 *Mirage* 2000B; 39 *Mirage* 2000C
   FGA 135: 62 *Mirage* 2000D; 6 F-1B *Mirage*; 22 F-1CT *Mirage*; 21 *Rafale* B F3; 24 *Rafale* C F3
   ISR 29 F-1CR *Mirage**
   ELINT 2 C-160G *Gabriel* (ESM)
   TRG 91 *Alpha Jet**;
UAV • ISR • Heavy 3 *Harfang*
MSL
   AAM IRAAM R-550 *Magic* 2 **IIR AAM** *Mica IR*
   SARH AAM *Super* 530D **ARH AAM** *Mica* RF
   ASM AS-30L; *Apache* AASM
   LACM SCALP
BOMBS
   Laser-guided: GBU-12 *Paveway* II

FACILITIES

Trg School   2 with *Alphajet*

Air Mobility Brigade

FORCES BY ROLE

SAR/Tpt/ Trg	7 (light) sqn with CN-235M; DHC-6 *Twin Otter*; *Falcon* 7X (VIP); *Falcon* 50 (VIP); *Falcon* 900 (VIP); TBM-700; EC 725 *Caracal*; AS-555 *Fennec*

Tkr/Tpt   6 sqn with C-130H *Hercules*; C-130H-30;
C-160 *Transall*; C-160NG *Transall*

Tpt   1 (heavy) sqn with A-310-300; A-319; A-340-
200 (on lease)

Tpt Hel   5 sqn with AS-332 *Super Puma*; SA-330 *Puma*;
AS-532 *Cougar* (tpt/VIP); AS-555 *Fennec*

OCU   1 sqn with SA-330 *Puma*; AS-555 *Fennec*; 1
unit with C-160 *Transall*

EQUIPMENT BY TYPE
AIRCRAFT
TKR/TPT 15 C-160NG *Transall*
TPT 125: **Medium** 56: 5 C-130H *Hercules*; 9 C-130H-30
Hercules; 42 C-160 *Transall* **Light** 55: 17 CN-235M; 4
DHC-6 *Twin Otter*; 25 EMB-121 *Xingu*; 9 TBM-700;
PAX 14: 3 A310-300; 2 A319 (VIP); 2 A340-200 (on
lease); 2 *Falcon 7X*; 3 *Falcon 50* (VIP); 2 *Falcon 900* (VIP)
HELICOPTERS
MRH 37 AS-555 *Fennec*
TPT 36 **Heavy** 6 EC-725 *Caracal* **Light** 30: 5 AS-332
Super Puma; 3 AS-532 *Cougar* (tpt/VIP); 22 SA-330
Puma

FORCES BY ROLE
Trg School   1 with EMB-121 *Xingu*

Air Space Control Brigade
FORCES BY ROLE
Space   1 (*Helios* satellite obs) sqn

AEW&C   1 (Surveillance & Control) sqn with E-3F
Sentry

AD   3 sqn with *Crotale* NG; SAMP/T; 2 sqn with
SAMP/T

Radar   5 (Control)

EQUIPMENT BY TYPE
SATELLITES 3 (*Helios*-1A/2A/2B)
AIRCRAFT• AEW&C 4 E-3F *Sentry*
AD
SAM *Crotale* NG; SAMP/*T*
GUNS 20mm 76T2
SYSTEMS STRIDA (Control)

Security and Intervention Brigade
24 protection units
30 fire fighting and rescue sections
3 intervention paratroop commandos

Air Training Command
Over 6,000 personnel
FORCES BY ROLE
Trg   Some sqn with CAP 10; Grob G120A-F; TB-30
Epsilon

EQUIPMENT BY TYPE
AIRCRAFT
TRG 48: 5 CAP 10; 18 Grob G120A-F; 25 TB-30 *Epsilon*
(incl many in storage)

Reserves 5,186 reservists

Paramilitary 103,376

Gendarmerie 103,376, 1,925 civilians. 40,000 reservist
3,193 (Headquarters); 4,092 (Administration); 2,051 (Maritime Air (personnel drawn from other departments)); 16,754 (Mobile); 4,999 (Republican Guard, Air Tpt, Arsenals); 5,444 (Schools); 63,162 (Territorial); 1,925 (civilians); 3,640 (Overseas); 41 opcon Strategic Nuclear Forces

EQUIPMENT BY TYPE
LT TK 28 VBC-90
APC (W) 153 VBRG-170
ARTY MOR 157+ **60mm**; **81mm**
PATROL AND COASTAL COMBATANTS 33
PCO 1 *Fulmar*
PB 32: 1 *Patra* (possibly to be decommissioned in 2011); 4 *Géranium*; 3 VSC 14; 24 VSCM (8 EBSLP patrol boats in build; expected ISD 2011)
HELICOPTERS • TPT 35: 20 EC-135; 15 EC-145

DEPLOYMENT

Legal provisions for foreign deployment:
Constitution: Codified constitution (1958)
Specific legislation: 'Order of 7 January 1959'
Decision on deployment of troops abroad: De jure: by the minister of defence, under authority of the PM and on agreement in council of ministers ('Order of 7 January 1959', Art. 16, Art.20-1 of constitution)

AFGHANISTAN
NATO • ISAF/OEF-A 3,750; 1 mech inf bde HQ; 1 (Marine) inf BG; 1 inf BG; 8 AMX 10 RC; 10 VBCI; 449 VAB APC; 76 VBL; 15 PVP; 3 *Mirage* 2000D; 3 Mirage F1; 3 *Harfang* UAV; 1 cbt hel bn (3 AS-665 *TigerAH*, 2 AS-532 *Cougar*, 3 EC-725; 3 *Gazelle* AHl)

ARABIAN SEA
Coalition Maritime Forces • CTF-150: 1 DDGHM
Navy: ISSN; ICVN; 2 DDGHM; 1 AORH

BOSNIA-HERZEGOVINA
EU • EUFOR • *Operation Althea* (*Operation Astrée*) 4
OSCE • Bosnia and Herzegovina 3

CENTRAL AFRICAN REPUBLIC
Operation Boali 240; 1 inf coy; 1 spt det

CHAD
Operation Epervier 634; 1 mech inf BG with (elm 1 mech inf regt; elm 1 armd cav regt); 1 hel det with 4 SA-330 *Puma*

CÔTE D'IVOIRE
Operation Licorne 772; 1 (Marine) mech inf BG with (elm 1 mech inf regt; elm 1 armd cav regt); 1 hel unit with 3 SA-330 *Puma*
UN • UNOCI 7

DEMOCRATIC REPUBLIC OF THE CONGO
UN • MONUSCO 5 obs

DJIBOUTI
Army 1,690; 1 (Foreign Legion) BG with (1 engr coy, 1 arty bty, 2 recce sqn, 2 inf coy); 1 (Marine) combined arms regt with (1 engr coy, 1 arty bty, 2 recce sqn, 2 inf coy)
Navy: 1 LCT

Air Force: 1 Air unit with 10 M-2000C/D *Mirage*; 1 C-160 *Transall*; 2 SA-330 *Puma*; 1 AS-555 *Fennec*

EGYPT
MFO 2

FRENCH GUIANA
Army 1,435 1 (Foreign Legion) inf regt; 1 (Marine) inf regt; 1 SMA regt
Navy 150; 2 PCC
Air Force 1 tpt unit; 1 DHC-6; 4 SA-330 *Puma*; 3 AS-555 *Fennec*
Gendarmerie 3 coy; 1 AS-350 *Ecureuil*

FRENCH POLYNESIA
Army 640 (incl Centre d'Expérimentation du Pacifique); 1 (Marine) inf regt; 3 SMA coy
Navy 710; 1 HQ at Papeete; 1 FFGHM with 1 AS-565SA *Panther* ASW hel; 4 PCC; 2 LST; 1 AOT; 3 Falcon 200 *Gardian*
Air Force 1 tpt unit; 3 CN-235M; 1 AS-332 *Super Puma*; 1 AS-555 *Fennec*

FRENCH WEST INDIES
Army 729; 1 (Marine) inf regt; 1 (Marine) inf bn; 2 SMA regt
Navy 450; 1 FFGHM; 1 PCC; 1 LST: 1 naval base at Fort de France (Martinique)
Air Force 1 tpt unit; 3 CN-235M; 2 SA-330 *Puma*; 1 AS-555SN *Fennec*
Gendarmerie 4 coy; 2 AS-350 *Ecureuil*

GABON
Army 645; 1 recce pl with ERC-90F1 *Lynx*; 1 (Marine) inf bn; 4 SA-330 *Puma*

GERMANY
Army 2,800 (incl elm Eurocorps and FRA/GER bde (2,500)); 1 (FRA/GER) army bde (1 army HQ, 1 armd cav regt, 1 mech inf regt)

GULF OF ADEN & INDIAN OCEAN
EU • *Operation Atalanta* 1 DDGHM; 1 FFGH; 1 FSM; 1 *Atlantique* 2; 1 *Falcon 20*

HAITI
UN • MINUSTAH 2

INDIAN OCEAN
Army 866 (incl La Réunion and TAAF); 1 (Marine) para regt; 1 (Foreign Legion) inf det; 1 SMA regt
Navy 1 base at Dzaoudzi (Mayotte), 1 HQ at Port-des-Galets (La Réunion); 1 FFGHM with 2 AS-55 *Fennec*; 1 PSO; LST
Air Force 1 tpt unit; 2 C-160 *Transall*; 2 AS-555 *Fennec*
Gendarmerie 5 coy; 1 SA-319 *Alouette III*

LEBANON
UN • UNIFIL 1,575; 1 armd inf bn; 1 armd sqn; 1 arty coy; 13 *Leclerc*; 36 AMX-10P; 14 PVP ; 72 VAB ; 5 AU-F1 155mm ; 6 *Mistral*; 2 *Cobra* radar

LIBERIA
UN • UNMIL 1

MIDDLE EAST
UN • UNTSO 2 obs

MOLDOVA
OSCE • Moldova 1

NEW CALEDONIA
Army 723; 1 (Marine) mech inf regt; 2 SMA coy; 6 ERC-90F1 *Lynx*
Navy 510; 1 base with 2 Falcon 200 *Gardian* at Nouméa
Air Force some air det; 1 tpt unit; 3 CN-235 MPA; 4 SA-330 *Puma*; 1 AS-555 *Fennec*
Gendarmerie 4 coy; 2 AS-350 *Ecureuil*

SENEGAL
Army 575; 1 (Marine) mech inf bn; 1 recce sqn with ERC-90F1 *Lynx*
Navy 230; 1 LCT; 1 *Atlantique*
Air Force 1 C-160 *Transall*; 1 AS-555 *Fennec*

SERBIA
NATO • KFOR 743; 1 armd cav BG
OSCE • Serbia 1
OSCE • Kosovo 6

UAE
86: 3 *Mirage* 2000-5, 1 KC-135F at al-Dhafra (To operate alongside UAE *Mirage*-9s)

UGANDA
EU • EUTM 25

WESTERN SAHARA
UN • MINURSO 13 obs

FOREIGN FORCES

Belgium Air Force: 29 *Alpha Jet* trg ac located at Cazaux/Tours
Germany Army: 209 (GER elm Eurocorps)
Singapore Air Force: 200; 1 trg sqn with 5 A-4SU *Super Skyhawk*; 11 TA-4SU *Super Skyhawk*

Georgia GEO

Georgian Lari		2009	2010	2011
GDP	lari	17.9bn	20.3bn	
	US$	10.7bn	11.3bn	
per capita	US$	2,522	2,690	
Growth	%	-4.0	4.5	
Inflation	%	1.7	6.4	
Def exp	lari	1.01bn		
	US$	604m		
Def bdgt	lari	897m	750m	
	US$	537m	420m	
FMA (US)	US$	11.0m	16.0m	16.0m
US$1=lari		1.67	1.78	

Population	4,219,191

Age	0 – 14	15 – 19	20 – 24	25 – 29	30 – 64	65 plus
Male	8.4%	3.5%	4.1%	3.7%	21.7%	6.4%
Female	7.3%	3.3%	4.0%	3.9%	24.2%	9.7%

Capabilities

ACTIVE 20,655 (Army 17,767 Air 1,310 National Guard 1,578) **Paramilitary 11,700**

Terms of service conscription, 18 months

ORGANISATIONS BY SERVICE

Army 14,000; 3,767 conscript (total 17,767)

FORCES BY ROLE

Inf	5 bde
SF	1 bde
Marine Inf	2 bn (1 cadre)
Arty	2 bde

EQUIPMENT BY TYPE

MBT 93 T-72; (3 T-72 & 23 T-55 in store)
AIFV 63: 17 BMP-1; 45 BMP-2; 1 BRM-1K; (8 BMP-1 & 1 BMP-2 in store)
APC 137
 APC (T) 45 MT-LB; (21 MT-LB in store)
 APC (W) 92: 25 BTR-70 (1 in store); 17 BTR-80 (2 in store); 50 *Ejder* (15 in store)
ARTY 185
 SP 35: **152mm** 32 DANA; 13 2S3; 1 2S19; **203mm** 1 2S7
 TOWED 68: **122mm** 55 D-30; (3 D-30 in store); **152mm** 13: 3 2A36; 10 2A65
 MRL 122mm 37: 13 BM-21; 6 GRADLAR; 18 RM-70
 MOR 120mm 43: 13 2S12; 21 M-75; 9 M-120; (1 2S12, 13 M-75 & 9 M-120 in store)
AT ε50
 MSL ε10
 GUNS ε40
AD • SAM • SP 9K35 *Strela*-10 (SA-13 *Gopher*)

Air Force 1,310 (incl 290 conscript)

1 avn base, 1 hel air base
AIRCRAFT 12 combat capable
 ATK 12: 3 Su-25 *Frogfoot*; 7 Su-25K *Frogfoot A*; 2 Su-25UB *Frogfoot* B
 TPT • Light 9: 6 An-2 *Colt*; 1 Tu-134A *Crusty* (VIP); 2 Yak-40 *Codling*
 TRG 9 L-29 *Delfin*
HELICOPTERS
 TPT 29 Medium 17 Mi-8T *Hip* **Light** 12 Bell 205 (UH-1H *Iroquois*)
AD • SAM 1–2 bn 9K37 *Buk*-M1 (SA-11 *Gadfly*), 8 9K33 *Osa*-AK (SA-8B *Gecko*) (two bty), 6-10 9K33 *Osa*-AKM updated SAM systems.

National Guard 1,578 active reservists opcon Army

MRR	1 bde (plus trg centre)

Paramilitary 11,700

Border Guard 5,400

Coast Guard

HQ at Poti. Significant damage sustained to Navy and Coast Guard units during the August 2008 war. The Navy was subsequently merged with the Coast Guard in 2009 under the auspices of the Georgian Border Guard, within the Ministry of the Interior.
PATROL AND COASTAL COMBATANTS 17
PBF 1 *Kaan 33*
PB 16: 7 *Zhuk* (3 ex-UKR); 2 *Point*; 2 *Dauntless*; 2 *Dilos* (ex-GRC); 1 *Akhmeta* (up to 20 patrol launches also in service)
AMPHIBIOUS • LANDING CRAFT • LCU 1 *Vydra* (ex-BUL)
LOGISTIC AND SUPPORT • YTL 1
FACILITIES
Bases Located at Poti, Batumi

Ministry of Interior Troops 6,300

DEPLOYMENT

Legal provisions for foreign deployment of armed forces:
Constitution: Codified constitution (1995)
Decision on deployment of troops abroad: By the presidency upon parliamentary approval (Art. 100)

AFGHANISTAN
NATO • ISAF 925; 1 inf bn

SERBIA
OSCE • Serbia 1
OSCE • Kosovo 4

TERRITORY WHERE THE GOVERNMENT DOES NOT EXERCISE EFFECTIVE CONTROL

Following the August 2008 war between Russia and Georgia, the areas of Abkhazia and South Ossetia declared themselves independent. Data presented here represent the de facto situation and do not imply international recognition as sovereign states.

FOREIGN FORCES

Russia Army 7,000; 2 MR bde; at locations incl Gudauta (Abkhazia), Djava and Tskhinvali (S. Ossetia)

Germany GER

Euro €		2009	2010	2011
GDP	€	2.40tr	2.53tr	
	US$	3.34tr	3.35tr	
per capita	US$	40,775	40,781	
Growth	%	-4.9	1.3	
Inflation	%	0.3	1.3	
Def exp[a]	€	34.1bn		
	US$	47.5bn		
Def bdgt	€	31.2bn	31.1bn	31.5bn
	US$	43.5bn	41.2bn	
US$1=€		0.72	0.76	

[a] including military pensions

Population   82,056,775

Age	0–14	15–19	20–24	25–29	30–64	65 plus
Male	6.9%	2.6%	3.1%	3.0%	25.0%	8.6%
Female	6.5%	2.5%	2.9%	2.9%	24.2%	11.8%

Capabilities

ACTIVE 251,465 (Army 105,291 Navy 19,179 Air 44,565 Joint Support Service 57,495 Joint Medical Service 24,935)

Terms of service 6 months; up to 23 months voluntary Conscription to be phased out from mid-2011.

RESERVE 40,396 (Army 15,351 Navy 1,867 Air 4,914 Joint Support Service 12,871 Joint Medical Service 4,970 MoD 423)

ORGANISATIONS BY SERVICE

Army 105,291

Germany contributes staff to all multinational Corps HQs in Europe and is the Framework Nation for European Corps, (Strasbourg), the German-Netherlands Corps (Münster) and the Multinational Corps Northeast (Szczecin). The forces will be specifically trained and equipped for their respective missions. Their overall capability will be enhanced as required from the Army, Air Force, Navy, Joint Support Service and Joint Medical Service. The Army forces consist of five divisional headquarters, three of them are deployable, and a total of twelve brigades. Forces are tailored to form Response Forces (1st Armd Div & FRA/GER Bde), 1 bde Special Forces, 1 air mobile div and four stabilisation brigades. The Response Forces brigades are structured to fight in a divisional context supported by the capabilities of the divisional troops. The stabilisation brigades would normally deploy under the command of the Air Mobile Div HQ and receive any additional capability from its Army Support Arms bde. The Special Operations Division Headquarters is designed to provide a multinational special forces headquarters at command level. Its airborne brigades are generally capable of concurrently conducting operations against irregular forces and military evacuation operations.

The Joint Support Service assists the individual services in terms of logistics, command support and protection. Its assets include psyops capabilities, logistic follow on support, communication systems and EW-capabilities. Medical support is provided by the Joint Medical Service.

FORCES BY ROLE

Armd   1 div (1st) (RF) with (1 armd bde with (2 armd bn; 1 armd inf bn; 1 SP arty bn, 1 log bn, 1 armd recce coy); 1 armd bde with (1 armd bn; 1 armd inf bn; 1 SP arty bn; 1 log bn, 1 armd recce coy); 1 armd recce bn; 1 arty regt; 1 engr regt; 1 AD regt; 1 NBC bn); 1 div (10th) (StF) with (1 armd bde with (1 armd bn; 2 armd inf bn; 1 armd recce bn; 1 engr bn, 1 log bn); 1 mtn inf bde with (3 mtn inf bn; 1 recce bn; 1 engr bn, 1 log bn))

Mech   1 (13th) div (StF) with 2 bde (each: 1 armd bn, 2 armd inf bn, 1 recce bn, 1 engr bn, 1 sig bn, 1 log bn)

Spec Ops   1 div (RF) with (2 (26th & 31st) AB bde (each: 2 para bn, 1 log bn, 1 recce coy, 1 engr coy), 1 SF bde, 1 AD bn, 1 sigs bn)

Air Mob   1 div (RF) with 1 (air manoeuvre) bde with (1 atk hel bn, 1 spt hel bn, 1 air mob inf regt) 1 air tpt bde (2 tpt hel regt, 1 lt tpt hel regt), 1 spt bde with (1 arty regt, 1 AD bn, 1 NBC regt)

Lt Inf   2 bn (GER/FRA Bde)

Arty   1 bn (GER/FRA Bde)

Engr   1 coy (GER/FRA Bde)

EQUIPMENT BY TYPE

MBT 768 *Leopard* 2 (350 to be upgraded to A6); (384 *Leopard* 1A3/A4/A5 in store)

RECCE 298: 212 *Fennek* (incl 24 engr recce, 10 fires spt); 86 Tpz-1 *Fuchs* (CBRN)

AIFV 2,044: 1,648 *Marder* 1A2/A3; 5 *Puma* (test); 108 *Wiesel* (with 20mm gun)

APC 2,157

  APC (T) 1,113: 370 Bv-206D/S; 816 M-113 (inc 109 arty obs and other variants)

  APC (W) 1,044: 279 APV-2 *Dingo II*; 765 TPz-1 *Fuchs* (incl variants)

ARTY 824

  SP • 155mm 460: 288 M-109A3G; 172 PzH 2000

  TOWED 25 **105mm** 10 M-101; **155mm** 15 FH-70

  MRL • 227mm 109 MLRS

  MOR • 120mm 230 *Tampella*

AT • MSL 476

  SP 100 *Wiesel* (TOW)

  MANPATS 376 *Milan*

AMPHIBIOUS 27 LCM (river engr)

HELICOPTERS

  MRH/ISR 150 Bo-105 M/Bo-105P PAH-1 (with HOT)

  TPT 188 **Heavy** 89 CH-53G *Stallion* **Light** 99: 85 Bell 205 (UH-1D *Iroquois*); 14 EC-135;

UAV • ISR 12 **Medium** 6 KZO **Light** 6 *LUNA*

AD • SAM

  SP 50 ASRAD *Ozelot* (with FIM-92A *Stinger*)

  MANPAD: some FIM-92A *Stinger*

RADARS 136: 7 *Cobra*; 8 LÜR; 3 NBR; 73 RASIT (veh, arty); 45 RATAC (veh, arty)

Europe

Navy 19,179

Previous Type Comds have been merged into two Flotillas. Flotilla I combines SS, MCM, PBF and SF whilst Flotilla II comprises 2 FF and Aux squadrons.

EQUIPMENT BY TYPE

SUBMARINES • TACTICAL • SSK 4:
 4 Type 212A (2 further vessels on order) each with 6 single 533mm TT with 12 A4 *Seehecht* DM2 HWT

PRINCIPAL SURFACE COMBATANTS 20
 DESTROYERS • DDGHM 7
  4 *Brandenburg* each with 2 twin lnchr (4 eff.) each with MM-38 *Exocet* AShM, 1 16 cell Mk 41 VLS with RIM-7M/P, 2 Mk49 GMLS each with RIM-116 *RAM* SAM, 4 single 324mm ASTT each with Mk 46 LWT, 1 76mm gun, (capacity: 2 *Sea Lynx* Mk88/Mk88A ASW hel)
  3 *Sachsen* each with 2 quad Mk 141 lnchr (8 eff.) each with RGM-84F *Harpoon* AShM, 1 32 cell Mk 41 VLS with SM-2MR/RIM-162B *Sea Sparrow* SAM, 2 Mk 49 GMLS each with 21 RIM-116 *RAM* SAM; (capacity; 2 NH-90/*Lynx* hel)
 FRIGATES 13
  FFGHM 8 *Bremen* each with 2 quad Mk 141 lnchr (8 eff.) with RGM-84A/C *Harpoon* AShM, 1 octuple Mk29 GMLS with RIM-7M/P *Sea Sparrow* SAM, 2 Mk 49 GMLS each with RIM-116 *RAM* SAM, 2 twin 324mm ASTT (4 eff.) each with Mk 46 LWT, 1 76mm gun, (capacity either 2 MK88 *Sea Lynx* ASW hel or 2 *Sea Lynx* MK88A ASW)
  FFGM 5 *Braunschweig* (K130) each with 2 twin lnchr (4 eff.) each with RBS-15 AShM, 2 M49 GMLS each with RIM-116 *RAM* SAM, 1 76mm gun, 1 hel landing platform

PATROL AND COASTAL COMBATANTS • PCGM 10
 10 *Gepard* each with 2 twin lnchr (4 eff.) each with MM-38 *Exocet* AShM, 1 Mk 49 GMLS with RIM-116 *RAM* SAM, 1 76mm gun

MINE WARFARE • MINE COUNTERMEASURES 37:
 MHO 14: 9 *Frankenthal*; 5 *Kulmbach*
 MSO 5 *Ensdorf*
 MSD 18 *Seehund*

AMPHIBIOUS 3
 LCM 1
 LCU 2 Type 521

LOGISTICS AND SUPPORT 31
 AO 2 *Walchensee* Type 703
 AOT 2 *Spessart* Type 704
 AFH 2 *Berlin* Type 702 (capacity either 2 NH-90 utl hel or 2 *Sea King* MK41 SAR hel; 2 RAMs)
 AE 1 *Westerwald* Type 760
 AG 6: 3 *Schwedeneck* Type 748; 3 *Stollergrund* Type 745
 AGOR 1 *Planet* Type 751
 AGI 3 *Oste* Type 423
 AT 5
 AX 1
 SPT 6 *Elbe* Type 404 (2 specified for PFM support; 1 specified for SSK support; 3 specified for MHC/MSC support)
 Trial Ship 2

FACILITIES
Bases   Located at Olpenitz, Wilhelmshaven, Glücksburg (Maritime HQ), Warnemünde, Eckernförde, Kiel

Naval Aviation 2,227

AIRCRAFT 8 combat capable
 ASW 8 AP-3C *Orion*
 TPT • Light 2 Do-228 (pollution control)
HELICOPTERS
 ASW 22 *Lynx* Mk88A
 SAR 21 *Sea King* Mk41
MSL AShM *Sea Skua*

Air Force 44, 565

Flying hours   140 hrs/year (plus 40 hrs high-fidelity simulator)

Air Force Command

FORCES BY ROLE

Ftr	1 wg with (2 sqn with F-4F *Phantom II*); 2 wg with Eurofighter *Typhoon*
FGA	1 wg with (2 sqn with *Tornado* IDS); 1 wg with (2 sqn with *Tornado* ECR/IDS) 1 wg (2 sqn *Typhoon*)
ISR	1 wg with (2 recce sqn with *Tornado* IDS; 1 UAV sqn with *Heron*)
AD	3 wg (each 2 SAM gp) with *Patriot*
Radar	4 (tac air ctrl) gp

EQUIPMENT BY TYPE

AIRCRAFT 318 combat capable
 FTR 109: 58 Eurofighter *Typhoon*; 51 F-4F *Phantom* II
 FGA 175 *Tornado* IDS
 EW/FGA 34 *Tornado* ECR*
UAV • ISR • Heavy 3 *Heron*
AD • SAM • TOWED 24 *Patriot* PAC-3
MSL
 AAM • IR AAM AIM-9L/Li *Sidewinder*; IIR AAM LFK *Iris*-T; ARH AAM AIM 120A/B AMRAAM
 LACM KEPD 350
 AShM *Kormoran* 2
 ARM AGM-88B HARM
BOMBS
 LGB: GBU-24 *Paveway* III, GBU-54 JDAM (Being integrated on *Tornado*)

Transport Command

FORCES BY ROLE

Tkr/tpt	1 (special air mission) wg with A310MRT; A-310MRTT; AS-532U2 *Cougar II* (VIP); CL-601 *Challenger*
Tpt	3 wg with (4 sqn with Bell 205 (UH-1D *Iroquois*); 3 sqn with C-160 *Transall*)

EQUIPMENT BY TYPE

AIRCRAFT
 TKR/TPT 4 A310 MRTT
 TPT 88 **Medium** 80 C-160 *Transall* **PAX** 8: 1 A310 MRT; 1 A340 (VIP); 2 A-319; 4 CL-601 *Challenger* (VIP);

Europe

HELICOPTERS • TPT 48: **Medium** 4 AS-532U2 *Cougar II* (VIP) INH90 **Light** 44 Bell 205 (UH-1D *Iroquois*) (SAR, Tpt)

Training Command
FORCES BY ROLE

Trg   1 sqn located at Holloman AFB (US) with *Tornado* IDS; 1 unit (ENJJPT) located at Sheppard AFB (US) with T-6 *Texan* TII, 40 T-38A; 1 (hel trg) unit located at Fassberg; 1 (msl) unit located at Fort Bliss (US) with *Patriot*

EQUIPMENT BY TYPE
AIRCRAFT 24 combat capable
  FGA 24 *Tornado* IDS
  TRG 109: 69 T-6 *Texan* TII, 40 T-38A
AD • SAM *Patriot*

Joint Support Services 57,495
FORCES BY ROLE
Sigs   3 regt
MP   6 bn
Log   1 bde; 3 regt

Joint Medical Services 24,935
FORCES BY ROLE
Med   7 regt; 5 fd hospital unit

DEPLOYMENT

Legal provisions for foreign deployment:
Constitution: Codified constitution ('Basic Law', 1949)
Specific legislation: 'Parlamentsbeteiligungsgesetz' (2005)
Decision on deployment of troops abroad: a) By parliament: in general and in the case of military intervention; b) by government: in urgent cases of threat or emergency (parliamentary consent a posteriori), or for preparatory measures or humanitarian interventions; c) simplified procedure for 'missions of low intensity' or if the government seeks an extension of parliamentary approval (§§ 1–5 of the 2005 law)

AFGHANISTAN
NATO • ISAF 4,388; 1 div HQ; 2 mtn inf bn; *Marder* AIFV; *Fennek* (Recce); TPz-1 *Fuchs* APC; *Dingo* II APC; PzH 2000 155mm SP arty; *Wiesel* (TOW) SP AT; KZO UAV; LUNA UAV **Air Force:** 6 *Tornado* ECR (SEAD); CH-53 tpt hel; C-160 tpt ac; Heron UAV
UN • UNAMA 1 obs

BOSNIA-HERZEGOVINA
EU • EUFOR • *Operation Althea* 111
OSCE • Bosnia and Herzegovina 4

FRANCE
Army 400 (incl GER elm Eurocorps)

GULF OF ADEN & INDIAN OCEAN
EU • *Operation Atalanta* 1 FFGHM; 1 AOL

LEBANON
UN •UNIFIL 249; 2 PC; 1 SPT

MEDITERRANEAN SEA
NATO • *Operation Active Endeavour* 1 FFGHM
NATO • SNMCMG 2: 1 MHO

NORTH SEA
NATO • SNMCMG 1: 1 MHO

POLAND
Army 67 (GER elm Corps HQ (multinational))

SERBIA
NATO • KFOR 1,355; 1 inf bn HQ; 1 inf coy; 1 sigs coy; 1 spt bn; elm 1 MP coy; 1 med unit; elm 1 hel gp; 16 TPz-1 *Fuchs*; 7 UH-1D *Iroquois*
OSCE • Serbia 3
OSCE • Kosovo 10

SUDAN
UN • UNAMID 3
UN • UNMIS 5; 25 obs

UGANDA
EU • EUTM 13

UNITED STATES
Air Force: trg units at Goodyear AFB (AZ)/Sheppard AFB (TX) with 40 T-38 *Talon* trg ac; 69 T-6A *Texan* II; 1 trg sqn Holloman AFB (NM) with 24 *Tornado* IDS; NAS Pensacola (FL); Fort Rucker (AL) • Missile trg located at Fort Bliss (TX)

UZBEKISTAN
NATO • ISAF 106

FOREIGN FORCES

Canada NATO 287
France Army: 1 (FRA/GER) army bde (1 army HQ, 1 armd cav rgt, 1 mech inf regt); 2,800 (incl elm Eurocorps and FRA/GER bde (2,500))
United Kingdom Army 18,230; 1 army corps HQ (multinational); 1 armd div **Royal Navy** 40; **Air Force** 260
United States
US Africa Command: **Army**; 1 HQ at Stuttgart **USAF**; 1 HQ (17th Air Force) at Ramstein AB.
US European Command: 53,130; 1 combined service HQ (EUCOM) at Stuttgart-Vaihingen
  Army 37,828; 1 HQ (US Army Europe (USAREUR) at Heidelberg; 2 armd inf bde; 1 (hvy) cbt avn bde (1 mech inf SBCT currently deployed to AFG); 1 engr bde; 1 spt bde; 1 int bde; 2 sigs bde; 1 (APS) armd HBCT eqpt. set (transforming); some M-1 *Abrams*; some M-2/M-3 *Bradley*; some *Stryker*; some M-109; some MLRS; some AH-64 *Apache*; some CH-47 *Chinook*; some UH-60 *Black Hawk*
  Navy 225
  USAF 14,708; 1 HQ (US Airforce Europe (USAFE)) at Ramstein AB; 1 HQ (3rd Air Force) at Ramstein AB; 1 ftr wg at Spangdahlem AB with (1 atk sqn with 12 A-10 *Thunderbolt II*; 6 OA-10 *Thunderbolt II*, 1 ftr sqn with 24 F-16C *Fighting Falcon*); 1 airlift wg at Ramstein AB with 16 C-130E/J *Hercules*; 2 C-20 Gulfstream; 9 C-21 Learjet; 1 CT-43 *Boeing 737*
  USMC 369

Greece GRC

Euro €		2009	2010	2011
GDP	€	238bn	231bn	
	US$	331bn	306bn	
per capita	US$	29,378	27,339	
Growth	%	-2.0	-4.0	
Inflation	%	1.2	4.6	
Def exp[a]	€	7.25bn		
	US$	10.1bn		
Def bdgt	€	7.82bn	7.3bn	6.7bn
	US$	10.9bn	9.66bn	
US$1=€		0.72	0.76	

[a] including military pensions and procurement

Population   11,183,393

Age	0–14	15–19	20–24	25–29	30–64	65 plus
Male	7.3%	2.5%	2.7%	3.2%	24.7%	8.6%
Female	6.9%	2.3%	2.6%	3.2%	25.0%	11.0%

Capabilities

ACTIVE 138,936 (Army 78,836 Navy 20,000 Air 28,500 Joint 11,600) **Paramilitary 4,000**

Terms of service: Conscripts in all services up to 9 months

RESERVE 250,876 (Army 193,876 Navy 23,000 Air 34,000)

ORGANISATIONS BY SERVICE

Army 47,459; 31,337 conscripts (78,836 total)

FORCES BY ROLE
Field army to re-org. Units are manned at 3 different levels – Cat A 85% fully ready, Cat B 60% ready in 24 hours, Cat C 20% ready in 48 hours (requiring reserve mobilisation). There are 3 military regions

Comd	4 corps HQ (incl NDC-GR)
Armd	1 div HQ; 4 bde (each: 1 mech inf bn, 1 SP arty bn, 2 armd bn)
Recce	5 bn
Mech Inf	3 div HQ; 7 bde (each: 1 armd bn, 1 SP arty bn, 2 mech bn)
Inf	1 div HQ; 2 div; 5 bde (each: 1 armd bn, 1 arty regt, 3 inf regt)
SF	1 comd with (1 (cdo) amph bde; 1 cdo para bde)
Marine	1 bde
Arty	1 regt with (1 arty bn; 2 MRL bn)
Air Mob	1 bde
AD	3 bn (2 I-*HAWK*, 1 *Tor* M1)
Log	1 corps HQ; 1 div with (4 bde)
Avn	1 bde with (1 hel regt with (2 atk hel bn), 2 tpt hel bn, 4 hel bn)

EQUIPMENT BY TYPE
MBT 1,590: 170 *Leopard* 2A6HEL; 183 *Leopard* 2A4; 527 *Leopard* 1; 205 M-60A1/A3; 505 M-48A5
RECCE 242 VBL
AIFV 401 BMP-1
APC (T) 1,778: 86 *Leonidas* Mk1/2; 1,692 M-113A1/A2
ARTY 3,156
  SP 346: **155mm** 219: 195 M-109A1B/A2/A3GEA1/A5; 24 PzH 2000; **203mm** 127 M-110A2
  TOWED 410: **105mm** 281: 263 M-101; 18 M-56; **155mm** 129 M-114
  MRL 148: **122mm** 112 RM-70 *Dana*; **227mm** 36 MLRS (incl ATACMS)
  MOR 2,252: **81mm** 1,632; **107mm** 620 M-30 (incl 231 SP)
AT
  MSL 1,008
    SP 528: 196 9P163 *Kornet-E*; 290 M-901; 42 *Milan* HMMWV
    MANPATS 580: 262 9K111 *Fagot* (AT-4 *Spigot*); 248 *Milan*; 70 TOW
  RCL 4,150:
    SP 106mm 925 M-40A1
    MANPATS 3,225 **84mm** 2,019 *Carl Gustav*; **90mm** 1,206 EM-67
AIRCRAFT • TPT • Light 37: 3 Beech 200 *King Air* (C-12C/R/AP *Huron*); 34 Cessna 185 (U-17A)
HELICOPTERS
  ATK 30: 19 AH-64A *Apache*; 11 AH-64D *Apache*
  TPT 124 **Heavy** 15 CH-47D *Chinook* **Light** 109: 95 Bell 205 (UH-1H *Iroquois*); 14 Bell 206 (AB-206) *JetRanger*
UAV • ISR • Medium 2 *Sperwer*
AD
  SAM 1,722
    SP 113: 21 *Tor*-M1 (SA-15 *Gauntlet*); 38 9K33 Osa-M (SA-8B *Gecko*); 54 ASRAD HMMWV
    TOWED 42 I-HAWK MIM-23B
    MANPAD 1,567 FIM-92A *Stinger*
  GUNS
    TOWED 747: **20mm** 207 Rh 202; **23mm** 523 ZU-23-2
RADAR • LAND 76: 3 ARTHUR, 5 AN/TPQ-36 *Firefinder* (arty, mor); 8 AN/TPQ-37(V)3; 40 BOR-A; 20 MARGOT

National Guard 32,988 reservists
Internal security role

Inf	1 div
Para	1 regt
Arty	8 bn
AD	4 bn
Avn	1 bn

Navy 16,900; 3,100 conscript; (total 20,000)

EQUIPMENT BY TYPE
SUBMARINES • TACTICAL • SSK 9:
  4 *Glavkos* (GER T-209) each with 8 single 533mm TT each with SUT HWT
  4 *Glavkos* (GER T-209) each with 8 single 533mm TT each with UGM-84C *Harpoon* AShM/SUT HWT

1 *Papanikolis* (GER T-214) with 8 single 533mm TT each with UGM-84C *Harpoon* AShM/SUT HWT

PRINCIPAL SURFACE COMBATANTS 14

FRIGATES • FFGHM 14:

4 *Elli* Batch I (NLD *Kortenaer* Batch 2) each with 2 quad Mk 141 lnchr (8 eff.) each with RGM-84A/C *Harpoon* AShM, 1 octuple Mk29 GMLS with RIM-7M/P *Sea Sparrow* SAM, 2 twin 324mm ASTT (4 eff.) each with Mk 46 LWT, 1 76mm gun, (capacity: 2 Bell 212 (AB-212) hel)

2 *Elli* Batch II (NLD *Kortenaer* Batch 2) each with 2 quad Mk 141 lnchr (8 eff.) each with RGM-84A/C *Harpoon* AShM, 1 octuple Mk29 GMLS with RIM-7M/P *Sea Sparrow* SAM, 2 twin 324mm ASTT (4 eff.) each with Mk46 LWT, 2 76mm gun, (capacity 2 Bell 212 (AB-212) hel)

4 *Elli* Batch III (NLD *Kortenaer* Batch 2) each with 2 quad Mk 141 lnchr (8 eff.) each with RGM-84A/C *Harpoon* AShM, 1 octuple Mk29 lnchr with RIM-7M/P *Sea Sparrow* SAM, 2 twin 324mm ASTT (4 eff.) each with Mk46 LWT, 1 76mm gun, (capacity 2 Bell 212 (AB-212) utl hel)

4 *Hydra* (GER MEKO 200) each with 2 quad lnchr (8 eff.) each with RGM-84G *Harpoon* AShM, 1 16 cell Mk48 Mod 5 VLS with RIM-7M *Sea Sparrow* SAM, 2 triple 324mm ASTT (6 eff.) each with Mk46 LWT, 1 127mm gun, (capacity 1 S-70B *Seahawk* ASW hel)

PATROL AND COASTAL COMBATANTS 32

CORVETTES • FSGM 3 *Roussen* (*Super Vita*) each with 2 quad lnchr (8 eff.) each with MM-40 *Exocet* AShM, 1 Mk49 GMLS with RIM-116 *RAM* SAM, 1 76mm gun (4 additional vessels in build)

PCFG 15:

5 *Kavaloudis* (FRA *La Combattante* II, III, IIIB) each with 6 RB 12 *Penguin* AShM, 2 single 533mm TT each with SST-4 HWT, 2 76mm gun

4 *Laskos* (FRA *La Combattante* II, III, IIIB) each with 4 MM-38 *Exocet* tactical SSM, 2 single 533mm TT each with SST-4 HWT, 2 76mm gun

2 *Votsis* (FRA *La Combattante*) each with 2 Mk-141 *Harpoon* twin each with RGM-84C *Harpoon* AShM, 1 76mm gun

4 *Votsis* (FRA *La Combattante* IIA) each with 4 MM-38 *Exocet* AShM, 1 76mm gun

PCO 8:

2 *Armatolos* (DNK *Osprey*) each with 1 76mm gun

2 *Kasos* each with 1 76mm gun

4 *Machitis* each with 1 76mm gun

PB 6: 4 *Andromeda* (NOR *Nasty*); 2 *Stamou*; 2 *Tolmi*

MINE COUNTERMEASURES 11

MHO 4: 2 *Evropi* (UK *Hunt*); 2 *Evniki* (US *Osprey*)

MSC 3 *Alkyon* (US MSC-294)

AMPHIBIOUS

LANDING SHIPS • LST 5:

5 *Chios* (capacity 4 LCVP; 300 troops) each with 1 hel landing platform (for med hel)

LANDING CRAFT 7

LCU 4

LCAC 3 *Kefallinia* (*Zubr*) (capacity either 3 MBT or 10 APC (T); 230 troops)

LOGISTICS AND SUPPORT 40:

AORH 1 AE *Etna*

AOT 4

AE 2 (ex-GER *Luneburg*)

AWT 6

AGHS 3

TPT 2

TRG • AXL 1

YTL 2

YTM 19

FACILITIES

Bases Located at Salamis, Patras, Soudha Bay

Naval Aviation

FORCES BY ROLE

ASW 1 div with S-70B *Seahawk*; Bell 212 (AB-212) ASW; SA-319 *Alouette III*

MP 2 sqn with P-3B *Orion*

EQUIPMENT BY TYPE

AIRCRAFT 6 combat capable

ASW 6 P-3B *Orion*

HELICOPTERS

ASW 19: 8 Bell 212 (AB-212) ASW; 11 S-70B *Seahawk*

MRH 2 SA-319 *Alouette III*

MSL

ASM AGM-119 *Penguin*

ASSM MM-40 *Exocet*

Air Force 28,500

Tactical Air Force

FORCES BY ROLE

Ftr/FGA 1 sqn with A/TA-7E/H *Corsair II*; 2 sqn with F-4E *Phantom II*; 4 sqn with F-16CG/DG Block 30/50, *Fighting Falcon*; 4 sqn with F-16CG/DG Block 52+ *Fighting Falcon*; 1 sqn with *Mirage* 2000-5 Mk2; 1 sqn with *Mirage* 2000E/BGM

ISR 1 sqn with RF-4E *Phantom II*

AEW 1 sqn with EMB-145H *Erieye*

EQUIPMENT BY TYPE

AIRCRAFT 303 combat capable

FGA 241: 35 F-4E *Phantom II*; 72 F-16CG/DG Block 30/50 *Fighting Falcon*; 38 F-16CG/DG Block 52+; 51 F-16C Block 52+ *Fighting Falcon*; 25 *Mirage* 2000-5 Mk2; 20 *Mirage* 2000EG/BG

ATK 43 A/TA-7E/H *Corsair II*

ISR 19 RF-4E *Phantom II**

AEW 4 EMB-145AEW (EMB-145H) *Erieye*

MSL

AAM IR AAM AIM-9L/AIM-9P *Sidewinder*; R-550 *Magic* 2; IIR AAM *Iris-T*; *Mica* IR; SARH AAM *Super 530*; ARH AAM AIM-120B/C, *Mica* RF

ASM AGM-65A/B/G *Maverick*

LACM SCALP EG

AShM AM 39 *Exocet*

ARM AGM-88 HARM

BOMBS

Conventional: GBU-8B HOBOS; AGM-154 JSOW; GBU-31 JDAM

Laser-guided: GBU-12/GBU-16 *Paveway* II; GBU-24 *Paveway* III

Air Defence
FORCES BY ROLE

SAM   6 sqn/bty PAC-3 *Patriot* with 36 launchers [MIM-104 (A/B SOJC/D GEM)]; 2 sqn/bty with S-300 PMU-1 (SA-10 *Grumble*/SA-20 *Gargoyle*) with 12 launchers; 12 bty *Skyguard* with *Sparrow* RIM-7/GUNS; 9 *Crotale* NG/GR; 4 *Tor* M-1 (SA-15 *Gauntlet*)

EQUIPMENT BY TYPE
AD
   SAM TOWED 61+: 36 PAC-3 *Patriot*; 12 S-300 PMU-1 (SA-10/20 *Grumble*/*Gargoyle*); 9 *Crotale* NG/GR; 4 9K331 *Tor*-M1 (SA-15 *Gauntlet*); some *Skyguard*/ *Sparrow*
   GUNS 35+ 35mm

Air Support Command
FORCES BY ROLE

Tpt   1 sqn with C-27J *Spartan*; 1 sqn with C-47 *Skytrain*; C-130B *Hercules*; C-130H *Hercules*; YS-11-200; 1 sqn with EMB-135; Gulfstream V

Hel   1 sqn with AS-332 *Super Puma* (SAR/CSAR); AB-205A (Bell 205A) (SAR); AB-212 (Bell 212) (VIP, tpt)

EQUIPMENT BY TYPE
AIRCRAFT
   TPT 33: **Medium** 27: 12 C-27J *Spartan* (being delivered; 8 AT and 4 AAR); 5 C-130B *Hercules*; 10 C-130H *Hercules* **Light** 5: 2 C-47 *Skytrain*; 2 EMB-135; 1 YS-11-200 **PAX** 1 Gulfstream V
HELICOPTERS
   TPT 27: **Medium** 10 AS-332 *Super Puma* **Light** 17: 13 Bell 205A (AB-205A) (SAR); 4 Bell 212 (AB-212) (VIP, Tpt)

Air Training Command
FORCES BY ROLE

Trg   5 sqn with T-2C/E *Buckeye*; T-6A/B *Texan II*; T-41 D

EQUIPMENT BY TYPE
AIRCRAFT • TRG 104: 40 T-2C/E *Buckeye*; 20 T-6A *Texan II*; 25 T-6B *Texan II*; 19 T-41D

Paramilitary • Coast Guard and Customs 4,000
EQUIPMENT BY TYPE
PATROL AND COASTAL COMBATANTS 128: **PCC** 3; **PBF** 54; **PB** 71
AIRCRAFT • TPT • Light 4: 2 Cessna 172RG *Cutlass*; 2 TB-20 *Trinidad*

DEPLOYMENT
Legal provisions for foreign deployment:
Constitution: Codified constitution (1975/1986/2001)
Specific legislation: 'Law 2295/95' (1995))
Decision on deployment of troops abroad: By the Government Council on Foreign Affairs and Defence

AFGHANISTAN
NATO • ISAF 80 1 engr coy **Air Force:** 1 C-130

BOSNIA-HERZEGOVINA
EU • EUFOR • *Operation Althea* 49
OSCE • Bosnia and Herzegovina 4

CYPRUS
Army 950 (ELDYK army); ε200 (officers/NCO seconded to Greek-Cypriot National Guard) (total 1,150)
1 mech bde with (1 armd bn, 2 mech inf bn, 1 arty bn); 61 M-48A5 MOLF MBT; 80 *Leonidas* APC; 12 M-114 arty; 6 M-107 arty; 6 M-110A2 arty

LEBANON
UN • UNIFIL 59; 1 PB

MEDITERRANEAN SEA
NATO • *Operation Active Endeavour* 1 FFGHM
NATO • SNMCMG 2: 1 AE; 1 MHO

SERBIA
OSCE • Serbia 1
NATO • KFOR • *Joint Enterprise* 711; 1 mech inf bn
OSCE • Kosovo 5

SUDAN
UN • UNMIS 1; 2 obs

UGANDA
EU • EUTM 2

WESTERN SAHARA
UN • MINURSO 1 obs

FOREIGN FORCES
United States US European Command: 346; 1 naval base at Makri; 1 naval base at Soudha Bay; 1 air base at Iraklion

Hungary HUN

Hungarian Forint f		2009	2010	2011
GDP	f	26.1tr	26.9tr	
	US$	130bn	130bn	
per capita	US$	12,971	13,011	
Growth	%	-6.3	0.5	
Inflation	%	4.2	4.5	
Def exp	f	296bn		
	US$	1.48bn		
Def bdgt	f	327bn	281bn	275bn
	US$	1.63bn	1.35bn	
FMA (US)	US$	1.0m	1.0m	1.0m
US$1=f		200.72	207.50	

Population	9,973,141					
Age	0–14	15–19	20–24	25–29	30–64	65 plus
Male	7.7%	3.1%	3.2%	3.2%	24.2%	6.2%
Female	7.2%	2.9%	3.1%	3.1%	25.4%	10.6%

Capabilities

ACTIVE 29,626 (Army 10,100, Air 5,806 Joint 13,720) **Paramilitary 12,000**

RESERVE 44,000 (Army 35,200 Air 8,800)

ORGANISATIONS BY SERVICE

Hungary's armed forces have reorganised into a joint force.

Joint Component 13,720

FORCES BY ROLE

Sigs   1 (HQ) regt

Land Component 10,100 (incl riverine element)

FORCES BY ROLE

Mech Inf   2 bde (total: 4 mech inf, 1 lt inf, 1 mixed bn, 2 log bn)
SF   1 bn
Engr   1 regt
Spt   1 bde
CBRN   1 regt
EOD/Rvn   1 regt

EQUIPMENT BY TYPE

MBT 29 T-72
AIFV/APC (W) 380 BTR-80/BTR-80A
ARTY 68
  TOWED 152mm 18 D-20
  MOR 82mm 50
AT • MSL • MANPATS 130: 30 9K111 *Fagot* (AT-4 *Spigot*); 100 9K113 *Konkurs* (AT-5 *Spandrel*)
PATROL AND COASTAL COMBATANTS • PBR 2

FACILITIES

Training Centre 2

Air Component 5,806

Flying hours   50 hrs/yr

FORCES BY ROLE

C&C   1 (Comd and Air Surv) rgt
FGA   1 sqn with *Gripen C/D*
Tpt   1 sqn with An-26 *Curl*; (NATO Hy Airlift Wg with 3 C-17A *Globemaster* based at Papa)
Trg   1 sqn with; Yak-52
Atk Hel   1 (cbt) bn with Mi-24 *Hind*
Tpt Hel   1 bn with Mi-8 *Hip*; Mi-17 *Hip H*;
AD   1 regt with (9 bty with *Mistral*; 3 bty with 2K12 *Kub* (SA-6 *Gainful*))

EQUIPMENT BY TYPE

AIRCRAFT 14 combat capable
  FGA14: 12 *Gripen* C; 2 *Gripen* D
  TPT • Light 5 An-26 *Curl*
  TRG 9 Yak-52

HELICOPTERS
  ATK 12 Mi-24 *Hind*
  MRH 7 Mi-17 *Hip H*
  TPT • Medium 10 Mi-8 *Hip*
AD • SAM 61
  SP 16 2K12 *Kub* (SA-6 *Gainful)*
  MANPAD 45 *Mistral*
  RADAR: 3 RAT-31DL, 6 P-18: 6 SZT-68U; 14 P-37
MSL
  AAM • IR AAM AIM-9 *Sidewinder*; R-73 (AA-11 *Archer*)
  SARH AAM R-27 (AA-10 *Alamo* A) **ARH AAM** AIM 120C AMRAAM (on order)
  ASM 20 AGM-65 *Maverick*; 150 AT-2 *Swatter*; 80 AT-6

FACILITIES

Air bases   1 hel base (Szolnok), 2 air bases (Kecskemet, Papa)

Paramilitary 12,000

Border Guards 12,000 (to reduce)

Ministry of Interior

FORCES BY ROLE

Paramilitary 1 (Budapest) district (7 Rapid Reaction coy); 11 (regt/district) regt

EQUIPMENT BY TYPE
APC (W) 68 BTR-80

DEPLOYMENT

Legal provisions for foreign deployment:
Constitution: Codified constitution (1949)
Decision on deployment of troops abroad: By gov in case of NATO/EU operations (Art. 40/C para 1). Otherwise, by parliament (Art. 19, para 3 point j)

AFGHANISTAN
NATO • ISAF 507; 1 lt inf coy

ARMENIA/AZERBAIJAN
OSCE • Minsk Conference 2

BOSNIA-HERZEGOVINA
EU • EUFOR • *Operation Althea* 166; 1 inf coy
OSCE • Bosnia and Herzegovina 2

CYPRUS
UN • UNFICYP 84; 1 inf pl

EGYPT
MFO 38; 1 MP unit

IRAQ
NATO • NTM-I 3

LEBANON
UN • UNIFIL 4

SERBIA
NATO • KFOR 242; 1 inf coy
OSCE • Serbia 2
OSCE • Kosovo 3

UGANDA

EU • EUTM 4

WESTERN SAHARA

UN • MINURSO 7 obs

Iceland ISL

Icelandic Krona K		2009	2010	2011
GDP	K	1.50tr	1.60tr	
	US$	12.2bn	12.9bn	
per capita	US$	38,095	39,265	
Growth	%	-6.5	-2.2	
Inflation	%	12.0	5.7	
Sy Bdgt[a]	K	4bn		
	US$	32m		
US$1=K		123.47	123.60	

[a] Iceland has no armed forces. Budget is mainly for coast guard.

Population   329,279

Age	0–14	15–19	20–24	25–29	30–64	65 plus
Male	10.3%	3.8%	3.8%	3.5%	22.9%	5.8%
Female	10.0%	3.7%	3.6%	3.5%	22.4%	6.9%

Capabilities

ACTIVE NIL Paramilitary 130

ORGANISATIONS BY SERVICE

Paramilitary

Iceland Coast Guard 130

EQUIPMENT BY TYPE
PATROL AND COASTAL COMBATANTS • PSOH: 2
Aegir
LOGISTICS AND SUPPORT • AGS 1 *Baldur*
AIRCRAFT • TPT • Light 1 DHC-8-300
HELICOPTERS
   MRH 1 AS-365N *Dauphin 2*
   TPT • Medium 2 AS-322L1 *Super Puma*
FACILITIES
Base   Located at Reykjavik

FOREIGN FORCES

NATO • Iceland Air Policing: Aircraft and personnel from various NATO members on a rotating basis.

Ireland IRL

Euro €		2009	2010	2011
GDP	€	160bn	156bn	
	US$	222bn	207bn	
per capita	US$	49,963	45,030	
Growth	%	-6.0	-1.3	
Inflation	%	-4.5	-1.6	
Def exp	€	1.01bn		
	US$	1.4bn		
Def bdgt	€	1.03bn	909m	
	US$	1.44bn	1.2bn	
US$1=€		0.72	0.76	

Population   4,589,002

Age	0 – 14	15 – 19	20 – 24	25 – 29	30 – 64	65 plus
Male	10.8%	3.0%	3.2%	4.0%	23.6%	5.3%
Female	10.4%	2.9%	3.2%	4.1%	23.2%	6.3%

Capabilities

ACTIVE 10,460 (Army 8,500 Navy 1,110 Air 850)

RESERVE 14,875 (Army 14,500 Navy 300 Air 75)

ORGANISATIONS BY SERVICE

Army ε8,500

FORCES BY ROLE

Armd Recce	1 sqn
Inf	3 bde (each: 3 inf bn, 1 cav recce sqn, 1 fd arty regt (2 fd arty bty), 1 fd engr coy, 1 log bn)
Ranger	1 coy
AD	1 regt (1 AD bty)
Constr Engr	1 coy

EQUIPMENT BY TYPE
LT TK 14 *Scorpion*
RECCE 52: 15 *Piranha* IIIH; 18 AML-20; 19 AML-90
APC (W) 67: 65 *Piranha* III; 2 XA-180 *Sisu*
ARTY 495
   TOWED 24: **105mm** 24 L-118 Light Gun
   MOR 471: **81mm** 400; **120mm** 71
AT
   MSL • MANPATS 57: 36 *Javelin*; 21 *Milan*
   RCL **84mm** 444 *Carl Gustav*
   RL **84mm** AT-4
AD
   SAM • MANPAD 7 RBS-70
   GUNS • TOWED **40mm** 32 L/70 each with 8 *Flycatcher*

Reserves 14,500 reservists
The Reserve consists of two levels. Of these the 'Integrated' Reserve would provide nine rifle companies (one per regular infantry battalion, three cavalry troops (one per regular squadron) and three field batteries (one

per regular field artillery regiment) on mobilisation. The three reserve brigades form the 'Non-Integrated' Reserve and unlike the regular infantry battalions their component battalions have a variable number of rifle companies, five having four companies each, three having three and one having only two.

Cav	3 tps (integrated)
Inf	3 bde (non integrated) (each: 1 fd arty regt (2 fd arty bty), 1 fd engr coy, 1 cav recce sqn,1 log bn)
Inf	9 coy (integrated); 9 inf bn (non integrated 31 coy)
SF	1 coy (2 aslt pl, 1 spt pl)
Arty	3 bty (integrated)
Log	1 bn
AD	3 bty

Navy 1,110

EQUIPMENT BY TYPE
PATROL AND COASTAL COMBATANTS 8
PSOH 1 *Eithne* with 1 hel landing platform
PSO 2 *Roisin* each with 1 76mm gun
PCO 5: 3 *Emer*; 2 *Orla* (UK *Peacock*) each with 1 76mm gun;

FACILITIES
Bases   Located at Cork, Haulbowline

Air Corps 850

FORCES BY ROLE
Air   2 ops wg; 2 spt wg; 1 comms and info sqn

EQUIPMENT BY TYPE
AIRCRAFT
MP 2 CN-235 MPA
TPT 9 **Light** 8: 1 Beech 200 *King Air*; 1 BN-2 *Defender* 4000 (police spt); 5 Cessna FR-172H; 1 Learjet 45 (VIP)
PAX 1 Gulfstream GIV
TRG 8 PC-9M
HELICOPTERS:
MRH 6 AW-139
TPT • **Light** 4: 1 AS-355N *Twin Squirrel* (police spt); 2 EC-135 P2 (incl trg/medevac); 1 EC-135 T2

DEPLOYMENT

Legal provisions for foreign deployment:
Constitution: Codified constitution (1937)
Specific legislation: 'Defence (Amendment) Act' 2006
Decision on deployment of troops abroad: a) By parliament; b) by government if scenario for deployment corresponds with conditions laid out in Art.3 of 2006 'Defence (Amendment) Act' which exempts from parliamentary approval deployments for purposes of participation in exercises abroad; monitoring, observation, advisory or reconnaissance missions; and 'humanitarian operations 'in response to actual or potential disasters or emergencies.

AFGHANISTAN
NATO • ISAF 7

BOSNIA-HERZEGOVINA
EU • EUFOR • *Operation Althea* 43
OSCE • Bosnia and Herzegovina 3

CENTRAL AFRICAN REPUBLIC/CHAD
UN • MINURCAT 10

CÔTE D'IVOIRE
UN • UNOCI 2 obs

DEMOCRATIC REPUBLIC OF THE CONGO
UN • MONUSCO 3 obs

LEBANON
UN • UNIFIL 8

MIDDLE EAST
UN • UNTSO 12 obs

SERBIA
NATO • KFOR 22
OSCE • Serbia 2
OSCE • Kosovo 5

UGANDA
EU • EUTM 5

WESTERN SAHARA
UN • MINURSO 3 obs

Italy ITA

Euro €		2009	2010	2011
GDP	€	1.52tr	1.56tr	
	US$	2.13tr	2.06tr	
per capita	US$	35,175	34,304	
Growth	%	-5.0	0.6	
Inflation	%	0.8	1.6	
Def exp[a]	€	21.9bn		
	US$	30.5bn		
Def bdgt	€	15.5bn	15.5bn	15.5bn
	US$	21.5bn	20.5bn	
US$1=€		0.72	0.76	

[a] including military pensions

Population   60,097,564

Age	0–14	15–19	20–24	25–29	30–64	65 plus
Male	6.9%	2.4%	2.5%	2.8%	25.8%	8.6%
Female	6.5%	2.3%	2.4%	2.6%	25.2%	12.0%

Capabilities

ACTIVE 184,609 (Army 107,500 Navy 34,000 Air 43,109) **Paramilitary 142,330**

Terms of service all professional

RESERVES 42,153 (Army 38,284 Navy 4,229)

ORGANISATIONS BY SERVICE

Army 107,500

FORCES BY ROLE

Comd	1 corps HQ (NRDC-IT) with (1 sigs bde, 1 spt regt)
Mech	1 (*Mantova*) div (1st FOD) with (1 (*Ariete*) armd bde with (3 tk regt, 2 mech inf regt, 1 arty regt, 1 engr regt, 1 log bn); 1 (*Pozzuolo del Friuli*) cav bde with (3 cav regt, 1 amph regt, 1 arty regt); 1 (*Folgore*) AB bde with (1 SF regt, 1 SF RSTA regt, 3 para regt, 1 cbt engr regt);1 (*Friuli*) air mob bde with (1 cav regt, 1 air mob regt, 2 avn regt))
	1 (*Acqui*) div (2nd FOD) with: (1 (*Pinerolo*) mech bde with (1 tk regt, 3 mech inf regt, 1 SP arty regt, 1 cbt engr regt); 1 (*Granatieri*) mech bde with (1 cav regt, 2 mech inf regt, 1 SP arty regt); 1 (*Garibaldi* Bersaglieri) mech bde with (1 tk regt, 1 cav regt, 2 hy mech inf regt, 1 SP arty regt, 1 cbt engr regt); 1 (*Aosta*) mech bde with (1 cav regt, 3 mech inf regt, 1 SP arty regt, 1 cbt engr regt); 1 (*Sassari*) lt mech bde with (2 mech inf regt, 1 cbt engr regt))
Mtn Inf	1 (*Tridentina*) mtn div with (1 (*Taurinense*) mtn bde with (3 mtn inf regt (2nd, 3rd, 9th), 1 cav regt (3rd *Nizza Cavalleria*), 1 arty regt, 1 mtn cbt engr regt, 1 spt bn); 1 (*Julia*) mtn bde with (3 mtn inf regt (5th, 7th, 8th), 1 arty regt, 1 mtn cbt engr regt, 1 spt bn); 1 (6th) mtn inf trg regt))
SF	1 regt (4th *Alpini*)
Arty	1 arty bde with (1 hy arty regt, 2 arty regt, 1 psyops regt, 1 NBC regt)
AD	1 bde with (2 (*HAWK*) AD regt, 2 (SHORAD) AD regt)
Engr	1 engr bde with (3 engr regt, 1 CIMIC regt)
EW	1 (CIS/EW) comd HQ with (1 EW/ISTAR bde with (1 ISTAR bn, 1 EW bn, 1 (HUMINT) int bn); 1 sigs bde with (6 sigs bn))
Spt	1 regt
Log	1 log div with (4 (manoeuvre) log regt, 4 tpt regt)
Avn	1 avn bde with (3 avn regt, 1 avn bn)

EQUIPMENT BY TYPE

MBT 320: 200 C1 *Ariete*; 120 *Leopard* 1A5
RECCE 300 B-1 *Centauro*
AIFV 243: 200 VCC-80 *Dardo*; 43 VBM 8x8 *Freccia*
APC
  APC (T) 2,398: 230 Bv-206; 396 M-113 (incl variants); 1,772 VCC-1 *Camillino*/VCC-2
  APC (W) 617: 57 Fiat 6614; 560 *Puma*
AAV 16: 14 AAVP-7; 1 AAVC-7; 1 AAVR-7
ARTY 953
  SP 155mm 186: 124 M-109L; 62 PzH 2000
  TOWED 155mm 164 FH-70
  MRL 227mm 22 MLRS

MOR 581: **81mm** 253; **120mm** 328: 183 *BRANDT*; 145 RT-F1
AT
  MSL • MANPATS 1,327: 32 *SPIKE*; 1,000 *Milan*; 295 I-TOW
  RCL 80mm 482 *Folgore*
  RL 110mm 2,000 Pzf 3 *Panzerfaust 3*
AIRCRAFT • TPT • Light 6: 3 Do-228 (ACTL-1); 3 P-180 *Avanti*
HELICOPTERS
  ATK 59 AW-129 ESS *Mangusta*
  MRH 41: 21 Bell 412 (AB-412) *Twin Huey*; 20 AW-109
  TPT 129 **Heavy** 18 CH-47C *Chinook* **Medium** 9 NH-90
  TTH Light 102: 41 Bell 205 (AB-205); 43 Bell 206 *Jet Ranger* (AB-206); 18 Bell 212 (AB-212)
AD
  SAM 132
    TOWED 68: 36 MIM-23 *HAWK*; 32 *Skyguard/Aspide*
    MANPAD 64 FIM-92A *Stinger*
  GUNS • SP 25mm 64 SIDAM

Navy 34,000

FORCES BY ROLE

Fleet	1 Fleet Commander CINCNAV with 6 subordinate operational commands
Navy	COMFORAL (Front – Line Forces located at Taranto), COMFORPAT (Patrol Forces located at Augusta), COMFORDRAG (MCM Forces located at La Spezia), COMFORSUB (Submarine Forces located at Taranto), COMFORAER (Naval Aviation Forces located at Rome), COMFORSBARC (Amphibious/ Landing Forces located at Brindisi).
Maritime	1 High Readiness Forces HQ

EQUIPMENT BY TYPE

SUBMARINES • TACTICAL • SSK 6:
  4 *Pelosi* (imp *Sauro*, 3rd and 4th series) each with 6 single 533mm TT each with Type A-184 HWT
  2 *Salvatore Todaro* (Type U212A) each with 6 single 533mm TT each with Type A-184 HWT/DM2A4 HWT
PRINCIPAL SURFACE COMBATANTS 18
  AIRCRAFT CARRIERS • CVS 2:
  1 *G. Garibaldi* with 2 octuple *Albatros* lnchr (16 eff.) each with *Aspide* SAM, 2 triple 324mm ASTT (6 eff.) each with Mk46 LWT, (capacity: mixed air group of either 12-18 AV-8B *Harrier II*; 17 SH-3D *Sea King* or AW-101 *Merlin* - LHA role planned post 2013-14 refit)
  1 *Cavour* with 1 32-cell VLS with Aster 15 SAM, 2 76mm gun, (capacity: mixed air group of 18–20 aircraft of AV-8B *Harrier II*; 12 AW-101 *Merlin*)
  DESTROYERS • DDGHM 4:
  2 *Andrea Doria* each with 2 quad lnchr (8 eff.) each with *Otomat Mk2A* AShM, 1 48-cell VLS with *Aster* 15/*Aster* 30 SAM, 2 twin 324mm ASTT (4 eff.) each with MU-90, 3 76mm gun, (capacity 1 AW-101 *Merlin*/NH90 TTH hel)

Europe

2 *Luigi Durand de la Penne* (ex-*Animoso*) each with 2 quad lnchr (8 eff.) each with *Milas* AS/*Otomat* Mk 2A AShM, 1 Mk13 GMLS with SM-1MR SAM, 1 octuple *Albatros* lnchr with *Aspide* SAM, 2 triple 324mm ASTT (6 eff.) each with Mk46 LWT, 1 127mm gun, (capacity: 1 Bell 212 (AB-212) hel)

FRIGATES • FFGHM 12:

4 *Artigliere* each with 8 single each with *Otomat* Mk 2 AShM, 1 octuple *Albatros* lnchr with *Aspide* SAM, 1 127mm gun, (capacity: 1 Bell 212 (AB-212) hel)

8 *Maestrale* each with 4 single lnchr each with *Otomat* Mk2 AShM, 1 octuple *Albatros* lnchr with *Aspide* SAM, 2 triple 324mm ASTT (6 eff.) each with Mk46 LWT, 1 127mm gun, (capacity: 2 Bell 212 (AB-212) hel)

PATROL AND COASTAL COMBATANTS 22

CORVETTES • FS 8 *Minerva* each with 1 76mm gun

PSOH 6:

4 *Comandante Cigala Fuligosi* each with 1 76mm gun, (capacity 1 Bell 212 (AB-212)/NH-90 hel)

2 *Comandante Cigala Fuligosi* (capacity 1 Bell 212 (AB-212)/NH-90 hel)

PCO 4 *Cassiopea* each with 1 76mm gun, (capacity: 1 Bell 212 (AB-212) hel)

PB 4 *Esploratore*

MINE WARFARE • MINE COUNTERMEASURES 12

MHO 12: 8 *Gaeta*; 4 *Lerici*

AMPHIBIOUS

PRINCIPAL AMPHIBIOUS SHIPS • LPD 3

2 *San Giorgio* each with 1 76mm gun (capacity 3-5 AW-101/NH-90/SH3-D/Bell 212; 1 CH-47 *Chinook* tpt hel; 3 LCM 2 LCVP; 30 trucks; 36 APC (T); 350 troops)

1 *San Giusto* with 1 76mm gun, (capacity 4 AW-101 *Merlin*; 1 CH-47 *Chinook* tpt hel; 3 LCM 2 LCVP; 30 trucks; 36 APC (T); 350 troops)

LANDING CRAFT 26: 17 **LCVP**; 9 **LCM**

LOGISTICS AND SUPPORT 90

AORH 3: 1 *Etna* (capacity 1 AW-101/NH-90); 2 *Stromboli* (capacity 1 AW-101/NH-90)

AOT 4

ARS 1

AKSL 6

AWT 3

AG 2

AGI 1

AGS 3: 1; 2 (coastal)

ABU 5

ATS 7

AT 9 (coastal)

TRG 12: 4 **AXL**; 8 **AXS**

YDT 2

YTL 32

FACILITIES

Bases Located at La Spezia (HQ), Taranto (HQ), Brindisi, Augusta

Naval Aviation 2,200

FORCES BY ROLE

FGA 1 unit with AV-8B *Harrier II*

ASW 5 sqn with AW-101 *Merlin* ASW; Bell 212 ASW (AB-212AS); SH-3D *Sea King;* NH-90

Trg 1 flt with TAV-8B *Harrier*

Tpt Hel Some (aslt) sqn with Bell 212 (AB-212); SH-3D *Sea King;* AW-101 *Merlin;* P-180

EQUIPMENT BY TYPE

AIRCRAFT 16 combat capable

FGA 16: 14 AV-8B *Harrier III;* 2 TAV-8B *Harrier*

HELICOPTERS

ASW 41: 8 AW-101 *Merlin* ASW; 25 Bell 212 ASW; 8 SH-3D *Sea King*

AEW 4 AW-101 *Merlin*

TPT 22 **Medium** 16: 8 AW-101 *Merlin;* 8 SH-3D *Sea King;* **Light** 6 Bell 212 (AB-212)

MSL

AAM • IR AAM AIM-9L *Sidewinder* **ARH AAM** AIM-120 AMRAAM

ASM AGM-65 *Maverick*

AShM: *Marte* Mk 2

Marines 2,000

FORCES BY ROLE

Op 1 San Marco regt (1,300 Marine)

Log 1 regt

LC 1 gp

EQUIPMENT BY TYPE

APC (T) 40 VCC-2

AAV 18 AAV-7

ARTY • MOR 12: **81mm** 8 *Brandt;* **120mm** 4 *Brandt*

AT • MSL• MANPATS 6 *Milan*

AD • SAM • MANPAD FIM-92A *Stinger*

Special Forces Command

FORCES BY ROLE

Diving 1 op

Navy SF 1 op

SF 1 comd

FACILITIES

Centre 1 (Research)

School 1

Air Force 43,109

4 Commands – Air Sqn Cmd (air defence, attack, recce, mobility, support, force protection, EW ops); Training; Logistics; Operations (national and international exercises)

FORCES BY ROLE

Ftr 4 sqn with Eurofighter *Typhoon;* 2 sqn with F-16A/B *Fighting Falcon* on lease

FGA 2 sqn with AMX *Ghibli;* 1 (SEAD/EW) sqn with *Tornado* ECR; 2 sqn with *Tornado* IDS

FGA/ISR 1 sqn with AMX *Ghibli*

MP 1 sqn (opcon Navy) with *Atlantic*

Tkr/Tpt 1 sqn with B-767MRTT; G-222/G-222VS (EW)

CSAR 4 sqn with HH-3F *Pelican*

SAR 2 det with Bell 212 (AB-212)

Tpt	2 (VIP) sqn with A319CJ; *Falcon 50*; *Falcon 900 Easy*; *Falcon 900EX*; SH-3D *Sea King*; 2 sqn with C-130J *Hercules*; 1 sqn with C-27J *Spartan*; 1 (calibration) sqn with P-166-DL3; P-180 *Avanti*; 1 sqn with AB-212
Trg	1 sqn with Eurofighter *Typhoon*; 1 sqn with MB-339A (aerobatic team); 1 sqn with NH-500D; 1 sqn with *Tornado* (A200-A buddy-buddy tanker); 1 sqn with AMX-T *Ghibli*; 1 sqn with MB-339A; 1 sqn with MB-339CD*; 1 sqn with SF-260EA; 1 sqn with *Atlantic*; 1 sqn with HH-3F/AB-212
Tpt Hel	1 sqn with AB-212 ICO
ISR UAV	1 sqn with RQ-1B *Predator*
AD	7 bty with *Spada* towed SAM

EQUIPMENT BY TYPE

AIRCRAFT 252 combat capable

FTR 73: 46 Eurofighter *Typhoon*; 24 F-16A *Fighting Falcon*; 3 F-16B *Fighting Falcon* (F-16A/B on lease to 2012)

FGA 150: 68 *Tornado* IDS; 69 AMX *Ghibli*; 13 AMX-T *Ghibli*

EW/SEAD 16 *Tornado* ECR

ASW 7 *Atlantic*

TKR/TPT 1 B-767MRTT

TPT 88: **Medium** 37: 21 C-130J *Hercules*; 12 C-27J *Spartan*; 4 G-222/G-222VS; **Light** 41: 6 P-166-DL3; 15 P-180 *Avanti*; 20 S-208 (liason) **PAX** 10: 3 A319CJ; 2 *Falcon* 50 (VIP); 2 *Falcon* 900 *Easy*; 3 *Falcon* 900EX (VIP)

TRG 108: 49 MB-339A (18 aero team, 31 trg); 29 MB-339CD*; 30 SF-260M

HELICOPTERS

MRH 48 MD-500D (NH-500D)

SAR 22 HH-3F *Pelican*

TPT • Light 34 Bell 212 (AB-212)/AB-212 ICO (of which 29 for SAR); 2 SH-3D *Sea King* (liaison/VIP)

UAV • ISR • Heavy 6 RQ-1B *Predator*

AD • SAM

TOWED *Spada*

MSL

AAM • IR AAM AIM-9L *Sidewinder* **IIR AAM** *IRIS*-T

ARH AAM AIM-120 AMRAAM

ARM AGM-88 HARM

LACM SCALP EG/*Storm Shadow*

BOMBS

Laser-guided/GPS: Enhanced *Paveway* II; Enhanced *Paveway* III

FACILITIES

School	5
Center of Excellence	1

Paramilitary 142,330

Carabinieri 107,967

The Carabinieri are organisationally under the MoD. They are a separate service in the Italian Armed Forces as well as a police force with judicial competence. As a military force they carry out military police and security tasks in support of the armed forces in Italy and abroad.

As a national police force they report to the Minister of the Interior and are tasked with the maintainance of public order and law enforcement, as well as criminal investigations, counter terrorism and counter organised crime. The Carabinieri Territorial Command Structure is based on 5 Inter-Regional Commands; 5 Regional Commands; 102 Provincial Commands; and one Group Command. In addition there are 17 Territorial Depts; 18 Group Comd; 538 Company Comd; 44 Lieutenancy Comd; 4,624 Station Comd.

Mobile and Specialised Branch

FORCES BY ROLE

Comd	1 HQ
Spec Ops	1 gp (ROS)
Mobile	1 div with (1 bde (1st) with (1 horsed cav regt, 11 mobile bn); 1 bde (2nd) with (1 (1st) AB regt, 1 (Special Intervention) GIS gp, 2 (7th & 13th) Mobile regt))
Specialised	1 div (1 Ministry of Foreign Affairs Carabinieri HQ; 9 Carabinieri HQ (spt to Civil Ministries))
Hel	1 gp

EQUIPMENT BY TYPE

RECCE 18 Fiat 6616

APC 37

APC (T) 25: 10 VCC-1 *Camillino*; 15 VCC-2

APC (W) 12 *Puma*

AIRCRAFT • TPT • Light: 1 P-180 *Avanti*

HELICOPTERS

MRH 33 Bell 412 (AB-412)

TPT • Light 61: 40 AW-109; 21 Bell 206 (AB-206) *JetRanger*

Training

FORCES BY ROLE

Trg	1 HQ

Customs

(Servizio Navale Guardia Di Finanza)

PATROL AND COASTAL COMBATANTS 147:

PCF 1 *Antonio Zara*

PBF 123: 24 *Bigliani*; 24 *Corrubia*; 9 *Mazzei*; 34 V-2000; 32 V-5000/V-6000

PB 23 Buratti; 16 *Meatini*

Coast Guard 11,266

(Guardia Costiera – Capitanerie Di Porto)

PATROL AND COASTAL COMBATANTS 188:

PCC 6 *Saettia*

PBF 103

PB 79

LOGISTICS AND SUPPORT • TRG 1 (ex-US *Bannock*)

AIRCRAFT

MP 2 ATR-42 MP *Surveyor*

TPT • Light 7 P-166-DL3

HELICOPTERS • MRH 9 Bell 412SP (AB-412SP *Griffin*)

DEPLOYMENT

Legal provisions for foreign deployment:
Constitution: Codified constitution (1949)
Decision on deployment of troops abroad: By the government upon approval by the parliament

AFGHANISTAN
NATO • ISAF 3,330; 1 mtn inf bde HQ; 3 mtn inf regt; some AIFV *Dardo*; some A-129 *Mangusta*; some CH-47; some *Tornado*; some C-130
UN • UNAMA 1 obs

ALBANIA
Delegazione Italiana Esperti (DIE) 27

BOSNIA-HERZEGOVINA
EU • EUFOR • *Operation Althea* 193
OSCE • Bosnia and Herzegovina 5

EGYPT
MFO 78; 1 coastal patrol unit

GULF OF ADEN & INDIAN OCEAN
EU • *Operation Atalanta* 1 FFGHM

GULF OF ADEN & SOMALI BASIN
NATO • *Operation Ocean Shield* 1 FFGHM

INDIA/PAKISTAN
UN • UNMOGIP 7 obs

IRAQ
NATO • NTM-I 84

LEBANON
UN • UNIFIL 1,734; 1 armd recce bn; 1 armd inf bn; 1 inf coy; 1 hel bn; 1 sigs coy; 1 CIMIC coy; 1 FFG

MALTA
Air Force 35; 2 Bell 212 (AB-212)

MEDITERRANEAN SEA
NATO • *Operation Active Endeavour* 1 FFGHM
NATO • SNMCMG 2: 1 MHO

MIDDLE EAST
UN • UNTSO 7 obs

MOLDOVA
OSCE • Moldova 1

SERBIA
NATO • KFOR 1,247; 1 inf BG HQ; 1 engr unit; 1 hel unit; 1 sigs unit; 1 CSS unit; 1 Carabinieri regt
OSCE • Serbia 1
OSCE • Kosovo 16

SUDAN
UN • UNAMID 2

UGANDA
EU • EUTM 17

WESTERN SAHARA
UN • MINURSO 5 obs

FOREIGN FORCES
Germany 3 MP ac (in ELMAS/Sardinia)
United States US European Command: 9,665
Army 3,321; some M-119; some M-198; (1 AB IBCT currently deployed to AFG)
Navy 2,155; 1 HQ (US Navy Europe (USNAVEUR)) at Naples; 1 HQ (6th Fleet) at Gaeta; 1 MR Sqn eq. with 9 P-3C *Orion* at Sigonella
USAF 4,131; 1 ftr wg with (2 ftr sqn with 21 F-16C *Fighting Falcon*/F-16D *Fighting Falcon* at Aviano)
USMC 58

Latvia LVA

Latvian Lat L		2009	2010	2011
GDP	L	13.1bn	12.6bn	
	US$	26.0bn	23.5bn	
per capita	US$	11,519	10,508	
Growth	%	-18.0	-3.5	
Inflation	%	3.5	-1.4	
Def exp	L	159m		
	US$	316m		
Def bdgt	L	172m	134m	
	US$	341m	250m	
FMA (US)	US$	1.5m	2.5m	3.0m
US$1=L		0.50	0.54	

Population   2,240,265

Age	0–14	15–19	20–24	25–29	30–64	65 plus
Male	6.9%	2.8%	4.1%	4.0%	23.0%	5.5%
Female	6.6%	2.7%	4.0%	3.9%	25.0%	11.4%

Capabilities

ACTIVE 5,745 (Army 1,058 Navy 587 Air 319 Joint Staff 3,202 National Guard 579)

RESERVE 10,866 (Army Volunteer Reservist 10,866)

ORGANISATIONS BY SERVICE

Joint 3,202
FORCES BY ROLE
Comd   1 Joint HQ (1 Staff bn)
          1 log HQ (1 tpt bn, 1 log bn)
          1 Trg and Doctrine Comd
SF   1 Ranger bn, 1 cbt diver unit, 1 anti-terrorist unit
Security 1 MP unit

Army 1,058
FORCES BY ROLE
Inf   1 bde (2 inf bn)

National Guard 579; 10,866 part-time (11,445 in total)

Inf	14 bn
Fd Arty	1 bn
AD	1 bn
Engr	1 bn
NBC	1 bn

EQUIPMENT BY TYPE
MBT 3 T-55 (trg)
RECCE 2 BRDM-2
ARTY 56
   TOWED 100mm 26 K-53
   MOR 120mm 30 M-120
   AT
      RL 73mm RPG-7 *Knout*; **84mm** AT-4; **90mm**
      GUNS 143: **76mm** 3; **90mm** 140
AD
   SAM • MANPAD 5 *Strela* 2M (SA-7) *Grail*
   GUNS • TOWED 52: **14.5mm** 2 ZPU-4; **20mm** 10 FK-20;
   23mm 16 GSH-23; **30mm** 2: 1; 1 AK-230; **40mm** 22 L/70

Navy 587 (incl Coast Guard)

1 Naval HQ commands a Naval Forces Flotilla separated into two squadrons: an MCM squadron and a Patrol Boat squadron. LVA, EST and LTU have set up a joint Naval unit* BALTRON with bases at Liepaja, Riga, Ventspils (LVA), Tallinn (EST), Klaipeda (LTU).*Each nation contributes 1–2 MCMVs

EQUIPMENT BY TYPE
PATROL AND COASTAL COMBATANTS 4PB 4 *Storm* (NOR) each with 1 76mm gun **MINE WARFARE • MINE COUNTERMEASURES** 5
   MHO 4 *Imanta* (NLD *Alkmaar/Tripartite*)
   MCCS 1 *Vidar* (NOR)
   LOGISTICS AND SUPPORT 2
   AXL 1 *Varonis* (C3 and support ship, ex-*Buyskes*, NLD)
   ATA 1 *Goliat* (FSU)

FACILITIES
Bases   Located at Liepaja, Daugavgriva (Riga – Coast Guard)

Coast Guard

Under command of the Latvian Naval Forces.
PATROL AND COASTAL COMBATANTS
PB 6: 1 *Astra*; 5 KBV 236 (SWE)

Air Force 319

Main tasks are air space control and defence, maritime and land SAR and air transportation.

FORCES BY ROLE

Tpt	1 sqn
AD	1 bn
Radar	1 sqn (radar/air ctrl)

AIRCRAFT • TPT • Light 3: 2 An-2 *Colt*; 1 L-410 *Turbolet*
HELICOPTERS
   MRH 4 Mi-17 *Hip H*
   TPT • Light 2 PZL Mi-2 *Hoplite*

Paramilitary

State Border Guard
PATROL AND COASTAL COMBATANTS
PB 2: 1 *Valpas* (FIN); 1 *Lokki*

DEPLOYMENT

Legal provisions for foreign deployment:
Constitution: Codified constitution (1922)
Specific legislation: 'Law on Participation of the National Armed Forces of Latvia in International Operations' (1995) (Annex of 21 Jan 2009 allows Latvian armed forces to take part in quick response units formed by NATO/EU)
Decision on deployment of troops abroad: a) By parliament (Section 5 I of the 1995 'Law on Participation', in combination with Art. 73 of constitution); b) by cabinet, if deployment is for rescue or humanitarian operations (Section 5 II of the 1995 law) or for military exercises (Section 9 of the 1995 law)

AFGHANISTAN
NATO • ISAF 155

MOLDOVA
OSCE • Moldova 2

Lithuania LTU

Lithuanian Litas L		2009	2010	2011
GDP	L	92.0bn	94.4bn	
	US$	37.1bn	35.9bn	
per capita	US$	11,120	11,022	
Growth	%	-15.0	0.5	
Inflation	%	4.5	1.0	
Def exp	L	996m		
	US$	402m		
Def bdgt	L	1.2bn	850m	990m
	US$	484m	323m	
FMA (US)	US$	1.7m	2.7m	3.3m
US$1=L		2.48	2.63	

Population   3,255,324

Ethnic groups: Lithuanian 84.6%; Polish 6.3%; Russian 5.1%; Belarussian 1.1%

Age	0–14	15–19	20–24	25–29	30–64	65 plus
Male	7.1%	3.2%	4.0%	3.9%	23.2%	5.7%
Female	6.7%	3.1%	3.8%	3.8%	24.8%	10.8%

Capabilities

ACTIVE 10,640 (Army 8,200 Navy 530 Air 980 Joint 1,804) **Paramilitary 14,600**
Terms of service 12 months.

RESERVE 6,700 (Army 6,700)

ORGANISATIONS BY SERVICE

Army 3,500; 4,700 active reserves (total 8,200)

FORCES BY ROLE

Rapid Reaction	1 bde (2 mech inf bn, 2 mot inf bn, 1 arty bn)
Engr	1 bn
Sy	1 MP bn
Trg	1 regt

EQUIPMENT BY TYPE
RECCE 10 BRDM-2
APC (T) 187 Bv 206/M-113A1
ARTY 133
   TOWED 105mm 72 M-101
   MOR 120mm 61 M-43
AT • MSL
   SP 10 M1025A2 HMMWV with *Javelin*
   MANPATS *Javelin*
RCL 84mm *Carl Gustav*
AD • SAM • MANPAD *Stinger*

Reserves

National Defence Voluntary Forces 4,700 active reservists

Territorial Def	5 regt; 36 bn (total: 150 def coy)
Trg	1 bn
Avn	1 sqn

Special Operation Force

SF	1 gp (1 CT unit; 1 Jaeger bn, 1 cbt diver unit)

Navy 410; 120 conscript (total 530)

LVA, EST and LTU established a joint naval unit BALTRON with bases at Liepaja, Riga, Ventpils (LVA), Tallinn (EST), Klaipeda (LTU), HQ at Tallinn

EQUIPMENT BY TYPE
PATROL AND COASTAL COMBATANTS 4
   PCC 3 *Standard Flex 300* (DNK *Flyvefisken*) with 1 76mm gun
   PB 1 *Storm*(NOR)
MINE WARFARE • MINE COUNTERMEASURES 3
   MHC 2 *Sūduvis* (GER *Lindau*)
   MCCS 1 *Vidar* (NOR)
LOGISTICS AND SUPPORT 4
   AG 1 (FSU)
   AAR 1
   YDT 1 *Lokys* (DNK)
   YTL 1 (FSU)

FACILITIES

Base   Located at Klaipeda

Air Force 980 (plus 190 civilian)

Flying hours   120 hrs/year

FORCES BY ROLE

AD	1 bn

FACILITIES

Air base   1

Air base, Airspace Surveillance and Control Command (ASSCC), AD btn, armament and equipment repair depot

EQUIPMENT BY TYPE
AIRCRAFT
   TPT 5 **Medium** 3 C-27J *Spartan* **Light** 2 L-410 *Turbolet*
   TRG 2 L-39ZA *Albatros*
HELICOPTERS • TPT • Medium 9 Mi-8 *Hip* (tpt/SAR)
AD • SAM RBS-70

Joint Logistics Support Command 1,070

FORCES BY ROLE

Log	1 bn

Joint Training and Doctrine Command (TRADOC) 734

FORCES BY ROLE

1 regt	Trg

FACILITIES

3 trg school (one per service)

Paramilitary 14,600

Riflemen Union 9,600

State Border Guard Service 5,000

Ministry of Internal Affairs

Coast Guard 540

PATROL AND COASTAL COMBATANTS • PB 3: 1 *Lokki* (FIN); 1 KBV 041 (SWE); 1 KBV 101 (SWE)
AMPHIBIOUS • LANDING CRAFT • UCAC 1 *Christina* (*Griffon* 2000)

DEPLOYMENT

Legal provisions for foreign deployment:
Constitution: Codified constitution (1992)
Decision on deployment of troops abroad: By parliament (Art. 67, 138, 142)

AFGHANISTAN
NATO • ISAF 220

BOSNIA-HERZEGOVINA
EU • EUFOR • *Operation Althea* 1

IRAQ
NATO • NTM-I 2

FOREIGN FORCES

United States NATO Baltic Air Policing 4 F-15C *Eagle*

Europe

Luxembourg LUX

Euro €		2009	2010	2011
GDP	€	37.6bn	40.1bn	
	US$	52.4bn	53.1bn	
per capita	US$	105,316	107,927	
Growth	%	-3.4	1.5	
Inflation	%	0.4	3.0	
Def exp	€	179m		
	US$	249m		
Def bdgt	€		420m	200m
	US$		556m	
US$1=€		0.72	0.76	

Population   491,772

Foreign citizens: ε124,000

Age	0–14	15–19	20–24	25–29	30–64	65 plus
Male	9.4%	3.2%	3.1%	3.2%	24.1%	6.2%
Female	8.8%	3.0%	3.1%	3.2%	23.9%	8.7%

Capabilities

ACTIVE 900 (Army 900) Paramilitary 612

ORGANISATIONS BY SERVICE

Army 900

FORCES BY ROLE

Recce   2 coy (1 to Eurocorps/BEL div, 1 to NATO pool of deployable forces)

Lt Inf   1 bn

EQUIPMENT BY TYPE
ARTY • MOR 81mm 6
AT • MSL• MANPATS 6 TOW
  RL 66mm M-72 *LAW*

Air Force

FORCES BY ROLE
None, but for legal purposes NATO's E-3A AEW ac have LUX registration

AEW&C   1 sqn with 3 B-707 (trg); 17 E-3A *Sentry* (NATO standard)

EQUIPMENT BY TYPE
AIRCRAFT
  AEW&C 17 E-3A *Sentry* (NATO standard)
  TPT • PAX 3 B-707 (trg)

Paramilitary 612

Gendarmerie 612

DEPLOYMENT

Legal provisions for foreign deployment:
Constitution: Codified constitution (1868)
Specific legislation: 'Loi du 27 juillet 1992 relatif à la participation du Grand-Duché de Luxembourg à des opérations pour le maintien de la paix (OMP) dans le cadre d'organisations internationales'
Decision on deployment of troops abroad: By government after formal consultation of relevant parliamentary committees and the Council of State (Art. 1–2 of the 1992 law)

AFGHANISTAN
NATO • ISAF 9

BOSNIA-HERZEGOVINA
EU • EUFOR • *Operation Althea* 1

SERBIA
NATO • KFOR 23

UGANDA
EU• EUTM 1

Macedonia, Former Yugoslav Republic FYROM

Macedonian Denar d		2009	2010	2011
GDP	d	413bn	431bn	
	US$	9.40bn	9.27bn	
per capita	US$	4,601	4,538	
Growth	%	-0.7	1.9	
Inflation	%	-0.3	1.9	
Def exp	d	7bn		
	US$	159m		
Def bdgt	d	8.54bn	6.52bn	6.05bn
	US$	194m	140m	
FMA (US)	US$	2.8m	4.0m	5.0m
US$1=d		43.98	46.53	

Population   2,043,360

Age	0–14	15–19	20–24	25–29	30–64	65 plus
Male	9.6%	3.7%	3.9%	4.0%	23.7%	5.0%
Female	8.9%	3.5%	3.7%	3.8%	23.7%	6.6%

Capabilities

ACTIVE 8,000 (Joint 8,000)

RESERVE 4,850

ORGANISATIONS BY SERVICE

Joint Operational Command 8,000

Army

FORCES BY ROLE
2 corps HQ (cadre)
Tk   1 bn
Inf   2 bde
SF   1 (Special Purpose) unit with (1 SF bn; 1 Ranger bn)
Arty   1 (mixed) regt
AD   1 coy
Sig   1 bn

NBC	1 coy
Sy	1 MP bn

Logistic Support Command

Log	3 bn
Engr	1 bn (1 active coy)

EQUIPMENT BY TYPE
MBT 31: 31 T-72A
RECCE 51: 10 BRDM-2; 41 M-1114 HMMWV
AIFV 11: 10 BMP-2; 1 BMP-2K
APC 201
    APC (T) 47: 9 *Leonidas*; 28 M-113A; 10 MT-LB
    APC (W) 154: 58 BTR-70; 12 BTR-80; 84 TM-170 *Hermelin*
ARTY 126
    TOWED 70: **105mm** 14 M-56; **122mm** 56 M-30 M-1938
    MRL 17: **122mm** 6 BM-21; **128mm** 11
    MOR 39: **120mm** 39
AT • MSL • MANPATS 12 *Milan*
RCL 57mm; **82mm** M60A
AD
    SAM 13: 8 9K35 *Strela*-10 (SA-13 *Gopher*)
    MANPAD 5 9K310 *Igla*-1 (SA-16 *Gimlet*)
    Guns 40mm 36 L20

Reserves
Inf   1 bde

Marine Wing
PATROL AND COASTAL COMBATANTS • PBR 2

Air Wing
Air Wg is directly under Joint Operational Cmd

FORCES BY ROLE
Tpt	1 (VIP) sqn with An-2 *Colt*
Trg	1 sqn with Bell 205 (UH-1H *Iroquois*); 1 sqn with Z-242
Atk Hel	1 sqn with Mi-24K *Hind* G2; Mi-24V *Hind* E
Tpt Hel	1 sqn with Mi-8MTV *Hip*; Mi-17 *Hip* H

EQUIPMENT BY TYPE
AIRCRAFT
    TPT • Light 1 An-2 *Colt*
    TRG 3 Z-242
HELICOPTERS
    ATK 14: 2 Mi-24K *Hind* G2 (being modernised by Elbit); 12 Mi-24V *Hind* E
    MRH 6: 4 Mi-8MTV *Hip* (being modernised by Elbit); 2 Mi-17 *Hip* H
    TPT • Light 2 Bell 205 (UH-1H *Iroquois*)

Paramilitary

Police 7,600 (some 5,000 armed)
incl 2 SF units

EQUIPMENT BY TYPE
APC BTR APC (W)/M-113A APC (T)
HELICOPTERS 3
    MRH 1 Bell 412EP *Twin Huey*
    TPT • Light 2: 1 Bell 206B (AB-206B) *JetRanger II*; 1 Bell 212 (AB-212)

DEPLOYMENT

Legal provisions for foreign deployment of armed forces:
Constitution: Codified constitution (1991)
Specific legislation: 'Defence Law' (2005)
Decision on deployment of troops abroad: a) by the government is deployment is for humanitarian missions or military exercises; b) by the parliament if for peacekeeping operations ('Defence Law', Art. 41)

AFGHANISTAN
NATO • ISAF 161

BOSNIA-HERZEGOVINA
EU • EUFOR • *Operation Althea* 12

LEBANON
UN • UNIFIL 1

SERBIA
OSCE • Kosovo 4

Malta MLT

Maltese Lira ML		2009	2010	2011
GDP	ML	5.75bn	5.97bn	
	US$	8.01bn	7.90bn	
per capita	US$	19,299	19,259	
Growth	%	-2.1	3.8	
Inflation	%	2.1	1.9	
Def exp	ML	43m		
	US$	59m		
Def bdgt	ML	36m	43m	43m
	US$	50m	57m	
FMA (US)	US$	0.1m	0.455m	0.6m
US$1=ML		0.72	0.76	

Population   409,999

Age	0 – 14	15 – 19	20 – 24	25 – 29	30 – 64	65 plus
Male	8.0%	3.3%	3.6%	3.7%	24.3%	6.9%
Female	7.6%	3.1%	3.4%	3.4%	23.9%	8.9%

Capabilities

ACTIVE 1,954 (Armed Forces 1,954)

RESERVE 167 (Emergency Volunteer Reserve Force 120 Individual Reserve 47)

ORGANISATIONS BY SERVICE

Armed Forces of Malta 1,954
FORCES BY ROLE
Inf	1 regt (1st) with (2 inf coy, 1 AD/spt coy)
Log	1 regt (3rd) with (1 engr sqn); 1 regt (4th) with (1 sigs coy, 1 sy coy (Revenue Security Corps))

Maritime Squadron

The AFM maritime element is organised into 5 Divisions: Offshore Patrol; Inshore Patrol; Rapid Deployment and Training; Marine Engineering and Logistics.

EQUIPMENT BY TYPE
PATROL AND COASTAL COMBATANTS 8
  PCC 1 *Diciotti*
  PB 7: 4 Austal 21m; 2 *Marine Protector*; 1 *Bremse* (GER)
LOGISTICS AND SUPPORT 2
  AAR 2 *Cantieri Vittoria*

Air Wing

1 Base Party. 1 Flt Ops Div; 1 Maint Div; 1 Integrated Logs Div; 1 Rescue Section

EQUIPMENT BY TYPE
AIRCRAFT
  TPT • Light 2 BN-2B *Islander*
  TRG 5 *Bulldog* T MK1
HELICOPTERS
  MRH 7: 2 Hughes 500M; 5 SA-316B *Alouette* III
  TRG 1 Bell 47G2

DEPLOYMENT

Legal provisions for foreign deployment:
Constitution: Codified constitution (1964)
Decision on deployment of troops abroad: The constitution does not regulate any responsibilities and mechanisms with regard to the use of armed forces abroad.

SERBIA
OSCE • Kosovo 1

UGANDA
EU • EUTM 3

FOREIGN FORCES

Italy Air Force: 35; 2 Bell 212 (SAR) hel

Moldova MDA

Moldovan Leu L		2009	2010	2011
GDP	L	60.0bn	66.9bn	
	US$	5.41bn	5.38bn	
per capita	US$	1,501	1,505	
Growth	%	-6.5	2.5	
Inflation	%	-0.1	7.4	
Def exp	L	223m		
	US$	20m		
Def bdgt	L	223m	205m	
	US$	20m	16m	
FMA (US)	US$	0.5m	0.75m	1.5m
US$1=L		11.10	12.44	

Population	3,575,574					
Age	0 – 14	15 – 19	20 – 24	25 – 29	30 – 64	65 plus
Male	8.0%	3.5%	4.6%	4.8%	22.9%	3.8%
Female	7.6%	3.4%	4.5%	4.7%	25.5%	6.6%

Capabilities

ACTIVE 5,354 (Army 3,231 Air 826 Logistic Support 1,297) **Paramilitary 2,379**
Terms of service 12 months

RESERVE 57,971 (Joint 57,971)

ORGANISATIONS BY SERVICE

Army 1,297; 1,934 conscript (total 3,231)
FORCES BY ROLE

Mot Inf	3 bde (1st, 2nd & 3rd); 1 bn (22nd Peacekeeping)
SF	1 bn
Arty	1 bn
Engr	1 bn
Sy	1 (Guard) bn
Sigs	1 coy
NBC	1 coy

EQUIPMENT BY TYPE
AIFV 44 BMD-1
APC 164
  APC (T) 64: 9 BTR-D; 55 MT-LB
  APC (W) 100: 11 BTR-80; 89 TAB-71
ARTY 148
  TOWED 69: **122mm** 17 (M-30) *M-1938*; **152mm** 52: 21 2A36; 31 D-20
  GUN/MOR • SP 120mm 9 2S9 *Anona*
  MRL 220mm 11 9P140 *Uragan*
  MOR 59: **82mm** 52; **120mm** 7 M-120
AT
  MSL • MANPATS 120: 72 9K111 *Fagot* (AT-4 *Spigot*); 21 9K113 *Konkurs* (AT-5 *Spandrel*); 27 9K114 *Shturm* (AT-6 *Spiral*)
  RCL 73mm 138 SPG-9
  GUNS 100mm 36 MT-12
AD • GUNS • TOWED 39: **23mm** 28 ZU-23; **57mm** 11 S-60
RADAR • LAND 4: 2 ARK-1; 2 SNAR-10

Air Force 826 (incl 259 conscripts)
1 Air Force base, 1 AD regt
FORCES BY ROLE

Tpt	2 sqn with An-2; An-26; An-72; Mi-8PS *Hip*; Yak-18
SAM	1 regt with S-125 *Neva* (SA-3 *Goa*)

EQUIPMENT BY TYPE
AIRCRAFT
  TPT • Light 6: 2 An-2 *Colt*; 1 An-26 *Curl*; 2 An-72 *Coaler* 1 Yak-18
HELICOPTERS
  MRH 4 Mi-17-1V *Hip*
  TPT • Medium 2 Mi-8PS *Hip*
AD • SAM 12 S-125 *Neva* SA-3 (*Goa*)

Paramilitary 2,379
Ministry of Interior

OPON 900 (riot police)
Ministry of Interior

DEPLOYMENT

Legal provisions for foreign deployment:
Constitution: Codified constitution (1994)
Decision on deployment of troops abroad: By the parliament (Art. 66)

CÔTE D'IVOIRE
UN • UNOCI 3 obs

LIBERIA
UN • UNMIL 2 obs

SERBIA
OSCE • Serbia 1
OSCE • Kosovo 1

SUDAN
UN • UNMIS 2 obs

FOREIGN FORCES

Bulgaria OSCE 1
Estonia OSCE 2
France OSCE 1
Italy OSCE 1
Latvia OSCE 2
Poland OSCE 1
Sweden OSCE 1
Russia ε1,500 (including 335 peacekeepers) Military Air Forces 7 Mi-24 *Hind*/Mi-8 *Hip*
Ukraine 10 mil obs (Joint Peacekeeping Force)
United Kingdom OSCE 1
United States OSCE 2

Montenegro MNE

Euro €		2009	2010	2011
GDP	€	2.98bn	2.97bn	
	US$	4.15bn	3.93bn	
per capita	US$	6,651	6,280	
Growth	%	-7.0	-0.6	
Inflation	%	3.4	0.6	
Def exp	€	41m		
	US$	57m		
Def bdgt	€	41m	27m	
	US$	57m	35m	
FMA (US)	US$	0.8m	1.2m	1.8m
US$1=€		0.72	0.76	

Population   625,516

Age	0 – 14	15 – 19	20 – 24	25 – 29	30 – 64	65 plus
Male	7.6%	2.7%	3.7%	4.6%	25.9%	5.4%
Female	8.0%	2.9%	3.5%	3.8%	23.9%	8.1%

Capabilities

ACTIVE 3,127 (Army 2,500 Navy 401 Air Force 226)
Paramilitary 10,100

ORGANISATIONS BY SERVICE

Army ε2,500

FORCES BY ROLE

Comd	1 op comd
Mot inf	2 bde (2 inf regt (2 inf bn))
Lt Inf	1 bde
SF	1 unit (forming)
Arty	1 coastal bn
Security	1 MP bn

EQUIPMENT BY TYPE
APC (W) 8 BOV-VP M-86
ARTY 138
  SP 18: **130mm** 18 M46
  TOWED 12: **122mm** 12 D-30
  MRL 128mm 18 M63 *Plamen*/M 94 *Plamen* (SP)
  MOR 90: **82mm** 47; **120mm** 43
AT
  SP 10 BOV-1
  MSL • MANPATS 117: 71 AT-4 9K111 *Spigot*; 19 AT-5 9K113 *Spandrel*; 27 AT-6 9K114 *Spiral*
  GUNS 100mm 36 MT-12

Navy 401

A new armed forces organisational structure is under development (1 Naval Cmd HQ with 4 Operational Naval Units (Patrol Boat; Coastal Surveillance; Maritime Detachment and SAR) with additional Sig, Log and Trg units with a separate Coast Guard Element). Some listed units are in the process of decommissioning or sale.

EQUIPMENT BY TYPE
SUBMARINES • SDV 2 † (*Mala*)
PATROL AND COASTAL COMBATANTS 5
  PSO 1 *Kotor* with 1 twin (2 eff.) 76mm gun
  PCFG 2 *Rade Končar* each with 2 single lnchr each with P-15 *Termit* (SS-N-2B Styx) AShM
  PB 2 *Mirna* (Type 140) (Police units)
AMPHIBIOUS • LANDING CRAFT 5
  LCU 5: 3 (Type 21); 2 (Type 22)
LOGISTICS AND SUPPORT 3
AOTL 1 *Drina*; **AET** 1 *Lubin*; **AXS** 1 *Jadran*
FACILITIES
Base   Located at Bar

Air Force 226

Golubovci (Podgorica) air base under army command.
FORCES BY ROLE
FGA/Trg 1 (mixed) sqn with G-4 *Super Galeb*; Utva-75
Tpt Hel   1 sqn with SA-341 *Gazelle*; SA-342L *Gazelle*

EQUIPMENT BY TYPE

AIRCRAFT • TRG 18: 15 G-4 *Super Galeb* (7–8 serviceable);
3 Utva-75 (basic trg).

HELICOPTERS

  MRH 15 SA 341/SA 342L *Gazelle* (7–8 serviceable)

  TPT • Medium (1 Mi-8T stored awaiting overhaul)

Paramilitary ε10,100

Montenegrin Ministry of Interior Personnel ε6,000

Special Police Units ε4,100

DEPLOYMENT

AFGHANISTAN

NATO • ISAF 31

LIBERIA

UN • UNMIL 2 obs

SERBIA

OSCE • Kosovo 1

Netherlands NLD

Euro €		2009	2010	2011
GDP	€	572bn	589bn	
	US$	797bn	780bn	
per capita	US$	48,190	46,822	
Growth	%	-4.0	1.2	
Inflation	%	1.2	1.3	
Def exp	€	8.71bn		
	US$	12.1bn		
Def bdgt	€	8.7bn	8.5bn	8.4bn
	US$	12.1bn	11.3bn	
US$1=€		0.72	0.76	

Population	16,653,346					
Age	0–14	15–19	20–24	25–29	30–64	65 plus
Male	8.7%	3.1%	3.2%	3.0%	24.7%	6.8%
Female	8.3%	3.0%	3.1%	3.0%	24.4%	8.8%

Capabilities

ACTIVE 37,368 (Army 20,836; Navy 8,502; Air 8,030)
Military Constabulary 5,911

CIVILIAN 3,485 (Army 2,336; Navy 650; Air 499)
Military Constabulary 543

RESERVE 3,189 (Army 2,686; Navy 82; Air 421)
Military Constabulary 84
Soldiers/sailors to age 35, NCOs to 40, officers to 45

ORGANISATIONS BY SERVICE

Army 20,836

FORCES BY ROLE

Comd	elm 1 (GER/NLD) Corps HQ
Armd Inf	2 (Mech) bde (13th & 43rd) (each: 1 armd bn. 2 armd inf bn, 1 SP arty bn (2 bty), 1 engr bn, 1 armd recce sqn, 1 maint coy, 1 medical coy)
Air Mob	1 bde (11th) with (3 air mob inf bn, 1 mor coy, 1 AD coy, 1 engr coy, 1 med coy, 1 supply coy, 1 maint coy)
SF	5 coy (4 land; 1 maritime)
AD	1 comd with (3 bty)
ISR	1 bn with (2 armd recce sqn, 1 EW coy, 1 arty bty, 1 UAV bty)
Engr	1 bn
CIS	1 bn
CIMIC	1 bn
Log/Tpt	2 tpt bn
Maint	3 coy
Med	1 bn
EOD	48 teams

EQUIPMENT BY TYPE

MBT 44 *Leopard* 2A6; (16 more in store)

RECCE 296 *Fennek*

AIFV 151 CV9035

APC • APC (W) 16 M577A1

LFV 67 *Bushmaster* IMV

ARTY 67:

  SP 155mm 24 PzH 2000

  MOR 43: **81mm** 27 L16/M1 **120mm** 16 *Brandt*

AT

  MSL

    SP 96 *Fennek* MRAT

    MANPATS 297 MR *Spike (Gil)*

  RL 1381 Pzf

AD

  SAM

    SP 18 *Fennek* with FIM-92A *Stinger*; 18 MB with FIM-92A *Stinger*

    MANPAD 18 FIM-92A *Stinger*

  GUNS• SP35mm 60 *Gepard* (in store for sale)

RADAR • LAND 6+: 6 AN/TPQ-36 *Firefinder* (arty, mor); WALS; *SQUIRE*

UAV • ISR • Medium 14 *Sperwer*

Reserves 2,686 reservists

National Command

Cadre bde and corps tps completed by call-up of reservists (incl Territorial Comd)

FORCES BY ROLE

  Inf   5 bn (Could be mob for territorial defence).

Navy 8,502 (incl Marines)

EQUIPMENT BY TYPE

SUBMARINES • TACTICAL • SSK 4:

  4 *Walrus* each with 4 single 533mm TT each with Mk48 *Sea Arrow* HWT (equipped for UGM-84C *Harpoon* AShM, but none embarked)

PRINCIPAL SURFACE COMBATANTS 6

DESTROYERS • DDGHM 4:

4 *Zeven Provinciën* each with 2 quad Mk 141 lnchr (8 eff.) each with RGM-84F *Harpoon* AShM, 1 40 cell Mk 41 VLS with SM-2MR/ESSM SAM, 2 twin 324mm ASTT (4 eff.) each with Mk46 LWT, 1 127mm gun, (capacity 1 *Lynx*/NH-90 hel)

FRIGATES • FFGHM 2:

2 *Karel Doorman* each with 2 quad Mk 141 lnchr (8 eff.) each with RGM-84A/C *Harpoon* AShM, 1 Mk 48 VLS with RIM-7P *Sea Sparrow* SAM, 2 twin 324mm ASTT (4 eff.) each with Mk46 LWT, 1 76mm gun, (capacity 1 *Lynx*/NH-90 hel)

MINE WARFARE • MINE COUNTERMEASURES • MHO 10 *Alkmaar* (tripartite)

AMPHIBIOUS

PRINCIPAL AMPHIBIOUS SHIPS • LPD 2:

1 *Rotterdam* (capacity either 6 *Lynx* hel or 4 NH-90/AS-532 *Cougar* hel; either 6 LCVP or 2 LCU and 3 LCVP; either 170 APC (T) or 33 MBT; 538 troops)

1 *Johan de Witt* (capacity 6 NH-90 utl hel or 4 AW-101 *Merlin*/AS-532 *Cougar* hel; either 6 LCVP or 2 LCU and 3 LCVP; either 170 APC (T) or 33 MBT; 700 troops)

CRAFT 17: 5 **LCU**; 12 **LCVP**

LOGISTICS AND SUPPORT 16

AORH 1 *Amsterdam* (capacity: 4 *Lynx* or 2 NH-90 hel)

AOLH 1 *Zuiderkruis* (capacity: 2 *Lynx*/NH-90 hel)

AGS 2

TRG 2

SPT 1 *Pelikaan*

TRV 1 *Mercuur*

YDT 4

YFS 4

FACILITIES

| Bases | Located at Den Helder, Willemstad (Dutch Antilles) |
| Naval air base | Located at De Kooy (hel) |

Marines 2,654

FORCES BY ROLE

Marine	2 amph bn (1 bn integrated with UK 3 Cdo Bde to form UK/NLD Amphibious Landing Force)
CS	1 amphibious support bn (1 recce coy, 2 mor coy, 1 AD plt, 2 amph beach units, 1 (Maritime Joint Effect) bty, 1 AD pl, some SF units)
CSS	1 bn (2 CSS units, 1 Sea Based Support gp, 2 medical facility)

EQUIPMENT BY TYPE

APC (T) 156: 87 Bv-206D; 69 BvS-10 *Viking*

ARTY • MOR 18: **81mm** 12 L16/M-1; **120mm** 6 *Brandt*

AT • MSL • MANPATS 24 MRAT *Gil*

    RL 84mm 144 *Pantserfaust* III Dynarange 2000

AD • SAM • MANPAD 4 FIM-92A *Stinger*

Air Force 8,030

Flying hours   180 hrs/year

FORCES BY ROLE

FGA	5 (multi role) sqn with F-16AM/BM *Fighting Falcon*
ASW/SAR	1 sqn with *Lynx* SH-14D
SAR	1 sqn with Bell 412SP (AB-412SP *Griffin*)
Tpt	1 sqn with; C-130H-30 *Hercules*; DC-10/KDC-10; Gulfstream IV
Trg	1 sqn with PC-7 *Turbo Trainer*
Atk Hel	1 sqn with AH-64D *Apache*
Tpt Hel	1 sqn with AS-532U2 *Cougar II*; 1 sqn with CH-47D *Chinook*
AD	4 sqn (total: 7 AD Team. 4 AD bty with MIM-104 *Patriot* (TMD capable))

EQUIPMENT BY TYPE

AIRCRAFT 72 combat capable

FTR 72 F-16AM/BM *Fighting Falcon*

TKR 2 KDC-10

TPT 6 **Medium** 4 C-130H-30 *Hercules*; **PAX** 2: 1 DC-10; 1 Gulfstream IV

TRG 13 PC-7 *Turbo Trainer*

HELICOPTERS

ATK 29 AH-64D *Apache*

ASW 5 *Lynx* SH-14D (to be replaced by NH-90)

MRH 7: 3 Bell 412 (AB-412SP *Griffin*); 4 SA-316 *Alouette III*

TPT 28 **Heavy** 11 CH-47D *Chinook* **Medium** 17 AS-532U2 *Cougar II*

AD • SAM

TOWED 20 MIM-104 *Patriot* (TMD Capable/PAC-3 msl)

MANPAD FIM-92A *Stinger*

MSL

AAM • IR AAM AIM-9L/M/N **ARH AAM** AIM-120B AMRAAM

ASM AGM-114K *Hellfire*; AGM-65D/G *Maverick*

BOMBS

Conventional Mk 82; Mk 84

Laser-guided GBU-10/GBU-12 *Paveway* II; GBU-24 *Paveway* III (all supported by LANTIRN)

FACILITIES

Air Bases 6: 2 F-16, 1 land hel, 1 maritime hel, 1 tpt,1 trg; Euro Air Tpt Coord centre in Eindhoven

Paramlilitary

Royal Military Constabulary 5,911

Subordinate to the Ministry of Defence, but performs most of its work under the authority of other ministries.

FORCES BY ROLE

| Paramilitary | 6 district (total: 60 Paramilitary 'bde') |

EQUIPMENT BY TYPE

AIFV 24 YPR-765

DEPLOYMENT

Legal provisions for foreign deployment:

Constitution: Codified constitution (1815)

Decision on deployment of troops abroad: By the government (Art. 98)

AFGHANISTAN

NATO • ISAF 380

BOSNIA-HERZEGOVINA
EU • EUFOR • *Operation Althea* 75
OSCE • Bosnia and Herzegovina 2

GULF OF ADEN & INDIAN OCEAN
EU • *Operation Atalanta* 1 AORH

IRAQ
NATO • NTM-I 7

MEDITERRANEAN SEA
NATO • *Operation Active Endeavour* 1 DDGHM

MIDDLE EAST
UN • UNTSO 12 obs

NORTH SEA
NATO • SNMCMG 1: 1 MHO

SERBIA
NATO • KFOR 8
OSCE • Serbia 2
OSCE • Kosovo 3

SUDAN
UN • UNAMID 2
UN • UNMIS 2; 12 obs

FOREIGN FORCES

United Kingdom Air Force 120
United States US European Command: 477

Norway NOR

Norwegian Kroner kr		2009	2010	2011
GDP	kr	2.38tr	2.53tr	
	US$	381bn	418bn	
per capita	US$	78,858	86,082	
Growth	%	-1.6	1.2	
Inflation	%	2.2	2.5	
Def exp	kr	38.8bn		
	US$	6.2bn		
Def bdgt	kr	33.5bn	34.9bn	39.2bn
	US$	5.36bn	5.77bn	
US$1=kr		6.25	6.05	

Population	4,855,315					

Age	0–14	15–19	20–24	25–29	30–64	65 plus
Male	9.2%	3.4%	3.3%	3.0%	23.7%	7.0%
Female	8.8%	3.3%	3.2%	2.9%	23.2%	9.0%

Capabilities

ACTIVE 26,450 (Army 8,900, Navy 3,750, Air 5,550, Central Support 7,750, Home Guard 500)
Terms of service: conscription with maximum 18 months of duty. Conscripts initially serve 12 months at the age of 19 to 21, and then up to 4–5 refresher training periods until the age of 35, 44, 55 or 60 depending on rank and function. Numbers above include conscripts during initial service.

RESERVE 45,250 (Army 270, Navy 320, Central Support 350, Home Guard 44,250)
Reserves: readiness varies from a few hours to several days

ORGANISATIONS BY SERVICE

Army 4,500; 4,400 conscript (total 8,900)

The Norwegian Army consists of one mechanised brigade – Brigade North – one border guard battalion, one guard infantry battalion (His Majesty The King's Guard), one special operations regiment and one joint logistic/support centre. Brigade North trains new personnel of all categories, provides units for international operations, and is a low readiness brigade. At any time around 1/3 of the brigade will be trained and ready to conduct operations across the whole spectrum of operations. The Brigade also includes one high readiness mechanised battalion (Telemark Battalion) with combat support and combat service support units on high readiness. Other organisational elements are the Army Land Warfare Centre, the Army Special Operations Command and the Army Military Academy. Joint Command is exercised from The Norwegian National Joint Headquarters.

FORCES BY ROLE

Recce	1 (Border Guard) lt bn with (3 coy (HQ/ Garrison, Border Control & Trg))
Mech Inf	1 bde (2 mech inf bn, 1 lt inf bn, 1 arty bn, 1 ISTAR bn, 1 engr bn, 1 CIS bn, 1 spt bn, 1 med bn, 1 MP coy)
Inf	1 bn (His Majesty The King's Guards)
SF	1 (SOF) comd with (1 regt)

EQUIPMENT BY TYPE
MBT 72: 52 *Leopard* 2A4; 20 *Leopard* 1A5NO (for trg only)
AIFV 104 CV9030N
APC 390
  APC (T) 315 M-113 (incl variants)
  APC (W) 75 XA-186 *Sisu*/XA-200 *Sisu*
ARTY 316
  SP 155mm 54 M-109A3GN
  MOR 262:
  SP 36: 81mm 24 M-106A1; 12 M-125A2
  81mm 226 L-16
AT
  MANPATS 514: 424 *Eryx*; 90 *Javelin*
  RCL 84mm 2,517 *Carl Gustav*
  RL 66mm M-72 *LAW*
RADAR • LAND 12 ARTHUR
FACILITIES
Bases 5 (Finnmark, Østerdalen, Oslo, Romerike and Tromso)

Navy 2,300; 1,450 conscripts (total 3,750)

Joint Command – Norwegian National Joint Headquarters. The Royal Norwegian Navy is organised into four elements under the command of the Chief of Staff of the Navy; the naval units '*Kysteskadren*', the schools '*Sjoforsvarets Skoler*', the naval bases and the coast guard '*Kystvakten*'.

FORCES BY ROLE
SF   1 Sqn

ISTAR   1 coy (Coastal Rangers)
EOD   1 plt

EQUIPMENT BY TYPE
SUBMARINES • TACTICAL • SSK 6 *Ulla* each with 8 single 533mm TT each with A3 *Seal* DM2 HWT
PRINCIPAL SURFACE COMBATANTS •
DESTROYERS 5
   DDGHM 5 *Fridjof Nansen* each with 2 quad (8 eff.) each with NSM AShM (under acquisition), 1 8 cell Mk41 VLS with ESSM SAM, 2 twin 324mm ASTT (4 eff.) each with *Sting Ray* LWT, 1 76mm, (capacity NH-90 TTH hel)
PATROL AND COASTAL COMBATANTS • PCFGM 6
   6 *Skjold* each with 8 NSM AShM; 1 twin lnchr (2 eff.) with *Mistral* SAM; 1 76mm gun
MINE WARFARE 6
   MINE COUNTERMEASURES • MSC 3 *Alta* **MHC** 3 *Oksoy*
AMPHIBIOUS • LANDING CRAFT 12
   LCP 12 S90N
LOGISTICS AND SUPPORT 13
   ATS 1 *Valkyrien*
   AGI 1 *Marjata*
   AGS 1 *HU Sverdrup II*
   RY 1 *Norge*
   TRG 2 *Hessa*
   YDT 7

FACILITIES
Bases   Located at Bergen, Ramsund and Trondenes and Sortland (Coast Guard)

Coast Guard
PATROL AND COASTAL COMBATANTS 14
   PSO 8: 3 *Barentshav*; 1 *Svalbard* with 1 hel landing platform; 1 *Harstad*; 3 *Nordkapp* each with 1 hel landing platform
   PCO 6: 1 *Aalesund*; 5 *Nornen*;

Air Force 2,700; 850 conscript (total 3,550)
Joint Command – Norwegian National HQ

Flying hours   180 hrs/year

FORCES BY ROLE
FGA   3 sqn with F-16AM/BM *Fighting Falcon*
MP   1 sqn with P-3C *Orion*; P-3N *Orion* (pilot trg)
EW   1 sqn with *Falcon* 20C (EW, Flight Inspection Service)
SAR   1 sqn with *Sea King* MK43B
Tpt   1 sqn with C-130J *Hercules*
Trg   1 sqn with MFI-15 SAAB *Safari*
Tpt Hel   2 sqn with Bell 412SP; 1 sqn with *Lynx* Mk86
SAM   1 reinforced bty with NASAMS II

EQUIPMENT BY TYPE
AIRCRAFT 63 combat capable
   FTR 57 F-16AM/F-16BM *Fighting Falcon*
   ASW 6: 4 P-3C *Orion*; 2 P-3N *Orion* (pilot trg)
   EW 3 *Falcon* 20C
   TPT • Medium 4 C-130J *Hercules*
   TRG 15 MFI-15 *Safari*
HELICOPTERS
   ASW 6 *Lynx* Mk86 (to be replaced by 14 NH-90 from 2012)

   SAR 12 *Sea King* Mk43B
   MRH 18 Bell 412SP
AD
   SAM
      TOWED NASAMS
   MSL
      AAM • IR AAM AIM-9L *Sidewinder;* **IIR AAM** *IRIS-T*
      ARH AAM AIM-120B AMRAAM
BOMBS
   Laser-guided: EGBU-12 *Paveway* II
   INS/GPS guided: JDAM

FACILITIES
Bases: Rygge, Bodo, Ørland, Bardufoss, Gardemoen, Andoeya

Central Support, Administration and Command 6,750; 1,000 conscripts (total 7,750)

Central Support, Administration and Command includes military personnel in all joint elements including, among others, the Ministry of Defence, the NJHQ, the Norwegian Defence Logistics Organisation (NDLO), the Norwegian Armed Forces Medical Services, the Defence Command and Staff College, the CIS and intelligence communities. Several of these elements do not provide forces as such, but others do, and they are responsible for logistics and CIS in support of all forces in Norway and abroad

Home Guard 500 (total 500 – with 46,000 reserves)

The Home Guard is a separate organisation, but closely cooperates with all services. The Home Guard can be mobilised on very short notice for local security operations. The main body of the Home Guard are land forces, but it also includes smaller elements for naval and air operations support. The Home Guard relies on recruitment and basic training conducted in the services, while basic officer training is partly done within the Home Guard organisation. The Home Guard has its own tactics and weapons centre.

Land Home Guard 42,650 with reserves

11 Home Guard Districts with mobile Rapid Reaction Forces (5,000 troops in total) as well as reinforcements and follow-on forces (37,150 troops in total). The reinforcements and follow-on forces are organised in company size 'Home Guard Areas', mainly intended for local security operations

Naval Home Guard 1,900 with reserves

Consisting of Rapid Reaction Forces with a total of 500 troops, and 17 'Naval Home Guard Areas' with a total of 1,250 troops. The Naval Home Guard is equipped with 2 vessels of the *Reine* class and 12 smaller vessels, deployed along the Norwegian coastline. In addition, a number of civilian vessels can be requisitioned as required.

Air Home Guard 1,450 with reserves

Provides force protection and security detachments for air bases.

DEPLOYMENT

Legal provisions for foreign deployment:
Constitution: Codified constitution (1814)
Decision on deployment of troops abroad: By royal prerogative exercised by the government (Art. 25, 26)

AFGHANISTAN
NATO • ISAF 351; 1 mech inf coy; 1 spt coy
UN • UNAMA 2 obs

BOSNIA-HERZEGOVINA
OSCE • Bosnia and Herzegovina 1

CENTRAL AFRICAN REPUBLIC/CHAD
UN • MINURCAT 1

DEMOCRATIC REPUBLIC OF THE CONGO
UN • MONUSCO 1 obs

EGYPT
MFO 3

MIDDLE EAST
UN • UNTSO 13 obs

NORTH SEA
NATO • SNMCMG 1: 1 MHC

SERBIA
NATO • KFOR 5
OSCE • Serbia 3
UN • UNMIK 1

SUDAN
UN • UNMIS 6; 13 obs

FOREIGN FORCES

United States US European Command: 1 (APS) 155mm SP Arty bn eqpt. set
NATO Joint Warfare Centre (JWC)/ACT situated Stavanger; E-3A Fwd Op Location at Ørland air base

Poland POL

Polish Zloty z		2009	2010	2011
GDP	z	1.34tr	1.40tr	
	US$	434bn	463bn	
per capita	US$	11,376	12,163	
Growth	%	1.7	3.1	
Inflation	%	3.9	2.4	
Def exp	z	22.6bn		
	US$	7.3bn		
Def bdgt	z	22.8bn	25.2bn	25.3bn
	US$	7.36bn	8.35bn	
FMA (US)	US$	27.0m	47.0m	42.0m
US$1=z		3.10	3.02	

Population	38,038,094					

Age	0–14	15–19	20–24	25–29	30–64	65 plus
Male	7.6%	3.1%	3.6%	4.3%	24.6%	5.2%
Female	7.1%	3.0%	3.5%	4.2%	25.3%	8.4%

Capabilities

ACTIVE 100,000 (Army 47,300, Navy 8,000, Air 17,500, Special Forces 1,650, Joint 25,550)
Paramilitary 21,400

ORGANISATIONS BY SERVICE

Land Forces Command 47,300

Land Forces Command directly controls airmobile bdes and their avn. Transition to lighter forces is continuing but is hampered by lack of funds.

FORCES BY ROLE

Comd	1 (2nd) mech corps HQ; elm 1 (MNC NE) corps HQ
Armd	1 (armd cav) div (11th) with (2 armd cav bde, 1 mech bde, 1 recce bn, 1 arty bn, 2 AD regt, 1 engr bn)
Recce	3 regt
Mech	1 div (1st) with (1 armd bde, 1 mech bde, 1 mtn bde, 1 recce bn, 1 arty regt, 1 AD regt, 1 engr bn); 1 div (12th) with (2 mech bde, 1 (coastal) mech bde, 1 arty regt, 2 AD regt, 1 engr bn); 1 div (16th) with (1 armd cav bde, 2 mech bde, 1 recce bn, 1 arty regt, 1 AD regt, 1 AT regt, 1 engr bn)
Air Mob	1 (air aslt) bde (6th) with (2 air aslt, 1 para bn), 1 (air cav) bde (25th) (2 tpt hel bn, 2 air cav bn, 1 (casevac) med unit)
Arty	2 bde
Engr	2 bde; 1 regt
Chemical	1 regt, 1 bn
Avn	1 (cbt) regt (49th) with (3 atk hel sqn with Mi-24, 1 ISR sqn with Mi-2); 1 (cbt) regt (56th) with (1 atk hel sqn with Mi-24V; 2 ISR sqn with Mi-2; 1 tpt hel sqn with Mi-2)

EQUIPMENT BY TYPE
MBT 946: 128 *Leopard* 2 2A4; 232 PT-91 *Twardy*; 586 T-72/T-72M1D/T-72M1
RECCE 376 BRDM-2
AIFV 1,536: 1,297 BMP-1; 239 *Rosomak (Patria)*
APC • APC (W) 40 *Cougar*
ARTY 1,136
  SP 608: **122mm** 522 2S1 *Carnation*; **152mm** 86 M-77 *Dana*
  MRL 122mm 291: 205 BM-21; 30 RM-70; 56 WR-40 *Langusta*
  MOR 237: **98mm** 99 M-98; **120mm** 138 M-120
AT • MSL • MANPATS 327: 129 9K11 *Malyutka* (AT-3 *Sagger*); 77 9K111 *Fagot* (AT-4 *Spigot*); 18 9K113 *Konkurs* (AT-5 *Spandrel*); 7 9K115 *Metis* (AT-7 *Saxhorn*); 96 *Spike* LR
AD
  SAM 971
    SP 144: 80 GROM *Poprad*; 64 9K33 *Osa-AK* (SA-8 *Gecko)*
    MANPAD 582: 246 9K32 *Strela-2* (SA-7 *Grail*), 336 GROM
  GUNS 441
    SP 23mm 37: 36 ZSU-23-4; 1 SPAAG

TOWED 23mm 404 ZU-23-2
RADAR • LAND SNAR-10 *Big Fred* (veh, arty)
HELICOPTERS
  ATK 31 Mi-24D *Hind D*
  MRH 35: 13 Mi-17T/U *Hip H*; 22 PZL Mi-2URP *Hoplite*
  MRH/TPT 37 PZL W-3A *Sokol* (med tpt)/W-3W *Sokol* (MRH)
  TPT 78: **Medium** 17 Mi-8T/U *Hip* **Light** 61: 24 PZL Mi-2 *Hoplite*

Navy 8,000

Comd	Navy HQ
	1 Surface Combatant Flotilla
	1 Coastal Defence Flotilla
	1 Naval Aviation bde (3 Naval Sqn)

EQUIPMENT BY TYPE
SUBMARINES • TACTICAL 5
  SSK 5:
    4 *Sokol* (Type-207) each with 8 single 533mm TT
    1 *Orzel* (ex-*Kilo*) with 6 single 533mm TT each with T-53/T-65 HWT
PRINCIPAL SURFACE COMBATANTS 8
  FRIGATES 2
    FFGHM 2 *Pulaski* (US *Oliver Hazard Perry* class) each with 1 Mk 13 GMLS with RGM-84D/F *Harpoon* AShM/SM-1MR SAM, 2 triple 324mm ASTT (6 eff.) each with A244 LWT, 1 76mm gun, (capacity: 2 SH-2G *Super Seasprite* ASW hel)
PATROL AND COASTAL COMBATANTS 6:
  CORVETTES • FSM 1 *Kaszub* with 1 quad lnchr (4 eff.) with 9K32 *Strela*-2 (SA-N-5 *Grail*) SAM, 2 twin 533mm ASTT (4 eff.) with SET-53 HWT, 2 RBU 6000 *Smerch 2* (24 eff.), 1 76mm gun
  PCFGM 5:
    3 *Orkan* (GDR *Sassnitz*. Refit programme in progress) each with 2 quad lnchr (8 eff.) each with RBS-15 Mk2 AShM 1 quad lnchr (manual aiming) with *Strela*-2 (SA-N-5 *Grail*) SAM, 1 76mm gun
    2 *Tarantul* each with 2 twin lnchr (4 eff.) each with P-15M *Termit-M* (SS-N-2C *Styx*) AShM, 1 quad lnchr (manual aiming) with 9K32 *Strela*-2 (SA-N-5 *Grail*) SAM, 1 76mm gun
MINE WARFARE • MINE COUNTERMEASURES 20
  MHO 3 *Krogulec*
  MHI 4 *Mamry*
  MSI 13 *Goplo*
AMPHIBIOUS 8
  LANDING SHIPS • LSM 5 *Lublin* (capacity 9 tanks; 135 troops)
  LANDING CRAFT • LCU 3 *Deba* (capacity 50 troops)
LOGISTICS AND SUPPORT 33
  AORL 1
  AOL 1
  MRV 1 Project 890
  ARS 4
  AGI 2 *Moma*
  AGS 8: 2; 6 (coastal)
  ATF 3
  TRG 6: 1 AXS

YDG 2
YTM 5
FACILITIES
Bases Located at Kolobrzeg, Gdynia (HQ), Swinoujscie, Hel Peninsula (Spt), Gdynia-Babie Doly

Naval Aviation 1,300

FORCES BY ROLE

ASW/ SAR	1 sqn with MI-14PL *Haze A*; MI-14PS *Haze C*; 1 sqn with PZL W-3RM *Anakonda*; SH-2G *Super Seasprite*
Tpt	1 sqn with An-28B1R; An-28E; 1 sqn with An-28TD; Mi-17 *Hip H*; PZL Mi-2 *Hoplite*; PZL W-3RM; PZL W-3TT

EQUIPMENT BY TYPE
AIRCRAFT
  MP 10: 8 An-28B1R *Bryza*; 2 An-28E *Bryza* (ecological monitoring)
  TPT • Light 2 An-28TD *Bryza*
HELICOPTERS
  ASW 12: 8 Mi-14PL *Haze*; 4 SH-2G *Super Seasprite*
  MRH 2 Mi-17 *Hip H*;
  SAR 9: 2 Mi-14PS *Haze C*; 7 PZL W-3RM *Anakonda*
  TPT 4 **Medium** 2 PZL W-3T *Sokol* **Light** 2 PZL Mi-2 *Hoplite*

Air Force 17,500

Flying hours   160 to 200 hrs/year

FORCES BY ROLE
2 tac air wg: 1st (5 sqn); 2nd (3 sqn); 1 tpt air wg: 3rd (4 sqn); 1 spec air tpt: 36th
2 rocket AD bdes (1st & 3rd), 2 rocket AD regt (61st & 78th)

Ftr	2 sqn with MiG-29A/UB *Fulcrum*
FGA	3 sqn with F-16C/D Block 52+ *Fighting Falcon*
FGA/ISR	3 sqn with Su-22M-4 *Fitter*
Tpt	4 sqn with C-130E; C-295M; PZL M-28 *Bryza*. 1 regt with Tu-154M; Yak-40
Trg	Some units with An-28 *Cash*; PZL-130 *Orlik*; TS-11 *Iskra*
Tpt Hel	2 sqn with Bell 412 *Twin Huey* Mi-2; Mi-17; PZL W-3 *Sokol*; SW-4 *Puszczyk* (trg)
SAM	2 bde with S-125 *Neva* (SA-3 *Goa*); 1 indep regt with S-125 *Neva* (SA-3 *Goa*); S-200 *Angara* (SA-5 *Gammon*); 1 indep regt with 2K11 *Krug* (SA-4 *Ganef*)

EQUIPMENT BY TYPE
AIRCRAFT 125 combat capable
  FTR 32: 26 MiG-29A *Fulcrum*; 6 MiG-29UB *Fulcrum*
  FGA 83: 36 F-16C Block 52+ *Fighting Falcon*; 12 F-16D Block 52+ *Fighting Falcon*; 35 Su-22M-4 *Fitter*
  TPT 34 **Medium** 2 C-130E *Hercules* **Light** 33: 11 C-295M; 16 M-28 *Bryza* TD; 4 Yak-40 *Codling* **PAX** 1 Tu-154 *Careless*
  TRG 72: 28 PZL-130 *Orlik*; 44 TS-11 *Iskra*
HELICOPTERS
  MRH 11: 1 Bell 412 *Twin Huey*; 10 Mi-17 *Hip H*

TPT 65 **Medium** 19 PZL W-3 *Sokol*; **Light** 46: 22 PZL Mi-2 Hoplite; 24 SW-4 *Puszczyk* (trg)
AD • SAM 90 S-125 *Neva* (SA-3 *Goa*)
SP 78; 60 S-125 *Neva* (SA-3 Goa), 14 2K11 *Krug* (SA-4 *Ganef*)
STATIC 12 S-200 *Vega* (SA-5 *Gammon*)
MSL
AAM • IR AAM R-60 (AA-8 *Aphid*); R-73 (AA-11 *Archer*), AIM-9 *Sidewinder*, **ARH AAM** AIM-120C AMRAAM
ASM Kh-23 (AS-7 *Kerry*)†; AGM-65J/G *Maverick*
FACILITIES
4 Control and Reporting Centres

Special Forces 1,650

FORCES BY ROLE
SF   3 units (GROM, FORMOZA & Cdo)
Spt   1 Cbt Spt/Spt unit

Paramilitary 21,400

Border Guards 14,100
Ministry of Interior and Administration

Maritime Border Guard
PATROL AND COASTAL COMBATANTS 19:2 PCC; 6 **PBF**; 8 **PB**
AMPHIBIOUS • LANDING CRAFT • UCAC 2

Prevention Units of Police 6,300; 1,000 conscript (total 7,300)
OPP–Ministry of Interior

DEPLOYMENT

Legal provisions for foreign deployment:
Constitution: Codified constitution (1997)
Decision on deployment of troops abroad: a) By president on request of prime minister in cases of direct threat (Art. 136);
b) in general, specified by ratified international agreement or statute (both must be passed by parliament, Art. 117)

AFGHANISTAN
NATO • ISAF 2,417; 1 armd bde HQ with (2 inf BG); 35 *Rosomak*; 68 other IFV; 6 Mi-24 *Hind*; 4 Mi-17 *Hip*
UN • UNAMA 1 obs

ARMENIA/AZERBAIJAN
OSCE • Minsk Conference 1

BOSNIA-HERZEGOVINA
EU • EUFOR • *Operation Althea* 184; 1 inf coy

CENTRAL AFRICAN REPUBLIC/CHAD
UN • MINURCAT 2

CÔTE D'IVOIRE
UN • UNOCI 3 obs

DEMOCRATIC REPUBLIC OF THE CONGO
UN • MONUSCO 3 obs

IRAQ
NATO • NTM-I 3

LIBERIA
UN • UNMIL 2 obs

MOLDOVA
OSCE • Moldova 1

NORTH SEA
NATO • SNMCMG 1: 1 MRV

SERBIA
NATO • KFOR 152; 1 inf coy
OSCE • Kosovo 4
UN • UNMIK 1 obs

SUDAN
UN • UNMIS 1 obs

WESTERN SAHARA
UN • MINURSO 1 obs

FOREIGN FORCES
Germany Army: 67 (GER elm Corps HQ (multinational))

Portugal PRT

Euro €		2009	2010	2011
GDP	€	168bn	171bn	
	US$	233bn	226bn	
per capita	US$	21,960	21,099	
Growth	%	-2.7	0.2	
Inflation	%	-0.8	0.9	
Def exp[a]	€	2.66bn		
	US$	3.71bn		
Def bdgt	€	1.82bn	2.41bn	2.42bn
	US$	2.54bn	3.19bn	
US$1=€		0.72	0.76	

[a] including military pensions

Population	10,732,357

Age	0–14	15–19	20–24	25–29	30–64	65 plus
Male	8.5%	3.0%	3.2%	3.5%	23.3%	7.4%
Female	7.8%	2.6%	2.8%	3.1%	24.3%	10.6%

Capabilities

ACTIVE 43,340 (Army 26,700 Navy10,540 Air 7,100)
Paramilitary 47,700

RESERVE 210,900 (Army 210,000 Navy 900)
Reserve obligation to age 35

ORGANISATIONS BY SERVICE

Army 26,700
5 Territorial Comd (2 mil region, 1 mil district, 2 mil zone)

FORCES BY ROLE

Rapid Reaction	1 bde with (1 (RI 3) inf bn, 1 AT coy, 1 recce sqn, 1 AD bty, 1 engr coy, 1 fd arty bn, 2 (RI 10 and 15) para bn)
Mech inf	1 bde with (1 (RC4) tk regt, 2 (1st and 2nd) mech inf bn)
Lt inf	1 (intervention) bde with (1 (RC 6) cav regt, 1 (RE3) engr bn, 1 (RAAA 1) AD bn, 1 (RA4) fd arty bn, 3 (RI13,14 and 19) inf bn)
Spec Ops	1 unit
Cdo	1 bn
MP	1 regt
Garrison	2 (Madeira and Azores) gp (Madeira 2 inf bn (RG 1 and RG 2), Azores 1 inf bn (RG 3) 1 AD unit)

Reserves 210,000 reservists

Territorial Def   3 bde (on mob)

EQUIPMENT BY TYPE

MBT 225: 38 *Leopard* 2A6; 86 M-60A3; 8 M-60A4; 7 M-60; 86 M-48A5
RECCE 40: 15 V-150 *Chaimite*; 25 ULTRAV M-11
APC 473
  APC (T) 280: 240 M-113; 40 M-577 A2
  APC (W) 193: 73 V-200 *Chaimite*; 120 *Pandur II*
ARTY 350+
  SP 155mm 20: 6 M-109A2; 14 M-109A5
  TOWED 135: **105mm** 97: 21 L-119; 52 M-101; 24 M-56; **155mm** 38 M-114A1
  COASTAL 21: **150mm** 9; **152mm** 6; **234mm** 6 (inactive)
  MOR 174+: **81mm** (incl 21 SP); **107mm** 76 M-30 (incl 14 SP); **120mm** 98 *Tampella*
AT
  MSL • MANPATS 118: 68 *Milan* (incl 6 ULTRAV-11); 50 TOW (incl 18 M-113, 4 M-901)
  RCL 402: **106mm** 128 M-40; **84mm** 162 *Carl Gustav*; **90mm** 112
AD
  SAM • MANPAD 52: 37 *Chaparral*; 15 FIM-92A *Stinger*
  GUNS • TOWED 93: **20mm** 31 Rh 202; **40mm** 62 L/60

Navy 9,110; (total 10,540) incl Marines

EQUIPMENT BY TYPE

SUBMARINES • TACTICAL • SSK 1 *Tridente* (GER Type 209) with 8 533mm TT (2nd vessel awaiting commissioning)
PRINCIPAL SURFACE COMBATANTS • FRIGATES • FFGHM 5
  3 *Vasco Da Gama* each with 2 Mk 141 *Harpoon* quad (8 eff.) with RGM-84C *Harpoon* AShM, 1 octuple Mk 29 GMLS with RIM-7M *Sea Sparrow* SAM, 2 Mk36 triple 324mm ASTT each with Mk 46 LWT, 1 100mm gun, (capacity 2 *Lynx* Mk95 (*Super Lynx*) hel)
  2 *Karel Dorman* class (*ex*-NLD) each with 2 quad Mk 141 lnchr (8 eff.) each with RGM-84C *Harpoon* AShM, 1 Mk48 VLS with RIM-7M *Sea Sparrow* SAM, 2 Mk32 twin 324mm ASTT each with Mk46 LWT, 1 76mm gun, (capacity: 1 *Lynx* Mk95 (*Super Lynx*) hel)

PATROL AND COASTAL COMBATANTS 24
  CORVETTES • FSH 7
    3 *Baptista de Andrade* each with 1 100mm gun, 1 hel landing platform
    4 *Joao Coutinho* each with 1 twin 76mm gun (2 eff.), 1 hel landing platform
  PSO 2 *Viana do Castelo* each with 1 hel landing platform (2 additional vessels in build)
  PCC 3 *Cacine*
  PBR 12: 2 *Albatroz*; 5 *Argos*; 4 *Centauro*; 1 *Rio Minho*
AMPHIBIOUS • LANDING CRAFT • LCU 1
LOGISTICS AND SUPPORT 10:
  AORL 1 *Bérrio* (ex UK *Rover*) with 1 hel landing platform (for medium hel)
  AGS 4
  ABU 2
  TRG 3 AXS

FACILITIES

Base	Located at Lisbon
Naval air base	Located at Montijo
Support bases	Leca da Palmeira (North), Portimao (South), Funchal (Madiera), Ponta Delgada (Azores)

Marines 1,430

FORCES BY ROLE

Police	1 det
Lt inf	2 bn
Spec Ops	1 det
Fire spt	1 coy

EQUIPMENT BY TYPE

APC(W) 4 *Pandur* II
ARTY •MOR 15 120mm

Naval Aviation

HELICOPTERS • ASW 5 *Lynx* Mk95 (*Super Lynx*)

Air Force 7,100

Flying hours   180 hrs/year on F-16 *Fighting Falcon*

FORCES BY ROLE

1 (op) COFA comd; 5 (op) gp

FGA	1 sqn with F-16A/B *Fighting Falcon*; 1 sqn with F-16 MLU *Fighting Falcon*
MP	1 sqn with P-3P/C *Orion*
ISR	1 (survey) sqn with CASA 212B *Aviocar*
CSAR/SAR	1 sqn with with AW-101 *Merlin*; SA-330S *Puma*
Tpt	1 sqn with C-130H *Hercules*; 1 sqn with C-212 *Aviocar* (to be replaced by CN-295M); 1 (liaison) sqn with FTB-337; 1 sqn with *Falcon* 50
Trg	1 sqn with *Alpha Jet*; 1 sqn with SA-316 *Alouette III*; 1 sqn with TB-30 *Epsilon*

EQUIPMENT BY TYPE

AIRCRAFT 70 combat capable
  FTR 39: 16 F-16A *Fighting Falcon*; 3 F-16B *Fighting Falcon*; (20 F-16 MLU)
  ASW 6 P-3P *Orion*
  ISR 14: 2 C-212B *Aviocar*; 12 FTB-337 (being phased out)

TPT 34: **Medium** 6 C-130H *Hercules* (tpt/SAR) **Light** 25: 24 C-212A *Aviocar* (tpt/SAR, Nav/ECM trg, fisheries protection); 1 C-295 (11 more on order) **PAX** 3 *Falcon 50* (tpt/VIP)
TRG 41: 25 *Alpha Jet** (FGA/trg); 16 TB-30 *Epsilon*
HELICOPTERS
  MRH 18 SA-316 *Alouette III* (trg, utl)
  TPT • Medium 16: 12 AW-101 *Merlin* (6 SAR, 4 CSAR, 2 fishery protection); 4 SA-330S *Puma* (SAR)
UAV • Unknown 34 *Armor X7*
MSL
  AAM IRAAM AIM-9J/AIM-9L/AIM-9P *Sidewinder*; **SARH AAM** AIM-7M *Sparrow*; **ARH AAM** AIM-120 AMRAAM
  ASM AGM-65A *Maverick*; AShM AGM-84A *Harpoon*
BOMBS
  Laser-guided: *Paveway* II

Paramilitary 47,700

National Republican Guard 26,100
APC (W): some *Commando* Mk III (*Bravia*)
HELICOPTERS • MRH 7 SA-315 *Lama*

Public Security Police 21,600

DEPLOYMENT

Legal provisions for foreign deployment:
Constitution: Codified constitution (1976)
Decision on deployment of troops abroad: By government

AFGHANISTAN
NATO • ISAF 26
UN • UNAMA 1 obs

BOSNIA-HERZEGOVINA
EU • EUFOR • *Operation Althea* 51
OSCE • Bosnia and Herzegovina 2

LEBANON
UN • UNIFIL 146; 1 engr coy

SERBIA
NATO • KFOR 301; 1 AB bn (KTM)
OSCE • Kosovo 4

TIMOR LESTE
UN • UNMIT 3 obs

UGANDA
EU • EUTM 15

FOREIGN FORCES

United States US European Command: 705; 1 spt facility at Lajes

Romania ROM

Lei		2009	2010	2011
GDP	lei	491bn	511bn	
	US$	162bn	162bn	
per capita	US$	7,519	7,627	
Growth	%	-8.5	-0.5	
Inflation	%	5.6	5.9	
Def exp	lei	6.77bn		
	US$	2.23bn		
Def bdgt	lei	6.96bn	6.78bn	7.16bn
	US$	2.29bn	2.14bn	
FMA (US)	US$	12.0m	13.0m	16.5m
US$1=lei		3.04	3.17	

Population   21,190,154

Ethnic groups: Hungarian 9%

Age	0–14	15–19	20–24	25–29	30–64	65 plus
Male	7.6%	2.8%	3.8%	3.8%	24.7%	6.0%
Female	7.2%	2.7%	3.6%	3.6%	25.3%	8.8%

Capabilities

ACTIVE 71,745 (Army 42,500, Navy 7,345, Air 8,400, Joint 13,500) **Paramilitary 79,900**

RESERVE 45,000 (Joint 45,000)

ORGANISATIONS BY SERVICE

Army 42,500
FORCES BY ROLE
Readiness is reported as 70–90% for NATO designated forces and 40–70% for other forces)

Comd	3 div HQ (1 NATO designated)
Mech Inf	5 bde (1 NATO designated)
Inf	2 bde (1 NATO designated)
Mtn Inf	2 bde (1 NATO designated)
Arty	1 bde; 3 regt
AD	2 regt
Engr	1 bde

EQUIPMENT BY TYPE
MBT 345: 249 T-55; 42 TR-580; 54 TR-85 M1
AIFV 20 MLI-84
APC 1,616
  APC (T) 75 MLVM
  APC (W 988: 69 B33 TAB *Zimbru*; 31 *Piranha III*; 374 TAB-71; 150 TAB-77; 364 TABC-79
  TYPE VARIANTS 553 APC
ARTY 870
  SP 122mm 24: 6 2S1 *Carnation*; 18 Model 89
  TOWED 388: **122mm** 40 (M-30) M-1938 (A-19); **152mm** 348: 245 M-1981 Model 81; 103 M-1985

Europe

MRL 122mm 187: 133 APR-40; 54 LAROM
MOR 120mm 271 M-1982
AT
MSL • SP 138: 12 9P122 BRDM-2 *Malyutka*; 78 9P133
BRDM-2 *Malyutka*; 48 9P148 BRDM-2 *Konkurs*
GUNS 100mm 231: 208 M1977 Gun 77; 23 SU-100 SP
AD • GUNS 78
SP 35mm 36 *Gepard*
TOWED 42: **35mm** 24 GDF-203; **37mm** 18
RADARS • LAND 8 SNAR-10 *Big Fred*

Navy 7,345

Navy HQ with 1 Naval Operational Component, 1 Fleet
Command, 1 Frigate Flotilla, 1 Riverine Flotilla (Danube
based)

EQUIPMENT BY TYPE
PRINCIPAL SURFACE COMBATANTS 3
DESTROYERS 3:
DDGH 1 *Marasesti* with 4 twin lnchr (8 eff.) each with
P-15M *Termit-M* (SS-N-2C *Styx*) AShM, 2 triple 533mm
ASTT (6 eff.) with RUS 53–65 ASW, 2 RBU 6000 *Smerch*
2 (24 eff.), 2 twin 76mm gun (4 eff.), (capacity 2 SA-316
(IAR-316) *Alouette III* hel)
DDH 2 *Regele Ferdinand* (ex UK Type-22), each with
1 76mm gun (capacity 1 SA330 (IAR-330) *Puma* –
platforms undergoing upgrades)
PATROL AND COASTAL COMBATANTS 21
CORVETTES 4:
FSH 2 *Tetal II* each with 2 twin 533mm ASTT (4 eff.), 2
RBU 6000 *Smerch* 2 (24 eff.), 1 76mm gun, (capacity 1
SA-316 (IAR-316) *Alouette III* hel)
FS 2 *Tetal I* each with 2 twin 533mm ASTT (4 eff.) with
RUS 53-65 ASW, 2 RBU 2500 *Smerch* 1 (32 eff.), 2 twin
76mm gun (4 eff.)
PCFG 3 *Zborul* each with 2 twin lnchr (4 eff.) each with
P-15M *Termit-M* (SS-N-2C *Styx*) AShM, 1 76mm gun
PCR 8:
1 *Brutar* I with 1 BM-21 MRL RL, 1 100mm gun
4 *Brutar* II each with 1 BM-21 MRL RL, 1 100mm gun
3 *Kogalniceanu* each with 2 100mm gun
PBR 6 VD 141 (ex MSI now used for river patrol)
MINE WARFARE 11
MINE COUNTERMEASURES 10
MSO 4 *Musca*
MSI 6 VD 141 (used for river MCM)
MINELAYERS • ML 1 *Corsar* with up to 100 mines
LOGISTICS AND SUPPORT 12: 3 **AOL**; 2 **AGF**; 1 **AGOR**;
1 **AK**; 1 **AXS**; 1 **ADG**; 1 **ARS**; 2 **YTL**
FACILITIES
Base   Located at Tulcea, Braila (Danube),
             Mangalia, Constanta (coast)

Naval Infantry
FORCES BY ROLE
Naval inf 1 bn

EQUIPMENT BY TYPE
APC (W) 14: 11 ABC-79M; 3 TABC-79M

Air Force 8,400

Flying hours 120 hrs/year

FORCES BY ROLE
Ftr   2 sqn with MiG-21 *Lancer* C
FGA   1 sqn with MiG-21 *Lancer* A/*Lancer* B
Tpt   1 sqn with, An-26 *Curl*, An-30 *Clank*; C-27J
            Spartan; 1 tpt sqn with C-130B/H *Hercules*,
Trg   1 sqn with An-2 Colt; 1 sqn with IAR-99
            *Soim**; 1 sqn with SA-316B *Alouette III* (IAR-
            316B);1 sqn with Yak-52 (Iak-52)
Tpt Hel   2 (multi-role) sqns with IAR-330 *Puma*
            SOCAT; 3 sqn with SA-330 *Puma* (IAR-330)
AD   1 bde
Engr   1 regt

EQUIPMENT BY TYPE
AIRCRAFT 70 combat capable
FGA 49: 29 MiG-21 *Lancer* A/B; 20 MiG-21 *Lancer* C
ISR 1 An-30 *Clank*
TPT 20 **Medium** 7: 2 C-27J *Spartan* (5 more on order);
3 C-130B *Hercules*; 2 C-130H *Hercules*; **Light** 13: 9 An-2
Colt; 4 An-26 *Curl*
TRG 33: 10 IAR-99 *Soim**; 11 IAR-99C *Soim**; 12 Yak-52
(Iak-52)
HELICOPTERS
MRH 29: 23 IAR-330 SOCAT *Puma*; 6 SA-316B *Alouette
III* (IAR-316B)
TPT • Medium 35 SA-330 *Puma* (IAR-330)
AD • SAM 6 S-75M3 *Volkhov* (SA-2 *Guideline*); 8 HAWK
PIP III
MSL
AAM • IR AAM R-550 *Magic* 2; *Python* 3;
ASM SPIKE-ER
FACILITIES
Air bases   3 cbt air bases with *Lancer* and *Puma*.
            1 tpt air base
            1 trg air base

Paramilitary 79,900

Border Guards 22,900 (incl conscripts)
Ministry of Interior

Gendarmerie ε57,000
Ministry of Interior

DEPLOYMENT

Legal provisions for foreign deployment:
Constitution: Codified constitution (1991)
Decision on deployment of troops abroad: By parliament
(Art. 62); or b) by president upon parliamentary approval
(Art. 92)

AFGHANISTAN
NATO • ISAF 1,648; 1 inf bn; some TAB-77; some TABC-
79; some *Piranha* IIIC

BOSNIA-HERZEGOVINA
**EU • EUFOR • *Operation Althea* 64
**OSCE • Bosnia and Herzegovina 3

CÔTE D'IVOIRE
UN • UNOCI 6 obs

DEMOCRATIC REPUBLIC OF THE CONGO
UN • MONUSCO 21 obs

IRAQ
NATO • NTM-I 3

LIBERIA
UN • UNMIL 2 obs

NEPAL
UN • UNMIN 7 obs

SERBIA
NATO • KFOR 139; 1 inf coy
OSCE • Kosovo 3
UN • UNMIK 1 obs

SUDAN
UN • UNMIS 10 obs

Serbia SER

Serbian Dinar d		2009	2010	2011
GDP	d	2.90tr	3.10tr	
	US$	43.4bn	40.2bn	
per capita	US$	5,925	4,081	
Growth	%	-2.9	1.6	
Inflation	%	7.8	4.6	
Def exp	d	64.9bn		
	US$	969m		
Def bdgt	d	67.1bn	70.7bn	
	US$	1bn	918m	
FMA (US)	US$	0.8m	1.0m	2.5m
US$1=d		63.1		

Population 9,855,857

Age	0 – 14	15 – 19	20 – 24	25 – 29	30 – 64	65 plus
Male	7.8%	3.0%	3.3%	3.5%	24.5%	6.7%
Female	7.3%	2.8%	3.1%	3.4%	24.9%	9.7%

Capabilities

ACTIVE 29,125 (Army 12,260, Air Force and Air Defence 4,262, Training Command 6,212, MoD 6,391)

RESERVE 50,171
Terms of service 6 months

ORGANISATIONS BY SERVICE

Army 10,460; 1,800 conscripts (12,260 in total)
Reconstruction continues
FORCES BY ROLE
Mech   3 bde (2nd, 3rd and 4th) (each: 1 tk bn, 1 MRL bn, 1 SP arty bn, 1 AD bn, 1 inf bn, 2 mech inf bn,); 1 (1st) bde (2 mech inf bn, 1 inf bn, 1 SP arty bn, 1 MRL bn, 1 AD bn, 1 engr bn)

Gd   1 (ceremonial) bde with (2 MP bn, 1 anti terrorist bn)
SF   1 bde with (1 anti terrorist bn, 1 cdo bn, 1 para bn)
Engr   4 bn
Sig   1 bn
Arty   1 (mixed) bde with (3 arty bn, 1 MRL bn); 7 bn
Riverine 2 det (under review), 2 pontoon br bn
NBC   1 bn

EQUIPMENT BY TYPE
MBT 212: 199 M-84; 13 T-72
RECCE 46: 46 BRDM-2
AIFV 323 M-80
APC 39 BOV VP M-86
ARTY 515
   SP 122mm 67 2S1 *Carnation*
   TOWED 204: **122mm** 78 D-30; **130mm** 18 M-46; **152mm** 36 M-84; **155mm** 72: 66 M-1; 6 M-65
   MRL 81: **128mm** 78: 18 M-63 *Plamen*; 60 M-77 *Organj*; **262mm** 3 *Orkan*
   MOR 163: **82mm** 106 M-69; **120mm** 57: M-74/M-75
AT • MSL
   SP 48 BOV-1 (M-83) AT-3 9K11 *Sagger*
   MANPATS 168: 99 AT-3 9K11 *Sagger*; 69 AT-4 9K111 *Fagot* (*Spigot*)
   RCL 6: 90mm 6 M-79;
AD • SAM 156
   SP 77 2K12 Kub (SA-6 *Gainful*); 12 S-1M (SA-9 *Gaskin*); 5 *SAVA S10M*;
   MANPADS 62: 8 S-2M (SA-7 *Grail*); 54 *Šilo* (SA-16 *Gimlet*)
GUNS 36
   TOWED 40mm: 36 L70 Bofors

River Flotilla
The Serbian-Montenegrin navy was transferred to Montenegro upon independence in 2006, but the Danube flotilla remained in Serbian control. The flotilla is subordinate to the Land Forces.
EQUIPMENT BY TYPE
PATROL AND COASTAL COMBATANTS • PBR 5
MINE WARFARE • MINE COUNTERMEASURES • MSI 4 *Nestin*
AMPHIBOUS • LANDING CRAFT • LCU 5 Type 22
LOGISTICS AND SUPPORT 4:
   ADG 1 *Šabac*
   AGF 1 *Kozara*
   AOL 1
   YTL 1

Reserve Organisations
Territorial brigades 8.

Air Force and Air Defence 3,785 (plus 477 conscripts) Total 4,262
Comprises a Cmd HQ, 2 air bases (Batajnica near Belgrade and Ladevci, central Serbia), 1 SAM bde; 1 centre for early warning and reporting, 1 comms bn and 1 eng bn.

Flying hours: Ftr – 40 per yr

FORCES BY ROLE

Ftr 1 sqn with MiG-21bis *Fishbed*; MiG-29 *Fulcrum*

FGA 1 sqn with G-4 *Super Galeb**; J-22 *Orao*

ISR 2 flt with IJ-22 *Orao 1**; MiG-21R *Fishbed H**

Tpt 1 sqn with An-2; An-26; Do-28; Yak-40 (Jak-40),

Trg 1 sqn with G-4 *Super Galeb** (adv trg/light atk); SA-341/342 *Gazelle*; Utva-75 (basic trg);

Atk Hel 1 sqn with Hn-42/45 and Mi-24

Tpt Hel 1 sqn with Mi-8; Mi-17; Mi-24

AD 1 bde (4 bn) with S-125 *Pechora* (SA-3 *Goa*); 2K12 *Buk* (SA-6 *Gainful*); 9K32 *Strela*-2 (SA-7 *Grail*); 9K310 *Igla*-1 (SA-16 *Gimlet*)

Radar 2 bn (for early warning and reporting)

EQUIPMENT BY TYPE

AIRCRAFT 83 combat capable

FTR 29: 20 MiG-21bis *Fishbed L & N*; 5 MiG-21UM *Mongol B*; 3 MiG-29 *Fulcrum*; 1 MiG-29UB *Fulcrum*

FGA 22 J-22 *Orao 1*

ISR 12: 10 IJ-22R *Orao 1**; 2 MiG-21R *Fishbed H**

TPT • Light 8: 1 An-2 *Colt*; 4 An-26 *Curl*; 1 Do-28 *Skyservant*; 2 Yak-40 (Jak-40)

TRG 28: 20 G-4 *Super Galeb**; 8 Utva-75

HELICOPTERS

ATK 2 Mi-24 *Hind*

MRH 54: 2 Mi-17 *Hip H*; 2 SA-341H *Gazelle* (HI-42); 34 SA-341H *Gazelle* (HN-42)/SA-342L *Gazelle* (HN-45); 16 SA-341H *Gazelle* (HO-42)/SA-342L1 *Gazelle* (HO-45);

TPT • Medium 9 Mi-8T *Hip* (HT-40)

AD

SAM 15: 6 S-125 *Pechora* (SA-3 *Goa*); 2K12 *Kub* (SA-6 *Gainful*)

MANPAD 156; 9K32 *Strela*-2 (SA-7 *Grail*); 9K310 *Igla*-1 (SA-16 *Gimlet*)

GUNS • 40mm 24 L-70 Bofors

MSL

AAM IR AAM R-60 (AA-8 *Aphid*)

ASM AGM-65 *Maverick*; A-77 *Thunder*

DEPLOYMENT

Legal provisions for foreign deployment:
Constitution: Codified constitution (2006)
Decision on deployment of troops abroad: By parliament (Art. 140)

CENTRAL AFRICAN REPUBLIC/CHAD
UN • MINURCAT 14

CÔTE D'IVOIRE
UN • UNOCI 3 obs

DEMOCRATIC REPUBLIC OF THE CONGO
UN • MONUSCO 6 (Air Medical Evacuation Team); 2 obs

LIBERIA
UN • UNMIL 4 obs

FOREIGN FORCES

All OSCE.
Austria 1
Bosnia-Herzegovina 1
Canada 1
Croatia 1
France 1
Georgia 1
Germany 3
Greece 1
Hungary 2
Ireland 2
Italy 1
Moldova 1
Netherlands 2
Norway 3
Slovenia 1
Spain 1
Sweden 2
Turkey 1
Ukraine 1
United Kingdom 3
United States 5

TERRITORY WHERE THE GOVERNMENT DOES NOT EXERCISE EFFECTIVE CONTROL

Data presented here represent the *de facto* situation in Kosovo. This does not imply international recognition as a sovereign state. In February 2008 Kosovo declared itself independent. Serbia remains opposed to this, and while Kosovo has not been admitted to the United Nations, a number of states have recognised Kosovo's self-declared status.

Kosovo Security Force 2,500; reserves 800

The Kosovo Security Force was formed in January 2009 as a non-military organisation with responsibility for crisis response, civil protection and explosive ordnance disposal. The force is armed with small arms and light vehicles only. A July 2010 law created a reserve force.

FOREIGN FORCES

All under Kosovo Force (KFOR) comd. unless otherwise specified.
Albania 3
Armenia 35• OSCE (Kosovo) 1
Austria 437; 1 inf coy; elm 1 MP coy; elm 1 hel gp • OSCE (Kosovo) 13
Azerbaijan OSCE (Kosovo) 2
Belarus OSCE (Kosovo) 2
Belgium OSCE (Kosovo) 1
Bosnia-Herzegovina OSCE (Kosovo) 8
Bulgaria 3
Canada 5 • OSCE (Kosovo) 4

Croatia 20 • OSCE (Kosovo) 8
Czech Republic 103; elm 1 engr bn • UNMIK 1 obs
Denmark 152 • UNMIK 1 obs
Estonia 1
Finland 196
France 743; 1 armd cav BG • OSCE (Kosovo) 6
Georgia OSCE (Kosovo) 4
Germany 1,355; 1 inf bn HQ; 1 inf coy; 1 sigs coy; 1 spt bn; elm 1 MP coy; 1 med unit elm 1 hel gp; 26 C2 Leopard MBT; 17 SPz-2 Luchs recce; 25 Marder 1 AIFV; 21 APC (T); 54 TPz-1 Fuchs APC (W); 10 M-109A3G 155mm SP; 6 Wiesel (TOW) msl; 3 CH-53G Stallion hel; 9 UH-1D Iroquois hel • OSCE (Kosovo) 10
Greece 711; 1 mech inf bn • OSCE (Kosovo) 5
Hungary 242; 1 inf coy • OSCE (Kosovo) 3
Ireland 22 • OSCE (Kosovo) 5
Italy 1,247; 1 inf BG HQ; 1 engr unit;1 hel unit; 1 sigs unit; 1 CSS unit; 1 Carabinieri regt • OSCE (Kosovo) 16
Luxembourg 23
Macedonia, Former Yugoslav Republic of OSCE (Kosovo) 4
Malta OSCE (Kosovo) 1
Moldova OSCE (Kosovo) 1
Montenegro OSCE (Kosovo) 1
Morocco 210; 1 inf unit
Netherlands 8 • OSCE (Kosovo) 3
Norway 5 • UNMIK 1 obs
Poland 152; 1 inf coy • UNMIK 1 obs • OSCE (Kosovo) 4
Portugal 301; 1 AB bn (KTM) • OSCE (Kosovo) 4
Romania 139; 1 inf coy • UNMIK 1 obs • OSCE (Kosovo) 3
Russia OSCE (Kosovo) 2
Slovakia 141; 1 inf coy • OSCE (Kosovo) 1
Slovenia 331; 1 inf bn HQ; 2 mot inf coy; 1 engr gp
Spain 3 • OSCE (Kosovo) 10 • UNMIK 1 obs
Sweden 246; 1 inf coy • OSCE (Kosovo) 4
Switzerland 200; 1 inf coy; elm 1 MP coy; elm 1 hel gp
Turkey 479; 1 inf coy; elm 1 MP coy • OSCE (Kosovo) 12
Ukraine 127; 1 inf coy • UNMIK 2 obs • OSCE (Kosovo) 2
United Kingdom 4 • OSCE (Kosovo) 10
United States 810; 1 ARNG cbt spt bde • OSCE (Kosovo) 18
Uzbekistan OSCE (Kosovo) 2

Slovakia SVK

Slovak Koruna Ks		2009	2010	2011
GDP	Ks	63.3bn	66.8bn	
	US$	88.2bn	88.4bn	
per capita	US$	16,280	16,331	
Growth	%	-6.2	3.6	
Inflation	%	1.6	0.8	
Def exp	Ks	969m		
	US$	1.35bn		
Def bdgt	Ks	1.1bn	820m	760m
	US$	1.53bn	1.09bn	
FMA (US)	US$	1.0m	1.25m	1.5m
US$1=Ks/€ from 2009		0.72	0.76	

Population	5,411,640

Age	0–14	15–19	20–24	25–29	30–64	65 plus
Male	8.0%	3.2%	3.7%	4.1%	24.7%	4.8%
Female	7.6%	3.1%	3.6%	3.9%	25.3%	8.0%

Capabilities

ACTIVE 16,531 (Army 7,322 Air 4,190 Cental Staff 1,462 Support and Training 3,557)
Terms of service 6 months

ORGANISATIONS BY SERVICE

Army 7,322
1 Land Forces Comd HQ

FORCES BY ROLE

Mech inf	1 bde (1st)(3 mech inf bn (11th, 12th 13th), 1 log spt bn); 1 bde (2nd) (2 mech inf bn (21st 22nd), 1 tk bn, 1 mixed SP arty bn, 1 log spt bn)
Recce	1 (5th Special) regt
Arty	1 MBL bn
Engr	1 bn
NBC	1 bn

EQUIPMENT BY TYPE
MBT 245 T-72M
AIFV 383: 292 BMP-1; 91 BMP-2
APC 132:
　APC (T) 108 OT-90
　APC (W) 24: 17 OT-64; 7 Tatrapan (6x6)
ARTY 340
　SP 193:**122mm** 1 2S1 Carnation; 45 in store; **152mm** 131: 119 M-77 Dana; 12 in store; **155mm** 16 M-2000 Zuzana
　TOWED 122mm 51 D-30
　MRL 84: **122mm** 59 RM-70; **122/227mm** 25 RM-70/85 MODULAR
　MOR 120mm 12: 8 M-1982; 4 PRAM SPM
AT
　MANPATS 425: AT-3 9K11 Sagger/AT-5 9K113 Spandrel
　SP 9S428 with Malyutka Sagger on BMP-1; 9P135 Fagot on BMP-2; 9P148 with Spandrel on BRDM

AD

SAM • TOWED
SP 48 9K35 *Strela*-10 (SA-13 *Gopher*)
MANPADS 9K32 *Strela*-2 (SA-7 *Grail*); 9K310 *Igla*-1 (SA-16 *Gimlet*)
RADAR • LAND SNAR-10 *Big Fred* (veh, arty)

Air Force 4,190

Flying hours 90 hrs/yr for MiG-29 pilots (NATO Integrated AD System); 140 hrs/yr for Mi-8/17 crews (reserved for EU & NATO), min 20hrs/yr for remainder

Air Bases Sliac tac wg; Presov hel wg; Kuchyna tpt wg

FORCES BY ROLE

Ftr 1 wg with MiG-29/Mi-29UB/MiG-29AS/MiG-29SD *Fulcrum*

Atk Hel/ 1 wg with Mi-8 *Hip*; Mi-17 *Hip H*; Mi-24D *Hind D/*
Tpt Hel Mi-24V *Hind E*; PZL MI-2 *Hoplite*

AD 1 bde with 2K12 *Kub* (SA-6 *Gainful*); 9K32 *Strela*-2 (SA-7 *Grail*); S-300 (SA-10B *Grumble*)

EQUIPMENT BY TYPE
AIRCRAFT 22 combat capable
  FTR 22 MiG-29/MiG-29UB *Fulcrum* (12 MiG-29SD/AS modernised to NATO standard)
  TRG 15 L-39 *Albatross*
HELICOPTERS
  ATK 16 Mi-24D *Hind D*/Mi-24V *Hind E*
  MRH 14 Mi-17 *Hip H*
  TPT 7 **Medium** 1 Mi-8 *Hip* **Light** 6 PZL MI-2 *Hoplite*
AD • SAM
  SP S-300 (SA-10B *Grumble*); 2K12 *Kub* (SA-6 *Gainful*)
  MANPAD 9K32 *Strela*-2 (SA-7 *Grail*)
MSL
  AAM • IR AAM R-60 (AA-8 *Aphid*); R-73 (AA-11 *Archer*); **SARH AAM** R-27 (AA-10 *Alamo*)
  ASM S5K/S5KO (57mm rockets); S8KP/S8KOM (80mm rockets)

DEPLOYMENT

Legal provisions for foreign deployment:
Constitution: Codified constitution (1992)
Decision on deployment of troops abroad: By the parliament (Art. 86)

AFGHANISTAN
NATO • ISAF 300

BOSNIA-HERZEGOVINA
EU • EUFOR • *Operation Althea* 40
OSCE • Bosnia and Herzegovina 3

CYPRUS
UN • UNFICYP 198; elm 1 inf coy; 1 engr pl

MIDDLE EAST
UN • UNTSO 2 obs

SERBIA
NATO • KFOR 141; 1 inf coy
OSCE • Kosovo 1

Slovenia SVN

Slovenian Tolar t		2009	2010	2011
GDP	t/€	34.9bn	35.5bn	
	US$	48.6bn	47.0bn	
per capita	US$	23,786	23,216	
Growth	%	-7.8	1.4	
Inflation	%	0.9	1.5	
Def exp	t	569m		
	US$	793m		
Def bdgt	t	550m	508m	483m
	US$	766m	672m	
FMA (US)	US$	0.4m	0.5m	0.75m
US$1=€		0.72	0.76	

Population	2,024,912

Age	0–14	15–19	20–24	25–29	30–64	65 plus
Male	6.9%	2.5%	3.1%	3.5%	26.0%	6.6%
Female	6.5%	2.4%	3.0%	3.4%	25.9%	10.2%

Capabilities

ACTIVE 7,600 (Army 7,600) **Paramilitary 4,500**

RESERVE 1,700 (Army 1,700)

ORGANISATIONS BY SERVICE

Army 7,600
FORCES BY ROLE

Inf 1 bde with (3 mot inf bn, 1 arty bn, 1 log bn, 1 recce coy)
SF 1 unit
ISTAR 1 bn
Engr 1 bn
Sigs 1 bn
CBRN 1 bn
MP 1 bn

EQUIPMENT BY TYPE
MBT 45 M-84
APC (W) 112: 85 *Pandur 6x6* (*Valuk*); 27 *Patria 8x8* (*Svarun*)
ARTY 74
  TOWED • 155mm 18 TN-90
  MOR 120mm 56: 8 M-52; 16 M-74; 32 MN-9
AT • MSL
  SP 24: 12 BOV-3 9K11 *Malyutka* (AT-3 *Sagger*); 12 BOV-3 9K111 *Fagot* (AT-4 *Spigot*)
  MANPATS 9K11 *Malyutka* (AT-3 *Sagger*); 9K111 *Fagot* (AT-4 *Spigot*)

Reserves
FORCES BY ROLE
Tk 1 bn
Mtn Inf 1 bn with (6 Coy)

Army Maritime Element 47

FORCES BY ROLE
Maritime   1 bn (part of Sp Comd)

EQUIPMENT BY TYPE
PATROL AND COASTAL COMBATANTS • PBF 1
Super Dvora MkII

FACILITIES
Base   Located at Koper

Air Element 530

FORCES BY ROLE
1 fixed wg sqn; 1 rotary wg sqn; 1 AD bn; 1 airspace
control bn; 1 avn school; 1 air maintenance coy; 1 mil
ATC coy. All at Cerklje air base except airspace control
bn at Brnik air base.

EQUIPMENT BY TYPE
AIRCRAFT 9 combat capable
  TPT • Light 3: 1 L-410 *Turbolet*; 2 PC-6 *Turbo-Porter*
  TRG 11: 2 PC-9; 9 PC-9M*
HELICOPTERS
  MRH 8 Bell 412 *Twin Huey* (some armed)
  TPT 8 **Medium** 4 AS 532AL *Cougar* **Light** 4 Bell 206 *Jet Ranger* (AB-206)
AD
  SAM 138
    SP 6 *Roland* II
    MANPAD 132: 36 9K310 *Igla*-1 (SA-16 *Gimlet*); 96
    9K38 Igla (SA-18 *Grouse*)

Paramilitary 4,500

Police 4,500 (armed); 5,000 reservists (total
9,500)
PATROL AND COASTAL COMBATANTS • PBF 1
HELICOPTERS
MRH 1 Bell 412 *Twin Huey*
TPT • Light 4: 1 AW-109; 2 Bell 206 (AB-206) *Jet Ranger*;
1 Bell 212 (AB-212)

DEPLOYMENT

Legal provisions for foreign deployment:
Constitution: Codified constitution (1991)
Decision on deployment of troops abroad: By
government (Art. 84 of Defence Act)

AFGHANISTAN
NATO • ISAF 72

BOSNIA-HERZEGOVINA
EU • EUFOR • *Operation Althea* 29
OSCE • Bosnia and Herzegovina 1

LEBANON
UN • UNIFIL 14; 1 inf pl

MIDDLE EAST
UN • UNTSO 2 obs

SERBIA
NATO • KFOR 331; 1 inf bn HQ; 2 mot inf coy; 1 engr gp
OSCE • Serbia 1

Spain ESP

Euro €		2009	2010	2011
GDP	€	1.054tr	1.051tr	
	US$	1.47tr	1.39tr	
per capita	US$	31,940	30,708	
Growth	%	-3.6	-0.8	
Inflation	%	-0.4	1.4	
Def exp[a]	€	12.2bn		
	US$	16.9bn		
Def bdgt	€	7.84bn	7.69bn	7.15bn
	US$	10.9bn	10.2bn	
US$1=€		0.72	0.76	

[a] including military pensions plus extra budgetary expenditure

Population   45,316,586

Age	0–14	15–19	20–24	25–29	30–64	65 plus
Male	7.8%	2.4%	2.8%	3.4%	25.7%	7.2%
Female	7.3%	2.3%	2.6%	3.1%	25.5%	9.9%

Capabilities

ACTIVE 142,212 (Army 78,121 Navy 21,606 Air
21,172 Joint 21,313) **Paramilitary 80,210**

CIVILIAN 17,429 (Army 8,029 Navy 3,990 Air Force
5,410)

RESERVE 319,000 (Army 265,000 Navy 9,000 Air
45,000)

ORGANISATIONS BY SERVICE

Army 78,121; 8,029 civilian

The Army Force is organised in Land Forces High
Readiness HQ, Land Force, Operational Logistic Force and
the Canary Islands Command. The principal deployable
elements are the Heavy Forces (FUP) consisting of 2 mech
bde and 1 Armd bde, and the Light Forces (FUL) consisting
of 1 Cav, 1 Legion, 1 AB and 2 lt bde. The Land Forces
High Readiness HQ Spain provides one NATO Rapid
Deployment Corps HQ (NRDC-SP).

FORCES BY ROLE
Infantry regiments usually comprise 2 bn. Spain deploys
its main battle tanks within its armd/mech inf formations,
and its armd cav regt

Comd	1 corps HQ (CGTAD) with (1 HQ bn, 1 int regt, 1 MP bn); 2 div HQ (coordinative role)
Armd	1 bde (12th) with (1 HQ bn, 1 armd inf regt, 1 mech inf regt, 1 SP arty bn, 1 recce sqn, 1 engr bn, 1 log bn, 1 sigs coy)
Armd Cav	1 bde (2nd) with (1 HQ bn, 3 lt armd cav regt, 1 fd arty regt, 1 engr bn, 1 log bn, 1 sigs coy)

Europe

Mech Inf	2 bde (10th & 11th) (each: 1 HQ bn, 1 mech inf regt, 1 armd inf bn, 1 recce sqn, 1 SP arty bn, 1 engr bn, 1 log bn, 1 sigs coy)
Mtn Inf	1 comd (1st) with (3 mtn inf regt)
Lt inf	2 bde (2nd/La Legion & 7th) with (1 HQ bn, 2 inf regt, 1 recce bn, 1 fd arty bn, 1 engr bn, 1 log bn, 1 sigs coy); 1 bde (5th) with (1 HQ bn, 2 lt inf regt))
SF	1 comd with (1 HQ bn, 3 Spec Ops bn, 1 sigs coy)
AB	1 bde (6th) with (1 HQ bn, 2 para bn,, 1 air mob bn, 1 fd arty bn, 1 engr bn, 1 log bn, 1 sigs coy)
Arty	1 comd with (3 arty regt)
Coastal Arty	1 comd with (1 coastal arty regt. 1 sigs unit,)
AD	1 comd with (5 ADA regt, 1 sigs unit)
Engr	1 comd with (2 engr regt, 1 engr bridging regt)
Sigs/ EW	1 bde with (2 sigs regt, 2 EW regt)
Avn	1 comd (FAMET) with (1 atk hel bn, 2 spt hel bn, 1 tpt hel bn, 1 log unit (1 spt coy, 1 supply coy), 1 sigs bn)
Log	1 comd; 1 bde with (5 log regt)
NBC	1 regt
Medical	1 bde with (1 log unit, 3 medical regt, 1 field hospital unit)
CIMIC	1 bn
Territorial	1 (Canary Islands) comd with (1 lt inf bde (1 HQ bn, 3 lt inf regt, 1 fd arty regt, 1 log bn, 1 sigs coy); 1 AD regt; 1 spt hel bn); 1 (Balearic Islands) comd with (1 inf regt); 2 (Ceuta and Melilla) comd (each: 1 HQ bn, 2 inf regt, 1 cav regt, 1 arty regt, 1 engr bn, 1 log bn, 1 sigs coy)

EQUIPMENT BY TYPE
MBT 447: 108 *Leopard* 2A4; 155 *Leopard* 2A5E (64 more on order); 184 M-60A3TTS
RECCE 292: 84 B-1 *Centauro*; 208 VEC-3562 *BMR-VEC*
AIFV 144 *Pizarro* (incl 22 comd; 190 more on order)
APC 1,997
  APC (T) 1,314 M-113 (incl variants)
  APC (W) 683 BMR-600/BMR-600M1
ARTY 1,854
  SP 155mm 96 M-109A5
  TOWED 308 **105mm** 226: 56 L-118 light gun; 170 Model 56 pack howitzer; **155mm** 82: 60 M-114; 22 SBT 155/52 SIAC (42 more on order)
  COASTAL 155mm 18 SBT 155/52 APU SBT V07
  MRL 140mm 14 *Teruel*
  MOR 1,418:
    SP 288: **81mm** 83; **120mm** 205
    81mm 890; **120mm** 240
AT
  MSL
    SP 187: 113 *Milan*; 74 *TOW*
    MANPATS 500: 39 *Spike LR* (197 more on order); 335 *Milan*; 126 *TOW*

HELICOPTERS
ATK 6 AS-665 *Tiger* (18 more on order)
MRH 25 BO-105 HOT
TPT 119 **Heavy** 17 CH-47D *Chinook* (HT-17D) **Medium** 33: 16AS-332 *Super Puma* (HU-21); 17 AS-532UL *Cougar* **Light** 69: 31 Bell-205 (HU-10B *Iroquois*); 6 Bell 212 (HU.18); 7 Bo-105
UAV • ISR • Medium 4 *Searcher* Mk II-J (PASI)
AD
  SAM 263
    SP 18 *Roland*
    TOWED 65: 36 I *HAWK* Phase III MIM-23B; 13 *Skyguard/Aspide*; 8 NASAMS; 8 PAC-2 *Patriot*
    MANPAD 180 *Mistral*
  GUNS • TOWED 35mm 92 GDF-002
RADAR • LAND 6: 4 ARTHUR; 2 AN/TPQ-36 *Firefinder*

Reserves 265,000 reservists

Cadre units	
Railway	1 regt
Armd Cav	1 bde
Inf	3 bde

Navy 21,606 (incl Naval Aviation and Marines); 3,990 civilian

HQ located at Madrid

FORCES BY ROLE

Navy	1 Strike Group
	2 Frigate Squadrons
	1 Submarine Flotilla
	1 MCM Flotilla
	1 Naval Aviation Flotilla

EQUIPMENT BY TYPE
SUBMARINES • TACTICAL • SSK 4:
  4 *Galerna* each with 4 single 533mm TT each with F17 Mod 2/L5 HWT
PRINCIPAL SURFACE COMBATANTS 12
  AIRCRAFT CARRIERS • CVS 1 *Principe de Asturias* (capacity: 10 AV-8B *Harrier II*/AV-8B *Harrier II Plus* FGA ac; 8 SH-3 *Sea King* ASW hel; 2 Bell 212 (HU-18) hel)
  DESTROYERS • DDGHM 4
    4 *Alvaro de Bazan* each with Baseline 5 *Aegis* C&C, 2 quad Mk 141 lnchr (8 eff.) each with RGM-84F *Harpoon* AShM, 1 48 cell Mk 41 VLS (LAM capable) with SM-2MR/RIM-162B *Sea Sparrow* SAM (quad packs), 2 twin 324mm ASTT (4 eff.) each with Mk46 LWT, 1 127mm gun, (capacity 1 SH-60B *Seahawk* ASW hel)
  FRIGATES • FFGHM 6:
    6 *Santa Maria* each with 1 Mk 13 GMLS with RGM-84C *Harpoon* AShM/SM-1MR SAM, 2 Mk32 triple 324mm ASTT each with Mk46 LWT, 1 76mm gun, (capacity 2 SH-60B *Seahawk* ASW hel)
AMPHIBIOUS
  PRINCIPAL AMPHIBIOUS SHIPS 3
    LHD 1 *Juan Carlos I* (capacity 4 LCM; 42 APC; 46 MBT; 700 troops; able to operate as alternate platform for CVS aviation group)
    LPD 2 *Galicia* (capacity 6 Bell-212 or 4 SH-3D *Sea King*; 4 LCM or 6 LCVP; 130 APC or 33 MBT; 450 troops)

LANDING SHIPS • LST 1 *Pizarro* (2nd of class in reserve)
LANDING CRAFT • LCM 14
LOGISTICS AND SUPPORT 3
AORH 2: 1 *Patino*; 1 *Cantabria* (expected ISD '09)
AO 1 *Marques de la Ensenada*

FACILITIES

| Bases | Located at El Ferrol, Rota (Fleet HQ), Cartagena (ALMART HQ, Maritime Action), Las Palmas (Canary Islands), Mahon (Menorca), Porto Pi (Mallorca) |
| Naval Air Stations | Located at Mahón (Menorca), Porto Pi (Mallorca) |

Navy – Maritime Action Force

FORCES BY ROLE

| Navy | Canary Islands Maritime Command (Cadiz) Maritime Action Units Command (Ferrol) Maritime Action Command, Balear Islands Maritime Area |

PATROL AND COASTAL COMBATANTS 24
PSO 11:
   3 *Alboran* each with 1 hel landing platform
   1 *Chilreu*
   4 *Descubierta*
   3 *Meteoro* each with 1 hel landing platform (*Buquesde Accion Maritime* – 1 additional vessels on order)
PCO 4 *Serviola*
PCC 4 *Anaga*
PB 2 *Toralla*
PBR 3
MINE WARFARE • MINE COUNTERMEASURES 7
MCCS 1 *Diana*
MHO 6 *Segura*
LOGISTICS AND SUPPORT 29:
AGOR 2 (with ice strengthened hull, for polar research duties in Antarctica)
AGHS 4
AGI 1
ATF 3
AK 3
YDT 1
TRG 15: 8 **AXL**; 7 **AXS**

Naval Aviation 814

| Flying hours | 150 hrs/year on AV-8B *Harrier II* FGA ac; 200 hrs/year on hel |

FORCES BY ROLE

FGA	1 sqn with AV-8B *Harrier II*; AV-8B *Harrier II Plus*
ASW	1 sqn with SH-60B *Seahawk*
AEW	1 sqn with SH-3H AEW *Sea King*
Tpt	1 sqn with SH-3D *Sea King*, 1 sqn with Bell 212 (HU-18),
Tpt	1 (liason) sqn with Cessna 550 *Citation II*; Cessna 650 *Citation* VII
Trg	1 sqn with Hughes 500MD; 1 flt with 1 TAV-8B *Harrier*

EQUIPMENT BY TYPE
AIRCRAFT 24 combat capable
FGA 17: 4 AV-8B *Harrier II*; 12 AV-8B *Harrier II Plus*; 1 TAV-8B *Harrier* (on lease from USMC)
ASW 7 P-3 *Orion*
TPT • Light 4: 3 Cessna 550 *Citation II*; 1 Cessna 650 *Citation VII*
HELICOPTERS
ASW 20: 8 SH-3D *Sea King*; 12 SH-60B *Seahawk*
MRH 9 Hughes 500MD
AEW 3 SH-3H AEW *Sea King*
TPT • Light 8 Bell 212 (HU-18)
MSL
AAM • IR AAM AIM-9L *Sidewinder* **ARH AAM** AIM-120 AMRAAM
ASM AGM-65G *Maverick*
AShM AGM-119 *Penguin*

Marines 5,300

FORCES BY ROLE

| Marine | 1 bde (2,500) with (1 mech inf bn, 2 inf bn, 1 arty bn, 1 log bn, 1 recce unit, 1 spec ops unit) |
| Marine Garrison | 5 gp |

EQUIPMENT BY TYPE
MBT 16 M-60A3TTS
APC (W) 22 *Piranha*
AAV 19: 16 AAV-7A1/AAVP-7A1; 2 AAVC-7A1; 1 AAVR-7A1
ARTY 18
SP 155mm 6 M-109A2
TOWED 105mm 12 M-56 (pack)
AT • MSL • MANPATS 24 TOW-2
RL 90mm C-90C
AD • SAM • MANPAD 12 *Mistral*

Air Force 21,172; plus 5,410 civilian

The Spanish Air Force is organised in 3 commands – General Air Command, Combat Air Command and Canary Islands Air Command

| Flying hours | 120 hrs/year on hel/tpt ac; 180 hrs/year on FGA/ftr |

FORCES BY ROLE

Ftr	2 sqn with Eurofighter *Typhoon*; 2 sqn with *Mirage* F-1C (F-1CE); *Mirage* F-1E (F-1EE); Mirage F-1EDA
FGA	5 sqn with F/A-18A/B *Hornet* (EF-18A/B)
MP	1 sqn with P-3A *Orion*; P-3B *Orion* 1 sqn with CN-235
EW	3 sqn with B-707; C- 212 *Aviocar*; *Falcon* 20
SAR	1 sqn with AS-332 *Super Puma* (HU-21); C-212 *Aviocar*; 1 sqn with AS-332 *Super Puma* (HU-21); F-27 *Friendship*; 1 sqn with C-212 *Aviocar*; SA-330 *Puma* (AS-330)
Tkr/Tpt	1 sqn with B-707 Tkr; 1 sqn with KC-130H *Hercules*
Tkr	1 sqn with A310; B-707 Tkr

Tpt   1 sqn with A310; *Falcon* 900; 1 sqn with
                   AS-332 *Super Puma* (HU-21); Beech C90
                   King Air (VIP); 1 sqn with B-707; 1 sqn with
                   C-130H/C-130H-30 *Hercules*; 1 sqn with
                   C-212 *Aviocar*; 1 (spt) sqn with C-212 *Aviocar*;
                   Canadair CL-215; Cessna 550 *Citation V*
                   (ISR); 1 sqn with CN-235

OCU   Eurofighter *Typhoon* OCU; 1 sqn with F/A-
                   18A/B (EF-18A/B) *Hornet*

Trg   1 sqn with Beech F33C *Bonanza* (trg); 2 sqn
                   with C-101 *Aviojet*; 1 sqn with C-212 *Aviocar*;
                   2 sqn with EC-120 *Colibri*; S-76C; 2 (LIFT)
                   sqn with F-5B *Freedom Fighter*; 1 sqn with
                   T-35 *Pillan* (E-26)

EQUIPMENT BY TYPE

AIRCRAFT 179 combat capable
   FTR 54: 34 Eurofighter *Typhoon*; 20 F-5B *Freedom Fighter*
   FGA 119: 86 F/A-18A/B *Hornet* (EF-18A/B - 67 being given
   MLU); 33 *Mirage* F-1C (F-1CE)/F-1EDA/F-1E (F-1EE)
   ASW 6: 2 P-3A *Orion*; 2 P-3B *Orion*; 2 P-3M *Orion*
   MP 6 CN-235 MPA
   TKR 7: 5 KC-130H *Hercules*, 2 B-707 Tkr
   TPT 97: Medium 7 C-130H/H-30 *Hercules*; **Light** 77: 4
   Beech C90 *King Air*; 22 Beech F33C *Bonanza*; 18 C-212
   Aviocar; 13 C-295; 14 CN-235 (12 tpt, 2 VIP); 3 Cessna
   550 *Citation V* (recce); 3 F-27 *Friendship* (SAR); **PAX** 13:
   2 A310; 4 B-707 (incl EW); 2 *Falcon* 20 (EW, NAVAID); 5
   Falcon 900 (VIP)
   TRG 108: 71 C-101 *Aviojet*; 37 T-35 *Pillan* (E-26)
HELICOPTERS
   TPT 46 Medium 23: 15 AS-332 *Super Puma* (HU-21); 2
   AS-532 *Cougar* (VIP); 6 SA-330 *Puma* (AS-330) **Light** 23:
   15 EC-120 *Colibri*; 8 S-76C
AD
   SAM *Mistral*; R-530
   TOWED *Skyguard/Aspide*
MSL
   AAM • IR AAM AIM-9L/AIM-9M/AIM-9N/AIM-9P
   Sidewinder; **SARH AAM** AIM-7F/M *Sparrow*, R-530;
   ARH AAM AIM-120B/C AMRAAM
   ARM AGM-88A HARM
   ASM AGM-65A/G *Maverick*
   AShM AGM-84C/D *Harpoon*
   LACM *Taurus* KEPD 350
BOMBS
   Conventional: Mk 82; Mk 83; Mk 84; BLU-109; BPG-
   2000; BR-250; BR-500;
      BME-330B/AP; CBU-100 (anti-tank)
   Laser-guided: GBU-10/16 *Paveway* II; GBU-24 *Paveway*
   III; EGBU-16 *Paveway* II

Emergencies Military Unit (UME)

FORCES BY ROLE

HQ   1 (div)
Air   1 gp with Firefighting planes belonging
               to the Air Force; 1 emergency hel bn
               belonging to Army Aviation (FAMET)
Emergency 5 bn
Intervention

Paramilitary 80,210

Guardia Civil 79,950
9 regions, 56 Rural Comds
FORCES BY ROLE
Inf   17 (Tercios) regt
Spec Op   10 (rural) gp
Sy   6 (traffic) gp; 1 (Special) bn
EQUIPMENT BY TYPE
APC (W) 18 BLR
HELICOPTERS
   MRH 26 Bo-105ATH
   TPT • Light 12: 8 BK-117; 4 EC-135P2

Guardia Civil Del Mar 760
PATROL AND COASTAL COMBATANTS 53
   PCC 15
   PCI 1
   PBF 22
   PB 15

DEPLOYMENT

Legal provisions for foreign deployment:
Constitution: Codified constitution (1978)
Specific legislation: 'Ley Orgánica de la Defensa
Nacional' (2005)
Decision on deployment of troops abroad: a) By
the government (Art. 6 of the 'Defence Law'); b)
parliamentary approval is required for military operations
'which are not directly related to the defence of Spain or
national interests' (Art. 17 of the 'Defence Law')

AFGHANISTAN
NATO • ISAF 1,537; 1 AB bn

BOSNIA-HERZEGOVINA
OSCE • Bosnia and Herzegovina 3

DEMOCRATIC REPUBLIC OF THE CONGO
UN • MONUSCO 3 obs

GULF OF ADEN & INDIAN OCEAN
EU • *Operation Atalanta* 1 PSOH; 1 LPD; 1 CN-235

LEBANON
UN • UNIFIL 1,064; 1 armd inf bn

MEDITERRANEAN SEA
NATO • SNMCMG 2: 1 MHO

SERBIA
NATO • KFOR 3
OSCE • Serbia 1
OSCE • Kosovo 10
UN • UNMIK 1 obs

UGANDA
EU • EUTM 38

FOREIGN FORCES

United States US European Command: 1,256 1 air base at
Morón; 1 naval base at Rota

Sweden SWE

Swedish Krona Skr		2009	2010	2011
GDP	Skr	3.11tr	3.27tr	
	US$	408bn	450bn	
per capita	US$	43,910	48,427	
Growth	%	-4.9	1.6	
Inflation	%	-0.3	1.8	
Def exp	Skr	40.3bn		
	US$	5.3bn		
Def bdgt [a]	Skr	36.4bn	40.3bn	40.6bn
	US$	4.78bn	5.54bn	
US$1=Skr		7.61	7.27	

[a] Excluding Civil Defence

Population   9,293,026

Capabilities

ACTIVE 21,070 (Army 7,332 Navy 3,423 Air 3,770 Staff 6,545) **Paramilitary 800 Voluntary Auxiliary Organisations 30,000**

Terms of service: conscription abolished from 1st July 2010

RESERVE 200,000

ORGANISATIONS BY SERVICE

Army 5,165; 2,167 conscript (total 7,332)

FORCES BY ROLE

1 Joint Forces Comd, 22 Training Detachments whose main task is to provide support to the Home Guard and other voluntary defence organisations; the Military Districts were disbanded in 2005. The army has been transformed to provide brigade-sized task forces depending on the operational requirement. Sweden provided the majority of forces to the EU Nordic Battlegroup.

Comd	1 div HQ (on mobilisation); 2 bde HQ
Armd	2 bn
Mech	8 bn
Arty	2 bn
AD	2 bn
Engr	2 bn
Log	3 bn
Home Guard	60 bn

EQUIPMENT BY TYPE

MBT 280: 120 *Leopard* 2 (Strv 122); 160 *Leopard* 2A4 (Strv-121)
AIFV 354 CV9040 (Strf 9040)
APC 489
  APC (T) 286: 214 Pbv 302; 72 Pbv 401A
  APC (W) 203: 34 XA-180 *Sisu*; 20 XA-202 *Sisu*; 149 XA-203 *Sisu*
ARTY 280
  SP 155mm 24 *Archer* (being delivered)
  TOWED 155mm 49 FH-77B

MOR 120mm 207
AT
  MSL • MANPATS RB-55; RB-56 *Bill*
  RCL 84mm *Carl Gustav*
  RL 84mm AT-4
AD
  SAM
    SP 16 RBS-70
    TOWED RBS-90
    MANPAD RBS-70
  GUNS • SP 40mm 30 Strv 90LV
RADAR • LAND ARTHUR (arty); M-113 A1GE *Green Archer* (mor)
UAV • ISR • Medium 3 *Sperwer*

Navy 1,842; 543 (Amphibious); 1,083 conscript; (total 3,423)

FORCES BY ROLE

Maritime forces restructured

Navy	2 Surface flotillas
Maritime	1 Surveillance and info bn
Amph	1 Amph bde (1 Amph bn)
SS	1 Submarine flotilla
Log	1 bn

EQUIPMENT BY TYPE
SUBMARINES 6
  TACTICAL • SSK 5:
    3 *Gotland* (AIP fitted) each with 2 single 400mm TT with Tp432/Tp 451, 4 single 533mm TT with Tp613/Tp62
    2 *Sodermanland* (AIP fitted) each with 6 single 533mm TT each with Tp432/Tp451/Tp613/Tp62
  SSI 1 *Spiggen* II
PATROL AND COASTAL COMBATANTS 19
  CORVETTES • FSG 5 *Visby* with 8 RBS-15 AShM, 4 single 400mm ASTT each with Tp45 LWT, 1 hel landing plaform; (2 operational in 2010)
  PCG 2:
    2 *Göteborg* each with 4 twin lnchr (8 eff.) each with RBS-15 Mk2 AShM, 4 single 400mm ASTT each with Tp431 LWT, 4 Saab 601 A/S mor (36 eff.)
    2 *Stockholm* each with 4 twin lnchr (8 eff.) each with RBS-15 Mk2 AShM, 4 Saab 601 mortars, 4 single ASTT each with Tp431 LWT
  PBR 12 *Tapper*
MINE WARFARE • MINE COUNTERMEASURES 6
  MCC 5 *Koster*
  MCD 1 *Styrso*
AMPHIBIOUS • LANDING CRAFT 164
  LCM 17 *Trossbat*
  LCPL 147 *Combatboat* 90
LOGISTICS AND SUPPORT 17:
  ARS 1 *Furusund* (former ML)
  AG 2: 1 *Carlskrona* with 1 hel landing platform (former ML); 1 *Trosso* (Spt ship for corvettes and patrol vessels but can also be used as HQ ship)
  AK 1 *Visborg*
  AGI 1
  AGS 2 (Government Maritime Forces)
  TRG 7: 5 **AXS**; 2 (other)

TRV 1
YDT 2

FACILITIES

Bases   Located Karlskrona, naval det at Muskö

Support base Located at Muskö

Amphibious 543

FORCES BY ROLE

Amph   1 bde; 1 bn

EQUIPMENT BY TYPE

ARTY • MOR 81mm 12

MSL • SSM 8 RBS-17 *Hellfire*

Air Force 3,059; 711 conscript (total 3,770)

Flying hours   100 to 150 hrs/year

Units: F 7, Skaraborg Wing in Såtenäs; F 17, Blekinge Wing in Ronneby; F 21, Norrbotten Wing in Luleå; Helicopter Wing in Linköping (also operates in Luleå, Såtenäs and Ronneby; Air Combat School (LSS) in Uppsala

FORCES BY ROLE

Ftr/FGA/ISR	4 sqn with JAS 39A/B/C/D *Gripen*
SIGINT	1 sqn with Gulfstream IV SRA-4 (S-102B)
AEW&C	1 sqn with S-100B *Argus*
Tpt	1 sqn with C-130E *Hercules*/C-130H *Hercules* (Tp-84)
1 trg unit with SK 60 Radar	1 (fighter control and air surv) bn

EQUIPMENT BY TYPE

AIRCRAFT 130 combat capable

FGA 130 JAS39 (A/B/C/D mdels)

ELINT 2 Gulfstream IV SRA-4 (S-102B)

AEW&C 2 S-100B *Argus*

TPT 14: **Medium** 8 C-130E *Hercules*/C-130H *Hercules* (Tp-84) (7 tpt, 1 tkr); **Light** 4 Saab 340 (Tp-100A – 1 VIP); PAX 2 Gulfstream IV (Tp-102A)

TRG 80 SK-60

MSL

ASM RB-75 (AGM-65) *Maverick*

AShM RB-15F

AAM • IR AAM AIM-9L *Sidewinder* (RB-74) ARH AAM AIM-120B *AMRAAM* (RB-99))

BOMB BK-39

FACILITIES

Trg School   1 with SK-60

Armed Forces Hel Wing (included in Air Force figures)

FORCES BY ROLE

Tpt Hel	1 bn with AS-332 *Super Puma* (HKP-10); AW-109M (HKP-15); Bo-105CB (HKP-9A); NH 90 TTH (HKP-14)

EQUIPMENT BY TYPE

HELICOPTERS

TPT 51: **Medium** 12: 9 AS-332 *Super Puma* (HKP-10 - SAR); 3 NH 90 TTH (HKP-14) **Light** 39: 20 AW-109M (HKP-15); 19 Bo-105CB (HKP-9A - trg)

Paramilitary 800

Coast Guard 800

PATROL AND COASTAL COMBATANTS 30

PSO 5: 3 KBV-001; 1 KBV-181 (fishery protection)

PCC 2 KBV-201

PB 23: 3 KBV-101; 6 KBV-281; 3 KBV-288; 11 KBV-301

AMPHIBIOUS • LANDING CRAFT • LCAC 3 Griffon 2000 TDX (KBV-591)

LOGISTICS AND SUPPORT 12 AG (MARPOL-CRAFT)

Air Arm

AIRCRAFT • TPT • Light 3 DHC-8Q-300

DEPLOYMENT

Legal provisions for foreign deployment:

Constitution: Constitution consists of four fundamental laws; the most important is 'The Instrument of Government' (1974)

Decision on deployment of troops abroad: By the government upon parliamentary approval (Ch. 10, Art. 9)

AFGHANISTAN

NATO • ISAF 500

UN • UNAMA 1 obs

BOSNIA-HERZEGOVINA

EU • EUFOR • *Operation Althea* 1

OSCE • Bosnia and Herzegovina 2

DEMOCRATIC REPUBLIC OF THE CONGO

UN • MONUSCO 4 obs

GULF OF ADEN & INDIAN OCEAN

EU• *Operation Atalanta* 1 AG

INDIA/PAKISTAN

UN • UNMOGIP 6 obs

KOREA, REPUBLIC OF

NNSC • 5 obs

MIDDLE EAST

UN • UNTSO 5 obs

MOLDOVA

OSCE • Moldova 1

NEPAL

UN • UNMIN 2 obs

SERBIA

NATO • KFOR 246; 1 inf coy (to withdraw by end 2010)

OSCE • Serbia 2

OSCE • Kosovo 4

SUDAN

UN • UNMIS 5 obs

UGANDA

EU • EUTM 4

Switzerland CHE

Swiss Franc fr		2009	2010	2011
GDP	fr	535bn	555bn	
	US$	494bn	526bn	
per capita	US$	63,930	69,294	
Growth	%	-1.5	1.8	
Inflation	%	-0.5	0.9	
Def exp	fr	4.41bn		
	US$	4.07bn		
Def bdgt	fr	4.52bn	4.81bn	4.09bn
	US$	4.17bn	4.57bn	
US$1=fr		1.08	1.05	

Population   7,594,561

Age	0 – 14	15 – 19	20 – 24	25 – 29	30 – 64	65 plus
Male	7.9%	3.1%	3.2%	3.1%	24.7%	7.1%
Female	7.3%	2.9%	3.0%	3.2%	24.5%	9.8%

Capabilities

ACTIVE 25,620 (Joint 25,620)

RESERVE 171,891 (Army 121,998, Air 26,436, Armed Forces Logistic Organisation 9,321, Command Support Organisation 14,136)

Civil Defence 80,000

Terms of service 18 weeks compulsory recruit trg at age 19–20 (19,000 (2006)), followed by 7 refresher trg courses (3 weeks each) over a 10-year period between ages 20–30. (189,000 continuation trg (2006))

ORGANISATIONS BY SERVICE

Joint 3,711 active; 21,909 conscript (197,511 on mobilisation)

Land Forces (Army) 121,998 on mobilisation

With the exception of military security all units are non-active.

FORCES BY ROLE

4 Territorial Regions

Comd	4 regional comd (each: 1 sig bn, 2 engr bn)
Armd	1 bde (1st) with (2 armd bn, 1 recce bn, 2 armd inf bn, 1 sp arty bn, 2 engr bn, 1 sigs bn); 1 bde (11th) with (2 tk bn, 1 recce bn, 2 armd inf bn, 1 inf bn, 2 SP arty bn, 1 engr bn, 1 sigs bn)
Armd/Arty	1 trg unit
Inf	1 bde (2nd) with (1 recce bn, 4 inf bn, 2 SP arty bn, 1 engr bn, 1 sigs bn); 1 bde (5th) with (1 recce bn, 3 inf bn, 2 SP arty bn, 1 engr bn, 1 sigs bn); 1 (reserve) bde (7th) with (3 recce bn, 3 inf bn, 2 mtn inf bn, 1 sigs bn); 1 trg unit
Mtn Inf	1 bde (9th) with (5 mtn inf bn, 1 SP Arty bn, 1 sigs bn); 1 bde (12th) with (2 inf bn, 3 mtn inf bn, 1 (fortress) arty bn, 1 sigs bn); 1 (reserve) bde (10th) with (2 armd bn, 1 recce bn, 3 inf bn, 2 mtn inf bn, 2 SP arty bn, 2 sigs bn)
Engr Rescue	1 bde (trg)
Sigs	1 bde (trg)
Supply	1 bde (trg)
Sy	1 bde

EQUIPMENT BY TYPE

MBT 344 *Leopard 2* (Pz-87 *Leo*)
RECCE 446 *Eagle II*
AIFV 154 CV9030
APC • APC (W) 346 *Piranha* II
AIFV/APC look-a-likes 573: M-113/*Piranha* I/II(8x8)/ IIIC(8x8)/CV 9030 CP
ARTY 498
  SP 155mm 200 M-109
  MOR SP 81mm 298 M-113 with M-72/91
AT
  MSL • SP 110 TOW-2 SP *Piranha* I 6x6
  RL 67mm 12,916 PZF 44 *Panzerfaust*
AD • SAM • MANPAD FIM-92A *Stinger*
UAV • ISR • Medium ADS-95 *Ranger*
PATROL AND COASTAL COMBATANTS • PBR 7 *Aquarius*

Air Force 26,436 (incl air defence units and military airfield guard units)

Flying hours   200–250 hrs/year

FORCES BY ROLE

Ftr	3 sqn with F-5E/F *Tiger II*; 3 sqn with F/A-18C/D *Hornet*
Tpt	1 sqn with Beech 350 *King Air*; Beech 1900D; Cessna 560XL *Citation*; DHC-6 *Twin Otter*; Falcon 50; PC-6 *Turbo-Porter*; PC-12
Trg	1 sqn with PC-7 *Turbo Trainer*; PC-21; 1 sqn with PC-9 (tgt towing)
Tpt Hel	6 sqn with AS-332 *Super Puma*; AS-532 *Cougar*; EC-635; SA-316 *Alouette III*
ISR UAV	1 bn with ADS 95 *Ranger*

EQUIPMENT BY TYPE

AIRCRAFT 87 combat capable
  FTR 54: 42 F-5E *Tiger II*; 12 F-5F *Tiger II*
  FGA 33: 26 F/A-18C *Hornet*; 7 F/A-18D *Hornet*
  TPT 22: **Light** 21: 1 Beech 350 *King Air*; 1 Beech1900D; 1 Cessna 560XL *Citation*; 1 DHC-6 *Twin Otter*; 15 PC-6 *Turbo-Porter*; 1 PC-6 (owned by armasuisse, civil registration); 1 PC-12 (owned by armasuisse, civil registration) **PAX** 1 *Falcon 50*
  TRG 49: 32 PC-7 *Turbo Trainer*; 11 PC-9; 6 PC-21
HELICOPTERS
  MRH 12 SA-316 *Alouette III*;
  TPT 47 **Medium** 27: 15 AS-332 *Super Puma*; 12 AS-532 *Cougar* **Light** 20 EC-635
UAV • ISR • Medium 4 ADS 95 *Ranger* systems

MSL • **AAM** • IR AAM AIM-9P/9X *Sidewinder* **ARH AAM** AIM-120B *AMRAAM*

Ground Based Air Defence (GBAD)

GBAD assets can be used to form AD clusters to be deployed independently as task forces within Swiss territory.

EQUIPMENT BY TYPE
AD
  SAM
    TOWED *Rapier*
    MANPAD FIM-92A *Stinger*
  GUNS 35mm
  RADARS • **AD RADARS** *Skyguard*

Armed Forces Logistic Organisation 9,321 on mobilisation

FORCES BY ROLE
Log   1 bde

Command Support Organisation 14,136 on mobilisation

FORCES BY ROLE
Spt   1 (comd) bde

Civil Defence 80,000

(not part of armed forces)

DEPLOYMENT

Legal provisions for foreign deployment:
Constitution: Codified constitution (1999)
Decision on deployment of troops abroad:
Peace promotion (66, 66a, 66b Swiss Mil Law): UN.OSCE mandate. Decision by govt; if over 100 tps deployed or op over 3 weeks Fed Assembly must agree first, except in emergency.
Support service abroad (69, 60 Swiss Mil Law): Decision by govt; if over 2,000 tps or op over 3 weeks Fed Assembly must agree in next official session

BOSNIA-HERZEGOVINA
EU • EUFOR • *Operation Althea* 20

BURUNDI
UN • BINUB 1 mil advisor

DEMOCRATIC REPUBLIC OF THE CONGO
UN • MONUSCO 3 obs

KOREA, REPUBLIC OF
NNSC • 5 officers

MIDDLE EAST
UN • UNTSO 13 obs

NEPAL
UN • UNMIN 3 monitors

SERBIA
NATO • KFOR 200 (military volunteers); 1 inf coy; elm 1 MP coy; elm 1 hel gp; 2 hel

SUDAN
UN • UNMIS 2 obs

Turkey TUR

New Turkish Lira L		2009	2010	2011
GDP	L	953bn	1.11tr	
	US$	616bn	737bn	
per capita	US$	8,233	9,730	
Growth	%	-4.7	6.3	
Inflation	%	6.3	8.7	
Def exp[a]	L	16.8bn		
	US$	10.9bn		
Def bdgt	L	15.4bn	15.8bn	17bn
	US$	9.95bn	10.5bn	
FMA (US)	US$	1.0m	-	-
US$1=L		1.55	1.51	

[a] including coast guard and gendarmerie

Population   75,705,147

Age	0-14	15-19	20-24	25-29	30-64	65 plus
Male	13.6%	4.4%	4.4%	4.5%	20.6%	2.9%
Female	13.0%	4.2%	4.3%	4.3%	20.4%	3.4%

Capabilities

ACTIVE 510,600 (Army 402,000 Navy 48,600 Air 60,000) Paramilitary 102,200
Terms of service 15 months. Reserve service to age of 41 for all services. Active figure reducing

RESERVE 378,700 (Army 258,700 Navy 55,000 Air 65,000) Paramilitary 50,000

ORGANISATIONS BY SERVICE

Army ε77,000; ε325,000 conscript (total 402,000)

FORCES BY ROLE
4 army HQ; 10 corps HQ

Armd	17 bde
Mech inf	15 bde
Inf	2 div; 11 bde
Trg/inf	4 bde
SF	1 comd HQ with (4 cdo bde)
Cbt hel	1 bn
Avn	4 regt; 3 bn (total: 1 tpt bn, 2 trg bn)
Trg/arty	4 bde

EQUIPMENT BY TYPE
MBT 4,503: 298 *Leopard* 2A4; 170 *Leopard* 1A4; 227 *Leopard* 1A3; 274 M-60A1; 658 M-60A3; 2,876 M-48A5 T1/M-48A5 T2 (1,300 to be stored)
RECCE 250+: ε250 *Akrep;* ARSV *Cobra*
AIFV 650
APC (T) 3,643: 830 AAPC; 2,813 M-113/M-113 A1/M-113A2
ARTY 7,450+

SP 868+: **105mm** 391: 26 M-108T; 365 M-52T; **155mm** 222 M-44T1; TU SpH Storm (K-9) *Thunder*; **175mm** 36 M-107; **203mm** 219 M-110A2

TOWED 685+: **105mm** M-101A1; **155mm** 523: 517 M-114A1/M-114A2; 6 *Panter*; **203mm** 162 M-115

MRL 84+: **70mm** 24; **107mm** 48; **122mm** T-122; **227mm** 12 MLRS (incl ATACMS)

MOR 5,813+
  SP 1,443+: **81mm**; **107mm** 1,264 M-30; **120mm** 179
  TOWED 4,370: **81mm** 3,792; **120mm** 578

AT
  MSL 1,363
    SP 365 *TOW*
    MANPATS 998: 80 *Kornet*; 186 *Cobra*; ε340 *Eryx*; 392 *Milan*
  RCL 3,869: **106mm** 2,329 M-40A1; **57mm** 923 M-18; **75mm** 617
  RL 66mm M-72 *LAW*

AIRCRAFT
  TPT • Light 105: 4 Beech 200 *Super King Air*; 98 Cessna 185 (U-17B); 3 Cessna 421
  TRG 63: 34 *Citabria*; 25 T-41D *Mescalero*; 4 T-42A *Cochise*

HELICOPTERS
  ATK 37 AH-1P/W *Cobra*
  MRH 37: 9 Bell 412 *Twin Huey*; 28 Hughes 300C
  ISR 3 OH-58B *Kiowa*
  TPT 222 **Medium** 60: 10 AS-532UL *Cougar*; 50 S-70B *Black Hawk* **Light** 162: 12 Bell 204B (AB-204B); ε45 Bell 205 (UH-1H *Iroquois*); 64 Bell 205A (AB-205A); 20 Bell 206 *Jet Ranger*; 2 Bell 212 (AB-212)

UAV • ISR 946+: **Heavy** some *Falcon* 600/*Firebee* **Medium** 196+: some CL-89; 196 *Gnat* **Light** 750 *Harpy*

AD
  SAM SP 148: 70 *Altigan* PMADS octuple *Stinger*, 78 *Zipkin* PMADS quad *Stinger* lnchr
  MANPAD 935: 789 FIM-43 *Redeye* (being withdrawn); 146 FIM-92A *Stinger*
  GUNS 1,664
    SP 40mm 262 M42A1
    TOWED 1,402: **20mm** 439 GAI-D01; **35mm** 120 GDF-001/GDF-003; **40mm** 843: 803 L/60/L/70; 40 T-1

RADAR • LAND AN/TPQ-36 *Firefinder*

Navy 14,100; 34,500 conscript (total 48,600 including 2,200 Coast Guard and 3,100 Marines)

Naval Forces Comd HQ at Ankara, Trg HQ at Altinovayalova, Fleet HQ at Gölcük, Northern Sea Area HQ at Istanbul, Southern Sea Area HQ at Izmir

EQUIPMENT BY TYPE
SUBMARINES • TACTICAL • SSK 14:
  6 *Atilay* (GER Type 209/1200) each with 8 single 533mm ASTT each with SST-4 HWT
  8 *Preveze/Gur* (GER Type 209/1400) each with 8 single 533mm ASTT each with UGM-84 *Harpoon* AShM/*Tigerfish* HWT
PRINCIPAL SURFACE COMBATANTS • FRIGATES • FFGHM 17:
  2 *Barbaros* (mod GER MEKO 200 F244 & F245) each with 2 quad Mk 141 lnchr (8 eff.) each with RGM-84C *Harpoon*

AShM, 1 octuple Mk29 lnchr with *Aspide* SAM, 2 Mk32 triple 324mm ASTT (6 eff.) with Mk46 LWT, 1 127mm gun, (capacity: 1 Bell 212 (AB-212) hel)
  2 *Barbaros* (mod GER MEKO 200 F246 & F247) each with 2 quad Mk 141 lnchr (8 eff.) each with RGM-84C *Harpoon* AShM, 1 8 cell Mk 41 VLS with *Aspide* SAM, 2 Mk32 triple 324mm ASTT with Mk 46 LWT, 1 127mm gun (capacity: 1 Bell 212 (AB-212) hel)
  8 *Gaziantep* (ex-US *Oliver Hazard Perry*-class) each with 1 Mk 13 GMLS with RGM-84C *Harpoon* AShM/SM-1MR SAM, 2 Mk32 triple 324mm ASTT (6 eff.) each with Mk46 LWT, 1 76mm gun, (capacity: 1 S-70B *Seahawk* ASW hel)
  1 *Muavenet* (ex-US *Knox*-class) with 1 octuple Mk16 lnchr with ASROC/RGM-84C *Harpoon* AShM, 2 twin 324mm ASTT (4 eff.) each with Mk46 LWT, 1 127mm gun, (capacity: 1 Bell 212 (AB-212) utl hel)
  4 *Yavuz* (GER MEKO 200TN) each with 2 quad Mk 141 lnchr (8 eff.) each with RGM-84C *Harpoon* AShM, 1 octuple Mk29 GMLS with *Aspide* SAM, 2 Mk32 triple 324mm ASTT (6 eff.) each with Mk46 LWT, 1 127mm gun, (capacity: 1 Bell 212 (AB-212) hel)

PATROL AND COASTAL COMBATANTS 52
  CORVETTES • FSGM 6
    6 *Burak* (FRA *d'Estienne d'Orves*) each with 2 single lnchr each with MM-38 *Exocet*AShM, 1 twin *Simbad* lnchr (manual aiming) with *Mistral* SAM, 4 single 533mm ASTT each with L5 HWT, 1 100mm gun
  PCFG 26:
    8 *Dogan* (GER *Lurssen*-57) each with 2 quad lnchr (8 eff.) with RGM-84A/C *Harpoon* AShM, 1 76mm gun
    8 *Kartal* (GER *Jaguar*) each with 4 single lnchr each with RB 12 *Penguin* AShM 2 single 533mm TT
    8 *Kilic* each with 2 quad Mk 141 lnchr (8 eff.) each with RGM-84C *Harpoon* AShM, 1 76mm gun (1 additional vessels in build)
    2 *Yildiz* each with 2 quad lnchr (8 eff.) each with RGM-84A/C *Harpoon* AShM, 1 76mm gun
  PCC 8: 1 *Hisar*; 6 *Karamursel* (GER *Vegesack*); 1 *Trabzon*;
  PBF 2 Kaan 15
  PB 10: 4 PGM-71; 6 *Turk*

MINE WARFARE • MINE COUNTERMEASURES 27
  MCM SPT 8 (tenders)
  MHO 10: 5 *Edineik* (FRA *Circe*); 5 *Aydin* (additional vessel on order)
  MSC 5 *Silifke* (US *Adjutant*)
  MSI 4 *Foca* (US *Cape*)

AMPHIBIOUS
  LANDING SHIPS • LST 5:
    2 *Ertugrul* (capacity 18 tanks; 400 troops) (US *Terrebonne Parish*)
    1 *Osman Gazi* (capacity 4 LCVP; 17 tanks; 980 troops;)
    2 *Sarucabey* (capacity 11 tanks; 600 troops)
  LANDING CRAFT 41: 25 LCT; 16 LCM
LOGISTICS AND SUPPORT 49:
  AORH 2
  AORL 1
  AOT 2
  AOL 1
  AO 1 (harbour)
  AGS 3
  ARS 1

Europe

ASR 1
AWT 15: 12; 3 (harbour)
ABU 2
ATF 3
TPT 1
TRG 10
TRV 3
YTM 17

FACILITIES

Bases   Located at Gölcük, Erdek, Canakkale,
               Eregli, Bartin, Izmir, Istanbul, Foka, Aksaz,
               Antalya, Mersin, Iskanderun

Marines 3,100

FORCES BY ROLE

Arty   1 bn (18 guns)
Marine   1 HQ; 1 regt; 3 bn

Naval Aviation

FORCES BY ROLE

ASW   Some sqn with Bell 204AS (Bell 204AS); Bell 212
       (AB-212); S-70B Seahawk
Trg   1 sqn with CN-235; ATR-72

EQUIPMENT BY TYPE

AIRCRAFT • TPT • Light 7: 1 ATR-72 (additional ac on
order); 6 CN-235
HELICOPTERS
   ASW 10: 3 Bell 204AS (AB-204AS); 7 S-70B Seahawk
   TPT • Light 11 Bell 212 (AB-212)

Air Force 60,000

2 tac air forces (divided between east and west)

Flying hours   180 hrs/year

FORCES BY ROLE

Ftr   2 sqn with F-4E Phantom II; 2 sqn with F-5A/B
          Freedom Fighter; 3 sqn with F-16C/D Fighting
          Falcon
FGA   2 sqn with F-4E Phantom II; 5 sqn with F-16C/D
          Fighting Falcon
ISR   2 sqn with RF-4E Phantom II
AEW&C   1 sqn (forming) with B-737 AEW&C
SAR   1 sqn with AS-532 Cougar
Tkr   1 sqn with KC-135R Stratotanker
Tpt   1 sqn with C-130B Hercules/C-130E Hercules; 1
          sqn with C-160 Transall;1 (VIP) sqn with Cessna
          560 Citation (UC-35); CN-235; 2 sqn with CN-
          235; Gulfstream III (C-20); 10 (liaison) flt with
          Bell 205 (UH-1H Iroquois); CN-235
OCU   1 sqn with F-4E Phantom II; 1 sqn with F-5A/B
          Freedom Fighter; 1 sqn with F-16C/D Fighting
          Falcon;
Trg   1 sqn with SF-260D; 1 sqn with T-37B Tweet/T-
          37C Tweet; T-38A Talon; 1 sqn with T-41
          Mescalero
SAM   4 sqn with 92 MIM-14 Nike Hercules; 2 sqn with
          86 Rapier; 8 (firing) unit with MIM-23 HAWK

EQUIPMENT BY TYPE

AIRCRAFT 426 combat capable
   FTR 87 F-5A/B Freedom Fighter; (48 being upgraded as
   LIFT)
   FGA 339: 126 F-4E Phantom II (52 upgraded to Phantom
   2020); 213 F-16C/D Fighting Falcon (all being upgraded to
   Block 50 standard; further 30 F-16 Block 52+ on order);
   ISR 35 RF-4E Phantom II
   AEW&C 1 B-737 AEW&C (3 more on order)
   TKR 7 KC-135R Stratotanker
   TPT 77+ **Medium** 29: 13 C-130B/E Hercules; 16 C-160D
   Transall **Light** 48: 2 Cessna 560 Citation (UC-35 - VIP); 46
   CN-235 (tpt/EW) **PAX** some Gulfstream III (C-20);
   TRG 198: 40 SF-260D; 60 T-37B/C Tweet; 70 T-38A Talon;
   28 T-41 Mescalero
HELICOPTERS
   TPT 40 **Medium** 20 AS-532 Cougar (14 SAR/6 CSAR)
   Light 20 Bell 205 (UH-1H Iroquois)
UAV • ISR 28: **Heavy** 10 Heron **Medium** 18 Gnat 750
AD
   SAM 178+: 86 Rapier
      TOWED: MIM-23 HAWK
      STATIC 92 MIM-14 Nike Hercules
MSL
   AAM • IR AAM AIM-9S Sidewinder; Shafrir 2(‡)
   SARH AAM AIM-7E Sparrow **ARH AAM** AIM-120A/B
   AMRAAM
   ARM AGM-88A HARM
   ASM AGM-65A/G Maverick; Popeye I
BOMBS
   Conventional BLU-107; GBU-8B HOBOS (GBU-15)
   Infra-Red 40 AN/AAQ 14 LANTIRN; 40 AN/AAQ 13
   LANTIRN
   Laser-guided Paveway I; Paveway II

Paramilitary

Gendarmerie/National Guard 100,000; 50,000 reservists (total 150,000)

Ministry of Interior; Ministry of Defence in war

FORCES BY ROLE

Army   1 (Border) div; 2 bde
Cdo   1 bde

EQUIPMENT BY TYPE

RECCE Akrep
APC (W) 560: 535 BTR-60/BTR-80; 25 Condor
AIRCRAFT
   ISR Some O-1E Bird Dog
   TPT • Light 2 Do-28D
HELICOPTERS
   MRH 19 Mi-17 Hip H
   TPT 37: Medium 14 S-70A Black Hawk; **Light** 23: 8 Bell
   204B (AB-204B); 6 Bell 205A (AB-205A); 8 Bell 206A
   (AB-206A) JetRanger; 1 Bell 212 (AB-212)

Coast Guard 800 (Coast Guard Regular element); 1,050 (from Navy); 1,400 conscript (total 3,250)

PATROL AND COASTAL COMBATANTS 72:
   PBF 43
   PB 29

AIRCRAFT • MP 3 CN-235 MPA
HELICOPTERS • MRH 8 Bell 412EP (AB-412EP - SAR)

DEPLOYMENT

Legal provisions for foreign deployment:
Constitution: Codified constitution (1985)
Decision on deployment of troops abroad: a) In general, by parliament (Art. 92); b) in cases of sudden aggression and if parliament is unable to convene, by president (Art. 92, 104b)

AFGHANISTAN
NATO • ISAF 1,790; 1 inf bde HQ; 2 inf bn

ARABIAN SEA & GULF OF ADEN
Combined Maritime Forces • CTF-151: 1 FFGHM

BOSNIA-HERZEGOVINA
EU • EUFOR • *Operation Althea* 280; 1 inf coy
OSCE • Bosnia and Herzegovina 2

CYPRUS (NORTHERN)
Army ε36,000
1 army corps HQ; some air det; 1 armd bde; 1 indep mech inf bde; 2 inf div; 1 cdo regt; 1 arty bde; 1 avn comd; 8 M-48A2 training; 441 M-48A5T1/M-48A5T2; 361 AAPC (incl variants); 266 M-113 (incl variants); (towed arty) 102: **105mm** 72 M-101A1; **155mm** 18 M-114A2; **203mm** 12 M-115; (SP) **155mm** 90 M-44T; (MRL) **122mm** 6 T-122; (MOR) 450: **81mm** 175; **107mm** 148 M-30; **120mm** 127 HY-12; (AT MSL) 114: 66 *Milan*; 48 TOW; (RCL) **106mm** 192 M-40A1; **90mm** M-67; **RL 66mm** M-72 *LAW*; (AD towed) **20mm** Rh 202; **35mm** GDF 16 GDF-003; **40mm** 48 M-1; 3 U-17 ac; 1 AS-532UL *Cougar*; 3 UH-1H *Iroquois* hel; 1 **PB**

IRAQ
NATO • NTM-I 2

LEBANON
UN • UNIFIL 504; 1 engr coy; 1 PB

MEDITERRANEAN SEA
NATO • *Operation Active Endeavour* 1 FFGHM
NATO • SNMCMG 2: 1 MHO

SERBIA
NATO • KFOR 479; 1 inf coy; elm 1 MP coy
OSCE • Serbia 1
OSCE • Kosovo 12

SUDAN
UN • UNMIS 3

FOREIGN FORCES

Israel Air Force: up to 1 ftr det (occasional) located at Akinci with F-16 *Fighting Falcon* (current status uncertain)
United States US European Command: 1,560; 1 spt facility at Izmir; 1 spt facility at Ankara; 1 air base at Incirlik
• US Strategic Command: 1 Spacetrack Radar at Incirlik

Ukraine UKR

Ukrainian Hryvnia h		2009	2010	2011
GDP	h	915bn	1.08tr	
	US$	117bn	137bn	
per capita	US$	2,553	3,005	
Growth	%	-15.1	3.0	
Inflation	%	15.9	9.8	
Def bdgt[a]	h	11bn	11.3bn	13.2bn
	US$	1.41bn	1.43bn	
FMA (US)	US$	7.0m	11.0m	15.0m
US$1=h		7.79	7.93	

[a] = excluding military pensions

Population   45,433,415

Age	0 – 14	15 – 19	20 – 24	25 – 29	30 – 64	65 plus
Male	7.1%	2.9%	3.9%	4.2%	22.8%	5.1%
Female	6.7%	2.8%	3.7%	4.1%	26.3%	10.4%

Capabilities

ACTIVE 129,925 (Army 70,753 Navy 13,932 Air 45,240) Paramilitary 84,900
Terms of Service Army, Air Force 18 months, Navy 2 years. Currently contract servicemen comprise about 50% of the Ukrainian armed forces.

RESERVE 1,000,000 (Joint 1,000,000)
mil service within 5 years

ORGANISATIONS BY SERVICE

Ground Forces (Army) 70,753
The three army mechanised corps are now under command of Army HQ and the territorial commands will be disbanded. Transformation of the army is due to be completed by 2015. The proposed structure is: a Joint Rapid Reaction Force; a Main Defence Force; and Strategic Reserve. Some units will become subordinate to Army HQ namely a msl bde, SF and a NBC protection group. The resulting 3 corps (div) formation organisation is:

Comd	1 (ground forces) comd (1 AM bde, 1 SSM bde, 2 SF regts, 1 Presidential Guard regt, 1 engr regt); 1 (MoD) gp (1 engr bde, 1 sy bde)
6 Corps	1 tk bde, 3 mech bde, 1 AB bde, 1 arty bde, 1 MRL regt, 1 AD regt
8 Corps	1 tk bde, 2 mech bde, 1 AM bde, 1 arty bde, 1 AD regt
13 Corps	3 mech bde, 1 mech regt, 1 AM regt, 1 arty bde, 1 MRL regt, 1 AD regt

FORCES BY ROLE:

Tk	2 bde
Mech	8 bde, 1 regt
AB	1 bde
Air Mob	2 bde, 1 regt

Arty	3 bde, 2 MRL regt
AD	3 regt
SF	2 regt
SSM	1 bde

EQUIPMENT BY TYPE
MBT 2,988: 10 T-84 *Oplot* (development complete); 167 T-80; 1,032 T-72; 1,667 T-64; 112 T-55
RECCE 600+ BRDM-2
AIFV 3,028: 60 BMD-1; 78 BMD-2; 994 BMP-1; 1,434 BMP-2; 4 BMP-3; 458 BRM-1K
APC 1,432
  APC (T) 44 BTR-D
  APC (W) 1,398: up to 10 BTR 4; 136 BTR-60; 857 BTR-70; 395 BTR-80
ARTY 3,351
  SP 1,226: **122mm** 600 2S1 *Carnation*; **152mm** 527: 40 2S19 *Farm*; 463 2S3; 24 2S5; **203mm** 99 2S7
  TOWED 1,065: **122mm** 371: 369 D-30; 2 (M-30) *M-1938*; **152mm** 694: 287 2A36; 185 2A65; 215 D-20; 7 ML-70
  GUN/MOR 120mm 69:
    SP 67 2S9 *Anona*
    TOWED 2 2B16 *NONA-K*
  MRL 554: **122mm** 335: 20 9P138; 315 BM-21; **132mm** 2 BM-13; **220mm** 137 9P140 *Uragan*; **300mm** 80 9A52 *Smerch*
  MOR 120mm 437: 318 2S12; 119 PM-38
AT • MSL • MANPATS AT-4 9K111 *Spigot*/AT-5 9K113 *Spandrel*/AT-6 9K114 *Spiral*
  GUNS 100mm ε500 MT-12/T-12
HELICOPTERS
  ATK 139 Mi-24 *Hind*
  TPT • Medium 38 Mi-8 *Hip*
AD • SAM • SP 435: 60 9K37 *Buk*-1 (SA-11 *Gadfly*); ε150 9K35 *Strela*-10(SA-13 *Gopher*); 100 *Krug* 2K11 (SA-4 *Ganef*); 125 9K33 *Osa* (SA-8 *Gecko*); S-300V (SA-12 *Gladiator*)
  GUNS 470:
    SP 30mm 70 2S6
    TOWED 57mm ε400 S-60
RADAR • LAND *Small Fred/Small Yawn/SNAR-10 Big Fred* (arty)
MSL • SSM 212: 50 FROG; 90 SS-21 *Scarab (Tochka)*; 72 *Scud-B*

Navy 11,932; 2,000 conscript (total 13,932 incl Naval Aviation and Naval Infantry)

After intergovernmental agreement in 1997, the Russian Federation Fleet currently leases bases in Sevastopol and Karantinnaya Bays and also shares facilities jointly with Ukr warships at Streletskaya Bay. The overall serviceability of the fleet is assessed as low.

EQUIPMENT BY TYPE
SUBMARINES • TACTICAL • SSK 1 *Foxtrot* (T-641)†
PRINCIPAL SURFACE COMBATANTS • FRIGATES 1
  FFHM 1 *Hetman Sagaidachny* (RUS *Krivak* III) with 1 twin lnchr (2 eff.) with *Osa-M* (SA-N-4 *Gecko*) SAM, 2 quad 533mm ASTT (8 eff.) each with T-53 HWT, 1 100mm gun, (capacity 1 Ka-27 *Helix* ASW hel)
PATROL AND COASTAL COMBATANTS 10
  CORVETTES • FSM 3 *Grisha* (II/V) each with 1 twin lnchr (2 eff.) with *Osa-M* (SA-N-4 *Gecko*) SAM, 2 twin 533mm ASTT (4 eff.) each with SAET-60 HWT, 1 to 2 RBU 6000 *Smerch* 2 (12-24 eff.), 1 76mm gun
  PCFGM 2 *Tarantul II* each with 2 twin lnchr each with P-15 Termit-R (SS-N-2D *Styx*) AShM; 1 quad lnchr (manual aiming) with 9K32 *Strela-2* (SA-N-5 *Grail*); 1 76mm gun
  PHG 2 *Matka* each with 2 single lnchr each with P-15 Termit-M/R (SS-N-2C *Styx*/SS-N-2D *Styx*) AShM, 1 76mm gun
  PCMT 2 *Pauk* I each with 1 quad lnchr (manual aiming) with 9K32 Strela-2 (SA-N-5 *Grail*) SAM, 4 single 406mm TT, 2 RBU-1200 (10 eff.), 1 76mm gun
  PB 1 *Zhuk*
MINE WARFARE • MINE COUNTERMEASURES 5
  MHI 1 *Yevgenya*
  MSO 2 *Natya*
  MSC 2 *Sonya*
AMPHIBIOUS
  LANDING SHIPS 2:
    LSM 1 *Polnochny* C (capacity 6 MBT; 180 troops)
    LST 1 *Ropucha* with 4 quad lnchr (16 eff.) each with 9K32 *Strela-2* (SA-N-5 *Grail*) SAM, 92 mine, (capacity either 10 MBT or 190 troops; either 24 APC (T) or 170 troops)
  LANDING CRAFT • LCAC 1 *Pomornik* (*Zubr*) each with 2 quad lnchr (8 eff.) each with 9K32 *Strela-2* (SA-N-5 *Grail*) SAM, (capacity 230 troops; either 3 MBT or 10 APC (T))
LOGISTICS AND SUPPORT 29
  AGF 1 *Bambuk*
  AR 1 *Amur* (can also act as a comd. ship or as a spt ship for surface ships and submarines)
  AWT 1
  AGS 2: 1 *Moma* (mod); 1 *Biya*
  ABU 1
  TRG • 3 AXL
  YDG 1
  YDT 13: 1 *Yelva*; 12
  YTM 6
FACILITIES

Bases	Located at Sevastopol, Kerch, Donuzlav, Chernomorskoye, Odessa, Ochakov
Construction and Repair Yards	Located at Nikolaev, Balaklava

Naval Aviation ε2,500

AIRCRAFT 10 combat capable
  ASW 10 Be-12 *Mail*
  TPT 16 **Medium** 5 An-12 *Cub* **Light** 10: 1 An-24 *Coke*; 8 An-26 *Curl*; 1 Tu-134 *Crusty* **PAX** 1 Il-18 *Coot*
HELICOPTERS
  ASW 72: 28 Ka-25 *Hormone*; 2 Ka-27E *Helix*; 42 Mi-14 *Haze*
  TPT • Heavy 5 Mi-6 *Hook*

Naval Infantry 3,000

Naval inf 1 bde

Air Forces 45,240

| Air | 3 air cmd – West, South, Centre plus Task Force 'Crimea'. Flying hours 40-50hrs/yr |

FORCES BY ROLE

Ftr	5 bde with MiG-29 *Fulcrum*; Su-27 *Flanker*
FGA	2 bde with Su-24M *Fencer*; Su-25 *Frogfoot*
ISR	2 sqn with Su-24MR *Fencer-E**
Tpt	3 bde with An-24; An-26; An-30; Il-76 *Candid*; Tu-134 *Crusty*;
Trg	Some sqn with L-39 *Albatros*
Tpt Hel	Some sqn with Mi-8; Mi-9; PZL Mi-2 *Hoplite*

EQUIPMENT BY TYPE
AIRCRAFT 211 combat capable
  FTR 80 MiG-29 *Fulcrum*
  FGA 72: 36 Su-24 *Fencer*; 36 Su-27 *Flanker*
  ATK 36 Su-25 *Frogfoot*
  ISR 26: 3 An-30 *Clank*; 23 Su-24MR *Fencer-E**
  TPT 46 **Heavy** 20 Il-76 *Candid* **Medium** 26: 3 An-24 *Coke*; 21 An-26 *Curl*; 2 Tu-134 *Crusty*
  TRG 39 L-39 *Albatros*
HELICOPTERS
  C&C 4 Mi-9;
  TPT 34 **Medium** 31 Mi-8 *Hip* **Light** 3 PZL Mi-2 *Hoplite*
AD • SAM 825 S-300PS (SA-10 *Grumble*) (quad)/SA-11 *Gadfly*/S-75 Volkhov (SA-2 *Guideline*) (towed)/S-125 *Pechora* (SA-3 *Goa*) (towed)/S-200V *Angara* (SA-5 *Gammon*) (static)
MSL
  ASM: Kh-25 (AS-10 *Karen*); Kh-59 (AS-13 *Kingbolt*); Kh-29 (AS-14 *Kedge*);
  ARM: Kh-58 (AS-11 *Kilter*); Kh-25MP (AS-12 *Kegler*); Kh-28 (AS-9 *Kyle*)
  AAM:IR AAM R-60 (AA-8 *Aphid*); R-73 (AA-11 *Archer*); SARH AAM R-27 (AA-10A *Alamo*)

Paramilitary

MVS ε39,900 active
(Ministry of Internal Affairs)

FORCES BY ROLE

| Mil Region | 4 tps |
| MP | 1 (Internal Security) tps |

Border Guard 45,000 active

Maritime Border Guard
The Maritime Border Guard is an independent subdivision of the State Comission for Border Guards and is not part of the navy.

FORCES BY ROLE

Air Wing	1 (gunship) sqn
Air	3 sqn
MCM	1 sqn
Paramilitary	2 (river) bde; 1 (aux ship) gp; 4 (cutter) bde
Trg	1 div

EQUIPMENT BY TYPE
PATROL AND COASTAL COMBATANTS 30
  PCFT 10 *Stenka* each with 4 single 406mm TT

PCT 3 *Pauk* I each with 4 single 406mm TT, 2 RBU-1200 (10 eff.), 1 76mm gun
PHT 1 *Muravey* with 2 single 406mm TT, 1 76mm gun
PB 12 *Zhuk*
PBR 4
LOGISTICS AND SUPPORT • AGF 1
AIRCRAFT • TPT Medium An-8 *Camp* **Light** An-24 *Coke*; An-26 *Curl*; An-72 *Coaler*
HELICOPTERS • ASW: Ka-27 *Helix A*

Civil Defence Troops 9,500+ (civilian)
(Ministry of Emergency Situations) Army
4 indep bde; 4 indep regt

DEPLOYMENT

Legal provisions for foreign deployment:
Constitution: Codified constitution (1996)
Specific legislation: 'On the procedures to deploy Armed Forces of Ukraine units abroad' (1518-III, March 2000).
Decision on deployment of troops abroad: Parliament authorised to approve decision to provide military assistance, deploy troops abroad and allow foreign military presence in Ukraine (Art. 85, para 23); Also, in accordance with Art. 7 of the specific legislation (above), president is authorised to take a decision to deploy troops abroad and at the same time to submit a draft law to the Parliament of Ukraine for approval

AFGHANISTAN
NATO • ISAF 31

BOSNIA-HERZEGOVINA
OSCE• Bosnia and Herzegovina 1

DEMOCRATIC REPUBLIC OF THE CONGO
UN • MONUSCO 12 obs

IRAQ
NATO • NTM-I 9

LIBERIA
UN • UNMIL 277; 2 obs; 1 avn coy

MEDITERRANEAN SEA
NATO • *Operation Active Endeavour* 1 FSM

MOLDOVA
10 mil obs

SERBIA
NATO • KFOR 127; 1 inf coy
OSCE • Serbia 1
OSCE • Kosovo 2
UN • UNMIK 2 obs

SUDAN
UN • UNMIS 9 obs

FOREIGN FORCES

Russia ε13,000 Navy 1 Fleet HQ at Sevastopol; 1 indep naval inf regt; 102 AIFV/APC (T)/APC (W); 24 arty

United Kingdom UK

British Pound £		2009	2010	2011
GDP	£	1.39tr	1.46tr	
	US$	2.18tr	2.25tr	
per capita	US$	35,235	36,427	
Growth	%	-4.9	1.2	
Inflation	%	-0.6	3.0	
Def exp[b]	£	37.8bn		
	US$	59.1bn		
Def bdgt[a]	£	38.7bn	36.7bn	32.9bn
	US$	60.5bn	56.5bn	
US$1=£		0.64	0.65	

[a] Resource Accounting and Budgeting terms. Figure for 2011 excludes cost of capital charge included in previous years

[b] NATO definition

Population   61,899,272

Age	0–14	15–19	20–24	25–29	30–64	65 plus
Male	8.9%	3.2%	3.5%	3.5%	23.3%	7.3%
Female	8.5%	3.1%	3.4%	3.3%	22.9%	9.2%

Capabilities

ACTIVE 178,470 (Army 102,600, Navy 35,480 Air 40,390)

RESERVE 82,274 (Regular Reserve ε51,000 incl 5,420 RAF; Volunteer Reserve 31,274 (Army 27,010; Navy 2,785; Air 1,479)
Includes both trained and those currently under training within the Regular Forces, excluding university cadet units.

ORGANISATIONS BY SERVICE

Strategic Forces 1,000

Armed Forces
RADAR • STRATEGIC 1 Ballistic Missile Early Warning System *BMEWS* at Fylingdales Moor

Royal Navy
SUBMARINES • STRATEGIC • SSBN 4:
    4 *Vanguard* each with 4 533mm TT each with *Spearfish* HWT, up to 16 UGM-133A *Trident D-5* SLBM (Each boat will not deploy with more than 48 warheads, but each missile could carry up to 12 MIRV, some *Trident D-5* capable of being configured for sub-strategic role)
MSL • STRATEGIC 48 SLBM (Fewer than 160 declared operational warheads)

Army 99,100; 3,500 (Gurkhas) (total 102,600)
Regt normally bn size
FORCES BY ROLE
1 Land Comd HQ, 1 multinational corps HQ, 3 deployable div HQ, 7 deployable bde HQ and 1 tri-service Joint Hel Comd. The UK Field Army has a capability to form 46 battlegroups drawing on 5 armd regts, 5 armd recce regts, 8 armd inf bn, 3 mech inf bn, 21 lt inf bn, 2 para bns and 2 air asslt bns. Additional spt is provided from theatre troops.

Comd	1 (Allied Command Europe Rapid Reaction Corps - ARRC) multinational corps HQ, 1 (6th) div HQ
Armd	1 div (1st) with (2 armd bde (7th and 20th) (each: 1 armd regt, 1 armd recce regt, 2 armd inf bn, 1 lt inf bn); 1 mech bde (4th) with (1 armd regt, 1 armd recce regt, 1 armd inf bn, 1 mech inf bn, 2 lt inf bn, 1 (Gurhka) lt inf bn); 1 cbt spt gp with (3 SP arty regt; 1 AD regt; 3 cbt engr))
Mech	1 div (3rd) with (1 mech bde (1st) with (1 armd regt, 1 armd recce regt, 1 armd inf bn 1 mech inf bn, 2 lt inf bn); 1 mech bde (12th) with (1 armd regt, 1 armd recce regt, 1 armd inf bn, 1 mech inf bn, 3 lt inf bn); 1 lt inf bde (19th) with (4 lt inf bn); 1 cbt spt gp with (2 SP arty regt; 1 arty regt; 1 AD regt; 2 cbt engr regt; 2 engr regt))
Lt Inf	3 bn (London District); 2 bn (Cyprus); 1 (Gurkha) bn (Brunei)
SF	1 (SAS) regt; 1 (specl recce reg) regt; 1 (SF spt) gp (based on para bn)
Air Aslt	1 bde (16th) with (2 para bn, 2 air aslt bn, 1 arty regt, 1 engr regt, 2 atk hel regt, 1 lt hel regt)
Arty	1 bde HQ
STA	1 regt
MRL	1 (MLRS) regt
AD	1 bde HQ (opcon RAF); 1 regt
Engr	1 force engr bde (4 EOD regt/bn, 1 Air Spt); 1 EOD bn
Log	2 log bde, 1 (log spt) bde
Trg	1 BG (based on 1 armd inf bn)
Avn	2 hel regt, 1 indep sqn, 3 indep flt
ISR UAV	1 regt

Home Service Forces • Gibraltar 200 reservists; 150 active reservists (total 350)

Reserves

Territorial Army 27,010 reservists
The Territorial Army has been reorganised to enable the regular army to receive relevant manpower support from their associated territorial unit.

Armd	2 regt
Armd Recce	2 regt
Lt Inf	13 bn
SF	2 (SAS) regt
Para	1 bn
Arty	3 lt regt
STA	1 regt
MRL	1 (MLRS) regt
AD	1 regt

Engr	5 regt, 1 (EOD) regt, 1 sqn, 1 (geo) sqn, 1 (cdo) sqn
Avn	1 regt
ISR UAV	1 regt

EQUIPMENT BY TYPE
MBT 325 CR2 *Challenger 2*
RECCE 738: 150 *Jackal*; 110 *Jackal 2*; 140 *Jackal* 2A; 327 *Scimitar*; 11 Tpz-1 *Fuchs*
AIFV 526 *Warrior*
APC 2,059+
  APC (T) 1,535: 646 AFV432; 380 *Bulldog* Mk3; 394 FV 103 *Spartan;* 115 *Warthog* being delivered
  APC (W) 524+: 109 AT105 *Saxon* (Northern Ireland only); 277 *Mastiff* (4x4); 118 *Ridgeback*; 20+ *Wolfhound* (6x6)
LFV 401 *Panther*
ARTY 670
  SP 155mm 130 AS-90 *Braveheart*
  TOWED 105mm 118 L-118 *Light gun*
  MRL 227mm 51 MLRS/GMLRS
  MOR 371: **81mm SP** 11; **81mm** 360
AT • MSL • MANPATS *Javelin*
AIRCRAFT • TPT • Light 1 Beech *King Air* 350ER (3 more on order); 3 BN-2T-4S *Defender* (4th on order)
HELICOPTERS
  ATK 66 AH-64D *Apache*
  MRH 232: 77 *Lynx* AH MK7; 22 *Lynx* AH MK9; 133 SA-341 *Gazelle*
UAV • ISR • Medium *Hermes* 450; *Watchkeeper* (In Test – ISD expected 2011)
AD • SAM 338+
  SP 134 FV4333 *Stormer*
  TOWED 57+ *Rapier* FSC
  MANPAD 147 *Starstreak* (LML)
RADAR • LAND 157: 4-7 *Cobra*; 150 MSTAR
AMPHIBIOUS 6 LCVP
LOGISTICS AND SUPPORT 5 RCL

Royal Navy 35,480

EQUIPMENT BY TYPE
SUBMARINES 11
  STRATEGIC • SSBN 4:
    4 *Vanguard*, opcon Strategic Forces, each with up to 16 UGM-133A *Trident* D-5 SLBM, 4 single 533mm TT each with *Spearfish* HWT, (Each boat will not deploy with more than 48 warheads, but each missile could carry up to 12 MIRV; some *Trident* D-5 capable of being configured for sub strategic role)
  TACTICAL • SSN 7:
    6 *Trafalgar* each with 5 single 533mm TT each with *Spearfish* HWT/*Tomahawk* tactical LACM/UGM 84 *Harpoon* AShM
    1 *Astute* with 6 single 533mm TT with *Spearfish* HWT/UGM-84 *Harpoon* AShM/*Tomahawk* tactical LACM (additional vessels in build)
PRINCIPAL SURFACE COMBATANTS 25
  AIRCRAFT CARRIERS • CVS 1
    1 *Invincible* with 3 single Mk15 *Phalanx*-1B/*Goalkeeper* CIWS, (capacity 'tailored air group' 8–12 *Harrier* GR9A; 4 AW-101 *Merlin* ASW (HM Mk1) hel; 4 *Sea King* AEW Mk7 AEW hel)

DESTROYERS • DDHM 7
  2 *Daring* (Type-45) each with 1 48 cell VLS with Aster 15/Aster 30 SAM, 1 114mm gun, (capacity 1 *Lynx*/AW-101 *Merlin* hel - additional vessels in build)
  1 *Sheffield* (Type-42 Batch 2) each with 1 twin lnchr (2 eff.) with *Sea Dart* SAM, 2 single Mk15 *Phalanx* CIWS, 1 114mm gun, (capacity 1 *Lynx* hel)
  4 *Sheffield* (Type-42 Batch 3) each with 1 twin lnchr (2 eff.) with *Sea Dart* SAM, 2 single Mk15 *Phalanx*-1B CIWS, 1 114mm gun, (capacity 1 *Lynx* hel)
FRIGATES • FFG 17
  4 *Cornwall* (Type-22 Batch 3) each with 2 quad Mk141 lnchr (8 eff.) each with RGM-84C *Harpoon* AShM, 2 sextuple lnchr (12 eff.) each with *Sea Wolf* SAM, 1 *Goalkeeper* CIWS, 1 114mm gun, (capacity 2 *Lynx* hel) (all to be retired by April 2011)
  13 *Norfolk* (Type-23) each with 2 quad Mk141 lnchr (8 eff.) each with RGM-84C *Harpoon* AShM, 1 32 cell VLS with *Sea Wolf* SAM, 2 twin 324mm ASTT (4 eff.) each with *Sting Ray* LWT, 1 114mm gun, (capacity either 2 *Lynx* or 1 AW-101 *Merlin* ASW (HM Mk1) hel)
PATROL AND COASTAL COMBATANTS 22
  PSO 4: 3 *River*; 1 *River* (mod) with 1 hel landing platform
  PB 18: 16 *Archer* (trg); 2 *Scimitar*
MINE WARFARE • MINE COUNTERMEASURES 16
  MCO 8 *Hunt* (incl 4 mod *Hunt*)
  MHC 8 *Sandown* (1 decommissioned and used in trg role)
AMPHIBIOUS
  PRINCIPAL AMPHIBIOUS SHIPS 3
    LPD 2 *Albion* (capacity 2 med hel; 4 LCVP; 6 MBT; 300 troops) (1 to be transferred to extended readiness by Nov 2011)
    LPH 1 *Ocean* (capacity 18 hel; 4 LCU or 2 LCAC; 4 LCVP; 800 troops)
  LANDING CRAFT 36: 13 **LCU**; 23 **LCVP**
LOGISTICS AND SUPPORT 5
  AGOBH 1 *Endurance* (capacity 2 *Lynx* hel)
  AGHS 3: 1 *Scott*; 2 *Echo*
  AGS 1 *Gleaner* (inshore/coastal)

FORCES BY ROLE
Navy/Marine 1 party located at Diego Garcia, BIOT

FACILITIES

Bases	Located at Portsmouth (Fleet HQ), Faslane, Devonport, Gibraltar
Naval air bases	Located at Prestwick, Culdrose, Yeovilton

Royal Fleet Auxiliary

Support and Miscellaneous vessels are mostly manned and maintained by the Royal Fleet Auxiliary (RFA), a civilian fleet owned by the UK MoD, which has approximately 2,500 personnel with type comd under CINCFLEET.

AMPHIBIOUS • PRINCIPAL AMPHIBIOUS SHIPS
  LSD 4 *Bay* (capacity 4 LCU; 2 LCVP; 1 LCU; 24 CR2 *Challenger* 2 MBT; 350 troops) (one to be decommissioned by Apr 2011)

LOGISTICS AND SUPPORT 18

AORH 4: 2 *Wave*; 2 *Fort Victoria* (1 to be decommissioned by Apr 2011)

AOR 2 *Leaf* (1 to be decommissioned by Apr 2011)

AORLH 2 *Rover*

AFSH 2 *Fort Rosalie*

ARH 1 *Diligence*

AG 1 *Argus* (aviation trg ship with secondary role as primarily casualty receiving ship)

AKR 6 *Point* (Not RFA manned)

Naval Aviation (Fleet Air Arm) 5,520

FORCES BY ROLE

ASW	4 sqn with AW-101 ASW *Merlin* (HM Mk1); 1 sqn with *Lynx* HAS Mk3/*Lynx* HMA Mk8; 1 flt with *Lynx* Mk3
AEW	3 sqn with *Sea King* AEW Mk7
SAR	1 sqn (and detached flt) with *Sea King* HU MK5
Spt	some (Fleet) sqn with Beech 55 *Baron* (civil registration); Cessna 441 *Conquest* (civil registration); *Falcon* 20 (civil registration); G-115 (op under contract); 1 sqn with *Lynx* AH MK7 (incl in Royal Marines entry); 3 sqn with *Sea King* HC Mk4
Trg	1 (operational evaluation) sqn with AW-101 ASW *Merlin* (HM Mk1); *Sea King* HC Mk4; 1 sqn with *Jetstream* T Mk2/3; 1 sqn with *Lynx* Mk3

EQUIPMENT BY TYPE

AIRCRAFT 12 combat capable

TPT 21 Light 2: 1 Beech 55 *Baron* (civil registration); 1 Cessna 441 *Conquest II* (civil registration); **PAX** 19 *Falcon* 20 (civil registration)

TRG 27: 5 G-115 (op under contract); 12 *Hawk* T Mk1*; 10 *Jetstream* T Mk2/T Mk3

HELICOPTERS

ASW 113: 71 *Lynx* HAS Mk3/*Lynx* HMA Mk8; 42 AW-101 ASW *Merlin* (HM Mk1)

MRH 6 *Lynx* AH Mk7 (incl in Royal Marines entry)

AEW 13 *Sea King* AEW Mk7

TPT • Medium 52: 37 *Sea King* HC MK4 (for RM); 15 *Sea King* HU Mk5

MSL • AShM *Sea Skua*

Royal Marines 6,840

FORCES BY ROLE

LCA	3 sqn opcon Royal Navy; 1 sqn (539 Aslt Sqn RM)
Sy	1 Fleet Protection Group, opcon Royal Navy
SF	1 (SBS) regt
Cdo	1 bde (3 cdo (bn sized), 1 recce tp, 1 lt inf bn (army) 1 cdo arty regt (army))
AD	1 bty (army)
Engr	1 regt (army)
Logistic	1 regt
Tpt Hel	2 sqn opcon Royal Navy

EQUIPMENT BY TYPE

APC (T) 142: 118 BvS-10 *Viking*; 24 BvS-10 Mk2 *Viking*

ARTY 18+

TOWED 105mm 18 L-118

MOR 81mm some

AT • MSL • MANPATS *Javelin*

AMPHIBIOUS • LANDING CRAFT • LCAC 4 *Griffon* 2400TD

HELICOPTERS

MRH 6 *Lynx* AH Mk7

TPT • Medium 37 *Sea King* HC Mk4

AD • SAM • HVM

RADAR • LAND 4 MAMBA (*Arthur*)

Royal Marines Reserve 600

Royal Air Force 40,390

Flying hours   210/yr on fast jets; 290 on tpt ac; 240 on support hels; 90 on *Sea King*

FORCES BY ROLE

Ftr	1 sqn with *Tornado* F-3 (OSD March 2011)
FGA	5 sqn with *Tornado* GR4/GR4A; 4 sqn (incl 1 Op Eval Unit) with *Typhoon*
ISR	1 sqn with Beech 350 *Shadow* R1; *Sentinel* RMk1 (To be withdrawn from role post-Afghanistan)
ELINT	1 sqn with *Nimrod* R1 (OSD March 2011)
AEW&C	2 sqn with E-3D *Sentry*
SAR	2 sqn with *Sea King* HAR-3/3A
Tkr/tpt	1 sqn with L-1011-500 *Tristar* C2; *Tristar* K1; *Tristar* KC1; 1 sqn with VC-10C1K; VC-10K3; VC-10K4
Tpt	1 (comms) sqn with AS-355 *Squirrel*; BAe-125; BAe-146; BN-2A *Islander* CC2; 1 sqn with C-17 *Globemaster*; 4 sqn with C-130J/C-130K *Hercules*
OCU	2 sqn with *Typhoon*; *Tornado* GR4
Trg	Units (including postgraduate training on 203(R) sqn) with Beech 200 *King Air*; *Dominie* T1; EMB -312 *Tucano* (T Mk1); Grob 115E *Tutor*; *Hawk* T Mk1/1A/1W; *Sea King* HAR-3/3A; T67M/M260 *Firefly*
Tpt Hel	2 sqn with AW-101 *Merlin* (HC Mk3);1 sqn Bell 412EP *Griffin*; 3 sqn with CH-47 *Chinook*; 2 sqn with SA-330 *Puma*; 3 sqn with *Sea King* HAR-3
Cbt ISR UAV	1 sqn with MQ-9 *Reaper*
NBC	1 (joint service) regt

EQUIPMENT BY TYPE

AIRCRAFT 334 combat capable

FTR 12 *Tornado* F-3 (to be withdrawn from service by end Mar 2011)

FGA 177: 105 *Tornado* GR4/GR4A; 72 *Typhoon*

ISR 9: 4 Beech 350 *Shadow* R1; 5 *Sentinel* RMK1

ELINT 2 *Nimrod* R1 (OSD March 2011)

AEW&C 6 E-3D *Sentry*

TKR/TPT 22: 2 *Tristar* K1; 4 *Tristar* KC1; 10 VC-10C1K; 4 VC-10K3; 2 VC-10K4

TPT 70: **Heavy** 7 C-17A *Globemaster*; **Medium** 43: 10 C-130J *Hercules)*; 14 C-130J-30 *Hercules*; 3 C-130K *Hercules*; 16 C-130K-30 *Hercules*; **Light** 9: 7 Beech 200 *King Air* (on lease); 2 BN-2A *Islander* CC2/3 **PAX** 11: 6 BAe-125 CC-3 5; 2 BAe-146 MkII; 3 L-1011-500 *Tristar* C2

TRG 366: 9 *Dominie* T1; 95 EMB-312 *Tucano* T1; 101 G-115E *Tutor*; 28 *Hawk* 128*; 117 *Hawk* T Mk1/1A/1W*; 38 T67M/M260 *Firefly*

HELICOPTERS

MRH 47: 31 AS-355 *Squirrel*; 4 Bell 412EP *Griffin* HAR-2; 12 Bell 412EP *Griffin* HT1

TPT 128: **Heavy** 41: 40 CH-47 HC2/2A *Chinook*; 1 CH-47 HC3 *Chinook* in test; **Medium** 87: 28 AW-101 *Merlin* (HC Mk3); 34 SA-330 *Puma* HC1; 25 *Sea King* HAR-3A

UAV • CBT/ISR • Heavy 5+ MQ-9 *Reaper*

MSL

AAM • IR AAM AIM-9L/AIM-9L/I *Sidewinder;* **IIR AAM** ASRAAM; SARH AAM *Skyflash;* **ARH AAM** AIM-120B/AIM-120 C5 AMRAAM

ARM ALARM

ASM *Brimstone; Dual-Mode Brimstone;* AGM-65G2 *Maverick*

LACM Storm Shadow

BOMBS

Conventional Mk 82; CRV-7

Laser-Guided/GPS: *Paveway* II; GBU-10 *Paveway* III; Enhanced *Paveway* II/III; GBU-24 *Paveway* IV

Royal Air Force Regiment

FORCES BY ROLE

Air	3 (tactical Survival To Operate (STO)) sqn + HQ; 7 (fd) sqn
Trg	1 (joint) unit (with army) with *Rapier* C

Tri-Service Defence Hel School

HELICOPTERS: 28 AS-350 *Ecureuil*; 7 *Griffin* HT1

Volunteer Reserve Air Forces

(Royal Auxiliary Air Force/RAF Reserve)

Air	1 (air movements) sqn; 2 (intelligence) sqn; 5 (field) sqn; 1 (HQ augmentation) sqn; 1 (C-130 Reserve Aircrew) flt
Medical	1 sqn

DEPLOYMENT

Legal provisions for foreign deployment:
Constitution: Uncodified constitution which includes constitutional statutes, case law, international treaties and unwritten conventions
Decision on deployment of troops abroad: By the government

AFGHANISTAN

NATO • ISAF 9,500;

Army: 1 div HQ (6th); 1 air aslt bde HQ (16th) with (1 recce regt; 2 para bn; 2 air aslt bn; 2 lt inf bn); *Jackal; Scimitar; Warrior; Spartan; Mastiff; Ridgeback; Warthog*

Wolfhound; L-118; GMLRS; AH-64D *Apache; Lynx; Hermes* 450

Royal Navy: *Sea King* HC Mk4

Air Force: *Tornado* GR4/GR4A; C-130 *Hercules*; CH-47 *Chinook*; HC Mk3 *Merlin*; Beech *King Air* 350 *Shadow* R1; MQ-9 *Reaper*

ARABIAN SEA

Combined Maritime Forces • TF-53: 1 ARH
Combined Maritime Forces • CTF-150: 1 FFGHM

ARABIAN SEA & GULF OF ADEN

Combined Maritime Forces • CTF-151: 1 AORH

ARMENIA/AZERBAIJAN

OSCE • Minsk Conference 1

ASCENSION ISLAND

Air Force 23

ATLANTIC (NORTH)

Royal Navy 1 DD/FF; 1 AO

ATLANTIC (SOUTH)

Royal Navy 1 DD/FF; 1 AO

BAHRAIN

Royal Navy 100; Air Force 1 BAe-125, 1 BAe-146

BELIZE

Army 70

BOSNIA-HERZEGOVINA

EU • EUFOR • *Operation Althea* 4
OSCE • Bosnia and Herzegovina 2

BRITISH INDIAN OCEAN TERRITORY

Royal Navy 40; 1 Navy/Marine party at Diego Garcia

BRUNEI

Army 550; 1 Gurkha bn; 1 jungle trg centre; 1 hel flt with 3 hel

CANADA

Army 370; 2 trg units Royal Navy 10: Air Force 10

CYPRUS

Army 1,700; 2 inf bn
Navy 20
Air Force 870; 1 SAR sqn with 4 Bell 412 *Twin Huey*; 1 radar (on det)
UN • UNFICYP 271; 1 inf coy

DEMOCRATIC REPUBLIC OF THE CONGO

UN • MONUC 4 obs

FALKLAND ISLANDS

Army 420; 1 AD det with *Rapier* FSC
Navy 420; 1 OPV
Air Force 680; 1 ftr flt with 4 E-F *Typhoon* FGR.4; 1 SAR sqn with *Sea King* HAR-3A/*Sea King* HAR-3; 1 tkr/tpt flt with C-130 *Hercules*; VC-10 K3/4

GERMANY

Army 18,230; 1 corps HQ, 1 armd div with (2 armd bde)
Navy 40
Air Force 260

GIBRALTAR

Army 270 (incl 175 pers of Gibraltar regt)

Air Force 70 some (periodic) AEW det

GULF OF ADEN & SOMALI BASIN

NATO • *Operation Ocean Shield* 1 FFGHM

IRAQ

Royal Navy: 75; 1 Navy Transition Team (training the Iraqi Riverine Patrol Service (IRPS))

NATO • NTM-I 15

UN • UNAMI 1 obs

KENYA

Army trg team 120

KUWAIT

Army 30

MOLDOVA

OSCE • Moldova 1

NEPAL

Army 280 (Gurkha trg org)

NETHERLANDS

Air Force 100

NORTH SEA

NATO • SNMCMG1: 1 MHC

OMAN

Army 40

Royal Navy 30

Air Force 20: 1 *Sentinel*; 1 *Tristar* tkr

PERSIAN GULF

Combined Maritime Forces • CTF-152: 2 MCO; 2 MHC; 2 LSD; 1 AOT

QATAR

Air Force 4 C-130J

SERBIA

NATO • KFOR 4

OSCE • Serbia 3

OSCE • Kosovo 10

SIERRA LEONE

IMATT 30

SUDAN

UN • UNMIS 5 obs

UGANDA

EU • EUTM 2

UNITED STATES

Army/Royal Navy/Air Force ε540

FOREIGN FORCES

United States

US European Command: 9,221; 1 ftr wg at RAF Lakenheath with (1 ftr sqn with 24 F-15C *Eagle*/F-15D *Eagle*, 2 ftr sqn with 24 F-15E *Strike Eagle*); 1 tkr wg at RAF Mildenhall with 15 KC-135 *Stratotanker*; 1 Special Ops gp at RAF Mildenhall with 5 MC-130H *Combat Talon II*; 5 MC-130P *Combat Shadow*; 1 C-130E *Hercules*

US Strategic Command: 1 Ballistic Missile Early Warning System (*BMEWS*) at Fylingdales Moor; 1 Spacetrack radar at Fylingdales Moor;

Table 12 **Selected Arms Procurements and Deliveries, Europe**

Designation	Type	Quantity	Contract Value	Supplier Country	Prime Contractor	Order Date	First Delivery Due	Notes
Albania (ALB)								
AS-532 AL Cougar	Tpt Hel	5	€78.6m	Int'l	Eurocopter	2009	n.k.	To be delivered by 2013
Belgium (BEL)								
Piranha IIIC	APC (W)	242	€700m (US$844m)	CHE	Mowag	2006	2010	First batch (138 veh) due by 2010. Second (81) and third batches (23) due 2010–15. Option on further 104
Dingo II	APC (W)	220	€170m	GER	KMW	2005	2005	Option on further 132. Deliveries ongoing
A-400M	Tpt ac	7	n.k.	Int'l	Airbus	2003	2014/5 (org 2010)	In development. Official unit cost US$80m. First delivery delayed
NH-90	ASW/Tpt Hel	10	€293m (US$400m)	Int'l	EADS	2007	n.k.	6 TTH, 4 NFH. Delivery status unclear
Bulgaria (BLG)								
C-27J Spartan	Tpt ac	4	US$133m	ITA	Alenia	2006	2007	To replace An-26. Order reduced from 5 ac. 2 ac delivered by Aug 2010
AS-565 Panther	MRH Hel	6	See notes	Int'l	Eurocopter	2005	2010	For navy. €360m (US$460m) incl 12 AS-532. BLG wishes to reduce order to 3 units due to budget issues
AW-139	MRH Hel	1	n.k.	ITA/UK	Agusta-Westland	2009	n.k.	For Border Police. Delivery status unclear
AS-532 Cougar	Tpt Hel	12	See notes	Int'l	Eurocopter	2005	2006	€360m (US$460m) incl 6 AS-565. 11 delivered by early 2010. Option on 7 more
AW-109	Tpt Hel	3	n.k.	ITA/UK	Agusta-Westland	2010	2010	For Border Police. Delivery status unclear
Croatia (CRO)								
Patria 8×8	APC (W)	126	€170m (US$218m)	CRO/FIN	Patria	2007	2012	Contract extended from 84 to 126 veh Jul 2010. 15 delivered by Jul 2010. Delivery extended until 2012
Cyprus (CYP)								
T-80	MBT	41	€115m (US$156m)	RUS	Rosoboron-export	2010	n.k.	27 T-80U MBT and 14 T-80UK comd veh. To be delivered by mid-2011. Option on a further 41
Czech Republic (CZE)								
Pandur II 8×8	APC (W)	107	US$828m	AUT	General Dynamics	2008	2009	To replace OT-64 SKOT. No reduced from 199 veh. 72 in IFV and APC role; 16 recce, 11 CP, 4 ARV and 4 armoured ambulance variants. Final delivery due 2013
C-295M	Tpt ac	4	CZK3.5 bn (US$167m)	ESP	EADS CASA	2009	2009	Contract value incorporates an aircraft exchange. First ac delivered Jan 2010. Final delivery due 2011
Denmark (DNK)								
CV9035 MkIII	AIFV	45	DKK1.68bn (US$273m)	SWE	BAE	2005	2007	Offset deal concluded 2009. 16 to be delivered
Iver Huitfeldt-class	DDG	3	DKK4.3bn (US$471m)	NLD	n.k.	2006	2012	Projekt Patruljeskib. First delivery due early 2011

Table 12 **Selected Arms Procurements and Deliveries, Europe**

Designation	Type	Quantity	Contract Value	Supplier Country	Prime Contractor	Order Date	First Delivery Due	Notes
Estonia (EST)								
XA-188	APC(W)	80	€20m	NLD	n.k.	2010	2010	Second hand Dutch veh. Delivery to be completed in 2015
Ground Master 403	Radar	2	n.k.	FRA/US	Thales-Raytheon	2009	2012	Acquired as part of agreement with FIN. Air surveillance for W and SE EST
Finland (FIN)								
RG-32M	APC (W)	16	GB£6m (US$8.1m)	RSA/UK	BAE Land Systems	2010	2010	Delivery to be complete by early 2011
Norwegian Advanced Surface-to-Air Missile System (NASAMS)	SAM	n.k.	NOK3bn (US$458m)	FIN/US	Kongsberg/ Raytheon	2009	2009	To replace Buk-M1 (SA-11 *Gadfly*). Delivery status unclear
RBS-70 SAM	MANPAD	n.k.	€26m (US$36m)	SWE	Saab	2010	2012	–
2010 Project vessel	MCM	3	€244.8m (US$315m)	GER/ITA	Intermarine	2006	2010	Final delivery due 2012. First vessel, *Katanpaa*, launched Jun 2009
F/A-18C *Hornet*	FGA Upgrade	10	US$30 m	US	Boeing	2008	2009	AN/AAQ-28 *Litening* ATP upgrade. Block 2 pods for MLU 2 programme
C-295M	Tpt ac	1	€112m (US$144.6m)	ESP	CASA	2010	2013	To replace Fokker F27s
Hawk Mk 51/51A	Trg ac	30/45	€20m (US$26.3m)	US	Patria	2007	2010	Avionics upgrade. 30 ac receive level 1 upgrade, a further 15 ac to receive level 2 upgrade. First deliverd Jun 2009
NH-90 TTH	Tpt Hel	20	€370m	NLD	NH Industries	2001	2004	8 delivered by late 2010
AW-119Ke	Tpt Hel	4	n.k.	ITA/UK	Agusta-Westland	2008	2010	For Border Guard. Fourth added to order in Jan 2010. First delivered Aug 2010
France (FRA)								
M51	SLBM	n.k.	more than €3bn	FRA	EADS	2004	2010	To replace M-45. Development phase from 2000–04. Final delivery due 2014
VBCI 8x8	AIFV	630	n.k.	FRA	Nexter	2000	2008	To replace AMX10P. Total requirement of 630 VBCIs (520 VCIs, 110 VPCs), another 332 ordered in 2009. Final delivery due 2015
BvS10 Mk II	APC (T)	53	n.k.	UK/SWE	BAE Systems	2009	2010	Options for further 76 vehicles
Petits Véhicules Protégé (PVP)	LFV	933	€150m (US$239m)	FRA	Panhard	2004	2008	Delivery in progress
CAESAR	SP 155mm Arty	72	€300m (US$362m)	FRA	Nextar	2004	2008	Final delivery due 2011. 66 delivered by Apr 2010
Barracuda	SSN	6	€8bn (US$10.5bn)	FRA	DCNS	2006	2016	One SSN to be delivered every two years until 2027. First to enter service 2017
FREMM (*Aquitaine*-class)	FFG	11	US$23.6bn	FRA/ITA	DCNS	2002	2012	Multi mission FFG. First-of-class FNS *Aquitaine* launched 2010; scheduled for commissioning 2012. Further 3 ordered in Oct 2009 (2 anti-air warfare, 1 ASW). Final delivery due 2022
Mistral-class	LHD	1	€420m (US$554m)	FRA	STX France Cruise	2009	2012	Expected ISD 2012

Table 12 **Selected Arms Procurements and Deliveries, Europe**

Designation	Type	Quantity	Contract Value	Supplier Country	Prime Contractor	Order Date	First Delivery Due	Notes
SCALP Naval	LACM	200	See notes	Int'l	MBDA	2007	2013	Original cotnract value €910m (US$1.2bn) for 250 msl. Test fired Mar 2010. To be deployed on *Barracuda*-class SSN and *Aquitaine*-class FFG
Rafale F3	FGA ac	180	n.k.	FRA	Dassault	1984	2006	Order increased to 180 in 2009, but annual production rate slowed
A-400M	Tpt ac	50	See notes	Int'l	Airbus	2003	2009	In development. Official unit cost US$80m. First deliveries delayed until at least 2013
CN-235	Tpt ac	8	€225m (US$305m)	Int'l	Airbus	2010	2011	Delivery to be complete by mid-2013
AS-665 *Tiger*	Atk Hel	80	n.k.	FRA/GER	Eurocopter	1999	2005	40 HAD, 40 HAP variant. 30 delivered by late 2010
NH-90 NFH	ASW Hel	27	n.k.	Int'l	NH Industries	2000	2010 (org 2009)	For navy. First delivery Apr 2010. Final delivery due 2019
NH-90 TTH	Tpt Hel	34	See notes	Int'l	NH Industries	2007	2012	For army avn. 12 ordered 2007 with option for a further 56. 22 more ordered Jan 2009. €1.8bn if all options taken. First flight Dec 2010
EC-725 *Super Cougar*	Tpt Hel	14	n.k.	Int'l	Eurocopter	2009	2010	Final delivery due 2012 (6 air force; 8 army – delivered)
Eagle 1/SIDM	UAV	n.k.	See notes	Int'l	EADS	2001	2009	In development. Total programme cost: US$1.4 bn
AGM-114 *Hellfire* II	ASM	n.k.	n.k.	US	Lockheed Martin	2007	n.k.	For 40 *Tiger*. Final delivery due 2012. Msl no. and contract value undisclosed; projected requirement of 680
EGBU-12 Enhanced *Paveway* II	LGB	n.k.	US$22m	US	Raytheon	2008	n.k.	For *Mirage* 2000D

Germany (GER)								
Puma	AIFV	405	€3 bn (US$4.3 bn)	GER	PSM	2007	2010	To replace *Marder* 1A3/A4/A5 AIFVs. To be fitted with *Spike* LR ATGW launcher. Final delivery 2020
Wiesel 2	APC (T)	8	€61.5m	GER	Rhein-metall	2009	n.k.	For use in AFG. 120mm mortar. Option for further 2 C2 vehicles
Boxer (8×8)	APC (W)	272	€1.5bn (US$2.1bn)	GER/NLD	ARTEC GmbH	2006	2009	135 APC, 65 CP variants, 72 heavy armoured ambulances. First delivery in Sept 2009
Fennek	APC (W)	20	US$94m	GER/NLD	ARGE Fennek	2007	2009	Joint fire support role (JFSR) configuration. Second batch ordered in Aug 2009 (US$48m), to be delivered in late 2011
Dingo 2	APC (W)	98	€73.6m	GER	KMW	2008	2008	50 in standard ptrl veh config and 48 in battle damage repair veh config
Dingo 2	APC (W)	85	n.k.	GER	KMW	2010	2010	41 in standard ptrl veh config and 44 in battle damage repair veh config. All to be delivered by end 2010
Spike LR	AT msl	311	€35m (US$49m)	GER	Eurospike	2009	n.k.	For *Puma* AIFV. Option for further 1,160 for est €120m
Skyshield 35/NBS	AD	2	€136m	GER	Rhein-metall	2009	2011	In development, original contract from 2007. Each consists of six *Skyshield* 35 mm guns, two sensor units and C2 centre

Table 12 **Selected Arms Procurements and Deliveries, Europe**

Designation	Type	Quantity	Contract Value	Supplier Country	Prime Contractor	Order Date	First Delivery Due	Notes
IRIS-T SLS	SAM	–	€123m (US$166m)	GER	Diehl BGT	2007	2012	Surface-launched variant of infra-red guided IRIS-T AAM. ISD from 2012. Secondary msl for army MEADS
Type 212A	SSK	2	n.k.	GER	HDW	2006	n.k.	Due to enter service from 2012
F125 (*Baden-Württemberg*-class)	DDGHM	4	€2bn	GER	TKMS	2007	2016	Final delivery due late 2018
K130 (*Braun-schweig*-class)	FS	5	n.k.	GER	TMS	2001	2008	*Erfurt, Oldenburg*, and *Ludwigshafen* in trials mid-2009
Berlin-class (Type 702)	AFH	1	€245m US$330m	GER	ARGE shipbuilding	2008	2013	–
Eurofighter *Typhoon*	FGA	143	n.k.	Int'l	Eurofighter GmbH	2004	2008	31 aircraft Tranche 3A order signed in 2009
A-400M	Tpt ac	53	See notes	Int'l	Airbus	2003	2010	In development. Official unit cost US$80m. Order reduced from 60 aircraft; delivery delayed
A319/ Bombardier *Global 5000*	Tpt ac	6	US$270m	GER	Airbus	2007	2010	2 AC-319J delivered 2010, 4 *Global 5000* to be delivered 2011. To replace CL-601 fleet
AS-665 *Tiger* (UHT variant)	Atk Hel	80	US$2.6bn	GER	Eurocopter	1984	2005	Deliveries suspended in 2010 due to technical problems. Overall procurement number now uncertain
NH-90 TTH	Tpt Hel	80	n.k.	NLD	NH Industries	2000	2007	50 for army, 30 for air force. Deliveries in progress to trials and test
NH-90 TTH	Tpt Hel	42	n.k.	NLD	NH Industries	2007	n.k.	30 for army air corps and 12 for air force
Eurohawk	ISR UAV	5	€430m (US$559m)	Int'l	EADS/ Northrop Grumman	2007	2010	Final delivery due 2015
Greece (GRC)								
Katsonis-class (Type 214)	SSK	6	Est. €1.67bn	GER	TMS/HDW	2000	2005	First commissioned Dec 2010. All scheduled to be in service by 2018
Roussen/Super Vita	PFM	2	€299m (US$405m)	GRC	Elefsis/VT	2008	2010	Further order to bring total to 7. Delivery now expected 2012–13
AH-64A *Apache*	Atk hel Upgrade	20	n.k.	US	n.k.	2008	2012	Upgrade to D standard to commence 2010; 4 to have *Longbow* radar
AS-332C1 *Super Puma*	SAR Hel	2	n.k.	Int'l	Eurocopter	2010	n.k.	Delivery to be complete by 2012
NH-90 TTH	Tpt Hel	20	€657m	NLD	EADS	2002	2005	16 tac tpt variants and 4 Special Op variants. Option on further 14. Delivery now expected to begin 2011 and conclude 2015
Hungary (HUN)								
Cougar	APC (W)	3	US$1.3m	US	Force Protection	2009	n.k.	Contract value incl spares and trg
Ireland (IRL)								
RG-32M	APC (W)	27	n.k.	RSA/UK	BAE	2008	2010	Delivery status unclear

Table 12 **Selected Arms Procurements and Deliveries, Europe**

Designation	Type	Quantity	Contract Value	Supplier Country	Prime Contractor	Order Date	First Delivery Due	Notes
Italy (ITA)								
PzH 2000	SP 155mm arty	70	n.k.	GER	OTO Melara/ KMW	1999	2004	62 delivered by Oct 2010
ARTHUR	Radar	5	SEK475m (US$30m)	ITA/SWE	Saab/Selex Systemi Integrati	2009	n.k.	Deliveries to be complete by end 2012
Todaro-class (Type 212A)	SSK	2	€915m (US$1.34 bn)	ITA	Fincantieri	2008	2015	Second batch – option exercised from 1996 contract. With AIP
FREMM	FFG	6	€1,628m (US$2,361m)	FRA/ITA	Orizzonte Sistemi Navali	2002	2010	Batch 1 (2 vessels) in production. Batch 2 (4 vessels) had funding confirmed Mar 2008 – first vessel to be launched 2011; deliveries due 2014–17
Eurofighter *Typhoon*	FGA ac	96	n.k.	Int'l	Eurofighter GmbH	1985	2004	21 ac Tranche 3A order signed in 2009
KC-767	Tkr/Tpt ac	4	n.k.	US	Boeing	2002	2008	First delivery delayed
ATR-42MP	MP ac	1	n.k.	ITA	Alenia	2008	2010	For MSO
ATR-72MP	MP ac	4	€360–400m	ITA	Alenia Aeronautica	2009	2012	To be fitted with long-range surv suite. Final delivery due 2014
M-346 *Master*	Trg ac	6	€220m (US$330m)	ITA	Alenia	2009	2010	Part of agreement for 15. First delivery due by end-2010
AW139	MRH Hel	2	n.k.	ITA/UK	Agusta Westland	2008	2009	For SAR role. Likely to replace current fleet of Agusta-Bell 412HP hel. First delivery May 2010
CH-47F *Chinook*	Tpt Hel	16	€900m	US	Agusta Westland	2009	2013	For army. Final delivery due 2017
NH-90 TTH	Tpt Hel	116	n.k.	NLD	Agusta Westland	1987	2007	60 for army; 56 for navy. 9 delivered to army as of late 2010
RQ-7B *Shadow*	ISR UAV	16	€80m (US$109m)	US	AAI	2010	2011	
Lithuania (LTU)								
Hunt-class	MCM	2	€55m	UK	Thales	2008	2010	Ex-UK stock. Former HMS *Cottesmore* and HMS *Dulverton*. Expected to transfer in 2011
Luxembourg (LUX)								
Dingo 2	ASRV	48	n.k.	GER	Thales/KMW	2008	2010	To meet Protected Recce Vehicle requirement and be deployed in AFG
A-400M	Tpt ac	1	See notes	Int'l	Airbus	2003	2010	In development. Official unit cost US$80m. First deliveries delayed
Netherlands (NLD)								
CV90	AIFV	184	€749m (US$981m)	SWE	Hagglunds	2004	2007	CV9035NL version. 150 in IFV role and 34 in CP role. Final delivery due 2011
Boxer (8×8)	APC (W)	200	€595m (US$747m)	GER/NLD	ARTEC GmbH	2006	2011	19 cargo/C2, 27 cargo, 55 CP variants, 58 ambulances and 41 engr. To replace YPR 765
PzH 2000	155mm SP arty	57	US$420m	GER	KMW	2000	2004	Deliveries ongoing
Walrus-class	SSK Upgrade	4	€50–150m (US$77–232m)	NLD	n.k.	2011	2018	SLEP. Incl combat systems and nav upgrades.

Table 12 **Selected Arms Procurements and Deliveries, Europe**

Designation	Type	Quantity	Contract Value	Supplier Country	Prime Contractor	Order Date	First Delivery Due	Notes
Holland-class	PSOH	4	€365m	NLD	Schelde and Thales	2007	2011	Holland & Zeeland launched 2010; Groningen & Friesland still under construction
Joint Logistics Support Ship (JSS)	AFSH	1	€364m (US$545m)	NLD	Damen Schelde (DSNS)	2009	2014	To replace HrMS Zuiderkruis
NH-90	ASW/Tpt Hel	20	n.k.	Int'l	NH Industries	1987	2007	12 NFH, 8 TTH. First NFH delivered Apr 2010. Final 4 due 2013
Ch-47F Chinook	Tpt Hel	6	US$335m	US	Boeing	2007	2009	Final delivery due 2010
Enhanced Paveway II	LGB	200	n.k.	US	Raytheon	2008	n.k.	For upgraded F-16AMs. EGBU-12 (GBU-49/B) 500lb
Norway (NOR)								
Hisnorsat	Sat	24	€300m (US$368m)	ESP	Hisdesat	2010	2013	Military communications satellite
FH-77 BW L52 Archer 6×6	155mm SP arty	24	£135m (US$200m)	SWE/UK	BAE Systems Bofors	2010	2011	Contract value is for combined 48 unit NWG/SWE order
Fridtjof Nansen-class	FFG	5	n.k.	ESP	Navantia	2000	2006	Four vessels delivered. Final vessel due for commissioning 2010/11
Naval Strike Missile (NSM)	SSM	n.k.	NOK2.2746bn (US$466m)	NOR	KDA	2007	2010	Final delivery due 2014. For 5 Fridtjof Nansen-class FF and 6 Skjold-class fast strike craft
Sting Ray Mod 1	AS Torp	n.k.	GB£99m (US$144m)	UK	BAE	2009	2010	For Fridtjof Nansen-class, NH90 ASW hel and P-3 Orion
Oksoy-class/ Alta-class	MCM Upgrade	2	n.k.	FRA	Thales	2007	n.k.	Sonar upgrade involving the delivery of 6 TSM2022 MK3 N hull mounted sonars
P-3 Orion	ASW ac upgrade	6	US$95m	US	Lockheed Martin	2007	2009	SLEP. Final delivery due Mar 2010. Delivery status unclear
NH90	ASW/Tpt Hel	14	n.k.	Int'l	Eurocopter	2001	2005	First delivery due 2010. Delivery status unclear; 6 for ASW, 8 for coast guard. Option for further 10 in SAR configuration
Poland (POL)								
AMV XC-360P	APC (W)	690	US$1.7bn	FIN	Patria	2003	2004	Final delivery due 2014.
BM-21 launchers	MRL upgrade	36	PLN97m (US$43.9m)	POL	Centrum Produkcji Wojskowej	2008	2010	Upgrade to WR-40 Langusta MRL standard
Spike-LR	MANPAT	264	PLN1.487bn (US$512m)	FRA	Rafael/ZM Mesko	2003	2004	264 launchers and 2,675 msl. Manufactured under licence
Project 621-Gawron	FFGM	2	PLN77m (US$24.8m)	POL	SMW	2004	2008	Based on GER MEKO A100. Project suspended in Sept 2009; may be restarted
RBS 15 Mk 3	AShM	36	PLN560m (US$178m)	SWE	ZM Mesko	2006	2009	For Orkan-class and Gawron-class. Incl, spares, spt, trg and simulator. Final delivery due 2012
Naval Strike Missile (NSM)	AShM	12	NOK800m (US$115m)	NOR	Kongsberg Defence & Aerospace	2008	2012	Contact value incl 6 firing veh
M28B-1R/bis (Bryza-1R/bis)	MP ac	3/4	n.k.	POL	PZL	n.k.	2008	Delivery due end 2010. Delivery status unclear
C-130 E Hercules	Tpt ac	5	US$98.4m	US	SAIC	2006	2007	Refurbished ex-US aircraft. First ac delivered Mar 2009. Second delivered Apr 2010

Table 12 **Selected Arms Procurements and Deliveries, Europe**

Designation	Type	Quantity	Contract Value	Supplier Country	Prime Contractor	Order Date	First Delivery Due	Notes
M-28B/PT *Bryza*	Tpt ac	8	PLN399m	US	Polskie Zaklady Lotnicze	2008	2010	For air force. Order reduced from 12 to 8 ac in 2009 due to budget cuts. Final delivery due 2013
Aerostar	ISR UAV	8	PLN89m ($30m)	ISR	Aeronautics Ltd	2010	–	4 for use in AFG, remainder for trg
Portugal (PRT)								
Pandur II 8×8	APC (W)	260	€344.3m (US$415m)	AUT	Steyr Daimler Puch Spezial-fahrzeug GmbH	2005	2006	240 for army in 11 config. 20 for marines in 4 config. 120 and 4 respectively deilvered. Final delivery delayed from 2010 to 2013
Type 209PN	SSK	2	€800m (US$958m)	GER	TKMS	2004	2009	To replace 3 *Albacora*-class SS. *Tridente* delivered Aug 2010; *Arpão* launched Jun 2009, delivery due 2011
Viana do Castelo-class (NPO2000)	PSO	10	n.k.	PRT	ENVC	2002	2006	2 Pollution Control Vessels, 8 PSOH. First delivery expected early 2010. Final delivery due 2015
C-295M/C-295 MPA	MP/Tpt ac	12	€270m (US$326m)	Int'l	EADS CASA	2006	2008	To replace C-212. 7 ac in tpt role, 2 in maritime surv role and 3 in *Persuader* config. 5 delivered by Nov 2009. Delivery status unclear
Romania (ROM)								
MICA (VL MICA)	SAM	n.k.	n.k.	FRA	MBDA	2009	n.k.	Launch customer for land-based version
C-27J *Spartan*	Tpt ac	7	€220m (US$293m)	ITA	Alenia	2006	2007	To replace An-26. Incl log and trg support. 2 delivered; 1 more due 2010, 2 in 2011 and final 2 in 2012
Serbia (SER)								
Lasta 95	Trg ac	15	n.k.	SER	Utva	n.k.	2010	Delivery to be complete by end 2012
Slovakia (SVK)								
C-27J *Spartan*	Tpt ac	2 to 3	€120m (US$167m)	ITA	Alenia Aeronautica	2008	n.k.	Procurement suspended until 2011 due to budget cuts
Slovenia (SVN)								
Patria 8×8	APC (W)	135	SIT66.61bn (US$365.9m)	FIN	Patria	2007	2007	SVN seeking to reduce order total. 13 APCs and 3 Command Posts delivered by Mar 2010. Final delivery due 2013
Spain (ESP)								
Paz (Peace) satellite	Sat	2	€160m	ESP	Hidesat/ EADS CASA	2008	2012	–
Leopard 2E	MBT	239	€1.94bn (US$2.34bn)	ESP/GER	General Dynamics SBS	1998	2003	ESP version of 2A6. Incl 16 ARV and 4 trg tk.
Pizarro	AIFV	212	€707m (US$853m)	ESP	General Dynamics SBS	2003	2005	In five variants. Delivery status unclear
Piranha IIIC	APC (W)	21	n.k.	CHE/ESP/ US	GDELS/ MOWAG	2007	2010	Delivery to be complete by 2013. First four delivered

Table 12 **Selected Arms Procurements and Deliveries, Europe**

Designation	Type	Quantity	Contract Value	Supplier Country	Prime Contractor	Order Date	First Delivery Due	Notes
RG-31 Mk 5E	APC (W)	100	€75m (US$118m)	RSA	GDSBS	2008	2009	85 in APC role, 10 ambulance and 5 CP versions. Delivery ongoing
SBT (V07)	Towed 155mm arty	70	€181m (US$216m)	ESP	General Dynamics	2005	n.k.	4 155/52 APU SBT (V07) how, plus design and production of 66 how (SIAC). Also retrofit of 12 APU SBT how from V06 to V07 version and 82 towing vehicles
Spike-LR	MANPAT	See notes	US$424.5m	US	General Dynamics SBS	2007	2007	260 launchers, 2,600 msl and spt service. Deliveries ongoing
National Advanced Surface-to-Air Missile System (NASAMS)	SAM	4	n.k.	ESP/US	Raytheon	2003	n.k.	Four units each with 3D radar, control unit and 2 six-round truck-mounted launchers. In devt. Successfully tested 2008
ARTHUR (Artillery Hunting Radar)	Radar	See notes	€69m	SWE	SAAB Microwave	2006	2007	Contract incl 4 remote control units, trg sys and log spt. Final delivery Apr 2009
S-80A	SSK	4	n.k.	ESP	Navantia	2003	2013	First vessel, S-81, due for delivery Dec 2013
Alvaro de Bazan-class F-100	DDGHM	1	€71.5m (US$105.4m)	ESP	Navantia	2005	2012	*Cristóbal Colón*. Option for one more vessel. Launched Nov 2010 delivery due summer 2012
Aegis	C&C	1	US$117m	US	Lockheed Martin	2007	2012	For F-100
Buques de Accion Maritima-class (BAM)	PSO	4	€1.1 bn (US$1.4bn)	ESP	Navantia	2005	2009	Deliveries delayed by over 1 year. Final keel laid May 2010. First delivery scheduled end 2010. Addl vessels ordered 2009
Eurofighter *Typhoon*	FGA	74	n.k.	Int'l	Eurofighter GmbH	1994	2004	21 aircraft Tranche 3A order signed 2009
AV-8B *Harrier* II	FGA upgrade	4	€11.5m (US$17.8m)	ESP	EADS	2008	2011	Upgrade to AV-8B *Harrier* II Plus standard
CN-235-300 MPA	MPA ac	2	n.k.	Int'l	EADS CASA	2007	2008	For Guardia Civil maritime patrol duties
A-400M	Tpt ac	27	See notes	Int'l	Airbus	2003	2010	In development. Official unit cost US$80m. First deliveries delayed
AS-665 *Tiger* (HAD)	Atk Hel	24	€1.4bn	FRA	Eurocopter	2003	2007	First 3 hel delivered May 2007, second 3 by 2008. Final delivery due 2011
NH-90 TTH	Tpt Hel	45	n.k.	Int'l	NH Industries	2007	2010	First flight December 2010. Deliveries scheduled to begin in 2012
AS 532AL *Cougar*	Tpt Hel	5	€116m (US$171m)	Int'l	Eurocopter	2008	n.k.	3 for army air wing. 2 for Emergencies Military Unit
EC-135	Tpt Hel	12	n.k.	Int'l	Eurocopter	2010	2010	6 for National Police, 6 for Guarda Civil. Delivery to be completed in 2012
EC-135	Tpt Hel	9	€85m (US$113m)	Int'l	Eurocopter	2010	2010	5 to be delivered in 2010, remainder in 2011
Sweden (SWE)								
RG32M	APC (W)	60	€18m (US$24m)	UK/RSA	BAE	2008	2010	–
Armoured Modular Vehicle (AMV)	APC (W)	113	€240m (US$338m)	FIN	Patria	2009	2011	79 APCs and 34 other variants. Further 113 req. To be delivered 2011-13 Was subject to contractual dispute

Europe

Table 12 **Selected Arms Procurements and Deliveries, Europe**

Designation	Type	Quantity	Contract Value	Supplier Country	Prime Contractor	Order Date	First Delivery Due	Notes
FH-77 BW L52 Archer 6×6 155mm	155mm SP Arty	24	£135m (US$200m)	UK/SWE	BAE Systems Bofors	2010	2011	Contract value is for combined 48 unit NOR/SWE order
AMOS 120mm	120mm Mor	2	SKR30m (approx US$4m)	Int'l	n.k.	2006	2011	Two prototypes to be mounted on Vv90 tracked chassis
Koster-class	MCC upgrade	5	US$133m	Dom	Kockums	2007	2009	MLU. HMS Koster and Vinga re-commissioned Mar 2009. Upgrades for HMS Ivön, Kullen and Ven delayed; programme schedule now unclear
CB 90H	LCPL Upgrade	145	n.k.	Dom	n.k.	2008	n.k.	Upgrade from 90H to 90HS
JAS 39A/B Gripen	FGA Upgrade	31	SEK3.9bn (US$611m)	Dom	SAAB	2007	2012	Upgrade: 18 to become JAS 39Cs and 13 to become JAS 39D two-seaters
NH-90	ASW/Tpt Hel	18	n.k.	Int'l	Eurocopter	2001	2007	13 TTT/SAR hel and 5 ASW variants. Option for 7 further hel. Deliveries ongoing
RQ-7 Shadow	ISR UAV	8	SEK500m (US$63.5m)	SWE/US	Saab/AAI	2010	n.k.	Delivery to be complete by end 2011
Switzerland (CHE)								
Piranha I	APC	160	n.k.	Dom	Mowag	2006	2008	Re-role of Piranha I tank hunter APC to protected comd vehicles. Final delivery due 2010
Piranha IIIC	NBC Recce	12	See notes	Dom	Mowag	2008	2010	CHF260m (€167m) incl 232 DURO IIIP. Final delivery due 2012
Duro IIIP	APC (W)	232	See notes	Dom	Mowag	2008	2010	CHF260m (€167m) incl 12 Piranha IIIC. Order quantity incl 12 NBC laboratory vehicles. Final delivery due 2012
Turkey (TUR)								
Gokturk (recce & SURV sat)	Sat	1	€270m (US$380m)	ITA	Telespazio/ Thales Alenia Space	2009	2013	Thales Alenia Space responsible for sat. Dom companies involved in design and development stage & supply of subsystems
Altay	MBT	250	See notes	ROK/TUR	Otokar	2007	n.k.	4 initial prototypes by 2014 for approx US$500m. To be followed by an order for 250 units following testing
Firtina 155mm/52-cal	155mm SP arty	350	n.k.	ROK/TUR	Samsung	2001	2003	ROK Techwin K9 Thunder. Total requirement of 350. Deliveries ongoing (81 delivered by May 2009)
Type-214	SSK	6	€1.96bn (US$2.9bn)	GER	HDW, TKMS and MFI	2009	2015	To be built at Golcuk shipyard.
Ada-class	FFGHM	8	n.k.	TUR	Istanbul Naval Shipyard	1996	2011	First of class, TCG Heybeliada conducting sea trials; ISD 2011. Part of Milgem project which incl requirement for 4 F-100 class FFG
Dost-class	PSOH	4	€352.5m	TUR	RMK Marine	2007	2011	Based on Sirio-class PCO design. For coast guard. First vessel launched Jun 2010. Final delivery due 2011
NTPB (New Type Patrol Boat)	PCC	16	€402m (US$545m)	TUR	Dearsan	2007	2010	First delivery scheduled for Dec 2010. Final delivery due 2015

Table 12 **Selected Arms Procurements and Deliveries, Europe**

Designation	Type	Quantity	Contract Value	Supplier Country	Prime Contractor	Order Date	First Delivery Due	Notes
F-16C/D Block 50 *Fighting Falcon*	FGA ac	30	US$1.78bn	TUR/US	Lockheed Martin	2009	2011	14 F-16C and 16 F-16D variants. Final assembly in TUR. First delivery due Mar 2011. Final delivery due 2014
F-16C/D *Fighting Falcon*	FGA ac Upgrade	216	US$635m	US	Lockheed Martin/TAI	2006	n.k.	Upgrade. 216 modernisation kits, flight testing, training, technical spt and sustainment activities
ATR-72 MP	MP ac	10	US$210m	ITA	Alenia Aeronautica	2005	2010	First five deliveries by 2010. Final delivery due 2012
B-737 AEW	AEW&C ac	4	US$1bn	US	Boeing	2002	2009	*Peace Eagle* programme. Option for a further 2. First aircraft to be delivered 2011
A-400M	Tpt ac	10	See notes	Int'l	Airbus	2003	2012	In development. Official unit cost US$80m. First deliveries delayed
KT-1 *Woong-Bee*	Trg ac	40	US$500m	ROK/TUR	KAI/TAI	2007	2009	To replace T-37 trg ac. Option for 15 further ac. First due to be delivered Nov 2010
T129 (AW129 *Mangusta*)	Atk Hel	51	US$3bn	TUR	TAI/Aselsan/ Agusta Westland	2007	2013	Option on further 41. Serial production planned for 2013
T129 (AW129 *Mangusta*)	Atk Hel	9	€150m (US$208m)	ITA/TUR/UK	TAI/Aselsan/ Agusta Westland	2010	2012	Interim measure to fill capability gap until large scale production of T129 begins
S-70B *Seahawk*	ASW Hel	17	n.k.	US	Sikorsky	2006	2009	Delivery status unclear
CH-47F *Chinook*	Tpt Hel	14	US$1.2bn	US	Boeing	2009	–	10 for army, 4 for Special Forces Comd
Heron	ISR UAV	10	US$183m	ISR	Israel UAV Partnership	2005	2009	Navy to receive 2, army 4 and navy 4. 2 delivered; undergoing further upgrades
AGM-84H SLAM-ER	ASM	48	US$79.1m	US	McDonnell Douglas	2007	2008	Incl 3 SLAM-ER instrumented recoverable air test vehicles and 59 msl containers. Final delivery due 2011
Ukraine (UKR)								
An-70	Tpt ac	5	n.k.	RUS	Antonov	1991	2010	Limited serial production started. First delivery due 2010
United Kingdom (UK)								
ASCOD 2 SV	Recce	7	GB£500m	UK	General Dynamics UK	2010	n.k.	Prototype phase of FRES SV
Cougar	APC (W)	157	US$94m	US	Force Protection	2008	n.k.	To be converted to *Ridgeback* by NP Aerospace
Wolfhound	APC (W)	125	GB£160m	US	Force Protection	2009	2010	First delivered to AFG in Oct 2010. Delivery to be complete by Autumn 2011
Cougar Mastiff	APC (W)	23	US$16m	US	Force Protection	2010	2010	EOD vehiicles. First 5 delivered Feb 2010
Cougar Mastiff	APC (W)	37	n.k.	US	Force Protection	2010	n.k.	Delivery status unclear
Ocelot (*Foxhound*)	APC (W)	200	GB£180m	US	Force Protection	2010	2011	–
Astute-class	SSN	6	See notes	UK	BAE	1994	2008	First vessel commissioned 2010. To be fitted with *Tomahawk* Block IV SLCM

Europe

Table 12 **Selected Arms Procurements and Deliveries, Europe**

Designation	Type	Quantity	Contract Value	Supplier Country	Prime Contractor	Order Date	First Delivery Due	Notes
Queen Elizabeth-class	CV	2	GB£3.9bn (US$8bn)	UK	BAE Systems	2007	2014	ISD delayed until 2020 (HMS Queen Elizabeth) and 2022 (HMS Prince of Wales) as a result of 2010 SDSR. One to be fitted with catapults and arrestor traps; other to be mothballed.
Daring-class (Type 45)	DDGHM	6	See notes	UK	VT Group and BAE	2001	2008	Initial budget projection: GB£5.47bn. Overall cost now expected to be GB£6.46bn (US$12.7bn). First 2 vessels in service; 3rd awaiting commissioning
Eurofighter Typhoon	FGA ac	160	n.k.	Int'l	Eurofighter GmbH	1984	2003	40 aircraft Tranche 3A order signed in 2009
F-35B Lightning II	FGA ac	3	US$600m	US	Lockheed Martin	2009	n.k.	STOVL version. Contractual commitment to purchase 3 STOVL ac.
A330-200	Tkr/Tpt ac	14	GB£13bn (US$26 bn)	Int'l	AirTanker consortium	2008	2011	First ac arrived at Getafe facility Jul 2009 for avionics and aerial refuelling equipment. Due Oct 2011.
RC-135 Rivet Joint	ELINT ac	3	est GB£700m (US$1bn)	US	Boeing	2010	2014	–
A-400M	Tpt ac	22	See notes	Int'l	Airbus	2003	2010	In development. First deliveries delayed. Order reduced by 3 aircraft to 22
AW-159 Lynx Wildcat	MRH Hel	62	GB£1bn (US$1.8bn)	ITA/UK	Agusta Westland	2006	2014	34 for army, 28 for navy. Option for a further 10 hel, 5 for army and 5 for navy. Final delivery due 2015
Chinook HC.3	Tpt hel	8	GB£62m (US$124m)	US	Boeing	2007	2009	Conversion to HC.2/2A standard. Delivery in progress
Chinook HC.2/2A (Project Julius)	Tpt Hel Upgrade	48	US$656m	UK	Honeywell/ Thales	2009	n.k.	Upgrade with T55-L-714 engines and Thales TopDeck cockpits for op requirements
SA 330E Puma HC.1	Tpt Hel Upgrade	28	US$479m	UK	Eurocopter	2009	2011	Life-extension programme. First 14 due to be in service by late 2012, Final delivery due 2014. Option on two more
Hermes 450	ISR UAV	n.k.	US$110m	Int'l	Thales	2007	2010	Contract incl trg, log spt and management services
MQ-9 Reaper	Cbt ISR UAV	5	GB£135m (US$213m)	US	General Atomics	2010	n.k.	Delivery to be complete by 2013. Contract includes 4 ground stations

Chapter Five
Russia

Structural change continues

The Russian military has continued the ambitious reform programme launched in September 2008. The motivations behind Defence Minister Anatoly Serdyukov's plan for fundamental change, and the aspirations that the Russian Ministry of Defence (MoD) has for it, were detailed in *The Military Balance 2010* (pp. 211–16). However, so far the results of the process are mixed. Although a major plank of the army's transformation to a brigade-based structure – namely, the dissolution of the established army/corps/division organisational structure – had been officially completed by 1 December 2009, the precise composition of the new brigades remains under development. Indeed, Russian ground forces appear to have embarked on a modernisation process that is being tested and adjusted as it proceeds.

While this may, at first glance, seem to indicate problems in executing the changes, this adaptive process could, paradoxically, be the very means by which the Russian military arrives at improved structures. Structures are now being tested in exercise conditions and, if found wanting, are altered or discarded. What is clear is that, with the adoption of the brigade structure and the end of cadre units, the pre-revolutionary and Soviet system of a military force based on large-scale mobilisation has ended, with the stress now on transitioning to forces capable of being held (at least in theory) at high readiness.

Overall, the process of reform is proving flexible and is developing with impressive speed. However, in some areas it has not run smoothly. Coming after a lengthy period of relative stagnation, the implementation of, and adjustment to, fundamental changes in the nature of the Russian military has left some senior Russian servicemen – including those who support reform – expressing disorientation and bewilderment at the pace of change and at the constant stream of instructions in adjusting its course. Further significant changes should be expected during 2011.

Reforming central headquarters

Defence Minister Serdyukov focused much attention during 2010 on reforming the central headquarters and related staffs. This stemmed from a desire to improve effectiveness by functionally dividing responsibilities between the MoD and the General Staff of the Armed Forces. The MoD is now considered a civilian institution with the task of implementing overall strategic direction and ensuring managerial competence. The General Staff is intended to focus on planning, command and control, military training and, of course, delivering military effect under the overall direction of the MoD and higher state command. This change in the decision-making structure of the ministry is designed at least in part to enable civilian control over financial matters – particularly regarding the procurement of armaments and associated military equipment – where there has traditionally been a high level of corruption. Previously, the post of first deputy minister of defence was occupied by a general who was responsible for the training of soldiers and their military service; the post is now occupied by a civil servant (currently a retired general) whose main task is to fulfil the State Defence Order and implement the State Armament Programme (see 'Rearmament' section, p. 179).

While sharpening the focus of the bodies in charge of Russia's armed forces, Serdyukov has also concentrated minds by continuing to reshuffle high-ranking military personnel. Since he assumed his post in 2007 almost all deputy ministers of defence, commanders-in-chief of armed services and branches, and commanders of military districts and fleets have been replaced, as was the chief of the main intelligence directorate of the Russian General Staff. Seven of the nine deputy ministers are now civilians, and five of these previously worked with Serdyukov in the Federal Tax Service. The individuals who remain in post, or have been appointed under Serdyukov, share his views and those of Chief of General Staff Army General Nikolay Makarov on the necessity of military reform; they are willing to assist in the far-reaching modernisation process now under way.

Other structural changes in 2010 have included the generation of a new Armed Forces Logistics and Procurement Command (*Material'no-tekhnicheskoye obespecheniye vooruzhennykh sil*, MTO). This body unifies the armed forces' logistics services and is intended to control operations and maintenance tasks. While the development of similar joint logistic commands has been enacted and tested by foreign militaries, and this has informed Russian thinking, it remains to be seen how effective the command will be.

Reforming military administration

The general headquarters (*Glavkomat*) of the army, air force and navy have so far been left unchanged in the new armed-forces structure, although there are continuing reductions in the number of managerial levels within the headquarters. Similar reductions are also being made in service commands, military district and fleet headquarters, as well as in general and central directorates of the defence ministry. The exact number affected remains unclear, although it has been reported that personnel serving in central directorates and headquarters will ultimately be reduced from around 10,500 to 3,000. It was also planned that the number of staff officers up to and including the rank of general in the various service commands would fall from 300 to 100 during 2010; at the time of writing this lower figure had not been reached.

In line with staff reductions, the functions of the service headquarters have been cut back, with some tasks being transferred to other command structures. According to one source, the headquarters now have only four tasks, all specific to the respective service: organisational development; training; education; and equipment repair.

Overall, Chief of General Staff (CGS) Makarov has said that 700 of a total 1,200 generals' positions have already been cut. Some analysts have criticised these reductions in the higher ranks, saying that command and control may have been affected. Meanwhile, the pension and resettlement costs associated with the continuing retirement of large numbers of senior officers will have a substantial financial impact.

New command structures

On 6 July 2010 President Dmitry Medvedev issued a decree entitled 'Strategic Military Territorial Formations of the Russian Federation', establishing four joint strategic commands. July also saw the MoD begin the establishment of four military districts (in place of the previous six), a move that was formalised on 20 September when Medvedev signed a decree entitled 'On the Military Administrative Division of the Russian Federation'. These moves are part of a bid to streamline command and control within the

Russian armed forces; Makarov has said that enacting these formations will reduce the number of echelons of command from 11 to three. However, according to the draft of a further 'Statute on the Military District of the Russian Armed Forces', the military district will remain the main organisational division in peacetime, and the joint strategic-command function will only come into effect 'during special periods', i.e., during military exercises or in time of war. The activation of the joint strategic command would therefore serve as a significant indicator of imminent major activity by the Russian armed forces.

These joint strategic commands, based geographically on the new military districts, would also be led by the military district commanders, who are to combine both command responsibilities. All military units stationed on the territory of a joint strategic command, including navy, air-force and air-defence units – excepting strategic missile forces and space forces – are under the direct control of this commander. This individual also has operational command over Interior Ministry and Emergency Ministry units, border guards and other military formations. Airborne troops, meanwhile, remain a separate arm of service, while Long-Range Aviation (previously the 37th Air Army) and Military Transport Aviation (previously the 61st Air Army) continue to report to the commander-in-chief of the Russian Air Force.

The four new joint strategic commands are:

- Joint Strategic Command West, headquartered in St Petersburg, which combines units located in the old Moscow and Leningrad Military Districts, as well as the Baltic and Northern Fleets, and forces in Kaliningrad Oblast;
- Joint Strategic Command South, headquartered in Rostov-on-Don, which is based on units in the North Caucasus Military District, together with the Black Sea Fleet, the Caspian Flotilla, Military Base 102 in Gyumri (Armenia) and the Russian military bases in Abkhazia and South Ossetia;
- Joint Strategic Command Centre, with headquarters in Yekaterinburg, which combines the Volga–Urals Military District with the western part of the Siberian Military District as well as Military Base 4 on the outskirts of Dushanbe, Tajikistan, and the air-force base in Kant, Kyrgyzstan; and
- Joint Strategic Command East, headquartered in Khabarovsk, which combines the

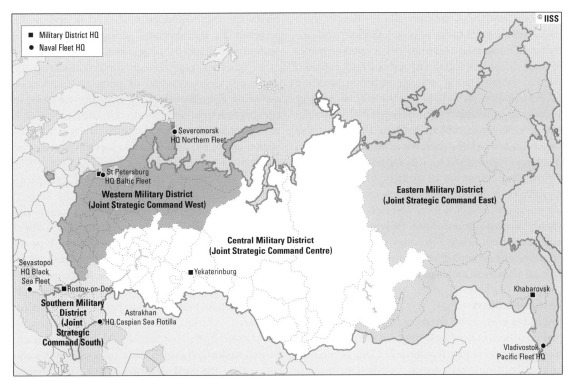

Map 3 **Russian Military Commands**

eastern part of the Siberian Military District with the Far Eastern Military District, and also includes the Pacific Fleet and forces in the Kamchatka Special Territorial Region.

CGS Makarov has said that these organisational changes have streamlined the command and control of the armed forces by eradicating duplication. However, no precise definition has yet been released of the four commanders' role in the context of operations (as commander of a joint strategic command) and administration (as commander of a military district). Moscow has said it plans to minimise the administrative responsibilities of each district by handing more of these to the central directorates of the MoD. Meanwhile, more authority on operational matters should be delegated to the military district/joint strategic command. But if the commander of a military district and of a joint strategic command are still the same individual, who remains responsible for both administrative and operational decision-making, this calls into question some of the aims of streamlining command and control by separating out administrative functions. The effectiveness of the reorganisation has yet to be tested under operational conditions.

Other developments have included the formation of three new combined-arms armies (at Chita, Stavropol and St Petersburg) that are intended to be integrated into a new three-level command-and-control system (joint strategic command/army/brigade) instead of the previous four levels (military district/army/division/regiment).

The brigade system in action
By the end of 2009 the long-established means of organising Russian ground forces by divisions and regiments had officially ended. Russia's adoption of the brigade structure saw 23 division formations disbanded, with the exception of the 18th Machine Gun Artillery Division stationed on the South Kuril Islands disputed with Japan. According to official guidelines, these new Russian army units are 95% manned, have complete stocks of military equipment and are considered as permanent-readiness units.

In total, 40 combined-arms permanent-readiness brigades were formed, comprising four tank brigades, 35 motor rifle brigades and one logistics brigade. Forty-five other brigades relate to other service branches, including missile, artillery, multiple-launch rocket system (MLRS), engineer, signals and radio-electronic warfare. A tank brigade consists of three tank battalions (31 tanks in each battalion) and one motor rifle battalion. A motor rifle brigade consists of three motor rifle battalions, and one tank battalion with 41 tanks. This is augmented by an auxiliary MLRS battalion, as well as two regimental artillery battalions, an auxiliary air-defence missile battalion and an air-defence artillery battalion. In reality, these new brigades broadly conform to structures seen in the former regiments of the Russian and Soviet armed forces, albeit reinforced by artillery, air-defence and logistics units. (An artillery brigade consists of three batteries, one of which is an anti-tank battery.) The storage and maintenance bases for weapons and military equipment (*Bazy khraneniya voyennoy tekhniki*) have been designated main reserve units; at present around 60 of these are planned.

Test and adjust

Unofficial assessments from the MoD have indicated that up to 60% of these new brigades are not combat-ready. Key reasons for this include a lack of modern military hardware and a dearth of up-to-date communications and combat-support systems, coupled with commanders' inability to exercise effective command and control using modern C4I (command, control, communications, computers and intelligence) systems. In a bid to address the latter problem, President Medvedev has directed that the army transforms its communications systems from analogue to digital by 2012. Although this could be technically achieved by the domestic defence industry, it is unclear if sufficient funding is available.

In addition, readiness is compromised by the continuing reorganisation of units and personnel, including the after-effects of reducing the term of conscription from two years to one. During the *Vostok 2010* exercise, for example, some units were 80% staffed with conscripts who had served less than two months.

The new brigades have been tested in a series of major exercises, of which *Vostok* was the largest. Following a post-exercise review, the MoD reassessed the developing brigade structures, and the General Staff has since put forward designs for three types of combined-arms brigades: heavy (formed mainly of tank units); medium/multi-purpose (equipped with armoured personnel carriers); and light air-assault and mountain brigades (equipped with wheeled, armoured vehicles). The heavy-brigade concept is being tested by the 21st Separate Motor Rifle Brigade located in the Orenburg Oblast; the medium-brigade concept by the 23rd Separate Motor Rifle Brigade located in Samara Oblast; and the light-brigade concept by the 56th Separate Air Assault Brigade in Volgograd Oblast.

Airborne troops remain organised according to a divisional structure. Within the order of battle there are two airborne divisions (the 98th and 106th), two air-assault divisions (the 7th and 76th), two indepen-

Developing the T-50

Russia's T-50 fifth-generation fighter prototype aircraft was flown for the first time in January 2010 in Russia's Far East. Designed from the outset to meet low-observable requirements, the aircraft is intended to provide the air force with a stealthy multi-role platform.

Developed by Russian aircraft manufacturer Sukhoi to meet the air force's PAK FA (*Perspectivny Aviatzionny Kompleks Frontovoy Aviatzii* or Future Tactical Aviation Aircraft System) requirement, the type is planned to enter service around 2016. As of the end of November 2010 only one prototype – the T-50-01 – was involved in the flight-test programme. It was anticipated that a second airframe would be ready to join the programme by around the turn of the year. A pre-production batch of up to ten aircraft could be ordered in 2012. The T-50 design was selected by the air force in 2002 as the basis for its future heavy fighter, in preference to a proposal from MiG.

The PAK FA project superseded the air force's MFI (*Mnogofunktsionalny Frontovoi Istrebitel* or Multi-Frontal Fighter) programme, an effort dating back to the 1980s to produce a successor to the Su-27 *Flanker*. Repeatedly delayed and hampered by a lack of funding, the MFI – which was being developed by MiG – was eventually abandoned in the late 1990s.

The PAK FA programme is of fundamental importance to the air force and to the Russian defence aerospace sector. It will provide the air force with a high-end replacement for the Su-27, at the same time as producing a successor to the *Flanker* for the export market. In October 2010 India indicated that it would become involved in the programme to meet what it terms its Fifth-Generation Fighter Aircraft (FGFA) programme.

The T-50 prototype has a chined forward fuselage, with planform edge alignment that now typifies low-observable designs. The twin-engine aircraft's air-intake geometry is such that it helps to reduce the radar visibility of the engine compressor blades. There are two main internal weapon bays in the tunnel between the engines, as well as what appear to be two smaller single-missile bays.

Other air-force developments

- Four new Yak-130 jet trainer/light attack aircraft arrived after January 2010, although these were grounded after an accident in May;
- Four Su-34 strike aircraft delivered in December 2010;
- One Su-30M2 arrived from a 64-aircraft contract agreed in 2006 (48 Su-35, 12 Su-27 and 4 Su-30M2); and
- The Russian air force received five light *Ansat* multi-purpose helicopters and will receive three more by the end of 2010. The delivery of five new Mi-8 AMTSh helicopters will bring the total number of this variant to 20. Around five Mi-28 (anti-armour) attack helicopters have been fielded, with this fleet rising to between eight and ten within a year.

dent air-assault brigades, two independent airborne regiments, a training centre and support units. The airborne command's proposal to reinforce airborne forces has been adopted, increasing the number of airborne regiments from two to three and creating an air-defence missile regiment in each airborne division. Plans also exist to attach a helicopter regiment (a full complement would be 60 helicopters) to an air-assault brigade through a bulk purchase of helicopters. While this may aid tactical mobility, mobility in general is a serious challenge for the airborne troops. With today's assets, Russia's air force can only transport one airborne regiment (plus equipment) over distance. And although military airlift is another priority for the military-reform project, the airlift fleet is decreasing.

Air force and strategic rocket forces

The Russian air force is also overhauling its basing structure, with the aim of reducing its overall number of airfields, in part by co-locating units at a far smaller number of 'combined air bases' that will support a number of satellite airfields. The air force has replaced its air-regiment structure with that of air bases, with air groups the equivalent of the former regiments. Voronezh, Chelyabinsk and Domna will be locations for early 'enlarged' bases. Air bases consist of a headquarters, between one and seven squadrons, an airfield-maintenance battalion and a communications unit. As of late 2009, these air bases were divided into three categories: the first is equivalent to the former air divisions, the second to a former air regiment, and the third category to an independent squadron.

Fifty-two air bases had been formed by the end of 2009, replacing 72 air regiments, 14 former air bases, 12 independent air squadrons and an unspecified number of air-force and air-defence units. (The total number of air-force units, meanwhile, fell to 180 from 340.) But further reductions are planned. The number of airfields in use is also to be reduced; there are currently 245 of these, each costing an average of one billion roubles (US$33.05 million) per year. It is envisaged that in future each air base will control two or three airfields, implying that more than half of those currently in use will close.

A further reform proposal is the creation of an aviation taskforce that would consist of bomber, close support, reconnaissance and fighter aircraft. Fielding the latest fifth-generation fighter technology would, of course, assist the effective generation of such capability, and Russia's contender for a fifth-generation multi-role fighter met with generally favourable comments after its maiden flight in January 2010. The Sukhoi T-50 stealth fighter is a key project (see box). The initial flight-test programme should end in 2013, while introduction into service is slated for 2015–16. However, testing has thus far been limited to the new air frame, while next-generation propulsion and some avionics have yet to be selected. Even when these have been decided, developing and producing the aircraft will be challenging. A shortage of technical specialists and of factories with serial-production techniques will hinder the fielding of the T-50.

The structure of the strategic rocket forces (SRF) has remained unchanged. Three rocket armies, consisting of 11 divisions, are the core of the SRF. However, it is planned that one of the armies (the 31st) will be disbanded by 2016 and the number of divisions will fall to nine. Instead of quantity, the SRF is focusing on increasing the quality of its missile systems. As the old R-36M2 and UR-100 UTTH multi-stage missiles are decommissioned, the light single-warhead *Topol*-M and RS-24 *Yars* missiles equipped with multiple independently targeted re-entry vehicles (MIRV) will comprise 80% of the SRF inventory. Further, it is reported that development work is proceeding on a new heavy MIRV-equipped intercontinental ballistic missile; this development work was confirmed in December 2009 by General Andrey Shvaychenko, then commander-in-chief of the SRF, who promised to put the missile into service by 2016. This new missile is reported to be liquid-fuelled, which would indicate that it is intended to be silo-based; liquid-fuelled propulsion would allow a greater throw-weight compared to solid-fuelled missiles.

Military doctrine

President Medvedev approved a new military doctrine of the Russian Federation in February 2010, superseding the 2000 version which had been approved by Vladimir Putin. The new doctrine contains a carefully nuanced treatment of NATO. The Alliance is not referred to as a threat, but specific NATO activities are noted as military dangers that could under certain circumstances lead to an immediate threat – in particular, the development of military infrastructure closer to the borders of Russia, and use of force globally 'in violation of international law'. Other problem areas for Russia are the militarisation of outer space, the deployment of advanced conventional precision-guided weapons, and the deployment of ballistic-missile defence systems. (However, at NATO's November 2010 Lisbon Summit, NATO and Russia agreed on a joint ballistic-missile threat assessment, decided to resume theatre missile-defence cooperation and began, according to NATO, 'a joint analysis of the future framework for broader missile-defence cooperation'.)

Belarus, which did not appear in the older doctrine, is mentioned as a main ally, and political–military cooperation with Minsk is declared a top priority. Other allies mentioned include the remaining member states of the Collective Security Treaty Organisation (CSTO) – Armenia, Kazakhstan, Kyrgyzstan, Tajikistan and Uzbekistan. Indeed, the mutual-defence provision of the Collective Security Treaty is reproduced in full in the new doctrine. This reinforces the obligations, spelled out elsewhere in the doctrine, for Russia to act militarily in support of its allies or its citizens abroad. Provisions for the use of Russian troops abroad reflect amendments to Russian legislation and a simplified procedure for presidential authorisation of operations outside Russia.

The doctrine was widely expected to contain a significant new provision for preventive or preemptive nuclear first strike. In fact, the section on nuclear weapons instead subtly raises the threshold for their use: Russia may now launch a nuclear strike only in response to weapons of mass destruction or otherwise 'when the very existence of the state is under threat'. The precise formulation of Russia's nuclear threshold is contained in a classified addendum to the doctrine.

Recruitment and manning

The MoD has halted, and indeed reversed, any growth in the number of contract personnel. From an official figure of 150,000 contract servicemen in late 2010, the number is expected to fall to 80,000 by 2015. This reflects continuing difficulties in managing and retaining professional servicemen, as well as a realisation of their true financial cost and, in part, the failure to launch the long-promised professional training for NCOs in any meaningful capacity. New professional training for career NCOs, intended to last up to two-and-a-half years, has proved difficult to implement while the concepts for employment of NCOs and the selection procedures for the training courses are still being developed. Meanwhile, most NCOs will continue to be one-year conscripts selected to complete a short 'sergeant's course', who will subsequently be expected to maintain order among the same draft with which they were recruited. While a corps of professional NCOs remains an aspiration, there is little evidence that Russia has fully grasped the depth of organisational and social change that this implies.

The bulk of servicemen, therefore, will continue to be conscripts. This promises further difficulties in future, especially as Russia's demographic situation leads to continuing sharp falls in the number of 18-year-olds available for conscription. In October 2010 Russia carried out a national census that it is widely hoped will, after decades of decline, show a slight upturn in the overall population – reflecting improvements in health care and recent social policies intended to encourage young families to have children. But this is of limited comfort to those planning military manpower in the short term. The 2011 conscription rounds will be drafting young men born in 1993, during the period of demographic collapse (1987–99) when the number of live male births in Russia fell by more than 50%. Thus, the pool of available manpower will continue to shrink drastically well into the 2020s, complicating aspirations to improve the average health and behaviour of conscripts through more stringent selection criteria.

Meanwhile, cuts in the number of mid-ranking officers continue, with a planned reduction to 150,000 by 2015. Although in some cases these are vacant posts that are being eliminated, the redundancy programme still affects tens of thousands of officers.

Military service and education

A key part of Defence Minister Serdyukov's plans to improve the image of the armed forces revolves

Global Navigation Satellite System

Russia's Global Navigation Satellite System (GLONASS) has received a surge in investment to address deficiencies, but the fruits of this extra funding have yet to be seen after a recent launch failure. The system's inadequacies had long been the subject of complaint, but were thrown into sharp focus during the Russia–Georgia conflict of August 2008. Lack of satellite navigation and guidance was identified as a specific problem for Russian forces during the conflict, with very low penetration of receiver and navigation equipment exacerbated by the lack of capacity and incomplete coverage of the GLONASS satellite system itself, particularly when compared to GPS systems used by Georgia.

A key problem was the insufficient number of satellites in orbit to ensure fully functioning coverage. In the wake of the conflict, there was a sudden burst of launch activity, with 15 of the 26 GLONASS satellites in orbit in early 2011 having been launched after the Georgia war. However, only 21 were working and three additional satellites, intended to bring the number of operational satellites to the 24 needed to fully deploy GLONASS, crashed into the sea during launch in December 2010. Experts estimate this has set Russia's plans for GLONASS back by six months.

Meanwhile, ground systems using GLONASS data are also rapidly being brought into testing. After suffering relative neglect, GLONASS is now seen as key to the introduction of advanced C2 systems, including the *Sozvezdiye* automated system, and the laptop-based Integrated Tactical-Echelon Command and Control System (YeSU TZ), currently being tested by Western Military District's 5th Motor-Rifle Brigade. But in the short term it appears unlikely that GLONASS usage will permeate the military to the extent that GPS systems have outside Russia, because of the relatively primitive nature, bulk and high power consumption of the receivers and navigation units built around it.

For the same reason, take-up of GLONASS services remains slow outside the military; commercial use is hampered by a lack of receivers suitable for car or handheld use; the smallest GLONASS receiver unit publicly available in Russia is a circuit board measuring 5×7cm and costing US$250.

around changes to the conditions of service for conscripts. However, administrative upheaval and the wholesale removal of units, headquarters and staff to other parts of the country have themselves had an impact on troops' quality of life.

One proposal is to fit all physical, combat and weapons training into a five-day week, with weekends treated as days off when conscripts can wear civilian clothes and leave base – a significant innovation in the Russian context. Serdyukov is also keen to outsource basic base administrative tasks, such as catering and cleaning, to commercial organisations. At present, external contractors provide catering services to 200 units, catering to more than 180,000 personnel, at a cost of R6.5bn (US$214.87m) per year. As well as catering, these companies are responsible for supporting laundry and bathing facilities, some military transportation activities, providing fuel services (including for aircraft) and logistical support for the navy.

The MoD views these developments positively and hopes to increase their application in the future. The *Vostok-2010* exercise saw the first trial of civilian contractor services in the field in simulated combat conditions.

There are also proposals to improve servicemen's quality of life by reforming the system of pay and allowances, the complexity of which provides broad scope for abuse. At the time of writing, it was unclear what form this overhaul would take, but continuing substantial pay rises have been proposed. Meanwhile, a scheme introduced in 2009 by Serdyukov to financially reward officers who meet specific criteria continues to prove corrosive and divisive.

In 2010, enrolment of officer cadets in military higher-education institutions was suspended for two years. In one sense a radical step to address an oversupply of junior officer graduates, this is also an attempt to 'reset' military education, creating space to overhaul curricula and reorganise the whole system. The number of educational establishments is to be reduced sharply: around 70 military higher-education institutions will be reduced and reorganised into just ten by 2013, the majority of them 'military–scientific centres' specific to individual arms of service.

Rearmament

Efforts to rationalise the system by which the Russian armed forces acquire arms and equipment appeared to be progressing. In July 2010 a deputy minister of defence for material and technical provision (*Material'no-tekhnicheskoye obespecheniye vooruzhennykh sil,* MTO) was appointed, heading a single new agency created to address what CGS Makarov called

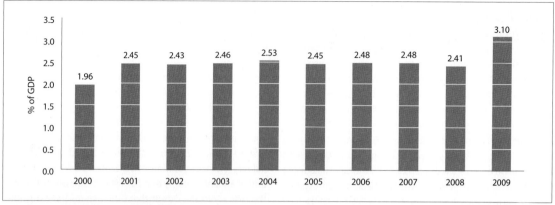

Figure 5 **Estimated Russian Defence Expenditure** as % of GDP

problems and failures of coordination in procurement resulting from there being one deputy minister for logistics and one for armaments. This move marked the end of the short-lived *Rosoboronpostavka*, the federal agency for the supply of weapons, military, special technology and material means, which was established by former Defence Minister Sergey Ivanov in 2007, and was intended to finance and order equipment required by the armed forces.

Ambitious spending plans continued to be put forward. First Deputy Minister of Defence Vladimir Popovkin announced in mid-2010 that funding for the State Armaments Programme for 2011–20 would be increased by 50%. As well as strategic nuclear forces, the funds would be spent on precision weaponry, automated command systems and a wide range of transport aircraft to enable rapid movements of units across Russia.

A stated aim to move away from the long-standing practice of modernising and upgrading old models, and a long-overdue reduction in the number of types in inventory, is supposed to release additional funds for the purchase of completely new equipment. But the rolling State Armaments Programme and its cousin, the State Defence Order, have rarely had successful outcomes; the armaments programme is not even binding, unlike the State Defence Order, which includes fiscal commitments. The State Armaments Programme 1996–2005 failed after a year: by 2000 the rate of 'modern' arms and equipment induction had decreased by up to 20%. The next programme, the State Armaments Programme 2001–10, focused on strategic nuclear forces and also turned out to be untenable. This latest State Armaments Programme for 2011–20, adopted in 2006, is the fourth since the end of the Soviet Union.

Priorities for the development of the armed forces have been established to:

- maintain strategic deterrent forces;
- purchase high-precision weapons, with targeting informed by space-based assets;
- provide the armed forces with C4I systems (all branch and service command C4I should be integrated in two to three years);
- restore the military airlift inventory; and
- recapitalise naval forces. This is a long-term programme requiring significant financial support. It is intended that the Black Sea Fleet, for instance, should acquire ten new surface ships (Project 22350 frigates) and five diesel submarines (*Lada*-class, Project 677) by 2020.

According to official statements, 1,500 new aircraft and helicopters (including T-50 stealth fighters, see box p. 176) and 200 anti-aircraft systems are to be procured under this programme. It is hoped that the production line for An-124 strategic air-lifters will be restarted, while purchases of Il-112, Il-476, Il-76M and An-70 aircraft are also desired. The plan is for the Russian Air Force to receive around 400 new and upgraded combat- and assault-transport helicopters, including the Mi-28, Ka-52 and Mi-8. Long-term contracts have been signed for 60 Su-34 and Su-35C fixed-wing aircraft. Deliveries have recently started, though progress is slow and only several fixed- and rotary-wing aircraft have been fielded. Further plans include the purchase of five battalions' worth of S-400 air-defence systems, although only two battalions have been delivered so far. Meanwhile, it is believed that ten *Pantsyr*-C combined short- to medium-range surface-to-air missile and anti-aircraft artillery systems have been inducted into air-force service.

Table 13 **Draft Russian National Defence Expenditure (Rm)**

A: Chapter 2 'National Defence'	2009	2010	2011
Armed Forces of the Russian Federation	894.6	952.2	1,115.3
Mobilisation of external forces	3.6	4.6	6.7
Mobilisation of the economy	4.6	4.9	4.9
Collective peacekeeping	0.6	7.7	0.45
Military nuclear programmes	19.1	18.8	27
International treaty obligations	4.8	4.05	4.8
Applied R&D	162.9	151.4	167
Other	121.7	133.15	194.6
Sub-total: Chapter 2 'National Defence'	1,211.9	1,276.8	1,520.8

B: Additional military-related expenditure	2009	2010	2011
Internal troops	58.2	66.9	71.9
Security organs of the state	178.9	196.5	233.4
Border troops	79.9	77.2	78.9
Subsidies to closed towns	n.a.	n.a.	n.a
Ministry of emergencies	57.2	125.1	72.6
Military pensions	223.2	240.8	237.24
Sub-total: Additional military-related expenditure	597.4	706.5	694
Total Defence-related Expenditure (A+B)	1,809.30	1,983.30	2,214.80
as % of GDP	4.63	4.41	4.34
as % of total outlays	18.2	19.2	-

The State Armaments Programme for 2011–20 runs to R19 trillion (US$628.09bn) for the MoD, with R3.5tr (US$115.7bn) to be spent in equipping other law-enforcement units. The programme is intended to provide for renewal of up to 9–11% of military hardware and weapon systems annually, which will enable the 70% increase in 'modern' arms and military equipment that Serdyukov has been advocating by 2020.

However, the amount of money allocated to arms procurement is invariably less than the amount planned in the State Armaments Programme. This situation is particularly affected by the forecast deflators included by the Ministry of Economic Development and Trade in each fiscal year; as a rule, these deflators are not proved accurate by the real rate of inflation.

The 2010 State Defence Order amounted to R1.15tr (US$38.01bn), according to Prime Minister Putin, with R375bn (US$12.39bn) spent on new military hardware. In the draft of the federal budget for 2011, and its planning for 2012–13, expenses on national defence are predicted to steadily increase from R1.52tr in 2011 to R1.66tr in 2012 and R2.1tr in 2013.

Until 2005 information on the funds allocated in the defence budget to purchase, maintain and repair – as well as to develop – new military equipment was included in a separate appendix to the federal budget. But in the following years, there was a hiatus in the publication of defence-budget data, during which it became the source of informed speculation among defence officials and military officers. The Defence Committee of the State Duma has now released figures for 2010–13. This development may point to a greater openness in defence financing; on the other hand, the reliability of the figures given is unclear, and the subject remains something of a grey area.

Expenses on the purchase, maintenance and repair of armaments (less R&D) are R380bn (US$12.56bn) in 2010, R460bn in 2011, R596bn in 2012, and R980bn in 2013. The percentage allocated to R&D is to fall from 22% in 2010 to 16% in 2013, and this has already led the MoD to cancel several procurement programmes that had not yielded effective capabilities. Meanwhile, the total spend on weapons is planned to be R487bn (US$16.09bn) in 2010, R574bn in 2011, R726bn in 2012 and R1.165tr in 2013.

Notwithstanding these plans, the capacity of the Russian defence industry to satisfy the increasing State Defence Order has been questioned, particularly in light of the financial crisis. Production capacities are ageing, as is the defence-industrial workforce, and defence businesses now compete for personnel on the open employment market. Moreover, high-tech production lines have only been developed in a very few cases. Indeed, some analysts say that the military-industrial complex has only survived because of work to maintain and modernise Soviet-era equipment.

Problems in serially manufacturing high-tech defence equipment are a key concern. Although design bureaus are often able to create modern platforms, turning the design into a production model can prove problematic. The government is attempting to create a culture of innovation through the decision to establish an Advanced and Venture Developments Funding Organisation; the hope is that this will be analogous to the US Defence Advanced Research Projects Agency.

Meanwhile, the inability of the domestic defence industry to fulfil military equipment plans has led the MoD to purchase foreign equipment, including

Israeli unmanned aerial vehicles. Negotiations with France about the purchase and/or licensed production of *Mistral*-class helicopter carriers reached a conclusion on 24 December with an agreement between the French and Russian governments that two of the vessels will be constructed in France, with a further two to be built in Russia. No value was assigned to the deal at time of writing, while the issue of technology transfer (relating to the systems onboard the vessels) also remained unclear. In early 2011, the KAMAZ factory in Tatarstan was due to start production of the Italian *Iveco* LMV M65. A minimum of 500 are due to be produced.

Estimating Russian military expenditure

Estimating the real scale of Russian military spending is fraught with difficulty, not least because of recent changes in the presentation of budget data. Taken at face value, the official national-defence allocation for 2009, R1,211bn (US$38.3bn), corresponded to 3.1% of GDP; however, as indicated in Table 13, this figure excludes funds made available for other military-related expenditures, such as pensions and paramilitary forces, not to mention the rising level of subsidies provided to the defence-industrial sector for which figures are unavailable. Including these additional budget allocations brings overall defence-

related expenditure for 2009 to around R1,809bn, or 4.63% of that year's GDP.

Using the prevailing market exchange rate for 2009, Russia's stated defence expenditure was worth US$38.3bn, or US$57.2bn with the additional expenditures factored in. However, when assessing macroeconomic data from countries in transition, the market exchange rate does not usually reflect the actual purchasing power of the domestic currency. Economists therefore use an alternative methodology to make currency conversions, known as Purchasing Power Parity (PPP). For example, in 2009 Russia's GDP measured US$1,236bn when converted at market exchange rates; however, the International Monetary Fund has also calculated that, in PPP terms, Russia's 2009 GDP was equivalent to US$2,116bn. If this crude methodology is applied to military spending, then total defence-related expenditure in 2009 would jump to the equivalent of US$97.9bn.

Note: Although PPP rates can be a useful tool for comparing macroeconomic data, such as GDP, of countries at different stages of development, because there is no specific PPP rate to apply to the military sector, its use in this context should be treated with caution. In addition, there is no definitive guide as to which elements of military spending should be calculated using available PPP rates.

Russia RUS

Russian Rouble r		2009	2010	2011
GDP	r	39.1tr	45.0tr	
	US$	1.24tr	1.49tr	
	US$ a	2.12tr	2.11tr	
per capita	US$	8,777	10,602	
Growth	%	-7.9	5.5	
Inflation	%	11.7	6.5	
Def exp	US$	57.2bn		
	US$ª	97.9bn		
Def bdgt	r	1.21tr	1.27tr	1.52tr
	US$	38.3bn	41.4bn	
	US$ª	65.5bn	61.8bn	
US$1=r	MER	31.62	30.25	
	PPP	18.48	20.29	

ª PPP estimate

Population   140,366,561

Ethnic groups: Tatar 4%; Ukrainian 3%; Chuvash 1%; Bashkir 1%; Belarussian 1%; Moldovan 1%; Other 8%;

Age	0–14	15–19	20–24	25–29	30–64	65 plus
Male	7.8%	2.7%	4.1%	4.2%	23.1%	3.9%
Female	7.4%	2.6%	4.0%	4.2%	26.7%	9.1%

Capabilities

ACTIVE 1,046,000 (Army 360,000 Airborne 35,000 Navy 161,000 Air 160,000 Strategic Deterrent Forces 80,000 Command and Support 250,000) **Paramilitary 449,000**

(Estimated 170,000 in the permanent readiness units)
Terms of service: 12 months conscription.

RESERVE 20,000,000 (all arms)

Some 2,000,000 with service within last 5 years; Reserve obligation to age 50.

ORGANISATIONS BY SERVICE

Strategic Deterrent Forces ε80,000 (incl personnel assigned from the Navy and Air Force)

Navy

SUBMARINES • STRATEGIC • SSBN 14
5 (1†) *Kalmar* (*Delta* III) each with 16 RSM-50 (SS-N-18 *Stingray*) strategic SLBM;
5 *Delfin* (*Delta* IV) each with 16 RSM-54 (SS-N-23 *Skiff*) strategic SLBM;
1 *Delfin* (*Delta* IV) in refit with 16 RSM-52 (SS-N-23 *Skiff*) strategic SLBM;
2 *Akula* (*Typhoon*) in reserve awaiting refit each with 20 RSM-52 (SS-N-20 *Sturgeon*) strategic SLBM;
1 *Akula* (*Typhoon*)† in reserve with capacity for 20 RSM-52 (SS-N-20) *Sturgeon* strategic SLBM/*Bulava* (SS-N-X-32) strategic SLBM (trials/testing);

(1 *Borey* limited OC undergoing sea trials; 2 additional units in build)

Strategic Rocket Force Troops

3 Rocket Armies operating silo and mobile launchers with 430 missiles and 1,605 nuclear warheads organised in 12 divs (reducing to 8). Launcher gps normally with 10 silos (6 for SS-18) and one control centre
MSL • STRATEGIC 376
ICBM 376: 60 RS-20 (SS-18 *Satan*) (mostly mod 4/5, 10 MIRV per msl); 170 RS12M (SS-25 *Sickle*) (mobile single warhead); 70 RS18 (SS-19 *Stiletto*) (mostly mod 3, 6 MIRV per msl.); 52 *Topol*-M (SS-27) silo-based/18 *Topol* M (SS-27) road mobile single warhead (5 regts); 6 RS-24 (MIRV)

Long-Range Aviation Command

FORCES BY ROLE

Bbr   1 sqn with Tu-160 *Blackjack*; 3 sqn with Tu-95MS *Bear*

EQUIPMENT BY TYPE
AIRCRAFT •
LRSA 79: 16 Tu-160 *Blackjack* each with up to 12 KH-55SM(AS-15B *Kent*) nuclear ALCM; 32 Tu-95MS6 (*Bear* H-6) each with up to 6 Kh-55 (AS-15A *Kent*) nuclear ALCM; 31 Tu-95MS16 (*Bear* H-16) each with up to 16 Kh-55 (AS-15A *Kent*) nuclear ALCM

Warning Forces 3rd Space and Missile Defence Army

ICBM/SLBM launch-detection capability. 3 operational satellites
RADAR (9 stations) 1 ABM engagement system located at Sofrino (Moscow). Russia leases ground-based radar stations in Baranovichi (Belarus); Balkhash (Kazakhstan); Gaballa (Azerbaijan). It also has radars on its own territory at Lekhtusi, (St. Petersburg); Armavir, (southern Russia); Olenegorsk (northwest Arctic); Pechora (northwest Urals); Mishelevka (east Siberia).
MISSILE DEFENCE 2,064: 32 SH-11 *Gorgon*; 68 SH-08 *Gazelle*; 1,900 S-300 (SA-10 *Grumble*); 64 S-400 (SA-21 *Growler*)

Space Forces 40,000

Formations and units withdrawn from Strategic Missile and Air Defence Forces to detect missile attack on the RF and its allies, to implement BMD, and to be responsible for military/dual-use spacecraft launch and control.

Army ε205,000 (incl 35,000 AB); ε190,000 conscript (total 395,000)

Transformation process continues; previous 6 Military Districts have been consolidated into 4 (West (HQ St Petersburg), Centre (HQ Yekaterinburg), South (HQ Rostov-on-Don) & East (HQ Khabarovsk), each with a unified Joint Strategic Command. Current plans call for the establishment of 28 new bdes (6 MR; 2 air aslt; 1 engr; 1 AD & 18 army avn), and for the restructuring of the existing MR brigades into new light, medium and heavy formations.

Russia

FORCES BY ROLE

Comd	10 army HQ (3 established 2010)
Tk	4 bde (each: 3 tk bn; 1 armd recce bn; 1 MR bn; 1 arty bn; 1 MRL bn; 2 AD bn; 1 engr bn; 1 EW coy; 1 NBC coy)
Recce	1 bde
MR	1 div (201st); 31 bde (each: 1 tk bn; 1 recce bn; 3 MR bn; 2 arty bn; 1 MRL bn; 1 AT bn; 2 AD bn; 1 engr bn; 1 EW coy; 1 NBC coy); 2 bde (each: 4-5 MR bn; 1 arty bn; 1 AD bn; 1 engr bn); 3 (lt/mtn) bde (each: 1 recce bn; 2 MR bn; 1 arty bn)
SF	7 (Spetsnaz) bde; 1 (AB Recce) regt
Air Aslt	3 bde
AB	4 (VdV) div (each: 2 para/air aslt regt; 1 arty regt; 1 AD regt); 1 (VdV) indep bde
Arty	8 bde
AD	10 bde
MRL	4 bde; 2 regt
SSM	1 bde with *Iskander-M/Tochka* (SS-21 *Scarab*); 8 bde each with *Tochka* (SS-21 *Scarab*) (to be replaced by *Iskander-M*)
MGA	1 div (18th) with (2 MGA regt; 1 arty regt; 1 tk bn; 2 AD bn)
Engr	1 bde

EQUIPMENT BY TYPE

MBT 2,800+: 1,500 T-72B/BA; 1,000 T-80BV/U; 300+ T-90/T-90A; (18,000 in store: 2,800 T-55; 2,500 T-62; 2,000 T-64A/T-64B; 7,500 T-72/T-72A/T-72B; 3,000 T-80B/T-80BV/T-80U; 200 T-90)

RECCE 1,200: 100+ *Dozor*, 100+ *Tigr*, 1,000 BRDM-2/2A; (1,000+ BRDM-2 in store)

AIFV 7,360+: 700 BMD-1; 600 BMD-2; 100 BMD-3; 60+ BMD-4; 1,000 BMP-1; 3,500 BMP-2; 500+ BMP-3; 700 BRM-1K; 200+ BTR-80A; (8,500 in store: 7,000 BMP-1; 1,500 BMP-2)

APC 9,700+

APC (T) 5,700: 700 BTR-D; 5,000 MT-LB; (2,000 MT-LB in store)

APC (W) 4,000+ BTR-60/70/80; (4,000 BTR-60/70 in store)

ARTY 5,436+

SP 1,820: **122mm** 400 2S1; **152mm** 1,400: 800 2S3; 150 2S5; 450 2S19; **203mm** 20 2S7; (4,050 in store: **122mm** 1,800 2S1; **152mm** 1,950: 1,000 2S3; 800 2S5; 150 2S19; **203mm** 300 2S7)

TOWED 550: **122mm** 400 D-30; **152mm** 150 2A65; (12,215 in store: **122mm** 7,950: 4,200 D-30; 3,750 M-30 *M-1938*; **130mm** 650 M-46; **152mm** 3,575: 1,100 2A36; 600 2A65; 1,075 D-20; 700 D-1 *M-1943*; 100 ML-20 M-1937; **203mm** 40 B-4M)

GUN/MOR 970+

SP 120mm 870+: 790 2S9 *NONA-S*; 30 2S23 *NONA-SVK*; 50+ 2S34

TOWED 120mm 100 2B16 *NONA-K*

MRL 1,106+ **122mm** 800 BM-21; **220mm** 200 9P140 *Uragan*; **300mm** 106 9A52 *Smerch*; (2,920 in store: **122mm** 2,120: 1,700 BM-21; 420 9P138; **132mm** 100 BM-13; **220mm** 700 9P140 *Uragan*)

MOR 990

SP 240mm 20 2S4; (410 2S4 in store)

TOWED 970+: **120mm** 970: 50+ 2B23; 920 2S12; (2,100 in store: **120mm** 1,800: 900 2S12; 900 PM-38; **160mm** 300 M-160)

AT

MSL • SP & MANPATS 9K11/9K14 *Malyutka* (AT-3 *Sagger*); 9K111 *Fagot* (AT-4 *Spigot*); 9K112 *Kobra* (AT-8 *Songster*); 9K113 *Konkurs* (AT-5 *Spandrel*); 9K114 *Shturm* (AT-6 *Spiral*); 9K115 *Metis* (AT-7 *Saxhorn*); 9K115-1 *Metis-M* (AT-13 *Saxhorn* 2); 9K116 *Bastion/Basnya* (AT-10 *Stabber*); 9K119 *Reflex/Svir* (AT-11 *Sniper*); 9K123 *Khrisantema* (AT-15 *Springer*); 9K135 *Kornet* (AT-14 *Spriggan*); 9M120 *Ataka* (AT-12 *Swinger*)

RCL 73mm SPG-9

RL 64mm RPG-18; **73mm** RPG-16/RPG-22/RPG-26/RPG-7; **105mm** RPG-27/RPG-29

GUNS 562+

SP: 125mm 36+ 2S25

TOWED 100mm 526 MT-12; (**100mm** 2,000 T-12/MT-12 in store)

AD

SAM 1,570+

SP 1,320+: 350+ *Buk* (SA-11/17 *Gadfly*); 450 *Osa-AK/AKM* (SA-8 *Gecko*); 400 *Strela-10* (SA-13 *Gopher*); 120+ *Tor* (SA-15 *Gauntlet*)

SPAAGM 250+ 2S6 *Tunguska* (SA-19 *Grison*)

MANPAD *Igla-1* (SA-16 *Gimlet*); *Igla* (SA-18 *Grouse*); *Igla-S* (SA-24 *Grinch*); *Strela-3* (SA-14 *Gremlin*)

GUNS

SP 23mm ZSU-23-4

TOWED 23mm ZU-23-2; **57mm** S-60

UAV • Heavy Tu-143 *Reys*; Tu-243 *Reys*/Tu-243 *Reys-D*; Tu-300 *Korshun* **Light** BLA-07; *Pchela-1*; *Pchela-2*

MSL • SSM 200+: 200 *Tochka* (SS-21 *Scarab*); some *Iskander* (SS-26 *Stone*); (some FROG in store; some *Scud* in store)

FACILITIES

Bases	1 in Abkhazia; 1 in South Ossetia, 1 in Tajikistan, 1 in Armenia

Reserves

Cadre formations, on mobilisation form

Tk	1 bde
MR	13 bde

Navy 161,000

4 major fleet organisations (Northern Fleet, Pacific Fleet, Baltic Fleet, Black Sea) and Caspian Sea Flotilla

EQUIPMENT BY TYPE

SUBMARINES 67

STRATEGIC • SSBN 14:

5 *Kalmar* (*Delta* III) (1†) each with 16 RSM-50 (SS-N-18 *Stingray*) strategic SLBM

5 *Delfin* (*Delta* IV) each with 16 RSM-54 (SS-N-23 *Skiff*) strategic SLBM

1 *Delfin* (*Delta* IV) in refit each with 16 RSM-52 (SS-N-23 *Skiff*) strategic SLBM

2 *Akula* (*Typhoon*) in reserve awaiting refit each with 40 RSM-52 (SS-N-20 *Sturgeon*) strategic SLBM

1 *Akula* (*Typhoon*)† in reserve for training with capacity for 20 RSM-52 (SS-N-20 *Sturgeon*) strategic SLBM/*Bulava* (SS-N-X-32) strategic SLBM (trials/testing)

(1 *Borey* sea trials completed in September 2010; *Bulava* (SS-N-X-32) SLBM not yet operational; 3 additional units in build)

TACTICAL 45
SSGN 8:
8 *Antyey* (*Oscar* II) (of which 3 in reserve) each with 2 single 650mm TT each with T-65 HWT, 4 single 553mm TT each with 3M45 *Granit* (SS-N-19 *Shipwreck*) AShM

SSN 17:
2 *Schuka-B* (*Akula* II) each with 4 single 533mm TT each with 3M10 *Granat* (SS-N-21 *Sampson*) SLCM, 4 single 650mm TT each with T-65 HWT

8 *Schuka-B* (*Akula* I) (of which 2 in reserve) each with 4 single 533mm TT each with 3M10 *Granat* (SS-N-21 *Sampson*) SLCM, 4 single 650mm TT each with T-65 HWT

2 *Kondor* (*Sierra* II) with 4 single 533mm TT each with,3M10 *Granat* (SS-N-21 *Sampson*) SLCM, 4 single 650mm TT each with T-65 HWT

1 *Barracuda* (*Sierra* I) with 4 single 533mm TT each with SS-N-21 *Sampson* SLCM, SS-N-15 *Starfish* and T-53 HWT, 4 single 650mm TT each with SS-N-16 *Stallion* AShM and T-65 HWT

4 *Schuka* (*Victor* III) (of which 1 in reserve) each with 4 single 533mm TT each with 3M10 *Granat* (SS-N-21 *Sampson*) SLCM, 2 single 650mm TT each with T-65 HWT

SSK 20:
15 *Paltus* (*Kilo*) each with 6 single 533mm TT each with T-53 HWT

4 *Varshavyanka* (*Kilo*) each with 6 single 533mm TT

1 *Lada* with 6 single 533mm TT (2 additional vessels in build)

SUPPORT 8
SSAN 7: 1 *Orenburg* (*Delta* III Stretch); 1 *Losharik*; 2 Project 1851 (*Paltus*); 3 *Kashalot* (*Uniform*)
SSA 1 *Sarov*

PRINCIPAL SURFACE COMBATANTS 32
AIRCRAFT CARRIERS • CV 1 *Orel* (*Kuznetsov*) with 1 12 cell VLS with 3M45 *Granit* (SS-N-19 *Shipwreck*) AShM, 4 sextuple VLS (24 eff.) each with 3K95 *Kindzhal* (SA-N-9 *Gauntlet*) SAM (capacity 18-24 Su-33 *Flanker D* FGA ac; 4 Su-25UTG *Frogfoot* ac, 15 Ka-27 *Helix* ASW hel, 2 Ka-31 *Helix* AEW hel)

CRUISERS 6
CGHMN 2:
2 *Orlan* (*Kirov*) with 10 twin VLS (20 eff.) each with 3M45 *Granit* (SS-N-19 *Shipwreck*) AShM, 2 twin lnchr (4 eff.) each with *Osa-M* (SA-N-4 *Gecko*) SAM, 12 single VLS each with *Fort/Fort* M (SA-N-6 *Grumble/SA-N-20 Gargoyle*) SAM, 2 octuple VLS (16 eff.) each with 3K95 *Kindzhal* (SA-N-9 *Gauntlet*) SAM, 10 single 533mm ASTT, 1 twin 130mm gun (2 eff.), (capacity 3 Ka-27 *Helix* ASW hel) (2nd *Orlan* undergoing extensive refit currently non operational)

CGHM 4:
1 *Berkot-B* (*Kara*), with 2 quad lnchr (8 eff.) each with *Rastrub* (SS-N-14 *Silex*) AShM/ASW, 2 twin lnchr (4 eff.) each with 4K60 *Shtorm* (SA-N-3 *Goblet*) SAM, 2 twin lnchr (4 eff.) each with *Osa-M* (SA-N-4 *Gecko*) SAM, 2 quintuple 533mm ASTT (10 eff.), 2 RBU 6000 (24 eff.), 2 twin 76mm gun (4 eff.), (capacity 1 Ka-27 *Helix* ASW hel) (2nd *Berkot-B* laid up awaiting decommissioning)

3 *Atlant* (*Slava*) each with 8 twin lnchr (16 eff.) each with 4K80 *Bazalt* (SS-N-12 *Sandbox*) AShM, 8 octuple VLS (64 eff.) each with 8 SA-N-6 *Grumble* SAM, 2 quintuple 533mm ASTT (10 eff.), 1 twin 130mm gun (2 eff.), (capacity 1 Ka-27 *Helix* ASW hel)

DESTROYERS 18
DDGHM 17:
8 *Sarych* (*Sovremenny*) (of which 3 in reserve) each with 2 quad lnchr (8 eff.) each with 3M80 *Moskit* (SS-N-22 *Sunburn*) AShM, 2 twin lnchr (4 eff.) each with *Uragan/Yezh* (SA-N-7 *Gadfly*/SA-N-12 *Grizzly*) SAM, 2 twin 533mm TT (4 eff.), 2 twin 130mm gun (4 eff.), (capacity 1 Ka-27 *Helix* ASW hel)

8 *Fregat* (*Udaloy* I) each with 2 quad lnchr (8 eff.) each with *Rastrub* (SS-N-14 *Silex*) AShM/ASW, 8 octuple VLS (64 eff.) each with 3K95 *Kindzhal* (SA-N-9 *Gauntlet* SAM), 2 quad 533mm ASTT (8 eff.), 2 100mm gun, (capacity 2 Ka-27 *Helix* ASW hel)

1 *Fregat* (*Udaloy* II) with 2 quad lnchr (8 eff.) each with 3M80 *Moskit* (SS-N-22 *Sunburn*) AShM, 8 octuple VLS (64 eff.) each with 3K95 *Kindzhal* (SA-N-9 *Gauntlet*) SAM, 2 CADS-N-1 CIWS with 9M311 *Kashtan* (SA-N-11 *Grisson*) SAM, 10 single 533mm ASTT, 2 100mm gun, (capacity 2 Ka-27 *Helix* ASW hel)

DDGM 1:
1 *Komsomolets Ukrainy* (*Kashin* mod) with 2 quad lnchr (8 eff.) each with 3M24 *Uran* (SS-N-25 *Switchblade*) AShM, 2 twin lnchr (4 eff.) each with *Volnya* (SA-N-1 *Goa*) SAM, 5 single 533mm ASTT, 1 twin 76mm gun (2 eff.)

FRIGATES 7
FFGHM 2:
2 *Jastreb* (*Neustrashimy*) each with 4 octuple VLS (32 eff.) each with 3K95 *Kindzhal* (SA-N-9 *Gauntlet*) SAM, 6 single 533mm ASTT, 1 RBU 12000 (10 eff.), 1 100mm gun, (capacity 1 Ka-27 *Helix* ASW) (3rd in build)

FFGM 4:
1 *Gepard* with 2 quad lnchr (8 eff.) each with 3M24 *Uran* (SS-N-25 *Switchblade*) AShM, 1 twin lnchr (2 eff.) with *Osa-M* (SA-N-4 *Gecko*) SAM, 2 30mm CIWS, 1 76mm gun, (2nd vessel on trials)

1 *Burevestnik* (*Krivak* I mod) with 1 quad lnchr (4 eff.) with *Rastrub* (SS-N-14 *Silex*) AShM/ASW, 1 twin lnchr (2 eff.) with *Osa-M* (SA-N-4 *Gecko*) SAM, 2 quad 533mm ASTT (8 eff.), 2 twin 76mm gun (4 eff.)

2 *Burevestnik* M (*Krivak* II) each with 1 quad lnchr (4 eff.) with *Rastrub* (SS-N-14 *Silex*) AShM/ASW, 2 twin lnchr (4 eff.) each with 10 *Osa-M* (SA-N-4 *Gecko* SAM), 2 quad 533mm ASTT (8 eff.), 2 RBU 6000 (24 eff.), 2 100mm gun

FFM 1:
  1 *Steregushchiy* with 2 quad lnchr (8 eff.) with *Kashtan* (SA-N-11 *Grisson*) SAM, 1 100mm gun, (4 additional vessels in build)

PATROL AND COASTAL COMBATANTS 78
  CORVETTES 47:
    FSGM 16:
      2 *Sivuchi* (*Dergach*) each with 2 quad lnchr (8 eff.) each with 3M80 *Moskit* (SS-N-22 *Sunburn*) AShM, 1 twin lnchr (2 eff.) with *Osa-M* (SA-N-4 *Gecko*) SAM, 1 76mm gun
      12 *Ovod* (*Nanuchka* III) each with 2 triple lnchr (6 eff.) each with P-120 *Malakhit* (SS-N-9 *Siren*) AShM, 1 twin lnchr (2 eff.) with *Osa-M* (SA-N-4 *Gecko*), 1 76mm gun
      1 *Ovod* (*Nanuchka* IV) with 2 triple lnchr (6 eff.) each with 3M55 *Onix* (SS-N-26) AShM, 1 twin lnchr (2 eff.) with *Osa-M* (SA-N-4 *Gecko*), 1 76mm gun
    FSM 31:
      3 *Albatros* (*Grisha* III) each with 1 twin lnchr (2 eff.) with *Osa-M* (SA-N-4 *Gecko*) SAM, 2 twin 533mm ASTT (4 eff.), 2 RBU 6000 *Smerch 2* (24 eff.)
      21 *Albatros* (*Grisha* V) each with 1 twin lnchr (2 eff.) with *Osa-M* (SA-N-4 *Gecko*) SAM, 2 twin 533mm ASTT (4 eff.), 1 RBU 6000 *Smerch 2* (12 eff.), 1 76mm gun
      8 *Parchim* II (one in reserve following a fire in 2008) each with 2 quad lnchr (8 eff.) each with *Strela-2* (SA-N-5 *Grail*) SAM, 2 twin 533mm ASTT (4 eff.), 2 RBU 6000 *Smerch 2* (24 eff.), 1 76mm gun
    PCFG 25:
      6 *Molnya* (*Tarantul* II) each with 2 twin lnchr (4 eff.) each with P-15M *Termit* (SS-N-2C/D *Styx*) AShM
      19 *Molnya* (*Tarantul* III) each with 2 twin lnchr (4 eff.) each with 3M80 *Moskit* (SS-N-22 *Sunburn*) AShM
    PHG 4 *Vekhr* (*Matka*) each with 2 single lnchr each with P-15M *Termit* (SS-N-2C/D *Styx*) AShM
    PHT 1 *Sokol* (*Mukha*) with 2 quad 406mm TT (8 eff.)
    PCM 1 *Buyan* (Project 21630) with some 9K310 *Igla-1* (SA-16 *Gimlet*) SAM, 1 100mm gun
  MINE WARFARE • MINE COUNTERMEASURES 50
    MHO 2 *Rubin* (*Gorya*)
    MSO 10 *Akvamaren* (*Natya*)
    MSC 23 *Yakhont* (*Sonya*)
    MHI 15: 9 *Sapfir* (*Lida*); 3 Project 696 (*Tolya*); 3 *Malakhit* (*Olya*)
  AMPHIBIOUS 38
    LANDING SHIPS 25
      LSM 6:
        6 Project 771 (*Polnochny* B) (of which 5 in reserve) (capacity 6 MBT; 180 troops)
      LST 19:
        4 *Tapir* (*Alligator*) (capacity 20 tanks; 300 troops)
        12 Project 775 (*Ropucha* I) (capacity either 10 MBT and 190 troops or 24 APC (T) and 170 troops)
        3 Project 775M (*Ropucha* II) (capacity either 10 MBT and 190 troops or 24 APC (T) and 170 troops)
        (1 *Tapir* (*Alligator* (mod)) (capacity 1 Ka-29 *Helix* B; 13 MBT; 300 troops) (expected ISD 2011)

LANDING CRAFT 13
  LCU 8: 1 *Dyagon*; 7 Project 11770 (*Serna*) (capacity 100 troops)
  LCAC 5:
    2 *Dzheryan* (*Aist*) (capacity 4 lt tk)
    3 *Pomornik* (*Zubr*) (capacity 230 troops; either 3 MBT or 10 APC (T))

LOGISTICS AND SUPPORT 249
A significant element of the RUS Auxiliary and Support Fleet (estimated at 370+ vessels) is either no longer active, at extended readiness or awaiting disposal.
AOR 5 *Boris Chilikin*
AOL 13: 2 *Dubna*; 5 *Uda*; 6 *Altay* (mod)
AORL 3: 1 *Kaliningradneft*; 2 *Olekma*
AWT 2 *Manych*
AS 1 Project 2020 (*Malina*); 2 *Amga* (msl spt ship)
ARS 14: 4 *Mikhail Rudnitsky*; 10 *Goryn*
AR 13 *Amur*
ARC 7: 4 *Emba*; 3 *Klasma*
AG 2 *Vytegrales*
ATF 48: 2 *Baklazhan*; 5 *Katun*; 3 *Ingul*; 2 *Neftegaz*; 14 *Okhtensky*; 18 *Prometey*; 1 *Prut*; 3 *Sliva*
AH 3 *Ob* †
AGOR 6: 2 *Akademik Krylov*; 2 *Sibiriyakov*, 2 *Vinograd*
AGE 2: 1 *Tchusovoy*; 1 *Zvezdochka* **AGSH** 4: 1 *Samara*; 3 *Vaygach*
AGI 12: 2 *Alpinist*; 2 *Balzam*; 2 *Moma*; 6 *Vishnya*
AGM 1 *Marshal Nedelin*
AGS 18: 3 BGK-797; 6 *Kamenka*; 9 *Onega*
AGS(I) 52: 8 *Biya*; 25 *Finik*; 7 *Moma*; 12 *Yug*
AGB 4 *Dobrynya Mikitich*
ABU 12: 8 *Kashtan*; 4 *Sura*
ATF 13 *Sorum*
AXL 12: 10 *Petrushka*; 2 *Smolny*

Naval Aviation ε35,000

4 Fleet Air Forces

Flying hours   ε40 hrs/year

FORCES BY ROLE

Bbr	Some sqn with Tu-22M *Backfire* C
Ftr/FGA	Some sqn with MiG-31 *Foxhound*; Su-24 *Fencer*; Su-27 *Flanker*; Su-33 *Flanker* D;
ASW	Some sqn with Ka-27 *Helix*; Mi-14 *Haze*-A; sqn with Be-12 *Mail*; Il-38 *May*; Tu-142 *Bear*
MP/EW	Some sqn with An-12 *Cub*; Il-20 RT *Coot-A*; Mi-8 *Hip*
Tpt	Some sqn with An-12 *Cub*/An-24 *Coke*/An-26 *Curl*
Trg	Some sqn with Su-25UTG *Frogfoot*
Atk Hel	Some sqns with Mi-24 *Hind*
Tpt Hel	Some sqns with Ka-25 PS *Hormone* C, Ka-27 PS *Helix* D; Mi-6 *Hook*; Mi-14 PS *Haze* C; Ka-29 *Helix*; Mi-8 *Hip*

EQUIPMENT BY TYPE

AIRCRAFT 276 combat capable
  BBR 56 Tu-22M *Backfire* C
  FTR 97: 49 Su-27 *Flanker*; 18 Su-33 *Flanker* D; 30 MiG-31 *Foxhound*
  FGA 47 Su-24 *Fencer*

ATK 5 Su-25UTG *Frogfoot*
ASW 27 Tu-142 *Bear* F/J*
MP 44: 15 Be-12 *Mail**; 29 Il-38 *May**
EW • ELINT 2 Il-20 RT *Coot-A*; 5 An-12 *Cub*
TPT 37: 37 An-12 *Cub*/An-24 *Coke*/An-26 *Curl*

HELICOPTERS

ATK 11 Mi-24 *Hind*
ASW 90: 70 Ka-27 *Helix*; 20 Mi-14 *Haze-A*
EW 8 Mi-8 *Hip J*
SAR 62: 22 Ka-25 PS *Hormone* C/Ka-27 PS *Hormone*-D; 40 Mi-14 PS *Haze* C
TPT 64 **Heavy** 10 Mi-6 *Hook* **Medium** 54: 28 Ka-29 *Helix*; 26 Mi-8 *Hip*

MSL

ASM Kh-25 (AS-10 *Karen)*; Kh-23 (AS-7 *Kerry‡)*; Kh-59 (AS-13 *Kingbolt*)
ARM Kh-58 (AS-11 *Kilter*); Kh-25MP (AS-12 *Kegler*)
LACM Kh-22 (AS-4 *Kitchen*)
AAM • IR AAM R-27T/ET (AA-10B/D *Alamo*); R-60 (AA-8 *Aphid*); R-73 (AA-11 *Archer*) SARH AAM R-27R/ER (AA-10A/C *Alamo*); R-33/33S (AA-9A/B *Amos*)

Coastal Defence • Naval Infantry (Marines) 9,500

FORCES BY ROLE

Naval inf 1 indep bde; 3 indep regt;

SF   3 (fleet) bde (1 op, 2 cadre) (each: 1 para bn, 1 spt elm, 2–3 underwater bn)

EQUIPMENT BY TYPE

MBT 160 T-55M/T-72/T-80
RECCE 60 BRDM-2 each with 9K11 (AT-3 *Sagger)*
AIFV 150+: ε150 BMP-2; BMP-3; BRM-1K
APC 750+
   APC (T) 250 MT-LB
   APC (W) 500+ BTR-60/BTR-70/BTR-80
ARTY 367
   SP 113: **122mm** 95 2S1 *Carnation*; **152mm** 18 2S3
   TOWED 122mm 45 D-30
   GUN/MOR 113
      SP 120mm 95: 20 2S23 *NONA-SVK*; 75 2S9 SP *NONA-S*
      TOWED 120mm 18 2B16 *NONA-K*
   MRL 122mm 96 9P138
AT • MSL • MANPATS 72 9K11 (AT-3 *Sagger)*/9K113 (AT-5 *Spandrel*)
   GUNS 100mm T-12
AD • SAM 320
      SP 70: 20 *Osa* (SA-8 *Gecko*); 50 *Strela-1*/*Strela-10* (SA-9 *Gaskin*/SA-13 *Gopher* [200 eff])
      MANPAD 250 *Strela-2* (SA-7 *Grail*)
      GUNS 23mm 60 ZSU-23-4

Coastal Defence Troops 2,000

FORCES BY ROLE

(All units reserve status)

Coastal Def 2 bde

Arty   2 regt

SAM   2 regt

EQUIPMENT BY TYPE

MBT 350 T-64
AIFV 450 BMP
APC 320
   APC (T) 40 MT-LB
   APC (W) 280 BTR-60/BTR-70/BTR-80
ARTY 364
   SP 152mm 48 2S5
   TOWED 280: **122mm** 140 D-30; **152mm** 140: 50 2A36; 50 2A65; 40 D-20
   MRL 122mm 36 BM-21
AD • SAM 50

Military Air Forces 160,000 reducing to 148,000 (incl conscripts)

Flying hours 80 to 100 hrs/year

HQ at Balashikha, near Moscow. A joint CIS Unified Air Defence System covers RUS, ARM, BLR, KAZ, KGZ, TJK, TKM, UKR and UZB. The Russian Air Force is currently undergoing a period of significant restructuring, both in terms of general organisation as well as air base and unit structure.

FORCES BY ROLE

Bbr	6 sqn with Tu-22M3/MR *Backfire C*; 3 sqn with Tu-95MS *Bear*; 1 sqn with Tu-160 *Blackjack*
Ftr	7 sqn with MiG-29 *Fulcrum*; 3 sqn with MiG-29SMT *Fulcrum*; 9 sqn with MiG-31/31BM *Foxhound*; 9 sqn with Su-27 *Flanker*; 4 sqn with Su-27SM *Flanker*
Atk	15 sqn with Su-24/Su-24M2 *Fencer*; 14 sqn with Su-25/SM *Frogfoot*
EW	1 sqn with Mi-8PPA *Hip*
ISR	1 sqn with MIG-25RB *Foxbat**; 4 sqn with Su-24MR *Fencer**; 1 flt with An-30 *Clank;*
AEW&C	1 sqn with A-50 *Mainstay*/A-50U *Mainstay*
Tkr	1 sqn with Il-78/Il-78M *Midas*
Tpt	7 (mixed) sqn with An-12 *Cub*/An-24 *Coke*/An-26 *Curl*/Mi-8 *Hip*/Tu-134 *Crusty*/Tu-154 *Careless*; 1 sqn with An-124 *Condor*/Il-76MD *Candid*; 1 sqn with An-12BK *Cub*/Il-76MD *Candid*; 1 sqn with An-22 *Cock*; 6 sqn with Il-76MD *Candid*
Atk Hel	10 sqn with Mi-24 *Hind*; 1 sqn (forming) with Mi-28 *Havoc*
Tpt Hel	16 sqn with Mi-8 *Hip*/Mi-26 *Halo*
SAM	35 regt with S-300PS (SA-10 *Grumble*) (quad); S-300PM (SA-20 *Gargoyle*) (quad); 3 bn with S-400 (SA-21 *Growler*) (five more planned by end 2010).

EQUIPMENT BY TYPE

AIRCRAFT 1,604 combat capable
   BBR 195: 116 Tu-22M-3/Tu-22MR *Backfire C*; 32 Tu-95MS6 *Bear*; 31 Tu-95MS16 *Bear*; 16 Tu-160 *Blackjack*
   FTR 707: 226 MiG-29 *Fulcrum*; 40 MiG-29UB *Fulcrum*; 188 MiG-31/31BM *Foxhound*; 232 Su-27 *Flanker*; 21 Su-27UB *Flanker*

FGA 337: 36 MiG-29 SMT *Fulcrum*; 212 Su-24 *Fencer*; 16 Su-24 *Fencer* (instructor trg); 12 Su-24M2 *Fencer*; 48 Su-27SM *Flanker*; 4 Su-30; 9 Su-34 *Fullback*
ATK 256: 241 Su-25/SM *Frogfoot*; 15 Su-25UB *Frogfoot*
ISR 113: 4 An-30 *Clank*; 30 MiG-25RB *Foxbat**; 79 Su-24MR *Fencer**
AEW&C 20 A-50 *Mainstay*/A-50U *Mainstay*
C&C 4 Il-87 *Maxdome*
TKR 20 IL-78 *Midas*/Il-78M *Midas*
TPT 298: **Heavy** 112: 12 An-124 *Condor*; 21 An-22 *Cock* (Under MoD control); 79 Il-76M/MD/MF *Candid*; **Medium** 50 An-12/An-12BK *Cub*; **Light** 105: 25 An-24 *Coke*; 80 An-26 Curl **PAX** 31: 30 Tu-134 *Crusty*; 1 Tu-154 *Careless*
TRG 193 L-39 *Albatros*
HELICOPTERS
ATK 325: 12 Ka-50 *Hokum*; 9 Ka-52A *Hokum B*; 280 Mi-24 *Hind* D/V/P; 24 Mi-28N *Havoc B*
EW 60 Mi-8PPA *Hip*
TPT 560: **Heavy** 40: 32 Mi-26 *Halo*; 8 Mi-6 *Hook*; **Medium** 520 Mi-17 (Mi-8MT) *Hip* H/Mi-8 *Hip*
UAV • **ISR** Some **Light** *Pchela*-1T
AD • **SAM** • **SP** 1,900+ S-300PS (SA-10 *Grumble*) (quad)/S-300PM (SA-20 *Gargoyle*) (quad)/S-400 (SA-21 *Growler*)
MSL •
AAM • **IR AAM** R-27T/ET (AA-10 *Alamo* B/D); R-73 (AA-11 *Archer*); R-60T (AA-8 *Aphid*) • **SARH AAM** R-27R/ER (AA-10 *Alamo* A/C); R-33/33S (AA-9 *Amos* A/B) • **ARH AAM** R-77 (A-12 *Adder*) R-37M (AA-X-13) • **PRH AAM** R-27P/EP (AA-10 *Alamo* E/F)
ARM Kh-58 (AS-11 *Kilter*); Kh-25MP (AS-12 *Kegler*); Kh-15P (AS-16 *Kickback*) Kh-31P (AS-17 *Krypton*)
ASM Kh-25 (AS-10 *Karen*); Kh-59/Kh-59M (AS-13 *Kingbolt*/AS-18 *Kazoo*) Kh-29 (AS-14 *Kedge*); Kh-31A (AS-17 *Krypton*); Kh-38 (AS-XX - in development)
LACM Kh-22 (AS-4 *Kitchen*); Kh-55/55SM (AS-15 *Kent* A/B); Kh-101; Kh-102; Kh-555
BOMBS • **Laser-guided** KAB-500; KAB-1500L • **TV-guided** KAB-500KR; KAB-1500KR; KAB-500OD;UPAB 1500

Russian Military Districts

Western Military District
(ex-Leningrad & Moscow Military Districts & Kaliningrad Special Region)
Combined   1 HQ at St Petersburg
Service

Army
FORCES BY ROLE

Comd	2 army HQ
Tk	2 bde
MR	5 bde
SF	2 (Spetsnaz) bde; 1 (AB Recce) bn
AB	3 (VdV) div
Arty	2 bde
AD	2 bde
MRL	1 bde

SSM	1 bde with *Iskander-M*/*Tochka* (SS-21 *Scarab)*; 2 bde with *Tochka* (SS-21 *Scarab*)

Reserves
FORCES BY ROLE

Tk	1 bde
MR	2 bde

Northern Fleet
EQUIPMENT BY TYPE
SUBMARINES 40
  STRATEGIC 9 **SSBN**
  TACTICAL 23: 3 **SSGN**; 13 **SSN**; 7 **SSK**
  SUPPORT 8: 7 **SSAN** (other roles); 1 **SSA**
PRINCIPAL SURFACE COMBATANTS 10: 1 **CV**; 1 **CGHMN**; 1 **CGHM**; 7 **DDGHM** (of which 1 in refit)
PATROL AND COASTAL COMBATANTS 12: 3 **FSGM**; 9 **FSM**
MINE WARFARE 11: 1 **MHSO**; 3 **MSO**; 7 **MSC**
AMPHIBIOUS 5: 4 **LST**; 1 **LSM**
LOGISTICS AND SUPPORT 20+
FACILITIES

Bases	Located at Severomorsk and Kola Peninsula

Naval Aviation
EQUIPMENT BY TYPE
AIRCRAFT
  BBR 39 Tu-22M *Backfire C*
  FTR 18 Su-33 *Flanker D*
  ATK 5 Su-25UTG *Frogfoot*
  ASW 13 Tu-142M/MR *Bear F/J*
  MP 14 Il-38 *May**
  TPT An-12 *Cub*/An-24 *Coke*/An-26 *Curl*
HELICOPTERS
  ASW Ka-27 *Helix A*
  TPT Ka-29 *Helix B*; Mi-8 *Hip*

Naval Infantry

Naval inf	1 regt

Coastal Defence

Coastal def	1 bde with 360 MT-LB; 134 arty
AD	1 regt

Baltic Fleet
EQUIPMENT BY TYPE
SUBMARINES • **TACTICAL** 3 **SSK**: 1 *Lada*; 2 *Paltus* (*Kilo*)
PRINCIPAL SURFACE COMBATANTS 6: 2 **DDGHM**; 2 **FFGHM**; 1 **FFGM**; 1 **FFM**
PATROL AND COASTAL COMBATANTS 19: 4 **FSGM**; 7 **FSM**; 8 **PCFG**
MINE WARFARE • **MINE COUNTERMEASURES** 15: 4 **MSC**; 11 **MHI**
AMPHIBIOUS 4 Project 775 (*Ropucha*)
LOGISTICS AND SUPPORT 8+

FACILITIES
Bases located at Kronstadt and Baltiysk

Naval Aviation
EQUIPMENT BY TYPE
AIRCRAFT
FTR 24 Su-27 *Flanker*
FGA 29 Su-24/Su-24MR *Fencer*
TPT An-12 *Cub*/An-24 *Coke*/An-26 *Curl*
HELICOPTERS
ATK 11 Mi-24 *Hind*
ASW Ka-27 *Helix*
TPT • Medium Ka-29 *Helix*; Mi-8 *Hip*

Naval Infantry
FORCES BY ROLE
Naval inf 1 regt

Coastal Defence
FORCES BY ROLE
Arty 2 regt
AShM 1 regt with P5/P-35 (SS-C-1B *Sepal*)

Military Air Forces

Special Purpose Aviation Command
(elm ex-16th Air Army)
FORCES BY ROLE
Comd 3 bde HQ
Ftr 3 sqn with MiG-29SMT *Fulcrum*; 2 sqn with MiG-31 *Foxhound*; 2 sqn with Su-27 *Flanker*
Atk 2 sqn with Su-24M *Fencer*; 3 sqn with Su-25 *Frogfoot*
ISR 1 sqn with MiG-25RB *Foxbat**
EQUIPMENT BY TYPE
AIRCRAFT
FTR 71: 41 MiG-31 *Foxhound*; 30 Su-27 *Flanker*
FGA 70: 36 MiG-29SMT *Fulcrum*; 6 MiG-29UB *Fulcrum*; 28 Su-24M/M2 *Fencer*
ATK 52 Su-25 *Frogfoot*
ISR 8 MiG-25RB *Foxbat**
AD • SAM 600

1st Air Force & Air Defence Command
(ex-6th & elm ex-16th Air Army)
FORCES BY ROLE
Comd 3 bde HQ
Ftr 2 sqn with MiG-31 *Foxhound*; 4 sqn with Su-27 *Flanker*
ISR 1 flt with A-30 *Clank*; 1 sqn with Su-24MR *Fencer-E*
EW 1 sqn with Mi-8PPA *Hip*
Tpt 1 sqn with An-12 *Cub*/An-26 *Curl*/Tu-134 *Crusty*
Atk Hel 4 sqn with Mi-24 *Hind*
Tpt Hel 4 sqn with Mi-8 *Hip*
EQUIPMENT BY TYPE
AIRCRAFT
FTR 89: 34 MiG-31 *Foxhound*; 55 Su-27 *Flanker*

ISR 18: 4 An-30 *Clank*; 14 Su-24MR *Fencer**
TPT 12 An-12/An-26/Tu-134
HELICOPTERS
ATK 48 Mi-24 *Hind*
EW 10 Mi-8
TPT • Medium 48 Mi-8 *Hip*
AD • SAM 525 incl S-300V

Central Military District
(ex-Volga-Ural & part ex-Siberia Military Districts)
Combined Service 1 HQ at Yekaterinburg

Army
FORCES BY ROLE
Comd 2 army HQ
Tk 1 bde
MR 1 div (201st); 7 bde
SF 1 (Spetsnaz) bde
AB 1 (VdV) bde
Arty 1 bde
AD 2 bde
MRL 1 regt
SSM 2 bde each with *Tochka* (SS-21 *Scarab*)

Reserves
FORCES BY ROLE
MR 3 Bde
FACILITIES
Training Centre 1 located at Kamshlov (district)

Military Air Force

2nd Air Force & Air Defence Command
(ex-5th & elm ex-14th Air Army)
FORCES BY ROLE
Comd 2 bde HQ
Ftr 4 sqn with MiG-31 *Foxhound*
Tpt 3 sqn with An-12 *Cub*/An-26 *Curl*/Tu-134 *Crusty*/Mi-8 *Hip*
Atk Hel 2 sqn with Mi-24 *Hind*
Tpt Hel 4 sqn with Mi-8 *Hip*/Mi-26 *Halo*
EQUIPMENT BY TYPE
AIRCRAFT
FTR 73 MiG-31 *Foxhound*
TPT 36 An-12/An-26 *Curl*/Tu-134 *Crusty*
HELICOPTERS
ATK 24 Mi-24 *Hind*
TPT 46: 6 Mi-26 *Halo*; 40 Mi-8 *Hip*
AD • SAM S-300

Southern Military District
(ex-North Caucasus Military District - including Trans-Caucasus Group of Forces (GRVZ))
Combined Service 1 HQ located at Rostov-on-Don

Army
FORCES BY ROLE
Comd 2 army HQ

Recce	1 bde
MR	7 bde; 3 (lt/mtn) bde; 2 bde (Armenia); 1 bde (Abkhazia); 1 bde (South Ossetia)
SF	2 (Spetsnaz) bde
Air Aslt	1 bde
AB	1 (VdV) div
Arty	1 bde
MRL	1 bde; 1 regt
SSM	1 bde with *Tochka* (SS-21 *Scarab*)

Black Sea Fleet

The RUS Fleet is leasing bases in Sevastopol and Karantinnaya Bay, and is based, jointly with UKR warships, at Streletskaya Bay. The Fleet's overall serviceability is assessed as medium.

EQUIPMENT BY TYPE
SUBMARINES • TACTICAL 1 **SSK** (also 1 *Som* (*Tango*) in reserve)
PRINCIPAL SURFACE COMBATANTS 5: 2 **CGHM** (1 in reserve awaiting decommissioning); 1 **DDGM**; 2 **FFGM**
PATROL AND COASTAL COMBATANTS 12: 4 **FSGM**; 6 **FSM**; 1 **PHM**; 1 **PHT**
MINE WARFARE • MINE COUNTERMEASURES 9: 1 **MCO**; 6 **MSO**; 2 **MSC**
AMPHIBIOUS 7: 4 Project 775 (*Ropucha*); 3 *Tapir* (*Alligator*)
LOGISTICS AND SUPPORT 6+

FACILITIES
Bases located at Sevastopol, Novorossiysk and Temryuk

Naval Aviation

EQUIPMENT BY TYPE
AIRCRAFT
  FGA 20 Su-24 *Fencer/Su-24MR*
  MP 15 Be-12 *Mail**
  TPT An-12 *Cub* (MR/EW); An-26
HELICOPTERS
  ASW Ka-27 *Helix*
  TPT • Medium Mi-8 *Hip* (MP/EW/Tpt)

Naval Infantry

FORCES BY ROLE
Naval inf   1 regt

Caspian Sea Flotilla

EQUIPMENT BY TYPE
PRINCIPAL SURFACE COMBATANTS 1 **FFGM**
PATROL AND COASTAL COMBATANTS 6: 2 **PCFG**; 3 **PHG**; 1 **PCM**
MINE WARFARE • MINE COUNTERMEASURES 6: 5 **MSC**; 1 **MHI**
AMPHIBIOUS 6
LOGISTICS AND SUPPORT 5+

FACILITIES
Bases located at Astrakhan, Kaspiysk and Makhachkala

Military Air Force

4th Air Force & Air Defence Command

(ex 4th Air Army)
FORCES BY ROLE

Comd	1 bde HQ
Ftr	3 sqn with MiG-29 *Fulcrum*; 1 sqn (Armenia) with MiG-29 *Fulcrum*; 3 sqn with Su-27 *Flanker*
Atk	5 sqn with Su-24M *Fencer*; 6 sqn with Su-25 *Frogfoot*
ISR	1 sqn with Su-24MR *Fencer-E*
Tpt	1 sqn with An-12 *Cub*/Mi-8 *Hip*
Atk Hel	2 sqn with Mi-24 *Hind*
Tpt Hel	3 sqn with Mi-8 *Hip*/Mi-26 *Halo*

EQUIPMENT BY TYPE
AIRCRAFT
  FTR 118: 60 MiG-29 *Fulcrum*; 58 Su-27 *Flanker*
  FGA 62 Su-24M *Fencer*
  ATK 77 Su-25 *Frogfoot*
  ISR 14 Su-24MR *Fencer**
  TPT 12 An-12 *Cub*
HELICOPTERS
  ATK 24 Mi-24 *Hind*
  TPT 72 **Heavy** 10 Mi-26 *Halo* **Medium** 28 Mi-8 *Hip*

Eastern Military District

(ex Far East & part ex-Siberia Military Districts)
Combined Service   1 HQ located at Khabarovsk

Army

FORCES BY ROLE

Comd	4 army HQ
Tk	1 bde
MR	10 bde
SF	2 bde
Air Aslt	2 bde
Arty	4 bde
AD	4 bde
MRL	2 bde
SSM	3 bde each with *Tochka* (SS-21 *Scarab*)
MGA	1 div

Reserves

FORCES BY ROLE
MR   8 bde

FACILITIES
Training Centre 1 located at Khabarovsk (district)

Pacific Fleet

EQUIPMENT BY TYPE
SUBMARINES 23
  STRATEGIC 5 **SSBN** (of which one in reserve)
  TACTICAL 18: 5 **SSGN**; 4 **SSN**; 9 **SSK**
PRINCIPAL SURFACE COMBATANTS 8: 1 **CGHM**; 7 **DDGHM**

PATROL AND COASTAL COMBATANTS 23: 4
FSGM; 9 FSM; 10 PCFG
MINE WARFARE 7: 2 MSO; 5 MSC
AMPHIBIOUS 4
LOGISTICS AND SUPPORT 15+

FACILITIES
Bases located at Fokino, Magadan, Petropavlovsk-
Kamchatsky, Sovetskya Gavan, Viliuchinsk and
Vladivostok

Naval Aviation
EQUIPMENT BY TYPE
AIRCRAFT
  BBR 17 Tu-22M *Backfire C*
  FTR 30 MiG-31 *Foxhound*
  ASW 14 Tu-142M/MR *Bear F/J*
  MP 15 Il-38 *May*
  TPT An-12 *Cub* (MR/EW); An-26 *Curl*
HELICOPTERS
  ASW Ka-27 *Helix*
  TPT • **Medium** Ka-29 *Helix*; Mi-8 *Hip*

Naval Infantry
FORCES BY ROLE
Naval Inf   1 bde with (1 tk bn, 3 inf bn, 1 arty bn)

Coastal Defence
FORCES BY ROLE
Coastal Def   1 bde

Military Air Force

3rd Air Force & Air Defence Command
ex 11th elms 14th AF and AD Army
FORCES BY ROLE
Comd   4 bde HQ
Ftr   3 sqn with MiG-29 *Fulcrum*; 1 sqn with
      MiG-31 *Foxhound*; 4 sqn with Su-27SM
      Flanker
Atk   8 sqn with Su-24M/M2 *Fencer*; 5 sqn with
      Su-25 *Frogfoot*
ISR   2 sqn with Su-24MR *Fencer-E*
Tpt   2 sqn with An-12 *Cub*/An-24 *Coke*/An-26
      Curl/Tu-134 *Crusty*/Tu-154 *Careless*
Atk Hel   2 sqn with Mi-24 *Hind*
Tpt Hel   5 sqn with Mi-8 *Hind*/Mi-26 *Halo*
EQUIPMENT BY TYPE
AIRCRAFT
  FTR 74: 60 MiG-29 *Fulcrum*; 14 MiG-31 *Foxhound*
  FGA 173: 115 Su-24M *Fencer*; 10 Su-24M2 *Fencer*;
  48 Su-27SM *Flanker*
  ATK 72 Su-25 *Frogfoot*
  ISR 28 Su-24MR *Fencer-E**
  TPT 22 An-12 *Cub*/An-24 *Coke*/An-26 *Curl*; 1 Tu-
  134 *Crusty*; 1 Tu-154 *Careless*
HELICOPTERS
  ATK 24 Mi-24 *Hind*
  TPT 48 **Heavy** 4 Mi-26 *Halo* **Medium** 56 Mi-8 *Hip*
AD • **SAM** S-300P

Direct Reporting Commands

Long-Range Aviation Command
Flying hours: 80–100 hrs/yr
FORCES BY ROLE
Bbr   1 sqn with Tu-160 *Blackjack*; 6 sqn with Tu-
      22M3/MR *Backfire C*; 3 sqn with Tu-95MS
      Bear
Tkr   1 sqn with 20 Il-78 *Midas*/Il-78M *Midas*
EQUIPMENT BY TYPE
AIRCRAFT
BBR 195: 116 Tu-22M-3/Tu-22MR *Backfire* C; 32 Tu-
95MS6 *Bear*; 31 Tu-95MS16 *Bear*; 16 Tu-160 *Blackjack*
TKR 20 IL-78 *Midas*/Il-78M *Midas*

Transport Aviation Command
Flying hours   60 hrs/year
FORCES BY ROLE
Tpt   1 sqn with An-124 *Condor*/Il-76MD
      Candid; 1 sqn with An-12BK *Cub*/Il-
      76MD *Candid*; 1 sqn with An-22 *Cock*; 6
      sqn with Il-76MD *Candid*
EQUIPMENT BY TYPE
AIRCRAFT • **TPT** 118 **Heavy** 112: 12 An-124 *Condor*;
21 An-22 *Cock* (Under MoD control); 79 Il-76M/MD/MF
Candid **Medium** 6 An-12BK *Cub*

Paramilitary 449,000

Federal Border Guard Service ε160,000 active
Directly subordinate to the President; now reportedly
all contract-based personnel
FORCES BY ROLE
10 regional directorates
Frontier   7 gp
EQUIPMENT BY TYPE
AIFV/APC (W) 1,000 BMP/BTR
ARTY • **SP** 90: **122mm** 2S1 *Carnation*; **120mm** 2S12;
120mm 2S9 *Anona*
PRINCIPAL SURFACE COMBATANTS 14
  FRIGATES 13
  FFGHM 7 *Nerey* (*Krivak* III) each with 1 twin (2 eff.)
  with *Osa-M* (SA-N-4 *Gecko*) naval SAM, 2 quad 533mm
  TT (8 eff.), 2 RBU 6000 *Smerch* 2 (24 eff.), (capacity 1 Ka-
  27 *Helix A* ASW hel; 1 100mm)
PATROL AND COASTAL COMBATANTS 180
  CORVETTES • **FSM** 3: 1 *Albatros* (*Grisha* II); 2 *Albatros*
  (*Grisha* III) **PCM** 46:
    2 *Molnya* II (*Pauk* II) each with 1 quad (4 eff.) with SA-
    N-5 *Grail* naval SAM, 2 twin 533mm TT (4 eff.), 2 RBU
    1200 (10 eff.), 1 76mm
    27 *Svetljak* (*Svetlyak*) each with 1 quad (4 eff.) with SA-
    N-5 *Grail* naval SAM, 2 single 406mm TT, 1 76mm
    17 *Molnya* I (*Pauk* I) each with 1 quad (4 eff.) with SA-
    N-5 *Grail* naval SAM, 4 single 406mm TT, 1 76mm
  PHT 2 *Antares* (*Muravey*)
  PCO 9: 8 Project 503 (*Alpinist*); 1 *Sprut*
  PSO 4 *Komandor*

PCC 13 *Tarantul* (*Stenka*)

PB 70: 9 Project 14310 (*Mirazh*); 27 *Type 1496*; 12 *Grif* (*Zhuk*); 2 *Antur*; 17 *Kulik*; 3 *Terrier* **PBR** 35: 3 *Ogonek*; 8 *Piyavka*; 15 *Shmel*; 7 *Moskit* (*Vosh*); 2 *Slepen* (*Yaz*)

PBF 38: 1 A-125; 2 *Enforcer II*; 6 *Mangust*; 1 *Mustang* (Project 18623); 15 *Saygak*; 12 *Sobol*; 1 *Sokzhoi*

LOGISTICS AND SUPPORT 42:

AO 1 *Baskunchak*

AK 10 *Neon Antonov*

AKSL 6 *Kanin*

AGS 2 *Yug* (primarily used as patrol ships)

AGB 5 *Ivan Susanin* (primarily used as patrol ships)

ATF 18 *Sorum* (primarily used as patrol ships)

AIRCRAFT • **TPT** ε86: 70 An-24 *Coke*/An-26 *Curl*/An-72 *Coaler*/Il-76 *Candid*/Tu-134 *Crusty*/Yak-40 *Codling*; 16 SM-92

HELICOPTERS: ε200 Ka-28 (Ka-27) *Helix* ASW/Mi-24 *Hind* Atk/Mi-26 *Halo* Spt/Mi-8 *Hip* Spt

Interior Troops 200,000 active

FORCES BY ROLE

7 Regional Commands: Central, Urals, North Caucasus, Volga, Eastern, North-Western and Siberian

Paramilitary	5 (special purpose) indep div (ODON) (each: 2–5 paramilitary regt); 6 div; 65 regt (bn – incl special motorised units); 10 (special designation) indep bde (OBRON) (each: 1 mor bn, 3 mech bn); 19 indep bde
Avn	gp

EQUIPMENT BY TYPE

MBT 9

AIFV/APC (W) 1,650 BMP-1/BMP-2/BTR-80

ARTY 35

  TOWED 122mm 20 D-30

  MOR 120mm 15 PM-38

HELICOPTERS • **ATK** 4 Mi-24 *Hind*

Federal Security Service ε4,000 active (armed)

Cdo	unit (incl Alfa and Vympel units)

Federal Protection Service ε10,000–30,000 active

Org include elm of ground forces (mech inf bde and AB regt)

Mech inf	1 bde
AB	1 regt
Presidential Guard	1 regt

Federal Communications and Information Agency ε55,000 active

MOD • Railway Troops ε50,000

Paramilitary 4 (rly) corps; 28 (rly) bde

Special Construction Troops 50,000

DEPLOYMENT

ARMENIA

Army 3,214; 2 MR bde; 74 MBT; 330 AIFV; 14 APC (T)/APC (W); 68 SP/towed arty; 8 mor; 8 MRL; 1 base

Military Air Forces 1 sqn with 18 MiG-29 *Fulcrum*; 2 AD bty with S-300V (SA-12A *Gladiator*); 1 AD bty with SA-6 *Gainful*; 1 air base at Yerevan

BELARUS

Strategic Deterrent Forces • Warning Forces 1 radar station at Baranovichi (*Volga* system; leased)

Navy 1 Naval Communications site

BOSNIA-HERZEGOVINA

OSCE • Bosnia and Herzegovina 3

CÔTE D'IVOIRE

UN • UNOCI 11 obs

CENTRAL AFRICAN REPUBLIC/CHAD

UN • MINURCAT 119; 1 hel pl with 4 Mi-17 (Mi-8MT) *Hip-H*

DEMOCRATIC REPUBLIC OF THE CONGO

UN • MONUSCO 28 obs

GEORGIA

Army 7000; Abkhazia 1 MR bde; South Ossetia 1 MR bde; Military Air Forces some atk hel

GULF OF ADEN

Navy: 1 DDGHM; 1 AORL; 1 ATF

KAZAKHSTAN

Strategic Deterrent Forces • Warning Forces 1 radar station at Balkash (*Dnepr* system; leased)

KYRGYZSTAN

Military Air Forces ε500; 5 Su-25 *Frogfoot*; 2 Mi-8 *Hip* spt hel

LIBERIA

UN • UNMIL 4 obs

MIDDLE EAST

UN • UNTSO 5 obs

MOLDOVA/TRANSDNESTR

Army ε1,500 (including 335 peacekeepers); 2 MR bn; 100 MBT/AIFV/APC;

Military Air Forces 7 Mi-24 *Hind*; some Mi-8 *Hip*

SERBIA

OSCE • Kosovo 2

SUDAN

UN • UNMIS 123; 13 obs; 1 hel coy

SYRIA

Army/Navy 150; 1 naval facility under renovation at Tartus

TAJIKISTAN

Army 5,000; 1 mil base (subord Volga-Ural MD) with (1 MR div (201st — understrength); 54 T-72; 300 BMP-2/BTR-80/MT-LB; 100 2S1/2S3/2S12/9P140 *Uragan*

Military Air Forces: 5 Su-25 *Frogfoot*; 4 Mi-8 *Hip*

UKRAINE

Navy • Coastal Defence • 13,000 including Naval Infantry (Marines) 1,100; 102 AIFV/APC: 24 arty
Navy Black Sea Fleet; 1 Fleet HQ located at Sevastopol:
Strategic Deterrent Forces. Warning Forces; 2 radar stations located at Sevastopol (*Dnepr* System, leased) and Mukachevo (*Dnepr* system, leased).

WESTERN SAHARA

UN • MINURSO 17 obs

Table 14 **Selected Arms Procurements and Deliveries, Russia**

Designation	Type	Quantity	Contract Value	Supplier Country	Prime Contractor	Order Date	First Delivery Due	Notes
Bulava 30 (SS-NX-30)	SLBM	n.k.	n.k.	RUS	n.k.	n.k.	2009	In development. For *Borey*-class SSBN
T-72 and T-80	MBT	180	n.k.	RUS	n.k.	2006	2007	Some to be modernised. Number may be subject to change
BTR-80 and BTR-90	APC (W)	100	n.k.	RUS	n.k.	2005	2006	Delivery status unclear
Almaz-Antey *Tor*-M2 (SA-15 *Gauntlet*)	SAM	n.k.	n.k.	RUS	n.k.	n.k.	2010	Bty formations. First AD regts due to be re-equipped by 2010–11
Buk-M2 (SA-17 *Grizzly*)	SAM	n.k.	n.k.	RUS	n.k.	n.k.	n.k.	To replace Buk-M1-2 systems in service with army AD
S-400 *Triumf* (SA-21 *Growler*)	SAM	18 bn	n.k.	RUS	n.k.	n.k.	2007	Three bn deployed by mid 2010; 5 more bn were due by end of 2010
Pantsir-S1	AD	n.k.	n.k.	RUS	KBP	n.k.	2010	Delivery status unclear
Project 955 *Borey*	SSBN	4	n.k.	RUS	Sevmash Shipyard	1996	2006	Lead vessel launched Feb 2008; remains in test
Project 885 *Yasen*	SSN	6	n.k.	RUS	Sevmash Shipyard	1993	2010	Construction of second vessel began 2009. First of class, *Severodvinsk*, launched Jun 2010, with expected ISD 2011. Delayed for financial reasons
Project 22350/ *Admiral Gorshkov*	FFGHM	1	US$400m	RUS	Severnaya Verf Shipyard	2005	2011	Navy estimates need for up to 20 vessels by 2015. Delayed. First launch due 2011
Project 20380/ *Steregushchiy*-class	FFM	4	n.k.	RUS	Severnaya Verf Shipyard	n.k.	2009	First vessel delivered. Second vessel (*Stoiky*) launched Mar 2010; expected ISD 2011. Up to 20 planned
Project 21631 *Buyan-M*	FSG	5	n.k.	RUS	Zelenodolsk Shipyard	2010	n.k.	For Caspian Flotilla
Mistral	LHD	4	n.k.	FRA	DCNS/STX	2011	2013	2 built in FRA; 2 in RUS
Dyugon	LCU	1	R200m (US$69m)	RUS	Volga Shipyard	2005	2007	Laid down 2006. Delivery status unclear
Seliger	AGOR	2	n.k.	RUS	Yantar Shipyard	2009	2011	First vessel expected ISD 2011
Tu-160 *Blackjack*	Bbr ac upgrade	15	–	RUS	UAC	2007	2012	Upgrade of 15 current Tu-160s
Su-34 *Fullback*	FGA ac	32	US$864m	RUS	Sukhoi	2008	n.k.	5 delivered. 4 more due for delivery late 2010, early 2011. Deliveries due to be complete by 2013
Su-35S *Flanker*	FGA ac	48	n.k.	RUS	Sukhoi	2009	2015	Upgrade with with new avionics, longer range air-to-air radar and more powerful engines
Su-27SM, Su-30MK2	FGA ac	16 (12 Su-27, 4 Su-30)	n.k.	RUS	Sukhoi	2009	2015	Combined with above deal in contract worth US$2.5bn
Yak-130 AJT (Advanced Jet Trainer)	Trg ac	200	n.k.	RUS	Yakolev	2005	2015	To replace current L-39.
Mi-28N *Night Hunter*	Atk Hel	8	n.k.	RUS	Rostvertol	2005	2009	Plans for 45 to 67 Mi-28N. Delivery status unclear
Ka-52 *Hokum-B*	Atk Hel	30	n.k.	RUS	Progress	2008	2009	Twin-seat version of Ka-50 *Black Shark* For air force. Final delivery 2012. Delivery status unclear
Searcher II	ISR UAV	n.k.	US$50m	ISR	IAI	2009	n.k.	Contract incl I-*View* 150 and *Bird-Eye* 400

Chapter Six
Asia

NORTHEAST ASIA

China

Although the global financial crisis has been felt most keenly outside East Asia, defence-budget growth in China has slowed after Beijing became concerned about a rapid increase in government spending in 2009 and began to rein in its expenditure. Yet China's defence-budget growth of 7.5% in 2010 was still more than most other countries'. Combined with its more muscular regional diplomacy, China's increased defence budget has continued to provoke concern over the implications of its defence modernisation. Increasingly, these concerns have spread beyond East Asia, as China has begun tentatively to explore operations further afield.

Maritime extroversion
The year 2010 began with a discussion of the extra-regional ambitions of the People's Liberation Army Navy (PLAN), following a December 2009 interview with Rear Admiral (retd.) Yin Zhou published on the Ministry of National Defence (MND) website. The retired naval officer suggested that the PLAN could set up China's first permanent overseas base in an unspecified location in the Middle East. The MND subsequently distanced itself from these comments, saying on 1 January that: 'China has no plans for an overseas naval base'. It then removed the Yin interview from its website. Nonetheless, Yin's comment, and subsequent debate among Chinese military officers and analysts over China's expanding overseas deployments, highlighted the continuing development of Beijing's power-projection capabilities. Two years after the PLAN deployed two destroyers and a supply ship on counter-piracy operations in the Gulf of Aden, it retains a flotilla in the region (see the box 'PLAN deployments to the Gulf of Aden', p. 196). In July 2010, it dispatched its relatively new Type 071 landing-platform dock, the *Kunlun Shan*, overseas for the first time.

These missions have allowed the PLAN to practise out-of-area activities, and in particular to engage in logistical tasks such as blue-water replenishment-at-sea (RAS), a key component of any navy's ability to sustain forces far from home. The navy has gradually extended its abilities in this realm, moving from fixed-shore facilities to shore-to-ship replenishment, to green-water RAS with small vessels, and finally to blue-water RAS with large ships such as destroyers. The ability to deliver fuel, ammunition and supplies on the high seas is a challenge for any navy, given the difficulties in maintaining a constant parallel course of two large vessels at a distance of perhaps 50 metres in open seas. Although it is impossible to gauge whether all replenishments were entirely successful, particularly as some involved replenishment of China's merchant fleet by helicopter, the fact that the flotillas have continued to undertake RAS indicates a modicum of success and useful training. This latter issue is one taken seriously by the PLAN, as the commander of a logistic-support flotilla suggested in a 2007 study into RAS when he stated: 'One minute on stage takes ten years of practice off stage.'

Meanwhile, there has been much foreign and unofficial domestic conjecture over the likely use of the former Soviet aircraft carrier, the *Varyag*. Having left its specially created dry dock in Dalian, northeastern China, in March 2010 – some 12 years after its purchase – the hull reportedly underwent steam testing to check its turbines and pipes. Satellite and hand-held photographic imagery of possible training areas for carrier-borne aircraft (a Su-33 variant likely to be dubbed the J-15) also emerged in late 2009 and 2010. These included a mock-up of the *Varyag*'s deck, ramp and bridge in Wuhan, central China, and a new airstrip at the naval air force's flight school in Xingcheng, 20 kilometres south of Huludao, in southwestern Liaoning Province. Given the *Varyag*'s age and continued lack of both propulsion and rudder, its most likely use is as a training vessel and for reverse engineering in support of an indigenous carrier programme, but the mounting of close-in weapons systems in late 2010 leaves open the possibility of a more operational role. While Beijing has not released a timetable for aircraft-carrier construction, the Pentagon's annual report on China's military power (this year titled *Military and Security Developments Involving the People's Republic of China – 2010*) suggested several vessels will be in service by 2020.

PLAN deployments to the Gulf of Aden

1st Flotilla (December 2008 – April 2009)

Wuhan	Type 052B DDG (Luyang)
Haikou	Type 052C DDG (Luyang II)
Weishanhu	Fuchi-class AOR

2nd Flotilla (April 2009 – August 2009)

Shenzhen	Type 051B DDG (Luhai)
Huangshan	Type 054A FFG (Jiangkai II)
Weishanhu	Fuchi-class AOR

3rd Flotilla (July 2009 – November 2009)

Zhoushan	Type 054A FFG (Jiangkai II)
Xuzhou	Type 054A FFG (Jiangkai II)
Qiandaohu	Fuchi-class AOR

4th Flotilla (November 2009 – March 2010)

Wenzhou	Type 054 FFG (Jiangkai I)
Ma'anshan	Type 054 FFG (Jiangkai I)
Qiandaohu	Fuchi-class AOR

5th Flotilla (March 2010 – July 2010)

Guangzhou	Type 052B DDG (Luyang)
Chaohu	Type 054A FFG (Jiangkai II)
Weishanhu	Fuchi-class AOR

6th Flotilla (July 2010 – November 2010)

Kunlun Shan	Type 071 LPD (Yuzhao)
Lanzhou	Type 052C DDG (Luyang II)
Weishanhu	Fuchi-class AOR

7th Flotilla (November 2010 –)

Zhoushan	Type 054A FFG (Jiangkai II)
Xuzhou	Type 054A FFG (Jiangkai II)
Qiandaohu	Fuchi-class AOR

Regional focus

The Gulf of Aden mission and the likely use of the *Varyag* as a test-bed for aircraft-carrier design and operation (as well as possible reverse engineering) are indicators of China's growing willingness and ability to develop blue-water capabilities; they both suggest a long-term desire to more frequently project power beyond China's littoral and immediate region. However, they are not the PLAN's main focus today. By and large, China remains a regional power with regional concerns, as demonstrated in 2010 by a series of exercises, construction projects and equipment purchases. In particular, the unresolved issue of Taiwan's sovereignty and maritime disputes in the East and South China Seas dominate the PLAN's planning and procurement decisions.

Two combined-arms exercises in 2010 reflected the PLAN's desire to exert its influence in regional seas and improve its interoperability. In early April, in the PLAN's first combined-fleet exercise, 16 warships from all three fleets (the North, East and South Sea Fleets) sailed within 140km of the Japanese island of Okinawa, through the Bashi Channel and towards the Malacca Strait. The ships conducted live-firing and anti-submarine drills along the Chinese coast, during which flotillas and air regiments from numerous PLAN bases simulated attacks on the training fleet. Simultaneously deploying underwater, surface and air assets, the exercise suggested that the PLAN is attempting to improve its forces' ability to operate jointly. However, joint-service PLA operations remain to be tested operationally.

In July, at least a dozen warships from all three fleets exercised in the South China Sea. With JH-7/7A aircraft in support, they included the most modern surface vessels and submarines: Type 051C *Luzhou*; Type 052B *Luyang* I and Type 052C *Luyang* II destroyers; Type 054A *Jiangkai* II frigates; all four of the East Sea Fleet's *Sovremenny* destroyers; and *Kilo*-class attack submarines. Numerous live-firing and missile tests were carried out. The exercise received widespread domestic media coverage and was attended by many high-ranking PLA personnel, including General Chen Bingde, a Central Military Commission member and chief of the General Staff department, who called upon the PLAN to 'pay close attention to [regional] situations, and be militarily prepared'. Amid tensions with other claimants to islands and maritime space in the South China Sea, this long-range combined-arms exercise sent a clear deterrent message. It displayed China's willingness and ability to project naval power in a flexible and comprehensive manner. It also showed that the PLAN is now assessing its capabilities in light of broader issues than simply a potential military resolution of the Taiwan issue.

The PLAN Marines force had its equipment upgraded in 2010. Assessments indicate that the 1st Marine Brigade received the latest Type 05 amphibious fighting vehicles, while the 2nd Marines (164th Brigade) were re-equipped with Type 063A vehicles handed down by the 1st Marines. In early November the 1st Marines conducted a large amphibious assault exercise, *Sea Dragon 2010*, in the South China Sea. This involved combined-arms units from a variety of military branches, and provided an opportunity for the

Map 4 **China: Military Regions and Major Formations**

Marines force to display its capabilities to 40 foreign military observers.

Asymmetric capabilities

The PLAN is aware that it is not yet the predominant naval power in the western Pacific, a position still held by the United States Seventh Fleet. For this reason, the PLAN has continued to develop and demonstrate sea-denial and anti-access capabilities. In July 2010, PLAN fleets conducted a series of drills in response to US–South Korean naval exercises in the Yellow Sea. Although Beijing understood that those bilateral exercises were a response to North Korea's alleged sinking of the South Korean corvette *Cheonan* in March, it still objected to the presence of the aircraft carrier USS *George Washington* so close to the Chinese coast. The first drill was conducted by Type 022 *Houbei*-class fast missile-attack vessels of the East

Sea Fleet's 16th Fast Attack Flotilla. The Type 022s, each of which carries eight YJ-83 long-range anti-ship missiles, are an important element of China's littoral defence capability.

The development of anti-access and area-denial capabilities is the most cost-effective manner by which China believes it can deter US involvement in regional contingencies. Anti-ship missiles are crucial, particularly in the Taiwan Strait, as they potentially allow Chinese forces to sink or cripple large vessels cost-effectively. The PLAN's anti-ship cruise missiles now include both Russian and nationally developed systems. Along with the *Raduga* 3M80 (SS-N-22 *Sunburn*) rocket/ramjet-powered missile that arms the Russian-built *Sovremenny*-class destroyer, and the *Novator* 3M54 (SS-N-27B *Sizzler*) fitted on the PLAN's Russian-designed *Kilo*-class submarines, the navy is now fielding the Chinese-built YJ-62 anti-ship

Table 15 **China – Estimated Total Military-Related Funding 2009**

	A RMB bn	B US$bn at market exchange rates	C US$bn incl PPP estimates[a]
Official PLA budget (Including local militia funding)	480.7	70.38	127.85[b]
Foreign weapons purchase (2002-2009 average)	12.2	1.79	1.79
Defence Industry Subsidies	See text in *The Military Balance* 2010, p. 392		
R&D	53.06	7.77	7.77
Government funded science and technology	39.19	5.74	5.74
People's Armed Police			
Central funding	67.91	9.94	18.06[b]
Local funding	18.72	2.74	4.97[b]
Total	**671.78**	**98.36**	**166.18**
% of GDP	1.97		

Sources: *China Statistical Yearbook 2010* and 'Conventional Arms Transfers to Developing Nations 2002–2009', Congressional Research Service.
[a]Where appropriate.
[b]Arms Includes PPP estimate.

Although the best indicator of the overall trend in military spending, China's official defence budget does not reflect the true level of resources devoted to the PLA. Table 15 includes estimates for additional military-related elements. Column A includes figures for the 2009 official budget plus estimates of foreign-weapons purchases, R&D and new product expenditure, and outlays on the PAP. This suggests total military-related spending amounted to RMB671.78bn (US$98.36bn), about 1.4 times greater than the official budget. However, exchange rates must also be considered. In 2009, for example, when converted at the average market exchange rate for the year, China's GDP measured US$4.98 trillion. However, the World Bank calculated that using PPP rates China's 2009 GDP was the equivalent of US$9.09 trillion. In the case of countries at different stages of economic development, it is conventional to use Purchasing Power Parity (PPP, see) to help compare macroeconomic data. So Table 15 uses two methods for calculating Chinese military spending. Column B converts the data from column A into US dollars using the 2009 market-exchange rate; column C uses a combination of market-exchange and PPP rates. Not surprisingly, this methodology dramatically boosts the size of Chinese military spending and partly explains the wide range of spending estimates available in the media.

During the past decade, the likely gap between the official budget and the true figure has narrowed. Whatever the true extent of China's military-related spending – and the Chinese government continues to insist that no spending exists outside the official budget – the continued fine-tuning of differing methodologies to determine a definitive figure, particularly one expressed in US dollars, is becoming a less revealing exercise than in the past. For information on PPP calculations, see Explanatory Notes on p. 483.

cruise missile on its Type 052C (*Luyang* II) destroyers to complement the shorter-range YJ-8 family of weapons. Another anti-ship capability that China is developing is a land-based anti-ship ballistic missile. The Commander of US Pacific Command said in August 2010 that this had undergone repeated tests. Probably a modified DF-21 (CSS-5) medium-range ballistic missile, it would, if deployed, be the only type of its kind in service anywhere. Likely targets would be aircraft carriers or large naval task forces, although the guidance systems currently used may be insufficient to guarantee a direct strike on any particular vessel.

Finally, submarines continue to constitute an important aspect of China's continuing sea-denial strategy. In October 2010, a possible hybrid derived from the *Yuan* and *Kilo* classes (Types 041 and 039) was reported, suggesting continued indigenous submarine development. The role envisaged for such patrol submarines would probably be in littoral and coastal operations, for blockades or attacks on larger surface combatants and submarines.

Force mobility
The PLA has also made efforts to extend the range of air-force operations; strategic airlift and airborne refuelling capabilities are still limited. In October 2010, the People's Liberation Army Air Force (PLAAF) made its most distant deployment to date, when four J-11 fighters flew to Konya, Turkey, to take part in the bilateral *Anatolian Eagle 2010* exercise. This was the first military exercise between China and a NATO member, leading the US to express fears over potential technology and knowledge transfer from Turkey to China, particularly given Ankara's substantial F-16 fleet. In the event, a US military spokeswoman claimed that Turkey had assured the US that it would take the 'utmost care' to avoid any such transfers, and 'to the best of our knowledge, US-made F-16s were not involved in the exercise'. Iran allowed the Chinese fighters and their Il-76 support aircraft over-flight rights, and refuelling facilities at Tabriz. The PLAAF also deployed four H-6 bombers, escorted by two J-10 fighters and a KJ-2000 airborne warning and control system (AWACS) aircraft, to Kazakhstan during the

Shanghai Cooperation Organisation's *Peace Mission 2010* in September. Elsewhere, the PLAAF and the People's Liberation Army Naval Air Force (PLANAF) halved the number of publicised exercises over the South China Sea in 2010 from approximately a dozen to around six. Coastal aviation units have instead conducted integration exercises with the three PLAN fleets.

PLA ground forces were focused in 2010 on internal issues such as border protection, disaster relief and training for internal-security operations. Improving the ability of the ground forces to project power domestically, by using military and civilian transport infrastructure, is crucial to force development. During exercises such as October's *Duty Action 2010*, light mechanised units have moved ever-longer distances by rail and road, while being subjected to simulated attack and electronic interference. This is seen by the PLA as the best way of testing the resilience of its ground units in fighting a 'modern war under informationised [sic] conditions', a primary goal mentioned in the 2004, 2006 and 2008 defence white papers. Meanwhile, the use of civil–military transport also allows the PLA to deploy some of its key formations faster, thus enhancing its ability to protect borders and to consolidate control in remote regions. These developments are noteworthy given the difficulties in using fixed-wing airlift in the Himalayan border region, and the lack of growth in airlift capabilities. A 2005 agreement to purchase 34 Il-76 transport aircraft from Russia remains frustrated by negotiations over contract value.

Civilian transport networks have been integrated into the PLA's logistical infrastructure and can provide troop transport with little notice. This has dramatically increased the mobility of PLA ground formations inside China, and is particularly important in southern Tibet, where the Qinghai–Tibet railway can rapidly move units from the Chengdu military region to Lhasa or to the disputed Sino-Indian border. These units would be used to reinforce the relatively few formations based in Tibet. PLA units in the southern military regions have also augmented their amphibious capabilities with large civilian ships, such as roll-on roll-off ferries, which would be helpful in any Taiwan scenario.

Smaller, more mobile forces
To improve rapid-reaction capabilities, most light mechanised units have been re-equipped with wheeled infantry fighting vehicles. Supporting combat

PLA brigade organisation

After the PLA started disbanding divisions in favour of brigades in the late 1990s, the mechanised brigade was seen as the main operational unit for the future (until the view gained traction that these doctrinal changes were best developed through creating flexible and modular battalions). There are now seven mechanised brigades in the PLA, out of which five – the 235th, 188th (27th GA), 58th (20th GA), 190th (39th GA), and 139th (47th GA) – are considered to be elite formations.

PLA mechanised brigades are divided into light and heavy: the former is equipped with wheeled APCs such as the Type 92/92A; the latter with tracked IFV/APCs such as the Type 63/89. All mechanised brigades have at least one battalion of tanks, while certain elite formations have two battalions each. These tank battalions are accompanied by three battalions of infantry. All Chinese battalions follow the 3+3 organisation of three companies with three platoons.

There is also a scaled-down artillery regiment under the direct control of the brigade commander. This consists of one battalion each of 122mm and 152mm howitzers and one company of 122mm MRLs. The guns are towed in light formations and self-propelled in the case of heavy. In addition to this, each infantry battalion also has an organic artillery company consisting of one platoon of 82mm/100mm mortars, and two platoons of 82mm/120mm recoilless rifles.

There is also a mixed air-defence battalion (towed/tracked AAA and MANPADS, and an anti-tank company with 100mm AT guns (towed/self-propelled) and two platoons of AT msl (HJ-8/HJ-73).

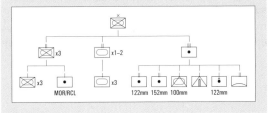

units have also been issued new weapons, including the self-propelled PTL-02 100mm assault gun and Type 95 SPAAG, which are now in service with anti-tank and air-defence battalions respectively. Although integrating new equipment has not always proved straightforward, the PLA has increasingly worked closely with industry when bringing new systems into service. The move towards smaller, more mobile forces continues a long-running doctrinal and organisational shift in the army. In the late 1990s, the PLA began disbanding dozens of heavy divisions and creating smaller brigades – producing a core of more mobile mechanised and motorised formations. This process was halted in 2003 because of a lack of officers experienced in commanding such formations. However, the PLA has since experimented with 'special-mission battalions', usually an infantry battalion of a mechanised or motorised brigade specifically trained for ad-hoc quick-reaction missions and rapid deployment. This trend towards special-mission battalions has intensified since the publication of the new military training and evaluation manual in 2006, with the formation of 'combined battalions', i.e., battalion battle groups formed from company-sized units from up to a dozen different branches of the armed forces.

According to the PLA, this reorganisation within the army is significantly improving operational flexibility, although China's continuing opacity in the military sphere complicates any objective assessment of the PLA's success in adapting to the new doctrine. The importance of the battalion-battle-group concept is highlighted by the use of elite units in the new combined battalions. Because they can adapt more easily than other, less-trained units of the PLA, units such as the elite 58th Mechanised Brigade (Jinan Military Region) and the 1st Armoured Division (Nanjing Military Region) are among those actively training in the new battalion battle groups.

The PLA's new operational concept was tested during September's *Peace Mission 2010* in Kazakhstan, in which a battalion battle group formed from light mechanised units of the Beijing Military Region took part. Armoured, mechanised and aviation units were supported by a range of artillery, assault-gun, electronic-warfare and logistical personnel. The PLA appeared more satisfied with this arrangement than with previously tested brigade-level formations, and has instigated widespread combined-battalion training. It is believed that the idea is not to make these combined battalions permanent, but merely to allow units within the PLA to form ad hoc battle groups as needs dictate, allowing for a more 'modular' army. The newly trained battalion commanders who emerge from the process should also mean that the process of downsizing most of the remaining 38 divisions to brigades can in future be resumed.

The requirement for smaller operational formations stems from the changing security environment in which the PLA finds itself. Just as the brigade experiments were a response to the end of the Soviet threat, the battalion battle group is largely a response to concern over domestic and other low-intensity threats. Smaller and faster-reacting units can better respond to domestic instability, as well as fight counter-insurgency campaigns. The move towards lighter and more mobile forces may slowly degrade the PLA's doctrinal preference for heavy armour. Currently, all PLA divisions retain an armoured regiment, even light rapid-reaction units such as the 149th in the 13th Group Army in Chengdu Military Region. Nevertheless, regional differences in the employment of armour suggest that military chiefs recognise that tanks are not necessarily suited to every contingency, with light troops being used in areas with developed road networks and tracked units in difficult terrain. For example, combined battalions in the Jinan Military Region usually include light mechanised units from the 58th Brigade with some tanks in support, while those in the Nanjing Military Region – opposite Taiwan – include many tanks and tracked infantry fighting vehicles.

MODERNISING CHINA'S DEFENCE INDUSTRY

China has set its sights on joining the ranks of the world's leading defence-industrial powers. It possesses many of the vital ingredients for success: ample funding, strong political support and selective access to foreign technologies. It also has an insatiable customer in the People's Liberation Army (PLA). A question remains as to whether this former bastion of autarkic central planning has the organisational capacity, management expertise, risk-taking culture, and research talent to carry out sustained and cutting-edge innovation. However, there has been a concerted drive since the late 1990s to build a market-based and research-driven regime that would provide the discipline and competition required to nurture these critical but neglected capabilities. This has produced noticeable gains in efficiency, profitability and the development of more capable weapons. With Chinese leaders urging the defence industry to catch up with the West within the next decade, the pace and intensity of modernisation may accelerate.

New-found dynamism in China's defence industry contrasts sharply with its struggle for survival only a decade ago. It suffered a prolonged downturn after China's economic reforms began in the late 1970s, when defence spending was sharply curtailed in favour of economic development. This situation was exacerbated by the unwillingness of conservative defence-industry leaders to reduce enormous waste, inefficiency and widespread obsolescence.

The defence industry's inability to meet the PLA's modernisation needs became a grave security concern from the early 1990s onwards, as tensions worsened between Beijing and Taiwan. The PLA had to look overseas, most notably to Russia, to meet urgent operational requirements, causing considerable consternation among Chinese decision-makers. This eventually led to far-reaching reforms in the late 1990s to tackle critical defence-industrial weaknesses.

Organisational reforms in the late 1990s allowed the PLA to gain primacy in guiding defence-science and -technology R&D. Previously, development of armaments was overwhelmingly driven by defence-industrial interests, while the PLA's requirements were secondary.

The General Armament Department (GAD), a principal command body of the PLA general headquarters, is responsible for ensuring that military end-user requirements are served. Created in 1998, the GAD quickly established itself as a powerful player in managing the competing interests of the military and the defence industry. One way that the GAD has been able to assert its authority has been to look abroad to acquire capabilities that best meet the PLA's requirements.

Also important is the GAD's role in coordinating military strategy and doctrinal planning with weapons and technology development. It works closely with the State Administration of Science, Technology and Industry for National Defence (SASTIND), the government's primary defence-industry regulator.

The role of corporations

The rise of China's ten major defence corporations is, however, marginalising the operational role of SASTIND, which is a remnant of the central-planning system. Over the past decade, these state-owned conglomerates – each controlling subsidiaries numbering from several dozen to more than 100 – have sought to transform themselves from bloated, loss-making, quasi-state bureaucracies into market-driven enterprises. They have been slimmed down, allowed to shed heavy debt burdens and given access to new sources of capital.

With increased defence and civilian orders over the past decade, these companies have become highly profitable; estimated defence-industry profits totalled around RMB 45 billion (US$6.75bn) in 2008, the highest ever. The aviation, space and missile, defence-electronics and naval sectors have benefited most from rising defence procurement, while the ordnance industry has benefited from selling civilian products such as motor vehicles. These corporations are now engaged in an ambitious expansion strategy, with the aim of becoming significant players in the global arms and strategic-technology sectors.

Key to this strategy is expanding these enterprises to compete with much larger Western rivals. Mergers and acquisitions in the past several years most notably included the 2008 merger of the aviation industry's two dominant companies into the Aviation Industry Corporation of China, which is now effectively a monopoly. Another important consolidation was the 2009 takeover of China Satellite Communications Corporation by China Aerospace Science and Technology Corporation, another leading aerospace group.

These mergers will help support the defence industry's concerted drive to export arms. Chinese firms have become increasingly active in the international arms market, regularly attending defence exhibitions and benefiting from the PLA's global defence diplomacy. China has had some major successes in selling competitively priced military equipment to Pakistan, Egypt, Nigeria, and other Asian and African states. Meanwhile, some defence firms have also developed their arms-sale relationships abroad by signing mining deals for raw materials, such as precious metals and oil, in Africa and Central Asia.

These merged corporations are vital elements in the defence industry's drive to become a leading innovator in defence technologies. Firstly, they now own and manage a growing segment of the national R&D apparatus. Secondly, their growing financial strength allows them to invest heavily in innovation. Thirdly, their collaboration with foreign companies, and engagement in foreign markets, makes them important conduits for external knowledge and technology. Fourthly, it is in the core interest of these firms to support institutional mechanisms that will safeguard their innovations, particularly through strengthening intellectual-property protection. Modest progress has been made in building legal and patent systems to safeguard local firms. However, the authorities have failed to protect the intellectual property of foreign companies, and have supported unauthorised copying and reverse engineering in cases involving critical foreign strategic technologies, as Russian defence firms have discovered.

Defence conglomerates also stand to benefit from moves to open up the defence sector to foreign investment through the capital markets. A key objective is to widen the sources of funding available to defence firms, thereby reducing their heavy reliance on the state. Chinese officials have said that limited access to investment funds has been a major factor constraining defence-industrial growth and technological modernisation. The authorities are eager to attract domestic state-owned, private and even foreign firms to acquire equity stakes in defence companies, as well as to allow them to list on stock markets. There are currently more than 60 defence-related firms listed on the Shenzhen, Shanghai and Hong Kong stock exchanges.

Focus on R&D

The defence R&D apparatus has been undergoing a far-reaching overhaul and expansion to overcome serious organisational, managerial and operational problems that have crippled its ability to conduct high-quality work for much of its 60-year history.

Developing a robust defence R&D system is a top priority in the country's 2006–2020 Medium and Long-Term Defence Science and Technology Development Plan (MLDP), which emphasises several key goals:

- *Shifting ownership and funding of key portions of the state-controlled defence R&D apparatus to the country's ten leading defence conglomerates.* The primary goals of this reform include: reducing the dependence of the R&D apparatus on state funding; increasing the investment that firms devote to R&D, especially in applied and commercial development; and speeding up exploitation and commercialisation of proprietary R&D output.

- *Developing an extensive defence-laboratory system to pave the way for long-term technological breakthroughs.* Around 90 research laboratories belonging to the defence industry and PLA have been established. However, the lack of experienced and highly rated scientific personnel means that these laboratories are still unable to conduct high-quality R&D.

- *Breaking down barriers that have kept the defence R&D system separate from the rest of the national R&D base, and forging close links with universities and civilian research institutes.* Considerable progress has been made in the past few years, with many top research establishments, such as Tsinghua University, establishing sponsored research facilities with the defence sector. Large sums have also been invested to upgrade the research standards of the science-and-technology universities directly under PLA and defence-industry control.

Since the beginning of the twenty-first century, a major initiative has sought to forge close links between the civilian and defence economies, so that the defence industry can gain access to more advanced civilian sectors. This has led to modest functional and geographical pockets of civil–military activity. The electronics, information technology, high-technology and automotive sectors have been in the vanguard, particularly through the efforts of China Electronics Technology Group Corporation, one of the top ten defence conglomerates, and non-state firms such as Huawei Technologies and Zhongxing Telecommunications Equipment. Cities such as Mianyang in Sichuan Province have been

Table 16 **China's First-Tier, State-Owned Defence Corporations**

Sector	Company	Weapons Systems
Aviation	Aviation Industry Corp. of China	J-10 fighter, J-11 fighter, JH-7 fighter-bomber
Ordnance	China North Industries Group Corp.	Type 99 main battle tank, armoured fighting vehicles
Ordnance	China South Industries Group Corp.	Type 95 self-propelled anti-aircraft artillery, small arms
Shipbuilding	China State Shipbuilding Industry Corp.	Nuclear (Type 93 nuclear attack) and conventional submarines, frigates (Type 54A *Jiangkai*), destroyers (Type 52C *Luyang*)
Shipbuilding	China Shipbuilding Industry Corp.	Submarines, frigates, destroyers, missile boats
Space	China Aerospace Industry Corp.	Strategic and tactical missiles
Space	China Aerospace Science & Technology Corp.	Strategic and tactical missiles, satellites, manned spacecraft
Nuclear	China National Nuclear Corp.	Nuclear reactors
Nuclear	China Nuclear Engineering Construction Corp.	Nuclear power-plant construction
Defence Electronics	China Electronics Technology Group Corp.	Radars, electronic-warfare equipment

designated as military-to-civilian science-and-technology zones because of their concentration of industries with significant potential in areas such as optical technology, composite materials, and space- and aviation-related technology. But civil–military integration overall has barely penetrated the Chinese economy: less than 1% of the country's civilian high-technology enterprises are estimated to participate in defence-related activities.

Relationship with Russia

The Chinese defence industry has been a semi-pariah in the global defence industry since the end of the 1980s, when Western countries imposed sanctions after the 1989 Tiananmen Square incident. This embargo looks set to continue for the foreseeable future, because of more recent strategic concerns, particularly in the United States, over China's growing military power.

However, Beijing has been able to sidestep this embargo by forging a close relationship with Russia, which has been a principal source of military technology, equipment and knowledge since the beginning of the 1990s. This has been a fruitful marriage of convenience for both countries. From 1992–2009, China acquired upwards of US$30bn worth of weapons and defence technologies from Russia, and this has played a vital role in enhancing the qualitative modernisation of both the PLA and the defence industry. These sales have also helped the struggling Russian defence industry to survive.

Although self-sufficiency is an oft-expressed goal in China's defence-technology and defence-industry modernisation goals, it is a long-term strategic aspiration. The operational focus over the next two decades is to pursue a dual-track development strategy of acquiring and absorbing foreign technology that both

complements and supports indigenous weapons R&D. The defence industry has employed several approaches in pursuing Russian and other foreign products and processes since the 1990s, ranging from off-the-shelf purchases to licensed production. The latter allowed the transfer of technology and manufacturing processes that were at least a generation ahead of existing Chinese technologies.

The approach that offers the greatest opportunities for technology transfers and nurturing of domestic industrial capabilities is joint design and development. Russia has been willing to pursue some joint projects with China, in order to retain close defence technological ties with a valued customer. However, Moscow has also been concerned that too much joint development would allow the Chinese defence industry to accelerate its work and rapidly catch up with Russian defence-technology levels.

Russian worries about Chinese intentions were confirmed when the Chinese defence industry was discovered to have been indigenously producing Russian weapons systems through unauthorised reverse engineering and the substitution of Russian components with Chinese parts. Platforms such as the Su-27 fighter and advanced defence-electronic systems like the radar and data-link systems for the *Sovremenny* II 956E destroyer and the *Fregat* M2EM 3D and *Mineral*-ME radar systems have all been successfully copied by China.

The Chinese defence industry appears to have made reverse engineering a central tenet of its near-term development approach, which led to a fall in Russian arms sales to China after 2007. Besides illicit reverse engineering, Chinese military, defence-industrial and civilian intelligence agencies have aggressively sought access to classified foreign technologies and knowledge via clandestine means.

Key sources of weakness

Despite progress in renewing the Chinese defence industry, serious structural weaknesses remain that could frustrate the goal of closing the technological gap with the West. One overarching problem is the widespread duplication and balkanisation of industrial and research facilities. The defence industry has around 1,400 large and medium-sized factories employing more than 1.6 million workers; these are scattered across the country, especially in the interior, and often possess outdated manufacturing and research attributes. Intense rivalry, local protectionism and huge geographical distances mean that there is little cooperation or coordination among these facilities, preventing economies of scale and hampering consolidation.

Weak links in critical technological sub-sectors are holding back broader progress. One of the biggest problems remains the aero-engine sector, which has struggled to develop and produce the state-of-the-art, high-performance power plants needed to equip new-generation military aircraft. This has forced the defence industry and People's Liberation Army Air Force (PLAAF) to depend on imported Russian engines for Chinese J-10 and J-11 fighters.

Medium- and long-term development plans

The Chinese defence industry, in conjunction with the PLA, has drawn up major plans to guide weapons, technological and industrial development over the next five to ten years. These include the 12th five-year defence-science and -technology programme drafted by SASTIND, covering 2011–15. It provides detailed programmatic and procurement guidelines for projects that are in advanced stages of development and are expected to be ready for service soon. The plans also include the 2006–20 MLDP noted earlier, which focuses on guiding defence-related basic and applied R&D. Alongside this sits another medium- and long-term science and technology development plan for the same period that also includes military projects. The principal aspiration of these two national plans is to attain the technological level of first-tier global military powers within the next ten to 15 years.

Three of the MLDP's 16 high-priority technology developments are unnamed classified military projects. Several other defence-industry-led projects

have potential dual-use applications. They include a new-generation nuclear power reactor and a 150-seat civilian airliner that is China's bid to break the duopoly enjoyed by the US and Europe in commercial aviation.

One of the top development priorities for the 12th five-year programme is a next-generation fighter aircraft. Although Chinese aircraft designers claim that they are capable of producing a platform as technologically sophisticated as US fifth-generation F-22 and F-35 fighters (with stealth, super-cruise and active electronically scanned array radar), it is more likely that the Chinese fighter would be closer to a 4.5-generation aircraft such as the French *Rafale*, Swedish *Gripen* or Eurofighter *Typhoon*.

This judgement stems from the Chinese defence industry's lack, so far, of the expertise and experience needed to develop the composite materials required in stealth technology, while it has yet to begin serial production of its own high-performance turbofan engines, such as the WS-10. Without extensive foreign assistance, the track record of the Chinese defence industry indicates that it has little chance of making the necessary technological breakthroughs to produce a fifth-generation fighter within the next decade. A more credible and fruitful near- to mid-term strategy is to pursue incremental upgrades to the J-10, which appears to be happening already.

The Chinese defence industry is making robust progress towards becoming a leading global player within the next two decades. This trajectory will continue as long as the national leadership is committed to building a world-class defence industry, funding remains plentiful and end-user demand stays strong. This is likely to be the case even as a new generation of leaders takes power in 2012–13; the view that having a world-class indigenous innovation capacity is critical to China's long-term national security and economic competitiveness is widely held among China's political and military leadership. China's present approach appears to involve selectively targeting critical areas for accelerated development while the rest of the defence industry develops more slowly. But as the country grows more prosperous and technologically capable – and its security interests become more global and complex – this targeted strategy could be broadened.

Taiwan

The capability enhancements of the People's Liberation Army (PLA) are of concern to Taiwan, particularly as it can no longer afford to compete with China's rapid military modernisation. Hampered by sensitivities in the Sino-US relationship, Taiwan has struggled to procure the force-on-force capabilities it desires from Washington. Demands for eight diesel-electric submarines dating from 2001, and for 66 F-16 C/D fighter aircraft dating from 2006, have not been fulfilled, despite a US$6.4 billion deal being approved by the Obama administration in January 2010. Taiwan's 88-strong F-5 fleet is due to retire in 2014, leaving it to rely on its 146 F-16 A/B and 57 *Mirage* fighter aircraft and on its 128 *Ching Kuo* fighter ground-attack aircraft and *Tzu Ching* combat-capable trainers. A February 2010 US Defence Intelligence Assessment claimed the actual number of operational aircraft was far fewer given the age of the F-5 fleet and a lack of spare parts for the *Mirage*.

The January 2010 deal, which was part of a 2001 package agreed by then-President George W. Bush, focused on defensive and asymmetric systems, including 60 Sikorsky UH-60M *Black Hawk* helicopters, the second phase of the *Po Sheng* C4ISR/Link 16 programme, two *Osprey*-class minesweepers, *Patriot* Advanced Capability (PAC-3) air-defence systems and *Harpoon* anti-ship missiles. No funds were made available for the request to purchase diesel-electric submarines. In October, the ruling Kuomintang said it might attempt to postpone delivery of the PAC-3 batteries (from 2014 to 2017) and *Black Hawks* (from 2016 to 2019) because of budgetary constraints. The rest of the systems are awaiting delivery. (The Taiwanese request for F-16s, made in 2006, has yet to meet with a positive US response.)

The political and budgetary difficulties Taiwan faces in buying imported major weapons systems means the military has instead started to shift towards smaller, more flexible, high-tech forces, in a bid to disrupt any potential Chinese invasion. Taiwan's forces are undergoing a similar reform process to China's, developing asymmetric capabilities to deter a much larger competitor.

The most obvious example of such capabilities is the *Kwang Hua* 6 fast guided-missile patrol craft, the first squadron of which was commissioned in May 2010. Three ten-boat squadrons will be commissioned by 2012, each vessel armed with four *Hsiung Feng* 2E anti-ship missiles. Replacing the ageing *Hai Ou*-class boats, the *Kwang Hua* 6 is designed for hit-and-run attacks in littoral waters to disrupt shipping in a similar fashion to China's Type 22 fast patrol craft.

The Ma Ying Jeou administration plans to transform the armed forces into an all-volunteer military by 2014. In order to free up finance for this change, personnel numbers will fall from approximately 290,000 to 215,000, entrenching the shift towards smaller forces with high-tech force multipliers. According to a March 2010 Ministry of National Defence estimate, a 215,000-strong all-volunteer force would increase personnel costs by approximately TWD$4.2bn (US$133.33m), a small fraction of 2010's total budget of TWD$292.9bn (US$9.29bn).

With China's defence budget likely to increase commensurate with economic growth, such budgetary difficulties are going to make it even more difficult for Taipei to compete with Beijing's military development. Potential political difficulties in procuring advanced US weapons systems owing to sensitivities in the Sino-US relationship, particularly over the F-16 request, will further complicate matters.

North Korea

In terms of personnel numbers, the unified Korean People's Army (KPA) – comprising army, navy, air force, an artillery guidance bureau and special-operations forces – ranks as the fourth largest in the world, behind the forces of China, the United States and India. Approximately 5% of estimated population of 24m serve as active duty personnel. And these forces are equipped with a substantial array of military equipment, including a substantial ballistic-missile force, comprising short-range *Scud* B/C and medium-range *No-dong* ballistic missiles. Pyongyang is also pursuing the development of longer-range rockets, including space launch vehicles and intercontinental ballistic missiles. The KPA has a possible inventory of 2,500–5,000 tonnes of chemical weapons, an active biological-warfare research programme, and enough plutonium to produce four to eight warheads. North Korea is a proliferator of ballistic missiles, nuclear-weapons-related technologies and possibly chemical weapons. It continues to conduct provocative military and intelligence operations against South Korea.

An estimated 70% of the KPA's ground forces, and 50% of air and naval forces, are deployed within 100km of the Demilitarised Zone (DMZ) that has stood as a buffer zone between North and South Korea since 1953. These forward-deployed forces are protected by a network of more than 4,000 underground facilities and hardened artillery sites. (There are more than 11,000 underground facilities nation-wide). Such forward deployment and hardened positions give the KPA the capability to launch an invasion against South Korea with minimal preparation, or to defend the DMZ and the west coast in depth.

But as impressive as these characteristics and capabilities are, they belie the fact that the overall conventional capabilities of the KPA have declined over the past 20 years, because of the nation's economic collapse after the fall fo the Soviet Union. But the KPA remains a potent military threat to South Korea and Japan due to its ongoing doctrinal changes; inclination to take risks; and emphasis on asymmetric capabilities, including information warfare, ballistic missiles, long-range artillery, special-operations forces, midget submarines, and nuclear and chemical weapons.

In response to *Operation Desert Storm* in Iraq in 1991, the KPA began a comprehensive study of modern US and coalition combat operations to see what lessons could be learned for its forces and operations on the Korean peninsula. This seemingly limited objective quickly expanded following operations *Allied Force* in Kosovo in 1999, *Enduring Freedom* in Afghanistan in 2001 and *Iraqi Freedom* in 2003. Studies of these operations led to a series of strategic reviews that unambiguously emphasised the importance of asymmetric force in countering US and South Korean capabilities during any future war on the Korean Peninsula. Doctrinal changes were initiated that emphasised smaller, more mobile ground-force operational organisations, long-range and rocket artillery, ballistic missiles, reserve-force capabilities, 'electronic intelligence warfare' and special-operations forces. This led to the most far-reaching structural reorganisation of the KPA since the 1960s.

Force-structure developments included: the restructuring of two mechanised corps, one tank corps and one artillery corps into divisions, to provide greater operational flexibility; the acquisition and deployment of new tanks such as the *Chonma* (possibly a T-62 derivative) and *Pokpoong* (possibly a T-62/T-72 derivative) models, and long-range self-propelled artillery systems such as 240mm multiple rocket launchers and 170mm self-propelled guns; continued production and deployment of ballistic missiles; and the restructure and upgrade of reserve forces and the rear-area command structure.

Probably the two most significant changes, however, have been the growth in electronic intelligence warfare capabilities, as well as the KPA's special-operations forces. Even before these organi-sational changes, the KPA fielded one of the world's largest special-operations forces. Changes over the past decade have seen existing division-level light infantry battalions expand into regiments and seven infantry divisions reorganised into special-operations light infantry divisions. Urban, mountaineering and night-time training has been expanded for all special-operations units. However, because this force is composed of diverse units, presumably with varying degrees of training and quality of equipment, it remains unclear how many of these forces could be seen as 'special' as this term is understood by other militaries.

The idea of 'electronic intelligence warfare' was conceived in strategic reviews following *Operation Desert Storm*. The KPA described it as a new type of warfare, the essence of which was to disrupt or destroy the opponent's computer networks – thus paralysing command and control. Although this might at first appear to be analogous to information warfare, the KPA's understanding seems to include elements of reconnaissance, cryptanalysis (i.e., code-breaking), intelligence collection, electronic warfare and disin-formation operations. During any future conflict the KPA will probably employ information-warfare capabilities both to protect North Korea's C4ISR structure and to attack those of South Korea, the US and Japan. Meanwhile, the KPA expanded its electronic-warfare capabilities with the introduction of upgraded ELINT (electronic intelligence) equipment, jammers (such as communications and GPS) and radars. It is also believed to have fielded a hardened fibre-optic-based command-and-control system, to counter South Korean and US electronic-warfare capabilities.

The military threat posed by North Korea is exacerbated by its propensity for risky provocations. Tensions on the Korean Peninsula were heightened in 2010 by North Korea's 26 March torpedoing of the South Korean corvette *Cheonan*, killing 46 sailors (see South Korea section), and by its shelling of the South Korean island of Yeonpyeong on 23 November. The latter resulted in the death of four South Koreans (two marines and two civilians) when a number of rounds hit a military installation. Others were wounded.

The incident revealed further potential weaknesses in North Korea's conventional military capability. South Korea's military reported that of 170 rounds fired from the North, some 80 (i.e., fewer than half) landed on the island. The North Korean army has around 13,000 artillery pieces (not counting mortars), and it would be logical to assume that

Asian fighter procurement

As China continues to increase the modern combat aircraft in its inventory, and works on the design of a next-generation fighter, other states in the region are also recapitalising their fleets.

India is in the middle of its Medium Multi-role Combat Aircraft (MMRCA) procurement; Japan's nascent F-X competition seeks a replacement for its remaining F-4EJ *Phantoms*. Having taken delivery of its final Su-30MKMs in August 2009, Malaysia is still considering the purchase of F-18E/Fs. South Korea's F-X III project could yet lead to a competition, and in July 2010 Seoul signed an MoU with Indonesia for the joint development of a new, 4.5-generation fighter under the F-X programme. Indonesia will provide 20% of the development costs over ten years and will procure approximately 50 of the fighters. March 2010 also saw delivery of the firstF-15SGs to Singapore and the first F/A-18Fs to Australia. (Twelve of the RAAF's F/A-18Fs will be wired to provide the capability to be upgraded to the EA-18G *Growler*.) Thailand, meanwhile, is due to take delivery of its first six *Gripen* C/Ds in early 2011.

The Boeing F/A-18E/F is one of six contenders for India's MMRCA programme, along with the Dassault *Rafale*, Eurofighter *Typhoon*, Lockheed Martin F-16, MiG-35, and the Saab *Gripen*. In-country evaluation of the candidate platforms was concluded in mid-2010. India may well opt to reduce the number of contenders – possibly to three – before finally selecting the type to meet the 126 aircraft requirement. New Delhi also indicated in October 2010 that it planned to purchase up to 250 of the Russian aircraft being developed to meet Moscow's PAK FA (Future Tactical Aviation Aircraft System) requirement for a fighter to replace the Su-27 *Flanker*.

In Japan, a request for proposals for its F-X project may finally emerge in the first or second quarter of 2011, depending on the outcome of the revised National Defence Programme Guidelines (NDPG) and Mid-Term Defence Programme (which details spending plans). The F/A-18E/F and the *Typhoon* are probable contestants, while the Lockheed Martin F-35 may also be considered. For the F-X programme, however, the timing of the F-35 project is an issue since the F-4 is due to be replaced in 2014–15. Some 40–50 aircraft could be bought to meet the F-X requirement. The F-35 remains a candidate for broader future Japanese combat aircraft needs.

Asia

artillery batteries will have detailed coordinates of many South Korean and US installations. Therefore, if so many rounds missed their targets, judgements about North Korean capability (often based on numbers alone) have to be more nuanced.

The US Director of National Intelligence voiced doubts over North Korean capabilities in his department's 2010 Annual Threat Assessment, when he talked of an 'increasing diversion of the military to infrastructure support, inflexible leadership, corruption, low morale, obsolescent weapons, a weak logistical system, and problems with command and control'. But while Pyongyang's conventional capabilities may be lower than the raw data suggest, one cannot forget its growing asymmetric capabilities. These include its missile forces and nuclear programme, which in November 2010 was dramatically demonstrated to include a modern-looking uranium-enrichment plant with 2,000 apparently second-generation centrifuges.

Influencing and compounding the volatility of the situation are three political factors: the national policy known as *Songun*, or 'Military First'; the prominence of the National Defence Commission; and the continuing transition of power from Kim Jong-il to his 27-year old son Kim Jong-un, sometimes called the 'Brilliant Comrade' or 'Morning Star General'. Instituted by Kim Jong-il in 1995, the 'Military First'

policy places the KPA and its leadership at the centre of power and resource allocation within North Korea.

The apex of power in North Korea is the National Defence Commission (NDC), consisting of 12 members with Kim Jong-il as chair. With minimal interference from a middle-level infrastructure, the commission's members control North Korea's political, economic, military and intelligence resources and capabilities. The initial phase of the transition from Kim Jong-il to Kim Jong-un appears to have been settled by the son's debut in September 2010 as a newly minted four-star general and vice chairman of the Central Military Commission of the ruling Workers' Party of Korea (WPK). The succession issue, however, has influenced manoeuvres among the DPRK's elite for the past ten years and will continue to dominate the domestic political scene for years.

The most significant organisational changes during 2009–10 were of the intelligence and internal-security community. Among these changes, the North Korean military's Reconnaissance Bureau was reorganised into the Reconnaissance General Bureau (RGB) through absorbing the WPK's Operations Bureau and Office No. 35. South Korean intelligence claims that the RGB was responsible for the July 2010 sinking of the *Cheonan* (some analysts say by a *Yeono*-class midget submarine).

South Korea

The exchange of artillery fire between the armed forces of North and South Korea on 23 November 2010 revealed problems in precision targeting by some of North Korea's artillery inventory (see earlier section). But – like the sinking of the South Korean naval ship *Cheonan* in March – it also raised questions about Seoul's responsiveness. After the *Cheonan* sinking, the scheduled transfer of wartime operational control from US to South Korean forces was put back three years. In the wake of the November shelling, Defence Minister Kim Dae-jung was forced to step down and South Korea's rules of engagement were changed.

Questions about the Republic of Korea's (ROK) military focus were first raised after 26 March, when the *Cheonan*, a *Pohang*-class corvette, was sunk in the vicinity of Baeknyeong Island, near the Northern Limit Line (the disputed maritime boundary with North Korea). Forty-six of the 104 crew members died when an explosion split the vessel in half. The cause of the explosion was initially unclear. But after the vessel was raised and studied by an international commission, a report released on 20 May blamed a shockwave and high-pressure bubble caused by a North Korean CHT-02D torpedo. The commission's report said the torpedo had detonated three metres from the hull, effectively breaking the back of the ship. Pyongyang has continued to deny any involvement in the attack.

The sinking highlighted possible weaknesses in South Korean anti-submarine warfare (ASW) capabilities. In its recent pursuit of a blue-water navy capable of operating on the high seas, the ROK has concentrated on commissioning large, capital ships, including the *Dokdo*-class landing-platform dock in 2007, six KDX-II (*Chungmugong Yi Sunshin*) destroyers from 2003–08 and two KDX-III (*Sejong the Great*) cruisers in 2007 and 2010 (three have been ordered in total). In the past decade, no new ASW-focused surface vessel, either corvette or frigate, has been commissioned. In fact, three *Donghae*-class corvettes with ASW capabilities have been decommissioned since June 2009.

Though three out of an eventual nine KSS-2 submarines (German Type 214s) have been commissioned in the past decade, and a new frigate class will be commissioned from 2011, the emphasis in recent years has been on larger ships with an air-defence or amphibious role. According to Kim Hee-sang, the former head of the National Emergency Planning Commission, 'because of the blue-water navy plan, the focus shifted away from the North Korean navy'.

The *Cheonan* incident, however, turned attention back to the threat from the North in general, and the threat from submarines and sea-denial capabilities in particular. On 24 May, the navy admitted that it had started mass production of the *Hong Sangeo* ship-to-submarine missile/torpedo to be used on the KDX-II and KDX-III platforms; 70 of the two-stage anti-submarine missiles had been ordered in 2009. Two days later, the cabinet approved 35.2bn won (US$30.2m) to purchase communications equipment, sonar, sound-surveillance systems and 3D radar. It is expected that the 2011 defence budget will be heavily weighted towards measures to counter North Korean asymmetric threats, as well as towards artillery and submarines. General force-structure improvements will be designed to fulfil the existing Defence Reform 2020 plan.

The 2010 defence budget of KRW29.6 trillion (US$25.45bn) was a 3.6% rise over the previous year, while the 2010 budget allocation for the Force Improvement Programme, at KRW9.1tr (US$7.82bn), was a 5.7% increase. As part of this programme, key investments are expected in ballistic-missile early-warning radar, *Aegis* destroyers, F-15K and SAM-X aircraft, new-generation multiple rocket launch systems (MLRS) and the K-21 infantry fighting vehicle programme. It was reported that the government was seeking an increase for the 2011 budget of KRW31.2tr (US$27.51bn), which would be an increase of 6% on the 2010 figure.

Exercises immediately after the *Cheonan* sinking concentrated on improving ASW capabilities. The largest-ever South Korean ASW exercise was held in the Yellow Sea (also known as the West Sea) from 4–9 August, involving approximately 4,500 personnel, 29 ships and 50 combat aircraft. A US–South Korean exercise, *Invincible Spirit*, was held in the Sea of Japan (East Sea) from 24–28 July, again with a focus on ASW and live-fire exercises against a mock North Korean submarine. Further US–South Korean ASW exercises were held from 27 September–1 October, this time in the West Sea, albeit far south of the Northern Limit Line.

The annual *Hoguk* joint exercise between the US and South Korea was due to begin on 23 November, initially involving some 70,000 South Korean troops as well as the US 31st Marine Expeditionary Unit and 7th Air Force. However, US Marines pulled out of the exercise a week beforehand, claiming a scheduling conflict. Pyongyang objected to the exercise, which it regards as training for an attack on its soil.

In the afternoon of 23 November, while South Korean live-fire exercises were under way, North Korea fired 170 rounds towards the island of Yeonpyeong. Eighty of them found their target, killing four South Koreans (two marines and two civilians) and injuring 18. In response, the six K-9 155mm self-propelled guns on Yeonpyeong fired 80 rounds. Six F-15 aircraft were also scrambled. At the time of writing, the Ministry of National Defence had refused to confirm how many rounds had struck North Korean territory.

By then, Kim Dae-jung had already been forced to step down as defence minister, amid criticism of his handling of the incident and criticism of the existing rules of engagement, which required approval from the president's office before aircraft could launch counter-attacks. After Kim Kwan-jin was appointed as the new defence minister, extensive changes to the rules of engagement were announced. In future, the Ministry of Defence said, the South would deploy different weapons and use different levels of response depending on the targets North Korea threatens. 'The rules of engagement we have now can be rather passive as they are focused on preventing an escalation, so it was agreed to devise a fresh set of rules based on a new paradigm for countering the North's provocations,' a spokesman for President Lee Myung Bak was reported as saying.

Along with revising the rules of engagement, Seoul bolstered its defences on the five islands in the West Sea near the disputed maritime border, including Yeonpyeong and Baeknyeong. Plans from 2006 to reduce Marine troops on the five West Sea islands were scrapped, and reinforcements ordered for the 4,000 troops already there. Firepower was also set to increase, with further K-9s to be deployed to Yeonpyeong, 105mm howitzers on the island will be replaced by more K-9s and more weapons to come. The US and South Korea also announced another naval exercise in the West Sea from 28 November–1 December, in which the USS *George Washington* carrier strike group participated; this passed off without incident.

Before he left the Defence Ministry in November, Kim Dae-jung met US Secretary of Defence Robert Gates for the 42nd Security Consultative Meeting to discuss details of future defence cooperation. This meeting, on 8 October, built on discussions between US President Barack Obama and President Lee Myung-bak at the Toronto G20 summit in June, during which the transfer of wartime operational control from US to South Korean forces was delayed until December 2015.

Although peacetime operational control had been transferred to South Korean forces in 1994, wartime operational control (OPCON) had not been scheduled for handover in 2012. But, General Walter Sharp, commander of US Forces Korea, said in early July: 'If OPCON transition had occurred in 2012, ROK forces would have had to rely on some US bridging capabilities.' By adjusting the transfer to 2015 – in a plan called Strategic Alliance 2015 – South Korea would have 'time to field many of the critical organic systems in [its] Defence Reform plan to lead the war-fight', Sharp claimed. The US has further said that the plan 'covers a broad range of other initiatives, including developing new war plans, reviewing military organisational structures and timing the movement of US forces south of Seoul'.

The final communiqué of October's Security Consultative Meeting 'reaffirmed the continued US commitment to provide and strengthen extended deterrence for the ROK, using the full range of military capabilities, to include the US nuclear umbrella, conventional strike, and missile-defence capabilities'. Moreover, Secretary Gates and Minister Kim agreed to institutionalise an Extended Deterrence Policy Committee, as a cooperation mechanism to enhance the effectiveness of extended deterrence.

Meanwhile, US forces in Korea were continuing to change organisational structures and relocate some US forces south of the demilitarised zone (as noted in previous editions of *The Military Balance*). US Forces Korea became US Korea Command (double-hatted with Combined Forces Command) while the 8th Army was to transition from an army service component command to an operational war-fighting headquarters as a field army.

Japan

Japan's defence policy was expected to change after the Democratic Party of Japan (DPJ) defeated the Liberal Democratic Party (LDP) in the September 2009 elections – ending 50 years of almost unbroken LDP rule. However, a year into the new administration the DPJ's defence policy is proving little different from its predecessor's. Indeed, the first DPJ prime minister, Yukio Hatoyama, felt compelled to step down in June 2010 over his inability to change the status quo on the island of Okinawa. Accidents, crime, noise pollution and environmental impacts have made the heavy US military presence on the island increasingly unpopular among locals, with the US Marine Corps (USMC) Futenma Air Station in the centre of Ginowan city particularly disputed. After previously inconclusive deals, Tokyo and Washington signed an agreement in 2006 under which the base would move to Okinawa's less-populated Cape Henoko, while another 8,000 marines on Okinawa would be transferred to Guam, east of the Philippines.

However, the DPJ and Hatoyama objected to the agreement on the grounds that it would consolidate, rather than relieve, the US base burden on the main island of Okinawa. Throughout late 2009 and early 2010, the DPJ-led government suggested alternative sites within and outside Japan, from the smaller Ie and Shimoji islands in the Okinawa chain, to Tokunoshima Island in Kagoshima Prefecture, and Guam. The US refused to accommodate DPJ plans, not least because there seemed no feasible alternative to Henoko and any hold-up on Futenma would jeopardise other marine relocations from Okinawa to Guam. The DPJ's failure to make progress on the matter, and the accompanying domestic-policy dispute, eventually led Hatoyama to conclude that Japan had to adhere to the existing agreement – and that he had to resign.

When then-Finance Minister Naoto Kan replaced Hatoyama as DPJ leader and prime minister in June, he confirmed that Japan would essentially follow the existing relocation plans. But the issue is far from resolved. Domestic political opinion in Okinawa has turned against the existing agreement, and Japan and the US continue to discuss details of the relocation.

The DPJ's focus on the alliance relationship and Futenma meant it had limited energy to reconsider broader defence policy. Moreover, Japan's external security environment has provided little breathing space. Japan viewed the sinking of the South Korean naval ship *Cheonan* as confirmation of the continuing threat from North Korea. It also became increasingly concerned about China's maritime activities, including the passage of Chinese naval vessels close to Japan's southern territorial waters in April. Japan–China tensions continued throughout 2010 over disputed gas fields and islands in the East China Sea. These flared into open confrontation from September onwards, after the Japanese coastguard detained (and later released) a Chinese trawler captain whose fishing boat attempted to collide with Japanese patrol ships near the Senkaku/Diaoyu islands. China responded by curtailing diplomatic interactions and the export of rare earth minerals to Japan. Japan quickly sought

guarantees from the US that the two countries' bilateral security treaty extended to the disputed islands, only further aggravating China's irritation with Japan by bringing a third party into the dispute. Relations between Japan and China were patched up somewhat afterwards, but remained testy at the end of 2010.

The DPJ did launch its own defence review at the end of 2009, despite an LDP review earlier that year, and it postponed the Defence Ministry's revision of the National Defence Programme Guidelines (NDPG) scheduled for the end of 2009. However, in September 2010 when the prime minister's office released its advisory defence report – a document designed to inform the MoD's revision of the NDPG – it was strikingly similar to earlier reports produced under the LDP.

The prime minister's advisory group recommended that Japan should seek to abandon its Basic Defence Force concept, a legacy of the Cold War whereby forces were structured mainly to repel aggression against Japan itself. Instead, it said, Japan should continue the work of previous NDPGs in converting the Japan Self Defence Force into a more flexible military able to mobilise, if necessary, outside Japan itself for 'dynamic deterrence'. The group revisited past defence reviews by recommending that Japan might – for the purposes of ballistic-missile defence and to help defend its US ally – consider breaching its ban on the exercise of collective self-defence. It also recommended reviewing Tokyo's ban on the export of weapons-related technology to help Japan's domestic defence industry form international partnerships.

This latter measure was endorsed by the DPJ itself in late November 2010, though revision of the ban was not written into the NDPG. The draft advisory report even considered softening one of Japan's non-nuclear principles – prohibiting the introduction of nuclear weapons onto its territory – in order to facilitate US nuclear strategy. However, this was absent from the final version.

Meanwhile, the new DPJ government's defence-procurement programme demonstrated considerable continuity with that of previous LDP governments, although the budgetary environment has become progressively more severe. The defence budget was trimmed by 0.4% in 2010, to ¥4.68tr (US$52.8bn), and some analysts consider that the DPJ may look for larger cuts in 2011. The DPJ government consented in 2009 to the Maritime Self Defence Force's (MSDF) acquisition of the DDH-22, a new 20,000 tonne light helicopter carrier. This vessel, one-third bigger than its *Hyuga*-class predecessors, is the largest vessel ever built for the MSDF.

The DPJ further remained committed to Japan's *Aegis* and *Patriot* Advanced Capability-3 ballistic-missile-defence programmes. In its 2011 budget request, the MoD sought to procure the first of its new 2,900t submarines; the indigenous P-1 maritime patrol aircraft; unmanned aerial vehicles (UAVs or drones), the C-2 transport aircraft; and a new UH-X helicopter. It also wanted investment for research into a stealth destroyer and fighter technologies. Reflecting concerns about China's growing assertiveness in areas of territorial dispute, the MoD is seeking funds to investigate the stationing of units of the Ground Self Defence Force in Japan's more distant southern islands. Indeed, the MoD is reported to have considered the idea of establishing Japan's own version of a Marine Corps for enhanced amphibious operations.

These concerns were also reflected in the NDPG, released in mid-December. Discussing the security environment surrounding Japan, Tokyo noted the 'destabilising effect' of North Korea's nuclear and missile programmes, Chinese military modernisation and 'insufficient transparency', as well as Russia's 'increasingly robust' military activities. In response, Japan pledged to build a 'Dynamic Defence Force' designed to increase the credibility of Japan's deterrent capability. Legacy equipments such as tanks and artillery would be reduced, while submarines and destroyers were projected to increase in number, as were early-warning squadrons, *Aegis* destroyers and SAM – possibly *Patriot* – units. Military forces on Japan's southwestern islands were to be bolstered by personnel enhancements and improvements in capability.

In procurement terms, though, Japan's main dilemma remains the F-X replacement for its F-4 fighter-bombers, due to retire in 2014–15. Currently, Japan's preferred long-term option appears to be the F-35. But – although the government may finally take a decision in the revised NDPG or shortly after in 2011 – Tokyo still appears uncertain over the options for the F-X. Upgrades to current inventory types and extended production lines have been considered as an alternative, or an adjunct, to an interim fighter purchase. The Boeing F/A-18E/F and the Eurofighter *Typhoon* are two candidates that meet the F-X requirement, or more likely the interim F-X requirement before the F-35 becomes available, if present timelines are adhered to. The near-term acquisition of a further

fighter type, mainly to meet the air-superiority role, would also provide badly needed work to help sustain the domestic combat-aircraft manufacturing base.

SOUTH ASIA

India

Although India still perceives the rise of China as essentially peaceful, the view expressed by Foreign Minister Pranab Mukherjee in November 2008 that it is nevertheless a key security 'challenge and priority' for India is beginning to gain traction. While in 2010 New Delhi turned its attention to countering China's growing presence and influence in South Asia, its much-criticised defence-procurement practices also came to the fore, when the troubled project to purchase and refit an ex-Soviet aircraft carrier for the Indian navy got into even deeper water. By August 2010, the final cost of the INS *Vikramaditya* had more than doubled to around US$2.9bn and the delivery date had been pushed back at least four years. However, the army did place a large order for the indigenous *Arjun* tank, and the *Agni*-III ballistic missile was confirmed ready for induction into the army's missile regiments.

After Maoist Naxalite rebels carried out the deadliest attack in their 43-year history, in Chhattisgarh state in April 2010, there were media calls to bring the army or air force into the counter-insurgency campaign. New Delhi resisted these, but did deploy extra paramilitary police and tested unmanned aerial vehicles, reportedly including some indigenously developed prototypes, in surveillance operations.

During the year, the Integrated Defence Staff (IDS) Headquarters released four classified joint doctrines on: electronic warfare; maritime air operations; perception management and psychological operations; and air and land operations. A fifth declassified joint doctrine on sub-conventional operations emphasised that employing the armed forces was not the natural choice for countering internal threats. In April 2010, Minister of Defence A.K. Antony confirmed his approval of 'jointness' within the military as the IDS HQ neared completion of its first Long Term 15-year Integrated Perspective Plan. This is intended to provide priorities for acquisition and spin-ons from common electronic operating systems for the three services. The MoD is also coordinating efforts to counter cyber-security threats after the defence minister called in April 2010 for a crisis-management action plan in this sphere.

Perceptions of China

Indian security officials are concerned by what they see as China's recent assertiveness in the two countries' long-standing border dispute, and by a change in policy towards India's dispute with Pakistan over Kashmir, and they have reacted accordingly. They are also suspicious of China's bolstered military presence in Tibet and of its involvement in infrastructure projects in South Asia with the potential for dual civil–military use. India sees these as an attempt to contain and encircle it strategically, while China gains permanent access to the Indian Ocean for the first time through the Chinese-built port of Gwadar on Pakistan's Baluchistan coast. This led Indian Prime Minister Manmohan Singh to note with uncharacteristic forthrightness in September 2010 that India should be prepared to deal with 'a new assertiveness among the Chinese' and with China's desire for a 'foothold in South Asia' – although both New Delhi and Beijing subsequently attempted to downplay these remarks.

India is concerned that new Chinese roads, rail lines and airports near the two countries' 4,000km de facto border – or Line of Actual Control (LAC) – will provide China's armed forces with enhanced access to the region. India and China view the LAC very differently. Whereas New Delhi considers it to be the boundary separating India's Arunachal Pradesh from China's Tibet, China claims that most of Arunachal Pradesh is Chinese territory, as an extension of southern Tibet. In the western sector of the LAC, India claims Aksai Chin as part of its Ladakh region, which China disputes. As a result, there are regular border incursions across the LAC by both sides, although these are rarely serious. Before work began in September 2010 to extend the world's highest railway line onwards from the Tibetan capital Lhasa west to the second-largest city, Xigaze, near the Nepalese border, China had already announced another rail extension east to Nyingchi, less than 50km from the LAC in Arunachal Pradesh. Tibet's fifth airport, in Xigaze, began operations in November 2010.

China has also established trade ties with Pakistan, Myanmar and Sri Lanka, and offered military training to Nepal for national army personnel. India has responded to this perceived Chinese assertiveness and growing influence in South Asia with a mix of rhetorical, diplomatic, infrastructural and defence-led initiatives. India's military chiefs have begun publicly to voice their concerns about China's rising military proficiency. In August 2009, the navy chief said that India had neither the military capability nor the intention 'to match China force for force' and advocated the use of maritime domain awareness and network-centric operations 'along with a reliable stand-off deterrent' in response to China's military rise. In December 2009, the Times of India reported that the army was revising its doctrine to fight a two-front war with both Pakistan and China, quoting the then-army chief, General Deepak Kapoor, on the shape of the new doctrine. In October 2010, Kapoor's successor, General V.K. Singh, described Pakistan and China as the 'two irritants' to India's national security.

In August 2009, Defence Minister Antony announced that nearly US$200m, double the previous year's amount, had been allocated in 2009–10 to build roads near the border with China. The Indian Supreme Court gave clearance in April 2010 for the construction of two strategic roads in the Indian state of Sikkim near the borders with Tibet and Bhutan; these are due to be finished in 2012.

India has nearly finished raising two new mountain divisions of 36,000 troops each (announced in 2008). Two new battalions of Arunachal Pradesh and Sikkim scouts, comprising 5,000 locally recruited troops, are also being raised, with plans for a new mountain strike corps and a third artillery division for the area. Meanwhile, the Indian air force has begun to deploy two squadrons of Su-30MKI aircraft to Tezpur air base, close to the LAC with China. It is also upgrading six airstrips in Arunachal Pradesh, as it has already started to do in the Ladakh region of Jammu & Kashmir bordering Pakistan-administered Kashmir. Along with the acquisition of AWACS aircraft, ground-based air defence close to the LAC has reportedly been bolstered with 19 low-altitude transportable medium-power radars.

The Indian navy also plans to strengthen its eastern fleet, notably by basing an aircraft carrier in the Bay of Bengal. At the same time, India has stepped up its naval interactions with the US and with Southeast and East Asian states. An increased Chinese naval presence in the Indian Ocean is being countered by bilateral Indian naval exercises with Singapore and Vietnam in the South China Sea, and with trilateral exercises with the US and Japan off Okinawa.

The Indian navy's new maritime doctrine in August 2009 made a clear distinction between its primary and secondary areas of maritime interest. These secondary areas of maritime interest included, for the first time, the 'South China Sea, other areas of the west Pacific Ocean and friendly littoral countries located herein', along with 'other areas of national

Table 17 **Indian Defence Budget by Function, 2007–10**

Current Rupees bn Personnel, Operations and Maintenance	2007 outturn	2009 budget	2009 outturn	2010 budget
MoD	23.9	31.7	35.8	34.3
Defence Pensions	202.3	217.9	240	250
Army	481.9	585.5	579	573.3
Navy	80.3	83.2	93.1	93.3
Air Force	122	143.2	146.8	152.1
Defence Service – R&D	38.4	47.5	43.5	52.3
Defence Ordnance factories	89.7	105.8	110	115.5
Recoveries and Receipts	-76.5	-97.5	-88.14	-113
Sub-total	962	1117.3	1160	1157.8
Procurement and Construction				
Tri-Service R&D	30.9	37.2	41.6	45.8
Army	111.1	177.6	126.5	169.7
Navy	89.3	109.6	116.2	113.4
Air Force	169.3	199.4	185	249.5
Other	9.4	24.4	8.9	21.6
Sub-total	410	548.2	478.2	600
Total Defence Budget	**1,372.0**	**1,665.5**	**1,638.2**	**1,757.8**

interest based on considerations of diaspora and overseas investments'. While the Indian navy now regularly exercises and trains with Western and Southeast Asian navies, the Chinese navy is consolidating its relations with the Pakistani navy.

Defence spending and defence industry
During the global economic downturn, Indian economic growth dipped to 6.7% in 2008–09, down from 9% the previous year, but this began to accelerate to 7.2% in 2009–10 and an estimated 8.4% in 2010–11. The budget estimate in February 2010 anticipated a 2010 budget figure of INR1.76tr (US$38.4bn), a rise of 5.5% and equivalent to 2.5% of GDP. Capital expenditure was expected to increase to INR600bn (US$13.2bn). But nearly US$450m from the 2009–10 allocation had still not been spent, notwithstanding continuing procurement demands from the three armed services to recapitalise inventories and improve combat capabilities. As noted in *The Military Balance 2010* (p. 349): 'The under-spending and procurement malpractice that has plagued the Ministry of Defence (MoD) for a generation remains chronic and between 2002 and 2008 a combination of bureaucratic delay, inefficiency and corruption in the procurement process saw the MoD return some INR225bn (US$5.5bn) of procurement funds to the Treasury.'

While the nine-year-old 26% cap on foreign direct investment (FDI) may have reduced the number of defence joint ventures, in September 2010 Hindustan Aeronautics Limited and Russia's United Aircraft Corporation/Rosoboronexport announced a US$600m joint venture to produce multi-role transport aircraft (see following 'Service developments' section). Earlier, in February, Defense Land Systems India, the joint venture between BAE Systems and Mahindra & Mahindra, unveiled its first product, the Mine Protected Vehicle India (MPVI). In an attempt to promote India's defence-industrial reforms, the heads of defence and trade promotion groups from the US, the UK, France, Germany and Canada wrote to the Defence Minister on 25 August with reference to India's current procurement and investment rules. This included recommending increased FDI in the defence sector by endorsing an earlier recommendation of the Indian Ministry of Commerce and Industry to increase the FDI cap to 74%, even though majority equity would suffice. Analysts argue that India needs to raise the FDI cap to over 50% if it is to provide a technological and productivity boost to its inefficient domestic public-sector defence industries. At the same time, India's relatively new private defence-industrial companies faced teething problems; Larsen & Toubro warned that its planned ship-manufacturing project in Kattupalli, Tamil Nadu, might be wasted as the government had not issued it with any major order. A new Defence Procurement Policy is expected in 2011.

Service developments

The navy was allocated just under 15% of overall defence expenditure planned for in 2010–11, amounting to INR214.67bn (US$4.73bn). This is, in effect, a flat budget compared with 2009–10. Almost half of the funding is intended for acquisition and modernisation programmes, including surface ships, submarines and aviation. While delivery of the MiG-29K carrier-borne fighter began in 2010, the navy will not now commission the INS *Vikramaditya* aircraft carrier until the end of 2012, as the saga of the conversion of the ex-Russian *Admiral Gorshkov* continues. This programme, to remodel the Kiev-class carrier *Gorshkov* into a full carrier and rename it *Vikramaditya*, has proved more protracted and expensive than first anticipated. The *Gorshkov* was only capable of operating short-take off/vertical landing fixed-wing aircraft, requiring an extensive redesign to be able to operate the MiG-29K fighters. While the navy has delayed the retirement of its sole current carrier, INS *Viraat* (ex-HMS *Hermes*) until 2012, these delays mean that there is a possibility that India could have a gap in its carrier capability. Under a revised project agreement in March 2010, India agreed to pay US$2.9bn for the refit.

Also in August 2010, a report by the Indian Comptroller and Auditor General highlighted the procurement and manufacturing shortcomings and delays that had combined to undermine India's naval aviation capabilities. According to the report, the 'availability of aircraft was a mere 26% of asset strength, on account of the high number of aircraft undergoing repair/overhaul and sluggish progress in acquisition programme'. The report recommended that the government speed the completion and approval of the navy's 15-year Long Term Perspective Plan 2012–27, so that firm direction could be given on aircraft acquisition and induction into service, as well as on the management of assets and the flow of funds. In late 2010, this recommendation had yet to be implemented.

The *Vikramaditya* is due to be followed into service in 2015 by the INS *Vikrant* (formerly the Air Defence Ship, or ADS, project). The 37,500t ship will be India's first locally manufactured aircraft carrier. The ADS project has been under way for two decades, with the ambition to eventually field two or three carriers in this class. The *Vikrant* will be equipped with MiG-29K fighters and the naval variant of India's much delayed *Tejas* light fighter; a carrier-version *Tejas* prototype was unveiled in July 2010. As a result of further procure-

ment problems, the submarine service faces a fall in its inventory. The first of six French *Scorpene* submarines ordered in 2005 will enter service in 2014–15 at the earliest. The slow pace of the acquisition is due to initial delays in procurement decision-making, problems in absorbing the technology and the lack of suitable infrastructure. In consequence, India's operationally available submarine fleet will fall, with the number of diesel-electric boats reducing from 16 to eight or nine by 2012. In a bid to address this problem, a request for information (RFI) for a second batch of six Russian Project-75I submarines was issued on 7 September 2010. At an estimated cost of US$10.72bn, this would be one of India's largest arms deals. Meanwhile, the lease of the Russian *Akula*-II nuclear-powered submarine was postponed until March 2011, with further tests required after one of the vessels was involved in a fatal accident during trials with a Russian crew in November 2008. Meanwhile INS *Arihant*, India's first locally built, nuclear-powered submarine, is expected to undergo two to three years of sea trials before commissioning; the vessel was launched in July 2009.

Coastal security continues to be a priority for the Indian navy and coastguard in the wake of the Mumbai attacks of November 2008. A Coastal Security Scheme (CSS) has aimed to provide infrastructure assistance to nine states so that their ability to patrol the littoral zone can be improved. The second phase of the CSS was scheduled to begin in April 2011, with the objective of improving boats, police stations, jetties, vehicles and equipment, as well as personnel training. In addition, there has been greater focus on gathering and coordinating intelligence; a new chain of 46 coastal radar stations is near completion.

Meanwhile, the navy held bilateral exercises with the Singaporean, Omani, British, French and US navies, to improve interoperability. In 2010, it held the annual *Milan* naval gathering at Port Blair in the Andaman and Nicobar Islands. Eleven South and Southeast Asian nations were represented, as well as Australia and New Zealand, with the exercises and lectures focusing on humanitarian assistance and disaster relief. The navy continued to deploy a guided-missile frigate or destroyer on rotation to the Gulf of Aden, in support of the UN-sanctioned counter-piracy mission.

The air force budget increased by a fifth to INR404.62bn (US$8.95bn), with 60% of this allocated to capital expenditure. In October 2010, the government indicated a desire to purchase up to 250 combat

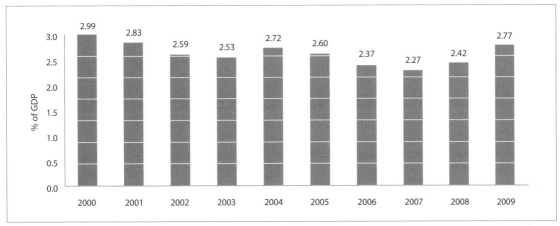

Figure 6 **South and Central Asia Regional Defence Expenditure** as % of GDP

aircraft from Russia to meet its fifth-generation fighter aircraft requirement, with the Sukhoi T-50 prototype now in development for the Russian air force the likely target for an eventual procurement programme. New Delhi also intends to acquire 45 of the multi-role transport aircraft being developed with Russia in the $600m joint venture the two countries announced in September. The air force was also looking to procure an additional 42 Su-30MKI combat aircraft from Russia for delivery in 2014–18. The last of three Il-76 AWACS aircraft built by Russia and equipped by Israel was delivered in November 2010, significantly upgrading India's air-defence capabilities. The operational clearance for the induction of the *Tejas* light combat aircraft into the air force is expected in early 2011.

During British Prime Minister David Cameron's visit to India in July 2010, a follow-on contract (valued at US$780m) for 57 *Hawk* Advanced Trainers was signed with BAE Systems; 17 are for the navy. Later, in November, US President Obama publicly acknowledged a 'preliminary agreement' for the sale of ten C-17 *Globemaster* III transport aircraft at the same time as the Indian air force chief indicated the possible acquisition of an additional six aircraft. However, protracted negotiations over three key technology-transfer and equipment-exchange agreements continue with the US. These agreements (the Logistics Support Agreement, Communication Interoperability and Security Memorandum of Agreement, and the Basic Exchange and Cooperation Agreement for Geo-Spatial Cooperation) influence the technical conditions under which India and the US can operate and trade high-technology equipment and exchange services with each other.

In November, the Indian-designed Kaveri engine (originally developed for both versions of the *Tejas*) made its maiden flight in Russia. Although the Kaveri had been replaced by a US power plant for the *Tejas*, it could still feature on India's future Medium Multi-role Combat Aircraft (MMRCA). Given the *Tejas* delay, and in the face of an ageing – and depleting – MiG fleet, the air force issued a proposal for the acquisition of 126 medium combat aircraft. Amid considerable media speculation, the MoD said on 27 July that 'commercial proposals have not been opened' for the procurement of the aircraft, estimated to cost $10-12bn. It was reported that evaluations of all six contenders – Lockheed Martin's F-16IN, Boeing's F/A-18 E/F, Dassault's *Rafale*, the Eurofighter *Typhoon*, Saab's *Gripen* and Russia's MiG-35 – had been completed, with these aircraft operating in diversified topographical and climatic conditions. Meanwhile, the air-launched version of the *Brahmos* cruise missile planned for the Su-30 MKI is due to be ready for deployment in 2012; the missile is already in service with the army and navy.

The army received a total of INR740bn (US$16.38bn), or half the 2010–11 defence budget, just 5% more than the previous year. Despite criticism of the indigenous *Arjun* tanks and the continuing deployment of the T-90S tanks, in August the army placed a follow-on order for 124 *Arjun* MkIIs, worth INR17bn (US$390m). This doubled the total order for *Arjun* and came after the tank had – according to the army – outperformed the T-90S in a desert trial. This was seen as a milestone, despite the project having been under way for more than 30 years, and despite concerns over the tank's price and weight, as well as its night capabilities. The MoD reissued an RFI on 23 July for 1,580 155mm towed guns. There had been no significant acquisition of artillery since the late-1980s Bofors acquisition, and this development effectively cancelled a tender stalled since 2009 when seven foreign firms were blacklisted in the wake of corruption allegations. In March, the indigenous multi-role light combat helicopter made its inaugural flight; flight testing continues ahead of its planned induction in 2012. Meanwhile, the army continues to suffer disproportionally from under-staffing in the officer cadre. With 11,500 out of 46,614 posts vacant, these shortages affect key operational tasks including staffing brigade and divisional officer posts.

India continued its missile development and deployment programme. In 2010, the 3,000km-range *Agni*-III ballistic missile was confirmed as ready for induction into the army's missile regiments, even though only three successful flight tests had been carried out. The first flight test of the 5,000km-range *Agni*-V is expected in 2011. The navy confirmed plans to deploy the joint Indo-Russian *Brahmos* supersonic cruise missile on surface ships, possibly including the INS *Rajput* and *Ranvir*; the army was reported to have begun deploying the Block II-variant with two additional missile regiments. As well as the three successful tests of *Agni* missiles between January and May 2010, one *Prithvi*-II and a *Danush* missile were tested in March. But problems in these missile programmes remain: a *Prithvi*-II test failed in September 2010, following a failed missile interception in March.

Pakistan

The unprecedented flooding in the Indus valley in August 2010 increased pressure on the Islamabad government's attempts to maintain domestic security and stability. Current estimates of the likely financial damage range between US$25bn and US$40bn, while the affected population (estimated as 20m) faced deteriorating sanitary conditions, health problems and food shortages. The turmoil caused by the flooding provided an opportunity for militant-affiliated groups to increase their support, while terrorism remains a key security threat, particularly with increasing foreign involvement in aid and relief operations. Approximately 60,000 Pakistani troops and 45 helicopters were deployed to assist with relief operations in flood-affected areas, with international support including US helicopters and C-130 aircraft. Disaster-relief operations increased the strains on the Pakistani military, and led to some personnel being reassigned from existing posts, even as the military

struggled to maintain its deployment of an estimated 160,000 troops against militants along the Afghan border. It has been reported that civilians' perception of the army has been bolstered in light of its flood-assistance efforts. The US government reassessed the Kerry–Lugar Act (see *The Military Balance 2010*, p. 337) so that it could ensure that 'the needs of the Pakistani people are appropriately addressed in the aftermath of the flood disaster'.

Pakistan continued to deploy significant numbers of its military and security personnel in Khyber Pakhtunkhwa (formerly North West Frontier Province) and the Federally Administered Tribal Areas (FATA). XI Corps, which has operational responsibility for the area, comprises two infantry divisions – the 7th and 9th – and these have been reinforced by elements of two additional divisions drawn from I and II Corps on a rotational basis. Factoring in other local military and paramilitary forces, the total strength available to the government is approximately 160,000. The Pakistani army now has a presence in six of the seven tribal agencies, with the exception of North Waziristan, where most insurgents are now bottled up. (North Waziristan was the target of 104 of the 118 UAV strikes launched by the CIA in 2010.)

In early June 2010, Pakistan's defence budget increased by nearly 30% to PKR442,173m (US$5.2bn). As the country suffers double-digit inflation, this increase is not as substantial in real terms as it might initially appear. However, as noted in *The Military Balance 2010* (p. 354), the official defence budget in Pakistan does not include all military-related expenditure; it omits items such as military pensions, benefits for retired and serving personnel, military aid from Gulf states, space and nuclear programmes, and income generated by the armed forces' diverse business interests.

Furthermore, because of its special relationship with China, Pakistan is able to procure Chinese-produced weapons at favourable prices. Defence agreements between Pakistan and China have enabled the transfer of funds for military training. On 25 May, Islamabad announced that it was to receive RMB6om (US$8.8m) from China for unspecified training purposes, and that the two countries had agreed to conduct joint military exercises.

Meanwhile, the US currently offers Pakistan $300m annually as part of its Foreign Military Financing arrangements, through which Pakistan can procure equipment from US companies. It also continues to receive security-related support through the Pakistan Counterinsurgency Capability Fund (PCCF). In FY11, this assistance will be worth at least $1.7bn. Aimed at enhancing the capabilities of the Pakistani security forces against Afghan and Pakistani Taliban-affiliated militants, the fund focuses on air mobility, command and control, night operations and combat logistics.

Modernisation of Pakistan's air force continues, with acquisitions from both the US and China. At the 2010 Farnborough air show, the jointly developed Chengdu/Pakistan Aeronautical Complex (PAC) FC-1/JF-17 combat aircraft was displayed for the first time. The Pakistan Air Force is reportedly seeking to acquire up to 250 of these aircraft in the next five to ten years. Egypt is believed to be in talks with Pakistan over joint production of the JF-17, while Pakistan is reported to have reached a $1.4bn deal with China to buy 36 more advanced Chengdu J-10 fighters. Meanwhile, three Lockheed Martin F-16C/D Block 52+ fighters arrived in June; Pakistan had requested these in 2008 through the US Foreign Military Sales (FMS) programme. These are the first of a total order of 12 F-16Cs and 6 F-16Ds, all of which were scheduled to be delivered before the end of 2010.

Also under FMS, Lockheed Martin delivered the first two of seven upgraded P-3C *Orion* maritime surveillance aircraft to the Pakistani Navy, while Pakistan has urged the US to approve the transfer of advanced technologies related to unmanned aerial vehicles and supply Pakistan with 12 RQ-7 *Shadow* UAVs. Meanwhile, the air force was expected to receive both its second *Erieye* radar equipped Saab 2000 and its first Shaanxi ZDK-03 AWACS aircraft before the end of 2010.

On 31 August, the Pakistani Navy took delivery of the ex-US Navy *Oliver Hazard Perry*-class frigate USS *McInerney*. The ship is to be refitted in the US before being renamed PNS *Alamgir* and delivered to Pakistan in early 2011. In February 2010, the second of four *Sword*-class (F-22P) frigates ordered from China in 2005 entered service. Additionally, China's Vice Premier Zhang Dejiang met with civil and military leaders in Pakistan in June to discuss the possibility of Pakistan buying at least three Chinese submarines, potentially as an alternative to German Type-214s or French *Scorpenes*.

Pakistan undertook several offensive-capability demonstrations during 2010, involving its air, land and sea forces. In addition, it successfully tested the short range *Hatf*-III and medium range *Hatf*-IV ballistic missiles in May.

Sri Lanka

Sri Lanka's defence budget has continued to rise, even though the 26-year civil war against the Liberation Tigers of Tamil Eelam (LTTE, or Tamil Tigers) ended in May 2009 with a government military victory. Presenting his forecast budgetary allocations to parliament in mid-October 2010, Prime Minister DM Jayaratne said spending on the armed forces and police would be around Rs217bn for the 2011 calendar year – roughly a fifth of the national budget. This is a 2% increase on the Rs212 defence allocation for 2010 (slightly higher than the figure first announced).

A government spokesman was reported as claiming that this rise in spending was necessary because the government was still paying for military hardware bought in the last phase of the war against the LTTE. Although no detailed breakdown of the defence budget was provided, another major outgoing is widely believed to be the payroll for the 160,000 members of the armed forces. There is apparently no prospect of demobilisation in the short-term. Indeed, in 2009, the government announced that it wished to recruit another 50,000 troops to increase security in the northern areas of Sri Lanka once controlled by the rebels, where it will build new military posts. Two permanent security headquarters have already been established at Kilinochchi and Mullaithivu.

Fearing a possible re-emergence of terrorism, the government has repeatedly extended the state of emergency in force in Sri Lanka. In May, it relaxed some of the restrictions in force, including curbs on meetings and publications, as well as the military's power to cordon and search premises. However, the Prevention of Terrorism Act and many other restrictions remained in force.

General Sarath Fonseka, the former army chief who spearheaded the military defeat of the LTTE, decided in late 2009 to run for the presidency. He was runner-up in the polls and was reported as having fallen out with President Rajapaksa. Fonseka was arrested in February 2010 and in August was found guilty by a court martial of participating in politics while in uniform and stripped of his military rank.

There have been repeated calls, led by international human-rights groups, for an independent, third-party investigation into allegations of war crimes committed during the final phase of the war against the LTTE. These calls have been rejected by President Rajapaksa's government, which instead established its own Lessons Learned and Reconciliation

Commission in August 2010. The UN Secretary General set up a panel of experts in June 2010 to 'advise him on the issue of accountability with regard to any alleged violations of international human rights and humanitarian law during the final stages of the conflict in Sri Lanka'.

The army continued to search and clear areas of the remnants of the conflict with the LTTE; these include substantial numbers of mines. In August, the US gave LKR56m (US$500,000) to the Sri Lankan Army to 'purchase more heavy vehicles' including six ambulances, and nine armoured personnel carriers to aid the demining process.

Turning to both Russia and China for additional economic and military assistance, the government signed a deal in February with Russia, providing it with 'credit worth up of US$300m to purchase Russian-made military equipment and technology, although no equipment to date has been acquired. Further, it was reported that the air force placed an order for six MA60 transport aircraft from the China National Aero-Technology Import and Export Corporation (CATIC). Sri Lanka was due to receive two by the end of 2010, with the remainder due for delivery in 2011.

The Sri Lankan navy said it expected the end of the conflict to 'radically' change the maritime environment. Nevertheless, at the end of his first year as naval commander, Vice Admiral Thisara Samarasinghe said he saw 'no case for downsizing the navy', because problems remained with the widespread illegal exploitation of marine resources and with Indian fisherman entering Sri Lankan waters. The latter he described as 'a major source of bilateral tensions'. The first phase of the new commercial sea port in Hambantota, built with Chinese assistance, was inaugurated on 15 August.

SOUTHEAST ASIA AND AUSTRALASIA

Southeast Asian governments have continued efforts to improve their military capabilities against a backdrop of strategic uncertainty, especially given the evolving roles of major powers in the region; there has been particular anxiety over China's growing military power and Beijing's assertiveness over its territorial claims in the South China Sea. Heightened threat perceptions were most clear in **Vietnam**, which like China claims the entire Spratly islands group; Hanoi also claims the Paracel Islands, which China seized from the South Vietnamese regime in 1974. Vietnam was the victim of Chinese aggression in 1979, when the People's Liberation Army crossed into northern Vietnam, sparking a brief border war. Vietnam's fast-growing economy – 6.5% growth is expected in 2010 – has allowed the government to increase defence spending and to fund substantial defence procurement, which will particularly benefit the country's navy and air force. Most importantly, during a visit to Moscow in December 2009 President Nguyen Tan Dung signed a major arms deal, which will see Russia supply Vietnam with six *Kilo*-class Project 636 submarines, together with their associated weapons and equipment. Moscow will also provide assistance with the construction of a submarine base and deliver eight Su-30MK2V combat aircraft. Russian sources estimate the total value of the agreement at US$2.1bn. In February 2010, Vietnam agreed a contract with Russia for a further 12 Su-30MK2Vs. When delivered in 2011–12, these will operate alongside 11 similar (although older) Su-27s, enabling partial replacement of Vietnam's large but ageing force of Soviet-supplied MiG-21 fighters.

Meanwhile, the two 2,000t *Gepard* 3.9-class frigates ordered in 2006 were launched at the Admiralty Shipyards in St Petersburg in December 2009 and March 2010. Vietnam's determination to boost its maritime capabilities is also evident in its May 2010 order for six Canadian-built DHC-6 *Twin Otter* amphibian aircraft, three of these being the *Guardian* 400 maritime-patrol variant. Significantly, this was Hanoi's first major order for defence equipment from a Western source. Vietnam's efforts to develop its forces (particularly a well-equipped submarine flotilla) are apparently aimed at eventually helping to deter China from using force to assert its South China Sea claims, and they have provoked a reaction from Beijing; in meetings with Western interlocutors during early 2010 Chinese academics and researchers frequently warned that 'some Southeast Asian states' were developing 'destabilising' military capabilities.

In **Thailand**, the armed forces face quite different challenges. No resolution is in sight to the continuing violence in the country's four southernmost provinces, which has resulted in more than 4,400 deaths since 2004. Vendetta-type conflict between elements of the Thai security forces and local gangs has apparently become a significant element in the poor internal-security environment, alongside the organised insurgency of the Barisan Revolusi Nasional–Coordinate and other Malay Muslim nationalist groups. Approximately 30,000 troops, including 10,000

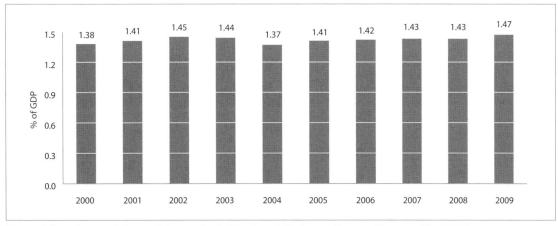

Figure 7 **Southeast Asia and Australasia Regional Defence Expenditure** as % of GDP

personnel belonging to the army paramilitary border force (the *ThahanPhran*, or 'hunter-soldiers'), were still deployed in the region in late 2010. Earlier, in 2009, the army's Internal Security Operations Command received a US$1.8bn special budget to pay for security and development operations in the south until 2012. This budget is helping to pay for the replacement of the army's M-16 assault rifles with the Israeli-produced *Tavor*, which is judged more suitable for use by troops deployed in the local version of the US High Mobility Multipurpose Wheeled Vehicle (HMMWV or Humvee).

Meanwhile, Thailand's drawn-out national political crisis erupted into urban violence during the first half of the year. Opposition remained widespread to Prime Minister Abhisit Vejjajiva's government from 'red-shirt' supporters of the United Front for Democracy against Dictatorship (UDD), which is allied with exiled former premier Thaksin Shinawatra. However, because many police personnel sympathised with the UDD and Thaksin (himself a former senior policeman), the army had to lead efforts to contain anti-government protests.In February 2010, the government deployed 5,000 troops to prevent UDD protestors from entering Bangkok. Ninety-two people were subsequently killed in Bangkok in the most violent clashes between the army and protesters since 1992. Most were civilians, although some troops also died. On 10 April, 24 people (including five soldiers) died at Phan Fah bridge in Bangkok. The army later admitted that troops had fired live rounds directly at protesters, who used rocks, petrol bombs and, the army claimed, firearms and grenades. The army was unable to take the site and retreated in disarray, leaving behind substantial quantities of arms and other equipment, including assault rifles, heavy machine-guns and APCs.

On 13 May, troops and police prepared to surround the main red-shirt camp in central Bangkok and its several thousand protesters, but met heavy resistance. A sniper – presumably from the security forces, although this has not been proved – fatally wounded the red-shirts' unofficial security chief, Major-General Khattiya Sawasdipol. Sawasdipol was an outspoken special-operations officer and Thaksin supporter, who recruited many well-trained former members of the *ThahanPhran* as the core of a UDD militia, after he was suspended from the army in January 2010. Central Bangkok effectively became a war zone. After several days of skirmishing, and Khattiya's eventual death four days after he was shot, on 19 May troops (mainly drawn from 2nd and 3rd army region units, and from the Special Operations Command) launched a long-delayed assault on the protesters' encampment using APCs. UDD leaders surrendered in order to avoid further casualties.

Although a hardline core of red-shirts continued to resist, and there were disturbances in provincial centres in the north and northeast, violent protest had subsided by 22 May. Observers in Bangkok provided mixed assessments of the army's performance in responding to what amounted to an urban insurgency. While some pointed to weaknesses in army tactics, others emphasised troops' restraint compared to previous efforts to suppress major anti-government protests in 1976 and 1992. Nevertheless, with the rift between Thailand's two main political camps deeper than ever, the prospect of continuing domestic conflict, and possibly more violence, was one that presented serious challenges for Thailand's army. While the majority of the officer corps was believed to be royalist and conservative in its political orientation, a significant proportion of rank-and-file troops were drawn from poor areas in the north and northeast, the heartland of support for Thaksin and the red-shirt movement. In November 2010, fears of disloyalty and potential subversion among troops led army commander-in-chief General Prayuth Chan-ocha to order a taskforce within the Internal Security Operations Command to escalate its surveillance of soldiers' telephone and internet usage, to control leaking of army secrets and to 'keep tabs on acts of lèse-majesté' (offences against the monarchy).

Despite these serious domestic challenges for the military, the Thai government has increased its use of the armed forces as a foreign-policy instrument. Importantly, two large international deployments began in late 2010. The first involved sending the frigate HTMS *Pattani*, supported by the replenishment vessel HTMS *Similan*, to take part in counter-piracy activities in the Gulf of Aden, as part of Combined Task Force-151. Among other achievements, in early November the Thai taskforce rescued the crew of a Thai trawler sunk by pirates. In mid-November, the first element of Task Force 980, the Thai army's contribution to the UN–African Union mission in Darfur (UNAMID), was outlined. The troops will be deployed in southern Darfur, with the main roles of building military installations for UNAMID in the towns of Mukhjar and Um-Dukhum, and protecting peacekeeping convoys. At the same time, the Thai military command's huge political influence over the Abhisit government meant that it could continue to count on substantial financial allocations, from which it has continued to fund major arms procurement. Between 2006 (when a military coup overthrew Thaksin Shinawatra's populist government) and 2009, the defence budget doubled from US$2.4bn to US$4.8bn. Although the economic slowdown led to a US$574m budget cut in 2010, the 2011 defence budget amounted to THB170bn, approximately US$5.6bn. The most significant procurement to be funded under this latest budget is an additional batch of six *Gripen* combat aircraft, which will follow the first six aircraft and a Saab 340 airborne early-warning and control (AEWAC) aircraft due for delivery by early 2011.

Thailand's government and military command remain concerned about the potential for tensions on the borders with Myanmar and Cambodia to escalate into armed conflict. In February 2001 an intentional incursion by Myanmar government forces into Thai territory in pursuit of Karen insurgents led to the 'Battle of Border Post 9631', the most serious outbreak of fighting so far between two members of the Association of Southeast Asian Nations (ASEAN). Concern over potential instability in **Myanmar** after its November 2010 elections led the Thai armed forces to step up border patrols to prevent incursions by ethnic-minority insurgent groups and Myanmar's army, while the Thai navy's 3rd Fleet made efforts to tighten maritime security in the Andaman Sea. On polling day, 7 November, fighting between troops from the Myanmar army's Military Operations Command 19 and the Democratic Karen Buddhist Army's 5th Brigade, centred on the town of Myawaddy, led almost 20,000 civilians to seek temporary refuge in the Thai border town of Mae Sot, which was itself hit by a stray rocket-propelled grenade. Within days, fighting near the Three Pagodas Pass led to renewed, although smaller, movements of displaced people.

With the military regime having maintained its hold on power through the November election (the declared victor being its proxy, the United Solidarity and Development Party), and with junta leaders influenced by the example set by the Sri Lankan armed forces' military defeat of the LTTE, ethnic-minority insurgents were convinced that a major military offensive would soon be launched to attempt to eradicate their armed resistance once and for all. Over the last year, Myanmar's military procurement indicated a continuing drive to improve both the conventional warfare and counter-insurgency capabilities of its armed forces. An additional 50 K-8 armed light trainers – eminently suitable for low-intensity combat operations – were ordered from China in November 2009, with deliveries beginning in mid-2010. An arms package agreed with Russia in December 2009 covered the supply of 20 MiG-29SMT fighter aircraft (with delivery scheduled for the second half of 2010, 50 Mi-35 attack helicopters (to equip four squadrons), and Mi-2 transport helicopters. Earlier, in September 2009, the armed forces established a Directorate of Missiles to exercise control over the growing inventory of medium-range ballistic missiles (such as the *Scud*-type *Hwasong*-6 supplied by North Korea) and multiple-launch rocket systems such as the 240mm M1191 system, also supplied by Pyongyang. Controversy among analysts has continued over whether Myanmar's nuclear-energy programme, supported by North Korea, has a weapons dimension.

Thailand also remained concerned about continuing tensions on its eastern border with

Cambodia, where the dispute over 26 sq km of territory around the Preah Vihear temple continues. In September 2010, Cambodia's foreign ministry announced the imminent delivery of 50 T-55 main battle tanks and 44 BTR-60PB APCs from an unspecified East European supplier, the intention being 'to strengthen our military capacity to defend territorial integrity and to prevent any … invasion from another country'. In July, China donated 257 military trucks to Cambodia as substitutes for a similar number of army vehicles that the United States had refused to supply after Phnom Penh deported 20 Uighur asylum-seekers at Beijing's request.

Australia's overseas military deployments reflected its overriding security preoccupations with alliance management and the stability of fragile states in its near neighbourhood. Canberra has forces stationed in the Middle East (particularly Iraq), in Afghanistan, and closer to home in East Timor and Solomon Islands.

The most important development in Australia's military capabilities has been the delivery of the first 12 F/A-18F *Super Hornet* strike aircraft, with the remaining 12 due for delivery in 2011. The *Super Hornets* are intended to bridge the gap between the retirement of the F-111 fleet in early December 2010 and the introduction of the F-35 Joint Strike Fighter from 2018. Meanwhile, the air force took delivery of all four Boeing 737 *Wedgetail* AEWAC aircraft, which are expected to be fully operational by the end of 2011 and, in October 2010, the first KC-30A multi-role tanker-transport aircraft – a modified A330.

Meanwhile, the 2009 Defence White Paper continued to provoke debate. Critics in the Australian media have expressed doubts over whether the force structure proposed in the White Paper was adequately costed or, indeed, is affordable at all. Concern has also been voiced that future governments might trim the defence budget, particularly in the wake of the global financial crisis which, while it did not send Australia into recession, has made the government more conscious of public expenditure. The Australian Strategic Policy Institute has observed that A$8.8billion (US$8bn) of defence spending was deferred in the 2009–10 budget; this amount appears not to have resurfaced in the 2010–11 budget. But defence spending is a set to increase from A$25.6bn (US$19.7bn) in 2009–10 to A$26.9bn (US$24.5bn) in

2010-11, and A$1.1bn of additional funding has been allocated for improved personnel protection capability in Afghanistan in 2010-11 – including 'the acquisition of a Counter-Rocket, Artillery and Mortar sense and warn capability'. The delivery of the force outlined in the White Paper is also heavily dependent on the defence department's Strategic Reform Programme. This aims to make A$20bn in efficiency savings – particularly through slimming down the civilian workforce and targeting waste in maintenance, logistics and administration costs – and will be essential if the costs outlined over the next decade are to be met.

In November 2010, **New Zealand** released its first Defence White Paper since 1997. The White Paper identifies the principal roles of the New Zealand Defence Force (NZDF) as protecting domestic territory and citizens, conducting and leading missions in the South Pacific, and contributing to international security operations. To that third end, the document emphasised increasing New Zealand's expeditionary power-projection capabilities and underscored the importance of security relations with the US. The main capability initiatives include: introducing short-range maritime-patrol aircraft; upgrading the self-defence capacity of the two ANZAC frigates; replacing or upgrading *Seasprite* naval helicopters; renewing the army's vehicle fleet; procuring a modern army command-and-control system; replacing the littoral warfare support ship; and replacing the navy's fleet tanker. It also foreshadows replacement of the C-130 *Hercules* transport and P-3 *Orion* maritime patrol aircraft, as well as the ANZAC frigates, with more details to be published in a strategic review in 2015. The New Zealand government proposes to fund these projects largely through 'redistributing existing resources and by prioritising the capability programme' within the NZDF. Two days after the Defence White Paper was released, the Wellington Declaration signed by Foreign Minister Murray McCully and US Secretary of State Hillary Clinton established a new 'strategic partnership' between New Zealand and the US, which will see increased defence cooperation and more regular high-level security dialogue. The Declaration promises 'a new focus on practical cooperation in the Pacific region; and enhanced political and subject-matter dialogue – including regular Foreign Ministers' meetings and political-military discussions'.

Afghanistan AFG

New Afghan Afghani Afs		2009	2010	2011
GDP	US$	14.1bn	16.9bn	
per capita	US$	472	579	
Growth	%	15.7	8.9	
Inflation	%	-13.2	0.4	
Def exp[a]	US$	252m		
Def bdgt	Afs	10.4bn		
	US$	205m		
US$1=Afs			50.76	46.61

[a] Domestic budget only

Population   29,117,489

Ethnic groups: Pashtun 38%; Tajik 25%; Hazara 19%; Uzbek 12%; Aimaq 4%; Baluchi 0.5%

Age	0–14	15–19	20–24	25–29	30–64	65 plus
Male	21.7%	6.2%	5.0%	3.8%	13.4%	1.2%
Female	20.6%	5.8%	4.7%	3.5%	12.9%	1.3%

Capabilities

ACTIVE 136,106 (Army 131,906 Air Force 4,200)
Paramlitary 119,639

ORGANISATIONS BY SERVICE

Afghan National Army (ANA) 131,906

The ANA is expanding rapidly but suffers from high wastage and poor retention.

FORCES BY ROLE

5 regional comd

Inf   1 corps (201st) with (2 inf bde (1st & 2nd); 1 mech bde (3rd)); 3 corps (203rd, 209th & 215th) (each: 3 inf bde); 1 corps (205th) with (4 inf bde);1 corps (207th) with (2 inf bde); 1 div (111th Capital) with (2 inf bde; 1 sy bde)

Cdo   1 bde with (2–3 bn); 6 indep bn (one per corps)

EQUIPMENT BY TYPE

MBT T-62; T-55
RECCE BRDM-1/BRDM-2
AIFV BMP-1/BMP-2
APC (T) 173 M-113A2
APC (W) BTR-40/BTR-60/BTR-70/BTR-80
ARTY
  TOWED 76mm M-1938; ZIS-3 M-1942; 122mm D-30; M-30 M-1938; BM 21; 130mm M-46; 140mm BM 14; 152mm D-1; 220 mm BM1 Oragan
  MRL 122mm BM-21; 140mm BM-14; 220mm 9P140 Uragan
  MOR 82mm M-37; 107mm; 120mm M-43
AT • MSL • MANPATS Milan; AT4 9K111 Spigot
  RCL 73mm SPG9; 82mm B-10
  GUNS 85mm D-48
AD • SAM
  SP 9K35 Strela-10 (SA-13 Gopher)‡

MANPAD 9K32 Strela-2 (SA-7 Grail)‡
GUNS
  SP ZSU-23-4
  TOWED 12.7mm; 14.5mm; 23mm ZU-23; 37mm M-139; 57mm S-60; 85mm M-1939 KS-12; 100mm KS-19
MSL • SSM FROG-7; SS-1 Scud

Afghan Air Force (AAF) 4,200

3 bases – Kabul North, Kandahar and Shindand

EQUIPMENT BY TYPE

AIRCRAFT
  TPT 14: Medium 8 G-222 (C-27A) (10 more on order)
  Light 6: 1 An-26 Curl; 5 An-32B Cline
  TRG 2 L-39 Albatros†
HELICOPTERS
  ATK 9 Mi-35
  MRH 27 Mi-17

Paramilitary 119,639

Afghan National Police 119,639

Under control of Interior Ministry.

FOREIGN FORCES

All under ISAF comd unless otherwise specified. ISAF HQ resembles a static HQ with contributing NATO countries filling identified posts.

Albania 257; 1 inf coy

Armenia 40

Australia 1,550; 1 inf BG with (1 mot inf coy; 1 armd recce sqn); 1 cdo BG (elm 2 cdo bn); elm 1 arty regt; 1 hel gp with 2 CH-47D; 1 UAV det with Scaneagle; 25 Bushmaster IMV LFV; 3 C-130J Hercules • UNAMA 3 obs

Austria 3

Azerbaijan 90

Belgium 491; 6 F-16 (reinforce Dutch F-16s)

Bosnia – Herzegovina 45

Bulgaria 516; 1 mech inf coy

Canada (Op Athena/Archer) 2,922; 1 lt inf BG with (3 lt inf coy; 1 armd sqn; 1 armd recce sqn; 1 arty bty; 1 UAV flt; 1 cbt engr regt; 1 MP coy; 20 Leopard C2 MBT; some LAV III Kodiak; some LAV-25 Coyote; 6 M-777; 6 CH-147 Chinook; 8 CH-146 Griffon; CU-170 Heron UAV • UNAMA (Op Accius) 2 obs

Croatia 300

Czech Republic 468; 19 IVECO DV LMV Panther

Denmark 750; 1 mech inf BG with (2 mech inf coy; 1 tk pl) • UNAMA 1 obs

Estonia 136; 1 mech inf coy with 14 XA-180 Sisu; 1 mor det with 3 81mm

Finland 150

France (Operation Epidote/Pamir) 3,750; 1 mech inf bde HQ; 1 (Marine) inf BG; 1 inf BG; 3 Mirage 2000D; 3 Mirage F1; 1 cbt hel bn with (3 AS-665 Tiger; 2 AS-532 Cougar; 3 EC-725; 3 Gazelle)

Georgia 925; 1 inf bn

Germany 4,388; 1 div HQ; 2 mtn inf bn Army: 100 APV-2 *Dingo II* APC (W); some CH-53G *Stallion* tpt hel Air Force: 6 *Tornado* ECR SEAD ac; C-160 *Transall* tpt ac • UNAMA 1 obs

Greece 80; 1 engr coy; 1 C-130 *Hercules* tpt ac

Hungary 507; 1 lt inf coy

Ireland 7

Italy 3,300; 1 mtn inf bde HQ; 3 mtn inf regt; some *Dardo* AIFV; 6 A-129 *Mangusta*; 3 CH-47; 2 RQ-1 *Predator* Air Force: 2 C-27J; some C-130 • UNAMA 1 obs

Korea, Republic of 246 • UNAMA 1 obs

Latvia 155

Lithuania 220

Luxembourg 9

Macedonia, Former Yugoslav Republic of 161

Malaysia 40

Mongolia 36

Montenegro 31

Netherlands 380; 4 F-16 *Fighting Falcon*

New Zealand 231 • UNAMA 1 obs

Norway 351; 1 mech inf coy; 1 spt coy • UNAMA 2 obs

Poland 2,417; 1 armd bde HQ; 2 inf BG; 35 Rosomak AIFV; 68 IFV; 6 Mi-24; 4 Mi-17 • UNAMA 1 obs

Portugal 26 • UNAMA 1 obs

Romania 1,648; 1 inf bn; some TAB-77; some TAB-79; some Piranha IIIC • *Op Enduring Freedom-Afghanistan* 37

Singapore 36

Slovakia 300

Slovenia 72

Spain 1,537; 1 AB bn

Sweden 500 • UNAMA 1 obs

Turkey 1,790; 1 inf bde HQ; 2 inf bn

Ukraine 31

United Arab Emirates 35

United Kingdom 9,500; Army: 1 div HQ (6th); 1 air aslt bde HQ (16th) with (1 recce regt; 2 para bn; 2 air aslt bn; 2 lt inf bn; 1 fd arty regt; 1 engr regt); 1 GMLRS tp; 2 UAV bty; 1 EOD unit (bn sized); 1 spt bn; 1 theatre log spt gp; 1 medical bn; 29 *Warrior*; 130 *Mastiff*; 12 L-118; 4 GMLRS; 8 AH-64D *Apache*; 5 *Lynx*; some *Hermes* 450; some *Predator* B; some *Desert Hawk* Navy: 55 *Viking*; 6 *Sea King* HC MK 4 Air Force: 8 *Tornado* GR4; 4 C-130 *Hercules*; 8 CH-47 *Chinook*; 6 HC Mk3 *Merlin*; 4 *Shadow R1* (Beech *King Air 350*)

United States 90,000; 1 corps HQ; 1 div HQ; 1 armd HBCT; 1 mech inf SBCT; 1 lt inf IBCT; 4 air aslt IBCT; 1 AB IBCT; 1 BfSB; 3 cbt avn bde; 1 MEF with (2 RCT); some AH-64 *Apache*; some OH-58 *Kiowa*; some CH-47 *Chinook*; some M1A1 *Abrams*; some Stryker; some M-ATV; 3,200 MRAP; some M119; some M198 some EA-6B *Prowler* some F-15E *Strike Eagle*; some A-10 *Thunderbolt II*; some EC-130H *Compass Call*; some C-130 *Hercules*; some HH-60 *Pave Hawk*; some MQ-1 *Predator*; some MQ-9 *Reaper* (Equipment includes both ISAF and OEF-A forces) some MV-22B *Osprey*; some AV-8B *Harrier*; some AH-1W *Cobra*; some CH-53 *Sea Stallion*; some UH-1N *Iroquois*; some RQ-7B *Shadow* • *Operation Enduring Freedom – Afghanistan* ε7,000

Uruguay UNAMA 1 obs

Australia AUS

Australian Dollar A$		2009	2010	2011
GDP	A$	1.26tr	1.37tr	
	US$	967bn	1.24tr	
per capita	US$	44,184	57,686	
Growth	%	1.3	3.4	
Inflation	%	1.8	3.0	
Def exp[a]	A$	25.4bn		
	US$	19.5bn		
Def bdgt	A$	25.6bn	26.9bn	25.9bn
	US$	19.7bn	24.5bn	
US$1=A$		1.3	1.1	

[a] Including military pensions

Population	21,511,888

Age	0–14	15–19	20–24	25–29	30–64	65 plus
Male	9.4%	3.4%	3.6%	3.7%	23.7%	6.4%
Female	8.9%	3.2%	3.4%	3.5%	23.3%	7.6%

Capabilities

ACTIVE 56,552 (Army 28,246 Navy 14,250 Air 14,056)

RESERVE 20,440 (Army 15,840 Navy 2,000 Air 2,600)

The High Readiness Reserve of 2,800 army and 1,400 air force personnel is intended to strengthen the Australian Defence Force (ADF) with members trained to the same skill levels as the Regular Force. Integrated units are formed from a mix of reserve and regular personnel. All ADF operations are now controlled by Headquarters Joint Operations Command (HQJOC).

ORGANISATIONS BY SERVICE

Army 28,246

Under its Adaptive Army initiative, the army has reorganised into a structure consisting of Army HQ and three functional commands: HQ 1 Div; Special Operations Command and Forces Command.

Forces Command

FORCES BY ROLE

Comd	1 div HQ (1st) with 1 sigs regt; 1 bde HQ (6th – CS/ISTAR)
Mech Inf	1 bde HQ (1st) with (1 armd regt, 1 recce regt, 2 (5th & 7th) mech inf bn, 1 arty regt, 1 cbt engr regt, 1 sigs regt, 1 CSS bn)
Lt Inf	1 bde HQ (3rd) with (1 recce regt, 3 inf bn, 1 (IMV) mot inf sqn, 1 arty regt, 1 cbt engr regt, 1 sigs regt, 1 CSS bn)
Mot Inf	1 bde HQ (7th) with (1 recce regt, 2 mot inf bn, (incl 1 lt inf bn (8/9th) op by 2010), 1 arty regt, 1 cbt engr regt, 1 CSS bn, 1 sig sqn)

Asia

STA	1 (20th) regt with (1 STA bty, 1 UAV bty, 1 CSS bty)
AD	1 regt (16th) (integrated)
Engr	1 regt with (2 (construction) sqn, 1 (topographic) sqn)
Int	1 bn
Surv	3 (regional force) units (integrated)
EW	1 (7th) regt
CSS	1 bde HQ (17th) (3 log bn, 3 health bn (integrated), 1 MP bn)
Hel	1 bde HQ (16th) with (1 avn regt (1st) with (2 recce hel sqn), 1 avn regt (5th) with (2 tpt hel sqn, 1 spt hel sqn), 1 avn regt (6th) with (1 Special Ops sqn, 1 (FW) surv sqn))

FACILITIES

Trg Centre   5

Special Operations Command

FORCES BY ROLE

1 SF trg centre located at Singleton.

SF	1 (SAS) regt
Cdo	2 bn (1st & 2nd)
Incident Response	1 regt
Sigs	3 sqn (incl 1 reserve)
CSS	1 sqn

FACILITIES

Trg centre   1 at Singleton

Reserve Organisations

Force Command 15,840 reservists

FORCES BY ROLE

Comd	1 div HQ (2nd)
Inf	6 bde HQ (4th, 5th, 8th, 9th, 11th & 13th) (each: 2–3 inf bn, 1 recce unit, some CS/CSS units)
Engr	2 (construction) regt

EQUIPMENT BY TYPE

MBT 59 M1-A1 *Abrams*
AIFV 257 ASLAV-25 (all variants)
APC (T) 606: 598 M-113A1 (350 to be upgraded to AS3); 8 M-113AS4 (Test); (119 more M-113A1 in store)
LFV 657 *Bushmaster* IMV
ARTY 330
    TOWED 145: **105mm** 109 L-118 Light Gun; **155mm** 36 M-198
    MOR 81mm 185
AT
    MSL • MANPATS *Javelin*
    RCL • 84mm 514 *Carl Gustav*
AMPHIBIOUS 21: 15 LCM-8 (capacity either 1 MBT or 200 troops); 6 LCM-2000 (not yet operational)
AIRCRAFT • TPT • Light 3 Beech 350 *King Air* (on lease)

HELICOPTERS
ATK 16 AS-665 *Tiger* (6 more due to be delivered by end 2010)
TPT 97: **Heavy** 6 CH-47D *Chinook* **Medium** 50: 15 NH-90 TTH (MRH-90 TTH) (25 more on order); 35 S-70A *Black Hawk* **Light** 41 Bell 206B-1 *Kiowa* (being replaced by *Tiger*); (20 Bell-205 (UH-1H *Iroquois*) in store/decommissioned)
UAV • ISR • Heavy 8 *Heron* (leased)
AD • SAM • MANPAD 30 RBS-70
RADAR • LAND 21: 7 AN/TPQ-36 *Firefinder* (arty, mor); 14 RASIT (veh, arty)

Navy 14,250

Fleet Comd HQ located at Stirling; Naval Systems Comd located at Canberra

EQUIPMENT BY TYPE

SUBMARINES • TACTICAL • SSK 6 *Collins* each with 6 single 533mm TT each with Mk48 *Sea Arrow* ADCAP HWT/UGM-84C *Harpoon* AShM
PRINCIPAL SURFACE COMBATANTS • FRIGATES 12 **FFGHM** 12
    4 *Adelaide* (Mod) each with 1 Mk13 GMLS with RGM-84C *Harpoon* AShM/SM-2 MR SAM, 1 8 cell Mk41 VLS (32 eff.) with RIM-162 Evolved *Sea Sparrow* SAM, 2 triple Mk32 324mm ASTT each with MU90 LWT, 1 76mm gun, (capacity 2 S-70B *Seahawk* ASW hel)
    8 *Anzac* (GER MEKO 200) each with 2 quad Mk141 lnchr (8 eff.) each with RGM-84C *Harpoon* AShM, 1 8 cell Mk41 VLS (32 eff.) each with RIM-162 *Evolved Sea Sparrow* SAM, 2 triple 324mm ASTT each with MU90 LWT, 1 127mm gun, (capacity 1 S-70B *Seahawk* ASW hel ASW hel), (capability upgrades in progress)
PATROL AND COASTAL COMBATANTS • PHSC 14 *Armidale*
MINE WARFARE • MINE COUNTERMEASURES 9
    MHO 6 *Huon*
    MSD 3
AMPHIBIOUS
    PRINCIPAL AMPHIBIOUS SHIPS 3:
        LSL 1 *Tobruk* (capacity 2 *Sea King* Mk50A hel; 2 LCM; 2 LCVP; 40 APC and 18 MBT; 500 troops)
        LSTH 2 *Kanimbla* (capacity either 4 UH-60 *Black Hawk* hel or 3 *Sea King* Mk50A hel; 2 LCM; 21 MBT; 450 troops)
    LANDING CRAFT 10:
        LCH 6 *Balikpapan* (capacity 3 MBT or 13 APC)
        LCVP 4
LOGISTICS AND SUPPORT 24
    AE 3 *Wattle*
    AGSH 2 *Leeuwin*
    AGS 4 *Paluma*
    AORH 1 *Success*
    AOR 1 *Sirius*
    AOL 4 *Warrigal*
    ASR 3
    TRG 3: 1 **AXL**; 2 **AXS**
    YPT 3

Naval Aviation 990

FORCES BY ROLE

ASW	1 sqn
ASuW	1 sqn
Trg/Spt	1 sqn

EQUIPMENT BY TYPE

HELICOPTERS

ASW 24: 2 NH-90 NFH (MRH-90) (additional ac on order); 16 S-70B-2 *Seahawk*; 6 *Sea King* Mk50A

TPT • Light 16: 13 AS-350BA *Ecureuil*; 3 AW-109E *Power*

FACILITIES

Bases   Located at Sydney (NSW), Darwin (NT), Cairns (QLD), Garden Island (WA), Jervis Bay (NSW), Nowra (NSW), Flinders (SA).

Air Force 14,056

Flying hours   175 hrs/year on F/A-18 *Hornet*

FORCES BY ROLE

Air Comd coordinates air force operations. HQ Air Comd is responsible for developing and delivering the capability to command and control air operations. The air commander controls the activities of six subordinate Force Element Groups – Air Cbt, Air Lift, Aerospace Ops Support, Combat Support, Surveillance and Response, Air Force Training.

FGA	3 sqn with F/A-18A/B *Hornet*; 2 sqn (forming) with F/A-18F *Super Hornet*
ASW	2 sqn with AP-3C *Orion*
AEW&C	1 sqn with Boeing 737-700 *Wedgetail* (being delivered)
Tkr/Tpt	1 tkr/tpt sqn with KC-30B MRTT (being delivered)
Tpt	1 (special purpose/VIP)tpt sqn with B-737 BBJ; CL-604 *Challenger*, 1 sqn with C-17 *Globemaster*; 1 sqn with C-130H *Hercules*/C-130J *Hercules*
Trg	2 (LIFT) sqn with *Hawk* MK127*; 1 (fwd air cbt dev) unit with PC-9/A(F); 10 (reserve) sqn

FACILITIES

Trg School   2 with PC-9/A

EQUIPMENT BY TYPE

AIRCRAFT 138 combat capable

FGA 86: 55 F/A-18A *Hornet*; 16 F/A-18B *Hornet*; 15 F/A-18F *Super Hornet* (9 more to be delivered)

ASW 19 AP-3C *Orion*

AEW&C 6 B-737 *Wedgetail* (being delivered)

TKR/TPT 5 KC-30B MRTT (being delivered)

TPT 41: **Heavy** 4 C-17 *Globemaster*; **Medium** 24: 12 C-130H *Hercules*; 12 C-130J *Hercules* **Light** 8 Beech 300 *King Air* (navigation trg); **PAX** 5: 2 B-737 BBJ (VIP); 3 CL-604 *Challenger* (VIP)

TRG 95: 33 *Hawk* Mk127*; 62 PC-9/A (incl 4 PC-9/A(F) for tgt marking)

HELICOPTERS • TPT • Light 5–7 S-76 (civil contract)

RADAR • AD RADAR 8

OTH-B *Jindalee* 4

Tactical 4

MSL

AShM AGM-84A *Harpoon*

ASM AGM-142E *Raptor*; AGM-158 JASSM (on order)

AAM • IR AAM AIM-9M *Sidewinder*; **IIR AAM** ASRAAM: **SARH AAM** AIM-7M *Sparrow*; **ARH AAM** AIM-120 *AMRAAM*

BOMBS

Conventional Mk 82 500lb GP; Mk 84 2,000lb GP; BLU-109/B 2,000lb penetrator

Laser-guided *Paveway* II/IV

INS/GPS guided JDAM (on order)

Paramilitary

Border Protection Command

Has responsibility for operational coordination and control of both civil and military maritime enforcement activities within Australia's Exclusive Economic Zone (EEZ). The BPC is staffed by military and civilian officials from Defence, Customs, the Australian Fisheries Management Authority (AFMA) and the Australian Quarantine Inspection Service (AQIS).

PATROL AND COASTAL COMBATANTS 10:

PSOH 1 *Triton*

PSO 1

PCC 8 *Bay*

AIRCRAFT

TPT • Light 15: 6 BN-2B *Islander*; 1 *Commander* (AC50 *Shrike*); 5 DHC-8 *Dash 8*; 3 F-406 *Caravan II*

HELICOPTERS • TPT 2 **Medium** 1 Bell 214 **Light** 1 Bell 206L *Long Ranger*

DEPLOYMENT

AFGHANISTAN

NATO • ISAF 1,550; 1 inf BG with (1 mot inf coy; 1 armd recce sqn); 1 cdo BG with (elm 2 cdo bn); elms 1 arty regt; 1 hel gp with 2 CH-47D; 1 UAV det with *Scaneagle*; 25 *Bushmaster* IMV

UN • UNAMA 3 obs

ARABIAN SEA

Combined Maritime Forces • CTF-150 1 FFGHM

EGYPT

MFO (*Operation Mazurka*) 25

IRAQ

Army 35; 1 sy det

UN • UNAMI 2 obs

MALAYSIA

Army 115; 1 inf coy (on 3-month rotational tours)

Air force 13; 1 AP-3C *Orion* crew

MIDDLE EAST

UN • UNTSO 11 obs;

Air Force 313; 1 tpt det with 3 C-130 *Hercules*; 1 MP det with 2 AP-3C *Orion*

PAPUA NEW GUINEA
Army 38; 1 trg unit

SOLOMON ISLANDS
RAMSI (Operation Anode) 80; 1 inf pl; 4 OH-58 Kiowa; 2 S-70 Black Hawk; 2 Armidale PCC; 2 DHC-4 Caribou

SUDAN
UN • UNMIS 9; 6 obs

TIMOR LESTE
ISF (Operation Astute) 404; 1 inf bn HQ; 2 inf coy; 1 AD bty; elm 1 cbt engr regt; 1 hel det with 4 S-70 Black Hawk; 3 C-130
UN • UNMIT 4 obs

FOREIGN FORCES
New Zealand Army: 9 (air navigation) trg
Singapore Air Force 230: 1 school at Pearce with PC-21 trg ac; 1 op trg sqn at Oakey with 12 AS-332 Super Puma/AS-532 Cougar
United States US Pacific Command: 129; 1 SEWS at Pine Gap; 1 comms facility at NW Cape; 1 SIGINT stn at Pine Gap

Bangladesh BGD

Bangladeshi Taka Tk		2009	2010	2011
GDP	Tk	6.53tr	7.31tr	
	US$	94.5bn	105bn	
per capita	US$	583	640	
Growth	%	5.9	6.0	
Inflation	%	5.4	8.5	
Def exp	Tk	70.2bn		
	US$	1.02bn		
Def bdgt	Tk	78.8bn	91.8bn	
	US$	1.14bn	1.32bn	
FMA (US)	US$	0.59m	1.5m	1.5m
US$1=Tk		69.04	69.47	

Population 164,425,491

Religious groups: Muslim 90%; Hindu 9%; Buddhist 1%

Age	0–14	15–19	20–24	25–29	30–64	65 plus
Male	17.4%	4.8%	4.0%	3.5%	16.7%	2.3%
Female	16.9%	5.2%	4.8%	4.3%	17.8%	2.4%

Capabilities

ACTIVE 157,053 (Army 126,153 Navy 16,900 Air 14,000) Paramilitary 63,900

ORGANISATIONS BY SERVICE

Army 126,153
FORCES BY ROLE
Armd   1 bde (1 armd regt); 6 regt

Inf	7 div HQ; 17 bde (total: 68 inf bn)
Cdo	1 bn
Arty	20 regt
Engr	1 bde
Sigs	1 bde
Avn	1 regt (2 sqn)
AD	1 bde

EQUIPMENT BY TYPE
MBT 232: 58 Type-69/Type-69G; 174 Type-59
LT TK 8 Type-62
APC 226
  APC (T) 134 MT-LB
  APC (W) 92: 75 BTR-80; 17 Otocar
ARTY 815+
  TOWED 343+: 105mm 170: 56 Model 56A1; 114 Model 56/L 10A1 pack howitzer; 122mm 111: 57 Type-54/54-1 (M-30), 54 T96 (D-30), 130mm 62 Type-59-1 (M-46)
  MOR 472: 81mm 11 M-29A1; 82mm 366 Type-53/87/M-31 (M-1937); 120mm 95 MO-120-AM-50 M67/UBM 52
AT • RCL 106mm 238 M-40A1
AIRCRAFT • TPT • Light 6: 5 Cessna 152; 1 PA-31T Cheyenne
AD • SAM • MANPAD QW-2; 20 HN-5A (being replaced by QW-2)
  GUNS • TOWED 164: 37mm 132 Type 65/74 57mm 34 Type 59 (S-60)

Navy 16,900
Navy HQ at Dhaka
EQUIPMENT BY TYPE
PRINCIPAL SURFACE COMBATANTS • FRIGATES 5
  FFGHM 1:
    1 Bangabandhu (ROK Modified Ulsan) with 2 twin lnchr (4 eff.) each with Otomat Mk 2 AShM, 2 triple 324mm TT, 1 76mm gun (capacity: 1 AW-109E hel)
  FFG 1:
    1 Osman (PRC Jianghu I) with 2 quad lnchr (8 eff.) each with HY-2 (CSS-N-2) Silkworm AShM, 2 RBU 1200 (10 eff.), 2 twin 100mm gun (4 eff.)
  FF 3:
    2 Abu Bakr† (UK Leopard) each with 2 115mm twin gun (4 eff.)
    1 Umar Farooq† (UK Salisbury – trg role) with 3 Squid, 1 115mm twin gun (2 eff.)
PATROL AND COASTAL COMBATANTS 40
  PCFG 4 Durdarsha (PRC Huangfeng) each with 4 single lnchr each with HY-2 (CSS-N-2) Silkworm AShM
  PCO 6: 1 Madhumati (Sea Dragon); 5 Kapatakhaya (UK Island class)
  PCC 3: 2 Meghna (fishery protection); 1 Nirbhoy (PRC Hainan) with 4 RBU 1200 (20 eff.)
  PBFG 5 Durbar (PRC Hegu) each with 2 single lnchr each with SY-1 AShM
  PBFT 4 Huchuan (PRC) each with 2 single 533mm TT each with YU 1 Type 53 HWT
  PBF 4 Titas (ROK Sea Dolphin)

PB 14: 2 *Akshay*; 1 *Barkat* (PRC *Shanghai III*); 1 *Bishkali*;
2 *Karnaphuli*; 1 *Salam* (PRC *Huangfen*); 7 *Shaheed Daulat*
(PRC *Shanghai II*)

MINE WARFARE • MINE COUNTERMEASURES 5

MSO 5: 1 *Sagar*; 4 *Shapla* (UK *River*)

AMPHIBIOUS 10

LANDING SHIPS • LSL 1

LANDING CRAFT 9:

LCU 2†
LCVP 3†
LCM 4 *Yuchin*

LOGISTICS AND SUPPORT 10

AOR 2 (coastal)
AR 1†
AG 1
ATF 1†
AGHS 1 *Agradoot*
TRG 1 *Shaheed Ruhul Amin*
YTM 3

FACILITIES

Bases   Located at Chittagong, Dhaka, Kaptai,
             Khulna, Mangla

Air Force 14,000

Three major bases - Bashar AB (consists of Dhaka-Tejgaon
and Dhaka-Kurmitola); Matiur Rahman AB (Jessore) and
Zahurul Haque AB (Chittagong). Kurmitola is the main fast
jet fighter/FGA base. Tejgaon houses two helicopter squadrons. Jessore houses the transport squadrons, the Air Force
Academy and the Flying Training Wing. Bogra houses the
flying instructors' school; Chittagong has a combat train-
ing/light attack squadron plus a helicopter squadron.

Flying hours   17,000+ flying hrs/year

FORCES BY ROLE

Ftr   1 sqn with MiG-29B/MiG-29UB *Fulcrum*
FGA   2 sqn with F-7MB/F-7BG/FT-7BG/FT-7B
           Airguard; A-5C (Q-5III) *Fantan*
Tpt   1 sqn with An-32 *Club*; 1 sqn with C-130B
           Hercules
Hel   5 sqn with Mi-17/MI-171/MI-17MI-IV *Hip*;
           Bell 206L *Long Ranger*-4; Bell 212 *Huey*
Trg   1 (OCU) unit with L-39ZA *Albatros*; FT-6
           (MiG-19UTI) *Farmer*

FACILITIES

Trg School   1 trg school with PT-6 (basic trg); T-37B
              Tweet (jet conversion trg); Bell 206L *Long
              Ranger*-4 (hel trg)

EQUIPMENT BY TYPE†

AIRCRAFT 74 combat capable

FTR 48: 30 F-7MB/F-7BG (recce capable)/FT-7BG/FT-7B
Airguard; 10 FT-6 *Farmer*; 6 MiG-29 *Fulcrum*; 2 MiG-29UB
Fulcrum

ATK 18 A-5C *Fantan*

TPT 7: **Medium** 4 C-130B *Hercules* **Light** 3 An-32 *Club* †

TRG 30: 8 L-39ZA *Albatros**; 10 PT-6; 12 T-37B *Tweet*

HELICOPTERS

MRH/TPT 17 Mi-17/MI-171 (med tpt)/MI-17MI-IV *Hip*

TPT • **Light** 13: 2 Bell 206 *Long Ranger*; 11 Bell 212
MSL • **AAM** R-3 (AA-2 Atoll)

Paramilitary 63,900

Ansars 20,000+
Security Guards

Armed Police 5,000
Rapid action force (forming)

Border Guard Bangladesh 38,000
Border Guard
Paramilitary   41 bn

Coast Guard 900
PATROL AND COASTAL COMBATANTS 9
PB 4: 1 *Ruposhi Bangla*; 1 *Shaheed Daulat*; 2 *Shetgang*
PBR 5 *Pabna*

DEPLOYMENTS

CENTRAL AFRICAN REPUBLIC/CHAD
UN • MINURCAT 138; 2 obs; 2 hel pl

CÔTE D'IVOIRE
UN • UNOCI 2,090; 9 obs; 2 inf bn; 1 engr coy; 1 sigs coy;
1 fd hospital

DEMOCRATIC REPUBLIC OF THE CONGO
UN • MONUSCO 2,521; 30 obs; 2 mech inf bn; 1 engr coy;
2 avn unit

LEBANON
UN • UNIFIL 325

LIBERIA
UN • UNMIL 1,441; 12 obs; 1 inf bn; 2 engr coy; 1 sigs coy;
1 log coy; 1 MP coy; 1 fd hospital

SUDAN
UN • UNAMID 580; 6 obs; 1 log coy
UN • UNMIS 1,621; 6 obs; 1 inf bn; 1 engr coy; 1 tpt coy; 1
rvn coy; 1 MP coy; 1 de-mining pl; 1 fd hospital

TIMOR LESTE
UN • UNMIT 4 obs

WESTERN SAHARA
UN • MINURSO 9 obs

Brunei BRN

Brunei Dollar B$		2009	2010	2011
GDP	B$	15.1bn	16.5bn	
	US$	10.4bn	12.0bn	
per capita	US$	26,059	29,478	
Growth	%	0.2	1.1	
Inflation	%	1.8	1.8	
Def exp	B$	482m		
	US$	332m		
Def bdgt	B$	550m	512m	
	US$	378m	372m	
US$1=B$		1.45	1.37	

Population 407,045

Ethnic groups: Malay, Kedayan, Tutong, Belait, Bisaya, Dusun, Murut 66.3%; Chinese 11.2%; Iban, Dayak, Kelabit 6%; Other 11.8%

Age	0–14	15–19	20–24	25–29	30–64	65 plus
Male	13.2%	4.3%	4.5%	4.6%	21.7%	1.7%
Female	12.4%	4.3%	4.7%	5.0%	21.8%	1.8%

Capabilities

ACTIVE 7,000 (Army 4,900 Navy 1,000 Air 1,100) **Paramilitary 2,250**

RESERVE 700 (Army 700)

ORGANISATIONS BY SERVICE

Army 4,900

FORCES BY ROLE

Inf	3 bn
Spt	1 bn with (1 armd recce sqn, 1 engr sqn)
Reserves	1 bn

EQUIPMENT BY TYPE
LT TK 20 *Scorpion* (16 to be upgraded)
APC (W) 45 VAB
ARTY • MOR 81mm 24
AT • RL 67mm *Armbrust*

Navy 1,000

FORCES BY ROLE

SF 1 sqn

EQUIPMENT BY TYPE
PATROL AND COASTAL COMBATANTS 12
  PSO 2 *Darvssalam* being delivered (3rd vessel expected ISD Aug 2011)
  PCC 4 *Itjihad*
  PBG 3 *Waspada* to be replaced by *Darvssalam* class and transferred to IDN) each with 2 MM-38 *Exocet* AShM
  PB 3 *Perwira*
AMPHIBIOUS • LANDING CRAFT • LCU 4: 2 *Teraban*; 2 *Cheverton Loadmaster*

Air Force 1,100

FORCES BY ROLE

MP	1 sqn with 1 CN-235M
Trg	1 sqn with PC-7 *Turbo Trainer*; Bell 206B *Jet Ranger II*
Tpt Hel	1 sqn with Bell 212; Bell 214 (SAR); S-70A *Black Hawk*; 1 sqn with Bo-105
AD	2 sqn with *Mistral*

EQUIPMENT BY TYPE
AIRCRAFT
  MP 1 CN-235M
  TRG 4 PC-7 *Turbo Trainer*
HELICOPTERS
  TPT 23 **Medium** 5: 1 Bell 214 (SAR); 4 S-70A *Black Hawk***Light** 18: 2 Bell 206B *Jet Ranger II*; 10 Bell 212; 6 Bo-105 (armed, 81mm rockets)
AD • SAM 12 *Mistral*

Paramilitary ε2,250

Gurkha Reserve Unit 400-500

FORCES BY ROLE

Inf   2 bn

Royal Brunei Police 1,750

EQUIPMENT BY TYPE
PATROL AND COASTAL COMBATANTS • PB 10: 3 *Bendaharu*; 7 PDB-type

DEPLOYMENT

LEBANON
UN • UNIFIL 9

PHILIPPINES
IMT 15

FOREIGN FORCES

Singapore Army: 1 trg camp with infanty units on rotation Air Force; trg school; 1 hel det with AS 332 *Super Puma*
United Kingdom Army: 550; 1 Gurhka bn; 1 trg unit; 1 hel flt with 3 hel

Cambodia CAM

Cambodian Riel r		2009	2010	2011
GDP	r	44.8tr	47.4tr	
	US$	10.8bn	11.3bn	
per capita	US$	732	748	
Growth	%	-2.1	5.0	
Inflation	%	-0.7	4.0	
Def exp	r	1.14tr		
	US$	275m		
Def bdgt	r	923bn	1.15tr	1.22tr
	US$	223m	274m	
FMA (US)	US$	1.0m	1.0m	1.0m
US$1=r		4139.15	4204.07	

Population   15,053,112

Ethnic groups: Khmer 90%; Vietnamese 5%; Chinese 1%

Age	0–14	15–19	20–24	25–29	30–64	65 plus
Male	16.2%	5.5%	5.7%	5.0%	14.6%	1.4%
Female	16.0%	5.6%	5.8%	5.1%	16.9%	2.3%

Capabilities

ACTIVE 124,300 (Army 75,000 Navy 2,800 Air 1,500 Provincial Forces 45,000) **Paramilitary 67,000**

Terms of service conscription authorised but not implemented since 1993

ORGANISATIONS BY SERVICE

Army ε75,000

FORCES BY ROLE
6 Military Regions (incl 1 special zone for capital)

Armd	3 bn
Recce	some indep bn
Inf	12 (drawing down to 7) div (established str 3,500; actual str under 1,500); 3 indep bde; 9 indep regt
AB/SF	1 regt
Arty	some bn
Protection	1 bde (4 bn)
Engr construction	1 regt
Fd engr	3 regt
AD	some bn

EQUIPMENT BY TYPE
MBT 150+: 50 Type-59; 100+ T-54/T-55
LT TK 20+: Type-62; 20 Type-63
RECCE BRDM-2
AIFV 70 BMP-1
APC 190+
  APC (T) M-113
  APC (W) 190: 160 BTR-60/BTR-152; 30 OT-64
ARTY 428+

TOWED 400+ **76mm** ZIS-3 *M-1942*/**122mm** D-30/**122mm** M-30 *M-1938*/**130mm** Type-59-I
MRL 28+: **107mm** Type-63; **122mm** 8 BM-21; **132mm** BM-13-16 (BM-13); **140mm** 20 BM-14-16 (BM-14)
MOR 82mm M-37; **120mm** M-43; **160mm** M-160
AT • RCL 82mm B-10; **107mm** B-11
AD • GUNS • TOWED 14.5mm ZPU-1/ZPU-2/ZPU-4; **37mm** M-1939; **57mm** S-60

Navy ε2,800 (incl 1,500 Naval Infantry)

EQUIPMENT BY TYPE
PATROL AND COASTAL COMBATANTS 11
  PBF 2 *Stenka*
  PB 7: 4 (PRC 46m); 3 (PRC 20m)
  PBR 2 *Kaoh Chhlam*

FACILITIES

Bases	Located at Phnom Penh (river), Ream (maritime)

Naval Infantry 1,500

Inf	7 bn
Arty	1 bn

Air Force 1,500

FORCES BY ROLE

Ftr	1 sqn with MiG-21bis *Fishbed L & N*†; MiG-21UM *Mongol B*†
ISR/Trg	some sqn with P-92 *Echo* (pilot trg/recce); 5 L-39 *Albatros** (lead-in trg)
Tpt	1 (VIP (reporting to Council of Ministers)) sqn with 2 An-24RV *Coke*; 1 AS-350 *Ecureuil*; 1 AS-365 *Dauphin 2*; 1 sqn with 1 BN-2 *Islander*; 1 Cessna 421; 2 Y-12
Tpt Hel	1 sqn with 1 Mi-8P *Hip K* (VIP); 2 Mi-26 *Halo*; 13 Mi-17 (Mi-8MT) *Hip H*/Mi-8 *Hip*

EQUIPMENT BY TYPE
AIRCRAFT 24 combat capable
  FGA 19: 14 MiG-21bis *Fishbed L & N*†; 5 MiG-21UM *Mongol B*†
  TPT • Light 11: 2 An-24RV *Coke*; 1 BN-2 *Islander*; 1 Cessna 421; 5 P-92 *Echo* (pilot trg/recce); 2 Y-12
  TRG 5 L-39 *Albatros** (lead-in trg)
HELICOPTERS
  MRH 14: 1 AS-365 *Dauphin 2*; 13 MI-17 (Mi-8MT) *Hip H*/Mi-8 *Hip*
  TPT 4: **Heavy** 2 Mi-26 *Halo* **Medium** 1 Mi-8P *Hip* (VIP) **Light** 1 AS-350 *Ecureuil*

Provincial Forces 45,000+

Reports of at least 1 inf regt per province, with varying numbers of inf bn (with lt wpn)

Paramilitary

Police 67,000 (including gendarmerie)

DEPLOYMENT

LEBANON
UN • UNIFIL 1

SUDAN
UN • UNMIS 51; 3 obs; 1 de-mining pl

China, People's Republic of PRC

Chinese Yuan Renminbi Y		2009	2010	2011
GDP	Y	34.1tr	38.9tr	
	US$	4.98tr	5.73tr	
	US$ᵃ	9.09tr	10.1tr	
per capita	US$	3,744	4,234	
Growth	%	9.1	9.6	
Inflation	%	-0.7	3.2	
Def exp	Y	671.78bn		
	US$	98.36bn		
	US$ᵃ	166.18bn		
Def bdgtᵇ	Y	480.7bn	519bn	
	US$	70.4bn	76.4bn	
US$1=Y	MER	6.83	6.79	
	PPP	3.76	3.86	

ᵃ PPP estimate

ᵇ Official defence budget at market exchange rates

Population   1,354,146,443

Ethnic groups: Tibetan, Uighur and other non-Han 8%

Age	0–14	15–19	20–24	25–29	30–64	65 plus
Male	9.5%	4.0%	4.8%	4.0%	25.0%	4.3%
Female	8.1%	3.5%	4.4%	3.8%	24.0%	4.6%

Capabilities

ACTIVE 2,285,000 (Army 1,600,000 Navy 255,000
Air 300,000-330,000 Strategic Missile Forces 100,000)
Paramilitary 660,000

Terms of service selective conscription; all services 2 years

RESERVE ε510,000

Overall organisation: Army leadership is exercised by the four general headquarters/departments. A military region exercises direct leadership over the Army units under it. Each of the Navy, Air Force and Second Artillery Force have a leading body consisting of the headquarters, political department, logistics department and armaments department. These direct the military, political, logistical and equipment work of their respective troops, and take part in the command of joint operations.

ORGANISATIONS BY SERVICE

Strategic Missile Forces (100,000+)

Offensive

The Second Artillery Force organises and commands its own troops to launch nuclear counterattacks with strategic missiles and to conduct operations with conventional missiles. It comprises missile and training bases, and relevant support troops

Org as 27 launch bdes subordinate to 6 army-level msl bases; org varies by msl type; one testing and one trg base

MSL • STRATEGIC 442
  ICBM 66: ε12 DF-31 (CSS-9) (1 bde); ε24 DF31A (CSS-9 Mod 2) (2 bde); ε10 DF-4 (CSS-3) (1 bde); 20 DF-5A (CSS-4 Mod 2) (3 bdes)
  IRBM 118: ε80 DF-21 (CSS-5) (5 bde); ε36 DF21C (CSS-5 Mod 3) (2 bde); ε2 DF-3A (CSS-2 Mod) (1 bde)
  SRBM 204
    108 DF-11A/M-11A (CSS-7 Mod 2) (4 bde); 96 DF-15/M-9 (CSS-6) (6 bde)
  LACM ε54 CJ-10 (DH-10); (2 bde)

Navy

SUBMARINES • STRATEGIC • SSBN 3:
  1 Xia equipped with 12 JL-1 (CSS-N-3) strategic SLBM
  2 Jin equipped with up to 12 JL-2 (CSS-NX-4) strategic SLBM (full operational status unknown; 3rd and 4th vessels in build)

Defensive

RADAR • STRATEGIC: some phased array radar; some detection and tracking radars (covering Central Asia and Shanxi (northern border)) located at Xinjiang

People's Liberation Army ε800,000; ε800,000 conscript (reductions continue) (total ε1,600,000)

Ground forces are organised into eight service arms (branches)—infantry, armour, artillery, air defence, aviation, engineering, chemical defence and communications—as well as other specialised units, including electronic counter-measures (ECM), reconnaissance and mapping. 7 military region comds are sub-divided into 28 Military Districts. 18 Group Armies, org varies, normally with 2–3 mech/mot inf div/bde, 1 armd div/bde, 1 arty div/bde, 1 SAM/AAA or AAA bde (reorg to bde structure still in progress). Five Regions have rapid reaction units (RRU). The PLA Air Force has 3 RRU airborne divisions and the Navy two marine bde.

FORCES BY ROLE

Comd	7 mil regions (MR)
Armd	9 div; 7 bde; 1 (amph) bde; 1 (OPFOR) bde
Mech Inf	7 div; 2 (high alt) div; 5 bde; 1 (high alt) bde; 2 indep regt
Amph	2 (mech) div
Mot Inf	10 div; 3 (high alt) div; 1 (jungle) div; 19 mot inf bde; 2 (high alt) bde
Mtn Inf	2 bde
SF	7 units
AB	1 (manned by AF) corps with (3 AB div (35,000))
Arty	2 arty div, 17 arty bde
SSM/AShM	2 indep bde; 9 (coastal defence) regt
AD	21 bde; 1 indep regt

Engr	1 indep bde; 13 regt;
EW	5 regt
Sigs	50 regt
Sy	2 (Guard) div
Avn	1 bde; 9 avn regt, 2 (indep) regt (trg)

EQUIPMENT BY TYPE

MBT 7,050: 4,300 Type-59/Type-59D/Type-59-II; 300 Type-79; 500 Type-88A/B; 1,500 Type-96/Type-96A; 450 Type-98A/Type-99

LT TK 800: 200 Type-05 AAAV *ZTD-05*; 400 Type-62; 200 Type-63A

AIFV 2,390: 40 Type-03 (ZBD-03); 500 Type-04 (ZBD-04); 250 Type-05 AAAV (ZBD-05); 700 Type-86/Type-86A (WZ-501); 750 Type-92; 150 Type-92A

APC 2,700
  APC (T) 2,000: 1,650 Type-63/Type-63C; 350 Type-89
  APC (W) 700: 100 Type-09 (ZBL-09); 500 Type-92B; 100 WZ-523

ARTY 12,462+
  SP 1,710: **122mm** 1,296 Type-70-I/Type-89/Type-07 PLZ-07 **152mm** 324 Type-83; **155mm** 90 Type-05 PLZ-05
  TOWED 6,246: **122mm** 3,870 Type-54-1 (M-30) *M-1938*/Type-83/Type-60 (D-74)/Type-96 (D-30); **130mm** 270 Type-59 (M-46)/Type-59-I; **152mm** 2,106 Type-54 (D-1)/Type-66 (D-20); **155mm** 150 Type 88 WAC-21
  GUN/MOR 150+: **120mm** 150+: 100 2S23 *NONA-SVK*; 50+ PLL-05
  MRL 1,770+
    SP 1,716+: **107mm** some **122mm** 1,620 Type-81/Type-89; **300mm** 96 Type-03 *PHL-03*
    TOWED • 107mm 54 Type-63
  MOR 2,586
    TOWED 81mm Type-W87; **82mm** Type-53 (M-37)/Type-67/Type-82; **100mm** Type-71 (reported); **120mm** Type-55 (incl SP); **160mm** Type-56 (M-160)

AT
  MSL
    SP 276 HJ-9 *Red Arrow 9*
    MANPATS HJ-73A/HJ-73B/HJ-73C/HJ-8A/HJ-8C/HJ-8E
  RCL 3,966: **75mm** Type-56; **82mm** Type-65 (B-10)/Type-78; **105mm** Type-75; **120mm** Type-98
  RL 62mm Type-70-1
  GUNS 1,730: **100mm** 1,658: 1,308 Type-73 (T-12)/Type-86; 350 Type-02 *PTL02* **120mm** up to 72 Type-89 SP

HELICOPTERS

ATK 6-10 WZ-10
MRH 248: 22 Mi-17 *Hip H*; 12 Mi-17V7; 8 SA-316 *Alouette III*; 80 Z-9/9B; 100 Z-9 WA; 26 Z-9W
TPT 251 **Heavy** 14: 3 Mi-6 *Hook*; 4 Mi-26 *Halo*; 7 SA-321 *Super Frelon* **Medium** 184: 50 Mi-8T *Hip*; 57 Mi-171; 9 Mi-171V; 42 Mi-171V5; 8 Mi-172; 18 S-70C2 (S-70C) *Black Hawk* **Light** 53 AS-350 *Ecureuil*
UAV • ISR • Heavy BZK-005; WZ-5 **Medium** ASN-105; ASN-206 **Light** ASN-104; W-50 **Unknown** WZ-6 *BZK-006*

AD

SAM 290+:
  SP 290: 200 HQ-7A; 60 9K331 *Tor-M1* (SA-15 *Gauntlet*); 30 HQ-6D *Red Leader*

  MANPAD HN-5A/HN-5B *Hong Nu*; FN-6/QW-1/QW-2
GUNS 7,700+
  SP 25mm Type-95/Type-04; **37mm** Type-88; **57mm** Type-80
  TOWED 23mm Type-80 (ZU-23-2); **25mm** Type-85; **35mm** Type-90 (GDF-002); **37mm** Type-55 (M-1939)/Type-65/Type-74; **57mm** Type-59 (S-60); **85mm** Type-56 (M-1939) *KS-12*; **100mm** Type-59 (KS-19)

RADAR • LAND *Cheetah*; RASIT; Type-378

MSL
  AShM HY-1 (CSS-N-2) *Silkworm*; HY-2 (CSS-C-3) *Seersucker*; HY-4 (CSS-C-7) *Sadsack*
  ASM KD-10

Reserves

Armd	2 regt
Inf	18 div; 4 bde; 3 regt
Arty	3 div; 7 bde
AD	17 div; 8 bde; 8 regt
Engr	1 (pontoon bridging) bde; 15 regt; 3 (pontoon bridging) regt
Logistic	9 bde; 1 regt
Sigs	10 regt
Chemical	7 regt

Navy ε215,000; 40,000 conscript (total 255,000)

The PLA Navy organises and commands maritime operations conducted independently by its troops or in support of maritime operations. The PLA Navy is organised into five service arms: submarine, surface, naval aviation, coastal defence and marine corps, as well as other specialised units. There are three fleets, the Beihai Fleet (North Sea), Donghai Fleet (East Sea) and Nanhai Fleet (South Sea).

SUBMARINES 71

STRATEGIC • SSBN 3:
  1 *Xia* (Type 092) equipped with 12 JL-1 (CSS-N-3) strategic SLBM
  2 *Jin* (Type 094) each equipped with up to 12 JL-2 (CSS-NX-4) strategic SLBM (full operational status unknown; 2 additional vessels in build)

TACTICAL 68
  SSN 6:
    4 *Han* (Type 091) each with YJ-82 SSM, 6 single 533mm TT
    2 *Shang* (Type 093), 6 single 533mm TT (full operational status unknown, 3rd vessel in build)
  SSG 1 mod *Romeo* (Type SSG) with 6 YJ-1 (CSS-N-4) *Sardine* SSM, 8 single 533mm TT (test platform)
  SSK 60:
    12 *Kilo* (2 Project 877, 2 Project 636, 8 Project 636N) each with 3M54 *Klub* (SS-N-27 *Sizzler*) ASCM; 6 single 533mm TT with up to 18 *Test-71/96* HWT
    20 *Ming* (4 Type 035, 12 Type 035G, 4 Type 035B) each with 8 single 533mm TT
    8 *Romeo*† (Type 033) each with 8 533mm TT

16 *Song* (Type 039/039G) each with YJ-82 (CSS-N-8) *Saccade* ASCM, 6 single 533mm TT

4 *Yuan* (Type 39A/B) each with 6 533mm TT (2 further vessels launched in 2010; expected ISD 2011)

SS 1 *Golf* (SLBM trials)

PRINCIPAL SURFACE COMBATANTS 78

DESTROYERS 13

DDGHM 11:

4 *Hangzhou* (RF *Sovremenny*) each with 2 quad lnchr (8 eff.) each with 3M80/3M82 *Moskit* (SS-N-22 *Sunburn*) AShM, 2 3K90 *Uragan* (SA-N-7 *Grizzly*) SAM, 2 twin 533mm ASTT (4 eff.), 2 RBU 1000 *Smerch* 3, 2 twin 130mm gun (4 eff.), (capacity either 1 Z-9C (AS-565SA *Panther*) hel or 1 Ka-28 *Helix* A hel)

2 *Luyang* (Type 052B) each with 4 quad lnchr (16 eff.) each with YJ-83 AShM, 2 single lnchr each with 3K90 *Uragan* (SA-N-7 *Grizzly*) SAM, 2 triple 324mm TT (6 eff.) each with Yu-7 LWT, 1 100mm gun, (capacity 1 Ka-28 *Helix* A hel)

2 *Luyang II* (Type 052C) each with 2 quad lnchr (8 eff.) each with YJ-62 AShM, 8 sextuple VLS (48 eff.) each with HHQ-9 SAM, 2 triple 324mm TT (6 eff.) each with Yu-7 LWT, 1 100mm gun, (capacity 2 Ka-28 *Helix* A hel)

1 *Luhai* (Type 051B) with 4 quad lnchr (16 eff.) each with YJ-83 AShM, 1 octuple lnchr (8 eff.) with HQ-7 SAM, 2 triple 324mm ASTT (6 eff.) each with Yu-7 LWT, 1 twin 100mm gun (2 eff.), (capacity 2 Z-9C (AS-565SA *Panther*)/Ka-28 *Helix* A hel)

2 *Luhu* (Type 052) each with 4 quad lnchr (16 eff.) each with YJ-83 AShM, 1 octuple lnchr (8 eff.) with HQ-7 SAM, 2 triple 324mm ASTT (6 eff.) each with Yu-7 LWT, 2 FQF 2500 (24 eff.), 1 twin 100mm gun (2 eff.), (capacity 2 Z-9C (AS-565SA *Panther*) hel)

DDGM 2:

2 *Luzhou* (Type 051C) each with 2 quad lnchr (8 eff.) each with YJ-83 (C-803) AShM; 6 sextulpe VLS each with SA-N-20 *Grumble* SAM, 1 100mm gun, 1 hel landing platform

FRIGATES 65

FFGHM 23:

2 *Jiangkai* (Type 054) each with 2 quad lnchr (8 eff.) each with YJ-83 AShM, 1 octuple lnchr (8 eff.) with HQ-7 SAM, 2 triple 324mm TT (6 eff.) each with Yu-7 LWT, 2 RBU 1200 (10 eff.), 1 100mm gun, (capacity 1 Ka-28 *Helix* A/Z-9C (AS-565SA *Panther*) hel)

7 *Jiangkai II* (Type 054A) each with 2 quad lnchr (8 eff.) each with YJ-83 AShM, 1 VLS (32 eff.) with HQ-16 SAM (reported), 2 triple 324mm TT (6 eff.) each with Yu-7 LWT, 2 RBU 1200 (10 eff.), 1 76mm gun, (capacity 1 Ka-28 *Helix* A/Z-9C (AS-565SA *Panther*) hel)

4 *Jiangwei I* (Type 053H2G) each with 2 triple lnchr (6 eff.) each with YJ-83 AShM, 1 sextuple lnchr (6 eff.) with 1 HQ-61 (CSA-N-2) SAM, 2 RBU 1200 (10 eff.), 1 twin 100mm gun (2 eff.), (capacity: 2 Z-9C (AS-565SA *Panther*) hel)

10 *Jiangwei II* (Type 053H3) each with 2 quad lnchr (8 eff.) each with YJ-83 AShM, 1 octuple lnchr (8 eff.) with HQ-7 SAM, 2 RBU 1200 (10 eff.), 2 100mm gun, (capacity: 2 Z-9C (AS-565SA *Panther*) hel)

FFGH 1:

1 *Jianghu IV* (Type 053H1Q - trg role) with 1 triple lnchr (3 eff.) with SY-1 (CSS-N-1) *Scrubbrush* AShM, 4 RBU 1200 (20 eff.), 1 100mm gun, (capacity: 1 Z-9C (AS-565SA *Panther*) hel)

FFGM 2:

2 *Luda mod* (Type-051DT) each with 2 quad lnchr (8 eff.) each with YJ-1 (CSS-N-4) *Sardine* AShM, 1 octuple lnchr (8 eff.) with HQ-7 *Crotale* SAM, 2 FQF 2500 (24 eff.), 2 twin 130mm guns (4 eff.), (mine laying capability)

FFG 39:

11 *Jianghu I* (Type 053H) each with 2 triple lnchr (6 eff.) each with SY-1 (CSS-N-1) *Scrubbrush* AShM, 4 RBU 1200 (20 eff.), 2 100mm gun

8 *Jianghu II* (Type 053H1) each with 1 triple lnchr (3 eff.) with SY-1 (CSS-N-1) *Scrubbrush* AShM, 2 RBU 1200 (10 eff.), 1 twin 100mm gun (2 eff.), (capacity 1 Z-9C (AS-565SA) *Panther* hel)

3 *Jianghu III* (Type 053H2) each with 8 YJ-1 (CSS-N-4) *Sardine* AShM, 4 RBU 1200 (20 eff.), 2 twin 100mm gun (4 eff.)

6 *Jianghu V* (Type 053H1G) each with 1 triple lnchr (3 eff.) with SY-1 (CSS-N-1) *Scrubbrush* AShM, 2 RBU 1200 (10 eff.), 1 twin 100mm gun (2 eff.)

9 *Luda* (Type-051/051D/051Z) each with 2 triple 324mm ASTT (6 eff.), 2 FQF 2500 (24 eff.), 2 twin 130mm gun (4 eff.)

1 *Luda II* (Type 051G) with 2 triple lnchr (6 eff.) each with HY-2 (CSS-N-2) *Silkworm* AShM, 2 triple 324mm ASTT (6 eff.), 1 twin 130mm gun (2 eff.), (mine-laying capability)

1 *Luda III* (Type 051G II) with 2 triple lnchr (6 eff.) each with HY-2 (CSS-N-2) *Silkworm*/YJ-1 (CSS-N-4) *Sardine* AShM, 4 twin lnchr (8 eff.) each with YJ-1 (CSS-N-4) *Sardine* AShM, 2 triple 324mm ASTT (6 eff.), 2 twin 130mm gun (4 eff.)

PATROL AND COASTAL COMBATANTS 211+

PCFG 76+

65+ *Houbei* (Type 022) each with 2 quad lanchr (8 eff.) each with YJ-83 (C-803) AShM

11 *Huangfen* (Type 021) each with 2 twin lnchr (4 eff.) each with HY-2 (CSS-N-3 *Seersucker*) AShM

PCG 26

6 *Houjian* (Type 037/II) each with 2 triple lnchr (6 eff.) each with YJ-1 (CSS-N-4 *Sardine*) AShM

20 *Houxin* (Type 037/IG) each with 2 twin lnchr (4 eff.) each with YJ-1 (CSS-N-4 *Sardine*) AShM

PCC 75

3 *Haijui* (Type 037/I) each with 4 RBU 1200 (20 eff.)

50 *Hainan* (Type 037) each with ε4 RBU 1200 (20 eff.)

22 *Haiqing* (Type 037/IS) each with 2 type-87 (12 eff.)

PB 34+ *Haizui/Shanghai III* (Type 062/I)

MINE WARFARE 73

MINE COUNTERMEASURES 88

MCO 7: 6 *Wochi*; 1 *Wozang*

MSO 16 T-43

MSC 16 *Wosao*

MSD 49: 4 *Futi*-class (Type 312); 42 in reserve; 3 (other)

MINELAYERS • ML 1 *Wolei*

AMPHIBIOUS
PRINCIPAL AMPHIBIOUS VESSELS • LPD 1 *Yuzhao* (Type 071) (capacity 2 LCAC or 4 UCAC plus supporting vehicles; 500–800 troops; 2 hel) [1 further vessel launched in 2010, expected ISD 2011]

LANDING SHIPS 87
LSM 61:
10 *Yubei* (capacity 10 tanks or 150 troops)
1 *Yudeng* (Type 073) (capacity 6 tk; 180 troops)
10 *Yuhai* (capacity 2 tk; 250 troops)
30 *Yuliang* (Type 079) (capacity 5 tk; 250 troops)
10 *Yunshu* (Type 073A) (capacity 6 tk)
LST 26:
7 *Yukan* (capacity 10 tk; 200 troops)
9 *Yuting* (capacity 10 tk; 250 troops; 2 hel)
10 *Yuting* II (capacity 4 LCVP; 10 tk; 250 troops)
LANDING CRAFT 151
LCU 120 *Yunnan*
LCM 20 *Yuchin*
LCAC 1
UCAC 10

LOGISTICS AND SUPPORT 205
AORH 5: 2 *Fuqing*; 2 *Fuchi*; 1 *Nanyun*
AOT 50: 7 *Danlin*; 20 *Fulin*; 2 *Shengli*; 3 *Jinyou*; 18 *Fuzhou*
AO L 5 *Guangzhou*
AS 8: 1 *Dazhi*; 5 *Dalang*; 2 *Dazhou*
ASR 1 *Dajiang* (capacity: 2 SA-321 *Super Frelon*)
ARS 2: 1 *Dadong*; 1 *Dadao*
AG 6: 4 *Qiongsha* (capacity 400 troops); 2 *Qiongsha* (hospital conversion)
AK 23: 2 *Yantai*; 2 *Dayun*; 6 *Danlin*; 7 *Dandao*; 6 *Hongqi*
AWT 18: 10 *Leizhou*; 8 *Fuzhou*
AGOR 5: 1 *Dahua*; 2 *Kan*; 1 *Bin Hai*; 1 *Shuguang*
AGI 1 *Dadie*
AGM 5 (space and missile tracking)
AGS 6: 5 *Yenlai*; 1 *Ganzhu*
AGB 4: 1 *Yanbing*; 3 *Yanha*
ABU 7 *Yannan*
ATF 51: 4 *Tuzhong*; 10 *Hujiu*; 1 *Daozha*; 17 *Gromovoy*; 19 *Roslavl*
AH 1 *Daishan*
TRG 2: 1 *Shichang*; 1 *Daxin*
YDG 5 *Yen Pai*
MSL • AShM 72 YJ-62 (coastal defence) (3 regt)

Naval Aviation 26,000
FORCES BY ROLE
Bbr	2 regt with H-6G, 1 regt with H-5/H-6DU/ H-6G/Y-8X
Ftr	1 regt with J-7, 1 regt with J-7E, 1 regt J-8F, 1 regt with J-8H
FGA	1 regt with Su-30Mk2
Atk	2 regt with JH-7; 1 regt with JH-7A; 1 regt with JH-7A/Q-5C
ELINT/ISR	1 regt with SH-5; 1 regt with Y-8J/Y-8JB
Tpt	2 regt with Y-7; Y-8
Trg	1 regt with HY-7/JL-8; 1 regt with HY-7/HJ-5; 1 regt with CJ-6; 1 regt with JJ-6/JJ-7

Hel	2 regt with Ka-28 Helix A; Mi-8 Hip; Z-8; Z-8A; Z-8JH; Z-8S; Z-9C

AIRCRAFT 311 combat capable
BBR 50: 20 H-5; 30 H-6G
FTR 84: 36 J-7/J-7E *Fishbed* (being retired); 48 J-8F/H *Finback*
FGA 108: 84 JH-7/JH-7A; 24 Su-30Mk2 *Flanker*
ATK 30 Q-5 *Fantan*
ASW 4 SH-5
RECCE 13: 7 HZ-5; 6 Y-8J/Y-8JB *High New 2*
MP 4 Y-8X
TKR 3 H-6DU
TPT 66: **Medium** 4 Y-8 **Light** 62: 50 Y-5; 4 Y-7; 6 Y-7H; 2 Yak-42
TRG 94: 38 CJ-6; 5 HJ-5*; 21 HY-7; 14 JJ-6*; 4 JJ-7*; 12 JL-8*
HELICOPTERS
ASW 28: 13 Ka-28 *Helix A* (6 additional ac on order); 25 Z-9C
AEW 2 Ka-31
TPT 48 **Heavy** 40: 15 SA-321 *Super Frelon*; 20 Z-8/Z-8A; 3 Z-8JH; 2 Z-8S (SAR) **Medium** 8 Mi-8 *Hip*
MSL
AAM • IR AAM PL-5; PL-9; R-73 (AA-11 *Archer*) **SARH AAM** PL-11 **IR/SARH AAM** R-27 (AA-10 *Alamo*) **ARH AAM** R-77 (AA-12 *Adder*)
ASM Kh-31A (AS-17 *Krypton*); YJ-61 (CAS-1 (improved) *Kraken*); YJ-8K (CSS-N-4 *Sardine*); YJ-83K (CSSC-8 *Saccade*)
BOMBS
Conventional: Type-200-4/Type-200A
Laser-Guided: LS-500J;
TV-Guided: KAB-500KR; KAB-1500KR

Marines ε10,000
FORCES BY ROLE
Marine inf	2 bde (each: 2 tk bn, 1 recce bn, 4 mech inf bn, 1 arty bn, 1 comms bn, 1 eng bn,1 msl (AT/AD) bn; 1 spec ops bn; 1 SF amph recce bn)

EQUIPMENT BY TYPE
LT TK 124: 62 Type-63A; 62 Type-05 AAAV *ZTD-05*
APC (T) 248: 62 Type-63C; 62 Type-86; 124 Type-05 AAAV *ZBD-05*
ARTY 40+
SP 122mm 40+: 20+ Type-07; 20+ Type 89
MRL 107mm Type-63
MOR 82mm
AT
MSL • MANPATS HJ-73; HJ-8
RCL 120mm Type-98
AD • SAM • MANPAD HN-5 *Hong Nu/Red Cherry*

Air Force 300,000–330,000
The PLA Air Force (PLAAF) is organised into four service branches: aviation, SAM, AD and airborne. It also has comms, radar, ECM, chemical defence, tech recce and other specialised units. The PLAAF organises and commands air and AD operations throughout China, as

well as airborne operations. The PLAAF organises its command through seven military region air forces (MRAF) – Shenyang, Beijing, Lanzhou, Jinan, Nanjing, Guangzhou and Chengdu – and 14 div-level command posts. Under the command of the MRAF are 29 air div, surface-to-air missile and anti-aircraft artillery units, radar units, and other support troops.

Flying hours Ftr, ground attack and bbr pilots average 100-150 hrs/yr. Tpt pilots average 200+ per year. Each regt has two quotas to meet during the year – a total number of hours, and the percentage of flight time dedicated to tactics trg.

FORCES BY ROLE

Bbr	3 regt with H-6A/M; 2 regt with H-6H with YJ-63; 1 (nuclear ready) regt with H-6E
Ftr	10 regt with J-7 *Fishbed*; 10 regt with J-7E *Fishbed*; 4 regt with J-7G *Fishbed*; 3 regt with J-8B *Finback*; 3 regt with J-8D *Finback*; 2 regt with J-8F *Finback*; 2 regt with J-8H *Finback*; 8 regt with J-11/J-11B/Su-27SK *Flanker*
FGA	3 regt with Su-30MKK *Flanker*; 6 regt with J-10
Atk	3 regt with JH-7A; 5 regt with Q-5/Q-5D/Q-5E *Fantan*
ISR	2 regt with JZ-6*; 1 regt with JZ-8 *Finback*;1 regt with JZ-6/JZ-8F *Finback*; 1 regt with Y-8H1
EW	1 regt with Y-8G
AEW&C	1 regt with KJ-200/KJ-2000
CSAR	1 regt with Mi-171; Z-8
Tkr	1 regt with H-6U
Tpt	3 (VIP) regt with Il-76MD; Tu-154M; B-737-200; Y-8; An-30; 2 regt with Il-76MD *Candid B* (to support 15th and 16th Airborne armies); 1 regt with Y-7; Y-8; 1 regt with Y-7
Trg	1 regt with 12 H-6H; some regt with CJ-6/-6A/-6B; H-5; HJ-5; Y-7; JL-8 (K-8); JJ-5; JJ-6; JJ-7
Tpt Hel	Some regts with AS-332 *Super Puma* (VIP); Mi-8 *Hip*; Z-9 (AS-365N) *Dauphin 2*; Bell 214
AD	3 SAM div; 2 mixed AD div; 9 SAM bde; 2 mixed AD bde; 2 ADA bde; 9 indep SAM regt; 1 indep ADA regt; 4 indep SAM bn

EQUIPMENT BY TYPE

AIRCRAFT 1,687 combat capable
  BBR up to 82 H-6A/E/H/M
  FTR 986: 240 J-7 *Fishbed*; 240 J-7E *Fishbed*; 96 J-7G *Fishbed*; 72 J-8B *Finback*; 72 J-8D *Finback*; 48 J-8F *Finback*; 48 J-8H *Finback*; 95 J-11; 43 Su-27SK *Flanker*; 32 Su-27UBK *Flanker*
  FGA 313+: 144+ J-10; 24+ J-11B *Flanker*; 72 JH-7/JH-7A; 73 Su-30MKK *Flanker*
  ATK 120 Q-5/Q-5D/Q-5E *Fantan*
  EW 10 Y-8G
  ISR 99: 60 JZ-6*; 24 JZ-8 *Finback*; 12 JZ-8F *Finback*; 3 Y-8H1
  AEW&C 8+: 4+ KJ-200; 4 KJ-2000

TKR 10 H-6U
TPT 336+ **Heavy** 18 Il-76MD *Candid B* **Medium** 40+ Y-8; **Light** 239: 170 Y-5; 41 Y-7/Y-7H; 20 Y-11; 8 Y-12 **PAX** 39: 15 B-737-200 (VIP); 5 CL-601 *Challenger*; 2 Il-18 *Coot*; 17 Tu-154M *Careless*
TRG 490: 400 CJ-6/-6A/-6B; 50 JJ-7*; 40 JL-8*
HELICOPTERS
MRH 20 Z-9
TPT 60+: **Heavy** Some Z-8 (SA-321) **Medium** 6+ AS-332 *Super Puma* (VIP); 4 Bell 214; 50 Mi-8 *Hip*; some Mi-171
UAV • ISR • Heavy CH-1 *Chang Hong*; *Chang Kong* 1; *Firebee* **Light** *Harpy*
AD
  SAM 600+
    SP 300+: 24 HD-6D; 60+ HQ-7; 32 HQ-9; 24 HQ-12 (KS-1A); 32 S-300PMU (SA-10B)/64 S-300PMU1 (SA-10C) *Grumble*/64 S-300PMU2 (SA-10C) *Grumble*
    TOWED 300+ HQ-2 (SA-2) *Guideline* Towed/HQ-2A/HQ-2B(A)
  GUNS 16,000 **100mm/85mm**
MSL
  AAM • IR AAM PL-2B‡; PL-5B/C; PL-8; R-73 (AA-11 *Archer*); **SARH AAM** PL-11; **IR/SARH AAM** R-27 (AA-10 *Alamo*); **ARH AAM** PL-12; R-77 (AA-12 *Adder*)
  ASM KD-88; Kh-29 (AS-14 *Kedge*); Kh-31A/P (AS-17 *Krypton*); Kh-59 (AS-18 *Kazoo*); YJ-91 (Domestically produced Kh-31P variant)
  LACM YJ(KD)-63; CJ-10 (in development)

Military Regions

Direct Reporting Units

Air Force Headquarters
1 air div (34th, VIP Tpt) with (3 regt with An-30, B-747, CRJ200, Il-76MD, Tu-154M, B-747, Y-8, Y-7, An-30; 1 (flight test) regt)

Shenyang MR (North East)

Land Forces
3 Group Army (16th, 39th & 40th) (Heilongjiang, Jilin, Liaoning MD): 1 GA (16th) with (1 armd div, 2 mot inf div, 2 mot inf bde, 1 arty bde, 1 AD bde, 1 engr regt); 1 GA (39th) with (1 armd div, 1 mech inf div, 1 mot inf div; 1 mech inf bde, 1 arty bde, 1 AD bde, 1 avn regt); 1 GA (40th) with (1 armd bde, 2 mot inf bde, 1 arty bde, 1 AD bde, 1 engr regt); 1 mot inf bde; 1 EW regt; 1 SF unit.

Shenyang MRAF
1 air div (1st ftr) with (1 ftr regt with J-11/J-11B; 1 FGA regt with J-10; 1 ftr regt with J-8A); 1 air div (11th atk) with (1 atk regt with JH-7A; 1 atk regt with Q-5D); 1 air div (21st ftr) with (1 ftr regt with J-7E; 1 ftr regt with J-8H; 1 ftr regt with J-8B); 1 air div (30th ftr) with (2 ftr regt with J-7E; 1 ftr regt with J-8E); 1 indep recce regt with JZ-8; 3 trg schools with An-30/CJ-6/H-5/HJ-5/JJ-5/K-8/Y-7; 1 (mixed) AD bde; 1 SAM bde

Beijing MR (North)

Land Forces

3 Group Army (27th, 38th & 65th) (Beijing, Tianjin Garrison, Inner Mongolia, Hebei, Shanxi MD): 1 GA (27th) with (1 (OPFOR) armd bde, 2 mech inf bde, 2 mot inf bde, 1 arty bde, 1 AD bde, 1 engr regt); 1 GA (38th) with (1 armd div, 2 mech inf div, 1 arty bde, 1 AD bde, 1 engr regt, 1 avn regt); 1 GA (65th) with (1 armd div, 1 mech inf div, 1 mot inf bde, 1 arty bde, 1 AD bde, 1 engr regt, 1 avn regt); 2 (Beijing) sy div; 1 mot inf bde; 1 ADA bde; 1 SF unit.

Beijing MRAF

1 air div (7th ftr) with (1 ftr regt with J-11; 1 ftr regt with J-7G); 1 air div (15th ftr/atk) with (2 ftr regt with J-7; 1 atk regt with Q-5); 1 air div (24th ftr) with (1 ftr regt with J-8; 1 FGA regt with J-10); 1 Flight Test Centre with Su-30, Su-27/J-11, J-8C, J-10, J-7E, JJ-7 (on rotation); 1 trg base with J-7B, JJ-7; 2 trg schools with CJ-6/JJ-5/K-8; 3 SAM div; 1 (mixed) AD div

Lanzhou MR (West)

Land Forces

2 Group Army (21st & 47th) (Ningxia, Shaanxi, Gansu, Qing-hai, Xinjiang, South Xinjiang MD): 1 GA (21st) with (1 armd div, 1 mot inf div (RRU), 1 arty bde, 1 AD bde, 1 engr regt); 1 GA (47th) with (1 armd bde, 1 mech inf bde, 2 (high alt) mot inf bde, 1 arty bde, 1 AD bde, 1 engr regt); Xinjiang MD with (1 (high alt) mech div, 3 (high alt) mot div, 1 arty bde, 1 AD bde, 2 indep mech inf regt, 1 engr regt, 1 avn bde); 1 EW regt; 1 SF unit.

Lanzhou MRAF

1 air div (6th ftr) with (1 ftr regt with J-11; 1 ftr regt with J-7E; 1 ftr regt with J-7); 1 air div (36th bbr) with (1 surv regt with Y8H-1; 1 bbr regt with H-6M; 1 bbr regt with H-6H); 1 air div (37th ftr) with (1 ftr regt with J-8H; 1 ftr regt with J-7G; 1 ftr regt with J-7E); 2 trg schools with CJ-6, JJ-5; PLAAF Msl Testing Regt with JJ-6, J-7B; 1 (mixed) AD div; 1 SAM bde; 4 indep SAM regt

Jinan MR (Centre)

Land Forces

3 Group Army (20th, 26th & 54th) (Shandong, Henan MD): 1 GA (20th) with (1 armd bde, 1 mech inf bde, 1 mot inf bde, 1 arty bde, 1 AD bde, 1 engr regt); 1 GA (26th) with (1 armd div, 3 mot inf bde, 1 arty bde, 1 AD bde, 1 avn regt); 1 GA (54th) with (1 armd div, 2 mech inf div (RRU), 1 arty bde, 1 AD bde, 1 avn regt); 1 EW regt; 1 SF unit

North Sea Fleet

Coastal defence from DPRK border (Yalu River) to south of Lianyungang (approx 35°10′N); equates to Shenyang, Beijing and Jinan MR, and to seaward; HQ at Qingdao; support bases at Lushun, Qingdao. 9 coastal defence districts

2 **SSBN**; 4 **SSN**; 23 **SS**; 2 **DDGHM**; 2 **DDGM**; 2 **FFGHM**; 2 **FFGM**; 1 **FFGH**; 10 **FFG**; 1 **ML**; ε20 **PCFG/PCG**; 9 **LS**; ε7 **MCMV**

Jinan MRAF

1 air div (5th atk) with (1 atk regt with Q-5E; 1 atk regt with JH-7A); 1 air div (12th ftr) with (2 ftr regt with J-8B; 1 ftr regt with J-7G); 1 air div (19th ftr) with (1 ftr regt with Su-27SK; 1 ftr regt with J-7; 1 ftr regt with J-7E); 1 indep recce regt with JZ-6; 4 SAM bn

Nanjing MR (East)

Land Forces

3 Group Army (1st, 12th & 31st) (Shanghai Garrison, Jiangsu, Zhejiang, Fujian, Jiangxi, Anhui MD): 1 GA (1st) with (1 amph div, 1 arty div, 1 armd bde, 1 mot inf bde, 1 AD bde, 1 engr regt, 1 avn regt); 1 GA (12th) with (1 armd div, 3 mot inf bde (1 RRU), 1 arty bde, 1 AD bde, 1 engr regt); 1 GA (31st) (2 mot inf div (1 RRU), 1 (amph) armd bde, 1 mot inf bde, 1 arty bde, 1 AD bde, 1 avn regt); 1 SSM bde; 1 SF unit.

East Sea Fleet

Coastal defence from south of Lianyungang to Dongshan (approx 35°10′N to 23°30′N); equates to Nanjing Military Region, and to seaward; HQ at Ningbo; support bases at Fujian, Zhoushan, Ningbo. 7 coastal defence districts

16 **SS**; 4 **DDGHM**; 13 **FFGHM**; 14 **FFG**; ε35 **PCFG/PCG**; 27 **LS**; ε22 **MCMV**

Nanjing MRAF

1 air div (3rd ftr) with (1 FGA regt with J-10; 1 ftr regt with J-7E; 1 FGA regt with Su-30MKK); 1 air div (10th bbr) with (2 bbr regt with H-6E; 1 EW regt with Y-8D); 1 air div (14th ftr) with (1 ftr regt with J-11; 1 ftr regt with J-7E); 1 air div (26th Special Mission) with (1 AEW&C regt with KJ-2000/KJ-200; 1 CSAR regt with M-171/Z-8; 1 recce regt with JZ-8F); 1 air div (28th atk) with (1 atk regt with JH-7A; 2 atk regt with Q-5D); 1 air div (29th ftr) with (1 FGA regt with Su-30MKK; 1 ftr regt with J-11; 1 ftr regt with J-8D); 1 trg school with K-8, JJ-5, CJ-6; 3 SAM bde; 1 ADA bde; 2 indep SAM regt

Guangzhou MR (South)

Land Forces

2 Group Army (41st & 42nd) (Hubei, Hunan, Guang-dong, Guangxi, Hainan MD): 1 GA (41st) with (1 mech inf div (RRU), 1 mot inf div, 1 armd bde, 1 arty bde, 1 AD bde, 1 engr regt); 1 GA (42nd) with (1 amph div (RRU), 1 mot inf div, 1 arty div, 1 armd bde, 1 AD bde, 1 avn regt); 1 mot inf bde; 1 (composite) mot inf bde (Composed of units drawn from across the PLA and deployed to Hong Kong on a rotational basis); 1 AD bde; 1 SSM bde; 1 EW regt; 1 SF unit

South Sea Fleet

Coastal defence from Dongshan (approx 23°30′N) to VNM border; equates to Guangzhou MR, and to

seaward (including Paracel and Spratly Islands); HQ at Zuanjiang; support bases at Yulin, Guangzhou
1 **SSBN**; 2 **SSN**; 18 **SS**; 5 **DDGHM**; 8 **FFGHM**; 15 **FFG**; ε40 **PCFG/PCG**; 1 **LPD**; 51 **LS**; ε10 **MCMV**

Guangzhou MRAF

1 air div (2nd ftr) with (1 ftr regt with J-7G; 1 FGA regt with J-10; 1 ftr regt with Su-27SK/J-11); 1 air div (8th bbr/tkr) with (1 tkr regt with H-6U; 1 bbr regt with H-6H; 1 bbr regt with H-6E); 1 air div (9th ftr) with (1 FGA regt with J-10; 2 ftr regt with J-8D); 1 air div (13th airlift) with (2 tpt regt with IL-76MD; 1 tpt regt with Y-7/Y-8); 1 air div (18th ftr) with (1 ftr regt with J-7; 1 FGA regt with Su-30MKK); 1 air div (42nd ftr) with (2 ftr regt with J-7); 1 indep recce regt with JZ-6; 4 SAM Bde, 1 ADA bde, 1 indep ADA regt

Chengdu MR (South-West)

Land Forces

2 Group Army (13th & 14th) (Chongqing Garrison, Sichuan, Guizhou, Yunnan, Tibet MD): 1 GA(13th) with (1 (high alt) mech inf div (RRU), 1 mot inf div, 1 armd bde, 1 arty bde, 1 AD bde, 1 avn regt, 1 engr regt); 1 GA (14th) with (1 (jungle) mot inf div, 1 mot inf div, 1 armd bde, 1 arty bde, 1 AD bde); 1 (high alt) indep mech inf bde; 2 indep mtn inf bde; 1 EW regt; 1 SF unit.

Chengdu MRAF

1 air div (4th airlift) with Y-7/Mi-17; 1 air div (33rd ftr) with (1 ftr regt with J-7E; 1 ftr regt with J-11; 1 ftr regt with J-7); 1 air div (44th ftr) with (2 ftr regt with J-7; 1 FGA regt with J-10); 1 trg school with H-5, HJ-5, CJ-6; 1 (mixed) AD bde; 3 indep SAM regt

Paramilitary 660,000+ active

People's Armed Police ε660,000

Internal Security Forces ε400,000

Security   14 (mobile) div; 22 (mobile) indep regt; some (firefighting & garrison) units

Border Defence Force (incl Coast Guard) ε260,000

Border   30 div HQ; 110 (border) regt; 20 (marine)
Guard   regt

PATROL AND COASTAL COMBATANTS 154+
PCO 16; **PB/PBF** 138+

China Maritime Surveillance

Patrols China's EEZ
PATROL AND COASTAL COMBATANTS 68+
PSO 6; **PCO** 14; **PB/PBF** 48+

Maritime Safety Administration (MSA)

Various tasks including aid to navigation
PATROL AND COASTAL COMBATANTS 207+
PB 207+

Fisheries Law Enforcement Command (FLEC)

Enforces Chinese fishery regulations
PATROL AND COASTAL COMBATANTS 133+
PSO 4; **PCO** 11; **PB/PBF** 118+

DEPLOYMENT

CÔTE D'IVOIRE
UN • UNOCI 6 obs

DEMOCRATIC REPUBLIC OF THE CONGO
UN • MONUSCO; 218; 16 obs; 1 engr coy; 1 fd hospital

GULF OF ADEN
Navy: 1 DDGHM; 1 LPD; 1 AORH

LEBANON
UN • UNIFIL 344; 1 engr coy; 1 fd hospital

LIBERIA
UN • UNMIL 564; 2 obs; 1 engr coy; 1 tpt coy; 1 fd hospital

MIDDLE EAST
UN • UNTSO 5 obs

SUDAN
UN • UNAMID 319; 2 obs; 1 engr coy
UN • UNMIS 437; 12 obs; 1 engr coy; 1 tpt coy; 1 fd hospital

TIMOR LESTE
UN • UNMIT 2 obs

WESTERN SAHARA
UN • MINURSO 5 obs

Fiji FJI

Fijian Dollar F$		2009	2010	2011
GDP	F$	5.77bn	6.24bn	
	US$	2.96bn	3.20bn	
per capita	US$	3,480	3,746	
Growth	%	-2.5	2.0	
Inflation	%	3.7	6.0	
Def bdgt	F$	100m	108m	100m
	US$	51m	55m	
US$1=F$		1.95	1.95	

Population   854,098

Ethnic groups: Fijian 51%; Indian 44%; European/Others 5%

Age	0–14	15–19	20–24	25–29	30–64	65 plus
Male	14.8%	4.7%	4.5%	4.5%	20.0%	2.4%
Female	14.1%	4.5%	4.2%	4.2%	19.3%	2.8%

Capabilities

ACTIVE 3,500 (Army 3,200 Navy 300)

RESERVE ε6,000
(to age 45)

ORGANISATIONS BY SERVICE

Army 3,200 (incl 300 recalled reserves)
FORCES BY ROLE

Inf	3 inf bn; 4 reserve inf bn.
Spec Ops	1 coy
Arty	1 bty
Engr	1 bn

EQUIPMENT BY TYPE
ARTY 16
    TOWED 85mm 4 25-pdr (ceremonial)
    MOR 81mm 12
HELICOPTERS
    MRH 1 AS-365 *Dauphin 2*
    TPT • **Light** 1 AS-355 *Ecureuil*

Navy 300
EQUIPMENT BY TYPE
PATROL AND COASTAL COMBATANTS • PB 7: 3 *Kula*; 2 *Levuka*; 2 *Vai*
LOGISTICS AND SUPPORT • TRG 1 *Cagi Donu* (Presidential Yacht)
FACILITIES

Bases	Located at Viti (trg), Walu Bay

DEPLOYMENT

EGYPT
MFO 338; 1 inf bn

IRAQ
UN • UNAMI 221; 3 sy unit

SUDAN
UN • UNMIS 6 obs

TIMOR LESTE
UN • UNMIT 1 obs

India IND

Indian Rupee Rs		2009	2010	2011
GDP	Rs	59.5tr	70.8tr	
	US$	1.23tr	1.55tr	
per capita	US$	1,065	1,273	
Growth	%	7.2	8.5	
Inflation	%	10.9	13.2	
Def exp	Rs	1.85tr		
	US$	38.3bn		
Def bdgt	Rs	1.67tr	1.76tr	
	US$	34.4bn	38.4bn	
US$1=Rs		48.37	45.84	

Population   1,214,464,312

Religious groups: Hindu 80%; Muslim 14%; Christian 2%; Sikh 2%

Age	0–14	15–19	20–24	25–29	30–64	65 plus
Male	15.8%	5.0%	4.6%	4.4%	19.5%	2.6%
Female	13.9%	4.4%	4.2%	4.0%	18.7%	2.9%

Capabilities

ACTIVE 1,325,000 (Army 1,129,900, Navy 58,350 Air 127,200, Coast Guard 9,550) **Paramilitary 1,300,586**

RESERVE 1,155,000 (Army 960,000 Navy 55,000 Air 140,000) **Paramilitary 987,821**
Army first line reserves (300,000) within 5 years of full time service, further 500,000 have commitment to the age of 50.

ORGANISATIONS BY SERVICE

Strategic Forces Command
India's Nuclear Command Authority (NCA) controls the nation's nuclear weapons. The NCA comprises a Political Council and an Executive Council. The Political Council, chaired by the Prime Minister, is the only body that can authorise nuclear weapons use; the Executive Council, chaired by the National Security Advisor to the Prime Minister, provides inputs for decision making by the NCA and executes directives given by the Political Council. Strategic Forces Command (SFC) is a tri-service command established in 2003. The Commander-in-Chief of SFC, a senior three-star military officer, manages and administers all Strategic Forces through separate Army and Air Force chains of command, with the army responsible for all nuclear-capable land-based ballistic missiles and the air force responsible for all nuclear-capable fixed-wing aircraft (the navy is not yet nuclear-capable). The navy is also establishing its own chain of comd, following the launch of INS *Arihant* in July 2009. The C-in-C SFC reports directly to the Chairman, Chiefs of Staff Committee.

FORCES BY ROLE

Msl 2 Gps with SS-150/SS-250 *Prithvi*
    1 Gp with *Agni* I
    1 Gp with *Agni*-II

EQUIPMENT BY TYPE

MSL • STRATEGIC

IRBM 80–100 *Agni* I; 20–25 *Agni*-II; *Agni*-III (successfully tested)

SRBM 60 msl produced 1993–1999. Up to 20 SS-150 *Prithvi* I/SS-250 *Prithvi* II msl produced each year; SS-350 *Dhanush* (naval testbed)

Some Indian Air Force assets (such as *Mirage* 2000H or Su-30MKI) could be tasked with a strategic role

Army 1,129,900

FORCES BY ROLE

6 Regional Comd HQ (Northern, Western, Central, Southern, Eastern, South Western), 1 Training Comd (ARTRAC), 13 corps HQ (3 (1st, 2nd, 21st) strike corps, 10 (3th, 4th, 9th–11th, 12th (Desert), 14th–16th, 33rd), 'holding' corps

Armd	3 div (each: 2–3 armd bde, 1 SP arty bde (1 medium regt, 1 SP arty regt)); 8 indep bde; (total: 13 regt with T-55; 35 regt with T-72M1; 5 regt with T-90S; 14 regt with *Vijayanta*)
Mech Inf	4 RAPID div (each: 2 mech inf, 1 armd bde); 2 indep bde (25 bn in total)
Inf	18 div (each: 1 arty bde, 2–5 inf bde); 7 indep bde; (319 bn in total)
Mtn Inf	10 div (each: 3–4 mtn inf bde, 3-4 arty regt); 2 indep bde
SF	5-7 bn
AB	1 para bde, 5 bn
Arty	2 div (each: 2 arty bde (each: 3 med arty, 1 composite regt (1 SATA/MRL regt))
Med Arty	63 regt (bn)
SP Med Arty	1 regt (bn)
Fd Arty	118 regt
SP Fd Arty	3 regt (bn)
MRL	4 regt (bn)
Mor	15 regt
SSM	2 (*Prithvi*) regt; 1 (*Agni*) regt; 2-3 PJ-10 (*BrahMos*) regt
Engr	4 bde
Hel	14 sqn
AD	6 bde; 5 'flak' regt with 320 ZU-23-2 (some SP); 30 'flak' regt with 1,920 L40/70 (each: 4 AD bty); 35+ regt
SAM	12 regt; 2 gp (each: 2–5 SAM bty)

EQUIPMENT BY TYPE

MBT 4,117+ (ε1,133 in reserve): 320+ T-90S (to replace *Vijayanta* and T-55); 124 *Arjun*; 1,950 T-72M1; 1,008 *Vijayanta* (modified) 715 T-55 (modifications similar to *Vijayanta*)

RECCE 110 BRDM-2 each with AT-4 *Spigot*/AT-5 *Spandrel*; *Ferret* (used for internal security duties along with some indigenously built armd cars)

AIFV 1,455+: 350+ BMP-1; 980 *Sarath* (BMP-2); 125 BMP-2K

APC 331+

    APC (W) 331+: ε160 *Casspir*; 157+ OT-62/OT-64; 14 *Yukthirath* MPV (of 327 order)

ARTY 10,758+

    SP 20+: **130mm** 20 M-46 *Catapult*; **152mm** 2S19 *Farm*

    TOWED 4,010+: **105mm** 1,350+: 600+ IFG Mk1/Mk2/Mk3 (being replaced); up to 700 LFG; 50 M-56 **122mm** 550 D-30; **130mm** 1,700: 1,200 M-46; 500 (in process of upgrading to 155mm); (500 in store) **155mm** 410 FH-77B

    MRL 208: **122mm** ε150 BM-21/LRAR **214mm** 30 *Pinaka* (non operational) **300mm** 28 9A52 *Smerch*

    MOR 6,520+

        SP 120mm E1

        TOWED 6520+: **81mm** 5,000+ E1 **120mm** ε1,500 AM-50/E1 **160mm** 20 M-58 *Tampella*

AT • MSL

    SP 9K111 (AT-4 *Spigot*); 9K113 (AT-5 *Spandrel*)

    MANPATS 9K11 (AT-3 *Sagger*) (being phased out); 9K111 (AT-4 *Spigot*); 9K113 (AT-5 *Spandrel*); *Milan* 2

    RCL 84mm *Carl Gustav*; **106mm** 3,000+ M-40A1 (10 per inf bn)

HELICOPTERS

MRH 222: 30 *Dhruv*; 12 *Lancer*; 120 SA-315B *Lama* (*Cheetah*); 60 SA-316B *Alouette III* (*Chetak*)

AD • SAM 3,500+

    SP 880+: 180 2K12 *Kub* (SA-6 *Gainful*); 50+ 9K33 *Osa* (SA-8B *Gecko*); 400 9K31 *Strela*-1 (SA-9 *Gaskin*); 250 9K35 *Strela*-10 (SA-13 *Gopher*)

    MANPAD 2,620+: 620 9K32 *Strela*-2 (SA-7 *Grail* – being phased out)‡; 2,000+ 9K31 *Igla*-1 (SA-16 *Gimlet*)

    GUNS 2,395+

        SP 155+: **23mm** 75 ZSU-23-4; ZU-23-2 (truck-mounted); **30mm** 20-80 2S6 *Tunguska*

        TOWED 2,240+: **20mm** Oerlikon (reported); **23mm** 320 ZU-23-2; **40mm** 1,920 L40/70

UAV • ISR • Medium 26: 14 *Nishant*; 12 *SearcherMk* I/*Searcher* Mk II

RADAR • LAND 12+: 12 AN/TPQ-37 *Firefinder*; BSR Mk.2; *Cymbeline*; EL/M-2140; M-113 A1GE *Green Archer* (mor); MUFAR; *Stentor*

AMPHIBIOUS 2 LCVP

MSL • SSM 8–10 PJ-10 *BrahMos*; 80–100 *Agni* I; 20–25 *Agni* II; *Agni* III; up to 20 SS-150 *Prithvi* I/SS-250 *Prithvi* II msl produced each year

Reserve Organisations

Reserves 300,000 reservists (1st line reserve within 5 years full time service); 500,000 reservists (commitment until age of 50) (total 800,000)

Territorial Army 160,000 reservists (only 40,000 regular establishment)

Army	6 Ecological bn; 37 Non-departmental units (raised from government ministries)
Inf	25 bn
AD	20 'flak' regt with 1,280 L40/60

Navy 58,350 (incl 7,000 Naval Avn and 1,200 Marines)

Fleet HQ New Delhi; Commands located at Mumbai, Vishakhapatnam, Kochi & Port Blair

EQUIPMENT BY TYPE

SUBMARINES • TACTICAL 16

SSN 1 *Chakra* (RUS *Nerpa*) each with 4 single 533mm TT each with 3M54 *Klub* (SS-N-27 *Sizzler*) SLCM, 4 single 650mm TT each with T-65 HWT; (RUS lease agreement - under trials; not at full OC)

SSK 15:

4 *Shishumar* (GER T-209/1500) each with 1 single 533mm TT

4 *Sindhughosh* (FSU *Kilo*) each with 6 single 533mm TT (of which 2 undergoing phased refit of 3M54 *Klub* (SS-N-27 *Sizzler*) SLCM)

6 *Sindhughosh* (FSU *Kilo*) with 6 single 533mm TT each with 3M54 *Klub* (SS-N-27 *Sizzler*) SLCM

1 *Vela* (FSU *Foxtrot* – to be decommissioned) with 10 single 533mm TT (6 forward, 4 aft)

PRINCIPAL SURFACE COMBATANTS 23

AIRCRAFT CARRIERS • CVS 1 *Viraat* (UK *Hermes*) (capacity 30 Sea Harrier FRS 1 (*Sea Harrier* FRS MK51) FGA ac; 7 Ka-27 *Helix* ASW hel/*Sea King* Mk42B ASW hel)

DESTROYERS 10:

DDGHM 5:

3 *Delhi* each with 4 quad lnchr (16 eff.) each with 3M-24 *Uran* (SS-N-25 *Switchblade*) AShM, 2 single lnchr each with 3K90 *Uragan* (SA-N-7 *Gadfly*) SAM, 5 single 533mm ASTT, 1 100mm gun, (capacity either 2 *Dhruv* hel/*Sea King* Mk42A ASW hel)

2 *Shivalik* each with 1 octuple VLS (8 eff.) with 3M54 *Klub* (SS-N-27 *Sizzler*) ASCM, 1 octuple VLS (8 eff.) with *Barak* SAM, 6 single lnchr with 3K90 *Uragan* (SA-N-7 *Gadfly*) SAM, 1 76mm gun, (capacity 1 *Sea King* Mk42B ASW hel) (3rd vessel expected ISD 2011)

DDGM 5:

2 *Rajput* (FSU *Kashin*) each with 2 twin lnchr (4 eff.) each with R-15M *Termit M* (SS-N-2C *Styx*) AShM, 2 twin lnchr (4 eff.) each with M-1 *Volna* (SA-N-1 *Goa*) SAM, 5 single 533mm ASTT, 2 RBU 6000 *Smerch* 2 (24 eff.), 1 76mm gun, (capacity 1 Ka-25 *Hormone*/ Ka-28 *Helix A* hel)

1 *Rajput* (FSU *Kashin*) each with 2 twin lnchr (4 eff.) each with PJ-10 BrahMos ASCM, 2 twin lnchr (4 eff.) each with R-15M *Termit M* (SS-N-2C *Styx*) AShM, 2 twin lnchr (4 eff.) each with M-1 *Volna* (SA-N-1 *Goa*) SAM, 5 single 533mm ASTT, 2 RBU 6000 *Smerch* 2 (24 eff.), 1 76mm gun, (capacity 1 Ka-25 *Hormone*/ Ka-28 *Helix A* hel)

2 *Rajput* (FSU *Kashin*) each with 1 octuple VLS (8 eff.) with PJ-10 *BrahMos* ASCM, 2 twin lnchr (4 eff.) each with R-15M *Termit M* (SS-N-2C *Styx*) AShM, 2 octuple VLS (16 eff.) each with *Barak* SAM. 1 twin lnchr (2 eff.) with M-1 *Volna* (SA-N-1 *Goa*) SAM, 5 single 533mm ASTT, 2 RBU 6000 *Smerch* 2 (24 eff.), 1 76mm gun, (capacity 1 Ka-25 *Hormone*/Ka-28 *Helix A* hel)

FRIGATES 12:

FFGHM 9:

3 *Brahmaputra* each with 4 quad lnchr (16 eff.) each with SS-N-25 *Switchblade* AShM, 1 octuple VLS (8 eff.) with *Barak* SAM, 2 triple 324mm ASTT (6 eff.), 1 76mm gun, (capacity 2 SA-316B *Alouette III* (*Chetak*)/ *Sea King* Mk42 ASW hel)

3 *Godavari* each with 4 single lnchr each with R-15 *Termit M* (SS-N-2D *Styx*) AShM, 1 octuple VLS (8 eff.) with *Barak* SAM, 2 triple 324mm ASTT (6 eff.), 1 76mm gun, (capacity 2 SA-316B *Alouette III* (*Chetak*)/ *Sea King* MK42 ASW hel)

3 *Talwar I* each with 1 octuple VLS (8 eff.) with 3M54 Klub (SS-N-27 *Sizzler*) AShM, 6 single lnchr each with 3K90 *Uragan* (SA-N-7 *Gadfly*) SAM, 2 twin 533mm ASTT (4 eff.), 2 RBU 6000 *Smerch* 2 (24 eff.), 2 CADS-N-1 *Kashtan* CIWS, 1 100mm gun, (capacity 1 *Dhruv*/Ka-31 *Helix B* AEW hel/Ka-28 *Helix A* ASW hel)

FFH 3:

3 *Nilgri* each with 2 triple (6 eff.) 324mm ASTT, 2 twin (4 eff.) 114mm gun (capacity 1 SA-316B *Alouette III* (*Chetak*) hel/*Sea King* Mk42 ASW hel)

PATROL AND COASTAL COMBATANTS 49

CORVETTES 24:

FSGM 20:

4 *Khukri* each with 2 twin lnchr (4 eff.) each with R-15M *Termit M* (SS-N-2C *Styx*) AShM, 2 twin lnchr (4 eff.) each with 9K32M *Strela*-2M (SA-N-5 *Grail*) SAM, 1 76mm gun, 1 hel landing platform (For *Dhruv*/SA-316 *Alouette III* (*Chetak*))

4 *Kora* each with 4 quad lnchr (16 eff.) each with 3M24 *Uran* (SS-N-25 *Switchblade*) AShM, 1 quad (4 eff.) with 9K32M *Strela*-2M (SA-N-5 *Grail*) SAM, 1 76mm gun, 1 hel landing platform (For *Dhruv*/SA-316 *Alouette III* (*Chetak*))

10 *Veer* (FSU *Tarantul*) each with 4 single lnchr each with R-15 *Termit M* (SS-N-2D *Styx*) AShM, 2 quad lnchr (8 eff. - manual aiming) each with 9K32M *Strela*-2M (SA-N-5 *Grail*), 1 76mm gun

2 *Prabal* (mod *Veer*) each with 4 quad lnchr (16 eff.) each with 3M24 *Uran* (SS-N-25 *Switchblade*) AShM, 1 quad lnchr (manual aiming) with 9K32M *Strela*-2M (SA-N-5 *Grail*) SAM, 1 76mm gun

FSM 4:

4 *Abhay* (FSU *Pauk* II) each with 1 quad lnchr (manual aiming) with 9K32M *Strela*-2M (SA-N-5 *Grail*) SAM, 2 single 533mm ASTT (twin), 2 RBU 1200 (10 eff.), 1 76mm gun

PSOH 6 *Sukanya* (capacity 1 SA-316 *Alouette III* (*Chetak*))

PCC 13: 7 *Car Nicobar*; 6 *Trinkat* (SDB Mk5)

PBF 7 *Super Dvora*

PB 2 SDB Mk3

MINE WARFARE • MINE COUNTERMEASURES 10

MSO 10 *Pondicherry* (FSU *Natya*)

AMPHIBIOUS 17

PRINCIPAL AMPHIBIOUS VESSELS • LPD 1

Jalashwa (US *Austin*) (capacity up to 6 med spt hel; either 9 LCM or 4 LCM and 2 LCAC; 4 LCVP; 930 troops)

LANDING SHIPS 10
LSM 5 *Kumbhir* (FSU *Polnocny* C) (capacity 5 MBT or 5 APC; 160 troops)
LST 5:
2 *Magar* (capacity 15 MBT or 8 APC or 10 trucks; 500 troops)
3 *Magar* mod (capacity 11 MBT or 8 APC or 10 trucks; 500 troops)
LANDING CRAFT • LCU 6 *Vasco de Gama* Mk2/3 LC (capacity 2 APC; 120 troops)
LOGISTICS AND SUPPORT 48
AORH 3: 1 *Aditya* (mod *Deepak*); 1 *Deepak*; 1 *Jyoti*
AOL 6
ASR 1
AWT 2
AGOR 1 *Sagardhwani*
AGHS 8 *Sandhayak*
AGS 1 *Makar*
ATF 1
TPT 3 *Nicobar*
TRG 4: 1 *Krishna* (UK *Leander*) 1 *Tir*; 2 AXS
TRV 1
YDT 3
YTL/YTM 14

FACILITIES

Bases   Located at Mumbai, Karwar (under construction), Calcutta, Vishakhapatnam, Port Blair (Andaman Is), Kochi
Naval air base Located at Arakonam, Goa

Naval Aviation 7,000

Flying hours   125–150 hrs/year on *Sea Harrier*

FORCES BY ROLE

FGA   1 sqn with MiG-29K *Fulcrum*; 1 sqn with *Sea Harrier* FRS 1 (Mk51); *Sea Harrier* T-4N (T-60)

ASW   5 sqn with Ka-25 *Hormone*; Ka-28 *Helix A*; Ka-31 *Helix B*; SA-316B *Alouette III* (*Chetak*); *Sea King* Mk42A/*Sea King* Mk42B

MP   2 sqn with BN-2 *Islander*; Do-228-101; Il-38 *May*; Tu-142M *Bear F*

SAR   1 sqn with SA-316B *Alouette III* (*Chetak*); *Sea King* Mk42C

Tpt   1 (comms) sqn with Do-228; 1 sqn with HS-748M (HAL-784M); 1 sqn with UH-3H *Sea King*

Trg   2 sqn with HJT-16 MkI *Kiran*; HJT-16 MkII *Kiran II*; HPT-32 *Deepak*

ISR UAV   1 sqn with *Heron*; *Searcher* MkII

EQUIPMENT BY TYPE

AIRCRAFT 26 combat capable
FTR 6 MiG-29K *Fulcrum*
FGA 11: 9 *Sea Harrier* FRS 1 (Mk51); 2 *Sea Harrier* T-4N (T-60)
ASW 9: 5 Il-38 *May*; 4 Tu-142M *Bear F*
MP 14 Do-228-101
TPT 37: **Light** 27: 17 BN-2 *Islander*; 10 Do-228 **PAX** 10 HS-748M (HAL-784M)

TRG 20: 6 HJT-16 MkI *Kiran*; 6 HJT-16 MkII *Kiran II*; 8 HPT-32 *Deepak*
HELICOPTERS
ASW 54: 7 Ka-25 *Hormone*; 12 Ka-28 *Helix A*; 21 *Sea King* Mk42A; 14 *Sea King* Mk42B
MRH 53: 4 *Dhruv*; 26 SA-316B *Alouette III* (*Chetak*); 23 SA-319 *Alouette III*
AEW 9 KA-31 *Helix B*
TPT • Medium 11: 5 *Sea King* Mk42C; up to 6 UH-3H *Sea King*
UAV • ISR 12 **Heavy** 4 *Heron* **Medium** 8 *Searcher* Mk II
MSL
AShM *Sea Eagle*; KH-35/*Sea Skua* (*Bear* and *May* a/c cleared to fire *Sea Eagle* and Kh-35)
ASCM PJ-10 *BrahMos*
AAM • IR AAM R-550 *Magic 2*/R-550 *Magic*; R-73 (AA-11 *Archer*) **IR/SARH AAM** R-27 (AA-10 *Alamo*) **ARH AAM** *Derby*; R-77 (AA-12 *Adder*)

Marines ε1,200 (Additional 1,000 for SPB duties)

As a consequence of the Mumbai attacks, the Sagar Prahari Bal (SPB) was established to protect critical maritime infrastructure. The estimated force strength is 1,000 pers with 80 PBF

FORCES BY ROLE

Amph   1 bde
Cdo   1 (marine) force

Air Force 127,200

5 regional air comds: Western (New Delhi), South-Western (Gandhinagar), Eastern (Shillong), Central (Allahabad), Southern (Trivandrum). Maintenance Cmd (Nagpur), Trg Comd (Bangalore)

Flying hours   180 hrs/year

FORCES BY ROLE

Ftr   3 sqn with MiG-29 *Fulcrum*; MiG-29UB *Fulcrum*

FGA   4 sqn with *Jaguar* IB/IS; 8 sqn with MiG-21bis/*Bison*; 4 sqn with MiG-21M/MF *Fishbed*; 6 sqn with MiG-27ML *Flogger*; 3 sqn with *Mirage* 2000E (2000H); *Mirage* 2000ED (2000TH) (secondary ECM role); 6 sqn with Su-30 MKI *Flanker*

ASuW   1 sqn with *Jaguar* IS with *Sea Eagle* AShM

ISR   1 sqn with Gulfstream IV SRA-4

AEW&C   1 sqn with IL-76 TD *Phalcon*

Tkr   1 sqn with Il-78 *Midas*

Tpt   7 sqn with An-32 *Cline*; 1 sqn with B-737; B-737 BBJ; EMB-145BJ; 4 sqns with Do-228; HS-748; 2 sqn with Il-76 *Candid*; 1 flt with EMB-135BJ

Trg   Some units with An-32; Do-228; *Hawk* Mk 132*; HJT-16 *Kiran*; HPT-32 *Deepak*; *Jaguar* IS/IM; MiG-21bis; MiG-21FL; MiG-21M/MF; MiG-27ML*; SA-316B *Alouette III* (*Chetak*)

Atk Hel   2 sqn with Mi-25 *Hind*; Mi-35 *Hind*

Tpt Hel	2 sqn with *Dhruv*; 9 sqn with Mi-8 Hip; 6 sqn with Mi-17 *Hip* H/Mi-17 IV; 1 sqn with Mi-26 *Halo*; 3 sqn with SA-315B *Lama* (*Cheetah*); 5 sqn *with* SA-316B *Alouette III* (*Chetak*)
ISR UAV	5 sqn with *Searcher* Mk II
AD	25 sqn with S-125 *Pechora* (SA-3B *Goa*); 6 sqn with 9K33 *Osa-AK* (SA-8B *Gecko*); 10 flt with SA-18 *Gimlet*

EQUIPMENT BY TYPE

AIRCRAFT 665 combat capable

FTR 112: 64 MiG-29 *Fulcrum*/MiG-29UB *Fulcrum*; 48 MiG-21FL

FGA 517: 83 *Jaguar* IS; 10 *Jaguar* IM; 31 MiG-21bis; 121 MiG-21 *Bison*; 55 MiG-21M; 16 MiG-21MF/PFMA *Fishbed*; 127 MiG-27ML *Flogger J2*; 40 *Mirage* 2000E (2000H); 12 *Mirage* 2000ED (2000TH); 122 Su-30 MKI *Flanker*

ISR 3 Gulfstream IV SRA-4

AEW&C 2 IL-76 TD *Phalcon* (1 more on order)

TKR 6 Il-78 *Midas*

TPT 217 **Heavy** 24 Il-76 *Candid* **Light** 160: 105 An-32 *Cline*; 51 Do-228; 4 EMB-135BJ **PAX** 33: 6 B-707; 4 B-737; 3 BBJ; 20 HS-748

TRG 282: 36 *Hawk* Mk132*; 120 HJT-16 MkI *Kiran*; 56 HJT-16 MkII *Kiran II*; 70 HPT-32 *Deepak*

HELICOPTERS

ATK 20 Mi-25 *Hind* D/Mi-35 *Hind*

MRH 200: 20 *Dhruv* (150 on order); 72 Mi-17 *Hip* H/Mi-17 IV; 60 SA-315B *Lama* (*Cheetah*); 48 SA-316B *Alouette III* (*Chetak*)

TPT 106 **Heavy** 4 Mi-26 *Halo* **Medium** 102 Mi-8

UAV • ISR • Medium some *Searcher* Mk II

AD • SAM S-125 *Pechora* (SA-3B *Goa*)

SP 9K33 *Osa-AK* (SA-8B *Gecko*)

MANPAD 9K310 *Igla-1* (SA-16 *Gimlet*)

MSL

AAM • IR AAM R-60 (AA-8 *Aphid*); R-73 (AA-11 *Archer*) R-550 *Magic* **IR/SARH AAM** R-23/24 *(AA-7 Apex)*; R-27 *(AA-10 Alamo)*; **SARH AAM** Super 530D

ARH AAM R-77 (AA-12 *Adder*)

AShM AM-39 *Exocet*; *Sea Eagle*

ASM AS-11; AS-11B (ATGW); Kh-59 (AS-13 *Kingbolt*); Kh-59M (AS-18 *Kazoo*); Kh-31A (AS-17 *Krypton*); AS-30; AS-7 *Kerry* ‡

ARM Kh-25MP (AS-12 *Kegler*); Kh-31A (AP-17 *Krypton*)

Coast Guard 9,550

Control of the Coast Guard is exercised through the Director General under the Ministry of Defence (HQ Delhi). The CG is organised into 11 districts with three regional Command Head Quarters at Mumbai, Chennai, Port Blair; in addition there are two principal air stations at Daman and Chennai with additional air stations at Mumbai, Goa, Kochi, Kolkata and Port Blair for maritime surveillance with a total of 9 Air Squadrons.

EQUIPMENT BY TYPE

PATROL AND COASTAL COMBATANTS 57

PSOH 7: 2 *Sankalp* (Additional vessels in build*)*; 4 *Samar*; 1 *Vishwast*

PCO 7 *Vikram*

PCC 16: 8 *Priyadarshini*; 1 *Rani Abbakka* (additional vessels in build); 7 *Sarojini-Naid*

PB 27: 7 *Jija Bai* mod 1; 6 *Tara Bai*; 14 (various)

AMPHIBIOUS • UCAC 6 *Griffon 8000*

AIRCRAFT • TPT • Light 24 Do-228

HELICOPTERS • MRH 17 SA-316B *Alouette III* (*Chetak*)

Paramilitary 1,300,586

Rashtriya Rifles 65,000

Ministry of Defence
Paramilitary   65 bn (in 15 sector HQ)

Assam Rifles 63,883

Ministry of Home Affairs. Security within north-eastern states, mainly army-officered; better trained than BSF

FORCES BY ROLE

Equipped to roughly same standard as an army inf bn
Paramilitary   7 HQ; 42 bn each with 6 81mm mor

EQUIPMENT BY TYPE

ARTY • MOR 81mm 240

Border Security Force 208,422

Ministry of Home Affairs.

FORCES BY ROLE

Paramilitary   157+ bn each with 6 81mm

EQUIPMENT BY TYPE

Small arms, lt arty, some anti-tank weapons

ARTY • MOR 81mm 942+

AIRCRAFT • TPT some (air spt)

Central Industrial Security Force 94,347 (lightly armed security guards only)

Ministry of Home Affairs. Guards public-sector locations

Central Reserve Police Force 229,699

Ministry of Home Affairs. Internal security duties, only lightly armed, deployable throughout the country
Paramilitary   2 Mahila (female) bn; 125 bn; 13 rapid action force bn

Defence Security Corps 31,000

Provides security at Defence Ministry sites

Indo–Tibetan Border Police 36,324

Ministry of Home Affairs. Tibetan border security
SF/guerrilla warfare and high-altitude warfare specialists; 30 bn

National Security Guards 7,357

Anti-terrorism contingency deployment force, comprising elements of the armed forces, CRPF and Border Security Force

Railway Protection Forces 70,000

Sashastra Seema Bal 31,554

Guards Indo-Nepal/Bhutan borders

Special Frontier Force 10,000
Mainly ethnic Tibetans

Special Protection Group 3,000
Protection of VVIP

State Armed Police 450,000
For duty primarily in home state only, but can be moved to other states. Some bn with GPMG and army standard infantry weapons and equipment
Paramilitary 24 (India Reserve Police (cdo-trained)) bn

Reserve Organisations

Civil Defence 500,000 reservists
Operate in 225 categorised towns in 32 states. Some units for NBC defence

Home Guard 487,821 reservists (515,000 authorised str)
In all states except Arunachal Pradesh and Kerala; men on reserve lists, no trg. Not armed in peacetime. Used for civil defence, rescue and fire-fighting provision in wartime; 6 bn (created to protect tea plantations in Assam)

DEPLOYMENT

AFGHANISTAN
400 ε2 cdo coy (Protection for road construction project)

CÔTE D'IVOIRE
UN • UNOCI 6 obs

DEMOCRATIC REPUBLIC OF THE CONGO
UN • MONUSCO 4,243; 60 obs; 3 mech inf bn; 1 inf bn; 1 atk hel coy; 1 hel coy; 1 fd hospital

GULF OF ADEN
Navy: 1 DDGHM

LEBANON
UN • UNIFIL 910; 1 mech inf bn; elm 1 fd hospital

SUDAN
UN • UNMIS 2,633; 18 obs; 2 inf bn; 1 engr coy; 1 tpt coy; 1 avn coy; 1 fd hospital

SYRIA/ISRAEL
UN • UNDOF 190; elm 1 log bn

TAJIKISTAN
Air Force: 1 IAF Forward Op Base, Farkhar

TIMOR LESTE
UN • UNMIT 1 obs

FOREIGN FORCES
Total numbers for UNMOGIP mission in India and Pakistan
Chile 2 obs
Croatia 9 obs
Finland 5 obs
Italy 7 obs

Korea, Republic of 9 obs
Sweden 6 obs
Uruguay 2 obs

Indonesia IDN

Indonesian Rupiah Rp		2009	2010	2011
GDP	Rp	5,613tr	6,311tr	
	US$	544bn	693bn	
per capita	US$	2,364	2,981	
Growth	%	4.5	6.1	
Inflation	%	4.6	5.2	
Def exp[a]	Rp	49.8tr		
	US$	4.82bn		
Def bdgt	Rp	33.6tr	40.7tr	60.0tr
	US$	3.25bn	4.47bn	
FMA (US)	US$	15.7m	20.0m	22.0m
US$1=Rp		10324.53	9106.13	

[a] including extra-budgetary funding estimate

Population   232,516,771

Ethnic groups: Javanese 45%; Sundanese 14%; Madurese 8%; Malay 8%; Chinese 3%; other 22%

Age	0–14	15–19	20–24	25–29	30–64	65 plus
Male	13.9%	4.5%	4.3%	4.2%	20.4%	2.7%
Female	13.4%	4.4%	4.1%	4.1%	20.5%	3.4%

Capabilities

ACTIVE 302,000 (Army 233,000 Navy 45,000 Air 24,000) Paramilitary 280,000
Terms of service 2 years selective conscription authorised

RESERVE 400,000
Army cadre units; numerical str n.k., obligation to age 45 for officers

ORGANISATIONS BY SERVICE

Army ε233,000

11 Mil Area Command (KODAM) 150,000
Provincial (KOREM) and District (KODIM) Comd
Cav	8 bn
Inf	2 bde (6 bn); 60 bn
AB	5 bn
Fd Arty	10 bn
Engr	7 bn
Avn	1 (composite) sqn
Hel	1 sqn
AD	7 bn

Special Forces Command (KOPASSUS) ε5,000
SF 3 gp (total: 2 cdo/para unit, 1 counter-terrorist unit (Unit 81), 1 trg unit, 1 (int) SF unit)

Strategic Reserve Command (KOSTRAD)
40,000

Comd	2 div HQ
Armd	2 bn
Inf	4 bde (9 bn)
AB	2 bde; 1 (3rd) indep bde
Fd Arty	2 regt (6 bn)
AD	1 regt (2 bn)
Engr	2 bn

EQUIPMENT BY TYPE
LT TK 350: 275 AMX-13 (to be upgraded); 15 PT-76; 60 *Scorpion* 90

RECCE 142: 55 *Ferret* (13 upgraded); 69 *Saladin* (16 upgraded); 18 VBL

AIFV 11 BMP-2

APC 356

    APC (T) 115: 75 AMX-VCI; 40 FV4333 *Stormer*

    APC (W) 241: 80 BTR-40; 34 BTR-50PK; 22 *Commando Ranger*; 45 FV603 *Saracen* (14 upgraded); 60 LAV-150 *Commando*

ARTY 1,010

    TOWED 135: **105mm** 130: 120 M-101; 10 M-56; **155mm** 5 FH-2000

    MOR 875: **81mm** 800; **120mm** 75 Brandt

    AT • RCL 135: **106mm** 45 M-40A1; **90mm** 90 M-67

    RL 89mm 700 LRAC

AIRCRAFT • TPT • Light 11: 3 DHC-5 *Buffalo*; 6 C-212 *Aviocar* (NC-212); 2 *Turbo Commander* 680

HELICOPTERS
    ATK 6 Mi-35P *Hind*

    MRH 28: 12 Bell 412 *Twin Huey* (NB-412); 16 Mi-17 *Hip*

    TPT • Light 25: 8 Bell 205A; 17 Bo-105 (NBo-105)

    TRG 12 Hughes 300C

AD • SAM 68: 51 *Rapier*; 17 RBS-70

    GUNS • TOWED 413: **20mm** 121 Rh 202; **40mm** 36 L/70; **57mm** 256 S-60

Navy ε45,000 (including Marines and Aviation)

Two fleets: East (Surabaya), West (Jakarta). Planned to change to 3 commands: Riau (West); Papua (East); Makassar (Central). 2 Forward Operating Bases at Kupang (West Timor) & Tahuna (North Sulawesi)

EQUIPMENT BY TYPE
SUBMARINES • TACTICAL • SSK 2 *Cakra*† each with 8 single 533mm TT each with SUT HWT

PRINCIPAL SURFACE COMBATANTS 11

    FRIGATES 11

        FFGHM 7

        6 *Ahmad Yani* each with 2 quad Mk 141 lnchr (8 eff.) each with RGM-84A *Harpoon* AShM, 2 SIMBAD twin lnchr (4 eff. - manual) each with *Mistral* SAM, 2 triple 324mm ASTT (6 eff.) each with Mk 46 LWT, 1 76mm gun, (capacity 1 Bo-105 (NBo-105) hel/*Wasp* HAS-1 ASW hel)

        1 *Hajar Dewantara* (trg role) with 2 twin lnchr (4 eff.) each with MM-38 *Exocet* AShM, 2 single 533mm ASTT each with SUT HWT, (capacity 1 Bo-105 (NBo-105) hel)

        FFGM 4:

        4 *Sigma* each with 2 twin (4 eff.) each with MM-40 *Exocet* Block II AShM, 2 quad *Tetral* lnchr (8eff.) each with *Mistral* SAM, 2 triple 324mm ASTT (6 eff.), 1 76mm gun, 1 hel landing platform

PATROL AND COASTAL COMBATANTS 66

    CORVETTES 19:

        FSGH 1:

        1 *Nala* with 2 twin lnchr (4 eff.) each with MM-38 *Exocet* AShM, 1 twin 375mm A/S mor (2 eff.), 1 120mm gun (capacity 1 lt hel)

        FSG 2:

        2 *Fatahillah* each with 2 twin lnchr (4 eff.) each with MM-38 *Exocet* AShM, 2 triple B515 *ILAS-3*/Mk32 324mm ASTT (6 eff.) with A244/Mk46 LWT, 1 twin 375mm A/S mor (2 eff.), 1 120mm gun

        FSM 16:

        16 *Kapitan Patimura*† (GDR *Parchim* I) each with 2 quad lnchr (8 eff.) each with 9K32M *Strela*-2 (SA-N-5 *Grail*) SAM, 4 single 400mm ASTT, 2 RBU 6000 *Smerch* 2 (24 eff.)

    PCFG 4 *Mandau* each with 4 single lnchr each with MM-38 *Exocet* AShM

    PCT 4 *Singa* each with 2 single 533mm TT (capability upgrade programme in progress)

    PCC 8: 4 *Kakap*; 4 *Todak*

    PB 31: 1 *Cucut*; 13 *Kobra*; 8 *Sibarau*; 9 *Viper*

MINE WARFARE • MINE COUNTERMEASURES 11

    MCO 2 *Pulau Rengat*

    MSC 9 *Palau Rote*†

AMPHIBIOUS

    PRINCIPAL AMPHIBIOUS VESSELS • LPD 4: 1 *Dr Soeharso* (Ex-*Tanjung Dalpele*; capacity 2 LCU/LCVP; 13 tanks; 500 troops; 2 AS-332L *Super Puma*); 3 *Makassar* (capacity 2 LCU/LCVP; 13 tanks; 500 troops; 2 AS-332L *Super Puma*); (1 additional vessel in build)

    LANDING SHIPS • LST 26: 1 *Teluk Amboina* (capacity 16 tanks; 200 troops); 12 *Teluk Gilimanuk*; 7 *Teluk Langsa* (capacity 16 tanks; 200 troops); 6 *Teluk Semangka* (capacity 17 tanks; 200 troops)

    LANDING CRAFT 54 LCU

LOGISTICS AND SUPPORT 32

    AGF 1 *Multatuli*

    AORLH 1 *Arun* (UK *Rover*)

    AOT 3: 2 *Khobi*; 1 *Sorong*

    AKSL 4

    AGOR 7: 5 *Baruna Jaya*; 1 *Jalanidhi*; 1 *Burujulasad*

    AGHS 1

    ATF 2

    TRG • AXS 2

    TPT 8: 1 *Tanjung Kambani* (troop transport); 2 *Tanjung Nusanive* (troop transport); 5 *Karang Pilang* (troop transport)

    YTM 3

Naval Aviation ε1,000

AIRCRAFT
    MP 24: 2 CN-235 MPA; 16 N-22B *Searchmaster B*; 6 N-22SL *Searchmaster L*

    TPT • Light 17: 4 C-212-200 *Aviocar*; 3 CN-235M; 4 *Commander* 100†; 2 DHC-5 *Buffalo*; 4 PA-34 *Seneca*

TRG 6 PA-38 *Tomahawk*
HELICOPTERS
ASW 9 *Wasp* HAS.1†
MRH 8: 4 Bell 412 (NB-412) *Twin Huey*; 4 Mi-17 (additional ac on order)
TPT 20: **Medium** 3 AS-332L *Super Puma* (NAS-322L); **Light** 17: 3 EC-120B *Colibri* (6 more on order); 6 Bo-105 (NBo-105); 8 PZL Mi-2 *Hoplite*

Marines ε20,000
FORCES BY ROLE
SF   1 bn

Marine   1st marine corps gp (total: 3 marine bn) based Surabaya; 1 indep marine corp gp (total: 3 bn) based Jakarta; 1 marine bde (total: 3 bn) based Teluk, Rata and Sumatra

Cbt spt   1 regt (arty, AD)

EQUIPMENT BY TYPE
LT TK 55 PT-76†
RECCE 21 BRDM
AIFV 34: 24 AMX-10P; 10 AMX-10 PAC 90
APC (W) 100 BTR-50P
ARTY 62+
 TOWED 50+: **105mm** 22 LG1 MK II; **122mm** 28 M-38 M-1938
 MRL 140mm 12 BM-14
 MOR 81mm
AD • GUNS 150: **40mm** 5 L/60/L/70; **57mm** S-60

Air Force 24,000
2 operational comd (East and West) plus trg comd. Only 45% of ac op

FORCES BY ROLE
Ftr   1 sqn with F-5E/F *Tiger II*; 1 sqn with F-16A/B *Fighting Falcon*

Ftr/FGA   1 sqn with Su-30 MKI *Flanker*; Su-27SK *Flanker*; 1 sqn with A-4E/TA-4H*/TA-4J* *Skyhawk*; 2 sqn with *Hawk* Mk109*/Mk209*

MP   1 sqn with B-737-200

ISR   1 (FAC) flt with OV-10F *Bronco** (mostly non-operational)

Tpt/Tkr   5 sqn with B-707; C-130B *Hercules*; C-130H *Hercules*; C-130H-30 *Hercules*; C-212 *Aviocar* (NC-212); Cessna 207 *Stationair*; Cessna 401/402; CN-235-110; F-27-400M *Troopship*; F-28-1000; F-28-3000; KC-130B *Hercules*; L-100-30; SC.7 3M *Skyvan* (survey)

Trg   3 sqn with Cessna 172; AS-202 *Bravo*; *Hawk* MK53*; KT-1B; SF-260M/SF-260W *Warrior*; T-34C *Turbo Mentor*; T-41D *Mescalero*

Tpt Hel   3 sqn with S-58T; AS-332L *Super Puma* (NAS-332L) (VIP/CSAR); SA-330 *Puma* (NAS-330SM VIP); EC-120B *Colibri*

EQUIPMENT BY TYPE
AIRCRAFT 100 combat capable
 FTR 27: 8 F-5E *Tiger II*; 4 F-5F *Tiger II*; 7 F-16A *Fighting Falcon*; 3 F-16B *Fighting Falcon*; 5 Su-27SK *Flanker*

FGA 5 Su-30 MKI *Flanker*
ATK 14: 11 A-4E *Skyhawk*; 1 TA-4H *Skyhawk*; 2 TA-4J *Skyhawk*
ISR 12 OV-10F *Bronco** (mostly non-operational)
TKR 2 KC-130B *Hercules*
TPT 67 **Medium** 18: 8 C-130B *Hercules*; 4 C-130H *Hercules*; 6 C-130H-30 *Hercules* **Light** 42: 2 L-100-30; 10 C-212 *Aviocar* (NC-212); 2 Cessna 172; 4 Cessna 207 *Stationair*; 5 Cessna 401; 2 Cessna 402; 10 CN-235-110; 6 F-27-400M *Troopship*; 1 SC.7 3M *Skyvan* (survey) **PAX** 7: 1 B-707; 3 B-737-200; 1 F-28-1000; 2 F-28-3000
TRG 133: 39 AS-202 *Bravo*; 7 *Hawk* Mk53*; 7 *Hawk* Mk109*; 28 *Hawk* Mk209*; 7 KT-1B; 19 SF-260M/SF-260W *Warrior*; 20 T-34C *Turbo Mentor*; 6 T-41D *Mescalero*
HELICOPTERS
SAR 10 S-58T
TPT 28 **Medium** 16: 5 AS-332 *Super Puma* (NAS-332L) (VIP/CSAR); 11 SA-330 *Puma* (NAS-330) (incl1 NAS-330SM VIP) **Light** 12 EC-120B *Colibri*
MSL • TACTICAL
ASM AGM-65G *Maverick*
AAM • IR AAM AIM-9P *Sidewinder*; R-73 (AA-11 *Archer*)
IR/SARH AAM R-27 (AA-10 *Alamo*)

Special Forces (Paskhasau)
Special Ops 3 (PASKHASAU) wg (total: 6 special ops sqn); 4 indep coy

Paramilitary ε280,000 active

Naval Auxiliary Service
PATROL AND COASTAL COMBATANTS • PB 71: 6 *Carpentaria*; 65 *Kal Kangean*

Customs
PATROL AND COASTAL COMBATANTS 65
 PBF 15
 PB 50

Marine Police
PATROL AND COASTAL COMBATANTS 28
 PSO 2 *Bisma*
 PB 26: 14 *Bango*; 12 (various)

Police ε280,000 (including 14,000 police 'mobile bde' (BRIMOB) org in 56 coy, incl CT unit (Gegana))
APC (W) 34 *Tactica*
AIRCRAFT • TPT • Light 5: 2 Beech 18; 2 C-212 *Aviocar* (NC-212); 1 *Turbo Commander 680*
HELICOPTERS • TPT • Light 22: 3 Bell 206 *Jet Ranger*; 19 Bo-105 (NBo-105)

KPLP (Coast and Seaward Defence Command)
Responsible to Military Sea Communications Agency
PATROL AND COASTAL COMBATANTS 11
 PCO 2 *Arda Dedali*
 PB 9: 4 *Golok* (SAR); 5 *Kujang*
LOGISTICS AND SUPPORT • ABU 1 *Jadayat*

Reserve Organisations

Kamra People's Security ε40,000 (report for 3 weeks' basic training each year; part time police auxiliary)

DEPLOYMENT

DEMOCRATIC REPUBLIC OF THE CONGO
UN • MONUSCO 175; 16 obs; 1 engr coy

LEBANON
UN • UNIFIL 1,324; 1 mech inf bn; 1 MP coy; elm 1 fd hospital

LIBERIA
UN • UNMIL 1 obs

NEPAL
UN • UNMIN 4 obs

SUDAN
UN • UNAMID 1; 2 obs
UN • UNMIS 9 obs

Japan JPN

Japanese Yen ¥		2009	2010	2011
GDP	¥	474tr	477tr	
	US$	5.08tr	5.39tr	
per capita	US$	39,786	42,422	
Growth	%	-5.2	2.5	
Inflation	%	-1.4	-1.0	
Def exp	¥	4.77tr		
	US$	51.1bn		
Def bdgt	¥	4.70tr	4.68tr	5.03tr
	US$	50.3bn	52.8bn	
US$1=¥		93.45	88.60	

Population 126,995,411

Ethnic groups: Korean <1%

Age	0–14	15–19	20–24	25–29	30–64	65 plus
Male	6.7%	2.5%	2.6%	3.0%	24.3%	9.7%
Female	6.4%	2.3%	2.5%	2.8%	24.1%	13.2%

Capabilities

ACTIVE 247,746 (Ground Self-Defense Force 151,641; Maritime Self- Defense Force 45,518; Air Self-Defense Force 47,123; Central Staff 3,464) Paramilitary 12,636

CIVILIAN 22,242

RESERVE 56,379 (General Reserve Army (GSDF) 46,000; Ready Reserve Army (GSDF) 8,479; Navy 1,100; Air 800)

ORGANISATIONS BY SERVICE

Space Defence
4 recce satellites (2 radar, 2 optical)

Ground Self-Defense Force 151,641

FORCES BY ROLE
5 Army HQ (regional comds)

Composite	1 bde
Armd Inf	8 div, 5 bde
Armd	1 div
Spec Ops	1 unit
AB	1 bde
Arty	1 bde; 2 unit
Engr	4 bde; 1 unit
Hel	1 bde
Trg	2 bde; 2 regt
AD	2 bde; 4 gp

EQUIPMENT BY TYPE
MBT 850: 13 Type 10; 517 Type-74; 320 Type-90
RECCE 100 Type-87
AIFV 70 Type-89
APC 780
  APC (T) 310 Type-73
  APC (W) 470: 220 Type-82; 250 Type-96
ARTY 1,880
  SP 210: **155mm** 130: 80 Type-75; 50 Type-99; **203mm** 80 M-110A2
  TOWED 155mm 420 FH-70
  MRL 227mm 100 MLRS
  MOR 1,150
    SP 120mm 20
    TOWED 1,130: **81mm** 670; **107mm** 50; **120mm** 410
AT
  MSL • MANPATS 630: 190 Type-79 *Jyu-MAT*; 440 Type-87 *Chu-MAT*
  RCL 2,740: **SP 106mm** 30 Type-60; **84mm** 2,710 *Carl Gustav*
  RL 230 **89mm**
AIRCRAFT
  TPT • Light 12 MU-2 (LR-1)/Beech 350 *King Air* (LR-2)
HELICOPTERS
  ATK 185: 78 AH-1S *Cobra*; 7 AH-64D *Apache*; 26 OH-1
  ISR 118 OH-6D
  TPT 236 **Heavy** 54 CH-47D *Chinook* (CH-47J)/CH-47JA *Chinook* **Medium** 34: 3 AS-332L *Puma*; 3 EC-225LP *Super Puma MkII+* (VIP); 28 UH-60L *Black Hawk* (UH-60JA) **Light** 148 Bell-205 (UH-1J)
AD • SAM 740
  SP 170: 60 Type-81 *Tan-SAM*; 110 Type-93 *Kin-SAM*
  TOWED 190: 180 MTM-23B *I-HAWK*; 10 Type-03 *Chu-SAM*
  MANPAD 380: 50 FIM-92A *Stinger*; 330 Type-91 *Kin-SAM*
  GUNS 60
    SP 35mm 50 Type-87 SP
    TOWED 35mm 10 (twin)
MSL • SSM • COASTAL 100 Type-88

Maritime Self-Defense Force 45,518

Surface units organised into 4 Escort Flotillas with a mix of 7–8 warships each. Bases at Yokosuka, Kure, Sasebo, Maizuru, Ominato. SSK organised into 2 Flotillas with bases at Kure and Yokosuka. Remaining units assigned to 5 regional districts.

EQUIPMENT BY TYPE

SUBMARINES • TACTICAL • SSK 18:

5 *Harushio* (incl 2 in trg role) each with 6 single 533mm TT each with T-89 HWT/UGM-84C *Harpoon* AShM

11 *Oyashio* each with 6 single 533mm TT each with T-89 HWT/UGM-84C *Harpoon* AShM

2 *Soryu* (AIP fitted) each with 6 single 533mm TT each with T-89 HWT/UGM-84C *Harpoon* AShM (additional vessels in build)

PRINCIPAL SURFACE COMBATANTS 49

AIRCRAFT CARRIERS • CVH 1:

1 *Hyuga* with 1 Mk41 VLS (16 eff.) with ASROC/RIM-162/ESSM *Sea Sparrow*, 2 triple 324mm TT (6 eff.) each with Mk46 LWT, 2 20mm CIWS gun, (normal ac capacity 3 SH-60 *Seahawk* ASW hel; plus additional ac embarkation up to 7 SH-60 *Seahawk* or 7 MCH-101) (additional vessel in build)

CRUISERS • CGHM 2:

2 *Atago* (*Aegis* Base Line 7) each with 2 quad lnchr (8 eff.) with SSM-1B AShM, 1 Mk41 VLS (64 eff.) with SM-2 MR SAM/ASROC, 1 Mk41 VLS (32 eff.) with SM-2 MR SAM, 2 triple 324mm ASTT (6 eff.) each with Mk46 LWT, 1 127mm gun, (capacity 1 SH-60 *Seahawk* ASW hel)

DESTROYERS 30:

DDGHM 20:

6 *Asagiri* each with 2 quad Mk141 lnchr (8 eff.) each with RGM-84C *Harpoon* AShM, 1 octuple Mk29 lnchr (8 eff.) with *Sea Sparrow* SAM, 2 triple 324mm ASTT (6 eff.) each with Mk46 LWT, 1 octuple Mk112 lnchr (8 eff.) with ASROC, 1 76mm gun, (capacity 1 SH-60 *Seahawk* ASW hel)

9 *Murasame* each with 2 quad lnchr (8 eff.) each with SSM-1B AShM, 1 Mk48 VLS (16 eff.) with RIM-7M *Sea Sparrow* SAM, 2 triple 324mm TT (6 eff.) each with Mk 46 LWT, 1 Mk 41 VLS (16 eff.) with ASROC, 2 76mm gun, (capacity 1 SH-60 *Seahawk* ASW hel)

5 *Takanami* (improved *Murasame*) each with 2 quad lnchr (8 eff.) each with SSM-1B AShM, 1 Mk41 VLS (32 eff.) with tactical ASROC/RIM-7M/ESSM *Sea Sparrow* SAM, 2 triple 324mm TT (6 eff.) each with Mk 46 LWT, 1 127mm gun, (capacity 1 SH-60 *Seahawk* ASW hel)

DDGM 7:

2 *Hatakaze* each with 2 quad Mk 141 lnchr (8 eff.) each with RGM-84C *Harpoon* AShM, 1 Mk 13 GMLS with SM-1 MR SAM, 2 triple 324mm ASTT (6 eff.), 2 127mm gun, 1 hel landing platform

4 *Kongou* (*Aegis* Baseline 4/5) each with 2 quad Mk141 lnchr (8 eff.) each with RGM-84C *Harpoon* AShM, 1 Mk41 VLS (29 eff.) with SM-2 MR SAM/ASROC, 1 Mk 41 VLS (61 eff.) with SM-2 MR SAM/ASROC, 2 triple 324mm ASTT (6 eff.), 1 127mm gun

1 *Tachikaze* each with 1 Mk13 GMLS with RGM-84C *Harpoon* AShM/SM-1 MR SAM, 2 triple 324mm ASTT (6 eff.) each with Mk 46 LWT, 1 octuple Mk112 lnchr (8 eff.) with ASROC, 1 127mm gun

DDM 3:

1 *Haruna* each with, 1 octuple Mk29 lnchr with RIM-7F/M *Sea Sparrow* SAM, 2 triple ASTT (6 eff.) each with Mk 46 LWT, 1 octuple Mk 112 lnchr (8 eff.) with ASROC, 2 127mm gun, (capacity 3 SH-60 *Seahawk* ASW hel)

2 *Shirane* each with 1 octuple Mk 112 lnchr (8 eff.) with tactical ASROC, 1+ Mk 29 *Sea Sparrow* octuple with 24+ RIM-162A *Sea Sparrow* SAM, 2 triple ASTT (6 eff.) each with Mk 46 LWT, 2 127mm gun, (capacity 3 SH-60 *Seahawk* ASW hel)

FRIGATES • FFGM 16:

6 *Abukuma* each with 2 quad Mk 141 lnchr (8 eff.) each with RGM-84C *Harpoon* AShM, 2 triple ASTT (6 eff.) each with Mk 46 LWT, 1 Mk 112 octuple (8 eff.) with ASROC, 1 76mm gun

10 *Hatsuyuki* each with 2 quad Mk 141 lnchr (8 eff.) each with RGM-84C *Harpoon* AShM, 1 octuple Mk29 lnchr (8 eff.) with RIM-7F/M *Sea Sparrow* SAM, 2 triple ASTT (6 eff.) each with Mk46 LWT, 1 octuple Mk 112 lnchr (8 eff.) with ASROC, 1 76mm gun, (capacity 1 SH-60 *Seahawk* ASW hel)

PATROL AND COASTAL COMBATANTS 6

PBFG 6 *Hayabusa* each with 4 SSM-1B AShM, 1 76mm gun

MINE WARFARE • MINE COUNTERMEASURES 37

MCM SPT 4:

2 *Nijma*

2 *Uraga* each with 1 hel landing platform (for MH-53E)

MSO 27: 3 *Hirashima*; 12 *Sugashima*; 9 *Uwajima*; 3 *Yaeyama*

MSD 6

AMPHIBIOUS

LS • LST 5:

3 *Osumi* each with 1 hel landing platform (for 2 x CH-47) (capacity 10 Type-90 MBTs; 2 LCAC(L) ACV; 330 troops)

2 *Yura* (capacity 70 troops)

LANDING CRAFT 20

LCU 2 *Yusotei*

LCM 12

ACV 6 **LCAC(L)** (capacity either 1 MBT or 60 troops)

LOGISTICS AND SUPPORT 77:

AOE 5: 2 *Mashuu*; 3 *Towada*

AS 1 *Chiyoda* (submarine rescue facilities)

ASR 1 *Chihaya*

ARC 1 *Muroto*

AG 2: 1 *Kurihama*; 1 *Asuka* (wpn trials)

AGOS 2 *Hibiki*

AGS 4: 1 *Futami*; 1 *Nichinan*; 1 *Shonan*; 1 *Suma*

AGB 1 *Shirase*

ATF 22

TRG 6: 1 *Kashima*; 1 *Shimayuki*; 2 *Yamagiri* TV35 with, 1 octuple Mk 112 lnchr (8 eff.) with ASROC, 2 triple ASTT (6 eff.) each with Mk 46 LWT, 1 Type 71/4 tube Mitsubshi

375mm Bofors (4 eff.), 4 76mm gun; 1 *Tenryu* (trg spt ship); 1 *Kurobe* (trg spt ship)
SPT 5 *Hiuchi*
YAC 1 *Hashidate*
YDT 6
YTM 20

FACILITIES

Bases Located at Kure, Sasebo, Yokosuka, Maizuru, Ominato

Naval Aviation ε9,800

FORCES BY ROLE

7 Air Groups

ASW/ ASuW	7 sqn (shipboard/trg) with SH-60B (SH-60J)/ SH-60K *Seahawk*
MR	6 sqn (1 trg) with P-1; P-3C *Orion*
EW	1 sqn with EP-3 *Orion*
MCM	1 sqn with MH-53E *Sea Dragon*; MCH-101
SAR	1 sqn with *Shin Meiwa* US-1A; 2 sqn with UH-60J *Black Hawk*
Tpt	1 sqn with AW-101 *Merlin* (CH-101); Beech 90 *King Air* (LC-90); YS-11M
Trg	1 sqn with OH-6D; OH-6DA; 3 sqn with T-5; Beech 90 *King Air* (TC-90); YS-11T

EQUIPMENT BY TYPE
AIRCRAFT 95 combat capable
  ASW 95: 2 P-1 (additional ac on order); 93 P-3C *Orion*
  ELINT 5 EP-3C *Orion*
  SAR 7: 4 *Shin Meiwa* US-1A; 3 *Shin Meiwa* US-2
  TPT • **Light** 39: 4 YS-11M; 6 YS-11T; 5 Beech 90 *King Air* (LC-90); 24 Beech 90 *King Air* (TC-90)
  TRG 33 T-5
HELICOPTERS
  ASW 93: 61 SH-60B *Seahawk* (SH-60J); 31 SH-60K *Seahawk*; 1 USH-60K *Seahawk*
  MCM 11: 9 MH-53E *Sea Dragon*; 2 MCH-101
  ISR 8: 3 OH-6D; 5 OH-6DA
  SAR 18 UH-60J *Black Hawk*
  TPT 9 **Medium** 7: 4 AW-101 *Merlin* (CH-101) (additional ac being delivered); 3 S-61A; **Light** 2 EC-135

Air Self-Defense Force 47,123

Flying hours   150 hrs/year

FORCES BY ROLE

7 cbt wings

Ftr	7 sqn with F-15J *Eagle*; 2 sqn with F-4EJ (F-4E) *Phantom II*; 3 sqn with Mitsubishi F-2
EW	2 sqn with Kawasaki EC-1; YS-11E
ISR	1 sqn with RF-4EJ (RF-4E) *Phantom II**
AEW&C	2 sqn with E-2C *Hawkeye*; E-767
SAR	1 wg with U-125A *Peace Krypton*; MU-2 (LR-1); UH-60J *Black Hawk*
Tkr	1 sqn with KC-767J
Tpt	1 (VIP) sqn with B-747-400; 3 sqn with C-1; C-130H *Hercules*; YS-11; some (liaison) sqn with Gulfstream IV (U-4); T-4 *

CAL	1 sqn with U-125-800 *Peace Krypton*; YS-11
Test	1 wg with F-15J *Eagle*; T-4*
Trg	1 (aggressor) sqn with F-15J *Eagle*
Tpt Hel	4 flt with CH-47 *Chinook*

FACILITIES

Trg	5 with T-7 (basic); F-2B and T-4* (advanced);
School	Beech T-400

EQUIPMENT BY TYPE
AIRCRAFT 374 combat capable
  FTR 202 F-15J *Eagle*
  FGA 159: 87 F-2/F-2B*; 72 F-4E *Phantom II* (F-4EJ)
  EW 11: 1 Kawasaki EC-1; 10 YS-11E
  ISR: 13 RF-4E *Phantom II** (RF-4J)
  AEW&C 17: 13 E-2C *Hawkeye*; 4 E-767
  SAR 26 U-125A *Peace Krypton*
  TKR 4 KC-767J
  TPT 60 **Medium** 16 C-130H *Hercules* **PAX** 44: 13 Beech T-400; 26 C-1; 5 Gulfstream IV (U-4)
  TRG 248: 199 T-4*; 49 T-7
HELICOPTERS
  SAR 38 UH-60J *Black Hawk*
  TPT • **Heavy** 15 CH-47 *Chinook*

Air Defence

FORCES BY ROLE

ac control and warning

AD	4 wg; 28 radar sites; 1 (Air Base Defence) gp with Type-81 *Tan-SAM*; FIM-92A *Stinger*; Type-91 *Kin-SAM*; M-167 *Vulcan*
SAM	6 gp, comprising 24 SAM bty each with 5 launchers MIM-104 *Patriot*, 16+ bty of PAC-3 (incl 4 bty for trg)

EQUIPMENT BY TYPE
AD • **SAM** 208+
  SP Type-81 *Tan-SAM*
  TOWED 208+: 120 MIM-104 *Patriot*; 16+ PAC-3
  MANPAD FIM-92A *Stinger*; Type-91 *Kei-SAM*
  GUNS • **TOWED 20mm** M-167 *Vulcan*
MSL
  ASM ASM-1Type-80; ASM-2 Type-93
  AAM AAM-4 (Type-99); AIM-7 *Sparrow*; AIM-9 *Sidewinder*; Type-90 (AAM-3)

FACILITIES

Radar stn   28 (ac control and warning)

Paramilitary 12,636

Coast Guard

Ministry of Land, Transport, Infrastructure and Tourism (no cbt role)
PATROL AND COASTAL COMBATANTS 351
  PSOH 13: 2 *Mizuho*; 1 *Shikishima*; 10 *Soya*
  PSO 29: 3 *Hida*; 1 *Izu*; 1 *Kojima* (trg); 1 *Miura*; 1 *Nojima*; 7 *Ojika*; 15 *Shiretoko*
  PCO 35: 3 *Aso*; 7 *Bihoro*; 9 *Hateruma*; 2 *Takatori*; 14 *Teshio*
  PCC 16: 4 *Amani*; 12 *Tokara*

PBF 34: 12 *Hayagumo*; 5 *Mihashi*; 9 *Raizan*; 2 *Takatsuki*; 6 *Tsuruugi*

PB 224: 5 *Akagi*; 9 *Akizuki*; 4 *Asogiri*; 170 CL-Type; 15 *Hayanami*; 1 *Matsunami*; 13 *Murakumo*; 2 *Natsugiri*; 1 *Shikinami*; 4 *Yodo*

LOGISTICS AND SUPPORT 27:

ABU 2

AGHS 13

AKSL 9

TRG 3

AIRCRAFT

MP 2 *Falcon 900 MPA*

ISR 2 Beech 200T

TPT 21 **Light** 12: 10 Beech 350 *King Air* (LR-2); 1 Cessna 206 *Stationair* (U-206G); 1 YS-11A **PAX** 9: 3 CL-300; 2 Gulfstream V (MP); 4 Saab 340B

HELICOPTERS

MRH 7 Bell 412 *Twin Huey*

TPT 39 **Medium** 6: 4 AS-332 *Super Puma*; 2 EC-225 *Super Puma* **Light** 33: 5 AW-139; 4 Bell 206B *Jet Ranger II*; 20 Bell 212; 4 S-76C

DEPLOYMENT

GULF OF ADEN & INDIAN OCEAN
MSDF: 2 DDGHM; 2 P-3C Orion

HAITI
UN • MINUSTAH 225; 1 engr coy

NEPAL
UN • UNMIN 6 obs

SUDAN
UN • UNMIS 2

SYRIA/ISRAEL
UN • UNDOF 31; elm 1 log bn

TIMOR LESTE
UN • UNMIT 2 obs

FOREIGN FORCES

United States US Pacific Command: 35,598
  Army 2,677; 1 HQ (9th Theater Army Area Command) at Zama
  Navy 3,539; 1 CVN; 2 CG; 8 DDG; 1 LCC; 2 MCM; 1 LHD; 2 LSD; 1 base at Sasebo; 1 base at Yokosuka
  USAF: 12,380; 1 HQ (5th Air Force) at Okinawa–Kadena AB; 1 ftr wg at Okinawa–Kadena AB (2 ftr sqn with total of 18 F-16 *Fighting Falcon* at Misawa AB); 1 ftr wg at Okinawa–Kadena AB (1 SAR sqn with 8 HH-60G *Pave Hawk*, 1 AEW sqn with 2 E-3B *Sentry*, 2 ftr sqn with total of 24 F-15C *Eagle*/F-15D *Eagle*); 1 airlift wg at Yokota AB with 10 C-130E *Hercules*; 2 C-21J; 1 spec ops gp at Okinawa–Kadena AB
  USMC 17,002; 1 Marine div (3rd); 1 ftr sqn with 12 F/A-18D *Hornet*; 1 tkr sqn with 12 KC-130J *Hercules*; 2 tpt hel sqn with 12 CH-46E *Sea Knight*; 1 tpt hel sqn with 12 MV-22B *Osprey*; 3 tpt hel sqn with 10 CH-53E *Sea Stallion*

Kazakhstan KAZ

Kazakhstani Tenge t		2009	2010	2011
GDP	t	15.9tr	18.8tr	
	US$	108bn	127bn	
per capita	US$	6,815	8,081	
Growth	%	1.2	6.0	
Inflation	%	-0.2	7.6	
Def exp	t	199bn		
	US$	1.35bn		
Def bdgt	t	139bn	165bn	
	US$	948m	1.12bn	
FMA (US)	US$	4.5m	3.0m	2.4m
US$1=t		146.97	147.33	

Population   15,753,460

Ethnic groups: Kazakh 51%; Russian 32%; Ukrainian 5%; German 2%; Tatar 2%; Uzbek 13%

Age	0–14	15–19	20–24	25–29	30–64	65 plus
Male	11.0%	4.3%	5.2%	4.7%	20.3%	2.5%
Female	10.5%	4.1%	5.1%	4.7%	22.5%	4.9%

Capabilities

ACTIVE 49,000 (Army 30,000 Navy 3,000 Air 12,000 MoD 4,000) **Paramilitary 31,500**
Terms of service 24 months

ORGANISATIONS BY SERVICE

Army 30,000

4 regional comd: Astana, East, West and Southern.

FORCES BY ROLE

Mech Inf	10 bde (1 Bde Astana Region, 4 Bde East Region, 5 bde South Region)
Air Aslt	4 bde
Arty	7 bde
MRL	2 (102nd, 402nd) bde with total of 180 BM 27 9P140 *Uragan*
AT	2 bde
SSM	1 bde
Coastal Def	1 (West Region) bde
Cbt Engr	3 bde
SSM	1 bde
Peacekeeping	1 (KAZBRIG) bde

EQUIPMENT BY TYPE
MBT 980 T-72
RECCE 280: 140 BRDM; 140 BRM
AIFV 1,520: 730 BMP-1; 700 BMP-2; 90 BTR-80A
APC 370
  APC (T) 180 MT-LB
  APC (W) 190 BTR-70/BTR-80
ARTY 1,460
  SP 240: **122mm** 120 2S1 *Carnation*; **152mm** 120 2S3

TOWED 670: **122mm** 400 D-30; **152mm** 270: 180 2A36; 90 2A65
GUN/MOR 120mm 25 2S9 *Anona*
MRL 380: **122mm** 200: 150 BM-21 *Grad*, 50 in store; **220mm** 180 9P140 *Uragan*
MOR 120mm 145 2B11/M-120
AT • MSL • MANPATS 9K111 (AT-4 *Spigot*); 9K113 (AT-5 *Spandrel*); 9K115 (AT-6 *Spiral*)
　RL 73mm RPG-7 *Knout*
　GUNS 100mm 68 MT-12/T-12
MSL • SSM 12 SS-21 *Tochka* (*Scarab*)
FACILITIES
Training centre　1

Navy 3,000

PATROL AND COASTAL COMBATANTS 17
　PB 17: 4 *Almaty*; 1 *Dauntless*; 5 *Guardian*; 3 *Sea Dolphin*; 2 *Turk* (AB25); 2 *Zhuk*

Air Force 12,000 (incl Air Defence)

Flying hours　100 hrs/year

FORCES BY ROLE

Comd　regt with Tu-134 *Crusty*; Tu-154 *Careless*
Ftr　1 regt with MiG-29/MiG-29UB *Fulcrum*; 1 regt with MiG-25 *Foxbat*; MiG-31 *Foxhound*
FGA　1 regt with Su-24 *Fencer*; 1 regt with Su-25 *Frogfoot*; 1 regt with Su-27 *Flanker*
Recce　1 regt with Su-24 *Fencer**
Trg　some regt with L-39 *Albatros*; Yak-18 *Max*
Atk hel　some regt with Mi-24V
Tpt Hel　some regt with Mi-171V5, Mi-8 *Hip*, UH-1H
SAM　some regt with 100 S-75M *Volkhov* (*SA-2 Guideline*)/S-125 *Neva* (*SA-3 Goa*); S-300 (*SA-10 Grumble*) (quad); 2K11 *Krug* (*SA-4 Ganef*)/S-200 *Angara* (*SA-5 Gammon*); 2K12 *Kub* (*SA-6 Gainful*) (60 eff.)

EQUIPMENT BY TYPE
AIRCRAFT 162 combat capable
　FTR 97: 16 MiG-25 *Foxbat*; 39 MiG-29/MiG-29UB *Fulcrum*; 42 MiG-31/MiG-31BM *Foxhound*
　FGA 39: 14 Su-24 *Fencer*; 25 Su-27 *Flanker*
　ATK 14 Su-25 *Frogfoot*
　ISR 12 Su-24MR *Fencer-E**
　TPT 3: **Light** 2 Tu-134 *Crusty*; **PAX** 1 Tu-154 *Careless*
　TRG 16: 12 L-39 *Albatros*; 4 Yak-18 *Max*
HELICOPTERS
　ATK 40+ Mi-24V (first 9 upgraded)
　TPT 76 **Medium** 70: 50 Mi-8 *Hip*; 20 Mi-171V5 **Light** 6 Bell-205 (UH-1H)
AD • SAM 147+
　SP 47+: 20 2K12 *Kub* (*SA-6 Gainful*); 27+ 2K11 *Krug* (*SA-4 Ganef*)/S-200 *Angara* (*SA-5 Gammon*); static; S-300 (*SA-10 Grumble*) (quad)
　TOWED 100 S-75M *Volkhov* (*SA-2 Guideline*); S-125 *Neva* (*SA-3 Goa*)
MSL
　ASM Kh-23 (AS-7 *Kerry*); Kh-25 (AS-10 *Karen*); Kh-29 (AS-14 *Kedge*)

　ARM Kh-28 (AS-9 *Kyle*); Kh-58 (AS-11 *Kilter*)
　AAM • IR AAM R-60 (AA-8 *Aphid*); R-73 (AA-11 *Archer*) **IR/SARH AAM** R-27 (AA-10 *Alamo*) **SARH AAM** R-33 (AA-9 *Amos*) **ARH AAM** R-77 (AA-12 *Adder* - on MiG-31BM)

Paramilitary 31,500

Government Guard 500

Internal Security Troops ε20,000
Ministry of Interior

Presidential Guard 2,000

State Border Protection Forces ε9,000
Ministry of Interior.
HEL • TPT • Medium 1 Mi-171

DEPLOYMENT

ARMENIA/AZERBAIJAN
OSCE • Minsk Conference 1

Korea, Democratic People's Republic of DPRK

North Korean Won		2009	2010	2011
GDP	US$			
per capita	US$			
Def exp	won	ε611bn		
	US$	ε4.38bn		

US$1=won

definitive economic data not available

Population　23,990,703

Age	0–14	15–19	20–24	25–29	30–64	65 plus
Male	10.5%	4.0%	4.1%	3.8%	22.4%	3.9%
Female	10.3%	3.9%	4.0%	3.7%	23.3%	6.0%

Capabilities

ACTIVE 1,190,000 (Army ε1,020,000 Navy 60,000 Air 110,000) **Paramilitary 189,000**
Terms of service Army 5–12 years Navy 5–10 years Air Force 3–4 years, followed by compulsory part-time service to age 40. Thereafter service in the Worker/Peasant Red Guard to age 60.

RESERVE ε600,000 (Armed Forces ε600,000), **Paramilitary 5,700,000**
Reservists are assigned to units (see also Paramilitary)

ORGANISATIONS BY SERVICE

Strategic Forces
North Korea's *No-dong* missiles and H-5 (Il-28) bombers could in future be used to deliver nuclear warheads or

bombs. At present, however, there is no conclusive evidence to suggest that North Korea has successfully produced a warhead or bomb capable of being delivered by either of these systems.

Army ε1,020,000

FORCES BY ROLE

Armd	1 div; 15 bde
Mech	2 corps; 4 div
Inf	9 corps; 27 div; 14 bde
Arty	1 div; 21 bde
MRL	9 bde
SSM	1 Scud SSM bde; 1 (FROG) SSM regt
Capital Defence	1 corps

Special Purpose Forces Command 88,000

Army	6 sniper bde
Recce	17 bn
Amph	2 sniper bde
SF	8 Reconnaissance General Bureau bn
Lt inf	9 bde
AB	2 sniper bde; 3 bde; 1 bn

Reserves 600,000

Inf 40 div; 18 bde

EQUIPMENT BY TYPE (ε)

MBT 3,500+ T-34/T-54/T-55/T-62/Type-59/*Chonma/Pokpoong*
LT TK 560+: 560 PT-76; M-1985
APC 2,500+
 APC (T) Type-531 (Type-63); VTT-323
 APC (W) 2,500 BTR-40/BTR-50/BTR-60/BTR-80A/BTR-152
ARTY 21,000+
 SP/TOWED 8,500: **SP 122mm** M-1977/M-1981/M-1985/M-1991; **130mm** M-1975/M-1981/M-1991; **152mm** M-1974/M-1977; **170mm** M-1978/M-1989
 TOWED 122mm D-30/D-74/M-1931/37; **130mm** M-46; **152mm** M-1937/M-1938/M-1943
 GUN/MOR 120mm (reported)
 MRL 5,100: **107mm** Type-63; **122mm** BM-11/M-1977 (BM-21)/M-1985/M-1992/M-1993; **240mm** M-1985/M-1989/M-1991
 MOR 7,500: **82mm** M-37; **120mm** M-43; **160mm** M-43
AT • MSL
 SP 9K11 (AT-3 *Sagger*)
 MANPATS AT-1 *Snapper*; 9K111 (AT-4 *Spigot*); 9K113 (AT-5 *Spandrel*)
 RCL 82mm 1,700 B-10
AD • SAM • MANPAD 9K310 *Igla*-1 (SA-16 *Gimlet*)/9K32 *Strela*-2 (SA-7 *Grail*)‡
 GUNS 11,000
  SP 14.5mm M-1984; **23mm** M-1992; **37mm** M-1992; **57mm** M-1985
  TOWED 11,000: **14.5mm** ZPU-1/ZPU-2/ZPU-4; **23mm** ZU-23; **37mm** M-1939; **57mm** S-60; **85mm** M-1939 *KS-12*; **100mm** KS-19

MSL

SSM 64+: 24 FROG-3/FROG-5/FROG-7; some *Musudan*; ε10 *No-dong* (ε90+ msl); 30+ *Scud*-B/*Scud*-C (ε200+ msl)

Navy ε60,000

FORCES BY ROLE

Navy 2 (Fleet) HQ located at Tasa-ri; 1 HQ located at Nampo; 1 HQ located at Toejo Dong

EQUIPMENT BY TYPE

SUBMARINES • TACTICAL 70
 SSK 22 PRC Type-031/FSU *Romeo*† each with 8 single 533mm TT with 14 SAET-60 HWT
 SSC 28 *Sang-O*† each with 2 single 533mm TT each with Russian 53–65 ASW
 SSW 20† (some *Yugo*, each with 2 single 406mm TT; some *Yeono*)
PRINCIPAL SURFACE COMBATANTS 3
 FRIGATES • FFG 3:
  2 *Najin* each with 2 single lnchr each with P-15 *Termit* (SS-N-2) AShM, 2 RBU 1200 (10 eff.), 2 100mm gun
  1 *Soho* with 4 single lnchr each with P-15 *Termit* (SS-N-2) AShM, 2 RBU 1200 (10 eff.), 1 100mm gun, 1 hel landing platform (for med hel)
PATROL AND COASTAL COMBATANTS 383
 PCG 18
  8 *Osa* II each with 2 single each with P-15 *Termit* (SS-N-2) AShM
  10 *Soju* each with 4 single each with P-15 *Termit* (SS-N-2) AShM
 PCO 5: 4 *Sariwon*; 1 *Tral* each with 1 85mm gun
 PCC 18:
  6 *Hainan* each with 4 RBU 1200 (20 eff.)
  12 *Taechong* each with 2 RBU 1200 (10 eff.), 1 100mm gun
 PBFG 16:
  4 *Huangfen* each with 4 single each with P-15 *Termit* (SS-N-2) AShM
  6 *Komar* each with 2 single lnchr each with P-15 *Termit* (SS-N-2) AShM
  6 *Sohung* each with 2 single lnchr each with P-15 *Termit* (SS-N-2) AShM
 PBF 229: 54 *Chong-Jin*; 142 *Ku Song/Sin Hung/Sin Hung (mod)*; 33 *Sinpo*
 PB 97
  59 *Chaho*
  6 *Chong-Ju* each with 2 RBU 1200 (10 eff.), 1 85mm gun
  13 *Shanghai* II
  19 SO-1
MINE WARFARE • MINE COUNTERMEASURES 24: 19 *Yukto* I; 5 *Yukto* II
AMPHIBIOUS
 LANDING SHIPS • LSM 10 *Hantae* (capacity 3 tanks; 350 troops)
 LANDING CRAFT 257:
  LCPL 96 *Nampo* (capacity 35 troops)
  LCM 25
  LCVP 136 (capacity 50 troops)
LOGISTICS AND SUPPORT 23:
 AS 8 (converted cargo ships); **ASR** 1 Kowan; **AGI** 14 (converted fishing vessels)

FACILITIES

Bases Located at Tasa-ri, Koampo, Chodo-ri, Sagon-ni, Pipa Got, Nampo (West Coast); Puam-Dong, Toejo Dong, Chaho Nodongjagu, Mayang-do, Mugye-po, Najin, Songjon-pardo, Changjon, Munchon (East Coast)

Coastal Defence

FORCES BY ROLE

AShM   2 regt with HY-1 (CSS-N-2) *Silkworm*; (6 sites, and probably some mobile launchers); KN-01 in development

EQUIPMENT BY TYPE

ARTY • TOWED 122mm M-1931/37; 152mm M-1937 COASTAL 130mm M-1992; SM-4-1

MSL • AShM HY-1 (CSS-N-2) *Silkworm*; KN-01 in development

Air Force 110,000

4 air divs. 1st, 2nd and 3rd Air Divs (cbt) responsible for N, E and S air defence sectors respectively. 8th Air Div (trg) responsible for NE sector. 33 regts (11 ftr/fga, 2 bbr, 7 hel, 7 pt, 6 trg) plus 3 indep air bns (recce/EW, test and evaluation, naval spt). The AF controls the national airline. Approx 70 full time/contingency air bases.

Flying hours   20 hrs/year on ac

FORCES BY ROLE

Bbr   3 (lt) regt with H-5 *Beagle*

Ftr/FGA   1 regt with F-7B *Airguard*; 6 regt with J-5; 4 regt with J-6; 5 regt with J-7; 1 regt with MiG-23 *Flogger* ML/P; 1 regt with MiG-29 *Fulcrum*; 1 regt with Su-7 *Fitter*; 1 regt with Su-25 *Frogfoot*

Tpt   regts with Y-5 (to infiltrate 2 air force sniper brigades deep into ROK rear areas (possibly grounded)); An-24 *Coke*; Il-18 *Coot*; Il-62M *Classic*; Tu-134 *Crusty*; Tu-154 *Careless*

Trg   regts with CJ-6; FT-2; MiG-21 *Fishbed*

Atk hel   regt with Mi-24 *Hind*

Tpt Hel   some regt with Hughes 500D; Mi-8 *Hip*/Mi-17 *Hip H*; PZL Mi-2 *Hoplite*; Z-5

SAM   19 bde with S-125 *Pechora* (SA-3 *Goa*); S-75 *Dvina* (SA-2 *Guideline*); S-200 *Angara* (SA-5 *Gammon*); 9K36 *Strela*-3 (SA-14 *Gremlin*); 9K310 *Igla*-1 (SA-16 *Gimlet*); 9K32 *Strela*-2 (SA-7 *Grail*)‡; (New medium-range SAM system shown in 2010 – designation unk.)

EQUIPMENT BY TYPE

AIRCRAFT 620 combat capable

BBR 80 H-5†

FTR 458: 40 F-7B *Airguard*; 107 J-5; 100 J-6; 120 J-7†; 46 MiG-23ML *Flogger*; 10 MiG-23P *Flogger*; ε35 MiG-29A/S *Fulcrum*

FGA 48: 30 MiG-21bis *Fishbed*†; 18 Su-7 *Fitter*

ATK 34 Su-25 *Frogfoot*

TPT 217: Light 208: 6 An-24 *Coke*; 2 Tu-134 *Crusty*; ε200 Y-5 PAX 9: 2 Il-18 *Coot*; 2 Il-62M *Classic*; 4 Tu-154 *Careless*; 1 Tu-204-300

TRG 215: 180 CJ-6; 35 FT-2

HELICOPTERS

ATK 20 Mi-24 *Hind*

MRH 80 Hughes 500D

TPT 202 Medium 63: 15 Mi-8 *Hip*/Mi-17 *Hip H*; 48 Z-5 Light 139 PZL Mi-2 *Hoplite*

UAV • ISR • Light *Pchela*-1 (*Shmel*)

AD • SAM 3400+

TOWED 312+: 179+ S-75 *Dvina* (SA-2 *Guideline*); 133 S-125 *Pechora* (SA-3 *Goa*)

STATIC/SHELTER 38 S-200 (SA-5 *Gammon*)

MANPAD 3,050+ 9K32 *Strela*-2 (SA-7 *Grail*)‡; 9K36 *Strela*-3 (SA-14 *Gremlin*); 9K310 *Igla*-1 (SA-16 *Gimlet*)

MSL

ASM Kh-23 (AS-7 *Kerry*); Kh-25 (AS-10 *Karen*)

AAM • IR AAM R-3 (AA-2 *Atoll*)‡; R-60 (AA-8 *Aphid*); R-73 (AA-11 *Archer*); PL-5; PL-7

Paramilitary 189,000 active

Security Troops 189,000 (incl border guards, public safety personnel)

Ministry of Public Security

Worker/Peasant Red Guard ε5,700,000 reservists

Org on a provincial/town/village basis; comd structure is bde–bn–coy–pl; small arms with some mor and AD guns (but many units unarmed)

Korea, Republic of ROK

South Korean Won		2009	2010	2011
GDP	won	1,063tr	1,154tr	
	US$	837bn	992bn	
per capita	US$	17,170	20,457	
Growth	%	0.2	6.0	
Inflation	%	2.8	3.0	
Def exp	won	28.5tr		
	US$	22.4bn		
Def bdgt	won	28.5tr	29.6tr	25.6tr
	US$	22.5bn	25.4bn	
US$1=won		1270.09	1163.25	

Population	48,500,717

Age	0–14	15–19	20–24	25–29	30–64	65 plus
Male	8.2%	3.8%	3.4%	3.9%	26.2%	4.6%
Female	7.5%	3.3%	3.0%	3.5%	25.9%	6.8%

Capabilities

ACTIVE 655,000 (Army 522,000 Navy 68,000 Air 65,000) Paramilitary 4,500

Terms of service conscription: Army, Navy and Air Force 26 months

RESERVE 4,500,000

Reserve obligation of three days per year. First Combat Forces (Mobilisation Reserve Forces) or Regional Combat Forces (Homeland Defence Forces) to age 33

Paramilitary 3,000,000

Being reorganised

ORGANISATIONS BY SERVICE

Army 522,000

FORCES BY ROLE

Comd	2 army HQ; 8 corps HQ; 1 (Capital Defence) comd
Armd	4 indep bde
Mech Inf	5 div (each: 2 mech inf bde, 1 armd bde, 1 recce bn, 1 fd arty bde, 1 engr bn)
Inf	17 div (each: 1 arty regt (4 arty bn), 1 recce bn, 1 engr bn, 1 tk bn, 3 inf regt); 2 indep bde
SF	1 (Special Warfare) comd; 7 bde
Air aslt	1 bde
Counter-Infiltration	3 bde
AD	3 ADA bde; 3 SAM bn with I HAWK; 2 SAM bn with Nike Hercules;
SSM	3 bn
Hel	1 (army avn) comd

EQUIPMENT BY TYPE

MBT 2,414: 1,000 K1; 484 K1A1; 253 M-48; 597 M-48A5; 80 T-80U; (400 M-47 in store)
AIFV 100+: 40 BMP-3; 60+ K21
APC 2,780
  APC (T) 2,560: 300 Bv 206; 1,700 KIFV; 420 M-113; 140 M-577
  APC (W) 220: 20 BTR-80; 200 KM-900/-901 (Fiat 6614)
ARTY 11,038+
  SP 1,353+: **155mm** 1,340: ε300 K-9 *Thunder*; 1,040 M-109A2 (K55/K55A1); **175mm** some M-107; **203mm** 13 M-110
  TOWED 3,500+: **105mm** 1,700 M-101/KH-178; **155mm** 1,800+ KH-179/M-114/M-115
  MRL 185: **130mm** 156 *Kooryong*; **227mm** 29 MLRS (all ATACMS capable)
  MOR 6,000: **81mm** KM-29 (M-29); **107mm** M-30
AT • MSL • MANPATS AT-7 9K115 *Saxhorn*; TOW-2A
  RCL 57mm; 75mm; 90mm M-67; **106mm** M-40A2
  RL 67mm PZF 44 *Panzerfaust*
  GUNS 58
    SP 90mm 50 M-36
    TOWED 76mm 8 M-18 *Hellcat* (AT gun)
HELICOPTERS
  ATK 60 AH-1F *Cobra*/AH-1J *Cobra*
  MRH 175: 130 Hughes 500D; 45 MD-500
  TPT 189 **Heavy** 24: 18 CH-47D *Chinook*; 6 MH-47E *Chinook* **Medium** 133: 3 AS-332L *Super Puma*; 130 UH-60P *Black Hawk* **Light** 32: 20 Bell-205 (UH-1H *Iroquois*); 12 Bo-105
AD • SAM 1,138+
  SP *Chun Ma Pegasus*

TOWED 158 I-*HAWK* MIM-23B; 48 *Patriot* to be delivered
STATIC 200 MIM-14 *Nike Hercules*
MANPAD 780+: 60 FIM-43 *Redeye*; ε200 FIM-92A *Stinger*; 350 *Javelin*; 170 *Mistral*; 9K31 *Igla*-1 (SA-16 *Gimlet*)
GUNS 330+
  SP 170: **20mm** ε150 KIFV *Vulcan* SPAAG; **30mm** 20 BIHO *Flying Tiger*
  TOWED 160: **20mm** 60 M-167 *Vulcan*; **35mm** 20 GDF-003; **40mm** 80 L/60/L/70; M1
RADAR • LAND AN/TPQ-36 *Firefinder* (arty, mor); AN/TPQ-37 *Firefinder* (arty); RASIT (veh, arty)
MSL • SSM 30 NHK-I/-II *Hyonmu*

Reserves

FORCES BY ROLE

Comd	1 army HQ
Inf	24 div

Navy 68,000 (incl marines)

Naval HQ (CNOROK) located at Gyeryongdae, with an Operational Cmd HQ (CINCROKFLT) located at Jinhae with 3 Separate Fleet Elements; 1st Fleet Donghae (East Sea – Sea of Japan); 2nd Fleet Pyeongtaek (West Sea – Yellow Sea); 3rd Fleet Busan (South Sea – Korea Strait); additional 3 Flotillas (incl SF, mine warfare, amphibious and spt elements) and 1 Naval Air Wing (3 gp plus Spt gp)

EQUIPMENT BY TYPE

SUBMARINES • TACTICAL 23
  SSK 12:
    9 *Chang Bogo* each with 8 single 533mm TT each with SUT HWT
    3 *Son Won-ill* (KSS-2; AIP fitted) each with 8 single 533mm TT each with SUT HWT (additional vessels in build)
  SSI 11: 9 *Cosmos*; 2 *Dolgorae* (KSS-1) each with 2 single 406mm TT
PRINCIPAL SURFACE COMBATANTS 47
  CRUISERS • CGHM 1
    1 *Sejong* (KDX-3) with 2 quad Mk141 lnchr (8 eff.) each with RGM-84 *Harpoon* AShM, 1 48-cell Mk41 VLS with SM-2MR SAM, 1 32-cell Mk41 VLS with SM-2MR SAM, 1 Mk49 GMLS with RIM-116, 2 triple 324mm ASTT (6 eff.) each with K745 LWT, 1 32-cell VLS with ASROC (intednd for *Cheon Ryong* LACM), 1 127mm gun, (capacity 2 *Lynx* Mk99 hel); (additional 2 of class in build)
  DESTROYERS • DDGHM 6:
    6 *Chungmugong Yi Sun-Jhin* (KDX-2) each with 2 quad Mk141 lnchr (8 eff.) each with RGM-84C *Harpoon* AShM, 2 32-cell Mk41 VLS (64 eff.) each with SM-2 MR SAM/ASROC, 2 triple 324mm ASTT (6 eff.) each with Mk46 LWT,1 127mm gun (capacity 1 *Lynx* Mk99 hel)
  FRIGATES 12
  FFGHM 3:
    3 *Gwanggaeto Daewang* (KDX-1) each with 2 quad Mk141 lnchr (8 eff.) each with RGM-84 *Harpoon* AShM, 1 16 cell Mk48 VLS with *Sea Sparrow* SAM, 2 triple 324mm ASTT (6 eff.) each with Mk46 LWT, 1 127mm gun, (capacity 1 *Lynx* Mk99 hel)

FFGM 9:

9 *Ulsan* each with 2 quad Mk141 lnchr (8 eff.) each with RGM-84C *Harpoon* AShM, 2 triple 324mm ASTT (6 eff.) each with Mk46 LWT, 2 76mm gun

PATROL AND COASTAL COMBATANTS 111

CORVETTES 30

FSG 7:

3 *Gumdoksuri* each with 2 twin lnchr each with RGM-84 *Harpoon* AShM, 1 76mm gun (additional vessel in build)

4 *Po Hang* each with 2 single lnchr each with MM-38 *Exocet* AShM, 2 triple ASTT (6 eff.) each with Mk 46 LWT, 1 76mm gun

FS 23:

4 *Dong Hae* each with 2 triple ASTT (6 eff.) each with Mk 46 LWT, 1 76mm gun

19 *Po Hang* each with 2 triple ASTT (6 eff.) each with Mk 46 LWT, 2 76mm gun

PBF 81 *Sea Dolphin*

MINE WARFARE 10

MINE COUNTERMEASURES 9

MHO 6 *Kan Kyeong*

MSO 3 *Yang Yang*

MINELAYERS • ML 1 *Won San*

AMPHIBIOUS

PRINCIPAL AMPHIBIOUS SHIPS 1:

LPD 1 *Dokdo* (capacity 2 LCVP; 10 tanks; 700 troops; 10 UH-60 hel)

LANDING SHIPS 5:

LST 5: 3 *Alligator* (capacity 20 tanks; 300 troops); 2 *Un Bong* (capacity 16 tanks; 200 troops)

LANDING CRAFT 41:

LCAC 5: 3 *Tsaplya* (capacity 1 MBT; 130 troops); 2 LSF-II

LCM 10 LCM-8

LCT 6

LCVP 20

LOGISTICS AND SUPPORT 24

AORH 3 *Chun Jee*

ARS 1

AG 1 *Sunjin* (trials spt)

ATS 2

AGOR 17 (civil manned, funded by the Ministry of Transport)

FACILITIES

Bases   Located at Pusan, Mukho, Cheju, Pohang, Mokpo, Jinhae (Fleet HQ and 3rd Fleet), Donghae (1st Fleet), Pyongtaek (2nd Fleet)

Naval Aviation

AIRCRAFT 8 combat capable

ASW 8 P-3C *Orion*

TPT • Light 5 Cessna F406 *Caravan II*

HELICOPTERS

ASW 24: 11 *Lynx* Mk99; 13 *Lynx* Mk99-A

MRH 5 SA-316 *Alouette III* (IAR-316)

Marines 27,000

FORCES BY ROLE

Marine 2 div (each 3 mne regt; 1 arty regt; 1 tk bn; 1 amph bn; 1 recce bn; 1 engr bn); 1 bde

Spt   some unit

EQUIPMENT BY TYPE

MBT 100 50 KIAI; 50 M-48

AAV 166 AAV-7A1

ARTY TOWED: 105mm; 155mm

LNCHR: some single (truck mounted) each with RGM-84A *Harpoon* AShM

Air Force 65,000

FORCES BY ROLE

4 Cmds (Ops, Southern Combat, Logs, Trg), Tac Airlift Wg and Composite Wg are all responsible to ROK Air Force HQ.

FGA/Ftr	1 wg with F-15K; 2 wg with F-16C/D *Fighting Falcon* (KF-16C/D); F-4E *Phantom II*; 3 wg with F-5E *Tiger II*; F-5F *Tiger II*
ISR	1 wg with KO-1; 1 gp with Hawker 800RA; RF-4C *Phantom II**; RF-5A *Tiger II**; *Harpy*; *Searcher*
SIGINT	1 sqn with Hawker 800XP
SAR	1 sqn with Bell-205 (UH-1H *Iroquois*); Bell 212
Tpt	some wg with AS-332 *Super Puma*; B-737-300 (VIP); BAe-748 (VIP); C-130H *Hercules*; CH-47 *Chinook*; CN-235-220/CN-235M; Ka-32 *Helix C* (SAR); S-92A *Superhawk* (VIP); UH-60 *Black Hawk* (Spec Ops)
Trg	1 wg (equipping) with T-50 *Golden Eagle**; some schools/sqn with F-5B *Freedom Fighter*; *Hawk* MK67; KT-1; T-38 *Talon*; Il-103

EQUIPMENT BY TYPE

AIRCRAFT 490 combat capable

FTR 233: 20 F-5B *Freedom Fighter*; 142 F-5E *Tiger II*; 32 F-5F *Tiger II*

FGA 234: 70 F-4E *Phantom II*; 39 F-15K *Eagle* (20 more on order 2010–2012); 118 F-16C *Fighting Falcon* (KF-16C); 46 F-16D *Fighting Falcon* (KF-16D); (some F-4D *Phantom* II in store)

ISR 47: 4 Hawker 800RA; 20 KO-1; 17 RF-4C *Phantom II**; 5 RF-5A *Tiger II**

SIGINT 4 Hawker 800SIG

TPT 33 **Medium** 10 C-130H *Hercules*; **Light** 20 CN-235-220/CN-235M **PAX** 3: 1 B-737-300 (VIP); 2 BAe-748 (VIP)

TRG 150: 17 *Hawk* Mk67*; 15 Il-103; 83 KT-1; 10 T-38 *Talon* (being returned to the USAF); 25 T-50 *Golden Eagle**

HELICOPTERS

TPT 56 **Heavy** 6 CH-47 *Chinook* **Medium** 40: 2 AS-332 *Super Puma*; 7 Ka-32 *Helix C*; 3 S-92A *Superhawk*; 28 UH-60 *Black Hawk* **Light** 10: 5 Bell-205 (UH-1H *Iroquois*) 5 Bell 212/Bell 412 *Twin Huey*

UAV • ISR 103+ **Medium** 3+: some *Night Intruder*; 3 *Searcher* **Light** 100 *Harpy*

MSL • TACTICAL

ASM AGM-130; AGM-142 *Popeye*

AGM AGM-65A *Maverick*; AGM-84 *Harpoon*; AGM-84-H SLAM-ER

ARM AGM-88 *HARM*

AAM • IR AAM AIM-9 *Sidewinder*; SARH AAM AIM-7 *Sparrow*; ARH AAM AIM-120B *AMRAAM*/AIM-120C5 *AMRAAM*

Paramilitary ε4,500 active

Civilian Defence Corps 3,000,000 reservists (to age 50)

Maritime Police ε4,500
PATROL AND COASTAL COMBATANTS 69:
  PSO 5: 1 *Sumjinkang*; 3 *Mazinger*; 1 *Sambongho*
  PCO 7: 1 *Han Kang*; 6 *Sea Dragon/Whale*;
  PCC 32: 4 *Bukhansan*; 22 *Sea Wolf/Shark*; 6 *(430 tonne)*
  PB 25: 5 Hyundai Type; ε20 (various)
LOGISTICS AND SUPPORT • ARS 13
HELICOPTERS
  MRH 9 Hughes 500
  TPT • Light 2 AW-139

DEPLOYMENT

AFGHANISTAN
NATO • ISAF 246
UN • UNAMA 1 obs

ARABIAN SEA & GULF OF ADEN
Combined Maritime Forces • CTF-151: 1 DDGHM

CÔTE D'IVOIRE
UN • UNOCI 2 obs

HAITI
UN • MINUSTAH 242; 1 engr coy

INDIA/PAKISTAN
UN • UNMOGIP 9 obs

LEBANON
UN • UNIFIL 368; 1 mech inf bn

LIBERIA
UN • UNMIL 1; 1 obs

NEPAL
UN • UNMIN 4 obs

SUDAN
UN • UNMIS 1; 6 obs
UN • UNAMID 2

UAE
130-150 SOF for training activities at UAE Special Operations School at Al-Ain (due to deploy Jan 2011)

WESTERN SAHARA
UN • MINURSO 2 obs

FOREIGN FORCES

Sweden NNSC: 5 obs
Switzerland NNSC: 5 obs
United States US Pacific Command: 25,374
  Army 17,130; 1 HQ (8th Army) at Seoul; 1 div HQ (2nd Inf) at Tongduchon; 1 armd HBCT; 1 cbt avn bde; 1 arty

(fires) bde; 1 AD bde with MIM 104 *Patriot*/FIM-92A *Avenger*; some M-1 *Abrams* MBT; some M-2/M-3 *Bradley* AIFV; some M-109 SP arty; some MLRS; some AH-64 *Apache*; some CH-47 *Chinook*; some UH-60 *Black Hawk*
Navy 254
USAF 7,857; 1 HQ (7th Air Force) at Osan AB; 1 ftr wg at Kunsan AB (1 ftr sqn with 20 F-16C *Fighting Falcon*/F-16D *Fighting Falcon*); 1 ftr wg at Kunsan AB (1 ftr sqn with 20 F-16C *Fighting Falcon*/F-16D *Fighting Falcon*, 1 ftr sqn with 24 A-10 *Thunderbolt II*/OA-10 *Thunderbolt II* (12 of each type) at Osan AB)
USMC 133

Kyrgyzstan KGZ

Kyrgyzstani Som s		2009	2010	2011
GDP	s	196bn	207bn	
	US$	4.58bn	4.53bn	
per capita	US$	86	815	
Growth	%	2.3	2.2	
Inflation	%	6.9	4.8	
Def exp	s	1.05bn		
	US$	24m		
Def bdgt	s	1.9bn	4.39bn	
	US$	44m	96m	
FMA (US)	US$	0.9m	3.5m	2.4m
US$1=s		42.87	45.76	

Population 5,550,239

Ethnic groups: Kyrgyz 56%; Russian 17%; Uzbek 13%; Ukrainian 3%

Age	0–14	15–19	20–24	25–29	30–64	65 plus
Male	14.9%	5.2%	5.4%	4.7%	16.8%	2.0%
Female	14.3%	5.0%	5.3%	4.7%	18.5%	3.2%

Capabilities

ACTIVE 10,900 (Army 8,500 Air 2,400) Paramilitary 9,500
Terms of service 18 months

ORGANISATIONS BY SERVICE

Army 8,500
FORCES BY ROLE
MR   2 bde; 1 (mtn) bde
SF   1 bde
Arty 1 bde
AD   1 bde

EQUIPMENT BY TYPE
MBT 150 T-72
RECCE 30 BRDM-2
AIFV 320: 230 BMP-1; 90 BMP-2
APC (W) 35: 25 BTR-70; 10 BTR-80
ARTY 246

SP **122mm** 18 2S1 *Carnation*

TOWED 141: **100mm** 18 M-1944; **122mm** 107: 72 D-30; 35 M-30 *M-1938*; **152mm** 16 D-1

GUN/MOR 120mm 12 2S9 *Anona*

MRL 21: **122mm** 15 BM-21; **220mm** 6 9P140 *Uragan*

MOR 120mm 54: 6 2S12; 48 M-120

AT • MSL • MANPATS 26+: 26 9K11 (AT-3 *Sagger*); 9K111 (AT-4 *Spigot*); 9K113 (AT-5 *Spandrel*)

RCL 73mm SPG-9

RL 73mm RPG-7 *Knout*

GUNS 100mm 18 MT-12/T-12

AD • SAM • MANPAD 9K32 *Strela-2* (SA-7 *Grail*)‡

GUNS 48

SP **23mm** 24 ZSU-23-4

TOWED 57mm 24 S-60

Air Force 2,400

FORCES BY ROLE

Ftr/Tpt   1 regt with L-39 *Albatros*; 1 (comp avn) regt with MiG-21 *Fishbed*; An-12 *Cub*; An-26 *Curl*

Ftr   1 regt with L-39 *Albatros*

Atk Hel/   1 regt with Mi-24 *Hind*; Mi-8 *Hip*
Tpt Hel

SAM   some regt with S-125 *Pechora* (SA-3 *Goa*); 2K11 *Krug* (SA-4 *Ganef*); S-75 *Dvina* (SA-2 *Guideline*)

EQUIPMENT BY TYPE

AIRCRAFT 52 combat capable

FGA 48 MiG-21 *Fishbed*; (24 more in store)

TPT 4 **Medium** 2 An-12 *Cub* **Light** 2 An-26 *Curl*

TRG 4 L-39 *Albatros**; (24 more in store)

HELICOPTERS

ATK 9 Mi-24 *Hind*

TPT • Medium 23 Mi-8 *Hip*

AD • SAM

SP **2K11** *Krug* (SA-4 *Ganef*)

TOWED S-75 *Dvina* (SA-2 *Guideline*); S-125 *Pechora* (SA-3 *Goa*)

Paramilitary 9,500

Border Guards 5,000 (KGZ conscript, RUS officers)

Interior Troops 3,500

National Guard 1,000

DEPLOYMENT

BOSNIA-HERZEGOVINA

OSCE • Bosnia and Herzegovina 1

LIBERIA

UN • UNMIL 3 obs

SUDAN

UN • UNMIS 7 obs

FOREIGN FORCES

Russia ε500 Military Air Forces: 5 Su-25 *Frogfoot*; 2 Mi-8 *Hip*

Laos LAO

New Lao Kip		2009	2010	2011
GDP	kip	47.6tr	53.7tr	
	US$	5.59bn	6.42bn	
per capita	US$	884	997	
Growth	%	6.4	7.4	
Inflation	%	0.04	5.4	
Def exp	kip	ε119bn		
	US$	ε14m		
US$1=kip		8515.97	8369.29	

Population   6,436,093

Ethnic groups: Lao 55%; Khmou 11%; Hmong 8%

Age	0–14	15–19	20–24	25–29	30–64	65 plus
Male	18.5%	5.6%	4.9%	4.2%	14.7%	1.7%
Female	18.2%	5.6%	5.0%	4.2%	15.2%	2.0%

Capabilities

ACTIVE 29,100 (Army 25,600 Air 3,500) **Paramilitary 100,000**

Terms of service 18 month minimum conscription

ORGANISATIONS BY SERVICE

Army 25,600

FORCES BY ROLE

4 Mil Regions

Armd   1 bn

Inf   5 div; 7 indep regt; 65 indep coy

Arty   5 bn

ADA   9 bn

Engr   1 regt

Avn   1 (liaison) lt flt

Engr   2 regt
construction

EQUIPMENT BY TYPE

MBT 25: 15 T-54/T-55; 10 T-34/85

LT TK 10 PT-76

APC (W) 50: 30 BTR-40/BTR-60; 20 BTR-152

ARTY 62+

TOWED 62: **105mm** 20 M-101; **122mm** 20 D-30/M-30 M-1938; **130mm** 10 M-46; **155mm** 12 M-114

MOR 81mm; **82mm**; **107mm** M-1938/M-2A1; **120mm** M-43

AT • RCL 57mm M-18/A1; **75mm** M-20; **106mm** M-40; **107mm** B-11

RL 73mm RPG-7 *Knout*

AD • SAM • MANPAD 9K32 *Strela-2* (SA-7 *Grail*)‡

GUNS

SP **23mm** ZSU-23-4

TOWED **14.5mm** ZPU-1/ZPU-4; **23mm** ZU-23; **37mm** M-1939; **57mm** S-60

Army Marine Section ε600
PATROL AND COASTAL COMBATANTS 52
    PBR 52
AMPHIBIOUS LCM 4

Air Force 3,500
FORCES BY ROLE

FGA   2 sqn with MiG-21bis *Fishbed L* & N†; MiG-21UM *Mongol B*†

Tpt   1 sqn with An-2 *Colt*; An-26 *Curl*; An-74 *Coaler*; Y-7; Y-12; Yak-40 *Codling* (VIP)

Trg   1 sqn with Yak-18 *Max*

Tpt   1 sqn with Ka-32T *Helix C*; Mi-6 *Hook*; Mi-8 *Hip*; Mi-
Hel   17 *Hip H*; 1 Mi-26 *Halo*; SA-360 *Dauphin*

EQUIPMENT BY TYPE
AIRCRAFT 24 combat capable
    FGA 24: up to 22 MiG-21bis *Fishbed L & N*†; up to 2 MiG-21UM *Mongol B*†
    TPT • Light 15: 4 An-2 *Colt*; 3 An-26 *Curl*; 1 An-74 *Coaler*; 5 Y-7; 1 Y-12; 1 Yak-40 *Codling* (VIP)
    TRG 8 Yak-18 *Max*
HELICOPTERS
    MRH 12 Mi-17 *Hip H*
    TPT 15 **Heavy** 2: 1 Mi-6 *Hook*; 1 Mi-26 *Halo* **Medium** 10: 1 Ka-32T *Helix C* (5 more on order); 9 Mi-8 *Hip* **Light** 3 SA-360 *Dauphin*
MSL • AAM • IR AAM R-3 (AA-2 *Atoll*)†

Paramilitary

Militia Self-Defence Forces 100,000+
Village 'home guard' or local defence

Malaysia MYS

Malaysian Ringgit RM		2009	2010	2011
GDP	RM	680bn	744bn	
	US$	193bn	230bn	
per capita	US$	7,025	8,237	
Growth	%	-1.7	5.7	
Inflation	%	0.6	2.2	
Def exp	RM	13.7bn		
	US$	3.88bn		
Def bdgt	RM	10.7bn	9.1bn	
	US$	3.02bn	2.81bn	
US$1=RM		3.52	3.24	

Population   27,913,990

Ethnic groups: Malay and other indigenous (Bunipatre) 64%; Chinese 27%; Indian 9%

Age	0–14	15–19	20–24	25–29	30–64	65 plus
Male	15.2%	4.6%	4.2%	4.2%	20.3%	2.3%
Female	14.4%	4.4%	4.2%	4.1%	19.5%	2.6%

Capabilities

ACTIVE 109,000 (Army 80,000 Navy 14,000 Air 15,000) Paramilitary 24,600

RESERVE 51,600 (Army 50,000, Navy 1,000 Air Force 600) Paramilitary 244,700

ORGANISATIONS BY SERVICE

Army 80,000 (to be 60–70,000)
FORCES BY ROLE
2 mil regions, 1 HQ fd comd, 4 area comd (div)

Tk	1 regt
Armd	5 regt
Mech Inf	1 bde (3 mech bn)
Inf	9 bde (36 bn)
SF	1 bde (3 SF bn)
AB	1 bde (10th) (Rapid Deployment Force) with (1 lt tk sqn, 1 light arty regt, 3 AB bn)
Med Arty	2 regt
Fd Arty	7 regt
MRL	1 regt
AD	3 ADA regt
Engr	5 regt
Avn	1 hel sqn
Arty Loc	1 regt

EQUIPMENT BY TYPE
MBT 48 PT-91M *Twardy* (plus 10 variants)
LT TK 90 *Scorpion* (21 upgraded, some †)
RECCE 394: 140 AML-60/AML-90; 92 *Ferret* (60 mod); 82 SIBMAS (some †)
AIFV 44: 31 ACV300 *Adnan* (25mm *Bushmaster*); 13 ACV300 *Adnan* AGL
APC 731
    APC (T) 281: 149 ACV300 *Adnan* (incl 77 variants); 25 FV4333 *Stormer* (13 upgraded); 107 K-200A (incl 9 variants)
    APC (W) 450: 400 *Condor* (incl variants); 50 LAV-150 *Commando*
ARTY 454
    TOWED 164: **105mm** 130 Model 56 pack howitzer; **155mm** 34: 12 FH-70; 22 G-5
    MRL 36 *ASTROS* II (equipped with 127mm SS-30)
    MOR 254: **81mm SP** 14: 4 K281A1; 10 ACV300; **120mm SP** 8 ACV-S **81mm**: 232
AT MSL
    SP 8 ACV300 *Baktar Shikan*
    MANPATS 60+: 18 AT-7 9K115 *Saxhorn*; 24 *Eryx*; 18 *Baktar Shihan* (HJ-8); METIS-M; C90-CRRB
    RCL 260: **84mm** 236 *Carl Gustav*; **106mm** 24 M-40
    RL 73mm 584 RPG-7 *Knout*
AMPHIBIOUS • LCA 165 *Damen* Assault Craft 540 (capacity 10 troops)
HELICOPTERS
    TPT • Light 11 AW-109
AD SAM 15 *Jernas* (*Rapier 2000*)

MANPAD 48+: 48 *Starburst*; *Anza*; HY-6 (FN-6); 9K38
Igla (SA-18 *Grouse*)
GUNS • TOWED 60: 35mm 24 GDF-005; 40mm 36
L40/70

Reserves

Territorial Army
Some paramilitary forces to be incorporated into a re-
organised territorial organisation.
5 highway sy bn
Border Security 2 bde (being created from existing
Territorial units)
Inf   16 regt

Navy 14,000
1 Naval HQ located at Lumut with 3 additional Regional
Commands (Reg Cmd); Reg Cmd 1 Kuantan – East Coast;
Reg Cmd 2 Kota Kinabalu – Borneo; Reg Cmd 3 Langkawi
– West Coast

EQUIPMENT BY TYPE
SUBMARINES • TACTICAL • SSK 2 *Tunku Abdul
Rahman (Scorpene)* each with 6 single 533mm TT for WASS
Black Shark LWT
PRINCIPAL SURFACE COMBATANTS 8
FRIGATES 8:
FFGHM 2:
   2 *Lekiu* each with 2 quad lnchr (8 eff.) each with MM-
   40 *Exocet* AShM, 1 16-cell VLS with *Sea Wolf* SAM,
   2 B515 *ILAS*-3 triple 324mm ASTT (6 eff.) each with
   Sting Ray LWT, (capacity 1 *Super Lynx* hel)
FFG 2:
   2 *Kasturi* each with 2 twin lnchr (4 eff.) each with
   MM-38 *Exocet* AShM, 1 twin 375mm A/S mor (2 eff.),
   1 100mm gun, 1 hel landing platform
FF 4:
   4 *Kedah* (MEKO) each with 1 76mm gun, 1 hel landing
   platform, (fitted for MM-40 *Exocet* AShM & RAM
   CIWS; Further 2 of class in build)
PATROL AND COASTAL COMBATANTS 37
CORVETTES • FSGM 4:
   4 *Laksamana* each with 3 twin lnchr (6 eff.) each with
   Mk 2 *Otomat* AShM, 1 quad (4 eff.) with *Aspide* SAM, 2
   B515 *ILAS*-3 triple 324mm (6 eff.) each with A244 LWT,
   1 76mm gun
PCFG 4 *Perdana* (*Combattante* II) each with 2 single lnchr
each with MM-38 *Exocet* AShM
PBG 4 *Handalan* (*Spica*-M) each with 2 twin lnchr (4 eff.)
each with MM-38 *Exocet* AShM
PBF 17 *Tempur*
PB 8: 6 *Jerong* (Lurssen 45); 2 *Sri Perlis*
MINE WARFARE • MINE COUNTERMEASURES
MCO 4 *Mahamiru*
AMPHIBIOUS
LANDING SHIPS 1:
   LST 1 *Alligator* (On loan from ROK; capacity 20 tanks;
   300 troops)
LANDING CRAFT 115 LCM/LCU
LOGISTICS AND SUPPORT 15
AOR 2; AOL 4; AG 1; ARS 2; AGS 2; AX 1; AXS 1; TPT
2

FACILITIES
Bases   Located at Tanjung Pengelih, Semporna, Langkawi
        (under construction), Lumut, Labuan, Kuantan,
        Sepanggar Bay (under construction)

Naval Aviation 160
HELICOPTERS
   ASW 6 *Super Lynx 300*
   MRH 6 AS-555 *Fennec*
MSL
   ASM *Sea Skua*

Special Forces
Mne cdo   1 unit

Air Force 15,000
1 Air Op HQ, 2 Air Div, 1 trg and Log Cmd, 1 Intergrated
Area Def Systems HQ

Flying hours   60 hrs/year

FORCES BY ROLE

Ftr	1 sqn with MiG-29 (MiG-29N)/Mig-29UB *Fulcrum*(MiG-29NUB) (to be withdrawn from service)
FGA	1 sqn with F/A-18D *Hornet*; 1 sqn with Su-30MKM; 2 sqn with *Hawk* MK108*/Mk208*
FGA/ISR	1 sqn with F-5E *Tiger II*/F-5F *Tiger II*; RF-5E *Tigereye**
MP	1 sqn with Beech 200T
Tkr/Tpt	2 sqn with KC-130H *Hercules* (tkr); C-130H *Hercules*; C-130H-30 *Hercules*; Cessna 402B
Tpt	1 (VIP) sqn with Airbus A319CT; AW-109; B-737-700 BBJ; BD700 *Global Express*; F-28 *Fellowship*; *Falcon* 900; S-61N; S-70A *Black Hawk*; 1 sqn with CN-235
Tpt Hel	4 (tpt/SAR) sqn with S-61A-4 *Nuri*; S-61N; S-70A *Black Hawk*
SF	1 (Air Force Commando) unit (airfield defence/SAR)
SAM	1 sqn with *Starburst*

FACILTIES
Trg School 1 with MB-339A/C; MD3-160 *Aero Tiga*; PC-7/
PC-7 MK II *Turbo Trainer*; SA-316 *Alouette III*

EQUIPMENT BY TYPE
AIRCRAFT 82 combat capable
   FTR 31: 13 F-5E *Tiger II*/F-5F *Tiger II*; 16 MiG-29 *Fulcrum*
   (MiG-29N); 2 MiG-29UB *Fulcrum* (MIG-29NUB) (MiG-29
   to be withdrawn from service)
   FGA 26: 8 F/A-18D *Hornet*; 18 Su-30MKM
   ISR 4 Beech 200T; 2 RF-5E *Tigereye**
   TKR 2 KC-130H *Hercules*
   TPT 32 Medium 12: 4 C-130H *Hercules*; 8 C-130H-30
   Hercules; Light 15: 6 CN-235 (incl 2 VIP); 9 Cessna 402B
   (2 modified for aerial survey) PAX 5: 1 Airbus A319CT; 1
   B-737-700 BBJ; 1 BD700 *Global Express*; 1 F-28 *Fellowship*;
   1 *Falcon* 900

TRG 107: 8 *Hawk* Mk108*; 15 *Hawk* Mk208*; 8 MB-339AB; 8 MB-339C; 20 MD3-160 *Aero Tiga*; 30 PC-7; 18 PC-7 Mk II *Turbo Trainer*

HELICOPTERS
MRH 17 SA-316 *Alouette III*
TPT 29 **Medium** 28: 20 S-61A-4 *Nuri*; 4 S-61N; 4 S-70A *Black Hawk* **Light** 1 AW-109
UAV • ISR 3+ **Heavy** 3 *Eagle* ARV **Medium** *Aludra*
AD • SAM •MANPAD *Starburst*
MSL
ASM AGM-65 *Maverick*; AGM-84D *Harpoon*
AAM • IR AAM AIM-9 *Sidewinder*; R-73 (AA-11 *Archer*)
IR/SARH AAM R-27 (AA-10 *Alamo*); **SARH AAM** AIM-7 *Sparrow*

Paramilitary ε24,600

Police-General Ops Force 18,000

FORCES BY ROLE
Police   5 bde HQ; 2 (Aboriginal) bn; 19 bn; 4 indep coy
Spec Ops 1 bn

EQUIPMENT BY TYPE
RECCE ε100 S52 *Shorland*
APC (W) 170: 140 AT105 *Saxon*; ε30 SB-301

Malaysian Maritime Enforcement Agency (MMEA) ε4,500

1 MMEA HQ Putrajaya with designated control for the Malaysian Maritime Zone, which is divided into 5 Maritime Regions (Northern Peninsula; Southern Peninsula; Eastern Peninsula; Sarawak; Sabah) and subdivided into a further 18 Maritime Districts. Supported by one provisional MMEA Air Unit.

EQUIPMENT BY TYPE
PATROL AND COASTAL COMBATANTS 66:
   PSO 2 *Langkawi* each with 1 100mm gun, 1 hel landing platform
   PB 64: 15 *Gagah*; 4 *Malawali*; 2 *Nusa*; 1 *Peninjau*; 5 *Ramunia*; 2 *Rhu*; 4 *Semilang*; 15 *Sipadan* (ex-*Kris/Sabah*); 16 (various)
LOGISTICS AND SUPPORT • TRG 1 *Marlin*
AIRCRAFT • MP 2 Bombardier 415MP
HELICOPTERS
   MRH 3 AS-365 *Dauphin*

Marine Police 2,100

EQUIPMENT BY TYPE
PATROL AND COASTAL COMBATANTS 132
   PBF 12: 6 *Sangitan*; 6 Stan Patrol 1500
   PB/PBR 120

FACILITIES
Bases Located at Kuala Kemaman, Penang, Tampoi, Sandakan

Police Air Unit

AIRCRAFT
   TPT • Light 17: 4 Cessna 206 *Stationair*; 6 Cessna 208 *Caravan*; 7 PC-6 *Turbo-Porter*

HELICOPTERS
   TPT • Light 3: 1 Bell 206L *Long Ranger*; 2 AS-355F *Ecureuil II*

Area Security Units (R) 3,500
(Auxiliary General Ops Force)
Paramilitary   89 unit

Border Scouts (R) 1,200
in Sabah, Sarawak

People's Volunteer Corps 240,000 reservists (some 17,500 armed)
RELA

Customs Service
PATROL AND COASTAL COMBATANTS 23
   PBF 10
   PB 13

DEPLOYMENT

AFGHANISTAN
NATO • ISAF 40

DEMOCRATIC REPUBLIC OF THE CONGO
UN • MONUSCO 17 obs

LEBANON
UN • UNIFIL 744; 1 mech inf bn

LIBERIA
UN • UNMIL 5 obs

NEPAL
UN • UNMIN 7 obs

SUDAN
UN • UNAMID 12; 1 obs
UN • UNMIS 2; 6 obs

TIMOR LESTE
UN • UNMIT 2 obs

WESTERN SAHARA
UN • MINURSO 20; 12 obs; 1 fd hospital

FOREIGN FORCES

Australia Air Force: 13 with 1 AP-3C *Orion* crew; Army: 115; 1 inf coy (on 3-month rotational tours)

Mongolia MNG

Mongolian Tugrik t		2009	2010	2011
GDP	t	6.06tr	7.91tr	
	US$	4.22bn	5.72bn	
per capita	US$	1,579	2,116	
Growth	%	-1.6	7.0	
Inflation	%	6.3	7.9	
Def exp	t	ε54.8bn		
	US$	ε38m		
FMA (US)	US$	1.0m	4.5m	5.0m
US$1=t		1436.21	1384.16	

Population 2,701,117

Ethnic groups: Khalka 80%; Kazakh 6%

Age	0–14	15–19	20–24	25–29	30–64	65 plus
Male	14.0%	4.8%	5.5%	4.9%	19.1%	1.7%
Female	13.4%	4.6%	5.4%	4.8%	19.5%	2.3%

Capabilities

ACTIVE 10,000 (Army 8,900 Air 800 Construction Troops 300) **Paramilitary 7,200**

Terms of service conscription: one year (males aged 18–25)

RESERVE 137,000 (Army 137,000)

ORGANISATIONS BY SERVICE

Army 5,600; 3,300 conscript (total 8,900)
FORCES BY ROLE

MR 6 (under strength) regt

Lt Inf 1 bn (rapid deployment – 2nd bn to form)

AB 1 bn

Arty 1 regt

EQUIPMENT BY TYPE
MBT 370 T-54/T-55
RECCE 120 BRDM-2
AIFV 310 BMP-1
APC (W) 150 BTR-60
ARTY 570
  TOWED ε300: **122mm** D-30/M-30 *M-1938*; **130mm** M-46; **152mm** ML-20 *M-1937*
  MRL 122mm 130 BM-21
  MOR 140: **120mm**; **160mm**; **82mm**
AT • GUNS 200: **85mm** D-44/D-48; **100mm** M-1944/MT-12

Air Force 800
FORCES BY ROLE

Tpt 1 sqn with A-310-300; An-2 *Colt*; An-26 *Curl*; B-737

AtkHel/ 1 sqn with Mi-8 *Hip*; Mi-24 *Hind*; Mi-171 (SAR)
Tpt Hel

AD 2 regt with 150 S-60/ZPU-4/ZU-23

EQUIPMENT BY TYPE
AIRCRAFT • TPT 9 **Light** 7: 6 An-2 *Colt*; 1 An-26 *Curl*; **PAX** 2: 1 A-310-300; 1 B-737
HELICOPTERS
  ATK 11 Mi-24 *Hind*
  TPT • Medium 13: 11 Mi-8 *Hip*; 2 Mi-171
AD • GUNS • TOWED 150: **14.5mm** ZPU-4; **23mm** ZU-23; **57mm** S-60

Paramilitary 7,200 active

Border Guard 1,300; 4,700 conscript (total 6,000)

Internal Security Troops 400; 800 conscript (total 1,200)
Gd 4 unit

Construction Troops 300

DEPLOYMENT

AFGHANISTAN
NATO • ISAF 36

CENTRAL AFRICAN REPUBLIC/CHAD
UN • MINURCAT 268; 1 inf coy

DEMOCRATIC REPUBLIC OF THE CONGO
UN • MONUSCO 2 obs

LIBERIA
UN • UNMIL 150

SUDAN
UN • UNMIS 2 obs

WESTERN SAHARA
UN • MINURSO 4 obs

Asia

Myanmar MMR

Myanmar Kyat K		2009	2010	2011
GDP	K	32.2tr	36.2tr	
	US$	34.3bn	35.7bn	
	US$[a]	129bn	145bn	
per capita	US$	685	706	
	US$[a]	2,551	2,868	
Growth	%	4.3	5.0	
Inflation	%	1.5	7.9	
Def bdgt	K	ε1.79tr		
	US$	ε1.9bn		
US$1=K[b]	Official Rate	6.57	6.56	
	Unofficial Rate	ε941.05	ε1015.74	

[a] PPP estimate

[b] GDP figures above calculated using the estimated unofficial rate.

Population   50,495,672

Ethnic groups: Burmese 68%; Shan 9%; Karen 7%; Rakhine 4%; Chinese 3+%; Other Chin, Kachin, Kayan, Lahu, Mon, Palaung, Pao, Wa, 9%

Age	0–14	15–19	20–24	25–29	30–64	65 plus
Male	14.0%	4.9%	4.8%	4.6%	19.3%	2.2%
Female	13.5%	4.7%	4.7%	4.5%	20.0%	2.8%

Capabilities

ACTIVE 406,000 (Army 375,000 Navy 16,000 Air 15,000) **Paramilitary 107,250**

ORGANISATIONS BY SERVICE

Army ε375,000

FORCES BY ROLE

12 regional comd, 4 regional op comd, 14 military op comd, 34 tactical op comd (TDC)

Armd   10 bn

Inf   100 bn; 337 bn (regional comd)

Lt Inf   10 div

Arty   7 bn; 37 indep coy

AD   7 bn

EQUIPMENT BY TYPE

MBT 150: 50 T-72; 100 Type-69-II

LT TK 105 Type-63 (ε60 serviceable)

RECCE 115: 45 *Ferret*; 40 Humber *Pig*; 30 Mazda

APC 325

   APC (T) 305: 250 Type-85; 55 Type-90

   APC (W) 20 *Hino*

ARTY 238+

   TOWED 128+: **105mm** 96 M-101; **122mm**; **130mm** 16 M-46; **140mm**; **155mm** 16 *Soltam*

   MRL 30+: **107mm** 30 Type-63; **122mm** BM-21 (reported); **240mm** M-1991 (reported)

MOR 80+: **82mm**Type-53 (M-37); **120mm** 80+: 80 *Soltam*; Type-53 (M-1943)

AT

   RCL 1,000+: **106mm** M-40A1; **84mm** ε1,000 *Carl Gustav*

   RL 73mm RPG-7 *Knout*

   GUNS 60: **57mm** 6-pdr; **76.2mm** 17-pdr

AD • SAM • MANPAD HN-5 *Hong Nu/Red Cherry* (reported); 9K310 *Igla*-1 (SA-16 *Gimlet*)

   GUNS 46

      SP 57mm 12 Type-80

      TOWED 34: **37mm** 24 Type-74; **40mm** 10 M-1

MSL • SSM some *Hwasong*-6 (reported)

Navy ε16,000

Naval Forces experienced considerable damage during Tropical Cyclone Nargis in 2008 with up to 30 vessels destroyed.

EQUIPMENT BY TYPE

PATROL AND COASTAL COMBATANTS 70

   CORVETTES • FS 3 *Anawrahta* each with 1 76mm gun

   PCG 6 *Houxin* each with 2 twin lnchr (4 eff.) each with C-801 (CSS-N-4 *Sardine*) AShM

   PCO 2 *Indaw*

   PCC 9 *Hainan*

   PBG 9 *Myanmar* each with 2 twin lnchr (4 eff.) each with 4 C-801 (CSS-N-4 *Sardine*) AShM

   PB 18: 3 PB-90; 6 PGM 401; 6 PGM 412; 3 *Swift*

   PBR 23: 4 *Sagu*; 9 Y-301; 1 Y-301 (Imp); 9 (various)

AMPHIBIOUS • CRAFT 18: 8 LCU 10 LCM

LOGISTICS AND SUPPORT 10

   AOT 1; **AK** 1; **AKSL** 5; **AGS** 2; **ABU** 1

FACILITIES

Bases   Located at Bassein, Mergui, Moulmein, Seikyi, Rangoon (Monkey Point), Sittwe

Naval Infantry 800

Navy 1 bn

Air Force ε15,000

FORCES BY ROLE

Ftr	3 sqn with F-7 *Airguard*; FT-7; MiG-29B *Fulcrum*; MiG-29UB *Fulcrum*
Atk	2 sqn with A-5M *Fantan*
Tpt	1 sqn with An-12 *Cub*; F-27 *Friendship*; FH-227; PC-6A *Turbo Porter*/PC-6B *Turbo Porter*
Trg	2 sqn with G-4 *Super Galeb**; PC-7 *Turbo Trainer**; PC-9*; 1 (trg/liaison) sqn with Ce-550 *Citation II*; Cessna 180 *Skywagon*; K-8 *Karakorum**
Tpt Hel	4 sqn with Bell 205; Bell 206 *Jet Ranger*; Mi-17 *Hip H*; PZL Mi-2 *Hoplite*; PZL W-3 *Sokol*; SA-316 *Alouette III*

EQUIPMENT BY TYPE

AIRCRAFT 136 combat capable

   FTR 69: 49 F-7 *Airguard*; 10 FT-7*; 8 MiG-29B *Fulcrum*; 2 MiG-29UB *Fulcrum*;

   ATK 22 A-5M *Fantan*

TPT 19 **Light** 15: 2 An-12 *Cub*; 4 Cessna 180 *Skywagon*; 1 Cessna 550 *Citation II*; 3 F-27 *Friendship*; 5 PC-6A *Turbo Porter/PC-6B Turbo Porter* **PAX** 4 FH-227
TRG 45+: 12 G-4 *Super Galeb**; 12+ K-8 *Karakorum**; 12 PC-7 *Turbo Trainer**; 9 PC-9*

HELICOPTERS
MRH 20: 11 Mi-17 *Hip H*; 9 SA-316 *Alouette III*
TPT 46: **Medium** 10 PZL W-3 *Sokol* **Light** 36: 12 Bell 205; 6 Bell 206 *Jet Ranger*; 18 PZL Mi-2 *Hoplite*

MSL • AAM • IR AAM Pl-5; R-73 (AA-11 *Archer*) **IR/SARH AAM** R-27 (AA-10 *Alamo*)

Paramilitary 107,250

People's Police Force 72,000

People's Militia 35,000

People's Pearl and Fishery Ministry ε250
PATROL AND COASTAL COMBATANTS • **PBR** 6 *Carpentaria*

Nepal NPL

Nepalese Rupee NR		2009	2010	2011
GDP	NR	991bn	1.13tr	
	US$	12.8bn	15.4bn	
per capita	US$	436	515	
Growth	%	4.7	3.5	
Inflation	%	13.2	10.5	
Def exp	NR	14.3bn		
	US$	184m		
Def bdgt	NR	15.5bn	18bn	
	US$	200m	245m	
FMA (US)	US$	-	0.8m	0.9m
US$1=NR		77.48	73.35	

Population 29,852,682

Religious groups: Hindu 90%; Buddhist 5%; Muslim 3%

Age	0–14	15–19	20–24	25–29	30–64	65 plus
Male	17.6%	6.2%	4.9%	3.7%	14.6%	2.0%
Female	17.0%	6.0%	5.1%	4.3%	16.3%	2.3%

Capabilities

ACTIVE 95,753 (Army 95,753) **Paramilitary 62,000**
Nepal is attempting to integrate the 23,500-strong (Maoist) People's Liberation Army (PLA) into the national army. This process has been delayed.

ORGANISATIONS BY SERVICE

Army 95,753
FORCES BY ROLE

Comd	6 inf div HQ; 1 (valley) comd
Inf	16 bde (total: 63 inf bn); 32 indep coy
SF	1 bde (1 AB, 1 mech inf, 1 indep SF bn)

Ranger	1 bn
Arty	1 HQ (4 arty regt,)
AD	1 HQ (2 AD regt, 4 indep AD coy)
Engr	1 HQ (5 engr bn)

EQUIPMENT BY TYPE
RECCE 40 *Ferret*
APC (W) 40 *Casspir*
ARTY 109+
 TOWED 39: **75mm** 6 pack; **94mm** 5 3.7in (mtn trg); **105mm** 28: 8 L-118 Lt Gun; 14 Pack Howitzer (6 non-operational)
 MOR 70+: **81mm**; **120mm** 70 M-43 (est 12 op)
AD • GUNS • TOWED 32+: **14.5mm** 30 Type-56 (ZPU-4); **37mm** (PRC); **40mm** 2 L/60

Air Wing 320
AIRCRAFT • TPT 5 **Light** 4: 2 BN-2T *Islander*; 2 M-28 *Skytruck* **PAX** 1 BAe-748
HELICOPTERS
 MRH 9: 1 *Dhruv*; 2 *Lancer*; 3 Mi-17 1V/V5; 1 SA-315B *Lama* (*Cheetah*); 2 SA-316B *Alouette III*
 TPT 3 **Medium** 1 SA-330J *Super Puma* **Light** 2 AS-350 *Ecureuil* B2/B3

Paramilitary 62,000

Armed Police Force 15,000
Ministry of Home Affairs

Police Force 47,000

DEPLOYMENT

CENTRAL AFRICAN REPUBLIC/CHAD
UN • MINURCAT 581; 1 obs; 1 inf coy

CÔTE D'IVOIRE
UN • UNOCI 1; 3 obs

DEMOCRATIC REPUBLIC OF THE CONGO
UN • MONUSCO 1,025; 24 obs; 1 inf bn; 1 engr coy

HAITI
UN • MINUSTAH 1,074; 1 mech inf bn; 1 inf bn

IRAQ
UN • UNAMI 1 obs

LEBANON
UN • UNIFIL 1,020; 1 inf bn

LIBERIA
UN • UNMIL 18; 2 obs; 1 MP sect

MIDDLE EAST
UN • UNTSO 4 obs

SUDAN
UN • UNAMID 346; 16 obs ; 2 inf coy
UN • UNMIS 7; 5 obs

TIMOR LESTE
UN • UNMIT 1 obs

WESTERN SAHARA
UN • MINURSO 2 obs

FOREIGN FORCES

(all opcon UNMIN unless stated)

Austria 2 obs
Brazil 6 obs
Egypt 3 obs
Guatemala 1 obs
Indonesia 4 obs
Japan 6 obs
Jordan 4 obs
Korea, Republic of 4 obs
Malaysia 7 obs
Nigeria 5 obs
Paraguay 4 obs
Romania 7 obs
Sierra Leone 2 obs
South Africa 1 obs
Sweden 2 obs
Switzerland 3 obs
United Kingdom Army 280 (Gurkha trg org)
Uruguay 2 obs
Zambia 1 obs
Zimbabwe 4 obs

New Zealand NZL

New Zealand Dollar NZ$		2009	2010	2011
GDP	NZ$	186bn	195bn	
	US$	118bn	141bn	
per capita	US$	27,348	32,654	
Growth	%	-0.5	3.0	
Inflation	%	1.4	2.2	
Def exp	NZ$	2.14bn		
	US$	1.36bn		
Def bdgt	NZ$	2.14bn	2.21bn	
	US$	1.36bn	1.59bn	
US$1=NZ$			1.57	1.39

Population 4,303,457

Ethnic groups: NZ European 58%; Maori 15%; Other European 13%; Other Polynesian 5%; Chinese 2%; Indian 1%; Other 6%

Age	0–14	15–19	20–24	25–29	30–64	65 plus
Male	10.4%	3.7%	3.6%	3.2%	22.8%	6.1%
Female	9.9%	3.5%	3.5%	3.2%	23.0%	7.2%

Capabilities

ACTIVE 9,673 (Army 4,905 Navy 2,161 Air 2,607)

RESERVE 2,314 (Army 1,789 Navy 339 Air Force 186)

ORGANISATIONS BY SERVICE

Army 4,905

FORCES BY ROLE

Comd	2 Gp HQ
Recce	1 sqn
Mech Inf	2 bn (1 being converted)
SF	1 gp
Arty	1 regt (2 arty bty, 1 AD tp)
Engr	1 regt (under strength)

EQUIPMENT BY TYPE

AIFV 105 NZLAV-25
LFAV 188 *Pinzgauer*
ARTY 74
   TOWED 105mm 24 L-118 Light Gun
   MOR 81mm 50
AT • MSL 24 *Javelin*
   RCL 84mm 42 *Carl Gustav*
AD • SAM • MANPAD 12 *Mistral*

Reserves

Territorial Force 1,789 reservists
Responsible for providing trained individuals for incrementing deployed forces
Trg 6 (Territorial Force Regional) regt

Navy 2,161

Fleet HQ at Auckland

EQUIPMENT BY TYPE

PRINCIPAL SURFACE COMBATANTS • FRIGATES • FFHM 2
   2 *Anzac* each with 1 Mk41 VLS (8 eff.) with RIM-7M *Sea Sparrow* SAM, 2 triple 324mm TT (6 eff.), 1 Mk15 *Phalanx* CIWS gun, 1 127mm gun, (capacity: 1 SH-2G (NZ) *Super Seasprite* ASW hel)
PATROL AND COASTAL COMBATANTS 6:
   PSOH 2 *Otago* (capacity 1 SH-2G *Super Seasprite* ASW hel)
   PCC 4 *Rotoiti*
AMPHIBIOUS • LANDING CRAFT • LCM 2
LOGISTICS AND SUPPORT 5
   MRV 1 *Canterbury* (capacity 4 NH90 tpt hel; 1 SH-2G *Super Seasprite* ASW hel; 2 LCM; 16 NZLAV; 14 NZLOV; 20 trucks; 250 troops)
   AO 1 *Endeavour*
   AGHS (SVY) 1 *Resolution*
   YDT/spt 1 *Manawanui*

FACILITIES

Base   1 at Auckland

Air Force 2,607

3 air bases – Whenuapai, Ohakea and Woodbourne

Flying hours   190

FORCES BY ROLE

MP	1 sqn with P-3K *Orion* (being progressively upgraded)
Tpt	1 sqn with B-757-200 (upgraded); C-130H *Hercules* (being progressively upgraded)

ASuW/1 (RNZAF/RNZN) sqn with SH-2G *Super Seasprite*
ASW (SH-2G(NZ))

Trg 1 wg with CT-4E *Airtrainer* (leased); Beech 200 *King Air* (leased); Bell 47G

Tpt Hel1 sqn with Bell 205 (UH-1H *Iroquois*) (to be replaced by 8 NH90 in 2010/11)

EQUIPMENT BY TYPE
AIRCRAFT 6 combat capable
  ASW 6 P-3K *Orion*
  TPT 12 **Medium** 5 C-130H *Hercules* (being upgraded)
  Light 5 Beech 200 *King Air* (leased, to be replaced) **PAX** 2 B-757-200 (upgraded)
  TRG 13 CT-4E *Airtrainer* (leased)
HELICOPTERS
  ASW 5 SH-2G *Super Seasprite* (SH-2G(NZ))
  TPT • Light 13 Bell 205 (UH-1H *Iroquois*) (to be replaced by 8 NH90 from 2011)
  TRG 5 Bell 47G (to be replaced by 5 AW-109 from 2011)
MSL • ASM AGM-65B/G *Maverick*

DEPLOYMENT

AFGHANISTAN
NATO • ISAF 231
UN • UNAMA 1 obs

EGYPT
MFO 28; 1 trg unit; 1 tpt unit

IRAQ
UN • UNAMI 1 obs

MIDDLE EAST
UN • UNTSO 7 obs

SOLOMON ISLANDS
RAMSI 5

SUDAN
UN • UNMIS 2; 2 obs

TIMOR LESTE
ISF *(Operation Astute)* 80; 1 inf coy
UN • UNMIT 1 obs

Pakistan PAK

Pakistani Rupee Rs		2009	2010	2011
GDP	Rs	12.8tr	14.7tr	
	US$	156bn	172bn	
per capita	US$	919	933	
Growth	%	3.7	3.0	
Inflation	%	13.6	11.7	
Def exp	Rs	311bn		
	US$	3.81bn		
Def bdgt	Rs	343bn	442bn	394bn
	US$	4.2bn	5.2bn	
FMA (US)[a]	US$	300m	238m	296m
US$1=Rs		81.68	85.09	

[a] FMA figure does not include the Pakistan Counter-Insurgency Capability Fund, the 2011 request for which amounted to US$1.2bn.

Population 184,753,300

Religious groups: Hindu less than 3%

Age	0–14	15–19	20–24	25–29	30–64	65 plus
Male	18.2%	5.9%	5.3%	4.4%	15.6%	2.0%
Female	17.2%	5.5%	5.0%	4.1%	14.6%	2.2%

Capabilities

ACTIVE 617,000 (Army 550,000 Navy 22,000 Air 45,000) **Paramilitary 304,000**

ORGANISATIONS BY SERVICE

Strategic Forces

The National Command Authority (NCA) formulates nuclear policy and is the key decision-making body for the employment and development of strategic systems. The NCA has two committees: the Employment Control Committee and the Development Control Committee. The Strategic Plans Division (SPD) acts as the secretariat, and among other duties formulates nuclear policy, strategy and doctrine and strategic and operational plans for deployment and employment. While operational control rests with the NCA, Army and Air Force strategic forces are responsible for technical aspects, training and administrative control of the services' nuclear assets.

Army Strategic Forces Command 12,000-15,000 personnel

(Commands all land-based strategic nuclear forces)
MSL • TACTICAL • SSM 190: 105 *Hatf*-1; *Abdali/Hatf*-2; 50 *Hatf*-3 (PRC M-11); up to 10 *Shaheen*-1/*Hatf*-4; up to 25 *Hatf*-5/*Ghauri*; *Ghauri* II • **LACM** *Hatf*-7 (in development)
  Some Pakistan Air Force assets (such as *Mirage* or F-16) could be tasked with a strategic role

Army 550,000

FORCES BY ROLE

Army	9 corps HQ
Armd	2 div; 7 (indep) bde
Mech	1 (indep) bde
Inf	1 (area) comd; 18 div; 6 bde
SF	1 gp (3 SF bn)
Arty	9 (corps) bde; 5 bde
Engr	7 bde
Avn	1 (VIP) sqn; 5 (composite) sqn
Hel	10 sqn
AD	1 comd (3 AD gp (total: 8 AD bde))

EQUIPMENT BY TYPE

MBT 2,386+: 240 MBT 2000 *Al-Khalid*; 320 T-80UD; 51 T-54/T-55; 1,100 Type-59; 400 Type-69; 275+ Type-85; 270 M-48A5 in store
APC 1,266
  APC (T) 1,100 M-113
  APC (W) 166: 120 BTR-70/BTR-80; 46 UR-416
ARTY 4,521+
  SP 490: **155mm** 430: 200 M-109/M-109A2; 230 M-109A5 **203mm** 60 M-110A2/M-110
  TOWED 1,629: **105mm** 329: 216 M-101; 113 M-56; **122mm** 570: 80 D-30 (PRC); 490 Type-54 M-1938; **130mm** 410 Type-59-I; **155mm** 292: 144 M-114; 148 M-198; **203mm** 28 M-115
  MRL 52+ **122mm** 52 *Azar* (Type-83) **300mm** some A-100
  MOR 2,350+: **81mm**; **120mm** AM-50; M-61
AT
  MSL 10,500+
    SP M-901 TOW
    MANPATS 10,500 HJ-8/TOW
  RCL 3,700: **75mm** Type-52; **106mm** M-40A1
  RL 73mm RPG-7 *Knout*; **89mm** M-20
  GUNS 85mm 200 Type-56 (D-44)
AIRCRAFT
  ISR 30 Cessna O-1E *Bird Dog*
  TPT • Light 4: 1 Cessna 421; 3 Y-12(II)
  TRG 90 Saab 91 *Safir* (50 obs; 40 liaison)
HELICOPTERS
  ATK 26: 25 AH-1F *Cobra* with TOW; 1 Mi-24 *Hind*
  MRH 71: 26 Bell-412 *Twin Huey*; 13 Mi-17 *Hip H*; 12 SA-315B *Lama*; 20 SA-319 *Alouette III*
  TPT 64 **Medium** 41: 31 SA-330 *Puma*; 10 Mi-8 *Hip* **Light** 23: 5 Bell-205 (UH-1H *Iroquois*); 5 Bell 205A-1 (AB-205A-1); 13 Bell 206B *Jet Ranger II*
  TRG 22: 12 Bell 47G; 10 Hughes 300C
UAV • ISR • Light *Bravo*; *Jasoos*; *Vector*
AD
  SAM • MANPAD 2,990+: 2,500 Mk1/Mk2; 60 FIM-92A *Stinger*; HN-5A; 230 *Mistral*; 200 RBS-70
  GUNS • TOWED 1,900: **14.5mm** 981; **35mm** 215 GDF-002/GDF-005; **37mm** 310 Type-55 (M-1939)/Type-65; **40mm** 50 L/60; **57mm** 144 Type-59 (S-60); **85mm** 200 Type-72 (M-1939) *KS-12*
RADAR • LAND AN/TPQ-36 *Firefinder* (arty, mor); RASIT (veh, arty)

MSL • TACTICAL • SSM 190: 105 *Hatf-1*; *Abdali/Hatf-2*; 50 *Hatf-3* (PRC M-11); up to 10 *Shaheen-1/Hatf-4*; up to 25 *Hatf-5/Ghauri*; *Ghauri* II

Navy 22,000 (incl ε1,400 Marines and ε2,000 Maritime Security Agency (see Paramilitary))

EQUIPMENT BY TYPE

SUBMARINES • TACTICAL 8
  SSK 5:
    2 *Hashmat* (FRA *Agosta* 70) each with 4 single 533mm ASTT each with F17P HWT/UGM- 84 *Harpoon* AShM
    3 *Khalid* (FRA *Agosta* 90B – 1 with AIP) each with 4 single 533mm ASTT each with F17 Mod 2 HWT/SM-39 *Exocet* AShM
  SSI 3 MG110 (SF delivery) each with 2 single 53mm TT
PRINCIPAL SURFACE COMBATANTS • FRIGATES 9
  FFGHM 3:
    3 *Sword* (PRC Type 054) each with 2 quad lnchr (8 eff.) each with YJ-83 AShM, 1 octuple lnchr (8 eff.) with HQ-7 SAM, 2 triple 324mm ASTT (6 eff.) each with Mk 46 LWT, 1 76mm gun, (capacity 1 Z-9C *Haitun* hel)
  FFGH 4:
    4 *Tariq* (UK *Amazon*) each with 2 twin Mk141 lnchr each with RGM-84D *Harpoon* AShM, 2 single each with TP 45 LWT, 1 114mm gun, (capacity 1 hel)
  FFHM 2:
    2 *Tariq* each with 1 sextuple lnchr (6 eff.) with LY-60 (*Aspide*) SAM, 2 triple 324mm ASTT (6 eff.) each with Mk 46 LWT, 1 114mm gun, (capacity 1 hel)
PATROL AND COASTAL COMBATANTS 10
  PBFG 2 *Zarrar* each with 4 single each with RGM-84 *Harpoon* AShM
  PBG 4:
    2 *Jalalat* II each with 2 twin lnchr (4 eff.) each with C-802 (CSS-N-8 *Saccade*) AShM
    2 *Jurrat* each with 2 twin lnchr (4 eff.) each with C-802 (CSS-N-8 *Saccade*) AShM
  PBF 2 *Kaan* 15
  PB 2: 1 *Larkana*; 1 *Rajshahi*
MINE WARFARE • MINE COUNTERMEASURES • MHC 3 *Munsif* (FRA *Eridan*)
AMPHIBIOUS
  LANDING CRAFT • UCAC 4 Griffon 2000
LOGISTICS AND SUPPORT 11
  AORH 2:
    1 *Fuqing* (capacity 1 SA-319 *Alouette III* utl hel)
    1 *Moawin* (capacity 1 *Sea King* MK45 ASW hel)
  AOT 3: 1 *Attock*; 2 *Gwadar*
  AGS 1 *Behr Paima*
  YTM 5

FACILITIES

Bases   Located at Ormara, Gwadar, Karachi

Marines ε1,400

Cdo 1 gp

Naval Aviation

AIRCRAFT 7 ac combat capable
  ASW 7: 3 *Atlantic*; 4 P-3C *Orion* (additional 6 ac on order)

MP 5 F-27-200 MPA
HELICOPTERS
ASW 6: 5 *Sea King* Mk45; 1 Z-9C *Haitun* (additional ac on order)
MRH 4 SA-319B *Alouette III* (additonal ac on order)
MSL • AShM AM-39 *Exocet*

Air Force 45,000

FORCES BY ROLE
3 regional comds: Northern (Peshawar) Central (Sargodha) Southern (Masroor). The Composite Air Tpt Wg, Combat Cadres School and PAF Academy are Direct Reporting Units.

Ftr   4 sqn with F-7 (F-7P *Skybolt);* 3 sqn with F-7MG *Airguard* (F-7PG); 2 sqn with F-16A/B *Fighting Falcon;* 1 sqn with *Mirage* IIID (IIIOD)/IIIE (IIIEP)
FGA   1 sqn with FC-1 (JF-17 *Thunder*); 1 sqn with F-16C/D Block 52 *Fighting Falcon;* 3 sqn with *Mirage* 5 (5PA)/5PA2/5PA3
Atk   1 sqn with A-5C *Fantan*
ASuW   1 sqn with *Mirage* IIIE (IIIEP) with AM-39 *Exocet* AShM
EW/ELINT   1 sqn with *Falcon* 20
ISR   1 sqn with *Mirage* IIIR* (*Mirage* IIIRP)
AEW&C   1 sqn with Saab 2000 *Erieye*
SAR   6 sqn with SA-316 *Alouette III;* 1 sqn with Mi-171 (SAR/liaison)
Tkr   1 sqn with Il-78 *Midas*
Tpt   1 sqn with C-130B/C-130E *Hercules;* L-100 *Hercules;* some sqn with An-26 *Curl;* B-707; Beech 33 *Bonanza;* Beech 200 *King Air;* CN-235; F-27-200 *Friendship; Falcon* 20; Y-12
Trg   Some sqn with FT-5; FT-6; FT-7; K-8 *Karakorum*;* MFI-17B *Mushshak; Mirage* 5D (5DPA)/5DPA2; *Mirage* IIIB; *Mirage* IIID (IIIOD); T-37C *Tweet*
SAM   1 bty with CSA-1 (SA-2 *Guideline*); 9K310 *Igla*-1 (SA-16 *Gimlet*); 6 bty with *Crotale*

EQUIPMENT BY TYPE
AIRCRAFT 426 combat capable
FTR 236: 54 F-7MG (F-7PG) *Airguard;* 75 F-7(F-7P *Skybolt*); 46 F-16A/F-16B *Fighting Falcon* (all to be given mid-life update); 25 FT-5; 15 FT-6; 19 FT-7; 2 *Mirage* IIIB
FGA 151: 12 F-16C/D Block 52 *Fighting Falcon* (6 more on order); 16 FC-1 (JF-17 *Thunder*); 150+ on order); 7 *Mirage* IIID (*Mirage* IIIOD); 63 *Mirage* IIIE (IIIEP); 40 *Mirage* 5 (5PA)/5PA2; 3 *Mirage* 5D (5DPA)/5DPA2; 10 *Mirage* 5PA3 (ASuW)
ATK 41 A-5C *Fantan*
ISR 15 *Mirage* IIIR* (*Mirage* IIIRP)
ELINT 2 *Falcon* 20
AEW&C 3: 2 Saab 2000 *Erieye* (2 more on order); 1 ZDK-03
TKR 2 Il-78 *Midas* (2 more on order)
TPT 26: **Medium** 12: 11 C-130B *Hercules*/C-130E *Hercules;* 1 L-100 *Hercules;* **Light** 10: 1 An-26 *Curl;* 1 Beech 33 *Bonanza;* 1 Beech 200 *King Air;* 4 CN-235; 2 F-27-200 *Friendship;* 1 Y-12 **PAX** 4: 3 B-707; 1 *Falcon* 20

TRG 112: 12 K-8 *Karakorum*;* 80 MFI-17B *Mushshak;* 20 T-37C *Tweet*
HELICOPTERS
MRH 15 SA-316 *Alouette III*
TPT • Medium 4 Mi-171
AD • SAM 150+
TOWED 150: 6 CSA-1 (SA-2 *Guideline*); 144 *Crotale*
MANPAD 9K310 *Igla*-1 (SA-16 *Gimlet*)
RADAR • LAND 51+: 6 AR-1 (AD radar low level); some *Condor* (AD radar high level); some FPS-89/100 (AD radar high level)
MPDR 45 MPDR/MPDR 60 MPDR 90 (AD radar low level)
TPS-43G Type 514 some (AD radar high level)
MSL
ASM: AGM-65 *Maverick; Raptor II*
AShM AM-39 *Exocet*
LACM *Raad* (in development)
AAM • IR AAM AIM-9L *Sidewinder*/AIM-9P *Sidewinder*; *U-Darter;* PL-5; **SARH AAM** Super 530; **ARH AAM** PL-12 (SD-10 – on order for the FC-1 (JF-17))

FACILITIES
Radar air control sectors   4
Radar control and reporting station   7

Paramilitary up to 304,000 active

Coast Guard
PATROL AND COASTAL COMBATANTS 5
PBF 4
PB 1

Frontier Corps up to 65,000 (reported)
Ministry of Interior
FORCES BY ROLE
Armd recce   1 indep sqn
Paramilitary 11 regt (total: 40 paramilitary bn)

EQUIPMENT BY TYPE
APC (W) 45 UR-416

Maritime Security Agency ε2,000
PRINCIPAL SURFACE COMBATANTS DESTROYERS
DD 1 *Nazim* (US *Gearing*) with 2 triple 324mm TT, 1 twin 127mm gun (2 eff.)
PATROL AND COASTAL COMBATANTS 10:
PCC 4 *Barkat*
PB 6: 2 *Subqat* (PRC *Shanghai II*); 1 *Sadaqat* (ex-PRC *Huangfen*); 3 (various)

National Guard 185,000
Incl *Janbaz* Force; *Mujahid* Force; National Cadet Corps; Women Guards

Northern Light Infantry ε12,000
Paramilitary 3 bn

Pakistan Rangers up to 40,000
Ministry of Interior

DEPLOYMENT

BURUNDI
UN • BINUB 1 obs

CENTRAL AFRICAN REPUBLIC/CHAD
UN • MINURCAT 4; 2 obs

CÔTE D'IVOIRE
UN • UNOCI 1,140; 11 obs; 1 inf bn; 1 engr coy; 1 tpt coy

DEMOCRATIC REPUBLIC OF THE CONGO
UN • MONUSCO 3,571; 55 obs; 3 mech inf bn; 1 inf bn

LIBERIA
UN • UNMIL 2,953; 7 obs; 3 inf bn; 3 engr coy; 1 fd hospital

SUDAN
UN • UNAMID 502; 5 obs; 1 engr coy
UN • UNMIS 1,479; 16 obs; 1inf bn; 1 engr coy; 2 avn coy; 1 tpt coy; 1 de-mining pl; 1 fd hospital

TIMOR LESTE
UN • UNMIT 4 obs

WESTERN SAHARA
UN • MINURSO 11 obs

FOREIGN FORCES

Unless specified, figures represent total numbers for UNMOGIP mission in India and Pakistan
Chile 2 obs
Croatia 9 obs
Finland 5 obs
Italy 7 obs
Korea, Republic of 9 obs
Sweden 6 obs
United Kingdom some (fwd mounting base) air elm located at Karachi
Uruguay 2 obs

Papua New Guinea PNG

Papua New Guinea Kina K		2009	2010	2011
GDP	K	21.8bn	24.6bn	
	US$	8.07bn	9.08bn	
per capita	US$	1,198	1,318	
Growth	%	4.5	5.5	
Inflation	%	6.9	7.1	
Def exp	K	109m		
	US$	40m		
Def bdgt	K	133m	116m	
	US$	49m	43m	
US$1=K		2.70	2.71	

Population	6,888,387					
Age	0–14	15–19	20–24	25–29	30–64	65 plus
Male	18.5%	5.2%	4.5%	3.9%	17.1%	2.0%
Female	17.9%	5.1%	4.4%	3.8%	15.8%	1.7%

Capabilities

ACTIVE 3,100 (Army 2,500 Air 200 Maritime Element 400)

ORGANISATIONS BY SERVICE

Army ε2,500
FORCES BY ROLE
Inf   2 bn
Engr 1 bn

EQUIPMENT BY TYPE
ARTY • MOR 3+: **81mm**; **120mm** 3

Maritime Element ε400
1 HQ located at Port Moresby
EQUIPMENT BY TYPE
PATROL AND COASTAL COMBATANTS 4:
  PB 4 *Pacific*
AMPHIBIOUS 2:
  LANDING SHIPS • LSM 2 *Salamaua*
FACILITIES
Bases   Located at Alotau (forward), Kieta (forward), Lombrun (Manus Island), Port Moresby

Air Force 200
FORCES BY ROLE
Tpt   1 sqn with C-212 *Aviocar*; CN-235; IAI-201 *Arava*
Tpt Hel 1 sqn with Bell 205 (UH-1H *Iroquois*)†

EQUIPMENT BY TYPE
AIRCRAFT • TPT • Light 6: 1 CASA 212 *Aviocar*; 2 CN-235; 3 IAI-201 *Arava*
HELICOPTERS • TPT • Light 4 Bell 205 (UH-1H *Iroquois*)†

FOREIGN FORCES
Australia Army 38; 1 trg unit

Philippines PHL

Philippine Peso P		2009	2010	2011
GDP	P	7.68tr	8.58tr	
	US$	161bn	188bn	
per capita	US$	1,751	2,009	
Growth	%	0.9	6.2	
Inflation	%	3.2	4.5	
Def exp	P	65bn		
	US$	1.36bn		
Def bdgt	P	54.2bn	97.2bn	105bn
	US$	1.14bn	2.13bn	
FMA (US)	US$	30.0m	32.0m	15.0m
US$1=P		47.67	45.59	

Population	93,616,853

Age	0–14	15–19	20–24	25–29	30–64	65 plus
Male	17.7%	5.1%	4.7%	4.4%	16.4%	1.8%
Female	17.0%	4.9%	4.6%	4.2%	16.9%	2.4%

Capabilities

ACTIVE 125,000 (Army 86,000 Navy 24,000 Air 15,000) Paramilitary 40,500

RESERVE 131,000 (Army 100,000 Navy 15,000 Air 16,000) Paramilitary 40,000 (to age 49)

ORGANISATIONS BY SERVICE

Army 86,000
FORCES BY ROLE
5 Area Unified Comd (joint service), 1 National Capital Region Comd

Armd	1 lt armd div with (3 lt armd bn; 3 lt armd coy; 4 mech inf bn; 4 armd cav tp; 1 avn bn; 1 cbt engr coy)
Spec Ops	1 comd (1 Scout Ranger regt, 1 SF regt, 1 lt reaction bn)
Lt Inf	10 div (each: 1 arty bn, 3 inf bde)
Arty	1 regt HQ
Engr	5 bde
Presidential Guard	1 gp

EQUIPMENT BY TYPE
LT TK 7 *Scorpion*
AIFV 36: 2 YPR-765; 34 M-113A1 FSV
APC 293
  APC (T) 70 M-113
  APC (W) 223: 77 LAV-150 *Commando*; 146 *Simba*
ARTY 254+
  TOWED 214: **105mm** 204 M-101/M-102/M-26/M-56; **155mm** 10 M-114/M-68
  MOR 40+: **81mm** M-29; **107mm** 40 M-30
AT • RCL 75mm M-20; **90mm** M-67; **106mm** M-40A1

AIRCRAFT
TPT • Light 4: 1 Beech 80 *Queen Air*; 1 Cessna 170; 1 Cessna 172; 1 Cessna P206A
UAV • ISR • Medium *Blue Horizon*

Navy 24,000
EQUIPMENT BY TYPE
PRINCIPAL SURFACE COMBATANTS • FRIGATES
  FF 1 *Rajah Humabon* with 3 76mm gun
PATROL AND COASTAL COMBATANTS 65
  PCF 1 *Cyclone*
  PCO 13:
    3 *Emilio Jacinto* each with 1 76mm gun
    8 *Miguel Malvar* (1†) each with 1 76mm gun
    2 *Rizal* each with 2 76mm gun
  PBF 18: 10 *Conrado Yap*; 8 *Tomas Batilo*
  PB 33: 2 *Aguinaldo*; 22 *Jose Andrada*; 3 *Kagitingan*; 2 *Point*; 4 *Swift* Mk3
AMPHIBIOUS
  LANDING SHIPS • LST 7:
    2 *Bacolod City* (*Besson*-class) each with 1 hel landing platform (capacity 32 tanks; 150 troops)
    5 *Zamboanga del Sur* (capacity 16 tanks; 200 troops)
  LANDING CRAFT 26: 8 LCU; 2 LCVP; 16 LCM
LOGISTICS AND SUPPORT 7: **AOL** 2; **AR** 1; **AK** 1; **AWT** 2; **TPT** 1
FACILITIES
Bases Located at Sangley Point/Cavite, Zamboanga, Cebu

Naval Aviation
AIRCRAFT • TPT • Light 6: 4 BN-2A *Defender* 2 Cessna 177 *Cardinal*
HELICOPTERS • TPT • Light 4 Bo-105

Marines 8,300
FORCES BY ROLE
Marine	4 bde (total: 12 marine bn)
CSS	1 bde (with 6 bn)

EQUIPMENT BY TYPE
APC (W) 24 LAV-300
AAV 85: 30 LVTP-5; 55 LVTP-7
ARTY 31+
  TOWED 105mm 31: 23 M-101; 8 M-26
  MOR 107mm M-30

Air Force 15,000
FORCES BY ROLE
PAF HQ, 5 Cmds (AD, tac ops, air ed and trg, air log and spt, air res)

Ftr	1 sqn with S-211*
MP	1 sqn with F-27-200 MPA; N-22SL *Searchmaster*
ISR	1 sqn with OV-10 *Bronco**
SAR	4 (SAR/Comms) sqn with Bell 205 (UH-1M *Iroquois*); AUH-76

Tpt	1 sqn with C-130/L-100B; C-130H *Hercules*; C-130K *Hercules*; 1 sqn with Cessna 210 *Centurion*; N-22B *Nomad*; 1 sqn with F-27-200 *Friendship*
Trg	1 sqn with SF-260TP; 1 sqn with T-41D *Mescalero*; 1 sqn with R172 *Hawk* XP
Tpt Hel	4 sqn with UH-1H *Iroquois*; 1 (VIP) sqn with S-70A *Black Hawk* (S-70A-5); 1 sqn with Bell 412EP *Twin Huey*; 1 sqn with MD-520MG

EQUIPMENT BY TYPE

AIRCRAFT 34 combat capable
MP 4: 2 F-27-200 MPA; 2 N-22SL *Searchmaster*
ISR 7 OV-10 *Bronco**
TPT 7 **Medium** 3 C-130/L-100B **Light** 4: 1 F-27-200 *Friendship*; 2 N-22B *Nomad*; 1 *Turbo Commander* 690A
TRG 26: 10 SF-260M; 6 SF-260TP; 10 T-41B/D/K *Mescalero*
HELICOPTERS
MRH 20: 4 AUH-76; 5 Bell 412EP *Twin Huey*; 11 MD-520MG
TPT 40 **Medium** 1: 1 S-70A *Black Hawk* (S-70A-5) **Light** 39 Bell 205 (UH-1H *Iroquois*)
UAV • ISR • Medium 2 *Blue Horizon* II
MSL • AAM • IR AAM AIM-9B *Sidewinder*‡

Paramilitary

Philippine National Police 40,500

Deptartment of Interior and Local Government

FORCES BY ROLE

Regional   15 comd
Provincial   73 comd
Aux   62,000

EQUIPMENT BY TYPE

PATROL AND COASTAL COMBATANTS • PB 14 Rodman
AIRCRAFT
   TPT • Light 5: 2 BN-2 *Islander*; 3 Lancair 320

Coast Guard

PATROL AND COASTAL COMBATANTS 61
   PCO 5: 4 *San Juan*; 1 *Balsam*
   PCC 2 *Tirad*
   PB 43: 4 *Agusan*; 3 *De Haviland*; 4 *Ilocos Norte*; 32 (various)
   PBR 11
HELICOPTERS 3 SAR

Citizen Armed Force Geographical Units 50,000 reservists

CAFGU
Militia 56 bn (part-time units which can be called up for extended periods)

DEPLOYMENT

CÔTE D'IVOIRE

UN • UNOCI 3; 3 obs

HAITI

UN • MINUSTAH 157; 1 HQ coy

LIBERIA

UN • UNMIL 117; 2 obs; 1 inf coy

SUDAN

UN • UNMIS 11 obs

SYRIA

UN • UNDOF 349; 1 inf bn

TIMOR LESTE

UN • UNMIT 3 obs

FOREIGN FORCES

Brunei IMT 15
Libya IMT 6
United States US Pacific Command: 117

Singapore SGP

Singapore Dollar S$		2009	2010	2011
GDP	S$	265bn	300bn	
	US$	182bn	218bn	
per capita	US$	36,573	45,071	
Growth	%	-4.0	14.0	
Inflation	%	0.2	3.0	
Def exp	S$	11.4bn		
	US$	7.83bn		
Def bdgt	S$	11.5bn	11.5bn	12.3bn
	US$	7.88bn	8.34bn	
US$1=S$		1.45	1.37	

Population   4,836,691

Ethnic groups: Chinese 76%; Malay 15%; Indian 6%

Age	0–14	15–19	20–24	25–29	30–64	65 plus
Male	7.1%	2.9%	3.2%	3.3%	28.0%	4.1%
Female	6.6%	2.8%	3.1%	3.5%	30.2%	5.1%

Capabilities

ACTIVE 72,500 (Army 50,000 Navy 9,000 Air 13,500) Paramilitary 75,100
Terms of service conscription 24 months

RESERVE 312,500 (Army 300,000 Navy 5,000 Air 7,500) Paramilitary 44,000
Annual trg to age of 40 for army other ranks, 50 for officers

ORGANISATIONS BY SERVICE

Army 15,000; 35,000 conscript (total 50,000)

FORCES BY ROLE

| Combined Arms | 3 div (mixed active/reserve formations) (each: 2 inf bde (each: 3 inf bn), 1 armd bde, 1 recce bn, 1 AD bn, 1 engr bn, 2 arty bn) |

Rapid Reaction	1 div (mixed active/reserve formations) (1 amph bde (3 amph bn), 1 air mob bde, 1 inf bde)
Recce/Lt Armd	4 bn
Inf	8 bn
Cdo	1 bn
Arty	4 bn
Engr	4 bn
MI	1 bn

Reserves

9 inf bde incl in mixed active/inactive reserve formations listed above; 1 op reserve div with additional inf bde; People's Defence Force Comd (homeland defence) with inf bn 12

Mech Inf	6 bn
Recce/Lt Armd	ε6 bn
Inf	ε56 bn
Cdo	ε1 bn
Arty	ε12 bn
Engr	ε8 bn

EQUIPMENT BY TYPE

MBT 196: 96 *Leopard* 2A4; 80–100 *Tempest* (*Centurion*) (being replaced)
LT TK ε350 AMX-13 SM1
RECCE 22 AMX-10 PAC 90
AIFV 272+: 22 AMX-10P; 250 IFV-25; M-113A1/M-113A2 (some with 40mm AGL, some with 25mm gun)
APC 1,280+
  APC (T) 1,000+: 250 IFV-40/50; 750+ M-113A1/M-113A2; ATTC *Bronco*
  APC (W) 280: 250 LAV-150 *Commando*/V-200 *Commando*; 30 V-100 *Commando*
ARTY 353
  SP 155mm 18: ε18 SSPH-1 *Primus*
  TOWED 125: **105mm** 37 LG1 (in store); **155mm** 70: 18 FH-2000; ε18 *Pegasus*; 52 FH-88
  MRL 227mm 18 HIMARS being delivered
  MOR 192+
    SP 90+ **81mm; 120mm** 90: 40 on *Bronco*; 50 on M-113
    TOWED 160mm 12 M-58 *Tampella*
AT • MSL • MANPATS 30+ *Milan/Spike MR*
  RCL 290: **84mm** ε200 *Carl Gustav*; **106mm** 90 M-40A1
  RL 67mm *Armbrust*; **89mm** M-20
AD • SAM 75+
  SP *Mistral*; RBS-70; 9K38 *Igla* (SA-18 *Grouse*) (on V-200/M-113)
  MANPAD *Mistral*; RBS-70; 9K38 *Igla* (SA-18 *Grouse*)
  GUNS 30
    SP 20mm GAI-C01
    TOWED 20mm GAI-C01
UAV • ISR • Light *Skylark*
RADAR • LAND AN/TPQ-36 *Firefinder*; AN/TPQ-37 *Firefinder* (arty, mor)

FACILITIES

Training camp 3 located in Taiwan (Republic of China) incl inf and arty, 1 located in Thailand, 1 located in Brunei

Navy 3,000; 1,000 conscript; ε5,000 active reservists (total 9,000)

EQUIPMENT BY TYPE

SUBMARINES • TACTICAL • SSK 5:
  3 *Challenger* each with 4 single 533mm TT
  1 *Challenger* (trg role) each with 4 single 533mm TT
  1 *Archer* (SWE *Västergötland* class) (AIP fitted) each with 6 single 533mm TT for *WASS Black Shark* LWT (Undergoing sea trials; 2nd vessel expected ISD 2011)
PRINCIPAL SURFACE COMBATANTS 6:
  FRIGATES • FFGHM 6 *Formidable* each with 2 quad lnchr (8 eff.) each with RGM-84 *Harpoon* AShM, 4 octuple VLS (32 eff.) with *Aster 15* SAM, 2 triple 324mm ASTT, 1 76mm gun, (capacity 1 S-70B *Sea Hawk* hel)
PATROL AND COASTAL COMBATANTS 35:
  CORVETTES • FSGM 6
    6 *Victory* each with 2 quad Mk140 lnchr (8 eff.) each with RGM-84C *Harpoon* AShM, 2 octuple lnchr (16 eff.) each with *Barak* SAM, 2 triple 32mm ASTT (6 eff.), 1 76mm gun
  PCO 11 *Fearless* each with 2 sextuple *Sadral* lnchr (12 eff.) each with *Mistral* SAM, 1 76mm gun
  PBF 6
  PB 12
MINE WARFARE • MINE COUNTERMEASURES
  MHC 4 *Bedok*
AMPHIBIOUS
  PRINCIPAL AMPHIBIOUS SHIPS • LPD 4 *Endurance* each with 2 twin lnchr (4 eff.) each with *Mistral* SAM, 1 76mm gun (capacity 2 hel; 4 LCVP; 18 MBT; 350 troops)
  LANDING CRAFT 34 LCU 100 LCVP
LOGISTICS AND SUPPORT 2
  AR 1 *Swift Rescue*
  TRG 1

FACILITIES

Bases Located at Changi, Tuas (Jurong)

Air Force 13,500 (incl 3,000 conscript)

5 Cmds: Air Defence and Operations Comd (includes Air Operations Control Group, Air Defence Group, and Air Surveillance and Control Group); Unmanned Aerial Vehicle (UAV) Comd; Participation Comd (includes Helicopter Group and Tactical Air Support Group: coordinates airlift, close air support and maritime air surveillance, and also raises, trains and sustains RSAF helicopters, divisional ground-based air-defence systems and tactical support elements); Air Combat Comd (includes Fighter Group and Transport Group); Air Power Generation Comd (controls air base support units including Field Defence Sqns).

FORCES BY ROLE

FGA	2 sqn with F-5S *Tiger II*; F-5T *Tiger II*; 1 sqn with F-15SG *Eagle*; 3 sqn with F-16C/F-16D *Fighting Falcon* (some used for ISR with pods)
ISR	1 recce sqn with RF-5
MP/Tpt	1 sqn with F-50
AEW&C	1 sqn with E-2C *Hawkeye*

Tkr	1 sqn with KC-135R *Stratotanker*
Tkr/Tpt	1 sqn with KC-130B *Hercules*; KC-130H *Hercules*; C-130H *Hercules*
Trg	1 sqn with A-4SU *Super Skyhawk*; TA-4SU *Super Skyhawk*; 1 (US based) sqn with AH-64D *Apache*; CH-47D *Chinook*; F-15SG: F-16C/D; 1 sqn with PC-21
Atk Hel	1 sqn with AH-64D *Apache*
Tpt Hel	1 sqn with CH-47SD *Super D Chinook*; 2 sqn with AS-332M *Super Puma*; AS-532UL *Cougar*
ISR UAV	2 sqn with *Searcher* Mk II; 1 sqn with *Hermes* 450 (Staffed by personnel from all three services)

EQUIPMENT BY TYPE
AIRCRAFT 148 combat capable
  FTR 37: 28 F-5S *Tiger II*; 9 F-5T *Tiger II*
  FGA 65: 5 F-15SG *Eagle* (19 more to be delivered by 2012); 60 F-16C/D *Fighting Falcon* (incl reserves)
  ATK 14: 4 A-4SU *Super Skyhawk*; 10 TA-4SU *Super Skyhawk*
  MP 5 F-50 *Maritime Enforcer**
  AEW&C 4 E-2C *Hawkeye*
  TKR 5: 1 KC-130H *Hercules*; 4 KC-135R *Stratotanker*
  TKR/TPT 4 KC-130B *Hercules*
  TPT 9 **Medium** 5 C-130H *Hercules* (2 ELINT) **PAX** 4 F-50
  TRG 27+: some PC-21; 27 S-211*
HELICOPTERS
  ATK 11 AH-64D *Apache*
  ASW 6 S-70B *Seahawk*
  TPT 40+ **Heavy** 16+: 6+ CH-47D *Chinook*; 10 CH-47SD *Super D Chinook* **Medium** 30: 18 AS-332M *Super Puma* (incl 5 SAR); 12 AS-532UL *Cougar*
  TRG 12 EC-120B *Colibri* (leased)
UAV • ISR 40+ **Heavy** some *Hermes* 450 **Medium** 40 *Searcher* MkII
MSL • TACTICAL
  ASM: *Hellfire*; AGM-65B/G *Maverick*;
  AShM AGM-84 *Harpoon*; AM-39 *Exocet*
  ARM AGM-45 *Shrike*
  AAM • IR AAM AIM-9N *Sidewinder*/AIM-9P *Sidewinder*; *Python 4* (reported) **SARH AAM** AIM-7P *Sparrow*; AIM-120C *AMRAAM* in store (US)

Air Defence Group
FORCES BY ROLE
4 (field def) sqn

Air Defence Bde
FORCES BY ROLE
Air	Some bde (total: 1 AD sqn with Oerlikon, 1 AD sqn with 18+ MIM-23 *HAWK*, 1 AD sqn with *Rapier-Blindfire*)

Air Force Systems Bde
Air	bde (total: 1 AD sqn with radar (mobile), 1 AD sqn with LORADS)

Divisional Air Def Arty Bde
Attached to army divs
FORCES BY ROLE
AD	Bde (total: 1 AD bn with 36 *Mistral*, 1 AD bn with 9K38 *Igla* (SA-18 *Grouse*); 3 AD bn with RBS-70)
EQUIPMENT BY TYPE
AD • SAM 36+
  TOWED *Mistral*; RBS-70
  MANPAD 9K38 *Igla* (SA-18 *Grouse*)

Paramilitary 75,100 active

Civil Defence Force 1,600 regulars; 3,200 conscript; 54,000+ volunteers; 1 construction bde (2,500 conscript) (total 61,300+); 23,000 reservists

Singapore Police Force (including Coast Guard) 8,500; 3,500 conscript; (total 12,000); 21,000 reservists
EQUIPMENT BY TYPE
PATROL AND COASTAL COMBATANTS 100
  PBF 72 (various)
  PB 28: 2 *Manta Ray*; 7 *Shark*; 19 (various)

Singapore Gurkha Contingent (under police) 1,800
6 coy

DEPLOYMENT

AFGHANISTAN
NATO • ISAF 36

AUSTRALIA
Air force: 2 trg schools – 1 with 12 AS-332 *Super Puma*/AS-532 *Cougar* (flying trg) located at Oakey; 1 with 27 S-211 (flying trg) located at Pearce. Army: prepositional AFVs and heavy equipment at Shoalwater Bay training area.

BRUNEI
Army 1 trg camp with infantry units on rotation
Air force; 1 hel det with AS-332 *Super Puma*

FRANCE
Air force 200: 1 trg sqn with 4 A-4SU Super Skyhawk; 10 TA-4SU *Super Skyhawk*

TAIWAN (REPUBLIC OF CHINA)
Army 3 trg camp (incl inf and arty)

THAILAND
Army 1 trg camp (arty, cbt engr)

TIMOR LESTE
UN • UNMIT 2 obs

UNITED STATES
Air force trg units at Luke AFB (AZ) with F-16 C/D; Mountain Home AFB (ID) with F-15E (F-15 SG from 2009);

AH-64D *Apache* at Marana (AZ); 6+ CH-47D *Chinook* hel at Grand Prairie (TX)

FOREIGN FORCES

United States US Pacific Command: 122; 1 naval spt facility at Changi naval base; 1 USAF log spt sqn at Paya Lebar air base

Sri Lanka LKA

Sri Lankan Rupee Rs		2009	2010	2011
GDP	Rs	4.83tr	5.50tr	
	US$	42.0bn	48.5bn	
per capita	US$	2,068	2,376	
Growth	%	3.5	5.8	
Inflation	%	3.4	6.5	
Def exp	Rs	171bn		
	US$	1.48bn		
Def bdgt[a]	Rs	169bn	163bn	164bn
	US$	1.47bn	1.44bn	
FMA (US)	US$	-	1.0m	1.0m
US$1=Rs		114.94	113.40	

Population   20,409,946

[a] Excludes Coast Guard and Departments of Police, Immigration and Emigration, Civil Security, Coast Conservation and Registry of Persons

Age	0–14	15–19	20–24	25–29	30–64	65 plus
Male	12.0%	4.0%	3.9%	4.2%	21.2%	3.9%
Female	11.5%	3.8%	3.8%	4.2%	23.0%	4.6%

Capabilities

ACTIVE 160,900 (Army 117,900 Navy 15,000 Air 28,000) **Paramilitary 62,200**

RESERVE 5,500 (Army 1,100 Navy 2,400 Air Force 2,000) **Paramilitary 30,400**

ORGANISATIONS BY SERVICE

Army 78,000; 39,900 active reservists (recalled) (total 117,900)

FORCES BY ROLE
9 Div HQ

Armd	3 regt
Armd Recce	3 regt (bn)
Air Mob	1 bde
Inf	33 bde
SF	1 indep bde
Cdo	1 bde
Fd Arty	1 light regt; 2 (med) regt
Fd Engr	3 regt

EQUIPMENT BY TYPE
MBT 62 T-55AM2/T-55A
RECCE 15 *Saladin*
AIFV 62: 13 BMP-1; 49 BMP-2
APC 217
  APC (T) 35 Type-85
  APC (W) 182: 31 *Buffel*; 21 FV603 *Saracen*; 105 *Unicorn*; 25 BTR-80/BTR-80A
ARTY 460
  TOWED 154: **122mm** 74; **130mm** 40 Type-59-I; **152mm** 40 Type-66 (D-20)
  MRL 122mm 22 RM-70 *Dana*
  MOR 784: **81mm** 520; **82mm** 209; **120mm** 55 M-43
AT • RCL 40: **105mm** ε10 M-65; **106mm** ε30 M-40
  GUNS 85mm 8 Type-56 (D-44)
UAV • ISR • Medium 1 *Seeker*
RADAR • LAND 2 AN/TPQ-36 *Firefinder* (arty)

Navy 15,000 (incl 2,400 recalled reservists)
1 (HQ and Western comd) located at Colombo
EQUIPMENT BY TYPE
PATROL AND COASTAL COMBATANTS 134
  PSOH 1 *Sayura* (IND *Vigraha*)
  PCG 2 *Nandimithra* (ISR *Sa'ar* 4) each with 3 single lnchr each with 1 GII *Gabriel II* AShM, 1 76mm gun
  PCO 3: 1 *Reliance*; 2 *Sagara* (IND *Vikram*)
  PCC 1 *Jayesagara*
  PBF 67: 27 *Colombo*; 3 *Dvora*; 3 *Killer* (ROK); 6 *Shaldag*; 9 *Super Dvora* (Mk1/II/III); 3 *Simonneau*; 5 *Trinity Marine*; 11 *Wave Rider*
  PB 15: 4 *Cheverton*; 2 *Prathapa* (PRC mod *Haizhui*); 3 *Ranajaya* (PRC *Haizhui*); 1 *Ranarisi* (PRC *Shanghai* II (mod)); 5 *Weeraya* (PRC *Shanghai II*)
  PBR 45
AMPHIBIOUS
  LANDING SHIPS • LSM 1 *Yuhai* (capacity 2 tanks; 250 troops)
  LANDING CRAFT 8
    LCU 2 *Yunnan*
    LCM 2
    LCP 3 *Hansaya*
    UCAC 1 M 10 (capacity 56 troops)
LOGISTICS AND SUPPORT 2: 1 **TPT**; 1 **TRG**
FACILITIES
Bases	Located at Trincomalee (Main base and Eastern Comd), Kankesanthurai (Northern Comd), Galle (Southern Comd), Medawachiya (North Central Comd) and Colombo (HQ and Western Comd)

Air Force 28,000 (incl SLAF Regt)
FORCES BY ROLE
Ftr	1 sqn with F-7BS/G; FT-7
FGA	1 sqn with MiG-23UB *Flogger* C; MiG-27M *Flogger* J2; 1 sqn with *Kfir* C-2/C-7/TC-2; 1 sqn with K-8 *Karakoram**
Tpt	1 sqn with An-32B *Cline*; C-130K *Hercules*; Cessna 421C *Golden Eagle*; 1 (light) sqn with Beech B200 *King Air*, Y-12 (II)

Trg   1 wg with PT-6, Cessna 150L

Atk hel   1 sqn with Mi-24V *Hind*; Mi-35P *Hind*

Tpt Hel   1 sqn with Mi-17, Mi-17-IV, Mi-171; 1 sqn with
            Bell 206A/B (incl basic trg), Bell 212; 1 (VIP) sqn
            with Bell206A/B *Jet Ranger*, Bell 412/412EP *Twin
            Huey*; Mi-17

ISR UAV   2 sqn with *Searcher* II; *Blue Horizon*-2

Inf   1 (SLAF) regt

EQUIPMENT BY TYPE

AIRCRAFT 23 combat capable

FTR 4: 3 F-7BS/G; 1 FT-7

FGA 16: 7 *Kfir* C-2; 2 *Kfir* C-7; 2 *Kfir* TC-2; 4 MiG-27M *Flogger J2*; 1 MiG-23UB *Flogger C* (conversion trg)

TPT 18 **Medium** 2 C-130K *Hercules*; **Light** 16: 7 An-32B *Cline*; 5 Cessna 150L; 1 Cessna 421C *Golden Eagle*; 3 Y-12 (II)

TRG 10: 3 K-8 *Karakoram**; 7 PT-6

HELICOPTERS

ATK 13: 1 Mi-24V *Hind E*; 12 Mi-35P *Hind*

MRH 9: 3 Mi-17 *Hip H* (3 more in store); 6 Bell 412 *Twin Huey* (VIP)

UTL 15: 5 Bell 206 *Jet Ranger*; 10 Bell 212

UAV • ISR • Medium 2+: some Blue-Horizon II; 2 Searcher Mk II

AD • GUNS • TOWED 27: **40mm** 24 L/40; **94mm** 3 (3.7in)

Paramilitary ε62,200

Home Guard 13,000

National Guard ε15,000

Police Force 30,200; 1,000 (women) (total 31,200) 30,400 reservists

Ministry of Defence

Special Task Force 3,000

Anti-guerrilla unit

DEPLOYMENT

CENTRAL AFRICAN REPUBLIC/CHAD
UN • MINURCAT 74

DEMOCRATIC REPUBLIC OF THE CONGO
UN • MONUSCO 4 obs

HAITI
UN • MINUSTAH 958; 1 inf bn; 1 log coy

SUDAN
UN • UNMIS 6 obs

WESTERN SAHARA
UN • MINURSO 3 obs

Taiwan (Republic of China) ROC

New Taiwan Dollar NT$		2009	2010	2011
GDP	NT$	12.5tr	13.6tr	
	US$	379bn	433bn	
per capita	US$	16,508	18,853	
Growth	%	4.1	7.7	
Inflation	%	-0.9	1.5	
Def exp	NT$	313bn		
	US$	9.5bn		
Def bdgt	NT$	316bn	293bn	297bn
	US$	9.6bn	9.3bn	
US$1=NT$		32.99	31.50	

Population   22,974,347

Ethnic groups: Taiwanese 84%; mainland Chinese 14%

Age	0–14	15–19	20–24	25–29	30–64	65 plus
Male	8.1%	3.6%	3.6%	4.0%	25.8%	5.2%
Female	7.5%	3.3%	3.3%	3.9%	25.9%	5.7%

Capabilities

ACTIVE 290,000 (Army 200,000 Navy 45,000 Air 45,000) **Paramilitary 17,000**

Terms of service 12 months

RESERVE 1,657,000 (Army 1,500,000 Navy 67,000 Air Force 90,000)

Army reservists have some obligation to age 30

ORGANISATIONS BY SERVICE

Army ε200,000 (incl MP)

FORCES BY ROLE

Comd   4 defence HQ

Army   3 corps

Armd   5 bde

Armd Inf   1 bde

Inf   28 bde

Avn/SF   1 comd (1 spec war bde, 3 avn bde)

Mot Inf   3 bde

SSM   1 coastal def bn

Missile Command

AD 1 AD msl comd (2 AD/SAM gp (total: 6 SAM bn with total of 100 MIM-23 *HAWK*; with up to 6 PAC-3 *Patriot* (systems); up to 6 Tien Kung I *Sky Bow*/ Tien Kung II *Sky Bow*))

Reserves

Lt Inf   7 div

EQUIPMENT BY TYPE

MBT 926+: 376 M-60A3; 100 M-48A5; 450+ M-48H *Brave Tiger*

LT TK 905: 230 M-24 *Chaffee* (90mm gun); 675 M-41/Type-64

AIFV 225 CM-25 (M-113 with 20–30mm cannon)

APC 950

    APC (T) 650 M-113

    APC (W) 300 LAV-150 *Commando*

ARTY 1,815+

    SP 405: **105mm** 100 M-108; **155mm** 245: 225 M-109A2/M-109A5; 20 T-69; **203mm** 60 M-110

    TOWED 1,060+: **105mm** 650 T-64 (M-101); **155mm** 340+: 90 M-59; 250 T-65 (M-114); M-44; **203mm** 70 M-115

    COASTAL 127mm ε50 US Mk 32 (reported)

    MRL 300+: **117mm** *Kung Feng* VI; **126mm** *Kung Feng* III/*Kung Feng* IV; RT 2000 *Thunder* (KF towed and SP)

    MOR

        SP 81mm M-29

        TOWED 81mm M-29; **107mm**

AT MSL 1,060: **SP** TOW

        MANPATS 60 *Javelin*; TOW

    RCL 500+: **90mm** M-67; **106mm** 500+: 500 M-40A1; Type-51

HELICOPTERS

    ATK 62 AH-1W *Cobra*

    MRH 39 OH-58D *Kiowa Warrior*

    TPT 89 **Heavy** 9 CH-47SD *Super D Chinook* **Light** 80 Bell 205 (UH-1H *Iroquois*)

    TRG 30 TH-67 *Creek*

UAV • ISR • Light *Mastiff* III

AD • SAM up to 678+

    SP 76: 74 FIM-92A *Avenger*; 2 M-48 *Chaparral*

    TOWED up to 137: 25 MIM-104 *Patriot*; 100 MIM-23 *HAWK*; up to 6 PAC-3 *Patriot* (systems); up to 6 *Tien Kung* I *Sky Bow*/Tien Kung II *Sky Bow*

    MANPAD 465+ FIM-92A *Stinger*

    GUNS 400

    SP 40mm M-42

    TOWED 40mm L/70

MSL • SSM *Ching Feng*

Navy 45,000

3 district; 1 (ASW) HQ located at Hualein; 1 Fleet HQ located at Tsoying; 1 New East Coast Fleet

EQUIPMENT BY TYPE

SUBMARINES • TACTICAL • SSK 4:

    2 *Hai Lung* each with 6 single 533mm TT each with SUT HWT

    2 *Hai Shih* (trg role) each with 10 single 533mm TT (6 fwd, 4aft) each with SUT HWT

PRINCIPAL SURFACE COMBATANTS 26

    CRUISERS • CGHM 4 *Keelung* (ex US *Kidd*) each with 1 quad lnchr with RGM-84L *Harpoon* AShM, 2 twin Mk26 lnchr (4 eff) each with SM-2MR SAM, 2 octuple Mk112 lnchr (16 eff.) with ASROC, 2 127mm gun, (capacity 2 med hel)

    FRIGATES 22

        FFGHM 20:

        8 *Cheng Kung* each with 2 quad lnchr (8 eff.) each with *Hsiung Feng* AShM, 1 Mk13 GMLS with SM-1MR SAM, 2 triple 324mm ASTT (6 eff.) each with Mk 46 LWT, 1 76mm gun, (capacity 2 S-70C ASW hel)

        6 *Chin Yang* each with 1 octuple Mk112 lnchr with ASROC/RGM-84C *Harpoon* AShM, 2 triple lnchr (6 eff.) each with SM-1 MR SAM, 2 twin (4 eff.) each with SM-1 MR SAM, 2 twin 324mm ASTT (4 eff.) each with Mk 46 LWT, 1 127mm gun, (capacity 1 MD-500 hel)

        6 *Kang Ding* each with 2 quad lnchr (8 eff.) each with *Hsiung Feng* AShM, 1 quad (4 eff.) with *Sea Chaparral* SAM, 2 triple 324mm ASTT (6 eff.) each with Mk 46 LWT, 1 76mm gun, (capacity 1 S-70C ASW hel)

        FFGH 2:

        2 *Chin Yang* each with 1 octuple Mk112 lnchr with ASROC/RGM-84C *Harpoon* AShM, 2 twin 324mm ASTT (4 eff.) each with Mk 46 LWT, 1 127mm gun, (capacity 1 MD-500 hel)

PATROL AND COASTAL COMBATANTS 73

    PCFG 2 *Lung Chiang* each with 4 single lnchr each with *Hsiung Feng* AShM

    PCG 59:

        47 *Hai Ou* each with 2 single lnchr each with *Hsiung Feng* AShM

        12 *Jinn Chiang* each with 1 quad lnchr (4 eff.) with *Hsiung Feng* AShM

    PBG 4 *Kwang Hua* each with 2 twin lnchr (4 eff.) each with *Hsiung Feng* II AShM (additional vessels in build)

    PBF 8 *Ning Hai*

MINE WARFARE • MINE COUNTERMEASURES 12

    MSC 8: 4 *Yung Chuan*; 4 *Yung Feng*

    MSO 4 *Aggressive* (Ex US)

COMMAND SHIPS • LCC 1 *Kao Hsiung*

AMPHIBIOUS

    PRINCIPAL AMPHIBIOUS SHIPS • LSD 2:

        1 *Shiu Hai* (capacity either 2 LCU or 18 LCM; 360 troops) with 1 hel landing platform

        1 *Chung Cheng* with 1 quad lnchr with *Sea Chapparal* SAM (capacity 3 LCU or 18 LCM)

    LANDING SHIPS 13

        LST 13: 11 *Chung Hai* (capacity 16 tanks; 200 troops); 2 *Newport* (capacity 3 LCVP, 400 troops)

    LANDING CRAFT 288: 18 LCU; 100 **LCVP**; 170 **LCM**

LOGISTICS AND SUPPORT 13:

    AOE 1 *WuYi* with 1 hel landing platform

    ARS 6

    AK 3 *Wu Kang* with 1 hel landing platform (capacity 1,400 troops)

    AGOR 1 *Ta Kuan*

    AG 1

    AGS 1

FACILITIES

Bases   Located at Makung (Pescadores), Keelung, Tsoying, Hualein, Suo

Marines 15,000

FORCES BY ROLE

Marine 3 bde

Spt   some amph elm

EQUIPMENT BY TYPE
AAV 204: 54 AAV-7A1; 150 LVTP-5A1
ARTY • TOWED 105mm; 155mm
AT • RCL 106mm

Naval Aviation

FORCES BY ROLE

ASW   3 sqn with S-70C *Seahawk* (S-70C *Defender*)

MP   2 sqn with S-2E *Tracker*; S-2G *Tracker*

EQUIPMENT BY TYPE

AIRCRAFT 32 combat capable
  ASW 32: 24 S-2E *Tracker*; 8 S-2G *Tracker*
HELICOPTERS • ASW 20 S-70C-*Seahawk* (S-70C *Defender*)

Air Force 55,000

Flying hours   180 hrs/year

Four Cmds: Air Cbt Comd (Air Tac Ctrl Wg; Comms & Avn Ctrl Wg; Weather Wg); Log Comd (1st Log Depot (Pingtung); 2nd Log Depot (Taichung); 3rd Log Depot (Kangshan); Air Defence & Security Comd; Education, Trg & Doctrine Devt Comd

Tactical Fighter Wings

1st (443rd) Tactical Fighter Wing (TFW)(Tainan)incl 3 Tac Ftr Gp (TFG) (1st, 3rd, 9th) with F-CK-1A/B
2nd (499th) TFW (Hsinchu) incl 2 TFG (41st, 42nd) with *Mirage* 2000-5Di/Ei; 1 Trg Gp (48th) with *Mirage* 2000-5Di/Ei
3rd (427th) TFW (Ching Chuan Kang) incl 2 TFG (7th, 28th) with F-CK-1A/B
4th (455th) TFW (Chiayi) incl 3 TFG (21st, 22nd, 23rd) with F-16A/B; 1 Air Rescue Gp with S-70C
5th (401st) TFW (Hualien) incl 3 TFG (17th, 26th, 27th) with F-16A/B; 1 Tac Recce Sqn (12th) with RF-16A
7th (737th) TFW (Taitung) with 1 TFG (7th) incl 3 ftr sqn (44th, 45th, 46th (Aggressor)) with F-5E/F

Composite Wing

439th Composite Wg (Pingtung) with 10th Tac Airlift Gp incl 2 airlift sqn (101st, 102nd) with C-130H; 1 EW Gp (20th); 1 EW Sqn (2nd) with E-2T/E-2T *Hawkeye* 2000; 1 EW Sqn (6th) with C-130HE

Air base Commands

Sungshan Air Base Comd incl Spec Tpt Sqn with Beech 1900C, Fokker 50; Presidential Flt Sect with Boeing 737, Fokker 50 • Makung Air Base Command incl 1 Det with F-CK-1A/B

Air Force Academy

incl Basic Trg Gp with T-34C; Ftr Trg Gp with AT-3; Airlift Trg Gp with Beech 1900C 2

FORCES BY ROLE

Ftr   3 sqn with *Mirage* 2000-5E (2000-5EI)/*Mirage* 2000-5D (2000-5DI)

FGA   1 sqn with AT-3A/B *Tzu-Chung**; 3 sqn with F-5E/F-5F *Tiger II*; 6 sqn with F-16A/F-16B *Fighting Falcon*; 5 sqn with F-CK-1A/B *Ching Kuo*

EW   1 sqn with C-130HE *Tien Gian*

ISR   1 sqn with RF-16A *Fighting Falcon*

AEW&C   1 sqn with E-2T *Hawkeye*

SAR   1 sqn with S-70C *Black Hawk*

Tpt   2 sqn with C-130H *Hercules*; 1 (VIP) sqn with B-727-100; B-737-800; Beech 1900; Fokker 50

Tpt Hel   1 sqn with CH-47 *Chinook*; S-70 *Black Hawk*; S-62A (VIP)

FACILTIES

Trg School   1 with T-34C *Turbo Mentor*; AT-3A/B *Tzu-Chung**

EQUIPMENT BY TYPE

AIRCRAFT 477 combat capable
  FTR 291: 88 F-5E *Tiger II*/F-5F *Tiger II* (some in store); 146 F-16A/F-16B *Fighting Falcon*; 10 *Mirage* 2000-5D (2000-5DI); 47 *Mirage* 2000-5E (2000-5EI)
  FGA 128 F-CK-1A/B *Ching Kuo*
  ISR 8 RF-5E *Tigereye*
  EW 2 C-130HE *Tien Gian*
  AEW&C 6 E-2T *Hawkeye*
  TPT 39 **Medium** 19 C-130H *Hercules* (1 EW); **Light** 12: 10 Beech 1900; 2 C-47 *Skytrain* (CC-47) **PAX** 8: 4 B-727-100; 1 B-737-800; 3 F-50
  TRG 100: 58 AT-3A/B *Tzu-Chung**; 42 T-34C *Turbo Mentor*
HELICOPTERS
  TPT 35: **Heavy** 3 CH-47 *Chinook*; **Medium** 32: 1 S-62A (VIP); 14 S-70; 17 S-70C *Black Hawk*
MSL
  ASM AGM-65A *Maverick*
  AShM AGM-84 *Harpoon*
  ARM *Sky Sword* IIA
  AAM • IR AAM AIM-9J *Sidewinder*/AIM-9P *Sidewinder*; R-550 *Magic* 2; *Shafrir*; *Sky Sword* I; **IR/ARH AAM** MICA; **ARH AAM** AIM-120C *AMRAAM*; *Sky Sword* II

Paramilitary 17,000

Coast Guard 17,000

New service formed with the merging of agencies from the ministry of finance, customs and marine police.

EQUIPMENT BY TYPE

PATROL AND COASTAL COMBATANTS 96
  PSO 2 *Ho Hsing*;
  PCO 16: 2 *Chin Hsing*; 2 *Kinmen*; 2 *Mou Hsing*; 1 *Shun Hu 1*; 2 *Shun Hu 2/3*; 4 *Taichung*; 2 *Taipei*; 1 *Yun Hsing*
  PBF 36 (various)
  PB 42: 4 *Hai Cheng*; 4 *Hai Ying*; 2 *Shun Hu 5/6*; 32 (various)

FOREIGN FORCES

Singapore Army: 3 trg camp (incl inf and arty)

Tajikistan TJK

Tajikistani Somoni Tr		2009	2010	2011
GDP	Tr	20.6bn	25.0bn	
	US$	5.01bn	5.72bn	
per capita	US$	720	808	
Growth	%	3.4	5.5	
Inflation	%	6.4	7.0	
Def exp	Tr	ε200m		
	US$	ε49m		
Def bdgt	Tr	363m	367m	
	US$	88m	84m	
FMA (US)	US$	0.74m	1.5m	1.2m
US$1=Tr		4.12	4.37	

Population 7,074,845

Ethnic groups: Tajik 67%; Uzbek 25%; Russian 2%; Tatar 2%

Age	0–14	15–19	20–24	25–29	30–64	65 plus
Male	17.3%	5.2%	5.6%	4.8%	15.4%	1.4%
Female	16.7%	5.1%	5.5%	4.7%	16.4%	1.9%

Capabilities

ACTIVE 8,800 (Army 7,300, Air Force/Air Defence 1,500) **Paramilitary 7,500**

Terms of service 24 months

ORGANISATIONS BY SERVICE

Army 7,300

FORCES BY ROLE

MR	3 bde with 1 trg centre
Air Aslt	1 bde
Arty	1 bde
SAM	1 regt

EQUIPMENT BY TYPE

MBT 37: 30 T-72; 7 T-62
AIFV 23: 8 BMP-1; 15 BMP-2
APC (W) 23 BTR-60/BTR-70/BTR-80
ARTY 23
    TOWED 122mm 10 D-30
    MRL 122mm 3 BM-21
    MOR 120mm 10
AD • SAM 20+
    TOWED 20 S-75 *Dvina* (SA-2 *Guideline*); S-125 *Pechora* (SA-3 *Goa*)
    MANPAD FIM-92A *Stinger* (reported); 9K32 *Strela-2* (SA-7 *Grail*)‡

Air Force/Air Defence 1,500

FORCES BY ROLE

Tpt	1 sqn with Tu-134A *Crusty*
Atk Hel/Tpt Hel	1 sqn with Mi-24 *Hind*; Mi-8 *Hip*/Mi-17TM *Hip H*

EQUIPMENT BY TYPE
AIRCRAFT • TPT • Light 1 Tu-134A *Crusty*
HELICOPTERS
    ATK 4 Mi-24 *Hind*
    TPT • Medium 12 Mi-8 *Hip*/Mi-17TM *Hip H*

Paramilitary 7,500

Interior Troops 3,800

National Guard 1,200

Emergencies Ministry 2,500

Border Guards

DEPLOYMENT

BOSNIA-HERZEGOVINA
OSCE • Bosnia and Herzegovina 1

FOREIGN FORCES

India Air Force: 1 Fwd Op Base located at Farkhar
Russia 5,000 Army: 1 mil base (subord Central MD) with (1 MR div (201st - understrength); 54 T-72; 300 BMP-2/BTR-80/MT-LB; 100 2S1/2S3/2S12/9P140 Uragan • Military Air Forces: 5 Su-25 *Frogfoot*; 4 Mi-8 *Hip*

Thailand THA

Thai Baht b		2009	2010	2011
GDP	b	9.05tr	10.0tr	
	US$	264bn	314bn	
per capita	US$	3,898	4,602	
Growth	%	-2.3	7.0	
Inflation	%	-0.8	3.2	
Def exp	b	162bn		
	US$	4.73bn		
Def bdgt	b	170bn	154bn	170bn
	US$	4.97bn	4.81bn	
FMA (US)	US$	1.6m	1.6m	1.06m
US$1=b		34.27	31.99	

Population 68,139,238

Ethnic and religious groups: Thai 75%; Chinese 14%; Muslim 4%

Age	0–14	15–19	20–24	25–29	30–64	65 plus
Male	10.1%	3.9%	3.7%	3.9%	23.9%	4.1%
Female	9.6%	3.8%	3.6%	3.9%	24.6%	5.0%

Capabilities

ACTIVE 305,860 (Army 190,000 Navy 69,860 Air 46,000) **Paramilitary 113,700**

Terms of service 2 years

RESERVE 200,000 Paramilitary 45,000

ORGANISATIONS BY SERVICE

Army 120,000; ε70,000 conscript (total 190,000)

4 Regional Army HQ, 2 Corps HQ

FORCES BY ROLE

Armd Air Cav	1 regt (3 air mob coy)
Rapid Reaction	1 force (1 bn per region forming)
Cav	2 div; 1 indep regt
Recce	4 coy
Armd Inf	3 div
Mech Inf	2 div
Inf	8 indep bn
SF	2 div
Lt Inf	1 div
Arty	1 div
AD	1 ADA div with (6 bn)
Engr	1 div
Hel	some flt
Economic development	4 div

EQUIPMENT BY TYPE

MBT 283: 53 M-60A1; 125 M-60A3; (50 Type-69 (trg) in store); 105 M-48A5

LT TK 465: 255 M-41; 104 *Scorpion* (50 in store); 106 *Stingray*

RECCE 32+: 32 S52 Mk 3; M1114 HMMWV

APC 950

    APC (T) 790: 340 M-113A1/M-113A3; 450 Type-85

    APC (W) 160: 18 *Condor*; 142 LAV-150 *Commando*

ARTY 2,479+

    SP 155mm 26: 6 CAESAR; 20 M-109A2

    TOWED 553: **105mm** 353: 24 LG1 MK II; 285 M-101/-Mod; 12 M-102; 32 M-618A2; **130mm** 15 Type-59-I; **155mm** 185: 42 GHN-45 A1; 50 M-114; 61 M-198; 32 M-71

    MRL 130mm Type-85 (reported)

    MOR 1,900

        SP 33: **81mm** 21 M-125A3; **120mm** 12 M-1064A3

        TOWED 1,867: **81mm**; **107mm** M-106A1

AT • MSL 318+

    SP 18+ M-901A5 (TOW)

    MANPATS 300 M47 *Dragon*

RCL 180: **75mm** 30 M-20; **106mm** 150 M-40

RL 66mm M-72 *LAW*

AIRCRAFT

ISR 40 Cessna O-1A *Bird Dog*

TPT • Light 20: 2 Beech 1900C; 2 Beech 200 *King Air*; 2 C-212 *Aviocar*; 10 Cessna A185E (U-17B); 2 *Jetstream* 41; 2 Short 330UTT

TRG 33: 18 MX-7-235 *Star Rocket*; 15 T-41B *Mescalero*

HELICOPTERS

ATK 5 AH-1F *Cobra*

TPT 167 **Heavy** 6 CH-47D *Chinook* **Medium** 2 UH-60L *Black Hawk* **Light** 159: 92 Bell 205 (UH-1H *Iroquois*); 65 Bell 206 *Jet Ranger*/Bell 212 (AB-212)/Bell 214/Bell 412 *Twin Huey*

TRG 42 Hughes 300C

UAV • ISR • Medium *Searcher*

AD • SAM

    STATIC *Aspide*

    MANPAD FIM-43 *Redeye*; HN-5A

    GUNS 202+

    SP 54: **20mm** 24 M-163 *Vulcan*; **40mm** 30 M-1/M-42 SP

    TOWED 148+: **20mm** 24 M-167 *Vulcan*; **37mm** 52 Type-74; **40mm** 48 L/70; **57mm** 24+: ε6 Type-59 (S-60); 18+ non-operational

RADAR • LAND AN/TPQ-36 *Firefinder* (arty, mor); RASIT (veh, arty)

Reserves

Inf   4 div HQ

Navy 44,011 (incl Naval Aviation, Marines, Coastal Defence); 25,849 conscript (total 69,860)

FORCES BY ROLE

Air wing   1 div

Navy   1 (Fleet) HQ located at Sattahip; Mekong River Operating Unit HQ located at Nakhon Phanom

EQUIPMENT BY TYPE

PRINCIPAL SURFACE COMBATANTS 10

    AIRCRAFT CARRIERS • CVS 1:

        1 *Chakri Naruebet* (capacity 9 AV-8A *Harrier*† FGA ac; 6 S-70B *Seahawk* ASW hel)

    FRIGATES 10

        FFGHM 2:

        2 *Naresuan* each with 2 quad Mk141 lnchr (8 eff.) each with RGM-84A *Harpoon* AShM, 1 8 cell Mk41 VLS with RIM-7M *Sea Sparrow* SAM, 2 triple 324mm TT (6 eff.), 1 127mm gun, (capacity 1 *Super Lynx 300* hel)

        FFGM 4:

        2 *Chao Phraya* each with 4 twin lnchr (8 eff.) each with C-801 (CSS-N-4 *Sardine*) AShM, 2 twin lnchr (4 eff.) each with HQ-61 (CSA-N-2) SAM (non-operational), 2 RBU 1200 (10 eff.), 2 twin 100mm gun (4 eff.)

        2 *Kraburi* each with 4 twin lnchr (8 eff.) each with C-801 (CSS-N-4 *Sardine*) AShM, 2 twin lnchr (4 eff.) with HQ-61 (CSA-N-2) SAM, 2 RBU 1200 (10 eff.), 1 twin 100mm gun (2 eff.), 1 hel landing platform

        FFGH 2:

        2 *Phuttha Yotfa Chulalok* (leased from US) each with 1 octuple Mk112 lnchr with RGM-84C *Harpoon* AShM/ ASROC, 2 twin 324mm ASTT (4 eff.) each with Mk 46 LWT, 1 127mm gun, (capacity 1 Bell 212 (AB-212) utl hel)

        FF 2:

        1 *Makut Rajakumarn* with 2 triple 34mm ASTT (6 eff.), 2 114mm gun

        1 *Pin Klao* (trg role) with 6 single 324mm ASTT, 3 76mm gun

PATROL AND COASTAL COMBATANTS 82
  CORVETTES 7
    FSG 2 *Rattanakosin* each with 2 quad Mk140 lnchr (8 eff.) each with RGM-84A *Harpoon* AShM, 1 octuple *Albatros* lnchr with *Aspide* SAM, 2 triple 324mm ASTT (6 eff.), 1 76mm gun
    FS 5:
      3 *Khamronsin* each with 2 triple 324mm ASTT (6 eff.), 1 76mm gun
      2 *Tapi* each with 6 single 324mm ASTT each with Mk 46 LWT, 1 76mm gun
  PCFG 6:
    3 *Prabparapak* each with 2 single lnchr each with 1 GI *Gabriel I* AShM, 1 triple lnchr (3 eff.) with GI *Gabriel I* AShM
    3 *Ratcharit* each with 2 twin lnchr (4 eff.) each with MM-38 *Exocet* AShM, 1 76mm gun
  PCO 5: 3 *Hua Hin* each with 1 76mm gun; 2 *Pattani* each with 1 76mm gun
  PCC 9: 3 *Chon Buri* each with 2 76mm gun; 6 *Sattahip* each with 1 76mm gun
  PBF 4
  PB 51: 10 T-11; 9 *Swift*; 3 T-81; 9 T-91; 3 T-210; 13 T-213; 1 T-227; 3 T-991
MINE WARFARE • MINE COUNTERMEASURES 19
  MCM SPT 1 *Thalang*
  MCO 2 *Lat Ya*
  MCC 2 *Bang Rachan*
  MSC 2 *Bangkeo*
  MSR 12
AMPHIBIOUS
  LANDING SHIPS 8:
    LS 2 *Prab*
    LST 6:
      4 *Chang* each with 6 40mm gun (capacity 16 tanks; 200 troops)
      2 *Sichang* training each with 2 40mm gun, 1 hel landing platform (capacity 14 tanks; 300 troops)
  LANDING CRAFT 16:
    LCU 13: 3 *Man Nok*; 6 *Mataphun* (capacity either 3–4 MBT or 250 troops); 4 *Thong Kaeo*
    UCAC 3 Griffon 1000TD
LOGISTICS AND SUPPORT 14
  AORH 1 *Similan* (capacity 1 hel)
  AOR 1 *Chula*
  AOL 5: 4 *Prong*; 1 *Samui*
  AWT 1
  AGOR 1
  AGS 2
  ABU 1
  TRG 1
  TPT 1

FACILITIES
Bases Located at Bangkok, Sattahip, Songkhla, Phang Nga, Nakhon Phanom

Naval Aviation 1,200
  AIRCRAFT 39 combat capable
    FGA 9: 7 AV-8A *Harrier II*†; 2 TAV-8A *Harrier*†
    ATK 18: 14 TA-7 *Corsair*; 4 TA-7C *Corsair II*

    ASW 3 P-3A *Orion* (P-3T)
    RECCE 9 *Sentry* 02-337
    MP 3 F-27-200 MPA*
    TPT • Light 12: 6 Do-228-212*; 2 F-27-400M *Troopship*; 5 N-24A *Searchmaster*; 1 UP-3A *Orion* (UP-3T)
  HELICOPTERS
    ASW 8: 6 S-70B *Seahawk*; 2 *Super Lynx 300*
    MRH 2 *Super Lynx*
    TPT 15 **Medium** 5 Bell 214ST (AB-214ST) **Light** 8: 4 Bell 212 (AB-212); 4 S-76B
  MSL • AShM: AGM-84 *Harpoon*

Marines 23,000

FORCES BY ROLE

Recce	1 bn
Amph Aslt	1 bn
Inf	2 regt (6 bn)
Arty	1 regt (1 ADA bn, 3 fd arty bn)
Marine	1 div HQ

EQUIPMENT BY TYPE
APC (W) 24 LAV-150 *Commando*
AAV 33 LVTP-7
ARTY • TOWED 48: **105mm** 36 (reported); **155mm** 12 GC-45
AT • MSL 24+
  TOWED 24 HMMWV TOW
  MANPATS M47 *Dragon*; TOW
AD • GUNS 12.7mm 14

Air Force ε46,000

4 air divs, one flying trg school
Flying hours 100 hrs/year

FORCES BY ROLE

Ftr	3 sqn with F-16A/B *Fighting Falcon;* 1 sqn with L-39ZA/MP *Albatros**; 4 sqn (1 aggressor) with F-5B *Tiger;* F-5E/5F *Tiger II*
Atk	1 sqn with *Alpha Jet**; 1 sqn with AU-23A *Peacemaker*, 1 sqn with L-39ZA/MP *Albatros**
ISR/ELINT	1 sqn with IAI-201 *Arava*, Learjet 35A; 1 (Survey) sqn with SA-226AT *Merlin IV/IVA;* N-22B *Nomad*
Tpt	1 (Royal Flight) sqn with A-310-324; Airbus A319CJ; AS-332L *Super Puma;* AS-532A2 *Cougar MkII;* B-737-200; BAe-748; B737-400; Beech 200 *King Air;* Bell 412 *Twin Huey;* SA-226AT *Merlin IV/IVA;* 1 sqn with Basler *Turbo-67;* GAF N-22B *Nomad;* 1 sqn with BAe-748; G-222; 1 (liaison) sqn with Beech 65 *Queen Air;* Beech E90 *King Air; Commander* 500; Cessna 150; T-41D *Mescalero;* 1 sqn with C-130H *Hercules;* C-130H-30 *Hercules*
Tpt Hel	1 sqn with Bell 205 (UH-1H *Iroquois*); 1 sqn with Bell 212

FACILITIES

Trg School	1 with CT-4B/E *Airtrainer;* PC-9; Bell 206B *Jet Ranger II*

EQUIPMENT BY TYPE

AIRCRAFT 165 combat capable

FTR 87: 35 F-5E *Tiger II*/F-5F *Tiger II* (32 being upgraded), 2 F-5B *Tiger* (to be replaced by 4 JAS-39C/2 JAS-39D *Gripen* from 2011); 41 F-16A *Fighting Falcon*; 9 F-16B *Fighting Falcon*

ATK 22 AU-23A *Peacemaker*

TPT 79 **Medium** 15: 7 C-130H *Hercules*; 5 C-130H-30 *Hercules*; 3 G-222; **Light** 44: 1 ATR-72; 2 Beech 200 *King Air*; 2 Beech 65 *Queen Air*; 1 Beech E90 *King Air*; 3 Cessna 150; 3 *Commander* 500; 3 IAI-201 *Arava*; 2 *Learjet* 35A; 18 N-22B *Nomad*; 9 SA-226AT *Merlin IV/IVA* **PAX** 20: 1 A-310-324; 1 A-319CJ; 1 B-737-200; 2 B-737-400; 6 BAe-748; 9 Basler BT-67

TRG 123: 10 *Alpha Jet**; 29 CT-4B/E *Airtrainer*; 46 L-39ZA/MP *Albatros**; 23 PC-9; 12 T-41D *Mescalero*

HELICOPTERS

MRH 2 Bell 412 *Twin Huey*

TPT 45 **Medium** 6: 3 AS-332L *Super Puma*; 3 AS-532A2 *Cougar MKII*; **Light** 39: 20 Bell 205 (UH-1H *Iroquois*); 6 Bell 206B *Jet Ranger II*; 13 Bell 212

MSL

AAM • IR AAM AIM-9B *Sidewinder*/AIM-9J *Sidewinder*; *Python* III **ARH AAM** AIM-120 AMRAAM

ASM: AGM-65 *Maverick*

Paramilitary ε113,700 active

Border Patrol Police 41,000

Marine Police 2,200

PATROL AND COASTAL COMBATANTS 89

PCO 1 *Srinakrin*

PCC 2 *Hameln*

PB 86: 1 *Burespadoongkit*; 2 *Chasanyabadee*; 3 *Cutlass*; 1 *Sriyanont*; 1 *Yokohama*; 78 (various)

National Security Volunteer Corps 45,000 – Reserves

Police Aviation 500

AIRCRAFT 6 combat capable

ATK 6 AU-23A *Peacemaker*

TPT 16 **Light** 15: 2 CN-235; 8 PC-6 *Turbo-Porter*; 3 SC-7 3M *Skyvan*; 2 Short 330UTT **PAX** 1 F-50

HELICOPTERS

MRH 6 Bell 412 *Twin Huey*

TPT • Light 67: 27 Bell 205A; 14 Bell 206 *Jet Ranger*; 20 Bell 212 (AB-212)

Provincial Police 50,000 (incl est. 500 Special Action Force)

Thahan Phran (Hunter Soldiers) ε20,000

Volunteer irregular force

Paramilitary   13 regt (each: 107 paramilitary coy)

DEPLOYMENT

ARABIAN SEA & GULF OF ADEN

Combined Maritime Forces • CTF-151: 1 PCO; 1 AORH

SUDAN

UN • UNAMID 7; 2 obs

FOREIGN FORCES

United States US Pacific Command: 122

Timor Leste TLS

Timorian Escudo TPE		2009	2010	2011
Population	1,040,880			

Age	0–14	15–19	20–24	25–29	30–64	65 plus
Male	19%	6%	5%	3%	16%	1%
Female	18%	6%	5%	3%	16%	2%

Capabilities

ACTIVE 1,332 (Army 1,250 Naval Element 82)

ORGANISATIONS BY SERVICE

Army 1,250

Training began in Jan 2001 with the aim of deploying 1,500 full-time personnel and 1,500 reservists. Authorities are engaged in developing security structures with international assistance.

Inf   2 bn

Naval Element 82

PATROL AND COASTAL COMBATANTS 4

PB 4: 2 *Albatros*; 2 *Shanghai* II

FOREIGN FORCES

Australia ISF (*Operation Astute*) 404; 1 bn HQ; 2 inf coy; 1 AD bty; elm 1 cbt engr regt; 1 hel det with 5 S-70A-9 (S-70A) *Black Hawk*; 4 OH-58 *Kiowa*; 3 C-130; • UNMIT 4 obs

Bangladesh UNMIT 4 obs

Brazil UNMIT 4 obs

China, People's Republic of UNMIT 2 obs

Fiji UNMIT 1 obs

India UNMIT 1 obs

Japan UNMIT 2 obs

Malaysia UNMIT 2 obs

Nepal UNMIT 1 obs

New Zealand ISF (*Operation Astute*) 80; 1 inf coy • UNMIT 1 obs

Pakistan UNMIT 4 obs

Philippines UNMIT 3 obs

Portugal UNMIT 3 obs

Sierra Leone UNMIT 1 obs

Singapore UNMIT 2 obs

Turkmenistan TKM

Turkmen Manat TMM		2009	2010	2011
GDP	TMM	52.7bn	56.8bn	
	US$	18.5bn	19.9bn	
per capita	US$	3,616	3,849	
Growth	%	8.0	11.0	
Inflation	%	-2.7	3.9	
Def exp	TMM	ε863m		
	US$	ε303m		
Def bdgt	TMM	712m	744m	
	US$	250m	261m	
FMA (US)	US$	0.15m	2.0m	1.2m
USD1=TMM		2.85	2.85	

Population 5,176,502

Ethnic groups: Turkmen 77%; Uzbek 9%; Russian 7%; Kazak 2%

Age	0–14	15–19	20–24	25–29	30–64	65 plus
Male	13.9%	5.5%	5.4%	4.7%	18.2%	1.8%
Female	13.6%	5.5%	5.4%	4.7%	18.9%	2.3%

Capabilities

ACTIVE 22,000 (Army 18,500 Navy 500 Air 3,000)

Terms of service 24 months

ORGANISATIONS BY SERVICE

Army 18,500

FORCES BY ROLE

5 Mil Districts

MR	3 div; 2 bde; 1 div (trg)
Air Aslt	1 indep bn
Arty	1 bde
MRL	1 regt
AT	1 regt
Engr	1 regt
SAM	2 bde
Msl	1 (Scud) bde

EQUIPMENT BY TYPE †

MBT 680: 10 T-90S; 670 T-72

RECCE 170 BRDM/BRDM-2

AIFV 942: 930 BMP-1/BMP-2; 12 BRM

APC (W) 829 BTR-60/BTR-70/BTR-80

ARTY 564

  SP 56: **122mm** 40 2S1 *Carnation;* **152mm** 16 2S3

  TOWED 269: **122mm** 180 D-30; **152mm** 89: 17 D-1; 72 D-20

  GUN/MOR 120mm 17 2S9 *Anona*

  MRL 131: **122mm** 65: 9 9P138; 56 BM-21; **220mm** 60 9P140 *Uragan*

  300mm 6 BM 9A52 *Smerch*

  MOR 97: **82mm** 31; **120mm** 66 PM-38

AT

  MSL • MANPATS 100 9K11 (AT-3 *Sagger*); 9K111 (AT-4 *Spigot*); 9K113 (AT-5 *Spandrel*); 9K115 (AT-6 *Spiral*)

  RL 73mm RPG-7 *Knout*

  GUNS 100mm 72 MT-12/T-12

AD • SAM 53+

  SP 53: 40 9K33 *Osa* (SA-8 *Gecko*); 13 9K35 *Strela-10* (SA-13 *Gopher*)

  MANPAD 9K32 *Strela-2* (SA-7 *Grail*)‡

  GUNS 70

  SP 23mm 48 ZSU-23-4

  TOWED 57mm 22 S-60

MSL • SSM 10 SS-1 *Scud*

Navy 500

Intention to form a combined navy/coast guard and currently has a minor base at Turkmenbashy. Caspian Sea Flotilla (see Russia) is operating as a joint RUS, KAZ, TKM flotilla under RUS comd based at Astrakhan.

EQUIPMENT BY TYPE

PATROL AND COASTAL COMBATANTS 6

  PBF 5 *Grif-T*

  PB 1 *Point*

FACILITIES

Minor base   Located at Turkmenbashy

Air Force 3,000

incl Air Defence

FORCES BY ROLE

Ftr / FGA	2 sqn with MiG-29 *Fulcrum*; MiG-29UB *Fulcrum*; Su-17 *Fitter*; Su-25MK *Frogfoot*
Tpt	1 sqn with An-26 *Curl*; Mi-8 *Hip*; Mi-24 *Hind*
Trg	1 unit with Su-7B *Fitter-A*; L-39 *Albatros*
AD	Some sqns with S-75 *Dvina* (SA-2 *Guideline*); S-125 *Pechora* (SA-3 *Goa*); S-200 *Angara* (SA-5 *Gammon*)

EQUIPMENT BY TYPE

AIRCRAFT 94 combat capable

  FTR 24: 22 MiG-29 *Fulcrum*; 2 MiG-29UB *Fulcrum*

  FGA 68: 3 Su-7B *Fitter-A*; 65 Su-17 *Fitter-B*;

  ATK 2 Su-25MK *Frogfoot* (41 more being refurbished)

  TPT • Light 1 An-26 *Curl*

  TRG 7: 2 L-39 *Albatros*

HELICOPTERS

  ATK 10 Mi-24 *Hind*

  TPT • Medium 8 Mi-8 *Hip*

AD • SAM 50 S-75 *Dvina* (SA-2 *Guideline*)/S-125 *Pechora* (SA-3 *Goa*)/S-200 *Angara* (SA-5 *Gammon*)

Asia

Uzbekistan UZB

Uzbekistani Som s		2009	2010	2011
GDP	s	48.1tr	59.7tr	
	US$	32.7bn	37.6bn	
per capita	US$	1,178	1,352	
Growth	%	8.1	8.2	
Inflation	%	14.1	10.6	
Def exp	s	ε1.15tr		
	US$	ε780m		
Def bdgt	s	1.82tr	2.26tr	
	US$	1.24bn	1.42bn	
US$1=s		1470.59	1587.30	

Population   27,794,296

Ethnic groups: Uzbek 73%; Russian 6%; Tajik 5%; Kazakh 4%; Karakalpak 2%; Tatar 2%; Korean <1%; Ukrainian <1%

Age	0–14	15–19	20–24	25–29	30–64	65 plus
Male	13.6%	5.6%	5.6%	4.9%	18.1%	2.0%
Female	12.9%	5.5%	5.5%	4.8%	18.9%	2.7%

Capabilities

ACTIVE 67,000 (Army 50,000 Air 17,000)
Paramilitary 20,000
Terms of service conscription 12 months

ORGANISATIONS BY SERVICE

Army 50,000
FORCES BY ROLE
4 Mil Districts; 2 op comd; 1 Tashkent Comd
Tk   1 bde
MR   11 bde
Mtn Inf   1 (lt) bde
Air Aslt 3 bde
AB   1 bde
SF   1 bde
Arty   6 bde
MRL   1 bde

EQUIPMENT BY TYPE
MBT 340: 70 T-72; 100 T-64; 170 T-62
RECCE 19: 13 BRDM-2; 6 BRM
AIFV 399: 120 BMD-1; 9 BMD-2; 270 BMP-2
APC 309
  APC (T) 50 BTR-D
  APC (W) 259: 24 BTR-60; 25 BTR-70; 210 BTR-80
ARTY 487+
  SP 83+: **122mm** 18 2S1 *Carnation*; **152mm** 17+: 17 2S3; 2S5 (reported); **203mm** 48 2S7
  TOWED 200: **122mm** 60 D-30; **152mm** 140 2A36
  GUN/MOR 120mm 54 2S9 *Anona*
  MRL 108: **122mm** 60: 24 9P138; 36 BM-21; **220mm** 48 9P140 *Uragan*
  MOR 120mm 42: 5 2B11; 19 2S12; 18 PM-120

AT • MSL • MANPATS 9K11 (AT-3 *Sagger*); 9K111 (AT-4 *Spigot*)
  GUNS 100mm 36 MT-12/T-12

Air Force 17,000
FORCES BY ROLE
7 fixed wg and hel regts.
Ftr   1 regt with MiG-29 *Fulcrum*/MiG-29UB *Fulcrum*; Su-27 *Flanker*/Su-27UB *Flanker C*
FGA/Atk   1 regt with Su-24 *Fencer*; Su-24MP *Fencer-F** (ISR); 1 regt with Su-25 *Frogfoot*/Su-25BM *Frogfoot*; Su-17M (Su-17MZ) *Fitter C*/Su-17UM-3 (Su-17UMZ) *Fitter G*
ELINT/Tpt 1 regt with An-12 *Cub*/An-12PP *Cub*; An-26 *Curl*/An-26RKR *Curl*
Tpt   Some sqns with An-24 *Coke*; Tu-134 *Crusty*
Trg   Some sqns with L-39 *Albatros*
Atk Hel/Tpt 1 regt with Mi-24 *Hind* (attack); Mi-26 *Halo*
Hel   (tpt); Mi-8 *Hip* (aslt/tpt); 1 regt with Mi-6 *Hook* (tpt); Mi-6AYa *Hook -C* (C2)

EQUIPMENT BY TYPE
AIRCRAFT 135 combat capable
  FTR 30 MiG-29 *Fulcrum*/MiG-29UB *Fulcrum*
  FGA 74: 26 Su-17M (Su-17MZ) *Fitter C*/Su-17UM-3 (Su-17UMZ) *Fitter G*; 23 Su-24 *Fencer*; 25 Su-27 *Flanker*/Su-27UB *Flanker C*
  ATK 20 Su-25/Su-25BM *Frogfoot*
  EW/Tpt 26 An-12 *Cub* (med tpt)/An-12PP *Cub* (EW)
  ELINT 11 Su-24MP *Fencer F**
  ELINT/Tpt 13 An-26 *Curl* (lt tpt)/An-26RKR *Curl* (ELINT)
  TPT • Light 2: 1 An-24 *Coke*; 1 Tu-134 *Crusty*
  TRG 5 L-39 *Albatros* (9 more in store)
HELICOPTERS
  ATK 29 Mi-24 *Hind*
  C2 2 Mi-6AYa *Hook*
  TPT 79 **Heavy** 27: 26 Mi-6 *Hook*; 1 Mi-26 *Halo* **Medium** 52 Mi-8 *Hip*
AD • SAM 45
  TOWED S-75 *Dvina* (SA-2 *Guideline*); S-125 *Pechora* (SA-3 *Goa*)
  STATIC S-200 *Angara* (SA-5 *Gammon*)
MSL
  ASM Kh-23 (AS-7 *Kerry*); Kh-25 (AS-10 *Karen*)
  ARM Kh-25P (AS-12 *Kegler*); Kh -28 (AS-9 *Kyle*); Kh-58 (AS-11 *Kilter*)
  AAM • IR AAM R-60 (AA-8 *Aphid*); R-73 (AA-11 *Archer*); **IR/SARH AAM** R-27 (AA-10 *Alamo*)

Paramilitary up to 20,000

Internal Security Troops up to 19,000
Ministry of Interior

National Guard 1,000
Ministry of Defence

DEPLOYMENT

SERBIA
OSCE • Kosovo 2

FOREIGN FORCES

Germany 163; some C-160 *Transall*

Vietnam VNM

Vietnamese Dong d		2009	2010	2011
GDP	d	1,658tr	1,934tr	
	US$	97bn	105bn	
per capita	US$	1,114	1,178	
Growth	%	5.5	6.7	
Inflation	%	7.0	8.4	
Def exp	d	36.5tr		
	US$	2.14bn		
Def bdgt	d	50.0tr	44.4tr	
	US$	2.93bn	2.41bn	
FMA (US)	US$	0.5m	2.0m	1.35m
US$1=d		17060.96	18450.48	

Population   89,028,741

Ethnic groups: Chinese 3%

Age	0–14	15–19	20–24	25–29	30–64	65 plus
Male	13.2%	4.9%	5.1%	5.0%	19.6%	2.1%
Female	12.0%	4.6%	4.8%	4.8%	20.6%	3.4%

Capabilities

ACTIVE 482,000 (Army 412,000 Navy 40,000 Air 30,000) **Paramilitary 40,000**

Terms of service 2 years Army and Air Defence, 3 years Air Force and Navy, specialists 3 years, some ethnic minorities 2 years

RESERVES 5,000,000

ORGANISATIONS BY SERVICE

Army ε412,000

9 Mil Regions (incl capital), 14 corps HQ

FORCES BY ROLE

Armd	10 bde
Mech inf	3 div
Inf	58 div (div strength varies from 5,000 to 12,500); 15 indep regt
SF	1 bde (1 AB bde, 1 demolition engr regt)
Fd arty	10+ bde
Engr	8 div; 20 indep bde
Economic construction	10–16 div

EQUIPMENT BY TYPE

MBT 1,315: 70 T-62; 350 Type-59; 850 T-54/T-55; 45 T-34
LT TK 620: 300 PT-76; 320 Type-62/Type-63
RECCE 100 BRDM-1/BRDM-2
AIFV 300 BMP-1/BMP-2
APC 1,380
  APC (T) 280: 200 M-113 (to be upgraded); 80 Type-63

APC (W) 1,100 BTR-40/BTR-50/BTR-60/BTR-152
ARTY 3,040+
  SP 30+: **152mm** 30 2S3; **175mm** M-107
  TOWED 2,300 **100mm** M-1944; **105mm** M-101/M-102; **122mm** D-30/Type-54 (M-30) *M-1938*/Type-60 (D-74); **130mm** M-46; **152mm** D-20; **155mm** M-114
  GUN/MOR 120mm 2S9 *Anona* (reported)
  MRL 710+: **107mm** 360 Type-63; **122mm** 350 BM-21; **140mm** BM-14
  MOR 82mm; **120mm** M-43; **160mm** M-43
AT • MSL • MANPATS 9K11 (AT-3 *Sagger*)
  RCL 75mm Type-56; **82mm** Type-65 (B-10); **87mm** Type-51
  GUNS
    SP 100mm Su-100; **122mm** Su-122
    TOWED 100mm T-12 (arty)
AD • SAM • MANPAD 9K32 *Strela*-2 (SA-7 *Grail*)‡; 9K310 *Igla*-1 (SA-16 *Gimlet*); 9K38 *Igla* (SA-18 *Grouse*)
  GUNS 12,000
    SP 23mm ZSU-23-4
    TOWED 14.5mm/30mm/37mm/57mm/85mm/100mm
MSL • SSM *Scud*-B/*Scud*-C (reported)

Navy ε40,000 (incl ε27,000 Naval Infantry)

FORCES BY ROLE

Navy 1 HQ located at Haiphong

EQUIPMENT BY TYPE

SUBMARINES • TACTICAL • SSI 2 *Yugo*† (DPRK)
PATROL AND COASTAL COMBATANTS 56
  CORVETTES 7:
    FSG 2:
    2 BPS-500 each with 2 quad lnchr (8 eff.) each with 3M24 *Uran* (SS-N-25 *Switchblade*) AShM (non-operational), 9K32 *Strela*-2M (SA-N-5 *Grail*) SAM (manually operated), 1 76mm gun
    FSG 5:
    3 *Petya* II (FSU) each with 1 quintuple 406mm ASTT (5 eff.), 4 RBU 6000 *Smerch* 2 (48 eff.), 4 76mm gun
    2 *Petya* III (FSU) each with 1 triple 533mm ASTT (3 eff.), 4 RBU 2500 *Smerch* 1 (64 eff.), 4 76mm gun
  PCFGM 7:
    4 *Tarantul* (FSU) each with 2 twin lnchr (4 eff.) each with P-15 *Termit* (SS-N-2D *Styx*) AShM, 1 quad lnchr (4 eff.) with SA-N-5 *Grail* SAM (manually operated), 1 76mm gun
    3 *Tarantul* V each with 4 quad lnchr (16 eff.) each with 3M24 *Uran* (SS-N-25 *Switchblade*) AShM; 1 quad lnchr (4 eff.) with SA-N-5 Grail SAM (manually operated), 1 76mm gun
  PCC 2 *Svetlyak* (Further 2 on order)
  PBFG 8 *Osa* II each with 4 single each with 1 SS-N-2 tactical SSM
  PBFT 3 *Shershen*† (FSU) each with 4 single 533mm TT
  PHT 3 *Turya*† each with 4 single 533mm TT
  PH 2 *Turya*†
  PB 20: 2 *Poluchat* (FSU); 14 *Zhuk*†; 4 *Zhuk* (mod)
  PBR 4 *Stolkraft*
MINE WARFARE • MINE COUNTERMEASURES 13
  MSO 2 *Yurka*
  MSC 4 *Sonya*

MHI 2 *Yevgenya*
MSR 5 K-8
AMPHIBIOUS
  LANDING SHIPS 6
    LSM 3:
      1 *Polnochny* A† (capacity 6 MBT; 180 troops)
      2 *Polnochny* B† (capacity 6 MBT; 180 troops)
    LST 3 LST-510-511 (US) (capacity 16 tanks; 200 troops)
  LANDING CRAFT 30: 15 **LCU**; 12 **LCM**; 3 **LCVP**
LOGISTICS AND SUPPORT 25:
  AKSL 20; **AWT** 1; **AGS** 1; **AT** 1; **SPT** 2 (floating dock)

Naval Infantry ε27,000

FACILITIES
  Bases Located at Hanoi, Ho Chi Minh City, Da Nang, Cam Ranh Bay, Ha Tou, Haiphong, Can Tho

Air Force 30,000

3 air divs (each with 3 regts), a tpt bde

FORCES BY ROLE

Ftr   7 regt with MiG-21bis *Fishbed L*

FGA   2 regt with Su-22M-3/Su-22M-4 *Fitter* (some ISR designated); Su-27SK/Su-27UBK *Flanker*; Su-30MKK *Flanker*

ASW/   1 regt (The PAF also maintains VNM naval air
SAR   arm) with Ka-25 *Hormone*; Ka-28 (Ka-27PL) *Helix A*; KA-32 *Helix C*; PZLW-3 *Sokol*

MP   1 regt with Be-12 *Mail*

Tpt   3 regt with An-2 *Colt*; An-26 *Curl*; Mi-6 *Hook*; Mi-8 *Hip*; Mi-17 *Hip H*; Bell 205 (UH-1H *Iroquois*); Yak-40 *Codling* (VIP)

Trg   1 regt with L-39 *Albatros*; MiG-21UM *Mongol B**; BT-6

Atk Hel   1 regt with Mi-24 *Hind*

AD   4 bde with 100mm; 130mm; 37mm; 57mm; 85mm; some (People's Regional) force (total: ε1,000 AD unit, 6 radar bde with 100 radar stn)

EQUIPMENT BY TYPE
AIRCRAFT 223 combat capable
  FGA 219: 140 MiG-21bis *Fishbed L & N*; 10 MiG-21UM *Mongol B*; 53 Su-22M-3/M-4 *Fitter* (some ISR); 7 Su-27SK *Flanker*; 5 Su-27UBK *Flanker*; 4 Su-30MKK *Flanker*
  ASW 4 Be-12 *Mail*
  TPT • Light 28: 12 An-2 *Colt*; 12 An-26 *Curl*; 4 Yak-40 *Codling* (VIP)
  TRG 43: 10 BT-6; 18 L-39 *Albatros*
HELICOPTERS
  ATK 26 Mi-24 *Hind*
  ASW 13: 3 Ka-25 *Hormone*; 10 Ka-28 *Helix A*
  MRH/Tpt 30 Mi-8 *Hip*/Mi-17 *Hip H*
  TPT 48 **Heavy** 4 Mi-6 *Hook* **Medium** 2 KA-32 *Helix C*; 4 PZL W-3 *Sokol* **Light** 12 Bell 205 (UH-1H *Iroquois*)
AD • SAM
  SP 2K12 *Kub* (SA-6 *Gainful*)
  TOWED S-75 *Dvina* (SA-2 *Guideline*); S-125 *Pechora* (SA-3 *Goa*)
  MANPAD 9K32 *Strela-2* (SA-7 *Grail*)‡; 9K310 *Igla-1* (SA-16 *Gimlet*)
  GUNS 37mm; 57mm; 85mm; 100mm; 130mm
MSL
  ASM Kh-29 (AS-14 *Kedge*); Kh-31A (AS-17 *Krypton*); Kh-59M (AS-18 *Kazoo*)
  ARM Kh-28 (AS-9 *Kyle*); Kh-31P (AS-17 *Krypton*)
  AAM • IR AAM R-3 (AA-2 *Atoll*)‡; R-60 (AA-8 *Aphid*); R-73 (AA-11 *Archer*); **IR/SARH AAM** R-27 (AA-10 *Alamo*)
FACILITIES
  SAM site   66 with 9K310 *Igla-1* (SA-16 *Gimlet*); S-75 *Dvina* (SA-2 *Guideline*); S-125 *Pechora* (SA-3 *Goa*); 2K12 *Kub* (SA-6 *Gainful*); 9K32 *Strela-2* (SA-7 *Grail*)‡

Paramilitary 40,000 active

Border Defence Corps ε40,000

Local Forces ε5,000,000 reservists

Incl People's Self-Defence Force (urban units), People's Militia (rural units); comprises of static and mobile cbt units, log spt and village protection pl; some arty, mor and AD guns; acts as reserve.

Table 18 **Selected Arms Procurements and Deliveries, Asia**

Designation	Type	Quantity	Contract Value	Supplier Country	Prime Contractor	Order Date	First Delivery Due	Notes
Afghanistan (AFG)								
G-222 (C-27A)	Tpt ac	18	US$257m	ITA	Alenia Aeronautica	2008	2009	ITA stock ordered by US. Refurbished and modernised by Alenia Aeronautica. First delivered Jul 2009
G-222 (C-27A)	Tpt ac	2	US$287m	ITA	Alenia Aeronautica	2010	n.k	To be delivered by 2011
Mi-24 *Hind*	Atk Hel	6	n.k.	CZE	n.k.	2007	2008	Ex-CZE stock. Modernised at NATO expense. Delivery status unclear
Australia (AUS)								
M113A1	APC upgrade	269	A$590m	AUS	BAE	2002	2010	Upgrade to AS3/AS4 (S) standard. Deliveries ongoing
M113A1	APC upgrade	81	n.k.	AUS	BAE	2008	n.k.	in addition to the above order
Bushmaster	LFV	293	n.k.	AUS	Thales Australia	2008	n.k.	Deliveries ongoing. Final delivery June 2012
Hobart-class	DDGHM	3	US$8bn	AUS/ESP	AWD Alliance	2007	2014	Aka *Air Warfare Destroyer* (AWD). Second to be delivered 2016, third 2017. Option on fourth. All to be fitted with *Aegis* system
Anzac	FFGHM Upgrade	8	A$260m	AUS	CEA Technologies	2005	2009	Upgrade: CEA-FAR Anti-Ship Missile Defence. Completion due 2012
Canberra-class	LHD	2	A$3.1bn (US$2.8bn)	AUS/ESP	Navantia	2007	2012	To replace HMAS *Tobruk* and 1 *Kanimbla*-class amphib tpt. To be named *Canberra* and *Adelaide*
RIM-162 ESSM	SAM	n.k.	See notes	US	Raytheon	2007	2010	Part of US$223m NATO *SeaSparrow* Consortium contract for collective purchase of 294 ESSM. Delivery in progress
F/A-18F Block II *Super Hornet*	FGA ac	24	A$6bn (US$4.6bn)	US	Boeing	2007	2010	To replace current F-111. Advanced targeting forward-looking infrared (ATFLIR) pods for 18 F/A-18F. First delivered March 2010. 12 to be in *Growler* configuration. Delivery in progress
B-737 AEW *Wedgetail*	AEW&C ac	6	A$3.6bn (US$3.4bn)	US	Boeing	2000	2006	2 delivered May 2010; 3 more due to be delivered by end 2010. Final delivery due 2011
A330-200 (MRTT)	Tkr/Tpt ac	5	A$1.5bn (US$1.4 bn)	Int'l	EADS	2004	2010	(KC-30B). First ac IOC mid-2010
Tiger ARH	Atk Hel	22	n.k.	FRA/GER	Eurocopter	2001	2010	16 delivered by mid-2010
NH90	Tpt hel	46	A$2bn (US$1.47bn)	AUS/Int'l	NH Industries	2005 2006	2007	Replacement programme. 6 for navy 40 for army. AUS variant of NH90. First 4 built in Europe; remainder in AUS. Option for a further 26. Deliveries ongoing
CH-47F *Chinook*	Tpt Hel	7	A$755m (US$670m)	US	Boeing	2010	2014	All to be operational by 2017. To replace CH-47Ds
Bangladesh (BGD)								
AW-109	Tpt Hel	2	n.k.	ITA	Agusta-Westland	2010	2011	–
Cambodia (CAM)								
T-55	MBT	50	n.k.	n.k.	n.k.	2010	n.k.	Second hand from unknown Eastern European country
BTR-60	APC(W)	44	n.k.	n.k.	n.k.	2010	n.k.	Second hand from unknown Eastern European country

Asia

Table 18 **Selected Arms Procurements and Deliveries, Asia**

Designation	Type	Quantity	Contract Value	Supplier Country	Prime Contractor	Order Date	First Delivery Due	Notes
China, People's Republic of (PRC)								
JL-2/CSS-NX-5	SLBM	n.k.	n.k.	PRC	n.k.	1985	2009	In development; range 8,000km. Reportedly to equip new Type 094 SSBN. ISD uncertain
Jin class (Type 094)	SSBN	5	n.k.	PRC	n.k.	1985	2008	Commissioning status unclear; 2 vessels belived to be in service; 3 more awaiting commissioning
Zubr-class hovercraft	LCAC	4	US$315m	PRC/UKR	PLAN/Morye Shipyard	2009	–	Deal finalised in July 2010; 2 to be constructed in Ukraine, 2 in China, with blueprints also transferred to China
Be-103	Tpt ac	6	n.k.	RUS	n.k.	2007	n.k.	Amphibious ac
Ka-28 ASW	ASW Hel	9	n.k.	RUS	Kumertau Aviation Production Enterprise	n.k.	2009	For navy. Six delivered by end-2009
Ka-28 ASW	ASW Hel	9	n.k.	RUS	Rosoboron-export	2010	n.k.	Delivery status unclear
Ka-31	AEW Hel	9	n.k.	RUS	Rosoboron-export	2010	n.k.	Delivery status unclear
Mi-171	Tpt Hel	32	n.k.	RUS	Rosoboron-export	2009	n.k.	Delivery to be complete by end 2011
India (IND)								
Agni III	IRBM	n.k.	n.k.	IND	DRDO	n.k.	2010	In development. Designed to carry 200–250 KT warhead with a range of 3,000km
Agni V	IRBM	n.k.	n.k.	IND	DRDO	n.k.	2012	In development. Est 5,000km range
Prithvi II	SRBM	54	INR12.13bn	IND	Bharat Dynamics	2006	n.k.	For air force
Sagarika K-15	SLBM	n.k.	n.k.	IND	Bharat Dynamics	1991	n.k.	In development. First test reported successful; est 700km range with 1 ton payload
BrahMos Block II (Land Attack)	AShM/ LACM	134 msl	INR83.52bn (US$1.64bn)	IND/RUS	Brahmos Aerospace	2006	2009	10 launchers entered test regime; 2 accepted Mar 2009
BrahMos Block II (Land Attack)	AShM/ LACM	n.k.	US$1.73bn	IND/RUS	Brahmos Aerospace	2010	n.k.	2 regiments' worth
Nirbhay	ALCM	n.k.	n.k.	IND	DRDO	n.k.	n.k.	In development. First flight test due 2009. Designed for air, land and sea platforms. Est 1,000km range
T-90S *Bhishma*	MBT	347	US$1.23bn	IND/RUS	Avadi Heavy Vehicles	2007	n.k.	Delivery in progress
Arjun	MBT	124	n.k.	IND	ICVRDE	2010	n.k.	Delivery status unclear
Akash	SAM	36	INR12bn (US$244m)	IND	DRDO	2009	2009	To equip two squadrons. Final delivery due 2012
Akash	SAM	12 bty	INR125 bn (US$2.77bn)	IND	DRDO	2009	2009	To equip 3 army regiments
Akash	SAM	96	INR42.7bn	IND	DRDO	2010	n.k.	To equip 6 squadrons. For the IAF
Medium -range SAM	SAM/AD	18 units	US$1.4bn	ISR	IAI	2009	2016	For air-force. Development and procurement contract for a medium range version of the *Barak* long-range naval AD system
Advanced Technology Vessel (ATV)	SSBN	5	n.k.	IND	DRDO	n.k.	n.k.	SLBM development programme. INS *Arihant* launched Jul 2009; 2 yr of sea trials expected
Akula-class (Type 971)	SSN	1	approx US$700m	RUS	Rosoboron-export	2004	2009	10 year lease from RUS. *Nerpa* in RUS service, to be renamed INS *Chakra*. Delivery delayed until March 2011

Table 18 **Selected Arms Procurements and Deliveries, Asia**

Designation	Type	Quantity	Contract Value	Supplier Country	Prime Contractor	Order Date	First Delivery Due	Notes
Scorpene	SSK	6	INR235.62bn	FRA/IND	DCNS	2005	2012	First delivery delayed until 2014–15. Option for a further 6 SSK
*Sindhughosh-*class	SSK Upgrade	10	n.k.	RUS	ORDTB/ Rosoboron-export	2002	n.k.	Upgrade incl mod to accept *Klub*-S 3M-14E msl. Delayed due to problems with msl system. 5 boats currently upgraded; all to be finished by 2015
*Kiev-*class *Admiral Gorshkov*	CV	1	US$2.5bn	RUS	Rosoboron-export	1999	2008	Incl 16 MiG 29 K. To be renamed INS *Vikramaditya*. Expected to be commissioned 2012.
Project 71/ Indigenous Aircraft Carrier	CV	1	US$730m	IND	Cochin Shipyard	2001	2012	To be named *Vikant*. Formerly known as Air Defence Ship (ADS). Expected ISD has slipped to 2015. Second vessel of class anticipated
Project 17 (*Shivalik-*class)	DDGHM	3	INR69bn	IND	Mazagon Dockyard	1999	2009	Lead vessel commissioned Apr 2010. INS *Sahyadri* and INS *Satpura* due for delivery 2011.
Project 15A (*Kolkata-*class)	DDGHM	3	US$1.75bn	IND	Mazagon Dockyard	2000	2013	First of class launched 2006, second launched in 2009. First delivery delayed, expected for 2013.
Project 17A (*Shivalik*)	DDGHM	7	INR450bn (US$9.24 bn)	IND	Mazagon Dockyard/ GRSE	2009	2014	Follow up to Project 17. Requires shipyard upgrade
Advanced Talwar	FFGHM	3	US$1.5bn	RUS	Yantar shipyard	2006	2011	Option exercised 2006. Expected to be commissioned from 2012
Project 28 (*Kamorta-*class)	FFGHM	4	INR70bn	IND	GRSE	2003	n.k.	ASW role. First of class launched Apr 2010
*Car Nicobar-*class	PCF	10	INR500m (US$10.m) per unit	IND	GRSE	n.k.	2009	INS *Cankarso*, INS *Kondul* & INS *Kalpeni* (fifth, sixth and seventh of class) commissioned 2010. Final commissioning due 2011.
*Deepak-*class	AORH	2	n.k.	ITA	Fincantieri	2007	n.k.	Second of class, INS *Shakti*, launched Oct 2010
High-speed interceptor boats	n.k.	15	INR2.8bn (US$54.2m)	IND	Bharati	2009	n.k.	For coast guard
3M14E *Klub*-S (SS-N-27 *Sizzler*)	SLCM	28	INR8.44bn (US$182m)	RUS	Novator	2006	n.k.	For a number of *Sindhughosh*-class SSK. Delivery status unclear
BrahMos PJ-10	ASCM	n.k.	US$2bn	IND/RUS	Brahmos Aerospace	2006	2010	Built jointly with RUS. For army, navy and air force. Air and submarine launch versions undergoing testing
Su-30 MKI	FGA ac	140	See notes	IND/RUS	Hindustan Aeronautics Ltd/ Rosoboron-export	2000	n.k.	Delivered in kit form and completed in IND under licence. Part of a 1996 US$8.5bn deal for 238 Su-30. Final delivery due 2015.
Su-30 MKI	FGA ac	40	US$1.6bn	RUS	Rosoboron-export	2007	2008	First 4 delivered early 2008.
Su-30 MKI	FGA ac	42	INR150bn (US$3.3bn)	RUS	Hindustan Aeronautics Ltd/ Rosoboron-export	2010	n.k.	Delivery to be complete by 2016–17. 40 + 2 accident replacements
MiG-29K *Fulcrum* D	FGA ac	16	US$600m	RUS	Rosoboron-export	2004	2007	Incl 4 two seat MiG-29KUB. For INS *Vitramaditya* (ex CV *Gorshkov*). Delivery in progress
MiG-29K *Fulcrum* D	FGA ac	29	US$1.5bn	RUS	Rosoboron-export	2010	n.k.	Delivery status unclear

Table 18 **Selected Arms Procurements and Deliveries, Asia**

Designation	Type	Quantity	Contract Value	Supplier Country	Prime Contractor	Order Date	First Delivery Due	Notes
Tejas	FGA ac	20	INR20bn US$445m	IND	HAL	2005	2011	Limited series production. To be delivered in initial op config. Option for a further 20 in full op config. Plans for 140
P-8I Poseidon	ASW ac	8	US$2.1bn	US	Boeing	2009	2013	To replace current Ilyushin Il-38 and Tupolev Tu-142M. Deliveries due 2013-5
Il-76TD Phalcon	AEW&C ac	3	US$1bn	ISR/RUS	IAI	2008	2012	Option on 2003 contract exercised. 2 delivered by end 2010; third due to be delivered 2011.
EMB-145	AEW&C ac	3	US$210m	BRZ	Embraer	2008	2011	Part of a INR18bn (US$400m) AEW&C project
C-130J Hercules	Tpt ac	6	INR40bn (US$1.02bn)	US	Lockheed Martin	2007	2012	For special forces ops. SF config with AN/AAR-47 msl approach warning sys and radar-warning receivers. First delivery allegedly now set for late 2010
Hawk Mk132 Advanced Jet Trainer	Trg ac	66	US$1.7bn	IND/UK	BAE/HAL	2004	2007	24 in fly-away condition and 42 built under licence. Final delivery due 2011.
Hawk Mk132 Advanced Jet Trainer	Trg ac	57	US$780m	IND	HAL	2010	n.k.	40 for air force and 17 for navy
Dhruv	MRH Hel	245	n.k.	IND	HAL	2004	2004	159 Dhruvs and 76 Dhruv-WSI. Deliveries ongoing
Mi-17 Hip-H	MRH Hel	80	INR58.41bn (US$1.2bn)	RUS	Rosoboron-export	2008	2010	To be weaponised and replace current Mi-8 fleet. Final delivery due 2014
Ka-31	AEW Hel	5	US$20m	RUS	Rosoboron-export	2009	n.k.	For navy. Delivery status unclear
AW-101	Tpt Hel	12	€560m	UK/ITA	Agusta-Westland	2010	n.k.	For air force VIP tpt. Delivery status unclear
Crystal Maze	ASM	n.k.	US$60m	ISR	Rafael	2010	n.k.	Delivery status unclear
AGM-84 Harpoon Block II	AShM	24	US$170m	US	Boeing	2010	n.k.	Delivery status unclear

Indonesia (IDN)								
Satellite	Sat	1	n.k.	PRC	n.k.	2009	n.k.	Remote-sensing sat, to monitor IDN seas
BMP-3F	AIFV	17-20	US$40m	RUS	Rosoboron-export	2008	2010	Petroleum supply offset; funding unconfirmed. To replace PT-76
Panser 6×6	APC	40	INR480bn (US$40m)	IDN	PT Pindad	n.k.	2010	Order reduced from 150 in Feb 2009.
LVTP7	AAV	Undis-closed	Value undisclosed	ROK	n.k.	2008	n.k.	Ex-ROK stock. Number undisclosed, but believed to be dozens. Delivery status uncertain
Makassar-class	LPD	4	US$150m	IDN/ROK	PT Pal/Dae Sun	2003	2008	3 vessels delivered. Fourth vessel launched 2009.
CN-235	Tpt ac	2	Value undisclosed	IDN	PT Dirgantara	2008	n.k.	Delivery status unclear
CN-235-220	Tpt ac	3	US$80m	IDN	PT Dirgantara	2009	n.k.	To be delivered by 2012
EMB-314 Super Tucano	Trg ac	8	US$142m	BRZ	Embraer	2010	2012	To replace OV-10F ac
AS-332 (NAS-332) Super Puma	Tpt Hel	10	n.k.	IDN	PT Dirgantara	1998	2004	Delays due to funding problems. Contract reduced to 10 in 2009. Delivery expected to be completed 2010; 6 more may be completed as AS-532 Cougar

Table 18 **Selected Arms Procurements and Deliveries, Asia**

Designation	Type	Quantity	Contract Value	Supplier Country	Prime Contractor	Order Date	First Delivery Due	Notes
Japan (JPN)								
Theatre Missile Defence System	BMD	n.k.	n.k.	JPN/US	n.k.	1997	n.k.	Joint development with US from 1998. Programme ongoing and incl SM-3 and PAC-3 systems
Soryu-class	SSK	6	n.k.	JPN	Kawasaki/ Mitsubishi	2004	2009	Second batch may be ordered. Second vessel (*Unryu*) delivered Mar 2010. Third vessel (Hauryu) launched Oct 2010; ISD expected 2011.
Hyuga-class	CVH	2	¥200bn	JPN	IHI Marine United	2001	2008	Second vessel (*Ise*) due for commissioning Mar 2011.
Akizuki-class (19DD)	DDGHM	4	¥84.8 bn (US$700m)	JPN	Mitsubishi Heavy Industries	2007	2011	To replace the oldest 5 *Hatsuyuki*-class. First vessel launched Oct 2010; ISD expected 2011
Hirashima-class (improved)	MSO	2	n.k.	JPN	Universal SB	n.k.	2012	–
Standard Missile 3 (SM-3)	SAM	9	US$458m	US	Raytheon	2006	–	Part of *Aegis* BMD System for *Kongou*-class DDGH
F-2A/F-2B	FGA ac	94	–	JPN/US	Mitsubishi Heavy Industries	1999	2000	Deliveries to conclude in 2011
AH-64D *Apache*	Atk Hel	13	n.k.	JPN	Boeing	2001	2006	Up to 6 in *Longbow* config. 10 delivered by early 2008. Deliveries ongoing
AW-101 *Merlin*/ MCH-101	ASW/MCM Hel	14	n.k.	ITA/JPN/UK	Agusta-Westland/ KHI	2003	2006	For JMSDF to replace MH-53E and S-61 hel under MCH-X programme. Deliveries ongoing
AW-139	MRH Hel	6	n.k.	ITA/UK	Agusta-Westland	2010	n.k.	For coast guard
Enstrom 480B	Trg Hel	30	n.k.	US	Enstrom Helicopter Corporation	2010	2010	Delivery to be complete by 2014. For JGSDF.
Kazakhstan (KAZ)								
S-300	AD	40	n.k.	RUS	Rosoboron-export	2009	2009	To equip each of up to 10 battalions with four missile launchers and support systems. Delivery status unclear
MiG-31	Ftr ac Upgrade	20	US$60m	RUS	Rosoboron-export	2007	2007	Upgrade to MiG-31BM configuration. 10 to be modernised in 2007, 10 in 2008. Delivery status unclear
Korea, Republic of (ROK)								
K2	MBT	up to 600	KRW3.9trn (US$2.6bn)	Dom	Hyandai Rotem	2007	n.k.	Delivery status unclear
K-21 NIFV	AIFV	500 (est)	US$3.5 m per unit	Dom	Doosan Infracore	2008	2009	Delivery in progress
(Multi-function Surface to Air Missile) M-SAM	SAM	n.k.	n.k.	Dom	n.k.	1998	2009	In development. To replace current army *HAWK* SAMs.
KSS-II (Type 214)	SSK	1	US$500m est	Dom	DSME	2008	2014	First vessel of a second batch of 6 KSS-II (with AIP) for which funding has been cleared, but orders for remaining 5 are pending
KSS-III	SSK	3	n.k.	Dom	n.k.	2006	2015	Construction due to start 2012. Further 3 or 6 SSK to follow in a second phase. To replace *Chang Bogo*-class (Type 209) KSS-I SSK

Table 18 **Selected Arms Procurements and Deliveries, Asia**

Designation	Type	Quantity	Contract Value	Supplier Country	Prime Contractor	Order Date	First Delivery Due	Notes
Sejong Daewang-class KDX-3	CGHM	3	n.k.	Dom	DSME	2002	2008	2 vessels commissioned. Final delivery due 2012. 3 additional vessels may be ordered.
Ulsan-1-class FFX	FFGHM	6	KRW1.7bn (US$1.8bn)	Dom	Hyundai Heavy Industries	2006	2015	To replace current *Isan*-class FFG. ISD by 2015. Up to 15 vessels may be built
Unknown class	PSO/PCO/PCC	5	KRW150bn (US$120m)	Dom	Hyundai Heavy Industries	2009	n.k.	1 PSO, 2 PCO & 2 PCC. For coast guard. Due to be completed by 2012
Gumdoksuri-class (PKX)	FSG	9	n.k.	Dom	Hyundai Heavy Industries/ STX Shipbuilding	n.k.	2008	Further batches considered. Final delivery due 2011. Delivery in progress
Haeseong (*Sea Star* – ASM/ SSM-700K)	ASCM	100	KRW270m (US$294m)	Dom	n.k.	2006	2010	Delivery status unclear
F-15K *Eagle*	FGA ac	20/21	US$2.2bn (KRW2.3trn)	US	Boeing	2008	2010	Exercised option of the 2002 contract. Final delivery due 2012.
737-700 AEW&C (E-737)	AEW&C ac	4	US$1.7bn	US	Boeing	2006	2011	E-X programme. First ac undergoing testing; ISD expected 2011
CN-235-110 MPA	MP ac	4	INR1trn (US$91m)	IDN	PT Dirgantara	2008	2010	Final delivery due 2011
AW-139	MRH Hel	1	n.k.	UK/ITA	Agusta-Westland	2009	n.k.	For coast guard
AIM-9X *Sidewinder*	AAM	102	US$31m	US	Raytheon	2008	n.k.	Contract value inc 26 containers.
Malaysia (MYS)								
Pars	APC (W)	250	n.k.	MYS/TUR/ UK/US	FNSS	2010	2012	Letter of intent signed Apr 2010
Vehiculo de Alta Movilidad Tactica (VAMATAC) 4×4 tactical vehicles	LFV	85	MYR60m (US$19.1m)	ESP/MYS	Urovesa	2008	n.k.	Incl 24 *Metis*-M ATGW carriers and 25 *Igla* MANPAD system self-launching unit carriers
2R2M	120mm Mor	8	n.k.	FRA	TDA Armaments	2010	n.k.	To be mounted on ACV-300s
Kedah-class MEKO A100-class	FF	6	n.k.	GER/MYS	Boustead Naval Shipyard	2008	n.k.	Second batch. To be built under licence in MYS. Final vessel, *Selangor*, expected ISD 2011
A-400M	Tpt ac	4	MYR907m (US$246m)	Int	EADS	2006	2013	In development. Official unit cost US$80m. First deliveries delayed until at least 2016
Mi-171Sh *Hip*	Tpt Hel	10	n.k.	RUS	Rosoboron-export	2003	2005	For CSAR. Delivery postponed pending decision on variant
EC 725 *Cougar*	Tpt Hel	12	MYR1.6bn (US$500m)	FRA	Eurocopter	2010	2012	Initial contract scrapped Oct 2008. Contract reinstated Apr 2010. 8 for air force, 4 for army. To be delivered 2012–13
ALUDRA	ISR UAV	n.k.	MYR5m (US$1.4m)	MYS	UST Consortium	2007	n.k.	In development. For army and navy
Myanmar (MMR)								
MiG-29 *Fulcrum*	Ftr ac	20	US$570m	RUS	Rosoboron-export	2009	2010	May be upgraded to SMT standard
MA60	Tpt ac	3	n.k.	PRC	AVIC	2010	2010	All to be delivered by end 2010
K-8	Trg ac	50	n.k.	PRC	Hongdu	2009	2010	Delivery status unclear

Table 18 **Selected Arms Procurements and Deliveries, Asia**

Designation	Type	Quantity	Contract Value	Supplier Country	Prime Contractor	Order Date	First Delivery Due	Notes
New Zealand (NZL)								
P-3K *Orion*	ASW ac Upgrade	6	n.k.	US	L-3 Spar	2005	2010	Mission systems, comms and nav equipment
C-130H *Hercules*	Tpt ac Upgrade	5	NZ$226m	CAN	L-3 Spar	2004	2010	SLEP. Life-extension programme. First delivery Nov 2010
C-130H *Hercules*	Tpt ac Upgrade	5	NZ$21.2m (US$15.6m)	US	L-3 Spar	2007	2007	Upgrade programme in addition to 2004 SLEP. EW Self-protection systems (EWSPS). Final delivery due 2011.
NH90	Hel	8	NZ$771m (US$477m)	FRA	NH Industries	2006	2010	Final delivery by 2013
AW-109	Hel	5	NZ$139m (US$109m)	Int'l	Agusta-Westland	2008	2011	Likely to replace Bell 47G-3B *Sioux*
Pakistan (PAK)								
Hatf 8 (Raad)	ALCM	n.k.	n.k.	PAK	n.k.	n.k.	n.k.	In development. Successfully test fired.
Al Khalid (MBT 2000)	MBT	460	–	PAK	Heavy Industries Taxila	1999	2001	Delivery status uncertain
Spada 2000	AD system	10	€415m	ITA	MBDA	2007	2009	Delivery in progress. Final delivery due 2013.
F-22P/*Sword*-class	FFGHM	4	See notes	PAK/PRC	Hudong-Zhonghua Shipyard	2005	2009	Improved version of *Jiangwei* II FF. Fourth ship to be built indigenously at Karachi. Deal worth est US$750m incl 6 Z-9EC hels. 3 vessels in service; Final delivery due 2013.
Oliver Hazard Perry-class	FF	1	US$65m	US	n.k.	2008	2010	ex-USS *McInerney*.To be refurbished for US$65m and delivered to Pakistan in 2011. Four-month modernisation begun Sep 2010.
SM-2 Block II AURS	Msl	10	n.k.	US	Raytheon	2006	n.k.	With 10 Mk 631
F-16C/D Block 50/52 *Fighting Falcon*	FGA ac	18	US$1.4bn	US	Lockheed Martin	2008	2010	12 single-seat C-model Block 52 ac and 6 two-seat D-model ac. Option for a further 18 dropped. Delivery in progress
FC-1 (JF-17)	FGA ac	up to 250	n.k.	PAK/PRC	PAC	2006	2008	Contract signed for 42 production ac in early 2009
J-10 (FC-20)	FGA ac	36	US$1.4bn	PRC	CAC	2006	2014	–
F-16 Block 15 *Fighting Falcon*	FGA ac Upgrade	42	US$75m	TUR	TAI	2009	2014	Upgrade to Block 40 standard. Will begin Oct 2010. Remainder to be upgraded in PAK.
P-3C *Orion*	ASW ac	8	US$970m	US	n.k.	2004	2007	Ex-US stock. First delivered Jan 2007. Final delivery due 2011. One for spares.
2000 *Erieye*	AEW&C ac	4	SEK8.3bn (US$1.05bn)	SWE	SAAB	2006	2009	Plus one tpt ac for trg. Order reduced from 6 ac. First ac delivered Dec 2009
ZDK-03 (KJ-200)	AEW&C ac	4	n.k.	PAK/PRC	n.k.	2008	2011	First ac delivered
Il-78 *Midas*	Tkr/Tpt ac	4	n.k.	UKR	n.k.	2008	2010	First two delivered Dec 2009
K-8	Trg ac	27	n.k.	PRC	JHA	2005	2008	Final delivery due 2011.
Z-9EC	ASW Hel	6	n.k.	PRC	Harbin	2007	2009	Anti-submarine warfare hels. Part of F-22P deal.
Bravo+	ISR UAV	n.k.	n.k.	PAK	Air Weapons Complex	2008	2009	For recce and info gathering missions. Delivery status unclear
Falco	ISR UAV	25	n.k.	ITA	Selex Galileo	2006	2009	For MALE recce and surv missions. Delivery status unclear

Asia

Table 18 **Selected Arms Procurements and Deliveries, Asia**

Designation	Type	Quantity	Contract Value	Supplier Country	Prime Contractor	Order Date	First Delivery Due	Notes
AIM-120 AMRAAM	AAM	500	See notes	US	Raytheon	2007	2008	US$284m incl 200 *Sidewinder* AAM. Final delivery due 2011
AIM-9M *Sidewinder*	AAM	200	See notes	US	Raytheon	2007	n.k.	US$284m inc 500 AMRAAM
Philippines (PHL)								
SF-260F/PAF	Trg ac	18	US$13.1m	ITA	Alenia Aermacchi	2008	2010	Contract renegotiated. First 4 delivered Nov 2010. Final delivery due 2012
W-3 *Sokol*	Tpt Hel	8	PHP2.8bn (US$59.8m)	POL	PZL	2010	2010	4 due for delivery in 2010; remainder to be delivered 2011
Singapore (SGP)								
Bedok-class	MCC Upgrade	4	unknown	FRA/SGP	Thales	2009	n.k.	SLEP. Incl upgraded sonar and C2
F-15SG *Eagle*	FGA ac	12	n.k.	US	Boeing	2005	2008	SGP trg sqn based at Mtn Home AB (US). First aircraft arrived in Singapore 2010
F-15SG *Eagle*	FGA ac	12	n.k.	US	Boeing	2007	2010	8 were option in original 2005 contract. Incl 28 GBU-10 and 56 GBU-12 PGM. Delivery to be complete in 2012
Gulfstream G550 CAEW	AEW ac	4	n.k.	ISR	IAI	2007	2008	To replace E-2C *Hawkeye*AEW ac. Final delivery due 2011.
Gulfstream G550	Tpt ac	1	US$73m	n.k.	ST Aerospace	2008	n.k.	Part of a 20 year trg contract
C-130 *Hercules*	Tpt ac Upgrade	10	n.k.	US	Rockwell Collins	2007	n.k.	Avionics upgrade. To be completed in 7 years
M-346	Trg ac	12	SGD543m (US$411m)	ITA/SGP	ST Aerospace	2010	2012	To be based at Cazuax in France
AIM-120 AMRAAM	AAM	100	n.k.	US	Raytheon	2006	2008	Delivery status unclear
Sri Lanka (LKA)								
MiG-29 *Fulcrum*	FGA ac	5	US$75m	RUS	Rosoboron-export	2008	n.k.	4 MiG-29SM and 1 MiG-29UB
MA60	Tpt ac	4	n.k.	PRC	AVIC	2010	2010	First two to be delivered in 2010; remainder in 2011
Taiwan (Republic of China) (ROC)								
Patriot PAC-3	AD	Up to 6	US$6bn	US	Raytheon	2009	n.k.	FMS purchase of at least 4 additional OFUs. 3 existing being upgraded PAC-2 - PAC-3
Patriot PAC-3 upgrade kits	AD Upgrade	n.k.	US$154m	US	Raytheon	2009	n.k.	Upgrade from config 2 to config 3
Patriot PAC-3	AD msl	330	US$3.1bn	US	Raytheon	2010	2014	–
P-3C *Orion*	ASW ac	12	US$1.3bn	US	Lockheed Martin	2010	2013	Refurbished by Lockheed Martin
E-2C *Hawkeye*	AEW ac Upgrade	6	US$154m	US	Northrop Grumman	2009	n.k.	Upgrade from Group II config to *Hawkeye* 2000 (H2K) export config. To be completed by 2013.
AH-64D Block III *Apache* *Longbow*	Atk Hel	30	US$2.5bn	US	Boeing	2010	2014	–
EC-225	Tpt Hel	3	US$111m	Int'l	Eurocopter	2010	n.k.	Option on up to 17 more

Table 18 **Selected Arms Procurements and Deliveries, Asia**

Designation	Type	Quantity	Contract Value	Supplier Country	Prime Contractor	Order Date	First Delivery Due	Notes
UH-60M *Blackhawk*	Tpt Hel	60	US$3.1bn	US	Sikorsky	2010	n.k.	FMS
AGM-84L *Harpoon* Block II	AShM	60	US$89m	US	Boeing	2007	2009	For F-16. Delivery status unclear
Hsiung Feng IIE	AShM	n.k.	n.k.	ROC	n.k.	2005	n.k.	In development
Thailand (THA)								
BTR-3E1 8×8	APC (W)	96	THB4bn (US$134m)	UKR	ADCOM	2007	n.k.	Amphibious APC. To be completed in 2–3 years. Order on hold since Oct 2007
WMZ 551	APC (W)	97	US$51.3m	PRC	NORINCO	2005	n.k.	Delivery date unknown
Type 25T *Naresuan*	FFGHM Upgrade	2	€5m (US$7m)	FRA	n.k.	2007	n.k.	Hel landing system upgrade.
OPV	PSO	1	n.k.	THA	Bangkok Dock	2009	2012	Built to BAE design.
141m landing platform dock	LPD	1	THB5bn (US$144m)	SGP	ST Marine	2008	2012	Contract value incl two 23m landing craft mechanised and two 13m landing craft vehicle and personnel
Gripen C/D	FGA ac	6	See notes	SWE	SAAB	2008	2010	SEK2bn (US$308m) incl one 340 *Erieye* and one Saab 340 ac. Four *Gripen* D, two *Gripen* C. To replace F-5B/E *Tiger* II ac. Final delivery due 2017.
Gripen C/D	FGA ac	6	See notes	SWE	SAAB	2010	n.k.	THB14.8bn (US$415.5m) incl one 340 *Erieye*
340 *Erieye*	AEW ac	1	See notes	SWE	SAAB	2010	n.k.	THB14.8bn (US$415.5m) incl 6 *Gripen*.
C-130H *Hercules*	Tpt ac	12	THB1bn	THA/US	Rockwell Collins	2007	n.k.	Phase 1: avionics upgrade. Phase 2: Comms, Nav, Surv/Air Traffic Management (CNS/ATM). Delivery status unclear
ATR-72-500	Tpt ac	4	n.k.	FRA/ITA	ATR Aircraft	2007	n.k.	First ac delivered Sep 2009
ERJ-135LR	Tpt ac	1	n.k.	BRZ	Embraer	2009	n.k.	Delivery status unclear
Enstrom 4080B	Trg Hel	16	n.k.	US	Enstrom Helicopter Corporation	2010	2010	Delivery status unclear
TSP-77 long-range air surv	Radar	1	n.k.	US	Lockheed Martin	2007	2009	Part of a multi-phase national AD system. Delivery status unclear
Timor Leste (TLS)								
Shanghai-II	PB	2	US$25m	PRC	Poly Technologies	2008	2010	To be launched June 2010
Turkmenistan (TKM)								
T-90S	MBT	10	US$30m	RUS	Rosoboronexport	2009	2009	Delivery in progress
Vietnam (VNM)								
VNREDSat-1	Sat	1	US$100m	VNM	n.k.	2009	2012	–
T-72	MBT	150	See notes	POL	Profus	2005	2005	Part of US$150m POL spt contract to supply ac, electronics and equipment. Delivery status unclear
Kilo-class	SSK	6	US$1.8bn	RUS	Rosoboronexport	2009	n.k.	Delivery status unclear

Table 18 **Selected Arms Procurements and Deliveries, Asia**

Designation	Type	Quantity	Contract Value	Supplier Country	Prime Contractor	Order Date	First Delivery Due	Notes
Gepard-class	FFGM	2	US$300m	RUS	Rosoboron-export	2005	2010	Second vessel launched Mar 2010. Undergoing testing before delivery
Su-30MK2	FGA ac	8	US$500m	RUS	Rosoboron-export	2009	2010	First 4 due to be delivered Dec 2010
Su-30MK2	FGA ac	12	US$1bn	RUS	Rosoboron-export	2010	2011	Procurement contract does not include weaponary
PZL M-28B *Bryza*-1R/ *Skytruck*	MP ac	10	n.k.	POL	Profus	2005	2005	Part of POL spt contract. 1 ac in service. Plans for up to 12 ac. Owned by coast guard but operated by air force. Deliveries ongoing
DHC-6 *Twin Otter*	Tpt ac	6	n.k	CAN	Viking Air	2010	2012	For MP role. To be delivered 2012–14
Yak-52 (Iak-52)	Trg ac	10	n.k.	ROM	Aerostar	2008	n.k.	Delivery status unclear

Chapter Seven
Middle East and North Africa

IRAQ

On 31 August 2010, the United States military ceased combat missions in Iraq, leaving primary responsibility for the imposition of order across the country to its indigenous security forces. The US military had already withdrawn from Iraq's towns and cities in June 2009, in accordance with the Status of Forces Agreement (SOFA) negotiated between the Iraqi and American governments in the dying days of the George W. Bush administration. The SOFA also set the deadline for all US forces to be removed from the country by 31 December 2011. The interim deadline of August 2010 for the end of combat missions was set by President Barack Obama in order to align the speed of the troop drawdown with the promises he made during his election campaign.

This step change in US relations with Iraq was signalled by major policy and personnel changes. The American ambassador to Baghdad, Christopher Hill, was replaced by James Jeffrey; unlike his predecessor, Jeffrey has substantial experience in dealing with Iraqi politics. On the military side, General Raymond Odierno, another long-serving veteran of the US campaign in Iraq, was replaced as head of the remaining American military mission by General Lloyd Austin.

The August 2010 deadline transformed the American role in the country from a kinetic to a training mission. The three separate military commands – Multi-National Force-Iraq, Multi-National Corps-Iraq and Multi-National Security Transition Command-Iraq – were merged into one organisation, the Iraq Training and Advisory Mission (ITAM). US troop numbers, which at their peak had numbered 176,000, were reduced to 49,775. The working logic of American commanders on the ground assumes that numbers will shrink to the 'tens or low hundreds' as the final SOFA deadline approaches. ITAM's time-constrained goal is to train and mentor the Iraqi security forces in the hope that they can reach what the US government has termed the 'minimum essential capability' standards needed to replace all US forces by 31 December 2011.

This rapid reduction in the number and role of US troops, and the increase in indigenous responsibility for the provision of order, was not universally welcomed in Iraq. The aged Iraqi politician Adnan Pachachi, who served as Iraq's foreign minister before the Ba'ath Party seized power in 1968, argued that American politicians were 'deluding themselves' if they thought that Iraq's security forces were ready to defend the country. Tariq Aziz, former deputy prime minister under Saddam Hussein, was even more forthright, declaring from his prison cell that Obama's withdrawal of troops was 'leaving Iraq to the wolves'.

Of greater concern were the comments made by General Babakir Zebari, Iraq's chief of staff. Citing the Ministry of Defence's own strategic planning, Zebari argued that if he had been consulted about a timetable for withdrawal (which he was not), he would have told his political masters 'the US army must stay until the Iraqi army is fully ready in 2020'. Zebari's comments were shaped by his ambitious plans to transform the strategic posture of Iraq's armed forces as US troops depart. In the aftermath of the American decision to disband the old Iraqi army in May 2003, a new indigenous military force was rapidly rebuilt with the primary task of counter-insurgency. As the number of US troops along with their military capacity in the country is reduced, the Iraqi government has embarked on far-reaching changes to the role of the Iraqi army. The Federal Police, the paramilitary force run by the Ministry of Interior, has been designated to take over the major counter-insurgency role, leaving the army to withdraw from Iraq's cities and adopt a more conventional military role. The timetable needed for this transformation runs through to 2020. A similar timeframe is envisaged before the nascent Iraqi air force will be able to defend Iraq's airspace.

However, during the period between August 2010 and 2020 the primary role of Iraq's security forces will to be impose order on the country itself, rather than to defend its borders. The troops needed to carry out this function are split between the Ministry of Defence – with 250,000 personnel – and the Ministry of Interior, with 410,000. The Ministry of Defence has managerial responsibility for the air force and navy, as well as the army. Its central role in rebuilding all three of

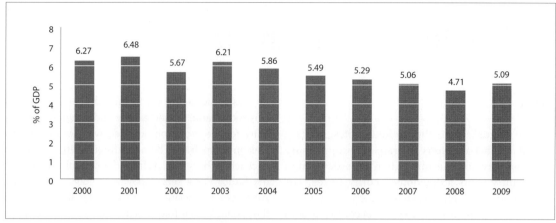

Figure 8 **Middle East and North Africa Regional Defence Expenditure** as % of GDP

these services is reflected in its budget, which rose by a yearly average of 28% from 2005–09. However, in 2009 a wider governmental funding squeeze saw its budget frozen at US$4.1 billion. The MoD's budget for 2010 once again rose by 20%, totalling US$4.9bn.

The new Iraqi army is organised into 14 divisions and support forces. It is indicative of its hasty reconstruction that by the end of 2009 it had only managed to recruit 82% of its target for officers and 55% for non-commissioned officers. This may partially explain why the MoD has, since 2008, been rehiring former officers and soldiers from the army disbanded after regime change. By March 2010, this process had seen 20,400 soldiers rehired, with a large proportion re-enlisting from the old officer corps. Current estimates suggest that as many as 60% of the new officer corps served in the old army.

The US Department of Defense is optimistic that, with the exception of logistics and support, the Iraqi army can reach the minimum essential capacity standard needed for it to shoulder its responsibilities once the US military training effort ends in December 2011. However, a number of independent analysts have pointed to a broad set of problems that continue to undermine the Iraqi army. The first, recognised by the US training mission, involves weaknesses in management. The MoD in Baghdad has a well-deserved reputation for red tape and an inefficient bureaucracy that is unresponsive to requests from the field. This has led to poor management of the ministry's budget, as well as weaknesses in logistics and strategic planning. However, beyond these bureaucratic problems there are wider ideological issues. A divide has opened up between older, more senior officers trained under the Ba'athist regime and younger colleagues who have

been promoted within the new army. The inflexible approach to leadership by senior military figures and their unwillingness to delegate continues to stifle innovation and independent decision-making further down the chain of command. Furthermore, there remains a problem of loyalty to the state as the influence of sectarian and ethnically based political parties is still felt at all levels of the army. The MoD has made sustained progress in challenging this by, for example, repeatedly moving locally raised forces to break their links with political parties, but this is very much a work in progress and leaves the loyalty of the army still open to question.

With plans to shift the Iraqi army's main role to border defence, the Ministry of Interior is increasingly responsible not only for law and order, but also paramilitary counter-insurgency. The potential risks involved in this strategy are very much evident in Iraq's recent history. Between 2005 and 2006, Ministry of Interior forces became one of the main groups that drove Iraq into civil war. The Ministry's Special Police Commandos (later renamed the Federal Police) were asserted to have acted as a sectarian death squad, frequently resorting to extra-judicial execution and torture. Complaints reached their peak in November 2005, when US forces raided a Ministry of Interior detention facility and found 170 detainees (166 of whom were Sunnis) held in appalling conditions and bearing signs of repeated torture. Following this, a number of secret detention facilities and the widespread use of torture came to light and resulted in an inquiry led by retired US General James Jones; the findings were published in September 2007. Jones's recommendation that the Federal Police be disbanded was not accepted by either the Iraqi government or the American military. Instead, the Federal Police was purged of the most egregious sectarian actors and 60,000 officers were dismissed. In addition, the force was greatly expanded and restructured.

The Federal Police is currently regarded as one of the most efficient fighting forces in Iraq. It has 46,580 members, with plans to expand to 86,000 by 2012. At present, the Federal Police consists of four divisions made up of 17 brigades, with plans to add two more. The expansion plans will see five provincial Emergency Response Units integrated into the Federal Police, allowing the force to have a brigade-sized group in each of Iraq's provinces. But in spite of extensive purges, restructuring and sustained expansion, the force is still plagued by corruption and sectarianism. The insidious effects of bribery at Federal Police checkpoints were highlighted by the ability of al-Qaeda in Mesopotamia to deliver truck bombs into the centre of Baghdad on numerous occasions throughout 2009 and 2010. The movement of these highly destructive cargos must have been facilitated by the bribing of Federal Police officers who staff the checkpoints surrounding the central government district. Beyond this, payroll fraud, corruption in the awarding of contracts and the acceptance of bribery to release detainees remain commonplace. There is also evidence that the Federal Police is unable to eliminate the influence of sectarian politics from its ranks. At the end of 2009, a series of reports demonstrated that 1,500 recruits to the force had been nominated by Iraq's political parties, indicating political interference not only in hiring and promotion, but also in policy formation.

In the last two years, the negative and corrosive influence of Iraq's politicians on its security services has reached its peak in the country's intelligence services and counter-terrorism special forces. The Iraqi National Counter Terrorism Force has over 6,000 men in its ranks, organised into two brigades, and is considered to be one of the best-trained forces across the Middle East. It operates its own detention centres and intelligence gathering, and has surveillance cells in every governorate. In April 2007, as managerial responsibility for it was transferred from the US Special Forces who had created it to the Iraqi government, Prime Minister Nuri al-Maliki set up a ministerial body, the Counter-Terrorism Bureau, to control it. This effectively removed the force from the oversight of parliament, the Ministry of Interior or Ministry of Defence. Since then the force has become known as the 'Fedayeen al-Maliki', a reference to its reputation

as the prime minister's tool for covert action against his rivals, as well as an ironic comparison to Saddam's militia.

Iraq's intelligence services have been similarly politicised. Maliki's attempt to gain personal control over them has directly contributed to their inability to independently collect and analyse intelligence without close US support. The struggle to dominate the intelligence services became apparent in the conflict between Mohammed al-Shahwani, who was the head of the National Intelligence Service (NIS), and Sherwan al-Waeli, who was appointed by Maliki in 2006 to be the minister of state for national security affairs. The NIS was set up by the US Central Intelligence Agency and Shahwani enjoyed a long and close working relationship with Washington. Waeli, conversely, although considered to be close to the prime minister, is alleged to also have links to Tehran. Things came to a head in August 2009 after a series of major bombs in the centre of Baghdad. Shahwani argued in the Iraqi press that there was clear evidence linking the attacks to Iran. In the subsequent fallout surrounding the incident, Shahwani was forced to resign. But fears that the NIS would lose more staff in the wake of his departure have yet to materialise.

The problems of politicisation in the military go well beyond the Federal Police and intelligence services. Since 2006, Maliki has used a number of tactics to secure his personal grip over Iraq's armed forces. Firstly, he used the Office of the Commander in Chief to control overall security policy, thus undermining the independent chains of command within the Ministries of Interior and Defence (see *The Military Balance* 2008, p. 228). Maliki then forced technocratic senior commanders aside, appointing those close to him into positions of influence in both ministries. These appointments have been labelled 'temporary' to avoid parliamentary oversight. Finally, Maliki has set up nine joint operational commands. These consolidate, under one commanding officer, the management of all the security services operating in individual unstable provinces. These officers are appointed and managed from a central office in Baghdad that Maliki controls. Through the use of joint operational commands, Maliki has bypassed his security ministers and their senior commanders, securing control over the operational level of Iraq's armed forces. Overall, Maliki's control of his country's security forces has made a military coup in Iraq highly unlikely, but this has come at the expense of the coherence of the chain of command, the promotion of political cronies over talented commanders and a break in the military's esprit de corps.

Weapons programmes

Beyond the damaging effects of politics, the ability of Iraq's armed forces to impose order on the country after 2011 will depend on extensive and continued investment in weapons systems and equipment. Force development in Iraq has already been constrained by budgetary problems. Oil is Iraq's only major source of revenue, so global prices directly affect the government's ability to build up its armed forces. From 2007 to 2010 the Iraqi government invested US$43.51bn in the Ministries of Defence and Interior. However, a global drop in the price for oil resulted in a budgetary crisis in 2009 and a 25% cut in government expenditure. The result was a recruitment freeze for both the army and police force, as well as delays in purchasing tanks and artillery. Though the situation has now eased, the problems during 2009 highlight Iraq's dependence, and especially that of its military, on a high oil price.

In spite of budgetary problems, Iraq continues to invest in new military hardware. The first of 140 M1 *Abrams* tanks purchased from America arrived in August 2010. In addition, Iraq has ordered 18 F-16IQ fighters from the US and has already taken delivery of 3 T-6A *Texan* training aircraft. The F-16 package, according to the notification issued by the US Defense Security Cooperation Agency, also included a raft of electronic systems and munitions, including *Sidewinder*, *Sparrow* and *Maverick* missiles as well as GBU-10, GBU-12 and GBU-24 laser-guided bombs. In 2010 Iraq's foreign military sales increased from US$1bn to US$1.5bn with the total value of its current order book amounting to US$13bn.

Baghdad's capacity to control the country between August 2010 (the end of US combat missions) and the total withdrawal of US forces in December 2011 is almost certainly strong enough to stop a slide back into the civil war that dominated the country in 2005–06. However, it is not the technical capacity of Iraq's armed forces that will guarantee the stability of the country after 2012. That will depend on the political settlement arrived at in the wake of the March 2010 national elections. The many months it took to find the compromise needed to form a working government indicates a deep instability animating Iraqi politics. Iraq's post-regime-change stability cannot be guaranteed in spite of the undoubted progress its armed forces have made since 2007.

IRAN

Iran's security environment has changed dramatically over the past decade with the neutralisation by the US of its two greatest external threats, Saddam Hussein's Ba'athist regime in Iraq and the Taliban in Afghanistan. However, while Tehran's traditional security threats no longer exist, the presence of US military forces in Iraq, Afghanistan and in Gulf waters presents new challenges. Faced with the possibility of a pre-emptive attack against its nuclear facilities, the Iranian regime has reason to reassess its national security strategies, rethink its military doctrine, and restructure its forces and weapons-acquisition plans to counter the potential threat posed by the US and its regional allies.

Iran's conventional military inventory is dominated by obsolete weapons systems purchased before the 1978–79 Iranian Revolution. Its military forces have almost no modern armour, artillery, aircraft or major combat ships, and UN sanctions will likely obstruct the purchase of high-technology weapons for the foreseeable future. Nascent indigenous arms industries have been successful in developing and building some niche weaponry, such as unmanned aerial vehicles, ballistic missiles and small naval craft, but these systems do not provide Iran with the capacity to conduct large-scale conventional offensive operations. Consequently, the military is not organised or trained to project power against its neighbours or across the Gulf.

Although Iran's conventional forces have limited capabilities, the military does maintain a robust capacity to conduct irregular warfare. The regime's strategic philosophy, therefore, emphasises and threatens the use of asymmetric operations to intimidate its neighbours and deter potential aggressors. And, should deterrence fail, the Iranian Revolutionary Guard Corps (IRGC) is structured and equipped to engage in wars of attrition using asymmetric military actions aimed at degrading an adversary's will, and increasing the cost and risks of aggression. Founded in the wake of the revolution, the IRGC maintains separate military forces from the regular Iranian military (the Artesh) and is often the recipient of the lion's share of modern defence equipment and appropriations in Iran, stemming in part from its general involvement in asymmetric operations but also from the depth of its ties within the Iranian political and security establishment and its substantial involvement in the Iranian business sector. Iran has proven its ability to threaten, intimidate and conduct significant low-level military operations or terrorist attacks, directly or through surrogates, such as Hizbullah, Hamas or militant groups in Iraq. This capability can be applied locally or globally, against regional rivals or major powers.

Iran's Quds Force has proved to be a key vehicle with which to project military force abroad. As noted in the IISS *Strategic Comment* 'Iranian influence in Iraq' (vol. 13, no. 10), the Quds Force – a paramilitary arm of the IRGC with a mission to export the ideals of the revolution that is directly answerable to the Supreme Leader – established relationships with Shia and Kurdish resistance groups in Iraq some time before the 2003 invasion. The IRCG created the Badr Corps as a vehicle for Iranian foreign policy in Iraq and has since maintained very close ties within it; the IRGC also arranged for Lebanese Hizbullah (itself created by the Quds Force in 1982) to begin training Iraq's Jaish al-Mahdi (JAM), a Shia paramilitary group. After JAM forces suffered heavy losses in their uprising of spring 2004, IRGC support for JAM intensified. In 2004, the IRGC started supplying JAM with lethal explosively formed projectiles. By 2005, Hizbullah was training JAM members in Iran. The Quds Force along with Hizbullah has been a powerful means for Iran to exert its influence and foment violence in Iraq.

Iran's burgeoning ballistic-missile facilities, and its potential to develop nuclear weapons, play a critical role in the regime's deterrence and intimidation strategy. The ample stocks of *Shahab*-1 and *Shahab*-2 short-range missiles, the medium-range *Ghadr*-1 and the *Sajjil*-2, which is under development, enhance the regime's capacity to threaten targets well beyond its borders. These missile systems are operated by the IRGC Air Force. While they have limited military utility because of their poor accuracy, they could be used to hit urban targets, sow terror and potentially weaken an adversary's political resolve. While there is no compelling evidence to date that Iran has made a decision to produce nuclear weapons, it seeks the capability to do so and the ambiguity created by the country's uranium-enrichment programme further strengthens the regime's ability to deter and intimidate.

Doctrine

Iranian military doctrine is primarily defensive, based on deterring potential aggressors, including the technologically superior forces of the US. And while doctrine continues to evolve, its main tenets were established in 2005 by General Mohammad Jafari, then-director of the IRGC's Centre for Strategy, and now the commander of the IRGC. Known as 'mosaic defence', this doctrine emphasises flexibility and the use of layered defences. It avoids direct confrontation with superior forces whenever possible. Instead, it seeks to capitalise on Iran's advantages in manpower, strategic depth, challenging terrain, and the regime's willingness to accept greater risk and the burdens of prolonged battle.

Implementation of the mosaic doctrine has resulted in an overhaul of the command-and-control structure of the IRGC's land forces into a network of 31 separate command elements, one for each of Iran's 30 provinces and one for Tehran itself. This devolution of responsibility and authority offers local commanders greater independence and flexibility in responding to local events and countering threats. Against invading forces, for example, it would take advantage of the country's strategic depth and rugged frontier terrain to mount insurgent attacks, interdict the opposition's logistic operations and to engage in wars of attrition. This evolving doctrine, however, has not succeeded in overcoming longstanding institutional and bureaucratic rivalries. Iran's overall military capabilities, for example, are significantly degraded by poor coordination between the IRGC and the Artesh.

Budgets and acquisitions

Iran's defence expenditures are dwarfed by those of its neighbours. The annual defence budget is estimated at US$10bn, but this does not account for money allocated to Iran's defence-manufacturing infrastructure. Nor does it include the cost of supporting proxies, non-state groups and foreign military aid or Iran's investment in its nuclear- and missile-development programmes. The overall budget is, therefore, thought to exceed US$13–14bn. Iran continues to find it difficult to acquire advanced weaponry and military technologies from the West. UN sanctions have severely constrained Tehran's ability to import necessary equipment from alternative suppliers although Iranian procurement networks continue in their attempts to circumvent these sanctions.

Army

Despite claims of success in indigenously producing major weapons systems, Iran is unable to produce heavy weaponry in significant quantities. To date,

Tehran has manufactured and deployed some 100 *Zulfiqar* main battle tanks and a small number of *Towsan* light tanks, about 140 *Boragh* armoured personnel carriers and a small number of self-propelled artillery pieces. Iran has produced large numbers of towed artillery and short- to long-range artillery rockets, including the *Fajr, Zelzal* and *Fateh-110*, to enhance its firepower. With Chinese assistance, Iran has established factories to produce short-range anti-tank weapons, man-portable surface-to-air missiles and anti-ship weapons. A variety of unmanned aerial vehicles, some designed to carry conventional bombs, have been recently introduced, including the *Karrar*. In general, however, the army is not well equipped, though it does have the size and capacity to defend Iranian territory. Neither the IRGC nor Artesh is sufficiently well-organised, -equipped or -trained to conduct sustained battle beyond Iran's borders. IRGC military exercises, which feature simulated ambushes against armoured columns of an advancing force, provide further evidence of the predominantly defensive nature of Iran's forces.

Navy

The naval branch of the IRGC oversees operations in the Gulf. Its capabilities, however, are severely constrained by the paucity of combat-capable surface ships. Presently, the Iranian navy operates only seven corvettes, all obtained before the revolution and thus out-dated and poorly equipped. Iran is believed to be building domestically a *Mowaj*-class corvette to redress this shortcoming over the long term, but to date the new ship is a prototype and has not yet achieved operational status.

The IRGC maintains more than 100 ships, including 25 *Peykaap* II-class boats armed with *Kosar* anti-ship missiles, and about 15 *Peykaap* I-class torpedo boats, as well as scores of smaller coastal patrol speedboats. These small, elusive boats are difficult to detect with radar and can easily out-manoeuvre the large surface combatants deployed by the US. Thus, they can avoid direct confrontation with the superior American forces. They can be used to disperse smart mines, launch long-range torpedoes, fire short-range missiles and employ swarm tactics to threaten, harass and disrupt US naval operations in the Gulf. The IRGC and the navy regularly conduct military exercises that employ small craft (domestically produced *Seraj-1* and *Zulfiqar*) and *Bavar* wing-in-ground-effect craft to simulate ambushing attacks on shipping, offshore facilities and key onshore infrastructure.

Despite sanctions, Iran has acquired a wide array of modern weapons to support asymmetric naval operations, including magnetic, acoustic and pressure-sensitive mines, ship-launched missiles produced in China and Iran, and four to seven North Korean- and Iranian-manufactured (*Ghadir*) *Yono* and *Nahang*-class miniature submarines. Iran is believed to be producing four additional submarines. The regime's three *Kilo*-class submarines, meanwhile, are a potentially potent foe with the capacity to launch attacks using torpedoes and mines. The IRGC maintains onshore batteries armed with HY-2, C-801 and C-802 anti-ship cruise missiles, and a range of domestically produced anti-ship cruise missiles. In addition to protecting the shoreline, these anti-ship weapons could be used to disrupt the flow of oil from the Gulf by threatening or attacking commercial ships transiting through the Straits of Hormuz. The IRGC Navy and Iran's regular naval forces (with some 18,000 personnel) pose the most serious threat to the US Navy and its allies in the Gulf.

Air-defence and air forces

Iran's air-defence and air forces are designed to defend its airspace, deter aggression, and protect critical infrastructure and strategic facilities throughout the country. Iranian pilots are relatively well trained and capable, but they are operating an ageing and deteriorating fleet of aircraft, most of which were purchased before the revolution, or were captured when Iraqi pilots fled to Iran during *Operation Desert Storm* in 1991. Of the 300+ warplanes, consisting of US-made F-4s, F-5s and F-14s, French *Mirages*, Chinese F-7s and Soviet Su-24, Su-25 and MiG-29s, only about half are operational at any given moment, primarily because of inadequate maintenance and lack of spare parts. Although the planes are poorly supported and obsolete, Iran has attempted to offset these deficiencies by obtaining modern Russian air-to-air missiles. Its engineers have also worked to develop more capable air defences by converting US-produced ground-to-air *Hawk* missiles for use as long-range air-to-air missiles.

The regime has attempted to modernise its air force through the purchase of Russian and Chinese fighters, but these efforts have been frustrated by UN sanctions. As an alternative, Iran has produced its own aircraft, the *Saegeh* and *Azarakhsh* light fighters, some of which may have been deployed to the air force. But their numbers and precise capability remain uncertain, and these warplanes would be little threat to the

Air defence

After several years of claim and counter-claim, in September 2010 Russian President Dmitry Medvedev blocked a deal to sell Iran the S-300 (SA-10 *Grumble*/SA-20 *Gargoyle*) surface-to-air missile (SAM) system.

Israel and the US opposed the delivery of the S-300, which would have provided Tehran with a considerable improvement in its capability, and a valuable asset in improving extended air defence of its nuclear facilities. But even if the S-300s had been acquired, their effectiveness would have been severely compromised by Iran's inadequate command-and-control structure and the lack of advanced radars distributed across the country to cue the S-300 missiles.

Iran displayed a crude mock-up of what Tehran claimed was its own developmental equivalent of the S-300 SAM system, during a military parade in April 2010. Iranian officials claim such a capability is being developed indigenously.

The failure to secure the sale leaves Iran dependent on a mix of predominantly ageing SAM systems, including the S-200 (SA-5 *Gammon*) and a variant of the US *Hawk*. Its most modern system is the *Tor* mobile short-range system (SA-15 *Gauntlet*), of which it reportedly has 29.

However, its older systems are all vulnerable to modern electronic countermeasures and air-launched anti-radiation missiles. Notwithstanding reports that Iran has recently established an 'air-defence command' to coordinate existing services, overall performance is also constrained by poor integration of the individual air-defence batteries and inadequate system-wide command and control.

advanced systems operated by the US and its allies in the Gulf. Iran is also producing unmanned aerial vehicles to support air-force operations, for reconnaissance operations and recently for land-attack missions.

SYRIA, LEBANON AND HIZBULLAH

Syria continues a drive to modernise its military forces, with efforts focused on building up air-defence capabilities. This is perhaps unsurprising: the 2007 air raid that destroyed a facility reportedly involved in nuclear-related activities and that was widely asserted to have been carried out by Israeli forces, saw Syria's integrated air defences rendered ineffective. In mid-2009, it was alleged that Syria had received from Iran a sophisticated radar system capable of providing early warning of Israeli air-force sorties.

In September 2010 Moscow confirmed that it would proceed with a US$300 million arms deal concluded with Damascus in 2007 despite US and Israeli objections. This deal would see the delivery of at least 2 *Bastion* coastal-defence systems to Syria, with each system including up to 36 *Yakhont* anti-ship cruise missiles. As noted by the IISS at the time of the deal, 'delivery of the *Bastion* system to Syria will mark a considerable improvement in capability over the obsolescent P-5 and P-15 systems which Russia also previously provided. *Bastion* uses the 3M-55 ramjet-powered missile, which has a launch weight of about 3 tonnes and a speed of around twice the speed of sound at low altitude, presenting a challenging target for ship-based air defence systems. This will be a particular concern for Israel.'

In April 2010, Syria was alleged to have transferred *Scud*-D ballistic missiles to Hizbullah. The *Scuds* are believed to have a range of more than 435 miles, placing Jerusalem, Tel Aviv and Israeli nuclear installations within the range of Hizbullah's military forces. Syria denied the report, while Hizbullah reacted ambiguously. Syria is alleged to have already supplied Hizbullah with M-600 missiles, a Syrian variant of the Iranian *Fateh*-110. With a range of up to 300km, a solid-fuel propellant and 500kg warhead, the M-600 would be a powerful addition to Hizbullah's arsenal.

Allegations that Hizbullah pursued its rearmament and training efforts in violation of UN resolutions during 2010 were rife. Under Resolution 1701 which ended the 2006 war, only personnel from the UN Interim Force in Lebanon (UNIFIL) and the Lebanese Armed Forces (LAF) are permitted to operate in the area south of the Litani River. Yet the explosion of two unmarked weapons-storage facilities in the villages of Khirbat Salim (14 July 2010) and Shehabiya (3 September 2010), both south of the Litani River, strongly suggests that Hizbullah has been storing weaponry there. A staged clash also took place between UNIFIL peacekeepers and villagers in a Hizbullah-friendly area of southern Lebanon. In order to prevent the inspection of a suspected weapons cache, a UN armoured personnel carrier and a light armoured vehicle were blocked by civilians, who pelted the vehicle with stones, resulting in the injury of one UN peacekeeper.

Cooperation on weapons transfer has also apparently increased between Hizbullah and its Iranian and Syrian allies. Media reports asserted that

Across the Middle East and North Africa

- The US and Israel signed two key agreements in 2010 relating to missile-defence systems. In July, the two states agreed to jointly develop a high-altitude *Arrow*-3 interceptor and integrate it with Israel's missile-defence systems, while in September an agreement was signed for the development of the *David's Sling* weapon system, to 'advance efforts to develop an Israeli capability against short-range and theatre ballistic missiles.'

- March saw the US government award Lockheed Martin US$213m 'for long-lead tasks for the production of 20 new Advanced Block 52 F-16 aircraft for Egypt'.

- Israel launched the *Ofeq*-9 surveillance satellite in late June.

- The UAE signed a contract for the acquisition of six C-17 aircraft with Boeing in January 2010. Four are due for delivery in 2011, and two in 2012. Qatar's C-17 aircraft (it has two in its inventory) were deployed in early 2010 as part of the government's response to the January earthquake in Haiti.

- South Korea planned to deploy 130–150 special-operations forces personnel to the UAE before the end of January 2011, on a six-month rotation cycle. The group will be located within the UAE Special Operations Command School in Al Ain. According to the South Korean defence ministry, the mission of the unit will be 'to support education and training of the UAE special forces, conduct combined training and exercises and protect ROK nationals in case of emergency.' In late 2009, a South Korean consortium won a deal to build four nuclear power plants in the UAE by 2020. France, as noted in last year's *Military Balance*, also maintains a military presence in the UAE. However, the UAE has yet to decide on a replacement aircraft for its existing *Mirage* fleet, with the French *Rafale* and the US F/A-18 *Super Hornet* believed to be the leading contenders.

- In October, Egypt signed a contract with Airbus Military for three C-295 transport aircraft, to be delivered from 2011.

- The UAE in November requested from the US the possible sale of 30 AH-64D Block II lot 10 *Apaches*, remanufactured to Block III configuration, as well as 30 Block III *Apaches*, along with a substantial package of supporting equipment.

- The second corvette built by BAE Systems for the Royal Navy of Oman under the *Project Khareef* contract was commissioned in July 2010 at Portsmouth. The *Al-Rahmani* joins *Al-Shamikh*, which was commissioned in 2009 and was reported by BAE Systems to have started sea trials in December 2010.

- Qatar's navy is to procure a batch of *Exocet* MM40 Block 3 anti-ship missiles for its four *Vita*-class boats, upgrading its existing *Exocet* capability.

- Algeria continues to recapitalise both its fixed-wing combat aircraft and rotary inventories, with ongoing procurements from Russian and European manufacturers, respectively. The air force reportedly placed a follow-on order for a further 16 Su-30MKA fighter aircraft to supplement its original order of 28 of the type, the last of which was delivered in 2009. Alongside the Su-30MKA, the air force continues to operate the Su-24 *Fencer* in the strike role, and the MiG-29 *Fulcrum* in the fighter role. The air force has also reportedly ordered 16 Yakovlev Yak-130 advanced jet trainers.

- Algeria is also revamping its rotary-wing inventory with a number of types from AgustaWestland, including the *Super Lynx* light maritime helicopter and the AW101 medium utility helicopter.

- Morocco is also improving its combat-aircraft inventory with the addition of 24 Lockheed Martin F-16 block 52 fighters. All but two of the total number of aircraft are expected to be delivered from mid-2011 until the end of 2012. The last two of the 24-strong order will be delivered in 2013.

- January 2011 saw the Tunisian military deploy troops and armour across the country after the declaration of a state of emergency after the departure of President Zine al-Abidine Ben Ali. Ben Ali fled the country in the wake of serious civil disturbances in a number of locations across the country, culminating in demonstrations in Tunis. An interim government of national unity was formed following Ben Ali's departure, but at the time of writing the security situation in the country remained fluid.

three Hizbullah logistical units based in Syria and Lebanon were overseeing the safe delivery of Iranian-sponsored weapons to the Shia militant group. It was alleged that as a result of these units' operations Hizbullah was in possession of over 40,000 rockets and missiles. In the 1 November 2010 report to the UN Security Council, it was noted that 'under its mandate, UNIFIL cannot search private houses and properties unless there is credible evidence of a violation of resolution 1701 (2006), including an imminent threat of hostile activity emanating from that specific location. To date, UNIFIL has neither been provided with, nor found, evidence of the unauthorized transfer of arms into its area of operations.' However, while the UN also said that there was no evidence of the reactivation of old weapons dumps or new facilities, the November report went on to say that 'attacks with explosive devices against UNIFIL and discoveries of weapons, ammunitions and related materiel have demonstrated the presence of weapons and hostile armed elements ready to use them in the area south of the Litani River.'

A key issue for Hizbullah – a group that now appears to have both guerrilla and 'conventional' military organisation – is how to train on and maintain these weapons systems. Given Israel's near-constant air surveillance over southern Lebanon (UAV flights, as well as fighter overflights, are a regular occurrence), along with covert and electronic surveillance methods, it has to be assumed that any overt training with advanced weaponry would be detected. It has been alleged, as a consequence of this, that training activities for some Hizbullah personnel take place outside Lebanon.

Perhaps the most serious incident of 2010 took place on 3 August. A dispute over the trimming of a tree on the Israeli side of the Blue Line, but close to the Lebanese village of Adaisseh, escalated into a firefight between the LAF and the Israel Defense Forces (IDF). Despite the pleas of UNIFIL personnel, a sniper from the LAF shot an Israeli colonel to death. Two Lebanese soldiers and a Lebanese journalist were subsequently killed. Though the incident had the potential to escalate further, swift diplomatic intervention by the US and France contained the risks, while Israel showed restraint after the initial exchanges. US military assistance to Lebanon, already under criticism in Congressional circles for fear that US-supplied armaments may fall into the hands of Hizbullah, was jeopardised as a result. (In recent years the US has delivered systems to the LAF including M-113 armoured personnel carriers.) Senior US legislators put a scheduled US$100m in assistance on hold, though this was later lifted after heavy pressure by the Obama administration. Indeed, despite Lebanese criticism about the quality of the materiel supplied, the US remains the principal source of military aid to Lebanon.

ISRAEL

Given that the 2006 war in southern Lebanon exposed its vulnerability to missiles and rockets, Israel is reportedly in the final stages of developing its *Iron Dome* mobile air-defence system, designed to inter-

cept 155mm artillery shells and rockets with ranges of 5–70km. The system has three central components: a detection and tracking radar system, a battle-management and weapons-control system and a missile firing unit equipped with a *Tamir* interceptor missile. The Israel Defense Forces have established a new battalion under the Israeli Air Force Defense Division to operate the *Iron Dome* system.

In May 2010, the US Congress approved US$205m in funding to spur the production and deployment of *Iron Dome*, whose cost is estimated at between US$200–215m. In July 2010, the system underwent successful initial tests in the Negev Desert by intercepting multiple rocket barrages that mimicked the *Qassam* and *Katyusha* rockets typically fired into Israel. The *Iron Dome* project has been criticised by some Israeli defence analysts for not being cost-effective, given that each *Iron Dome* defence missile costs an estimated US$100,000, while *Kassam* rockets cost up to several hundred dollars to produce. Critics have also questioned the inability of the system to intercept rockets with a range of less than 4.5km, nor those that explode in under 15 seconds, the estimated time required for the *Tamir* missile to identify and intercept a target.

Israel's planned procurement of F-35 *Lightning* II aircraft proceeded with a final agreement signed in Washington for 20 aircraft. With funding provided by the US Foreign Military Financing provision, the total value of the deal has been estimated at US$2.75bn. Each aircraft, including engines, costs US$96m; the deal also includes training, simulation, spare parts and the building of maintenance facilities. According to the IDF, delivery should take two years from 2015, though this depends on the progress of the programme in the US. According to the CEO of the defence ministry, who signed the deal in October, Israel has an option to order more aircraft. The IDF, meanwhile, saw an additional capability development with the reported upgrade to the IAI-1124 *Seascan* aircraft with improved surveillance and communications packages, at a reported cost of NIS22m (US$5.85m).

OTHER DEVELOPMENTS

Nations in the Gulf region remain preoccupied by Iran's ballistic-missile development programme. As noted in *The Military Balance 2010*, this concern has prompted moves to develop ballistic-missile defence. While the air-defence capacities of regional states have long been documented in *The Military Balance*, the capability enhancements in recent years are noteworthy. The **United Arab Emirates**, which requested *Patriot* missiles, has seen the deployment of these systems move closer, with the announcement by Raytheon that with the upgrade of a *Patriot* radar to PAC-3 configuration, it 'now had the necessary support systems in place to begin the design verification and validation testing' for the UAE's programme. It had, however, been stated by US Defense Secretary Robert Gates in a March 2010 press conference in Abu Dhabi, that the US had deployed two *Patriot* batteries to the UAE. Meanwhile, Executive Director of the US Missile Defense Agency David Altwegg said in February 2010 that the US was 'preparing an FMS [Foreign Military Sales] case for three THAAD [Terminal High Altitude Area Defense] batteries for the United Arab Emirates'. The UAE had requested the THAAD sale in 2008.

As noted in previous editions of this book, the US has been keen to encourage cooperative defence arrangements in the region. At the 2009 IISS Manama Dialogue in Bahrain, then-CENTCOM commander General David Petraeus said that such cooperation has taken many forms: 'air and ballistic missile defense, shared early warning, counter-terrorism, maritime freedom of navigation and counter-piracy, counter proliferation, sharing of a common operational picture, and whole of governments approaches to countering extremism'. He continued by noting how 'multi-bilateralism', as well as initiatives in a multilateral and coalition context, were of key importance. Indeed, he said that this was the process by which CENTCOM sought to integrate bilateral activities to achieve multilateral effects. 'We see this in particular in certain key areas – especially in shared early warning, air and missile defense, and achievement of a common operational picture.'

In 2010 **Saudi Arabia** continued its move to substantially modernise its inventories. A notification for a large deal worth US$29.43bn (if all options are exercised) was made in October to the US Congress by the US Defense Security Cooperation Agency. If this deal were to proceed, the Royal Saudi Air Force could receive 84 F-15SA aircraft, substantial quantities of supporting equipment and munitions (including dual-mode laser/GPS munitions, laser-guided bombs and joint-direct attack munitions, *Harpoon* and HARM missiles), as well as upgrades to the existing fleet of F-15S to F-15SA configuration. On the same day, a further notification was made of a request by the Saudi Arabian National Guard for 26 Block III *Apache*, 72 UH-60M *Blackhawk* and 36 AH-6i *Little Bird* helicopters, 20 *Longbow* fire-control radars and 2,592 AGM-114R *Hellfire* missiles, among other equipment. While the Saudi armed forces will undoubtedly be keen to replace munitions expended in military actions against Houthi rebels who crossed into Saudi Arabia from Yemen in late 2009, the above equipment will constitute a substantial capability enhancement once integrated into the armed forces. Meanwhile, work on the A330 multi-role tanker transport aircraft ordered by Saudi Arabia and the UAE is proceeding at the EADS facility; the type received its military certification in late 2009, before delivery to its launch customer, the Royal Australian Air Force.

Algeria ALG

Algerian Dinar D		2009	2010	2011
GDP	D	10.1tr	12.0tr	
	US$	140bn	161bn	
per capita	US$	3,998	4,553	
Growth	%	2.1	4.6	
Inflation	%	5.7	5.5	
Def bdgt	D	384bn	422bn	
	US$	5.28bn	5.67bn	
US$1=D			72.64	74.40

Population	35,422,589

Age	0–14	15–19	20–24	25–29	30–64	65 plus
Male	12.3%	5.2%	5.2%	5.2%	20.0%	2.4%
Female	11.8%	5.0%	5.1%	5.2%	19.8%	2.8%

Capabilities

ACTIVE 147,000 (Army 127,000 Navy 6,000 Air 14,000) **Paramilitary 187,200**

Terms of service Conscription in army only, 18 months (6 months basic, 12 months wth regular army often involving civil projects)

RESERVE 150,000 (Army 150,000) to age 50

ORGANISATIONS BY SERVICE

Army 47,000; ε80,000 conscript (total 127,000)

FORCES BY ROLE

6 Mil Regions; re-org into div structure on hold

Armd	2 div (each: 3 tk regt, 1 mech regt); 1 indep bde
Mech	3 div (each: 1 tk regt, 3 mech regt)
Mech Inf/ Mot Inf	5 indep bde
AB/SF	1 (Rapid Reaction) div with (5 para regt (18th SF, and 1st, 4th, 5th 12th))
Arty	7 regt
AD	5 bn
Engr	4 indep bn

EQUIPMENT BY TYPE

MBT 1,082: 187 T-90S; 325 T-72; 300 T-62; 270 T-54/T-55
RECCE 90: 26 BRDM-2; 64 BRDM-2M each with 9M133 *Kornet* (AT-14 *Spriggan*)
AIFV 1,040: 100 BMP-3; 260 BMP-2M each with 9M133 *Kornet* (AT-14 *Spriggan*); 680 BMP-1
APC (W) 750: 300 BTR-60; 150 BTR-80; 150 OT-64; 50 M-3 *Panhard;* 100 TH 390 *Fahd*
ARTY 1,019
  SP 170: **122mm** 140 2S1 *Carnation;* **152mm** 30 2S3
  TOWED 375: **122mm** 160 D-30; 25 D-74; 100 M-1931/37; 60 M-30 *M-1938;* **130mm** 10 M-46; **152mm** 20 ML-20 M-1937
  MRL 144: **122mm** 48 BM-21; **140mm** 48 BM-14/16; **240mm** 30 BM-24; **300mm** 18 9A52 *Smerch*

MOR 330: **82mm** 150 M-37; **120mm** 120 M-1943; **160mm** 60 M-1943
AT
  MSL • MANPATS 200+: 200 *Milan; Kornet*-E being delivered; *Metis-M1* being delivered; AT-3 9K11 *Sagger;* AT-4 9K111 *Spigot;* AT-5 9K113 *Spandrel*
  RCL 180: **107mm** 60 B-11; **82mm** 120 B-10
  GUNS 250: **57mm** 160 ZIS-2 M-1943; **85mm** 80 D-44: **100mm** 10 T-12; (50 SU-100 SP in store)
AD • SAM 288+
  SP 68: ε48 9K-33 OSA (SA-8 *Gecko*); ε20 9K31 *Strela*-1 (SA-9 *Gaskin*)
  MANPAD 220+: ε220 9K32 *Strela*-2 (SA-7A/B *Grail*); 9K36 *Strela*-3 (SA-14 *Gremlin*); 9K310 *Igla*-1 (SA-16 *Gimlet*)
  GUNS ε875
    SP ε225 ZSU-23-4
    TOWED ε650: **14.5mm** 100: 60 ZPU-2; 40 ZPU-4; **20mm** 100; **23mm** 100 ZU-23; **37mm** ε100 M-1939; **57mm** 70 S-60; **85mm** 20 M-1939 *KS-12;* **100mm** 150 KS-19; **130mm** 10 KS-30

Navy ε6,000 (incl 500 officers)

EQUIPMENT BY TYPE
SUBMARINES • TACTICAL • SSK 3
  2 *Kilo* (FSU *Paltus*) each with 6 single 533mm TT with Test-71ME HWT
  1 *Improved Kilo* (FSU *Varshavyanka*) with 6 single 533mm TT (one additional vessel delivered; expected ISD 2011)
PRINCIPAL SURFACE COMBATANTS 3
  FRIGATES • FFM 3
    2 *Mourad Rais* (FSU *Koni*) each with 1 twin lnchr (2 eff.) with 9M33 *Osa*-M (SA-N-4 *Gecko*) SAM, 2 RBU 6000 *Smerch* 2 (24 eff.), 2 twin 76mm gun (4 eff.)(undergoing modernisation programme)
    1 *Mourad Rais* (FSU *Koni*) with 1 twin lnchr (2 eff.) with 9M33 *Osa*-M (SA-N-4 *Gecko)* SAM, 2 twin 53mm TT (4 eff.), 2 RBU 6000 *Smerch* 2 (24 eff.), 2 twin 76mm gun (4 eff.)
PATROL AND COASTAL COMBATANTS 20
  CORVETTES 6
    FSGM 3:
      2 *Rais Hamidou* (FSU *Nanuchka* II) each with 4 single lnchr each withP-15 *Termit*-M (SS-N-2C *Styx*) AShM, 1 twin lnchr (2 eff.) with 9M33 *Osa*-M (SA-N-4 *Gecko*) SAM
      1 *Rais Hamidou* (FSU *Nanuchka* II) with 4 quad lnchr (16 eff.) with 3M24 *Uran* (SS-N-25 *Switchblade*) AShM, 1 twin lnchr (2 eff.) with 20 9M33 *Osa*-M (SA-N-4 *Gecko*) SAM
    FSG 3 *Djebel Chenona* each with 2 twin (4 eff.) each with C-802 (CSS-N-8 *Saccade*) tactical AShM, 1 76mm gun
  PBFG 9 *Osa* II (3†) each with 4 single lnchr each with P-15 *Termit* (SS-N-2B *Styx*) AShM
  PB 9 *Kebir*
AMPHIBIOUS • LS 3
  LSM 1 *Polnochny B* (capacity 6 MBT; 180 troops)
  LST 2 *Kalaat beni Hammad* (capacity 7 tanks; 240 troops) each with 1 med hel landing platform
LOGISTICS AND SUPPORT 3
  AGS 1 *El Idrissi*

Middle East and North Africa

AX 1 *Daxin*
YPT 1 *Poluchat I* (used for SAR)

FACILITIES

Bases   Located at Mers el Kebir, Algiers, Annaba, Jijel

Coast Guard ε500

PATROL AND COASTAL COMBATANTS 41
  PBF 6 *Baglietto 20*
  PB 35: 6 *Baglietto Mangusta*; 12 *Jebel Antar*; 7 *Deneb* (9
  additional vessels on order); 4 *El Mounkid*; 6 *Kebir*
LOGISTICS AND SUPPORT 8
  ARL 1 *El Mourafek*
  TRG • AXL 7 *El Mouderrib* (PRC *Chui-E)* (2 in reserve†)

Air Force 14,000

Flying hours   150 hrs/year

FORCES BY ROLE

Ftr   2 sqn with MiG-23MF/MS/U *Flogger*; 2 sqn with
        MiG-25 *Foxbat*; 4 sqn with MiG-29C *Fulcrum*/
        MiG-29UB *Fulcrum*

FGA   2 sqn with MiG-23BN *Flogger*; 2 sqn each with
        Su-24M *Fencer*/Su-24MK *Fencer D*; 1 sqn with
        Su-30MKA

MP   2 sqn with Beech 200T

ISR   1 sqn with Su-24E *Fencer**; 1 sqn with MiG-25R
        Foxbat

Tkr   1 sqn with Il-78 *Midas*

Tpt   2 sqn with C-130H *Hercules*; C-130H-30 *Hercules*;
        Gulfstream IV-SP; Gulfstream V; Il-76MD *Candid*
        B; Il-76TD *Candid*; L-100-30; 2 (VIP) sqn with F-27
        Friendship; *Falcon* 900

Trg   2 sqn with Z-142; 1 sqn with Yak-130; 2 sqn 36
        L-39ZA; L-39C *Albatros*; 1 (hel) sqn with 28 PZL
        Mi-2 *Hoplite*

Atk Hel 4 sqn with Mi-24 *Hind*

Tpt Hel 7 sqn with AS-355 *Ecureuil*; Mi-8 *Hip*; Mi-17 *Hip*
        H; Mi-171

AD   3 (ADA) bde with 85mm guns/100mm/130mm;
        3 (SAM) regt with S-75 *Dvina* (SA-2
        Guideline)/S-125 *Neva* (SA-3 *Goa*)/2K12 *Kub* (SA-6
        Gainful)l/9K33 *Osa* (SA-8 *Gecko*)

EQUIPMENT BY TYPE
AIRCRAFT 163 combat capable
  FTR 37: 12 MiG-25 *Foxbat*; 25 MiG-29C *Fulcrum*/MiG-
  29UB *Fulcrum*
  FGA 118: 28 Su-30MKA; 34 Su-24M/Su-24MK *Fencer D*;
  38 MiG-23BN *Flogger*; 18 MiG-23MF/MS/U *Flogger*
  ISR 8: 4 MiG-25R *Foxbat**; 4 Su-24E *Fencer**
  TKR 6 Il-78 *Midas*
  TPT 51 **Heavy** 9: 3 Il-76MD *Candid B*; 6 Il-76TD *Candid*;
  Medium 19: 9 C-130H; 8 C-130H-30 *Hercules*; 2 L-100-
  30 **Light** 15: 6 Beech 200T (additional units on order); 6
  Beech 1900D (electronic surv); 3 F-27 *Friendship* **PAX** 8: 3
  Falcon 900; 4 Gulfstream IV-SP; 1 Gulfstream V
  TRG 99: 36 L-39ZA *Albatros*; 7 L-39C; 16 Yak-130 being
  delivered; 40 Z-142
HELICOPTERS
  ATK 33 Mi-24 *Hind*

MRH/TPT 64 Mi-8 *Hip* (med tpt)/Mi-17 *Hip H*
TPT 78 **Medium** 42 Mi-171 **Light** 36: 8 AS-355 *Ecureuil*;
28 PZL Mi-2 *Hoplite*
AD
  SAM ε140 SA-2 *Guideline* Towed/SA-3 *Goa*/SA-6 *Gainful*
  SP/SA-8 *Gecko* SP (140–840 eff.)
  GUNS 725 **100mm/130mm/85mm**
MSL
  ASM Kh-25 (AS-10 *Karen*); Kh-29 (AS-14 *Kedge*); Kh-31
  (AS-17 *Krypton*); Kh-23 (AS-7 *Kerry*)
  ARM Kh-25MP (AS-12 *Kegler*)
  AAM • IR AAM R-3 (AA-2 *Atoll*)‡; R-60 (AA-8 *Aphid*);
  R-73 (A-11 *Archer*) **IR/SARH AAM** R-40/46 (AA-6 *Acrid*)
  R-23/24 (AA-7 *Apex*) **IR/SARH AAM** R-27 (AA-10 *Alamo*)

Paramilitary ε187,200

Gendarmerie 20,000
Ministry of Defence

FORCES BY ROLE

Army   6 region

EQUIPMENT BY TYPE
RECCE AML-60/110 M-3 *Panhard* APC (W)
APC (W) 100 TH 390 *Fahd*
HELICOPTERS • TPT • Light Some PZL Mi-2 *Hoplite*

National Security Forces 16,000
Directorate of National Security. Small arms

Republican Guard 1,200
EQUIPMENT BY TYPE
RECCE AML-60
APC (T) M-3

Legitimate Defence Groups ε150,000
Self-defence militia, communal guards (60,000)

Bahrain BHR

Bahraini Dinar D		2009	2010	2011
GDP	D	7.74bn	8.17bn	
	US$	20.6bn	21.7bn	
per capita	US$	26,022	26,931	
Growth	%	3	3.5	
Inflation	%	2.8	2.6	
Def exp	D	279m		
	US$	742m		
Def bdgt	D	265m	279m	
	US$	705m	742m	
FMA (US)	US$	8m	19.0m	19.5m
US$1=D		0.38	0.38	

Population	807,131

Ethnic groups: Nationals 64%; Asian 13%; other Arab 10%; Iranian 8%; European 1%

Age	0–14	15–19	20–24	25–29	30–64	65 plus
Male	12.6%	4.4%	4.2%	3.8%	27.8%	2.4%
Female	12.4%	4.3%	4.0%	3.5%	18.6%	2.0%

Capabilities

ACTIVE 8,200 (Army 6,000 Navy 700 Air 1,500)
Paramilitary 11,260

ORGANISATIONS BY SERVICE

Army 6,000

FORCES BY ROLE

Armd	1 bde under strength (2 armd bn, 1 recce bn)
Inf	1 bde (2 mech inf bn, 1 mot inf bn)
SF	1 bn
Arty	1 bde (1 lt arty bty, 1 hy arty bty, 1 MRL bty, 2 med arty bty)
Gd	1 (Amiri) bn
AD	1 bn (1 ADA bty, 2 SAM bty)

EQUIPMENT BY TYPE
MBT 180 M-60A3
RECCE 30: 22 AML-90; 8 S52 *Shorland*; (8 *Ferret* in store); (8 *Saladin* in store)
AIFV 25 YPR-765 (with 25mm)
APC 325+
APC (T) 205 M-113A2
APC (W) 120+: 10+ AT105 *Saxon*; 110 M-3 *Panhard*
ARTY 92
  SP 33: **155mm** 20 M109A5; **203mm** 13 M-110
  TOWED 26: **105mm** 8 L-118 Light Gun; **155mm** 18 M-198
  MRL 227mm 9 MLRS (with 30 ATACMS)
  MOR 24: **SP 120mm** 12
  81mm 12
AT • MSL • MANPATS 60 *Javelin*
  RCL 31: **106mm** 25 M-40A1; **120mm** 6 MOBAT
AD • SAM 93
  SP 7 *Crotale*
  TOWED 8 I-HAWK *MIM-23B*
  MANPAD 78: 18 FIM-92A *Stinger*; 60 RBS-70
  GUNS 27: **35mm** 15 Oerlikon; **40mm** 12 L/70

Navy 700

EQUIPMENT BY TYPE
PRINCIPAL SURFACE COMBATANTS 1
  FRIGATES • FFGHM 1 *Sabha* (US *Oliver Hazard Perry*) with 1 Mk13 GMLS with SM-1MR SAM/RGM-84C *Harpoon* AShM, 2 triple 324mm ASTT (6 eff.), 1 76mm gun, (capacity 1 Bo-105 hel)
PATROL AND COASTAL COMBATANTS 10
  CORVETTES • FSG 2 *Al Manama* (GER Lurssen 62m) each with 2 twin lnchr (4 eff.) each with MM-40 *Exocet* AShM, 1 76mm gun, 1 hel landing platform
  PCFG 4 *Ahmed el Fateh* (GER Lurssen 45m) each with 2 twin lnchr (4 eff.) each with MM-40 *Exocet* AShM, 1 76mm gun
  PB 4: 2 *Al Jarim* (US *Swift* FPB-20); 2 *Al Riffa* (GER Lurssen 38m)
AMPHIBIOUS • CRAFT 9
  LCU 9: 1 *Loadmaster*; 4 *Mashtan*; 2 ADSB 16m; 2 ADSB 42m;

LOGISTICS AND SUPPORT 4
  YFU 1 *Ajeera*
  YFL 3
FACILITIES
Base Mina Salman

Naval Aviation
EQUIPMENT BY TYPE
HELICOPTERS • TPT • Light 2 Bo-105

Air Force 1,500

FORCES BY ROLE

Ftr	2 sqn with F-16C/F-16D *Fighting Falcon*
FGA	1 sqn with F-5E/F-5F *Tiger II*
Tpt	Some sqn with B-727; BAe-146-200 (RJ-85); Gulfstream II; Gulfstream III (VIP)
Trg	some sqn with *Hawk* Mk-129*; T-67M *Firefly*,
Atk Hel	3 sqn with AH-1E *Cobra*; TAH-1P *Cobra*
Tpt Hel	1 sqn with Bell 212 (AB-212); 1 (VIP) unit with Bo-105; S-70A *Black Hawk*; UH-60L *Black Hawk*

EQUIPMENT BY TYPE
AIRCRAFT 39 combat capable
  FTR 12: 8 F-5E *Tiger II*; 4 F-5F *Tiger II*
  FGA 21: 17 F-16C *Fighting Falcon*; 4 F-16D *Fighting Falcon*
  TPT • PAX 4: PAX 1 B-727; 1 Gulfstream II; 1 Gulfstream III (VIP); 1 BAe-146-200 (RJ-85)
  TRG 9: 6 *Hawk* Mk-129*; 3 T-67M *Firefly*
HELICOPTERS
  ATK 22 AH-1E *Cobra*
  TPT 19 **Medium** 4: 3 S-70A *Black Hawk*; 1 UH-60L *Black Hawk* **Light** 15: 12 Bell 212 (AB-212); 3 Bo-105
  TRG 6 TAH-1P *Cobra*
MSL
  ASM AGM-65D/G *Maverick*
  AAM • IR AAM AIM-9P *Sidewinder* **SARH AAM** AIM-7 *Sparrow*
AT • MSL some TOW

Paramilitary ε11,260

Police 9,000
Ministry of Interior
HELICOPTERS
  MRH 2 Bell 412 *Twin Huey*
  ISR 2 Hughes 500
  TPT • Light 1 Bo-105

National Guard ε2,000
Paramilitary 3 bn

Coast Guard ε260
Ministry of Interior
PATROL AND COASTAL COMBATANTS • PB 23 (a further 29 small patrol vessels are in service)
AMPHIBIOUS • LANDING CRAFT • LCU 1 *Loadmaster II*
LOGISTICS AND SUPPORT 1 YA G

FOREIGN FORCES

United Kingdom Air Force 1 BAe-125 CC-3; 1 BAe-146 MKII

United States US Central Commmand: 1,339; 1 HQ (5th Fleet)

Egypt EGY

Egyptian Pound E£		2009	2010	2011
GDP	E£	1.04tr	1.20tr	
	US$	187bn	215bn	
per capita	US$	2,257	2,549	
Growth	%	4.7	5.4	
Inflation	%	11.8	11.7	
Def exp	E£	22.8bn		
	US$	4.12bn		
Def bdgt	E£	32.4bn	34.7bn	42.1bn
	US$	5.84bn	6.24bn	
FMA (US)	US$	1.30bn	1.30bn	1.30bn
US$1=E£		5.54	5.56	

Population   84,474,427

Age	0–14	15–19	20–24	25–29	30–64	65 plus
Male	16.7%	4.8%	4.8%	4.9%	17.5%	2.0%
Female	16.0%	4.6%	4.5%	4.6%	17.3%	2.5%

Capabilities

ACTIVE 468,500 (Army 340,000 Navy 18,500 Air 30,000 Air Defence Command 80,000) **Paramilitary 397,000**

Terms of service 12 months-3 years (followed by refresher training over a period of up to 9 years)

RESERVE 479,000 (Army 375,000 Navy 14,000 Air 20,000 Air Defence 70,000)

ORGANISATIONS BY SERVICE

Army 90,000–120,000; 190,000–220,000 conscript (total 280,000–340,000)

FORCES BY ROLE

Armd	4 div (each: 2 armd bde, 1 mech bde, 1 arty bde); 1 (Republican Guard) bde; 4 indep bde
Mech Inf	7 div (each: 1 arty bde, 1 armd bde, 2 mech inf bde); 4 indep bde
Air Mob	2 bde
Inf	1 div, 2 indep bde
Cdo	1 HQ (5 cdo gp, 1 counter-terrorist unit, str 300.)
Para	1 bde
Arty	15 indep bde
SSM	1 bde with 9 FROG-7; 1 bde with 9 Scud-B

EQUIPMENT BY TYPE

MBT 2,383: 973 M1A1 *Abrams*; 300 M-60A1; 850 M-60A3; 260 *Ramses II* (mod T-54/55); (840 T-54/T-55 in store); (500 T-62 in store)

RECCE 412: 300 BRDM-2; 112 *Commando Scout*

AIFV 390 YPR-765 (with 25mm); (220 BMP-1 in store)

APC 4,160

  APC (T) 2,600 M-113A2 (incl variants); (500 BTR-50/OT-62 in store)

  APC (W) 1,560: 250 BMP-600P; 250 BTR-60; 410 *Fahd-30/ TH* 390 *Fahd*; 650 *Walid*

ARTY 4,432

  SP 492: **122mm** 124 SP 122; **155mm** 368: 164 M-109A2; 204 M-109A5

  TOWED 962: **122mm** 526: 190 D-30M; 36 M-1931/37; 300 M-30 *M-1938*; **130mm** 420 M-46; **155mm** 16 GH-52

  MRL 450: **122mm** 356: 96 BM-11; 60 BM-21; 50 *Sakr*-10; 50 *Sakr*-18; 100 *Sakr*-36; **130mm** 36 *Kooryong*; **140mm** 32 BM-14; **227mm** 26 MLRS; **240mm** (48 BM-24 in store)

  MOR 2,528

    SP 100: **107mm** 65 M-106A1; 35 M-106A2

    81mm 50 M-125A2; **82mm** 500; **120mm** 1,848: 1,800 M-1943; 48 Brandt; **160mm** 30 M-160

AT • MSL 2,362

  SP 262: 52 M-901, 210 YPR 765 PRAT

  MANPATS 2,100: 1,200 AT-3 *Sagger* (incl BRDM-2); 200 *Milan*; 700 TOW-2

  RCL 107mm 520 B-11

UAV • ISR • Heavy R4E-50 *Skyeye*

AD • SAM 2,096+

  SP 96: 50 FIM-92A *Avenger*; 26 M-54 *Chaparral*; 20 9K31 *Strela*-1 (SA-9 *Gaskin*)

  MANPAD 2,000+: 2,000 *Ayn al-Saqr*/9K32 *Strela*-2 (SA-7 *Grail*)‡; FIM-92A *Stinger*

  GUNS 705+

    SP 205: **23mm** 165: 45 Sinai-23; 120 ZSU-23-4; **57mm** 40 ZSU-57-2

    TOWED 500+: **14.5mm** 300 ZPU-4; **23mm** 200 ZU-23-2; **57mm** S-60

RADAR • LAND AN/TPQ-36 *Firefinder*; AN/TPQ-37 *Firefinder* (arty/mor)

MSL • TACTICAL • SSM 42+: 9 FROG-7; 24 *Sakr*-80; some (trials); 9 *Scud*-B

Navy ε8,500 (incl 2,000 Coast Guard); 10,000 conscript (total 18,500)

Two Fleets: Mediterranean (HQ located at Alexandria) and Red Sea (HQ at Safaqa). Naval Organisation: 1 Submarine Bde, 1 Destroyer Bde, 1 Patrol Bde, 1 Fast Attack Bde and 1 Special Ops Bde.

EQUIPMENT BY TYPE

SUBMARINES • TACTICAL • SSK 4 *Romeo*† (PRC *Type 033*) each with 8 single 533mm TT each with UGM-84C *Harpoon* AShM

PRINCIPAL SURFACE COMBATANTS 8

  FRIGATES 8:

    FFGHM 4 *Mubarak* (US *Oliver Hazard Perry*) each with 1 Mk13 GMLS with RGM-84C *Harpoon* AShM/SM-1MP SAM, 1 76mm gun, (capacity 2 SH-2G *Super Seasprite* ASW hel)

FFGH 2 *Damyat* (US *Knox*) each with 1 octuple Mk16 GMLS with RGM-84C *Harpoon* AShM/ASROC, 2 twin 324mm TT (4 eff.), 1 127mm gun, (capacity 1 SH-2G *Super Seasprite* ASW hel)

FFG 2 *Najim Al Zaffer* (PRC *Jianghu* I) each with 2 twin lnchr (4 eff.) each with HY-2 (CSS-N-2 *Silkworm*) AShM, 2 RBU 1200 (10 eff.)

PATROL AND COASTAL COMBATANTS 50

CORVETTES • FSGM 2

2 *Abu Qir* (ESP *Descubierta*) each with 2 quad Mk141 lnchr (8 eff.) each with RGM-84C *Harpoon* AShM, 1 octuple lnchr with *Aspide* SAM, 2 triple 324mm ASTT (6 eff.) each with *Sting Ray* LWT, 1 twin 375mm A/S mor (2 eff.), 1 76mm gun

PCFG 11

6 *Ramadan* each with 4 single lnchr each with *Otomat* AShM

5 *Tiger* class each with 2 single lnchr each with *Otomat* AShM

PCC 5

5 *Hainan* (PRC) each with 2 triple 324mm TT (6 eff.), 4 single RL (3 more in reserve†)

PBFG 21

4 *Hegu* (*Komar* type) (PRC) each with 2 single lnchr each with SY-1 AShM

5 *October* (FSU *Komar* - 1†) each with 2 single lnchr each with SY-1 AShM

12 *Osa* I (FSU - 3†) each with 4 single lnchr each with P-15 *Termit* (SS-N-2A *Styx*) AShM

PBFM 5

4 *Shershen* (FSU) each with 1 9K32 *Strela-2* (SA-N-5 *Grail*) SAM (manual aiming), 1 12 tube BM-24 MRL (12 eff.)

PB 6

4 *Shanghai* II (PRC)

2 *Shershen* (FSU - 1†) each with 4 single 533mm TT, 1 8 tube BM-21 MRL (8 eff.)

MINE WARFARE • MINE COUNTERMEASURES 14

MHC 5: 2 *Osprey*; 3 *Dat Assawari* (US Swiftships)

MSI 2 *Safaga* (US Swiftships)

MSO 7: 3 *Assiout* (FSU T-43 class); 4 *Aswan* (FSU *Yurka*)

AMPHIBIOUS 12

LANDING SHIPS • LSM 3 *Polnochny* A (FSU) (capacity 6 MBT; 180 troops)

LANDING CRAFT • LCU 9 *Vydra* (capacity either 3 AMX-30 MBT or 100 troops)

LOGISTICS AND SUPPORT 25:

AOT 7 *Toplivo* (1 additional in reserve)

AE 1 *Halaib* (*Westerwald*-class)

AK 2

ARL 1 *Shaledin* (*Luneberg*-class)

ATA 5† *Okhtensky*

AX 5: 1 *El Fateh*† (UK 'Z' class); 1 *El Horriya* (also used as the Presidential yacht); 1 *Al Kousser*; 1 *Intishat*; 1 other

YPT 2 *Poluchat* 1

YDT 2

FACILITIES

Bases   Alexandria, Port Said, Mersa Matruh, Port Tewfig, Safaqa, Hurghada, Suez, Al Ghardaqah

Coastal Defence

Army tps, Navy control

MSL • TACTICAL • SSM SSC-2B *Samlet*

LNCHR 3:

3 twin each with 1 Mk 2 *Otomat* SSM

GUN 100mm; **130mm** SM-4-1; **152mm**

Naval Aviation

All aircraft operated by Air Force

AIRCRAFT • TPT • Light 4 Beech 1900C (Maritime Surveillance)

HELICOPTERS

ASW 14: 10 SH-2G *Super Seasprite* with Mk 46 LWT; 4 *Sea King* Mk47

MRH 5 SA-342 *Gazelle*

UAV • ISR • Light 2 *Camcopter* 5.1

Coast Guard 2,000

PATROL AND COASTAL COMBATANTS 74

PBF 15: 6 *Crestitalia*; 6 *Swift Protector*; 3 (various)

PB 59: 5 *Nisr*; 12 *Sea Spectre MkIII*; 9 Swiftships; 21 *Timsah*; 3 Type 83; 9 (various)

Air Force 30,000 (incl 10,000 conscript)

FORCES BY ROLE

Ftr	2 sqn with F-16A *Fighting Falcon*; 7 sqn with F-16C *Fighting Falcon*; 6 sqn with MiG-21 *Fishbed*; 2 sqn with *Mirage* 5D/E; 1 sqn with *Mirage* 2000C
FGA	1 sqn with *Alpha Jet**; 2 sqn with F-4E *Phantom II*; 2 sqn with J-6; 1 sqn with *Mirage* 5E2
ASW	2 sqn with SH-2G *Super Seasprite*; *Sea King* MK47; SA-342L *Gazelle*
MP	1 sqn with Beech 1900C
EW	1 sqn with Beech 1900 (ELINT); C-130H *Hercules* (ELINT); *Commando* Mk2E (ECM)
ISR	2 sqn with MiG-21R *Fishbed H**; *Mirage* 5R (5SDR)*
AEW	1 sqn with E-2C *Hawkeye*
Tpt	1 regt with An-74TK-200A; B-707-366C; B-737-100; Beech 200 *Super King Air*; C-130H *Hercules*; DHC-5D *Buffalo*; Falcon 20; Gulfstream III; Gulfstream IV; Gulfstream G-IVSP
Trg	Some sqn with *Alpha Jet**; DHC-5 *Buffalo*; EMB-312 *Tucano*; F-16B *Fighting Falcon**; F-16D *Fighting Falcon**; *Gomhouria*; Grob 115EG; JJ-6; K-8 *Karakorum**; L-29 *Delfin*; L-39 *Albatros*; L-59E *Albatros**; M-2000B *Mirage**; MiG-21U *Mongol A**
Atk hel	6 sqn with AH-64A *Apache*; SA-342K *Gazelle* (with HOT)
Tpt Hel	Some sqn with AS-61; CH-47C *Chinook*; CH-47D *Chinook*; *Commando*; Mi-6 *Hook*; Mi-8 *Hip*; S-70 *Black Hawk*; UH-12E; UH-60A *Black Hawk*; UH-60L *Black Hawk*
ISR UAV	sqn with R4E-50 *Skyeye*; Teledyne-Ryan 324 *Scarab*

EQUIPMENT BY TYPE

AIRCRAFT 565 combat capable

FTR 156: 26 F-16A *Fighting Falcon*; 12 F-16B *Fighting Falcon*; 44 J-6; 74 J-7

FGA 238: 29 F-4E *Phantom II*; 113 F-16C *Fighting Falcon*; 6 F-16D *Fighting Falcon*; 3 *Mirage* 2000B; 18 *Mirage* 2000C; 53 *Mirage* 5D/E; 16 *Mirage* 5E2;

ISR 20: 14 MiG-21R *Fishbed H**; 6 *Mirage* 5R (5SDR)*

AEW&C 6 E-2C *Hawkeye*

TPT 59 **Medium** 24: 22 C-130H *Hercules*; 2 C-130H *Hercules* (ELINT) **Light** 18: 3 An-74TK-200A (3 more on order); 1 Beech 200 *King Air*; 1 Beech 1900 (ELINT); 4 Beech 1900C; 4 DHC-5; 5 DHC-5D *Buffalo* **PAX** 17: 3 B-707-366C; 1 B-737-100; 3 *Falcon* 20; 3 Gulfstream III; 3 Gulfstream IV; 4 Gulfstream G-45P

TRG 331: 36 *Alpha Jet**; 34 EMB-312 *Tucano*; 36 *Gomhouria*; 74 Grob 115EG; 80 K-8 *Karakorum* *; 26 L-29 *Delfin*; 10 L-39 *Albatros*; 35 L-59E *Albatros**

HELICOPTERS

ATK 105: 35 AH-64A *Apache*

ASW 15: 10 SH-2G *Super Seasprite* (opcon Navy); 5 *Sea King* Mk47 (opcon Navy)

ELINT 4 *Commando* Mk2E (ECM)

MRH 70: 65 SA-342K *Gazelle* (some with HOT); 5 SA-342L *Gazelle* (opcon Navy)

TPT 100: Heavy 3 CH-47C *Chinook*; 16 CH-47D *Chinook*; 12 Mi-6 *Hook*; **Medium** 78: 2 AS-61; 25 *Commando* (of which 3 VIP); 40 Mi-8 *Hip*; 4 S-70 *Black Hawk* (VIP); 2 UH-60A *Black Hawk*; 5 UH-60L *Black Hawk* (VIP)

TRG 17 UH-12E

UAV • ISR • Heavy 49: 20 R4E-50 *Skyeye*; 29 Teledyne-Ryan 324 *Scarab*

MSL

ASM 245+: 80 AGM-65A *Maverick*; 123 AGM-65D *Maverick*; 12 AGM-65F *Maverick*; 30 AGM-65G *Maverick*; AGM-119 *Hellfire*; AGM-84 *Harpoon*; AM-39 *Exocet*; AS-30L HOT

ARM *Armat*; Kh-25MP (AS-12 *Kegler*)

AAM • IR AAM R-3(AA-2 *Atoll*)‡; AIM-9F *Sidewinder*/AIM-9L *Sidewinder*/AIM-9P *Sidewinder*; R-550 *Magic*;

SARH AAM AIM-7E *Sparrow*/AIM-7F *Sparrow*/AIM-7M *Sparrow*; R530

Air Defence Command 80,000 conscript; 70,000 reservists (total 150,000)

FORCES BY ROLE

AD 5 div (geographically based) (total: 12 SAM bty with M-48 *Chaparral*, 12 radar bn, 12 ADA bde (total: 100 ADA bn), 12 SAM bty with I-HAWK MIM-23B, 14 SAM bty with *Crotale*, 18 SAM bn with *Skyguard*, 110 SAM bn with S-125 *Pechora*-M (SA-3A) 2K12 *Kub* (SA-6 *Gainful*); S-75M *Volkhov* (SA-2 *Guideline*)

EQUIPMENT BY TYPE

AD

SYSTEMS 72+: *Amoun* each with RIM-7F *Sea Sparrow* SAM, 36+ quad SAM (144 eff.), *Skyguard* towed SAM, 36+ twin 35mm guns (72 eff.)

SAM 702+

SP 130+: 24+ *Crotale*; 50+ M-48 *Chaparral*; 56+ SA-6 *Gainful*

TOWED 572+: 78+ I-HAWK *MIM-23B*; S-75M *Volkhov* (SA-2 *Guideline*) 282+ *Skyguard*; 212+ S-125 *Pechora*-M (SA-3A *Goa*)

GUNS 1,566+

SP • 23mm 266+: 36+ *Sinai*-23 (SPAAG) each with *Ayn al-Saqr* MANPAD, Dassault 6SD-20S land; 230 ZSU-23-4 **TOWED 57mm** 600 S-60; **85mm** 400 M-1939 *KS-12*; **100mm** 300 KS-19

Paramilitary ε397,000 active

Central Security Forces 325,000

Ministry of Interior; Includes conscripts

APC (W) 100+: 100 *Hussar*; *Walid*

National Guard 60,000

Lt wpns only

FORCES BY ROLE

Paramilitary 8 (cadre status) bde (each: 3 paramilitary bn)

EQUIPMENT BY TYPE

APC (W) 250 *Walid*

Border Guard Forces 12,000

Ministry of Interior; lt wpns only

18 (Border Guard) regt

DEPLOYMENT

CENTRAL AFRICAN REPUBLIC/CHAD

UN • MINURCAT 2 obs

CÔTE D'IVOIRE

UN • UNOCI 176; 1 engr coy

DEMOCRATIC REPUBLIC OF THE CONGO

UN • MONUSCO 999; 25 obs; 1 inf bn; 1 SF coy

LIBERIA

UN • UNMIL 5 obs

NEPAL

UN • UNMIN 3 obs

SUDAN

UN • UNAMID 2,394; 24 obs; 2 inf bn; 1 engr coy; 1 sigs coy; 1 tpt coy

UN • UNMIS 1,503; 15 obs; 1 inf bn; 2 engr coy; 2 tpt coy; 1 med bn; 1 de-mining pl

WESTERN SAHARA

UN • MINURSO 21 obs

FOREIGN FORCES

Australia MFO (*Operation Mazurka*) 25

Canada MFO 28

Colombia MFO 354; 1 inf bn

Czech Republic MFO 3

Fiji MFO 338; 1 inf bn

France MFO 2

Hungary MFO 38; 1 MP unit

Italy MFO 78; 1 coastal ptl unit

New Zealand MFO 28 1 trg unit; 1 tpt unit

Norway MFO 3

United States MFO 688; 1 inf bn; 1 spt bn (1 EOD coy, 1 medical coy, 1 spt hel coy)

Uruguay MFO 58 1 engr/tpt unit

Iran IRN

Iranian Rial r		2009	2010	2011
GDP	r	3,233tr	3,639tr	
	US$	328bn	356bn	
per capita	US$	4,497	4,739	
Growth	%	1.8	3.0	
Inflation	%	13.5	9.5	
Def bdgt[a]	r	85.2tr	92.2tr	113tr
	US$	8.64bn	9.02bn	
US$1=r			9862.98	10227.88

[a] Excluding defence industry funding

Population 75,077,547

Ethnic groups: Persian 51%; Azeri 24%; Gilaki/Mazandarani 8%; Kurdish 7%; Arab 3%; Lur 2%; Baloch 2%; Turkman 2%

Age	0–14	15–19	20–24	25–29	30–64	65 plus
Male	12.3%	5.1%	6.2%	5.6%	19.1%	2.4%
Female	11.7%	4.8%	5.8%	5.4%	18.8%	2.6%

Capabilities

ACTIVE 523,000 (Army 350,000 Islamic Revolutionary Guard Corps 125,000 Navy 18,000 Air 30,000) Paramilitary 40,000

Armed Forces General Staff coordinates two parallel organisations: Regular Armed Forces and Revolutionary Guard Corps

RESERVE 350,000 (Army 350,000, ex-service volunteers)

ORGANISATIONS BY SERVICE

Army 130,000; 220,000 conscript (total 350,000)

FORCES BY ROLE
5 Corps-Level Regional HQ

Armd	4 div (each: 2 armd, 1 mech bde, 1 recce, 1 SP arty bn); 1 indep bde
Mech Inf	2 div (each: 1 armd, 2–3 mech inf bde, 1 recce bn, 1 SP arty, 1 arty bn)
Inf	4 div (each: 3–4 inf, 1 arty bde); 1 indep bde
SF	1 bde
Cdo	1 div; 3 bde
AB	1 div
Arty	6 gp
Avn	some gp

EQUIPMENT BY TYPE
Totals incl those held by Islamic Revolutionary Guard Corps Ground Forces. Some equipment serviceability in doubt

MBT 1,613+: ε100 Zulfiqar; 480 T-72; 150 M-60A1; 75+ T-62; 100 Chieftain Mk3/Mk5; 540 T-54/T-55/Type-59; 168 M-47/M-48

LT TK 80+: 80 Scorpion; Towsan

RECCE 35 EE-9 Cascavel

AIFV 610: 210 BMP-1; 400 BMP-2

APC 640
  APC (T) 340: 140 Boragh; 200 M-113
  APC (W) 300 BTR-50/BTR-60

ARTY 8,196+
  SP 310+: 122mm 60+: 60 2S1 Carnation; Thunder 1; 155mm 180+: 180 M-109; Thunder 2; 170mm 10 M-1978; 175mm 30 M-107; 203mm 30 M-110
  TOWED 2,010+; 105mm 130 M-101A1; 122mm 640: 540 D-30; 100 Type-54 (M-30) M-1938; 130mm 985 M-46; 152mm 30 D-20; 155mm 205: 120 GHN-45; 70 M-114; 15 Type 88 WAC-21; 203mm 20 M-115
  MRL 876+: 107mm 700+: 700 Type-63; Fadjr 1; HASEB; 122mm 157: 7 BM-11; 100 BM-21; 50 Arash/Hadid/Noor; 240mm 19: ε10 Fadjr 3; 9 M-1985; 333mm Fadjr 5
  MOR 5,000: 60mm; 81mm; 82mm; 107mm M-30; 120mm M-65

AT
  MSL • MANPATS 75 9K11 (AT-3 Sagger); 9K111 (AT-4 Spigot); 9K113 (AT-5 Spandrel); Saeqhe 1; Saeqhe 2; Toophan; some 9K111 (TOW); Toophan (TOW)
  RCL 200+: 75mm M-20; 82mm B-10; 106mm ε200 M-40; 107mm B-11
  RL 73mm RPG-7 Knout

AIRCRAFT • TPT 17 Light 16: 10 Cessna 185; 2 F-27 Friendship; 4 Turbo Commander 690 PAX 1 Falcon 20

HELICOPTERS
  ATK 50 AH-1J Cobra
  TPT 148 Heavy 20 CH-47C Chinook Light 128: 68 Bell 205A (AB-205A); 10 Bell 206 Jet Ranger (AB-206); 50 Bell 214
  MRH/Tpt 25 Mi-8 Hip (med tpt)/Mi-17 Hip H

UAV • ISR • Medium Mohajer IV Light Mohajer II/ Mohajer III

AD • SAM
  SP HQ-7 (reported); 10 Pantsyr S-1E (SA-22 Greyhound)
  MANPAD 9K36 Strela-3 (SA-14 Gremlin); 9K32 Strela-2 (SA-7 Grail)‡; Misaq (QW-1)
  GUNS 1,700
    SP 23mm ZSU-23-4; 57mm ZSU-57-2
    TOWED 14.5mm ZPU-2; ZPU-4; 23mm ZU-23; 35mm; 37mm M-1939; 57mm S-60
MSL • TACTICAL • SSM ε30 CSS-8 (175 msl); Shahin-1/ Shahin-2; Nazeat; Oghab

Iranian Revolutionary Guard Corps 125,000+

Iranian Revolutionary Guard Corps Ground Forces 100,000+

Controls Basij paramilitary forces. Lightly manned in peacetime. Primary role: internal security; secondary role: external defence, in conjunction with regular armed forces.

FORCES BY ROLE

Comd   31 (provincial) corps HQ (2 in Tehran)

Inf   Up to 15 div (Some divs are designated as
        armd or mech but all are predominantly
        infantry); some indep bde (each bde allocated
        10 bn Basij militia for ops)

AB   1 indep bde

Iranian Revolutionary Guard Corps Naval Forces 20,000+ (incl 5,000 Marines)

FORCES BY ROLE

Arty   some bty

AShM   some bty with HY-2 (CSS-C-3 *Seersucker*) AShM

EQUIPMENT BY TYPE

In addition to the vessels listed the IRGC operates a substantial number of patrol boats with a full-load displacement below 10 tonnes, including ε40 *Boghammar*-class vessels and small *Bavar*-class wing-in-ground effect air vehicles

PATROL AND COASTAL COMBATANTS 95

PBFG 40:

5 *China Cat* each with 2 twin lnchr (4 eff.) FL-10 AShM/C-701 *Kowsar* AShM

10 *Thondor* (PRC *Houdong*) each with 2 twin lnchr (4 eff.) each with C-802 (CSS-N-8 *Saccade*) AShM

25 *Peykaap II* (IPS-16 mod) each with 2 single each with C-701 *Kosar* AShM

PBF 35: 15 *Peykaap I* (IPS -16); 10 *Tir* (IPS 18); ε10 *Pashe* (MIG-G-1900)

PB ε 20 *Ghaem*

AMPHIBIOUS

LANDING SHIPS 4

2 *Hejaz* (mine-laying capacity)

2 MIG-S-5000

MSL • TACTICAL • SSM HY-2 (CSS-C-3 *Seersucker*)

FACILITIES

Bases Located at Bandar-e Abbas, Khorramshahr, Larak, Abu Musa, Al Farsiyah, Halul (oil platform), Sirri

Iranian Revolutionary Guard Corps Marines 5,000+

FORCES BY ROLE

Marine 1 bde

Iranian Revolutionary Guard Corps Air Force

Controls Iran's strategic missile force.

FORCES BY ROLE

Msl   ε1 bde *Shahab-1/2* with 12–18 launchers; ε1 bn
        with 6 launchers for *Shahab-3* strategic IRBM;
        some *Ghadr-1*; *Sajjil-2* (in devt)

EQUIPMENT BY TYPE

LAUNCHER 24: 12–18 for *Shahab-1/2* (ε200–300 msl); 6+ launchers for *Shahab-3* IRBM; some for *Ghadr-1*; *Sajjil-2* (in devt)

Navy 18,000

HQ at Bandar-e Abbas

EQUIPMENT BY TYPE

In addition to the vessels listed the Iranian Navy operates a substantial number of patrol boats with a full-load displacement below 10 tonnes.

SUBMARINES 23

TACTICAL 15

SSK 3 *Kilo* (RUS Type 877) each with 6 single 533mm TT

SSW 12: 11 *Qadir* (additional vessels in build); 1 *Nahang*

SDV 8: 5 *Al Sabehat* (SF insertion and mine-laying capacity); 3 (other)

PATROL AND COASTAL COMBATANTS 100+

CORVETTES 6

FSGM 1 *Jamaran* (UK Vosper Mk 5) with 2 twin lnchr (4 eff.) each with CSS-N-4 *Sardine* AShM, 2 lnchr with SM-1 SAM, 2 triple 324mm ASTT (6 eff.), 1 76mm gun, 1 hel landing platform (1 more under construction at Bandar-e Abbas, expected ISD 2013)

FSG 4

3 *Alvand* (UK Vosper Mk 5) each with 2 twin lnchr (4 eff.) each with CSS-N-4 *Sardine* AShM, 2 triple 324mm ASTT (6 eff.), 1 114mm gun

1 *Bayandor* (US PF-103) with 2 twin lnchr (4 eff.) each with C-802 AShM, 2 triple 324mm ASTT (6 eff.), 2 76mm gun

FS 1 *Bayandor* (US PF-103) with 2 76mm gun

PCFG 13 *Kaman* (FRA *Combattante II*) each with 1-2 twin lcnhr (2–4 eff.) each with CSS-N-4 *Sardine* AShM

PBFG ε4 Mk13 each with 2 single lnchr each with Kosar AShM

PBF 21: 3 (semi-submersible craft); 18 (various)

PB 56: 4 *China Cat*; 3 *Parvin*; 49 (various)

MINE WARFARE • MINE COUNTERMEASURES 5

MSC 3: 2 Type-292; 1 *Shahrokh* (in Caspian Sea as trg ship)

MSI 2 *Riazi* (US *Cape*)

AMPHIBIOUS

LANDING SHIPS 13

LSM 3 *Farsi* (ROK) (capacity 9 tanks; 140 troops)

LST 4 *Hengam* each with up to 1 hel (capacity 9 tanks; 225 troops)

LSL 6 *Fouque*

LANDING CRAFT 10

LCT 2

LCU 1 *Liyan 110*

UCAC 7: 6 *Wellington*; 1 *Iran*

LOGISTICS AND SUPPORT 26

AORH 3: 2 *Bandar Abbas*; 1 *Kharg*

AWT 5: 4 *Kangan*; 1 *Delvar*

AE 2 *Delvar*

AK 3 *Delvar*

AG 1 *Hamzah*

AB 12 *Hendijan* (also used for coastal patrol)

MSL • AshM C-802; *Kosar*; *Nasr*; *Ra'ad* (reported; coastal defence)

FACILITIES

Bases Located at Bandar-e Abbas, Bushehr, Kharg
Island, Bandar-e Anzelli, Bandar-e Khomeini,
Bandar-e Mahshahr, Chah Bahar, Jask

Marines 2,600

FORCES BY ROLE
Marine   2 bde

Naval Aviation 2,600

EQUIPMENT BY TYPE
AIRCRAFT 3 combat capable
  ASW 3 P-3F *Orion*
  TPT 16 **Light** 13: 5 Do-228; 4 F-27 *Friendship*; 4 *Turbo
  Commander* 680 **PAX** 3 *Falcon* 20 (ELINT)
HELICOPTERS
  ASW ε10 SH-3D *Sea King*
  MCM 3 RH-53D *Sea Stallion*
  TPT • Light 17: 5 Bell 205A (AB-205A); 2 Bell 206
  JetRanger (AB-206); 10 Bell 212 (AB-212)

Air Force 30,000 (incl 12,000 Air Defence)

FORCES BY ROLE
Serviceability probably about 60% for US ac types and about
80% for PRC/Russian ac. Includes Iranian Revolutionary
Guard Corps Air Force equipment.

Ftr   1 sqn with F-7M *Airguard*; 2 sqn with F-14
        Tomcat; 2 sqn with MiG-29A *Fulcrum A*/MiG-
        29UB *Fulcrum*

FGA   1 sqn with *Mirage* F-1E; Su-24MK *Fencer D*; 4
        sqn with F-4D/F-4E *Phantom II*; Su-25K *Frogfoot
        A*; 4 sqn with F-5E/F-5F *Tiger II*

MP   1 sqn with P-3MP *Orion**

ISR   1 (det) sqn with RF-4E *Phantom II**

Tkr/Tpt 1 sqn with B-707; B-747

Tpt   5 sqn with B-727; B-747F; C-130E *Hercules*/C-
        130H *Hercules*; F-27 *Friendship*; *Falcon* 20; Il-76
        Candid; *Iran-140*; L-1329 *Jetstar*; PC-6B *Turbo
        Porter*; *Turbo Commander* 680; Y-7; Y-12

Trg   trg units with Beech F33A *Bonanza*/Beech F33C
        Bonanza; EMB-312 *Tucano*; F-5B *Freedom Fighter*;
        JJ-7 *Mongol A**; MFI-17 *Mushshak*; PC-7 *Turbo
        Trainer*; TB-21 *Trinidad*; TB-200 *Tobago*

Hel   sqn with CH-47 *Chinook*; Bell 206A *JetRanger*
        (AB-206A); Bell-214C (AB-214C); *Shabaviz* 2-75;
        Shabaviz 2061

SAM   16 bn each with ε150 I-HAWK MIM-23B;
        5 sqn with FM-80 (*Crotale*); 30 *Rapier*; 15 *Tigercat*;
        45 S-75M *Volkhov* (SA-2 *Guideline*); 10 S-200
        Angara (SA-5 *Gammon*); FIM-92A *Stinger*; 9K32
        Strela-2 (SA-7 *Grail*)‡; 29 9K331 *Tor-M1* (SA-15
        Gauntlet) (reported)

EQUIPMENT BY TYPE
AIRCRAFT 336 combat capable
  FTR 189+: 20 F-5B *Freedom Fighter*; 60+ F-5E *Tiger II*/F-5F
  Tiger II; 24 F-7M *Airguard*; 44 F-14 *Tomcat*; 35 MiG-29A/
  UB/U *Fulcrum*; up to 6 *Azarakhsh* reported
  FGA 108: 65 F-4D *Phantom II*/F-4E *Phantom II*; 10 *Mirage*
  F-1E; 30 Su-24MK *Fencer D*; up to 3 *Saegheh* reported

  ATK 13 Su-25K/T/UBK *Frogfoot*
  ASW 5 P-3MP *Orion*
  ISR: 6+ RF-4E *Phantom II**
  TPT 116: **Heavy** 12 Il-76 *Candid* **Medium** 19 C-130E
  Hercules/C-130H *Hercules*; **Light** 75: 11 An-72; 5 An-140
  (Iran-140 *Faraz*) (45 projected); 10 F-27 *Friendship*; 1 L-1329
  Jetstar; 10 PC-6B *Turbo Porter*; 8 TB-21 *Trinidad*; 4 TB-200
  Tobago; 3 *Turbo Commander* 680; 14 Y-7; 9 Y-12; **PAX** 10: 3
  B-707; 1 B-727; 1 B-747; 4 B-747F; 1 *Falcon* 20
  TRG 169: 25 Beech F33A *Bonanza*/Beech F33C *Bonanza*; 23
  EMB-312 *Tucano*; 15 JJ-7*; 25 MFI-17 *Mushshak*; 12 *Parastu*;
  15 PC-6; 45 PC-7 *Turbo Trainer*; 9 T-33
HELICOPTERS
  MRH 30 Bell 214C (AB-214C)
  TPT 4+ Heavy 2+ CH-47 *Chinook*; Light 2+: 2 Bell 206A
  Jet Ranger (AB-206A); some *Shabaviz* 2-75 (indigenous
  versions in production); some *Shabaviz* 2061
AD • SAM 279+: FM-80 (*Crotale*); 30 *Rapier*; 15 *Tigercat*;
  150+ I-HAWK MIM-23B; 45 S-75 *Dvina* (SA-2 *Guideline*);
  10 S-200 *Angara* (SA-5 *Gammon*); 29 9K331 *Tor-M1* (SA-15
  Gauntlet) (reported)
  MANPAD FIM-92A *Stinger*; 9K32 *Strela*-2 (SA-7 *Grail*)‡
  GUNS • TOWED 23mm ZU-23; **37mm** Oerlikon
MSL
  ASM AGM-65A *Maverick*; Kh-25 (AS-10 *Karen*); Kh-29
  (AS-14 *Kedge*); C-801K (CSS-N-4 *Sardine*) AShM
  ARM Kh-58 (AS-11 *Kilter*)
  AAM • IR AAM PL-2A‡; PL-7; R-60 (AA-8 *Aphid*); R-73
  (AA-11 *Archer*): AIM-9 *Sidewinder*; **IR/SARH AAM** R-27
  (AA-10 *Alamo*) **SARH AAM** AIM-54 *Phoenix*; AIM-7
  Sparrow

Air Defence Command
A new air defence command has been established to coordinate Army, Air Force and IRGC air-defence assets

Paramilitary 40,000-60,000

Law-Enforcement Forces 40,000 – 60,000 (border and security troops); 450,000 on mobilisation (incl conscripts)
Part of armed forces in wartime
PATROL AND COASTAL COMBATANTS • PB ε 90
AIRCRAFT • TPT: 2 *Iran*-140; some Cessna 185/Cessna
310
HELICOPTERS • UTL ε24 AB-205 (Bell 205)/AB-206
(Bell 206) *Jet Ranger*

Basij Resistance Force up to ε1,000,000 on mobilisation
Paramilitary militia, with claimed membership of 12.6
million; perhaps 1 million combat capable; in the process
of closer integration with Iranian Revolutionary Guard
Corps Ground Forces.

Militia 2,500 bn (claimed, limited permanent
  membership)

DEPLOYMENT

GULF OF ADEN AND SOMALI BASIN
Navy: 1 FSG; 1 AORH

SUDAN

UN • UNMIS 2 obs

Iraq IRQ

Iraqi Dinar D		2009	2010	2011
GDP	D	77.0tr	98.4tr	
	US$	65.2bn	84.3bn	
per capita	US$	2,071	2,679	
Growth	%	4.2		
Inflation	%	-2.8	5.1	
Def bdgt[a]	D	4.84tr	5.72tr	
	US$	4.1bn	4.9bn	
US$1=D		1180.80	1167.92	

Population   31,466,698

Ethnic and religious groups: Arab 75–80% (of which Shi'a Muslim 55%, Sunni Muslim 45%) Kurdish 20–25%

Age	0–14	15–19	20–24	25–29	30–64	65 plus
Male	19.4%	5.2%	4.9%	4.6%	15.2%	1.4%
Female	18.7%	5.1%	4.8%	4.4%	14.8%	1.6%

Capabilities

ACTIVE 245,782 (Army 238,010 Navy 2,605 Air 5,167) Ministry of Interior 413,613

ORGANISATIONS BY SERVICE

Military Forces

Figures for Iraqi security forces reflect ongoing changes in organisation and manpower.

Army ε238,010 (incl trg + spt)

FORCES BY ROLE

Armd   1 div with (3 armd bde, 1 lt mech bde)

Mot Inf 8 div (each: 4 mot inf bde); 2 div (each: 3 mot inf bde); 2 (Presidential) bde; 1 (Baghdad) indep bde

Inf   1 div with (1 mech inf bde, 2 inf bde, 1 air mob inf bde); 1 div with (3 inf bde)

Lt Inf   1 div with (4 lt inf bde)

SOF   2 bde

EQUIPMENT BY TYPE

MBT 212: 77+ T-72; 72 T-55; 63 M1-A1 *Abrams*

RECCE 478: 35 EE-9 *Cascavel*; 18 BRDM 2; 425 LAV *Cougar*

AIFV 434 BMP-1

APC 1,479

  APC (T) 383: 100 FV 103 *Spartan*; 233 M-113 A1; 50 M-113A2

  APC (W) 698: 98 BTR-80; 600 *DZIK-3*

ARTY • **MOR** M-252

Navy ε2,605

Iraqi Coastal Defence Force (ICDF)

EQUIPMENT BY TYPE

PATROL AND COASTAL COMBATANTS 38+:
  PCC 4 *Saettia* (ITA *Diciotti*)
  PB 11: 5 *Predator* (PRC-27m); 2 Type-200; 4 Type-2010

FACILITIES

Base Located at Umm Qasr

Iraqi Air Force ε5,167

FORCES BY ROLE

ISR   1 sqn with SB7 L -360 *Seeker* located at Basra; 1 sqn with SB7L-360 *Seeker* (infrastructure patrols); Cessna 208B *Grand Caravan* located at Kirkuk

Tpt   1 sqn with C-130E *Hercules*; Beech 350 *King Air* (VIP tpt/trainer) located at New al-Muthanna

Tpt Hel 4 sqn with Bell 205 (UH-1H *Huey* II); Bell 206-B3 *Jet Ranger*; Mi-17 *Hip H*; PZL W-3W *Sokol* located at Taji

FACILITIES

Trg school   1 with Cessna 172 located at Kirkuk

EQUIPMENT BY TYPE

AIRCRAFT 6 combat capable
  ISR 8: 6 Cessna AC-208B *Combat Caravan**; 2 SB7L-360 *Seeker*
  TPT 22: **Medium** 3 C-130E *Hercules*; **Light** 19: 6 Beech 350 *King Air*; 8 Cessna 172; 5 Comp Air 7SL
  TRG 26: 8 CH-2000 *Sama*; 3 *Lasta*-95; 15T-6A
HELICOPTERS
  MRH 32+: 26 Mi-17 *Hip H*; 2 PZL W-3WA *Sokol*; 4+ SA-342 *Gazelle*
  ISR 10 OH-58 *Kiowa*
  TPT 36: **Medium** 8 Mi-171Sh **Light** 38: 16 Bell 205 (UH-1H *Huey* II); 10 Bell 206-B3 *Jet Ranger*; 2 PZL W-3 *Sokol*
MSL
  ASM AGM-114 *Hellfire*

Ministry of Interior Forces ε413,613 (incl Civil Intervention Force, Emergency Response Unit, Border Enforcement (40,205) and Dignitary Protection)

Iraqi Police Service ε298,540 (incl Highway Patrol)

National Police ε43,511

FOREIGN FORCES

Australia 35; 1 sy det with ASLAV • UNAMI 2 obs
Bulgaria NTM-I 2
Denmark 23 (sy forces) • NTM-I 6 • UNAMI 2 obs
Estonia NTM-I 2
Fiji UNAMI 221; 3 sy unit

Hungary NTM-I 3
Italy NTM-I 84
Jordan UNAMI 2 obs
Lithuania NTM-I 2
Nepal UNAMI 1 obs
Netherlands NTM-I 7
New Zealand UNAMI 1 obs
Poland NTM-I 3
Romania NTM-I 3
Turkey NTM-I 2
Ukraine NTM-I 9
United Kingdom 75; 1 Navy Transition Team (training the Iraqi Riverine Patrol Service (IRPS)) • NTM-I 15 • UNAMI 1 obs
United States *Operation New Dawn* 49,775; 1 corps HQ; 3 div HQ; 3 armd HBCT (AAB); 1 armd HBCT HQ (AAB); 1 armd cav regt (AAB); 1 mech inf SBCT (AAB); 1 lt inf IBCT (AAB); 1 ARNG lt inf IBCT (LoC duties); some M1 *Abrams*; some M2/M3 *Bradley*; some *Stryker*; some M109; some M198; 9,341 MRAP; some AH-64 *Apache*; some OH-58 *Kiowa*; some UH-60 *Black Hawk*; some CH-47 *Chinook*; some F-16D *Fighting Falcon*; some A-10 *Thunderbolt II*; some C-130 *Hercules*; some C-17 *Globemaster*; Some HH-60G *Pave Hawk*; some RQ-1B *Predator* • NTM-I 12 • UNAMI 4 obs

Israel ISR

New Israeli Shekel NS		2009	2010	2011
GDP	NS	768bn	825bn	
	US$	196bn	219bn	
per capita	US$	26,298	30,126	
Growth	%	0.7	-3.4	
Inflation	%	3.3	2.3	
Def exp	NS	53.1bn		
	US$	13.5bn		
Def bdgt	NS	58.4bn	58.8bn	54.1bn
	US$	14.9bn	15.6bn	
FMA (US)	US$	2.55bn	2.78bn	3.0bn
US$1=NS		3.93	3.76	

Population	7,285,033					
Age	0–14	15–19	20–24	25–29	30–64	65 plus
Male	14.1%	4.1%	4.0%	3.8%	19.7%	4.4%
Female	13.5%	3.9%	3.8%	3.7%	19.3%	5.7%

Capabilities

ACTIVE 176,500 (Army 133,000 Navy 9,500 Air 34,000) **Paramilitary 8,050**

RESERVE 565,000 (Army 500,000 Navy 10,000 Air 55,000)
Terms of service officers 48 months, other ranks 36 months, women 24 months (Jews and Druze only; Christians, Circassians and Muslims may volunteer). Annual trg as cbt reservists to age 41 (some specialists to age 54) for men, 24 (or marriage) for women

ORGANISATIONS BY SERVICE

Strategic Forces
Israel is widely believed to have a nuclear capability – delivery means include ac, *Jericho* 1 and *Jericho* 2 (IRBM and SRBM)
MSL • STRATEGIC
  IRBM: *Jericho* 2
  SRBM: *Jericho* 1
WARHEADS up to 200 nuclear warheads

Strategic Defences
17 batteries MIM-23B Improved HAWK
6 batteries MIM-104 *Patriot*
3 batteries (24 launchers) *Arrow/Arrow* 2 ATBM with *Green Pine* radar and *Citrus Tree* command post. Launchers sited Hadera and Palmachim (N and C Israel)
1 US EUCOM AN/TPY-2 X-band radar at Nevatim, SE of Beersheba

Army 26,000; 107,000 conscript; 500,000+ on mobilisation; (total 133,000–633,000)
Organisation and structure of formations may vary according to op situations. Equipment includes that required for reserve forces on mobilisation.

FORCES BY ROLE
3 regional commands each with 2 regular div; 1–2 regional/territorial div; 2 regular bde

Armd	2 div; 15 bde
Inf	4 div; 12 bde
Para	8 bde
Arty	4 regt
SP arty	8 regt

EQUIPMENT BY TYPE
MBT 3,501: 441 *Merkava* Mk1; 455 *Merkava* MkII; 454 *Merkava* MkIII; 175 *Merkava* MkIV; 111 *Magach-7*; 261 Ti-67 (T-55 mod); 711 M-60/M-60A1/M-60A3; 206 *Centurion*; 126 T-54/T-55/T-62S; 561 M-48A5
RECCE 408: ε400 RBY-1 RAMTA; ε8 Tpz-1 *Fuchs*
APC 10,484+
  APC (T) 10,418+: up to 45 *Namer*; 276 *Achzarit* (modified T-55 chassis); 6,131 M-113A1/M-113A2; 180 M-2 (some in store); 3,386 M-3 half-track (some in store); ε400 *Nagmachon* (*Centurion* chassis); *Nakpadon*
  APC (W) 46: 34 BTR-152; 6 BTR-40; 6 *Puma* (*Centurion*)
ARTY 5,432
  SP 620: **155mm** 548: 148 L-33; 350 M-109A1; 50 M-50; **175mm** 36 M-107; **203mm** 36 M-110
  TOWED 456: **105mm** 70 M-101A1; **122mm** 5 D-30; **130mm** 100 M-46; **155mm** 281: 50 M-114A1 in reserve; 100 M-46; 50 M-68/M-71; 81 M-839P/M-845P
  MRL 224: **122mm** 58 BM-21; **160mm** 50 LAR-160; **227mm** 60 MLRS; **240mm** 36 BM-24; **290mm** 20 LAR-290

MOR 4,132: **52mm** 2,000; **81mm** 1,358; **120mm** 652 (towed); **160mm** 122: 104 M-43 in reserve; 18 M-66 *Soltam*

AT

MSL • MANPATS 1,225+: 900 M47 *Dragon*; 9K11 (AT-3 *Sagger*); 25 IMI MAPATS; *Gil/Spike*; 300 TOW-2A/TOW-2B (incl *Ramta* (M-113) SP)

RCL 106mm 250 M-40A1

RL 82mm B-300

AD • SAM 1,270

SP 20 *Machbet*

MANPAD 1,250: 1,000 FIM-43 *Redeye*; 250 FIM-92A *Stinger*

RADAR • LAND AN/PPS-15 (arty); AN/TPQ-37 *Firefinder* (arty); EL/M-2140 (veh)

MSL 107

STRATEGIC ε100 *Jericho* 1 SRBM/*Jericho* 2 IRBM

TACTICAL • SSM (7 *Lance* in store)

Navy 7,000; 2,500 conscript; 10,000 on mobilisation (total 9,500–19,500)

EQUIPMENT BY TYPE

SUBMARINES • TACTICAL • SSK 3 *Dolphin* (GER Type-212 variant) each with 6 single 533mm TT each with UGM-84C *Harpoon* AShM/HWT, 4 single 650mm TT

PATROL AND COASTAL COMBATANTS 57

CORVETTES • FSGHM 3

3 *Eilat* (*Sa'ar* 5) each with 2 quad Mk140 lnchr (8 eff.) each with RGM-84C *Harpoon* AShM, 2 32 cell VLS (64 eff.) each with *Barak* SAM, 2 triple 324mm TT (6 eff.) each with Mk 46 LWT, 1 76mm gun, (capacity either 1 AS-565SA *Panther* ASW hel or 1 AS-366G *Dauphin II* SAR hel)

PCGM 8 *Hetz* (*Sa'ar* 4.5) each with 6 single lnchr each with GII *Gabriel II* AShM, 2 twin Mk140 lnchr (4 eff.) each with RGM-84C *Harpoon* AShM, 1 16-32 Cell Mk56 VLS (16-32 eff.) with *Barak* SAM, 1 76mm gun

PCG 2 *Reshef* (*Sa'ar* 4) each with 4–6 single lnchr each with GII *Gabriel II* AShM, 1 twin Mk140 lnchr (2 eff.) with RGM-84C *Harpoon* AShM, 1 76mm gun

PBFT 13 *Super Dvora* MKI and II each with 2 single 324mm TT each with Mk 46 LWT (SSM may also be fitted)

PBT 15 *Dabur* each with 2 single 324mm TT each with Mk 46 LWT

PBF 16: 5 *Shaldag*; 3 *Stingray*; 8 *Super Dvora* MK III (SSM & TT may be fitted)

AMPHIBIOUS • LANDING CRAFT • LCT 1 *Ashdod*

LOGISTICS AND SUPPORT 3

AG 2 (ex German Type T45)

TRG 1

FACILITIES

Bases Located at Haifa, Atlit (Naval Commandos), Eilat, Ashdod

Naval Aviation

AC • TPT • *Medium* 2 C-130 *Hercules*

HELICOPTERS

ASW 7 AS-565SA *Panther*

SAR 2 SA-366G *Dauphin II*

TPT • Light 17 Bell 212

Naval Commandos ε300

Air Force 34,000

Responsible for Air and Space Coordination

FORCES BY ROLE

Ftr/FGA	2 sqn with F-15A/F-15B *Eagle*; F-15C/F-15D *Eagle*; 1 sqn with F-15I *Ra'am*; 8 sqn with F-16A/F-16B *Fighting Falcon*; F-16C/F-16D *Fighting Falcon*; 4 sqn with F-16I *Sufa*; (3 sqn with A-4N *Skyhawk*/F-4 *Phantom II*/*Kfir* C-7 in reserve)
ASW	Some sqn with AS-565SA *Panther* (missions flown by IAF but with non-rated aircrew)
MP	1 sqn with IAI-1124 *Seascan*
EW	Some sqn with RC-12D *Guardrail*; Beech 200CT *King Air*; EC-130H *Hercules* (ELINT); Do-28; EC/RC-707 (ELINT/ECM) (being replaced by Gulfstream G550 *Shavit*); IAI-202 *Arava*
AEW&C	1 sqn with B-707 *Phalcon* (being replaced with Gulfstream G550 *Eitam*)
Tkr/Tpt	1 sqn with KC-707
Tkr	1 sqn with KC-130H *Hercules*
Tpt	1 sqn with DC-3 (C-47 *Skytrain*); 1 (liaison) sqn with BN-2 *Islander*; Beech 80 *Queen Air*; Cessna U206 *Stationair*
Trg	Some units with Beech 80 *Queen Air*; G-Grob 120; T-6A (replacing CM-170 *Magister*); TA-4H *Skyhawk*; TA-4J *Skyhawk*
Atk Hel	4 sqn with AH-1E *Cobra*; AH-1F *Cobra*; AH-64A *Apache*; AH-64D *Apache*
Tpt Hel	6 sqn with Bell 206 *Jet Ranger*; Bell 212; CH-53D *Sea Stallion*; S-70A *Black Hawk*; UH-60A *Black Hawk*; UH-60L *Black Hawk*
ISR UAV	1 sqn with *Firebee*; *Harpy*; *Hermes* 450; *Heron* TP (*Eitan*); *Heron* (*Shoval*); RQ-5A *Hunter*; *Samson*; *Scout*; *Searcher* I/II
AD	2 bty each with 9 *Arrow* II; 17 bty with MIM-23 *HAWK*; 5 bty with MIM-104 *Patriot*; 35 M-163 *Vulcan* 3 bty each with 16 PAC-2

EQUIPMENT BY TYPE

AIRCRAFT 460 combat capable

FTR 168: 27 F-15A *Eagle*; 7 F-15B *Eagle*; 17 F-15C *Eagle*; 11 F-15D *Eagle*; 90 F-16A *Fighting Falcon*; 16 F-16B *Fighting Falcon*

FGA 227: 25 F-15I *Ra'am*; 52 F-16C *Fighting Falcon*; 49 F-16D *Fighting Falcon*; 101 F-16I *Sufa*

ATK 65: 39 A-4N *Skyhawk*;10 TA-4H *Skyhawk*; 16 TA-4J *Skyhawk*

FTR/FGA/ATK (200+ A-4N *Skyhawk*/F-4 *Phantom II*/*Kfir* C-7 in reserve)

MP 3 IAI-1124 *Seascan*

ISR 6 RC-12D *Guardrail*

ELINT 5: 3 EC/RC-707 (ELINT/ECM); 2 EC-130H *Hercules*;3 Gulfstream G550 *Shavit*;

AEW 4: 3 B-707 *Phalcon*; 1 Gulfstream G550 *Eitam* (2 more on order)

TKR/TPT 9:5 KC-130H *Hercules*; 4 KC-707

TPT 77: **Medium** 5 C-130 *Hercules*; **Light** 72: 2 BN-2 *Islander*; 12 Beech 80 *Queen Air*; 4 Beech 200CT *King Air*;

22 Beech A36 *Bonanza* (*Hofit*); 1 DC-3 (*C-47 Skytrain*); 9 IAI-202 *Arava*; 22 TB-21 *Trinidad* (*Pashosh*)
TRG 37: 17 Grob G-120; 20 T-6A
HELICOPTERS
ATK 81: 33 AH-1E/AH-1F *Cobra*; 30 AH-64A *Apache*; 18 *Sarat* (AH-64D *Apache*)
ASW 7 AS-565SA *Panther* (missions flown by IAF but with non-rated aircrew)
TPT 200 **Heavy** 38 CH-53D *Sea Stallion* **Medium** 73: 49 S-70A *Black Hawk*; 10 UH-60A *Black Hawk*; 14 UH-60L *Black Hawk* **Light** 89: 34 Bell 206 *JetRanger*; 55 Bell 212;
UAV • ISR 26+ **Heavy** 4+: *Hermes 450*; *Heron* (*Shoval*); 4 *Heron TP* (*Eitan*); RQ-5A *Hunter* **Medium** 22 *Searcher* MkII (22+ in store) **Light** *Harpy*
AD
SAM • TOWED 48+: Some MIM-104 *Patriot*; Some MIM-23 HAWK; 48 PAC-2
GUNS 920
SP 165 **20mm** 105 M-163 Machbet *Vulcan*; **23mm** 60 ZSU-23-4
TOWED 755 **23mm** 150 ZU-23; **20mm/37mm** 455 M-167 *Vulcan* towed 20mm/M-1939 towed 37mm/TCM-20 towed 20mm; **40mm** 150 L/70
MSL
ASM AGM-114 *Hellfire*; AGM-62B *Walleye*; AGM-65 *Maverick*; Popeye I/Popeye II; *Delilah* AL
AAM • IR AAM AIM-9 *Sidewinder*; *Python* 4 **IIR AAM** *Python* 5 **ARH AAM** *Derby*; AIM-120A/C AMRAAM
BOMB • PGM • JDAM GBU-31; *Spice, Lizard, Opher, Griffon*

Airfield Defence 3,000 active; 15,000 reservists (total 18,000)

Regional/Territorial Forces
Can be mobilised in 72hrs
Inf 11 (territorial/regional) bde

Reserve Organisations
Reserves ε380,000 reservists
Armd   8 div (total: 15 armd bde, 6 arty regt, 4 inf bde, 6 mech inf bde)
Air Mob 1 div (3 air mob bde, 1 para bde)

Paramilitary ε8,000

Border Police ε8,000

DEPLOYMENT

TURKEY
Air Force up to 1 ftr det (occasional) located at Akinci, TUR, with F-16 *Fighting Falcon* (current status uncertain)

FOREIGN FORCES
UNTSO unless specified. Figures represent total numbers for mission in Israel, Syria & Lebanon
Argentina 5 obs
Australia 11 obs
Austria 7 obs

Belgium 2 obs
Canada 8 obs • 9 (*Operation Proteus*) USSC
Chile 3 obs
China 5 obs
Denmark 10 obs
Estonia 1 obs
Finland 14 obs
France 2 obs
Ireland 12 obs
Italy 7 obs
Nepal 4 obs
Netherlands 12 obs
New Zealand 7 obs
Norway 13 obs
Russia 5 obs
Slovakia 2 obs
Slovenia 2 obs
Sweden 5 obs
Switzerland 13 obs
United States 2 obs • US European Command; 1 AN/TPY-2 X-band radar at Nevatim

Jordan JOR

Jordanian Dinar D		2009	2010	2011
GDP	D	17.8bn	19.3bn	
	US$	25.3bn	27.5bn	
per capita	US$	4,251	4,249	
Growth	%	2.8	3.9	
Inflation	%	-0.7	5.5	
Def exp	D	981m		
	US$	1.39bn		
Def bdgt	D	1.64bn	1.77bn	
	US$	2.33bn	2.53bn	
FMA (US)	US$	335m	300m	300m
US$1=D		0.70	0.70	

Population   6,472,392
Ethnic groups: Palestinian ε50–60%

Age	0–14	15–19	20–24	25–29	30–64	65 plus
Male	18.1%	5.5%	4.9%	4.3%	15.6%	2.4%
Female	17.1%	5.2%	4.6%	4.2%	15.5%	2.5%

Capabilities

ACTIVE 100,500 (Army 88,000 Navy 500 Air 12,000)
Paramilitary 10,000

RESERVE 65,000 (Army 60,000 Joint 5,000)

ORGANISATIONS BY SERVICE

Army 88,000
Jordan has reorganised from a divisional structure to 4 commands, a strategic reserve and a special operations

command. The strategic reserve still has a divisional structure and special operations command is responsible for counter terrorism and unconventional operations. The Royal Guard also comes under this command.

FORCES BY ROLE

Armd   1 comd (Southern) (1 armd bde, 1 inf bde); 1 div (strategic reserve) (3 armd, 1 arty, 1 AD bde)

Mech   1 comd (Northern) (2 mech bde, 1 inf bde, 1 arty bde, 1 AD bde,); 1 comd (Eastern) (2 mech bde, 1 AD bde, 1 arty bde); 1 comd (Central) (1 mech bde, 1 lt inf bde, 1 AD bde, 1 arty bde)

Spec Ops 1 bde (2 ab bn, 1 ab arty bn, 1 psyops unit; 2 SF bn)

EQUIPMENT BY TYPE

MBT 1,044: 390 CR1 *Challenger 1* (*Al Hussein*); 274 FV4030/2 *Khalid*; 88 M-60 *Phoenix*; 292 *Tariq* (*Centurion* in store); (115 M-60A1/M-60A3 in store); (23 M-47/M-48A5 in store)
LT TK (39 *Scorpion* used as recce; in store)
RECCE 103 *Scimitar*
AIFV 303: 31 BMP-2; 259 *Ratel*-20; 13 YPR-765
APC • APC (T) 1,391: 1,072 M-113A1; 276 M-113A2 MK-1J; 3 YPR-765; 40 *Spartan*
ARTY 1,232
   SP 359: **105mm** 4 M-52; **155mm** 273: 253 M-109A1/M-109A2; 20 M-44; **203mm** 82 M-110A2
   TOWED 94: **105mm** 54: 36 M-102; 18 MOBAT; **155mm** 36: 18 M-1/M-59; 18 M-114; **203mm** 4 M-115
   MOR 779:
   SP 81mm 130
   TOWED 649: **81mm** 359; **107mm** 60 M-30; **120mm** 230 Brandt
AT • MSL 765
   SP 115: 70 M-901; 45 YPR-765 with *Milan*
   MANPATS 650: 30 *Javelin* (110 msl); 310 M47 *Dragon*; 310 TOW/TOW-2A
   RL 4,800+: **73mm** RPG-26; **94mm** 2,500 LAW-80; **112mm** 2,300 APILAS
AD
   SAM 942
   SP 152: 92 9K35 *Strela*-10 (SA-13 *Gopher*); 60 9K33 *Osa*-M (SA-8 *Gecko*)
   MANPAD 790: 250 FIM-43 *Redeye*; 9K32M *Strela*-2M (SA-7B2 *Grail*); 300 9K36 *Strela*-3 (SA-14 *Gremlin*); 240 9K310 *Igla*-1 (SA-16 *Gimlet*)
   GUNS • SP 395: **20mm** 139 M-163 *Vulcan*; **23mm** 40 ZSU-23-4; **40mm** 216 M-42 (not all op)
RADAR • LAND 7 AN/TPQ-36 *Firefinder*/AN/TPQ-37 *Firefinder* (arty, mor)

Navy ε500

EQUIPMENT BY TYPE
PATROL AND COASTAL COMBATANTS 7
   PB 3 *Al Hussein* (UK Vosper 30m); 4 *Abdullah* (US *Dauntless*)

FACILITIES
Bases Located at Aqaba

Air Force 12,000

Flying hours   180 hrs/year

FORCES BY ROLE

Ftr   1 sqn with F-16A/B *Fighting Falcon*; 1 sqn with *Mirage* F-1C (F-1CJ)/*Mirage* F-1BJ(F-1BJ)

FGA/ISR   3 sqn with F-5E *Tiger II*/F-5F *Tiger II*; 1 sqn with F-16AM/BM *Fighting Falcon*; 1 sqn with *Mirage* F-1E (F-1EJ)

ISR   Some sqn with RU-38A *Twin Condor*

Tpt   1 sqn with C-130H *Hercules*; C-212A *Aviocar*; CL-604 *Challenger*; CN-235; TB-20 *Trinidad*; 1 (Royal) flt with A-340-211; Gulfstream IV; L-1011 *Tristar*; S-70A *Black Hawk*

Trg   3 sqn with *Bulldog* 103 (being replaced by T-67M *Firefly*); C-101 *Aviojet*; Hughes 500D

Atk Hel   2 sqn with AH-1F *Cobra* with TOW

Tpt Hel   2 sqn with AS-332M *Super Puma*; Bell 205 (UH-1H *Iroquois*); Bo-105 (operated on behalf of the police); EC-635 (Tpt/SAR); 1 sqn (dedicated to SF)

ISR UAV   1 unit with *Seeker* SB7L

AD   1 comd (5–6 bty with PAC-2 *Patriot*; 5 bty with I-HAWK MIM-2BB Phase III; 6 bty with *Skyguard*/*Aspide*)

EQUIPMENT BY TYPE

AIRCRAFT 102 combat capable
   FTR 49: 25 F-5E *Tiger II*/F-5F *Tiger II*; 20 F-16A *Fighting Falcon*; 4 F-16B *Fighting Falcon*
   FGA 53: 8 F-16AM *Fighting Falcon*; 4 F-16BM *Fighting Falcon*; 11 F-16C/D *Fighting Falcon*; 15 *Mirage* F-1C (F-1CJ)/*Mirage* F-1B (F-1BJ); 15 *Mirage* F-1EJ (F-1E)
   ISR 2 RU-38A *Twin Condor*
   TPT 20 **Heavy** 2 Il-76 *Candid*; **Medium** 4 C-130H *Hercules*; **Light** 10: 2 C-212A *Aviocar*; 2 C-295; 2 CL-604 *Challenger*; 2 CN-235; 2 TB-20 *Trinidad* **PAX** 4: 1 A-340-211; 2 Gulfstream IV; 1 L-1011 *Tristar*
   TRG 25 15 *Bulldog* 103 (being replaced by 16 T-67M *Firefly*); 10 C-101 *Aviojet*
HELICOPTERS
   ATK 25 AH-1F *Cobra* (TOW)
   MRH 13 EC-635 (Tpt/SAR)
   TPT 78 **Medium** 26: 12 AS-332M *Super Puma*; 14 S-70A *Black Hawk* **Light** 52: 36 Bell 205 (UH-1H *Iroquois*); 5 BK-117; 3 Bo-105 (operated on behalf of the police); 8 Hughes 500D
UAV • ISR • Heavy 6 *Seeker* SB7L
AD • SAM 80+: 24 I-HAWK MIM-23B Phase III; 40 PAC-2 *Patriot*
MSL
   ASM AGM-65D *Maverick*
   AAM • IR AAM AIM-9 *Sidewinder*; R-550 *Magic*; **SARH AAM** AIM-7 *Sparrow*; R530; **ARH AAM** AIM-120C AMRAAM

Paramilitary 10,000 active

Public Security Directorate ε10,000 active
Ministry of Interior

FORCES BY ROLE
Sy   1

EQUIPMENT BY TYPE

LT TK: *Scorpion*

APC (W) 55+: 25+ EE-11 *Urutu*; 30 FV603 *Saracen*

Reserve Organisations 60,000 reservists

Armd   1 (Royal) div (1 arty bde, 1 AD bde,
3 armd bde)

Civil Militia 'People's Army' ε35,000 reservists

Men 16–65, women 16–45

DEPLOYMENT

CÔTE D'IVOIRE

UN • UNOCI 1,062; 7 obs ; 1 inf bn ; 1 SF coy

DEMOCRATIC REPUBLIC OF THE CONGO

UN • MONUSCO 218; 25 obs; 1 SF coy; 1 fd hospital

HAITI

UN • MINUSTAH 611; 1 inf bn

IRAQ

UN • UNAMI 2 obs

LIBERIA

UN • UNMIL 120; 4 obs; 1 fd hospital

NEPAL

UN • UNMIN 4 obs

SUDAN

UN • UNAMID 7; 5 obs

UN • UNMIS 6; 10 obs

WESTERN SAHARA

UN • MINURSO 1 obs

Kuwait KWT

Kuwaiti Dinar D		2009	2010	2011
GDP	D	28.2bn	33.7bn	
	US$	98.1bn	117bn	
per capita	US$	35,120	38,359	
Growth	%	-1.2	2.3	
Inflation	%	4.0	4.1	
Def exp	D	1.2bn		
	US$	4.18bn		
Def bdgt	D	1.1bn		1.21bn
	US$	3.81bn	3.91bn	
US$1=D		0.29	0.29	

Population   **3,050,744**

Ethnic groups: Nationals 35%; other Arab 35%; South Asian 9%; Iranian 4%; other 17%

Age	0–14	15–19	20–24	25–29	30–64	65 plus
Male	13.2%	3.6%	6.6%	10.4%	25.0%	1.9%
Female	12.7%	3.8%	5.2%	5.7%	10.7%	1.2%

Capabilities

ACTIVE 15,500 (Army 11,000 Navy 2,000 Air 2,500)

Paramilitary 7,100

Terms of service voluntary

RESERVE 23,700 (Joint 23,700)

Terms of service obligation to age 40; 1 month annual trg

ORGANISATIONS BY SERVICE

Army 11,000

FORCES BY ROLE

Army	1 (reserve) bde
Armd	3 bde
Mech/Recce	1 bde
Mech Inf	2 bde
SF	1 unit (forming)
Cdo	1 bn
Arty	1 bde
Engr	1 bde
Gd	1 (Amiri) bde
AD	1 comd (AD bty, 4 (HAWK Phase III), AD bty, 5 (*Patriot* PAC-2) AD bty, 6 (*Amoun* (*Skyguard/Aspide*)) AD bty)

EQUIPMENT BY TYPE

MBT 293: 218 M1-A2 *Abrams*; 75 M-84 (75 in store)

AIFV up to 450: up to 76 BMP-2; up to 120 BMP-3; 254 *Desert Warrior* (incl variants)

APC 321

    APC (T) 270: 230 M-113A2; 40 M-577

    APC (W) 11: 11 TPz-1 *Fuchs*; (40 TH 390 *Fahd* in store)

ARTY 218

    SP 155mm 95: 23 M-109A3; 18 (AMX) Mk F3; 54 PLZ45; (18 AU-F-1 in store)

    MRL 300mm 27 9A52 *Smerch*

    MOR 78: **81mm** 60; **107mm** 6 M-30; **120mm** ε12 RT-F1

AT • MSL 118+

    SP 74: 66 HMMWV TOW; 8 M-901

    MANPATS 44+: 44 TOW-2; M47 *Dragon*

    RCL 84mm ε200 *Carl Gustav*

AD • SAM 60+

    STATIC/SHELTER 12 *Aspide*

    MANPAD 48 *Starburst*; *Stinger*

    GUNS • TOWED 35mm 12+ Oerlikon

Navy ε2,000 (incl 500 Coast Guard)

EQUIPMENT BY TYPE

PATROL AND COASTAL COMBATANTS 10

    PCFG 2:

        1 *Al Sanbouk* (GER Lurssen TNC-45) with 2 twin lnchr (4 eff.) each with MM-40 *Exocet* AShM, 1 76mm gun

        1 *Istiqlal* (GER Lurssen FPB-57) with 2 twin lnchr (4 eff.) each with MM-40 *Exocet* AShM, 1 76mm gun

    PBG 8:

        8 *Um Almaradim* (FRA P-37 BRL) each with 2 twin lnchr (4 eff.) each with *Sea Skua* AShM, 1 sextuple lnchr (lnchr only)

LOGISTICS AND SUPPORT • SPT 1 *Sawahil*

FACILITIES

Base   Located at Ras al Qalaya

Air Force 2,500

Flying hours   210 hrs/year

FORCES BY ROLE

Ftr/FGA	2 sqn with F/A-18C/18D *Hornet*
Tpt	2 sqn with AS-332 *Super Puma* (Atk/Tpt/SAR); B-737; DC-9; L-100-30; SA-330 *Puma*
Trg	1 unit with EMB-312 *Tucano* (*Tucano* Mk52); *Hawk* Mk64*
Atk Hel	1 sqn with AH-64D *Apache*
Atk Hel/Trg Hel	1 sqn with SA-342 *Gazelle* with HOT
AD	1 comd (5–6 SAM bty with PAC-2 *Patriot*; 5 SAM bty with MIM-23B *I HAWK Phase III*; 6 SAM bty with *Skyguard/Aspide*)

EQUIPMENT BY TYPE

AIRCRAFT 50 combat capable

  FGA 39: 31 F/A-18C *Hornet*; 8 F/A-18D *Hornet*

  TPT 5 **Medium** 3 L-100-30 **PAX** 2: 1 B-737-200; 1 DC-9;

  TRG 19: 11 *Hawk* Mk64*; 8 EMB-312 *Tucano* (*Tucano* Mk52)*

HELICOPTERS

  ATK 12 AH-64D *Apache*

  MRH 13 SA-342 *Gazelle* with HOT

  TPT 10 **Medium** 5 AS-332 *Super Puma* (Atk/Tpt/SAR); 5 SA-330 *Puma*

MSL

  ASM AGM-65G *Maverick*; AGM-84A *Harpoon*; AGM-114K *Hellfire*

  AAM • IR AAM AIM-9 *Sidewinder*; R-550 *Magic*

  SARH AAM AIM-7F *Sparrow*

SAM 40 PAC-2 *Patriot*; 24 MIM-23B *I HAWK Phase III*; 12 *Skyguard/Aspide*

Paramilitary ε7,100 active

National Guard ε6,600 active

FORCES BY ROLE

Armd	1 (armd car) bn
SF	1 bn
Paramilitary	3 (national guard) bn
MP	1 bn

EQUIPMENT BY TYPE

RECCE 20 VBL

APC (W) 92: 70 *Pandur*; 22 S600 (incl variants)

Coast Guard 500

PATROL AND COASTAL COMBATANTS 32

  PBF 12 *Manta*

  PB 20: 3 *Al Shaheed*; 4 *Inttisar* (Austal 31.5m); 3 *Kassir* (Austal 22m); 10 *Subahi*

AMPHIBIOUS • CRAFT 4 LCU

LOGISTICS AND SUPPORT • SPT 1 *Sawahil*

FOREIGN FORCES

United Kingdom Army 35

United States United States Central Command: 2 AD bty with total of 16 PAC-3 *Patriot*; elm 1 (APS) HBCT eqpt. set (equipment in use). Remaining US log installations and units supporting US troops in Iraq.

Lebanon LBN

Lebanese Pound LP		2009	2010	2011
GDP	LP	52.1tr	59.0tr	
	US$	34.5bn	39.4bn	
per capita	US$	8,175	9,253	
Growth	%	8.0	6.0	
Inflation	%	3.4	5.0	
Def exp	LP	2.15tr		
	US$	1.43bn		
Def bdgt	LP	1.52tr	1.74tr	
	US$	1.01bn	1.16bn	
FMA (US)	US$	90m	100m	100m
US$1=LP		1507.50	1499.22	

Population   4,254,583

Ethnic and religious groups: Christian 30%; Druze 6%; Armenian 4%, excl ε300,000 Syrians and ε350,000 Palestinian refugees

Age	0–14	15–19	20–24	25–29	30–64	65 plus
Male	11.8%	4.6%	4.8%	4.5%	19.2%	4.2%
Female	11.2%	4.4%	4.6%	4.4%	21.5%	4.8%

Capabilities

ACTIVE 59,100 (Army 57,000 Navy 1,100 Air 1,000)

Paramilitary 20,000

The usual number of Lebanese troops in peacetime is around 59,100. This can increase to 291,735 if conscripts are recalled.

ORGANISATIONS BY SERVICE

Army 57,000

FORCES BY ROLE

Region	5 comd (Beirut, Bekaa Valley, Mount Lebanon, North, South)
Armd	2 regt
Mech inf	5 bde
Mot Inf	6 bde
Mne cdo	1 regt
SF	5 regt
Cdo	1 regt
AB	1 regt
Arty	2 regt
Security	5 intervention, 2 border sy regt
Presidential Guard	1 bde

MP	1 indep bde
Engr	1 indep regt
Logistics	1 indep bde
Medical	1 indep regt

EQUIPMENT BY TYPE
MBT 326: 233 T-54/T-55; 93 M-48A1/M-48A5
RECCE 54 AML
APC 1,240
  APC (T) 1,164 M-113A1/M-113A2
  APC (W) 76: 1 M-3VTT; 75 VAB VCT
LT VEH 379 M998 HMMVW
ARTY 492
  TOWED 136: **105mm** 13 M-101A1; **122mm** 41: 8 D-30; 33 M-30 M-1938; **130mm** 15 M-46; **155mm** 67: 18 M-114A1; 35 M-198; 14 Model-50
  MRL 122mm 22 BM-21
  MOR 334: **81mm** 134; **82mm** 112; **120mm** 88 Brandt
AT
  MSL • MANPATS 38: 26 *Milan*; 12 TOW
  RCL 106mm 113 M-40A1
  RL 73mm 3,263: 13 M-50; 3,250 RPG-7 *Knout*
  90mm 8 M-69
AD
  SAM • MANPAD 84 9K32 *Strela-2/2M* (SA-7A *Grail*/SA-7B *Grail*)‡
  GUNS 81
    TOWED 20mm 23; **23mm** 58 ZU-23
UAV • ISR • Medium 8 *Mohajer IV*

Navy 1,100

EQUIPMENT BY TYPE
PATROL AND COASTAL COMBATANTS 11
  PB 11: 1 *Aamchit* (GER *Bremen*); 1 *Al Kalamoun* (FRA *Avel Gwarlarn*); 5 *Attacker* (UK); 1 *Naquora* (GER *Bremen*); 1 *Tabarja* (GER *Bergen*); 2 *Tracker* (UK)
AMPHIBIOUS • LANDING CRAFT • LCT 2 *Sour* (FRA *Edic* - capacity 8 APC; 96 troops)

FACILITIES
Bases Located at Jounieh, Beirut

Air Force 1,000

3 air bases
FORCES BY ROLE

FGA	1 sqn with Hawker *Hunter* Mk6/Mk9/T66 at Rayak; Cessna AC-208 *Combat Caravan** at Beirut
Atk Hel	1 sqn with SA-342L *Gazelle* at Rayak
Tpt Hel	2 sqn with Bell 205 (UH-1H) at Beirut; 1 sqn with Bell 205(UH-1H) at Rayak; 1 sqn with Bell 205 (UH-1H) at Koleyate
Trg Hel	1 sqn with R-44 *Raven* II at Rayak

EQUIPMENT BY TYPE
AIRCRAFT 7 combat capable
  FGA 6 Hawker *Hunter* Mk6/Mk9/T66 (3 serviceable);
  ISR 1 Cessna AC-208 *Combat Caravan**
  TRG 3 *Bulldog* (could be refurbished)
HELICOPTERS
  MRH 9: 1 AW-139; 8 SA-342L *Gazelle* (plus 5 unserviceable – could be refurbished); (5 SA-316 *Alouette III* unserviceable – 3 could be refurbished); (1 SA-318 *Alouette II* unserviceable – could be refurbished)
  TPT 19 **Medium** 3: 3 S-61N (fire fighting); (5 SA-330 *Puma* unserviceable – 3 could be refurbished; 10 more expected from UAE) **Light** 16: 12 Bell 205 (UH-1H *Huey*) (+ 11 unserviceable); 4 R-44 *Raven* II (basic trg); (7 Bell 212 unserviceable – 6 could be refurbished)

Paramilitary ε20,000 active

Internal Security Force ε20,000
Ministry of Interior
FORCES BY ROLE

Police	1 (Judicial) unit
Regional	1 coy
Paramilitary	1 (Beirut Gendarmerie) coy

EQUIPMENT BY TYPE
APC (W) 60 V-200 *Chaimite*

Customs
PATROL AND COASTAL COMBATANTS 7
  PB 7: 5 *Aztec*; 2 *Tracker*

FOREIGN FORCES

Unless specified, figures refer to UNTSO and represent total numbers for the mission in Israel, Syria & Lebanon.
Argentina 5 obs
Australia 11 obs
Austria 7 obs
Bangladesh UNIFIL 325
Belgium 2 obs • UNIFIL 160 Army: 1 engr coy
Brunei UNIFIL 9
Cambodia UNIFIL 1
Canada 8 obs (*Op Jade*)
Chile 3 obs
China, People's Republic of 5 obs • UNIFIL 344; 1 engr bn; 1 fd hospital
Croatia UNIFIL 1
Cyprus UNIFIL 2
Denmark 10 obs • UNIFIL 142; 1 log bn
El Salvador UNIFIL 52; 1 inf pl
Estonia 1 obs
Finland 14 obs
France 2 obs • UNIFIL 1,575: Army: 1 armd inf bn; 1 armd sqn; 1 arty coy; 13 *Leclerc* MBT; 36 AMX-10P AIFV; 14 PVP; 72 VAB; 5 AU-F1 155mm; 6 *Mistral* MANPAD SAM; 2 *Cobra* radar
Germany UNIFIL 249: Navy: 2 PC; 1 SPT
Ghana UNIFIL 877; 1 mech inf bn
Greece UNIFIL 59: Navy: 1 PB
Guatemala UNIFIL 3
Hungary UNIFIL 4
India UNIFIL 910; 1 mech inf bn; elm 1 fd hospital
Indonesia UNIFIL 1,324; 1 mech inf bn; 1 MP coy; elm 1 fd hospital
Ireland 12 obs • UNIFIL 8

Italy 7 obs • UNIFIL 1,734: 1 armd recce bn; 1 armd inf bn; 1 hel bn; 1 sigs coy; 1 CIMIC coy; 1 FFG
Korea, Republic of UNIFIL 368; 1 mech inf bn
Macedonia, Former Yugoslav Republic of UNIFIL 1
Malaysia UNIFIL 744; 1 mech inf bn
Nepal 4 obs • UNIFIL 1,020; 1 inf bn
Netherlands 12 obs
New Zealand 7 obs
Nigeria UNIFIL 1
Norway 13 obs
Portugal UNIFIL 146; 1 engr coy
Qatar UNIFIL 3
Russia 5 obs
Sierra Leone UNIFIL 3
Slovakia 2 obs
Slovenia 2 obs • UNIFIL 14; 1 inf pl
Spain UNIFIL 1,046; 1 armd inf bn
Sweden 5 obs
Switzerland 13 obs
Tanzania UNIFIL 77; 1 MP coy
Turkey UNIFIL 504; 1 engr coy; 1 PB
United States 2 obs

Libya LBY

Libyan Dinar D		2009	2010	2011
GDP	D	75.3bn	97.4bn	
	US$	60.1bn	76.4bn	
per capita	US$	9,364	11,674	
Growth	%	2.1	5.2	
Inflation	%	2.5	4.5	
Def exp	D	2.14bn		
	US$	1.71bn		
FMA (US)	US$	-	0.15m	0.25m
US$1=D		1.25	1.27	

Population   6,545,619

Age	0–14	15–19	20–24	25–29	30–64	65 plus
Male	16.7%	4.6%	4.7%	4.7%	18.3%	2.2%
Female	16.0%	4.4%	4.5%	4.5%	17.1%	2.3%

Capabilities

ACTIVE 76,000 (Army 50,000 Navy 8,000 Air 18,000)
Terms of service selective conscription, 1–2 years

RESERVE ε40,000 (People's Militia)

ORGANISATIONS BY SERVICE

Army 25,000; ε25,000 conscript (total 50,000)
FORCES BY ROLE
11 Border Def and 4 Sy Zones
Army	1 (elite) bde (regime sy force)
Tk	10 bn
Mech inf	10 bn
Inf	18 bn
Cdo/para	6 bn
Arty	22 bn
SSM	4 bde
ADA	7 bn

EQUIPMENT BY TYPE
MBT 800: 200 T-72 (115 in store); 100 T-62 (70 in store); 500 T-55; (1,040 T-54/T-55 in store)
RECCE 120: 50 BRDM-2; 70 EE-9 *Cascavel*
AIFV 1,000+: 1,000 BMP-1; BMD
APC 945
  APC (T) 778: 28 M-113; 750 BTR-50/BTR-60
  APC (W) 167: 100 EE-11 *Urutu*; 67 OT-62/OT-64
ARTY 2,421+
  SP 444: **122mm** 130 2S1 *Carnation*; **152mm** 140: 60 2S3; 80 M-77 *Dana*; **155mm** 174: 14 M-109; 160 VCA 155 *Palmaria*
  TOWED 647+: **105mm** 42+ M-101; **122mm** 250: 190 D-30; 60 D-74; **130mm** 330 M-46; **152mm** 25 M-1937
  MRL 830: **107mm** ε300 Type-63; **122mm** 530: ε200 BM-11; ε230 BM-21; ε100 RM-70 *Dana*
  MOR 500: **82mm** 428; **120mm** ε48 M-43; **160mm** ε24 M-160
AT • MSL 3,000
  SP 40 9P122 BRDM-2 *Sagger*
  MANPATS 2,960: 620 AT-3 9K11 *Sagger*; 1,940 AT-3 9K11 *Sagger*/AT-4 9K111 *Spigot*/AT-5 9K113 *Spandrel*; 400 *Milan*
  RCL 620: **106mm** 220 M-40A1; **84mm** 400 *Carl Gustav*
  RL 73mm 2,300 RPG-7 *Knout*
AD • SAM • SP 424+: 24 *Crotale* (quad); 400 9K32 *Strela*-2 (SA-7 *Grail*)‡; 9K35 *Strela*-10 (SA-13 *Gopher*); 9K31 *Strela*-1 (SA-9 *Gaskin*)
  GUNS 490
    SP 23mm 250 ZSU-23-4
    TOWED 240: **14.5mm** 100 ZPU-2; **30mm** M-53/59; **40mm** 50 L/70; **57mm** 90 S-60
RADAR • LAND RASIT (veh, arty)
MSL • TACTICAL • SSM 45 FROG-7

Navy 8,000 (incl Coast Guard)
EQUIPMENT BY TYPE
SUBMARINES • TACTICAL • SSK 2 *Khyber*† (FSU *Foxtrot*) each with 10 533mm TT (6 fwd, 4 aft)
PRINCIPAL SURFACE COMBATANTS 2
  FRIGATES • FFGM 2 *Al Hani*† (FSU *Koni*) each with 2 twin lnchr (4 eff.) each with P-15 *Termit*-M (SS-N-2C *Styx*) AShM, 1 twin lnchr with 9K33 *Osa*-M (SA-N-4 *Gecko*) SAM, 2 twin 406mm ASTT (4 eff.) each with USET-95 Type 40 LWT, 1 RBU 6000 *Smerch* 2 (12 eff.), 2 twin 76mm gun (4 eff.)
PATROL AND COASTAL COMBATANTS 16
  CORVETTES • FSGM 1 *Tariq Ibin Ziyad* (FSU *Nanuchka* II) with 4 single lnchr each with P-15 *Termit*-M (SS-N-2C *Styx*) AShM, 1 twin lnchr with SA-N-4 *Gecko* SAM
  PBFG 11:
    4 *Al Zuara* (FSU *Osa* II) each with 4 single lnchr each with P-15 *Termit*-M (SS-N-2C *Styx*) AShM

7 *Sharaba* (FRA *Combattante* II) each with 4 single each with *Otomat* Mk 2 AShM, 1 76mm gun

PBF 4 PV-30LS (constabulary duties, additional units to follow)

MINE WARFARE • MINE COUNTERMEASURES • MSO 4 *Ras al Gelais* (FSU *Natya*)

AMPHIBIOUS 7

LANDING SHIPS • LST 2 *Ibn Harissa* (capacity 1 SA-316B *Alouette III* hel; 11 MBT; 240 troops)

LANDING CRAFT 5

LCT 3†

UCAC 2

LOGISTICS AND SUPPORT 12:

ARS 1

TPT 10 *El Temsah*

YDT 1

FACILITIES

Bases   Located at Tripoli, Benghazi, Tobruk, Khums

Minor bases Located at Derna, Zuwurah, Misonhah

Coastal Defence

FORCES BY ROLE

Msl 1 bty with SS-C-3 *Styx*

EQUIPMENT BY TYPE

MSL • TACTICAL • SSM: some SS-C-3 *Styx*

Naval Aviation

EQUIPMENT BY TYPE

HELICOPTERS • TPT • Heavy 7 SA-321 *Super Frelon* (air force assets)

Air Force 18,000

Flying hours   85 hrs/year

FORCES BY ROLE

Bbr	1 sqn with Tu-22 *Blinder*
Ftr	9+ sqn with MiG-21 *Fishbed*; MiG-23 *Flogger*; MiG-25 *Foxbat*; MiG-25U *Foxbat*; *Mirage* F-1B (F-1BD); *Mirage* F-1E (F-1ED)
FGA	7 sqn with MiG-23BN *Flogger H*; MiG-23U *Flogger*; *Mirage* F-1A (F-1AD); Su-17M-2 *Fitter D*/ Su-20 *Fitter C*; Su-24MK *Fencer D*
ISR	2 sqn with MiG-25R *Foxbat*; *Mirage* 5DP30
Tpt	7 sqn with An-26 *Curl*; An-124 *Condor*; C-130H *Hercules*; G-222; Il-76 *Candid*; L-100-20; L-100-30; L-410 *Turbolet*
Atk hel	Some sqn with Mi-25 *Hind D*; Mi-35 *Hind*
Tpt hel	Some sqn with Bell 206 *Jet Ranger* (AB-206); CH-47C *Chinook*; Mi-8 *Hip*; Mi-17 *Hip H*; SA-316 *Alouette III*
Trg	Some sqn with G-2 *Galeb*; L-39ZO *Albatros*; PZL Mi-2 *Hoplite*; SF-260WL *Warrior**; Tu-22 *Blinder*

EQUIPMENT BY TYPE

(many non-operational, many ac in store)

AIRCRAFT 394 combat capable

BBR 7 Tu-22 *Blinder*

FTR 187: 75 MiG-23 *Flogger*; 15 MiG-23U *Flogger*; 94 MiG-25 *Foxbat*; 3 MiG-25U *Foxbat*

FGA 180: 45 MiG-21 *Fishbed*; 40 MiG-23BN *Flogger H*; 4 *Mirage* 5DP30; 14 *Mirage* F-1A (F-1AD); 3 *Mirage* F-1B (F-1BD); 15 *Mirage* F-1E (F-1ED); 53 Su-17M-2 *Fitter D*/ Su-20 *Fitter C*; 6 Su-24MK *Fencer D*

ISR 7 MiG-25R *Foxbat*

TPT 85+: **Heavy** 27: 2 An-124 *Condor*; 25 Il-76 *Candid*; **Medium** 20+: 15 C-130H *Hercules*; Some G-222; 2 L-100-20; 3 L-100-30; **Light** 38: 23 An-26 *Curl*; 15 L-410 *Turbolet*

TRG 225: 90 G-2 *Galeb*; 115 L-39ZO *Albatros*; 20 SF-260WL *Warrior**

HELICOPTERS

ATK 35: 23 Mi-25 *Hind D*; 12 Mi-35 *Hind*

MRH 11 SA-316 *Alouette III*

MRH/TPT 35 Mi-8 *Hip* (med tpt)/Mi-17 *Hip H*

TPT 55: **Heavy** 4 CH-47C *Chinook*; **Light** 51: 5 Bell 206 *Jet Ranger* (AB-206); 46 PZL Mi-2 *Hoplite*

MSL

ASM; Kh-23 (AS-7 *Kerry*); 9M17 (AT-2 *Swatter*)

ARM Kh-28 (AS-9 *Kyle*); Kh-58 (AS-11 *Kilter*)

AAM • IR AAM R-3 (AA-2 *Atoll*)‡; R-60 (AA-8 *Aphid*); R-550 *Magic* **IR/SARH AAM** R-40/46 (AA-6 *Acrid*); R-23/24 (AA-7 *Apex*); R530

Air Defence Command

Senezh AD comd and control system

FORCES BY ROLE

AD 5 region (with ε3 AD bde each with 20–24 2K12 *Kub* (SA-6 *Gainful*)/9K33 *Osa* (SA-8 *Gecko*); 2–3 AD bde each with 12 S-125 *Pechora* (SA-3 *Goa*); 5–6 AD bde each with 18 S-75 *Volkhov* (SA-2 *Guideline*); 4 bde with S-200 *Angara* (SA-5A *Gammon*) (each: 1 radar coy, 2 AD bn with 6 launcher, 4+ ADA bn with guns)

EQUIPMENT BY TYPE

AD

SAM 216+:

SP 72 2K12 *Kub* (SA-6 *Gainful*)/9K33 *Osa* (SA-8 *Gecko*) (216–432 eff.)

TOWED 144: 108 s-75 *Volkhov* (SA-2 *Guideline*)

STATIC S-200 *Angara* (SA-5A *Gammon*); 36 S-125 *Pechora* (SA-3 *Goa*)

GUNS some

DEPLOYMENT

PHILIPPINES

IMT 6 obs

Mauritania MRT

Mauritanian Ouguiya OM		2009	2010	2011
GDP	OM	794bn	961bn	
	US$	3.02bn	3.66bn	
per capita	US$	919	1,088	
Growth	%	-1.1	4.9	
Inflation	%	2.2	6.1	
Def exp	OM	30.1bn		
	US$	115m		
US$1=OM			262.34	262.52

Population	3,365,675					

Age	0–14	15–19	20–24	25–29	30–64	65 plus
Male	20.3%	5.3%	4.5%	3.7%	12.9%	1.5%
Female	20.1%	5.4%	4.8%	4.2%	15.2%	2.0%

Capabilities

ACTIVE 15,870 (Army 15,000 Navy 620 Air 250)
Paramilitary 5,000

Terms of service conscription 24 months authorised

ORGANISATIONS BY SERVICE

Army 15,000

FORCES BY ROLE
6 Mil Regions

Army	2 (camel corps) bn
Armd	1 bn (T-54/55 MBT)
Armd recce	1 sqn
Inf	8 (garrison) bn
Mot inf	7 bn
Cdo/para	1 bn
Arty	3 bn
ADA	4 bty
Engr	1 coy
Gd	1 bn

EQUIPMENT BY TYPE
MBT 35 T-54/T-55
RECCE 70: 20 AML-60; 40 AML-90; 10 *Saladin*
APC
  APC (W) 25: 5 FV603 *Saracen*; ε20 M-3 *Panhard*
ARTY 194
  TOWED 80: **105mm** 36 HM-2/M-101A1; **122mm** 44: 20 D-30; 24 D-74
  MOR 114: **60mm** 24; **81mm** 60; **120mm** 30 *Brandt*
AT • MSL • MANPATS 24 *Milan*
  RCL 114: **75mm** ε24 M-20; **106mm** ε90 M-40A1
  RL 73mm ε48 RPG-7 *Knout*
AD • SAM 104
  SP ε4 SA-9 *Gaskin* (reported)
  MANPAD ε100 9K32 *Strela-2* (SA-7 *Grail*)‡

GUNS • TOWED 82: **14.5mm** 28: 16 ZPU-2; 12 ZPU-4; **23mm** 20 ZU-23-2; **37mm** 10 M-1939; **57mm** 12 S-60; **100mm** 12 KS-19

Navy ε620

EQUIPMENT BY TYPE
PATROL AND COASTAL COMBATANTS 12
  PCO 1 *Voum-Legleita*
  PCC 5: 1 *Abourbekr Ben Amer* (FRA OPV 54); 1 *Arguin*; 2 *Conjera*; 1 *Huangpu*
  PB 6: 1 *El Nasr* (FRA *Patra*); 4 *Mandovi*; 1 *Yacoub Ould Rajel*
FACILITIES
Bases Located at Nouadhibou, Nouakchott

Air Force 250

FORCES BY ROLE

Atk/ ISR	Some (COIN) sqn with FTB-337 *Milirole*; BN-2 *Defender*; Basler BT-67
MP	Some sqn with Cessna 337 *Skymaster*
Tpt	Some sqn with PA-31T *Navajo/Cheyenne II*; Y-12(II)

EQUIPMENT BY TYPE
AIRCRAFT 2 combat capable
  ISR 2 FTB-337 *Milirole**
  TPT 12 **Light** 11: 5 BN-2 *Defender*; 2 Cessna 337 *Skymaster*; 2 PA-31T *Navajo/Cheyenne II*; 2 Y-12(II) **PAX** 1 Basler BT-67
  TRG 4 SF-260E

Paramilitary ε5,000 active

Gendarmerie ε3,000
Ministry of Interior
Regional   6 coy

National Guard 2,000
Ministry of Interior
Aux   1,000

Customs
PATROL AND COASTAL COMBATANTS • PB 1 *Dah Ould Bah* (FRA *Amgram* 14)

Morocco MOR

Moroccan Dirham D		2009	2010	2011
GDP	D	736bn	777bn	
	US$	91.6bn	92.2bn	
per capita	US$	2,862	2,849	
Growth	%	5.0	-4.8	
Inflation	%	1.0	1.5	
Def bdgt	D	24.6bn	26.9bn	27.3bn
	US$	3.06bn	3.19bn	
FMA (US)	US$	3.6m	9.0m	9.0m
US$1=D		8.04	8.42	

Population   32,381,283

Age	0–14	15–19	20–24	25–29	30–64	65 plus
Male	14.1%	4.6%	4.7%	4.5%	18.5%	2.8%
Female	13.7%	4.6%	4.8%	4.7%	19.6%	3.3%

Capabilities

ACTIVE 195,800 (Army 175,000 Navy 7,800 Air 13,000) **Paramilitary 50,000**

Terms of service conscription 18 months authorised; most enlisted personnel are volunteers

RESERVE 150,000 (Army 150,000)

Terms of service obligation to age 50

ORGANISATIONS BY SERVICE

Army ε75,000; 100,000 conscript (total 175,000)

FORCES BY ROLE

2 Comd (Northern Zone, Southern Zone)

Sy	1 light bde
Armd	12 indep bn
Mech/Mot Inf	8 regt (each: 2–3 mech inf bn)
Mech Inf	3 bde
Inf	35 indep bn
Mot Inf	3 (camel corps) indep bn
Mtn Inf	1 indep bn
Cdo	4 indep unit
Para	2 bde
AB	2 indep bn
Arty	11 indep bn
Engr	7 indep bn
AD	1 indep bn

Royal Guard 1,500

Army	1 bn
Cav	1 sqn

EQUIPMENT BY TYPE

MBT 380: 40 T-72, 220 M-60A1; 120 M-60A3; (ε200 M-48A5 in store)

LT TK 116: 5 AMX-13; 111 SK-105 *Kuerassier*
RECCE 384: 38 AML-60-7; 190 AML-90; 80 AMX-10RC; 40 EBR-75; 16 *Eland*; 20 M1114 HMMWV
AIFV 70: 10 AMX-10P; 30 MK III-20 *Ratel*-20; 30 MK III-90 *Ratel*-90
APC 765
  APC (T) 400 M-113A1/A2
  APC (W) 365: 45 VAB VCI; 320 VAB VTT
ARTY 2,141
  SP 282: **105mm** 5 Mk 61; **155mm** 217: 84 M-109A1/M-109A1B; 43 M-109A2; 90 (AMX) Mk F3; **203mm** 60 M-110
  TOWED 118: **105mm** 50: 30 L-118 Light Gun; 20 M-101; **130mm** 18 M-46; **155mm** 50: 30 FH-70; 20 M-114
  MRL 35 BM-21
  MOR 1,706
    SP 56: **106mm** 32-36 M-106A2; **120mm** 20 (VAB APC)
    TOWED 1,650: **81mm** 1,100 Expal model LN; **120mm** 550 *Brandt*
AT • MSL 790
  SP 80 M-901
  MANPATS 710: 40 AT-3 9K11 *Sagger*; 440 M47 *Dragon*; 80 *Milan*; 150 TOW
  RCL 106mm 350 M-40A1
  RL 700: **66mm** 500 M-72 LAW; **89mm** 200 M-20
  GUNS 36
    SP 100mm 8 SU-100
    TOWED 90mm 28 M-56
UAV • Heavy R4E-50 *Skyeye*
AD • SAM 119
  SP 49: 12 9M311 *Tunguska* (SA-19 *Grison*) SPAAGM; 37 M-48 *Chaparral*
  MANPAD 70 9K32 *Strela*-2 (SA-7 *Grail*)‡
  GUNS 407
    SP 60 M-163 *Vulcan*
    TOWED 347: **14.5mm** 200: 150-180 ZPU-2; 20 ZPU-4; **20mm** 40 M-167 *Vulcan*; **23mm** 75-90 ZU-23-2; **100mm** 17 KS-19
RADAR • LAND: RASIT (veh, arty)

Navy 7,800 (incl 1,500 Marines)

EQUIPMENT BY TYPE
PRINCIPAL SURFACE COMBATANTS • FRIGATES • FFGH 2:
  2 *Mohammed V* (FRA *Floreal*) each with 2 single lnchr each with MM-38 *Exocet* SSM, 1 76mm gun, (capacity 1 AS-565SA *Panther*)
PATROL AND COASTAL COMBATANTS 39
  CORVETTES • FSGM 1
    1 *Lt Col Errhamani* (ESP *Descubierto*) with 2 twin lnchr (4 eff.) each with MM-38 *Exocet* AShM, 1 octuple *Albatros* lnchr with *Aspide* SAM, 2 triple 324mm ASTT (6 eff.) each with Mk 46 LWT, 1 76mm gun
  PCG 4 *Cdt El Khattabi* (ESP *Lazaga* 58m) each with 4 single lnchr each with MM-40 *Exocet* AShM, 1 76mm gun
  PCO 5 *Rais Bargach* (under control of fisheries dept)
  PCC 12:
    4 *El Hahiq* (DNK *Osprey* 55, incl 2 with customs)
    6 *LV Rabhi* (ESP 58m B-200D)

2 *Okba* (FRA PR-72) each with 1 76mm gun
PB 17: 6 *El Wacil* (FRA P-32); 11 (various)
AMPHIBIOUS
  LANDING SHIPS 4:
    LSM 3 *Ben Aicha* (FRA *Champlain* BATRAL) (capacity 7 tanks; 140 troops)
    LST 1 *Sidi Mohammed Ben Abdallah* (US *Newport*) (capacity 3 LCVP; 400 troops)
  LANDING CRAFT • LCM 1
LOGISTICS AND SUPPORT 4:
  AK 2; **AGOR** 1 (US lease); **YDT** 1

FACILITIES
Bases Located at Casablanca, Agadir, Al Hoceima, Dakhla, Tangier

Marines 1,500

FORCES BY ROLE
Naval inf   2 bn

Naval Aviation

EQUIPMENT BY TYPE
HELICOPTERS • ASW/ASUW 3 AS-565SA *Panther*

Air Force 13,000

Flying hours   100 hrs/year on F-1 *Mirage*/F-5A *Freedom Fighter Tiger*

FORCES BY ROLE
Ftr   1 sqn with *Mirage* F-1C (F-1CH)
FGA   1 sqn with F-5A/F-5B *Freedom Fighter*; 2 sqn with F-5E/F-5F *Tiger II*; 2 sqn with *Mirage* F-1E (F-1EH)
EW   sqn with C-130 *Hercules* (ELINT); *Falcon* 20 (ELINT)
ISR   Some sqn with OV-10 *Bronco**; C-130H *Hercules* (with side-looking radar)
Tkr   Some sqn with KC-130H *Hercules*; B-707
Tpt   Some sqn with Beech 100 *King Air*; Beech 200 *King Air*; C-130H *Hercules*; CN-235; Do-28; *Falcon* 20; *Falcon* 50 (VIP); Gulfstream II (VIP); Some (liaison) sqn with Beech 200 *King Air*
Trg   sqn with AS-202 *Bravo*; *Alpha Jet**; CAP 10; T-34C *Turbo Mentor*; T-37B *Tweet* (being replaced by K-8); CAP-231
Atk Hel   Some sqn with SA-342 *Gazelle* (Some with HOT)
Tpt Hel   Some sqn with Bell 205A (AB-205A); Bell 206 *Jet Ranger* (AB-206); Bell 212 (AB-212); CH-47D *Chinook*; SA-330 *Puma*; UH-60 *Black Hawk*

EQUIPMENT BY TYPE
AIRCRAFT 89 combat capable
  FTR 33: 8 F-5A *Freedom Fighter*; 2 F-5B *Freedom Fighter*; 20 F-5E *Tiger II*; 3 F-5F *Tiger II*;
  FGA 33: 19 *Mirage* F-1C (F-1CH); 14 *Mirage* F-1EH (F-1E)
  ISR 4 OV-10 *Bronco**
  TKR/TPT 2 KC-130H *Hercules*
  TPT 44 **Medium** 19: 2 C-130 *Hercules* (ELINT); 15 C-130H *Hercules*; 2 C-130H *Hercules* (with side-looking radar); **Light** 17: 4 Beech 100 *King Air*; 5 Beech 200 *King Air*; 6

CN-235; 2 Do-28; **PAX** 8: 1 B-707; 2 *Falcon* 20; 2 *Falcon* 20 (ELINT); 1 *Falcon* 50 (VIP); 2 Gulfstream II (VIP)
  TRG 51: 7 AS-202 *Bravo*; 19 *Alpha Jet**; 2 CAP-10; 9 T-34C *Turbo Mentor*; 14 T-37B *Tweet* (being replaced by K-8)
  TRIALS AND TEST 4 CAP-231
HELICOPTERS
  MRH 19 SA-342 *Gazelle* (7 with HOT, 12 with cannon)
  TPT 73: **Heavy** 8 CH-47D *Chinook* **Medium** 26: 24 SA-330 *Puma*; 2 UH-60 *Black Hawk* **Light** 39: 25 Bell 205A (AB-205A); 11 Bell 206 *Jet Ranger* (AB-206); 3 Bell 212 (AB-212)
MSL
  ASM AGM-62B *Walleye* (For F-5E); HOT
  AAM • IR AAM AIM-9B/D/J *Sidewinder*; R-550 *Magic* **SARH AAM** R530

Paramilitary 50,000 active

Gendarmerie Royale 20,000

FORCES BY ROLE
Coast Guard   1 unit
Para   1 sqn
Paramilitary 1 bde; 4 (mobile) gp
Avn   1 (air) sqn

EQUIPMENT BY TYPE
PATROL AND COASTAL COMBATANTS PB33
AIRCRAFT • TRG 2 R-235 *Guerrier*
HELICOPTERS
  MRH 14: 3 SA-315B *Lama*; 2 SA-316 *Alouette III*; 3 SA-318 *Alouette II*; 6 SA-342K *Gazelle*
  TPT 8 **Medium** 6 SA-330 *Puma* **Light** 2 SA-360 *Dauphin*

Force Auxiliaire 30,000 (incl 5,000 Mobile Intervention Corps)

Customs/Coast Guard
PATROL AND COASTAL COMBATANTS 11
  PB 11: 4 *Erraid*; 7 (SAR craft)

DEPLOYMENT

CÔTE D'IVOIRE
UN • UNOCI 726; 1 inf bn

DEMOCRATIC REPUBLIC OF THE CONGO
UN • MONUSCO 831; 4 obs; 1 mech inf bn; 1 fd hospital

SERBIA
NATO • KFOR 210; 1 inf unit

Oman OMN

Omani Rial R		2009	2010	2011
GDP	R	17.7bn	20.7bn	
	US$	46.1bn	53.8bn	
per capita	US$	16,207	18,513	
Growth	%	3.6	4.8	
Inflation	%	3.9	4.4	
Def bdgt	R	1.55bn		
	US$	4.02bn		
FMA (US)	US$	7.0m	11.85m	13.0m
US$1=R		0.38	0.38	

Population   2,905,114

Expatriates: 27%

Age	0–14	15–19	20–24	25–29	30–64	65 plus
Male	16.0%	5.2%	5.6%	6.3%	20.3%	1.6%
Female	15.2%	4.9%	4.9%	4.9%	13.6%	1.5%

Capabilities

ACTIVE 42,600 (Army 25,000 Navy 4,200 Air 5,000 Foreign Forces 2,000 Royal Household 6,400) Paramilitary 4,400

ORGANISATIONS BY SERVICE

Army 25,000

FORCES BY ROLE

(Regt are bn size)

Armd	1 bde HQ; 2 regt (each: 3 tk sqn)
Armd Recce	1 regt (3 armd recce sqn)
Inf	2 bde HQ; 8 regt
Rifle	1 indep coy (Musandam Security Force)
AB	1 regt
Inf Recce	1 regt (3 recce coy)
Med Arty	1 regt (2 med arty bty)
Fd Arty	2 regt
ADA	1 regt (2 ADA bty)
Fd Engr	1 regt (3 fd engr sqn)

EQUIPMENT BY TYPE

MBT 117: 38 CR2 *Challenger 2*; 6 M-60A1; 73 M-60A3
LT TK 37 *Scorpion*
RECCE 137: 13 *Sultan*; 124 VBL
APC 206
  APC (T) 16: 6 FV 103 *Spartan*; 10 FV4333 *Stormer*
  APC (W) 190: 175 *Piranha* (incl variants); 15 AT-105 *Saxon*
ARTY 233
  SP 155mm 24 G-6
  TOWED 108: **105mm** 42 ROF lt; **122mm** 30 D-30; **130mm** 24: 12 M-46; 12 Type-59-I; **155mm** 12 FH-70
  MOR 101: **81mm** 69; **107mm** 20 M-30; **120mm** 12 Brandt

AT • MSL 88
  SP 8 VBL (TOW)
  MANPATS 80: 30 *Javelin*; 32 *Milan*; 18 TOW/TOW-2A
  RL 73mm RPG-7 *Knout*; **94mm** LAW-80
AD • SAM 74+
  SP 20: up to 12 *Pantsyr* S1E SPAAGM; 8 *Mistral* 2
  MANPAD 54: 20 *Javelin*; 34 9K32 *Strela*-2 (SA-7 *Grail*)‡
  GUNS 26: **23mm** 4 ZU-23-2; **35mm** 10 GDF-005 (with *Skyguard*); **40mm** 12 L/60 (Towed)

Navy 4,200

EQUIPMENT BY TYPE

PATROL AND COASTAL COMBATANTS 11
  CORVETTES • FSGM 2
    2 *Qahir Al Amwaj* each with 2 quad (8 eff.) each with MM-40 *Exocet* AShM, 2 triple 324mm TT (6 eff.) (to be fitted), 1 octuple lnchr (8 eff.) with *Crotale* SAM, 1 76mm gun, 1 hel landing platform
  PCFG 3 *Dhofar* each with 2 quad lnchr (8 eff.) each with MM-40 *Exocet* AShM, 1 76mm gun
  PCC 4
    3 *Al Bushra* (FRA P-400) each with 4 single 406mm TT, 1 76mm gun
    1 *Dhofar* with 2 triple lnchr (6 eff.), 1 76mm gun
  PB 4 *Seeb* (UK Vosper 25m, under 100 tonnes)
AMPHIBIOUS
  LANDING SHIPS • LST 1 *Nasr el Bahr* (with hel deck) (capacity 7 tanks; 240 troops)
  LANDING CRAFT 5: 1 LCU; 3 LCM; 1 LCT
LOGISTICS AND SUPPORT 5
  AK 1 *Al Sultana*
  AGHS 1
  T-AP 2 *Shinas* (Commercial Tpt - Auxiliary military role only) (capacity 56 veh; 200 tps)
  TRG 1 *Al Mabrukah* (with hel deck, also used in OPV role)

FACILITIES

Bases   Located at Muaskar al Murtafaia (Seeb), Alwi, Main HQ located at Widam A'Sahil, Ghanam Island, Musandam, Salalah

Air Force 5,000

FORCES BY ROLE

Ftr/FGA	1 sqn with *Hawk* Mk103*; *Hawk* Mk203*
FGA	1 sqn with Block 50 F-16C *Fighting Falcon*/F-16D *Fighting Falcon*; 2 sqn with *Jaguar* OS/*Jaguar* OB
Tpt	1 sqn with C-130H *Hercules*; 1 sqn with SC.7 3M *Skyvan* (7 radar-equipped, for MP); 1 sqn with BAC-111
Tpt Hel	2 (med) sqn with AB-205 (Bell 205) *Jet Ranger*; AB-212 (Bell 212); *Lynx* Mk 300 *Super Lynx* (maritime/SAR)
Trg	1 sqn with AS-202-18 *Bravo*; MFI-17B *Mushshak*; PC-9*; SF-25 *Falke*; AB-206 hel
AD	2 sqn with 40 *Rapier*; 6 *Blindfire*; S713 *Martello*

EQUIPMENT BY TYPE

AIRCRAFT 54 combat capable

FGA 26: 8 F-16C Block 50 *Fighting Falcon*; 4 F-16D Block 50 *Fighting Falcon*; 12 Jaguar S (OS); 2 Jaguar B (OB)

TPT 16 **Medium** 3 C-130H *Hercules*; **Light** 10 SC.7 3M *Skyvan* (7 radar-equipped, for MP) **PAX** 3 BAC-111

TRG 26: 4 AS-202-18 *Bravo*; 4 *Hawk* Mk103*; 12 *Hawk* Mk203*; 8 MFI-17B *Mushshak*; 12 PC-9*; 2 SF-25

HELICOPTERS

MRH 16 *Lynx* Mk 300 *Super Lynx* (maritime/SAR)

TPT • Light 41: 19 Bell 205 (AB-205) (to be replaced by 20 NH-90); 3 Bell 206 (AB-206) *Jet Ranger*; 3 Bell 212 (AB-212)

AD • SAM 40 *Rapier*

RADAR • LAND 6+: 6 *Blindfire*; S713 *Martello*

MSL

AAM • IR AAM AIM-9LM *Sidewinder* **ARH AAM** AIM-120C AMRAAM

ASM 20 AGM-84D *Harpoon*; AGM-65 *Maverick*

Royal Household 6,400

(incl HQ staff)

SF   2 regt (1,000 men)

Royal Guard bde 5,000

LT TK 9 VBC-90

APC (W) 73: ε50 Type-92; 14 VAB VCI; 9 VAB VDAA

ARTY • MRL 122mm 6 Type-90A

AT • MSL • MANPATS *Milan*

AD • SAM • MANPAD 14 *Javelin*

GUNS • 20mm • SP 9: 9 VAB VDAA

Royal Yacht Squadron 150

PATROL AND COASTAL COMBATANTS • MISC BOATS/CRAFT • DHOW 1 *Zinat Al Bihaar*

LOGISTICS AND SUPPORT 2

RY 2: 1 *Al Said*; 1 (Royal Dhow)

TPT 1 *Fulk Al Salamah* (also veh tpt) with up to 2 AS-332C *Super Puma* spt hel

Royal Flight 250

AIRCRAFT • TPT • PAX 5: 2 B-747SP; 1 DC-8-73CF; 2 Gulfstream IV

HELICOPTERS • TPT • Medium 6: 3 SA-330 (AS-330) *Puma*; 2 AS-332F *Super Puma*; 1 AS-332L *Super Puma*

Paramilitary 4,400 active

Tribal Home Guard 4,000

org in teams of est 100

Police Coast Guard 400

PATROL AND COASTAL COMBATANTS 35

PCO 2

PBF 9

PB 24

Police Air Wing

AIRCRAFT • TPT • Light 4: 1 BN-2T *Turbine Islander*; 2 CN-235M; 1 Do-228

HELICOPTERS • TPT • Light 5: 2 Bell 205A; 3 Bell 214ST (AB-214ST)

FOREIGN FORCES

United Kingdom Army 40; Navy 20; Air Force 20; 1 *Tristar* tkr; 1 *Nimrod* MR2; 1 *Sentinel*

Palestinian Territories PT

New Israeli Shekel NS		2009*	2010	2011
GDP	US$			
per capita	US$			
Growth	%			
Inflation	%			

*definitive economic data unavailable

Population	4,409,392

Age	0–14	15–19	20–24	25–29	30–64	65 plus
Male	18.4%	5.9%	5.2%	4.2%	15.7%	1.5%
Female	17.4%	5.6%	4.9%	4.0%	15.0%	2.2%

Capabilities

ACTIVE 0 Paramilitary 56,000

Personnel strength figures for the various Palestinian groups are not known

ORGANISATIONS BY SERVICE

There is little data available on the status of the organisations mentioned below. Following internal fighting in June 2007, the Gaza Strip is under the de facto control of Hamas, while the West Bank is controlled by the emergency Palestinian Authority administration.

Paramilitary

National Forces ε56,000 (reported)

GENERAL SECURITY

Presidential security 3,000

SF 1,200

Police 9,000

Preventative Security n.k.

Civil Defence 1,000

AD • SAM • MANPAD 9K32 *Strela*-2 (SA-7 *Grail*)‡; *Stinger* reported

The **Al-Aqsa Brigades** profess loyalty to the Fatah group that dominates the Palestinian Authority. The strength of this group is not known.

Hamas maintains a security apparatus in the Gaza Strip that, although degraded in the aftermath of the military operation by Israeli forces in late 2008 and early 2009, *Operation Cast Lead*, still ensures that Hamas remains in control in the Gaza Strip. Hamas groupings include internal security groupings such as the **Executive Force** (est strength: 10–12,000; Major equipments include: artillery rockets, mortars, SALW) and the **al-Qassam Brigades** (Est strength: 10,000; Major equipments include: mines and IEDs, artillery rockets, mortars, SALW)

Qatar QTR

Qatari Riyal R		2009	2010	2011
GDP	R	358bn	461bn	
	US$	98.3bn	127bn	
per capita	US$	69,754	83,880	
Growth	%	11.5	28.7	
Inflation	%	-4.9	1.0	
Def exp	R	9.1bn		
	US$	2.5bn		
US$1=R		3.64	3.64	

Population   1,508,322

Ethnic groups: Nationals 25%; Expatriates 75% of which Indian 18%; Iranian 10%; Pakistani 18%

Age	0–14	15–19	20–24	25–29	30–64	65 plus
Male	11.2%	4.1%	5.3%	7.8%	37.1%	0.9%
Female	10.5%	3.0%	3.0%	3.1%	13.3%	0.6%

Capabilities

ACTIVE 11,800 (Army 8,500 Navy 1,800 Air 1,500)

ORGANISATIONS BY SERVICE

Army 8,500

FORCES BY ROLE

Tk	1 bde (1 tk bn, 1 mech inf bn, 1 mor sqn, 1 AT bn)
Mech inf	3 bn
SF	1 coy
Fd arty	1 bn
Royal Guard	1 bde (3 inf regt)

EQUIPMENT BY TYPE
MBT 30 AMX-30
RECCE 68: 12 AMX-10RC; 20 EE-9 *Cascavel*; 12 *Ferret*; 8 V-150 *Chaimite*; 16 VBL
AIFV 40 AMX-10P
APC 226
  APC (T) 30 AMX-VCI
  APC (W) 196: 36 *Piranha* II; 160 VAB
ARTY 89
  SP 155mm 28 (AMX) Mk F3
  TOWED 155mm 12 G-5
  MRL 4 ASTROS II
  MOR 45
    SP • 81mm 4: 4 VAB VPM 81
    81mm 26: 26 L16
    120mm 15: 15 *Brandt*
AT • MSL 148
    SP 24 VAB VCAC HOT

MANPATS 124: 24 HOT; 100 *Milan*
RCL 84mm ε40 *Carl Gustav*

Navy 1,800 (incl Marine Police)
1 HQ located at Doha
EQUIPMENT BY TYPE
PATROL AND COASTAL COMBATANTS 21
PCFG 7:
    4 *Barzan* (UK *Vita*) each with 2 quad lnchr (8 eff.) each with MM-40 *Exocet* AShM, 1 sextuple lnchr (6 eff.) with *Mistral* SAM, 1 76mm gun
    3 *Damsah* (FRA *Combattante* III) each with 2 quad lnchr (8 eff.) each with MM-40 *Exocet* AShM, 1 76mm gun
PBF 4 (operated by Marine Police)
PB 10: 3 Q-31 series; 7 (various; operated by Marine Police)
AMPHIBIOUS • LANDING CRAFT • LCT 1 *Rabha* (capacity 3 MBT; 110 troops)
FACILITIES
Bases	Located at Doha, Halul Island

Coastal Defence
FORCES BY ROLE
Msl	1 bty with 3 quad lnchr (12 eff.) each with MM-40 *Exocet* AShM

EQUIPMENT BY TYPE
LAUNCHER 3 quad lnchr each with MM-40 *Exocet* AShM

Air Force 1,500
FORCES BY ROLE
Ftr/FGA	1 sqn with *Alpha Jet**; 1 sqn with M-2000ED *Mirage*; M-2000D *Mirage*
Tpt	1 sqn with A-340; B-707; B-727; *Falcon* 900
Atk Hel	1 sqn with *Commando* Mk3 with *Exocet*; SA-342L *Gazelle* with HOT
Tpt Hel	Some sqn with *Commando* Mk2A; *Commando* Mk2C; SA-341 *Gazelle*

EQUIPMENT BY TYPE
AIRCRAFT 18 combat capable
  FGA 12: 9 *Mirage* M-2000ED; 3 *Mirage* M-2000D
  TPT 8 Heavy 2 C-17 *Globemaster* **PAX** 6: 1 A-340; 2 B-707; 1 B-727; 2 *Falcon* 900
  TRG 6 *Alpha Jet**
HELICOPTERS
  ASuW 8 *Commando* Mk3
  MRH 31: 18 AW-139 being delivered; 2 SA-341 *Gazelle*; 11 SA-342L *Gazelle*
  TPT • Medium 4: 3 *Commando* MK 2A; 1 *Commando* MK 2C
AD • SAM 75: 24 *Mistral*
  SP 9 *Roland* II
  MANPAD 42: 10 *Blowpipe*; 12 FIM-92A *Stinger*; 20 9K32 *Strela*-2 (SA-7 *Grail*)‡
MSL
  ASM AM-39 *Exocet*; *Apache*; HOT
  AAM • IR AAM R-550 *Magic* IIR/ARH AAM *Mica*

DEPLOYMENT

LEBANON
UN • UNIFIL 3

FOREIGN FORCES

United Kingdom Air Force: 4 C-130J
United States US Central Command: 531; elm 1 (APS)
HBCT set (equipment in use); USAF CAOC

Saudi Arabia SAU

Saudi Riyal R		2009	2010	2011
GDP	R	1.41tr	1.63tr	
	US$	376bn	434bn	
per capita	US$	14,800	16,531	
Growth	%	0.1	3.9	
Inflation	%	5.1	5.5	
Def exp	R	155bn		
	US$	41.3bn		
Def bdgt[a]	R	155bn	170bn	134bn
	US$	41.3bn	45.24	
US$1=R		3.75	3.75	

[a] Defence and security budget

Population 26,245,969

Ethnic groups: Nationals 73% of which Bedouin up to 10%, Shi'a 6%, Expatriates 27% of which Asians 20%, Arabs 6%, Africans 1%, Europeans <1%

Age	0–14	15–19	20–24	25–29	30–64	65 plus
Male	15.1%	5.0%	5.7%	6.0%	21.5%	1.5%
Female	14.4%	4.6%	4.6%	4.6%	15.5%	1.4%

Capabilities

ACTIVE 233,500 (Army 75,000 Navy 13,500 Air 20,000 Air Defence 16,000 Industrial Security Force 9,000 National Guard 100,000) Paramilitary 15,500

ORGANISATIONS BY SERVICE

Army 75,000

FORCES BY ROLE

Armd	3 bde (each: 3 tk bn, 1 mech bn, 1 fd arty bn, 1 recce bn, 1 AD bn, 1 AT bn)
Mech	5 bde (each: 1 tk bn, 3 mech bn, 1 fd arty bn, 1 AD bn, 1 spt bn,)
AB	1 bde (2 AB bn, 3 SF coy)
Arty	1 bde (5 fd arty bn, 2 (SP) MRL bn, 1 (SP) msl bn)
Avn	1 comd (1 atk hel bde, 1 hel bde)
Royal Guard	1 regt (3 lt inf bn)

EQUIPMENT BY TYPE

MBT 565: 115 M1-A2 *Abrams* (200 in store); 450 M-60A3; (145 AMX-30 in store)

RECCE 300 AML-60/AML-90
AIFV 780: 380 AMX-10P; 400 M-2 *Bradley* each with 2 TOW msl, 1 30mm gun
APC 1,840
   APC (T) 1,650 M-113A1/M-113A2/M-113A3 (incl variants)
   APC (W) 150: 150 M-3 *Panhard*; (ε40 AF-40-8-1 *Al-Fahd* in store)
ARTY 855
   SP 155mm 170: 60 AU-F-1; 110 M-109A1B/M-109A2
   TOWED 58: **105mm** (100 M-101/M-102 in store); **155mm** 50: 50 M-114; (40 FH-70 in store); (27 M-198 in store); **203mm** 8 M-115 in store
   MRL 60 ASTROS II
   MOR 400:
      SP 220: **81mm** 70; **107mm** 150 M-30
      TOWED 180: **81mm/107mm** M-30 70; **120mm** 110 Brandt
AT • MSL 2,240+
   SP 290+: 90+ AMX-10P (HOT); 200 VCC-1 *ITOW*
   MANPATS 1950: 1,000 M47 *Dragon*; 950 TOW-2A
   RCL 450: **84mm** 300 *Carl Gustav*; **106mm** 50 M-40A1; **90mm** 100 M-67
   RL 112mm ε200 APILAS
HELICOPTERS
   ATK 12 AH-64 *Apache*
   MRH 21: 6 AS-365N *Dauphin 2* (medevac); 15 Bell 406CS *Combat Scout*
   TPT • Medium 34: 12 S-70A-1 *Desert Hawk*; 22 UH-60A *Black Hawk* (4 medevac)
AD • SAM 1,000+
   SP *Crotale*
   MANPAD 1,000: 500 FIM-43 *Redeye*; 500 FIM-92A *Stinger*
RADAR • LAND AN/TPQ-36 *Firefinder*/AN/TPQ-37 *Firefinder* (arty, mor)
MSL • TACTICAL • SSM 10+ CSS-2 (40 msl)

Navy 13,500

Navy HQ at Riyadh; Eastern Fleet HQ at Jubail; Western FleetHQ at Jeddah

EQUIPMENT BY TYPE
PRINCIPAL SURFACE COMBATANTS 7
   DESTROYERS • DDGHM 3 *Al Riyadh* each with 2 quad lnchr (8 eff.) with MM-40 *Exocet* Block II AShM, 2 8 cell VLS (16 eff.) each with *Aster* 15 SAM, 4 single 533mm TT each with F17P HWT, 1 76mm gun, (capacity 1 AS-365N *Dauphin 2* hel)
   FRIGATES • FFGHM 4 *Madina* (FRA F-2000) each with 2 quad lnchr (8 eff.) each with *Otomat* Mk 2 AShM, 1 octuple lnchr (8 eff.) with *Crotale* SAM, 4 single 533mm ASTT each with F17P HWT, 1 100mm gun, (capacity 1 AS-365N *Dauphin 2* hel)
PATROL AND COASTAL COMBATANTS 30
   CORVETTES • FSG 4 *Badr* (US *Tacoma*) each with 2 Mk 140 *Harpoon* quad (8 eff.) each with RGM-84C *Harpoon* AShM, 2 triple 324mm ASTT (6 eff.) each with Mk 46 LWT, 1 76mm gun
   PCFG 9 *Al Siddiq* (US 58m) each with 2 twin Mk140 lnchr (4 eff.) each with RGM-84C *Harpoon* AShM, 1 76mm gun

PB 17 (US *Halter Marine*)
MINE WARFARE • MINE COUNTERMEASURES 7
    MCC 4 *Addriyah* (US MSC-322)
    MHC 3 *Al Jawf* (UK *Sandown*)
AMPHIBIOUS 8
    LCU 4 (capacity 120 troops)
    LCM 4 (capacity 80 troops)
LOGISTICS AND SUPPORT 5
    AORH 2 *Boraida* (mod FRA *Durance*) (capacity either 2 AS-365F *Dauphin* 2 utl hel or 1 AS-332C *Super Puma*)
    RY 2

FACILITIES

Bases   HQ (Eastern Fleet) located at Jubail; (HQ Western Fleet) Jeddah; (HQ Naval Forces) Riyadh; Dammam; Al Wajh; Ras al Mishab; Ras al Ghar

Naval Aviation

HELICOPTERS
    MRH 34: 6 AS-365N *Dauphin* 2; 15 AS-565 with AS-15TT ASM; 13 Bell 406CS *Combat Scout*
    TPT • Medium 12 AS-332F *Super Puma*/AS-532B *Super Puma* with AM-39 *Exocet* ASM

Marines 3,000

FORCES BY ROLE

Inf 1 regt (2 inf bn)

EQUIPMENT BY TYPE
APC (W) 140 BMP-600P

Air Force 20,000

FORCES BY ROLE

Ftr	1 sqn with *Tornado* ADV; 1 sqn with F-15S *Eagle*; 4 sqn with F-15C; F-15D *Eagle*
FGA	1 sqn with F-5B *Freedom Fighter*/F-5F *Tiger II*/RF-5E *Tigereye*; 2 sqn with F-15S *Eagle*; 3 sqn with *Tornado* GR1A; *Tornado* IDS; 1 sqn with *Typhoon* FGR.4
AEW&C	1 sqn with E-3A *Sentry*
Tpt	3 sqn with C-130E *Hercules*; C-130H *Hercules*; C-130H-30 *Hercules*; CN-235; L-100-30HS (hospital ac)
Tkr	Some sqn with KC-130H *Hercules* (tkr/tpt); KE-3A
Trg	2 (OCU) sqn with F-5B *Freedom Fighter*; 3 sqn with *Hawk* Mk65*; *Hawk* Mk65A*; 1 sqn with *Jetstream* MK31; Some sqn with MFI-17 *Mushshak*; 1 sqn with Cessna 172; 2 sqn with PC-9
Tpt Hel	2 sqn with AS-532 *Cougar* (CSAR); Bell 205 (ABell 205); Bell 206A (AB-206A) *JetRanger*; Bell 212 (AB-212); Bell 412 (AB-412) *Twin Huey* (SAR)

EQUIPMENT BY TYPE
AIRCRAFT 349 combat capable
    FTR 98: 14 F-5B *Freedom Fighter*; 66 F-15C *Eagle*; 18 F-15D *Eagle*; (15 *Tornado* ADV in store)
    FTR/ISR 22 F-5B *Freedom Fighter*/F-5F *Tiger II*/RF-5E *Tigereye**
    FGA 161: 70 F-15S *Eagle*; 75 *Tornado* IDS; 16 *Typhoon*
    ISR 10 *Tornado* GR1A*
    AEW&C 5 E-3A *Sentry*
    TKR/TPT 8 KC-130H *Hercules*
    TKR 7 KE-3A
    TPT 59 **Medium** 41: 7 C-130E *Hercules*; 29 C-130H; 2 C-130H-30 *Hercules*; 3 L-100-30HS (hospital ac) **Light** 18: 13 Cessna 172; 4 CN-235; 1 *Jetstream* Mk31
    TRG 108: 25 *Hawk* Mk65* (incl aerobatic team); 18 *Hawk* Mk65A*; 20 MFI-17 *Mushshak*; 45 PC-9
HELICOPTERS
    MRH 16 Bell 412 (AB-412) *Twin Huey* (SAR)
    TPT 62 **Medium** 10 AS-532 *Cougar* (CSAR) **Light** 52: 22 Bell 205 (AB-205); 13 Bell 206A (AB-206A) *Jet Ranger*; 17 Bell 212 (AB-212)
MSL
    ASM AGM-65 *Maverick*; *Sea Eagle*
    ARM ALARM
    AAM • IR AAM AIM-9J *Sidewinder*/AIM-9L *Sidewinder*/AIM-9P *Sidewinder* **SARH AAM** AIM-7 *Sparrow*; AIM-7M *Sparrow*; **ARH AAM** AIM-120 AMRAAM

Royal Flt

AIRCRAFT • TPT 16 **Medium** 4 VC-130H **Light** 3: 1 Cessna 310; 2 *Learjet* 35 **PAX** 9: 1 B-737-200; 2 B-747SP; 4 BAe-125-800; 2 Gulfstream III
HELICOPTERS • TPT 4+ **Medium** 4: 3 AS-61; 1 S-70 *Black Hawk* **Light** Some Bell 212 (AB-212)

Air Defence Forces 16,000

FORCES BY ROLE

SAM 16 bty with total of 96 PAC-2; 17 bty with total of 73 *Shahine*; with 50 AMX-30SA; 16 bty with total of 128 MIM-23B I-HAWK; 73 units (static defence) with total of 68 *Crotale/Shahine*

EQUIPMENT BY TYPE
AD • SAM 1,805
    SP 581: 40 *Crotale*; 400 FIM-92A *Avenger*; 73 *Shahine*; 68 *Crotale/Shahine*
    TOWED 224: 128 I-HAWK MIM-23B; 96 PAC-2
    MANPAD 500 FIM-43 *Redeye*
    NAVAL 500 *Mistral*
GUNS 1,220
    SP 942: **20mm** 92 M-163 *Vulcan*; **30mm** 850 AMX-30SA; **TOWED** 128: **35mm** 128 GDF *Oerlikon*; **40mm** (150 L/70 in store)
RADARS • AD RADAR 80: 17 AN/FPS-117; 28 AN/TPS-43; AN/TPS-59; 35 AN/TPS-63; AN/TPS-70

Industrial Security Force 9,000+

The force is part of a new security system that will incorporate surveillance and crisis management.

National Guard 75,000 active; 25,000 (tribal levies) (total 100,000)

FORCES BY ROLE

Cav   1 (ceremonial) sqn

Mech Inf 3 bde (each: 4 army bn (all arms))

Inf   5 bde (each: 1 Arty bn, 1 Supply bn, 3 (combined arms) bn)

EQUIPMENT BY TYPE
RECCE 450 LAV-25 *Coyote*
AIFV 1,117 IFV-25
APC • APC (W) 1,410: 1,120 *Piranha II*; 290 V-150 *Commando* (810 in store)
ARTY • TOWED 90: **105mm** 50 M-102; **155mm** 40 M-198
  MOR 81mm
AT • MSL • MANPATS 116+: 116 TOW-2A (2,000 msl); M47 *Dragon*
RCL • 106mm M-40A1
AD • GUNS • TOWED 160: **20mm** 30 M-167 *Vulcan*; **90mm** 130 (M-2)

Paramilitary 15,500+ active

Border Guard 10,500

FORCES BY ROLE
Subordinate to Ministry of Interior. HQ in Riyadh. 9 subordinate regional commands

Mobile Defence	some (long-range patrol/spt) units
MP	some units
Border Def	2 (patrol) units
Def	12 (infrastructure) units; 18 (harbour) units
Coastal Def	some units

EQUIPMENT BY TYPE
HELICOPTERS
  ASW 6 AS-332F *Super Puma* with AM-39 *Exocet* AShM
  TPT • Medium 6 AS-332B *Super Puma*

Coast Guard 4,500

EQUIPMENT BY TYPE
PATROL AND COASTAL COMBATANTS 53
  PBF 6: 4 *Al Jouf*; 2 *Sea Guard*
  PB 47: 39 *Simonneau*; 6 *StanPatrol 2606*; 2 *Al Jubatel*
AMPHIBIOUS • CRAFT 8: 3 UCAC; 5 LCAC
LOGISTICS AND SUPPORT 4: 1 AXL; 3 AO (small)
FACILITIES
Base   Located at Azizam

General Civil Defence Administration Units
HELICOPTERS • TPT • Medium 10 Boeing Vertol 107

Special Security Force 500
APC (W): UR-416

FOREIGN FORCES

United States US Central Command: 258

Syria SYR

Syrian Pound S£		2009	2010	2011
GDP	S£	2.44tr	2.77tr	
	US$	53.7bn	58.3bn	
per capita	US$	2,544	2,592	
Growth	%	4.0	4.0	
Inflation	%	2.9	5.0	
Def exp	S£	101bn		
	US$	2.23bn		
Def bdgt	S£	86.2bn	89.5bn	100bn
	US$	1.89bn	1.89bn	
US$1=S£		45.52	47.43	

Population   22,505,091

Age	0–14	15–19	20–24	25–29	30–64	65 plus
Male	18.1%	5.6%	5.4%	4.7%	15.4%	1.7%
Female	17.2%	5.3%	5.1%	4.5%	15.1%	2.0%

Capabilities

ACTIVE 295,000 (Army 220,000 Navy 5,000 Air 30,000 Air Defence 40,000) **Paramilitary 108,000**

RESERVE 314,000 (Army 280,000 Navy 4,000 Air 10,000 Air Defence 20,000)

Terms of service conscription, 30 months

ORGANISATIONS BY SERVICE

Army 220,000 (incl conscripts)

FORCES BY ROLE
3 Corps HQ

Armd	7 div (each: 3 armd; 1 mech; 1 arty bde)
Tk	1 indep regt
Mech	3 div (under strength) (each: 1 armd, 2 mech, 1 arty bde)
Inf	4 indep bde
SF	1 div (10 SF gp)
Arty	2 indep bde
AT	2 indep bde
SSM	1 (Coastal Def) bde with SS-C-1B *Sepal* and SS-C-3 *Styx*; 1 bde (3 SSM bn with FROG-7); 1 bde (3 SSM bn with SS-21); 1 bde (3 SSM bn with *Scud*-B/-C)
Border Guard	5 lt inf bde (under command of Mukhabarat for border sy)
Security	1 div (Republican Guard) (3 armd, 1 mech, 1 arty bde)

Reserves

Armd	1 div HQ; 4 bde; 2 regt
Inf	31 regt
Arty	3 regt

EQUIPMENT BY TYPE

MBT 4,950: 1,500–1,700 T-72 T-72M; 1,000 T-62K/T-62M; 2,250 T-55/T-55MV (some in store)

RECCE 590 BRDM-2

AIFV up to 2,450 BMP-1/BMP-2/BMP-3

APC (W) 1,500: 500 BTR-152; 1,000 BTR-50/BTR-60/BTR-70

ARTY up to 3,440+

SP 500+: **122mm** 450+: 400 2S1 *Carnation* (*Gvosdik*); 50+ D-30 (mounted on T34/85 chassis); **152mm** 50 2S3 (*Akatsiya*)

TOWED 2,030: **122mm** 1,150: 500 D-30; 150 (M-30) M1938; 500 in store (no given designation); **130mm** 700-800 M-46; **152mm** 70 D-20/ML-20 M1937; **180mm** 10 S23

MRL up to 500: **107mm** up to 200 Type-63; **122mm** up to 300 BM-21 (*Grad*)

MOR 410+: **82mm**; **120mm** circa 400 M-1943; **160mm** M-160 (hundreds); **240mm** up to 10 M-240

AT • MSL 2,600

SP 410 9P133 BRDM-2 *Sagger*

MANPATS 2190+: 150 AT-4 9K111 *Spigot*; 40 AT-5 9K113 *Spandrel*; AT-7 9K115 *Saxhorn*; 800 AT-10 9K116 *Stabber*; 1,000 AT-14 9M133 *Kornet*; 200 *Milan*

RL 73mm RPG-7 *Knout*; **105mm** RPG-29

AD • SAM 4,184+

SP 84: 14 9K33 *Osa* (SA-8 *Gecko*); 20 9K31 *Strela-1* (SA-9 *Gaskin*); 20 9K37 *Buk* (SA-11 *Gadfly*); 30 9K35 *Strela-10* (SA-13 *Gopher*)

MANPAD 4,100+: 4,000+ 9K32 *Strela-2* (SA-7 *Grail*)‡; 9K38 *Igla* (SA-18 *Grouse*); 100 9K36 *Strela-3* (SA-14 *Gremlin*)

GUNS 1,225+

SP ZSU-23-4

TOWED 23mm 600 ZU-23; **37mm** M-1939; **57mm** 600 S-60; **100mm** 25 KS-19

MSL • TACTICAL • SSM 94+: 18 Scud-B/Scud-C/Scud-D; 30 look-a-like; 18 FROG-7; 18+ SS-21 *Tochka* (*Scarab*); 4 P-35 (SS-C-1B *Sepal*); 6 P-15M *Termit*-R (SS-C-3 *Styx*) (ε850 SSM msl total)

Navy 5,000

EQUIPMENT BY TYPE

PATROL AND COASTAL COMBATANTS 32:

CORVETTES • FS 2 *Petya* III each with 1 triple 533mm ASTT (3 eff.) with SAET-60 HWT, 4 RBU 2500 *Smerch* 1 (64 eff.)†, 2 twin 76mm gun (4 eff.)

PBFG 22

16 *Osa* I/II each with 4 single lnchr each with P-15M *Termit*-M (SS-N-2C *Styx*) AShM

6 *Tir* each with 2 single lnchr with C-802 (CSS-N-8 *Saccade*) AShM

PB 8 *Zhuk*

MINE WARFARE • MINE COUNTERMEASURES 7:

MHC 1 *Sonya*

MSO 1 *Natya*

MSI 5 *Yevgenya*

AMPHIBIOUS • LANDING SHIPS • LSM 3 *Polnochny* B (capacity 6 MBT; 180 troops)

LOGISTICS AND SUPPORT • TRG 1

FACILITIES

Bases   Located at Latakia, Tartus, Minet el-Baida

Naval Aviation

HELICOPTER

ASW 13: 2 Ka-28 *Helix A* (air force manned); 11 Mi-14 *Haze*

Air Force 40,000 (incl 10,000 reserves); 60,000 Air Defence (incl 20,000 reserves) (total 100,000)

Flying hours   15 to 25 hrs/year on FGA/ftr; 70 hrs/year; 50 hrs/year on MBB-223 *Flamingo* trg ac

FORCES BY ROLE

Ftr   4 sqn with MiG-23 MLD *Flogger*; 4 sqn with MiG-25 *Foxbat*; 3 sqn with MiG-29A *Fulcrum A*

FGA   7 sqn with MiG-21 *Fishbed*; 2 sqn with MiG-23BN *Flogger H*; 5 sqn with Su-22 (Su-17M-2) *Fitter D*; 1 sqn with Su-24 *Fencer*

ISR   4 sqn with MiG-21H *Fishbed*/MiG-21J *Fishbed**; MiG-25R *Foxbat**

Tpt   Some sqn with An-24 *Coke*; An-26 *Curl*; *Falcon* 20; *Falcon* 900; Il-76 *Candid*; Mi-8 *Hip*; Mi-17 *Hip H*; PZL Mi-2 *Hoplite*; Yak-40 *Codling*

Atk hel   3 sqns with Mi-25 *Hind D*; SA-342L *Gazelle*

Trg   Some units with PA-31 *Navajo*; L-39 *Albatros*; MBB-223 *Flamingo* (basic); MFI-17 *Mushshak*; MiG-21U *Mongol A*; MiG-23UM; MiG-25U *Foxbat*

EQUIPMENT BY TYPE

AIRCRAFT 555 combat capable

FTR 158+: 80 MiG-23MLD *Flogger*; 6 MiG-23UM; 30 MiG-25 *Foxbat*; 2 MiG-25U *Foxbat*; 40+ MiG-29A *Fulcrum*

FGA 309: 159 MiG-21H *Fishbed*; 20 MiG-21U *Mongol A*; 60 MiG-23BN *Flogger H*; 50 Su-22 *Fitter D*; 20 Su-24 *Fencer*

ISR 48: 8 MiG-25R *Foxbat**; 40 MiG-21 H/J *Fishbed**

TPT 22 Heavy 4 Il-76 *Candid* **Light** 15: 1 An-24 *Coke*; 6 An-26 *Curl*; 2 PA-31 *Navajo*; 6 Yak-40 *Codling* **PAX** 3: 2 *Falcon* 20; 1 *Falcon* 900

TRG 111: 30 L-39 *Albatros*; 40 L-39 *Albatros**; 35 MBB-223 *Flamingo* (basic); 6 MFI-17 *Mushshak*

HELICOPTERS

ATK 36 Mi-25 *Hind D*

MRH 35 SA-342L *Gazelle*

MRH/TPT 100 Mi-8 *Hip* (med tpt)/Mi-17 *Hip H*

TPT • Light 20 PZL Mi-2 *Hoplite*

MSL

ASM Kh-25 (AS-7 *Kerry*); HOT

AAM • IR AAM R-3 (AA-2 *Atoll*)‡; R-60 (AA-8 *Aphid*); R-73 (AA-11 *Archer*) **IR/SARH AAM** R-40/46 (AA-6 *Acrid*); R-23/24 (AA-7 *Apex*); R-27 (AA-10 *Alamo*)

Air Defence Command 60,000

FORCES BY ROLE

AD   2 div (total: 25 AD bde (total: 150 SAM bty with total of 148 S-125 *Pechora* (SA-3 *Goa*); 195 2K12 *Kub* (SA-6 *Gainful*); 320 S-75 *Dvina* (SA-2 *Guideline*), some ADA bty with total of 4,000 9K32 *Strela*-2/M (SA-7A *Grail*/SA-7B *Grail*)‡)

SAM 2 regt (each: 2 SAM bn (each: 2 SAM bty with total of 44 S-200 *Angara* (SA-5 *Gammon*))

EQUIPMENT BY TYPE

AD • SAM 4,707
  SP 195 2K12 *Kub* (SA-6 *Gainful*)
  TOWED 468: 320 S-72 *Dvina* (SA-2 *Guideline*); 148 S-125 *Pechora* (SA-3 *Goa*)
  STATIC/SHELTER 44 S-200 *Angara* (SA-5 *Gammon*)
  MANPAD 4,000 9K32 *Strela*-2/2M (SA-7A *Grail*/SA-7B *Grail*)‡

Paramilitary ε108,000

Gendarmerie 8,000
Ministry of Interior

Workers' Militia ε100,000
People's Army (Ba'ath Party)

FOREIGN FORCES

UNTSO unless specified. Figures represent total numbers for mission in Israel, Syria and Lebanon.

Argentina 5 obs
Australia 11 obs
Austria 7 obs • UNDOF 378; elm 1 inf bn
Belgium 2 obs
Canada 8 obs • UNDOF 2
Chile 3 obs
China, People's Republic of 5 obs
Croatia UNDOF 94; 1 inf coy
Denmark 10 obs
Estonia 1 obs
Finland 14 obs
France 2 obs
India UNDOF 190; elm 1 log bn
Ireland 12 obs
Italy 7 obs
Japan UNDOF 31; elm 1 log bn
Nepal 4 obs
Netherlands 12 obs
New Zealand 7 obs
Norway 13 obs
Philippines UNDOF 349; 1 inf bn
Russia 5 obs • Army/Navy 150, naval facility reportedly under renovation at Tartus
Slovakia 2 obs
Slovenia 2 obs
Sweden 5 obs
Switzerland 13 obs
United States 2 obs

Tunisia TUN

Tunisian Dinar D		2009	2010	2011
GDP	D	58.8bn	65.1bn	
	US$	43.6bn	45.4bn	
per capita	US$	4,177	4,376	
Growth	%	3.1	4.0	
Inflation	%	6.3	4.5	
Def exp	D	718m		
	US$	532m		
FMA (US)	US$	12.0m	15.0m	4.9m
US$1=D		1.35	1.43	

Population	10,373,957					
Age	0-14	15-19	20-24	25-29	30-64	65 plus
Male	11.3%	4.6%	4.8%	5.0%	21.4%	3.4%
Female	10.6%	4.3%	4.5%	4.8%	21.5%	4.0%

Capabilities

ACTIVE 35,800 (Army 27,000 Navy 4,800 Air 4,000)
Paramilitary 12,000
Terms of service 12 months selective

ORGANISATIONS BY SERVICE

Army 5,000; 22,000 conscript (total 27,000)

FORCES BY ROLE

Mech   3 bde (each: 1 armd regt, 2 mech inf regt, 1 arty regt, 1 AD regt)
SF   1 (Sahara) bde; 1 bde
Engr   1 regt

EQUIPMENT BY TYPE

MBT 84: 30 M-60A1; 54 M-60A3
LT TK 48 SK-105 *Kuerassier*
RECCE 60: 40 AML-90; 20 *Saladin*
APC 268
  APC (T) 140 M-113A1/M-113A2
  APC (W) 128: 18 EE-11 *Urutu*; 110 Fiat 6614
ARTY 276
  TOWED 115: **105mm** 48 M-101A1/M-101A2; **155mm** 67: 12 M-114A1; 55 M-198
  MOR 161: **81mm** 95; **107mm** 48 (some SP); **120mm** 18 Brandt
AT • MSL 590
  SP 35 M-901 ITV TOW
  MANPATS 555: 500 *Milan*; 55 TOW
  RL 89mm 600: 300 LRAC; 300 M-20
AD • SAM 86
  SP 26 M-48 *Chaparral*
  MANPAD 60 RBS-70
  GUNS 127
    SP 40mm 12 M-42
    TOWED 115: **20mm** 100 M-55; **37mm** 15 Type-55 (M-1939)/Type-65
RADAR • LAND RASIT (veh, arty)

Navy ε4,800

EQUIPMENT BY TYPE

PATROL AND COASTAL COMBATANTS 25

  PCFG 3 *La Galite* (FRA *Combattante* III) each with 2 quad Mk140 lnchr (8 eff.) each with MM-40 *Exocet* AShM, 1 76mm gun

  PCG 3 *Bizerte* (FRA P-48) each with 8 SS 12M AShM

  PCF 6 *Albatros* (GER Type 143B) each with 2 single 533mm TT

  PB 13: 3 *Utique* (mod PRC *Haizhui* II); 10 (various)

LOGISTICS AND SUPPORT 6:

  AWT 1

  AGS 1

  ABU 3

  TRG 1 *Salambo* (US *Conrad*, survey)

FACILITIES

Bases Located at Bizerte, Sfax, Kelibia

Air Force 4,000

FORCES BY ROLE

FGA   1 sqn with F-5E/F-5F *Tiger* II

Tpt   1 sqn with C-130B *Hercules*; C-130E *Hercules*; C-130H *Hercules*; Falcon 20; G-222; L-410 *Turbolet*

Liaison 1 sqn with S-208A

Tpt/utl 2 sqn with AS-350A *Ecureuil*; AS-365 *Dauphin* 2;
hel   AB-205 (Bell 205); SA-313; SA-316 *Alouette III*; UH-1H *Iroquois*; UH-1N *Iroquois*; 1 sqn with HH-3E

Trg   2 sqn with L-59 *Albatros**; MB-326B; SF-260; 1 sqn with MB-326K; MB-326L

EQUIPMENT BY TYPE

AIRCRAFT 27 combat capable

  FTR 12 F-5E *Tiger II*/F-5F *Tiger II*

  ATK 3 MB-326K

  TPT 22 **Medium** 16: 8 C-130B *Hercules*; 1 C-130E *Hercules*; 2 C-130H *Hercules*; 5 G-222; **Light** 5: 3 L-410 *Turbolet*; 2 S-208A **PAX** 1 *Falcon* 20

  TRG 33: 12 L-59 *Albatros**; 4 MB-326B; 3 MB-326L; 14 SF-260

HELICOPTERS

  MRH 10: 1 AS-365 *Dauphin* 2; 6 SA-313; 3 SA-316 *Alouette III*

  SAR 11 HH-3 *Sea King*

  TPT • Light 33: 6 AS-350B *Ecureuil*; 15 Bell 205 (AB-205); 10 Bell 205 (UH-1H *Iroquois*); 2 Bell 212 (UH-1N *Iroquois*)

MSL • AAM • IR AAM AIM-9J *Sidewinder*

Paramilitary 12,000

National Guard 12,000

Ministry of Interior

PATROL AND COASTAL COMBATANTS 21

  PCC 6 *Kondor* I (GDR)

  PCI 15: 5 *Bremse* (GDR); 4 *Gabes*; 4 *Rodman*; 2 *Socomena*

HELICOPTERS • MRH 8 SA-318 *Alouette II*/SA-319 *Alouette III*

DEPLOYMENT

CENTRAL AFRICAN REPUBLIC/CHAD

UN • MINURCAT 2; 4 obs

CÔTE D'IVOIRE

UN • UNOCI 4; 7 obs

DEMOCRATIC REPUBLIC OF THE CONGO

UN • MONUSCO 46; 30 obs

United Arab Emirates UAE

Emirati Dirham D		2009	2010	2011
GDP	D	822bn	880bn	
	US$	224bn	240bn	
per capita	US$	48,683	50,910	
Growth	%	-0.7	-2.5	
Inflation	%	1.2	2.0	
Def exp	D	29.2bn		
	US$	7.96bn		
Def bdgt[a]	D	28.9bn	29.2bn	31.7bn
	US$	7.88bn	7.96bn	
US$1=D		3.67	3.67	

[a] Excludes possible extra-budgetary procurement funding

Population   4,707,307

Ethnic groups: Nationals 24%; Expatriates 76% of which Indian 30%, Pakistani 20%; other Arab 12%; other Asian 10%; UK 2%; other European 1%

Age	0–14	15–19	20–24	25–29	30–64	65 plus
Male	10.4%	2.9%	5.5%	10.7%	38.6%	0.6%
Female	10.0%	2.4%	3.3%	4.1%	11.2%	0.3%

Capabilities

ACTIVE 51,000 (Army 44,000 Navy 2,500 Air 4,500)

The Union Defence Force and the armed forces of the UAE (Abu Dhabi, Dubai, Ras al-Khaimah, Fujairah, Ajman, Umm al-Qawayn and Sharjah) were formally merged in 1976 and headquartered in Abu Dhabi. Dubai still maintains independent forces, as do other Emirates to a lesser degree.

ORGANISATIONS BY SERVICE

Army 44,000 (incl Dubai 15,000)

FORCES BY ROLE

GHQ Abu Dhabi

Armd   2 bde

Mech Inf 3 bde

Inf   2 bde

Arty   1 bde (3 arty regt)

Royal Guard 1 bde

Dubai Independent Forces

Mech inf 2 bde

EQUIPMENT BY TYPE

MBT 471: 390 *Leclerc*; 36 OF-40 Mk2 (*Lion*); 45 AMX-30

LT TK 76 *Scorpion*

RECCE 89: 49 AML-90; 24 VBL; 16 TPz-1 *Fuchs* (NBC); (20 *Ferret* in store); (20 *Saladin* in store)

AIFV 430: 15 AMX-10P; 415 BMP-3

APC 892

    APC (T) 136 AAPC (incl 53 engr plus other variants)

    APC (W) 756: 90 BTR-3U *Guardian*; 120 EE-11 *Urutu*; 370 M-3 *Panhard*; 80 VCR (incl variants); 20 VAB; 76 RG-31 *Nyala*

ARV 46

ARTY 561+

    SP 155mm 221: 78 G-6; 125 M-109A3; 18 Mk F3

    TOWED 93: **105mm** 73 ROF lt; **130mm** 20 Type-59-I

    MRL 92+: **70mm** 18 LAU-97; **122mm** 48+: 48 Firos-25 (est 24 op); Type-90 (reported); **227mm** 20 HIMARS being delivered; **300mm** 6 9A52 *Smerch*

    MOR 155: **81mm** 134: 20 Brandt; 114 L16; **120mm** 21 Brandt

AT • MSL 305+

    SP 20 HOT

    MANPATS 285+: 30 HOT; 230 *Milan*; 25 TOW; (*Vigilant* in store)

    RCL 262: **84mm** 250 *Carl Gustav*; **106mm** 12 M-40

AD • SAM • MANPAD 40+: 20+ *Blowpipe*; 20 *Mistral*

GUNS 62

    SP 20mm 42 M3 VDAA

    TOWED 30mm 20 GCF-BM2

MSL • TACTICAL • SSM 6 *Scud*-B (up to 20 msl)

Navy ε2,500

EQUIPMENT BY TYPE

PATROL AND COASTAL COMBATANTS 16

    CORVETTES • FSGM 2 *Muray Jib* (GER Lurssen 62m) each with 2 quad lnchr (8 eff.) each with MM-40 *Exocet* AShM, 1 octuple lnchr with *Crotale* SAM, 1 76mm gun, 1 hel landing platform

    PCFGM 2 *Mubarraz* (GER Lurssen 45m) each with 2 twin lnchr (4 eff.) each with MM-40 *Exocet* AShM, 1 sextuple lnchr with *Mistral* SAM, 1 76mm gun

    PCFG 6 *Ban Yas* (GER Lurssen TNC-45) each with 2 twin lnchr (4 eff.) each with MM-40 *Exocet* AShM, 1 76mm gun

    PB 6 *Ardhana* (UK Vosper 33m)

MINE WARFARE • MINE COUNTERMEASURES •

MHO 2 *Al Murjan* (*Frankenthal* Class Type 332)

AMPHIBIOUS • LANDING CRAFT 28

    LCP 16: 12 (capacity 40 troops); 4 (Fast Supply Vessel multi-purpose)

    LCU 5: 3 *Al Feyi* (capacity 56 troops); 2 (capacity 40 troops and additional vehicles)

    LCT 7

LOGISTICS AND SUPPORT 3: 1 YDT; 2 YTM

FACILITIES

Bases   Located at Mina Sakr (Sharjah), Mina Rashid, Khor Fakkan, Mina Zayed (Dubai), Dalma, Abu Dhabi (Main base), Mina Khalid, Mina Jabal (Ras al-Khaimah)

Naval Aviation

AIRCRAFT • TPT • Light 2 *Learjet* 35A

HELICOPTERS

    ASW 14: 7 AS-332F *Super Puma* (5 in ASUW role);

    MRH 11: 7 AS-565 *Panther*; 4 SA-316 *Alouette III*

Air Force 4,500

Incl Police Air Wing

Flying hours   110 hrs/year

FORCES BY ROLE

FGA   3 sqn with F-16E/F Block 60 *Fighting Falcon*; 3 sqn with *Mirage* 2000-9DAD/2000-9RAD; 1 sqn with *Mirage* M-2000DAD; 1 sqn with *Hawk* Mk63*/Mk63A*/Mk63C*; 1 sqn with *Hawk* Mk102*

ISR   1 sqn with *Mirage* M-2000 RAD*

SAR   1 sqn with AW-109K2; AW-139

Tpt   3 sqn with An-124 *Condor*; Beech 350 *King Air*; C-130H *Hercules*; C-130H-30 *Hercules*; CN-235M-100; DHC-6-300 *Twin Otter*; IL-76 *Candid* on lease; L-100-30

Trg   1 (OCU) unit with *Hawk* Mk61*; some sqn with Grob 115TA; PC-7 *Turbo Trainer*

Atk hel   2 sqn with AH-64A/D *Apache*; AS-550C3 *Fennec*; SA-342K *Gazelle* with HOT

Tpt hel   1 sqn with IAR-330 SOCAT *Puma*/SA-330 *Puma*; CH-47C *Chinook* (SF); AB-139 (VIP); AS-365F *Dauphin 2* (VIP); Bell 206 *Jet Ranger* trg; Bell 214; Bell 407; Bell 412 *Twin Huey*

EQUIPMENT BY TYPE

AIRCRAFT 184 combat capable

    FGA 142: 55 F-16E Block 60 *Fighting Falcon* (*Desert Eagle*); 25 F-16F Block 60 Fighting Falcon (13 to remain in US for trg); 18 *Mirage* 2000-9DAD; 44 *Mirage* 2000-9RAD

    ISR 7 *Mirage* 2000 RAD*

    TPT 23 **Heavy** 5: 1 An-124 *Condor*; 4 Il-76 *Candid* on lease; **Medium** 8: 4 C-130H *Hercules*; 2 C-130H-30 *Hercules*; 2 L-100-30 **Light** 10: 2 Beech 350 *King Air*; 7 CN-235M-100; 1 DHC-6-300 *Twin Otter*

    TRG 77: 12 Grob 115TA; 5 *Hawk* Mk61*; 17 *Hawk* Mk63A/*Hawk* Mk63C*; 13 *Hawk* Mk102*; 30 PC-7 *Turbo Trainer*

HELICOPTERS

    ATK 30 AH-64A *Apache* (being upgraded to AH-64D standard)

    MRH 23+: 4 AS-365F *Dauphin 2* (VIP); Some AS-550C3 *Fennec*; 9 Bell 412 *Twin Huey*; 10 SA-342K *Gazelle*

    TPT 51 **Heavy** 12 CH-47C *Chinook* (SF) **Medium** 15 IAR-330 SOCAT *Puma*/SA-330 *Puma* **Light** 24: 3 AW-109K2; 8 AW-139 (incl 2 VIP); 9 Bell 206 *Jet Ranger* trg; 3 Bell 214; 1 Bell 407

MSL

    ASM AGM-65G *Maverick*; AGM-114 *Hellfire*; Hydra-70; Hakeem 1/2/3 (A/B) HOT

    LACM *Black Shaheen* (*Storm Shadow*/SCALP EG variant)

    AAM • IR AAM AIM-9L *Sidewinder*; R-550 *Magic*

    IIR/ARH AAM *Mica* **ARH AAM** AIM-120 AMRAAM

Air Defence

FORCES BY ROLE

AD 2 bde (each: 3 bn with I-HAWK MIM-23B)

SAM 3 short-range bn with *Crotale*; *Mistral*; *Rapier*; RB-70; *Javelin*; 9K38 *Igla* (SA-18 *Grouse*)

EQUIPMENT BY TYPE

AD • SAM

  SP *Crotale*; RB-70

  TOWED I-HAWK MIM-23B; *Rapier*

  MANPAD *Javelin*; 9K38 Igla (SA-18 *Grouse*)

  NAVAL *Mistral*

Paramilitary • Coast Guard

Ministry of Interior

PATROL AND COASTAL COMBATANTS 51

  PBF 9 (ITA *Baglietto*)

  PB 42: 2 *Protector*; 16 (US Camcraft '65); 5 (US Camcraft '77); 19 (various)

DEPLOYMENT

AFGHANISTAN

NATO • ISAF 35

FOREIGN FORCES

France 86: 3 *Mirage* 2000-5, 1 KC-135F at al Dhafra (To operate alongside UAE *Mirage* 2000-9s)

South Korea: 130–150 SOF for training activities at UAE Special Operations School at Al-Ain (due to deploy Jan 2011)

United States: 2bty with MIM-104 *Patriot*

Yemen, Republic of YEM

Yemeni Rial R		2009	2010	2011
GDP	R	5.10tr	6.81tr	
	US$	25.1bn	30.7bn	
per capita	US$	1,066	1,264	
Growth	%	3.8	7.9	
Inflation	%	3.7	9.8	
Def bdgt	R	318bn	448bn	
	US$	1.57bn	2.02bn	
FMA (US)	US$	2.8m	12.5m	35.0m
US$1=R		202.81	222.01	

Population   24,255,928

Ethnic groups: Majority Arab, some African and South Asian

Age	0–14	15–19	20–24	25–29	30–64	65 plus
Male	21.9%	5.7%	5.0%	4.5%	12.4%	1.2%
Female	21.1%	5.5%	4.9%	4.1%	12.2%	1.4%

Capabilities

ACTIVE 66,700 (Army 60,000 Navy 1,700 Air Force 3,000, Air Defence 2,000) **Paramilitary 71,200**

Terms of service conscription, 2 years

ORGANISATIONS BY SERVICE

Army 60,000 (incl conscripts)

FORCES BY ROLE

Armd	8 bde
Mech	6 bde
Inf	16 bde
SF	1 bde
Cdo/AB	2 bde
Arty	3 bde
SSM	1 bde
Gd/Central Guard	1 force
AD	2 bn

EQUIPMENT BY TYPE

MBT 790: 50 M-60A1; 60 T-72; 200 T-62; 450 T-54/T-55; 30 T-34

RECCE 148: 80 AML-90; 18 YLAV *Cougar*; 50 BRDM-2

AIFV 200: 100 BMP-1; 100 BMP-2

APC 240

  APC (T) 60 M-113A

  APC (W) 180: 60 BTR-40; 100 BTR-60; 20 BTR-152; (470 BTR-40/BTR-60/BTR-152 in store)

ARTY 1,167

  SP 122mm 25 2S1 *Carnation*

  TOWED 310: **105mm** 25 M-101A1; **122mm** 200: 130 D-30; 30 M-1931/37; 40 M-30 M-1938; **130mm** 60 M-46; **152mm** 10 D-20; **155mm** 15 M-114

  COASTAL 130mm 36 SM-4-1

  MRL 294: **122mm** 280 BM-21 (150 op); **140mm** 14 BM-14

  MOR 502: **81mm** 200; **82mm** 90 M-43; **107mm** 12; **120mm** 100; **160mm** ε100

AT • MSL • MANPATS 71: 35 AT-3 9K11 *Sagger*; 24 M47 *Dragon*; 12 TOW

  RCL 75mm M-20; **82mm** B-10; **107mm** B-11

  RL 66mm M-72 LAW; **73mm** RPG-7 *Knout*

  GUNS 50+

    SP 100mm 30 SU-100

    TOWED 20+: **85mm** D-44; **100mm** 20 M-1944

AD • SAM ε800

    SP 9K31 *Strela*-1 (SA-9 *Gaskin*); 9K35 *Strela*-10 (SA-13 *Gopher*)

    MANPAD 9K32 *Strela*-2 (SA-7 *Grail*)‡; 9K36 *Strela*-3 (SA-14 *Gremlin*)

  GUNS 530

    SP 70: **20mm** 20 M-163 *Vulcan*; **23mm** 50 ZSU-23-4

    TOWED 460: **20mm** 50 M-167 *Vulcan*; **23mm** 100 ZU-23-2; **37mm** 150 M-1939; **57mm** 120 S-60; **85mm** 40 M-1939 KS-12

MSL • TACTICAL • SSM 28: 12 FROG-7; 10 SS-21 *Scarab* (*Tochka*); 6 *Scud*-B (ε33 msl)

Navy 1,700

EQUIPMENT BY TYPE

PATROL AND COASTAL COMBATANTS 20

  PCO 1 *Tarantul*† with 2 twin lnchr (4 eff. fitted for P-15 *Termit*-M (SS-N-2C *Styx*) AShM

  PBF 6 *Baklan*

PB 13: 3 *Hounan*† each with 4 single lnchr (fitted for C-801 (CSS-N-4 *Sardine*) AShM); 10 P-1000 (Austal 37.5m)

MINE WARFARE • MINE COUNTERMEASURES • MSO 1 *Natya* (FSU)

AMPHIBIOUS

LANDING SHIPS • LSM 1 NS-722 (capacity 5 MBT; 110 troops)

LANDING CRAFT • LCU 3 *Deba*

FACILITIES

Bases   Located at Aden, Hodeida

Minor   These have naval spt eqpt. located at Socotra,
Bases   Al-Mukalla, Perim Island

Air Force 3,000

FORCES BY ROLE

Ftr   3 sqn with F-5E *Tiger II*; MiG-21 *Fishbed*; MiG-29SMT/MiG-29UBT *Fulcrum*

FGA   1 sqn with Su-20 *Fitter C*/Su-22 *Fitter D*

Tpt   1 sqn with An-12 *Cub*; An-26 *Curl*; C-130H *Hercules*; Il-14 *Crate*; Il-76 *Candid*

Trg   1 trg school with F-5B *Freedom Fighter*†; L-39C; MiG-21U *Mongol A*; Yak-11; Z-242

Hel   1 sqn with Bell 47 (AB-47); Bell 212; Mi-8 *Hip*; Mi-35 *Hind*

EQUIPMENT BY TYPE

AIRCRAFT 79 combat capable

FTR 12: 2 F-5B *Freedom Fighter*†; 10 F-5E *Tiger II*

FGA 67: 15 MiG-21 *Fishbed*; 4 MiG-21U *Mongol A**; 16 MiG-29SMT *Fulcrum*; 2 MiG-29UBT; 30 Su-20 *Fitter C*/Su-22 *Fitter D*

TPT 18: 2 An-12 *Cub*; 6 An-26 *Curl*; 3 C-130H *Hercules*; 4 Il-14 *Crate* 4; 3 Il-76 *Candid*

TRG 44: 12 L-39C; 14 Yak-11 *Moose*; 12 Z-242

HELICOPTERS

ATK 8 Mi-35 *Hind*

TPT • Medium 9 Mi-8 *Hip* Light 2 Bell 212

TRG 1 Bell 47 (AB-47)

Air Defence 2,000

AD • SAM:

SP 2K12 *Kub* (SA-6 *Gainful*); 9K31 *Strela-1* (SA-9 *Gaskin*); 9K35 *Strela-10* (SA-13 *Gopher*)

TOWED S-75 *Dvina* (SA-2 *Guideline*); S-125 *Pechora* (SA-3 *Goa*)

MANPAD 9K32 *Strela-2* (SA-7 *Grail*); 9K36 *Strela-3* (SA-14 *Gremlin*)

MSL • IR AAM R-3 (AA-2 *Atoll*)‡; R-60 (AA-8 *Aphid*); AIM-9 *Sidewinder* IR/SARH AAM R-27 (AA-10 *Alamo*)

Paramilitary 71,200+

Ministry of the Interior Forces 50,000

Tribal Levies 20,000+

Yemeni Coast Guard Authority ε1,200

PATROL AND COASTAL COMBATANTS 12

PBF 4 *Archangel* (US)

PB 8

DEPLOYMENT

COTE D'IVOIRE

UN • UNOCI 1; 8 obs

DEMOCRATIC REPUBLIC OF THE CONGO

UN • MONUSCO 6 obs

LIBERIA

UN • UNMIL 1

SUDAN

UN • UNAMID 5; 22 obs

UN • UNMIS 21 obs

WESTERN SAHARA

UN • MINURSO 10 obs

Table 19 **Selected Arms Procurements and Deliveries, Middle East and North Africa**

Designation	Type	Quantity	Contract Value	Supplier Country	Prime Contractor	Order Date	First Delivery Due	Notes
Algeria (ALG)								
T-90S	MBT	300	US$1bn	RUS	Rosoboron-export	2006	n.k.	Deliveries ongoing
T-72	MBT Upgrade	250	US$200m	RUS	Rosoboron-export	2006	n.k.	Upgrade. Delivery status unclear due to order suspension in 2008
BMP-2	AIFV Upgrade	400	US$200m	RUS	Rosoboron-export	2006	n.k.	Upgrade. Delivery status unclear due to order suspension in 2008
Kornet-E (AT-14)	MANPATS	216	US450m	RUS	Rosoboron-export	2006	n.k.	Delivery status unclear due to order suspension in 2008
Metis- M1 (AT-13)	MANPATS	–	US$50m	RUS	Rosoboron-export	2006	n.k.	Delivery status unclear due to order suspension in 2008
S-300PMU-2	SAM	8	US$1bn	RUS	Rosoboron-export	2006	n.k.	8 bty. Delivery status unclear due to order suspension in 2008
Pantsyr-S1	AD	38	US$500m	RUS	Rosoboron-export	2006	2010	Delivery due 2010–11
FPB 98	PB	21	€135m (US$198m)	FRA	OCEA	2008	2009	For coast guard. 7 in service; Final delivery due 2012
Su-30 MKA	FGA ac	16	US$1bn	RUS	Rosoboron-export	2010	2011	Delivery to be complete by end 2012
Yak-130	Trg ac	16	US$250m	RUS	Rosoboron-export	2006	2009	Incl simulator. First delivery due 2011
AW-139	MRH Hel	4	US$635m	ALG/UK	Agusta Westland	2007	n.k.	Contract price includes 6 AW101s
AW-139	MRH Hel	5	n.k	ALG/UK	Agusta Westland	2009	2010	For use by Protection Civile force
AW101 Merlin	Tpt Hel	6	US$635m	ALG/UK	Agusta Westland	2007	n.k	For navy. Contract price includes 4 AW-139s
AW101 Merlin	Tpt Hel	42	n.k	ALG/UK	Agusta Westland	2009	2010	follow-on deal from 2007 supply of 6 AW101 Merlin and 4 Super Lynx Mk 130.Order currently on hold
AW-109	Tpt Hel	25	n.k	ALG/UK	Agusta Westland	2009	2010	15 for Gendarmerie Nationale's Border Protection Force; 10 for police
Bahrain (BHR)								
M113A2	APC Upgrade	n.k.	n.k.	TUR	FNSS	2007	n.k.	Refit with MKEK 81mm mortars
Landing Craft	LC	4	n.k.	UAE	ADSB	2008	2010	Two 16m Sea Keeper Fast Landing Craft delivered. Two 42m landing craft still on order for delivery 2010/11
UH-60M Blackhawk	Tpt Hel	9	n.k.	US	Sikorsky	2010	2011	All to be delivered by May 2011
Egypt (EGY)								
M1-A1 Abrams	MBT	125	US$349m	US	General Dynamics	2007	2009	Co-production with Cairo plant. Final delivery due Jul 2011
S-125 Pechora (SA-3 Goa)	SAM Upgrade	30	n.k.	RUS	Oboronit-elniye Sistemy	1999	n.k.	Upgrade to Pechora-2M. 30 btn to be ugraded in 3 stages. First stage completed 2006. 2nd stage ongoing
Ambassador Mk III	PCFG	4	US$1.3bn	US	VT Halter Marine	2008	2012	Phase II of the Fast Missile Craft (FMC) project
RAM Mk49	GMLS	3	US$24.75m	US	Raytheon	2005	2009	Upgrade for Fast Missile Craft. Mk49 RAM launchers and RAM Block 1A msl. Delivery status unclear
F-16C/D Fighting Falcon	FGA ac	20	n.k.	US	Lockheed Martin	2010	n.k.	16 F-16C and 4 F-16D. To be complete by 2013

Table 19 **Selected Arms Procurements and Deliveries, Middle East and North Africa**

Designation	Type	Quantity	Contract Value	Supplier Country	Prime Contractor	Order Date	First Delivery Due	Notes
E-2C *Hawkeye*	AEW&C ac Upgrade	1	US$38m	US	Northrop Grumman	2008	n.k.	Refurbishment and upgrade to *Hawkeye* 2000 (HE2K) standard
C-295	Tpt ac	3	n.k.	ESP	EADS CASA	2010	2011	–
Iran (IRN)								
T-72	MBT Upgrade	n.k.	See notes	RUS	Rosoboron-export	2005	n.k.	Upgrade. Part of a US$1.5bn procurement deal
MiG-29	Ftr ac Upgrade	n.k.	See notes	RUS	Rosoboron-export	2005	n.k.	Upgrade. Part of a US$1.5bn procurement deal
Su-24	FGA Upgrade	30	See notes	RUS	Rosoboron-export	2005	n.k.	Upgrade. Part of a US$1.5bn procurement deal
Iraq (IRQ)								
M1 *Abrams*	MBT	140	US$1.4bn	US	General Dynamics	2009	2010	Delivery in progress. M1A1 SA config. 140 further M1 may be ordered
ILAV	APC (W)	109	US$59m	UK/US	BAE Land Systems	2009	2010	Delivery expected by Oct 2010
BTR-4	APC (W)	420	US$2.5bn	UKR	Khariv Morozov	2010	n.k	Contract value includes 6 An-32 tpt ac
35PB1208 E-1455	PB	15	US$181m	US	Swiftships	2009	2012	35m PC for navy. Intial order was for 9 vessels. Option for further 6 subsequently exercised. First vessel commissioned Sep 2010. Further deliveries expected at 6 week intervals
Beech 350ER *King Air*	Tpt ac	6	US$10.5m	US	Hawker Beechcraft	2008	2010	5 Extended Range (ER) ISR ac; 1 lt tpt ac; plus spares and spt
C-130J *Super Hercules*	Tpt ac	4	US$292.8m	US	Lockheed Martin	2009	n.k.	For air force. FMS contract, ISD 2011
C-130J-30	Tpt ac	2	US$140.3m	US	Lockheed Martin	2009	n.k.	For air force. ISD 2011
An-32	Tpt ac	6	US$2.5bn	UKR	Antonov ASTC/Aviant	2010	n.k.	Contract value includes 420 BTR-4 APC
Lasta-95	Trg ac	20	see notes	SER	UTVA	2007	2010	Option for further 16. Part of US$230m deal. First 3 delivered Aug 2010
Hawker Beechcraft T-6A *Texan II*	Trg ac	8	US$86.6m	US	Hawker Beechcraft	2009	2010	For air force. Signed Aug 2009; First delivered Feb 2010
EC-635	Tpt Hel	24	€360m (US$490m)	FRA	Eurocopter	2009	n.k.	Cost incl training and maintenance
Mi-17CT	MRH Hel	22	US$80.6m	RUS	Aeronautical Radio Incorporated	2009	n.k.	Prime contractor is Aeronautical Radio Incorporated; Mi-17s to be supplied by Mil/Kazan
Bell 407	Tpt Hel	24	US$60.3m	US	Bell	2009	n.k.	For air force. FMS contract
Bell 407	Tpt Hel	3	US$6.93m	US	Bell	2009	2010	For air force. FMS contract
Israel (ISR)								
Arrow 2	ATBM/BMD	_	Undisclosed	ISR/US	IAI	2008	n.k.	Number and cost undisclosed.
Merkava Mk IV	MBT	up to 400	n.k.	ISR	n.k.	2001	2004	Estimated 50–60 tk per year over four years. Delivery status unclear
Dolphin (Type 800) class	SSK	2	€1bn (US$1.21bn)	GER	HDW	2006	2012	With Air-Independent Propulsion (AIP) system
F-35 *Lightning II*	FGA ac	20	US$2.75bn	US	Lockheed Martin	2010	2016	Option for a further 75

Table 19 **Selected Arms Procurements and Deliveries, Middle East and North Africa**

Designation	Type	Quantity	Contract Value	Supplier Country	Prime Contractor	Order Date	First Delivery Due	Notes
C-130J *Hercules*	Tpt ac	1	US$98.6m	US	Lockheed Martin	2010	2013	–
Skylark I-LE	ISR UAV	100	n.k.	ISR	Elbit Systems	2008	n.k.	Part of *Sky Rider* programme
Hermes 900	ISR UAV	n.k.	US$50m	ISR	Elbit Systems	2010	2010	Price includes additional *Hermes 450* UAVs. Deliveries to occur 2010-2013
AIM-120C-7	AAM	200	US$171m	US	Raytheon	2007	n.k.	Delivery status unclear
Joint Direct Attack Munitions (JDAM)	ASM	5,000	n.k.	US	Boeing	2004	n.k.	Deliveries ongoing
Jordan (JOR)								
YPR-765	AIFV	510	n.k.	NLD	n.k.	2010	2010	Order includes 69 M-577s and unknown number of YPR-806s. Deliveries to be complete by 2014
M109A2	155mm SP Arty	121	n.k.	NLD	n.k.	2010	2010	Deliveries to be complete by 2014
HIMARS	227mm MRL	12	$26.9m	US	Lockheed Martin	2010	n.k.	Delivery status unclear
F-16A/B Block 15	Ftr ac Upgrade	17	US$87m	TUR	Lockheed Martin	2005	2007	MLU. Deliveries ongoing
IL-76MF (*Candid*)	Tpt ac	2	US$100m	RUS	Rosoboron-export	2005	2007	2 delivered. Option for further 2 ac taken up in July 2007; delivery expected in 2011
Kuwait (KWT)								
Aspide	AD upgrade	n.k.	€65m (US$87.3m)	Int'l	MBDA	2007	n.k.	Upgrade to *Spada* 2000 config. To be completed over 3 years
MK V	PBF	10	US$461m	US	USMI	2009	n.k.	For navy. Final del due 2013
KC-130J	Tkr ac	3	US$245m	US	Lockheed Martin	2010	2013	Deliveries to be complete in early 2014
Lebanon (LBN)								
T-72	MBT	31	Free transfer	RUS	n.k.	2010	n.k.	Delivery status unclear
Mi-24 *Hind*	Atk Hel	6	Free transfer	RUS	n.k.	2010	2010	In place of previously offered MiG-29 *Fulcrum* ac
Libya (LBY)								
T-72	MBT Upgrade	145	n.k.	RUS	n.k.	2009	n.k.	Reportedly part of a cancellation of a US$4.5 billion debt to RUS. Upgrade of previously supplied MBTs. Upgrade may also include T-62, T-55 and T-54 fleet
Molniya-class	PCGM	3	est $150m–$200m	RUS	Vympel	2009	n.k.	Delivery status unclear
Yak-130	Trg ac	6	εUS$100m	RUS	Rosoboron-export	2010	2011	3 due 2011; 3 in 2012
Morocco (MOR)								
FREMM	DDGHM	1	€470m (US$676m)	FRA/ITA	DCNS	2008	2012	–
SIGMA	FFGHM	3	€600m (US$875m)	NLD	Schelde	2008	2011	(Ship Integrated Geometrical Modularity Approach) First vessel launched Jul 2010; ISD expected 2011. Final delivery due 2012

Table 19 **Selected Arms Procurements and Deliveries, Middle East and North Africa**

Designation	Type	Quantity	Contract Value	Supplier Country	Prime Contractor	Order Date	First Delivery Due	Notes
OPV-70	PSO	4	US$140m	FRA	STX	2008	2010	First vessel launched Aug 2010; delivery expected by Dec 2010
F-16C/D Block 52 Fighting Falcon	FGA ac	24	US$841.9m	US	Lockheed Martin	2008	n.k.	Inc. mission equipment and spt package. 18 Cs and 6 Ds. Deliveries due to begin late 2010
C-27J Spartan	Tpt ac	4	€130m (US$166m)	ITA	Alenia Aeronautica	2008	2010	First delivered Jul 2010
T-6C Texan	Trg ac	24	US$37m+	US	Hawker Beechcraft	2009	2010	FMS order
Oman (OMN)								
Project Khareef	FFG	3	GB£400m (US$785m)	UK	BAE Systems	2007	2010	First vessel (Al-Shamikh) launched Jul 2009; delivery expected 2011. Second vessel (Al-Rahmani) launched Jul 2010
A320	Tpt ac	2	n.k.	FRA	EADS	2007	n.k.	Delivery status unclear
C-130J-30 Hercules	Tpt ac	1	n.k.	US	Lockheed Martin	2009	2012	–
C-130J-30 Hercules	Tpt ac	2	n.k.	US	Lockheed Martin	2010	2013	Delivery due in 2013 and 2014
NH-90 TTH	Tpt Hel	20	n.k.	NLD	EADS	2003	2008	First 2 delivered Jun 2010. 2 more due for delivery Jul 2010
Qatar (QTR)								
C-130J-30 Hercules	Tpt ac	4	US$393.6m	US	Lockheed Martin	2008	2011	Contract value incl additional packages
AW-139	MRH Hel	18	€260m (US$413m)	ITA	Agusta-Westland	2008	2010	For air force. First delivered Nov 2009
Exocet MM40 Block 3	AShM	unk	unk	Int'l	MBDA	2010	unk	To equip Vita-class PCFG
Saudi Arabia (SAU)								
CAESAR 155mm	155mm SP arty	100	n.k.	FRA	Nexter Systems	2006	2009	For national guard; to replace M198. First four delivered March 2010. Deliveries to be completed by end 2011
LAV II	APC	724	US$2.2bn	CAN	General Dynamics (GDLS)	2009	2011	For SAU National Guard
M113	APC Upgrade	300	US$200m	TUR	FNSS	2007	2008	Upgrade. Follow-on contract could lead to upgrade of entire fleet of 2,000 M113. Delivery status unclear
Eurofighter Typhoon	FGA ac	72	GB£4.43bn (US$8.9bn)	Int'l	Eurofighter	2005	2008	Project Salam. 48 ac to be assembled in SAU. First delivered Jun 2009
E-3A Sentry	AEW&C ac Upgrade	5	US$16m	US	Data Link Solutions	2006	n.k.	Comms upgrade. Link 16 MIDS
A330 MRTT	Tkr/Tpt ac	6	US$600m	FRA	EADS	2008	2011	3 more purchased July 2009 for undisclosed fee. First delivery expected 2011
S-76	Tpt Hel	15	n.k.	US	Sikorsky	2007	n.k.	For Ministry of Interior
S-92	Tpt Hel	16	n.k.	US	Sikorsky	2007	n.k.	For Ministry of Interior
UH-60L Black Hawk	Hel	22	US$286 m	US	Sikorsky	2008	2010	Delivery status unclear
Schweizer S-434	Trg Hel	9	n.k.	US	Sikorsky	2007	n.k.	For Ministry of Interior. First 2 delivered Dec 2009

Table 19 **Selected Arms Procurements and Deliveries, Middle East and North Africa**

Designation	Type	Quantity	Contract Value	Supplier Country	Prime Contractor	Order Date	First Delivery Due	Notes
AIM-9X *Sidewinder*	AAM	250	US$164m	US	Raytheon	2009	n.k.	For F-15. Number and value undisclosed. FMS request was for 250 all-up-round AIM-9X *Sidewinder* short-range AAM, 84 AIM-9X captive air trg msl and 12 AIM-9X dummy air trg msl
AN/AAQ-33 *Sniper*	ATP	n.k.	n.k.	US	Lockheed Martin	2009	n.k.	FMS contract. Part of US$100m replacement of LANTIRN pods used by RSAF F-15s
AN/AAQ-33 *Sniper*	ATP	n.k.	US$41.9m	US	Lockheed Martin	2010	n.k.	Delivery status unclear
Syria (SYR)								
Buk-M2	SAM	n.k.	US$200m	RUS	Rosoboron-export	2007	2008	Delivery status unclear
96K6 *Pantsyr-S1E* (SA-22 *Greyhound*)	AD	36	US$730m	RUS	Rosoboron-export	n.k.	2007	Delivery reported to have begun in late 2009; delivery status unclear
Tunisia (TUN)								
C-130J *Hercules*	Tpt ac	2	n.k.	US	Lockheed Martin	2010	2013	To be delivered 2013–14
SA-342 *Gazelle*	MRH Hel	6	n.k.	FRA	Aerotec	2010	n.k.	Delivery status unclear
United Arab Emirates (UAE)								
Fuchs 2 NBC-RS	APC	32	€160m (US$205m)	GER	Rheinmetall	2005	2007	16 NBC recce vehicles, 8 BW detection vehicles, 8 mobile CP vehicles. Deliveries ongoing
Patria 8×8	APC	n.k.	n.k.	FIN	Patria	2008	n.k.	Contract value and number of units not declared.
Patriot Advanced Capability (PAC) 3	AD System	10 fire units, 172 msl	US$3.3bn	US	Raytheon	2008	2009	To replace HAWK. Incl 172 PAC-3 msl and 42 launcher mod packs, plus some GEM-T msl. Final delivery due 2012
96K6 *Pantsyr-S1E*	AD	50	US$734m	RUS	Rosoboron-export	2000	2004	To be mounted on MAN SX 45 8×8 trucks. First 4 delivered Mar 2009. Final delivery due end 2010
Agrab (*Scorpion*) 120mm MMS	120mm SP Mor	48	AED390m (US$106m)	RSA/SGP/ UAE/UK	IGG	2007	2008	Delivery status unclear
Javelin	MANPAT	100	(US$135m)	US	Raytheon/ Lockheed Martin	2008	2009	1,000 msl
Abu Dhabi-class	FFGHM	1	n.k.	ITA	Fincantieri	2009	2011	
Baynunah-class	FSGHM	6	AED3bn (US$820m)	FRA/UAE	ADSB	2003	2006	First of class built in FRA, others to be built in UAE. First vessel ISD due 2011. Delivery expected to be complete by 2014
Falaj II (*Commandante-*class)	FS	2	AED430m (US$117m)	ITA	Fincantieri	2009	2011	First vessel to be launched Dec 2011; second Apr 2012. Delivery of both vessels scheduled for late 2012
Project 'Ghannatha'	PBFG	12	AED771m	UAE	ADSB	2009	n.k.	Delivery status unclear
Project Al Saber	PB	12	AED127m (US$34.6m)	UAE	ADSB	2008	n.k.	For coast guard
340 *Erieye*	AEW ac	2	SEK1.5bn (US$234m)	SWE	Saab	2009	2010	Delivery scheduled for late 2010
A330 MRTT	Tkr/Tpt ac	3	n.k.	Int'l	EADS	2008	2011	Delivery now scheduled for 2012. Order for 3 more possible

Table 19 **Selected Arms Procurements and Deliveries, Middle East and North Africa**

Designation	Type	Quantity	Contract Value	Supplier Country	Prime Contractor	Order Date	First Delivery Due	Notes
C-17 *Globemaster III*	Tpt ac	4	AED4.3bn (US$1.2bn)	US	Boeing	2009	2011	Order placed
C-17 *Globemaster III*	Tpt ac	2	n.k.	US	Boeing	2010	2012	–
C-130 J-30 *Hercules*	Tpt ac	12	AED5.9bn	US	Lockheed Martin	2009	2013	–
PC-21	Trg ac	25	CHEfr500m ($492.4m)	CHE	Pilatus	2009	2011	–
AH-64D *Apache Longbow*	Hel Upgrade	30	n.k.	US	Boeing	2007	n.k.	Upgrade from AH-64A to D standard
UH-60M *Blackhawk*	Tpt Hel	10	n.k.	US	Sikorsky	2007	2010	Delivery status unclear
UH-60M *Blackhawk*	Tpt Hel	14	US$171m	US	Sikorsky	2009	n.k.	To be delivered by end 2012
Yemen, Republic of (YEM)								
MiG-29 SMT *Fulcrum*	FGA ac	32	US$1.3bn	RUS	Rosoboron-export	2006	n.k.	Delivery status unclear

Chapter Eight
Latin America and the Caribbean

Tensions in the Andes – previously the most serious threat to stability – were reduced somewhat in 2010, and further advances in multilateral cooperation were achieved across the region. But as noted in *The Military Balance 2010* (p. 53), while Latin American interest in the multilateral management of regional security may have revived, a considerable gap remained between ambition and reality. The improvement in relations in the Andean region appeared fragile and potentially short-lived. Overall gains were also set against the continuation of other disputes between governments both within the region and between regional and extra-regional governments, as well as some markedly regressive steps in civil–military relations and deteriorating levels of human security in many areas. And despite some improvements in transparency, military transformation and modernisation by various governments continued to provoke mistrust.

The diplomatic crisis between Colombia and neighbouring Venezuela and Ecuador, triggered in March 2008 by a Colombian raid on a guerrilla camp in Ecuador and intensified in 2009 by the signing of a US–Colombia defence agreement, was partly resolved over the course of 2010. This improvement had little to do with multilateral mediation. Other countries in the region were unable to go beyond offers of assistance to force each party to seriously address the other's grievance. Even Brazil was unable to force a solution: as Defence Minister Nelson Jobim conceded privately to US diplomats, for Brazil to acknowledge the presence in Venezuela of guerrillas from the Fuerzas Armadas Revolucionarias de Colombia (FARC) 'would ruin [its] ability to mediate'. Instead, the change of government in Colombia was pivotal. In spite of his reputation as the hawkish former defence minister responsible for the March 2008 attack, President Juan Manuel Santos, inaugurated in August, made it his priority to restore ties with Venezuela and Ecuador. Steps included handing over data seized during the March 2008 attack. Days after the outgoing administration of Alvaro Uribe had presented to the Organisation of American States (OAS) evidence that Venezuela had been harbouring

FARC, Santos offered an olive branch to Venezuelan President Hugo Chávez and began to back away from the US–Colombia defence agreement. While diplomatic relations had not been completely normalised with either Ecuador or Venezuela at the time of writing, specific economic and security gains had been achieved. Ecuador had cooperated in hostile actions against FARC camps in the border region; trade between Colombia and Venezuela had been restored; and the Venezuelan private sector had begun to pay back to Colombian exporters an approximate US$800 million debt incurred when Chávez broke off diplomatic relations in 2009.

Multilateral security developments
In parallel with these developments, there remained a keen interest in developing and refining multilateral security mechanisms. The most important of these was the South American Defence Council (SADC) of the Union of South American Nations (UNASUR), the founding charter of which had by the end of 2010 been ratified by enough countries to give the organisation legal status. In response to diplomatic tensions in the Andes, South American governments had worked out a set of shared goals during 2009 involving the automatic exchange of information on military capabilities; the adoption of a single methodology for calculating defence expenditure; prior notification in detail of all intra- or extra-mural defence or security agreements and military deployments or exercises on or near borders; cooperation against transnational threats; and firm guarantees of respect for the sovereignty and the constitutional order of member states.

Meetings in January and May 2010 then resulted in the development of a detailed *2010–2011 Action Plan* that sought to work towards these goals with an added emphasis on joint exercises for and participation in humanitarian and peacekeeping operations. A common format was worked out during the year to be used by all member states for classifying and notifying others of their defence capabilities and expenditure. In addition, earthquakes in Haiti and Chile at the beginning of the year put their pledges of multilateral humanitarian assistance to the test. In Haiti, Latin

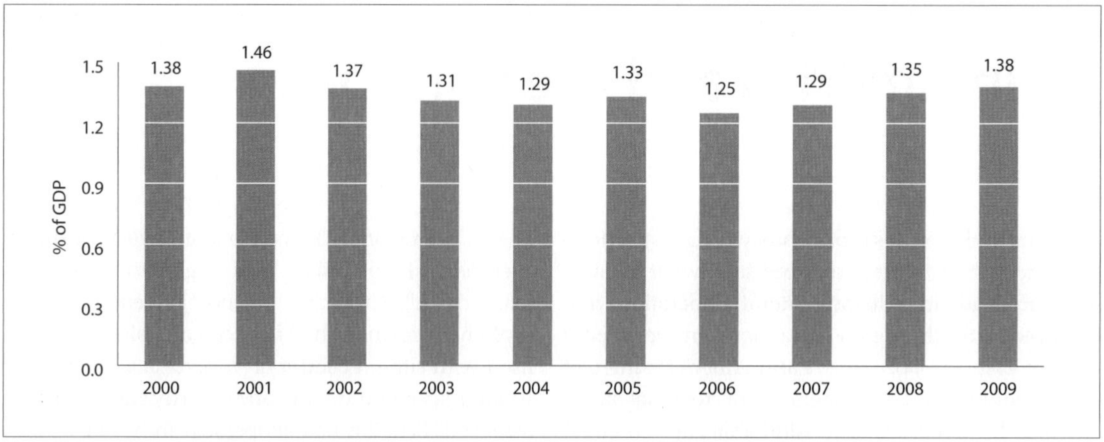

Figure 9 **Latin America and the Caribbean Regional Defence Expenditure** as % of GDP

American military and police forces had long formed the dominant contingent in the UN Stabilisation Mission in Haiti (MINUSTAH), which was itself decimated by the earthquake. Member countries of UNASUR not only took steps to ensure the recovery of the UN mission but also provided substantial additional medical and logistical assistance, and donated US$100m. With Ecuadorian leader Rafael Correa as pro-tem president of UNASUR, the re-establishment of MINUSTAH was hailed as indicative of a new era of south–south cooperation. After the quake in Chile, Argentina, Bolivia, Brazil, Peru, Uruguay and Venezuela all provided humanitarian assistance. Brazil and Argentina used C-130s to ferry aid to the stricken communities. In both cases, Venezuela and other countries also provided assistance under the umbrella of Alianza Bolivariana para los Pueblos de Nuestra América (The Bolivarian Alliance for the Peoples of our America (ALBA), with Cuba in particular sending substantial medical missions.

Finally, another important part of the SADC *Action Plan* was the development of a common agenda for the ninth Conference of Defence Ministers, held in Santa Cruz, Bolivia, in November 2010. All states in the hemisphere, apart from Honduras and Cuba, participated. Ministers met to discuss the development of greater military transparency and a common methodology for measuring defence expenditure as well as regional disaster-response capabilities. Although no specific further commitments were made on either issue, the final declarations recognised the SADC as the central forum for work in this respect.

Since UNASUR involves only South American states, no comparable momentum towards regional consensus on defence matters was achieved in Central America or the Caribbean. A range of factors, not least ongoing FARC presence on Venezuelan territory and deep ideological divisions, suggested that the rapprochement between Colombia and Venezuela would prove unsustainable. And while some bilateral conflicts showed signs of improvement, others continued to aggravate regional relations. In October 2010, for example, an incursion by a small group of Nicaraguan soldiers on Costa Rican territory at a disputed section of the border led to a diplomatic spat that the OAS was unable to resolve. Argentina responded to early indications of oil deposits in British waters around the Falkland Islands by increasing its level of diplomatic protest and more stringently regulating shipping to the islands.

In addition, 2010 saw some reversals in terms of democratic governance and civil–military relations. In Ecuador, the armed forces eventually intervened in a police revolt over wage reforms. During the stand-off, in which the president was held hostage for several hours, the armed forces appeared to prevaricate in suggesting that Correa should heed police grievances. In Paraguay, rumours abounded of possible coup attempts. In Venezuela, President Chávez dismissed international criticism of the head of the Operational Strategic Command, Major-General Henry Rángel Silva, a radical with ties to Colombian FARC guerrillas who had stated publicly that the armed forces would not support any opposition government elected in 2012. Chávez later promoted him to the position of general-in-chief. And protracted negotiations in the wake of the coup in Honduras in June 2009 failed to achieve any solution that could be internationally accepted, despite the continued exclusion of the new regime from the OAS.

In this context, economic constraints proved important in fostering better relations between states by encouraging both restraint in military spending and pragmatic engagement in pursuit of trade and other economic benefits. Many countries in the region, having entered the 2008–09 recession with comparatively less toxic debt and stronger domestic demand than their counterparts in the developed world, emerged from it in a relatively strong position; with the expectation that commodity prices would remain strong in the medium term; and with modest GDP growth in 2010 that is set to average 2.9% (3.3% excluding Haiti). The economic outlook, however, remains mixed. While the hemisphere need not necessarily fear a 'double-dip' recession, growth is expected to slow in 2011. Many economies in the region, particularly in Central America and the Caribbean, are heavily exposed to anticipated falls in both US and Chinese demand; monetary policies may need to be tightened in many cases to avoid overheating, something which several governments have already begun to do; and what Brazil called the ongoing 'currency war' between the US and China (as well as the related capital inflows into Latin America) is making currency appreciation problematic for the region's export competitiveness. In addition, Venezuela has so far defied the regional trend by remaining in recession: its GDP is expected to have fallen further in 2010. In general terms, this situation is reflected in the restraint with which governments have budgeted for defence in 2010. While year-on-year defence budget growth has returned to 15.5% (after a slower 2009 growth rate of 8.7%), countries have in general only looked to keep pace with GDP and overall budgets. Defence budgets both as a proportion of GDP as well as in relation to overall budgets in fact remained broadly the same, despite noticeable increases in five countries: Cuba, Ecuador, Honduras, Nicaragua and Paraguay. The proportion of funds allocated to defence by the major players remained static or actually fell slightly.

In addition, one common feature in the south and east of the region during the year was ongoing modernisation of defence ministries and relevant legislation to improve strategic planning – moves that sought to correct the distortions of post-authoritarian civil–military settlements. Similarly, all countries continued to emphasise their defensive outlook and interest in multilateral security cooperation and peacekeeping. However, long-term plans varied considerably. Chile, which enjoys substantial fiscal latitude, is not planning any major procurement or expansion; Argentina, conversely, intends to increase defence spending over the coming years and has urgent procurement and modernisation requirements, but little prospect of adequate funding; and Brazil, which has plans for substantial military reorganisation and expansion over the coming years, particularly in the naval dimension, arguably has the funding to implement these.

Brazil

Brazil's *National Defence Strategy* (NDS) was published in December 2008 as a guide for a 20-year transformation of Brazilian military capabilities and defence policy. The NDS seeks to consolidate Brazil's position as a dynamic middle power and the dominant force in South America. It outlines the redeployment and re-equipment of the military with modern hardware in pursuit of adequate 'monitoring, mobility and presence' capabilities, developing a 'strategic reserve' in the centre of the country and spreading out from Brazil's southern industrial heartland.

However, the NDS also lays claim to Brazil's future status as a great power in a multipolar world, designates the space, cybernetics and nuclear sectors as strategically important and looks to establish the beginnings of force projection outside Brazil. Although the strategy explicitly rejects the notion that capabilities should be developed in response to threats, both its focus on the protection of Brazil's Amazonian northwest and Atlantic oilfields and its emphasis on the need for the armed forces to develop 'elasticity' – the ability to rapidly expand if needed – are based on possible resource-motivated attacks by extra-regional powers. Mandatory military service is also maintained – both as a means of ensuring such 'elasticity' and as a key driver of social cohesion and nation-building. And the strategy is also in line with the constitutional and legal framework, which emphasises the defensive mandate of the armed forces but nevertheless allows for their participation in internal law enforcement when the civilian authorities judge that the police cannot enforce law and order alone. (The political sustainability of this distinction was put to the test in November 2010 when 800 troops were deployed with 1,800 police in a joint operation to tackle organised crime in Rio de Janeiro's Complexo do Alemão favela. Building on Brazil's experience in Haiti, the government would subsequently seek to describe this as domestic 'peacekeeping'.)

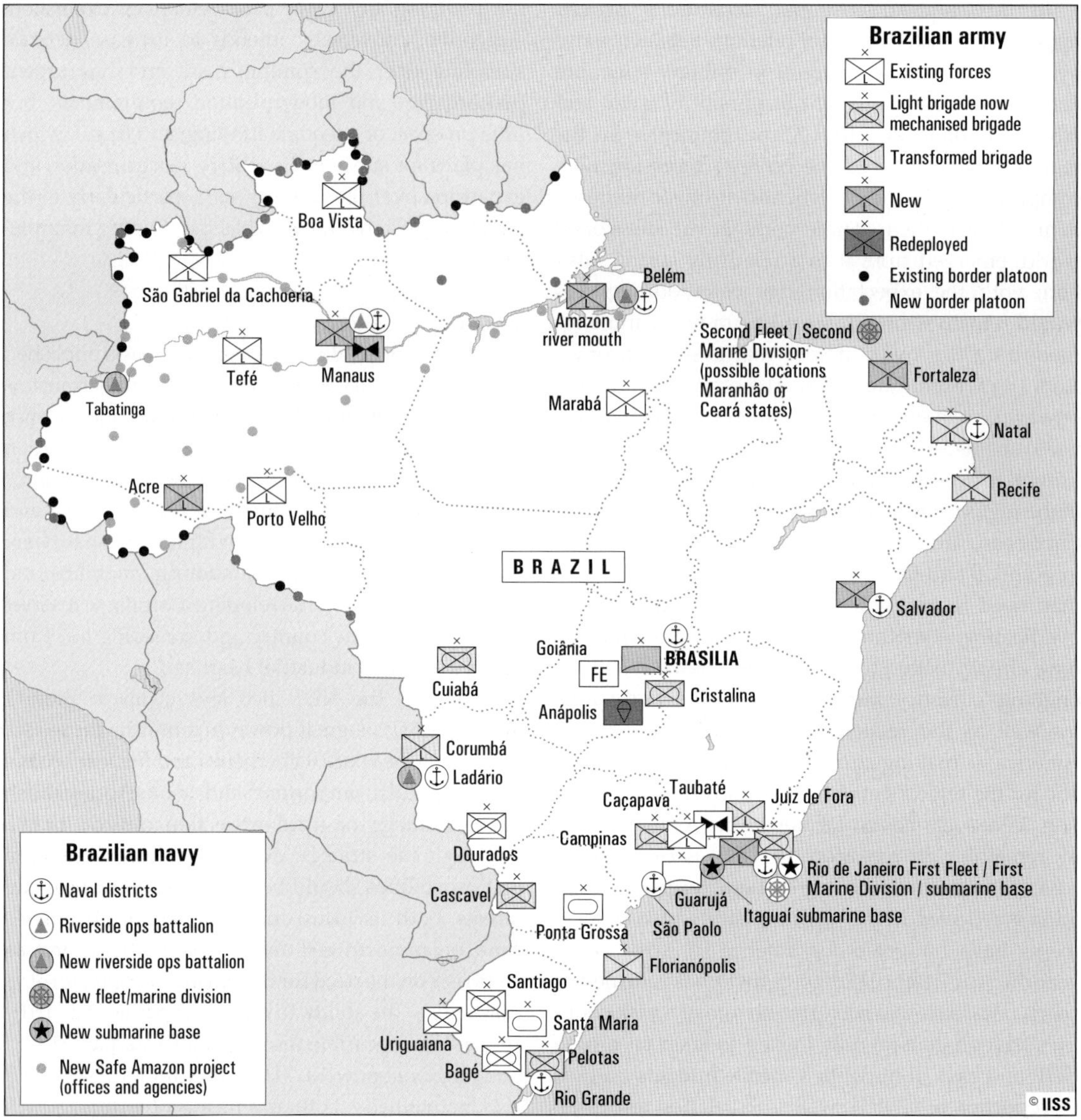
Brazilian army
Existing forces
Light brigade now mechanised brigade
Transformed brigade
New
Redeployed
Existing border platoon
New border platoon
Brazilian navy
Naval districts
Riverside ops battalion
New riverside ops battalion
New fleet/marine division
New submarine base
New Safe Amazon project (offices and agencies)
BRAZIL
Boa Vista
São Gabriel da Cachoeria
Tefé
Manaus
Tabatinga
Acre
Porto Velho
Belém
Amazon river mouth
Marabá
Second Fleet / Second Marine Division (possible locations Maranhâo or Ceará states)
Fortaleza
Natal
Recife
Salvador
Goiânia
BRASILIA
FE
Cristalina
Anápolis
Cuiabá
Corumbá
Ladário
Caçapava
Taubaté
Juiz de Fora
Campinas
Rio de Janeiro First Fleet / First Marine Division / submarine base
Guarujá
Itaguaí submarine base
São Paolo
Dourados
Cascavel
Ponta Grossa
Florianópolis
Santiago
Santa Maria
Uriguaiana
Bagé
Pelotas
Rio Grande
© IISS

Map 5 **Brazil's National Defence Strategy: Army and Navy Plans**

During 2010, Brazil's foreign policy seemed to express the same ambitions as the NDS more clearly than ever, with the government seeking to mediate in Iran's dispute with the West over uranium enrichment and leading opposition in the G20 to competitive currency devaluation. The Brazilian economy was also dynamic, rebounding strongly from the 2008–09 recession with GDP growth forecast to reach 6.5% in 2010.

The government strove to make measurable progress in implementing the NDS. In August 2010 the 'New Defence Law' was passed, introducing a package of measures required by the NDS to improve unified strategic command, civilian control of defence, and the strategic rationale and transparency of procurement. In addition, with Brazil one of the driving forces behind the emerging UNASUR consensus regarding the necessity of regular White Papers, the law also commits the government to the production of a White Paper on defence every four years, starting in 2012. The defence budget was also increased from R55.3bn (US$5.25bn) to R61.3bn (US$3.04bn), and the proportion allotted to investment was set at 14.9% (R$9.3bn), with R$6bn of that in turn destined specifically for the procurement plans mandated by the NDS.

All branches of the armed forces continued with their specific procurement and restructuring plans throughout the year. The army's two key tasks have been identified as the procurement of new hardware, costing approximately R51.7bn (US$29.23bn) over the period, and wholesale relocation/reorganisation. Firstly, the procurement plan has focused on replacing M-60 and M-41 tanks and transforming army mobility with a major armed personnel carrier (APC) purchase. In December 2008, Brazil signed an agreement with Germany through which the latter contracted out to Krauss-Maffei Wegmann the renovation of 269 *Leopard* 1A5s, including variants. The first delivery arrived in December 2009, and deliveries continued in 2010. Secondly, the army has committed to both modernise and more than double its APC inventory. In December 2007 Brazil contracted the Fiat subsidiary Iveco to develop a next-generation wheeled APC, and placed an initial order of 16 vehicles. The result, designed with the close involvement of the Ministry of Defence, is the VBTP-MR *Guaraní*. In order to gradually phase out most of its existing stock of ageing M-113s and EE-11 *Urutus*, in December 2009 the government signed a new R$6bn (US$ 3.04) contract with Iveco (effectively superseding the 2007 deal) for the production of up to 2,044 vehicles, with delivery beginning in 2012 and ending in 2030. As of December 2010, Iveco had not yet built the factory for production, but envisaged that the first prototypes would be tested in 2011. Beyond these, the army has also committed to procure a range of new and advanced equipment, including anti-aircraft defence systems and unmanned armed vehicles (UAVs).

In terms of relocation and reorganisation, the army has begun to implement two major programmes, 'Protected Amazon' and 'Homeland Guard'. The former will significantly increase the presence of the Amazon Military Command (CMA) along the length of Brazil's Amazonian border by modernising its Special Border Platoons (PEF), more than doubling them in number from 21 to 49, increasing personnel strength from approximately 25,000 to 48,000, and overhauling the operational and logistical capabilities of the CMA as a whole. Three light infantry brigades will be created to operate in the Amazon as part of this process. As of late 2010, the number of PEFs had not yet significantly increased, but work had begun to convert existing detachments into new PEFs. Furthermore, Brazilian army aviation capabilities in the Amazon will be expanded by the formation of a new aviation command.

'Homeland Guard', meanwhile, will reorganise the other six Military Commands. In this programme, several changes are to be made before 2014. The airborne infantry brigade will be moved from Rio de Janeiro to Aniápolis and a light infantry brigade created in Rio to replace it; and work will begin to transform several existing light and motorised infantry brigades into mechanised infantry brigades once the VBTP-MR *Guaranís* become available. The programme also anticipates the creation of three more light infantry brigades and one anti-aircraft artillery brigade. The anticipated result of all of the above changes in the long term is that the army will have 35 brigades in total (instead of the current 27) and approximately 242,500 troops. Though these plans to expand are still in place, in the short term the army is reported to be concentrating on enhancing the equipment, mobility and training of existing forces.

The air force has begun to implement changes of a similar magnitude and over the same 20-year timescale. Working closely with the army and navy, it will seek to guarantee air supremacy and enhanced deterrence, in particular in the Amazon basin and along Brazil's Atlantic coast. It is focusing its procurement efforts on modernising attack and transport capabilities. However, the Fighter Replacement Programme (FX2) is a central priority. It involves the purchase of 36 next-generation fighters by 2013 and 120 by 2025 – timed so as to avoid any gap in fighter capability. The competition is between Dassault's F-3 *Rafale*, Saab's *Gripen* NG, and the Boeing FA-18 *Super Hornet*. The US, Swedish and French governments were all closely involved in lobbying for the contract. The airforce reportedly preferred Saab's *Gripen*, though President Luis Inácio 'Lula' da Silva was reportedly inclined towards the *Rafale*. Lula delayed throughout late 2009 and 2010 without reaching a final decision, seeking to maximise benefits for Brazil in terms of technology transfer. In terms of transport, the air force is expected to play an important supporting role in enhancing army mobility, particularly in the Amazon region. Embraer's KC-390, a tanker/transport aircraft intended to compete internationally as a replacement for ageing C-130s, is important in this regard. Brazil's air force intends to buy 28 aircraft, with the first becoming available in 2015. The air force and Embraer signed a letter of intent for this deal at the 2010 Farnborough International Air Show. It has also contracted Airbus Military to modernise eight P-3A *Orions* acquired from the US Navy (with an option for one more). The *Orions* are being equipped with surveillance suites designed to detect submarines, in line with the emphasis of the NDS on protection of Brazil's Atlantic coast and maritime resources.

In total, between 2008 and 2031 the air force expects to spend R$58.5bn (US$33bn) on procurement of new aircraft, R$7.9bn (US$4.5bn) on modernisation of existing aircraft, and R$2.4bn (US$1.3bn) on new weapons systems, and to increase its personnel strength from 70,000 to over 100,000. Three new air bases will also be added at strategic locations along Brazil's Amazon border, and a significant proportion of resources will be devoted to protecting against transnational threats in the Amazon, including through the development of an unspecified number of UAVs.

Naval personnel are expected to almost double in number to approximately 115,000. Total procurement and modernisation costs between 2010 and 2030 are expected to exceed R$116bn (US$65.5bn). Some resources will be directed towards enhancing brownwater capabilities in the Amazon and Paraguay–Paraná river systems. In this respect, the navy plans to install three more riverine battalions at Tabatinga, Belem and Ladário (further to the existing battalion at Manaus) to cover the lower and uppermost reaches of the Brazilian Amazon and the Paraguay–Paraná basin respectively. A network of 34 small bases will also be developed throughout the tributary system of the Amazon basin.

In line with the NDS priority on effective protection of Brazil's Atlantic oilfields within a 350 nautical-mile margin, the navy has been tasked with developing an effective deterrent capability along Brazil's Atlantic coast and particularly around the Amazon estuary and the coastline between Santos and Vitória adjacent to the oil reserves. Its maritime capabilities are expected to progress from 'sea denial' to control and eventually to force projection. The discovery in 2010 of a further estimated 3.7–15 billion barrels in the 'presalt' Libra oilfield (matching the country's discovery of an equivalent amount in the Tupi oilfield in 2007) has enhanced the perceived importance of this goal. The Brazilian government's sensitivity in this respect was amply illustrated in September 2010 when Defence Minister Jobim pre-empted a forthcoming NATO summit by publicly expressing his opposition to any NATO interest in the South Atlantic.

The 'sea denial' objective is primarily to be pursued through the development of a substantial fleet of conventional and nuclear-powered submarines. In the long-term, the plan is to develop a fleet of 15 conventional submarines by 2037 and six nuclear submarines by 2047. Currently, the weapons and communications systems of Brazil's existing four Tupi-class and one Tikuna-class submarines are being modernised, with delivery expected to be completed in 2017; four diesel-electric submarines based on the Scorpène design are being built jointly by the French DCNS and Brazilian Odebrecht as a result of the 2008 France–Brazil defence cooperation agreement, with delivery between 2017 and 2021; and Brazil has embarked on the development of its first nuclear-powered submarine. With regard to the latter, France has agreed to jointly participate in its construction, but despite generous provisions on technology transfer, Brazil is responsible for learning how to solely manage the uranium fuel cycle, and building its own centrifuges for enrichment and pressurised water reactors (PWRs) for the submarines – all challenges that may incur unforeseen delays. Construction of the first nuclear-powered submarine is anticipated to take place between 2015 and 2023. In support of all of the above, a new shipyard and submarine base are currently being built at the port of Itaguaí, 80km from Rio de Janeiro.

The APC capability of the marines is being improved with the purchase from Mowag GmbH of 18 Piranha IIICs due from late 2010 onwards – to be used in UN peacekeeping operations. Naval aviation is also undergoing a major overhaul. Embraer is due to deliver modernised AF-1 and AF-1A Skyhawks between 2012 and 2014, Eurocopter EC-725 Cougars, and Sikorsky four S-70b helicopters before 2012.

Furthermore, the NDS argues that Brazil's peacetime defence policy should be subordinated to its overall economic and foreign-policy priorities, and that Brazil should develop an autonomous defence-industrial base through technology transfer and a series of strategic partnerships. The efforts of the Ministry of Defence under Nelson Jobim to boost Brazil's defence industry accelerated in 2010.

Brazil has also signed a number of defence agreements with other governments in 2010 that included a strong defence-industrial component granting preferential treatment of Brazilian defence and aerospace companies. The Brazilian government has initiated or augmented formal defence cooperation agreements during the year with Uruguay, Venezuela, Colombia and the Dominican Republic, as well as with a number of governments in Africa. It has also signed agreements with Spain, the United Kingdom, Poland, the Czech Republic and Israel, and deepened its existing association with China. Brazil also signed a defence cooperation agreement (DCA) with the US in April promoting collaboration in research, logistics, procurement and defence-industrial matters, education and intellectual exchange on peacekeeping and other issues, joint training and exercises, and naval visits. While the practical significance of the latter arrangement should not be exaggerated, its political importance is clear as an indicator of Washington's willingness to engage with Brasilia on its own terms and of Brazil's willingness to pursue deepened military ties with the US. Brazil has also sought to support its claims for international status during the year by increasing its participation in peacekeeping operations. Firstly, following the Haiti earthquake and the UN resolution to expand MINUSTAH, came the decision to commit a second infantry battalion to the mission, almost doubling its troop strength to 2,188. Secondly, the Brazilian government took initial steps to commit to participation in UNIFIL in south Lebanon following Italy's decision to withdraw. This would be its second major deployment after MINUSTAH, with the involvement of a naval force of 894 personnel (in line with the NDS's requirement that the navy develop an effective expeditionary force for peacekeeping), as well as 300 soldiers to help clear mines and unexploded munitions. At the time of writing, however, this deployment was awaiting the assent of the Brazilian senate. These moves were significant in light of Brazil's still-frustrated ambition to secure a permanent seat on the UN Security Council. Brazil's participation in multilateral military exercises outside the region was almost unique among Latin American nations. It sent a single *Niteroi*-class frigate to participate in both the NATO naval exercise *Joint Warrior*, held off the coast of Scotland in April, and *IBSAMAR* 2010, another joint exercise with India and South Africa held in the Indian Ocean east of Durban, intended to complement non-military cooperation between the three countries as the members of the IBSA Dialogue Forum. In addition, Brazil also participated in a number of multilateral exercises in Latin America, including the air force exercise *CRUZEX*, involving not only Argentina, Chile and Uruguay, but also France and the US (both with aircraft competing for the Brazilian fighter contract).

Brazilian defence policy is unlikely to change significantly over the medium term. Before the 2010 election to succeed Lula, his eventual successor Dilma Rousseff, who took office in January 2011, wrote an open letter as candidate to the armed forces promising 'to continue a work begun well' and referring

explicitly to the terms of the NDS. Defence Minister Nelson Jobim also continued in his post into the new government. However, the heavy financial commitment imposed by NDS-related procurement means that targets could be missed. This is particularly so given that this procurement has not yet entered its most expensive phase. Investment in air-force modernisation is set to double in 2011, rising from the 2010 total of R$1,179bn (US$666bn) to R$2,250bn (US$1,271bn). Naval investment is also set to climb very steeply after 2015.

Chile

The government in Santiago released a new defence White Paper in January 2010. This document sought to project a defensive strategic posture, emphasising deterrence, legitimate defence and peacekeeping/disaster response. While it did not provide detailed procurement schedules for the three forces, in other respects the document provided a useful model for a region which has recently recognised the value of such exercises for building confidence with neighbours. The White Paper also accounted for the major overhaul of the ministry of defence with which its publication coincided. In the last months of its tenure the outgoing Concertación government of President Michelle Bachelet presented and secured approval for a law that, inter alia, gave the minister of defence full authority over all defence policy and operations and removed advisory bodies that had operated in parallel. It created the Joint General Staff, a new body to be led by a three-star general with responsibility for unified strategic planning, joint training and doctrinal development; and rearranged the three subsecretariats responsible for the armed forces into two new equivalents with all-force functional responsibilities. These measures were aimed at improving efficiency, strengthening civilian control and creating a structure allowing for proper strategic consideration of long-term capability requirements, procurement and development.

Absent from these changes, however, was any reform of the 'Copper Law', a mechanism requiring 10% of the revenues of Chile's state-owned National Copper Corporation (CODELCO) to be transferred to the armed forces. As noted in previous editions of the *Military Balance*, these extra revenues have substantially augmented defence spending. Since 2004 they have increasingly been allowed to accumulate under civilian control in Ministry of Defence accounts. Indeed, in 2009, less than 25% found its way to the armed forces for procurement, and by early 2010 the accumulated savings had reached approximately $3.5bn. But the law is still seen as a drain on CODELCO's prospects for ongoing investment and growth, an added source of tension in relations with Peru, and (because of variable copper prices) an unwelcome element of uncertainty in military procurement and planning.

The Bachelet administration had introduced a bill to abolish the law in late 2009, but this was not approved before the change of government in March 2010. Since then, the new centre-right government of Sebastián Piñera has made clear that it will also seek to abolish the law. As of December 2010, the government was planning to submit a bill to Congress that would replace it with a multi-year (probably quadrennial) procurement budget including a contingency fund (as requested by the armed forces and the Defence Commission of the Chamber of Deputies). It has made this commitment in line with its generally cautious attitude towards military spending, indicating that it will seek only to maintain defence spending at around its current rate of 3.08% of GDP. In deciding on this figure, however, it appears to have considered funds collected via the Copper Law that have actually been passed to the armed forces for procurement in recent years. Indeed, the Piñera government has elected to divert around $1.2bn of the remaining accumulated funds to post-earthquake reconstruction. Although Chile's naval assets escaped the subsequent tsunami by rapidly deploying offshore – only the U-209 submarine *Simpson* was slightly damaged – the infrastructure of the Naval Armoury and Shipyards (ASMAR) at Talcahuano was severely damaged. Around half of the above reconstruction funds have therefore been allocated towards ASMAR repairs.

The Piñera government has also begun to seek 'strategic partners' in the international private sector willing to become involved with both ASMAR and the National Aeronautics Company. Unlike Brazil, however, while the state would retain majority control, such partners would invest in these businesses themselves rather than in specific projects; Chile does not see such partnerships as necessarily contingent on strategic association between governments. In fact, during 2010 Chile's extra-regional defence diplomacy was not comparable in energy and scope with that of Brazil, although Defence Minister Jaime Ravinet did meet with his Italian, French and Spanish counterparts to discuss defence-industrial and peacekeeping cooperation.

The Piñera administration has placed a high priority on improving security cooperation with several governments across the ideological spectrum. This is particularly true in the case of Peru, with bilateral ties at the beginning of the year in especially poor condition following Lima's decision in 2008 to take Chile to the International Court of Justice over the two countries' disputed maritime boundary, ensuing espionage scandals and Peruvian suspicions of Chilean procurement. The incoming Chilean government, closer ideologically to President Alan García than its predecessor, quickly sought to reach a new understanding, inviting Peru to jointly ratify the Convention on Cluster Munitions, making moves towards the joint adoption of a single methodology for measuring defence expenditure, and above all responding positively to a Peruvian request for Chile to cede its option on one or two Mi-17 helicopters from Russia. With Peru urgently needing these for counter-narcotics operations in the Apurímac and Ene River Valley (VRAE), but without any prospect of jumping the production queue, Piñera personally decided to transfer Chile's right to five aircraft, three more than had been requested. On the left, the Chilean Air Force (FACh) signed an agreement with its Ecuadorian counterpart to deepen their institutional contacts, and Santiago and Quito signed a five-year agreement for defence-industrial cooperation. In addition, the Chilean and Uruguayan Defence Ministries agreed to improve cooperation in peacekeeping and institutionalise annual meetings. Finally, Chile–Argentina relations had been boosted in late 2009 by the signing of the Treaty of Maipú, a strategic association providing for institutionalised cooperation across a broad range of areas, including defence. Building on this in 2010, the new Chilean government agreed with Argentina to create a commission to examine the possibility of the joint production of a single training aircraft to replace the Argentine *Mentor* and the Chilean *Pillán*; to allow direct cooperation between ASMAR and Argentina's Tandanor shipyards to help the former with its own production schedule, which had been severely affected by the earthquake; and to request UN recognition and integration from 2012 onwards of the binational Southern Cross peacekeeping force, conceived and developed over the past five years.

As noted in previous editions of *The Military Balance*, Chile is now approaching the end of a multi-year procurement cycle aimed at fully modernising its capabilities. In general, there were few major orders in 2010, but the air force and the navy did continue throughout the year to receive existing orders made as part of this cycle. The air force took delivery of some of the 12 Bell 412EP helicopters for use in disaster response, while deliveries of the 12 EMB-314 *Super Tucanos* ordered from Embraer for their training and light-attack/counter-insurgency capability continued during 2010, and the first of three KC-135E tanker/transport aircraft from the US was received in February 2010. The navy's original plan was to completely overhaul its fixed-wing maritime transport/patrol capabilities by phasing out its existing P-3 *Orions* and procuring eight C-295 *Persuaders* had been abandoned in favour of P-3 modernisation and the procurement of only three C-295s. Ordered from EADS in 2007, the first of these was delivered in April 2010. Similarly, construction by ASMAR of two Fassmer-design PSOs continued, with the first two from the batch of four on order already in operation; and the navy also took possession of the 42,000-ton tanker AO-52 *Almirante Montt*, purchased from the US.

In addition to these deliveries, moves were undertaken to improve the strength, flexibility and mobility of the marine infantry corps. The navy expressed an interest in buying a new multi-purpose vessel in 2011–12 to replace the LST-93 *Valdivia* and to be primarily used for marine deployment on the Chilean coast. Development of the EADS *Astrium* satellite for Chile's 'Satellite System for Earth Observation' (SSOT) programme continued, albeit with delays. After an initial launch date of February 2010 had passed, as of late 2010 the Chilean government was anticipating to launch within the first half of 2011. This system will have a range of uses, but is primarily planned to improve the armed forces' networked-warfare capabilities: during the course of the year, the Chilean navy progressed in talks with INDRA for the purchase of satellite communications systems for its *Scorpène* submarines to be linked to the SSOT.

Argentina

The government of Argentina matched its Brazilian and Chilean counterparts in its apparent zeal for transparency, launching in June 2010 the preparation of the first new White Paper in over a decade. Intended to be an inclusive process, this involved a series of seminars in which civilian members of the Ministry of Defence and external defence experts and stakeholders were heavily represented. Despite some perhaps over-optimistic predictions that the document could be ready by the end of 2010, as of

December the process was not yet complete. Unlike Brazil and Chile, however, Argentina remained slow in modernising its armed forces, and engaged in only minimal maintenance and procurement through the year.

The Ministry of Defence announced in June 2010 that the army's stock of TAM tanks would be overhauled. Secondly, two MI-17 transport helicopters were ordered from Rosoboronexport as part of a set of new deals with Russia. The planned purchase of five Bell 206 training helicopters for joint instruction of all armed forces and the modernisation/repair of existing stocks of *Huey* II and *Super Puma* helicopters had been announced earlier in March. The Ministry of Defence resumed discussions with Saab for the purchase of two early-warning aircraft; a programme for refurbishing the engines of the air force's existing stock of *Pucarás* and *Pampas* was heralded; and the manufacturer FAdeA embarked on the development of a training aircraft for *Pampa* pilots.

While Argentina has signed a declaration of intent for the future purchase of six KC-390s from Embraer, none of the above measures addressed the fact that the bulk of Argentina's stock of fixed- and rotary-wing aircraft is ageing without any replacement in sight. A shortfall in fighter-bomber capability in particular is looming. The air force's existing stock of 1970s-built *Mirages* is due for retirement in 2012, and while France has promised to sell Argentina a number of *Mirage* 2000s when it replaces these in due course, this has not yet occurred. An indication of Argentina's desperation in this respect was its unsuccessful request in April 2010 to rent *Mirage* F-1EJs from the Jordanian government for five to six years to fill the gap. In this context, a Spanish offer in 2008 to sell Argentina 12–16 *Mirage* F1Ms may be revisited, but the advanced age of these aircraft means that such a move would not resolve the essential problem. These difficulties can only be exacerbated by the high rate at which Argentine air force pilots move to the private sector, attracted by higher salaries.

In fact, the only major procurement during the year was naval. Construction of at least four Fassmer OPV 80 off-shore patrol vessels for the navy was finally announced as due to begin in August 2010.

While Argentina has recently reiterated its commitment to recover sovereignty over the Falkland Islands by non-violent and legal means, it did increase its level of diplomatic protest significantly during 2010 in response to UK oil exploration, and more generally the government is looking to assert Argentine claims over a swathe of South Atlantic and Antarctic territory. Such procurement as is occurring is directed explicitly at addressing Antarctic capabilities, as with the Mi-17s, or maritime control, as with the OPVs.

Budgetary constraints continue to play a central role in limiting Argentina's military capabilities. These constraints are partly the result of economic difficulties. Although Argentina began to recover from recession during 2010, helped by automobile exports to Brazil and high soft-commodity prices, this recovery was supported by expansionary monetary policies in a context of high inflation, and the country's public finances continued to be fragile. These constraints are also the legacy of tight civilian control of military spending since the country's transition to democracy. Although the Ministry of Defence received 4.7% of the budget in 2010, a relatively normal share for the region, the armed forces have been continuously obliged to prioritise salary, pension and operating costs over major procurement, which although equally necessary in the long term has been repeatedly deferred. Hence real direct investment comprised only 2.8% of defence expenditure in 2010. Argentina's hopes of benefiting from the development of its own once-substantial native defence industry are also uncertain. Instead of following Brazil's example – boosting private enterprise with substantial funding while maintaining strategic control over specific projects – the government has instead opted for nationalisation, as for example with FAdeA in 2006 (previously under concession to Lockheed Martin) and the Tandanor shipyards in 2007.

However, there are some indications that the outlook for defence spending and procurement in particular may change. The defence budget in 2011 is planned to increase on the previous year. While high inflation means that this may represent no increase in real terms, the government has announced that it plans to increase the defence budget from 0.9% to 1.5% of GDP over the coming years. This would go most of the way towards reversing the decline of recent decades. This move would be likely to meet with cross-party support regardless of the outcome of the presidential election due to be held in late 2011.

In addition, following recognition of the need for a comprehensive overhaul of defence policy from 2005 onwards, and previous initiatives – notably the *Argentine Army 2025* plan produced in 2006 – in 2009 the Ministry of Defence released a roadmap for the modernisation of all aspects of defence policy, including procurement, organisation and strategic planning. Legislative changes over the 2006–09 period have also required the Joint Staff to harmonise doctrine and procedures between the three forces; regularly gather detailed information from them on existing capabilities and submit it annually to the Ministry of Defence; and adopt a systematic approach to procurement and planning. Little information was as of December 2010 publicly available on the practical implementation of these changes – for example regular updates on capabilities submitted by the Joint Staff – but it is likely that the forthcoming White Paper will be used to launch any major reorganisation, expansion or procurement that may be considered necessary. The creation at the end of the year of a new Ministry of Security, to be headed by outgoing Defence Minister Nilda Garré, and the appointment of defence industry chief Arturo Puricelli in her place, also suggested that further significant changes were imminent.

Further north, diplomatic tensions between Colombia and its neighbours did not result in the emergence of an arms race, principally because of fiscal constraints on military spending. However, long-term military trends still suggested substantial potential for regional instability.

Venezuela

The government in Caracas was hampered somewhat in its quest for enhanced military capabilities, and in particular to improve its maritime and aerial defensive capabilities, by a parlous economic situation. While other countries in the region recovered strongly from recession, the Venezuelan economy contracted by 2.9% in 2010, with production of oil as Venezuela's main source of export revenue continuing to decline after years of under-investment and inflation running at over 25%. As of December 2010, Venezuela showed no sign of being able to benefit from freshly increasing oil prices. In this context, contractions in military spending were exacerbated by inflation that defeated the government's attempts to maintain fixed rates against the dollar. In dollar terms, therefore, the defence budget fell from US$4.18bn (Bs8.97bn) in 2009 to only US$3.3bn (Bs8.6bn) in 2010. Procurement plans became less certain and Venezuela's role as provider of defence cooperation in ALBA was reduced, with only the transfer of six out-of-service *Mirage* 50 fighter aircraft to Ecuador of any note in this respect.

However, during 2010 Venezuela's military capabilities continued to expand because of continuing deliveries on existing contracts with Spain and China and further procurement from Russia that was enabled by the extension of a generous credit line. During 2010 Venezuela's Coast Guard received two of four coastal patrol vessels (BVLs), the *Guaicamacuto* and the *Yavire*, from the Spanish contractor Navantia, as well as one of four ocean patrol vessels (POVZEEs). The government made clear its intentions to procure further aircraft and naval vessels in the future from China and Spanish firms, but these plans did not translate into new contracts during the year and may be constrained by budgetary limitations.

Venezuelan defence cooperation with Russia remained substantial during 2010. A visit by Chávez to Moscow in September 2009 had resulted in discussions over the possible purchase of 92 T-72 tanks and BM-30 *Smerch* surface-to-air missiles. This would be financed with US$2.2bn (Bs5.67bn) credit from Moscow. During 2010 discussions also took place over the posible purchase from Russia of an unspecified number of S-300 air-defence systems, ZU-23-2 anti-aircraft guns, anti-boat coastal defence missiles (type unknown), and possibly a further 35 tanks. Chávez revealed at the end of the year that his expensive Russian procurement programme was to be financed with further credit perhaps totalling as much as US$4bn (Bs10.32bn). Fiscal and political pressures at home restricted Chávez's ability to repay these substantial debts – possibly affecting his ability to secure future deals. But Chávez's continued dedication to enhancing the state's 'asymmetric warfare' capability and fully politicising the armed forces in favour of his government, despite Venezuela's high-profile cooperation with Moscow, probably has the greatest bearing on regional security. The development of a mass civilian militia and domestic production of Kalashnikov assault rifles (which came on-stream during the year as a result of previous technology transfer agreements with Russia), the extensive procurement of *Igla*-S MANPADs, and further erosion of the neutrality of the armed forces in open defiance of regional norms, are all ostensibly aimed at ensuring effective defence of Venezuelan sovereignty in the event of an extra-regional intervention by the US. However, with the prospect of such an intervention exceptionally remote, they also make democratic political change in Venezuela less likely and could possibly help establish conditions whereby Venezuela might become a source of illegal small arms and light weapons in the future.

Colombia

The government in Bogotá has not yet formulated a comprehensive defence strategy, continuing to rely instead on the external defence component of its 2003 'Policy of Defence and Democratic Security' (PDSD) and the 2007 'consolidation' update (PCSD) of this policy. The diplomatic turmoil of the past decade between Colombia, Venezuela and Ecuador, particularly since March 2008, has led to increasing recognition of the need to develop such a strategy. Politically, however, change in this respect has been slowed by the sheer popularity of the PDSD/PCSD as the perceived cornerstone of the government's success in delivering security. Furthermore, ongoing internal conflict and illegal drugs production and trafficking have ensured that the immediate national security priorities have remained counter-insurgency and counter-narcotics. Because of the importance it accorded to Colombia's relationship with the US, the previous government led by Alvaro Uribe was inclined to look north for adequate guarantees against a potentially belligerent Venezuela (this was, indeed, the behind-the-scenes focus of the 2009 US–Colombia base agreement).

Nevertheless, both in the last years of the Uribe government and now under President Juan Manuel Santos, Colombia has been seeking to match its non-state capabilities with adequate deterrence. Santos' interest in rebalancing Colombia's regional relationships – in counterpoint to a gradual decline in levels of US military and police aid to the country – will complement this change. With the armed forces' structure and hardware adapted to face non-state threats, the expansion of the defence establishment has slowed as it nears its fiscal limits, meaning that conventional defence capabilities cannot simply be added on. Neither military victory over FARC nor a peace deal seems imminent, despite some important successes against both FARC and organised crime networks during 2010, notably the killing of FARC's military chief 'Mono Jojoy' in September. (Some armed-forces chiefs put FARC's numbers as low as 7,000.) The defence ministry and President Santos are, therefore, showing interest in capabilities and organisational changes that could allow for a more flexible use of existing resources, such as the mooted rebranding of the army's counter-guerrilla battalions as 'land warfare' battalions. In November 2009 Colombia purchased 39 M-117 APCs from the US firm Textron. Similarly, during 2010 the government began to refer to the enhancement of aerial assets capable of responding to external threats as a priority. Deliveries of *Kfir* aircraft continued during 2010, and the year also saw the air force receive a tanker/transport Boeing KC-767 converted by Israel's IAI. In a more direct response to diplomatic tensions with Venezuela, Colombia created seven new army aviation battalions in December 2009 and chose to station two of these close to the border with Venezuela in La Guajira and Arauca, with plans to expand an existing outpost into a major military base. In general, however, both the outgoing Uribe government and the new Santos administration held back from embarking on any major programme of reactive procurement.

Mexico

The army continued its deployments against the country's drug gangs during 2010. While the violence had been confined to the northern states, particularly in northern cities such as Ciudad Juárez and Tijuana, 2010 saw this spread to other states. Though the government scored some notable successes, such as the death or capture of several leaders of drug cartels, this has not led to a notable fall in violent incidents. Indeed, government figures listed 15,273 murders during the year, making 2010 the most violent since President Felipe Calderón launched his offensive. The cartels continue campaigns designed to intimidate local populations as well as security forces, committing increasingly grisly murders. While Calderón previously acknowledged that deploying the army was an imperfect solution, there has been no viable alternative while local police forces remain weak. Amid fears that violence, as well as increased amounts of illegal drugs and greater numbers of illegal immigrants, could flow north of the border, the US announced in July 2010 that up to 1,200 National Guard troops were to be deployed along the southwest border with Mexico in support of the US Border Patrol and US Immigration and Customs Enforcement.

Antigua and Barbuda ATG

East Caribbean Dollar EC$		2009	2010	2011
GDP	EC$	3.02bn	2.97bn	
	US$	1.12bn	1.10bn	
per capita	US$	12,768	12,414	
Growth	%	-8.5	-1.4	
Inflation	%	2.4	2.0	
Def exp	EC$	22m		
	US$	8m		
Def bdgt	EC$	22m	90m	
	US$	8m	33m	
US$1=EC$		2.70	2.70	

Population   88,550

Age	0–14	15–19	20–24	25–29	30–64	65 plus
Male	13.1%	4.3%	3.7%	3.5%	19.9%	2.9%
Female	12.7%	4.4%	4.0%	3.9%	23.7%	3.9%

Capabilities

ACTIVE 170 (Army 125 Navy 45)
(all services form combined Antigua and Barbuda Defence Force)

RESERVE 75 (Joint 75)

ORGANISATIONS BY SERVICE

Army 125

Navy 45
EQUIPMENT BY TYPE
PATROL AND COASTAL COMBATANTS • PB 2: 1 *Dauntless*; 1 *Swift*
FACILITIES
Base   1 located at St Johns

FOREIGN FORCES

United States US Strategic Command: 1 detection and tracking radar at Antigua Air Station

Argentina ARG

Argentine Peso P		2009	2010	2011
GDP	P	1.14tr	1.48tr	
	US$	309bn	382bn	
per capita	US$	7,668	9,396	
Growth	%	0.9	4.8	
Inflation	%	6.3	10.6	
Def exp	P	8.72bn		
	US$	2.35bn		
Def bdgt	P	8.52bn	10.1bn	
	US$	2.3bn	2.60bn	
US$1=P		3.71	3.88	

Population   40,665,732

Age	0–14	15–19	20–24	25–29	30–64	65 plus
Male	13.0%	4.1%	4.1%	3.9%	19.7%	4.5%
Female	12.4%	3.9%	4.0%	3.9%	20.1%	6.5%

Capabilities

ACTIVE 73,100 (Army 38,500 Navy 20,000 Air 14,600) Paramilitary 31,240

CIVILIAN 21,100 (Army 7,000 Navy 7,200 Air 6,900)

RESERVE none formally established or trained

ORGANISATIONS BY SERVICE

Army 38,500; 7,000 civilian
A strategic reserve is made up of armd, AB and mech bdes normally subordinate to corps level.
FORCES BY ROLE
Comd	3 corps HQ (mob def)
Mobile Defence	1 (Northeast) force (1 jungle bde, 1 armd bde, 1 trg bde); 1 (Northern) force (1 AB bde (1 cdo coy), 1 mech inf bde, 1 mtn inf bde); 1 (Patagonia and Southern Atlantic) force (1 mtn inf bde, 1 armd bde, 3 mech inf bde)
Rapid Reaction	1 (rapid deployment) force (includes AB bde from corps level) (1 cdo coy)
Mot Cav	1 regt (presidential escort)
Mot Inf	1 bn (army HQ escort regt)
Arty	1 gp (bn)
ADA	2 gp
Engr	1 bn
Avn	1 gp

EQUIPMENT BY TYPE
MBT 213: 207 TAM, 6 TAM S21
LT TK 123: 112 SK-105A1 *Kuerassier*; 6 SK105A2 *Kuerassier*; 5 *Patagón*
RECCE 81: 47 AML-90; 34 M1025A2 HMMWV
AIFV 263 VCTP (incl variants); 114 M-113A2 (20mm cannon)

APC (T) 294: 70 M-113 A1-ACAV; 224 M-113A2
ARTY 1,103
  SP 155mm 37: 20 Mk F3; 17 VCA 155 *Palmaria*
  TOWED 179: **105mm** 70 M-56 (Oto Melara); **155mm**
  109: 25 M-77 *CITEFA*/M-81 *CITEFA*; 84 SOFMA L-33
  MRL 105mm 4 SLAM *Pampero*
  MOR 883: **81mm** 492; **120mm** 353 *Brandt*
    SP 38: 25 M-106A2; 13 TAM-VCTM
AT
  MSL • SP 3 HMMWV with total of 18 TOW-2A
  MANPATS msl
  RCL 150 M-1968
  RL 385+ **66mm** 385 M-72 *LAW*; **78mm** MARA
AIRCRAFT
  ISR 10: 10 OV-1D *Mohawk* (6 with SLAR)
  TPT 20 **Medium** 3 G-222; **Light** 17: 1 Beech 80 *Queen Air*;
  1 C-212-200 *Aviocar*; 3 Cessna 207 *Stationair*; 1 Cessna
  500 *Citation* (survey); 2 DHC-6 *Twin Otter*; 3 SA-226
  Merlin IIIA; 5 SA-226AT *Merlin IV/IVA*; 1 Sabreliner 75A
  (*Gaviao 75A*)
  TRG 5 T-41 *Mescalero*
HELICOPTERS
  MRH 5 SA-315B
  TPT Medium 3 AS-332B *Super Puma* **Light** 36: 5 AW-109;
  1 Bell 212; 24 UH-1H *Iroquois* (6 armed); 6 UH-1H-II *Huey II*
  TRG 8 UH-12E
AD
  SAM 6 RBS -70
  GUNS • TOWED 411: **20mm** 230 GAI-B01; **30mm** 21
  HS L81; **35mm** 12 GDF Oerlikon (*Skyguard* fire control);
  40mm 148: 24 L/60 training, 40 in store; 76 L/60; 8 L/70
  RADAR • AD RADAR 11: 5 Cardion AN/TPS-44;
  6 *Skyguard*
    LAND 18+: M-113 A1GE *Green Archer* (mor); 18
    RATRAS (veh, arty)

Navy 20,000; 7,200 civilian

Commands: Surface Fleet, Submarines, Naval Avn, Marines

EQUIPMENT BY TYPE
SUBMARINES • TACTICAL • SSK 3:
  1 *Salta* (GER T-209/1200) with 8 single 533mm TT each
  with Mk 37/SST-4 HWT
  2 *Santa Cruz* (GER TR-1700) each with 6 single 533mm
  TT each with SST-4 HWT
PRINCIPAL SURFACE COMBATANTS 11
  DESTROYERS 5:
    DDGHM 4 *Almirante Brown* (GER MEKO 360) each
    with 2 quad lnchr (8 eff.) with MM-40 *Exocet* AShM,
    2 triple B515 *ILAS-3* 324mm each with A244 LWT,
    1 127mm gun, (capacity 1 AS-555 *Fennec*/SA-316B
    Alouette III hel)
    DDH 1 *Hercules* (UK Type 42 - utilised as a fast troop
    transport ship), with 1 114mm gun, (capacity 1 SH-3H
    Sea King hel)
  FRIGATES • FFGHM 6:
    6 *Espora* (GER MEKO 140) each with 2 twin lnchr (4
    eff.) each with MM-38 *Exocet* AShM, 2 triple B515 *ILAS-
    3* 324mm ASTT each with A244 LWT, 1 76mm gun

(capacity either 1 SA-319 *Alouette III* utl hel or 1 AS-555
Fennec utl hel)
PATROL AND COASTAL COMBATANTS 17
  CORVETTES • FSG 3 *Drummond* (FRA A-69) each with
  2 twin lnchr (4 eff.) each with MM-38 *Exocet* AShM, 2
  triple Mk32 324mm ASTT each with A244 LWT,
  1 100mm gun
  PSO 3:
    2 *Irigoyen* (US *Cherokee* AT);
    1 *Teniente Olivieri* (ex-US oilfield tug)
  PCO 3:
    2 *Murature* (US *King* - trg/river patrol role) each with
    3 105mm gun
    1 *Sobral* (US *Sotoyomo* AT)
  PCGT 1 *Interpida* (GER Lurssen 45m) with 2 single lnchr
  each with MM-38 *Exocet* AShM, 2 single 533mm TT each
  with SST-4 HWT, 1 76mm gun
  PCT 1 *Interpida* (GER Lurssen 45m) with 2 single
  533mm TT each with SST-4 HWT, 1 76mm gun
  PB 6: 4 *Baradero* (*Dabur*); 2 Point
AMPHIBIOUS 18 LCVP
LOGISTICS AND SUPPORT 12
  AOR 1 *Patagonia* (FRA *Durance*) with 1 hel platform
  AORL 1 *Ingeniero Julio Krause*
  AK 3 *Costa Sur*
  AGOR 1 *Commodoro Rivadavia*
  AGHS 1 *Puerto Deseado* (ice breaking capability, used
  for polar research)
  AGB 1 *Almirante Irizar*
  ABU 3 *Red*
  TRG 1 *Libertad*

FACILITIES
Bases | Located at Ushuaio (HQ Centre), Mar del Plata (SS and HQ Atlantic), Buenos Aires, Puerto Belgrano (HQ Centre), Zarate (river craft)
Naval air bases | Located at Trelew, Punta Indio
Construction and Repair Yard | Located at Rio Santiago

Naval Aviation 2,000
AIRCRAFT 24 combat capable
  FGA 2 *Super Etendard* (9 more in store)
  ATK 1 AU-23 *Turbo-Porter*
  ASW 11: 5 S-2T *Tracker*; 6 P-3B *Orion*
  TPT 9 **Light** 7: 2 Beech 200F *King Air*; 5 Beech 200F/M
  King Air **PAX** 2 F-28 *Fellowship*
  TRG 10 T-34C *Turbo Mentor**
HELICOPTERS
  ASW 4 SH-3H (ASH-3H) *Sea King*
  MRH 9: 3 AS-555 *Fennec*; 6 SA-316B *Alouette* III
  TPT • Medium 4 UH-3H *Sea King*
MSL
  AAM • IR AAM R-550 *Magic*
  ASM AS-25K CITEFA *Martin Pescador*
  AShM AM-39 *Exocet*

Marines 2,500
FORCES BY ROLE
Spt/Amph   1 force (1 marine inf bn)

Marine   1 (fleet) force (1 arty bn, 1 AAV bn, 1 cdo
              gp, 1 ADA bn, 1 marine inf bn); 1 (fleet)
              force (2 marine inf bn, 2 navy det)

EQUIPMENT BY TYPE
RECCE 52: 12 ERC-90F *Sagaie*; 40 M1097 HMMWV
APC (W) 24 *Panhard VCR*
AAV 17: 10 LARC-5; 7 LVTP-7
ARTY 100
   TOWED 105mm 18: 6 M-101; 12 Model 56 pack
   howitzer
   MOR 82: 70 **81mm**; 12 **120mm**
AT
   MSL • MANPATS 50 *Cobra*/RB-53 *Bantam*
   RCL 105mm 30 M-1974 FMK-1
   RL 89mm 60 M-20
AD
   SAM 6 RBS-70
   GUNS 30mm 10 HS-816; **35mm** GDF-001

Air Force 14,600; 6,900 civilian

4 Major Comds – Air Operations, Personnel, Air Regions,
Logistics, 8 air bde

Air Operations Command

FORCES BY ROLE

Ftr/FGA   1 sqn with *Mirage* IIID/E (*Mirage* IIIEA/
             DA); 1 sqn with *Mirage* 5P *Mara*; 2 sqn with
             Nesher S/T (*Dagger* A/B);

Atk   2 sqn with A-4AR/OA-4AR *Skyhawk*; 2 (tac
             air) sqn with IA-58 *Pucara*; EMB-312 *Tucano*
             (on loan for border surv/interdiction)

ISR   1 sqn with *Learjet* 35A

SAR/Tpt   3 sqn with Bell 205 (UH-1H *Iroquois*); Bell
Hel   212; Bell 212 (UH-1N); *Hughes* 369; MD-500;
             SA-315B *Lama*

Tkr/Tpt   2 sqn with C-130B *Hercules*; C-130H
             Hercules; KC-130H *Hercules*; L-100-30;

Tpt   1 sqn with B-707; 1 sqn with DHC-6 *Twin
             Otter*; 1 sqn with F-27 *Friendship*; 1 sqn with
             F-28 *Fellowship*; *Learjet* 60; 1 (Pres) flt with
             B-757-23ER; S-70A *Black Hawk*, S-76B

FACILITIES

Trg School   1 with T-34 *Mentor* (basic); EMB-312 *Tucano*
             (primary); 3 MD-500; *Learjet* 35A (test and
             calibration)

EQUIPMENT BY TYPE
AIRCRAFT 121 combat capable
   FGA 29: 8 *Mirage* IIID/E (*Mirage* IIIEA/DA); 7 *Mirage*
   5P *Mara*; 11 *Nesher* S (*Dagger* A), 3 *Nesher* T (*Dagger* B);
   ATK 68: 34 A-4 (A-4AR)/OA-4 (OA-4AR) *Skyhawk*; 33
   IA-58 *Pucara*
   TKR 2 KC-130H *Hercules*
   TPT 38: **Medium** 9: 3 C-130B *Hercules*; 5 C-130H
   Hercules; 1 L-100-30 **Light** 22: 8 DHC-6 *Twin Otter*; 4
   F-27 *Friendship*; 5 Learjet 35A (test and calibration);
   1 *Learjet* 60; 4 Saab 340 **PAX** 7: 1 B-757-23ER; 6 F-28
   Fellowship

TRG 67: 18 AT-63 *Pampa** (LIFT); 19 EMB-312 *Tucano*; 6
EMB-312 *Tucano** (LIFT) (on loan from Brazil); 24 T-34
Mentor
HELICOPTERS
   MRH 25: 15 *Hughes* 369; 3 MD-500; 4 MD-500D; 3 SA-
   315B *Lama*
   TPT 7+ Medium Some S-70A *Black Hawk* **Light** 7: 6 Bell
   212; 1 S-76B
MSL
   AAM • IR AAM AIM-9L *Sidewinder*; R-550 *Magic*;
   Shafrir II ‡
AD
   GUNS 88: **20mm**: 86 Oerlikon/Rh-202 with 9 Elta
   EL/M-2106 radar; **35mm**: 2 Oerlikon GDF-001 with
   Skyguard radar
RADAR 6: 5 AN/TPS-43; 1 BPS-1000

Paramilitary 31,240

Gendarmerie 18,000
Ministry of Interior
FORCES BY ROLE
Region   5 comd
Paramilitary 16 bn

EQUIPMENT BY TYPE
RECCE S52 *Shorland*
APC (W) 87: 47 *Grenadier*; 40 UR-416
ARTY • MOR 81mm
AIRCRAFT
   TPT • Light 7: 1 Cessna 206; 3 PA-28-236 *Dakota*/PA-
   31P *Pressurized Navajo*; 3 PC-6 *Turbo-Porter*
HELICOPTERS
   MRH 3 MD-500C/D
   TPT • Light 8: 5 Bell 205 (UH-1H *Iroquois*); 3 AS-350
   Ecureuil

Prefectura Naval (Coast Guard) 13,240
PATROL AND COASTAL COMBATANTS 65:
   PCO 6: 1 *Delfin*; 5 *Mantilla* (F30 *Halcón*)
   PCC 1 *Mandubi*
   PB 57: 1 *Dorado*; 35 Estrellemar; 2 *Lynch* (US *Cape*); 18
   Mar del Plata (Z-28); 1 *Surel*
   PBR 1 *Tonina*
LOGISTICS & SUPPORT • TRG 4
AIRCRAFT
   TPT • Light 7: 5 C-212 *Aviocar*; 2 PC-12
HELICOPTERS
   SAR 1 AS-565MA
   MRH 2 AS-365 *Dauphin 2*
   TPT • Medium 1 SA-330L (AS-330L) *Puma*
   TRG 2 S-300C

DEPLOYMENT

CYPRUS
UN • UNFICYP 267; 2 inf coy; 1 avn pl; 2 Bell 212

HAITI
UN • MINUSTAH 708; 1 inf bn; 1 avn unit; 1 fd hospital

MIDDLE EAST
UN • UNTSO 5 obs

WESTERN SAHARA
UN • MINURSO 3 obs

Bahamas BHS

Bahamian Dollar B$		2009	2010	2011
GDP	B$	7.38bn	7.54bn	
	US$	7.38bn	7.54bn	
per capita	US$	21,588	21,803	
Growth	%	-3.9	-0.5	
Inflation	%	2.1	1.7	
Def exp	B$	49m		
	US$	49m		
Def bdgt	B$	49m	46m	49m
	US$	49m	46m	
FMA	US$	0.15m	0.15m	-
US$1=B$		1.00	1.00	

Population   345,736

Age	0–14	15–19	20–24	25–29	30–64	65 plus
Male	12.4%	4.6%	4.2%	4.0%	21.3%	2.4%
Female	12.0%	4.5%	4.1%	3.9%	22.7%	3.9%

Capabilities

ACTIVE 860 (Royal Bahamian Defence Force 860)

ORGANISATIONS BY SERVICE

Royal Bahamian Defence Force 860
FORCES BY ROLE
Marine   1 coy (Marines with internal and base sy duties)
EQUIPMENT BY TYPE
PATROL AND COASTAL COMBATANTS 9
  PCC 2 *Bahamas*
  PB 7: 2 *Dauntless*; 1 *Protector*; 4 (various)
AIRCRAFT • TPT • Light 6: 1 Beech A350 *King Air*; 1 Cessna 208 *Caravan*; 1 Cessna 404 *Titan*; 1 P-68 *Observer*; 2 PA-31
FACILITIES
Bases   Located at Coral Harbour, New Providence Island

FOREIGN FORCES

Guyana Navy: Base located at New Providence Island

Barbados BRB

Barbados Dollar B$		2009	2010	2011
GDP	B$	7.79bn	7.93bn	
	US$	3.90bn	3.96bn	
per capita	US$	15,222	15,445	
Growth	%	-3.0	1.7	
Inflation	%	3.6	5.0	
Def exp	B$	52m		
	US$	26m		
Def bdgt	B$	65m	68m	
	US$	33m	34m	
US$1=B$		2.00	2.00	

Population   256,552

Age	0–14	15–19	20–24	25–29	30–64	65 plus
Male	9.5%	3.4%	3.6%	3.8%	24.3%	3.8%
Female	9.5%	3.5%	3.5%	3.8%	25.4%	6.0%

Capabilities

ACTIVE 610 (Army 500 Navy 110)

RESERVE 430 (Joint 430)

ORGANISATIONS BY SERVICE

Army 500
Inf   1 bn (cadre)

Navy 110
HQ located at HMBS Pelican, Spring Garden
EQUIPMENT BY TYPE
PATROL AND COASTAL COMBATANTS • PB 6: 1 *Dauntless*; 2 *Enterprise*; 3 *Trident* (Damen Stan Patrol 4207)
FACILITIES
Base   located at HMBS Pelican, Spring Garden, secondary facilities St Ann's Fort, Bridgetown

Belize BLZ

Belize Dollar BZ$		2009	2010	2011
GDP	BZ$	2.70bn	2.86bn	
	US$	1.35bn	1.43bn	
per capita	US$	4,056	4,575	
Growth	%	-1.0	1.7	
Inflation	%	-1.1	2.8	
Def exp		27m		
		14m		
Def bdgt		43m	38m	33m
	US$	21m	19m	
FMA	US$	0.2m	0.2m	0.2m
US$1=BZ$		2.00	2.00	

Population   312,928

Age	0–14	15–19	20–24	25–29	30–64	65 plus
Male	18.8%	5.7%	5.1%	4.4%	14.9%	1.7%
Female	18.0%	5.5%	5.0%	4.2%	14.8%	1.9%

Capabilities

ACTIVE ε1,050 (Army ε1,050)

RESERVE 700 (Joint 700)

ORGANISATIONS BY SERVICE

Army ε1,050
FORCES BY ROLE

Inf	3 bn (each: 3 inf coy)
Spt	1 gp

EQUIPMENT BY TYPE
MOR 81mm 6
RCL 84mm 8 *Carl Gustav*

Maritime Wing

Air Wing
FORCES BY ROLE

MR/Tpt	1 sqn with BN-2A *Defender*; BN-2B *Defender*
Trg	1 unit with 1 Cessna 182 *Skylane*; 1 T-67M-200 *Firefly*

EQUIPMENT BY TYPE
AIRCRAFT
  TPT • Light 3: 1 BN-2A *Defender*; 1 BN-2B *Defender*; 1 Cessna 182 *Skylane*;
  TRG 1 T-67M-200 *Firefly*

Reserve

Inf	3 coy

FOREIGN FORCES

United Kingdom Army 30

Bolivia BOL

Bolivian Boliviano B		2009	2010	2011
GDP	B	122bn	134bn	
	US$	17.3bn	19.0bn	
per capita	US$	1,758	1,899	
Growth	%	3.4	4.2	
Inflation	%	3.3	1.7	
Def exp	B	2.01bn		
	US$	286m		
Def bdgt	B	1.7bn	2.5bn	
	US$	242m	357m	
US$1=B		7.02	7.02	

Population   10,030,832

Age	0–14	15–19	20–24	25–29	30–64	65 plus
Male	17.6%	5.3%	4.9%	4.4%	15.1%	2.1%
Female	17.0%	5.1%	4.9%	4.4%	16.5%	2.6%

Capabilities

ACTIVE 46,100 (Army 34,800 Navy 4,800 Air 6,500)
Paramilitary 37,100

ORGANISATIONS BY SERVICE

Army 9,800; 25,000 conscript (total 34,800)
FORCES BY ROLE
HQ: 6 Military Regions, 10 Div org; composition varies

Armd	1 bn
Cav	1 (aslt) gp; 5 (horsed) gp
Mech Inf	2 regt
Inf/Presidential Guard	1 regt
Inf	21 bn
Mech Cav	1 regt
SF	3 regt
AB	2 regt (bn)
Mot Cav	1 gp
Mot Inf	3 regt
Arty	6 regt (bn)
ADA	1 regt
Engr	6 bn
Avn	2 coy

EQUIPMENT BY TYPE
LT TK 54: 36 SK-105A1 *Kuerassier*; 18 SK-105A2 *Kuerassier*
RECCE 24 EE-9 *Cascavel*
APC 152+
  APC (T) 91+: 4 4K-4FA-SB20 *Greif*; 50+ M-113, 37 M9 half-track
  APC (W) 61: 24 EE-11 *Urutu*; 22 MOWAG *Roland*; 15 V-100 *Commando*
LT VEH 10: 10 *Koyak*
ARTY 311+

TOWED 61: **105mm** 25 M-101A1; **122mm** 36 (M-30) M-1938

MOR 250+: **60mm** M-224; **81mm** 250 M-29; Type-W87; **107mm** M-30; **120mm** M-120

AT • MSL • MANPATS 50+ HJ-8 (2 SP on *Koyak*)

RCL **106mm** M-40A1; **90mm** M-67

RL 200+: **66mm** M-72 *LAW*; **73mm** RPG-7V *Knout*; **89mm** 200+ M-20

AIRCRAFT

TPT • **Light** 2: Cessna 210 *Centurion*; 1 PA-34 *Seneca*

AD • GUNS • TOWED **37mm** 18 Type-65

Navy 4,800

Organised into 6 naval districts with HQ located at Puerto Guayaramerín

EQUIPMENT BY TYPE

PATROL AND COASTAL COMBATANTS • PBR 1 Santa Cruz

LOGISTICS AND SUPPORT 21:

AH 2

TPT 11 (river transports)

SPT 8

FACILITIES

Bases	Located at Riberalta, Tiquina, Puerto Busch, Puerto Guayaramerín, Puerto Villarroel, Trinidad, Puerto Suárez, Coral Harbour, Santa Cruz, Bermejo, Cochabamba, Puerto Villeroel

Marines 1,700 (incl 1,000 Naval Military Police)

Marine	6 inf bn (1 in each Naval District)
Mech inf	1 bn
MP	4 (naval MP) bn

Air Force 6,500 (incl conscripts)

FORCES BY ROLE

Atk	2 sqn with AT-33AN *Shooting Star*
Atk/ISR/Trg	1 sqn with PC-7 *Turbo Trainer*
ISR	1 sqn with Cessna 206; Cessna 402; *Learjet* 25B/25D (secondary VIP role)
SAR	1 sqn with HB-315B *Lama*, AS-532AC *Cougar*
Tpt	1 sqn with Beech 90 *King Air*; 2 sqn with C-130B/C-130H/RC-130A *Hercules*; DC-10; MA60; 1 sqn with *Aero-commander* 690; BAe-146-100 Beech-1900; CV-440; CV-580; F-27-400 *Friendship*; IAI-201 *Arava*; 3 sqn with Beech F33 *Bonanza*; Cessna 152; Cessna 206; Cessna 210; PA-32 *Saratoga*; PA-34 *Seneca*;
Trg	3 sqn with A-122; Cessna 152; Cessna 172; T-25; T-34B Beech *Turbo Mentor*
Tpt Hel	1 (anti-drug) sqn with Bell 205 (UH-1H *Iroquois)*
AD	1 regt with Oerlikon; Type-65

EQUIPMENT BY TYPE

AIRCRAFT 33 combat capable

ATK 15 AT-33AN *Shooting Star*

TPT 75: **Medium** 7 C-130B/C-130H/RC-130A *Hercules* **Light** 59: 1 *Aero-Commander* 690; 3 Beech 90 *King Air*; 1 Beech-1900; 3 C-212-100; 10 Cessna 152; 2 Cessna 172; 19 Cessna 206; 1 Cessna 210; 1 Cessna 212; 1 Cessna 402; 1 CV-440; 1 CV-580; 3 F-27-400 *Friendship*; 4 IAI-201 *Arava*; 2 Learjet 25B/D; 2 MA60; 1 PA-32 *Saratoga*; 3 PA-34 *Seneca*; **PAX** 9: 7 BAe-146-100; 1 DC-10; 1 Falcon 900EX (VIP)

TRG 53: 1 Beech F33 *Bonanza*; 28 A-122 *Uirapuru*; 6 T-25; 10 T-34B *Turbo Mentor*; 18 PC-7 *Turbo Trainer**

HELICOPTERS

MRH 2: 1 AS-532AC *Cougar*; 1 SB-315B (HB-315B) *Lama*

TPT • **Light** 17: 2 AS 350 B3 *Ecureuil*; 15 Bell 205 (UH-1H *Iroquois*)

AD • GUNS 18+: **20mm** *Oerlikon*; **37mm** 18 Type-65

Paramilitary 37,100+

National Police 31,100+

Frontier	27 unit
Paramilitary	9 bde; 2 (rapid action) regt

Narcotics Police 6,000+

FOE (700) - Special Operations Forces

DEPLOYMENT

CÔTE D'IVOIRE

UN • UNOCI 3 obs

DEMOCRATIC REPUBLIC OF THE CONGO

UN • MONUSCO 19; 10 obs

HAITI

UN • MINUSTAH 208; 1 mech inf coy

LIBERIA

UN • UNMIL 1; 2 obs

SUDAN

UN • UNAMID 1

UN • UNMIS 15 obs

Brazil BRZ

Brazilian Real R		2009	2010	2011
GDP	R	3.14tr	3.61tr	
	US$	1.59tr	2.04tr	
per capita	US$	8,217	10,435	
Growth	%	-0.2	6.4	
Inflation	%	4.9	5.0	
Def exp	R	51.3bn		
	US$	26bn		
Def bdgt	R	55.3bn	61.3bn	66.1bn
	US$	28bn	34.7bn	
US$1=R		1.97	1.77	

Population	195,423,252

Age	0–14	15–19	20–24	25–29	30–64	65 plus
Male	13.4%	4.2%	4.2%	4.3%	20.5%	2.8%
Female	12.9%	4.0%	4.1%	4.2%	21.5%	3.9%

Capabilities

ACTIVE 318,480 (Army 190,000 Navy 59,000 Air 69,480) Paramilitary 395,000

RESERVE 1,340,000

Terms of service 12 months (can be extended to 18)

ORGANISATIONS BY SERVICE

Army 120,000; 70,000 conscript (total 190,000)

FORCES BY ROLE

Comd	7 Mil Comd; 12 Mil Regions; 7 div HQ (2 with Regional HQ)
Armd	2 bde (each: 2 armd cav bn, 2 armd inf bn, 1 arty bn, 1 engr bn)
Mech Cav	4 bde (each: 1 armd cav bn, 2 mech cav bn, 1 arty bn)
Mot Inf	8 bde (total: 29 mot inf bn)
Lt Inf	2 bde (total: 6 lt inf bn)
Jungle Inf	5 bde (total: 15 bn)
SF	1 bde with (1 SF bn, 1 cdo bn, 1 SF training centre)
AB	1 bde (1 arty bn, 3 AB bn)
Arty	6 (med) gp; 4 (SP) gp
ADA	1 bde
Engr	2 gp (total: 11 engr bn)
Security	1 bde (total: 6 lt inf bn)
Hel	1 bde (4 hel bn (each: 2 hel sqn))

EQUIPMENT BY TYPE

MBT 267: 128 *Leopard* 1A1BE; 48 *Leopard* 1A5BR (172 more on order); 91 M-60A3/TTS
LT TK 152 M-41B/M-41C
RECCE 408: 408 EE-9 *Cascavel*
APC 807
   APC (T) 584 M-113

APC (W) 223 EE-11 *Urutu*
ARTY 1,805
   SP 109: **105mm** 72 M-108/M-7; **155mm** 37 M-109A3
   TOWED 431
      105mm 336: 233 M-101/M-102; 40 L-118 *Light Gun*; 63 Model 56 pack howitzer
      155mm 95 M-114
   MRL 20+: **70mm** SBAT-70; 20 ASTROS II
   MOR 1,245: **81mm** 1,168: 453 Royal Ordnance L-16, 715 M936 AGR; **120mm** 77 M2
AT
   MSL • MANPATS 30: 18 *Eryx*; 12 *Milan*
   RCL 343: **106mm** 194 M-40A1; **84mm** 149 *Carl Gustav*
   RL 84mm 540 AT-4
HELICOPTERS
   MRH 51: 32 AS-365 *Dauphin*; 19 AS-550U2 *Fennec* (armed)
   TPT 28 **Medium** 12: 8 AS-532 *Cougar;* 4 S-70A-36 *Black Hawk* **Light** 16 AS-350 LI *Ecureuil*
AD
   MANPAD 53 9K38 *Igla* (SA-18 *Grouse*)
   GUNS 66: **35mm** 39 GDF-001 towed (some with *Super Fledermaus* radar); **40mm** 27 L/70 (some with BOFI)
RADAR: 5 SABER M60

Navy 59,000

FORCES BY ROLE

Organised into 9 districts with HQ I Rio de Janeiro, HQ II Salvador, HQ III Natal, HQ IV Belém, HQ V Rio Grande, HQ VI Ladario, HQ VII Brasilia, HQ VIII Sao Paulo, HQ IX Manaus

EQUIPMENT BY TYPE

SUBMARINES • TACTICAL • SSK 5:
   4 *Tupi* (GER T-209/1400) each with 8 single 533mm TT each with MK 24 *Tigerfish* HWT
   1 *Tikuna* with 8 single 533mm TT each with MK 24 *Tigerfish* HWT
PRINCIPAL SURFACE COMBATANTS 15
   AIRCRAFT CARRIERS • CV 1:
   1 *Sao Paulo* (FRA *Clemenceau*) (capacity 15–18 A-4 *Skyhawk* atk ac; 4–6 SH-3D/SH-3A *Sea King* ASW hel; 3 AS-355F/AS-350BA *Ecureuil* hel; 2 AS-532 *Cougar* hel)
   DESTROYERS • DDGHM 3 *Greenhaigh* (UK *Broadsword*, 1 low readiness) each with 4 single lnchr each with MM-38 *Exocet* AShM, 2 sextuple lnchr (12 eff.) each with *Sea Wolf* SAM, 6 single 324mm ASTT each with Mk 46 LWT, (capacity 1 *Super Lynx* Mk21A hel)
   FRIGATES 11:
      FFGHM 6 *Niteroi* each with 2 twin lnchr (4 eff.) each with MM-40 *Exocet* AShM, 1 octuple *Albatros* lnchr with *Aspide* SAM, 2 triple 324mm ASTT (6 eff.) each with Mk 46 LWT, 1 twin 375mm A/S mor (2 eff.), 1 115mm gun, (capacity 1 *Super Lynx* Mk21A hel)
      FFGH 5:
         4 *Inhauma* each with 2 twin lnchr (4 eff.) each with MM-40 *Exocet* AShM, 2 triple 324mm ASTT (6 eff.) each with Mk 46 LWT, 1 115mm gun, (1 *Super Lynx* Mk21A hel)
         1 *Barroso* with 2 twin lnchr (4 eff.) each with MM-40 *Exocet* AShM, 2 triple 324mm ASTT (6 eff.) each with

Mk 46 LWT, 1 115mm gun, (capacity 1 *Super Lynx* Mk21A utl hel)

PATROL AND COASTAL COMBATANTS 42:

PCO 7: 4 *Bracui* (UK *River*); 2 *Imperial Marinheiro* with 1 76mm gun; 1 *Parnaiba* with 1 hel landing platform

PCC 2 *Macaé* (additional vessels in build)

PCR 5: 2 *Pedro Teixeira*; 3 *Roraima*

PB 28: 12 *Grajau*; 6 *Marlim*; 6 *Piratini* (US PGM); 4 *Tracker* (Marine Police)

MINE WARFARE • MINE COUNTERMEASURES • **MSC** 6 *Aratu* (GER *Schutze*)

AMPHIBIOUS

PRINCIPAL AMPHIBIOUS SHIPS • LSD 2:

2 *Ceara* (US *Thomaston*) (capacity either 21 LCM or 6 LCU; 345 troops)

LANDING SHIPS 3:

LST 1 *Mattoso Maia* (US *Newport*) (capacity 3 LCVP; 1 LCPL; 400 troops)

LSLH 2: 1 *Garcia D'Avila* (UK *Sir Galahad*) (capacity 1 hel; 16 MBT; 340 troops); 1 *Almirante Saboia* (UK *Sir Bedivere*) (capacity 1 med hel; 18 MBT; 340 troops)

LANDING CRAFT 46: 3 LCU; 35 LCVP; 8 LCM

LOGISTICS AND SUPPORT 39:

AOR 2: 1 *Gastao Motta*; 1 *Marajo*

ASR 1 *Felinto Perry* (NOR *Wildrake*)

AG 2: 1 (troop carrier); 1 (river spt)

AH 4: 2 *Oswaldo Cruz*; 1 *Dr Montenegro*; 1 *Tenente Maximiano*

AK 5

AGOR 3: 1 *Ary Rongel* (Ice-strengthened hull, used for polar research); 1 *Cruzeiro do Sul* (research); 1 *Almirante Maximiano*

AGHS 1 *Sirius*

AGS 4: 1 *Antares*; 3 *Amorim Do Valle* (UK *Rover*)

ABU 6: 1 *Almirante Graca Aranah* (lighthouse tender); 5 *Comandante Varella*

ATF 5: 3 *Tritao*; 2 *Almirante Guihem*

TPT 2: 1 *Paraguassu*; 1 *Piraim* (river transports)

TRG 4:

AXL 3 *Nascimento*

AXS 1

Naval Aviation 2,500

FORCES BY ROLE

Atk	1 sqn with A-4 *Skyhawk*; A-4M (A-4MB) *Skyhawk*; TA-4 *Skyhawk*; TA-4M (T-A4MB) *Skyhawk*
ASuW	1 sqn with *Super Lynx* Mk21A
ASW	1 sqn with SH-3G/H *Sea King*
Tpt Hel	1 sqn with AS-332 *Super Puma*; 4 sqn with AS-350 *Ecureuil* (armed); AS-355 *Ecureuil* (armed)
Trg	1 sqn with Bell 206B3 *Jet Ranger III*

EQUIPMENT BY TYPE

AIRCRAFT 12 combat capable

ATK 12 A-4 *Skyhawk*/A-4M (A-4MB) *Skyhawk*/TA-4 *Skyhawk*/TA-4M (TA-4MB) *Skyhawk**

HELICOPTERS

ASW 16: 12 *Super Lynx* Mk21A; 4 SH-3G/H *Sea King*

TPT 48: **Medium** 7 AS-332 *Super Puma*; **Light** 41: 18

AS-350 *Ecureuil* (armed); 8 AS-355 *Ecureuil* (armed); 15 Bell 206B3 *Jet Ranger III*

MSL • AShM: AM-39 *Exocet*; *Sea Skua*

Marines 15,000

FORCES BY ROLE

Amph	1 (Fleet Force) div (1 comd bn, 1 arty gp, 3 inf bn)
SF	1 bn
Marine	8+ (Regional) gp; 3 bn
Engr	1 bn

EQUIPMENT BY TYPE

LT TK 18 SK-105 *Kuerassier*

APC 42

APC (T) 30 M-113

APC (W) 12 Piranha IIIC (additional 18 on order)

AAV 25: 13 AAV-7A1; 12 LVTP-7

ARTY 59

TOWED 41: **105mm** 33: 18 L-118 Light Gun; 15 M-101; **155mm** 8 M-114

MOR 18 **81mm**

AT

MSL• MANPATS RB-56 *Bill*

RL 89mm M-20

AD • GUNS 40mm 6 L/70 (with BOFI)

Air Force 69,480

COMDABRA (aerospace defence), plus three general cmds – COMGAR (operations), COMGAP (logistics), COMGEP (personnel).

Brazilian air space is divided into 7 air regions, each of which is responsible for its designated air bases.

Air assets are divided among five designated air forces for operations (one temporarily deactivated).

I Air Force (HQ Natal) operates 3 avn gps (1st/5th, 2st/5th and 1st/11th GAV) and a Tactical Training Group (GITE) providing Air Combat Training for EMB-314 *Super Tucano* (A-29A/B) and EMB-312 *Tucano* (T-27) aircraft. I Air Force also operates the C-95 *Bandeirante* and AS350 (UH-50) helicopters.

II Air Force (HQ Rio de Janeiro) is organised into 3 Aviation Groups (7th, 8th and 10th GAVs). 7th GAV, responsible for coastal patrol, operates P-95A/B *Bandeirulhas* armed for ASV and ASW from 4 air bases. 8th and 10th GAVs, with H-60L *Blackhawk*, Mi-35M (AH-2) Bell 205 (H-1H), AS-332 *Super Puma* (CH-34) and AS350/AS355 *Ecureuil* (H-50/H-55) helicopters, are dedicated to SAR/utility, tpt ops and spec ops.

III Air Force (HQ Brasilia) 1st Air Defence Group is equipped with *Mirage* 2000B/C. The main light attack/armed recce force, with anti-narcotic and anti-terrorist roles, comprises 6 air groups with EMB-314 *Super Tucano* (A-29), AT-26 *Xavante* and AMX (A-1A/B); 6th GAV, with 5 EMB-145 AEW, 3 EMB-145RS, 3 Learjet 35A (R-35A) and 4 R-95 electronic recce aircraft, is responsible for electronic surveillance, AEW and reconnaissance.

V Air Force (HQ Rio de Janeiro) operates some 160 air transport and flight refuelling aircraft from 5 air bases. Six tpt gps operate C-295M, ERJ-135/ERJ-145, EMB-190 transports, C/KC-130E/H *Hercules* tkr/tpts and KC-137 tankers.

FORCES BY ROLE

Ftr   1 gp with *Mirage* 2000B/C, 2 sqn with F-5EM/ FM *Tiger II*

FGA   2 sqn with AMX (A-1A/B); 4 sqn with EMB-314 *Super Tucano* (A-29A/B)*

MP   4 sqn with EMB-110 (P-95A/P-95B)

ISR   1 sqn with AMX-R (RA-1)*; 1 sqn with *Learjet* 35 (R-35A); EMB-110B (R-95)

AEW&C   1 sqn with EMB-145RS (R-99); EMB-145SA (E-99)

Tkr   1 sqn with KC-130H, 1 sqn with KC-137

Tpt   1 sqn with A-319 (VC-1A); EMB-135 (VC-99A/B); EMB-190 (VC-2); Learjet 35 (VU-35); 2 sqn with C-130H/E *Hercules*; 2 sqn with C-295M (C-105A); 7 sqn with Cessna 208 (C-98); EMB-110 (C-95); EMB-120 (C-97); 1 sqn with ERJ-145 (C-99A); 1 sqn with EMB-120 (VC-97), EMB-121 (VU-9)

Trg   1 sqn with EMB-110 (C-95); 2 sqn with EMB-312 *Tucano* (T-27) (incl 1 air show sqn); 1 sqn with T-25

Tpt Hel   1 sqn with AS-332M *Super Puma* (H-34) (VIP); EC-135 (H-35); 1 sqn with AS350 *Ecureuil* (H-50); AS 355 *Ecureuil II* (H-55); 2 sqn with Bell 205 (H-1H); 1 sqn with UH-60L *Blackhawk* (H-60L)

EQUIPMENT BY TYPE

AIRCRAFT 256 combat aircraft

FTR 57: 6 F-5E *Tiger II*; 51 F-5EM/FM *Tiger II*

FGA 61: 38 AMX (A-1); 11 AMX-T (A-1B); 12 *Mirage* 2000B/C

ASW 9 P-3AM *Orion* (delivery in progress)

MP 19: 10 EMB-111 (P-95A *Bandeirulha*)*; 9 EMB-111 (P-95B *Bandeirulha*)*

ISR: 8: 4 AMX-R (RA-1)*; 4 EMB-110B (R-95)

ELINT 22: 9 EMB-110 (EC-95); 3 EMB-145RS (R-99); 3 Hawker 800XP (EU-93A); 4 HS-125 (EU-93); 3 Learjet 35A (R-35A)

AEW&C 5 EMB-145SA (E-99)

SAR 5: 4 EMB-110 (SC-95B), 1 SC-130E *Hercules*

TKR/TPT 5: 2 KC-130H; 3 KC-137 (1 more in store)

TPT 178 **Medium** 19: 6 C-130E *Hercules*; 13 C-130H *Hercules*; **Light** 156: 12 C-295M (C-105); 12 Cessna 208 (C-98); 13 Cessna 208-G1000 (C-98A); 53 EMB-110 (C-95A/B/C); 16 EMB-120 (C-97); 4 EMB-120 (VC-97); 6 EMB-121 (VU-9); 3 EMB-201 *Ipanema* (U-19); 6 ERJ-135 (VC-99C); 10 ERJ-145 (C-99A); 9 PA-34 *Seneca* (U-7); 12 U-42 *Regente* **PAX** 3: 1 A-319 (VC-1A); 2 EMB-190 (VC-2)

TRG 271: 105 EMB-312 *Tucano* (T-27); 40 EMB-314 *Super Tucano* (A-29A)*; 45 EMB-314 *Super Tucano* (A-29B)*; 81 T-25A/C

HELICOPTERS

ATK 6 Mi-35M *Hind* (AH-2)

TPT 70: **Medium** 16: 10 AS-332M *Super Puma* (H-34); 6 UH-60L *Blackhawk* (H-60L) (6 more on order) Light 24 AS-350B *Ecureuil* (H-50); 4 AS-355 *Ecureuil II* (H-55); 24 Bell 205 (H-1H); 2 EC-135 (H-35)

MSL • AAM • IR AAM MAA-1 *Piranha; Magic* 2; *Python* III; **SARH AAM** Super 530F **ARH AAM** Derby

ARM AMR-1 (in development)

Paramilitary 395,000 opcon Army

Public Security Forces 395,000

State police organisation technically under army control. However military control is reducing, with authority reverting to individual states.

EQUIPMENT BY TYPE

UAV • ISR • Heavy 3 *Heron* (deployed by Federal Police for Amazon and border patrols)

DEPLOYMENT

CÔTE D'IVOIRE

UN • UNOCI 3; 4 obs

CYPRUS

UN • UNFICYP 1

HAITI

UN • MINUSTAH 2,188; 2 inf bn; 1 engr coy

LIBERIA

UN • UNMIL 2; 2 obs

NEPAL

UN • UNMIN 6 obs

SUDAN

UN • UNMIS 2; 20 obs

TIMOR LESTE

UN • UNMIT 4 obs

WESTERN SAHARA

UN • MINURSO 11 obs

Chile CHL

Chilean Peso pCh		2009	2010	2011
GDP	pCh	91.5tr	105.3tr	
	US$	164bn	204bn	
per capita	US$	9,656	11,907	
Growth	%	-1.5	4.2	
Inflation	%	2.0	1.4	
Def exp[a]	pCh	2817bn		
	US$	5.04bn		
Def bdgt	pCh	1069bn	1068bn	
	US$	1.91bn	2.07bn	
FMA	US$	0.4m	0.4m	0.75m
US$1=pCh		558.49	515.98	

[a] Including estimates for military pensions, paramilitary and Copper Fund

Population	17,134,708

Age	0–14	15–19	20–24	25–29	30–64	65 plus
Male	11.4%	4.3%	4.3%	3.9%	21.5%	4.0%
Female	10.9%	4.1%	4.2%	3.8%	21.9%	5.6%

Capabilities

ACTIVE 59,059 (Army 35,000 Navy 16,299 Air 7,760)
Paramilitary 44,712

Terms of service Army 1 year Navy and Air Force 22 months. Voluntary since 2005

RESERVE 40,000 (Army 40,000)

ORGANISATIONS BY SERVICE

Army 24,000; 11,000 conscript (total 35,000)
FORCES BY ROLE

6 military administrative regions. Currently being reorganised into 4 armoured, 2 motorised, 2 mountain and 1 special forces brigade.

Comd	6 div (org, composition varies)
Composite	11 (reinforced) regt
Armd	4 bde
Armd Cav	2 regt
Inf	9 regt
SF	1 bde with (4 SF bn)
Arty	3 regt
Sigs	2 regt
Engr	2 regt
Avn	1 bde

EQUIPMENT BY TYPE
MBT 262: 122 *Leopard 1*; 140 *Leopard 2 A4*
AIFV 191: 173 *Marder*; 18 YPR-765
APC 436
  APC (T) 252 M-113A1/A2
  APC (W) 184 Cardoen *Piranha*
ARTY 1,016
  SP 155mm 35: 24 M-109A3; 11 (AMX) Mk F3
  TOWED 235: **105mm** 195: 90 M-101 105 Mod 56; **155mm** 40 M-68
  MRL 160mm 12 LAR-160
  MOR 734:
    81mm 650: 300 M-29; 150 Soltam; 200 FAMAE; **120mm** 170: 110 FAMAE; 60 Soltam M-65
    SP 120mm 84: 36 FAMAE (on *Piranha* 6x6); 48 M-5L1A
AT
  MSL• MANPATS 55 *Spike*
  RCL 106mm M-40A1; **84mm** *Carl Gustav*
AIRCRAFT
  TPT • Light 19: 1 Beech 58 *Baron*; 1 Beech 90 *King Air*; 5 C-212 *Aviocar*; 3 Cessna 208 *Caravan*; 1 Cessna 550 *Citation II*; 6 Cessna R172K *Hawk XP*; 2 CN-235
HELICOPTERS
  ISR 18 MD-530F *Lifter* (armed)
  TPT 17 Medium 8: 2 AS-332 *Super Puma*; 6 SA-330 *Puma*
  Light 9: 2 AS-350B2 *Ecureuil*; 6 AS-350B3 *Ecureuil*; 1 AS-355F *Ecureuil II*
AD
  SAM 24:
  MANPAD 24 *Mistral*
  GUNS 68:

    SP 18: **20mm** 18 *Piranha*/TCM-20; **35mm** 30 *Gepard* being delivered
    TOWED 50: **20mm** 50 M-167 *Vulcan*

Navy 15,492; 807 conscript (total 16,299)
Main Command: Fleet includes FF and SS flotilla; Naval Aviation, Marines, Seals and Transport Units. 5 Naval Zones; 1st Naval Zone and main HQ at Valparaiso (26°S-35°S); 2nd Naval Zone at Talcahuano (35°S-40°S); 3rd Naval Zone at Punta Arenas (49°S to Antarctica); 4th Naval Zone at Iquique (18°S-26°S); 5th Naval Zone at Puerto Montt (40°S-49°S)

EQUIPMENT BY TYPE
SUBMARINES • TACTICAL • SSK 4:
  2 *O'Higgins* (*Scorpene*) each with 6 single 533mm TT each with A-184 *Black Shark* HWT/SUT HWT/SM-39 *Exocet* AShM
  2 *Thompson* (GER T-209/1300) each with 8 single 533mm TT each with SUT HWT
PRINCIPAL SURFACE COMBATANTS 8
  DESTROYERS • DDGHM 1 *Almirante Williams* (UK Type 22) with 2 quad Mk141 lnchr (8 eff.) each with RGM-84 *Harpoon* AShM, 2 octuple VLS (16 eff.) each with *Barak* SAM; 2 triple 324mm ASTT (6 eff.) each with Mk46 LWT, 1 76mm gun (capacity 1 AS-532SC *Cougar*)
  FRIGATES 7:
    FFGHM 5:
      3 *Almirante Cochrane* (UK *Duke* class Type 23) each with 2 quad Mk141 lnchr (8 eff.) each with RGM-84C *Harpoon* AShM, 1 32 cell VLS with *Sea Wolf* SAM, 2 twin 324mm ASTT (4 eff.) each with Mk46 Mod2 LWT, 1 114mm gun, (capacity 1 AS-532SC *Cougar*)
      2 *Almirante Riveros* (NLD *Karel Doorman* class) each with 2 quad lnchr (8 eff.) each with RGM-84 *Harpoon* AShM, 1 octuple Mk 48 lnchr with RIM-7P *Sea Sparrow* SAM, 4 single Mk32 Mod9 324mm ASTT each with Mk46 Mod5 HWT, 1 76mm gun, (capacity 1 AS-532SC *Cougar*)
    FFGM 2:
      2 *Lattore* (NLD *Jacob Van Heemskerck* class) each with 2 quad Mk141 lnchr (8 eff.) each with RGM-84 *Harpoon* AShM, 1 Mk 13 GMLS with SM-1MR SAM, 1 octuple Mk48 lnchr with RIM-7P *Sea Sparrow* SAM, 2 twin 324mm ASTT (4 eff.) each with Mk 46 LWT
PATROL AND COASTAL COMBATANTS 13
  PCG 7:
    3 *Casma* (ISR *Sa'ar* 4) each with 8 GI *Gabriel I* AShM, 2 76mm gun
    4 *Tiger* (GER Type 148) each with 4 single lnchr each with MM-40 *Exocet* AShM, 1 76mm gun
  PCO 6 *Taitao*
AMPHIBIOUS • LANDING SHIPS 5
  LSM 2 *Elicura*
  LST 3: 2 *Maipo* (FRA *Batral* - capacity 7 tanks; 140 troops); 1 *Valdivia* (US *Newport* - capacity 400 troops)
LOGISTICS AND SUPPORT 9:
  AOR 2: 1 *Almirante Montt*; 1 *Araucano*
  AS 1 (also used as general spt ship)
  AGS 1 *Type 1200* (ice strengthened hull, ex-CAN)
  ATF 3: 2 *Veritas*; 1 *Smit Lloyd*

TPT 1
TRG • AXS 1
MSL • AShM MM-38 *Exocet*

FACILITIES

Bases   Located at Valparaiso, Talcahuano, Puerto Montt, Puerto Williams, Iquique, Punta Arenas

Naval Aviation 600

AIRCRAFT 20 combat capable
  ASW 3 P-3A *Orion*
  MP 6: 3 C-295MPA *Persuader*; 3 EMB-111 *Bandeirante**
  ISR 7 Cessna O-2A *Skymaster**
  TPT • Light 1 C-212A *Aviocar*
  TRG 7 PC-7 *Turbo Trainer**
HELICOPTERS
  ASW 5 AS-532SC *Cougar*
  MRH 8 AS-365 *Dauphin*
  TPT • Light 9: 5 Bell 206 *JetRanger*; 4 Bo-105S
MSL • AShM AM-39 *Exocet*

Marines 3,616

FORCES BY ROLE

Amph   1 bn

Marine   4 gp (total: 1 SSM bty (Excalibur Central Defence System), 2 trg bn, 4 inf bn, 4 ADA bty, 4 fd arty bty), 7 security det (one per naval zone)

EQUIPMENT BY TYPE
LT TK 15 *Scorpion*
APC (W) 25 MOWAG *Roland*
ARTY 26
  TOWED 18: **105mm** 4 KH-178; **155mm** 14 G-5
  MOR 8 **81mm**
AD • SAM • SP 18: 4 M998 HMMWV; 4 M1151A HMMWV; 10 M1097 HMMWV *Avenger*

Coast Guard

Integral part of the Navy
PATROL AND COASTAL COMBATANTS 47
  PSOH 2 *Piloto Pardo* (OPV-80)
  PB 45: 18 *Alacalufe* (*Protector* WPB class); 8 *Grumete Diaz* (*Dabor* class); 1 *Tokerau*; 18 (various)

Air Force 7,300; 460 conscript (total 7,760)

Flying hours   100 hrs/year

FORCES BY ROLE

Ftr/FGA   1 sqn with F-5E *Tiger III+*; F-5F *Tiger III+*; 1 sqn with F-16AM/F-16BM *Fighting Falcon*; 1 sqn withF-16C/F-16D Block 50 *Fighting Falcon* (*Puma*)

ISR   1 (photo) unit with; DHC-6-300 *Twin Otter*; *Learjet* 35A

Tpt   3 (tpt/liason) gp with B-737-300; B-737-500 (VIP); B-767ER; B-707 (AEW); Beech 99A7; C-130B *Hercules*; C-130H *Hercules*; C-212 *Aviocar*; Cessna O-2ADHC-6-100 *Twin Otter*; DHC-6-300; Gulfstream IV; KC-B5; *Learjet* 35A; PA-28-140 *Cherokee*

Trg   2 gp C-101CC *Aviojet* (A-36 *Halcón*); EMB-314 -*Super Tucano**; 1 gp with Bell 206A; Cessna 525 *Citation CJ1*; *Mirage* IIIBE; T-35A/B *Pillan*

Tpt Hel   3 gp with Bell 205 (UH-1H *Iroquois*); Bell 206B (trg); Bell 412 *Twin Huey*; Bo-105CBS-4; S-70A-39 *Black Hawk*

AD   1 regt (5 AD gp) with *Mygale*; *Mistral*; M-163 *Vulcan*/M-167 *Vulcan*; GDF-005; Oerlikon; *Crotale*

EQUIPMENT BY TYPE
AIRCRAFT 59 combat capable
  FTR 28: 12 F-5E/F *Tigre III+*; 16 F-16AM/BM *Fighting Falcon*; 6 F-16C,4 F-16 D Block 50
  FGA 10: 6 F-16C Block 50 *Fighting Falcon*; 4 F-16D Block 50 *Fighting Falcon*
  ATK 9: 9 C-101CC *Aviojet* (A-36 *Halcón*)
  ISR 6 Cessna O-2A
  ELINT 5: 3 Beech 99 *Petrel Alfa*; 2 Beech 99 *Petrel Beta*
  AEW&C 1 B-707 *Phalcon*
  TKR 1 KC-135
  TPT 37: **Medium** 3: 1 C-130B *Hercules*; 2 C-130H *Hercules*; **Light** 31: 4 C-212 *Aviocar*; 4 Cessna 525 *Citation CJ1*; 3 DHC-6-100 *Twin Otter*; 7 DHC-6-300 *Twin Otter*; 2 *Learjet* 35A; 11 PA-28-140 *Cherokee* **PAX** 3: 1 B-737-300; 1 B-737-500; 1 Gulfstream IV
  TRG 42: 12 EMB-314 *Super Turano**; 30 T-35A/B *Pillan*
HELICOPTERS
  MRH 16 Bell 412 *Twin Huey*
  TPT 17: **Medium** 1 S-70A-39 *Black Hawk*; **Light** 16: 13 Bell 205 (UH-1H *Iroquois*); 3 Bell 206B (trg)
AD
  SYSTEMS *Mygale*
  SAM *Mistral*
  SP 5 *Crotale*
  GUNS • TOWED 20mm M-163 *Vulcan* SP/M-167 *Vulcan*; **35mm** GDF-005 Oerlikon
MSL • AAM • IR AAM AIM-9J *Sidewinder*; *Python* III; *Shafrir*‡; **ARH AAM** *Derby*

Paramilitary 44,712

Carabineros 44,712

Ministry of Defence

FORCES BY ROLE

15 Zones

Paramilitary   36 district; 179 comisaria

EQUIPMENT BY TYPE
APC (W) 20 MOWAG *Roland*
MOR 60mm; 81mm
AIRCRAFT
  TPT • Light 12: 1 Beech 200 *King Air*; 2 Cessna 206; 1 Cessna 208; 3 Cessna 210 *Centurion*; 1 Cessna 550 *Citation V*; 4 PA-31T *Navajo/Cheyenne II*
HELICOPTERS • TPT • Light 12: 4 AW-109E *Power*; 1 Bell 206 *Jet Ranger*; 1 BK 117; 5 Bo-105; 1 EC-135

DEPLOYMENT

BOSNIA-HERZEGOVINA
EU • EUFOR • *Operation Althea* 21

CYPRUS
UN • UNFICYP 15

HAITI
UN • MINUSTAH 503; 1 inf bn; 1 avn coy; elm 1 engr coy

INDIA/PAKISTAN
UN • UNMOGIP 2 obs

MIDDLE EAST
UN • UNTSO 3 obs

Colombia COL

Colombian Peso pC		2009	2010	2011
GDP	pC	504.7tr	527.3tr	
	US$	235bn	278bn	
per capita	US$	5,149	6,003	
Growth	%	0.5	2.8	
Inflation	%	4.2	2.4	
Def exp a	pC	20.6tr		
	US$	9.6bn		
Def bdgt	pC	12.1tr	11.7tr	
	US$	5.64bn	6.18bn	
FMA	US$	53m	55.0	51.5
US$1=pC		2146.49	1897.13	

a including paramilitaries

Population   46,300,196

Age	0–14	15–19	20–24	25–29	30–64	65 plus
Male	13.7%	4.8%	4.6%	4.1%	19.7%	2.6%
Female	13.0%	4.6%	4.5%	4.0%	20.9%	3.5%

Capabilities

ACTIVE 283,004 (Army 235,798, Navy 33,138 Air 13,758) Paramilitary 158,824

RESERVE 61,900 (Army 54,700 Navy 4,800 Air 1,200 Joint 1,200)

ORGANISATIONS BY SERVICE

Army 235,798

FORCES BY ROLE

Mech — 1 (1st) div with (1 bde (2nd) (2 mech inf bn, 1 COIN bn, 1 mtn inf bn, 1 engr bn, 1 MP bn, 1 cbt spt bn, 2 Gaula anti-kidnap gp);1 bde (10th) (1 mech inf bn, 1 (med) tk bn, 1 mech cav bn, 1 mtn inf bn, 2 fd arty bn, 2 engr bn, 1 cbt spt bn, 2 Gaula anti-kidnap gp); 1 EOD gp

COIN — 1 div (2nd) with (1 bde (5th) (3 lt inf bn, 1 fd arty bn, 1 AD bn, 2 engr bn, 1 cbt spt bn, 1 Gaula anti-kidnap gp); 1 bde (18th) (1 airmob cav bn, 4 lt inf bn, 2 engr bn, 1 cbt spt bn); 1 bde (30th) (1 cav recce bn, 2 lt inf bn, 1 COIN bn, 1 engr bn, 1 cbt spt bn))

Rapid Reaction — 3 COIN mobile bde (each: 4 COIN bn, 1 cbt spt bn); 1 div (4th) with (1 airmob bde (2 airmob inf bn, 1 lt inf bn, 1 COIN bn, 1 SF (anti-terrorist) bn, 1 airmob engr bn, 1 cbt spt bn, 1 Gaula anti-kidnap gp); 1 bde (21st) with (3 lt inf bn)

Lt Inf — 1 div (3rd) with (1 bde (3rd) (1 cav recce bn, 3 lt inf bn, 1 mtn inf bn, 1 COIN bn, 1 Fd arty bn, 1 engr bn, 1 cbt spt bn, 1 MP bn, 1 Gaula anti-kidnap gp); 1 bde (8th) (2 lt inf bn, 1 COIN bn, 1 Fd arty bn, 1 engr bn, 1 Gaula anti-kidnap gp coy); 1 bde (29th) (1 mtn inf bn);

1 div (5th) with 1 bde (1st) (1 cav recce bn, 2 lt inf bn, 1 COIN bn, 1 fd arty bn, 2 engr bn, 1 cbt spt bn, 1 Gaula anti-kidnap gp); 1 bde (6th) (2 lt inf bn,1 mtn inf bn, 1 COIN bn, 1 cbt spt bn, 1 Gaula anti-kidnap gp); 1 bde (13th) (2 cav recce bn, 1 airmob inf bn, 2 lt inf bn, 1 mtn inf bn, 1 COIN bn, 1 Fd arty bn, 1 engr bn, 1 cbt spt bn, 2 MP bn);

1 div (6th) with 1 bde (12th) (2 lt inf bn, 1 mtn inf bn, 1 COIN bn, 1 engr bn, 1 cbt spt bn, 1 Gaula anti-kidnap gp); 1 (26th) jungle bde (1 lt jungle inf bn, 1 COIN bn, 1 cbt spt bn, 1 coast guard det); 1 (27th) bde (2 lt inf bn, 1 COIN bn, 2 engr bn, 1 cbt spt bn)

1 div (7th) with 1 bde (4th) (1 cav recce bn, 3 lt inf bn, 1 COIN bn, fd 1 arty bn, 2 engr bn, 1 cbt spt bn, 2 Gaula anti-kidnap gp, 1 SF (anti-terrorist) coy); 1 bde (11th) (1 airmob inf bn, 1 lt inf bn, 2 COIN bn, 1 engr bn, 1 cbt spt bn); 1 bde (14th) (3 lt inf bn, 2 COIN bn, 1 engr bn, 1 cbt spt bn); 1 bde (17th) (2 lt inf bn, 1 COIN bn, 1 engr bn, 1 cbt spt bn)1 div (8th) with 1 bde (16th) (1 mech cav recce bn, 1 lt inf bn, 3 COIN bn, 1 cbt spt bn, 1 Gaula anti-kidnap gp);1 (28th Jungle) bde (2 inf, 3 COIN, 2 marine (riverine) bn, 1 cbt spt bn);

EOD — 6 EOD gp (bn)

SF — 2 SF gp (bn); 1 SF anti-terrorist bn

Spt/Logistic — 2 bde (each: 1 spt bn, 1 maint bn, 1 supply bn, 1 tpt bn, 1 medical bn, 1 logistic bn)

Avn — 1 div; 1 bde (4 hel bn; 5 avn bn; 1 (SF) avn bn)

Counter-Narcotics — 1 indep bde (1 spt bn, 3 counter-narcotics bn)

EQUIPMENT BY TYPE
RECCE 226: 123 EE-9 *Cascavel*; 6 M-8 (anti-riot vehicle); 8 M-8 with 1 TOW; 39 M1117 *Guardian*; 50 VCL

APC 194

  APC (T) 54 TPM-113 (M-113A1)

  APC (W) 60: 56 EE-11 *Urutu*; 4 RG-31 *Nyala*

ARTY 622+

TOWED 101: **105mm** 86 M-101; **155mm** 15 155/52 APU SBT-1

MOR 521+: **81mm** 125 M-1; **107mm** 148 M-2; **120mm** 248+: 210 *Brandt*, 38 HY12, AM50

AT

MSL• SP 8+: 8 *TOW; Nimrod*

MANPATS 10+: 10 TOW; *SPIKE-ER, APILAS*

RCL **106mm** 63 M-40A1

RL 15+: **66mm** M-72 *LAW;* **73mm** RPG-22, **89mm** 15 M-20; **90mm** C-90C; **106mm** SR-106

AIRCRAFT

ELINT 3: 2 Beech B200 *King Air;* 1 Beech *King Air* 350

TPT • **Light** 13: 1 An-32B; 2 Beech 200 *King Air;* 1 Beech C90 *King Air;* 2 C-212 *Aviocar* (Medevac); 1 CV-580; 2 Cessna 208B *Grand Caravan;* 2 PA-34 *Seneca;* 2 *Turbo Commander 695A*

TRG 5 Utva-75

HELICOPTERS

MRH 22: 8 Mi-17-1V *Hip;* 9 Mi-17-MD; 5 Mi-17-V5 *Hip*

TPT 90 **Medium** 35 UH-60L *Black Hawk* **Light** 55: 30 Bell 205 (UH-1H *Iroquois);* 20 Bell 212 (UH-1N *Twin Huey);* 5 K-Max

AD

SAM • TOWED 3 *Skyguard/Sparrow*

GUNS 39+

SP **12.7mm** 18 M-8/M-55

TOWED 21+: **35mm** GDF Oerlikon; **40mm** 21 M-1A1 (with 7 *Eagle Eye* radar)

Navy 33,138; (incl 7,200 conscript)

HQ (Tri-Service Unified Eastern Command HQ) located at Puerto Carreño

EQUIPMENT BY TYPE

SUBMARINES • TACTICAL 4

SSK 2 *Pijao* (GER T-209/1200) each with 8 single 533mm TT each with SUT HWT

SSI 2 *Intrepido* (ITA SX-506, SF delivery)

PRINCIPAL SURFACE COMBATANTS 4

FRIGATES • FFG 4 *Almirante Padilla* (undergoing modernisation programme) each with 2 twin lnchr (4 eff.) each with MM-40 *Exocet* AShM, 2 twin *Simbad* lnchr each with *Mistral* SAM, 2 triple B515 *ILAS-3* 324mm ASTT each with A244 LWT, 1 76mm gun, (capacity 1 Bo-105/AS-555SN *Fennec* hel)

PATROL AND COASTAL COMBATANTS 48

PCO 2: 1 *Reliance* with 1 hel landing platform; 1 *San Andres*

PCC 3: 1 *Espartana* (ESP *Cormoran);* 2 *Lazaga*

PCR 14: 3 *Arauca;* 2 *Nodriza* (PAF-VII/VIII); 6 *Nodriza* (PAF-II) with hel landing platform; 3 LPR-40 (additional vessels on order)

PBF 1 *Quitasueño* (US *Asheville)* with 1 76mm gun

PB 12: 2 *Castillo Y Rada* (*Swiftships* 105); 2 *Jaime Gomez;* 2 *José Maria Palas* (*Swiftships* 110); 4 *Point;* 2 *Toledo*

PBR 16: 4 *Diligente;* 3 *Swiftships;* 9 *Tenerife*

AMPHIBIOUS 8:

LCM 1 LCM-8

LCU 7 *Morrosquillo* (LCU – 1466)

LOGISTICS AND SUPPORT 7:

AG 2 *Luneburg* (ex-GER, depot ship for patrol vessels)

AGOR 2 *Providencia*

AGS 1

ABU 1

TRG • AXS 1

FACILITIES

Bases   Located at Puerto Leguízamo, Buenaventura, (Pacific) Málaga, (Main HQ) Catagena, Barrancabermeja, Puerto Carreño, Leticia, Puerto Orocue, Puerto Inirida

Naval Aviation 146

AIRCRAFT

MP 3 CN-235 MPA *Persuader*

ISR 1 PA-31 *Navajo* (upgraded for ISR)

TPT • **Light** 8: 1 C-212 (Medevac); 4 Cessna 206; 2 Cessna 208 *Caravan;* 1 PA-31 *Navajo*

HELICOPTERS

MRH 6: 2 AS-555SN *Fennec;* 4 Bell 412

TPT • **Light** 4: 1 Bell 212; 1 BK 117; 2 Bo-105

Marines 14,000

FORCES BY ROLE

SF   1 bn; 2 (River) gp

Marine   1 bde (3 Marine bn, 2 COIN bn & 1 cmd & spt bn); 3 (River) bde (one with 3 marine inf bn; second with 3 marine inf bn, 3 assault inf bn & 1 cmd & spt bn; third with 4 marine inf bn)

EQUIPMENT BY TYPE

no hy equipment

APC (W) 8 BTR-80A (12 on order)

ARTY

MOR • **81mm** 20

Air Force 13,758

6 Combat Air Commands (CACOM) plus CACOM 7 (former Oriental Air Group) responsible for air ops in specific geographic area. Flts can be deployed or 'loaned' to a different CACOM

FORCES BY ROLE

Ftr/FGA/ ISR   1 sqn with A-37B/OA-37B; 1 sqn with AC-47T; *Hughes* 369; 1 sqn with EMB-312 *Tucano**; 1 sqn with EMB-314 *Super Tucano* (A-29); 1 sqn with *Kfir* C-2/C-10/C-12; 1 sqn with *Mirage-5* (5COAM); *Mirage-* 5 (5CODM) (used as comd post)

EW/ELINT   2 sqn with Schweizer SA-2-337, Cessna IV, Fairchild C-26B, Cessna 208, B-300 *Super King Air*

MP/ SAR   1 sqn with Bell 212, EMB-110P1 (C-95, *Queen Air,* T-41D*

Tpt   1 (Presidential) sqn with B-727; B-707 (tkr/tpt), B-737-700 (BBJ); B-767ER; Bell 212; Bell 412; C-295M; F-28 *Fellowship;* 1 sqn with C-130B, C-130H; 1 sqn with Beech C90 *King Air;* C-212; CN-235M; Do-328; IAI *Arava*

Hel   1 gp with AH-60L *Arpia* III; UH-60 (CSAR); 1 sqn with MD500; Bell 205 (UH-1H); 1 sqn with Hughes 369; 1 sqn with Bell 205 (UH-1H); Hughes 369; 1 sqn with Bell 206B3; Hughes 369; 2 (trg) sqn with Bell 206; Enstrom F-28F

Trg   1 (primary trg) sqn with Bell 205 (UH-1H *Iroquois*); PA-31 *Navajo*; PA-42 *Cheyenne*; 1 (basic trg) sqn with T-34 *Mentor*; 1 sqn with T-37B

EQUIPMENT BY TYPE

AIRCRAFT 86 combat capable

FGA 31: 10 *Kfir* C-2/C-10; 10 *Kfir* C-12; 4 *Kfir* TC-12; 5 *Mirage*-5 (5COAM); 2 *Mirage*-5D (5CODM)

ATK 18: 10 A-37B/OA-37B *Dragonfly*; 8 AC-47T *Spooky* (*Fantasma*)

ISR 20: 3 *Aero Commander*; 2 Beech B300 *King Air*; 4 C-26B *Metroliner*; 5 Cessna 650 *Citation* IV; 6 Schweizer SA-2-37

ELINT 2 Cessna 208 *Grand Caravan*

TKR/TPT 2: 1 KC-767, 1 B-707

TPT 51: **Medium** 7: 4 C-130B *Hercules* (3 more in store); 3 C-130H *Hercules*; **Light** 42: 2 Beech 300 *King Air* (medevac); 1 Beech 350C *King Air* (medevac); 1 Beech C90 *King Air*; 4 C-212; 4 C-295M; 1 Cessna 185; 1 Cessna 208; 2 Cessna 208B (medevac); 2 Cessna 210; 2 Cessna 337G/H; 1 Cessna 401; 3 Cessna 404; 1 Cessna 550; 3 CN-235M; 2 EMB-110P1 (C-95); 1 IAI-201 *Arava*; 2 PA-31 *Navajo*; 1 PA-31T *Navajo*; 4 PA-34 *Seneca*; 1 PA-42 *Cheyenne*; 1 PA-44 *Seminole*; 2 Turbo Commander 1000 **PAX** 2: 1 B-737-700 (BBJ); 1 F-28T *Fellowship*

TRG 83: 12 EMB-312 *Tucano**; 25 EMB-314 *Super Tucano* (A-29)*; 25 Lancair *Synergy* being delivered; 9 T-34 *Mentor*; 12 T-37B

HELICOPTERS

MRH 41: 14 AH-60L *Arpia* III; 2 Bell 412HP/SP; 7 Hughes 369HM; 10 Hughes 500C; 2 Hughes 500M; 1 Hughes 500ME; 1 MD-500MD *Defender*; 4 MD-530MG *Escorpion*

TPT 63 **Medium** 10: 8 UH-60A *Blackhawk*; 2 UH-60Q *Blackhawk* **Light** 53: 7 Bell 204 (UH-1P *Huey* II); 22 Bell 205 (UH-1H *Iroquois*); 11 Bell 206B3 JetRanger III; 13 Bell 212 *Twin Huey*

MSL•IR AAM *Python* III; R530, ARH AAM Derby

Paramilitary 144,097

National Police Force 136,097

AIRCRAFT

ELINT 3: 1 Cessna 208B, 2 C-26B *Metroliner*

TPT • Light 29: 6 Air Tractor AT-802; 2 Beech 200 *King Air*; 1 Beech 300 *King Air*; 1 Beech C99; 4 C-26 *Metroliner*; 3 Cessna C152; 5 Cessna 206; 5 Cessna 208 Caravan; 2 DHC 6 *Twin Otter*

HELICOPTERS

MRH 4: 1 Bell 412; 2 MD-500D; 1 MD-530F

TPT 54 **Medium** 7 UH-60L *Blackhawk* **Light** 47: 25 Bell 205 (UH-1H-II *Huey* II); 3 Bell 206B; 7 Bell 206L *Long Ranger*; 12 Bell 212

DEPLOYMENT

EGYPT

MFO 354; 1 inf bn

FOREIGN FORCES

United States US Southern Command: 65

Costa Rica CRI

Costa Rican Colon C		2009	2010	2011
GDP	C	16.8tr	18.4tr	
	US$	29.3bn	34.8bn	
per capita	US$	6,401	7,502	
Growth	%	-1.5	3.8	
Inflation	%	7.8	5.6	
Def exp	C	ε123bn		
	US$	ε215m		
Sy Bdgt	C	106bn	114bn	
	US$	184m	215m	
FMA	US$		0.325m	0.35m
US$1=C		573.13	528.54	

[a] No armed forces. Paramilitary budget

Population	4,639,827

Age	0–14	15–19	20–24	25–29	30–64	65 plus
Male	12.6%	4.7%	4.8%	4.6%	20.6%	3.0%
Female	12.0%	4.5%	4.6%	4.4%	20.8%	3.4%

Capabilities

Paramilitary 9,800

ORGANISATIONS BY SERVICE

Paramilitary 9,800

Civil Guard 4,500

Police	1 (tac) *comisaria*
Provincial	6 *comisaria*
Spec Ops	1 unit
Paramilitary	7 (Urban) *comisaria* (reinforced coy)

Border Police 2,500

FORCES BY ROLE

Sy   2 (Border) comd (8 *comisaria*)

Coast Guard Unit 400

EQUIPMENT BY TYPE

PATROL AND COASTAL COMBATANTS 8:

PB 8: 2 *Cabo Blanco*; 1 *Isla del Coco* (US *Swift* 32m); 3 *Point*; 1 *Primera Dama*; 1 *Puerto Quebos*

FACILITIES

Bases   Located at Golfito, Punta Arenas, Cuajiniquil, Quepos, Limbe, Moin

Air Surveillance Unit 400

AIRCRAFT •TPT • Light 10: 2 Cessna T210 *Centurion*; 4 Cessna U206G *Stationair*; 1 DHC-7 *Caribou*; 2 PA-31 *Navajo*; 1 PA-34 *Seneca*

HELICOPTERS • MRH 2 MD-500E

Rural Guard 2,000

Ministry of Government and Police. Small arms only

FORCES BY ROLE

Paramilitary 8 comd

Cuba CUB

Cuban Convertible Peso P		2009	2010	2011
GDP	P	66.0bn		
	US$	61.1bn		
per capita	US$	5,336		
Growth	%	1		
Inflation	%	4.3		
Def exp	US$	ε1.96bn		

Population	11,204,351					
Age	0–14	15–19	20–24	25–29	30–64	65 plus
Male	9.2%	3.3%	3.9%	3.4%	24.6%	5.4%
Female	8.7%	3.1%	3.7%	3.3%	24.9%	6.5%

Capabilities

ACTIVE 49,000 (Army 38,000 Navy 3,000 Air 8,000)
Paramilitary 26,500
Terms of service 2 years

RESERVE 39,000 (Army 39,000) **Paramilitary 1,120,000**
Ready Reserves (serve 45 days per year) to fill out Active and Reserve units; see also Paramilitary.

ORGANISATIONS BY SERVICE

Army ε38,000

FORCES BY ROLE

3 Regional comd HQ, 3 army comd HQ

Army	1 (frontier) bde; 14 (reserve) bde
Armd	up to 5 bde
Mech Inf	9 bde (each: 1 armd regt, 1 arty regt, 1 ADA regt, 3 mech inf regt)
AB	1 bde
ADA	1 regt
SAM	1 bde

EQUIPMENT BY TYPE†
MBT ε900 T-34/T-54/T-55/T-62
LT TK PT-76
RECCE BRDM-1/BRDM-2
AIFV ε 50 BMP-1
APC • APC (W) ε500 BTR-152/BTR-40/BTR-50/BTR-60
ARTY 1,730+
SP 40 2S1 *Carnation* **122mm**/2S3 **152mm**
TOWED 500 **152mm** D-1/**122mm** D-30/**152mm** M-1937/**122mm** M-30/**130mm** M-46/**76mm** ZIS-3 *M-1942*
MRL SP 175 **140mm** BM-14/**122mm** BM-21
MOR 1,000 **120mm** M-38/**82mm** M-41/**120mm** M-43/**82mm** M-43

STATIC 15 **122mm** 15 JS-2M (hy tk)
AT
MSL • MANPATS AT-1 *Snapper*; AT-3 9K11 *Sagger*
GUNS 700+: **100mm** 100 SU-100 SP; **85mm** D-44; **57mm** 600 M-1943
AD
SAM 200 9K35 *Strela-10* (SA-13 *Gopher*); 9K36 *Strela-3* (SA-14 *Gremlin* MANPAD); 9K310 *Igla-1* (SA-16 *Gimlet* MANPAD); 2K12 *Kub* (SA-6 *Gainful* SP); 9K32 *Strela-2* (SA-7 *Grail* MANPAD); 9K33 *Osa* (SA-8 *Gecko* SP); 9K31 *Strela-1* (SA-9 *Gaskin* SP) (300–1,800 eff.)
GUNS 400
SP **57mm** ZSU-57-2 SP/**23mm** ZSU-23-4 SP/**30mm** BTR-60P SP
TOWED **100mm** KS-19/M-1939/**85mm** KS-12/**57mm** S-60/**37mm** M-1939/**30mm** M-53/**23mm** ZU-23

Navy ε3,000

Western Comd HQ at Cabanas; Eastern Comd HQ at Holquin

EQUIPMENT BY TYPE
PATROL AND COASTAL COMBATANTS 7
PCM 1 *Pauk* II† (FSU) with 1 quad lnchr (manual aiming) with 9K32 *Strela-2* (SA-N-5 *Grail* SAM), 4 single ASTT, 2 RBU 1200 (10 eff.), 1 76mm gun
PBF 6 *Osa* II† (FSU) each with 4 single lnchr (for P-15 *Termit* (SS-N-2B *Styx*) AShM – missiles removed to coastal defence units)
MINE WARFARE AND MINE COUNTERMEASURES 5
MHI 3 *Yevgenya*† (FSU)
MSC 2 *Sonya*† (FSU)
LOGISTICS AND SUPPORT 1 AG; 1 ABU; 1 TRG

FACILITIES

Bases	Located at Cabanas, Havana, Cienfuegos, Holquin, Nicaro, Punta Movida, Mariel

Coastal Defence

ARTY • TOWED **122mm** M-1931/37; **130mm** M-46; **152mm** M-1937
MSL• AShM 2+: *Bandera* IV (reported); 2 P-15 *Rubezh* (SS-C-3 *Styx*)

Naval Infantry 550+

FORCES BY ROLE

Amph aslt   2 bn

Anti-aircraft Defence and Revolutionary Air Force ε8,000 (incl conscripts)

Air assets divided between Western Air Zone and Eastern Air Zone

Flying hours   50 hrs/year

FORCES BY ROLE

Ftr/ FGA	3 sqn with MiG-21ML *Fishbed*; MiG-23ML/MF/UM *Flogger*; MiG-29A/UB *Fulcrum*
Tpt	1 (exec) tpt sqn with An-24 *Coke*; Mi-8P *Hip*; Yak-40 (VIP)
Atk Hel	2 sqn with Mi-17 *Hip H*; Mi-35 *Hind*

Trg   2 tac trg sqns with L-39C *Albatros* (basic), MiG-21UM; Z-142 (primary)

EQUIPMENT BY TYPE

AIRCRAFT 45 combat capable

FTR 33: 16 MiG-23ML *Flogger*; 4 MiG-23MF *Flogger*; 4 MiG-23U *Flogger*; 4 MiG-23UM *Flogger*; 2 MiG-29A *Fulcrum*; 3 MiG-29UB *Fulcrum* (6 MiG-15UTI *Midget*; 4+ MiG-17 *Fresco*; 4 MiG-23MF *Flogger*; 6 MiG-23ML *Flogger*; 2 MiG-23UM *Flogger*; 2 MiG-29 *Fulcrum* in store)

FGA 12: 4 MiG-21ML Fishbed; 8 MiG-21U *Mongol A* (up to 70 MiG-21bis *Fishbed*; 30 MiG-21F *Fishbed*; 28 MiG-21PFM *Fishbed*; 7 MiG-21UM *Fishbed*; 20 MiG-23BN *Flogger* in store)

ISR 1 An-30 *Clank*

TPT 11: **Heavy** 2 Il-76 *Candid*; **Light** 9: 1 An-2 *Colt*; 3 An-24 *Coke*; 2 An-32 *Cline*; 3 Yak-40 (8 An-2 *Colt*; 18 An-26 *Curl* in store)

TRG 45: 25 L-39 *Albatros*; 20 Z-326 *Trener Master*

HELICOPTERS

ATK 4 Mi-35 *Hind* (8 more in store)

ASW (5 Mi-14 in store)

MRH 8 Mi-17 *Hip H* (12 more in store)

TPT • Medium 2 Mi-8P *Hip*

AD • SAM SA-3 *Goa*; SA-2 *Guideline* towed

MSL

ASM Kh-23 (AS-7 *Kerry*)‡

AAM IR AAM R-3 ‡ (AA-2 *Atoll*); R-60 (AA-8 *Aphid*); R-73 (AA-11 *Archer*) IR/SARH AAM R-23/24 ‡ (AA-7 *Apex*); R-27 (AA-10 *Alamo*)

FACILITIES

Surface To Air Missile Site   13 with S-125 *Pechora* (SA-3 *Goa* SAM); S-75 *Volkhov* (SA-2 *Guideline* Towed SAM) (active)

Paramilitary 26,500 active

State Security 20,000

Ministry of Interior

Border Guards 6,500

Ministry of Interior

PATROL AND COASTAL COMBATANTS 20

PCC: 2 *Stenka*

PB 18 *Zhuk*

Youth Labour Army 70,000 reservists

Civil Defence Force 50,000 reservists

Territorial Militia ε1,000,000 reservists

FOREIGN FORCES

United States US Southern Command: 886 at Guantánamo Bay

Dominican Republic DOM

Dominican Peso pRD		2009	2010	2011
GDP	pRD	1.68tr	1.88tr	
	US$	46.6bn	51.2bn	
per capita	US$	4,618	5,012	
Growth	%	3.5	4.0	
Inflation	%	1.4	6.9	
Def exp	pRD	9.54bn		
	US$	265m		
Def bdgt	pRD	11.5bn	12.3bn	
	US$	318m	335m	
FMA	US$	0.4m	1.0m	-
US$1=pRD		36.03	36.77	

Population   10,225,482

Age	0–14	15–19	20–24	25–29	30–64	65 plus
Male	15.0%	4.9%	4.6%	4.2%	19.0%	3.0%
Female	14.5%	4.7%	4.4%	4.0%	18.2%	3.5%

Capabilities

ACTIVE 24,500 (Army 15,000 Navy 4,000 Air 5,500) **Paramilitary 15,000**

ORGANISATIONS BY SERVICE

Army 15,000

FORCES BY ROLE

5 Defence Zones

Armd	1 bn
Air Cav	1 bde (1 cdo bn, 1 (6th) mtn regt, 1 sqn with *Bell* 205 (op by Air Force); OH-58 *Kiowa*; R-22; R-44 *Raven II*
Inf	6 bde: 1st and 3rd (each: 3 inf bn); 2nd (4 inf bn, 1 mtn inf bn); 4th and 5th (each: 2 bn); 6th (1 inf bn) (total: 16 inf bn)
SF	3 bn
Arty	2 bn
Engr	1 bn
Presidential Guard	1 regt
Security	1(MoD) bn

EQUIPMENT BY TYPE

LT TK 12 M-41B (76mm)

APC (W) 8 LAV-150 *Commando*

ARTY 104

    TOWED 105mm 16: 4 M-101; 12 *Reinosa* 105/26

    MOR 88: **81mm** 60 M-1; **107mm** 4 M-30; **120mm** 24 Expal Model L

AT

    RCL 106mm 20 M-40A1

    GUNS 37mm 20 M3

HELICOPTERS

    ISR 8: 4 OH-58A *Kiowa*; 4 OH-58C *Kiowa*

    TPT • Light 6: 4 R-22; 2 R-44 *Raven II*

Navy 4,000

HQ located at Santo Domingo

FORCES BY ROLE

Marine Sy   1 unit

SF   1 (SEAL) unit

EQUIPMENT BY TYPE

PATROL AND COASTAL COMBATANTS 16

  PCO 4: 2 *Balsam*

  PCC 2 *Tortuguero* (US ABU)

  PB 8: 2 *Altair* (Swiftships 35m); 4 *Bellatrix* (US Sewart
  Seacraft); 2 *Canopus*; 4 *Hamal* (Damen Stan 1505);
  3 *Point*

AMPHIBIOUS 1 *Neyba* (US LCU 1675)

LOGISTICS AND SUPPORT • AT 1

FACILITIES

Bases   Located at Santo Domingo, Las Calderas

Naval Aviation Unit

HELICOPTERS

  TPT • Light 2 Bell 206A-1 (CH-136)

Air Force 5,500

Flying hours   60 hrs/year

FORCES BY ROLE

Atk   1 sqn with EMB-314 *Super Tucano**

SAR/Tpt Hel 1 sqn with Bell 205 (UH-1H *Huey* II); Bell
             205 (UH-1H *Iroquois*); Bell 430 (VIP); OH-58
             Kiowa (CH-136); S-333

Tpt   1 sqn with C-212-400 *Aviocar*;
             Cessna 206; PA-31 *Navajo*

Trg   1 sqn with T-35B *Pillan*

AD   1 bn with 20mm guns

EQUIPMENT BY TYPE

AIRCRAFT 8 combat capable

  TPT • Light 5: 3 C-212-400 *Aviocar*; 1 Cessna 206; 1 PA-
  31 *Navajo*

  TRG 14: 8 EMB-314 *Super Tucano**; 6 T-35B *Pillan*

HELICOPTERS

  ISR 9 OH-58 *Kiowa* (CH-136)

  TPT • Light 25: 8 Bell 205 (UH-1H *Huey* II); 12 Bell 205
  (UH-1H *Iroquois*); 2 Bell 430 (VIP); 3 S-333

AD • GUNS 20mm 4

Paramilitary 15,000

National Police 15,000

Ecuador ECU

Ecuadorian Sucre ES		2009	2010	2011
GDP	ES	1,421tr	1,573tr	
	US$	55.6bn	61.5bn	
per capita	US$	4,077	4,464	
Growth	%	0.4	2.2	
Inflation	%	5.2	4.0	
Def bdgt	ES	27.7tr	37.5tr	
	US$	1.08bn	1.47bn	
FMA	US$	0.3m	0.3m	0.75m
US$1=ES		25587	25587	

Population   13,774,909

Age	0–14	15–19	20–24	25–29	30–64	65 plus
Male	15.3%	4.9%	4.6%	4.1%	17.7%	3.1%
Female	14.7%	4.8%	4.5%	4.2%	18.6%	3.3%

Capabilities

ACTIVE 58,483 (Army 46,500 Navy 7,283 Air 4,200)
Paramilitary 500

Terms of Service conscription 1 year, selective

RESERVE 118,000 (Joint 118,000)

Ages 18–55

ORGANISATIONS BY SERVICE

Army 46,500

FORCES BY ROLE

4 div (org, composition varies) (total: 1 armd bde, 1 SF
bde, 1 arty bde, 1 engr bde, 1 avn bde, 3 jungle bde, 5 inf
bde); 3 (hy mor) coy

Armd cav   1 bde

Armd Recce   3 sqn

Mech Inf   2 bn

Inf   13 bn; 10 (jungle) bn

AB/SF   6 bn

Arty   1 bde

SP Arty   1 gp

MRL   1 gp

ADA   1 gp

Engr   3 bn

Avn   5 bn

EQUIPMENT BY TYPE

MBT 30 *Leopard* 1V (from Chile, being delivered)

LT TK 24 AMX-13

RECCE 67: 25 AML-90; 10 EE-3 *Jararaca*; 32 EE-9 *Cascavel*

APC 123

  APC (T) 95: 80 AMX-VCI; 15 M-113

  APC (W) 28: 18 EE-11 *Urutu*; 10 UR-416

ARTY 541+

  SP 155mm 5 (AMX) Mk F3

  TOWED 100: **105mm** 78: 30 M-101; 24 M-2A2; 24 Model
  56 pack howitzer; **155mm** 22: 12 M-114; 10 M-198

MRL 24: 18 122mm BM-21, 6 RM-70
MOR 412+: **81mm** 400 M-29; **107mm** M-30 (4.2in); **160mm** 12 M-66 *Soltam*
AT
RCL 404: **106mm** 24 M-40A1; **90mm** 380 M-67
AIRCRAFT
TPT • Light 12: 1 Beech 100 *King Air*; 2 C-212; 2 CN-235; 1 Cessna 500 *Citation I*; 1 DHC-5D *Buffalo*; 4 IAI-201 *Arava*; 1 PC-6 *Turbo-Porter*
TRG 7: 2 CJ-6; 2 MX-7-235 *Star Rocket*; 3 T-41D *Mescalero*
HELICOPTERS
MRH 29: 9 Mi-17-1V *Hip*; 2 SA-315B *Lama*; 18 SA-342 *Gazelle* (13 with HOT for anti-armour role)
TPT 9 **Medium** 6 AS-332B *Super Puma*; (3 SA-330 *Puma* in store) **Light** 3 AS-350 *Ecureuil*
AD
SAM • MANPAD 185+: 75 *Blowpipe*; 20+ 9K32 *Strela-2* (SA-7 *Grail*)‡; 90 9K39 *Igla* (SA-18 *Grouse*)
GUNS 240
SP 44 M-163 *Vulcan*
TOWED 196: **14.5mm** 128 ZPU-1/-2; **20mm** 38: 28 M-1935, 10 M-167 *Vulcan*; **40mm** 30 L/70/M1A1

Navy 7,283 (incl Naval Aviation, Marines and Coast Guard)

EQUIPMENT BY TYPE
SUBMARINES • TACTICAL • SSK 2:
2 *Shyri*† (GER T-209/1300, undergoing refit in Chile) each with 8 single 533mm TT each with SUT HWT
PRINCIPAL SURFACE COMBATANTS 2
FRIGATES 2:
FFGHM 1 *Presidente Eloy Alfaro*† (ex-UK *Leander* batch II) each with 4 single lnchr each with MM-40 *Exocet* AShM, 3 twin lnchr (6 eff.) each with *Mistral* SAM, 1 twin 114mm gun (2 eff.), (capacity 1 Bell 206B *JetRanger II* hel)
FFGH 1 *Condell* (mod UK *Leander*; under transfer from Chile) with 4 single lnchr each with MM-40 *Exocet* AShM, 2 triple ASTT (6 eff.) each with Mk 46 LWT, 1 twin 114mm gun (2 eff.), (capacity 1 Bell 206B *JetRanger II* hel)
PATROL AND COASTAL COMBATANTS 9
CORVETTES • FSGM 6 *Esmeraldas* (4†) each with 2 triple lnchr (6 eff.) each with MM-40 *Exocet* AShM, 1 quad lnchr (4 eff.) with *Aspide* SAM, 2 triple B515 *ILAS-3* 324mm each with A244 LWT, 1 76mm gun, 1 hel landing platform (upgrade programme ongoing)
PCFG 3 *Quito* (GER Lurssen TNC-45 45m) each with 4 single lnchr each with MM-38 *Exocet* AShM, 1 76mm gun (upgrade programme ongoing)
LOGISTICS AND SUPPORT 8:
AOL 1 Taurus
AE 1
AG 1
AWT 2
AGOS 1 *Orion*
ATF 1
TRG • AXS 1
FACILITIES
Bases   Located at Guayaquil (main base), Galápagos Islands
Naval air base Jaramijo

Naval Aviation 375
AIRCRAFT
MP 1 CN-235-300M
ISR 3: 2 Beech 200T *King Air*; 1 Beech 300 *Catpass King Air*
TPT • Light 3: 1 Beech 200 *King Air*; 1 Beech 300 *King Air*; 1 CN-235-100
TRG 6: 2 T-34C *Turbo Mentor*; 4 T-35B *Pillan*
HELICOPTERS
TPT • Light 8: 3 Bell 206A; 3 Bell 206B; 2 Bell 230;
UAV • ISR 6: **Heavy** 2 *Heron* **Medium** 4 *Searcher* Mk.II

Marines 2,160
Cdo	1 unit (no hy wpn/veh)
Marine	5 bn (on garrison duties)

EQUIPMENT BY TYPE
ARTY • MOR 32+ 60mm/81mm/120mm
AD • SAM • MANPAD 64 *Mistral*/SA-18 *Grouse* (*Igla*)

Air Force 4,200

Operational Command
FORCES BY ROLE
Ftr	1 sqn with *Mirage* F-1B (F-1JB); *Mirage* F-1E (F-1JE)
FGA	1 sqn with A-37B *Dragonfly*; 1 sqn with *Kfir* CE; *Kfir* C-2; *Kfir* TC-2; 1 sqn with BAC-167 *Strikemaster**; 2 sqn with EMB-314 *Super Tucano**
Trg	1 sqn with A-37B *Dragonfly*; BAC-167 *Strikemaster**

Military Air Transport Group
FORCES BY ROLE
SAR/Tpt Hel	1 sqn with Bell 206B *JetRanger II*; *Dhruv*; SA-316B/SA-319 *Alouette III*
Tpt	4 sqn with B-727; C-130B *Hercules*, C-130H *Hercules*; DHC-6 *Twin Otter*; F-28 *Fellowship*; *Sabreliner* 40/60
Trg	Some units with Cessna 150; MXP-650; T-34C *Turbo Mentor*; T-41 *Mescalero*

EQUIPMENT BY TYPE
AIRCRAFT 80+ combat capable
FGA 62+: 25+ A-37B *Dragonfly*; 5 BAC-167 *Strikemaster*; 4 *Kfir* C.2; 7 *Kfir* C.10 (CE); 2 *Kfir* TC.2; 1 *Mirage* F-1B (F-1JB); 12 *Mirage* F-1E (F-1JE); 2 *Mirage* 50DV; 4 *Mirage* 50EV
TPT 44 **Medium** 5: 4 C-130B *Hercules*; 1 C-130H *Hercules* **Light** 27: 1 Beech E90 *King Air*; 16 Cessna 150; 3 DHC-6 *Twin Otter*; 2 EMB-170; 1 EMB-190; 1 Legacy 600; 1 MXP-650; 2 *Sabreliner* 40/60; **PAX** 12: 2 A-320; 3 B-727; 1 F-28 *Fellowship*; 6 HS-748
TRG 38: 18 EMB-314 *Super Tucano**; 15 T-34C *Turbo Mentor*; 5 T-41 *Mescalero*
HELICOPTERS
MRH 11: 6 *Dhruv*; 1 SA-315 *Lama* (HB-315B *Gaviao*); 4 SA-316B *Alouette III*/SA-319 *Alouette III*
TPT • Light 8 Bell 206B *Jet Ranger II*

MSL •**AAM** 60 *Python* III; 50 *Python* IV; R-550 *Magic*;
Super 530; *Shafrir*‡
AD
   SAM 7 M-48 *Chaparral*
      SP 6 9K33 *Osa* (SA-8 *Gecko*)
      MANPAD 185+: 75 *Blowpipe*; 9K32 *Strela-2* (SA-7
      Grail)‡; 20 9K310 *Igla-1* (SA-16) *Gimlet*; 90 9K38 *Igla*
      (SA-18 *Grouse*)
      RADARS: 2 CFTC gap fillers; 2 CETC 2D
   GUNS
      SP 28 M-35 with **20mm**
      TOWED 82: **23mm 34:** 34 ZU-23; **35mm** 30: 30
      GDF-002 (twin)

Paramilitary
All police forces; 39,500

Police Air Service
HELICOPTERS • TPT • Light 4: 1 AS-350B *Ecureuil*; 2
Bell 206B *Jet Ranger*, 1 R-22

Coast Guard 500
PATROL AND COASTAL COMBATANTS 21
   PCC 3 *Isla Fernandina* (*Vigilante*);
   PB 10: 4 10 *de Agosto*; 2 *Espada*; 1 *Isla Isabela*; 2 *Manta*
   (GER Lurssen 36m); 1 *Point*
   PBR 8: 2 *Río Esmeraldas*; 6 *Rio Puyango*

DEPLOYMENT

CÔTE D'IVOIRE
**UN • UNOCI 2 obs

HAITI
**UN • MINUSTAH 67; elm 1 engr coy

LIBERIA
**UN • UNMIL 1; 2 obs

SUDAN
**UN • UNMIS 17 obs

El Salvador SLV

El Salvador Colon C		2009	2010	2011
GDP	C	188bn	194bn	
	US$	21.1bn	21.8bn	
per capita	US$	3,537	3,519	
Growth	%	-2.5	1.2	
Inflation	%	1.1	1.1	
Def bdgt	C	1.16bn	1.13bn	
	US$	1.16bn	1.13bn	
FMA	US$	3.5m	1.0m	4.8m
US$1=C		8.92	8.92	

Population	6,194,126

Age	0–14	15–19	20–24	25–29	30–64	65 plus
Male	15.7%	5.7%	4.7%	3.9%	15.5%	2.9%
Female	14.9%	5.5%	4.8%	4.1%	18.8%	3.6%

Capabilities

ACTIVE 15,500 (Army 13,850 Navy 700 Air 771)
Paramilitary 17,000
Terms of Service conscription 18 months voluntary

RESERVE 9,900 (Joint 9,900)

ORGANISATIONS BY SERVICE

Army 9,850; 4,000 conscript (total 13,850)
FORCES BY ROLE
6 Military Zones

Armd cav	1 regt (2 armd cav bn)
Inf	5 bde (each: 3 inf bn)
Spec Ops	1 gp (1 SF coy, 1 para bn, 1 (naval inf) coy
Arty	1 bde (1 AD bn, 2 fd arty bn)
Engr	1 comd (2 engr bn)
Sy	1 (special sy) bde (2 border gd bn, 2 MP bn)

EQUIPMENT BY TYPE
RECCE 5 AML-90; 4 (in store)
APC (W) 38: 30M-37B1 *Cashuat* (mod); 8 UR-416
ARTY 217+
   TOWED 105mm 54: 36 M-102; 18 M-56 (FRY)
   MOR 163+: **81mm** 151 M-29; **120mm** 12+: M-74 in store;
   12 UBM 52
AT
   RCL 399: **106mm** 20 M-40A1 (incl 16 SP); **90mm** 379 M-67
   RL 94mm 791 LAW
AD • GUNS 35: **20mm** 31 M-55; 4 TCM-20

Navy 700 (incl some 90 Naval Inf and SF)
EQUIPMENT BY TYPE
PATROL AND COASTAL COMBATANTS 11
   PCO 1 *Balsam*
   PB 10: 3 *Camcraft* (30m);1 *Point;* 6 (various)
AMPHIBIOUS • LANDING CRAFT
   LCM 3
FACILITIES

Bases	Located at La Unîon
Minor Bases	Located at La Libertad, Acajutla, El Triunfo, Meanguera Is, Guija Lake

Naval Inf (SF Commandos) 90
SF	1 coy

Air Force 771 (incl 200 Air Defence)
Flying hours   90 hrs/year on A-37 *Dragonfly*

FORCES BY ROLE

FGA/ISR	1 sqn with A-37B *Dragonfly*; O-2A *Skymaster**
Tpt	1 sqn with BT-67; Cessna 210 *Centurion*; Cessna 337G; DC-3 (C-47R *Skytrain*); IAI-201 *Arava*; SA-226T *Merlin IIIB*
Trg	Some sqn with R-235GT *Guerrier*; T-35 *Pillan*; T-41D *Mescalero*; TH-300

Atk Hel   1 sqn with UH-1M *Iroquois*
Tpt Hel   1 sqn with Bell 205 (UH-1H *Iroquois*); Bell
            407; Bell 412 *Twin Huey*; MD-500

EQUIPMENT BY TYPE
AIRCRAFT 14 combat capable
  ATK 5 A-37B *Dragonfly*
  ISR 9: 7 O-2A/B *Skymaster**; 2 OA-37B *Dragonfly**
  TPT • Light 9: 2 BT-67; 2 Cessna 210 *Centurion*; 1 Cessna
  337G *Skymaster*; 1 DC-3 (C-47R *Skytrain*); 3 IAI-201 *Arav*
  TRG 11: 5 R-235GT *Guerrier*; 5 T-35 *Pillan*; 1 T-41D
  Mescalero
HELICOPTERS
  MRH 11: 4 Bell 412 *Twin Huey*; 5 MD-500; 2 UH-1M
  Iroquois
  TPT• Light 19: 18 Bell-205 (UH-1H *Iroquois*) (incl 4
  SAR); 1 Bell 407 (VIP tpt, govt owned)
  TRG 6 TH-300
MSL • AAM IR AAM *Shafrir* ‡

Paramilitary 17,000

National Civilian Police 17,000
Ministry of Public Security
AIRCRAFT • ISR 1 O-2A *Skymaster*
HELICOPTERS
  MRH 2: 1 MD-500D; 1 MD-520N
  TPT • Light 1 Bell 205 (UH-1H *Iroquois*)

DEPLOYMENT

CÔTE D'IVOIRE
UN • UNOCI 3 obs

LEBANON
UN • UNIFIL 52; 1 inf pl

LIBERIA
UN • UNMIL 2 obs

SUDAN
UN • UNMIS 1 obs

WESTERN SAHARA
UN • MINURSO 5 obs

FOREIGN FORCES

United States US Southern Command: 1 Forward
Operating Location (Military, DEA, USCG and Customs
personnel)

Guatemala GUA

Guatemalan Quetzal q		2009	2010	2011
GDP	q	307bn	330bn	
	US$	37.7bn	40.9bn	
per capita	US$	2,686	2,848	
Growth	%	0.4	2.0	
Inflation	%	1.9	3.9	
Def exp	q	1.35bn		
	US$	166m		
Def bdgt	q	1.3bn	1.36bn	
	US$	159m	169m	
FMA	US$	0.5m	1.765m	1.0m
US$1=q		8.16	8.07	

Population   14,376,881

Age	0–14	15–19	20–24	25–29	30–64	65 plus
Male	19.4%	6.0%	5.1%	4.0%	13.1%	1.8%
Female	18.7%	5.9%	5.2%	4.2%	14.6%	2.1%

Capabilities

ACTIVE 15,212 (Army 13,444 Navy 897 Air 871)
Paramilitary 19,000

RESERVE 63,863 (Navy 650 Air 900 Armed Forces
62,313)

(National Armed Forces are combined; the army provides
log spt for navy and air force)

ORGANISATIONS BY SERVICE

Army 13,444
The cavalry regts have a strength of 118 personnel, 7 AFV.
The arty gp is 3 bty of 4 guns.
FORCES BY ROLE
15 Military Zones

Armd	6 sqn
Cav	2 regt
Inf	1 (strategic) bde (2 inf bn, 1 SF pl, 1 recce sqn, 1 (lt) armd bn, 1 arty gp); 5 (regional) bde (each: 3 inf bn, 1 cav regt, 1 arty gp); 1 (frontier) det
SF	1 bde (1 trg bn, 1 SF bn)
AB	2 bn
Engr	2 bn
MP	1 bde (3 bn)
Sy	1 bn (Presidential Gd)
Trg	1 bn

EQUIPMENT BY TYPE
RECCE 7 M-8 in store
APC 52
  APC (T) 15: 10 M-113; 5 in store
  APC (W) 37: 30 *Armadillo*; 7 V-100 *Commando*

ARTY 161
TOWED 105mm 76: 12 M-101; 8 M-102; 56 M-56
MOR 85: 81mm 55 M-1; **107mm** 12 M-30 in store;
120mm 18 ECIA
AT
RCL 120+: 105mm 64 M-1974 FMK-1 (Arg); **106mm** 56
M-40A1; **75mm** M-20
RL 89mm M-20 in store (3.5in)
AD • GUNS • TOWED 32: **20mm** 16 GAI-D01; 16 M-55

Reserves
Inf   ε19 bn

Navy 897
EQUIPMENT BY TYPE
PATROL AND COASTAL COMBATANTS 10
   PB 10: 6 *Cutlass*; 1 *Dauntless*; 1 *Kukulkan* (US *Broadsword*
   32m); 2 *Sewart*
FACILITIES
Bases Located at Santo Tomás de Castilla, Puerto Quetzal

Marines 650 reservists
FORCES BY ROLE
Marine   2 bn under strength

Air Force 871
2 Air Commands, 3 air bases – Guatemala City, Santa Elena
Petén, Retalhuleu
FORCES BY ROLE
Serviceability of ac is less than 50%

FGA/Trg   1 sqn with A-37B *Dragonfly*; 1 sqn with PC-7
             *Turbo Trainer**
Tpt   1 sqn with Basler *Turbo-67*; Beech 100 *King
             Air*; Beech 90 *King Air*; F-27 *Friendship*; IAI-
             201 *Arava*; PA-31 *Navajo*
Liaison   1 sqn with Cessna 310; Cessna 206
Trg   Some sqn with Cessna R172K *Hawk XP*;
             T-35B
Hel   1 sqn with Bell 206 *Jet Ranger*; Bell 212
             (armed); Bell 412 *Twin Huey* (armed); UH-
             1H *Iroquois*

EQUIPMENT BY TYPE
AIRCRAFT 9 combat capable
   ATK 2 A-37B *Dragonfly*
   TPT • Light 22: 1 Beech 90 *King Air*; 1 Beech 100 *King
   Air*; 4 BT-67; 2 Cessna 206; 1 Cessna 208B; 1 Cessna 310;
   5 Cessna R172K *Hawk XP*; 2 F-27 *Friendship*; 4 IAI-201
   Arava; 1 PA-31 *Navajo*
   TRG 11: 7 PC-7 *Turbo Trainer**; 4 T-35B *Pillan*
HELICOPTERS
   MRH 1 Bell 412 *Twin Huey* (armed)
   TPT • Light 19: 3 Bell 205 (UH-1H *Iroquois*); 9 Bell 206 *Jet
   Ranger*; 7 Bell 212 (armed)

Tactical Security Group
Air Military Police
Armd   1 sqn

CCT   3 coy
AD   1 bty (army units for air-base sy)

Paramilitary 19,000 active (incl Treasury Police)

National Police 16,500
Army   1 (integrated task force) unit (incl mil and
             treasury police)
SF   1 bn
Paramilitary 21 (departments) region

Treasury Police 2,500

DEPLOYMENT

CÔTE D'IVOIRE
UN • UNOCI 5 obs

DEMOCRATIC REPUBLIC OF THE CONGO
UN • MONUSCO 150; 7 obs; 1 SF coy

HAITI
UN • MINUSTAH 147; 1 MP coy

LEBANON
UN • UNIFIL 3

NEPAL
UN • UNMIN 1 obs

SUDAN
UN • UNAMID 2
UN • UNMIS 1; 7 obs

Guyana GUY

Guyanese Dollar G$		2009	2010	2011
GDP	G$	420bn	449bn	
	US$	2.06bn	2.20bn	
per capita	US$	2,699	2,895	
Growth	%	3.1	3.5	
Inflation	%	2.9	3.7	
Def bdgt	G$		26.1bn	
	US$		128m	
FMA	US$	0.15m	0.3m	-
US$1=G$		203.95	203.77	

Population	761,442

Age	0–14	15–19	20–24	25–29	30–64	65 plus
Male	16.2%	5.7%	4.6%	3.8%	17.4%	2.0%
Female	15.7%	5.4%	4.3%	3.4%	18.5%	2.8%

Capabilities

ACTIVE 1,100 (Army 900 Navy 100 Air 100)
Paramilitary 1,500
Active numbers combined Guyana Defence Force

RESERVE 670 (Army 500 Navy 170)

ORGANISATIONS BY SERVICE

Army 900

FORCES BY ROLE

Inf	1 bn
SF	1 coy
Engr	1 coy
Spt	1 (spt wpn) coy
Presidential Guard	1 bn

EQUIPMENT BY TYPE

RECCE 9: 6 EE-9 *Cascavel* (reported); 3 S52 *Shorland*
ARTY 54
  TOWED 130mm 6 M-46†
  MOR 48: **81mm** 12 L16A1; **82mm**18 M-43; **120mm** 18 M-43

Navy 100

EQUIPMENT BY TYPE

PATROL AND COASTAL COMBATANTS 5
  PCO 1 *Essequibo* (ex-UK *River*)
  PB 4 *Barracuda*

FACILITIES

Bases Located at Georgetown (HQ), Benab, Morawhanna

Air Force 100

FORCES BY ROLE

Tpt   1 unit with Bell 206; Rotorway 162F; Y-12

EQUIPMENT BY TYPE

AIRCRAFT • TPT • **Light** 1 Y-12
HELICOPTERS
  MRH 1 Bell 412 *Twin Huey*†
  TPT • **Light** 3: 2 Bell 206; 1 Rotorway 162F

Paramilitary 1,500+

Guyana People's Militia 1,500+

Haiti HTI

Haitian Gourde G		2009	2010	2011
GDP	G	267bn	264bn	
	US$	6.48bn	6.65bn	
per capita	US$	646	653	
Growth	%	2.9	-8.5	
Inflation	%	-0.02	4.9	
FMA	US$	2.8m	1.6m	1.6m
US$1=G		39.66		

Population   10,188,175

Age	0–14	15–19	20–24	25–29	30–64	65 plus
Male	18.0%	5.7%	4.9%	4.2%	15.0%	1.8%
Female	17.9%	5.7%	5.0%	4.3%	15.4%	2.2%

Capabilities

No active armed forces. On 1 June 2004, following a period of armed conflict, the United Nations established a multi-national stabilisation mission in Haiti (MINUSTAH). The mission has an authorised strength of up to 8,940 military personnel and 4,391 civilian police. A National Police Force of some 2,000 pers remains operational.

FOREIGN FORCES

Argentina 708; 1 inf bn; 1 avn coy; 1 fd hospital
Bolivia 208; 1 mech inf coy
Brazil 2,188; 2 inf bn; 1 engr coy
Canada 8
Chile 503; 1 inf bn; 1 avn coy; elm 1 engr coy
Ecuador 67; elm 1 engr coy
France 2
Guatemala 147; 1 MP coy
India 1
Japan 225; 1 engr coy
Jordan 611; 1 inf bn
Korea, Republic of 242; 1 engr coy
Nepal 1,074; 1 mech inf bn; 1 inf bn
Paraguay 31
Peru 371; 1 inf coy
Philippines 157; 1 HQ coy
Sri Lanka 958; 1 inf bn; 1 log coy
United States 9
Uruguay 1,135; 2 inf bn; 1 mne coy, 1 avn sect

Honduras HND

Honduran Lempira L		2009	2010	2011
GDP	L	271bn	291bn	
	US$	14.3bn	15.4bn	
per capita	US$	1,918	2,021	
Growth	%	-2.0	2.1	
Inflation	%	5.5	4.6	
Def exp	L	2.1bn		
	US$	111m		
Def bdgt	L	1.93bn	2.6bn	
	US$	102m	138m	
FMA	US$	-	1.075m	1.3m
US$1=L		18.90	18.90	

Population   7,615,584

Age	0–14	15–19	20–24	25–29	30–64	65 plus
Male	18.8%	5.7%	5.1%	4.4%	14.6%	1.7%
Female	18.0%	5.5%	4.9%	4.3%	14.9%	2.1%

Capabilities

ACTIVE 12,000 (Army 8,300 Navy 1,400 Air 2,300)
Paramilitary 8,000

RESERVE 60,000 (Joint 60,000; Ex-servicemen registered)

ORGANISATIONS BY SERVICE

Army 8,300

FORCES BY ROLE
6 Military Zones

Armd cav	1 regt (1 lt tk sqn, 1 ADA bty, 1 arty bty, 1 recce sqn, 2 mech bn)
Inf	1 bde (3 inf bn); 3 bde (each: 1 arty bn, 3 inf bn)
Spec Ops	1 (special tac) gp (1 SF bn, 1 inf/AB bn)
Engr	1 bn
Presidential Guard	1 coy

EQUIPMENT BY TYPE
LT TK 12 *Scorpion*
RECCE 57: 13 RBY-1 *RAMTA*; 40 *Saladin*; 3 *Scimitar*; 1 *Sultan*
ARTY 118+
  TOWED 28: **105mm:** 24 M-102; **155mm:** 4 M-198
  MOR 90+: **60mm**; **81mm**; **120mm** 60 FMK-2; **160mm** 30 M-66 *Soltam*
AT • RCL 170: **106mm** 50 M-40A1; **84mm** 120 *Carl Gustav*
AD • GUNS 48: **20mm** 24 M-55A2; 24 TCM-20

Reserves

FORCES BY ROLE

Inf	1 bde

Navy 1,400

EQUIPMENT BY TYPE
PATROL AND COASTAL COMBATANTS 15
  PB 15: 1 *Chameleon* (*Swift* 26m); 1 *Tegucilgalpa* (US *Guardian* 32m); 4 *Guanaja*; 3 *Guaymuras* (*Swift* 31m); 6 *Nacaome* (*Swiftship*, 65)
AMPHIBIOUS • LCU 1 *Punta Caxinas*

FACILITIES

Bases	Located at Puerto Cortés, Puerto Castilla, Amapala

Marines 830

FORCES BY ROLE

Marine	3 indep coy

Air Force 2,300

FORCES BY ROLE

FGA	1 sqn with A-37B *Dragonfly*; 1 sqn with F-5E *Tiger II*
Tpt	1 sqn with C-130A *Hercules*; DC-3 (C-47 *Skytrain*); Some (liason) sqn with Cessna 185; Cessna 401; PA-31 *Navajo*; PA-32T *Saratoga*
Atk/ISR/Trg	Some sqn with Cessna 182 *Skylane*; EMB-312 *Tucano*; T-41B/D *Mescalero*
Tpt Hel	2 sqn with Bell 412SP *Twin Huey*; Hughes 500; UH-1H *Iroquois*

EQUIPMENT BY TYPE
AIRCRAFT 16 combat capable
  FTR 8 F-5E *Tiger II*
  ATK 8 A-37B *Dragonfly*
  TPT 12 **Medium** 1 C-130A *Hercules* **Light** 2 Cessna 182 *Skylane*; 4 Cessna 185; 1 Cessna 401; 2 DC-3 (C-47 *Skytrain*); 1 PA-31 *Navajo*; 1 PA-32T *Saratoga*
  TRG 14: 9 EMB-312 *Tucano*; 5 T-41B/D *Mescalero*
HELICOPTERS
  MRH 7: 5 Bell 412SP *Twin Huey*; 2 Hughes 500
  TPT • Light 2 Bell 205 (UH-1H *Iroquois*)
MSL • AAM IR AAM *Shafrir*‡

Paramilitary 8,000

Public Security Forces 8,000
Ministry of Public Security and Defence

Region	11 comd

DEPLOYMENT

WESTERN SAHARA
UN • MINURSO 12 obs

FOREIGN FORCES

United States US Southern Command: 397; 1 avn bn with CH-47 *Chinook*; UH-60 *Black Hawk*

Jamaica JAM

Jamaican Dollar J$		2009	2010	2011
GDP	J$	1.08tr	1.20tr	
	US$	12.3bn	13.7bn	
per capita	US$	4,569	5,000	
Growth	%	-2.6	0.3	
Inflation	%	9.6	12.7	
Def exp	J$	5.43bn		
	US$	62m		
Def bdgt	J$	8bn		
	US$	91m		
FMA	US$	0.4m	0.5m	-
US$1=J$		87.85	87.95	

Population	2,729,909

Age	0–14	15–19	20–24	25–29	30–64	65 plus
Male	15.3%	5.7%	5.2%	4.6%	15.4%	3.4%
Female	14.8%	5.6%	5.2%	4.7%	16.0%	4.2%

Capabilities

ACTIVE 2,830 (Army 2,500 Coast Guard 190 Air 140)
(combined Jamaican Defence Force)

RESERVE 953 (Army 877 Navy 60 Air 16)

ORGANISATIONS BY SERVICE

Army 2,500

FORCES BY ROLE

Inf   2 bn
Engr   1 regt (4 engr sqn)
Spt   1 bn

EQUIPMENT BY TYPE
APC (W) 4 LAV-150 *Commando*
MOR 81mm 12 L16A1

Reserves

FORCES BY ROLE
Inf   1 bn

Coast Guard 190

EQUIPMENT BY TYPE
PATROL AND COASTAL COMBATANTS 11
   PBF 3
   PB 8: 3 *Cornwall* (Damen Stan 4207); 4 *Dauntless*; 1 *Paul Bogle* (US 31m)
FACILITIES
Bases   Located at Port Royal, Pedro Cays
Minor Base   Located at Discovery Bay

Air Wing 140

Plus National Reserve

FORCES BY ROLE

MP/Tpt   1 flt with 1 BN-2A *Defender*; 1 Cessna 210M *Centurio*; 2 DA-40-180FP *Diamond Star* (trg)
SAR/Tpt Hel   2 flt with 4 AS-355N *Ecureuil*; 3 Bell 407; 3 Bell 412EP

EQUIPMENT BY TYPE
AIRCRAFT
   TPT • Light 4: 1 BN-2A *Defender*; 1 Cessna 210M *Centurion*; 2 DA40-180FP *Diamond Star*
HELICOPTERS
   MRH 3 Bell 412EP
   TPT • Light 7: 4 AS-355N *Ecureuil* II; 3 Bell 407

DEPLOYMENT

SIERRA LEONE
IMATT 1

Mexico MEX

Mexican Peso NP		2009	2010	2011
GDP	NP	11.8tr	12.9tr	
	US$	876bn	1.01tr	
per capita	US$	8,156	9,168	
Growth	%	-6.5	4.3	
Inflation	%	5.3	4.2	
Def exp	NP	64.3bn		
	US$	4.77bn		
Def bdgt[a]	NP	58.2bn	58.4bn	
	US$	4.31bn	4.6bn	
FMA (US)	US$	39m	265.25m	8.0m
US$1=NP		13.49	12.69	

[a] Excluding paramilitaries

Population   110,645,154

Age	0–14	15–19	20–24	25–29	30–64	65 plus
Male	14.4%	4.8%	4.5%	4.0%	18.3%	2.9%
Female	13.8%	4.7%	4.5%	4.2%	20.4%	3.6%

Capabilities

ACTIVE 280,250 (Army 212,000 Navy 56,500 Air 11,750) **Paramilitary 51,500**

Reserve 87,344 (National Military Service))

ORGANISATIONS BY SERVICE

Army 212,000

12 regions (total: 46 army zones). The Mexican Armed Forces have reorganised into a brigade structure. The Army consists of one manoeurvre corps (1st), with three inf bde and one armd bde, one SF corps one AB corps and one MP corps. Command and control functions have been redesigned and decentralised, allowing greater independence to each of the 12 Military Region commanders and establishing C4 units in every region.

FORCES BY ROLE

Armd   1 (1st) corps with (1 cbt engr bde (3 engr bn), 1 armd bde (2 armd recce bn, 2 lt armd recce bn, 1 (Canon) AT gp), 3 inf/rapid reaction bde (each: 3 inf bn, 1 arty regt, 1 (Canon) AT gp))
              2 bde (each: 2 armd recce bn, 2 lt armd recce bn, 1 (Canon) AT gp)
Armd Recce   3 regt
Lt Armd Recce 2 regt
Mot Recce   24 regt
Inf   107 indep inf bn; 12 indep inf coy
Lt Inf   3 indep lt inf bde each (2 lt inf bn, 1 AT (Canon) gp)
Arty   6 indep regt
Para   1 bde (3 bn, 1 GAFE SF gp,1 AT (Canon gp)

SF   3 bde (12 SF bn); 1 amph bde (5 SF bn)
Presidential 1 SF gp, 1 mech inf bde (2 inf bn, 1 aslt bn)
Guard   1 cbt engr bn, 1 MP bde (3 bn, 1 special ops
            anti-riot coy) 1 mne bn (Navy)
MP   2 bde (3 MP bn)

EQUIPMENT BY TYPE

RECCE 237: 124 ERC-90F1 *Lynx* (4 trg); 40 M-8; 41 MAC-1;
32 VBL

APC 709
  APC (T) 475: 398 DNC-1 (mod AMX-VCI); 40 HWK-11;
34 M-5A1 half-track; 3 M-32 *Recovery Sherman*
  APC (W) 234: 95 BDX; 25 DN-4; 19 DN-5 *Toro*; 26 LAV-
150 ST; 25 MOWAG *Roland*; 44 VCR (3 amb; 5 cmd post)

ARTY 1,390
  TOWED 123: **105mm** 123: 40 M-101; 40 M-56; 16 M-2A1,
14 M-3; 13 NORINCO M-90
  MOR 1,267: **81mm** 400 M-I, 400 *Brandt*, 300 SB
  120mm 167: 75 *Brandt*; 60 M-65; 32 RT61

AT
  MSL • SP 8 *Milan* (VBL)
  RL 1,187+
    SP 106mm M40A1
    64mm RPG-18 *Fly* **82mm** B-300 **73mm** RPG-16; **106mm**
M40A1
  GUNS 37mm 30 M3

AD
  GUNS 80
    TOWED 12.7mm 40 M-55; **20mm** 40 GAI-B01

Navy 56,500

HQ at Acapulco; HQ (exercise) at Vera Cruz. Two Fleet
Commands: Gulf (6 zones), Pacific (11 zones)

EQUIPMENT BY TYPE

PRINCIPAL SURFACE COMBATANTS 7
  FRIGATES 7:
    FFGHM 4 *Allende* (US *Knox*) each with 1 octuple Mk
112 lnchr with ASROC/RGM-84C *Harpoon* AShM, 1
Mk29 GMLS with *Sea Sparrow* SAM, 2 twin 324mm
ASTT (4 eff.) each with Mk46 LWT, 1 127mm gun,
(capacity 1 MD-902 hel)
    FF 3:
      1 *Quetzalcoatl* with 2 twin 127mm gun (4 eff.), 1 hel
landing platform
      2 *Bravo* (US *Bronstein*) each with 1 octuple Mk112
lnchr with ASROC, 2 triple 324mm ASTT (6 eff.)
each with Mk46 LWT, 1 twin 76mm gun (2 eff.), 1 hel
landing platform

PATROL AND COASTAL COMBATANTS 119
  PSOH 4 *Oaxaca* each with 1 76mm gun (capacity 1 AS-
565MB *Panther* hel)
  PCO 27:
    4 *Durango* (capacity 1 Bo-105 hel)
    4 *Holzinger* (capacity 1 MD-902 *Explorer*)
    10 *Leandro Valle* (US *Auk* MSF) each with 1 76mm gun
(being withdrawn from service; to be replaced with 4
additional *Oaxaca* class)
    3 *Sierra* (capacity 1 MD-902 *Explorer*)
    6 *Uribe* (ESP *Halcon*) (capacity 1 Bo-105 hel)

  PCG 2 *Huracan* (ISR *Aliya*) each with 4 single lnchr each
with *Gabriel* II AShM, 1 *Phalanx* CIWS
  PCC 2 *Democrata*
  PBF 69: 6 *Acuario*; 2 *Acuario B*; 4 *Isla* (US *Halter*); 48 *Polaris*
(SWE CB90); 9 *Polaris II* (SWE IC 16M; additional vessels
under construction)
  PB 15: 10 *Azteca*; 3 *Cabo* (US *Cape Higgon*); 2 *Punta* (US
Point)

AMPHIBIOUS • LS • LST 3: 2 *Papaloapan* (US *Newport*); 1
Panuco (ex US LST-1152)

LOGISTICS AND SUPPORT 17:
  AK 2
  AGOR 3: 2 *Robert D. Conrad*; 1 *Humboldt*
  AGS 4
  ATF 4
  TRG 4: 1 *Manuel Azuela*; 2 *Huasteco* (also serve as troop
transport, supply and hospital ships); **AXS** 1

FACILITIES

Bases   Located at Vera Cruz, Tampico, Chetumal,
               Ciudad del Carmen, Yukalpetén, Lerna,
               Frontera, Coatzacoalcos, Isla Mujéres,
               Acapulco, Ensenada, La Paz, Guaymas,
               Mayport (FL), US, Salina Cruz, Puerto
               Madero, Lazaro Cádenas, Puerto Vallarta

Naval Aviation 1,250

FORCES BY ROLE

MP   1 sqn with CASA 212PM *Aviocar**; CN-235
            MPA Persuader; 1 sqn with L-90 *Redigo*; 5 sqn
            with Beech 55 *Baron*; Beech F33C *Bonanza*;
            Cessna 404 *Titan*; MX-7 *Star Rocket*; Lancair
            IV-P

Tpt   1 sqn with An-32B *Cline*; 1 (VIP) sqn with
            Beech 90 *King Air*; DHC-8 *Dash 8*; Learjet 24;
            Turbo Commander 1000

Tpt Hel   5 sqn with Mi-8 *Hip*/Mi-17 *Hip H*; 2 sqn with
            AS-555 *Fennec*; AS-565MB *Panther*; MD-602;
            PZL Mi-2 *Hoplite*; 2 sqn with Bo-105 CBS-5

FACILITIES

Trg School   1 with Z-242L; R-44; MD-500E; *Schweizer*
               300C

EQUIPMENT BY TYPE

AIRCRAFT 7 combat capable
  ISR 7 CASA 212PM *Aviocar**
  MR 4 CN-235 MPA *Persuader*
  TPT • Light 32: 6 An-32B *Cline*; 4 Beech 55 *Baron*; 2
Beech 90 *King Air*; 2 C-295M; 1 Cessna 404 *Titan*; 1
DHC-8 *Dash 8*; 6 Lancair IV-P; 3 Learjet 24; 2 *Sabreliner*
60; 5 *Turbo Commander* 1000
  TRG 28: 4 Beech F33C *Bonanza*; 7 L-90TP *Redigo*; 9
MX-7 *Star Rocket*; 8 Z-242L

HELICOPTERS
  MRH 7: 2 AS-555 *Fennec*; 4 MD-500E; 1 Mi-17-V5 *Hip*
  MRH/TPT 22 Mi-8 *Hip* (med tpt)/Mi-17 *Hip H*
  SAR 4 AS-565MB *Panther*
  TPT 23 **Medium** 3 UH-60M *Black Hawk* being delivered
  Light 20: 11 Bo-105 CBS-5; 6 MD-902 (SAR role); 2 PZL
Mi-2 *Hoplite*; 1 R-44

Marines 19,533 (Expanding to 30,000)

FORCES BY ROLE

Inf	3 bn
Amphibious Reaction Force	2 bde
AB	1 bn
SF	2 coy
Presidential Guard	1 bn

EQUIPMENT BY TYPE

APC (W) 29: 3 BTR-60 (APC-60); 26 BTR-70 (APC-70)
ARTY 122
   TOWED 105mm 16 M-56
   MRL 122mm 6 Firos-25
   MOR 60mm/81mm 100
RCL 106mm M-40A1
AD • SAM • MANPAD 5+ 9K38 *Igla* (SA-18 *Grouse*)

Air Force 11,750

FORCES BY ROLE

Ftr	1 sqn with F-5E/F *Tiger II*
ISR	1 sqn with EMB-145AEW *Erieye*; EMB-145RS; SA-2-37B; 4 SA-227-BC Metro III (C-26B)
Anti-narc Spraying	1 sqn with Cessna T206H; Bell 206
Tpt	1 sqn with An-32B *Cline*; IAI-201/202 *Arava*; PC-6B; 1 (Presidential) gp with AS-332 *Super Puma*, B-757, B-737; EC-225; Gulfstream III; Learjet 35; *Turbo Commander*; 1 sqn with B-727; C-130E; C-130K; L-100-20; 1 (VIP) gp with Beech-200; Cessna 500 *Citation*; S-70; 6 (liaison) sqn with Cessna 182S; 1 (liaison) sqn with Cessna 206
Trg	4 sqn with PC-7*; PC-9M; 5 sqn with PT-17; SF-260EU; Beech F-33C *Bonanza*; PC-7
Tpt Hel	1 sqn with MD-530F; 1 sqn with S-70A-24 *Black Hawk*, S-65 *Yas'ur* 2000, B-412, SA-330S; 1 sqn with Mi-8T; Mi-17; Mi-26T; 3 sqn with Bell 212, Bell 206B; 1 sqn with Bell 206B; Bell 206L
ISR UAV	1 unit with *Hermes* 450; *Skylark* Mk.I

EQUIPMENT BY TYPE

AIRCRAFT 76 combat capable
  FTR 10: 8 F-5E *Tiger II*; 2 F-5F *Tiger II*
  ISR 6: 2 SA-2-37A; 4 SA-227-BC *Metro III* (C-26B)
  ELINT 2 EMB-145RS
  AEW&C 1 EMB-145AEW *Erieye*
  TPT 116 **Medium** 12: 2 C-130E Hercules; 4 C-130K Hercules; 5 C-130H Hercules; 1 L-100-20 **Light** 96: 1 An-32B *Cline*; 1 Beech 200 *King Air*; 5 C-295M; 59 Cessna 182; 3 Cessna 206; 8 Cessna T206H; 1 Cessna 500 *Citation*; 11 IAI-201/202 *Arava*; 2 Learjet 35; 4 PC-6B; 1 *Turbo Commander* 680 **PAX** 8: 3 B-727; 2 B-737; 1 B-757; 2 Gulfstream III
  TRG 119: 20 Beech F33C *Bonanza*; 64 PC-7*; 2 PC-9M*; 7 PT-17; 26 SF-260EU
HELICOPTERS
  MRH 31: 11 Bell 412EP; 20 Mi-17 *Hip H*

ISR 20 MD-530MF
TPT 106 **Heavy** 5: 1 Mi-26T *Halo*; 4 S-65C *Yas'ur* 2000 **Medium** 22: 4 AS-332L *Super Puma*; 2 EC-225 (VIP); 8 Mi-8T *Hip*; 6 S-70A-24 *Black Hawk*; 2 SA-330S *Puma* **Light** 79: 45 Bell 206; 13 Bell 206B *JetRanger II*; 7 Bell 206L; 14 Bell 212
UAV • ISR 4 **Medium** 2 *Hermes* 450 **Light** 2 *Skylark* Mk.I
MSL • AAM • IR AAM AIM-9J *Sidewinder*

Paramilitary 51,500

Federal Preventive Police 29,000

Public Security Secretariat
AIRCRAFT
  TPT 18 **Light** 17: 2 An-32B *Cline*; 1 CN-235M; 5 Cessna 182 *Skylane*; 1 Cessna 210 *Centurion*; 1 Cessna 404 *Titan*; 1 Learjet 24; 1 *Sabreliner* 60; 5 *Turbo Commander* 5 **PAX** 1 Gulfstream II
HELICOPTERS
  MRH 5: 1 AS-555 *Fennec*; 4 Mi-17 *Hip H*
  ISR 2 MD-530F *Lifter*
  TPT 38 **Medium** 9: 1 SA-330C *Puma*; 1 SA-330F *Puma*; 7 UH-60L *Blackhawk* (4 more on order) **Light** 29: 2 AS-350B *Ecureuil*; 14 Bell 206 *Jet Ranger*; 7 Bell 206B; 1 Bell 212; 5 EC-120;
UAV • ISR • Light 2 S4 *Ehécatl*

Federal Ministerial Police 4,500

HELICOPTERS
Anti-narcotics 44: 7 Bell 212; 26 Bell UH-1H; 11 Schweizer 333

Rural Defense Militia 18,000

Inf	13 units
Horsed Cav	13 units

Nicaragua NIC

Nicaraguan Gold Cordoba Co		2009	2010	2011
GDP	Co	125bn	136bn	
	US$	6.15bn	6.40bn	
per capita	US$	1,071	1,100	
Growth	%	-1.0	1.7	
Inflation	%	3.7	5.7	
Def exp	Co	819m		
	US$	40m		
Def bdgt	Co	837m	809m	
	US$	41m	38m	
FMA (US)	US$	0.4m	0.925m	0.8m
US$1=Co		20.34	21.27	

Population 5,822,265

Age	0–14	15–19	20–24	25–29	30–64	65 plus
Male	16.5%	5.8%	5.3%	4.7%	16.2%	1.5%
Female	15.9%	5.7%	5.2%	4.6%	16.7%	1.9%

Capabilities

ACTIVE 12,000 (Army 10,000 Navy 800 Air 1,200)

Terms of service voluntary, 18–36 months

ORGANISATIONS BY SERVICE

Army ε10,000

FORCES BY ROLE

Region 1 (Comandos Regionales Militares (CRM)) comd (3 inf bn); 5 (CRM) comd (each: 2 inf bn)

Comd 1 HQ (1 sy bn, 1 inf bn, 1 sigs bn, 1 int unit, 1 SF bde (3 SF bn))

Inf 2 det (total: 2 inf bn)

Mech 1 (lt) bde (1 tk bn, 1 mech inf bn, 1 recce bn, 1 AT gp, 1 fd arty gp (2 fd arty bn))

SF 1 bde (3 SF bn)

Engr 1 bn

Tpt 1 regt (1 (APC) army bn)

EQUIPMENT BY TYPE
MBT 62: 62 T-55 (65 in store)
LT TK 10 PT-76 in store
RECCE 20 BRDM-2
APC (W) 166: 102 BTR-152 in store; 64 BTR-60
ARTY 800
    TOWED 42: **122mm** 12 D-30; **152mm** 30 D-20 in store
    MRL 151: **107mm** 33 Type-63; **122mm** 118: 18 BM-21; 100 GRAD 1P (BM-21P) (single-tube rocket launcher, man portable)
    MOR 607: **82mm** 579; **120mm** 24 M-43; **160mm** 4 M-160 in store
AT
    MSL
        SP 12 BRDM-2 Sagger
        MANPATS AT-3 9K11 Sagger
RCL 82mm B-10
RL 73mm RPG-16/RPG-7 Knout
    GUNS 371: **100mm** 24 M-1944; **57mm** 264 ZIS-2 M-1943; 90 in store; **76mm** 83 ZIS-3
AD • SAM • MANPAD 200+ 9K36 Strela-3 (SA-14 Gremlin); 9K310 Igla-1 (SA-16 Gimlet); 9K32 Strela-2 (SA-7 Grail)‡

Navy ε800

EQUIPMENT BY TYPE
PATROL AND COASTAL COMBATANTS • PB 7: 3 Dabur; 4 Rodman 101
FACILITIES
Bases Located at Corinto, Puerto Cabezzas, El Bluff

Air Force 1,200

FORCES BY ROLE

Tpt Some sqn with An-2 Colt; An-26 Curl; Cessna 404 Titan (VIP)

Tpt/Trg Some sqn with T-41D Mescalero

Tpt Hel Some sqn with Mi-17 Hip H (VIP/tpt/armed)

AD 1 gp with ZU-23; C3-Morigla M1

EQUIPMENT BY TYPE
AIRCRAFT
    TPT • Light 6: 1 An-2 Colt; 4 An-26 Curl; 1 Cessna 404 Titan (VIP)
    TRG 1 T-41D Mescalero
HELICOPTERS • MRH 16: 3 Mi-17 Hip H (armed) (2 more on order); 12 Mi-17 Hip H (armed)†; 1 Mi-17 Hip H (VIP)
AD • GUNS 36: 18 ZU-23; 18 C3-Morigla M1
MSL • ASM AT-2 Swatter

Panama PAN

Panamanian Balboa B		2009	2010	2011
GDP	B	24.9bn	27.2bn	
	US$	24.9bn	27.2bn	
per capita	US$	7,197	7,752	
Growth	%	2.4	4.5	
Inflation	%	2.4	3.4	
Def exp	B	275m		
	US$	269m		
Def bdgt	B	269m	230m	
	US$	269m	230m	
FMA (US)	US$	1.0m	1.4m	2.1m
US$1=B		1.00	1.00	

Population 3,508,475

Age	0–14	15–19	20–24	25–29	30–64	65 plus
Male	14.6%	4.5%	4.3%	4.0%	19.5%	3.3%
Female	14.0%	4.4%	4.2%	3.9%	19.3%	3.9%

Latin America and the Caribbean

Capabilities

Paramilitary 12,000

ORGANISATIONS BY SERVICE

Paramilitary 12,000

National Police Force 11,000

No hy mil eqpt, small arms only

Police	18 coy
SF	1 unit (reported)
Paramilitary	8 coy
Presidential Guard	1 bn under strength
MP	1 bn

National Maritime Service ε600

EQUIPMENT BY TYPE
PATROL AND COASTAL COMBATANTS 18
  PCO 1 *Independencia* (US *Balsam class*)
  PB 17: 3 *Chiriqui* (US); 1 *Escudo de Veraguas*; 1 *Flamenco*; 1
  Naos; 1 *Negrita*; 1 *Nombre de Dios* (US MSB 5); 2 *Panama*;
  2 *Panquiaco* (UK Vosper 31.5m); 5 *Tres De Noviembre*
  (US *Point*)

FACILITIES
Bases   Located at Amador, Balboa, Colón

National Air Service 400

FORCES BY ROLE
Tpt   1 sqn with BN-2B *Islander*; C-212M *Aviocar*; PA-
       34 *Seneca*; 1 (Presidential) flt with Gulfstream II;
       S-76C

Trg   1 unit with Cessna 152; Cessna 172; T-35D *Pillan*

Tpt   1 sqn with Bell 205; Bell 205 (UH-1H *Iroquois*)
Hel   Bell 212

EQUIPMENT BY TYPE
AIRCRAFT
  TPT 11 **Light** 10: 1 BN-2B *Islander*; 5 C-212M *Aviocar*;
  1 Cessna 152, 1 Cessna 172; 2 PA-34 *Seneca* **PAX** 1
  Gulfstream II
  TRG 6 T-35D *Pillan*
HELICOPTERS
  TPT • Light 23: 2 Bell 205; 13 Bell 205 (UH-1H *Iroquois*);
  6 Bell 212; 2 S-76C

Paraguay PRY

Paraguayan Guarani Pg		2009	2010	2011
GDP	Pg	70.7tr	80.5tr	
	US$	14.2bn	16.9bn	
per capita	US$	2,244	2,618	
Growth	%	-3.8	5.1	
Inflation	%	2.6	4.6	
Def bdgt	Pg	625bn	678bn	
	US$	126m	142m	
FMA (US)	US$	-	-	0.75m
US$1=Pg		4962.16	4758.10	

Population   6,459,727

Age	0–14	15–19	20–24	25–29	30–64	65 plus
Male	14.5%	5.5%	4.9%	4.2%	18.2%	2.8%
Female	14.0%	5.4%	4.9%	4.2%	17.9%	3.3%

Capabilities

ACTIVE 10,650 (Army 7,600 Navy 1,950 Air 1,100)
Paramilitary 14,800
Terms of service 12 months Navy 2 years

RESERVE 164,500 (Joint 164,500)

ORGANISATIONS BY SERVICE

Army 6,100; 1,500 conscript (total 7,600)

The infantry regiments, each of which forms the major peacetime element of the six infantry divisions have a strength
of around 500. The three cavalry divisions each have two
regiments with a strength of approximately 750.

FORCES BY ROLE
3 corps HQ

Army	3 corps (each: 2 inf div, 1 cav div, 1 arty gp); 6 inf div in total; 20 (frontier) det
Armd Cav	3 regt
Cav	3 div (each: 2 (horse) regt)
Inf	6 regt (bn)
Arty	2 gp (bn); 1 gp divided between 2 of the corps
ADA	1 gp
Engr	6 bn
Presidential Guard	1 unit (1 inf bn, 1 SF bn, 1 arty bty, 1 MP bn, 1 (lt) armd sqn)

EQUIPMENT BY TYPE
MBT 5 M4A3 *Sherman*
LT TK 12 M-3A1 *Stuart*
RECCE 30 EE-9 *Cascavel*
APC (T) 20 M-9 half-track
APC (W) 10 EE-11 *Urutu*
ARTY 95
  TOWED 105mm 15 M-101
  MOR 81mm 80

AT
RCL 75mm M-20
RL 66mm M-72 *LAW*
AD • GUNS 19:
SP 20mm 3 M-9
TOWED 16: **40mm** 10 M-1A1, 6 L/60

Reserves

Cav 4 regt
Inf 14 regt

Navy 1,100; 850 conscript (total 1,950)

EQUIPMENT BY TYPE
PATROL AND COASTAL COMBATANTS 20
PCR 4: 1 *Itaipú*; 2 *Nanawa*†; 1 *Paraguay*† with 2 twin
120mm gun (4 eff.), 3 76mm gun
PBR 16: 1 *Capitan Cabral*; 2 *Capitan Ortiz* (ROC *Hai Ou*);
13 (various)
AMPHIBIOUS 3 LCVP
LOGISTICS AND SUPPORT • AKSL 1 (also serve as
river transport)
FACILITIES
Bases Located at Asunción (Puerto Sajonia), Bahía Negra,
Cuidad Del Este

Naval Aviation 100

FORCES BY ROLE

Tpt	1 (liason) sqn with Cessna 150; Cessna 210 *Centurion*; Cessna 310; Cessna 410
Tpt Hel	1 sqn with S-350 Ecureuil (HB-350 *Esquilo*); Bell 47 (OH-13 *Sioux*)

EQUIPMENT BY TYPE
AIRCRAFT • TPT • Light 6: 2 Cessna 150; 1 Cessna 210
Centurion; 2 Cessna 310; 1 Cessna 410
HELICOPTERS
TPT • Light 2 S-350 Ecureuil (HB-350 *Esquilo*)
TRG 1 Bell 47 (OH-13 *Sioux*)

Marines 700; 200 conscript (total 900)

FORCES BY ROLE

Marine	3 bn (under strength)

Air Force 900; 200 conscript (total 1,100)

FORCES BY ROLE

Atk	Some sqn with EMB-312 *Tucano**
SAR/Tpt	Some sqn with Beech 33 *Debonair*; Beech A36 *Bonanza*; Cessna 210 *Centurion*; Cessna 402B; 3 Cessna U206 *Stationair*; PA-32 *Cherokee* (EMB-720D *Minuano*); PA-32R *Saratoga*; PA-32R *Saratoga* (EMB-721C *Sertanejo*); PA-34 *Seneca* (EMB-810C); PZL-104 *Wilga 80*
Tpt	Some sqn with C-212 *Aviocar*; DC-3 (C-47 *Skytrain*); DHC-6 *Twin Otter*
Trg	Some sqn with T-25 *Universal*; T-35A *Pillan*; T-35B *Pillan*
Hel	Some sqn with AS-350 Ecureuil (HB-350 *Esquilo*); Bell 205 (UH-1H *Iroquois*)

EQUIPMENT BY TYPE
AIRCRAFT 6 combat capable
TPT 26: **Light** 24: 1 Beech 33 *Debonair*; 1 Beech 55 *Baron*
(army co-op); 2 Beech A36 *Bonanza*; 5 C-212 *Aviocar*;
1 Cessna 206 (army co-op); 1 Cessna 210 *Centurion*; 1
Cessna 310 (army co-op); 2 Cessna 402B; 3 Cessna U206
Stationair; 1 DHC-6 *Twin Otter*; 1 PA-32 *Cherokee* (EMB-
720D *Minuano*); 1 PA-32R *Saratoga* (EMB-721C *Sertanejo*);
1 PA-34 *Seneca* (EMB-810C); 2 PZL-104 *Wilga 80* **PAX** 1
B-707
TRG 19: 6 EMB-312 *Tucano**; 6 T-25 *Universal*; 3 T-35A
Pillan; 4 T-35B *Pillan*
HELICOPTERS • TPT • Light 9: 3 AS-350 Ecureuil
(HB-350 *Esquilo*); 6 Bell 205 (UH-1H *Iroquois*)

Paramilitary 14,800

Special Police Service 10,800; 4,000 conscript (total 14,800)

DEPLOYMENT

CÔTE D'IVOIRE
UN • UNOCI 2; 7 obs

CYPRUS
UN • UNFICYP 14

DEMOCRATIC REPUBLIC OF THE CONGO
UN • MONUSCO 17 obs

HAITI
UN • MINUSTAH 31

LIBERIA
UN • UNMIL 1; 2 obs

NEPAL
UN • UNMIN 4 obs

SUDAN
UN • UNMIS 9 obs

WESTERN SAHARA
UN • MINURSO 2 obs

Latin America and the Caribbean

Peru PER

Peruvian Nuevo Sol NS		2009	2010	2011
GDP	NS	382bn	430bn	
	US$	127bn	152bn	
per capita	US$	4,352	5,160	
Growth	%	0.9	6.1	
Inflation	%	2.9	1.7	
Def exp	NS	4.52bn		
	US$	1.5bn		
Def bdgt	NS	3.08bn	3.14bn	
	US$	1.03bn	1.11bn	
FMA (US)	US$	0.75m	1.5m	3.5m
US$1=NS		3.01	2.83	

Population	29,496,120					
Age	0–14	15–19	20–24	25–29	30–64	65 plus
Male	14.2%	5.1%	4.7%	4.1%	19.4%	2.8%
Female	13.7%	4.9%	4.5%	4.1%	19.3%	3.2%

Capabilities

ACTIVE 115,000 (Army 74,000 Navy 24,000 Air 17,000) **Paramilitary 77,000**

RESERVE 188,000 (Army 188,000)
Paramilitary 7,000

ORGANISATIONS BY SERVICE

Army 74,000

FORCES BY ROLE
4 Military Regions

North Region

Cav	1 bde (1st) (4 mech bn, 1 arty gp)
Inf	1 bde (1st reinforced) (1 tk bn, 3 inf bn, 1 arty gp); 2 bde (7th & 32nd) (each: 3 inf bn, 1 arty gp)
Jungle Inf	1 bde (6th) (4 jungle bn, 1 arty gp, 1 engr bn)

Central Region

Inf	1 bde (1st) (4 mech bn, 1 arty gp); 2 bde (2nd & 31st) (each: 3 mot inf bn, 1 arty gp); 1 bde (8th) (3 mot inf bn, 1 arty gp, 1 AD bn)
SF	1 bde (1st) (4 SF bn, 1 airmob arty gp); 1 bde (3rd) (3 cdo bn, 1 airmob arty gp, 1 AD gp)
Arty	1 gp (regional troops)
Avn	1 bde (1 atk hel/recce hel bn, 1 avn bn, 2 aslt hel/tpt hel bn)
Trg	1 armd bde (18th) (1 armd bn, 2 tk bn, 1 armd inf bn, 1 engr bn, 1 SP fd arty gp)

South Region

Armd	1 bde (3rd) (3 mech inf bn, 1 mot inf bn, 1 arty gp, 1 AD gp, 1 engr bn); 1 bde (3rd) (2 tk bn, 1 armd inf bn, 1 arty gp, 1 AD gp, 1 engr bn)
SF	1 gp (regional troops)
Mtn Inf	1 bde (4th) (1 armd regt, 3 mot inf bn, 1 arty gp); 1 bde (5th) (1 armd regt, 2 mot inf bn, 3 jungle coy, 1 arty gp)
Arty	1 gp (regional troops)
AD	1 gp (regional troops)
Engr	1 bn (regional troops)

Eastern Region

Jungle Inf	1 bde (5th) (1 SF gp, 3 jungle bn, 3 jungle coy, 1 jungle arty gp, 1 AD gp, 1 jungle engr bn)

EQUIPMENT BY TYPE
MBT 240: 165 T-55; 75†
LT TK 96 AMX-13
RECCE 95: 30 BRDM-2; 15 Fiat 6616; 50 M-9A1
APC 299
   APC (T) 120 M-113A1
   APC (W) 179: 150 UR-416; 25 Fiat 6614; 4 *Repontec*
ARTY 998
   SP • 155mm 12 M-109A2
   TOWED 290
     105mm 152: 44 M-101; 24 M-2A1; 60 M-56; 24 Model 56 pack howitzer; **122mm**; 36 D-30; **130mm** 36 M-46; **155mm** 66: 36 M-114, 30 Model 50
   MRL • 122mm 22 BM-21 *Grad*
   MOR 674+: **81mm/107mm** 350; **120mm** 300+ *Brandt/Expal Model L*
   SP 107mm 24 M-106A1
AT • MSL • MANPATS 838: 350 AT-3 9K11 *Sagger*/HJ-73C, 244 *Kornet*, 244 SPIKE-ER
   RCL 106mm M-40A1
AIRCRAFT
   TPT • Light 13: 2 An-28 *Cash*; 3 An-32B *Cline*; 1 Beech 350 *King Air*; 1 Cessna 208 *Caravan I*; 3 Cessna U206 *Stationair*; 2 PA-31T *Navajo/Cheyenne II*; 1 PA-34 *Seneca*
   TRG 4 IL-103
HELICOPTERS
   MRH 14 Mi-17 *Hip H* (8 more in store)
   TPT 12 **Heavy** 1 Mi-26T *Halo* (2 more in store) **Light** 11: 2 AW-109K2; 9 PZL Mi-2 *Hoplite*
   TRG 5 F-28F
AD
   SAM • MANPAD 298+: 70 9K36 *Strela-3* (SA-14 *Gremlin*); 128 9K310 *Igla-1* (SA-16 *Gimlet*); 100+ 9K32 *Strela-2* (SA-7 *Grail*)‡
   GUNS 165
     SP 23mm 35 ZSU-23-4
     TOWED 23mm 130: 80 ZU-23-2; 50 ZU-23

Navy 24,000 (incl 1,000 Coast Guard)

Commands: Pacific, Lake Titicaca, Amazon River
EQUIPMENT BY TYPE
SUBMARINES • TACTICAL • SSK 6:
   6 *Angamos* (GER T-209/1200 – 2 in refit/reserve) each with 6 single 533mm TT each with A-185 HWT

PRINCIPAL SURFACE COMBATANTS 9

CRUISERS • CG 1 *Almirante Grau* (NLD *De Ruyter*) with 8 single lnchr each with Otomat Mk 2 AShM, 4 twin 152mm gun (8 eff.)

FRIGATES • FFGHM 8:

4 *Aguirre* (ITA *Lupo*) each with 8 single lnchr each with Otomat Mk 2 AShM, 1 octuple *Albatros* lnchr with *Aspide* SAM, 2 triple 324mm ASTT (6 eff.) each with A244 LWT, 1 127mm gun, (capacity 1 Bell 212 (AB-212)/ SH-3D *Sea King*)

4 *Carvajal* (mod ITA *Lupo*) each with 8 single lnchr each with Otomat Mk 2 AShM, 1 octuple Mk29 lnchr with RIM-7P *Sea Sparrow* SAM, 2 triple 324mm ASTT (6 eff.) each with A244 LWT, 1 127mm gun, (capacity 1 Bell 212 (AB-212)/SH-3D *Sea King*)

PATROL AND COASTAL COMBATANTS 14

CORVETTES • FSG 6 *Velarde* (FRA PR-72 64m) each with 4 single lnchr each with MM-38 *Exocet* AShM, 1 76mm gun

PCR 5:

2 *Amazonas* each with 1 76mm gun

1 *Manuel Clavero* (additional vessel in build)

2 *Marañon* each with 2 76mm gun

PBR 3

AMPHIBIOUS • LS • LST 4 *Paita* (capacity 395 troops) (US *Terrebonne Parish*)

LOGISTICS AND SUPPORT 11:

AOR 1 *Mollendo*

AOT 2

ARS 1 *Guardian Rios*

AH 1

AGS 4: 1 *Carrasco*; 2 (coastal survey vessels); 1 (river survey vessel for the upper Amazon)

TRG • AXS 1

TRV 1

FACILITIES

Bases Located at Callao (Ocean), Puerto Maldonaldo (*River*), Iquitos (*River*), Talara (Ocean), Puno (Lake), Paita (Ocean), San Lorenzo Island (Ocean)

Naval Aviation ε800

FORCES BY ROLE

MP	1 sqn with Beech 200T; Bell 212 (AB-212); F-27 *Friendship*; F-60; SH-3D *Sea King*
Tpt	1 flt with An-32B *Cline*
Trg	1 sqn with F-28F; T-34C *Turbo Mentor*
Tpt Hel	1 (liaison) sqn with Bell 206B *Jet Ranger II*; Mi-8 *Hip*

EQUIPMENT BY TYPE

AIRCRAFT

MP 9: 5 Beech 200T; 4 F-60 (+2)

ELINT 1 F-27 *Friendship*

TPT Light 2 An-32B *Cline*

TRG 5 T-34C *Turbo Mentor*

HELICOPTERS

ASW 3 SH-3D *Sea King*

TPT 12: **Medium** 4 Mi-8 *Hip* **Light** 8: 5 Bell 206B *Jet Ranger II*; 3 Bell 212 (AB-212)

TRG 6 F-28F

MSL • AShM AM-39 *Exocet*

Marines 4,000

FORCES BY ROLE

Inf	1 (jungle) bn; 2 (indep) bn; 1 gp
Cdo	1 gp
Marine	1 bde (1 arty gp, 1 spec ops gp, 1 recce bn, 1 (amph veh) amph bn, 2 inf bn)

EQUIPMENT BY TYPE

APC (W) 35+: 20 BMR-600; V-100 *Commando*; 15 V-200 *Chaimite*

ARTY 18+

TOWED 122mm D-30

MOR 18+: **81mm**; **120mm** ε18

RCL 84mm *Carl Gustav*; **106mm** M-40A1

AD • GUNS 20mm SP (twin)

Air Force 17,000

FORCES BY ROLE

Air Force divided into five regions – North, Lima, South, Central and Amazon.

Ftr	1 sqn with MiG-29C *Fulcrum*; MiG-29SE *Fulcrum*; MiG-29UB *Fulcrum*
FGA	1 sqn with Mirage 2000E (2000P); Mirage 2000ED (2000DP); 1 sqn with A-37B *Dragonfly*; 3 sqn with Su-25A *Frogfoot A*†; Su-25UB *Frogfoot B*†
ISR	1 (photo-survey) unit with Learjet 36A; SA-227-BC *Metro III* (C-26B)
Tpt	sqn with An-32 *Cline*; B-737; DC-8-62F; DHC-6 *Twin Otter*; FH-227; L-100-20; PC-6 *Turbo-Porter*; Y-12(II); 1 (Presidential) flt with F-28 *Fellowship*, Falcon 20F; 1 (liason) sqn with Bell 205 (UH-1D *Iroquois*); PA-31T *Navajo/Cheyenne II*
Trg	Some (drug interdiction) sqn with EMB-312 *Tucano*; MB-339A*; T-41A/T-41D *Mescalero*; Z-242
Atk Hel	1 sqn with Mi-24 *Hind*/Mi-25 *Hind D*; Mi-17TM *Hip H*
Tpt Hel	3 sqn with Mi-17 *Hip H*; Bell 206 *Jet Ranger*; Bell 212 (AB-212); Bell 412 *Twin Huey*; Bo-105C; Schweizer 300C
AD	6 bn with S-125 *Pechora* (SA-3 *Goa*)

EQUIPMENT BY TYPE

AIRCRAFT 78 combat capable

FTR 20: 15 MiG-29C *Fulcrum*; 3 MiG-29SE *Fulcrum*; 2 MiG-29UB *Fulcrum*

FGA 12: 2 Mirage 2000ED (M-2000DP); 10 Mirage 2000E (2000P)

ATK 36: 18 A-37B *Dragonfly*; 10 Su-25A *Frogfoot A*†; 8 Su-25UB *Frogfoot B*†

ISR 6: 2 Learjet 36A; 4 SA-227-BC *Metro III* (C-26B)

TKR 1 KC-707-323C

TPT 31: **Medium** 5 L-100-20; **Light** 22: 6 An-32 *Cline*; 5 DHC-6 *Twin Otter*; 1 PA-31T *Navajo/Cheyenne II*; 8 PC-6 *Turbo-Porter*; 2 Y-12(II) (**PAX** 4: 1 B-737; 2 DC-8-62F; 1 Falcon 20F

TRG 50: 19 EMB-312 *Tucano*; 10 MB-339A*; 6 T-41A *Mescalero*/T-41D *Mescalero*; 15 Z-242

HELICOPTERS

ATK 16 Mi-24 *Hind*/Mi-25 *Hind D*

MRH 24: 1 Bell 412 *Twin Huey*; 13 Mi-17 (Mi-8MT) *Hip* H; 10 Mi-17TM *Hip* H

SPT 37: **Medium** 5 Mi-8 *Hip* **Light** 32: 8 Bell 206 *JetRanger*; 14 Bell 212 (AB-212); 10 Bo-105C

TRG 6 Schweizer 300C

AD

SAM 100+: S-125 *Pechora* (SA-3 *Goa*); 100+ *Javelin*

MSL

ASM AS-30

AAM IR AAM R-3 (AA-2 *Atoll*)‡; R-60 (AA-8 *Aphid*)‡; R-550 *Magic*; IR/SARH AAM R-27 (AA-10 *Alamo*); ARH AAM R-77 (AA-12 *Adder*)

Paramilitary • National Police 77,000 (100,000 reported)

APC (W) 100 MOWAG *Roland*

General Police 43,000

Security Police 21,000

Technical Police 13,000

Coast Guard 1,000

Personnel included as part of Navy

PATROL AND COASTAL COMBATANTS 12

PCC 5 *Rio Nepena*

PB 7: 3 *Dauntless*; 2 *Río Chira*; 2 *Río Santa*

AIRCRAFT

TPT • Light 2 F-27 *Friendship*

Rondas Campesinas ε7,000 gp

Peasant self-defence force. Perhaps 7,000 rondas 'gp', up to pl strength, some with small arms. Deployed mainly in emergency zone.

DEPLOYMENT

CÔTE D'IVOIRE

UN • UNOCI 3 obs

CYPRUS

UN • UNFICYP 2

DEMOCRATIC REPUBLIC OF THE CONGO

UN • MONUSCO 7 obs

HAITI

UN • MINUSTAH 371; 1 inf coy

LIBERIA

UN • UNMIL 2; 2 obs

SUDAN

UN • UNMIS 9 obs

Suriname SUR

Suriname Dollar gld		2009	2010	2011
GDP	gld	8.11bn	9.31bn	
	US$	2.96bn	3.39bn	
per capita	US$	5,686	6,464	
Growth	%	1.5	14.7	
Inflation	%	-0.1	6.4	
Def bdgt	gld	107bn	134bn	
	US$	39m	49m	
FMA (US)	US$	0.15m	0.3m	-
US$1=gld		2.74	2.75	

Population	524,345

Age	0–14	15–19	20–24	25–29	30–64	65 plus
Male	13.5%	4.3%	4.0%	4.7%	20.5%	2.7%
Female	12.9%	4.3%	4.1%	4.8%	20.6%	3.6%

Capabilities

ACTIVE 1,840 (Army 1,400 Navy 240 Air 200)

(All services form part of the army)

ORGANISATIONS BY SERVICE

Army 1,400

FORCES BY ROLE

Mech Cav   1 sqn

Inf   1 bn (4 inf coy)

MP   1 bn (coy)

EQUIPMENT BY TYPE

RECCE 6 EE-9 *Cascavel*

APC (W) 15 EE-11 *Urutu*

MOR 81mm 6

RCL 106mm: M-40A1

Navy ε240

EQUIPMENT BY TYPE

PATROL AND COASTAL COMBATANTS 8

PB 3 *Rodman 101*†

PBR 5

FACILITIES

Base   Located at Paramaribo

Air Force ε200

FORCES BY ROLE

Tpt/Trg   1 sqn with 1 BN-2 *Defender**; 1 PC-7 *Turbo Trainer**

EQUIPMENT BY TYPE

AIRCRAFT 4 combat capable

MP 2 C-212-400 *Aviocar**

TPT • Light 3: 1 BN-2 *Defender**; 1 Cessna 182; 1 Cessna U-206 *Stationair*;

TRG 1 PC-7 *Turbo Trainer**

Trinidad and Tobago TTO

Trinidad and Tobago Dollar TT$		2009	2010	2011
GDP	TT$	124bn	135bn	
	US$	19.6bn	21.2bn	
per capita	US$	14,660	15,794	
Growth	%	-4.4	2.2	
Inflation	%	7.0	9.4	
Def bdgt	TT$	1.06bn	1.1bn	1.12bn
	US$	167m	172m	
US$1=TT$		6.32	6.36	

Population   1,343,725

Age	0–14	15–19	20–24	25–29	30–64	65 plus
Male	9.9%	3.6%	4.4%	5.2%	24.0%	3.6%
Female	9.5%	3.3%	4.1%	4.9%	22.7%	4.8%

Capabilities

ACTIVE 4,063(Army 3,000 Coast Guard 1,063)

(All services form the Trinidad and Tobago Defence Force)

ORGANISATIONS BY SERVICE

Army ε3,000

FORCES BY ROLE

Inf	4 bn
SF	1 unit
Spt	1 bn

EQUIPMENT BY TYPE

MOR 6: **81mm** L16A1

AT

RCL **84mm** ε24 *Carl Gustav*

RL **82mm** 13 B-300

Coast Guard 1,063

FORCES BY ROLE

Marine   1 HQ located at Staubles Bay

EQUIPMENT BY TYPE

PATROL AND COASTAL COMBATANTS 20

PCO 1 *Nelson* (UK *Island*)

PB 19: 2 *Gasper Grande*; 1 *Matelot*; 4 *Plymouth*; 4 *Point*; 6 *Scarlet Ibis* (Austal 30m); 2 *Wasp*; (1 *Cascadura* (SWE *Karlskrona* 40m) non-operational)

FACILITIES

Bases   Located at Staubles Bay, Hart's Cut, Point Fortin, Tobago, Galeota

Air Wing 50

AIRCRAFT

TPT • Light 5: 1 Cessna 310; 2 PA-31 *Navajo*; 2 SA-227 *Metro III* (C-26)

HELICOPTERS

TPT • Light 9: 1 AS-355F *Ecureuil II*; 4 Bo-105 (NHS Ltd - 1 dedicated to support police); 1 S-76; 3 S-76 (NHS Ltd)

AIRSHIPS • ISR 2: 1 Aeros-40B *SkyDragon*; 1 Westinghouse *Skyship* 600

Uruguay URY

Uruguayan Peso pU		2009	2010	2011
GDP	pU	711bn	825bn	
	US$	31.6bn	41.1bn	
per capita	US$	9,460	12,196	
Growth	%	2.9	4.6	
Inflation	%	7.1	6.5	
Def exp	pU	11.1bn		
	US$	495m		
Def bdgt	pU	7.73bn	8.64bn	9.34bn
	US$	344m	431m	
FMA (US)	US$	-	-	0.57m
US$1=pU		22.47	20.06	

Population   3,372,222

Age	0–14	15–19	20–24	25–29	30–64	65 plus
Male	11.1%	3.9%	3.8%	3.6%	20.9%	5.4%
Female	10.7%	3.8%	3.7%	3.5%	21.6%	8.1%

Capabilities

ACTIVE 24,621 (Army 16,234 Navy 5,403 Air 2,984)
Paramilitary 818

ORGANISATIONS BY SERVICE

Army 16,234

Uruguayan units are sub-standard size, mostly around 30%. Div are at most bde size, while bn are of reinforced coy strength. Regts are also coy size, some bn size, with the largest formation being the 2nd Armd Cav Regt with 21 M-41A1UR and 16 M-113 A1.

FORCES BY ROLE

4 Military Regions/div HQ

Armd	2 (5th & 8th cav bdo) regt
Armd Inf	1 (2nd armd cav) regt
Mech Inf	5 (3rd, 4th, 6th, 7th & 10th mech cav) regt; 8 (mech inf) regt
Mot Inf	1 bn
Inf	5 bn
Para	1 bn
SF	1 trg centre
Arty	1 (Strategic Reserve) regt; 5 fd arty gp
Engr	1 (1st) bde with (2 engr bn)
Cbt engr	4 bn
AD	1 gp

EQUIPMENT BY TYPE

MBT 15 TI-67

LT TK 38: 16 M-24 *Chaffee*; 22 M-41A1UR

RECCE 110: 15 EE-9 *Cascavel*; 48 GAZ-39371 *Vodnik*; 47 OT-93;

AIFV 18 BMP-1

APC 176:

  APC (T) 29: 24 M-113A1UR; 3 M-93 (MT-LB); 2 PTS

  APC (W) 147: 54 *Condor*; 53 OT-64: 40 MOWAG *Piranha*

ARTY 185

  SP 122mm 6 2S1 *Carnation*

  TOWED 44: **105mm** 36: 28 M-101A1; 8 M-102; **155mm** 8 M-114A1

  MOR 135: **81mm** 91: 35 M1, 56 LN; **120mm** 44 SL

AT

  MSL • MANPATS 15 *Milan*

  RCL 69: **106mm** 69 M-40A1

UAV • ISR • Light 1 *Charrua*

AD • GUNS • TOWED 14: **20mm** 14: 6 M-167 *Vulcan*; 8TCM-20 (w/Elta M-2016 radar)

Navy 5,403 (incl 1,800 Prefectura Naval Coast Guard)

HQ at Montevideo

EQUIPMENT BY TYPE

PRINCIPAL SURFACE COMBATANTS • FRIGATES 2

  FF 2 *Uruguay* (PRT *Joao Belo*) with 2 triple 324mm ASTT (6 eff.) each with Mk46 LWT, 2 100mm gun

PATROL AND COASTAL COMBATANTS 18

  PB 18: 3 *15 de Noviembre* (FRA *Vigilante* 42m); 2 *Colonia* (US *Cape*); 1 *Paysandu*; 12 (various)

MINE WARFARE • MINE COUNTERMEASURES •

MSO 3 *Temerario* (*Kondor* II)

AMPHIBIOUS 3: 2 LCVP; 1 LCM

LOGISTICS AND SUPPORT 7:

  ARS 1 *Vanguardia*

  AR 1 *Artigas* (GER, *Freiburg*, general spt ship)

  AG 1 *Maldonado*

  AGHS 2: 1 *Helgoland*; 1 *Trieste*

  ABU 1 Sirius

  TRG • AXS 1

FACILITIES

Bases   Located at Montevideo (main base), Fray Bentos, Rio Negro (river)

Naval air bases   Located at La Paloma, Laguna del Sauce

Naval Aviation 211

FORCES BY ROLE

ASW   1 flt with *Beech* 200T*; *Jetstream* Mk2

SAR/Tpt Hel   1 sqn with AS 350B2 *Ecureuil* (*Esquilo*); Bo-105M; *Wessex* HC2/Mk60

Tpt/Trg   1 flt with T-34C *Turbo Mentor*

EQUIPMENT BY TYPE

AIRCRAFT 1 combat capable

  MP 2 *Jetstream* Mk2;

  ISR 1 Beech 200T*

  TRG 2 T-34C *Turbo Mentor*

HELICOPTERS

  MRH 6 Bo-105M

  TPT 2 **Medium** 1 *Wessex* HC2/Mk60 **Light** 1 AS 350B2 *Ecureuil* (*Esquilo*)

Naval Infantry 450

FORCES BY ROLE

Marine   1 bn (under strength)

Air Force 2,984

Flying hours   120 hrs/year

FORCES BY ROLE

FGA   1 sqn with A-37B *Dragonfly*, 1 sqn with IA-58B *Pucará*

ISR   1 flt with EMB–110 *Bandeirante*

Tpt   1 sqn with C–130B *Hércules*; C-212 *Aviocar*; EMB–110C *Bandeirante*; EMB–120 *Brasilia*; Some (liason) sqn with Cessna 206H; L–21 *Super Cub*; T–41D;

Trg   Some sqn with Beech 58 *Baron* (UB-58); PC-7U *Turbo Trainer*; SF–260EU

Tpt Hel   1 sqn with AS–365 *Dauphin*; Bell 205 (UH–1H *Iroquois*); Bell 212

EQUIPMENT BY TYPE

AIRCRAFT

  ATK 16: 11 A–37B *Dragonfly*; 5 IA–58 B *Pucará*

  ISR 1 EMB–110 *Bandeirante*

  TPT 21 **Medium** 2 C–130B *Hercules*; **Light** 19: 2 Beech 58 *Baron* (UB-58); 2 C–212 *Aviocar*; 11 Cessna 206H; 2 EMB–110C *Bandeirante*; 1 EMB-120 *Brasilia*; 1 L–21 *Super Cub*

  TRG 21: 5 PC-7U *Turbo Trainer*; 12 SF-260 EU; 4 T–41D *Mescalero*

HELICOPTERS

  MRH 1 AS–365 *Dauphin*;

  TPT • Light 10: 6 Bell 205 (UH–1H *Iroquois*); 4 Bell 212

Paramilitary 818

Guardia de Coraceros 368 (under Interior Ministry)

Guardia de Granaderos 450

DEPLOYMENT

AFGHANISTAN

UN • UNAMA 1 obs

CÔTE D'IVOIRE

UN • UNOCI 2 obs

DEMOCRATIC REPUBLIC OF THE CONGO

UN • MONUC 1,285; 46 obs; 1 inf bn; 1 engr coy; 1 mne coy; 1 hel pl

EGYPT

MFO 58; 1 engr/tpt unit

HAITI

UN • MINUSTAH 1,135; 2 inf bn; 1 mne coy, 1 avn sect

INDIA/PAKISTAN

UN • UNMOGIP 2 obs

NEPAL

UN • UNMIN 2 obs

WESTERN SAHARA

UN • MINURSO 1 obs

Venezuela VEN

Venezuelan Bolivar Bs		2009	2010	2011
GDP	Bs	700bn	984bn	
	US$	326bn	381bn	
per capita	US$	11,490	13,113	
Growth	%	-3.3	-2.9	
Inflation	%	28.6	29.2	
Def exp	Bs	7.12bn		
	US$	3.32bn		
Def bdgt	Bs	8.97bn	8.6bn	
	US$	4.18bn	3.33bn	
US$1=Bs		2.15	2.58	

Population   29,043,555

Age	0–14	15–19	20–24	25–29	30–64	65 plus
Male	15.0%	5.0%	4.4%	4.0%	18.6%	2.4%
Female	14.5%	4.9%	4.4%	4.1%	19.6%	3.0%

Capabilities

ACTIVE 115,000 (Army 63,000 Navy 17,500 Air 11,500 National Guard 23,000)

Terms of service 30 months selective, varies by region for all services

RESERVE 8,000 (Army 8,000)

ORGANISATIONS BY SERVICE

Army ε63,000

FORCES BY ROLE

Armd   1 div (4th) with (1 armd bde, 1 Lt armd bde, 1 mot cav bde, 1 AD bty)

Mot Cav   1 div (9th) with (1 mot cav bde, 1 ranger bde, 1 sec and spt bde)

Inf   1 div (1st) with (1 armd unit, 1 SF unit, 2 inf bde, 1 arty unit, 1 AAA bty, 1 spt unit); 1 div (2nd) with (2 inf bde, 2 ranger bde (each: 2 ranger bn), 1 AD Bty, 1 special dev and security bde); 1 div (3rd) with (1 inf bde, 1 ranger bde (2 ranger bn), 1 comms regt, 1 MP bde)

Lt Inf   1 div (5th) with (2 jungle inf bde each (3 jungle inf bn, 1 hy mor bty), 1 engr bn, 1 cav sqn)

AB   1 para bde

AD   1 bty with *Tor* M1

Cbt Engr 1 corps with (3 regt)

Avn   1 comd with (1 tpt bn, 1 atk hel bn, 1 recce bn)

Logistics 1 comd with (2 regt)

EQUIPMENT BY TYPE

MBT 81 AMX-30V

LT TK 109: 31AMX-13; 78 *Scorpion* 90

RECCE 431: 42 *Dragoon* 300 LFV2; 79 V-100/-150; 310 UR-53AR50 *Tiuna*

APC 91

  APC (T) 45: 25 AMX-VCI; 12 VCI-PC; 8 VACI-TB

  APC (W) 46: 36 *Dragoon* 300; 10 TPz-1 *Fuchs*

ARTY 370

  SP 155mm 12 (AMX) Mk F3

  TOWED 92: **105mm** 80: 40 M-101; 40 Model 56 pack howitzer; **155mm** 12 M-114

  MRL 160mm 20 LAR SP (LAR-160)

  MOR 246+: **81mm** 165; **120mm** 60 *Brandt*

    SP 21+: **81mm** 21 *Dragoon* 300PM; AMX-VTT

AT

  MSL • MANPATS 24 IMI MAPATS

  RCL 106mm 175 M-40A1

  RL 84mm AT-4

  GUNS 76mm 75 M-18 *Hellcat*

AD

  SAM 8 *Tor* M1 (SA-15 *Gauntlet*) (18 more to be delivered)

  MANPAD RBS-70; *Mistral*

  GUNS

    SP 40mm 6+ AMX-13 *Rafaga*

    TOWED 40mm M-1; L/70

AIRCRAFT

  TPT • Light 25: 2 Beech C90 *King Air*; 1 Cessna 172; 3 Cessna 182 *Skylane*; 2 Cessna 206; 2 Cessna 207 *Stationair*; 4 IAI-102/201/202 *Arava*; 11 M-28 *Skytruck*

HELICOPTERS

  ATK 10 Mi-35M2 *Hind*

  MRH 34: 10 Bell 412EP; 2 Bell 412SP; 22 Mi-17-1V *Hip*

  TPT 9 **Heavy** 3 Mi-26T2 *Halo* **Medium** 2 AS-61D **Light** 4: 3 Bell 206B *Jet Ranger*, 1 Bell 206L-3 *Long Ranger II*; (4 Bell 205 (UH-1H) & 1 Bell 205A-1 in store)

RADAR • LAND RASIT (veh, arty)

Reserve Organisations

Reserves 8,000 reservists

Armd	1 bn
Inf	4 bn
Ranger	1 bn
Arty	1 bn
Engr	2 regt

Navy ε14,300; ε3,200 conscript (total 17,500)

HQ at Caracas. Naval Commands: Fleet, Marines, Naval Aviation, Coast Guard, Fluvial (River Forces); HQ Arauca River at El Amparo; HQ Fluvial Forces at Ciudad Bolivar

EQUIPMENT BY TYPE

SUBMARINES • TACTICAL • SSK 2:

  2 *Sabalo* (GER T-209/1300) each with 8 single 533mm TT each with SST-4 HWT

PRINCIPAL SURFACE COMBATANTS • FRIGATES 6

FFGHM 6 *Mariscal Sucre* (ITA mod *Lupo*) each with 8 single lnchr each with *Otomat* Mk2 AShM, 1 octuple *Albatros* lnchr with *Aspide* SAM, 2 triple 324mm ASTT (6 eff.) with A244 LWT, 1 127mm gun, (capacity 1 Bell 212 (AB-212) hel)

PATROL AND COASTAL COMBATANTS 6:

PBG 3 *Federación* (UK Vosper 37m) each with 2 single lnchr each with *Otomat* Mk2 AShM

PB 3 *Constitucion* (UK Vosper 37m) each with 1 76mm gun

AMPHIBIOUS 7

LANDING SHIPS • LST 4 *Capana* (capacity 12 tanks; 200 troops) (FSU *Alligator*)

LANDING CRAFT 3:

  LCU 2 *Margarita* (river comd)

  UCAC 1 Griffon 2000TD

LOGISTICS AND SUPPORT 6

  AORH 1

  AGOR 1 *Punta Brava*

  AGHS 2

  ATF 1

  TRG • AXS 1

FACILITIES

Bases   Located at Puerto Caballo (SS, FF, amph and service sqn), Caracas, Punto Fijo (patrol sqn)

Minor Bases   Located at Maracaibo (Coast Guard), Ciudad Bolivar, El Amparo, La Guaira (Coast Guard)

Naval air bases Located at Turiamo, Puerto Hierro, La Orchila

Naval Aviation 500

FORCES BY ROLE

ASW   1 sqn with Bell 212 (AB-212)

MP   1 flt with C-212-200 MPA

Tpt   1 sqn with Beech 200 *King Air*; C-212 *Aviocar*; *Turbo Commander* 980C

Trg   1 sqn with Bell 206B *Jet Ranger II*; Bell TH-57A *Sea Ranger*; Cessna 210 *Centurion*; Cessna 310Q; Cessna 402

Tpt Hel 1 sqn with Bell 412EP *Twin Huey*; Mi-17V-5 *Hip*

EQUIPMENT BY TYPE

AIRCRAFT 10 combat capable

  MP 3 C-212-200 MPA*

  TPT • Light 12: 1 Beech C90 *King Air*; 1 Beech 200 *King Air*; 4 C-212 *Aviocar*; 1 Cessna 210 *Centurion*; 2 Cessna 310Q; 2 Cessna 402; 1 *Turbo Commander* 980C

HELICOPTERS

  MRH 4 Bell 412EP *Twin Huey*; 6 Mi-17V-5 *Hip*

  TPT • Light 8: 1 Bell 206B *Jet Ranger II* (trg); 7 Bell 212 (AB-212) (ASW)

  TRG 1 Bell TH-57A *Sea Ranger*

Marines ε7,000

FORCES BY ROLE

HQ   1 div HQ

Amph   1 (amph veh) bn

Inf   2 (river) bn; 6 bn

Arty   1 bn (1 AD bn, 3 fd arty bty)

Marine   1 (river) bde; 2 (landing) bde

Engr   1 BCT; 4 bn

EQUIPMENT BY TYPE

APC (W) 32 EE-11 *Urutu*

AAV 11 LVTP-7 (to be mod to -7A1)

ARTY • TOWED 105mm 18 M-56

  MOR 120mm 12 *Brandt*

AD • GUNS • SP 40mm 6 M-42

AD • SAM RBS-70

AT • AT-4 *Skip*

  RCL 84mm M3 *Carl Gustav*; **106mm** M-40A1

Coast Guard 1,000

EQUIPMENT BY TYPE

PATROL AND COASTAL COMBATANTS 47

  PSOH 2 *Guaicamacuto* each with 1 76 mm gun, (capacity 1 Bell 212 (AB-212) hel) (2 additional vessels in build)

  PB 20: 1 *Dianca*; 12 *Gavion*; 1 *Pegalo*; 4 *Petrel* (USCG *Point* class); 2 *Protector*

  PBR 25: 18 *Constancia*; 2 *Guaicapuro*; 2 *Manaure*; 3 *Terepaima* (*Cougar*)

LOGISTICS AND SUPPORT 5

  AG 2 *Los Tanques* (salvage ship)

  AKSL 1

  TPT 2

FACILITIES

Minor Base 1 (operates under Naval Comd and Control, but organisationally separate) located at La Guaira

Air Force 11,500

Flying hours   155 hrs/year

FORCES BY ROLE

Ftr/FGA   1 gp with F-5 *Freedom Fighter* (VF-5); 2 gp with F-16A/B *Fighting Falcon*; 2 gp with Su-30MKV

Atk/ISR   1 gp with OV-10A/E *Bronco**

EW   1 sqn with *Falcon* 20DC; SA-227 *Metro III* (C-26B)

Tpt   3 gp & 1 (Presidential) flt with A-319CJ; B-707; B-737; C-130H *Hercules*; G-222; Gulfstream III/ Gulfstream IV; HS-748; *Learjet* 24D

Tpt Hel   Some sqn with AS-332B *Super Puma*; AS-532 *Cougar*; Bell 204 (UH-1B); Bell 205 (UH-1H): Bell 212; Bell 212 (UH-1N); Bell 412SP

AD   1 bty with *Tor*-M1 (3 bty planned); *Barak*

EQUIPMENT BY TYPE

AIRCRAFT 99 combat capable

  FTR 31: 7 F-5 *Freedom Fighter* (VF-5), 3 F-5B *Freedom Fighter* (NF-5B); 17 F-16A *Fighting Falcon*; 4 F-16B *Fighting Falcon*

  FGA 24 Su-30MKV

  ISR 8 OV-10A/E *Bronco**

  EW 4: 2 *Falcon* 20DC; 2 SA-227 *Metro III* (C-26B)

  TPT 53 **Medium** 7: 6 C-130H *Hercules*; 1 G-222 **Light** 41: 2 Beech 65 *Queen Air*; 5 Beech 80 *Queen Air*; 5 Beech 200

King Air; 10 Cessna 182N *Skylane*; 6 Cessna 206 *Stationair*; 4 Cessna 208B *Caravan*; 1 Cessna 500 *Citation I*; 3 Cessna 550 *Citation II*; 1 Cessna *551*; 1 Learjet 24D; 1 Short 330; 2 Short 360 *Sherpa*; **PAX** 5: 1 A-319CJ; 2 B-707; 1 B-737; 1 *Falcon* 50 (VIP)

TRG 47: 18 EMB-312 *Tucano**; 17 K-8W *Karakorum** (deliveries in progress); 12 SF-260E

HELICOPTERS

MRH 10: 2 Bell 412SP; 8 Mi-17 (Mi-17VS) *Hip H*

TPT 32: **Medium** 20: 6 AS-332B *Super Puma*; 12 AS-532 *Cougar* (incl 2 VIP); 2 Mi-172 (VIP) **Light** 12: 3 Bell 204 (UH-1B); 9 Bell 205 (UH-1H)

AD

SAM 14+: 4 *Tor*-M1 (further 8 on order); 10+ *Barak*
   MANPAD 200 *Igla*-S; ADAMS; *Mistral*

GUNS

   TOWED 228+: **20mm**: 114 TCM-20; **35mm**; **40mm** 114 L/70

RADARS • LAND *Flycatcher*

MSL

ASM Kh-29 (AS-14 *Kedge*); Kh-31 A/P (AS-17 *Krypton*); KH-59M (AS-18 *Kazoo*)

AshM AM-39 *Exocet*

AAM • IR AAM AIM-9L/AIM-9P *Sidewinder*; R-73 (AA-11 *Archer*); *Python* 4; **SARH AAM** R-530 **ARH AAM** R-77(AA-12 *Adder*)

National Guard (Fuerzas Armadas de Cooperacion) 23,000

(Internal sy, customs) 8 regional comd

APC (W) 44: 24 Fiat 6614; 20 UR-416

MOR 50 **81mm**

PATROL AND COASTAL COMBATANTS • PB 34: 12 *Protector*; 12 *Punta*; 10 *Rio Orinoco II*

AIRCRAFT

TPT • Light 13: 1 Beech 55 *Baron*; 2 Beech 80 *Queen Air*; 1 Beech 90 *King Air*; 1 Beech 200C *Super King Air*; 3 Cessna 152 *Aerobat*; 2 Cessna 185; 2 Cessna 402C; 5 Cessna U206 *Stationair*; 4 IAI-201 *Arava*; 11 M-28 *Skytruck*;

TRG 3: 1 PZL 106 *Kruk*; 2 PLZ M26 *Isquierka*

HELICOPTERS

MRH 16: 10 Bell 412; 6 Mi-17 *Hip*

TPT • Light 26+: Some AS-350B *Ecureuil*; 9 AS-355F *Ecureuil II*; 4 AW-109; 12 Bell 206B/L *Jet Ranger*; 1 Bell 212 (AB 212);

TRG 6: 1 F-28C; 5 F-280C

Table 20 **Selected Arms Procurements and Deliveries, Latin America and the Caribbean**

Designation	Type	Quantity	Contract Value	Supplier Country	Prime Contractor	Order Date	First Delivery Due	Notes
Argentina (ARG)								
OPV 80	PSO	Up to 5	US$125m	ARG/GER	Astillero Rio Santiago	2009	2010	Based on Fassmer OPV 80 design. Patrulleros de Alta Mar (PAM) programme. Project currently suspended due to funding issues
Mi-17V-5 *Hip*	MRH Hel	2	US$27m	RUS	Rosoboron-export	2010	2011	–
Bolivia (BOL)								
K-8 *Karakorum*	Trg ac	6	US$57.8m	PRC	n.k.	2009	n.k.	In place of an original order for Czech L-159s held up by US export restrictions. For use in anti-drug operations.
Brazil (BRZ)								
Leopard 1A5	MBT	270	€8m	GER	n.k.	2006	2009	Ex-GER. 220 tk, plus 20 for spares and 30 in trg or engr role. 34 delivered Dec 2009 (from an intial batch of 19 MBTs, 7 ARVs, 4 Bridge layers and 7 engineer veh); 29 delivered March 2010
Piranha IIIC	APC (W)	18	n.k.	CHE	Mowag	2008	2010	For marines. 1 Ambulance, 14 APC, 1 ARV and 2 CP versions. First delivery due Sept 2010
VBTP-MR	APC (W)	up to 2044	R6bn (€2.5bn)	BRZ/ITA	IVECO Latin America	2009	2012	To replace EE-9 *Cascavel* and EE-11 *Urutu*; Delivery to be complete by 2030
SN-BR (Submarino Nuclear Brasileiro)	SSN	1	see notes	BRZ	DCNS	2009	2025	Part of €6.7bn (US$8.3bn) naval programme. Contract covers work on the non-nuclear sections of the submarine
S-BR (Submarino Brasileiro - *Scorpene*-class)	SSK	4	see notes	FRA	DCNS	2009	2017	Part of €6.7bn (US$8.3bn) naval programme. To be built by Itaguaí Construções Navais (JV between DCNS and Odebrecht). Delivery to be completed 2022
NAPA 500 (*Vigilante*-class 400 CL 54)	PCC	6	n.k.	BRZ/FRA	INACE/CMN/2nd batch: EISA	2006	2009	Delivery in progress. Call for tender for 3rd batch in early 2010
Marlim-class	PB	5	n.k.	BRZ	INACE	2007	n.k.	Delivery status unclear
P-3A *Orion*	ASW ac Upgrade	8	US$401m	ESP	EADS CASA	2005	n.k.	Upgrade to P-3AM. Option on a 9th ac. First ac upgraded by Apr 2009
Mi-35M *Hind* (AH-2 *Sabre*)	Atk Hel	12	US$150-300m	RUS	Rosoboron-export	2008	2009	Contract value incl spares and trg. First three delivered 2009. 3 more delivered 2010.
S-70B *Seahawk*	ASW Hel	4	US$195m	US	Sikorsky	2009	n.k.	Option for 2 more. To replace SH-3A/B *Sea King* hels. To be delivered by 2012
AS-365K *Panther*	MRH Hel	34	R376m (US$215m)	BRZ	EADS Brazil	2009	2011	To be manufactured in BRZ by Helibras. Final delivery due 2021
EC-725 *Super Cougar*	Tpt Hel	50	US$2bn	BRZ	EADS Brazil	2008	2010	First three to be built in FRA. Remainder to be manufactured in BRZ by Helibras
UH-60L *Black Hawk*	Tpt Hel	10	US$60.4m	US	Sikorsky	2009	2010	For air force SAR. Part of FMS programme
Heron-1	ISR UAV	14	US$350m	ISR	Israel Aerospace Industries	2009	2010	For Federal Police
Derby	BVRAAM	n.k.	n.k.	ISR	Rafael	2006	2006	For F-5M ftr. Delivery underway
A-*Darter*	AAM	n.k.	ZAR1bn (US$143m)	BRZ/RSA	Denel	2007	n.k.	As of 2009, AAM undergoing flight trials and delayed by budget problems. Intended to arm F-5M. Expected ISD 2015

Table 20 **Selected Arms Procurements and Deliveries, Latin America and the Caribbean**

Designation	Type	Quantity	Contract Value	Supplier Country	Prime Contractor	Order Date	First Delivery Due	Notes
Chile (CHL)								
Satellite	Sat	1	US$72m	FRA/GER	EADS	2008	2010	Role incl border surv and military uses. Financed by military
Piloto Pardo-class	PSO	4	See notes	CHL/GER	ASMAR	2005	2008	Fassmer OPV 80 design. First two in service with coast guard
F-16AM/BM *Fighting Falcon*	Ftr ac	18	US$270m	NLD	n.k.	2008	2010	Ex-NLD stock. To replace Northrop F-5E *Tiger* II (*Tigre* III). Delivery commenced Nov 2010
C-295 MPA	MP ac	3	US$120m	ESP	EADS CASA	2007	n.k.	For navy. Cost incl ASM and torp. Option for a further 5 MPA. First delivered Apr 2010
KC-135E	Tkr ac	3	n.k.	US	Boeing	2010	2010	Delivery in progress. One may be used for spares
Colombia (COL)								
M1117 *Guardian*	APC (W)	39	US$35m	US	Textron	2009	n.k.	Further requirement for 30 APCs. Delivery status unclear
LG1 Mk II, 105 mm	Towed 105mm Arty	20	n.k.	FRA	Nexter	2009	2010	Delivery to be completed by end 2010
July 20 class	PSO	1	n.k.	COL	Cotecmar shipyard	2008	2011	Based on Fassmer OPV 80 design. Launched July 2010. Due to commission 2011
n.k.	PCC	1	n.k.	GER	Fassmer	2010	n.k	Delivery status unclear
PAF-L (light)	PBR	10	n.k.	COL	Cotecmar shipyard	n.k.	2010	In development
Kfir C10	FGA ac	24	US$200m (est)	ISR	IAI	2008	2009	Ex ISR stock, upgraded from C7 to C10 by IAI. First delivery mid-2009; deliveries ongoing
Beech 350 *King Air*	Tpt ac	1	US$6.2m	US	Hawker Beechcraft	2010	2011	For ISR role
Ecuador (ECU)								
Leopard 1V	MBT	30	n.k.	CHL	n.k.	2009	2009	Ex-CHL stock. To replace 90 AMX-13. Deliveries ongoing
Shyri (Type 209/1300)	SSK Upgrade	2	US$120m	CHL	ASMAR/ DCNS	2008	2012	SLEP. To extend service life by 20 years
Cheetah C	FGA ac	12	n.k.	RSA	Denel	2010	n.k.	Second hand RSA ac. Delivery status unclear
XAC MA-60	Tpt Ac	4	US$60m	PRC	CATIC	2009	n.k.	For air force. To replace BAE 748-SRS-2A. Delivery status unclear
Mi-17 *Hip*	MRH Hel	2	n.k.	RUS	Rosoboron-export	2009	n.k.	Delivery status unclear
Heron + *Searcher*	ISR UAV	6	US$23m	ISR	IAI	2008	2009	2 *Heron*, 4 *Searcher*, plus radar, control stations, spares and trg. Delivery status unclear
Mexico (MEX)								
CN-235 MPA *Persuader*	MP ac	6	n.k.	ESP	EADS CASA	2008	2010	2 ordered under Merida Initiative; rest part of Mexican Navy order for 4 Cn-235s and 2 C-295s. 4 ac delivered
EC-725 *Super Cougar*	Tpt hel	6	n.k.	Int'l	Eurocopter	2009	2011	For tpt and civil sy missions
EC-725 *Super Cougar*	Tpt hel	6	n.k.	Int'l	Eurocopter	2010	n.k.	Follow on from similar order signed in 2009. Delivery status unclear
UH-60M *Black Hawk*	Tpt Hel	3	US$35.2m	US	Sikorsky	2010	n.k.	Contact to be completed by end 2012. Delivery status unclear

Table 20 **Selected Arms Procurements and Deliveries, Latin America and the Caribbean**

Designation	Type	Quantity	Contract Value	Supplier Country	Prime Contractor	Order Date	First Delivery Due	Notes
S4 *Ehecatl* (S4E)	ISR UAV	3	US$3m	MEX	Hydra Technologies	2009	n.k.	For navy. Primary anti-narcotics role & secondary SAR role. Delivery status unclear
Panama (PAN)								
AW-139	Tpt Hel	6	n.k.	ITA/UK	Agusta Westland	2010	n.k.	4 for national/public security roles, 1 for utility role, 1 for VIP tpt role. Delivery status unclear
Peru (PER)								
Clavero-class	PCC	2	n.k.	PER	Sima	n.k.	2008	First of class (CF-16) launched Jun 2008, commissioned 2010. Second of class expected to commission 2011
Newport-class	LST	2	n.k.	US	n.k.	2009	n.k.	Ex-US stock. USS *Fresno* (LST 1182) and USS *Racine* (LST 1191). Delivery status unclear
Mi-35 *Hind*	Atk Hel	2	see notes	RUS	Rosoboronexport	2010	2010	Part of εUS$250m order for 6 Mi-17 and 2 Mi-35. Delivery to be complete by end 2011
Mi-17 *Hip*	MRH Hel	6	see notes	RUS	Rosoboronexport	2010	2010	Part of εUS$250m order for 6 Mi-17 and 2 Mi-35. Delivery to be complete by end 2011
UH-3H *Sea King*	Tpt Hel	6	US$6m	US	n.k.	2009	n.k.	Ex-US stock. Likely to be for SAR. Delivery status unclear
Suriname (SUR)								
Dhruv	MRH Hel	3	INR750m (US$15.3m)	IND	HAL	2009	n.k.	For tpt role
Trinidad and Tobago (TTO)								
Port of Spain-class	PSO	3	GB£150m (US$296m)	UK	BAE Systems	2007	2010	Fist two launched 2009, but not delivered. Work on third hull stopped; order may be cancelled
AW-139	MRH Hel	4	US$348m	ITA/UK	Agusta Westland	2009	n.k.	For air guard (TTAG). Contract inc trg & log spt for 5 yrs. Delivery status unclear
Venezuela (VEN)								
T-72 M1M	MBT	92	n.k.	RUS	n.k.	2009	n.k.	Delivery status unclear. Financing reportedly from loan agreement with Moscow
Tor-M1	SAM	3 bty	n.k.	RUS	Rosoboronexport	2006	2007	First bty delivered Dec 2007. Further delivery status unclear
Project 636 (Imp *Kilo*)	SSK	1	n.k.	RUS	n.k.	2008	n.k.	*Varshavyanka* (Original procurement plan of 3 SSK reduced for financial reasons)
POVZEE	PSOH	4	See notes	ESP	Navantia	2005	2010	US$2.2bn incl 4 *Buque de Vigilancia de Litoral*-class coastal patrol ships. Final delivery due 2011. Contract may be extended to 6 vessels
BVL type	PSOH	4	See notes	ESP	Navantia	2005	2008	€1.2bn (USD1.5bn) incl 4 FS. To replace 6 *Constitution*-class. Final delivery due 2011. Contract may be extended to 6 vessels

Chapter Nine
Sub-Saharan Africa

AFRICAN PEACE AND SECURITY ARCHITECTURE

Moves to improve the capacities of African militaries for peacekeeping actions and other continental contingencies have been a preoccupation of many defence and foreign policy establishments in 2010. Specifically, governments in Africa and beyond keenly observed progress on the African Peace and Security Architecture (APSA) and the African Standby Force, though there was some concern about results of the final exercise cycle. In spite of the efforts of the African Union to enhance its diplomatic and military capabilities, African nations still lack the capacities to deal with many of the substantial challenges facing the continent. The biggest challenge for APSA is not disagreement on the need to intervene in complex emergencies, but rather the question of how to equip, fund and sustain such interventions.

Towards the African Standby Force (ASF)

As noted in *The Military Balance* 2010 (p. 284), the ASF is the African Union (AU)'s prescribed instrument for eventually meeting the military demands of the continent, with five brigades of roughly 6,500 soldiers planned. These brigades tend to be based on Africa's regional economic communities, such as the Southern African Development Community (SADC), but since membership of the economic organisations is not always determined by geographical location, and since members are not restricted to a single affiliation, the AU established 'Regional Mechanisms for Conflict Prevention, Management and Resolution'. 'The Policy Framework for the Establishment of the ASF' sets out six scenarios, designed as contingency-planning guidelines for the five regional brigades:

- **Scenario one**: AU/regional military advice to a political mission, deployment within 30 days of mandate;
- **Scenario two**: AU/regional observer mission co-deployed with UN mission, within 30 days of mandate;
- **Scenario three**: Standalone AU/regional observer mission, within 30 days of mandate;
- **Scenario four**: AU/regional peacekeeping force for preventive deployment missions and those mandated under Chapter VI of the UN Charter, within 30 days of mandate;
- **Scenario five**: AU peacekeeping force for complex multidimensional peacekeeping mission, including low-level spoilers (a feature of many current conflicts), within 30 days of mandate for military – 90 days for other elements;
- **Scenario six**: AU intervention within 14 days of mandate, for instance in genocide situations where prompt international action has been lacking.

According to the 2005 AU APSA roadmap, the Standby Force must be ready to implement all of the conflict and missions scenarios – especially scenario six. The implementation plan contained two phased targets; the first was assessed to have been completed by 30 June 2006. This included – for the AU – planning elements that would enable the management of political missions and an AU observer mission. Regions, meanwhile, were to stand up planning elements, brigade headquarters and regional standby arrangements. Implementation was at times problematic, with regional forces being selectively implemented for reasons of practicality; nonetheless, these planning elements existed in one form or another in all brigades. Phase-two objectives to develop the ability to manage complex missions as well as a roster of civilian experts, and the regions' ability to deploy a mission HQ for contingencies mandated under Chapter VI of the UN Charter, were to be completed by 30 June 2010.

To gauge the readiness of the brigades in relation to this roadmap, the AU prepared a major test exercise, *Amani Africa*, for October 2010, as part of a continental training cycle designed to accelerate and validate the ASF's state of operational readiness. In preparation for *Amani Africa*, the regional brigades

ASF Regional Brigades:

North African Regional Standby Brigade (NASBRIG – HQ: Tripoli, Libya): Algeria, Egypt, Libya, Mauritania, Tunisia, Western Sahara

Eastern Africa Standby Brigade (EASBRIG – HQ: Addis Ababa, Ethiopia): Burundi, Comoros, Djibouti, Eritrea, Ethiopia, Kenya, Madagascar, Mauritius, Rwanda, Seychelles, Somalia, Sudan, Tanzania, Uganda

Central African Multinational Force (*Force Multinationale de l'Afrique Centrale*) (FOMAC – HQ: Libreville, Gabon): Angola, Burundi, Cameroon, Central African Republic, Chad, Democratic Republic of the Congo, Equatorial Guinea, Gabon, Rwanda, São Tomé and Principe

Southern Africa Standby Brigade (SADCBRIG – HQ: Gabarone, Botswana): Angola, Botswana, Democratic Republic of the Congo, Lesotho, Madagascar, Malawi, Mozambique, Mauritius, Namibia, Seychelles, South Africa, Swaziland, Tanzania, Zambia, Zimbabwe

ECOWAS Standby Brigade (ECOBRIG – HQ: Abuja, Nigeria): Benin, Burkina Faso, Cape Verde, Côte d'Ivoire, Gambia, Ghana, Guinea, Guinea Bissau, Liberia, Mali, Niger, Nigeria, Senegal, Sierra Leone, Togo

were asked to plan and execute similar exercises during 2009 and 2010.

The September 2009 Southern Africa Standby Brigade (SADCBRIG) *Exercise Golfinho*, held in South Africa, was deemed a success. The field-training exercise (FTX) involving 7,000 troops from 12 countries, was preceded by a map exercise in Angola in January 2009 and a command-post exercise in Mozambique in April 2009. In an effort to prove its own operational competence, SADC decided not to draw on external support for the planning and execution of *Golfinho*; this was instead locally driven from the scenario-generation stage onwards. After the exercise, SADCBRIG declared that it could deploy to any location in Africa or even beyond, though the group did add the important caveat that this was dependent on available strategic lift and sustainable logistical support; two factors that remain substantial impediments for all Standby Brigade operations.

The Eastern African Standby Brigade (EASBRIG) conducted its FTX in Djibouti from 16–29 November 2009. Personnel from Burundi, Comoros, Djibouti, Ethiopia, Kenya, Rwanda, Sudan, Seychelles, Somalia and Uganda participated in training scenarios that included armed groups manning illegal vehicle check points, vehicle hijackings and roadblocks. The goal

was to learn how to work together to bring stability and peace during unstable situations and to overcome logistical obstacles. Police and civilian specialists also participated in the scenarios. Unlike the SADCBRIG exercise, the EASBRIG exercise relied heavily on international support from the EASBRIG partnership countries: France, Denmark, Germany, Finland, Japan, Norway, the United Kingdom and the United States. The success of the exercise was due in no small part to this international support. But, as noted in an IISS *Strategic Comment* on the issue, 'AU's Regional Force Still on Standby', vol. 16, December 2010), the establishment of the Eastern Africa Standby Force (EASF) has been hampered by inadequate funding and regional tensions which have limited contributions of troops, police and civilians. It has been difficult to coordinate the establishment of brigade headquarters, logistics and planning. In addition, the EASF relies on a weak legal framework. Although member states renew troop pledges each year, there are no binding arrangements for deployments. Communications between the AU and other bodies are poor.

The Economic Community of West African States (ECOWAS) had an initial objective to establish a 6,500-strong task force by 2010, though just over 2,700 were confirmed as available in 2009. The force is structured into two infantry battalions (western, led by Senegal; and eastern, led by Nigeria) and a composite logistics battalion, constituting a task force designed for rapid mobilisation and deployment, though at the June 2010 EU–ECOWAS Ministerial Dialogue in Brussels, ECOWAS indicated that the next step towards fulfilling the AU roadmap would involve further improving the task force's rapid deployment capacity. It is intended that the task force can be augmented by a main standby force, prepared to deploy at longer notice. A headquarters has been established in Abuja, Nigeria. Military and police components are operational, and training is carried out at centres in Nigeria, Ghana and Mali. A logistics depot that will boost regional capacity to undertake peace-support operations is planned for Freetown, Sierra Leone (with US support), while a second depot in Mali, according to ECOWAS, will be orientated towards responses to humanitarian crises. The ECOWAS Standby Force, supported by United States Africa Command (AFRICOM), executed *Exercise Cohesion Benin 2010* in Benin from 12–18 April 2010, with the objective of evaluating the eastern battalion's operational and logistical readiness (the western

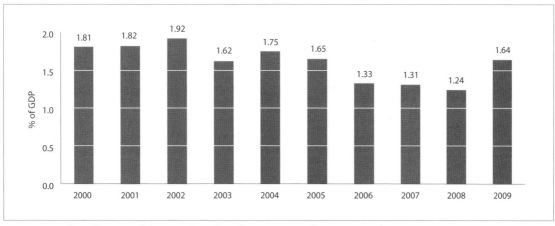

Figure 10 **Sub-Saharan Africa Regional Defence Expenditure** as % of GDP

and logistics battalion having been evaluated and validated in 2007 and 2009 respectively). Nearly 1,700 troops from Benin, Nigeria, Sierra Leone and Togo took part in the field training exercise, which ECOWAS deemed a success.

Meanwhile, soldiers, police officers and civilian staff of countries from the Economic Community of Central African States (ECCAS) conducted the *Kwanza 2010* exercise, from 22 May–10 June 2010 in Cabo Ledo, Angola. This exercise was designed to test the readiness for ASF status of the Central African Multinational Force (FOMAC), so that troops and relevant civilian components from its member states could be used in peace missions and humanitarian actions in Central Africa and beyond if required by the AU and the UN. Participants in the *Kwanza* exercise came from Angola, Burundi, Chad, Central African Republic, Cameroon, the Democratic Republic of the Congo, Equatorial Guinea, Gabon, and São Tomé and Principe. The focus of this exercise was on establishing security in scenarios based on African experiences, in which population security and health care were high priorities. According to US observers, participating troops took part in amphibious landings and parachute drops from a Cameroonian C-130, while also establishing two field hospitals to deliver health care to the local population. ECCAS has established a planning element, but has decided not to set up a permanent brigade headquarters; also, it has yet to develop a rapid-deployment capability.

According to the aforementioned IISS *Strategic Comment*, the North African Regional Capability (NARC) was created to fill a regional vacuum. The Arab Maghreb Union, which had become dormant following its establishment in 1989, proved difficult to

revitalise because of tensions among member states. Thus, there was a need to create a regional mechanism to enable North African countries to contribute to the ASF. Libya played a coordinating role in establishing the NARC, and at a meeting in Tripoli in 2008 it was agreed to locate an executive secretariat there. While all staff were initially Libyan, it was expected that staff from other member states would join in 2010. NARC is behind schedule in setting up its standby force. A brigade headquarters is to be established in Cairo, as well as logistic depots in Algiers and Cairo. Constitutional and legal regulations in some member states, such as Tunisia, have delayed ratification of a memorandum of understanding agreed in 2008 while the unresolved dispute over the status of the Western Sahara further complicates matters.

Towards *Amani Africa*

Exercise Amani Africa was opened on 13 October with a speech by Jean Ping, chair of the AU Commission. Ping reminded his audience of envoys, ambassadors, military dignitaries, commissioners and others of the ideals behind the establishment of the ASF. 'With the transformation from the Organization of African Unity into the African Union', he said, 'African leaders expressed both their desire and commitment to play a greater role in, and to take greater ownership of, peace and security on the African continent.' Ping said the lessons of the Cold War era and its aftermath had served as a reminder that, while partnership with the international community was important, the international community could not always be relied upon to address threats to peace and security on the African continent. 'Indeed', he went on, 'Somalia and Rwanda were painful lessons for us all. Within this

Sub-Saharan Africa

Standby Brigade optimal composition

- Brigade (Mission Level) HQ and support unit of up to 65 personnel and 16 vehicles
- HQ Company and support unit up to 120 personnel
- Four light infantry battalions, each composed of up to 750 personnel and 70 vehicles
- Engineer unit of up to 505 personnel
- Light signals unit of up to 135 personnel
- Reconnaissance company (Wheeled) of up to 150 personnel
- Helicopter unit of up to 80 personnel, 10 vehicles and 4 helicopters
- Military police unit of up to 48 personnel and 17 vehicles
- Light multi-role logistical unit of up to 190 personnel and 40 vehicles
- Level-2 medical unit of up to 35 personnel and 10 vehicles
- Military observer group of up to 120 officers
- Civilian support group consisting of logistical, administrative and budget components

Source 2005 ASF Roadmap

context, it became increasingly apparent that the AU would have to assume a greater responsibility for peace and security on the continent.'

To this end, the African Peace and Security Architecture (APSA), adopted by the AU Assembly in July 2002, consists of a Continental Early Warning System, a Panel of the Wise, the African Standby Force (ASF) and the Africa Peace Fund. A Post-Conflict Reconstruction and Development Framework was later included as an additional pillar. These instruments have given the AU the ability to analyse and manage conflicts through dialogue or intervention, and to assist societies to recover a sustainable and lasting peace.

International support has been vital in assisting the AU to progress more rapidly towards its goals. At the December 2007 Lisbon Summit, the European Union (EU) entered into a Strategic Partnership with the AU, recognising the importance of the AU's peace and security initiatives, as well as the importance to Europe of assisting peace and security in Africa given their geographical proximity. This partnership has centered on cooperation in the fields of peace and security, political relations, economic partnership and social development. Within the partnership framework, the EU has provided important support both to

the APSA and to the development and operationalisation of the ASF, which is seen as critical to the effective functioning of APSA. Without the ASF, AU Peace and Security Commission decisions regarding peace, security and stability in Africa could not be carried out effectively. To develop and test the AF concept, the AU and the EU decided to partner on the *Amani Africa* exercise cycle.

To assist this process, the EU has developed a new series of capacity-building exercises out of the Reinforcement of African Peace-keeping Capacities (RECAMP) initiative. EURORECAMP, as it is now called, supports the operational certification of the ASF at a continental level. France, the original proponent of the RECAMP cycles, remains the framework nation, as designated by the EU. According to the European Council's Special Adviser for Peace and Security, General Pierre-Michel Joana, speaking on 20 October 2010, the EU–Africa Peace and Security partnership aims to ensure 'adequate, coherent and sustainable support for the establishment and functioning of the African Peace and Security Architecture and for African-led efforts at all stages of the conflict cycle ... it also aims to promote long-term capacity building, including military and civilian crisis-management and coherent and coordinated support for the African Standby Forces'. EU support for the APSA has been helped by the establishment in 2004 of the African Peace Facility (APF), a funding mechanism which had channelled some €740 million (US$973.6m) in assistance by November 2010. The scope of this facility was broadened in 2007 to 'cover conflict prevention and post-conflict stabilisation' and, according to the EU, in terms of capacity building, the APF assists in bolstering the AU's Peace and Security Department, 'strengthening conflict prevention capacities, as well as reinforcing the planning and management capacities of the AU Commission, the Regional Economic Communities and the African Standby Force'.

Amani Africa was not a single exercise, but rather a cycle of exercises conducted since 2008. The primary objectives have been to test and evaluate the capacities and procedures for the engagement of the ASF in multidimensional peace support operations; to practise the establishment of a mission headquarters for an ASF deployment, including the production of an integrated mission plan; and to increase awareness of ASF capabilities, procedures and requirements among the senior leadership of the AU Commission and among member states. The main activities within the exercise cycle have included:

- A Strategic Decision-makers' Seminar in March 2009. This documented staff procedures and the decision-making process that were later developed into a Draft Aide Memoire to inform the subsequent major cycle activities and act as a planning document for deployment of the ASF.
- A Level I Decision-Making Exercise, or map exercise, in June 2009. This was the first major practical exercise of the *Amani Africa* cycle, comprising a series of studies, discussions and exercises practising all aspects of the deployment of an integrated AU mission.
- A Political-Strategic Seminar/Strategic Conference in November 2009. This tested the AU Commission's staff procedures for the planning and mandating of an AU mission and associated staff procedures. This conference produced the Mission Mandate and Draft Mission Plan for the AU Mission in Carana, a state on the fictitious island of Kisiwa, off the east coast of Africa. This was the scenario used for the final *Amani Africa* exercise.
- The cycle concluded with the Level II Decision-Making Exercise or Command Post Exercise (CPX) in Addis Ababa from 13–29 October 2010. The continental CPX was the culmination of the efforts to evaluate the entire ASF, and was aimed at evaluating the capacity and procedures for its engagement in a multidimensional peace-support operation. (This corresponds to the fourth scenario prescribed in the policy framework for the establishment of the ASF and the AU's Military Staff Committee) The exercise management consisted of a small directing staff responsible for achieving exercise objectives. As is often the case with such exercises, the exercise control team controlled the pace of the exercise (its 'battle rhythm') by 'injecting' incidents into the general flow of the exercise to test responses by the strategic and mission headquarters.

The CPX involved more than 200 people (120 military and police officers and 75 civilians) from the Eastern African Standby Brigade, the West African Brigade (ECOWAS Standby Force), the North African Brigade, the Southern African Brigade and the Central African Brigade, as well as personnel from EU partners. Chiefs of staff (CoS) of the regional standby force's planning elements and some other dignitaries were invited as observers to monitor the 'warm-up' phase from 20–23 October. While the exercise concluded on 29 October with Presidents' Day, when various dignitaries attended the final phase of the exercise, some exercise participants went into a fourth week with a report-writing stage.

These evaluation and first-impression reports were to be conducted in the first week of November, immediately after the CPX, while a final report incorporating a 'lessons learned' document was to be discussed at a conference in March 2011.

Evaluating the success of *Amani Africa*

The overall aim of the *Amani Africa* cycle was to test and evaluate the capacities and procedures for using the ASF in multidimensional peace-support operations (PSO). Joint deployment of participants from different countries during the exercises and specialisations (police, military or civilian), as well as the testing of procedures for the involvement of the AU's Peace and Security Council (PSC), Peace and Security Department, and Commission senior management, were assessed to have worked adequately. However, the exercise did not test the capacity of the AU's Peace Support Operations Department (PSOD) to organise and manage a PSO, as most of the relevant posts for the exercise cycle were occupied by non-PSOD staff. Furthermore, many personnel were found to be unfamiliar with the approved ASF guidance documentation, resulting in the use of national procedures and standards.

A further objective, according to Jean Ping, was to 'practise the establishment of a mission headquarters for an ASF deployment, including the production of an integrated mission plan'. Some analysts have reported that linguistic differences caused problems in establishing a functioning mission headquarters. This was despite the use of English as the mission's language. Communication problems also arose in relation to general mission correspondence as well as the unavailability of relevant communications infrastructure and – when this was present – unfamiliarity with such equipment. With regard to a further objective of the cycle, 'to increase awareness of the ASF capabilities, procedures and requirements among the senior leadership of the AU Commission and among Member States', the picture was again mixed. The involvement of regional chiefs of staff and others as observers on the VIP days (there were also press

Sub-Saharan Africa

days) has helped inform the general public and other stakeholders about the complexities of conducting PSO missions, while the direct involvement of senior AU personnel indicates that the AU is investing some political capital in this area. However, the AU and its Peace Support Operations Department could also invest in a more comprehensive ASF concept 'marketing plan' to continue the momentum established by *Amani Africa*. The relatively low numbers of African ambassadors attending exercise elements has indicated that more could be done to encourage 'ownership' of the ASF concept.

But the exercise cycle has resulted in the establishment of a body of knowledge that now requires development, for example, on AU doctrine, policies and procedures. A bigger pool of dedicated staff must be prepared, while training in mission planning (at the operational and strategic levels) could be increased. Training for and development related to peace-support operations should be conducted in accordance with AU/UN standards. Speaking at the end of the exercise, Jean Ping said further development of African PSO capacity was needed, particularly in terms of personnel and hardware. In future, though, the partnership with the EU and others (such as the US AFRICOM) will be increasingly important, to meet the challenge facing African states in broadening their pool of peacekeepers as well as their effectiveness. This can be achieved through improved training, better equipment and streamlined procedure, though substantial problems remain in acquiring and integrating the resources necessary to enable rapid deployment and to sustain such bodies of personnel.

The main benefits of the ASF development process include the emergence of common policy documents, an annual continental training programme and improved training standards, but these standby forces remain generally at an initial operational capability due to institutional and logistic factors. Meanwhile, the development of national rapid-deployment capabilities (the means by which nations are supposed to fill their ASF contingents) are advancing, though not at a uniform pace. Certain national developments, such as the Ugandan Rapid Deployment Force, have progressed, while developments are under way in national training (on top of the regional training offered by the established peacekeeping training centres). Botswana's three-year-old Defence Command and Staff College, for instance, is to move in 2012 to new purpose-built facilities north of Gabarone, where it will reportedly start taking students from other African countries.

Progress has also been made in better understanding the role of the police in peacekeeping, though forming a police component is more difficult at the regional level. But problems persist in operationalising a civilian component, due to a lack of understanding about the potential roles, functions, structures and composition of such a grouping. The view persists that peacekeeping missions should remain the purview of the military and/or other government staff. The civilian component should provide leadership and policy development, and coordinate and facilitate – in accordance with national norms – the work of other actors active from the fields of humanitarian aid, human rights, disarmament, demobilisation and reintegration (DDR), security-sector reform, and the safeguarding of vulnerable groups such as women and children. (This is perhaps at odds with the conception of civilian capacities now seen in some European states, where deployable civilian contingents are under development and are seen as an integral part of a civil–military response to existing and developing crisis situations.) Further tasks could include key support functions, finance, legal, contracting, procurement, conduct and discipline in AU and regional organisations, including ASF headquarters in the field.

Meanwhile, the strategic and policy environments have changed substantially since discussions began on the ASF concept: the original vision was that Standby Brigades could deploy on their own. The concept was focused on the military instrument, with a clear view that peacekeeping was essentially a military activity with other actors there to support the military force. But of the debate on the nature of peacekeeping is changing and the importance of integrated missions, combining military, civilian, and non-governmental efforts is no longer questioned. Some analysts have even argued that the original six scenarios set out in the policy framework for the establishment of the ASF need to be reviewed. It is thought that this would allow changes in the threats to African security to be addressed; it could also allow greater incorporation of multi-dimensional aspects, such as political factors, into conflict management. But a review would have a direct impact on the capabilities required for the ASF. Maritime threats, for instance, were not originally considered of great relevance, though these have now emerged as key issues.

In developing future work on the ASF roadmap, towards its development stage, Roadmap III

(Roadmap I set created basic policy documents for the ASF, while Roadmap II worked towards *Amani Africa* and ASF concept validation), policymakers may now have to consider a further set of issues: operationalising national rapid-deployment capacities; developing a coordination mechanism for police contingents; enabling the AU commission to manage civilian components; and coordinating ASF mission- and leadership-training.

When the ASF concept was first agreed in 2003, it was hoped that the forces could be operational by 2010. Notwithstanding the efforts that have taken place as part of the ASF process, and within the *Amani Africa* cycle, this has not been achieved; it is more doubtful still that continental forces could successfully intervene in a scenario-six action without substantial international assistance. Many African militaries lack the force enablers that would allow them to deploy, intervene and sustain their forces and, while there has been some progress in establishing the rapid deployment capacities required to staff the ASF brigades, maintaining this capability at a readiness-level that would enable rapid response remains a challenge; financing such capabilities remains a further challenge. But there is some progress, with international support important to further development.

International assistance

The lessons from the AU deployments into Darfur and Somalia have proved salutary. Deployment and sustainment have proved problematic, but in the case of the Somalia mission, filling the force has proved as troublesome. When originally deployed, the AMISOM deployment lacked a full complement of personnel, and this has continued. The UN provides substantial support to the mission through its United Nations Support Office to AMISOM (UNSOA). This provides, according to an October 2010 UN report, 'the delivery of rations, fuel, general stores and medical supplies; engineering and construction of key facilities; health and sanitation; medical evacuation and treatment services and medical equipment for AMISOM medical facilities; communications and information technology; information support services; aviation services for evacuations and troop rotations; vehicles and other equipment; and capacity-building. UNSOA is also providing training support to AU nations, particularly those deploying to the AMISOM mission, with some personnel embedded in the AMISOM planning and operations staff in Nairobi before deployment, while in Nairobi and Mogadishu UNSOA is engaged in training logistics personnel. The UN, meanwhile, conducts similar training and support activities as part of its other missions in Africa, while the EU – as discussed above in the context of the support it gives to the developing ASF concept – offers substantial assistance to other nations. Like the UN, the EU provides much financial and advisory support, as well as mounting its own missions. Back as far as *Operation Artemis* in 2003, and the EUFOR Tchad/RCA from 2008–09, Europe has been developing its contribution to the provision of personnel and equipment in a bid to more directly support peace and security in Africa. The most recent mission to be established is the training mission for Somalia (EUTM Somalia), based in Uganda, where Somali forces started training in May.

But important support is also provided by the United States. The troubled emergence of US Africa Command (AFRICOM) has been traced in previous editions of *The Military Balance*. The command still lacks an African home and is headquartered in Stuttgart, Germany (though Camp Lemonier, Djibouti – home to the Combined Joint Task Force-Horn of Africa – remains a key continental base). However, US forces are actively engaged across the continent, both on activities directed towards counter-terrorism and also in support of AFRICOM's wider agenda; that command's priorities are couched in inter-agency terms, stressing war prevention over war fighting, long-term capacity building and African ownership and responsibility, with an emphasis on creating stability on the continent.

One of AFRICOM's principal instruments remains the US Navy's Africa Partnership Station (APS), which now includes activities with nations in East Africa and the western Indian Ocean (initially, activity was focused in West Africa and the Gulf of Guinea). According to the 2010 Posture Statement of AFRICOM commander General William Ward, 'APS builds maritime security capabilities in our Africa partners using sea-based training platforms to provide predictable regional presence with a minimal footprint ashore'. But other navies are also involved: in recent years the UK's HMS *Ocean* and the Dutch vessel *Johan de Witt* have also participated. Planning stages for the 2011 APS deployment were under way in September 2010, with the final planning conferences for APS 2011 East and West taking place at the Naples headquarters of the US Sixth Fleet. The APS West Conference will be held in Libreville, Gabon, with the APS East conference in Dar Es Salaam, Tanzania. According to Rear

Admiral Gerard Hueber, US Naval Forces Europe–Africa deputy chief of staff for strategy, resources and plans: 'specifically in APS 2011, we are looking for more under-way operations, more exercises, rather than classroom training. African partners in their ships and boats, with their crews and teams patrolling their waters.' Other major US initiatives include the biennial *Natural Fire* exercise designed to address complex humanitarian emergencies – with the next due in late 2011 – as well as initiatives such as the African Land Forces Summit, which in May 2010 saw 44 African chiefs of staff gather in Washington to discuss the theme 'Adapting Land Forces to Twenty-first-Century Challenges.' But counter-terrorism remains another focus for US and partner activities in Africa.

SOMALIA

Recent editions of *The Military Balance* have analysed the activities of Islamist groups in Somalia, as well as the actions of the AU and other international actors (including the US) in addressing these groups. As detailed in a September 2010 *Strategic Comment* by the IISS, attacks in 2010 by the Somali group Harakat al-Shabaab al-Mujahideen (al-Shabaab) have demonstrated its ability to strike outside its usual territory and have stoked fears that it could be evolving into a transnational terror group. But these attacks have also indicated that the group's primary focus is on unseating Somalia's Western-supported Transitional Federal Government (TFG). On 11 July 2010, al-Shabaab bombed a restaurant and a rugby club in Kampala, Uganda, killing 76 people as they watched the FIFA World Cup final. The presence of Ugandan troops in AMISOM was the purported justification for the attack. Then, in late August, al-Shabaab launched a ten-day assault on Mogadishu in which over 100 people died, including 31 in a single suicide attack. On 10 September, suicide bombers attacked Mogadishu Airport, killing at least 14 people, including two AU soldiers. Following the Kampala bombings and al-Shabaab's August offensive in Mogadishu, the Ugandan government indicated that it was ready to send an additional 10,000 troops to Somalia if the US were to fund the deployment. Washington, which has already committed $185 million in support of AMISOM, immediately agreed to bankroll the deployment of another 1,000 Ugandan peacekeepers and called on other countries to provide additional manpower, equipment and financial support. The EU also announced that it would disburse €47m (US$61.8m) to support AMISOM, bringing its cumulative contribution to €142m (US$186.8m) – roughly on a par with the US commitment. However, a lack of mutual trust between the TFG and AMISOM limits the scope for AMISOM-based efforts to empower the TFG. Moreover, a dramatic increase in the foreign-troop presence in Somalia carries its own risks, as it gives jihadists an added pretext for violence.

Washington reviewed its Somalia policy in light of these incidents, and there appeared to be some possibility that AFRICOM would train TFG forces directly. Such a development would, however, constitute a significant shift in US policy, which has so far been limited to pre-deployment training for Ugandan and Burundian AMISOM troops in their countries of origin and for officers at the International Peace Support Training Centre in Kenya. Washington has also equipped the AMISOM soldiers, provided financial assistance and political support to the TFG and carried out occasional counter-terrorism operations in Somalia with TFG consent.

Targeted killings of prominent al-Shabaab figures by the US have included a May 2008 air-strike from an AC-130 that killed the group's then-leader, Aden Hashi Ayro, and the September 2009 killing of its military commander, Saleh Ali Saleh Nabhan, by a US Navy SEAL team inserted by helicopter. These operations have dealt short-term blows to jihadism in the region. Over the longer term, however, they have tended to intensify anti-American and anti-TFG attitudes among Somalis, as well as terrorist impulses, because of the civilian casualties resulting from some operations (for example, the June 2007 shelling by a US Navy destroyer of suspected terrorist training camps and a March 2008 US air-strike, targeting Nabhan, on the Somali town of Dobley). For now, the US and its major partners will probably intensify intelligence collection and the direct targeting of al-Shabaab militants with precision air-strikes and special-operations assaults, making sure to minimise any collateral damage that would turn the Somali population against the US and the TFG. The aim of such attacks would be to make Somalia a more dangerous place for al-Shabaab itself and a less attractive haven for jihadists from farther afield.

Piracy in Somalia

Despite the presence of three multinational naval task groups and assets from more than 15 countries deployed specifically to counter the threat to commer-

Map 6 **Piracy off the Coast of Somalia**

© IISS

Pirate attacks off Somalia increased in number and extent in 2010, despite the deployment of multinational and independent forces. As of 1 January 2011, according to the International Maritime Bureau, 27 vessels and 625 hostages were being held by pirates in Somalia. One problem for navies deployed to the region is the large area (more than 3.4 million km²) requiring patrols. Moreover, judicial difficulties occur when pirates are captured: Kenya has proven reluctant to prosecute all suspected pirates, and few other regional countries are willing to do so. As it stands, the cost-benefit analysis for the pirates weighs too heavily in favour of the benefits, with ransoms peaking at near US$9.5 million in 2010 and little judicial recourse if captured. As such, even with the various counter-piracy operations, Somali piracy seems set to continue in 2011.

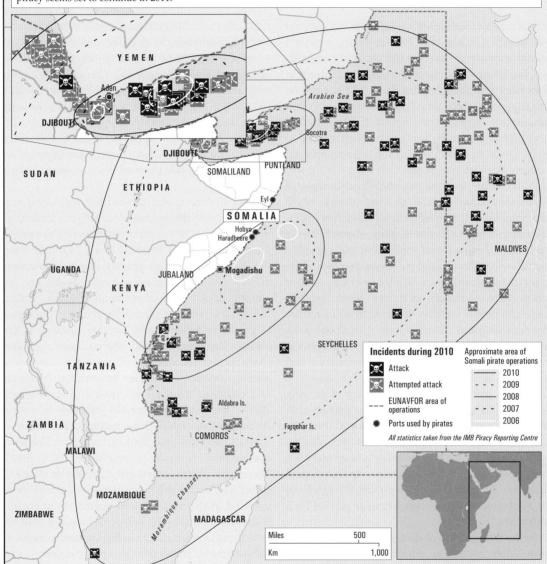

Incidents during 2010

- ☠ (black box) Attack
- ☠ (grey box) Attempted attack
- – – – EUNAVFOR area of operations
- ● Ports used by pirates

Approximate area of Somali pirate operations
- —— 2010
- – – – 2009
- –·–· 2008
- – – – 2007
- —— 2006

All statistics taken from the IMB Piracy Reporting Centre

2010 Timeline

11 Mar NATO extends *Operation Ocean Shield* until the end of 2012.

1 Apr Kenya announces that it will no longer take on trials of Somali pirates. Although trials continue, further obstructions throughout the year signal Nairobi's unwillingness to prosecute all suspected pirates.

27 Apr UNSCR 1918 calling on all states to criminalise piracy under their domestic laws is adopted unanimously.

6 May Russian special forces storm the Liberian-flagged *Moscow University*. Russian officials later announce that 10 pirates released by the navy in a skiff 300 nautical miles offshore are dead.

22 Jun The Netherlands announces the first deployment of a submarine in

anti-piracy operations – one of its four *Walrus*-class submarines joined *Ocean Shield* between September and November.

26 Aug French national Jack Lang appointed UN special adviser on legal issues related to Somali piracy.

7 Nov The largest-ever ransom of $9.5m is paid for the release of the *Samho Dream*, a South Korean oil tanker hijacked in April.

23 Nov UNSCR 1950 extends EUNAVFOR mission for another year.

23 Nov 10 Somalis go on trial in Hamburg for their attempt to hijack the German MS *Taipan* container ship in April, Germany's first such trial in 400 years.

24 Nov A Virginia court convicts five Somalis of attacking USS *Nicholas* in April, the first US piracy conviction in nearly 200 years.

cial shipping, piracy still reached record levels in 2010. According to the International Maritime Organisation, as of 4 November 438 sailors and 20 ships were being held by pirates off the coast of Somalia. According to the International Maritime Bureau, Somali pirates were responsible for 35 successful hijackings in the first nine months of the year. By comparison, 34 hijackings occurred globally in the same period in 2009.

The reasons for the continued growth in piracy are well known. The economic benefits to impoverished coastal societies of piracy, with its quick rewards and low set-up costs, are evident. In two ransoms in November 2010 alone, approximately US$12.3 million was supposedly paid for a South Korean tanker and Singaporean-flagged container ship. The former vessel, the *Samho Dream*, was a record ransom paid to pirates, with an initial demand for US$20m reduced through negotiation to $9.5m.

At the same time, the potential disadvantages of piracy are not high enough to deter activity. While some pirates have been killed in special-forces operations to free hijacked vessels, most suspects merely have their weapons and equipment and possibly mother-ship destroyed and are released on their skiffs to return to Somali shores. Efforts have been made to secure more convictions of pirates. More than 700 suspected pirates are now detained in 12 countries, and some regional countries have carried out prosecutions. Kenya has led the way with 50 convictions, the Seychelles has carried out 31 prosecutions and secured 22 convictions, as of November 2010. The low rate is partly down to the problem of proving suspected pirates' intent, which may be unclear until they board a ship at the time of hijacking. The presence of ladders and rocket-propelled grenades on board a skiff, which are obviously unnecessary for fishing purposes, has however helped to identify and subsequently detain suspected pirates, though these may constitute the conclusive evidence needed for a conviction.

In the face of these challenges, the naval deployments themselves can do little but address the piratical symptoms of the problems stemming from land-based ungoverned spaces. In a clear demonstration that their task is a difficult one to manage, EUNAVFOR, the European Union force tasked with addressing piracy, increased its area of operations in September 2010 further eastward into the Indian Ocean, acknowledging the 'balloon effect' of patrols and counter-piracy operations, whereby the activity of pirates is displaced to other areas of the Indian Ocean but not reduced.

In essence, the counter-piracy missions are unlikely to succeed in eliminating piracy until greater governance can be established in Somalia itself. To this end, the EU created a €5m (US$6.6m) training mission (EUTM Somalia) in January 2010, to enhance capacity building. Approximately 1,000 Somalis were to be trained by the end of 2010, and a further 1,000 in the first half of 2011. NATO has attempted to build a closer working relationship with the nascent Puntland coast guard, for example by providing fuel and embarking officers on HMS *Cornwall* and USS *Donald Cook* for short periods. The African Union Mission in Somalia (AMISOM) wants to train a further 6,000 security forces, but the problems of attempting such capacity building were made apparent when hundreds of Somalis trained in US-supported programmes in Djibouti and Uganda deserted in 2010 owing to a lack of funds.

Beyond dealing with piracy itself, there appear to have been side-effects to the counter-piracy missions in the Gulf of Aden, primarily through increasing interaction between various navies. Not only have the multinational deployments allowed collaboration of various countries' maritime assets, but the nations deploying independently (Russia, China, India, Malaysia and Japan) have also coordinated to greater or lesser extents with the missions in the region. The Bahrain-based Shared Awareness and Deconfliction (Shade) forum, created in December 2008 to coordinate activities between the coalitions and countries involved in regional counter-piracy efforts, has facilitated monthly discussions among its 26 member states. Three multinational missions and tactical communications systems have also been opened to all the navies present in the Gulf of Aden. Though the effects of these efforts on the incidence of piracy may be limited, they suggest a desire by those involved in the multinational operations to engage those nations deploying independently, not only for tactical purposes, but to open lines of communication between the militaries deployed in the region.

SUDAN

As the year drew to a close, attention both on the continent and abroad focused again on the situation in Sudan, notably in light of the referendum in South Sudan on independence from the North, which took place in early January 2011. Recent editions of *The*

Military Balance have highlighted the disputes that have led to instability in the south. The January 2005 Comprehensive Peace Agreement has been notable for its fragility, with tension rising in the face of the 2011 referendum; while in the north, low-level conflict has continued in Darfur.

According to the UN, the security situation in Darfur remains 'fragile and unpredictable'. The UN–AU mission in Darfur, UNAMID, has faced a series of attacks both from armed formations as well as criminal elements, and progress towards UNAMID's benchmarks remains mixed. Progress towards the first benchmark – achieving a political solution to the conflict through adherence to the Darfur Peace Agreement – has been limited by weak support for the agreement as well as the parties' failure to discuss subsequent agreements, the UN said. UNAMID's progress on the second of the four benchmarks, contributing to 'the restoration of a stable and secure environment throughout Darfur' is also problematic. The armed incidents that have affected the mission, as well as general restrictions on movement arising from instability, have limited progress. UNAMID remains hampered by the problem that has affected the mission since its inception: filling mission posts. As of September 2010, it was operating at 77% of its approved civilian strength of 5,516, while the military contingent – at 17,199 – was 87% of the authorised strength of 19,555.

But the most pressing issue in Sudan remains the referendum on self-determination for South Sudan, the culmination of the process initiated by the 2005 Comprehensive Peace Agreement (CPA). At the time of writing the result of the referendum was unclear, as were the security implications of a 'yes' vote. But, given the problems that the south has seen in recent years, in the event of a positive vote, it is certain that complex negotiations will need to take place over issues such as border demarcation, citizenship and oil revenue. It should be remembered that in July 2009, after a judgment by the Permanent Court of Arbitration in The Hague, the north was awarded the Bamboo and Heglig oilfields, the railway town of Meiram and a strip of grazing land, while the south was allowed to retain the high-production Diffra oilfield and more grazing area than the north preferred. Clashes in the disputed – and oil-rich – Abyei region have in recent years produced substantial movements of displaced persons, as well as a large number of fatalities. Abyei, and the promise of substantial oil revenues in the region, complicate current negotiations, and raise the stakes with regard to the durability of a final settlement. The Joint Integrated Units, composed of government and Somalia People's Liberation Army/Movement (SPLA/M) forces – the only mandated security forces in Abyei – were 32,900-strong in August 2010 – about 83% of their mandated strength of 39,639, according to the UN. Uncertainty over the post-referendum status of these groups will be a matter for the security working group established by the parties to the CPA.

Further complications arise from the still-undefined border between the two regions, with some analysts arguing that a 'soft' border allowing some freedom of movement, could lower tension. But military disputes persist, not just between Khartoum and the southern headquarters in Juba. Intra-SPLA disputes have led to armed incidents and fatalities in 2010, while the Lord's Resistance Army (LRA) was also reported to have attacked a number of villages along the southern border with the DRC and Uganda. The UN Mission in Sudan (UNMIS) has deployed extra security, logistical and technical personnel to assist the referendum commissions, and in April 2010 the UN Security Council further extended the mandate of UNMIS until 30 April 2011, with further extensions possible if required. However, the decision by New Delhi to withdraw the Indian Aviation Unit containing six Mi-17 helicopters by 31 October means that the tactical mobility of UNMIS would be eroded. The UN was subsequently reported to be attempting to negotiate a commercial contract in the event that the decision was carried out.

Should the south vote for secession, these issues will prove challenging for the military and security forces of the new state, based on the SPLA/M forces. Though these have retained security responsibility in the south since the CPA was signed, southern leaders are keen to modernise their forces. International support is important in enabling this and in enhancing the training levels of the south's military forces so that these forces move away from their former incarnation as guerrilla forces. Challenges will lie in improving force mobility as well as in matters such as training and military education. Here international support will be important. AFRICOM, for instance, deployed personnel in 2009 to help the South Sudanese establish an NCO training academy. According to AFRICOM, 'academy instruction will include professional military concepts such as humanitarian law, rules of land warfare, and civilian control of the military', and the graduates of the academy will form an NCO cadre that, it is hoped, will over time form the basis of an NCO corps.

THE GREAT LAKES

In May 2010 the UN Security Council voted to extend the mandate of its mission in the Democratic Republic of the Congo. However, the UN Organisation Mission in the DRC (MONUC), which had been the largest peacekeeping force in the world, did not survive the process wholly intact. The UN renamed it the UN Organisation Stabilisation Mission in the DRC (MONUSCO). Two thousand personnel were due to withdraw, but this did not address the main concern of DRC President Joseph Kabila, who was reportedly keen for the withdrawal of the entire force. Kabila said DRC forces could continue the activities previously undertaken by MONUC. MONUSCO had a new mandate defined by the Security Council: the protection of civilians, including supporting the efforts of the DRC government 'to ensure the protection of civilians from violations of international humanitarian law and human rights abuses, including all forms of sexual and gender-based violence' and to 'support the efforts of the Government of the Democratic Republic of the Congo to bring the ongoing military operations against the FDLR, the Lord's Resistance Army (LRA) and other armed groups, to a completion'. The mandate also outlined stabilisation and peace consolidation duties, including assisting the government in strengthening its military capacity, supporting police reform and combating the illegal exploitation of natural resources. MONUSCO had an initially authorised strength of 22,016, but as of 31 October 2010 the mission contained a total of 19,008 uniformed personnel. In terms of military reform, the UN report noted that many of these plans were stalled, with three draft laws on army reform not yet adopted by parliament. Some rehabilitation of infrastructure has continued, but the absence of legal frameworks impedes the generation of a domestic training doctrine.

Considerable instability and outbreaks of fighting continue to occur, particularly in the east of the country. As part of its bid to assist capacity-building in the Armed Forces of the DRC (FARDC), MONUSCO (and previously MONUC) is supporting the FARDC in a series of military operations in North and South Kivu provinces (*Kima* 1 and *Kima* 2, and then *Amani Leo*) aimed at countering the activities of the Forces Democratiques de Liberation du Rwanda and other armed groups in the area. According to the UN, reporting in October, 'military pressure continued to contribute to FDLR desertions and voluntary partici-

pation in the MONUSCO disarmament, demobilisation, repatriation, resettlement and reintegration process'. Since military operations began in January 2009, 5,238 FDLR elements have been repatriated to Rwanda, including 2,266 former combatants and 2,972 dependants. But while some FARDC units have been trained by MONUSCO to undertake 'hold' operations in areas in North Kivu from into which armed groups had been displaced, the UN reported that FARDC forces 'continued to face difficulties in holding ground, and several areas in Masisi, Rutshuru, Walikale, Shabunda and Mwenga territories were reoccupied by FDLR'. Complicating the picture further, the UN – while noting reports of attacks against civilians by the FDLR, and by the FDLR and other groups – alleged that 'human rights violations were also perpetrated by elements of the security forces of the Democratic Republic of the Congo'.

But the FARDC has to address security problems in regions other than the FDLR in the Kivus. FARDC launched military operations in June against the Allied Democratic Forces/National Army for the Liberation of Uganda. This Ugandan group, based in North Kivu, was targeted by a second operation in September. It was reported that around 100,000 civilians had been displaced as a result of the first operation alone. Meanwhile, the Lord's Resistance Army (LRA) continues to preoccupy security forces in the northeast of the country, where FARDC have conducted *Operation Rudia II*, while the Ugandan military conducted separate operations against the LRA, at times extending into the Central African Republic (CAR) and South Sudan. One positive development was the UN-sponsored meeting, on 2 June, to discuss the threat posed by the LRA. This included representatives of UN missions in the area, as well as the AU, and the meeting closed with agreements to improve information-sharing on the LRA and also improve inter-mission coordination. This was followed in July by a meeting of the chiefs of defence of the DRC, Uganda and the CAR – as well as the MONUSCO force commander – who agreed to set up a joint intelligence and operations centre to coordinate operations against the LRA.

Ugandan military actions against the LRA have been wide-ranging, though their effectiveness is harder to gauge given the LRA's tendency to cross borders in attempts to evade its pursuers, as well as the guerrilla tactics the group pursues. The persistence of LRA attacks and the failure – so far – to kill or capture key leaders would indicate that the group has substantial resilience. But the US has increased its security assistance to Uganda during the year. This includes logistical and intelligence support. The 17th Air Force, AFRICOM's air element, has – along with personnel from US Army Africa – trained Ugandan Air Force personnel in cargo loading and airdrop techniques, in a bid to improve its capacity to conduct airlift support using aircraft including the air force's L-130 *Hercules*. The 'Lord's Resistance Army Disarmament and Northern Uganda Recovery Act of 2009' has also led to the mobilisation of further US diplomatic and military resources, and up to $10m in financial resources, in an attempt to 'increase protection of civilians; apprehend or remove from the battlefield Joseph Kony and senior commanders; promote the defection, disarmament, demobilisation and reintegration of remaining LRA fighters; and increase humanitarian access and provide continued relief to affected communities'. But the difficulties of terrain and target identification, coupled with the resilience of the LRA and its mobility, indicate that attempts to combat the activities of this group will require concerted and long-term focus.

The disputed result of the 28 November presidential election in **Côte d'Ivoire** led to fresh instability in the country. Côte d'Ivoire has hosted international peacekeeping forces – as well as French military forces – after violence in 2002 that effectively left the country divided between the north, which is effectively controlled by the Forces Nouvelles, and the south controlled by President Laurent Gbagbo. While the presidential challenger, Alessane Outtara, secured many votes in the north, the constitutional council was reported as having annulled the votes from the north; Gbagbo was thus declared the winner. Outtara refused to accept this, declaring himself the winner. He was recognised as such by the UN, the EU and the AU, but was forced to take refuge in a hotel in Abidjan, surrounded by forces loyal to Gbagbo. While the danger of greater violence persisted at the time of writing, international action – with West African states prominent – has placed substantial economic and political pressure on Gbagbo, though this had not at the time of writing forced him to accede to international entreaties (including by a Joint ECOWAS–AU mission) to stand aside; in January he was reported as having rejected an offer by Outtara to form a unity government. A declaration following a 24 December meeting of ECOWAS heads of state, after demanding the 'immediate and peaceful handover of power by Mr Laurent Gbagbo to Mr Alassane Ouattara, in accord-

ance with the expressed wishes of the Ivorian people', continued with the following two provisions:

10. In the event that Mr Gbagbo fails to heed this immutable demand of ECOWAS, the Community would be left with no alternative but to take other measures, including the use of legitimate force, to achieve the goals of the Ivorian people.

11. Against the background of the parlous security situation, the Heads of State and Government hereby instruct the President of the ECOWAS Commission to convene without delay a meeting of the Committee of Chiefs of Defense Staff in order to plan future actions, including the provision of security along the Côte d'Ivoire-Liberia border, in the event that their message is not heeded.

By mid-January the likelihood of such intervention was receding. However, should a decision be taken to force entry to Côte d'Ivoire – possibly an opposed entry – the regional militaries could face challenges in deploying and sustaining an intervention force; Ghana, meanwhile, despite declaring its support for an ECOWAS intervention, declined to participate, saying its forces were overstretched. The direct effects of the crisis were also felt in neighbouring countries: on 11 January 2011 the UN reported that over 25,000 Ivorians were seeking refuge in Liberia, with 600 arriving daily.

SOUTH AFRICA

The South African National Defence Force (SANDF) remains one of the most capable on the continent, but the military is facing a number of severe challenges in its bid to retain high levels of combat effectiveness. Indeed, some of the major issues were highlighted in the Department of Defence's Annual Report 2009–10, and in the defence minister's statements around the time of the budget vote in May 2010.

Defence Minister Lindiwe Sisulu has proposed reforming employment law for the military, which has similar union rights to other sectors at present. The proposal follows, in particular, the incidents of 26 August 2009, which saw disorder erupt when unionised SANDF personnel marched on Union Buildings in Pretoria as part of a series of protests about pay and conditions. In her address to parliament during the budget debate, Sisulu said that the situation was partly a legacy of 1994, when power changed hands in South Africa after the first universal

Table 21 **South African Defence Budget by Programme, 2006–12**

Rand m	2006	2007	2008	Revised 2009	Budget 2010	Revised Budget 2010	Budget 2011	Budget 2012
Administration	2,012	2,154	2,480	2,881	3,142	3,247	3,617	3,992
Landward Defence	6,422	7,128	7,487	8,909	9,503	9,983	10,431	11,062
Air Defence	7,262	7,315	8,019	8,056	8,885	6,059	7,910	8,362
Maritime Defence	2,643	2,397	1,837	2,011	2,102	2,180	2,320	2,574
Military Health Support	1,705	1,878	2,177	2,483	2,606	2,770	2,961	3,201
Defence Intelligence	354	461	507	600	613	631	666	699
Joint Support	1,911	2,267	3,380	3,461	3,676	3,936	4,028	4,410
Force Employment	1,508	1,581	1,914	1,924	1,862	1,909	1,997	2,086
Total	23,818	25,180	27,801	30,325	32,389	30,715	33,931	36,387

Source: South African Defence Budget 2010

elections. 'In our quest to rein [in] the influence of the military,' she said, 'we developed regulations aimed at bringing down the power of the Defence Force. In doing so, we may have compromised its strength and capabilities.' However, the unions (South African National Defence Union (SANDU) and the South African Security Forces Union) have unsurprisingly resisted attempts at de-unionisation. The fate of the personnel who took part in the Pretoria dispute has also proved to be a particular sticking point. The SANDF had placed these individuals (over 1,000) on 'special leave', and was reported to have issued notices to the effect that, if they could not explain their location and actions on 26 August 2009, they would be dismissed (without facing formal disciplinary hearings). But in November and December 2010, legal action by SANDU halted such moves, on the reported basis that the dismissal notices had been issued without personnel being given the right to be heard. Sisulu was – at the end of 2010 – reported as being firm on her position that the armed forces should be de-unionised: the defence department was at time of writing intending to lodge an appeal against the court judgment, and Sisulu had been reported as saying that she would, if necessary, seek to change the constitution.

During the defence budget vote, Sisulu raised the possibility of introducing a bill to 'provide the necessary framework for the creation of national service'. Mindful of the association that many may have with the national military service of the apartheid-era, Sisulu was keen to stress that this would not be a compulsory military service, but rather 'an unavoidable national service'. The motivating factors seem social, rather than military, with most discussion focussing on the government's conception of national service as a tool that could be potentially useful in enhancing social cohesion and in educating young people. Sisulu said that if the idea proved popular, 'it would take the next two years to build up the capacity and infrastructure required for the numbers we are faced with'. Notwithstanding these comments, reintroducing national service – even if it were not overtly military in character – that would require the administrative and training resources of the defence establishment would likely pose a substantial challenge for the force in budgetary terms but also in terms of focus, given that recent stress has been on increasing professionalisation.

The defence minister also proposed further increasing military salaries. In her budget statement, she said the department of defence has lost a number of technical professionals in the SAAF (South African Air Force), Army, Navy and SAMHS (South African Medical Health Service) 'due to uncompetitive remuneration levels'. Junior ranks in particular had already seen a salary increase in late 2009, after intervention by President Jacob Zuma, with salary increases ranging from 2% to 65% for all members of the SANDF on certain salary levels. The Interim Service Commission has recommended that the salary increases (paid in December 2009) be backdated to 1 July 2009. However, Sisulu acknowledged that 'we did not have the budget then (neither do we have it now)', and that the soldiers would be paid their back pay incrementally. A further call on scarce financial resources will be made through the requirements of the Military Veterans Bill, approved by Cabinet in November 2010, though it has been reported that the bill was still being costed, according to the deputy defence minister.

Budgetary allocations have fluctuated in recent years, as the department seeks to realise savings in light of general pressures on public finances (see *The Military Balance* 2010, p. 290). Cost-saving measures have generally been low-level: limiting overseas visits, for example, and the fall in allocations to air defence in particular stems more from the cancellation of the A400M order than any administrative cost-saving measure. In that case, the requirement for a new airlift capability remains, so the cost will have to be borne at some future date. Increases over the next few years are largely due to the government's decision to adjust salaries upwards (the 2010 budget 'allocates R600m (US$81m), R370m (US$50m) and R850m (US$114.8m) over the medium term to implement the provisions of the new remuneration system'), implement the military skills development system, and shift focus from air to land modernisation. But the budget remains, according to the defence minister herself, 'woefully inadequate'. Sisulu continued by saying that the defence ministry had decided on a number of stop-gap measures: 'to trawl the existing budget to see where we can make temporary savings; to find innovative ways in which we can generate our own revenue; [and] to reprioritise the budget and transfer some funding to areas of critical shortage. We would like, for the current year, to prioritise our landward forces whose infrastructure and equipment has fallen into bad state of repairs.'

But force capability is suffering, and the Annual Report was clear in its comments. The South African Army, though it fulfilled its commitments, was 'overstretched, especially in the infantry, engineer and support capabilities' and, with the continuation of the partial acquisition approach, 'newly commissioned equipment is brought into preservation stores, as there is not sufficient ammunition to operate the system'. But the main problem remained the loss and continued shortage of critical skills as well as certain vehicle fleets and infrastructures. 'Owing to cost and time, [these challenges] will not be fully mitigated in the near future', the report said. Meanwhile, even though it also suffered funding constraints, the Navy moderately improved its personnel strength (skill shortage has been an issue for the navy, as well as other services). But there, the use of reserves has been 'crucial in supplementing critical vacancies'. The decrease in budgets up to 2009–10 was largely due to the end of the frigate and submarine procurement

programmes, while increases in the budgetary allocations until 2012 are primarily due to the planned acquisition of hydrographic vessels and the planned recruitment of personnel with niche skills, such as divers, technicians and engineers.

According to the Annual Report, the Air Force was 'to a large extent' still able to execute its mandate, but the 26 October report of the Portfolio Committee on Defence drew some bleak conclusions. Due to underfunding of technical skills, maintenance problems and obsolete equipment, the air force can effectively only operate the *Hawk* system 'with merely the current crew'. Furthermore, only a limited intake of *Gripen* pilots is possible. Meanwhile, notwithstanding these operational issues and funding problems, the Air Force continues to review its airlift options after pulling out of the European A400M programme in late 2009. It presently operates the C-130 and the smaller C-47 to provide airlift, a resource which is lacking in the south of the continent, and the air force has been looking to phase out its ageing C-130Bs by around 2013–14. The air force appears to be taking a two-tier approach to its airlift needs, looking to eventually purchase two types of aircraft to meet intra- and inter-theatre requirements. During 2010, it was briefed on the C-27J, the C-130J and even the C-17 by the US, though the last of these is likely to be well beyond the force's means. An alternative to the C-27J is the EADS/CASA C-295, while the A400M could also be reconsidered to meet the 'strategic' airlift capability, particularly if an attractive cost package could be worked out. Airlift is presently provided on an ad-hoc basis by leasing Il-76 capacity when required.

Project Saucepan and *Project Mesti* were notionally intended to meet requirements for airlift and for maritime surveillance using the same medium-size aircraft to fulfill both roles. A pallet-based mission system suite (where mission systems and workstations are contained within a discrete unit – such as an ISO container – that can be loaded and 'plugged into' an aircraft) was one approach being considered for the maritime-surveillance role. A further aircraft option is the Brazilian KC-390 project. South Africa and Brazil are forging closer defence links, including jointly funding the *A-Darter* imaging infrared air-to-air missile programme. Possible South African industrial participation in the KC-390 has been discussed during the course of 2010.

Angola ANG

New Angolan Kwanza AOA		2009	2010	2011
GDP	AOA	5.99tr	7.81tr	
	US$	75.7bn	85.1bn	
per capita	US$	4,093	4,479	
Growth	%	0.2	7.4	
Inflation	%	13.7	15.0	
Def exp	AOA	251bn		
	US$	3.17bn		
Def bdgt	AOA	237bn	251bn	342bn
	US$	3bn	2.74bn	
USD1=AOA		79.10	91.76	

Population   18,992,707

Ethnic groups: Ovimbundu 37%; Kimbundu 25%; Bakongo 13%

Age	0–14	15–19	20–24	25–29	30–64	65 plus
Male	21.8%	5.5%	4.7%	3.9%	13.4%	1.2%
Female	21.4%	5.4%	4.6%	3.7%	12.9%	1.5%

Capabilities

ACTIVE 107,000 (Army 100,000 Navy 1,000 Air 6,000) **Paramilitary 10,000**

ORGANISATIONS BY SERVICE

Army 100,000

FORCES BY ROLE

Armd/Inf   42 regt (dets/gps – strength varies)
Inf   16 indep bde

EQUIPMENT BY TYPE †

MBT 300+: ε200 T-54/T-55; 50 T-62; 50 T-72; T-80/T-84 (reported)
RECCE 600 BRDM-2
AIFV 250+: 250 BMP-1/BMP-2; BMD-3
APC (W) ε170 BTR-152/BTR-60/BTR-80
ARTY 1,408+
   SP 16+: **122mm** 2S1 Carnation; **152mm** 4 2S3; **203mm** 12 2S7
   TOWED 552: **122mm** 500 D-30; **130mm** 48 M-46; **152mm** 4 D-20
   MRL 90+: **122mm** 90: 50 BM-21; 40 RM-70 Dana; **240mm** BM-24
   MOR 750: **82mm** 250; **120mm** 500
AT • MSL • MANPATS 9K11 (AT-3 Sagger)
   RCL 500: 400 **82mm** B-10/**107mm** B-11 †; **106mm** 100†
   RL 73mm RPG-7 Knout†
   GUNS • SP 100mm SU-100†
AD • SAM • MANPAD 500 9K32 Strela-2 (SA-7 Grail)‡; 9K36 Strela-3 (SA-14 Gremlin); 9K 310 Igla-1 (SA-16 Gimlet)
   GUNS • TOWED 450+: **14.5mm** ZPU-4; **23mm** ZU-23-2; **37mm** M-1939; **57mm** S-60

Navy ε1,000

HQ located at Luanda

EQUIPMENT BY TYPE

PATROL AND COASTAL COMBATANTS • PBF 5 PVC-170

FACILITIES

Base   Located at Luanda

Coastal Defence

MSL • TACTICAL • SSM SS-C-1B Sepal (at Luanda base)

Air Force/Air Defence 6,000

FORCES BY ROLE

Ftr	Some sqn with MiG-21bis/MiG-21MF Fishbed; Su-27 Flanker; 2 sqn with MiG-23ML Flogger
FGA	Some sqn with MiG-23BN Flogger; Su-22 Fitter D; Su-24 Fencer; Su-25 Frogfoot
MP	1 sqn with F-27-200 MPA; CASA 212 Aviocar
Tpt	Some sqn An-12 Cub; An-24 Coke; An-26 Curl; An-32 Cline; An-72 Coaler; C-130 Hercules; C-212 Aviocar; with EMB-135BJ Legacy 600 (VIP); Il-62 Classic; Il-76TD Candid; PC-6B Turbo Porter; PC-7 Turbo Trainer/PC-9*
Trg	Some sqn with EMB-312 Tucano; L-29 Delfin
Atk Hel	Some sqn with Mi-24 Hind/Mi-35 Hind; SA-342M Gazelle (with HOT)
Tpt Hel	Some units with AS-565; Bell 212; Mi-8 Hip/Mi-17 Hip H; SA-316 Alouette III (IAR-316) (incl trg)
AD	5 bn; 10 bty each with 12 S-125 Pechora (SA-3 Goa); 10 9K35 Strela-10 (SA-13 Gopher)†; 25 2K12 Kub (SA-6 Gainful); 15 9K33 Osa (SA-8 Gecko); 20 9K31 Strela-1 (SA-9 Gaskin); 40 S-75M Volkhov (SA-2 Guideline)‡

EQUIPMENT BY TYPE

AIRCRAFT 103 combat capable
   FTR ε32: up to 14 Su-27 Flanker; 18 MiG-23ML Flogger
   FGA 54: 20 MiG-21bis/MiG-21MF Fishbed; 8 MiG-23BN Flogger; 14 Su-22 Fitter D; 12 Su-24 Fencer
   ATK 8 Su-25 Frogfoot
   MP 1 F-27-200 MPA
   TPT 51: **Heavy** 1 Il-76TD Candid; **Medium** 7: 6 An-12 Cub; 1 C-130 Hercules; **Light** 42: 2 An-24 Coke; 12 An-26 Curl; 3 An-32 Cline; 8 An-72 Coaler; 12 C-212 Aviocar (5 tpt and 7 MP); 1 EMB-135BJ Legacy 600 (VIP); 4 PC-6B Turbo Porter **PAX** 1 Il-62 Classic
   TRG 25: 8 EMB-312 Tucano; 6 L-29 Delfin; 2 L-39C Albatros; 9 PC-7 Turbo Trainer/PC-9*
HELICOPTERS
   ATK 14 Mi-24 Hind/Mi-35 Hind
   MRH 20: 8 AS-565 Panther; 10 SA-316 Alouette III (IAR-316) (incl trg); 2 SA-342M Gazelle
   MRH/TPT 27 Mi-8 Hip/Mi-17 Hip H
   TPT • Light 8 Bell 212
AD • SAM 122
   SP 70: 10 9K35 Strela-10 (SA-13 Gopher)†; 25 2K12 Kub (SA-6 Gainful); 15 9K33 Osa (SA-8 Gecko); 20 9K31 Strela-1 (SA-9 Gaskin)

TOWED 52: 40S-75M Volkhov (SA-2 *Guideline*)‡; 12 S-125 *Pechora* (SA-3 *Goa*)

MSL

ASM AT-2 *Swatter*; HOT
ARM Kh-28 (AS-9 *Kyle*)
AAM • IR AAM R-3 (AA-2 *Atoll*)‡; R-60 (AA-8 *Aphid*); R-73 (AA-11 *Archer*) IR/SARH AAM R-23/24 (AA-7 *Apex*)‡

Paramilitary 10,000

Rapid-Reaction Police 10,000

Benin BEN

CFA Franc BCEAO fr		2009	2010	2011
GDP	fr	3.13tr	3.30tr	
	US$	6.65bn	6.65bn	
per capita	US$	744	722	
Growth	%	3.8	3.5	
Inflation	%	2.2	3.3	
Def exp	fr	ε47.8bn		
	US$	ε101m		
Def bdgt	fr	35bn	26.5bn	
	US$	74m	53m	
US$1=fr		470.96	495.60	

Population   9,211,741

Age	0–14	15–19	20–24	25–29	30–64	65 plus
Male	22.8%	5.5%	4.6%	3.9%	12.3%	1.1%
Female	21.9%	5.3%	4.4%	3.8%	12.9%	1.6%

Capabilities

ACTIVE 4,750 (Army 4,300 Navy 200 Air 250)
Paramilitary 2,500
Terms of service conscription (selective), 18 months

ORGANISATIONS BY SERVICE

Army 4,300

FORCES BY ROLE

Armd	1 sqn
Inf	3 bn
Cdo/AB	1 bn
Arty	1 bty
Engr	1 bn

EQUIPMENT BY TYPE

LT TK 18 PT-76 (op status uncertain)
RECCE 31: 14 BRDM-2; 7 M-8; 10 VBL
APC (T): 22 M-113
ARTY 16+
TOWED 105mm 16: 12 L-118 Light Gun; 4 M-101
MOR 81mm
AT • RL 73mm RPG-7 *Knout*; 89mm LRAC

Navy ε200

EQUIPMENT BY TYPE
PATROL AND COASTAL COMBATANTS • PB 2 *Matelot Brice Kpomasse* (ex-PRC)
FACILITIES
Naval air base Located at Cotonou

Air Force 250

AIRCRAFT
TPT 11 Light 8: 2 An-26 *Curl*†; 2 DC-3 (C-47 *Skytrain*)†; 1 *Commander* 500B†; 1 DHC-6 *Twin Otter*†; 2 Do-128 *Skyservant*† PAX 3: 1 B-707-320† (VIP); 1 F-28 *Fellowship*† (VIP); 1 HS-748†
HELICOPTERS
MRH 1 SA-313B *Alouette II*†
TPT • Light 5: 4 AW-109BA; 1 AS-350B *Ecureuil*†

Paramilitary 2,500

Gendarmerie 2,500

4 (mobile) coy

DEPLOYMENT

CENTRAL AFRICAN REPUBLIC/CHAD
UN • MINURCAT 3 obs

CÔTE D'IVOIRE
UN • UNOCI 427; 6 obs; 1 inf bn

DEMOCRATIC REPUBLIC OF THE CONGO
UN • MONUSCO 450; 11 obs; 1 inf bn

LIBERIA
UN • UNMIL 1; 2 obs

SUDAN
UN • UNMIS 5 obs

Botswana BWA

Botswana Pula P		2009	2010	2011
GDP	P	83.2bn	92.7bn	
	US$	11.7bn	13.6bn	
per capita	US$	5,993	6,865	
Growth	%	-6.0	3.4	
Inflation	%	8.0	6.8	
Def exp	P	2.67bn		
	US$	375m		
Def bdgt	P		4.29bn	
	US$		628m	
FMA (US)	US$	-	0.2m	0.34m
US$1=P		7.12	6.83	

Population   1,977,569

Age	0–14	15–19	20–24	25–29	30–64	65 plus
Male	17.3%	5.6%	5.3%	5.1%	15.5%	1.6%
Female	16.6%	5.6%	5.5%	5.3%	14.3%	2.3%

Capabilities

ACTIVE 9,000 (Army 8,500 Air 500) Paramilitary 1,500

ORGANISATIONS BY SERVICE

Army 8,500

FORCES BY ROLE

Armd	1 bde (under strength)
Inf	2 bde (total: 1 cdo unit, 1 armd recce regt, 1 engr regt, 2 ADA regt, 4 inf bn)
Arty	1 bde
AD	1 bde (under strength)

EQUIPMENT BY TYPE
LT TK 55: ε30 SK-105 *Kuerassier*; 25 *Scorpion*
RECCE 72+: RAM-V-1; ε8 RAM-V-2; 64 VBL
APC 156
  APC (T) 6 FV 103 *Spartan*
  APC (W) 150: 50 BTR-60; 50 LAV-150 *Commando* (some with 90mm gun); 50 MOWAG *Piranha* III
ARTY 46
  TOWED 30: **105mm** 18: 12 L-118 Light Gun; 6 Model 56 pack howitzer; **155mm** 12 *Soltam*
  MOR 28: **81mm** 22; **120mm** 6 M-43
AT • MSL 6+
  SP V-150 TOW
  MANPATS 6 TOW
  RCL 84mm 30 *Carl Gustav*
  RL 73mm RPG-7 *Knout*
AD • SAM • MANPAD 27: 5 *Javelin*; 10 9K310 *Igla*-1 (SA-16 *Gimlet*); 12 9K32 *Strela*-2 (SA-7 *Grail*)‡
  GUNS • TOWED 20mm 7 M-167 *Vulcan*

Air Wing 500

FORCES BY ROLE

Ftr/FGA	1 sqn with F-5A *Freedom Fighter*; F-5D *Tiger II*
ISR	1 sqn with O-2 *Skymaster*
Tpt	2 sqn with BN-2 *Defender**; Beech 200 *Super King Air* (VIP); C-130B *Hercules*; C-212 *Aviocar*; CN-235; Gulfstream IV
Trg	1 sqn with PC-7 *Turbo Trainer**
Tpt Hel	1 sqn with AS-350B *Ecureuil*; Bell 412 *Twin Huey*; Bell 412EP *Twin Huey* (VIP); Bell 412SP *Twin Huey*

EQUIPMENT BY TYPE
AIRCRAFT 31 combat capable
  FTR 15: 10 F-5A *Freedom Fighter*; 5 F-5D *Tiger II*
  ISR 5 O-2 *Skymaster*
  TPT 19 **Medium** 3 C-130B *Hercules*; **Light** 15: 10 BN-2 *Defender**; 1 Beech 200 *King Air* (VIP); 2 C-212 *Aviocar*; 1 CN-235-100; 1 CN-235-300 **PAX** 1 Gulfstream IV
  TRG 6 PC-7 *Turbo Trainer**
HELICOPTERS
  MRH 7: 1 Bell 412 *Twin Huey*; 1 Bell 412EP *Twin Huey* (VIP); 5 Bell 412SP *Twin Huey*
  TPT • Light 8 AS-350B *Ecureuil*

Paramilitary 1,500

Police Mobile Unit 1,500 (org in territorial coy)

Burkina Faso BFA

CFA Franc BCEAO fr		2009	2010	2011
GDP	fr	3.97tr	4.23tr	
	US$	8.43bn	8.53bn	
per capita	US$	535	524	
Growth	%	3.5	4.4	
Inflation	%	2.6	2.6	
Def exp	fr	51.7bn		
	US$	110m		
Def bdgt	fr	55bn	48bn	
	US$	117m	97m	
US$1=fr		470.96	495.60	

Population   16,286,706

Age	0–14	15–19	20–24	25–29	30–64	65 plus
Male	23.0%	5.5%	4.5%	3.8%	12.0%	1.0%
Female	22.9%	5.4%	4.5%	3.7%	12.3%	1.5%

Capabilities

ACTIVE 11,200 (Army 6,400 Air 600 Gendarmerie 4,200) Paramilitary 250

ORGANISATIONS BY SERVICE

Army 6,400

FORCES BY ROLE
3 Mil Regions

Tk	1 bn (2 tk pl)
Inf	5 regt HQ (each: 3 inf bn (each: 1 inf coy (5 inf pl))
AB	1 regt HQ (1 AB bn, 2 AB coy)
Arty	1 bn (2 arty tps)
Engr	1 bn

EQUIPMENT BY TYPE
RECCE 83: 19 AML-60/AML-90; 24 EE-9 *Cascavel*; 30 *Ferret*; 2 M-20; 8 M-8
APC (W) 13 M-3 *Panhard*
ARTY 18+
  TOWED 14: **105mm** 8 M-101; **122mm** 6
  MRL 107mm ε4 Type-63
  MOR 81mm Brandt
AT
  RCL 75mm Type-52 (M-20); **84mm** *Carl Gustav*
  RL 89mm LRAC; M-20
AD • SAM • MANPAD 9K32 *Strela*-2 (SA-7 *Grail*‡)
  GUNS • TOWED 42: **14.5mm** 30 ZPU; **20mm** 12 TCM-20

Air Force 600

FORCES BY ROLE

Tpt   Some sqn with B-727 (VIP); Beech 200 *King Air*; *Commander* 500B; CN-235; HS-748; N-262 *Fregate*; Some (liaison) sqn with AS-350 *Ecureuil*; Cessna 172; Mi-8 *Hip*/Mi-17 *Hip H*; SA-316B *Alouette III*

Trg   Some sqn with SF-260W *Warrior*/SF-260WL *Warrior**

EQUIPMENT BY TYPE

AIRCRAFT Some combat capable
TPT 8 Light 1 Beech 200 *King Air*; 1 *Commander* 500B; 1 Cessna 172; 1 Cessna 337; 1 CN-235 **PAX** 1 B-727 (VIP); 1 HS-748; 1 N-262 *Fregate*
TRG Some SF-260WL *Warrior**
HELICOPTERS
ATK 2 Mi-35 *Hind*
MRH 1 SA-316B *Alouette III*
MRH/TPT 3 Mi-8 *Hip*/Mi-17 *Hip H*
TPT • Light 4: 1 AS-350 *Ecureuil*

Gendarmerie 4,200

Paramilitary 250

People's Militia (R) 45,000 reservists (trained)

Security Company 250

DEPLOYMENT

CENTRAL AFRICAN REPUBLIC/CHAD
UN • MINURCAT 2

DEMOCRATIC REPUBLIC OF THE CONGO
UN • MONUSCO 8 obs

SUDAN
UN • UNAMID 802; 7 obs; 1 inf bn
UN • UNMIS 6 obs

Burundi BDI

Burundi Franc fr		2009	2010	2011
GDP	fr	1.64tr	1.84tr	
	US$	1.33bn	1.50bn	
per capita	US$	160	176	
Growth	%	3.5	3.6	
Inflation	%	11.0	8.3	
Def exp	fr	52bn		
	US$	42m		
Def bdgt	fr	52.5bn	70.4bn	
	US$	43m	57m	
US$1=fr		1230.18	1230.36	

Population   8,518,862

Ethnic groups: Hutu 85%; Tutsi 14%

Age	0–14	15–19	20–24	25–29	30–64	65 plus
Male	23.1%	5.3%	4.5%	3.8%	11.8%	1.0%
Female	22.9%	5.3%	4.5%	3.8%	12.5%	1.5%

Capabilities

ACTIVE 20,000 (Army 20,000) **Paramilitary 31,050**

DDR efforts continue, while activity directed at improving professionalisation of the security forces have taken place, some sponsored by BINUB, the UN mission.

ORGANISATIONS BY SERVICE

Army 20,000
FORCES BY ROLE
Lt armd 2 bn (sqn)
Inf   7 bn; some indep coy
Arty   1 bn
Engr   1 bn
AD   1 bn

EQUIPMENT BY TYPE
RECCE 55: 6 AML-60; 12 AML-90; 30 BRDM-2; 7 S52 *Shorland*
APC (W) 57: 10 BTR 80; 20 BTR-40; 9 M-3 *Panhard*; 12 RG-31 *Nyala*; 6 *Walid*
ARTY 120
TOWED 122mm 18 D-30
MRL 122mm 12 BM-21
MOR 90: **82mm** 15 M-43; **120mm** ε75
AT
MSL • MANPATS *Milan* (reported)
RCL 75mm 60 Type-52 (M-20)
RL 83mm RL-83 *Blindicide*
AD • SAM • MANPAD ε30 9K32 *Strela-2* (SA-7 *Grail*)‡
GUNS • TOWED 150+: **14.5mm** 15 ZPU-4; 135+ **23mm** ZU-23/**37mm** Type-55 (M-1939)

Reserves
Army 10 (reported) bn

Air Wing 200
AIRCRAFT 2 combat capable
TPT 4 Light 2 Cessna 150L† **PAX** 2 DC-3
TRG 2 SF-260TP/SF-260W *Warrior**
HELICOPTERS
ATK 2 Mi-24 *Hind*
MRH 3 SA-316B *Alouette III*; 2 SA-342L *Gazelle*
TPT • Medium (4 Mi-8 *Hip* non-op)

Paramilitary 31,050

Marine Police 50
16 territorial districts
PATROL AND COASTAL COMBATANTS 3
PHT 3 *Huchuan*†
AMPHIBIOUS 1 LCT
LOGISTICS AND SUPPORT 1 SPT

General Administration of State Security ε1,000

Local Defence Militia ε30,000

DEPLOYMENT

CENTRAL AFRICAN REPUBLIC
ECCAS • MICOPAX 8

SOMALIA
AU • AMISOM 3,000; 3 inf bn

SUDAN
UN • UNAMID 2; 7 obs

FOREIGN FORCES

All forces part of BINUB unless otherwise stated.
Ghana 1 obs
Niger 1 obs
Pakistan 1 obs
Senegal 1 obs
Switzerland 1 obs

Cameroon CMR

CFA Franc BEAC fr		2009	2010	2011
GDP	fr	10.5tr	11.1tr	
	US$	22.2bn	22.4bn	
per capita	US$	1,139	1,123	
Growth	%	2.4	3.5	
Inflation	%	3.0	2.2	
Def exp	fr	162bn		
	US$	344m		
Def bdgt	fr		171bn	
	US$		346m	
US$1=fr		470.96	495.60	

Population	19,958,351

Age	0–14	15–19	20–24	25–29	30–64	65 plus
Male	20.4%	5.4%	5.0%	4.3%	13.6%	1.5%
Female	20.1%	5.3%	4.9%	4.1%	13.6%	1.8%

Capabilities

ACTIVE 14,100 (Army 12,500 Navy 1,300 Air 300)
Paramilitary 9,000

ORGANISATIONS BY SERVICE

Army 12,500

FORCES BY ROLE
3 Mil Regions

Armd Recce	1 bn
Inf	3 bn (under comd of Mil Regions); 5 bn; 1 bn (trg)
Cdo/AB	1 bn
Arty	1 bn (5 arty bty)
Engr	1 bn
Presidential Guard	1 bn

AD   1 bn (6 AD bty)

EQUIPMENT BY TYPE
RECCE 65: 31 AML-90; 6 AMX-10RC; 15 *Ferret*; 8 M-8; 5 VBL
AIFV 22: 8 LAV-150 *Commando* with 20mm gun; 14 LAV-150 *Commando* with 90mm gun
APC 33
  APC (T) 12 M-3 half-track
  APC (W) 21 LAV-150 *Commando*
ARTY 112+
  SP 18 ATMOS 2000
  TOWED 58: **75mm** 6 M-116 pack; **105mm** 20 M-101; **130mm** 24: 12 Model 1982 gun 82 (reported); 12 Type-59 (M-46); **155mm** 8 I1
  MRL 122mm 20 BM-21
  MOR 16+: **81mm** (some SP); **120mm** 16 Brandt
AT • MSL 49
  SP 24 TOW (on Jeeps)
  MANPATS 25 *Milan*
  RCL 53: **106mm** 40 M-40A2; **75mm** 13 Type-52 (M-20)
  RL 89mm LRAC
AD • GUNS • TOWED 54: **14.5mm** 18 Type-58 (ZPU-2); **35mm** 18 GDF-002; **37mm** 18 Type-63

Navy ε1,300

HQ located at Douala

EQUIPMENT BY TYPE
PATROL AND COASTAL COMBATANTS 11
  PCC 2: 1 *Bakassi* (FRA P-48); 1 *L'Audacieux* (FRA P-48)
  PB 7: 2 *Rodman* 101; 4 *Rodman* 46; 1 *Quartier*
  PBR 2 *Swift*-38
AMPHIBIOUS • LCU 2 (93 ft)

FACILITIES
Bases   Located at Douala, Limbe, Kribi

Air Force 300-400

FORCES BY ROLE
Air	1 composite sqn; 1 Presidential Fleet
FGA	Some sqn with MB-326K; *Alpha Jet*†; CM-170 *Magister**
MP	Some sqn with Do-128D-6 *Turbo SkyServant*
Tpt	Some sqn with B-707; C-130H-30 *Hercules*; DHC-4 *Caribou*; DHC-5D *Buffalo*; Gulfstream III; IAI-201 *Arava*; PA-23 *Aztec*
Atk Hel	Some sqn with Mi-24 *Hind*; SA-342 *Gazelle* (with HOT)
Tpt Hel	Some sqn with AS-332 *Super Puma*; AS-365 *Dauphin* 2; Bell 206 *Jet Ranger*; Bell 206 L-3; Bell 412; SA-313B *Alouette II*; SA-318 *Alouette II*; SA-319 *Alouette III*

EQUIPMENT BY TYPE
AIRCRAFT 15 combat capable
  ATK 6 MB-326K *Impala I/Impala II*
  TPT 15 **Medium** 3 C-130H-30 *Hercules* **Light** 10: 1 DHC-4 *Caribou*; 4 DHC-5D *Buffalo*; 2 Do-128D-6 *Turbo SkyServant*; 1 IAI-201 *Arava*; 2 PA-23 *Aztec* **PAX** 2: 1 B-707; 1 Gulfstream III
  TRG 9: 4 *Alpha Jet*†; 5 CM-170 *Magister**

HELICOPTERS
ATK 3 Mi-24 *Hind*
MRH 13: 1 AS-365 *Dauphin 2*; 2 Bell 412; 3 SA-313B *Alouette II*; 1 SA-318 *Alouette II*; 2 SA-319 *Alouette III*; 4 SA-342 *Gazelle* (with HOT)
TPT 6 **Medium** 1 AS-332 *Super Puma* **Light** 5: 3 Bell 206 *Jet Ranger*; 2 Bell 206L-3 *Long Ranger*

Paramilitary 9,000

Gendarmerie 9,000
Regional Spt 3 gp

DEPLOYMENT

CENTRAL AFRICAN REPUBLIC
ECCAS • MICOPAX 146

DEMOCRATIC REPUBLIC OF THE CONGO
UN • MONUSCO 5 obs

SUDAN
UN • UNAMID 3 obs

Cape Verde CPV

Cape Verde Escudo E		2009	2010	2011
GDP	E	125bn	134bn	
	US$	1.56bn	1.60bn	
per capita	US$	3,093	3,126	
Growth	%	2.8	5.1	
Inflation	%	1.0	2.5	
Def exp	E	682m		
	US$	9m		
Def bdgt	E	682m	674m	
	US$	9m	8m	
US$1=E			79.77	83.81

Population   512,582

Age	0–14	15–19	20–24	25–29	30–64	65 plus
Male	16.4%	5.8%	5.4%	4.5%	14.3%	2.1%
Female	16.2%	5.8%	5.4%	4.5%	16.2%	3.4%

Capabilities

ACTIVE 1,200 (Army 1,000 Coast Guard 100 Air 100)
Terms of service conscription (selective)

ORGANISATIONS BY SERVICE

Army 1,000
FORCES BY ROLE
Inf 2 bn (gp)

EQUIPMENT BY TYPE
RECCE 10 BRDM-2
ARTY 42
  TOWED 24: **75mm** 12; **76mm** 12

MOR 18: **82mm** 12; **120mm** 6 M-1943
AT • RL 73mm RPG-7 *Knout*; **89mm** (3.5in)
AD • SAM • MANPAD 50 SA-7 *Grail*‡
  GUNS • TOWED 30: **14.5mm** 18 ZPU-1; **23mm** 12 ZU-23

Coast Guard ε100
PATROL AND COASTAL COMBATANTS 3
PCC 1 *Kondor I*
PB 2: 1 *Espadarte*; 1 *Tainha* (PRC-27m)

Air Force up to 100
FORCES BY ROLE
MP   1 sqn with Do-228; EMB-110

EQUIPMENT BY TYPE
AIRCRAFT • TPT • Light 4: 1 Do-228; 1 EMB-110; 2 An-26 *Curl*†

Central African Republic CAR

CFA Franc BEAC fr		2009	2010	2011
GDP	fr	936bn	995bn	
	US$	1.99bn	2.01bn	
per capita	US$	449	446	
Growth	%	2.4	3.4	
Inflation	%	3.5	2.6	
Def exp	fr	17bn		
	US$	36m		
Def bdgt	fr	19bn	25.5bn	
	US$	40m	52m	
US$1=fr		470.96	495.60	

Population   4,505,945

Age	0–14	15–19	20–24	25–29	30–64	65 plus
Male	20.6%	5.4%	4.9%	4.0%	13.0%	1.5%
Female	20.4%	5.3%	4.8%	4.0%	13.7%	2.2%

Capabilities

ACTIVE 2,150 (Army 2,000 Air 150) **Paramilitary 1,000)**
Terms of service conscription (selective), 2 years; reserve obligation thereafter, term n.k.

ORGANISATIONS BY SERVICE

Joint
Combined Service 1 (Intervention and spt) bn

Army ε2,000
FORCES BY ROLE
HQ/Spt   1 regt
Army   1 (combined arms) regt (1 mech bn, 1 inf bn)
Territorial Def 1 regt (bn) (2 territorial bn (intervention))

EQUIPMENT BY TYPE
MBT 3 T-55†
RECCE 9: 8 Ferret†; 1 BRDM-2
AIFV 18 Ratel
APC (W) 39+: 4 BTR-152†; 25+ TPK 4.20 VSC ACMAT†; 10+ VAB†
ARTY • MOR 12+: 81mm†; 120mm 12 M-1943†
AT • RCL 106mm 14 M-40†
RL 73mm RPG-7 Knout†; 89mm LRAC†
PATROL AND COASTAL COMBATANTS 9 PBR†

Air Force 150

FORCES BY ROLE

Tpt   Some sqn with C-130 Hercules; Cessna 337 Skymaster; Falcon 20 (Mystère 20); 1 (liaison) sqn with AL-60

Tpt Hel Some sqn with AS-350 Ecureuil; Mi-8 Hip; SA-313B Alouette II

EQUIPMENT BY TYPE
AIRCRAFT • TPT 9 Medium 1 C-130 Hercules Light 7: AL-60; 1 Cessna 337 Skymaster PAX 1 Falcon 20 (Mystère 20)
HELICOPTERS
MRH 1 SA-313B Alouette II
TPT 3 Medium 2 Mi-8 Hip Light 1 AS-350 Ecureuil

Paramilitary

Gendarmerie ε1,000
3 Regional legions, 8 bde

FOREIGN FORCES

All forces part of MINURCAT unless otherwise stated, and due to withdraw by end Dec 2010. MINURCAT numbers represent total forces deployed in the Central African Republic and Chad unless stated.
Bangladesh 138; 2 obs; 2 hel pl
Benin 3 obs
Burkina Faso 2
Burundi MICOPAX 8
Cameroon MICOPAX 146
Chad MICOPAX 126
Congo MICOPAX 22
Democratic Republic of the Congo 1 • MICOPAX 107
Egypt 2 obs
Ethiopia 2
Equatorial Guinea MICOPAX 7
France Operation Boali 240; 1 inf coy; 1 spt det
Gabon MICOPAX 142
Ghana 527; 1 obs; 1 inf bn
Ireland 10
Kenya 3
Mali 1
Mongolia 268; 1 inf coy
Namibia 5
Nepal 581; 1 obs; 1 inf bn
Nigeria 4; 2 obs

Norway 1
Pakistan 4; 2 obs
Poland 2
Russia 119; 1 hel pl
Rwanda 1 obs
Senegal 10; 3 obs
Serbia 14
Sri Lanka 74
Togo 358; 2 inf coy
Tunisia 2; 4 obs
United States 2

Chad CHA

CFA Franc BEAC fr		2009	2010	2011
GDP	fr	3.23tr	3.81tr	
	US$	6.85bn	7.68bn	
per capita	US$	612	668	
Growth	%	1.6	2.1	
Inflation	%	10.1	3.0	
Def bdgt	fr	67.1bn	63.7bn	
	US$	142m	129m	
FMA (US)	US$	-	0.5m	0.4m
US$1=fr		470.96	495.60	

Population   11,506,130

Age	0–14	15–19	20–24	25–29	30–64	65 plus
Male	23.3%	5.5%	4.2%	3.4%	10.4%	1.2%
Female	22.7%	5.7%	4.8%	4.1%	13.0%	1.7%

Capabilities

ACTIVE 25,350 (Army 17,000–20,000 Air 350 Republican Guard 5,000) **Paramilitary 9,500**
Terms of service conscription authorised

ORGANISATIONS BY SERVICE

Army ε17,000–20,000 (being re-organised)
FORCES BY ROLE
7 Mil Regions
Armd 1 bn
Inf 7 bn
Arty 1 bn
Engr 1 bn

EQUIPMENT BY TYPE
MBT 60 T-55
RECCE 256: 132 AML-60/AML-90; ε100 BRDM-2; 20 EE-9 Cascavel; 4 ERC-90F Sagaie
AIFV 89: 80 BMP-1; 9 LAV-150 Commando (with 90mm gun)
APC (W) 52: 24 BTR-80; 8 BTR-3E; ε20 BTR-60
ARTY 7+
SP 122mm 2 2S1 Carnation
TOWED 105mm 5 M-2
MOR 81mm some; 120mm AM-50

AT • MSL • MANPATS *Eryx; Milan*
  RCL **106mm** M-40A1
  RL **112mm** APILAS; **73mm** RPG-7 *Knout*; **89mm** LRAC
AD • GUNS • TOWED **14.5mm** ZPU-1/ZPU-2/ZPU-4;
23mm ZU-23

Air Force 350

FORCES BY ROLE

Atk   1 unit with PC-7; PC-9; SF-260M *Warrior**; Su-25 *Frogfoot*

Tpt   Some sqn with An-26 *Curl*; C-130 *Hercules*; Mi-17 *Hip H*; 1 (Presidential) Flt with Beech 1900; DC-9-87

Atk Hel Some sqn with Mi-24V *Hind*; SA-316 *Alouette III*

EQUIPMENT BY TYPE
AIRCRAFT 7 combat capable
  ATK 4: 3 Su-25 *Frogfoot*; 1 Su-2SUB *Frogfoot*
  TPT 5: **Medium** 1 C-130H *Hercules* **Light** 3: 2 An-26 *Curl*; 1 Beech 1900 **PAX** 1 DC-9-87
  TRG 4: 2 PC-7 (only 1*); 1 PC-9 *Turbo Trainer**; 1 SF-260M *Warrior**
HELICOPTERS
  ATK 7 Mi-24V *Hind*
  MRH 8: 6 Mi-17 *Hip-H*; 2 SA-316 *Alouette III*
  TPT • **Medium** 2 Mi-171 *Hip-H*

Paramilitary 9,500 active

Republican Guard 5,000

Gendarmerie 4,500

DEPLOYMENT

CENTRAL AFRICAN REPUBLIC
ECCAS • MICOPAX 126

CÔTE D'IVOIRE
UN • UNOCI 1; 3 obs

FOREIGN FORCES

All forces part of MINURCAT unless otherwise stated, and due to withdraw by end Dec 2010. MINURCAT numbers represent total forces deployed in the Central African Republic and Chad unless stated.
Bangladesh 138; 2 obs; 2 hel pl
Benin 3 obs
Burkina Faso 2
Democratic Republic of the Congo 1
Egypt 2 obs
Ethiopia 2
France *Operation Epervier* 634; 1 mech inf BG with (elm 1 mech inf regt, elm 1 armd cav regt); 1 hel det with 4 SA-330 *Puma*
Ghana 527; 1 obs; 1 inf bn
Ireland 10
Kenya 3
Mali 1 obs
Mongolia 268; 1 inf coy
Namibia 5
Nepal 581; 1 obs; 1 inf bn
Nigeria 4; 2 obs
Norway 1
Pakistan 4; 2 obs
Poland 2
Russia 119; 1 hel pl
Rwanda 1 obs
Senegal 10; 3 obs
Serbia 14
Sri Lanka 74
Togo 358; 2 inf coy
Tunisia 2; 4 obs
United States 2

Congo COG

CFA Franc BEAC fr		2009	2010	2011
GDP	fr	4.52tr	5.96tr	
	US$	9.60bn	12.0bn	
per capita	US$	2,608	3,200	
Growth	%	7.6	1.9	
Inflation	%	5.0	5.3	
Def exp	fr	ε63bn		
	US$	ε134m		
Def bdgt	fr		108bn	
	US$		218m	
US$1=fr		470.96	495.60	

Population   3,758,678

Age	0–14	15–19	20–24	25–29	30–64	65 plus
Male	22.9%	5.6%	4.6%	3.7%	11.7%	1.1%
Female	22.6%	5.6%	4.6%	3.7%	12.1%	1.6%

Capabilities

ACTIVE 10,000 (Army 8,000 Navy 800 Air 1,200)
Paramilitary 2,000

ORGANISATIONS BY SERVICE

Army 8,000
FORCES BY ROLE
Armd   2 bn
Inf   1 bn; 2 bn (gp) (each: 1 lt tk tp, 1 (76mm gun) arty bty)
Cdo/AB 1 bn
Arty   1 gp (how, MRL)
Engr   1 bn

EQUIPMENT BY TYPE†
MBT 40+: 25 T-54/T-55; 15 Type-59; T-34 in store
LT TK 13: 3 PT-76; 10 Type-62
RECCE 25 BRDM-1/BRDM-2

APC (W) 68+: 20 BTR-152; 30 BTR-60; 18 *Mamba*; M-3 *Panhard*
ARTY 66+
  SP 122mm 3 2S1 *Carnation*
  TOWED 25+: **76mm** ZIS-3 *M-1942*; **100mm** 10 M-1944;
  122mm 10 D-30; **130mm** 5 M-46; **152mm** D-20
  MRL 10+: **122mm** 10 BM-21; **122mm** BM-14/**140mm**
  BM-16
  MOR 28+: **82mm**; **120mm** 28 M-43
AT • **RCL 57mm** M-18
  RL 73mm RPG-7 *Knout*
  GUNS 57mm 5 ZIS-2 *M-1943*
AD • **GUNS** 28+
  SP 23mm ZSU-23-4
  TOWED 14.5mm ZPU-2/ZPU-4; **37mm** 28 M-1939;
  57mm S-60; **100mm** KS-19

Navy ε800
EQUIPMENT BY TYPE
PATROL AND COASTAL COMBATANTS • **PB** 3 *Zhuk*†
FACILITIES
Base   Located at Pointe Noire

Air Force 1,200†
FORCES BY ROLE

FGA   Some sqn with MiG-21 *Fishbed* (non-op)
Tpt   Some sqn with An-24 *Coke*; An-26 *Curl*;
           B-727; N-2501 *Noratlas*
Trg   Some sqn with L-39 *Albatros*
Atk Hel/Tpt Some sqn with AS-365 *Dauphin 2*; Mi-8 *Hip*;
Hel   Mi-24 *Hind*; SA-316 *Alouette III*; SA-318
           Alouette II

EQUIPMENT BY TYPE†
AIRCRAFT
  FGA 8 *Mirage* F1 (12 MiG-21 *Fishbed* non-op)
  TPT 9 **Heavy** 1 An-12BK *Cub*; **Light** 7: 5 An-24 *Coke*; 1
  An-26 *Curl*; 1 N-2501 *Noratlas* **PAX** 1 B-727
  TRG 4 L-39 *Albatros*
HELICOPTERS†
  ATK (2 Mi-24 *Hind* in store)
  MRH 3: 1 AS-365 *Dauphin 2*; 1 SA-316 *Alouette III*; 1 SA-318 *Alouette II*
  TPT • **Medium** (3 Mi-8 *Hip* in store)
MSL • **AAM** R-3 (AA-2 *Atoll*)‡

Paramilitary 2,000 active
Gendarmerie 2,000
Paramilitary   20 coy
Presidential Guard some
Paramilitary   1 bn

DEPLOYMENT
CENTRAL AFRICAN REPUBLIC
ECCAS • MICOPAX 58

Côte D'Ivoire CIV

CFA Franc BCEAO fr		2009	2010	2011
GDP	fr	10.9tr	11.4tr	
	US$	23.1bn	22.9bn	
per capita	US$	1,096	1,063	
Growth	%	3.8	3.9	
Inflation	%	1.0	2.5	
Def exp	fr	ε155bn		
	US$	ε330m		
Def bdgt	fr	160bn		
	US$	340m		
US$1=fr		470.96	495.60	

Population   21,570,746

Age	0–14	15–19	20–24	25–29	30–64	65 plus
Male	20%	6%	5%	4%	14%	1%
Female	21%	6%	5%	4%	13%	1%

Capabilities
ACTIVE 17,050 (Army 6,500 Navy 900 Air 700
Presidential Guard 1,350 Gendarmerie 7,600)
Paramilitary 1,500

RESERVE 10,000 (Joint 10,000)

ORGANISATIONS BY SERVICE
Army 6,500
FORCES BY ROLE
4 Mil Regions
Armd   1 bn
Inf   3 bn
AB   1 gp
Arty   1 bn
ADA   1 coy
Engr   1 coy

EQUIPMENT BY TYPE
MBT 10 T-55†
LT TK 5 AMX-13
RECCE 34: 15 AML-60/AML-90; 13 BRDM-2; 6 ERC-90F4 *Sagaie*
AIFV 10 BMP-1/BMP-2†
APC (W) 41: 12 M-3 *Panhard*; 13 VAB; 6 BTR-80
ARTY 36+
  TOWED 4+: **105mm** 4 M-1950; **122mm** (reported)
  MRL 122mm 6 BM-21
  MOR 26+: **81mm**; **82mm** 10 M-37; **120mm** 16 AM-50
AT • **MSL** • **MANPATS** AT-14 9M133 *Kornet* (reported);
AT-5 9K113 *Spandrel* (reported)
  RCL 106mm ε12 M-40A1
  RL 73mm RPG-7 *Knout*; **89mm** LRAC
AD • **SAM** • **MANPAD** 9K32 *Strela*-2 (SA-7 *Grail*)‡
(reported)
  GUNS 21+

SP 20mm 6 M3 VDAA
TOWED 15+: **20mm** 10; **23mm** ZU-23-2; **40mm** 5 L/60
AIRCRAFT • TPT 1 An-12†

Navy ε900

EQUIPMENT BY TYPE
PATROL AND COASTAL COMBATANTS 3
PB 1 *Intrepide* (FRA *Patra*)
PBR 2 *Rodman* (fishery protection duties)
AMPHIBIOUS • 2 LCM

FACILITIES
Base Located at Locodjo (Abidjan)

Air Force 700

EQUIPMENT BY TYPE†
HELICOPTERS
ATK 1 Mi-24 (reported)
TPT • **Medium** 3 SA-330L *Puma* (IAR-330L)†

Paramilitary 10,450

Republican Guard 1,350
APC (W): 4 *Mamba*

Gendarmerie 7,600
APC (W): some VAB
PATROL AND COASTAL COMBATANTS 4 PB

Militia 1,500

FOREIGN FORCES

All forces part of UNOCI unless otherwise stated.
Bangladesh 2,090; 9 obs; 2 inf bn; 1 engr coy; 1 sigs coy; 1 fd hospital
Benin 427; 6 obs; 1 inf bn
Bolivia 3 obs
Brazil 3; 4 obs
Chad 1; 3 obs
China, People's Republic of 6 obs
Ecuador 2 obs
Egypt 176; 1 engr coy
El Salvador 3 obs
Ethiopia 2 obs
France 7 • *Operation Licorne* 772; **Army:** 1 (Marine) mech inf BG with (elm 1 mech inf regt, elm 1 armd cav regt); 1 hel unit with 3 SA-330 *Puma*
Gambia 3 obs
Ghana 507; 5 obs; 1 inf bn; 1 hel coy; 1 fd hospital
Guatemala 5 obs
Guinea 3 obs
India 6 obs
Ireland 2 obs
Jordan 1,062; 7 obs; 1 inf bn; 1 SF coy
Korea, Republic of 2 obs
Moldova 3 obs
Morocco 726; 1 inf bn
Namibia 1 obs

Nepal 1; 3 obs
Niger 393; 6 obs; 1 inf bn
Nigeria 7 obs
Pakistan 1,140; 11 obs; 1 inf bn; 1 engr coy; 1 tpt coy
Paraguay 2; 7 obs
Peru 3 obs
Philippines 3; 3 obs
Poland 3 obs
Romania 6 obs
Russia 11 obs
Senegal 324; 14 obs; 1 inf bn
Serbia 3 obs
Tanzania 2; 1 obs
Togo 315; 7 obs; 1 inf bn
Tunisia 4; 7 obs
Uganda 1; 2 obs
Uruguay 2 obs
Yemen, Republic of 1; 8 obs
Zambia 2 obs
Zimbabwe 3 obs

Democratic Republic of the Congo DRC

Congolese Franc fr		2009	2010	2011
GDP	fr	9.07tr	12.1tr	
	US$	11.3bn	13.4bn	
per capita	US$	171	197	
Growth	%	2.7	6.3	
Inflation	%	46.2	25.0	
Def exp	fr	99.1bn		
	US$	123m		
Def bdgt	fr		179bn	203bn
	US$		197m	
FMA (US)	US$	0.6m	1.45m	1.45m
US$1=fr		804.65	904.78	

Population	67,827,495					
Age	0–14	15–19	20–24	25–29	30–64	65 plus
Male	23.3%	5.6%	4.6%	3.7%	11.4%	1.0%
Female	23.1%	5.6%	4.6%	3.7%	11.7%	1.5%

Capabilities

ACTIVE ε144,000–159,000 (Central Staffs: ε14,000, Army 110–120,000 Republican Guard 6–8,000 Navy 6,703 Air 2,548)

ORGANISATIONS BY SERVICE

Army (Forces du Terre) ε110–120,000

The DRC has eleven Military Regions. A new draft Armed Forces law, which may have been partially implemented, would group these regions into three Defence Zones.

Forces in the Kinshasa region are detailed below. There are reports of small units in the 1st Military Region (Bandundu), an RG Bde and armoured units at Mbanza-Ngungu in the 2nd Military Region (Bas-Congo). In the 4th and 5th Military Regions, there there are reports of an integrated bde and log base. A possible five bdes have been reported in the 6th Military Region (Katanga), as well as the Kamina base and a number of armed groupings designated brigades (including the Kongolo Brigade) which are not under government control. The situation in the 7th Military Region (Maniema) as well as the 8th, 9th, and 10th Military Regions (North Kivu, Orientale, and South Kivu) is unclear. There are two commands in ongoing *Operation Amani Leo* operations; these parallel the 8th and 10th MR headquarters. Each command has two operations zones, each with a number of sectors, each including a number of small 'brigades', which can be bn-sized. Many of the former integrated bdes appear to have been broken up and dispersed. The 9th Military Region (Orientale) may include some of the integrated bdes plus newly reorganised smaller 'brigades'. There are also several cdo regts and at least two bn which have been formed and trained by foreign donors.

FORCES BY ROLE (elements)

Kinshasa

Rep Gd	1 bde; 1 special regt
Armd	1 regt (Rep Gd)
Arty	1 regt (Rep Gd)

EQUIPMENT BY TYPE†

MBT 49: 12–17 Type-59 †; 32 T-55
LT TK 40: 10 PT-76; 30 Type-62† (reportedly being refurbished)
RECCE up to 52: up to 17 AML-60; 14 AML-90; 19 EE-9 *Cascavel*; 2 RAM-V-2
AIFV 20 BMP-1
APC 138:
  APC (T) 3 BTR-50
  APC (W) 135: 30-70 BTR-60PB; 58 M-3 *Panhard*†; 7 TH 390 *Fahd*
ARTY 540+
  SP 122mm 6 2S1 *Carnation*
  TOWED 149: **75mm** 30 M-116 pack; **122mm** 77 (M-30) M-1938/D-30/Type-60; **130mm** 42 Type-59 (M-46)/Type-59 I
  MRL 57: **107mm** 12 Type-63; **122mm** 24 BM-21; **128mm** 6 M-51; **130mm** 3 Type-82; **132mm** 12
  MOR 328+: **81mm** 100; **82mm** 200; **107mm** M-30; **120mm** 28: 18; 10 Brandt
AT • RCL 36+: **57mm** M-18; **73mm** 10; **75mm** 10 M-20; **106mm** 16 M-40A1
  GUNS 85mm 10 Type-56 (D-44)
AD • SAM • MANPAD 20 9K32 *Strela*-2 (SA-7 *Grail*)‡
  GUNS • TOWED 114: **14.5mm** 12 ZPU-4; **37mm** 52 M-1939; **40mm** ε50 L/60† (probably out of service)

Republican Guard circa 6–8,000

FORCES BY ROLE

Armd	1 regt
Republican Guard	3 bde

Navy 6,703 (incl infantry and marines)

EQUIPMENT BY TYPE

PATROL AND COASTAL COMBATANTS 3
  PB 23: 1 *Shanghai* II; 2 Swiftships†; 20 various (all under 50ft)

FACILITIES

Bases   Located at Kinshasa (*River*), Boma (*River*), Lake Tanganyika, Matadi (*Coastal*)

Air Force 2,548

AIRCRAFT 5 combat capable
  FTR 2 MiG-23 *Flogger*
  ATK 3 Su-25 *Frogfoot*
  TPT 3 Light 1 An-26 *Curl* **PAX** 2 B-727
HELICOPTERS
  ATK 4 Mi-24/35 *Hind*
  TPT 36 **Heavy** 1 Mi-26 *Halo* (non op) **Medium** 35 Mi-8 *Hip* (very few serviceable)

Paramilitary

National Police Force

incl Rapid Intervention Police (National and Provincial forces)

People's Defence Force

DEPLOYMENT

CENTRAL AFRICAN REPUBLIC

ECCAS • MICOPAX 107

CENTRAL AFRICAN REPUBLIC/CHAD

UN • MINURCAT 1

FOREIGN FORCES

All part of MONUSCO unless otherwise specified.
Bangladesh 2,521; 30 obs; 2 mech inf bn; 1 engr coy; 2 avn unit
Belgium 22; 7 obs
Benin 450; 11 obs; 1 inf bn
Bolivia 19; 10 obs
Bosnia and Herzegovina 5 obs
Burkina Faso 8 obs
Cameroon 5 obs
Canada (*Operation Crocodile*) 10 obs
China, People's Republic of 218; 16 obs; 1 engr coy; 1 fd hospital
Czech Republic 3 obs
Denmark 2 obs
Egypt 999; 25 obs; 1 inf bn; 1 SF coy
France 5 obs
Ghana 462; 24 obs; 1 mech inf bn
Guatemala 150; 7 obs; 1 SF coy
India 4,243; 60 obs; 3 mech inf bn; 1 inf bn; 2 atk hel coy; 1 hel coy; 1 fd hospital
Indonesia 175; 16 obs; 1 engr coy
Ireland 3 obs
Jordan 218; 25 obs; 1 SF coy; 1 fd hospital
Kenya 24 obs

Malawi 50; 18 obs

Malaysia 17 obs

Mali 9 obs

Mongolia 2 obs

Morocco 831; 4 obs; 1 mech inf bn; 1 fd hospital

Mozambique 1 obs

Nepal 1,025; 24 obs; 1 inf bn; 1engr coy

Niger 16 obs

Nigeria 18 obs

Norway 1 obs

Pakistan 3,571; 55 obs; 3 mech inf bn; 1 inf bn

Paraguay 17 obs

Peru 7 obs

Poland 3 obs

Romania 21 obs

Russia 28 obs

Senegal 40; 23 obs

Serbia 6; 2 obs

South Africa (*Operation Mistral*) 1,205; 14 obs; 1 inf bn; 1 engr coy; 1 avn coy (air med evacuation team, air base control det) • *Operation Teutonic* 16

Spain 3 obs

Sri Lanka 4 obs

Sweden 4 obs

Switzerland 3 obs

Tanzania 2 obs

Tunisia 46; 30 obs

Ukraine 12 obs

United Kingdom 4 obs

United States 2 obs

Uruguay 1,285; 46 obs; 1 inf bn; 1 engr coy; 1 mne coy; 1 hel pl

Yemen, Republic of 6 obs

Zambia 16 obs

Djibouti DJB

Djiboutian Franc fr		2009	2010	2011
GDP	fr	186bn	202bn	
	US$	1.05bn	1.14bn	
per capita	US$	1,214	1,296	
Growth	%	5.0	3.9	
Inflation	%	5.5	3.8	
Def bdgt	fr	2.34bn	1.72bn	
	US$	13m	10m	
FMA (US)	US$	2.0m	2.0m	2.5m
US$1=fr		177.72	177.72	

Population 879,053

Ethnic groups: Somali 60%; Afar 35%

Age	0–14	15–19	20–24	25–29	30–64	65 plus
Male	17.5%	5.4%	4.9%	3.9%	13.0%	1.5%
Female	17.5%	5.8%	5.8%	5.2%	17.7%	1.8%

ACTIVE 10,450 (Army 8,000 Navy 200 Air 250 Gendarmerie 2,000) National Security Force 2,500

ORGANISATIONS BY SERVICE

Army ε8,000
FORCES BY ROLE

4 military districts (Tadjourah, Dikhil, Ali-Sabieh and Obock)

Rep Guard	1 regt (1 sy sqn, 1 spt sqn (arty, armd and motorcycle pls), 1 close prot sqn, 1 ceremonial sqn,1 comd and spt sqn; incl CT and cdo role)
Armd	1 regt (3 armd sqns, 1 *Ratel* sqn, 1 anti-smuggling coy)
Inf	4 joint regts (3–4 coys, comd and spt coy, training camp(s), 1 rapid reaction regt (4 coys, comd and spt coy, 1 hvy spt sect; incl CT and cdo/abn role)
Arty	1 regt
Engr	1 demining coy, 1 plant coy
Comd	1 HQ regt, 1 comms comd, 1 CIS sect
Spt	1 log sp regt

EQUIPMENT BY TYPE
RECCE 39: 4 AML-60†; 15 VBL; 16-20 *Ratel*
APC (W) 20: 8 BTR -80; 12 BTR-60†
ARTY 96
    TOWED 122mm 6 D-30
    MOR 45: 81mm 25; 120mm 20 Brandt
AT
    RCL 106mm 16 M-40A1
    RL 73mm RPG-7 *Knout*; 89mm LRAC
AD • GUNS 15+
    SP 20mm 5 M-693 (SP
    TOWED 10: 23mm 5 ZU-23; 40mm 5 L/70

Navy ε200
EQUIPMENT BY TYPE
PATROL AND COASTAL COMBATANTS 10
    PBF 2 Battalion-17
    PB 8
FACILITIES
Base   Located at Djibouti

Air Force 250
FORCES BY ROLE

Tpt	Some sqn with An-28 *Cash*; Cessna U206G *Stationair*; Cessna 208 *Caravan*; L-410UVP *Turbolet*
Atk Hel/ Tpt Hel	Some sqn with AS-355F *Ecureuil II*; Mi-17 *Hip H*; Mi-24 *Hind*
Trg	Some units with EMB-314 *Super Tucano**

EQUIPMENT BY TYPE
AIRCRAFT Some combat capable
    TPT • Light 5: 1 An-28 *Cash*; 1 Cessna U206G *Stationair*; 1 Cessna 208 *Caravan*; 2 L-410UVP *Turbolet*; (1 Cessna 402 in store)
    TRG Some EMB-314 *Super Tucano**
HELICOPTERS
    ATK 2 Mi-24 *Hind*

MRH 1 Mi-17 *Hip H*
TPT 1 **Medium** (1 Mi-8 *Hip* in store) **Light** 1 AS-355F *Ecureuil II*;

Gendarmerie 2,000 +
Ministry of Defence
FORCES BY ROLE
Paramilitary 1 bn
EQUIPMENT BY TYPE
PATROL AND COASTAL COMBATANTS 1 PB

Paramilitary ε2,500

National Security Force ε2,500
Ministry of Interior

DEPLOYMENT

WESTERN SAHARA
UN • MINURSO 2 obs

FOREIGN FORCES

France 1,501
Army 1 (Foreign Legion) BG with (1 engr coy, 1 arty bty, 2 recce sqn, 2 inf coy); 1 (Marine) combined arms regt with (1 engr coy, 1 arty bty, 2 recce sqn, 2 inf coy)
Navy 1 LCT
Air Force 1 air sqn with 10 M-2000C/D *Mirage*; 1 C-160 *Transall*; 2 SA-330 *Puma*; 1 AS-555 *Fennec*
United States US Africa Command: 1,285; 1 naval air base

Equatorial Guinea EQG

CFA Franc BEAC fr		2009	2010	2011
GDP	fr	5.77tr	7.30tr	
	US$	12.3bn	14.7bn	
per capita	US$	18,115	21,238	
Growth	%	-5.4	1.5	
Inflation	%	7.2	2.9	
Def exp	fr	ε3.8bn		
	US$	ε8m		
US$1=fr		470.96	495.60	

Population 693,385

Age	0–14	15–19	20–24	25–29	30–64	65 plus
Male	21.1%	5.3%	4.5%	3.8%	13.2%	1.8%
Female	20.4%	5.1%	4.4%	3.7%	14.4%	2.3%

Capabilities

ACTIVE 1,320 (Army 1,100 Navy 120 Air 100)

ORGANISATIONS BY SERVICE

Army 1,100

FORCES BY ROLE
Inf 3 bn
EQUIPMENT BY TYPE
RECCE 6 BRDM-2
AIFV 20 BMP-1
APC (W) 10 BTR-152

Navy ε120
EQUIPMENT BY TYPE†
PATROL AND COASTAL COMBATANTS • PB 6: 1 *Daphne*; 1 *Estuario de Muni*; 2 *Shaldag II*; 2 *Zhuk*
FACILITIES
Bases Located at Bata, Malabo (Santa Isabel)

Air Force 100
EQUIPMENT BY TYPE
AIRCRAFT 4 combat capable
ATK 6: 4 Su-25 *Frogfoot*; 2 Su-25UB *Frogfoot*
TPT 2 **Light** 2 An-72; 1 Cessna 337 *Skymaster* **PAX** 1 *Falcon* 900 (VIP)
TRG 2 L-39C
HELICOPTERS
ATK 3 Mi-24 *Hind*
MRH 3: 1 Mi-17 (Mi-8MT) *Hip-H*; 2 SA-316 *Alouette III*

Paramilitary

Guardia Civil some
2 coy

Coast Guard
PATROL AND COASTAL COMBATANTS • PB 1†

DEPLOYMENT

CENTRAL AFRICAN REPUBLIC
ECCAS • MICOPAX 7

Eritrea ERI

Eritrean Nakfa ERN		2009	2010	2011
GDP	ERN	28.8bn	34.7bn	
	US$	1.87bn	2.25bn	
per capita	US$	369	432	
Growth	%	4.2	1.4	
Inflation	%	34.7	14.5	
Def exp	ERN	ε1.2bn		
	US$	ε78m		
USD1=ERN		15.37	15.37	

Population 5,223,994
Ethnic groups: Tigrinya 50%; Tigre and Kunama 40%; Afar; Saho 3%

Age	0–14	15–19	20–24	25–29	30–64	65 plus
Male	21.2%	5.3%	4.5%	3.9%	12.9%	1.6%
Female	21.0%	5.3%	4.5%	4.0%	13.8%	2.0%

Capabilities

ACTIVE 201,750 (Army 200,000 Navy 1,400 Air 350)

Terms of service 16 months (4 month mil trg)

RESERVE 120,000 (Army ε120,000)

ORGANISATIONS BY SERVICE

Army ε200,000
FORCES BY ROLE

Army 4 corps
Mech 1 bde
Inf   19 div
Cdo   1 div

Reserve Organisations

Reserve ε 120,000 reported reservists
Inf   1 div

EQUIPMENT BY TYPE
MBT 270 T-54/T-55
RECCE 40 BRDM-1/BRDM-2
AIFV 15 BMP-1
APC • APC (W) 25 BTR-152 APC (W)/BTR-60 APC (W)
ARTY 208+
  SP 45: **122mm** 32 2S1 *Carnation*; **152mm** 13 2S5
  TOWED 19+: **122mm** D-30; **130mm** 19 M-46
  MRL 44: **122mm** 35 BM-21; **220mm** 9 BM-27/9P140 *Uragan*
  MOR 120mm/160mm 100+
AT
  MSL • MANPATS 200 AT-3 9K11 *Sagger*/AT-5 9K113 *Spandrel*
  RL 73mm RPG-7 *Knout*
  GUNS 85mm D-44
AD • SAM • MANPAD 9K32 *Strela*-2 (SA-7 *Grail*)‡
  GUNS 70+
    SP 23mm ZSU-23-4
    TOWED 23mm ZU-23

Navy 1,400
HQ located at Massawa
EQUIPMENT BY TYPE
PATROL AND COASTAL COMBATANTS 12
  PBF 9: 5 *Battalion*-17; 4 *Super Dvora*
  PB 3 Swiftships
AMPHIBIOUS
  LS • LST 2: 1 *Chamo*† (Ministry of Transport); 1 *Ashdod*†
FACILITIES
Bases   Located at Massawa, Assab, Dahlak

Air Force ε350
FORCES BY ROLE
Ftr/FGA Some sqn with MiG-21 *Fishbed*†; MiG-23 *Flogger*†; MiG-29 *Fulcrum*; MiG-29UB *Fulcrum**; Su-27 *Flanker*; Su-27UBK *Flanker**
Tpt   Some sqn with IAI-1125 *Astra*; Y-12(II)

Trg   Some sqn with L-90 *Redigo*; MB-339CE*
Atk Hel/ Some sqn with Mi-24-4 *Hind*; Mi-8 *Hip*; Mi-17
Tpt Hel   *Hip H*

EQUIPMENT BY TYPE
AIRCRAFT 31 combat capable
  FTR 14: 4 MiG-23 *Flogger*†; 8 MiG-29 *Fulcrum*; 2 MiG-29UB *Fulcrum*;
  FGA 13: 3 MiG-21 *Fishbed*†; 8 Su-27 *Flanker*; 2 Su-27UBK *Flanker*
  TPT • Light 4: 1 IAI-1125 *Astra*; 3 Y-12(II)
  TRG 12: 8 L-90 *Redigo*; 4 MB-339CE*
HELICOPTERS
  ATK 1 Mi-24-4 *Hind*
  MRH 4 Bell 412 *Twin Huey* (AB-412)
  MRH/TPT 4 Mi-8 *Hip*/Mi-17 *Hip H*
  MSL
    AAM • IR AAM R-60 (AA-8 *Aphid*); R-73 (AA-11 *Archer*) **IR/SARH AAM** R-27 (AA-10 *Alamo*)

Ethiopia ETH

Ethiopian Birr EB		2009	2010	2011
GDP	EB	336bn	399bn	
	US$	28.6bn	27.6bn	
per capita	US$	346	324	
Growth	%	8.7	9.7	
Inflation	%	8.5	7.7	
Def exp	EB	4.79bn		
	US$	408m		
Def bdgt	EB	4bn	4.5bn	
	US$	341m	311m	
FMA (US)	US$	0.8m	0.843m	2.0m
US$1=EB		11.73	14.48	

Population   84,975,606

Ethnic groups: Oromo 40%; Amhara and Tigrean 32%; Sidamo 9%; Shankella 6%; Somali 6%; Afar 4%

Age	0–14	15–19	20–24	25–29	30–64	65 plus
Male	23.1%	5.1%	4.4%	3.7%	11.8%	1.1%
Female	23.2%	5.1%	4.7%	3.9%	12.3%	1.5%

Capabilities

ACTIVE 138,000 (Army 135,000 Air 3,000)

ORGANISATIONS BY SERVICE

Army 135,000
FORCES BY ROLE
4 Mil Regional Commands (Northern, Western, Central, and Eastern) each acting as corps HQ and one functional (Support) Command; strategic reserve of 4 divs and 6 specialist bdes centred on Addis Ababa.

Army 4 corps HQ (each: 1 mech div, 4–6 inf div)

EQUIPMENT BY TYPE
MBT 246+ T-54/T-55/T-62

RECCE/AIFV/APC (W) ε450 BRDM/BMP/BTR-60/BTR-152/Type 89
ARTY 460+
  SP 10+: **122mm** 2S1 *Carnation*; **152mm** 10 2S19 *Farm*
  TOWED 400+: **76mm** ZIS-3 *M-1942*; **122mm** ε400 D-30/(M-30) *M-1938*; **130mm** M-46
  MRL 122mm ε50 BM-21
  MOR 81mm M-1/M-29; **82mm** M-1937; **120mm** M-1944
AT • MSL • MANPATS AT-3 9K11 *Sagger;* AT-4 9K111 *Spigot*
  RCL 82mm B-10; **107mm** B-11
  GUNS 85mm εD-44
AD • SAM ε370
  TOWED S-75 *Dvina* (SA-2 *Guideline*) S-125 *Pechora* (SA-3 *Goa*)
  MANPAD 9K32 *Strela-2* (SA-7 *Grail*)‡
GUNS
  SP 23mm ZSU-23-4
  TOWED 23mm ZU-23; **37mm** M-1939; **57mm** S-60

Air Force 3,000

FORCES BY ROLE

FGA   Some sqn with MiG-21MF *Fishbed J*; MiG-23BN *Flogger H*; Su-25T *Frogfoot*; Su-25UB *Frogfoot B*; Su-27 *Flanker*

Tpt   Some sqn with An-12 *Cub*; C-130B *Hercules*; DHC-6 *Twin Otter*; Mi-6 *Hook*; Y-12; Yak-40 *Codling* (VIP)

Trg   Some sqn with L-39 *Albatros*; SF-260

Atk Hel   Some sqn with Mi-24/Mi-35 *Hind*; Mi-14 *Haze*

Tpt hel   Some sqn with Mi-8 *Hip*/Mi-17 *Hip H*

EQUIPMENT BY TYPE
AIRCRAFT 42 combat capable
  FGA 38: 15 MiG-21MF *Fishbed J*; 12 MiG-23BN *Flogger H*; 11 Su-27 *Flanker*
  ATK 4: 2 Su-25T *Frogfoot*; 2 Su-25UB *Frogfoot B*
  TPT 17 **Medium** 12: 9 An-12 *Cub*; 3 C-130B *Hercules* **Light** 5: 2 DHC-6 *Twin Otter*; 2 Y-12; 1 Yak-40 *Codling* (VIP)
  TRG 16: 12 L-39 *Albatros*; 4 SF-260
HELICOPTERS
  ATK 18: 15 Mi-24 *Hind*; 3 Mi-35 *Hind*
  ASW 2 Mi-14 *Haze*
  MRH 8 SA316 *Alouette III*
  MRH/TPT 12 Mi-8 *Hip*/Mi-17 *Hip H*
  TPT • Heavy 10 Mi-6 *Hook*
  MSL
    AAM • IR AAM R-3 (AA-2 *Atoll*)‡; R-60 (AA-8 *Aphid*); R-73 (AA-11 *Archer*) **IR/SARH AAM** R-23/R-24 (AA-7 *Apex*) R-27 (AA-10 *Alamo*)

DEPLOYMENT

CENTRAL AFRICAN REPUBLIC/CHAD
UN • MINURCAT 2

COTE D'IVOIRE
UN • UNOCI 2 obs

LIBERIA
UN • UNMIL 4; 7 obs

SUDAN
UN • UNAMID 2,356; 10 obs; 2 inf bn; 1 recce coy; 1 log coy; 1 tpt coy; 1 hel coy

Gabon GAB

CFA Franc BEAC fr		2009	2010	2011
GDP	fr	5.20tr	6.38tr	
	US$	11.0bn	12.9bn	
per capita	US$	7,489	8,574	
Growth	%	-1.0	3.0	
Inflation	%	1.9	3.3	
Def bdgt	fr		124bn	
	US$		250m	
FMA (US)	US$	-	0.2m	0.2m
US$1=fr		470.96	495.60	

Population	1,501,266					
Age	0–14	15–19	20–24	25–29	30–64	65 plus
Male	21.2%	5.4%	4.8%	3.9%	12.8%	1.6%
Female	21.0%	5.4%	4.8%	3.9%	13.0%	2.2%

Capabilities

ACTIVE 4,700 (Army 3,200 Navy 500 Air 1,000)
Paramilitary 2,000

ORGANISATIONS BY SERVICE

Army 3,200
FORCES BY ROLE
Inf   8 coy
Cdo/AB   1 coy
Engr   1 coy
Presidential   1 (bn) gp (under direct presidential control)
Guard   (1 ADA bty, 1 arty bty, 1 armd/recce coy, 3 inf coy)

EQUIPMENT BY TYPE
RECCE 70: 24 AML-60/AML-90; 12 EE-3 *Jararaca*; 14 EE-9 *Cascavel*; 6 ERC-90F4 *Sagaie*; 14 VBL
AIFV 12 EE-11 *Urutu* (with 20mm gun)
APC (W) 28+: 9 LAV-150 *Commando*; 6 Type-92 (reported); 12 VXB-170; M-3 *Panhard*; 1 *Pandur* (Testing)
ARTY 51
  TOWED 105mm 4 M-101
  MRL 140mm 8 *Teruel*
  MOR 39: **81mm** 35; **120mm** 4 Brandt
AT • MSL • MANPATS 4 *Milan*
  RCL 106mm M-40A1
  RL 89mm LRAC
AD • GUNS 41
  SP 20mm 4 ERC-20
  TOWED 37: **23mm** 24 ZU-23-2; **37mm** 10 M-1939; **40mm** 3 L/70

Navy ε500
HQ located at Port Gentil

EQUIPMENT BY TYPE

PATROL AND COASTAL COMBATANTS 3

PCC 2 *General Ba'Oumar* (FRA P-400)

PBFG 1 *Patra* with 4 SS 12M AShM

AMPHIBIOUS

LANDING SHIPS • LST 1 *President Omar Bongo* (FRA *Batral*) (capacity 1 LCVP; 7 MBT; 140 troops) with 1 hel landing platform

LANDING CRAFT 12 **LCVP**

FACILITIES

Base   Located at Port Gentil

Air Force 1,000

FORCES BY ROLE

FGA   1 sqn with *Mirage* 5G/5DG; *Mirage* 5E2; *Mirage* F1-AZ

MP   1 sqn with EMB-111*

Tpt   1 (Presidential Guard) sqn with AS-332 *Super Puma*; ATR-42F; EMB-110 *Bandeirante*; *Falcon* 900 Some sqn with C-130H *Hercules*; CN-235; EMB-110 *Bandeirante*; YS-11A

Trg   1 (Presidential Guard) sqn with CM-170 *Magister*; T-34 *Turbo Mentor*

Atk Hel/ 1 sqn with SA-342 *Gazelle**; SA-330C *Puma*/SA-
Tpt Hel   330H *Puma*; SA-316 *Alouette III*/SA-319 *Alouette III*; AB-412 (Bell 412) *Twin Huey*

EQUIPMENT BY TYPE

AIRCRAFT 20 combat capable

FGA 19: 4 *Mirage* 5E2; 3 *Mirage* 5G/DG (*Mirage* 5); 12 *Mirage* F1-AZ

MP 1 EMB-111*

TPT 10 **Medium** 3 C-130H *Hercules* **Light** 6: 1 ATR-42F; 1 CN-235; 2 EMB-110 *Bandeirante*; 2 YS-11A **PAX** 1 *Falcon* 900

TRG 7: 4 CM-170 *Magister*; 3 T-34 *Turbo Mentor*

HELICOPTERS

MRH 10: 2 Bell 412 *Twin Huey*(AB-412); 3 SA-316 *Alouette III*/SA-319 *Alouette III*; 5 SA-342 *Gazelle*

TPT • Medium 4: 1 AS-332 *Super Puma*; 3 SA-330C *Puma*/SA-330H *Puma*

Paramilitary 2,000

Gendarmerie 2,000

FORCES BY ROLE

Armd   2 sqn

Paramilitary 3 bde; 11 coy

Avn   1 unit with AS-350 *Ecureuil*; AS-355 *Ecureuil*

EQUIPMENT BY TYPE

HELICOPTERS • TPT • Light 3: 2 AS-350 *Ecureuil*; 1 AS-355 *Ecureuil*

DEPLOYMENT

CENTRAL AFRICAN REPUBLIC

ECCAS • MICOPAX 142

FOREIGN FORCES

France • **Army** 645; 1 recce pl with ERC-90F1 *Lynx*; 1 (Marine) inf bn; 4 SA-330 *Puma*

Gambia GAM

Gambian Dalasi D		2009	2010	2011
GDP	D	25.8bn	28.4bn	
	US$	969m	1.04bn	
per capita	US$	568	597	
Growth	%	4.6	5.4	
Inflation	%	4.6	5.1	
Def bdgt	D	ε189m		
	US$	ε7m		
US$1=D		26.64	27.21	

Population   1,750,732

Age	0–14	15–19	20–24	25–29	30–64	65 plus
Male	21.7%	5.5%	4.6%	3.7%	13.0%	1.4%
Female	21.5%	5.4%	4.6%	3.8%	13.4%	1.5%

Capabilities

ACTIVE 800 (Army 800)

ORGANISATIONS BY SERVICE

Gambian National Army 800

Inf   2 bn
Engr   1 sqn
Presidential Guard   1 coy

Marine Unit ε70

EQUIPMENT BY TYPE

PATROL AND COASTAL COMBATANTS • PB 7: 1 *Bolong Kanta*; 2 *Fatimah* I; 4 *Taipei* (ROC *Hai Ou*)

FACILITIES

Base   Located at Banjul

Air Wing

EQUIPMENT BY TYPE

AIRCRAFT

ATK 1 Su-25 *Frogfoot*

TPT 3 **Light** 2 AT-802A **PAX** 1 Il-62M *Classic* (VIP)

FACILITIES

Base   Located at Banjul (Yundum Int'l Airport)

FACILITIES

Banjul-Yundum Int'l Airport

DEPLOYMENT

CÔTE D'IVOIRE

UN • UNOCI 3 obs

LIBERIA

UN • UNMIL 2 obs

SUDAN

UN • UNAMID 200; 1 obs; 1 inf coy

Ghana GHA

Ghanaian Cedi C		2009	2010	2011
GDP	C	21.7bn	25.9bn	
	US$	15.5bn	18.2bn	
per capita	US$	649	748	
Growth	%	3.5	6.4	
Inflation	%	19.3	12.2	
Def exp	C	159m		
	US$	113m		
Def bdgt	C	381m	179m	206m
	US$	271m	126m	
FMA (US)	US$	0.3m	0.35m	0.45m
US$1=C		1.41	1.42	

Population   24,332,755

Age	0–14	15–19	20–24	25–29	30–64	65 plus
Male	18.4%	5.4%	5.1%	4.4%	15.1%	1.6%
Female	18.0%	5.3%	5.1%	4.3%	15.3%	1.9%

Capabilities

ACTIVE 15,500 (Army 11,500 Navy 2,000 Air 2,000)

ORGANISATIONS BY SERVICE

Army 11,500

FORCES BY ROLE

2 Comd HQ

Army	6 inf bn
Recce	1 regt (3 recce sqn)
AB/SF	2 coy
Arty	1 regt (1 arty bty, 2 mor bty)
Fd engr	1 regt (bn)
Trg	1 bn

EQUIPMENT BY TYPE

RECCE 3 EE-9 Cascavel

AIFV 39: 24 Ratel FSC-90; 15 Ratel-20

APC (W) 50 Piranha

ARTY 84

TOWED 122mm 6 D-30

MOR 78: **81mm** 50; **120mm** 28 Tampella

AT • RCL 84mm 50 Carl Gustav

AD • SAM • MANPAD 9K32 Strela-2 (SA-7 Grail)‡

GUNS • TOWED 8+: **14.5mm** 4+: 4 ZPU-2; ZPU-4;

23mm 4 ZU-23-2

Navy 2,000

Naval HQ located at Accra; Western HQ located at
Sekondi; Eastern HQ located at Tema

EQUIPMENT BY TYPE

PATROL AND COASTAL COMBATANTS 7

PCO 2 Anzole (US)

PCC 4: 2 Achimota (GER Lurssen 57m); 2 Dzata (GER Lurssen 45m)

PB 1(US)

FACILITIES

Bases   Located at Sekondi, Tema

Air Force 2,000

Main base Accra. Tpt element at Takoradi

FORCES BY ROLE

Atk	1 sqn with K-8 Karakorum*; L-39ZO*: MB-326K; MB-339A*
Tpt	1 sqn with BN-2 Defender; Cessna 172; F-27 Friendship; F-28 Fellowship (VIP)
Hel	1 sqn with AW-109A; Bell 212 (AB-212); Mi-171V; SA-319 Alouette III

FACILITIES

Flying School 1 with Cessna 172

EQUIPMENT BY TYPE†

AIRCRAFT 11 combat capable

FGA 3 MB-326K

TPT 9 **Light** 8: 1 BN-2 Defender; 3 Cessna 172; 4 F-27 Friendship **PAX** 1 F-28 Fellowship (VIP)

TRG 8: 4 K-8 Karakorum*; 2 L-39ZO*; 2 MB-339A*

HELICOPTERS

MRH 2 SA-319 Alouette III

TPT 7 **Medium** 4 Mi-171V **Light** 3: 2 AW-109A; 1 Bell 212 (AB-212)

DEPLOYMENT

BURUNDI

UN • BINUB 1 obs

CENTRAL AFRICAN REPUBLIC/CHAD

UN • MINURCAT 527; 1 obs; 1 inf bn

CÔTE D'IVOIRE

UN • UNOCI 507; 5 obs; 1 inf bn; 1 hel coy; 1 fd hospital

DEMOCRATIC REPUBLIC OF THE CONGO

UN • MONUSCO 462; 24 obs; 1 mech inf bn

LEBANON

UN • UNIFIL 877; 1 inf bn

LIBERIA

UN • UNMIL 706; 11 obs; 1 inf bn

SUDAN

UN • UNAMID 6; 4 obs

WESTERN SAHARA

UN • MINURSO 7; 9 obs

Guinea GUI

Guinean Franc fr		2009	2010	2011
GDP	fr	21.7tr	25.4tr	
	US$	4.57bn	4.57bn	
per capita	US$	454	443	
Growth	%	-0.6	4.3	
Inflation	%	4.7	8.9	
Def exp	fr	ε355bn		
	US$	ε75m		
Def bdgt	fr	275bn		
	US$	58m		
US$1=fr		4761.90	5555.56	

Population 10,323,755

Age	0–14	15–19	20–24	25–29	30–64	65 plus
Male	21.5%	5.3%	4.5%	3.8%	13.5%	1.5%
Female	21.0%	5.2%	4.4%	3.7%	13.7%	2.0%

Capabilities

ACTIVE 12,300 (Army 8,500 Navy 400 Air 800
Gendarmerie 1,000 Republican Guard 1,600)
Paramilitary 7,000
Terms of service conscription, 2 years

ORGANISATIONS BY SERVICE

Army 8,500

FORCES BY ROLE

Armd	1 bn
Inf	5 bn
SF	1 bn
Ranger	1 bn
Cdo	1 bn
Arty	1 bn
Engr	1 bn
AD	1 bn

EQUIPMENT BY TYPE
MBT 38: 8 T-54; 30 T-34
LT TK 15 PT-76
RECCE 27: 2 AML-90; 25 BRDM-1/BRDM-2
APC (W) 40: 16 BTR-40; 10 BTR-50; 8 BTR-60; 6 BTR-152
ARTY 47+
    TOWED 24: **122mm** 12 M-1931/37; **130 mm** 12 M-46
    MRL 220mm 3 BM-27/9P140 *Uragan*
    MOR 20+: **82mm** M-43; **120mm** 20 M-1943/M-38
AT • MSL • MANPATS AT-3 9K11 *Sagger*; AT-5 9M113 *Spandrel*
    RCL 82mm B-10
    RL 73mm RPG-7 *Knout*
    GUNS 6+: **57mm** ZIS-2 *M-1943*; **85mm** 6 D-44
AD • SAM • MANPAD 9K32 *Strela*-2 (SA-7 *Grail*) ‡
    GUNS • TOWED 24+: **30mm** M-53 (twin); **37mm** 8
    M-1939; **57mm** 12 Type-59 (S-60); **100mm** 4 KS-19

Navy ε400

EQUIPMENT BY TYPE
PATROL AND COASTAL COMBATANTS • PB 2
Swiftships†
FACILITIES
Bases   Located at Conakry, Kakanda

Air Force 800

FORCES BY ROLE

FGA	1 sqn with MiG-17F *Fresco C* (non-op); MiG-21 *Fishbed* (non-op)
Tpt	1 sqn with An-14 *Clod*; An-24 *Coke*
Trg	1 sqn with MiG-15UTI *Midget*
Atk Hel/Tpt Hel	sqn with Mi-24 *Hind*; SA-342K *Gazelle*; SA-330 *Puma*; Mi-8 *Hip*

EQUIPMENT BY TYPE†
AIRCRAFT
    FTR (4 MiG-17F *Fresco C* non-op)
    FGA (3 MiG-21 *Fishbed* non-op)
    TPT • Light 7: 4 An-14 *Clod*; 1 An-24 *Coke*; 2 An-72 *Coaler*
    TRG 2 MiG-15UTI *Midget*
HELICOPTERS
    ATK 4 Mi-24 *Hind*
    MRH 1 SA-342K *Gazelle*
    TPT • Medium 3: 2 Mi-8 *Hip*; 1 SA-330 *Puma*†
MSL
    AAM • IR AAM R-3 (AA-2 *Atoll*)‡

Paramilitary 2,600 active

Gendarmerie 1,000

Republican Guard 1,600

People's Militia 7,000

DEPLOYMENT

CÔTE D'IVOIRE
UN • UNOCI 3 obs

SUDAN
UN • UNMIS 7 obs

WESTERN SAHARA
UN • MINURSO 3 obs

Sub-Saharan Africa

Guinea Bissau GNB

CFA Franc BCEAO fr		2009	2010	2011
GDP	fr	395bn	419bn	
	US$	839m	845m	
per capita	US$	521	513	
Growth	%	3.0	3.4	
Inflation	%	-1.7	2.5	
Def exp	fr	ε6.39bn		
	US$	ε14m		
US$1=fr		470.96	495.60	

Population   1,647,380

Age	0–14	15–19	20–24	25–29	30–64	65 plus
Male	20.2%	5.3%	4.7%	4.0%	13.3%	1.3%
Female	20.2%	5.4%	4.8%	4.1%	14.8%	1.9%

Capabilities

ACTIVE ε4,458 (Army ε4,000 (numbers reducing) Navy 350 Air 100) Gendarmerie 2,000
Terms of service conscription (selective).
Manpower and eqpt totals should be treated with caution. Recent governments have envisaged reducing the armed forces. A number of draft laws to restructure the armed services and police have been produced.

ORGANISATIONS BY SERVICE

Army ε4,000 (numbers reducing)
FORCES BY ROLE
Armd   1 bn (sqn)
Recce   1 coy
Inf   5 bn
Arty   1 bn
Engr   1 coy
EQUIPMENT BY TYPE
MBT 10 T-34
LT TK 15 PT-76
RECCE 10 BRDM-2
APC (W) 55: 35 BTR-40/BTR-60; 20 Type-56 (BTR-152)
ARTY 26+
   TOWED 122mm 18 D-30/*M-1938*
   MOR 8+: **82mm** M-43; **120mm** 8 M-1943
AT
   RCL 75mm Type-52 (M-20); **82mm** B-10
   RL 89mm M-20
   GUNS 85mm 8 D-44
AD • SAM • MANPAD 9K32 *Strela-2* (SA-7 *Grail*)‡
   GUNS • TOWED 34: **23mm** 18 ZU-23; **37mm** 6 M-1939; **57mm** 10 S-60

Navy ε350
EQUIPMENT BY TYPE
PATROL AND COASTAL COMBATANTS • PB 2 *Alfeite*†

FACILITIES
Base   Located at Bissau

Air Force 100
FORCES BY ROLE
Ftr/FGA   sqn with MiG-17 *Fresco*
Hel   sqn with SA-319 *Alouette III*; SA-341 *Gazelle*
EQUIPMENT BY TYPE
AIRCRAFT 2 combat capable
   FTR 2 MiG-17 *Fresco* †
HELICOPTERS • MRH 3: 2 SA-319 *Alouette III*; 1 SA-341 *Gazelle*

Paramilitary 2,000 active

Gendarmerie 2,000

Kenya KEN

Kenyan Shilling sh		2009	2010	2011
GDP	sh	2.27tr	2.51tr	
	US$	29.4bn	31.9bn	
per capita	US$	739	782	
Growth	%	2.2	3.6	
Inflation	%	9.2	7.3	
Def exp	sh	41.2bn		
	US$	533m		
Def bdgt	sh	58bn	56.7bn	55.9bn
	US$	750m	720m	
FMA (US)	US$	0.25m	1.0m	1.0m
US$1=sh		77.31	78.73	

Population   40,862,900

Ethnic groups: Kikuyu ε22–32%

Age	0–14	15–19	20–24	25–29	30–64	65 plus
Male	21.3%	5.0%	4.9%	4.5%	13.2%	1.2%
Female	20.9%	5.0%	4.8%	4.5%	13.2%	1.5%

Capabilities

ACTIVE 24,120 (Army 20,000 Navy 1,620 Air 2,500) Paramilitary 5,000
(incl HQ staff)

ORGANISATIONS BY SERVICE

Army 20,000
FORCES BY ROLE
Armd   1 bde (3 armd bn)
Air Cav   1 indep bn
Inf   1 bde (2 inf bn); 1 bde (3 inf bn); 1 indep bn
AB   1 bn
Arty   1 bde (2 arty bn)
ADA   1 bn
Engr   1 bde (2 engr bn)

EQUIPMENT BY TYPE
MBT 188: 110 T-72 (reported); 78 Vickers Mk 3
RECCE 92: 72 AML-60/AML-90; 12 *Ferret*; 8 S52 *Shorland*
APC (W) 94: 10 M-3 *Panhard* in store; 52 UR-416; 32 Type-92 (reported)
ARTY 115
  TOWED 105mm 48: 8 Model 56 pack howitzer; 40 lt Gun
  MRL 122mm 11 BM-21 (reported)
  MOR 62: **81mm** 50; **120mm** 12 Brandt
  AT • MSL • MANPATS 54: 40 *Milan*; 14 *Swingfire*
  RCL 84mm 80 *Carl Gustav*
  AD • GUNS • TOWED 94: **20mm** 81: 11 Oerlikon; ε70 TCM-20; **40mm** 13 L/70

Navy 1,620 (incl 120 marines)
EQUIPMENT BY TYPE
PATROL AND COASTAL COMBATANTS 5
  PCFG 2 *Nyayo* each with 2 twin lnchr (4 eff.) each with *Otomat* AShM, 1 76mm gun
  PCC 2 *Shujaa* each with 1 76mm gun
  PBF 1 *Archangel*
AMPHIBIOUS LCM 2 *Galana*
FACILITIES
Base Located at Mombasa

Air Force 2,500
FORCES BY ROLE
FGA Some sqn with F-5E *Tiger II*/F-5F *Tiger II*
Tpt Some sqn with DHC-5D *Buffalo*†; DHC-8 *Dash 8*†; F-70† (VIP); PA-31 *Navajo*†; Y-12(II)†
Trg Some sqn with *Bulldog* 103/*Bulldog* 127†; EMB-312 *Tucano*†*; *Hawk* Mk52†*; Hughes 500D†
Atk Hel Some sqn with Hughes 500M†; Hughes 500MD *Scout Defender*†(with TOW); Hughes 500ME†; Z-9W
Tpt Hel Some sqn with SA-330 *Puma*†
EQUIPMENT BY TYPE†
AIRCRAFT 42 combat capable
  FTR 22 F-5E *Tiger II*/F-5F *Tiger II*
  TPT 19 **Light** 18: 4 DHC-5D *Buffalo*†; 3 DHC-8 *Dash 8*†; 1 PA-31 *Navajo*†; 10 Y-12(II)†; (6 Do-28D-2† in store); **PAX** 1 F-70† (VIP)
  TRG up to 25: up to 5 *Bulldog* 103/*Bulldog* 127†; 12 EMB-312 *Tucano*†*; 8 *Hawk* Mk52†*
HELICOPTERS
  MRH 39+: 2 Hughes 500D†; 15 Hughes 500M†; 11 Hughes 500MD *Scout Defender*† (with TOW); 8 Hughes 500ME†; 3+ Z-9W
  TPT • Medium 11 SA-330 *Puma*†
MSL
  AAM • IR AAM AIM-9 *Sidewinder*
  ASM AGM-65 *Maverick*; TOW

Paramilitary 5,000
Police General Service Unit 5,000
PATROL AND COASTAL COMBATANTS • PB 5 (2 on Lake Victoria)

Air Wing
AIRCRAFT • TPT 7 *Cessna*
HELICOPTERS
  TPT • Light 1 Bell 206L *Long Ranger*
  TRG 2 Bell 47G

DEPLOYMENT
CENTRAL AFRICAN REPUBLIC/CHAD
UN • MINURCAT 3
DEMOCRATIC REPUBLIC OF THE CONGO
UN • MONUSCO 24 obs
SUDAN
UN • UNMIS 724; 4 obs; 1 inf bn; 1 de-mining coy
UN • UNAMID 82; 6 obs; 1 MP coy
UGANDA
EU • EUTM 9

FOREIGN FORCES
United Kingdom Army 52

Lesotho LSO

Lesotho Loti M		2009	2010	2011
GDP	M	13.8bn	15.4bn	
	US$	1.65bn	2.08bn	
per capita	US$	797	999	
Growth	%	2.1	2.3	
Inflation	%	7.2	5.5	
Def exp	M	452m		
	US$	54m		
US$1=M		8.35	7.40	

Population 2,084,182

Age	0–14	15–19	20–24	25–29	30–64	65 plus
Male	16.8%	5.0%	5.0%	5.0%	14.9%	2.6%
Female	16.7%	5.3%	5.7%	5.7%	14.6%	2.7%

Capabilities
ACTIVE 2,000 (Army 2,000)

ORGANISATIONS BY SERVICE
Army ε2,000
FORCES BY ROLE
Recce 1 coy
Inf 7 coy
Arty 1 bty under strength (with 2 x 105 guns)
Avn 1 sqn
Spt 1 coy (with 81mm mor)

EQUIPMENT BY TYPE

RECCE 22: 4 AML-90; 10 RBY-1 *RAMTA*; 8 S52 *Shorland*
ARTY 12
   TOWED 105mm 2
   MOR 81mm 10
AT • RCL 106mm 6 M-40

Air Wing 110

AIRCRAFT
   TPT • Light 4: 2 C-212-300 *Aviocar*; 1 C-212-400
   Aviocar; 1 GA-8 *Airvan*
HELICOPTERS
   MRH 3: 1 Bell 412EP *Twin Huey* (tpt, VIP tpt, SAR); 2
   Bell 412 SP
   TPT • Light 3 Bo-105LSA-3 (tpt, trg)

Liberia LBR

Liberian Dollar L$		2009	2010	2011
GDP	US$	879m	977m	
per capita	US$	222	238	
Growth	%	4.6	7.7	
Inflation	%	7.4	5.0	
Def bdgt	L$	110m		
	US$	1.59m		
FMA (US)	US$	1.5m	6.0m	9.0m
US$1=L$		68.98	72.06	

Population   4,101,767

Ethnic groups: Americo-Liberians 5%

Age	0–14	15–19	20–24	25–29	30–64	65 plus
Male	22.3%	4.2%	4.4%	4.2%	13.3%	1.5%
Female	22.0%	4.5%	4.5%	4.2%	13.4%	1.5%

Capabilities

ACTIVE 2,050 (Army 2,000, Coast Guard 50)

ORGANISATIONS BY SERVICE

Army 2,000

FORCES BY ROLE

Inf   1 inf bde (23rd) with (2 inf bn, 1 engr coy, 1 MP
        coy)
Trg   1 unit (forming)

FACILITIES

Bases   3 (Barclay Training Camp, Sandee S. Ware and
        Edward B. Kessely military barracks)

Coast Guard 50

8 craft (*Zodiac*) under 10t FLO

FOREIGN FORCES

All under UNMIL comd unless otherwise specified
Bangladesh 1,441; 12 obs; 1 inf bn; 2 engr coy; 1 sigs coy; 1
log coy; 1 MP unit; 1 fd hospital

Benin 1; 2 obs
Bolivia 1; 2 obs
Brazil 2; 2 obs
Bulgaria 2 obs
China, People's Republic of 564; 2 obs; 1 engr coy; 1 tpt
coy; 1 fd hospital
Croatia 2
Denmark 3; 2 obs
Ecuador 1; 2 obs
Egypt 5 obs
El Salvador 2 obs
Ethiopia 4; 7 obs
Finland 2
France 1
Gambia 2 obs
Ghana 706; 11 obs; 1 inf bn
Indonesia 1 obs
Jordan 120; 4 obs; 1 fd hospital
Korea, Republic of 1; 1 obs
Kyrgyzstan 3 obs
Malaysia 5 obs
Mali 1 obs
Moldova 2 obs
Mongolia 150
Montenegro 2 obs
Namibia 3; 1 obs
Nepal 18; 2 obs; 1 MP sect
Niger 2 obs
Nigeria 1,553; 13 obs; 1 inf bn; 1 sigs coy
Pakistan 2,953; 7 obs; 3 inf bn; 3 engr coy; 1 fd hospital
Paraguay 1; 2 obs
Peru 2; 2 obs
Philippines 117; 2 obs; 1 inf coy
Poland 2 obs
Romania 2 obs
Russia 4 obs
Senegal 1; 1 obs
Serbia 4 obs
Togo 1; 2 obs
Ukraine 277; 2 obs; 1 hel coy
United States 5; 4 obs
Yemen, Republic of 1
Zambia 3 obs
Zimbabwe 2 obs

Madagascar MDG

Malagsy Ariary fr		2009	2010	2011
GDP	fr	16.8tr	18.0tr	
	US$	8.59bn	8.52bn	
per capita	US$	438	423	
Growth	%	0.4	-0.4	
Inflation	%	9.0	9.1	
Def exp	fr	176bn		
	US$	90m		
Def bdgt	fr	176bn	119bn	
	US$	90m	56m	
US$1=fr		1955.52	2105.95	

Population   20,146,442

Age	0–14	15–19	20–24	25–29	30–64	65 plus
Male	21.7%	5.4%	4.6%	3.8%	12.9%	1.3%
Female	21.4%	5.4%	4.6%	3.8%	13.3%	1.7%

Capabilities

ACTIVE 13,500 (Army 12,500 Navy 500 Air 500)
Paramilitary 8,100
Terms of service conscription (incl for civil purposes) 18 months

ORGANISATIONS BY SERVICE

Army 12,500+
FORCES BY ROLE
Army 2 (gp) bn
Engr 1 regt

EQUIPMENT BY TYPE
LT TK 12 PT-76
RECCE 73: ε35 BRDM-2; 10 *Ferret*; ε20 M-3A1; 8 M-8
APC (T) ε30 M-3A1 half-track
ARTY 25+
  TOWED 17: **105mm** 5 M-101; **122mm** 12 D-30
  MOR 8+: **82mm** M-37; **120mm** 8 M-43
AT • RCL 106mm M-40A1
  RL 89mm LRAC
AD • GUNS • TOWED 70: **14.5mm** 50 ZPU-4; **37mm** 20 Type-55 (M-1939)

Navy 500 (incl some 100 Marines)
EQUIPMENT BY TYPE
PATROL AND COASTAL COMBATANTS 7
  PCC 1 *Chamois*
  PB 6 (USCG)
AMPHIBIOUS • LCT 1 (FRA *Edic*)
FACILITIES
Bases Located at Diégo Suarez, Tamatave, Fort Dauphin, Tuléar, Majunga

Air Force 500
FORCES BY ROLE
Tpt   Some sqn with An-26 *Curl*; BN-2 *Islander*; C-212 *Aviocar*; Yak-40 *Codling* (VIP); Some (liaison) sqn with Cessna 310; Cessna 337 *Skymaster*; PA-23 *Aztec*
Trg   Some sqn with Cessna 172
Tpt Hel   Some sqn with Mi-8 *Hip*; SA-318C *Alouette II*

EQUIPMENT BY TYPE
AIRCRAFT • TPT • Light 16: 1 An-26 *Curl*; 1 BN-2 *Islander*; 2 C-212 *Aviocar*; 4 Cessna 172; 1 Cessna 310; 2 Cessna 337 *Skymaster*; 1 PA-23 *Aztec*; 4 Yak-40 *Codling* (VIP)
HELICOPTERS
  MRH 4 SA-318C *Alouette II*
  TPT • Medium 5 Mi-8 *Hip*

Paramilitary 8,100

Gendarmerie 8,100
PATROL AND COASTAL COMBATANTS • 5 PB

Malawi MWI

Malawian Kwacha K		2009	2010	2011
GDP	K	667bn	764bn	
	US$	4.73bn	5.09bn	
per capita	US$	310	325	
Growth	%	7.7	6.0	
Inflation	%	8.4	8.8	
Def exp	K	ε7.2bn		
	US$	ε51m		
US$1=K		141.15	150.03	

Population   15,691,784

Age	0–14	15–19	20–24	25–29	30–64	65 plus
Male	22.6%	5.5%	4.7%	4.0%	11.8%	1.1%
Female	22.5%	5.5%	4.8%	4.0%	11.8%	1.5%

Capabilities

ACTIVE 5,300 (Army 5,300) **Paramilitary 1,500**

ORGANISATIONS BY SERVICE

Army 5,300
FORCES BY ROLE
Inf   3 bn
Para 1 indep bn
Spt   1 (general) bn (1+ marine coy 1 armd recce sqn, 1 engr unit, 2 lt arty bty)

EQUIPMENT BY TYPE
Less than 20% serviceability
RECCE 41: 13 *Eland*; 20 FV721 *Fox*; 8 *Ferret*
ARTY 17
  TOWED 105mm 9 lt
  MOR 81mm 8 L16
AD • SAM • MANPAD 15 *Blowpipe*
  GUNS • TOWED 14.5mm 40 ZPU-4

Maritime Wing 220

EQUIPMENT BY TYPE
PATROL AND COASTAL COMBATANTS • PB1
Kasungu†
FACILITIES
Base Located at Monkey Bay (Lake Nyasa)

Air Wing 200

FORCES BY ROLE

Tpt   1 sqn with Basler BT-67; Do-228; Hawker 800
Tpt hel 1 sqn with AS-332 *Super Puma* (VIP);
         AS-350L *Ecureuil*; SA-330F *Puma*

EQUIPMENT BY TYPE
AIRCRAFT • TPT 7 **Light** 4 Do-228; **PAX** 3: 2 Basler
BT-67; 1 Hawker 800
HELICOPTERS • TPT 3 **Medium** 2: 1 AS-332 *Super
Puma* (VIP); 1 SA-330F *Puma* **Light** 1 AS-350L *Ecureuil*

Paramilitary 1,500

Mobile Police Force 1,500

RECCE 8 S52 *Shorland*
AIRCRAFT
   TPT • Light 4: 3 BN-2T *Defender* (border patrol); 1
   SC.7 3M *Skyvan*
HELICOPTERS • MRH 2 AS-365 *Dauphin 2*

DEPLOYMENT

DEMOCRATIC REPUBLIC OF THE CONGO
UN • MONUSCO 50; 18 obs

SUDAN
UN • UNAMID 7; 8 obs

Mali MLI

CFA Franc BCEAO fr		2009	2010	2011
GDP	fr	4.23tr	4.61tr	
	US$	8.99bn	9.30bn	
per capita	US$	691	698	
Growth	%	4.3	4.6	
Inflation	%	2.2	1.9	
Def exp	fr	ε83.3bn		
	US$	ε177m		
Def bdgt	fr	80bn	103bn	
	US$	170m	208m	
FMA (US)	US$	-	0.2m	0.2m
US$1=fr		470.96	495.60	

Population   13,323,104

Ethnic groups: Tuareg 6-10%

Age	0–14	15–19	20–24	25–29	30–64	65 plus
Male	23.8%	5.2%	4.2%	3.5%	11.4%	1.4%
Female	23.5%	5.3%	4.4%	3.7%	12.0%	1.5%

Capabilities

ACTIVE 7,350 (Army 7,350) **Paramilitary 4,800**
Militia 3,000

ORGANISATIONS BY SERVICE

Army ε7,350

FORCES BY ROLE

Tk	2 bn
Inf	4 bn
SF	1 bn
AB	1 bn
Arty	2 bn
AD	2 bty
Engr	1 bn
SAM	1 bty

EQUIPMENT BY TYPE†
MBT 33: 12 T-54/T-55; 21 T-34
LT TK 18 Type-62
RECCE 64 BRDM-2
APC (W) 84: 44 BTR-60; 30 BTR-40; 10 BTR-152
ARTY 46+
   TOWED 14+: **100mm** 6 M-1944; **122mm** 8 D-30; **130mm**
   M-46 (reported)
   MRL 122mm 2 BM-21
   MOR 30+: **82mm** M-43; **120mm** 30 M-43
AT • MSL • MANPATS AT-3 9K11 *Sagger*
   RL 73mm RPG-7 *Knout*
   GUNS 85mm 6 D-44
AD • SAM 12+
   TOWED 12+ S-125 *Pechora* (SA-3 *Goa*)
   MANPAD 9K32 *Strela*-2 (SA-7 *Grail*)‡
   GUNS • TOWED 12: **37mm** 6 M-1939; **57mm** 6 S-60

Navy 50

EQUIPMENT BY TYPE
PATROL AND COASTAL COMBATANTS 3 **PBR**†
FACILITIES
Bases Located at Bamako, Mopti, Segou, Timbuktu

Air Force 400

FORCES BY ROLE

Ftr 1 sqn with MiG-21 *Fishbed*
Tpt Some regt with An-24 *Coke*; An-26 *Curl*; An-2 *Colt*
Trg Some sqn with L-29 *Delfin*; MiG-21UM *Mongol*;
     Yak-11 *Moose*; Yak-18 *Max*
Tpt Some sqn with AS-350 *Ecureuil*; Mi-8 *Hip*; Mi-24D
Hel *Hind*; Z-9

EQUIPMENT BY TYPE
AIRCRAFT 14 combat capable
   FGA 14: 13 MiG-21 *Fishbed*; 1 MiG-21UM *Mongol*
   TPT • Light 5: 2 An-2 *Colt*; 2 An-24 *Coke*; 1 An-26 *Curl*;
   TRG 13: 6 L-29 *Delfin*; 4 Yak-11 *Moose*; 2 Yak-18 *Max*
HELICOPTERS
   ATK 6 Mi-24D *Hind*

MRH 2 Z-9
TPT 2 **Medium** 1 Mi-8 *Hip* **Light** 1 AS-350 *Ecureuil*

Paramilitary 4,800 active

Gendarmerie 1,800
Paramilitary 8 coy

Republican Guard 2,000

National Police 1,000

Militia 3,000

DEPLOYMENT

CENTRAL AFRICAN REPUBLIC/CHAD
UN • MINURCAT 1 obs

DEMOCRATIC REPUBLIC OF THE CONGO
UN • MONUSCO 9 obs

LIBERIA
UN • UNMIL 1 obs

SUDAN
UN • UNMIS 1 obs
UN • UNAMID 2; 8 obs

Mauritius MUS

Mauritian Rupee R		2009	2010	2011
GDP	R	274bn	291bn	
	US$	8.61bn	9.44bn	
per capita	US$	6,750	7,284	
Growth	%	2.2	4.2	
Inflation	%	2.5	4.5	
Def bdgt	R	1.24bn		
	US$	41m		
US$1=R		31.89	30.86	

Population 1,296,569

Age	0–14	15–19	20–24	25–29	30–64	65 plus
Male	11.1%	4.1%	3.9%	3.8%	23.2%	3.0%
Female	10.7%	4.0%	3.8%	3.7%	24.0%	4.5%

Capabilities

ACTIVE NIL Paramilitary 2,000

ORGANISATIONS BY SERVICE

Paramilitary 2,000

Special Mobile Force ε1,500
FORCES BY ROLE
Rifle 6 coy
Paramilitary 2 (mob) coy
Engr 1 coy
Spt 1 pl

EQUIPMENT BY TYPE
RECCE BRDM-2; *Ferret*
AIFV 2 VAB with 20mm gun
APC (W) 16: 7 *Tactica*; 9 VAB
ARTY • MOR 81mm 2
AT • RL 89mm 4 LRAC

Coast Guard ε500
PATROL AND COASTAL COMBATANTS 5
PSOH 1 *Vigilant* (capacity 1 hel) (CAN *Guardian* design)
PB 4: 1 P-2000; 1 SDB-Mk3; 2 *Zhuk* (FSU)
AIRCRAFT • TPT • **Light** 3: 1 BN-2T *Defender*; 2 Do-228-101

Police Air Wing
HELICOPTERS
MRH 4 SA-316 *Alouette III*
TPT • **Light** 1 AS-355 *Ecureuil II*

Mozambique MOZ

Mozambique Metical M		2009	2010	2011
GDP	M	263bn	306bn	
	US$	9.55bn	9.08bn	
per capita	US$	417	388	
Growth	%	6.3	5.8	
Inflation	%	3.3	9.2	
Def exp	M	2.32bn		
	US$	84m		
Def bdgt	M	2.02bn		
	US$	73m		
US$1=M		27.56	33.72	

Population 23,405,670

Age	0–14	15–19	20–24	25–29	30–64	65 plus
Male	22.0%	6.0%	4.7%	3.3%	12.3%	1.2%
Female	21.8%	5.9%	4.8%	3.3%	13.0%	1.7%

Capabilities

ACTIVE 11,200 (Army 10,000 Navy 200 Air 1,000)
Terms of service conscription, 2 years

ORGANISATIONS BY SERVICE

Army ε9,000–10,000
FORCES BY ROLE
Inf 7 bn
SF 3 bn
Arty 2–3 bty
Engr 2 bn
Log 1 bn

EQUIPMENT BY TYPE†
Equipment at estimated 10% or less serviceability
MBT 60+ T-54

RECCE 30 BRDM-1/BRDM-2
AIFV 40 BMP-1
APC (W) 271: 160 BTR-60; 100 BTR-152; 11 *Casspir*
ARTY 126
 TOWED 62; **100mm** 20 M-1944; **105mm** 12 M-101;
 122mm 12 D-30; **130mm** 6 M-46; **152mm** 12 D-1
 MRL **122mm** 12 BM-21
 MOR 52: **82mm** 40 M-43; **120mm** 12 M-43
AT • MSL • MANPATS 290: 20 AT-3 9K11 *Sagger*; 120 in
store; 12 AT-4 9K111 *Spigot*; 138 in store
 RCL **75mm**; **82mm** B-10; **107mm** 24 B-12
 GUNS **85mm** 18: 6 D-48; 12 Type-56 (D-44)
AD • SAM • MANPAD 250: 20 9K32 *Strela*-2
(SA-7 *Grail*)‡; 230 in store
 GUNS 330+
 SP **57mm** 20 ZSU-57-2
 TOWED 310+: **20mm** M-55; **23mm** 120 ZU-23-2;
 37mm 100: 90 M-1939; 10 in store; **57mm** 90: 60 S-60;
 30 in store

Navy ε200

FACILITIES

Bases   Located at Pemba - Metangula (Lake Malawi),
 Nacala, Beira, Maputo

Air Force 1,000

FORCES BY ROLE
(incl AD units)

Tpt	1 sqn with An-26 *Curl*; C-212 *Aviocar*; PA-32 *Cherokee* (non-op)
Trg	sqn with Cessna 182 *Skylane*; Z-326 *Trener Master*
Atk Hel/Tpt Hel	Some sqn with Mi-24 *Hind*†; Mi-8 *Hip* (non-operational)
AD	Some bty with S-125 *Pechora* (SA-3 *Goa*) (non-op)‡; S-75 *Dvina* (SA-2 *Guideline*)†‡

EQUIPMENT BY TYPE
AIRCRAFT none combat capable
 FGA (some MiG-21bis *Fishbed L & N* non-op)
 TPT • Light 5: 2 An-26 *Curl*; 2 C-212 *Aviocar*; 1 Cessna
182 *Skylane*; 4 PA-32 *Cherokee* (non-op)
 TRG 7 Z-326 *Trener Master*
HELICOPTERS
 ATK 2 Mi-24 *Hind*†
 SPT 2 Mi-8 *Hip* (non-op)
AD • SAM 10+ S-125 *Pechora* SA-3 *Goa* (non-op)‡
 TOWED: S-75 *Dvina* (SA-2 *Guideline*)† ‡

DEPLOYMENT

DEMOCRATIC REPUBLIC OF THE CONGO
UN • MONUSCO 1 obs

SUDAN
UN • UNMIS 1 obs

Namibia NAM

Namibian Dollar N$		2009	2010	2011
GDP	N$	79.3bn	90.0bn	
	US$	9.49bn	12.0bn	
per capita	US$	4,370	5,439	
Growth	%	1.0	3.0	
Inflation	%	8.8	6.2	
Def bdgt	N$	2.6bn	3.02bn	3.1bn
	US$	311m	408m	
US$1=N$		8.35	7.40	

Population   2,212,037

Age	0–14	15–19	20–24	25–29	30–64	65 plus
Male	17.3%	6.0%	5.6%	5.1%	14.6%	1.8%
Female	17.0%	5.9%	5.5%	4.8%	14.2%	2.3%

Capabilities

ACTIVE 9,200 (Army 9,000 Navy 200) **Paramilitary
6,000**

ORGANISATIONS BY SERVICE

Army 9,000
The MOD plans to build new military bases including at
Luiperdsvallei outside Windhoek, Osana near Okahandja,
Keetmanshoop and Karibib

FORCES BY ROLE

Inf	6 bn
AT	1 regt
Cbt Spt	1 bde (1 arty regt)
Presidential Guard	1 bn
AD	1 regt

EQUIPMENT BY TYPE
MBT T-54/T-55†; T-34†
RECCE 12 BRDM-2
APC (W) 60: 10 BTR-60; 20 *Casspir*; 30 *Wolf Turbo* 2
ARTY 69
 TOWED 140mm 24 G2
 MRL 122mm 5 BM-21
 MOR 40: **81mm**; **82mm**
AT • RCL 82mm B-10
 GUNS 12+: **57mm**; **76mm** 12 ZIS-3
AD • SAM • MANPAD 74 9K32 *Strela*-2 (SA-7 *Grail*)‡
 GUNS 65
 SP 23mm 15 *Zumlac*
 TOWED 14.5mm 50 ZPU-4

Navy ε200
Fishery protection, part of the Ministry of Fisheries
EQUIPMENT BY TYPE
PATROL AND COASTAL COMBATANTS 8
 PCO 4: 1 *Imperial Marinheiro* with 76mm gun; 2
 Nathanael Maxwilili; 1 *Tobias Hainyenko*
 PCC 2: 1 *Oryx*; 1 *Brendan Simbwaye*

PB 2 *Tracker II* (additional vessels on order)
LOGISTICS AND SUPPORT • AGOR 4
AIRCRAFT • TPT • Light 1 F406 *Caravan II*
HELICOPTERS 1
FACILITIES

Base Located at Walvis Bay

Air Force

FORCES BY ROLE

FGA	Some sqn with MiG-23 *Flogger* (reported); F-7 (F-7NM); FT-7 (FT-7NG)
ISR	Some sqn with Cessna 337 *Skymaster*/O-2A *Skymaster*
Tpt	Some sqn with An-26 *Curl*; *Falcon* 900; *Learjet* 36; 2 Y-12
Trg	Some sqn with K-8 *Karakorum**
Atk Hel/ Tpt Hel	Some sqn with Mi-25 *Hind D*; Mi-17 *Hip H*; SA-319 *Alouette III*

EQUIPMENT BY TYPE
AIRCRAFT 24 combat capable
  FTR 12: 2 MiG-23 *Flogger* (reported); 8 F-7 (F-7NM); 2 FT-7 (FT-7NG)*
  ISR/TPT 5 Cessna 337 *Skymaster* (lt tpt)/O-2A *Skymaster*
  TPT 6: **Light** 5: 2 An-26 *Curl*; 1 *Learjet* 36; 2 Y-12 **PAX** 1 *Falcon* 900
  TRG 12 K-8 *Karakorum**
HELICOPTERS
  ATK 2 Mi-25 *Hind D*
  MRH 4: 2 Mi-17 (Mi-8MT) *Hip H*; 2 SA-319 *Alouette III*

Paramilitary 6,000

Police Force • Special Field Force 6,000 (incl Border Guard and Special Reserve Force)

DEPLOYMENT

CENTRAL AFRICAN REPUBLIC/CHAD
UN • MINURCAT 5

CÔTE D'IVOIRE
UN • UNOCI 1 obs

LIBERIA
UN • UNMIL 3; 1 obs

SUDAN
UN • UNMIS 7 obs
UN • UNAMID 2; 10 obs

Niger NER

CFA Franc BCEAO fr		2009	2010	2011
GDP	fr	2.48tr	2.69tr	
	US$	5.27bn	5.44bn	
per capita	US$	345	342	
Growth	%	1.0	3.2	
Inflation	%	4.3	3.3	
Def exp	fr	ε24bn		
	US$	ε51m		
Def bdgt	fr	30bn		
	US$	64m		
US$1=fr		470.96	495.60	

Population 15,891,482
Ethnic groups: Tuareg 8–10%

Age	0–14	15–19	20–24	25–29	30–64	65 plus
Male	25.1%	5.3%	4.3%	3.6%	10.9%	1.0%
Female	24.6%	5.1%	4.1%	3.4%	11.6%	1.3%

Capabilities

ACTIVE 5,300 (Army 5,200 Air 100) **Paramilitary 5,400**
Terms of service selective conscription (2 year)

ORGANISATIONS BY SERVICE

Army 5,200
FORCES BY ROLE
3 Mil Districts

Armd recce	4 sqn
Inf	7 coy
AB	2 coy
Engr	1 coy
AD	1 coy

EQUIPMENT BY TYPE
RECCE 132: 35 AML-20/AML-60; 90 AML-90; 7 VBL
APC (W) 22 M-3 *Panhard*
ARTY • MOR 40: **81mm** 19 Brandt; **82mm** 17; **120mm** 4 Brandt
AT • RCL 14: **75mm** 6 M-20; **106mm** 8 M-40
  RL 89mm 36 LRAC
AD • GUNS 39
  SP 10 M3 VDAA
  TOWED 20mm 29

Air Force 100
FORCES BY ROLE

Tpt	Some sqn with An-26 *Curl*; B-737-200 (VIP); C-130H *Hercules*; Do-28; 1 (liaison) sqn with Cessna 337D *Skymaster*
Atk Hel/Tpt Hel	Some sqn with Mi-24 *Hind*; Mi-17 *Hip H*

EQUIPMENT BY TYPE

AIRCRAFT

ISR 2 DA42 MPP *Twin Star*

TPT 6 **Medium** 1 C-130H *Hercules* **Light** 4: 1 An-26 *Curl*; 2 Cessna 337D *Skymaster*; 1 Do-28 **PAX** 1 B-737-200 (VIP)

HELICOPTERS

ATK 2 Mi-24 *Hind*

MRH 2 Mi-17 *Hip H*

Paramilitary 5,400

Gendarmerie 1,400

Republican Guard 2,500

National Police 1,500

DEPLOYMENT

BURUNDI

UN • BINUB 1 obs

CÔTE D'IVOIRE

UN • UNOCI 393; 6 obs; 1 inf bn

DEMOCRATIC REPUBLIC OF THE CONGO

UN • MONUSCO 16 obs

LIBERIA

UN • UNMIL 2 obs

Nigeria NGA

Nigerian Naira N		2009	2010	2011
GDP	N	25.1tr	31.0tr	
	US$	169bn	207bn	
per capita	US$	1,090	1,311	
Growth	%	2.9	4.4	
Inflation	%	12.4	9.3	
Def exp	N	224bn		
	US$	1.5bn		
Def bdgt	N	224bn	232bn	
	US$	1.5bn	1.55bn	
FMA (US)	US$	1.3m	1.35m	1.35m
US$1=N		148.88	149.32	

Population 158,258,917

Ethnic groups: North (Hausa and Fulani) South-west (Yoruba) South-east (Ibo); these tribes make up ε65% of population

Age	0–14	15–19	20–24	25–29	30–64	65 plus
Male	20.9%	5.5%	4.8%	4.2%	14.1%	1.5%
Female	20.0%	5.2%	4.6%	4.0%	13.6%	1.6%

Capabilities

ACTIVE 80,000 (Army 62,000 Navy 8,000 Air 10,000) **Paramilitary 82,000**

Reserves planned, none org

ORGANISATIONS BY SERVICE

Army 62,000

FORCES BY ROLE

Army	1 (comp) div (2 mot inf bde, 1 AB bn, 1 amph bde, 1 engr bde, 1 arty bde, 1 recce bde)
Armd	1 div (1 recce bn, 1 engr bde, 1 arty bde, 2 armd bde)
Mech	2 div (each: 1 engr bn, 1 mot inf bde, 1 mech bde, 1 recce bn, 1 arty bde)
Presidential Guard	1 bde (2 Gd bn)
AD	1 regt

EQUIPMENT BY TYPE

MBT 276: 176 Vickers Mk 3; 100 T-55†

LT TK 157 *Scorpion*

RECCE 452: 90 AML-60; 40 AML-90; 70 EE-9 *Cascavel*; 50 FV721 *Fox*; 20 *Saladin* Mk2; 72 VBL (reported); 110 *Cobra*

APC 484+

  APC (T) 317: 250 4K-7FA *Steyr*; 67 MT-LB

  APC (W) 167+: 10 FV603 *Saracen*; 110 *Piranha*; 47 BTR-3U; EE-11 *Urutu* (reported)

ARTY 506

  SP 155mm 39 VCA 155 *Palmaria*

  TOWED 112: **105mm** 50 M-56; **122mm** 31 D-30/D-74; **130mm** 7 M-46; **155mm** 24 FH-77B in store

  MRL 122mm 25 APR-21

  MOR 330+: **81mm** 200; **82mm** 100; **120mm** 30+

AT • MSL • MANPATS *Swingfire*

  RCL 84mm *Carl Gustav*; **106mm** M-40A1

AD • SAM 164

  SP 16 *Roland*

  MANPAD 148: 48 *Blowpipe* ε100 9K32 *Strela*-2 (SA-7 *Grail*)‡

  GUNS 90+

  SP 30 ZSU-23-4

  TOWED 60+: **20mm** 60+; **23mm** ZU-23; **40mm** L/70

RADAR • LAND: some RASIT (veh, arty)

Navy 8,000 (incl Coast Guard)

Western Comd HQ located at Apapa; Eastern Comd HQ located at Calabar;

EQUIPMENT BY TYPE

PRINCIPAL SURFACE COMBATANTS 1

  FRIGATES • FFGHM 1 *Aradu* (GER MEKO 360) with 8 single lnchr each with *Otomat* AShM, 1 octuple *Albatros* lnchr with *Aspide* SAM, 2 triple STWS 1B 324mm ASTT with A244 LWT, 1 127mm gun, (capacity 1 *Lynx* Mk89 hel)

PATROL AND COASTAL COMBATANTS 20

  CORVETTES • FSM 1 *Enymiri* (UK Vosper Mk 9) each with 1 triple lnchr with *Seacat* SAM, 1 twin 375mm A/S mor (2 eff.), 1 76mm gun

  PCFG 1 *Ayam* (FRA *Combattante*) each with 2 twin (4 eff.) each with 1 MM-38 *Exocet* AShM, 1 76mm gun (Additional 2 vessels†)

  PCO 4 *Balsam* (buoy tenders (US))

PCC 3 *Ekpe* (GER Lurssen 57m - 2†) with 1 76mm gun
PBF 5: 4 *Manta* (Suncraft 17m); 1 *Shaldag II*
PB 6: 2 *Sea Eagle* (Suncraft 38m; 4 additional vessels on order); 2 *Town*; 2 *Yola*
MINE WARFARE • MINE COUNTERMEASURES •
MCC 2 *Ohue* (mod ITA *Lerici*)
AMPHIBIOUS • LS • LST 1 *Ambe* (capacity 5 tanks; 220 troops) (GER)
LOGISTICS AND SUPPORT 5:
1 AGHS; 4 YTL

FACILITIES

Bases   Located at Lagos, Apapa, Calabar, Warri, Port Harcourt

Trg School   Located at Sapele, Delta State.

Naval Aviation
HELICOPTERS
ASW 2 *Lynx* Mk 89† (non-op)
MRH 2 AW-139 (AB-139)
TPT • Light 3 AW-109E *Power*†

Air Force 10,000
FORCES BY ROLE

Very limited op capability

Ftr/FGA   1 sqn with *Jaguar* S(N)† (non-op); *Jaguar* B(N)†; 1 sqn with *Alpha Jet*; 1 sqn with MiG-21bis/MiG-21FR*†; MiG-21MF†; MiG-21U†; F-7 (F-7NI); FT-7 (FT-NI)

Tpt   2 sqn with C-130H *Hercules*; C-130H-30 *Hercules*; Do-128D-6 *Turbo SkyServant*; Do-228-200 (incl 2 VIP); G-222; 1 (Presidential) flt with B-727; BAe-125-1000; *Falcon* 900; Gulfstream II/Gulfstream IV

Trg   Some sqns with *Air Beetle*†; AW-109; Hughes 300; L-39 *Albatros*†*; MB-339A* (all being upgraded)

Atk Hel/   Some sqns with Bo-105D†; AS-332 *Super Puma*;
Tpt Hel   Mi-24/Mi-35 *Hind*†; Mi-34 *Hermit* (trg); SA-330 *Puma*

EQUIPMENT BY TYPE†
AIRCRAFT 78 combat capable
FTR 15: 12 F-7 (F-7NI); 3 FT-7 (FT-NI)
FGA 9: 3 *Jaguar* B(N)†; 5 MiG-21MF *Fishbed J*†; 1 MiG-21U *Mongol A*†; (12 *Jaguar* S(N) non-op)
FGA/ISR 12 MiG-21bis *Fishbed L/N* (FGA)/MiG-21FR *Fishbed**† (ISR)
MP 2 ATR-42 MP
TPT 53: Medium 14: 5 C-130H-30 *Hercules* (4†); 3 C-130H-30 *Hercules*; 6 G-222† **Light** 33; 17 Do-128D-6 *Turbo SkyServant*; 16 Do-228-200 (incl 2 VIP); **PAX** 6: 1B-727; 1 BAe 125-1000 2 *Falcon* 900; 2 Gulfstream II/IV; 1 B-727
TRG 100: 58 *Air Beetle*† (up to 20 awaiting repair); 6 *Alpha Jet**; 24 L-39 *Albatros*†*; 12 MB-339AN* (all being upgraded)
HELICOPTERS
ATK 9: 2 Mi-24P *Hind*; 2 Mi-24V *Hind*; 5 Mi-35 *Hind*

TPT 20: **Medium** 13: 7 AS-332 *Super Puma*; 4 Mi-171 *Hip*; 2 SA-330 *Puma* **Light** 7: 2 AW-109; 5 Bo–105D†
TRG 18: 13 Hughes 300; 5 Mi-34 *Hermit*†
MSL • AAM IR AAM R-3 (AA-2 *Atoll*)‡; PL-9C

Paramilitary ε82,000

Coast Guard

Port Security Police ε2,000
PATROL AND COASTAL COMBATANTS • MISC BOATS/CRAFT 60+ boats
AMPHIBIOUS 5+ ACV

Security and Civil Defence Corps • Police 80,000
APC (W) 70+: 70+ AT105 *Saxon*†; UR-416
AIRCRAFT • TPT • Light 4: 1 Cessna 500 *Citation I*; 2 PA-31 *Navajo*; 1 PA-31-350 *Navajo Chieftain*
HELICOPTERS • TPT • Light 4: 2 Bell 212 (AB-212); 2 Bell 222 (AB-222)

DEPLOYMENT

CENTRAL AFRICAN REPUBLIC/CHAD
UN • MINURCAT 4; 2 obs

CÔTE D'IVOIRE
UN • UNOCI 7 obs

DEMOCRATIC REPUBLIC OF THE CONGO
UN • MONUSCO 18 obs

LEBANON
UN • UNIFIL 1

LIBERIA
UN • UNMIL 1,553; 13 obs; 1 inf bn; 1 sigs coy

NEPAL
UN • UNMIN 5 obs

SIERRA LEONE
IMATT 1

SUDAN
UN • UNMIS 5; 13 obs
UN • UNAMID 3,318; 12 obs; 4 inf bn; 1 fd hospital

WESTERN SAHARA
UN • MINURSO 6 obs

Rwanda RWA

Rwandan Franc fr		2009	2010	2011
GDP	fr	2.96tr	3.33tr	
	US$	5.22bn	5.73bn	
per capita	US$	522	557	
Growth	%	5.3	5.1	
Inflation	%	10.4	6.3	
Def exp	fr	64.1bn		
	US$	113m		
Def bdgt	fr	43.4bn	43.6bn	
	US$	76m	75m	
FMA (US)	US$	-	0.2m	0.4m
US$1=fr		568.15	582.04	

Population   10,277,212

Ethnic groups: Hutu 80%; Tutsi 19%

Age	0–14	15–19	20–24	25–29	30–64	65 plus
Male	21.6%	4.8%	4.8%	4.4%	13.2%	1.0%
Female	21.3%	4.8%	4.9%	4.4%	13.4%	1.5%

Capabilities

ACTIVE 33,000 (Army 32,000 Air 1,000) **Paramilitary 2,000**

ORGANISATIONS BY SERVICE

Army 32,000

FORCES BY ROLE

Army 4 div (each: 3 Army bde)

EQUIPMENT BY TYPE

MBT 24 T-54/T-55
RECCE 106: ε90 AML-60/AML-90/AML-245; 16 VBL
AIFV 35+: BMP; 15 *Ratel-90*; 20 *Ratel-60*
APC (W) 56+: 36 RG-31 *Nyala*; BTR; *Buffalo* (M-3 *Panhard*); 20 Type-92 (reported)
ARTY 155+
  TOWED 35+: **105mm** 29 Type-54 (D-1); **122mm** 6 D-30; **152mm**†
  MRL 122mm 5 RM-70 *Dana*
  MOR 115: **81mm**; **82mm**; **120mm**
AD • SAM • MANPAD 9K32 *Strela-2* (SA-7 *Grail*)‡
  GUNS ε150: **14.5mm**; **23mm**; **37mm**

Air Force ε1,000

FORCES BY ROLE

Tpt	Some sqn with An-2 *Colt*; An-8 *Camp*; B-707; BN-2A *Islander*
Trg	Some sqn with L-39 *Albatros*
Atk Hel /Tpt Hel	Some sqn with Mi-17MD *Hip H*; Mi-24V *Hind E*

EQUIPMENT BY TYPE

AIRCRAFT

TPT 5+ **Medium** 2–3 An-8 *Camp* **Light** 1+ some An-2 *Colt*; 1 BN-2A *Islander* **PAX** 1 B-707

TRG L-39 *Albatros*
HELICOPTERS
  ATK 5–7 Mi-24V *Hind E*
  MRH 8–12 Mi-17MD *Hip H*

Paramilitary

Local Defence Forces ε2,000

DEPLOYMENT

CENTRAL AFRICAN REPUBLIC/CHAD

UN • MINURCAT 1 obs

SUDAN

UN • UNMIS 257; 10 obs; 1 inf coy
UN • UNAMID 3,231 ; 9 obs; 4 inf bn

Senegal SEN

CFA Franc BCEAO fr		2009	2010	2011
GDP	fr	6.02tr	6.35tr	
	US$	12.8bn	12.8bn	
per capita	US$	1,020	996	
Growth	%	1.5	3.4	
Inflation	%	-1.1	2.2	
Def exp	fr	ε99.1bn		
	US$	ε210m		
Def bdgt	fr	97.2bn	98.7bn	
	US$	206m	199m	
FMA (US)	US$	-	0.3m	0.4m
US$1=fr		470.96	495.60	

Population   12,860,717

Ethnic groups: Wolof 36%; Fulani 17%; Serer 17%; Toucouleur 9%; Man-dingo 9%; Diola 9% (of which 30-60% in Casamance)

Age	0–14	15–19	20–24	25–29	30–64	65 plus
Male	21.7%	5.5%	4.7%	3.8%	11.3%	1.3%
Female	21.5%	5.5%	4.9%	4.2%	14.0%	1.5%

Capabilities

ACTIVE 13,620 (Army 11,900 Navy 950 Air 770) **Paramilitary 5,000**

Terms of service conscription, 2 years selective

ORGANISATIONS BY SERVICE

Army 11,900 (incl conscripts)

FORCES BY ROLE

4 Mil Zone HQ

Armd	3 bn
Inf	6 bn
Cdo/AB	1 bn
Arty	1 bn
Engr	1 bn

Presidential Guard   1 bn (horsed)

Construction   3 coy

EQUIPMENT BY TYPE

RECCE 118: 30 AML-60; 74 AML-90; 10 M-8; 4 M-20

APC 36+

  APC (T) 12 M-3 half-track

  APC (W) 24: 16 M-3 *Panhard*; 8 *Casspir*

ARTY 28

  TOWED 12: **105mm** 6 HM-2/M-101; **155mm** ε6 Model-50

  MOR 16: **81mm** 8 Brandt; **120mm** 8 Brandt

AT • MSL • MANPATS 4 *Milan*

  RL 89mm 31 LRAC

AD • GUNS • TOWED 33: **20mm** 21 M-693; **40mm** 12 L/60

Navy 950

EQUIPMENT BY TYPE

PATROL AND COASTAL COMBATANTS 10

  PCC 5: 1 *Fouta* (DNK *Osprey*); 1 *Njambour* (FRA SFCN 59m) with 2 76mm gun; 2 *Saint Louis*† (PR-48)

  PB 5: 2 *Alioune Samb*; 2 *Alphonse Faye*; 1 *Senegal* II

AMPHIBIOUS • LCT 2 *Edic* 700

FACILITIES

Bases Located at Dakar and Casamance

Air Force 770

FORCES BY ROLE

MP/SAR   1 sqn with C-212 *Aviocar*; Bell 205 (UH-1H *Iroquois*)

ISR   1 unit with BN-2T *Islander* (anti-smuggling patrols)

Tpt   1 sqn with B-727-200 (VIP); F-27-400M *Troopship*

Trg   Some sqn with R-235 *Guerrier**; TB-30 *Epsilon*

Atk Hel /   Some sqn with Mi-35P *Hind*; SA-318C *Alouette*
Tpt Hel   *II*; S355F *Ecureuil*; Bell 206

EQUIPMENT BY TYPE

AIRCRAFT 1 combat capable

  TPT 10: **Light** 9: 2 BN-2T *Islander* (govt owned, mil op); 1 C-212 *Aviocar*; 6 F-27-400M *Troopship* **PAX** 1 B-727-200 (VIP)

  TRG 3: 1 R-235 *Guerrier**; 2 TB-30 *Epsilon*

HELICOPTERS

  ATK 2 Mi-35P *Hind*

  MRH 2 SA-318C *Alouette II*

  TPT 18 **Medium** 2 Mi-171 *Hip*; **Light** 16: 1 AS355F *Ecureuil*; 1 Bell 205 (UH-1H *Iroquois*); 12 Bell 206; 2 Mi-2 *Hoplite*

Paramilitary 5,000

Gendarmerie 5,000

APC (W) 12 VXB-170

Customs

PATROL AND COASTAL COMBATANTS • PB 2 VCSM

DEPLOYMENT

BURUNDI

UN • BINUB 1 obs

CENTRAL AFRICAN REPUBLIC/CHAD

UN • MINURCAT 10; 3 obs

CÔTE D'IVOIRE

UN • UNOCI 324; 14 obs; 1 inf bn

DEMOCRATIC REPUBLIC OF THE CONGO

UN • MONUSCO 40; 23 obs

LIBERIA

UN • UNMIL 1; 1 obs

SUDAN

UN • UNAMID 1,010; 17 obs; 1 inf bn

FOREIGN FORCES

France

  Army 531; 1 (Marine) mech inf bn; 1 recce sqn with ERC-90F *Lynx*;

  Navy 230: 1 LCT; 1 *Atlantique*

  Air Force 1 C-160 *Transall*; 1 AS-555 *Fennec*

Seychelles SYC

Seychelles Rupee SR		2009	2010	2011
GDP	SR	10.7bn	11.2bn	
	US$	810m	935m	
per capita	US$	9,208	11,049	
Growth	%	-7.6	3.9	
Inflation	%	31.8	3.0	
Def exp	SR	82m		
	US$	6m		
Def bdgt	SR		87m	
	US$		7m	
US$1=SR		13.24	11.99	

Population	84,600

Age	0–14	15–19	20–24	25–29	30–64	65 plus
Male	11.2%	3.9%	4.1%	4.4%	24.7%	2.7%
Female	10.7%	3.7%	3.6%	3.9%	22.7%	4.5%

Capabilities

ACTIVE 200 (Army 200) Paramilitary 450

ORGANISATIONS BY SERVICE

Army 200

FORCES BY ROLE

Sy   1 unit

Inf   1 coy

Sub-Saharan Africa

EQUIPMENT BY TYPE†
RECCE 6 BRDM-2†
ARTY• MOR 82mm 6 M-43†
AT • RL 73mm RPG-7 Knout†
AD • SAM • MANPAD 10 9K32 Strela-2 (SA-7 Grail) ‡
    GUNS • TOWED 14.5mm ZPU-2†; ZPU-4†; 37mm M-1939†

Paramilitary

Coast Guard 200 (incl 80 Marines)
EQUIPMENT BY TYPE
PATROL AND COASTAL COMBATANTS 5
    PCC 2: 1 Andromache (ITA Pichiotti 42m); 1 Topaz
    PB 3: 2 Aries; 1 Junon
AMPHIBIOUS • LCT 1 Cinq Juin (govt owned but civilian op)
FACILITIES
Base   Located at Port Victoria

National Guard 250

Air Wing 20
AIRCRAFT
    TPT • Light 3: 1 BN-2 Islander; 1 Cessna 152; 1 F-406 Caravan II

FOREIGN FORCES

United States US Africa Command: some MQ-9 Reaper UAV

Sierra Leone SLE

Sierra Leonean Leone L		2009	2010	2011
GDP	L	6.33tr	7.58tr	
	US$	1.88bn	1.93bn	
per capita	US$	331	331	
Growth	%	4.0	4.0	
Inflation	%	9.2	9.1	
Def exp	L	40bn		
	US$	12m		
Def bdgt	L	40bn	50.4bn	57.6bn
	US$	12m	13m	
US$1=L		3361.85	3926.94	

Population   5,835,664

Age	0–14	15–19	20–24	25–29	30–64	65 plus
Male	20.8%	4.9%	4.5%	3.7%	13.0%	1.6%
Female	21.1%	5.2%	4.8%	4.0%	14.4%	2.0%

Capabilities

ACTIVE 10,500 (Joint 10,500)

ORGANISATIONS BY SERVICE

Armed Forces 10,500
UK-trained national army has formed, which has an initial target strength of 13–14,000. This initial strength is set to reduce to some 10,000 over a ten-year period.
ARTY • MOR 31: 81mm ε27; 82mm 2; 120mm 2
AT • RCL 84mm Carl Gustav
HELICOPTERS • MRH/TPT 2 Mi-17 (Mi-8MT) Hip H/ Mi-8 Hip†
AD • GUNS 7: 12.7mm 4; 14.5mm 3

Navy ε200
EQUIPMENT BY TYPE
PATROL AND COASTAL COMBATANTS • PB 1 Shanghai III
FACILITIES
    Base   Located at Freetown

DEPLOYMENT

LEBANON
UN • UNIFIL 3

NEPAL
UN • UNMIN 2 obs

SUDAN
UN • UNAMID 135; 6 obs; 1 recce coy
UN • UNMIS 6 obs

TIMOR LESTE
UN • UNMIT 1 obs

FOREIGN FORCES

Canada IMATT 8
Jamaica IMATT 1
Nigeria IMATT 1
United Kingdom IMATT 30
United States IMATT 3

Somalia SOM

Somali Shilling sh		2009	2010	2011
GDP	US$			
per capita	US$			

Definitive economic data unavailable

Population   9,358,602

Age	0–14	15–19	20–24	25–29	30–64	65 plus
Male	22.6%	4.8%	4.5%	3.5%	13.6%	1.0%
Female	22.5%	4.8%	4.6%	3.7%	13.2%	1.4%

Capabilities

No national armed forces since 1991. Transitional government attempting to establish armed forces but hampered by defections, financial difficulties, UN arms embargo and institutional deficiencies. Militia forces and armed groups within the country. Somaliland and Puntland have their own militias. Hy equipment in poor repair or inoperable.

MILITARY FORCES

Transitional Federal Government

Army ε2,000 (Ethiopian trained)

FOREIGN FORCES

Burundi AMISOM 3,000; 3 inf bn
Uganda AMISOM 4,250; 5 inf bn

TERRITORY WHERE THE RECOGNISED AUTHORITY (TFG) DOES NOT EXERCISE EFFECTIVE CONTROL

Data presented here represent the de facto situation. This does not imply international recognition as a sovereign state.

Somaliland
Population   3.5m

Militia unit strengths are not known. Equipment numbers are generalised assessments; most of this equipment is in poor repair or inoperable.

ORGANISATIONS BY SERVICE

Army ε15,000
FORCES BY ROLE

Armd	2 bde
Mech Inf	1 bde
Inf	14 bde
Arty	2 bde
Spt	1 bn

EQUIPMENT BY TYPE †
MBT 33: M47; T54/55
RECCE BTR-50; *Panhard* AML 90; BRDM-2
APC(W) 15-20 Fiat 6614
ARTY 69
  TOWED 122mm 12 D-30
  MOR MRL: 8-12 BM21
  45: **81mm**; **120mm**
AT
  RCL 106mm 16 M-40A1
  RL 73mm RPG-7 *Knout*
AD
  GUNS some†
  TOWED 20mm; **23mm** ZU-23

Coast Guard ε350

Ministry of the Interior
EQUIPMENT BY TYPE
PATROL AND COASTAL COMBATANTS 26

PB 7 *Dolphin 26*
PBR 19
FACILITIES
Base   Located at Berbera. Secondary regional bases at Zeylac and Mait

Puntland

Armed Forces ε5–10,000; coastguard

South Africa RSA

South African Rand R		2009	2010	2011
GDP	R	2.42tr	2.68tr	
	US$	290bn	362bn	
per capita	US$	5,881	7,166	
Growth	%	-1.8	2.4	
Inflation	%	7.1	5.8	
Def exp	R	35.9bn		
	US$	4.3bn		
Def bdgt	R	31.3bn	30.7bn	33.9bn
	US$	3.75bn	4.15bn	
FMA (US)	US$	-	0.8m	0.8m
US$1=R		8.35	7.40	

Population   50,492,408

Age	0–14	15–19	20–24	25–29	30–64	65 plus
Male	14.3%	5.1%	5.8%	5.3%	16.9%	2.3%
Female	14.2%	5.1%	5.5%	4.8%	17.2%	3.4%

Capabilities

ACTIVE 62,082 (Army 37,141 Navy 6,244 Air 10,653 South African Military Health Service 8,044)

CIVILIAN 12,382 (Army 6,452 Navy 2,000 Air 2,144 South African Military Health Service 1,786)

RESERVE 15,071 (Army 12,264 Navy 861 Air 831 South African Military Health Service Reserve 1,115)

ORGANISATIONS BY SERVICE

Army 37,141
FORCES BY ROLE
Formations under direct command and control of SANDF Chief of Joint Operations: 9 Joint Operational Tactical HQs, tps are provided when necessary by permanent and reserve force units from all services and SF Bde.

A new army structure is planned with 2 divisions (1 mechanised, 1 motorised) with 10 bdes (1 armd, 1 mech, 7 motorised and 1 rapid reaction). Training, Support and Land Commands are also planned, while Divisional HQ is to be re-established.

HQ	2 bde
Tk	1 bn
Armd recce	1 bn

Mech inf	2 bn
SF	1 bde (2 SF bn under strength)
Mot inf	10 bn (1 bn roles as AB, 1 as Amph)
Arty	1 bn
ADA	1 bn
Engr	1 regt

EQUIPMENT BY TYPE

MBT 34 *Olifant* 1A (133 *Olifant* 1B in store)
RECCE 82 *Rooikat*-76 (94 in store)
AIFV 534 *Ratel*-20 Mk III-20/*Ratel*-60 Mk III-60/*Ratel*-90 Mk III-90 FSV 90 (666 in store)
APC (W) 810: 370 *Casspir*; 440 *Mamba*
ARTY 1,255
  SP 155mm 2 G-6 (41 in store)
  TOWED 140mm (75 G2 in store); **155mm** 6 G-5 (66 in store)
  MRL 127mm 21: (26 *Valkiri* Mk I in store) (24 tube)); 21 *Valkiri* Mk II MARS *Bataleur* (40 tube); (4 in store (40 tube))
  MOR 1,226: **81mm** 1,190 (incl some SP); **120mm** 36
AT • MSL • MANPATS 59: 16 ZT-3 *Swift* (36 in store); 43 *Milan* ADT/ER
  RCL 106mm 100 M-40A1 (some SP)
  RL 92mm FT-5
AD • GUNS 76
  SP 23mm 36 *Zumlac*
  TOWED 35mm 40 GDF-002
UAV • ISR • Light up to 4 *Vulture*
RADAR • LAND ESR 220 *Kameelperd*; 2 Thales *Page*

Reserve Organisations

Regular Reserve 12,264 reservists (under strength)

Tk	3 bn
Armd Recce	2 bn
Recce	1 bn
Mech Inf	6 bn
Mot Inf	16 bn (incl 2 dual roles: 1 AB, 1 Amph
Lt Inf	3 converting to mot inf
AB	1 bn
Arty	7 regt
Engr	2 regt
AD	4 regt

Navy 6,244

Fleet HQ and Naval base located at Simon's Town; Naval stations located at Durban and Port Elizabeth

EQUIPMENT BY TYPE

SUBMARINES • TACTICAL • SSK 3 *Heroine* (Type 209) each with 8 533mm TT
PRINCIPAL SURFACE COMBATANTS • FRIGATES 4
  FFGHM 4 *Valour* (MEKO A200) each with 2 quad lnchr (8 eff.) each with MM-40 *Exocet* AShM (upgrade to Block III planned); 2 octuple VLS (16 eff.) each with *Umkhonto*-IR naval SAM, 1 76mm gun (capacity 1 *Super Lynx 300* hel)
PATROL AND COASTAL COMBATANTS 5:
  PCC 2 *Warrior* (ISR *Reshef*) each with 2 76mm gun

PCI 3 *Tobie*
MINE WARFARE • MINE COUNTERMEASURES 2
  MHC 2 *River* (GER *Navors*) (Limited operational roles; training and dive support); (additional vessel in reserve)
AMPHIBIOUS 6 LCU
LOGISTICS AND SUPPORT 6:
  AORH 1 *Drakensberg* with 1 spt hel (capacity 4 LCU; 100 troops)
  AGOS 1 (use for Antarctic survey, operated by private co. for Dept of Environment)
  AGHS 1 *Protea* (UK *Hecla*)
  YTM 3

FACILITIES

Bases	Located at Durban Salisbury Island (Naval Station); Port Elizabeth (Naval Station); Pretoria, Simon's Town

Air Force 10,653

Air Force office, Pretoria, and 4 op gps
Command & Control: 2 Airspace Control Sectors, 1 Mobile Deployment Wg
1 Air Force Command Post

FORCES BY ROLE

FGA	1 sqn with *Gripen* C/D (JAS-39C/D) (forming)
Tpt	1 (VIP) sqn with B-737 BBJ; Cessna 550 *Citation II*; Falcon 50; Falcon 900; 1 sqn with BT-67 (C-47TP); 2 sqns with C-130B/BZ *Hercules*; C-212; Cessna 185; CN-235; 9 (AF Reserve) sqn with ε130 private lt tpt ac
Trg	1 (Lead-in Ftr Trg) sqn with *Hawk* Mk120*
Atk Hel	1 (cbt spt) sqn with AH-2 *Rooivalk*
Tpt hel	4 (mixed) sqn with *Oryx*; BK-117; A109UH;

FACILITIES

Trg School	1 (tpt and trg) with Beech 200 *King Air*; Beech 300 *King Air*; Cessna 208 *Caravan I*; PC-12 *Aviocar*; 1 (basic flying trg) with PC-7 MkII *Astra*; 1 (hel trg) with *Oryx* and AW-109UH; 1 (air nav)

EQUIPMENT BY TYPE

AIRCRAFT 39 combat capable
  FGA 15: 6 *Gripen* C (JAS-39C); 9 *Gripen* D (JAS-39D) (further 11 *Gripen* C to be delivered by 2012)
  TPT 57 **Medium** 9 C-130B/BZ *Hercules*; **Light** 44: 3 Beech 200 *King Air*; 1 Beech 300 *King Air*; 10 BT-67 (C-47TP) (5 maritime, 3 tpt, 2 EW); 4 C-212 *Aviocar*; 10 Cessna 185; 12 Cessna 208 *Caravan*; 2 Cessna 550 *Citation II*; 1 CN-235; 1 PC-12 **PAX** 4: 1 B-737 BBJ; 2 *Falcon* 50; 1 *Falcon* 900
  TRG 74: 24 *Hawk* Mk120*; 50 PC-7 Mk II *Astra*
HELICOPTERS
  Atk 11 AH-2 *Rooivalk*
  MRH 4 *Super Lynx* 300
  TPT 76 **Medium** 39 *Oryx* **Light** 37: 29 AW-109; 8 BK-117
UAV • ISR • Medium *Seeker II*
MSL • AAM • IR AAM V3C *Darter*/**IIR AAM** IRIS-T

Ground Defence

FORCES BY ROLE

Air some SAAF regt (total: 12 (security) Air sqn)

EQUIPMENT BY TYPE

2 Radar (static) located at Ellisras and Mariepskop; 2 (mobile long-range); 4 (tactical mobile)

FACILITIES

Radar air   Located at Pretoria, Hoedspruit
control sectors

South African Military Health Service 8,044; ε1,115 reservists (total 9,159)

DEPLOYMENT

DEMOCRATIC REPUBLIC OF THE CONGO

UN • MONUSCO • *Operation Mistral* 1,205; 14 obs; 1 inf bn; 1 engr coy; 1 avn coy (air med evacuation team, air base control det)• *Operation Teutonic* 16

SUDAN

UN • UNAMID • *Operation Cordite* 775; 15 obs; 1 inf bn

Sudan SDN

Sudanese Dinar d		2009	2010	2011
GDP	d	126bn	153bn	
	US$	54.7bn	66.1bn	
per capita	US$	1,294	1,531	
Growth	%	4.0	5.4	
Inflation	%	11.2	9.1	
Def exp	d	ε1.6bn		
	US$	ε696m		
US$1=d			2.30	2.31

Population   43,192,438

Ethnic and religious groups: Muslim 70% mainly in North; Christian10% mainly in South; 52% mainly in South; Arab 39% mainly in North

Age	0–14	15–19	20–24	25–29	30–64	65 plus
Male	21.5%	5.7%	4.8%	3.9%	12.9%	1.4%
Female	20.6%	5.5%	4.7%	3.9%	13.8%	1.3%

Capabilities

ACTIVE 109,300 (Army 105,000 Navy 1,300 Air 3,000) Paramilitary 17,500

Terms of service conscription (males 18–30) 2 years

RESERVE NIL Paramilitary 85,000

ORGANISATIONS BY SERVICE

Army 85,000; ε20,000 conscripts (total 105,000)

FORCES BY ROLE

Armd   1 div
Mech inf   1 div; 1 indep bde

Inf   6 div; 7 indep bde
Recce   1 indep bde
SF   5 coy
AB   1 div
Arty   3 indep bde
Engr   1 div
Border Guard 1 bde

EQUIPMENT BY TYPE

MBT 360: 20 M-60A3; 60 Type-59/Type-59D; 270 T-54/T-55; 10 *Al-Bashier* (Type-85-IIM)
LT TK 115: 70 Type-62; 45 Type-63
RECCE 238: 6 AML-90; 60 BRDM-1/BRDM-2; 50–80 *Ferret*; 42 M1114 HMMWV; 30–50 *Saladin*
AIFV 75 BMP-1/BMP-2
APC 419
   APC (T) 66: 36 M-113; 20-30 BTR-50
   APC (W) 353: 55-80 V-150 *Commando*; 10 BTR 70; 7 BTR-80A; 50–80 BTR-152; 20 OT-62; 50 OT-64; 96 *Walid*; 10 Type-92 (reported)
ARTY 778+
   SP 20: **122mm** 10 2S1 *Carnation*; **155mm** 10 (AMX) Mk F3
   TOWED 123+ **105mm** 20 M-101; **122mm** 16+: 16 D-30; D-74; M-30; **130mm** 75 M-46/Type-59-I; 12 M-114A1
   MRL 635: **107mm** 477 Type-63; **122mm** 158: 90 BM-21; 50 *Saqr*; 18 Type-81
   MOR 81mm; **82mm**; **120mm** AM-49; M-43
AT • MSL • MANPATS 4+: 4 *Swingfire*; AT-3 9K11 *Sagger*
   RCL 106mm 40 M-40A1
   RL 73mm RPG-7 *Knout*
   GUNS 40+: 40 **76mm** ZIS-3/**100mm** M-1944; **85mm** D-44
AD • SAM • MANPAD 54 9K32 *Strela-2* ‡ (SA-7 *Grail*)
   GUNS 996+
   SP 20: **20mm** 8 M-163 *Vulcan*; 12 M3 VDAA
   TOWED 976+: 740+ **14.5mm** ZPU-2/**14.5mm** ZPU-4/**37mm** Type-63/**57mm** S-60/**85mm** M-1944; **20mm** 16 M-167 *Vulcan*; **23mm** 50 ZU-23-2; **37mm** 110: 80 M-1939; 30 unserviceable; **40mm** 60
RADAR • LAND RASIT (veh, arty)

Navy 1,300

HQ located at Port Sudan

EQUIPMENT BY TYPE

PATROL AND COASTAL COMBATANTS • PBR 4 *Kurmuk*
AMPHIBIOUS • LANDING CRAFT 7
   LCT 2 *Sobat*
   LCVP 5

FACILITIES

Bases   Located at Port Sudan, Flamingo Bay (Red Sea), Khartoum (Nile)

Air Force 3,000

The two main air bases are at Khartoum International Airport and Wadi Sayyidna north of Omdurman. The air force also has facilities at civilian airports - El Geneina, Nyala and El Fasher have been used for Darfur ops.

FORCES BY ROLE

incl Air Defence

FGA	Some sqns with A-5 *Fantan*; F-7; J-6; Su-25 *Frogfoot*; MiG-29SE/UB *Fulcrum*;
Tpt	Some sqns with An-26 *Curl** (modified for bombing); An-30 *Clank*; An-74TK-200/300; C-130H *Hercules*; DHC-5D *Buffalo*; Falcon 20 (VIP); Falcon 50 (VIP); F-27 (VIP;)Y-8
Trg	Some sqns with K-8 *Karakorum**
Atk Hel/ Tpt Hel	Some sqns with Mi-8 *Hip*; Mi-24V *Hind E*; Mi-171; SA-330 (IAR-330) *Puma*
AD	5 bty with S-75 *Dvina* (SA-2 *Guideline*) ‡

EQUIPMENT BY TYPE

AIRCRAFT 84 combat capable

FTR 39: 10 F-7; 6 J-6; 21 MiG-29SE *Fulcrum*; 2 MiG-29UB *Fulcrum*

FGA 3 MiG-23BN *Flogger H*

ATK 29: 15 A-5 *Fantan*; 14 Su-25 *Frogfoot*

ISR 1 An-30 *Clank*

TPT 14 **Medium** 6: 4 C-130H *Hercules*; 2 Y-8 **Light** 6: 1 An-26 *Curl** (modified for bombing); 1 An-74TK-200/300; 3 DHC-5D *Buffalo*; 1 F-27 (VIP) **PAX** 2: 1 *Falcon* 20 (VIP); 1 *Falcon* 50 (VIP);

TRG 12 K-8 *Karakorum**

HELICOPTERS

ATK 31 Mi-24V *Hind E*

TPT • **Medium** 21+: 20+ Mi-8/Mi-171 *Hip*; 1 SA-330 (IAR-330) *Puma* (10 more non op)

AD • **SAM** • **TOWED**: 90 S-75 *Dvina* (SA-2 *Guideline*) ‡

MSL • **AAM** • **IR AAM** R-3 (AA-2 *Atoll*)‡; R-60 (AA-8 *Aphid*)); R-73 (AA-11 *Archer*) **IR/SARH AAM** R-23/24 (AA-7 *Apex*) **ARH AAM** R-77 (AA-12 *Adder*)

Paramilitary 17,500

Popular Defence Force 17,500 (org in bn 1,000); 85,000 reservists (total 102,500)

mil wing of National Islamic Front

FOREIGN FORCES

(all UNMIS, unless otherwise indicated)

Australia 9; 6 obs

Bangladesh 1,621; 6 obs; 1 inf bn; 1 engr coy; 1 de-mining pl; 1 MP coy; 1 fd hospital; 1 tpt coy; 1 rvn coy • UNAMID 580; 6 obs; 1 inf coy; 1 log coy

Belgium 4 obs

Benin 5 obs

Bolivia 15 obs • UNAMID 1

Brazil 2; 20 obs

Burkina Faso 6 obs • UNAMID 802; 7 obs; 1 inf bn

Burundi UNAMID 2; 7 obs

Cambodia 51; 3 obs 1 de-mining pl

Canada 7; 20 obs (*Op Safari*) • UNAMID 5

China, People's Republic of 437; 12 obs; 1 engr coy; 1 tpt coy; 1 fd hospital • UNAMID 319; 2 obs; 1 engr coy

Croatia 4

Denmark 4; 5 obs

Ecuador 17 obs

Egypt 1,503; 15 obs; 1 inf bn; 2 engr coy; 2 tpt coy; 1 med bn; 1 de-mining pl • UNAMID 2,394; 24 obs; 2 inf bn; 1 engr coy; 1 sigs coy; 1 tpt coy

El Salvador 1 obs

Ethiopia UNAMID 2,356; 10 obs; 2 inf bn; 1 recce coy; 1 log coy; 1 tpt coy; 1 hel coy

Fiji 6 obs

Finland 1; 1 obs

Gambia UNAMID 200; 1 obs; 1 inf coy

Germany 5; 25 obs • UNAMID 3

Ghana UNAMID 6; 4 obs

Greece 1; 2 obs

Guatemala 1; 7 obs • UNAMID 2

Guinea 7 obs

India 2,633; 18 obs; 2 inf bn; 1 engr coy; 1 tpt coy; 1 hel coy; 1 fd hospital

Indonesia 9 obs • UNAMID 1; 2 obs

Iran 2 obs

Italy UNAMID 2

Japan 2

Jordan 6; 10 obs • UNAMID 7; 5 obs

Kenya 724; 4 obs; 1 inf bn; 1 de-mining pl • UNAMID 82; 6 obs; 1 MP coy

Korea, Republic of 1; 6 obs • UNAMID 2

Kyrgyzstan 7 obs

Malawi UNAMID 7; 8 obs

Malaysia 2; 6 obs • UNAMID 12; 1 obs

Mali 1 obs • UNAMID 2; 8 obs

Moldova 2 obs

Mongolia 2 obs

Mozambique 1 obs

Namibia 7 obs • UNAMID 2; 10 obs

Nepal 7; 5 obs • UNAMID 346; 16 obs; 2 inf coy

Netherlands 2; 12 obs • UNAMID 2

New Zealand 2; 2 obs

Nigeria 5; 13 obs • UNAMID 3,318; 12 obs; 4 inf bn; 1 fd hospital

Norway 6; 13 obs

Pakistan 1,479; 16 obs; 1 inf bn; 1 engr coy; 2 avn coy; 1 tpt coy; 1 de-mining pl; 1 fd hospital • UNAMID 502; 5 obs; 1 engr coy

Paraguay 9 obs

Peru 9 obs

Philippines 11 obs

Poland 1 obs

Romania 10 obs

Russia 123; 13 obs; 1 hel coy

Rwanda 257; 10 obs; 1 inf coy • UNAMID 3,231; 9 obs; 4 inf bn

Senegal UNAMID 1,010; 17 obs; 1 inf bn

Sierra Leone 6 obs • UNAMID 135; 6 obs; 1 recce coy

South Africa UNAMID 775; 15 obs; 1 inf bn

Sri Lanka 6 obs

Sweden 5 obs

Switzerland 2 obs

Tanzania 11 obs • UNAMID 816; 20 obs; 1 inf bn

Thailand 7; 2 obs

Togo UNAMID 7 obs

Turkey 3

Uganda 8 obs • UNAMID 1 obs

Ukraine 9 obs
United Kingdom 5 obs
Yemen, Republic of 21 obs • UNAMID 5; 22 obs
Zambia 544; 14 obs; 1 inf bn •UNAMID 7; 13 obs
Zimbabwe 9 obs • UNAMID 2; 9 obs

Tanzania TZA

Tanzanian Shilling sh		2009	2010	2011
GDP	sh	28.2tr	31.6tr	
	US$	21.4bn	22.7bn	
per capita	US$	489	504	
Growth	%	5.5	5.7	
Inflation	%	12.1	8.5	
Def exp	sh	ε326bn		
	US$	ε247m		
FMA (US)	US$	-	0.2m	0.2m
US$1=sh		1320.27	1393.20	

Population   45,039,573

Age	0–14	15–19	20–24	25–29	30–64	65 plus
Male	21.1%	5.8%	5.0%	4.2%	12.3%	1.3%
Female	20.9%	5.8%	5.0%	4.2%	12.9%	1.7%

Capabilities

ACTIVE 27,000 (Army 23,000 Navy 1,000 Air 3,000)
Paramilitary 1,400
Terms of service incl civil duties, 2 years

RESERVE 80,000 (Joint 80,000)

ORGANISATIONS BY SERVICE

Army ε23,000
FORCES BY ROLE
Tk   1 bde
Inf   5 bde
Arty   4 bn
Mor   1 bn
AT   2 bn
ADA   2 bn
Engr   1 regt (bn)

EQUIPMENT BY TYPE†
MBT 45: 30 T-54/T-55; 15 Type-59
LT TK 55: 30 *Scorpion*; 25 Type-62
RECCE 10 BRDM-2
APC (W) 14: ε10 BTR-40/BTR-152; 4 Type-92 (reported)
ARTY 378
    TOWED 170: **76mm** ε40 ZIS-3; **122mm** 100: 20 D-30; 80
    Type-54-1 (M-30) *M-1938*; **130mm** 30 Type-59-I
    MRL **122mm** 58 BM-21
    MOR 150: **82mm** 100 M-43; **120mm** 50 M-43
AT • RCL **75mm** Type-52 (M-20)
    RL **73mm** RPG-7 *Knout*
    GUNS **85mm** 75 Type-56 (D-44)

Navy ε1,000
EQUIPMENT BY TYPE
PATROL AND COASTAL COMBATANTS 8
    PHT 2 *Huchuan* each with 2 533mm ASTT
    PB 6: 2 *Ngunguri*; 2 *Shanghai II* (PRC); 2 VT 23m
AMPHIBIOUS • LCU 2 *Yuch'in*
FACILITIES
Bases Located at Dar es Salaam, Zanzibar, Mwanza (Lake
    Victoria)

Air Defence Command ε3,000;
FORCES BY ROLE
Ftr   3 sqn with J-5; J-6; J-7; K-8 *Karakorum*
Tpt   1 sqn with DHC-5D *Buffalo*;
           F-28 *Fellowship*; HS-125-700; HS-748; Y-5;
           Y-12(II); Some (liaison) sqn with Cessna 310;
           Cessna 404 *Titan*; Cessna U206 *Stationair*; Bell
           206B *Jet Ranger II*
Trg   sqn with PA-28-140 *Cherokee*; MiG-15UTI *Midget*
Hel   some sqn with 4 Bell 205 (AB-205); Bell 412; SA-
           316 *Alouette III*

EQUIPMENT BY TYPE†
Virtually no air defence assets serviceable.
AIRCRAFT 25 combat capable
    FTR 19: 3 J-5; 10 J-6; 6 J-7
    TPT 27: **Medium** 2 Y-8 **Light** 19: 5 Cessna 310; 2 Cessna
    404 *Titan*; 1 Cessna U206 *Stationair*; 3 DHC-5D *Buffalo*;
    5 PA-28-140 *Cherokee*; 1 Y-5; 2 Y-12(II) **PAX** 6: 2 F-28
    Fellowship; 1 HS-125-700; 3 HS-748
    TRG 8: 6 K-8 *Karakorum**; 2 MiG-15UTI *Midget*
HELICOPTERS
    MRH 8: 4 Bell 412; 4 SA-316 *Alouette III*
    TPT • **Light** 10: 4 AB-205 (Bell 205); 6 Bell 206B *Jet
    Ranger II*
AD
    SAM 160:
        SP 20 2K12 *Kub* (SA-6 *Gainful*)†; 20 S-125 *Pechora* (SA-
        3 *Goa*)†
        MANPAD 120 9K32 *Strela*-2 (SA-7 *Grail*)‡
    GUNS 200
        TOWED **14.5mm** 40 ZPU-2/ZPU-4†; **23mm** 40 ZU-23;
        37mm 120 M-1939

Paramilitary 1,400 active

Police Field Force 1,400
18 sub-units incl Police Marine Unit

Air Wing
AIRCRAFT • TPT • **Light** 1 Cessna U206 *Stationair*
HELICOPTERS
    TPT • **Light** 4: 2 Bell 206A *Jet Ranger* (AB-206A);
    2 Bell 206L *Long Ranger*
    TRG 2 Bell 47G (AB-47G)/Bell 47G2

Marine Unit 100
PATROL AND COASTAL COMBATANTS • MISC
BOATS/CRAFT: some boats

DEPLOYMENT

CÔTE D'IVOIRE
UN • UNOCI 2; 1 obs

DEMOCRATIC REPUBLIC OF THE CONGO
UN • MONUSCO 2 obs

LEBANON
UN • UNIFIL 77; 1 MP coy

SUDAN
UN • UNMIS 11 obs
UN • UNAMID 816; 20 obs; 1 inf bn

Togo TGO

CFA Franc BCEAO fr		2009	2010	2011
GDP	fr	1.48tr	1.56tr	
	US$	3.15bn	3.15bn	
per capita	US$	476	464	
Growth	%	2.5	2.5	
Inflation	%	2.0	2.4	
Def bdgt	fr	ε30bn		
	US$	ε67m		
US$1=fr		470.96	495.60	

Population	6,780,030

Age	0–14	15–19	20–24	25–29	30–64	65 plus
Male	20.5%	5.3%	4.9%	4.1%	13.4%	1.4%
Female	20.4%	5.3%	4.9%	4.2%	13.8%	1.8%

Capabilities

ACTIVE 8,550 (Army 8,100 Navy 200 Air 250)
Paramilitary 750
Terms of service conscription, 2 years (selective)

ORGANISATIONS BY SERVICE

Army 8,100+

FORCES BY ROLE
Inf	1 regt (some spt unit (trg), 2 armd sqn, 3 inf coy); 1 regt (1 mot inf bn, 1 mech inf bn)
Cdo/Para	1 regt (3 cdo/para coy)
Spt	1 regt (1 fd arty bty, 1 engr/log/tpt bn, 2 ADA bty)
Presidential	1 regt (1 Presidential Guard bn,
Guard	1 cdo bn, 2 Presidential Guard coy)

EQUIPMENT BY TYPE
MBT 2 T-54/T-55
LT TK 9 *Scorpion*
RECCE 61: 3 AML-60; 7 AML-90; 36 EE-9 *Cascavel*; 3 M-20; 4 M-3A1; 6 M-8; 2 VBL
AIFV 20 BMP-2
APC (W) 30 UR-416
ARTY 30

SP 122mm 6
TOWED 105mm 4 HM-2
MOR 82mm 20 M-43
AT • RCL 22: **75mm** 12 Type-52 (M-20)/Type-56; **82mm** 10 Type-65 (B-10)
  GUNS 57mm 5 ZIS-2
AD • GUNS • TOWED 43 **14.5mm** 38 ZPU-4; **37mm** 5 M-1939

Navy ε200 (incl Marine Infantry unit)

EQUIPMENT BY TYPE
PATROL AND COASTAL COMBATANTS • PB 2 *Kara* (FRA *Esterel*)

FACILITIES
Base   Located at Lomé

Air Force 250

FORCES BY ROLE
FGA	Some sqn with EMB-326G*; *Alpha Jet**
Tpt	Some sqn with B-707 (VIP); Beech 58 *Baron*; Cessna 337 *Skymaster*; DHC-5D *Buffalo*; Do-27; F-28-1000 (VIP);
Trg	Some sqn with TB-30 *Epsilon**
Tpt Hel	Some sqn with AS-332 *Super Puma*; SA-315 *Lama*; SA-319 *Alouette III*; SA-330 *Puma*

EQUIPMENT BY TYPE†
AIRCRAFT 10 combat capable
  TPT 8 **Light** 7 Beech 58 *Baron*; 2 Cessna 337 *Skymaster*; 2 DHC-5D *Buffalo*; 1 Do-27 **PAX** 2: 1 B-707 (VIP); 1 F-28-1000 (VIP)
  TRG 10: 3 *Alpha Jet**; 4 EMB-326G *; 3 TB-30 *Epsilon**
HELICOPTERS
  MRH 3: 2 SA-315 *Lama*; 1 SA-319 *Alouette III*
  TPT • Medium (1 AS-332 *Super Puma* in store); (1 SA-330 *Puma* in store)

Paramilitary 750

Gendarmerie 750
Ministry of Interior
FORCES BY ROLE
2 reg sections
Paramilitary   1 (mob) sqn

FACILITIES
School   1

DEPLOYMENT

CENTRAL AFRICAN REPUBLIC/CHAD
UN • MINURCAT 358; 2 inf coy

CÔTE D'IVOIRE
UN • UNOCI 315; 7 obs; 1 inf bn

LIBERIA
UN • UNMIL 1; 2 obs

SUDAN
UN • UNAMID 7 obs

Uganda UGA

Ugandan Shilling Ush		2009	2010	2011
GDP	Ush	30.1tr	34.4tr	
	US$	14.9bn	16.2bn	
per capita	US$	455	479	
Growth	%	7.1	7.4	
Inflation	%	12.7	8.9	
Def exp	Ush	593bn		
	US$	293m		
Def bdgt	Ush	488bn	489bn	499bn
	US$	241m	230m	
FMA (US)	US$	-	0.3m	0.3m
US$1=Ush		2023.82	2125.82	

Population   33,796,461

Age	0–14	15–19	20–24	25–29	30–64	65 plus
Male	25.1%	5.8%	4.7%	3.7%	10.0%	0.8%
Female	24.7%	5.7%	4.7%	3.6%	9.8%	1.2%

Capabilities

ACTIVE 45,000 (Ugandan People's Defence Force 45,000) **Paramilitary 1,800**

ORGANISATIONS BY SERVICE

Ugandan People's Defence Force ε40,000-45,000

FORCES BY ROLE

Army 5 div (each: up to 5 army bde)

Armd 1 bde

Arty   1 bde

EQUIPMENT BY TYPE†

MBT 185 T-54/T-55; 10 T-72

LT TK ε20 PT-76

RECCE 46: 40 *Eland*; 6 *Ferret*

AIFV 31 BMP-2

APC (W) 79: 15 BTR-60; 20 *Buffel*; 40 *Mamba*; 4 OT-64

ARTY 333+

   SP 155mm 6 ATMOS 2000

   TOWED 243+: **76mm** ZIS-3; **122mm** M-30; **130mm** 221; **155mm** 4 G-5; 18 M-839

   MRL 6+: **107mm** (12-tube); **122mm** 6+: BM-21; 6 RM-70

   MOR 78+: **81mm** L16; **82mm** M-43; **120mm** 78 *Soltam*

AD • SAM • MANPAD 200+: 200 9K32 *Strela*-2 (SA-7 Grail)‡; 9K310 *Igla*-1 (SA-16 *Gimlet*)

   GUNS • TOWED 20+: **14.5mm** ZPU-1/ZPU-2/ZPU-4; **37mm** 20 M-1939

Air Wing

FORCES BY ROLE

FGA   Some sqn with MiG-23 *Flogger*; MiG-21 *Fishbed*

Tpt   Some sqn with Y-12

Trg   Some sqn with L-39 *Albatros*†*; SF-260* (non-op)

Atk Hel Some sqn with Mi-24 *Hind*

Tpt Hel Some sqn with Bell 206 *Jet Ranger*; Bell 412 *Twin Huey*; Mi-17 *Hip H*; Mi-172 (VIP)

EQUIPMENT BY TYPE

AIRCRAFT 15 combat capable

   FTR 5 MiG-23 *Flogger*

   FGA 7 MiG-21 *Fishbed*

   TPT • Light 2 Y-12

   TRG 3 L-39 *Albatros*†*; (1 SF-260* non-op)

HELICOPTERS

   ATK 1 Mi-24 *Hind* (5 more non-op)

   MRH 5: 2 Bell 412 *Twin Huey*; 3 Mi-17 *Hip H* (1 more non-operational)

   TPT 4: **Medium** 1 Mi-172 (VIP) **Light** 3 Bell 206 *Jet Ranger*

Paramilitary ε1,800 active

Border Defence Unit ε600

Equipped with small arms only

Police Air Wing ε800

HELICOPTERS • TPT • Light 1 Bell 206 *Jet Ranger*

Marines ε400

PATROL AND COASTAL COMBATANTS 8 PBR

Local Militia Forces Amuka Group ε3,000; ε7,000 (reported under trg) (total 10,000)

DEPLOYMENT

CÔTE D'IVOIRE

UN • UNOCI 1; 2 obs

SOMALIA

AU • AMISOM 4,250; 5 inf bn

SUDAN

UN • UNMIS 8 obs

UN • UNAMID 1 obs

FOREIGN FORCES

(all EUTM, unless otherwise indicated)

Belgium 5

Finland 4

France 25

Germany 13

Greece 2

Hungary 4

Ireland 5

Italy 17

Kenya 9

Luxembourg 1

Malta 3

Portugal 15

Spain 38

Sweden 4

UK 2

Zambia ZMB

Zambian Kwacha K		2009	2010	2011
GDP	K	64.6tr	76.0tr	
	US$	12.9bn	15.8bn	
per capita	US$	995	1,193	
Growth	%	6.3	5.8	
Inflation	%	13.4	10.0	
Def exp	K	1.07tr		
	US$	213m		
Def bdgt	K	1.07tr	1.33tr	
	US$	213m	276m	
US$1=K		5022.56	4806.41	

Population   13,257,269

Age	0–14	15–19	20–24	25–29	30–64	65 plus
Male	23.4%	5.4%	4.6%	4.1%	11.5%	1.1%
Female	23.3%	5.4%	4.6%	4.0%	11.2%	1.4%

Capabilities

ACTIVE 15,100 (Army 13,500 Air 1,600) **Paramilitary 1,400**

RESERVE 3,000 (Army 3,000)

ORGANISATIONS BY SERVICE

Army 13,500

FORCES BY ROLE

Army   3 bde HQ

Armd   1 regt (1 tk bn, 1 armd recce bn)

Inf   6 bn

Arty   1 regt (1 MRL bn, 2 fd arty bn)

Engr   1 regt

EQUIPMENT BY TYPE

Some equipment†

MBT 30: 20 Type-59; 10 T-55

LT TK 30 PT-76

RECCE 70 BRDM-1/BRDM-2 (ε30 serviceable)

APC (W)33: 20 BTR-70; 13 BTR-60

ARTY 182

  TOWED 61: **105mm** 18 Model 56 pack howitzer; **122mm** 25 D-30; **130mm** 18 M-46

  MRL 122mm 30 BM-21 (ε12 serviceable)

  MOR 91: **81mm** 55; **82mm** 24; **120mm** 12

AT • MSL • MANPATS AT-3 9K11 *Sagger*

  RCL 12+: **57mm** 12 M-18; **75mm** M-20; **84mm** *Carl Gustav*

  RL 73mm RPG-7 *Knout*

AD • SAM • MANPAD 9K32 *Strela*-2 (SA-7 *Grail*)‡

  GUNS • TOWED 136: **20mm** 50 M-55 (triple); **37mm** 40 M-1939; **57mm** ε30 S-60; **85mm** 16 M-1939 *KS-12*

Reserve 3,000

Inf   3 bn

Air Force 1,600

FORCES BY ROLE

FGA   1 sqn with F-6; 1 sqn with MiG-21MF/MiG-21U; *Fishbed J*†

Tpt   1 sqn with An-26 *Curl*; DHC-5D *Buffalo*; MA60; Y-12(II)/(IV); 1 (VIP) unit with HS-748; Yak-40 *Codling*; Some (liaison)sqn with Do-28

Trg   sqns with FT-6*; K-8 *Karakorum**; SF-260TP; MFI-17

Tpt Hel   1 sqn with Mi-8 *Hip*; Some (liaison) sqn with Bell 47G; Bell 205 (UH-1H *Iroquois*/AB-205))

AD   3 bty with S-125 *Pechora* (SA-3 *Goa*)

EQUIPMENT BY TYPE†

Very low serviceability.

AIRCRAFT 28 combat capable

  FTR 10: 8 F-6; 2 FT-6*

  FGA 8 MiG-21MF *Fishbed J*; 2 MiG-21U *Mongol A*

  TPT 27: **Light** 4 An-26 *Curl*; 4 DHC-5D *Buffalo*; 5 Do-28; 2 MA60; 4 Y-12(II); 5 Y-12(IV); 2 Yak-40 *Codling* **PAX** 1 HS-748

  TRG 13+: 8 K-8 *Karakourm**; some MFI-17; 5 SF-260TP

HELICOPTERS

  MRH 4 Mi-17 *Hip*

  TPT • Light 13: 10 Bell 205 (UH-1H *Iroquois*/AB-205); 3 Bell 212

  TRG 5 Bell 47G

AD • SAM S-125 *Pechora* (SA-3 *Goa*)

MSL • ASM AT-3 *Sagger*

AAM • IR AAM • R-3 (AA-2 *Atoll*)‡; PL-2; *Python* 3

Paramilitary 1,400

Police Mobile Unit 700

Police 1 bn (4 Police coy)

Police Paramilitary Unit 700

Paramilitary   1 bn (3 Paramilitary coy)

DEPLOYMENT

CÔTE D'IVOIRE

UN • UNOCI 2 obs

DEMOCRATIC REPUBLIC OF THE CONGO

UN • MONUSCO 16 obs

LIBERIA

UN • UNMIL 3 obs

NEPAL

UN • UNMIN 1 obs

SUDAN

UN • UNMIS 544; 14 obs; 1 inf bn

UN • UNAMID 7; 13 obs

Zimbabwe ZWE

Zimbabwe Dollar Z$		2009	2010	2011
GDP	Z$	n.a.	n.a.	
	US$	ε4.62bn	ε5.57bn	
per capita	US$	369	441	
Growth	%	4.0	6.0	
Inflation	%	6.5	12.0	
Def bdgt	Z$	n.a.	n.a.	
	US$	67.1m	98.3m	
US$1=Z$		n.a.	n.a.	

Population   12,644,041

Age	0–14	15–19	20–24	25–29	30–64	65 plus
Male	21.2%	6.2%	4.3%	3.9%	11.0%	1.6%
Female	20.7%	6.2%	5.4%	5.2%	12.2%	2.2%

Capabilities

ACTIVE 29,000 (Army 25,000 Air 4,000) **Paramilitary 21,800**

ORGANISATIONS BY SERVICE

Army ε25,000

FORCES BY ROLE

Armd	1 sqn
Mech	1 bde HQ
Mech Inf	1 bn
Inf	5 bde HQ; 15 bn
Cdo	1 bn
Para	1 bn
Arty	1 bde
Fd arty	1 regt
Engr	2 regt
Gd	3 bn
Presidential Guard	1 gp
AD	1 regt

EQUIPMENT BY TYPE
MBT 40: 30 Type-59†; 10 Type-69†
RECCE 100: 20 *Eland*; 15 *Ferret*†; 80 EE-9 *Cascavel* (90mm)
APC 85
  APC (T) 30: 8 Type-63; 22 VTT-323
  APC (W) 55 TPK 4.20 VSC *ACMAT*
ARTY 242
  TOWED 122mm 20: 4 D-30; 16 Type-60 (D-74)
  MRL 76: **107mm** 16 Type-63; **122mm** 60 RM-70 *Dana*
  MOR 146: **81mm/82mm** ε140; **120mm** 6 M-43
AD • SAM • MANPAD 30 9K32 *Strela*-2 (SA-7 *Grail*) ‡
  GUNS • TOWED 116: **14.5mm** 36 ZPU-1/ZPU-2/ZPU-4;
  23mm 45 ZU-23; **37mm** 35 M-1939

Air Force 4,000

Flying hours   100 hrs/year

FORCES BY ROLE

Ftr	1 sqn with F-7M (F-7N) *Airguard*†; F-7II†; FT-7†
FGA	1 sqn with K-8 *Karakourm**; (1 sqn Hawker *Hunter* in store)
Atk/ISR	1 sqn with Cessna 337 *Skymaster**
ISR/Trg	1 sqn with SF-260M; SF-260TP*; SF-260W *Warrior**
Tpt	1 sqn with BN-2 *Islander*; CASA 212-200 *Aviocar* (VIP); Il-76 *Candid*
Atk Hel/Tpt Hel	1 sqn with Mi-35 *Hind*; Mi-35P *Hind* (liaison); SA-319 *Alouette III*; AS-532UL *Cougar* (VIP); 1 trg sqn with Bell 412 *Twin Huey*, SA-319 *Alouette III*
AD	1 sqn with 37mm guns; 57mm guns

FACILITIES
AD   1 with 37mm guns (not deployed); 57mm guns
School (not deployed); 100mm guns (not deployed)

EQUIPMENT BY TYPE
AIRCRAFT 45 combat capable
  FTR 9: 4 F-7M (F-7N) *Airguard*†; 3 F-7II†; 2 FT-7 †
  FGA (12 Hawker *Hunter* in store)
  TPT 28 **Heavy** 1 Il-76 *Candid* **Light** 27: 5 BN-2 *Islander*;
  8 C-212-200 *Aviocar* (VIP); 14 Cessna 337 *Skymaster**; (10
  C-47 *Skytrain* in store)
  TRG 32: 12 K-8 *Karakorum**; 5 SF-260M; 5 SF-260TP*; 5
  SF-260W *Warrior**; 5 SF-260F
HELICOPTERS
  ATK 6: 4 Mi-35 *Hind*; 2 Mi-35P *Hind*
  MRH 10: 8 Bell 412 *Twin Huey*; 2 SA-319 *Alouette III*;
  TPT • Medium 2 AS-532UL *Cougar* (VIP)
  MSL • AAM • IR AAM PL-2; PL-5
AD • GUNS 100mm (not deployed); **37mm** (not
deployed); **57mm** (not deployed)

Paramilitary 21,800

Zimbabwe Republic Police Force 19,500

incl Air Wg

Police Support Unit 2,300

DEPLOYMENT

CÔTE D'IVOIRE
UN • UNOCI 3 obs

LIBERIA
UN • UNMIL 2 obs

NEPAL
UN • UNMIN 4 obs

SUDAN
UN • UNMIS 9 obs
UN • UNAMID 2; 9 obs

Table 22 **Selected Arms Procurements and Deliveries, Sub-Saharan Africa**

Designation	Type	Quantity	Contract Value	Supplier Country	Prime Contractor	Order Date	First Delivery Due	Notes
Chad (CHA)								
Su-25 *Frogfoot*	Atk ac	6	n.k.	UKR	Sukhoi	2007	2008	Ex-UKR stock. Deliveries ongoing
Equatorial Guinea (EQG)								
Barroso-class	PSO	1	n.k.	BRZ	Emgepron	2010	n.k.	Delivery status unclear
Kenya (KEN)								
Z-9	MRH Hel	4	n.k.	PRC	HAMC	2009	2010	Delivery status unclear
Namibia (NAM)								
Chetak + *Cheetah*	MRH hel	3	US$10m	IND	Hindustan Aeronautic	2009	n.k.	2 *Chetak*, 1 *Cheetah*
Nigeria (NGA)								
Shaldag-class	PBF	2	US$25m	ISR	IAI	2009	n.k.	First delivered by mid-2009
ATR-42	MP ac	2	US$73m	ITA	Alenia	2007	n.k.	Second delivered March 2010
South Africa (RSA)								
AMV 8×8	APC (W)	264	ZAR8.8bn (US$1.2bn)	FIN/RSA	Patria/Denel	2007	n.k.	5 variants to be produced: cmd, mor, msl, section, and fire spt vehicles
JAS 39 C/D *Gripen*	FGA ac	26	US$1.47bn	SWE	SAAB	2000	2008	17 C single seat variant and 9 D twin seat variant. Final delivery due 2012. Deliveries ongoing
A-*Darter*	AAM	n.k.	n.k.	Int'l	Denel	2007	n.k.	As of 2009, AAM undergoing flight trials and delayed by budget problems. Intended to arm *Gripen*
Zimbabwe (ZWE)								
FC-1 *Xiaolong*	FGA ac	12	n.k.	PRC	n.k.	2004	n.k.	Delivery status unclear

Chapter Ten
Country comparisons – commitments, force levels and economics

Country comparisons

Table 23 **UN Deployments 2010–11**

Europe

Location	CYPRUS	
Operation	UN Peacekeeping Force in Cyprus (UNFICYP)	
Original Mandate:	Resolution 186 (4 Mar 1964)	
Mandate Renewed	Resolution 1930 (15 Jun 2010)	
Renewed Until:	15-Dec-10	
Mission:	Prevent a recurrence of conflict between Greek Cypriot and Turkish/Turkish Cypriot forces; help to maintain law and order	

Country	Forces by role	Troops
UK	1 inf coy	271
Argentina	2 inf coy, 1 hel flt	267
Slovakia	elms 1 inf coy, 1 engr pl	198
Hungary	1 inf pl	84
Chile		15
Paraguay		14
Austria		4
Croatia		2
Peru		2
Brazil		1
Canada		1
TOTAL (excluding police)		**859**

Location	SERBIA	
Operation	UN Mission in Kosovo (UNMIK)	
Original Mandate:	Resolution 1244 (10 Jun 1999)	
Renewed Until	Cancelled by the Security Council	
Mission:	Originally established to provide a transitional administration for Kosovo, and to oversee the development of democratic, self-governing institutions. UNMIK has subsequently scaled down and moved from an executive role to providing support for local institutions.	

Country		Military Observers
Ukraine		2
Czech Republic		1
Denmark		1
Norway		1
Poland		1
Romania		1
Spain		1
TOTAL (excluding police)		**8**

Asia

Location	AFGHANISTAN	
Operation	UN Assistance Mission in Afghanistan (UNAMA)	
Original Mandate	Resolution 1401 (28 Mar 2002)	
Mandate Renewed	Resolution 1943 (13 Oct 2010)	
Renewed Until	13-Oct-11	
Mission	Assist the Afghan government in developing and promoting good governance and the rule of law; support human rights; coordinating role for delivery of humanitarian aid; promote coherent support for Afghanistan from the international community.	

Location		Military Observers
Australia		3
Norway		2
Denmark		1
Germany		1
Italy		1
Korea, Republic of		1
New Zealand		1
Poland		1

Location	AFGHANISTAN (continued)	
Portugal		1
Sweden		1
Uruguay		1
TOTAL (excluding police)		**14**

Location	INDIA AND PAKISTAN	
Operation	UN Military Observer Group in India and Pakistan (UNMOGIP)	
Original Mandate	Resolution 47 (21 Apr 1948)	
Mandate Renewed	Resolution 307 (21 Dec 1971)	
Renewed Until	Cancelled by the Security Council	
Mission	Monitor the ceasefire between India and Pakistan in Kashmir.	

Country		Military Observers
Korea, Republic of		9
Croatia		9
Italy		7
Sweden		6
Finland		5
Chile		2
Uruguay		2
TOTAL (excluding police)		**40**

Location	NEPAL	
Operation	UN Mission in Nepal (UNMIN)	
Original Mandate	Resolution 1740 (23 Jan 2007)	
Mandate Renewed	Resolution 1939 (15 Sep 2010)	
Renewed Until	15-Jan-11	
Mission	UNMIN remains in Nepal to monitor the continued compliance of the Nepalese Army and the Maoist forces with the Comprehensive Peace Agreement. It also assists the OHCHR in monitoring the human rights situation, and aiding in the disposal of landmines and IEDs.	

Country		Military Observers
Malaysia		7
Romania		7
Brazil		6
Japan		6
Nigeria		5
Indonesia		4
Jordan		4
Korea, Republic of		4
Paraguay		4
Zimbabwe		4
Egypt		3
Switzerland		3
Austria		2
Sierra Leone		2
Sweden		2
Uruguay		2
Zambia		1
TOTAL (excluding police)		**66**

Table 23 **UN Deployments 2010–11**

Location	TIMOR LESTE
Operation	UNMIT
Original Mandate	Resolution 1704 (25 Aug 2005)
Mandate Renewed	Resolution 1912 (26 Feb 2010)
Renewed Until	26-Feb-11
Mission	Provide training and support to the Timorese National Police (PNTL) so that it can resume its policing responsibilities and enable a UNMIT policing drawdown. Also to provide assistance to the Timorese government and institutions and aid in the provision of economic assistance.

Country	Military Observers
Australia	4
Bangladesh	4
Brazil	4
Pakistan	4
Philippines	3
Portugal	3
China, People's Republic of	2
Japan	2
Malaysia	2
Singapore	2
Fiji	1
India	1
Nepal	1
New Zealand	1
Sierra Leone	1
TOTAL (excluding police)	**35**

Middle East and North Africa

Location	IRAQ
Operation	UN Mission Assistance Mission in Iraq (UNAMI)
Original Mandate	Resolution 1500 (14 Aug 2003)
Mandate Renewed	Resolution 1936 (5 Aug 2010)
Renewed Until	31-Jul-11
Mission	Support government and people of Iraq in the ongoing political process, help to provide humanitarian assitance to refugees and displaced persons, and promote human rights.

Country	Forces by role	Troops	Mil Obs
Fiji	3 Sy units	221	
United States			4
Australia			2
Denmark			2
Jordan			2
Nepal			1
New Zealand			1
UK			1
		221	13
TOTAL (excluding police)		**234**	

Location	ISRAEL, SYRIA AND LEBANON
Operation	UN Truce Supervision Organisation (UNTSO)
Original Mandate	Resolution 50 (29 May 1948)
Mandate Renewed	Resolution 339 (23 Oct 1973)
Renewed Until	Cancelled by the Security Council
Mission	Originally acting as supervisors for the armistice agreements signed between Israel and its Arab neighbours, UNTSO has subsequently undertaken a range of tasks including providing a channel for communication between hostile powers; it can provide the nucleus for establishing other peacekeeping operations at short notice.

Location	ISRAEL, SYRIA AND LEBANON (continued)
Country	Military Observers
Finland	14
Norway	13
Switzerland	13
Ireland	12
Netherlands	12
Australia	11
Denmark	10
Canada	8
Austria	7
Italy	7
New Zealand	7
Argentina	5
China, People's Republic of	5
Russia	5
Sweden	5
Nepal	4
Chile	3
Belgium	2
France	2
Slovakia	2
Slovenia	2
United States	2
Estonia	1
TOTAL (excluding police)	**152**

Location	LEBANON
Operation	UNIFIL
Original Mandate	Resolutions 425 and 426 (19 Mar 2008)
Mandate Renewed	Resolution 1937 (30 Aug 2010)
Renewed Until	31-Aug-11
Mission	Assist the Lebanese government in securing its borders and establishing a de-militarised zone in Southern Lebanon; help to ensure access for humanitarian aid.

Country	Forces by role	Troops
Italy	1 armd recce bn, 1 armd inf bn, 1 hel bn, 1 CIMIC coy, 1 sigs coy, 1 FF	1,734
France	1 armd inf bn, 1 armd sqn, 1 arty coy	1,575
Indonesia	1 mech inf bn, 1 MP coy, 1 fd hospital	1,324
Spain	1 armd inf bn	1,064
Nepal	1 inf bn	1,020
India	1 inf bn, elm 1 fd hospital	910
Ghana	1 mech inf bn	877
Malaysia	1 mech inf bn	744
Turkey	1 engr coy, 1 PB	504
Korea, Republic of	1 inf bn	368
China, People's Republic of	1 engr coy, 1 fd hospital	344
Bangladesh		325
Germany	2 PC, 1 Spt	249
Belgium	1 engr coy	160
Portugal	1 engr coy	146
Denmark	1 log bn	142
Tanzania	1 MP coy	77
Greece	1 PB	59
El Salvador	1 inf pl	52
Slovenia	1 inf pl	14
Brunei		9

Table 23 **UN Deployments 2010–11**

Location	LEBANON (continued)	
Ireland		8
Hungary		4
Guatemala		3
Qatar		3
Sierra Leone		3
Cyprus		2
Cambodia		1
Croatia		1
FYROM		1
Nigeria		1
TOTAL (excluding police)		**11,724**

Location	SYRIAN GOLAN HEIGHTS	
Operation	UN Disengagement Observer Force (UNDOF)	
Original Mandate	Resolution 350 (31 May 1974)	
Mandate Renewed	Resolution 1934 (30 June 2010)	
Renewed Until	31-Dec-10	
Mission	Supervise the continued implemetation of the disengagement of forces agreement signed by Israel and Syria after the war of October 1973.	
Country	**Forces by role**	**Troops**
Austria	elm 1 inf bn	378
Philippines	1 inf bn	349
India	elm 1 log bn	190
Croatia	1 inf coy	94
Japan	elm 1 log bn	31
Canada		2
TOTAL (excluding police)		**1,044**

Location	WESTERN SAHARA		
Operation	UN Mission for the Referendum in the Western Sahara (MINURSO)		
Original Mandate	Resolution 690 (29 Apr 1991)		
Mandate Renewed	Resolution 1920 (30 Apr 2010)		
Renewed Until	30-Apr-11		
Mission	Ensuring compliance with the ceasefire agreed between Morocco and POLISARIO whilst efforts continue to establish a longer term solution to the situation in Western Sahara.		
Country	**Forces by role**	**Troops**	**Mil Obs**
Malaysia	1 fd hospital	20	12
Egypt			21
Russia			17
Ghana		7	9
France			13
Honduras			12
Brazil			11
Pakistan			11
Yemen			10
Bangladesh			9
Croatia			7
Hungary			7
Nigeria			6
China, Peoples Republic of			5
El Salvador			5
Guinea			5
Italy			5
Mongolia			4
Argentina			3
Ireland			3
Sri Lanka			3
Austria			2

Location	WESTERN SAHARA (continued)	
Djibouti		2
Korea, Republic of		2
Nepal		2
Paraguay		2
Greece		1
Jordan		1
Poland		1
Uruguay		1
	27	192
TOTAL (excluding police)		**219**

Caribbean and Latin America

Location	HAITI	
Operation	UN Stabilisation Mission in Haiti (MINUSTAH)	
Original Mandate	Resolution 1542 (30 Apr 2004)	
Mandate Renewed	Resolution 1944 (14 Oct 2010)	
Renewed Until	15-Oct-11	
Mission	Support the political process, help to strengthen state institutions and support the work of both the Haitian National Police and the National Commission on Disarmament, Dismantlement and Reintegration. In addition, supporting the post-earthquake recovery, reconstruction and stability efforts in Haiti.	
	Forces by Role	**Troops**
Brazil	2 inf bn, 1 engr coy	2,188
Uruguay	2 inf bn, 1 mne coy, 1 hel sec	1,135
Nepal	1 mech inf bn, 1 inf bn	1,074
Sri Lanka	1 inf bn, 1 log coy	958
Argentina	1 inf bn, 1 hel coy, 1 fd hospital	708
Jordan	1 inf bn	611
Chile	1 inf bn, 1 hel coy, elms 1 engr coy	503
Peru	1 inf coy	371
Korea, Republic of	1 engr coy	242
Japan	1 engr coy	225
Bolivia	1 mech inf coy	208
Philippines	1 HQ coy	157
Guatemala	1 MP coy	147
Ecuador	elms 1 engr coy	67
Paraguay		31
United States		9
Canada		8
France		2
India		1
TOTAL (excluding police)		**8,645**

Sub-Saharan Africa

Location	BURUNDI	
Operation	UN Integrated Office in Burundi (BINUB)	
Original Mandate	Resolution 1719 (25 Oct 2006)	
Mandate Renewed	Resolution 1902 (17 Dec 2009)	
Renewed Until	31-Dec-10	
Mission	Support the government of Burundi in peace consolidation and democratic governance, disarmament and security sector reform, and the promotion of human rights.	
Country		**Military Observers**
Ghana		1
Niger		1
Pakistan		1
Senegal		1
Switzerland		1
TOTAL (excluding police)		**5**

Table 23 **UN Deployments 2010–11**

Location	CHAD AND THE CENTRAL AFRICAN REPUBLIC		
Operation	UN Mission in the Central African Republic and Chad (MINURCAT)		
Original Mandate	Resolution 1778 (25 Sep 2007)		
Mandate Renewed	Resolution 1923 (25 May 2010)		
Renewed Until	21-Dec-10		
Mission	Assist in the organisation and training of the Détachement integeré de sécurité (DIS) in Chad, as part of efforts to relocate refugee camps away from the border and to ensure that the rule of law and human rights are protected. To be withdrawn with the end of the mission madate in December 2010		

Country	Forces by Role	Troops	Mil Obs
Nepal	1 inf bn	581	1
Ghana	1 inf bn	527	1
Togo	2 inf coy	358	
Mongolia	1 inf coy	268	
Bangladesh	2 avn pl	138	2
Russia	1 avn pl	119	
Sri Lanka		74	
Serbia		14	
Senegal		10	3
Ireland		10	
Nigeria		4	2
Pakistan		4	2
Tunisia		2	4
Namibia		5	
Benin			3
Kenya		3	
Burkina Faso		2	
Ethiopia		2	
Poland		2	
United States		2	
Egypt			2
Democratic Republic of the Congo		1	
Norway		1	
Mali			1
Rwanda			1
		2,127	22
TOTAL (excluding police)		**2,149**	

Location	CÔTE D'IVOIRE		
Operation	UN Operation in Côte d'Ivoire (UNOCI)		
Original Mandate	Resolution 1528 (27 Feb 2004)		
Mandate Renewed	Resolution 1946 (15 Oct 2010)		
Renewed Until	30-Apr-11		
Mission	Tasked with monitoring the ceasefire agreement and arms embargo, assisting in the process of disarming militia groups, reform of the security sector, promoting and protecting human rights and law and order and providing technical and logistical support to the Independent Electoral Commission.		

	Forces by role	Troops	Mil Obs
Bangladesh	2 inf bn, 1 engr coy, 1 sigs coy, 1 fd hospital	2,090	9
Pakistan	1 inf bn, 1 engr coy, 1 tpt coy	1,140	11
Jordan	1 inf bn, 1 SF coy	1,062	7
Morocco	1 inf bn	726	
Ghana	1 inf bn, 1 hel coy, 1 fd hospital	507	5
Benin	1 inf bn	427	6
Niger	1 inf bn	393	6
Senegal	1 inf bn	324	14

Location	CÔTE D'IVOIRE (continued)		
Togo	1 inf bn	315	7
Egypt	1 engr coy	176	
Tunisia		4	7
Russia			11
Paraguay		2	7
Yemen		1	8
France		7	
Brazil		3	4
Nigeria			7
Philippines		3	3
China, People's Republic of			6
India			6
Romania			6
Guatemala			5
Nepal		1	3
Chad		1	3
Tanzania		2	1
Uganda		1	2
Bolivia			3
El Salvador			3
Gambia			3
Guinea			3
Moldova			3
Peru			3
Poland			3
Serbia			3
Zimbabwe			3
Ecuador			2
Ethiopia			2
Ireland			2
Korea, Republic of			2
Uruguay			2
Zambia			2
Namibia			1
		7,185	184
TOTAL (excluding police)		**7,369**	

Location	DEMOCRATIC REPUBLIC OF THE CONGO		
Operation	UN Organisation Stabilization Mission in the Democratic Republic of the Congo (MONUSCO)		
Original Mandate	Resolution 1279 (30 Nov 1999)		
Mandate Renewed	Resolution 1925 (28 May 2010)		
Renewed Until	30-Jun-11		
Mission	Protect civilians and UN staff, support Congolese military operations against armed groups and assist the Congolese government in military and police capacity building.		

	Forces by role	Troops	Mil Obs
India	3 mech inf bn, 1 inf bn, 2 atk hel coy, 1 hel coy, 1 fd hospital	4,243	60
Pakistan	3 mech inf bn, 1 inf bn	3,571	55
Bangladesh	2 mech inf bn, 1 engr coy, 2 hel coy	2,521	30
Uruguay	1 inf bn, 1 engr coy, 1 mne coy; 1 hel flt	1,285	46
South Africa	1 inf bn, 1 engr coy, 1 hel coy	1,205	14
Nepal	1 inf bn, 1 engr coy	1,025	24
Egypt	1 inf bn, 1 engr coy	999	25
Morocco	1 mech inf bn 1 fd hospital	831	4
Ghana	1 mech inf bn	462	24
Benin	1 inf bn	450	11
Jordan	1 SF coy, 1 fd hospital	218	25

Country comparisons

Table 23 **UN Deployments 2010–11**

Location	DEMOCRATIC REPUBLIC OF THE CONGO (cont.)		
China, Peoples Republic of	1 engr coy, 1 fd hospital	218	16
Indonesia	1 engr coy	175	16
Guatemala	1 SF coy	150	7
Tunisia		46	30
Malawi		50	18
Senegal		40	23
Belgium	1 avn flt	22	7
Bolivia		19	10
Russia			28
Kenya			24
Romania			21
Nigeria			18
Paraguay			17
Malaysia			17
Niger			16
Zambia			16
Ukraine			12
Canada			10
Mali			9
Serbia		6	2
Burkina Faso			8
Peru			7
Yemen			6
Bosnia-Herzegovina			5
Cameroon			5
France			5
Sri Lanka			4
Sweden			4
United Kingdom			4
Czech Republic			3
Ireland			3
Poland			3
Spain			3
Switzerland			3
Denmark			2
Mongolia			2
Tanzania			2
United States			2
Mozambique			1
Norway			1
		17,536	708
TOTAL (excluding police)			**18,244**

Location	LIBERIA		
Operation	UN Mission in Liberia (UNMIL)		
Original Mandate	Resolution 1509 (19 Sep 2003)		
Mandate Renewed	Resolution 1938 (15 Sep 2010)		
Renewed Until	30-Sep-11		
Mission	Provide support for the peace process and ceasefire agreement as well as humanitarian and security sector reform assistance.		
	Forces by role	Troops	Mil Obs
Pakistan	3 inf bn, 3 engr coy, 1 fd hospital	2,953	7
Nigeria	1 inf bn, 1 sigs coy	1,553	13
Bangladesh	1 inf bn, 2 engr coy, 1 log coy, 1 sigs coy, 1 MP coy, 1 fd hospital	1,441	12
Ghana	1 inf bn	706	11
China, Peoples Republic of	1 engr coy, 1 tpt coy, 1 fd hospital	564	2
Ukraine	1 hel coy	277	2

Location	LIBERIA (continued)		
Mongolia		150	
Jordan	1 fd hospital	120	4
Philippines	1 inf coy	117	2
Nepal	1 MP unit	18	2
Ethiopia		4	7
United States		5	4
Denmark		3	2
Egypt			5
Malaysia			5
Namibia		3	1
Brazil		2	2
Peru		2	2
Russia			4
Serbia			4
Benin		1	2
Bolivia		1	2
Ecuador		1	2
Paraguay		1	2
Togo		1	2
Kyrgyzstan			3
Zambia			3
Croatia		2	
Finland		2	
Korea, Republic of		1	1
Senegal		1	1
Bulgaria			2
El Salvador			2
Gambia			2
Moldova			2
Montenegro			2
Niger			2
Poland			2
Romania			2
Zimbabwe			2
France		1	
Yemen		1	
Indonesia			1
Mali			1
		7,931	129
TOTAL (excluding police)			**8,060**

Location	SUDAN		
Operation	UN Mission in Sudan (UNMIS)		
Original Mandate	Resolution 1590 (24 Mar 2005)		
Mandate Renewed	Resolution 1919 (29 Apr 2010)		
Renewed Until	30-Apr-11		
Mission	Monitor and verify the implementation of the Comprehensive Peace Agreement between the Sudanese Government and the Sudan People's Liberation Movement/Army; provide security conditions to enable the return of refugees and the provision of humanitarian assistance.		
	Forces by role	Troops	Mil Obs
India	2 inf bn, 1 engr coy, 1 hel coy, 1 tpt coy, 1 fd hospital	2,633	18
Bangladesh	1 inf bn, 1 engr coy, 1 MP coy, 1 tpt coy, 1 rvn coy, 1 de-mining pl, 1 fd hospital	1,621	6
Egypt	1 inf coy, 2 engr coy, 2 tpt coy, 1 med bn, 1 med coy, 1 de-mining pl	1,503	15
Pakistan	1 inf bn, 2 hel coy, 1 engr coy, 1 tpt coy, 1 de-mining pl, 1 fd hospital	1,479	16

Table 23 **UN Deployments 2010–11**

Location	LIBERIA (continued)		
Kenya	1 inf bn, 1 de-mining pl	724	4
Zambia	1 inf bn	544	14
China, People's Republic of	1 engr coy, 1 tpt coy, 1 fd hospital	437	12
Rwanda	1 inf coy	257	10
Russia	1 hel coy	123	13
Cambodia	1 de-mining pl		3
Germany		5	25
Canada		7	20
Brazil		2	20
Yemen			21
Norway		6	13
Nigeria		5	13
Ecuador			17
Jordan		6	10
Australia		9	6
Bolivia			15
Netherlands		2	12
Nepal		7	5
Philippines			11
Tanzania			11
Romania			10
Denmark		4	5
Indonesia			9
Paraguay			9
Peru			9
Ukraine			9
Zimbabwe			9
Malaysia		2	6
Guatemala		1	7
Uganda			8
Korea, Republic of		1	6
Guinea			7
Kyrgyzstan			7
Namibia			7
Burkina Faso			6
Fiji			6
Sierra Leone			6
Sri Lanka			6
Benin			5
Sweden			5
United Kingdom			5
Croatia		4	
New Zealand		2	2
Belgium			4
Turkey		3	
Greece		1	2
Japan		2	
Finland		1	1
Iran			2
Moldova			2
Mongolia			2
Switzerland			2
El Salvador			1
Mali			1
Mozambique			1
Poland			1
		9,442	478
TOTAL (excluding police)			**9,920**

Location	SUDAN (DARFUR REGION)		
Operation	UN-AU Mission in Darfur (UNAMID)		
Original Mandate	Resolution 1769 (31 Jul 2007)		
Mandate Renewed	Resolution 1945 (14 Oct 2010)		
Renewed Until	19-Oct-11		
Mission	Protect the local civilian population from violence, monitor the implementation of the various ceasefire agreements, establish a safe environment for the provision of humanitarian assistance and economic reconstruction, promote human rights and the rule of law and monitor the situation on Sudan's borders with Chad and the Central African Republic.		
	Forces by role	**Troops**	**Mil Obs**
Nigeria	4 inf bn, 1 fd hospital	3,318	12
Rwanda	4 inf bn	3,231	9
Egypt	2 inf bn, 1 engr coy, 1 sigs coy, 1 tpt coy	2,394	24
Ethiopia	2 inf bn, 1 recce coy, 1 hel coy, 1 log coy, 1 tpt coy	2,356	10
Senegal	1 inf bn	1,010	17
Tanzania	1 inf bn	816	20
Burkina Faso	1 inf bn	802	7
South Africa	1 inf bn	775	15
Bangladesh	1 inf coy, 1 log coy	580	6
Pakistan	1 engr coy	502	5
Nepal	2 inf coy	346	16
China, People's Republic of	1 engr coy	319	2
Gambia	1 inf coy	200	1
Sierra Leone	1 recce coy	135	6
Kenya	1 MP coy	82	6
Yemen		5	22
Zambia		7	13
Malawi		7	8
Malaysia		12	1
Jordan		7	5
Namibia		2	10
Zimbabwe		2	9
Ghana		6	4
Mali		2	8
Thailand		7	2
Burundi		2	7
Togo			7
Canada		5	
Germany		3	
Indonesia		1	2
Cameroon			3
Guatemala		2	
Italy		2	
Korea, Republic of		2	
Netherlands		2	
Bolivia		1	
Uganda			1
		16,943	258
TOTAL (excluding police)			**17,201**

Table 24 **Non-UN Deployments 2010–11**

Europe	
Location:	**ARMENIA AND AZERBAIJAN**
Operation:	The Personal Representative of the Chairman-in-Office on the Conflict Dealt with by the OSCE Minsk Conference
Primary Organisation:	OSCE
Mission:	Represent the OSCE in issues related to the Nagorno-Karabakh conflict, and assist in confidence-buliding and other measures contributing to the peace process.

Contributor:	Total:
Hungary	2
Bulgaria	1
Kazakhstan	1
Poland	1
UK	1
TOTAL	**6**

Location:	**BOSNIA-HERZEGOVINA**	
Operation:	EUFOR (Operation Althea)	
Primary Organisation:	EU	
Mission:	Ensure continued compliance with the Dayton/Paris agreement, and maintain security and stability within Bosnia-Herzegovina	

Contributor:	Forces by role (where known)	Total:
Austria	1 inf bn HQ, 1 inf coy, 1 recce pl	304
Turkey	1 inf coy	280
Italy		193
Poland	1 inf coy	184
Hungary	1 inf coy	166
Bulgaria		120
Germany		111
Netherlands		75
Romania		64
Portugal		51
Greece		49
Ireland		43
Slovakia		40
Slovenia		29
Chile		21
Switzerland		20
Albania		13
FYROM		12
Finland		4
France		4
UK		4
Czech Republic		2
Estonia		2
Lithuania		1
Luxembourg		1
Sweden		1
TOTAL		**1,794**

Location:	**BOSNIA-HERZEGOVINA**
Operation:	OSCE Mission to Bosnia and Herzegovina
Primary Organisation:	OSCE
Mission:	Promote human rights, democracy building and regional military stabilisation.

Contributor:	Total:
United States	9
Italy	5
Germany	4
Greece	4

Location:	**BOSNIA-HERZEGOVINA (continued)**
France	3
Ireland	3
Romania	3
Russia	3
Slovakia	3
Spain	3
Canada	2
Hungary	2
Netherlands	2
Portugal	2
Sweden	2
Turkey	2
UK	2
Armenia	1
Austria	1
Belarus	1
Belgium	1
Croatia	1
Czech Republic	1
Finland	1
Kyrgyzstan	1
Norway	1
Slovenia	1
Tajikistan	1
Ukraine	1
TOTAL:	**66**

Location:	**MOLDOVA**
Operation:	Transdniestr Peacekeeping Force
Primary Organisation:	Russia/Moldova/Ukraine
Mission:	Peacekeeping operations in the Trans-dniester region under the terms of the 1992 ceasefire agreement, with the aim of contributing to a negotiated settlement between the two sides.

Contributor	Obs/Troops
Moldova	453
Russia	335
Ukraine	10
TOTAL	**798**

Location:	**MOLDOVA**
Operation:	OSCE Mission to Moldova
Primary Organisation:	OSCE
Mission:	Main objective is to negotiate a lasting solution to the Trans-dniestrian conflict. Mission also deals with issues of human rights, democratisation and the removal and destruction of former Russian munitions.

Contributor:	Total:
Estonia	2
Latvia	2
United States	2
Bulgaria	1
France	1
Italy	1
Poland	1
Sweden	1
UK	1
TOTAL	**12**

Table 24 **Non-UN Deployments 2010–11**

Location:	SERBIA
Operation:	OSCE Mission to Serbia
Primary Organisation:	OSCE
Mission:	Assist Serbia to build democratic institutions, particularly in the fields of human rights and the rule of law.

Contributor:	Total:
United States	5
Germany	3
Norway	3
UK	3
Hungary	2
Ireland	2
Netherlands	2
Sweden	2
Austria	1
Bosnia-Herzegovina	1
Canada	1
Croatia	1
France	1
Georgia	1
Greece	1
Italy	1
Moldova	1
Slovenia	1
Spain	1
Turkey	1
Ukraine	1
TOTAL	35

Location:	SERBIA (KOSOVO)
Operation:	KFOR (Joint Enterprise)
Primary Organisation:	NATO
Mission:	Under UNSCR 1244 (10th June 1999) KFOR is mandated to enforce law and order in Kosovo until UNMIK can assume responsibility for this task. Since 2008, NATO has taken on the additional responsibility of supporting the development of multi-ethnic security forces.

Contributor:	Forces by role (where known)	Total:
Germany	1 inf bn HQ, 1 inf coy, 1 sigs coy, 1 spt bn, elms 1 hel gp, elms 1 MP coy, 1 med unit	1,355
Italy	1 inf BG HQ, 1 engr unit, 1 hel unit, 1 sigs unit, 1 CSS unit, 1 Carabinieri regt	1,247
United States	1 ARNG cbt spt bde	810
France	1 armd cav BG	743
Greece	1 mech inf bn	711
Turkey	1 inf coy, elms 1 MP coy	479
Austria	1 inf bn HQ, elm 1 MP coy, elm hel gp	437
Slovenia	1 inf bn HQ, 2 mot inf coy, 1 CSS coy	331
Portugal	1 AB bn (KTM)	301
Sweden	1 inf coy	246
Hungary	1 inf coy	242
Morocco	1 inf unit	210
Switzerland	1 inf coy, elm 1 MP coy, elm 1 hel gp	200
Finland		196
Poland	1 inf coy	152
Denmark		152
Slovakia	1 inf coy	141
Romania	1 inf coy	139
Ukraine	1 inf coy	127
Czech Republic	elm 1 engr bn	103
Armenia		35

Luxembourg	23
Ireland	22
Croatia	20
Netherlands	8
Canada	5
Norway	5
UK	4
Bulgaria	3
Albania	3
Spain	3
Estonia	1
TOTAL	8,454

Location:	SERBIA (KOSOVO)
Operation:	OSCE Mission in Kosovo
Primary Organisation:	OSCE
Mission:	Institution and democracy building in Kosovo, and promoting human rights and the rule of law.

Contributor:	Total:
United States	18
Italy	16
Austria	13
Turkey	12
Germany	10
Spain	10
UK	10
Bosnia-Herzegovina	8
Croatia	8
France	6
Greece	5
Ireland	5
Canada	4
Georgia	4
FYROM	4
Poland	4
Portugal	4
Sweden	4
Hungary	3
Netherlands	3
Romania	3
Azerbaijan	2
Belarus	2
Russia	2
Ukraine	2
Uzbekistan	2
Armenia	1
Belgium	1
Malta	1
Moldova	1
Montenegro	1
Slovakia	1
TOTAL	170

Table 24 **Non-UN Deployments 2010–11**

Location:	MEDITERRANEAN SEA
Operation:	*Active Endeavour*
Primary Organisation:	NATO
Mission:	Naval deployment to the eastern Mediterranean to provide a deterrent presence and surveillance of maritime traffic. (Standing NATO Maritime Group 2)

Contributor:	Forces:
Netherlands	1 DDGHM
Germany	1 FFGHM
Greece	1 FFGHM
Italy	1 FFGHM
Turkey	1 FFGHM
Ukraine	1 FSM

Asia

Location:	AFGHANISTAN
Operation:	ISAF/*Operation Enduring Freedom -Afghanistan* (OEF-A)
Primary Organisation:	NATO/United States
Mission:	Under UNSCR 1386 (Dec 2001), and its extension by subsequent resolutions, ISAF has a peace-enforcement mandate. In this capacity it undertakes a range of tasks, including counter-insurgency and counter-narcotics operations and the provision of training and support to the Afghan National Army. OEF-A conducts combat operations against al-Qaeda, and trains Afghan security forces.

Contributor:	Forces by role (where known)	Total:
United States (ISAF)	1 corps HQ; 1 div HQ, 1 HBCT, 1 SBCT, 5 IBCT, 1 ARNG IBCT, 3 cbt avn bde, 1 USMC MEF with (2 RCT)	90,000
United States (OEF-A)		7,000
UK	1 div HQ, 1 air aslt bde HQ, 6 lt inf bn, 1 recce regt	9,500
Germany	1 div HQ, 2 mtn inf bn	4,388
France	1 mech inf bde HQ, 1 (TdM) inf regt, 1 inf regt	3,750
Italy	1 mtn inf bde HQ; 3 mtn inf regt	3,300
Canada	1 inf BG	2,922
Poland	1 armd bde HQ, 2 inf bn	2,417
Turkey	1 inf bde HQ, 2 inf bn	1,790
Romania	1 inf bn	1,648
Australia	1 inf BG, 1 cdo BG	1,550
Spain	1 AB bn	1,537
Georgia	1 inf bn	925
Denmark	1 mech inf BG	750
Bulgaria	1 mech inf coy	516
Hungary	1 lt inf coy	507
Sweden		500
Belgium		491
Czech Republic		468
Netherlands		380
Norway	1 mech inf coy, 1 spt coy	351
Croatia		300
Slovakia		300
Albania	1 inf coy, 1 inf pl	257
Korea, Republic of		246
New Zealand		231
Lithuania		220
FYROM		161
Latvia		155
Finland		150

Location:	AFGHANISTAN (continued)	
Estonia	1 mech inf coy; 1 mor det	136
Azerbaijan		90
Greece	1 engr coy	80
Slovenia		72
Bosnia-Herzegovina		45
Armenia		40
Malaysia		40
Mongolia		36
Singapore		36
United Arab Emirates		35
Ukraine		31
Montenegro		31
Portugal		26
Luxembourg		9
Ireland		7
Austria		3
Iceland		5 (civilian)
TOTAL		137,427

Location:	NORTH/SOUTH KOREA	
Operation:	NNSC	
Mission:	Monitor the ceasefire between North and South Korea	

Contributor:		Total:
Sweden		5
Switzerland		5
TOTAL		10

Location:	PHILIPPINES	
Operation:	IMT	
Mission:	Monitor the ceasefire between the Philippines government and the Moro Islamic Liberation Front in Mindanao	

Contributor:	Forces by role (where known)	Total:
Brunei	1 inf pl	15
Libya	1 inf pl	6
TOTAL		21

Location:	SOLOMON ISLANDS	
Operation:	RAMSI	
Primary Organisation:	Coalition of 15 Pacific nations	
Mission:	Ensure the security and stability of the Solomon Islands, and help to rebuild the Islands' government and economy	

Contributor:	Forces by role (where known)	Total:
Australia	1 inf pl	80
Tonga	1 inf pl	34
New Zealand		5
TOTAL		119

Location:	TIMOR LESTE	
Operation:	ISF (*Operation Astute*)	
Primary Organisation:	International Coalition	
Mission:	Assisting the Timorese government in restoring peace and stability to the country	

Contributor:	Forces by role (where known)	Total:
Australia	1 bn HQ, 2 inf coy, 1 AD bty, elm 1 cbt engr regt, 1 hel det	404
New Zealand	1 inf coy	80
TOTAL		484

Table 24 **Non-UN Deployments 2010–11**

Middle East and North Africa

Location:	EGYPT	
Operation:	MFO	
Mission:	Supervising implementation of the Egyptian–Israeli peace treaty's security provisions.	
Contributor:	Forces by role (where known)	Total:
United States	1 inf bn, 1 spt bn	688
Colombia	1 inf bn	354
Fiji	1 inf bn	338
Italy	1 coastal patrol unit	78
Uruguay	1 engr/tpt unit	58
Hungary	1 MP unit	38
Canada		28
New Zealand	1 trg unit, 1 tpt unit	28
Australia		25
Norway		3
Czech Republic		3
France		2
TOTAL		1,643

Location:	IRAQ
Operation:	New Dawn
Primary Organisation:	United States
Mission:	Advising and assisting Iraqi security forces in ensuring stability in Iraq.

Contributor	Forces by role (where known)	Total:
United States	1 corps HQ, 3 div HQ, 3 armd HBCT (AAB), 1 armd HBCT HQ (AAB), 1 armd cav regt (AAB), 1 mech inf SBCT (AAB), 1 lt inf IBCT (AAB), 1 (LoC) ARNG IBCT; 2 cbt avn bde	49,775

Location:	IRAQ
Operation:	NTM-I
Primary Organisation:	NATO
Mission:	Training the Iraqi security forces

Contributor:	Total:
Italy	84
UK	15
United States	12
Ukraine	9
Netherlands	7
Denmark	6
Hungary	3
Poland	3
Romania	3
Bulgaria	2
Estonia	2
Lithuania	2
Turkey	2
TOTAL	150

Location:	ARABIAN SEA
Operation:	TF-53
Primary Organisation:	Combined Maritime Forces
Mission:	Logistic Support to Combined Maritime Forces

Contributor	Forces by role
US	1 AE, 2 AKE, 1 AOH, 3 AO
UK	1 ARH

Location:	ARABIAN SEA
Operation:	CTF-150
Primary Organisation:	Combined Maritime Forces
Mission:	Maritime Security and Counter Terrorism operations in the Arabian Sea.

Contributor	Forces by role
France	1 DDGHM
Australia	1 FFGHM
UK	1 FFGHM

Location:	ARABIAN SEA & GULF OF ADEN
Operation:	CTF-151
Primary Organisation:	Combined Maritime Forces
Mission:	Anti-piracy operations off the coast of Somalia.

Contributor	Forces by role
United States	1 CGHM, 1 DDGHM, 1 FFH, 1 LPD, 1 LSD
Korea, Republic of	1 DDGHM
Turkey	1 FFGHM
Thailand	1 PCO, 1 AORH
UK	1 AORH

Location:	GULF OF ADEN & INDIAN OCEAN
Operation:	Atalanta
Primary Organisation:	EU
Mission:	Maritime Security Operations off the coast of Somalia.

Contributor	Forces by role
France	1 DDGHM, 1 FFGH, 1 FSM, 1 Atlantique 2, 1 Falcon 20
Germany	1 FFGHM, 1 AOL
Spain	1 PSOH, 1 LPD, 1 CN-235
Belgium	1 FFGHM
Italy	1 FFGHM
Netherlands	1 AORH
Sweden	1 AG

Location:	GULF OF ADEN & SOMALI BASIN
Operation:	Ocean Shield
Primary Organisation:	NATO
Mission:	Anti-piracy operations off the coast of Somalia. (Standing NATO Maritime Group 1)

Contributor	Forces by role
United States	1 DDGM, 1 FFH
Italy	1 FFGHM
UK	1 FFGHM
Denmark	1 AG

Location:	PERSIAN GULF
Operation:	CTF-152
Primary Organisation:	Combined Maritime Forces
Mission:	Counter-proliferation and maritime infrastructure protection.

Contributor	Forces by role
UK	2 MCO, 2 MHC, 2 LSD, 1 AOT
United States	4 MCO

Country comparisons

Table 24 **Non-UN Deployments 2010–11**

Sub-Saharan Africa

Country	CENTRAL AFRICAN REPUBLIC	
Operation:	*Boali*	
Primary Organisation:	France	
Mission:	Providing technical and operational support to the Central African armed forces.	
Contributor:	Forces by role	Total:
France	1 inf coy, 1 spt det	240

Location:	CENTRAL AFRICAN REPUBLIC	
Operation:	MICOPAX	
Primary Organisation:	Economic Community of Central African States (ECCAS)	
Mission:	Providing security, protecting civilians, contributing to the national reconciliation process and facilitating political dialogue.	
Contributor:		Total:
Cameroon		146
Gabon		142
Chad		126
Congo, Democratic Republic of		107
Congo, Republic of		22
Burundi		8
Equatorial Guinea		7
TOTAL		558

Location:	CHAD	
Operation:	*Epervier*	
Primary Organisation:	France	
Mission:	Providing technical support and military training to the armed forces of Chad, and acting in a support role for MINURCAT.	
Contributor:	Forces by role	Total:
France	1 mech inf BG; 1 avn gp; 1 hel det	634

Location:	CÔTE D'IVOIRE	
Operation:	*Licorne*	
Primary Organisation:	France (in support of UN)	
Mission:	Assist the UNOCI peacekeeping operation and provide the UNOCI force commander with a QRF.	
Contributor:	Forces by role	Total:
France	1 (Marine) mech inf BG, 1 hel unit, 1 Gendarme sqn.	772

Location:	DEMOCRATIC REPUBLIC OF THE CONGO	
Operation:	*Teutonic*	
Primary Organisation:	Bilateral	
Mission:	Assist the reconstuction of the Congolese armed forces.	
Contributor:		Total:
South Africa		16

Location:	SIERRA LEONE	
Operation:	IMATT	
Mission:	Train and advise the Sierra Leone army.	
Contributor:		Total:
UK		30
Canada		8
United States		3
Jamaica		1
Nigeria		1
TOTAL		43

Location:	SOMALIA	
Operation:	AMISOM	
Primary Organisation:	AU	
Mission:	Support the Transitional Federal Governement's efforts to stabilise the political and security situation in Somalia and facilitate the provision of humanitarian assistance.	
Contributor:	Forces by role (where known)	Total:
Uganda	5 inf bn	4,250
Burundi	3 inf bn	3,000
TOTAL		7,250

Location:	UGANDA	
Operation:	EUTM	
Primary Organisation:	EU	
Mission:	Train Somali Army personnel.	
Contributor:		Total:
Spain		38
France		25
Italy		17
Portugal		15
Germany		13
Kenya		9
Belgium		5
Ireland		5
Finland		4
Hungary		4
Sweden		4
Malta		3
Greece		2
UK		2
Luxembourg		1
TOTAL		147

Index of contributing nations

Malta
  Non-UN: EUTM; OSCE Kosovo
Moldova
  UN: UNMIL; UNMIS; UNOCI
  Non-UN: OSCE Kosovo; OSCE Serbia; Trans-dniester PKF
Mongolia
  UN: MINURCAT; MINURSO; MONUSCO; UNMIL; UNMIS
  Non-UN: ISAF
Montenegro
  UN: UNMIL
  Non-UN: ISAF; OSCE Kosovo
Morocco
  UN: MONUSCO; UNOCI
  Non-UN: KFOR
Mozambique
  UN: MONUSCO; UNMIS
Namibia
  UN: MINURCAT; UNAMID; UNMIL; UNMIS; UNOCI
Nepal
  UN: MINURCAT; MINURSO; MINUSTAH; MONUSCO; UNAMI; UNAMID; UNIFIL; UNMIL; UNMIS; UNMIT; UNOCI; UNTSO
Netherlands
  UN: UNAMID; UNMIS; UNTSO
  Non-UN: Active Endeavour; Atalanta; EUFOR Althea; ISAF; KFOR; NTM-I; OSCE Bosnia; OSCE Kosovo; OSCE Serbia
New Zealand
  UN: UNAMA; UNAMI; UNMIS; UNMIT; UNTSO
  Non-UN: ISAF; ISF; MFO; RAMSI
Niger
  UN: BINUB; MONUSCO; UNMIL; UNOCI
Nigeria
  UN: MINURCAT; MINURSO; MONUSCO; UNAMID; UNIFIL; UNMIL; UNMIN; UNMIS; UNOCI
  Non-UN: IMATT
Norway
  UN: MINURCAT; MONUSCO; UNAMA; UNMIK; UNMIS; UNTSO
  Non-UN: ISAF; KFOR; MFO; OSCE Bosnia; OSCE Serbia
Pakistan
  UN: BINUB; MINURCAT; MINURSO; MONUSCO; UNAMID; UNMIL; UNMIS; UNMIT; UNOCI
Paraguay
  UN: MINURSO; MINUSTAH; MONUSCO; UNFICYP; UNMIL; UNMIN; UNMIS; UNOCI
Peru
  UN: MINUSTAH; MONUSCO; UNFICYP; UNMIL; UNMIS; UNOCI
Philippines
  UN: MINUSTAH; UNDOF; UNMIL; UNMIS; UNMIT; UNOCI

Poland
  UN: MINURCAT; MINURSO; MONUSCO; UNMIK; UNMIL; UNMIS
  Non-UN: EUFOR Althea; ISAF; KFOR; NTM-I; OSCE Kosovo; OSCE Minsk Conf; OSCE Moldova
Portugal
  UN: UNAMA; UNIFIL; UNMIT
  Non-UN: EUFOR Althea; EUTM; ISAF; KFOR; OSCE Bosnia; OSCE Kosovo
Qatar
  UN: UNIFIL
Romania
  UN: MONUSCO; UNMIK; UNMIL; UNMIN; UNMIS; UNOCI
  Non-UN: EUFOR Althea; ISAF; KFOR; NTM-I; OSCE Bosnia; OSCE Kosovo
Russia
  UN: MINURCAT; MINURSO; MONUSCO; UNMIL; UNMIS; UNOCI; UNTSO
  Non-UN: OSCE Bosnia; OSCE Kosovo; Trans-dniester PKF
Rwanda
  UN: MINURCAT; UNAMID; UNMIS
Senegal
  UN: BINUB; MINURCAT; MONUSCO; UNAMID; UNMIL; UNOCI
Serbia
  UN: MINURCAT; MONUSCO; UNMIL; UNOCI
Sierra Leone
  UN: UNAMID; UNIFIL; UNMIN; UNMIS; UNMIT
Singapore
  UN: UNMIT
  Non-UN: ISAF
Slovakia
  UN: UNFICYP; UNTSO
  Non-UN: EUFOR Althea; ISAF; KFOR; OSCE Bosnia; OSCE Kosovo
Slovenia
  UN: UNIFIL; UNTSO
  Non-UN: EUFOR Althea; ISAF; KFOR; OSCE Bosnia; OSCE Serbia
South Africa
  UN: MONUSCO; UNAMID
  Non-UN: Teutonic
Spain
  UN: MONUSCO; UNIFIL; UNMIK
  Non-UN: Atalanta; EUTM; ISAF; KFOR; OSCE Bosnia; OSCE Kosovo; OSCE Serbia
Sri Lanka
  UN: MINURCAT; MINURSO; MINUSTAH; MONUSCO; UNMIS
Sweden
  UN: MONUSCO; UNAMA; UNMIN; UNMIS; UNMOGIP; UNTSO
  Non-UN: Atalanta; EUFOR Althea; EUTM; ISAF; KFOR; NNSC; OSCE Bosnia; OSCE Kosovo; OSCE Moldova; OSCE Serbia

Switzerland
  UN: BINUB; MONUSCO; UNMIN; UNMIS; UNTSO
  Non-UN: EUFOR Althea; KFOR; NNSC
Tajikistan
  Non-UN: OSCE Bosnia
Tanzania
  UN: MONUSCO; UNAMID; UNIFIL; UNMIS; UNOCI
Thailand
  UN: UNAMID
  Non-UN: CTF-151
Togo
  UN: MINURCAT; UNAMID; UNMIL; UNOCI
Tunisia
  UN: MINURCAT; MONUSCO; UNOCI
Turkey
  UN: UNIFIL; UNMIS
  Non-UN: Active Endeavour; CTF-151; EUFOR Althea; ISAF; KFOR; NTM-I; OSCE Bosnia; OSCE Kosovo; OSCE Serbia
Uganda
  UN: UNAMID; UNMIS; UNOCI
  Non-UN: AMISOM
Ukraine
  UN: MONUSCO; UNMIK; UNMIL; UNMIS
  Non-UN: Active Endeavour; ISAF; KFOR; NTM-I; OSCE Bosnia; OSCE Kosovo; OSCE Serbia; Trans-dniester PKF
United Arab Emirates
  Non-UN: ISAF
United Kingdom
  UN: MONUSCO; UNAMI; UNFICYP; UNMIS
  Non-UN: CTF-150; CTF-151; CTF-152; EUFOR Althea; EUTM; IMATT; ISAF; KFOR; NTM-I; Ocean Shield; OSCE Bosnia; OSCE Kosovo; OSCE Minsk Conf; OSCE Moldova; OSCE Serbia; TF-53
United States
  UN: MINURCAT; MINUSTAH; MONUSCO; UNAMI; UNMIL; UNTSO
  Non-UN: CTF-151; CTF-152; IMATT; ISAF; KFOR; MFO; New Dawn; NTM-1; Ocean Shield; OEF-A; OSCE Bosnia; OSCE Kosovo; OSCE Moldova; OSCE Serbia
Uruguay
  UN: MINURSO; MINUSTAH; MONUSCO; UNAMA; UNMIN; UNMOGIP; UNOCI
  Non-UN: MFO
Uzbekistan
  Non-UN: OSCE Kosovo
Yemen
  UN: MINURSO; MONUSCO; UNAMID; UNMIL; UNMIS; UNOCI
Zambia
  UN: MONUSCO; UNAMID; UNMIL; UNMIN; UNMIS; UNOCI
Zimbabwe
  UN: UNAMID; UNMIL; UNMIN; UNMIS; UNOCI

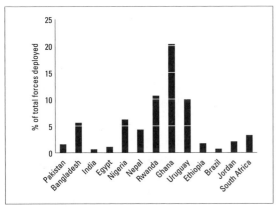

Figure 11 **UN Forces 2010** (Deployed %, in countries with over 2,000 deployed)

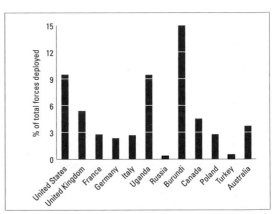

Figure 12 **Non-UN Forces 2010** (Deployed %, in countries with over 2,000 deployed)

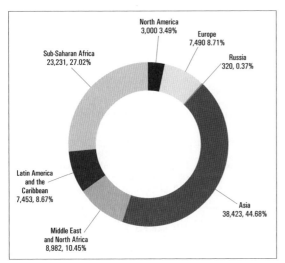

Figure 13 **Regional Share of UN-Deployed Armed Forces 2010**

Table 25 **Selected Training Activity 2010**

Date	Title	Location	Aim	Principal Participants/Remarks
North America (US and Canada)				
12–22 Feb 2010	SOUTHBOUND TROOPER X	US	Civil Affairs ex	CAN, UK, US
23 Jun–01 Aug 2010	RIMPAC 2010	US	Interop ex	AUS, CAN, CHL, COL, FRA, IDN, JPN, MYS, NLD, PER, ROK, SGP, THA, US
26 Jul–13 Aug 2010	EMPIRE CHALLENGE 2010	US	ISR interop ex	AUS, CAN, FRA, GER, JPN, NZL, US
06–26 Aug 2010	NANOOK 2010	CAN	Sovereignty and interop ex	CAN,DNK, US
08–11 Aug 2010	VIGILANT EAGLE	US	Interop ex	CAN, RUS, US
Europe				
06–16 Nov 2009	NUSRET 09	TUR	NAVEX	BLG, ESP, GER, GRC, TUR
05–24 Jan 2010	RED DEVIL	FRA	Air Interop ex	FRA, US
10–24 Feb 2010	NOBLE MANTA 2010	Ionian Sea	NATO ASWEX	CAN, ESP, FRA, GER, GRC, ITA, NOR, TUR, UK, US
17 Feb–04 Mar 2010	COLD RESPONSE 2010	NOR	Cold weather ex	AUT, FIN, GER, NLD, NOR, SWE, UK, US
09–27 Apr 2010	BLACKSEAFOR	Black Sea	Naval cooperation ex	BLG, ROM, RUS, TUR, UKR
10–23 Apr 2010	JOINT WARRIOR (SPRING)	UK	MAREX	BEL, BRZ, FRA, GER, ITA, NLD, NZL, UK, US
12–22 Apr 2010	BRILLIANT ARDENT 2010	GER	Air-Land NRF ex	CZE, FRA, GER, ITA, POL, TUR, USA
12–22 Apr 2010	BRILLIANT MARINER 2010	North Sea	Naval NRF ex	
01–21 May 2010	FLYING RHINO 2010	CZE	FAC ex	CZE, DNK, GER, LTU, SVK, UK, US
18–20 May 2010	PANOPTIS 2010	GRC	Cyber Defence ex	GRC
20 May–02 Jun 2010	CLEVER FERRET 2010	HUN	Interop ex	HUN, ITA, SVN
24 May–01 Jun 2010	PHOENIX EXPRESS 2010	Eastern Mediterranean Sea	MAREX	ALG, ESP, GRC, ITA, MLT, MOR, PRT, SEN, US
31 May–04 Jun 2010	BALTIC HOST 2010	EST/LTU/LVA	NATO rapid deployment ex	DNK, EST, GER, LTU, LVA, NOR, POL, US
04–15 Jun 2010	POMOR 2010	NOR	Naval interop ex	NOR, RUS
07–18 Jun 2010	ANATOLIAN EAGLE 2010/2	TUR	Air ex	ESP, ITA, JOR, TUR, UAE, US
07–18 Jun 2010	BALTOPS 2010	LVA	Naval interop ex	BEL, DNK, EST, FRA, GER, LVA, LTU, RUS, SWE, UK, US
09–30 Jun 2010	AZOR 2010	ESP	Hel Trg Ex	AUT, BEL, CZE, ESP, GER, SVN, SWE, UK
14–25 Jun 2010	GARUDA IV	FRA	Air Interop ex	FRA, IND, SGP
21–24 Jun 2010	PEACE FAIRWAY 2010	UKR	CPX	RUS, UKR
12–23 Jul 2010	SEA BREEZE 2010	UKR	NAVEX	AUT, AZE, BEL, DNK, GEO, GER, GRC, MDA, SWE, TUR, UKR, US
19–23 Jul 2010	FRUKUS 2010	Atlantic Ocean	NAVEX	FRA, RUS, UK, US
27 Aug–08 Sep 2010	OPEN SPIRIT 2010	Baltic Sea	MCMEX	BEL, EST, FIN, FRA, GER, LTU, LVA, NOR, POL, RUS
01–16 Sep 2010	COMBINED ENDEAVOUR 2010	GER	Comms Interop ex	AFG, ALB, ARM, AUT, AZE, BIH, BLG, CAN, CHE, CRO, CZE, DNK, ESP, EST, FIN, FRA, GEO, GER, HUN. IRE, IRQ, ITA, KAZ, LTU, MDA, MNE, NLD, NOR, POL, PRT, ROM, SER, SVK, SVN, TUR, UK, UKR, US
05–18 Sep 2010	RAPID TRIDENT 2010	UKR	Multinational CPX	ARM, AUT, AZE, CAN, FYROM, GEO, GER, MDA, NOR, POL, SWE, SVN, UK, US
13–20 Sep 2010	BLACK BEAR 10	CRO	Mil Pol ex	CRO, CZE, POL, SVK
13–23 Sep 2010	EUROPEAN ADVANCE 2010	AUT		AUT, CHE, FRA, GER, IRL, ITA, MNT, SER, SVN
13–27 Sep 2010	JACKAL STONE 10	POL & LTU	SOF ex	CRO, LVA, LTU, POL, ROM, US
13–24 Sep 2010	NORTHERN COASTS 10	FIN	NAVEX	BEL, DNK, EST, FIN, FRA, GER, LVA, NLD, NOR, POL, SWE, UK, US
29 Sep–04 Oct 2010	FRIENDSHIP SEA 2010	Eastern Mediterranean Sea	Naval Interop ex	EGY, TUR
04–22 Oct 2010	JOINT WARRIOR (AUTUMN)	UK	MAREX	BEL, CAN, DNK, EST, FRA, ITA, NLD, NOR, POL, SWE, TUR, UK, US
11–14 Oct 2010	MINOAS 2010	GRC	Air Interop ex	GRC, ISR
11–22 Oct 2010	ANATOLIAN EAGLE 2010/3	TUR	Air ex	PRC, TUR
18–30 Oct 2010	NEMESIS SWORD 2010	GER	CPX	FRA, GER, NLD, POL
06–13 Nov 2010	NUSRET 10	TUR	NAVEX	BLG, ESP, GER, GRC, ITA, TUR
08 Nov–15 Nov 2010	n.k.	TUR	Mountain ex	PRC, TUR

Table 25 **Selected Training Activity 2010**

Date	Title	Location	Aim	Principal Participants/Remarks
Russia				
29 Jun–08 Jul 2010	*VOSTOK 2010*	RUS	Test new military structures	RUS
01–15 Sep 2010	*DARKHAN-3*	RUS	CT ex	MNG, RUS
25–29 Oct 2010	*VZAIMODEISTVIE 2010*	RUS	CSTO RRF ex	ARM, KAZ, KGZ, RUS, TJK
Asia				
18–23 Nov 2009	*IRON FIST-2009*	PRC	Div level joint op ex	PRC
01–11 Feb 2010	*COBRA GOLD 2010*	THA	CPX, H/CA, FTX	IDN, JPN, ROK, SGP, THA, US
04–08 Feb 2010	*MILAN 2010*	IND	NAVEX	Ships: AUS, BGD, IND, IDN, MYS, MMR, SGP, LKA Reps: BRN, NZL, PHL, VNM
14 Feb–19 Mar 2010	*BALIKATAN 2010*	PHL	Civ-mil ex	PHL, US
01–27 Mar 2010	*BOLD KURUKSHETRA*	IND	Armd trg ex	IND, SGP
08–18 Mar 2010	*KEY RESOLVE/FOAL EAGLE*	ROK	OPLAN CPX; defensive FTX	ROK, US
25 Mar–10 Apr 2010	*MALINDO LATGABMA DARSASA 7AB/2010*	MYS	CT ex	IDN, MYS
03–16 Apr 2010	*SIMBEX 2010*	Andaman Sea/ Bay of Bengal	NAVEX	IND, SGP
08–23 Apr 2010	*CROIX DU SUD 10*	French New Caledonia	Civilian evacuation ex	AUS, FRA, PNG, NZL, Tonga, Vanuatu
22–26 Apr 2010	*RUBEZH 2010*	TJK	CP CSTO Response Force ex	KAZ, KGZ, RUS, TJK
26 Apr–07 May 2010	*BERSAMA SHIELD 10*	MYS	n.k.	AUS, MYS, NZL, SGP, UK
03–10 May 2010	*CARAT 2010*	THA	n.k.	BGD, BRN, CAM, IDN, MYS, PHL, SGP, THA, US
08–18 May 2010	*CASSOWARY 2010*	IDN	PB NAVEX	AUS, IDN
08–22 June 2010	*GARUDA SHIELD 2010*	IDN	n.k.	BGD, BRN, NPL, PHL, THA, US
19–26 Jun 2010	*CROCODILE 2010*	TLS	MAREX	AUS, NZL, TLS, US
03–10 Jul 2010	*FRIENDSHIP 2010*	PRC	CT ex	PAK, PRC
16 Jul–06 Aug 2010	*PITCH BLACK 2010*	AUS	Air Cbt Ex	AUS, NZL, SGP, THA
25–28 Jul 2010	*INVINCIBLE SPIRIT-1*	Sea of Japan	NAVEX	ROK, USA
03–08 Aug 2010	*VANGUARD 2010*	PRC	AD EX	PRC
08–29 Aug 2010	*KHAAN QUEST 2010*	MNG	Bilateral PKO ex	MNG, US
16–26 Aug 2010	*ULCHI FREEDOM GUARDIAN 2010*	ROK	Annual CPX	ROK, USA
16–27 Aug 2010	*STEPPE EAGLE 2010*	KAZ	PKO ex	KAZ, UK, US
27 Aug–01 Sep 2010	*PACIFIC REACH 2010*	JPN	Civ-mil ex	JPN, US
Aug 2010	*n.k.*	PRC	First PLA MOUT ex	PRC
09–25 Sep 2010	*PEACE MISSION 2010*	KAZ	CT ex	KAZ, KGZ, RUS, PRC, TJK, UZB
16 Sep 2010	*n.k.*	NZ	NAVEX	PRC, NZ
25 Sep 2010	*n.k.*	Yellow Sea	NAVEX, live fire	PRC, AUS
27 Sep – 01 Oct 2010	*INVINCIBLE SPIRIT-2*	Yellow Sea	ASW ex	ROK, US
10–29 Oct 2010	*BERSMA PADU 10*	Sea of Japan	Interoperability ex	AUS, MYS, NZL, SGP, UK
18 Oct–03 Nov 2010	*INDRADHANUSH*	IND	AIR ex	IND, UK
31 Oct–04 Nov 2010	*MISSION ACTION 2010*	PRC	3 div cross-regional ex	PRC
Nov 2010	*DRAGON 2010*	PRC	Amph aslt ex	PRC
Nov 2010	*FRIENDSHIP ACTION 2010*	PRC	Mt Ex, Interoperability	PRC, ROM
10 Nov–12 Nov 2010	*BLUE STRIKE 2010*	THA	Exchange, amph cbt, CT	PRC, THA
28 Nov–01 Dec 2010	*INVINCIBLE SPIRIT-3*	Yellow Sea	NAVEX	ROK, US
03–10 Dec 2010	*KEEN SWORD 2011*	JPN	Interop/AD/MD ex	JPN, US
Middle East and North Africa				
23 Apr–02 May 2010	*MALABAR 10*	Arabian Sea	NAVEX	IND, US
05–19 May 2010	*EAGLE RESOLVE 2010*	BHR	GCC-US milex	BHR, KWT, OMN, QTR, SAU, US
14 May–09 Jun 2010	*AFRICAN LION 2010*	MOR	Interop ex	MOR, US
18–20 May 2010	*n.k.*	Gulf of Aden	Naval Interop ex	FRA, YEM
19 –21 May 2010	*EAGLE SALUTE 2010*	Red Sea	NAVEX	EGY, US
08 Oct 2010	*BLUE SEA ANGEL 2010*	Gulf of Aden	NAVEX, medical	PRC
17–21 Oct 2010	*TABUK II*	EGY	EGY-SAU milex	EGY, SAU

Table 25 **Selected Training Activity 2010**

Date	Title	Location	Aim	Principal Participants/Remarks
Latin America and Caribbean				
15 Feb–10 Jun 2010	*BEYOND THE HORIZON 2010*	DOM, GUA, NIC, PAN, SLV	Civil assistance ex	DOM, GUA, NIC, PAN, SLV, US
12–26 Apr 2010	*TRADEWINDS 2010*	BLZ, JAM	MAREX; SAREX	ATG, BHS, BLZ, Dominica, DOM, Grenada, GUA, GUY, HTI, JAM, NIC, PAN, SLV, St Kitts & Nevis, St Lucia, St Vincent & Grenadines, SUR, UK, US
13–27 May 2010	*UNITAS ATLANTIC 2010*	ARG	MAREX	ARG, BRZ, MEX, US
16–24 Jun 2010	*FUERZAS ALIADAS COMANDO 2010*	DOM	CT ex	ARG, BLZ, BRZ, CHL, COL, CRI, DOM, ECU, GUA, GUY, JAM, NIC, PAN, PER, PRY, SLV, TTO, URY, US
Jun–Sep 2010	*NEW HORIZONS - HAITI 2010*	HTI	Civil assistance ex	HTI, US
02–24 Jul 2010	*PARTNERSHIP OF THE AMERICAS 2010/SOUTHERN EXCHANGE 2010*	PER	PKO, civil assistance ex	ARG, BRZ, CAN, COL, ECU, MEX, PER, PRY, URY, US
16–27 Aug 2010	*PANAMAX 2010*	PAN	infrastructure protection ex	ARG, BLZ, BRZ, CAN, CHL, COL, DOM, ECU, GUA, HON, MEX, NIC, PAN, PER, PRY, SLV, URY, US
23–27 Aug 2010	*BOLBRA I*	BOL	Joint Air Force ex	BOL, BRZ
27 Oct–10 Nov 2010	*ATLASUR*	ARG	MAREX	ARG, BRZ, RSA, URY
Sub-Saharan Africa				
01–04 Dec 2009	*n.k.*	DJB	East African Standby Bde (EASBRIG) FTX	BDI, Comoros, DJB, ETH, KEN, RWA, SYC, SOM, SDN, UGA
15 Feb–15 Mar 2010	*GOOD HOPE IV*	RSA	Naval/Air ex	GER, RSA
22–23 Feb 2010	*OBANGAME 2010*	Gulf of Guinea	Maritime Interdiction trg	CMR, COG, EQG, GAB, NGA, US
11–18 Apr 2010	*COHESION BENIN 2010*	BEN	Test Eastern Battalion of ECOWAS standby force	BEN, BFA, CIV, CPV, GAM, GHA, GUI, GNB, LBR, MLI, NER, NGA, SEN, SLE, TGO
02–23 May 2010	*FLINTLOCK 10*	BFA, CHA, MLI, MRT, NER, NGA, SEN	CT, interop ex	BFA, CHA, MLI, MRT, NER, NGA, SEN, US
22 May–06 Jun 2010	*KWANZA 2010*	ANG	Test regional standby bde	ECCAS
04–12 Aug 2010	*SHARED ACCORD 2010*	MOZ	Civil assistance ex	MOZ, US
09–20 Aug 2010	*AFRICA ENDEAVOUR 2010*	GHA	ASF C4I ex	AU, CHE, ECCA, ECOWAS, SWE, US, 36 African countries
10–26 Sep 2010	*IBSAMAR 2010*	RSA	Naval ex	BRZ, IND, RSA
20–29 Oct 2010	*AMANI AFRICA*	ETH	CPX to test Africa Standby force concept	Elm from all Standby Bdes, EU, US

Table 26 Strategic Forces Comparison

| | Delivery Systems | | | | | | | Operational Warheads[1] | | |
| | Land based msl lnchr | | | Sub based msl lnchr | | Aircraft[2] | | Strategic | Sub-strategic | Total |
	ICBM	IRBM	SSM	SLBM	SLCM[3]	Bbr ac	Strike ac			
Russia	376			176[4]	n.k.	251	249	2,700	2,000	4,700
United States	450			336	n.k.	155	1,142	2,200	500	2,700
France				64			108	280		280
China	66	118	54	36		132	150	180		180
United Kingdom[5]				64				160		160
Israel			100		n.k.		202	80–200		80–200
Pakistan			190				135	70–90		70–90
India		100–125	n.k.				267	60–80		60–80
North Korea[6]			10			80		4–8		4–8

[1] Numbers represent estimates based on available open source information. With the exception of Russia and the United States, all warheads are regarded as strategic. Warhead numbers for Israel, India, Pakistan and North Korea represent estimated total holdings

[2] Figures represent total holdings of theoretically nuclear-capable aircraft, not just those with a declared nuclear role

[3] As part of its 2010 Nuclear Posture Review the US is planning to withdraw the TLAM-N cruise missile from service. The status of Russia's 3M-10 (SS-N-21 *Sampson*) remains uncertain, though at least some may have been converted to the conventional land-attack role. There have been repeated press reports that Israel has a submarine-launched cruise missile capability

[4] Russia SLBM total does not include 3 *Akula* (*Typhoon*) class SSBN

[5] UK operational warheads reducing to no more than 120; only 50 *Trident* missiles currently in inventory

[6] North Korea's ability to produce a deliverable nuclear weapon remains in doubt

Table 27 Global Top Ten Defence Budgets

| | 2008 | | | | | 2009 | | | | | 2010 | | |
		DB	GDP	%			DB	GDP	%			DB	GDP	%
1	US	696.3	14,264	4.9	1	US	693.3	14,119	4.9	1	US	692.8	14,624	4.7
2	UK	71.4	2,670	2.7	2	China	70.4	4,984	1.4	2	China	76.4	5,733	1.3
3	China	60.1	4,422	1.4	3	UK	60.5	2,179	2.8	3	UK	56.5	2,255	2.5
4	Japan	46	4,926	0.9	4	Japan	50.3	5,075	1.0	4	Japan	52.8	5,387	1.0
5	France	44.6	2,863	1.6	5	France	46.0	2,656	1.7	5	Saudi Arabia	45.2	434	10.4
6	Germany	43.3	3,659	1.2	6	Germany	43.5	3,339	1.3	6	France	42.6	2,587	1.6
7	Russia	40.5	1,680	2.4	7	Saudi Arabia	41.3	376	11.0	7	Russia	41.4	1,488	2.8
8	Saudi Arabia	38.2	469	8.1	8	Russia	38.3	1,236	3.1	8	Germany	41.2	3,346	1.2
9	India	28.4	1,223	2.3	9	India	34.4	1,231	2.8	9	India	38.4	1,545	2.5
10	Italy	24.1	2,307	1.0	10	Brazil	28.0	1,592	1.8	10	Brazil	34.7	2,039	1.7

Table 28 **NATO Defence Budgets 2001–10** (US$m)

Country/Year	2001	2002	2003	2004	2005	2006	2007	2008	2009	2010
Albania	51	59	76	105	116	141	198	254	249	195
Belgium	2,292	2,497	3,051	3,300	3,326	3,363	3,774	4,200	3,969	3,640
Bulgaria	285	397	471	572	623	706	996	1,168	1,041	609
Canada	8,377	8,471	9,929	10,878	11,817	14,080	17,550	17,786	18,456	19,925
Croatia	467	553	596	606	600	693	837	1,090	972	863
Czech Republic	1,187	1,453	1,855	1,965	2,211	2,465	2,718	3,168	2,957	2,552
Denmark	2,054	2,185	2,679	3,171	3,170	3,343	4,178	4,468	4,115	3,661
Estonia	83	99	156	183	205	238	345	429	356	330
France	25,986	27,264	35,307	40,500	41,125	44,250	49,589	44,676	45,962	42,618
Germany	21,622	22,284	27,702	30,075	29,875	34,838	38,889	43,309	43,455	41,162
Greece	3,441	3,226	3,653	4,185	4,368	4,644	5,314	6,118	10,892	9,662
Hungary	825	1,142	1,404	1,611	1,448	1,533	1,869	2,062	1,630	1,354
Iceland	24	26	34	40	48	46	56	44	32	n.k.
Italy	15,914	12,896	15,682	17,685	17,048	15,133	19,288	24,154	21,528	20,510
Latvia	75	113	194	229	274	314	445	542	341	250
Lithuania	167	273	267	314	331	353	450	546	484	323
Luxembourg	147	154	206	245	261	254	360	176	n.k.	556
Netherlands	12,649	6,625	8,308	9,584	9,678	9,889	11,460	11,903	12,117	11,250
Norway	3,017	3,466	4,183	4,362	4,720	4,774	5,583	5,592	5,356	5,769
Poland	3,431	3,496	3,824	4,452	5,325	5,806	7,303	9,361	7,362	8,350
Portugal	1,577	1,536	1,883	2,148	2,408	2,386	2,579	2,632	2,539	3,192
Romania	989	1,068	1,345	1,530	1,948	2,374	3,141	3,324	2,288	2,142
Slovak Republic	346	464	626	717	828	966	1,257	1,465	1,532	1,085
Slovenia	276	275	378	519	502	568	750	803	766	672
Spain	5,470	5,964	7,059	8,433	8,738	8,904	10,542	11,971	10,920	10,178
Turkey	5,714	6,490	6,806	7,023	8,191	8,310	9,967	10,208	9,952	10,500
United Kingdom	35,534	40,895	50,592	60,213	61,415	63,046	74,774	71,443	60,545	56,497
United States	305,421	362,106	456,185	490,621	505,796	617,155	625,850	696,268	693,260	692,780

Table 29 **International Comparisons of Defence Expenditure and Military Manpower**

(Current US$ m)	Defence Expenditure US$ m			Defence Expenditure per capita US$			Defence Expenditure % of GDP			Number in Armed Forces (000)	Estimated Reservists (000)	Paramilitary (000)
	2007	2008	2009	2007	2008	2009	2007	2008	2009	2011	2011	2011
North America												
Canada	17,995	19,836	19,575	539	597	580	1.26	1.31	1.46	66	34	0
USA	625,850	696,268	661,049	2,077	2,290	2,153	4.53	4.88	4.68	1,564	871	0
Nato Europe												
Albania	198	254	248	55	70	79	1.83	1.90	2.03	14	0	1
Belgium	5,168	5,551	5,624	497	534	521	1.13	1.10	1.26	38	0	2
Bulgaria	1,206	1,315	905	165	181	119	3.03	2.62	1.92	31	303	34
Croatia	837	1,090	1,014	186	243	229	1.43	1.57	1.60	19	21	3
Czech Republic	2,539	3,165	3,127	248	310	298	1.48	1.46	1.63	23	0	3
Denmark	4,178	4,468	4,337	764	815	784	1.35	1.31	1.39	19	54	0
Estonia	388	450	356	295	344	266	1.86	1.94	1.84	5	30	0
France	61,838	67,185	54,446	1,012	1,049	870	2.38	2.35	2.05	239	34	103
Germany	42,589	46,943	47,466	517	570	580	1.28	1.28	1.42	251	40	0
Greece	8,215	10,141	10,091	767	946	894	2.63	2.85	3.04	139	251	4
Hungary	1,783	1,869	1,476	179	188	147	1.29	1.22	1.14	30	44	12
Iceland	n.a	n.a	n.a.	n.a	n.a	n.a.	n.a	n.a	n.a.	0	0	0
Italy	37,770	30,934	30,489	650	532	506	1.79	1.34	1.44	185	42	142
Latvia	447	542	316	198	241	140	1.55	1.60	1.22	6	11	0
Lithuania	453	547	402	127	153	120	1.16	1.16	1.08	11	7	15
Luxembourg	286	232	249	596	478	500	0.57	0.43	0.47	1	0	1
Netherlands	11,489	12,276	12,132	693	738	734	1.48	1.41	1.52	37	3	6
Norway	5,877	5,869	6,196	1,270	1,264	1,284	1.51	1.30	1.63	26	45	0
Poland	7,855	10,176	7,297	204	264	191	1.85	1.94	1.68	100	0	21
Portugal	3,312	3,729	3,710	311	349	349	1.48	1.53	1.59	43	211	48
Romania	2,616	3,005	2,225	117	135	104	1.57	1.53	1.38	72	45	80
Slovakia	1,239	1,477	1,350	227	271	249	1.52	1.55	1.53	17	0	0
Slovenia	741	834	793	369	415	388	1.64	1.53	1.63	8	2	5
Spain	16,738	19,263	16,944	414	476	369	1.16	1.20	1.15	142	319	80
Turkey	11,840	13,531	10,883	158	179	145	1.83	1.85	1.77	511	379	102
United Kingdom	68,868	60,794	59,131	1,133	998	956	2.46	2.28	2.71	178	82	0

Table 29 **International Comparisons of Defence Expenditure and Military Manpower**

(Current US$ m)	Defence Expenditure US$ m			Defence Expenditure per capita US$			Defence Expenditure % of GDP			Number in Armed Forces (000)	Estimated Reservists (000)	Paramilitary (000)
	2007	2008	2009	2007	2008	2009	2007	2008	2009	2011	2011	2011
Subtotal NATO Ex-US	315,434	324,134	300,782	550	562	509	1.75	1.65	1.71	2,229	1,956	661
Total NATO	941,284	1,020,402	961,831	1,076	1,158	1,071	2.96	3.01	3.04	3,793	2,827	661
Non-Nato Europe												
Armenia	296	396	401	99	133	130	3.13	3.32	4.67	49	210	7
Austria	3,603	3,193	2,800	439	389	335	0.97	0.77	0.73	26	195	0
Azerbaijan	936	1,585	1,500	115	194	171	2.96	3.23	3.49	67	300	15
Belarus	573	674	896	59	70	93	1.28	1.12	1.83	73	290	110
Bosnia	196	244	243	43	53	64	1.42	1.32	1.42	11	0	0
Cyprus	498	537	472	474	503	542	2.30	2.16	2.00	10	50	1
Finland	3,151	3,632	3,886	601	693	728	1.29	1.33	1.63	22	350	3
Georgia	573	1,037	604	123	224	142	5.60	8.13	5.63	21	0	12
Ireland	1,329	1,588	1,403	323	382	315	0.51	0.60	0.63	10	15	0
Macedonia	157	192	159	76	93	78	1.98	2.06	1.69	8	5	0
Malta	44	49	59	109	122	143	0.59	0.60	0.74	2	0	0
Moldova	19	22	20	4	5	6	0.44	0.36	0.37	5	58	2
Montenegro	55	71	58	80	105	93	2.11	2.31	1.39	3	0	10
Serbia	985	1,034	969	132	139	132	2.67	2.10	2.23	29	50	0
Sweden	6,773	6,659	5,298	750	736	570	1.49	1.39	1.30	21	200	1
Switzerland	3,526	4,110	4,075	467	542	527	0.83	0.83	0.82	26	172	0
Ukraine	1,877	1,804	1,414	41	39	31	1.32	1.00	1.20	130	1,000	85
Total	25,625	28,172	24,258	191	210	193	1.19	1.15	1.16	512	2,894	246
Russia ¹												
Russia	32,215	40,484	38,293	228	288	272	2.48	2.41	3.10	1,046	20,000	449
South and Central Asia												
Afghanistan	153	180	252	6	7	8	1.58	1.51	1.79	136	0	120
Bangladesh	998	1,195	1,016	7	8	6	1.45	1.50	1.07	157	0	64
India	26,513	31,540	38,278	24	28	33	2.32	2.58	3.11	1,325	1,155	1,301
Kazakhstan	1,164	1,608	1,353	76	105	85	1.12	1.18	1.25	49	0	32
Kyrgyzstan	44	47	44	8	9	8	1.17	0.92	0.8	11	0	10
Maldives	37	43	52	102	111	167	3.52	3.40	3.96	n/a	n/a	n/a

Table 29 **International Comparisons of Defence Expenditure and Military Manpower**

(Current US$ m)	Defence Expenditure US$ m			Defence Expenditure per capita US$			Defence Expenditure % of GDP			Number in Armed Forces (000)	Estimated Reservists (000)	Paramilitary (000)
	2007	2008	2009	2007	2008	2009	2007	2008	2009	2011	2011	2011
Nepal	167	176	184	6	6	6	3.34	3.48	1.44	96	0	62
Pakistan	4,530	4,422	3,811	27	26	22	3.15	2.97	2.44	617	0	304
Sri Lanka	1,383	1,793	1,485	66	85	73	4.25	4.15	3.54	161	6	62
Tajikistan	78	80	49	11	11	7	2.13	1.74	0.97	9	0	8
Turkmenistan	99	84	n.a.	21	17	n.a.	0.81	0.71	n.a.	22	0	0
Uzbekistan	n.a.	n.a.	n.a.	n.a	n.a	n.a.	n.a	n.a.	n.a.	67	0	20
Total	**35,166**	**41,167**	**46,524**	**22**	**26**	**29**	**2.27**	**2.42**	**2.79**	**2,650**	**1,161**	**1,981**
East Asia and Australasia												
Australia	20,216	22,194	19,515	974	1,056	892	2.24	2.24	2.02	57	20	0
Brunei	346	360	332	895	945	830	2.81	2.49	3.18	7	1	2
Cambodia	137	255	275	10	18	19	1.59	2.30	2.54	124	0	67
China [1]	46,174	60,187	70,381	35	45	54	1.36	1.36	1.45	2,285	510	660
Fiji	50	57	56	54	61	66	1.78	1.84	1.90	4	6	0
Indonesia	4,320	5,108	4,821	18	22	21	1.00	1.00	0.89	302	400	280
Japan	41,039	46,044	51,085	322	362	400	0.93	0.93	1.01	248	56	13
Korea, North	n.a	n.a	n.a.	n.a.	n.a.	n.a.	n.a.	n.a.	n.a.	1,190	600	189
Korea, South	26,588	24,182	22,439	551	500	460	2.53	2.60	2.68	655	4,500	5
Laos	15	17	14	2	3	2	0.36	0.32	0.25	29	0	100
Malaysia	3,979	4,370	3,883	160	173	141	2.13	1.97	2.01	109	52	25
Mongolia	43	52	38	15	17	14	1.04	1.10	0.91	10	137	7
Myanmar	n.a.	n.a.	n.a.	n.a.	n.a.	n.a.	n.a.	n.a.	n.a.	406	0	107
New Zealand	1,611	1,754	1,358	391	420	315	1.24	1.39	1.15	10	2	0
Papua New Guinea	37	35	40	6	6	6	0.74	0.56	0.50	3	0	0
Philippines	1,130	1,427	1,363	12	15	15	0.78	0.85	0.85	125	131	41
Singapore	7,007	7,662	7,831	1,539	1,663	1,570	4.22	4.20	4.29	73	313	75
Taiwan	9,015	10,495	9,500	389	458	414	2.32	2.76	2.50	290	1,657	17
Thailand	3,333	4,294	4,732	51	65	70	1.36	1.57	1.79	306	200	114
Timor Leste	n.a.	n.a.	n.a.	n.a.	n.a.	n.a.	n.a.	n.a.	n.a.	1	0	0
Vietnam	2,159	2,907	2,137	25	33	24	3.04	3.19	2.20	455	5,000	40

Table 29 International Comparisons of Defence Expenditure and Military Manpower

(Current US$ m)	Defence Expenditure US$ m			Defence Expenditure per capita US$			Defence Expenditure % of GDP			Number in Armed Forces (000)	Estimated Reservists (000)	Estimated Paramilitary (000)
	2007	2008	2009	2007	2008	2009	2007	2008	2009	2011	2011	2011
Total	167,199	191,400	199,803	78	88	92	1.45	1.44	1.44	6,688	13,585	1,741
Middle East and North Africa												
Algeria	4,270	5,179	5,281	128	153	151	3.18	3.03	3.78	147	150	187
Bahrain	579	553	742	816	768	938	3.28	2.76	3.60	8	0	11
Egypt	4,464	4,562	4,118	59	59	50	3.36	2.90	2.20	469	479	397
Iran	8,040	9,595	8,636	123	146	118	2.81	2.84	2.63	523	350	40
Iraq	n.a.	n.a.	4,118	n.a.	n.a.	131	n.a.	n.a.	6.31	246	0	414
Israel	11,607	14,772	13,516	1,806	2,077	1,816	7.07	7.41	6.91	177	565	8
Jordan	1,621	2,127	1,393	270	347	234	9.84	10.63	5.51	101	65	10
Kuwait	5,250	6,812	4,184	2,095	2,623	1,497	4.62	4.38	4.26	16	24	7
Lebanon	1,130	1,155	1,426	187	189	338	2.99	2.71	4.13	59	0	20
Libya	624	1,086	1,708	108	129	266	1.19	1.22	2.84	76	40	0
Mauritania	n.a.	119	115	6	7	35	0.72	0.69	3.80	16	0	5
Morocco	2,409	2,977	3,061	79	96	96	3.21	3.48	3.34	196	150	50
Oman	4,376	4,671	4,018	1,366	1,410	1,412	10.39	8.53	8.71	43	0	4
Palestinian Authority	n.a.	n.a.	n.a.	n.a.	n.a.	n.a.	n.a.	n.a.	n.a.	0	0	56
Qatar	1,266	1,756	2,500	1,554	2,129	1,774	1.79	1.75	2.54	12	0	0
Saudi Arabia	35,446	38,223	41,276	1,284	1,357	1,626	9.24	8.15	10.98	234	0	16
Syria	1,376	1,941	2,229	67	91	106	3.48	3.78	4.15	295	314	108
Tunisia	491	534	532	48	51	51	1.39	1.28	1.22	36	0	12
UAE	11,253	13,733	7,957	2,532	2,972	1730	5.67	5.09	3.55	51	0	0
Yemen	1,211	1,492	883	56	67	37	6.58	6.35	3.51	67	0	71
Total	95,068	110,498	107,694	269	306	284	5.06	4.71	5.09	2,768	2,137	1,416
Latin America and Caribbean												
Antigua and Barbuda	7	7	8	80	79	93	0.58	0.56	0.73	0	0	0
Argentina	2,093	2,031	2,352	52	50	58	0.80	0.61	0.76	73	0	31
Bahamas, The	50	49	49	166	161	144	0.67	0.65	0.67	1	0	0
Barbados	28	30	26	97	106	102	0.80	0.79	1.01	1	0	0
Belize	n.a.	n.a.	14	n.a.	n.a.	41	n.a.	n.a.	1.01	1	1	0
Bolivia	162	250	286	17	26	29	1.24	1.50	1.65	46	0	37

Table 29 International Comparisons of Defence Expenditure and Military Manpower

(Current US$ m)	Defence Expenditure US$ m			Defence Expenditure per capita US$			Defence Expenditure % of GDP			Number in Armed Forces (000) 2011	Estimated Reservists (000) 2011	Paramilitary (000) 2011
	2007	2008	2009	2007	2008	2009	2007	2008	2009			
Brazil	20,559	26,254	25,984	106	134	134	1.54	1.66	1.63	318	1,340	395
Chile	5,238	5,561	5,044	322	338	297	3.19	3.28	3.08	59	40	45
Colombia	6,806	9,546	9,603	160	221	210	3.96	3.91	4.08	283	62	159
Costa Rica	140	156	215	34	37	47	0.53	0.53	0.73	0	0	10
Cuba	2,148	2,296	1,960	188	201	175	4.00	4.00	3.13	49	39	27
Dominican Republic	270	278	265	29	29	26	0.66	0.60	0.57	25	0	15
Ecuador	773	1,105	1,915	55	77	141	1.80	1.99	3.45	58	118	1
El Salvador	111	115	135	16	16	22	0.55	0.52	0.64	16	10	17
Guatemala	166	180	166	13	14	12	0.48	0.42	0.44	15	64	19
Guyana	n.a.	n.a.	21	n.a.	n.a.	27	n.a.	n.a.	1.00	1	1	2
Haiti	n.a.	n.a.	11	n.a.	n.a.	1	n.a.	n.a.	0.17	0	0	0
Honduras	76	96	111	10	12	15	0.61	0.67	0.78	12	60	8
Jamaica	87	96	62	31	34	23	0.68	0.65	0.50	3	1	0
Mexico	3,982	4,346	4,769	37	40	44	0.39	0.40	0.54	280	87	52
Nicaragua	37	42	40	6	7	7	0.64	0.66	0.65	12	0	0
Panama	200	226	275	61	68	80	1.03	0.97	1.11	0	0	12
Paraguay	100	132	126	15	19	20	0.83	0.83	0.88	11	165	15
Peru	1,226	1,424	1,503	43	49	52	1.14	1.11	1.18	115	188	77
Suriname	26	31	31	54	65	60	1.16	1.33	1.05	2	0	0
Trinidad and Tobago	127	143	106	103	116	79	0.58	0.59	0.54	4	0	0
Uruguay	304	260	344	88	75	103	1.29	0.81	1.09	25	0	1
Venezuela	2,578	3,328	3,316	99	126	117	1.13	1.04	1.02	115	8	0
Total	**47,292**	**57,981**	**58,736**	**84**	**101**	**102**	**1.29**	**1.35**	**1.45**	**1,524**	**2,183**	**920**
Sub-Saharan Africa												
Angola	2,247	2,425	3,174	183	194	172	3.66	3.05	4.19	107	0	10
Benin	55	67	101	7	8	11	0.93	0.98	1.53	5	0	3
Botswana	317	293	375	166	150	193	2.57	2.19	3.21	9	0	2
Burkina Faso	95	112	110	7	7	7	1.34	1.21	1.30	11	0	0
Burundi	78	83	42	9	9	5	8.37	7.48	3.18	20	0	31
Cameroon	297	306	344	16	17	18	1.43	1.28	1.55	14	0	9

Country comparisons

Table 29 **International Comparisons of Defence Expenditure and Military Manpower**

(Current US$ m)	Defence Expenditure US$ m			Defence Expenditure per capita US$			Defence Expenditure % of GDP			Number in Armed Forces (000)	Estimated Reservists (000)	Paramilitary (000)
	2007	2008	2009	2007	2008	2009	2007	2008	2009	2011	2011	2011
Cape Verde	8	9	9	19	21	17	0.55	0.51	0.55	1	0	0
Central African Republic	18	20	36	4	5	8	0.99	0.95	1.82	2	0	1
Chad	89	145	437	9	14	39	1.35	1.78	6.37	26	0	10
Congo	94	112	134	25	29	36	1.23	0.89	1.39	10	0	2
Cote d'Ivoire	290	336	330	15	17	16	1.38	1.45	1.43	17	10	2
Democratic Republic of the Congo	166	168	123	3	3	2	1.71	1.49	1.09	159	0	0
Djibouti	18	15	37	25	22	42	1.98	1.46	3.49	10	0	3
Equatorial Guinea	8	11	8	15	18	12	0.07	0.06	0.07	1	0	0
Eritrea	n.a.	n.a.	78	n.a.	n.a.	15	n.a.	n.a.	4.17	202	120	0
Ethiopia	336	366	408	4	4	5	1.75	1.23	1.42	138	0	0
Gabon	123	134	132	85	90	89	1.06	0.89	1.19	5	0	2
Gambia	8	16	7	5	9	4	1.23	2.17	0.73	1	0	0
Ghana	104	105	113	5	4	5	0.70	0.69	0.73	16	0	0
Guinea	52	51	75	5	5	7	1.11	1.04	1.63	12	0	7
Guinea Bissau	15	18	14	10	12	8	3.94	3.74	1.62	4	0	2
Kenya	681	735	533	18	19	13	2.47	2.14	1.81	24	0	5
Lesotho	40	36	54	20	17	26	2.38	2.13	3.29	2	0	0
Liberia	n.a.	n.a.	8	n.a.	n.a.	2	n.a.	n.a.	0.94	2	0	0
Madagascar	82	103	90	4	5	5	1.12	1.09	1.05	14	0	8
Malawi	42	43	51	3	3	3	1.71	1.50	1.08	5	0	0
Mali	132	157	177	10	12	14	1.77	2.14	1.97	7	0	5
Mauritius	27	36	16	22	28	13	0.36	0.39	0.19	0	0	2
Mozambique	57	76	84	3	4	4	0.74	0.83	0.88	11	0	0
Namibia	239	287	311	116	137	143	2.70	3.25	3.28	9	0	6
Niger	48	58	51	3	4	3	1.09	1.08	0.97	5	0	5
Nigeria	980	1,339	1,505	7	9	10	0.59	0.66	0.89	80	0	82
Rwanda	62	71	113	6	7	11	1.82	1.83	2.16	33	0	2
Senegal	193	218	210	15	16	17	1.64	1.67	1.65	14	0	5
Seychelles	11	8	6	134	98	71	1.12	0.91	0.77	0	0	0
Sierra Leone	15	14	12	3	3	2	0.75	0.59	0.63	11	0	0

Table 29 International Comparisons of Defence Expenditure and Military Manpower

(Current US$ m)	Defence Expenditure US$ m			Defence Expenditure per capita US$			Defence Expenditure % of GDP			Number in Armed Forces (000)	Estimated Reservists (000)	Paramilitary (000)
	2007	2008	2009	2007	2008	2009	2007	2008	2009	2011	2011	2011
Somali Republic	n.a.	n.a.	44	n.a.	n.a.	5	n.a.	n.a.	n.a.	2	0	0
South Africa	3,577	3,359	4,296	74	69	87	1.26	1.22	1.48	62	0	15
Sudan	n.a.	n.a.	696	n.a.	n.a.	16	n.a.	n.a.	1.27	109	0	18
Tanzania	162	184	247	4	5	6	0.99	0.91	1.16	27	80	1
Togo	42	56	49	7	10	7	1.60	1.90	1.56	9	0	1
Uganda	232	277	293	8	9	9	1.71	1.68	1.97	45	0	2
Zambia	200	262	213	17	22	16	1.72	1.77	1.65	15	3	1
Zimbabwe	n.a.	n.a.	n.a.	n.a.	n.a.	n.a.	0.16	n.a.	n.a.	29	0	22
Total	11,242	12,113	15,146	14	15	18	1.31	1.24	1.62	1,286	213	262
Summary												
US	625,850	696,268	661,049	2,077	2,290	2,153	4.53	4.88	4.68	1,564	871	0
NATO Ex-US	315,434	324,134	300,782	550	562	509	1.75	1.65	1.71	2,229	1,956	661
Total NATO	941,284	1,020,402	961,831	1,076	1,158	1,071	2.96	3.01	3.04	3,793	2,827	661
Non-NATO Europe	25,625	28,172	24,258	191	210	193	1.19	1.15	1.16	512	2,894	246
Russia[1]	32,215	40,484	38,293	228	288	272	2.48	2.41	3.10	1,046	20,000	449
Middle East and North Africa	35,166	41,167	46,524	22	26	29	2.27	2.42	2.79	2,650	1,161	1,981
South and Central Asia	167,199	191,400	199,803	78	88	92	1.45	1.44	1.47	6,688	13,585	1,741
East Asia and Australasia	95,068	110,498	107,694	269	306	284	5.06	4.71	5.09	2,768	2,137	1,416
Latin America and Caribbean	47,292	57,981	58,736	84	101	102	1.29	1.35	1.45	1,524	2,183	920
Sub-Saharan Africa	11,242	12,113	15,146	14	15	18	1.31	1.24	1.62	1,286	213	262
Global totals	1,404,377	1,547,732	1,452,283	213	232	214	2.56	2.56	2.52	20,267	45,000	7,676

1. 'Official Budget' only at market exchange rates - excludes extra-budgetary funds

Table 30 **Arms Deliveries to Developing Nations** Leading Recipients in 2009

(current US$m)

1	Saudi Arabia	2,700
2	China	1,500
3	South Korea	1,400
4	Egypt	1,300
5	India	1,200
6	Israel	1,200
7	Pakistan	1,000
8	Venezuela	900
9	Algeria	900
10	Iraq	800

Table 31 **Arms Transfer Agreements with Developing Nations** Leading Recipients in 2009

(current US$m)

1	Brazil	7,200
2	Venezuela	6,400
3	Saudi Arabia	4,300
4	Taiwan	3,800
5	U.A.E.	3,600
6	Iraq	3,300
7	Egypt	3,000
8	Vietnam	2,400
9	India	2,400
10	Kuwait	1600

Table 32 **Global Arms Deliveries** Leading Suppliers in 2009

(current US$m)

1	United States	14,383
2	Russia	3,700
3	Germany	2,800
4	UK	2,200
5	China	1,800
6	France	1,200
7	Sweden	1,200
8	Canada	1,200
9	Austria	700
10	Israel	600
11	Italy	600

Table 33 **Global Arms Transfer Agreements** Leading Suppliers in 2009

(current US$m)

1	United States	22,610
2	Russia	10,400
3	France	7,400
4	Germany	3,700
5	Italy	2,700
6	Israel	2,100
7	China	1,700
8	United Kingdom	1,500
9	Ukraine	1,200
10	Spain	1,000

Table 34 **Value of Global Arms Transfer Agreements and Market Share by Supplier, 2002–09** (constant 2009US$m – % in italics)

	Total	Russia		US		UK		France		Germany		Italy		All Other European		China		Others	
2002	35,101	6,918	19.7	15,953	45.4	988	2.8	741	2.1	1,359	3.8	494	1.4	5,559	15.8	494	1.4	2,594	7.3
2003	36,924	5,198	14.0	17,463	47.2	3,626	9.8	3,385	9.1	846	2.2	725	1.9	2,659	7.2	725	1.9	2,297	6.2
2004	49,216	9,593	19.4	14,822	30.1	4,913	9.9	3,393	6.8	4,679	9.5	468	0.9	6,317	12.8	1,170	2.3	3,861	7.8
2005	51,148	9,203	17.9	14,336	28.0	3,255	6.3	6,622	12.9	2,245	4.3	1,684	3.2	8,530	16.6	3,255	6.3	2,020	3.9
2006	60,912	15,949	26.1	17,307	28.4	4,556	7.4	8,352	13.7	1,736	2.8	1,302	2.1	6,400	10.5	1,627	2.6	3,688	6.0
2007	63,271	11,180	17.6	25,722	40.6	10,336	16.3	2,109	3.3	2,004	3.1	1,371	2.1	5,590	8.8	2,531	4.0	2,426	3.8
2008	62,838	5,528	8.8	38,065	60.5	205	0.3	3,173	5.0	3,173	5.0	3,787	6.0	4,197	6.6	2,150	3.4	2,559	4.0
2009	57,510	10,400	18.0	22,610	39.3	1,500	2.6	7,400	12.8	3,700	6.4	2,700	4.6	4,500	7.8	1,700	2.9	3,000	5.2

Table 35 **Value of Global Arms Deliveries and Market Share by Supplier, 2002–09** (constant 2009US$m – % in italics)

	Total	Russia		US		UK		France		Germany		Italy		All Other European		China		Others	
2002	35,261	4,447	12.6	12,037	34.1	6,177	17.5	1,853	5.2	1,482	4.2	741	2.1	3,830	10.8	1,112	3.1	3,582	10.1
2003	41,635	5,077	12.1	13,109	31.4	8,220	19.7	2,901	6.9	3,022	7.2	484	1.1	4,956	11.9	967	2.3	2,901	6.9
2004	40,618	6,434	15.8	13,594	33.4	3,744	9.2	6,551	16.1	2,340	5.7	234	0.5	2,925	7.2	1,053	2.5	3,744	9.2
2005	35,441	3,704	10.4	13,219	37.3	4,153	11.7	3,030	8.5	2,132	6.0	1,122	3.1	3,479	9.8	1,235	3.4	3,367	9.5
2006	37,694	6,508	17.2	13,396	35.5	5,207	13.8	1,844	4.8	2,603	6.9	325	0.8	4,013	10.6	1,410	3.7	2,386	6.3
2007	36,735	5,379	14.6	13,003	35.4	2,109	5.7	2,426	6.6	3,059	8.3	844	2.3	4,430	12.0	2,215	6	3,270	8.9
2008	36,704	6,040	16.4	12,239	33.3	2,252	6.1	1,638	4.4	3,890	10.6	614	1.6	4,811	13.1	2,150	5.8	3,071	8.3
2009	35,083	3,700	10.5	14,383	41.0	2,200	6.2	1,200	3.4	2,800	7.9	600	1.7	4,700	13.4	1,800	5.1	3,700	10.5

US DoD Price Deflator. All data rounded to nearest $100m. Source: Richard F. Grimmett, Conventional Arms Transfers to Developing Nations 2002-2009 (Washington DC: Congressional Research Service)

Table 36 **Arms Deliveries to Middle East and North Africa, by Supplier**

(current US$m)

2002–05	US	Russia	China	Major West European*	All other European	Others	Total
Algeria		200	100			100	400
Bahrain	300						300
Egypt	6,100	100	400	100	200		6,900
Iran		100	100		100	300	600
Iraq					200	100	300
Israel	4,600				100		4,700
Jordan	400				100	100	600
Kuwait	800		200	100		200	1,300
Lebanon							–
Libya		100			100	100	300
Morocco				200		100	300
Oman	300			300			600
Qatar							–
Saudi Arabia	4,400			15,700	1,600	100	21,800
Syria		300			100	200	600
Tunisia				100			100
UAE	500	400		5,900	400	100	7,300
Yemen		600			200	100	900

2006–09	US	Russia	China	Major West European*	All other European	Others	Total
Algeria		2,800	500	100			3,400
Bahrain	300			100			400
Egypt	4,400	200	400		300		5,300
Iran		400	100				500
Iraq	1,700	100		100	200		2,100
Israel	5,200	200					5,400
Jordan	800	100	100		100		1,100
Kuwait	1,500						1,500
Lebanon	100						100
Libya		100			100		200
Morocco	100	100			100		300
Oman	500			300			800
Qatar							–
Saudi Arabia	5,000		800	4,300			10,100
Syria		800	1,000		100	300	2,200
Tunisia							–
UAE	600	100		400	200		1,300
Yemen		100					100

* Major West European includes UK, Germany, France and Italy

All data rounded to nearest $100m

Source: Richard F. Grimmett, *Conventional Arms Transfers to Developing Nations 2002–2009* (Washington DC: Congressional Research Service)

Country comparisons

Table 37 **Selected Operational Military Satellites 2011**

Country	Designations	Quantity	Orbit	Launch	Description and Remarks
Communications					
Australia	*Optus* C1	1	GSO	2003	dual use telecom satellites for civ/mil comms
China	*Fenghuo (Zhong Xing)*	4	GSO	2003–10	dual use telecom satellites for civ/mil comms
France	*Syracuse* 3	2	GSO	2005–06	secure comms; designed to integrate with UK *Skynet* and Italy *Sicral*
Germany	*COMSATBw-1/2*	2	GSO	2009–10	Bundeswehr secure relay platforms
Italy	*Sicral*	2	GSO	2001–09	Sicral 1 & 1B. Sicral 2 due for launch 2012-3
NATO	NATO-4	2	GSO	1993	military, diplomatic and data comms
Russia	*Molniya-1*	2	HEO	1997–2003	dual use telecom satellites for civ/mil comms
Russia	*Geizer/Potok 11*	1	GSO	2000	data relay
Russia	*Globus (Raduga-1)*	1	GSO	2007	
Russia	*Mod. Globus (Raduga-1M)*	2	GSO	2009–10	Modernised *Globus/Raduga*
Russia	*Strela*	11	LEO	2001–10	replacement by *Rodnik* reportedly underway
Russia	*Rodnik (Gonets-M)*	7	GSO	2005–09	reported to be replacing *Strela*
Russia	Meridian-1/2/3	3	HEO	2006–10	Replacements for *Molniya*-1
Spain	*Spainsat*	1	GSO	2006	secure comms
UK	*Skynet-4*	3	GSO	1990–2001	
UK	*Skynet-5*	3	GSO	2007–08	secure comms for mil and govt.
USA	DSCS-3	8	GSO	1989–2003	incl 1 in reserve
USA	*Milstar-1*	2	GSO	1994–95	
USA	*Milstar-2*	3	GSO	2001–03	
USA	PAN/P360	1	n.k.	2009	Operating agency unknown – military status questionable
USA	SDS-III	5	HEO/GSO	1998–2007	relay; polar replay functions may have moved to other satellites
USA	UFO	7	GSO	1995–2003	3 with Global Broadcast Service; due to be replaced by MUOS, of which first launch due 2010
USA	WGS SV2 (GS-F1, F2 & F3)	3	GSO	2007–09	first 3 of 5; will replace DSCS system
USA	AEFH-1	1	n.k.	2010	USAF communications satellite; first of four designed to replace *Milstar*-1/2
Navigation, Positioning and Timing					
China	*Beidou-1*	2	GSO	2000–03	
China	*Beidou-2 (M)*	1	MEO	2007	
China	*Beidou-2 (G)*	4	GSO	2009–10	
China	*Beidou-2 (IGSO)*	1	GSO	2010	2nd due for launch by end 2010
Russia	*Parus*	10	LEO	1999–2010	also relay
Russia	*GLONASS*	26	MEO	2004–10	an operational constellation needs 24 satellites; additions planned
USA	*Navstar GPS*	32	MEO	1989–2009	also carry a Nuclear Detonation Detection System; poss utility for precision guidance
Meteorology and Oceanography					
USA	DMSP-5	6	SSO/LEO	1995–2009	early warning
Intelligence, Surveillance and Reconnaissance					
China	*Haiyang 1B*	1	LEO	2007	*Haiyang* 2 and 3 series planned
China	*Yaogan Weixing*	12	LEO	2007–10	remote sensing
China	*Zhangguo Ziyuan (ZY-2)*	2	LEO	2002–04	recce/surv; remote sensing

Table 37 **Selected Operational Military Satellites 2011**

Country	Designations	Quantity	Orbit	Launch	Description and Remarks
China	*Shi Jian-6*	8	SSO	2004–10	4 pairs of 2 (A&B; C&D; E&F; G&H) reports of poss ELINT/SIGINT roles
France	*Helios-1A/2A/2B*	3	SSO	1995–2009	optical recce; partnership with Belgium, Germany, Italy & Spain
Germany	*SAR-Lupe (1-5)*	5	LEO	2006–08	surv
India	RISAT-2	1	LEO	2009	surv
Italy	*Cosmo (Skymed)*	4	LEO	2007–10	surv
Israel	Ofeq-5,7& 9	3	SSO/LEO	2002–10	recce/surv
Israel	*TecSAR 1 (Polaris)*	1	LEO	2008	recce
Japan	IGS-1/3/4/5	4	SSO	2003–09	optical recce
Russia	Liana (Lotos-S)	1	LEO	2009	To replace *Tselina* + US-PU systems
Russia	*Tselina-2*	1	LEO	2007	recce/surv; ELINT
Taiwan	*Rocsat-2*	1	SSO/LEO	2004	recce/surv
USA	*Keyhole (KH-12) (Crystal/ Misty)*	3	SSO/LEO	1999–2005	recce/surv; high-res surv
USA	*Lacrosse (Onyx)*	2	SSO/LEO	2000–05	recce/surv
USA	*Mentor 1/2/3 (Orion)*	3	GSO	1995–2003	ELINT
USA	*Advanced Mentor* (NROL-26)	1	GSO	2009	surv; SIGINT
USA	*Mercury*	2	GSO	1994–96	COMINT
USA	*TacSat-3*	1	LEO	2009	Real-time combat imagery data
USA	*Trumpet*	3	elliptic HEO	1997–2008	SIGINT; NROL-22 and -28; reports of poss SIGINT role
USA	SBWASS	8	LEO	2001–07	ocean and wide-area sigint; each paired with sub-satellite
USA	STSS DEMO-1/2	2	n.k.	2009	Missile Tracking
USA	NROL-32	1	elliptic HEO	2010	unknown; possibly SIGINT
USA	NROL-41	1	n.k.	2010	unknown
USA	SBSS	1	n.k.	2010	

Early Warning					
Russia	*Oko*	3	HEO/GSO	2007–10	
USA	DSP	4	GSO	1997–2004	an operational constellation needs 3 satellites
France	*Spirale*	2	elliptic	2009	future ballistic missile warning system

Orbit abbreviations: GSO – geosynchronous orbit; HEO – Earth orbit; LEO – low Earth orbit; MEO –mid Earth orbit; SSO – sun-synchronous orbit

Explanatory Notes

The Military Balance is updated each year to provide an accurate assessment of the military forces and defence expenditures of 170 countries and territories. Each edition contributes to the provision of a unique compilation of data and information, enabling the reader to discern trends through the examination of editions as far back as 1959. The data in the current edition are according to IISS assessments as at November 2010, unless specified. Inclusion of a territory, country or state in *The Military Balance* does not imply legal recognition or indicate support for any government.

GENERAL ARRANGEMENT AND CONTENTS

The Editor's Foreword contains a summary of the book and general comment on defence matters.

Part I of *The Military Balance* comprises the regional trends, military capabilities and defence economics data for countries grouped by region. Thus North America includes the US and Canada. Regional groupings are preceded by a short introduction describing the military issues facing the region. Essays at the front of the book analyse important defence trends or debates. Tables analysing aspects of defence activity including salient comparative analyses, selected major training exercises, non-UN and UN multinational deployments, international defence expenditure, and the international arms trade.

Part II comprises reference material.

There are maps showing selected deployments in Afghanistan, counter-piracy activities off Somalia, Russia's military regions and Brazil's National Defence Strategy.

The loose Chart of Conflict is updated for 2010 to show data on recent and current armed conflicts.

USING THE MILITARY BALANCE

The country entries in *The Military Balance* are an assessment of the personnel strengths and equipment holdings of the world's armed forces. Qualitative assessment is enabled by relating data, both quantitative and economic, to textual comment, as well as through close reference to qualitative judgements applied to inventory data. The strengths of forces and the numbers of weapons held are based on the most accurate data available or, failing that, on the best estimate that can be made. In estimating a country's total capabilities, old equipment may be counted where it is considered that it may still be deployable.

The data presented each year reflect judgements based on information available to the IISS at the time the book is compiled. Where information differs from previous editions, this is mainly because of changes in national forces, but it is sometimes because the IISS has reassessed the evidence supporting past entries. Given this, care must be taken in constructing time-series comparisons from information given in successive editions.

ABBREVIATIONS AND DEFINITIONS

Abbreviations are used throughout to save space and avoid repetition. The abbreviations may be either singular or plural; for example, 'elm' means 'element' or 'elements'. The qualification 'some' is used to indicate that while the IISS assesses that a country maintains a capability, a precise inventory is unavailable at time of press. 'About' means the total could be higher than given. In financial data, '$' refers to US dollars unless otherwise stated; billion (bn) signifies 1,000 million (m). The large quantity of data in *The Military Balance* has been compressed into a portable volume by the extensive employment of abbreviations. An essential tool is therefore the list of abbreviations for data sections, which appears on page 491.

Within the country entries, a number of caveats are employed to aid the reader in assessing military capabilities. The * symbol is used to denote aircraft counted by the IISS as combat-capable (see 'Air Forces', below); † is used when the IISS assesses that the serviceability of equipment is in doubt; and ‡ is used to denote equipment judged obsolescent (weapons the basic design of which is more than four decades old and which has not been significantly upgraded within the past decade); these latter two qualitative judgements should not be taken to imply that such equipment cannot be used.

COUNTRY ENTRIES

Information on each country is shown in a standard format, although the differing availability of information and differences in nomenclature result in some variations. Country entries include economic, demographic and military data. Population aggregates are based on the most recent official census data or, in their absence, demographic statistics taken from the US Census Bureau. Data on ethnic and religious minorities are also provided in some country entries. Military data include manpower, length of conscript service where relevant, outline organisation, number of formations and units and an inventory of the major equipment of each service. Details of national forces stationed abroad and of foreign forces stationed within the given country are also provided.

ARMS PROCUREMENTS AND DELIVERIES

Tables at the end of the regional texts show selected arms procurements (contracts and, in selected cases, major development programmes that may not yet be at contract stage) and deliveries listed by country buyer, together with additional information including, if known, the country supplier, cost, prime contractor and the date on which the first delivery was due to be made. While every effort has been made to ensure accuracy, some transactions may not be fulfilled or may differ – for instance in quantity – from those reported. The information is arranged in the following order: land; sea; and air.

DEFENCE ECONOMICS

Country entries include defence expenditures, selected economic performance indicators and demographic aggregates. There are also international comparisons of defence expenditure and military manpower, giving expenditure figures for the past three years in per capita terms and as a % of GDP. The aim is to provide an accurate measure of military expenditure and the allocation of economic resources to defence. All country entries are subject to revision each year as new information, particularly regarding defence expenditure, becomes available. The information is necessarily selective.

Individual country entries show economic performance over the past two years, and current demographic data. Where these data are unavailable, information from the last available year is provided. Where possible, official defence budgets for the current year and previous two years are shown, as well as an estimate of actual defence expenditures for those countries where true defence expenditure is thought to be higher than official budget figures suggest. Estimates of actual defence expenditure, however, are only made for those countries where there are sufficient data to justify such a measurement. Therefore, there will be several countries listed in The Military Balance for which only an official defence budget figure is provided but where, in reality, true defence-related expenditure is almost certainly higher.

All financial data in the country entries are shown both in national currency and US dollars at current year – not constant – prices. US-dollar conversions are generally, but not invariably, calculated from the exchange rates listed in the entry. In some cases a US-dollar purchasing power parity (PPP) rate is used in preference to official or market exchange rates and this is indicated in each case.

Definitions of terms

Despite efforts by NATO and the UN to develop a standardised definition of military expenditure, many countries prefer to use their own definitions (which are often not made public). In order to present a comprehensive picture, The Military Balance lists three different measures of military-related spending data.

- For most countries, an official defence budget figure is provided.
- For those countries where other military-related outlays, over and above the defence budget, are known, or can be reasonably estimated, an additional measurement referred to as defence expenditure is also provided. Defence expenditure figures will naturally be higher than official budget figures, depending on the range of additional factors included.
- For NATO countries, an official defence budget figure as well as a measure of defence expenditure (calculated using NATO's definition) is quoted.

NATO's definition of military expenditure, the most comprehensive, is defined as the cash outlays of central or federal governments to meet the costs of national armed forces. The term 'armed forces' includes strategic, land, naval, air, command, administration and support forces. It also includes other forces if these forces are trained, structured, and equipped to support defence forces and are realistically deployable. Defence expenditures are reported in four categories: Operating Costs, Procurement and Construction, Research and Development (R&D) and Other Expenditure. Operating Costs include salaries and pensions for military and civilian personnel; the cost of maintaining and training units, service organisations, headquarters and support elements; and the cost of servicing and repairing military equipment and infrastructure. Procurement and Construction expenditure covers national equipment and infrastructure spending, as well as common infrastructure programmes. R&D is defence expenditure up to the point at which new equipment can be put in service, regardless of whether new equipment is actually procured. Foreign Military Aid (FMA) contributions of more than US$1 million are also noted.

For many non-NATO countries the issue of transparency in reporting military budgets is fundamental. Not every UN member state reports defence budget data (even fewer real defence expenditures) to their electorates, the UN, the IMF or other multinational organisations. In the case of governments with a proven record of transparency, official figures generally conform to the standardised definition of defence budgeting, as adopted by the UN, and consistency problems are not usually a major issue. The IISS cites official defence budgets as reported by either national governments, the UN, the OSCE or the IMF.

For those countries where the official defence budget figure is considered to be an incomplete measure of total military-related spending, and appropriate additional data are available, the IISS will use data from a variety of sources to arrive at a more accurate estimate of true defence expenditure. The most frequent instances of budgetary manipulation or falsification typically involve equipment procurement, R&D, defence industrial investment, covert weapons programmes, pensions for retired military and civilian personnel, paramilitary forces and non-budgetary sources of revenue for the military arising from ownership of industrial, property and land assets.

The principal sources for national economic statistics cited in the country entries are the IMF, the Organisation for Economic Cooperation and Development (OECD), the World Bank and three regional banks (the Inter-American, Asian and African Development Banks). For some countries basic economic data are difficult to obtain. The Gross Domestic Product (GDP) figures are nominal (current) values at market prices. GDP growth is real, not nominal, growth, and inflation is the year-on-year change in consumer prices. Dollar exchange rates are annual averages for the year indicated, except 2010 where the latest market rate is used.

Calculating exchange rates

Typically, but not invariably, the exchange rates shown in the country entries are also used to calculate GDP and defence budget and expenditure dollar conversions. Where they are not used, it is because the use of exchange rate dollar conversions can misrepresent both GDP and defence expenditure. For some countries, PPP rather than market exchange rates are sometimes used for dollar conversions of both GDP and defence expenditures. Where PPP is used, it is annotated accordingly.

The arguments for using PPP are strongest for Russia and China. Both the UN and IMF have issued caveats concerning the reliability of official economic statistics on transitional economies, particularly those of Russia, some Eastern European and Central Asian countries. Non-reporting, lags in the publication of current statistics and frequent revisions of recent data (not always accompanied by timely revision of previously published figures in the same series) pose transparency and consistency problems. Another problem arises with certain transitional

economies whose productive capabilities are similar to those of developed economies, but where cost and price structures are often much lower than world levels. No specific PPP rate exists for the military sector, and its use for this purpose should be treated with caution. Furthermore, there is no definitive guide as to which elements of military spending should be calculated using the limited PPP rates available. The figures presented here are only intended to illustrate a range of possible outcomes depending on which input variables are used.

Arms trade

The source for data on the global and regional arms trade is the US Congressional Research Service (CRS). It is accepted that these data may vary in some cases from national declarations of defence exports, which is due in part to differences in the publication times of the various sets of data and national definitions of military-related equipment.

GENERAL MILITARY DATA

Manpower

The 'Active' total comprises all servicemen and women on full-time duty (including conscripts and long-term assignments from the Reserves). When a gendarmerie or equivalent is under control of the MoD, they may be included in the active total. Under the heading 'Terms of Service', only the length of conscript service is shown; where service is voluntary there is no entry. 'Reserve' describes formations and units not fully manned or operational in peacetime, but which can be mobilised by recalling reservists in an emergency. Unless otherwise indicated, the 'Reserves' entry includes all reservists committed to rejoining the armed forces in an emergency, except when national reserve service obligations following conscription last almost a lifetime. Some countries have more than one category of 'Reserves', often kept at varying degrees of readiness. Where possible, these differences are denoted using the national descriptive title, but always under the heading of 'Reserves' to distinguish them from full-time active forces.

Other forces

Many countries maintain paramilitary forces whose training, organisation, equipment and control suggest they may be used to support or replace regular military forces. These are detailed after the military forces of each country, but their manpower is not normally included in the Armed Forces totals at the start of each entry. Home Guard units are counted as paramilitary.

Non-state groups

The Military Balance includes detail on selected non-state groups that pose a militarily significant challenge to state and international security. This information appears in the essays and relevant regional chapters. Further detailed information may be obtained from the IISS Armed Conflict Database (http://www.iiss.org/acd).

Forces by Role and Equipment by Type

Quantities are shown by function (according to each nation's employment) and type, and represent what are believed to be total holdings, including active and reserve operational and training units. Inventory totals for missile systems – such as surface-to-surface missiles (SSM), surface-to-air missiles (SAM) and anti-tank guided weapons (ATGW) – relate to launchers and not to missiles. Equipment held 'in store' – that is, held in reserve and not assigned to either active or reserve units – is not counted in the main inventory totals. However, aircraft in excess of unit establishment holdings, held to allow for repair and modification or immediate replacement, are not shown 'in store'.

Deployments

The Military Balance mainly lists permanent bases and operational deployments including peacekeeping operations, which are often discussed in the text for each regional section. Information in the country data files detail deployments of troops and military observers and, where avail-

Units and formation strength

Company	100–200
Battalion	500–800
Brigade (Regiment)	3,000–5,000
Division	15,000–20,000
Corps (Army)	60,000–80,000

able, the role and equipment of deployed units; Tables 23 and 24 in the reference section constitute fuller listings of selected UN and non-UN deployments, not including police and civilian personnel. In these tables, deployments are detailed by region and by mission, with the largest troop contributing country at the head of the list.

Training activity

Selected exercises which involve military elements from two or more states and are designed to improve interoperability or test new doctrine, forces or equipment are detailed in tabular format. (Exceptions may be made for particularly important exercises held by single states which indicate novel capability developments or involve newly inducted equipments.)

Principal Ground Equipment Definitions

The Military Balance uses the following definitions of equipment:

Main Battle Tank (MBT): An armoured, tracked combat vehicle, weighing at least 16.5 metric tonnes unladen, that may be armed with a turret-mounted gun of at least 75mm calibre. Any new-wheeled combat vehicles that meet the latter two criteria will be considered MBTs.

Armoured Combat Vehicle (ACV): A self-propelled vehicle with armoured protection and cross-country capability. ACVs include:

Armoured Infantry Fighting Vehicle (AIFV): An armoured combat vehicle designed and equipped to transport an infantry squad, armed with an integral/organic cannon of at least 20mm calibre. Variants of AIFVs are also included and indicated as such.

Armoured Personnel Carrier (APC): A lightly armoured combat vehicle, designed and equipped to transport an infantry squad and armed with integral/organic weapons of less than 20mm calibre. Variants of APCs converted for other uses (such as weapons platforms, command posts and communications vehicles) are included and indicated as such.

(Look-a-like: The term 'look-a-like' is used to describe a quantity of equipment, the precise role of which is unknown, but which has the basic appearance – and often employing the chassis – of a known equipment type.)

Artillery: A weapon with a calibre greater than 100mm for artillery pieces, and 80mm and above for mortars, capable of engaging ground targets by delivering primarily indirect fire. The definition also applies to guns, howitzers, gun/howitzers, multiple-rocket launchers.

GROUND FORCES

The national designation is normally used for army forma-tions, while the manpower strength, equipment hold-ings and organisation of formations such as brigades and divisions differ widely from country to country. Also, the term 'regiment' can be misleading. It can mean essentially a brigade of all arms; a grouping of battalions of a single arm; or a battalion group. The sense intended is indicated in each case. Where there is no standard organisation, the intermediate levels of command are shown as headquar-ters (HQ), followed by the total numbers of units that could be allocated to them. Where possible, the normal compo-sition of formations is given in parentheses. It should be noted that where both divisions and brigades are listed, only independent or separate brigades are counted and not those included in divisions. Where a unit's title overstates its real capability, an estimate is given in parentheses of the unit size comparable with its true strength.

NAVAL FORCES

Classifying naval vessels according to role is increasingly complex. A post-war consensus on primary surface combat-ants revolved around a distinction between independently operating cruisers, air-defence escorts (destroyers) and anti-submarine warfare escorts (frigates). However, new ships are increasingly performing a range of roles; the Littoral Combat Ship produced by the US, for example, is a frigate-sized vessel that carries surface-to-air missiles and can be recon-figured for anti-submarine warfare, anti-surface warfare or a mine counter-measures role. For this reason, *The Military Balance* has drawn up a classification system based on full-load displacement (FLD) rather than role that will allow for greater international comparisons of navies through their tonnage. Older vessels will still often retain the primary role suggested by their type, but in more modern ships this will decreasingly be the case. This classification system thus does not assist comparison based on other important capabilities,

Principal Naval Equipment Definitions

To aid comparison between fleets, the following definitions, which do not necessarily conform to national definitions, are used:

Submarines: All vessels equipped for military operations and designed to operate primarily under water. Submarines with a dived displacement below 250 tonnes are classified as midget submarines; those below 500 tonnes are coastal submarines. Those vessels with submarine-launched ballistic missiles are also listed under 'Strategic Nuclear Forces'.

Principal surface combatants: All surface ships primarily designed for operations on the high seas, either as escorts or primary ships in a task force. These vessels usually have a FLD above 1,500 tonnes. Such ships will have offensive ship-to-ship capabilities and may include anti-submarine warfare and/or anti-air capabilities. Principal surface combatants include aircraft carriers (including helicopter carriers), cruisers (with a FLD above 9,750 tonnes), destroyers (with a FLD above 4,500 tonnes) and frigates (with a FLD above 1,500 tonnes).

Patrol and coastal combatants: All surface vessels designed for coastal or inshore operations, in an escort, protective or patrol role. These vessels include corvettes, which usually have a FLD between 500 and 1,500 tonnes and are distinguished from other patrol vessels by their heavier armaments, often including ship-to-ship and/or ship-to-air missiles. Also included in this category are offshore patrol ships, with a FLD greater than 1,500 tonnes, patrol craft, which have a full-load displacement between 250 and 1,500 tonnes and patrol boats with a FLD between ten and 250 tonnes. Fast patrol craft or boats have a top speed greater than 35 knots.

Mine warfare vessels: All surface vessels configured primarily for mine laying or counter-measures. Counter-measures vessels are either: sweepers, which are designed to locate and destroy mines in a maritime area; hunters, which are designed to locate and destroy individual mines; or counter-meas-ures vessels, which combine both roles.

Amphibious vessels: All surface vessels designed to transport personnel and/or equipment on to unpre-pared shorelines. Such vessels are classified as amphibious assault vessels, which can embark fixed-wing and/or rotary wing air assets as well as landing craft; landing platforms, which can embark

such as command systems, but eases comparisons across international naval fleets.

Given this system, *The Military Balance* designation will not necessarily conform to national definitions.

AIR FORCES

Aircraft listed in *The Military Balance* as combat capable are assessed as being equipped to deliver air-to-air or air-to-surface ordnance. The definition includes aircraft designated by type as Bomber, Fighter, Fighter Ground Attack, Ground Attack, and Anti-Submarine Warfare. Other aircraft considered to be combat capable are marked with an asterisk (*). Operational groupings of air forces are shown where known. Squadron aircraft strengths vary with aircraft types and from country to country.

When assessing missile ranges, *The Military Balance* uses the following range indicators: Short-Range Ballistic Missile (SRBM), less than 1,000km; Medium-Range Ballistic Missile (MRBM), 1,000–3,000km; Intermediate-Range Ballistic Missiles (IRBM), 3,000–5,000km; Intercontinental Ballistic Missiles (ICBM), over 5,000km.

ATTRIBUTION AND ACKNOWLEDGEMENTS

The International Institute for Strategic Studies owes no allegiance to any government, group of governments, or any political or other organisation. Its assessments are its own, based on the material available to it from a wide variety of sources. The cooperation of governments of all listed countries has been sought and, in many cases, received. However, some data in *The Military Balance* are estimates.

Care is taken to ensure that these data are as accurate and free from bias as possible. The Institute owes a considerable debt to a number of its own members, consultants and all those who help compile and check material. The Director-General and Chief Executive and staff of the Institute assume full responsibility for the data and judgements in this book. Comments and suggestions on the data and textual material contained within the book, as well as on the style and presentation of data, are welcomed and should be communicated to the Editor of *The Military Balance* at: IISS, 13–15 Arundel Street, London WC2R 3DX, UK, email: *dmap@iiss.org*. Copyright on all information in *The Military Balance* belongs strictly to the IISS. Application to reproduce limited amounts of data may be made to the publisher: Taylor & Francis, 4 Park Square, Milton Park, Abingdon, Oxon, OX14 4RN. Email: *permissionrequest@tandf.co.uk*. Unauthorised use of *Military Balance* data will be subject to legal action.

Principal Naval Equipment Definitions (continued)

rotary wing aircraft as well as landing craft; landing ships, which are amphibious vessels capable of ocean passage; and landing craft, which are smaller vessels designed to transport personnel and equipment from a vessel or across small stretches of water. Landing ships have a hold; landing craft are open vessels.

Auxiliary vessels: All ocean-going surface vessels performing an auxiliary military role, supporting combat ships or operations. Such vessels are either very lightly armed or unarmed. These generally fulfil five roles: underway replenishment (such as tankers and oilers); logistics (such as cargo ships); maintenance (such as cable repair ships or buoy tenders); research (such as survey ships); and special purpose (such as intelligence-collection ships and ocean-going tugs).

Yard craft/miscellaneous vessels: All surface vessels performing a support role in coastal waters or to ships not in service. These vessels often have harbour roles, such as tugs and tenders. Other miscellaneous craft, such as royal yachts, are also included here.

Weapons systems: Weapons are listed in the following order: land-attack missiles, ship-to-ship missiles, surface-to-air missiles, guns, torpedo tubes, anti-submarine weapons and aircraft. Missiles with a range less than 5km and guns with a calibre less than 76mm are generally not included, unless for some lightly armed minor combatants.

Organisations: Naval groupings such as fleets and squadrons frequently change and are shown only where doing so would add to qualitative judgements.

Principal Aviation Equipment Definitions

Countries regularly use military aircraft in a variety of roles, with determinants including platform equipment, weapons and systems fit, as well as crew training. The Military Balance uses the following main definitions as a guide.

Type and Role Definitions

Bomber (Bbr): Comparatively large platforms intended for the delivery of air-to-surface ordnance. Long-range bombers are those which have an un-refuelled combat radius of greater than 5,000km with a maximum weapons payload in excess of 10,000kg. Medium bombers have a range of between 1,000–5,000km. Bbr units are units equipped with bomber aircraft for the air-to-surface role

Fighter (Ftr): This term covers aircraft designed primarily for air-to-air combat, with the associated sensors, weapons and performance. It may include a limited air-to-surface capability. Ftr units are equipped with aircraft intended to provide air superiority, which may have a secondary and limited air-to-surface capability.

Fighter/Ground Attack (FGA): indicates a multi-role fighter-size platform with a significant air-to-surface capability, potentially including maritime attack, and some air-to-air capacity. FGA units are multi-role units equipped with aircraft capable of air-to-air and air-to surface attack with varying degrees of capability.

Ground Attack (Atk): is used to describe aircraft designed solely for the air-to-surface task, with limited or no air-to-air capability. Atk units are equipped with fixed-wing aircraft to undertake air-to-surface missions.

Attack Helicopter (Atk Hel): Rotary platforms designed for delivery of air-to-surface weapons, and fitted with an integrated fire control system.

Anti-Submarine Warfare (ASW): Fixed and rotary-wing platforms designed to locate and engage submarines, many with a secondary anti-surface warfare capacity. ASW units are equipped with fixed or rotary-wing aircraft for anti-submarine missions.

Anti-Surface Warfare (ASuW): units are equipped with fixed or rotary wing-aircraft intended for anti-surface warfare missions.

Maritime Patrol (MP): Fixed-wing aircraft and unmanned aerial vehicles intended for maritime surface surveillance, which may possess an anti-surface warfare capability. MP units are equipped with fixed-wing aircraft or unmanned aerial vehicles intended for maritime surveillance. May also have an ASuW/ASW capability.

Electronic Warfare (EW): Fixed and rotary-wing aircraft and unmanned aerial vehicles intended for electronic countermeasures. EW units are equipped with fixed or rotary wing aircraft or unmanned aerial vehicles used for electronic counter-measures.

Intelligence/Surveillance/Reconnaissance (ISR): Fixed and rotary-wing aircraft and unmanned air vehicles (UAVs) intended to provide radar, visible light, or infra-red imagery, or a mix thereof. ISR units are equipped with fixed or rotary wing aircraft or unmanned aerial vehicles intended for the ISR role.

Combat/Intelligence/Surveillance/Reconnaissance (CISR): is used to describe those UAVs which have the capability to deliver air to surface weapons, as well as undertaking ISR tasks. CISR units are equipped with armed UAVs for the ISR and air-to-surface missions.

COMINT/ELINT/SIGINT: Fixed and rotary-wing platforms and unmanned aerial vehicles capable of gathering electronic (ELINT), communication (COMINT) or signals intelligence (SIGINT). COMINT

Principal Aviation Equipment Definitions (continued)

units are equipped with fixed or rotary-wing aircraft or unmanned aerial vehicles intended for the communications intelligence task. ELINT units are equipped with fixed or rotary-wing aircraft or unmanned aerial vehicles used for gathering electronic intelligence. SIGINT units are equipped with fixed or rotary-wing aircraft or unmanned aerial vehicles used to collect signals intelligence.

Airborne Early Warning (& Control) (AEW (&C)): Fixed and rotary-wing platforms capable of providing airborne early warning, with a varying degree of onboard command and control depending on the platform. AEW&C units are equipped with fixed or rotary-wing aircraft to provide airborne early warning and command and control.

Search and Rescue (SAR): units are equipped with fixed or rotary-wing aircraft used to recover military personnel or civilians.

Combat Search and Rescue (CSAR): units are equipped with armed fixed or rotary wing aircraft for recovery of personnel from hostile territory.

Tanker (Tkr): Fixed and rotary-wing aircraft designed for air-to-air re-fuelling. Tkr units are equipped with fixed or rotary-wing aircraft used for air-to-air refuelling.

Tanker Transport (Tkr/Tpt): describes those platforms capable of both air-to-air refuelling and military airlift.

Transport (Tpt): Fixed or rotary wing aircraft intended for military airlift. Light transport aircraft are categorised as having a maximum payload of up to 11,340kg, medium up to 27,215kg, and heavy above 27,215kg. Medium transport helicopters have an internal payload of up to 4,535kg; heavy transport helicopters greater than 4,535kg. PAX aircraft are platforms are platforms generally unsuited for transporting cargo on the main deck. Tpt units are equipped with fixed- or rotary-wing platforms to transport personnel or cargo.

Trainer (Trg): A fixed or rotary-wing aircraft designed primarily for the training role, some also have the capacity to carry light-to-medium ordnance. Trg units are equipped with fixed or rotary wing training aircraft intended for pilot or other aircrew training.

Multi-role helicopter: Rotary-wing platforms designed to carry out a variety of military tasks including light transport, armed reconnaissance and battlefield support.

Unmanned Aerial Vehicles: Remotely piloted or controlled unmanned fixed-or-rotary wing systems. Light UAVs are those weighing between 20–150kg; medium are those from 150kg–600kg; and large are those weighing more than 600kg.

Reference

Table 38 **List of Abbreviations for Data Sections**

– part of unit is detached/less than
* combat capable
″ unit with overstated title/ship class nickname
+ unit reinforced/more than
< under 100 tonnes
† serviceability in doubt
‡ obsolete
ε estimated

AAA anti-aircraft artillery
AAB Advisory and Assistance Brigade
AAM air-to-air missile
AAV amphibious assault vehicle
AB airborne
ABM anti-ballistic missile
ABU sea-going buoy tender
ac aircraft
ACCS Air Command and Control System
ACM advanced cruise missile
ACP airborne command post
ACV air cushion vehicle/armoured combat vehicle
AD air defence
ADA air defence artillery
adj adjusted
AE auxiliary, ammunition carrier
AEW airborne early warning
AF Air Force
AFB Air Force Base/Station
AFS logistics ship
AG misc auxiliary
AGB icebreaker
AGF command ship
AGHS hydrographic survey vessel
AGI intelligence collection vessel
AGL automatic grenade launcher
AGM air-to-ground missile/missile range instrumentation ship
AGOR oceanographic research vessel
AGOS oceanographic surveillance vessel
AGS survey ship
AH hospital ship
AIFV armoured infantry fighting vehicle
AIP air independent propulsion
AK cargo ship
aka also known as
AKL cargo ship (light)
AKR roll-on/roll-off cargo ship

AKSL stores ship (light)
ALARM air-launched anti-radiation missile
ALCM air-launched cruise missile
amph amphibious/amphibian
AMRAAM advanced medium-range air-to-air missile
AO oiler
AOE fast combat support ship
AOR fleet replenishment oiler with RAS capability
AORH oiler with hel capacity
AORL replenishment oiler (light)
AORLH oiler light with hel deck
AOT oiler transport
AP armour-piercing/anti-personnel
APC armoured personnel carrier
AR repair ship
ARC cable repair ship
ARG amphibious ready group
ARH active radar homing
ARH AAM active radar homing air-to-air missile
ARL airborne reconnaissance low
ARM anti-radiation missile
armd armoured
ARS rescue and salvage ship
ARSV armoured reconnaissance/ surveillance vehicle
arty artillery
ARV armoured recovery vehicle
AS anti-submarine/submarine tender
ASaC airborne surveillance and control
AShM anti-ship missile
aslt assault
ASM air-to-surface missile
ASR submarine rescue craft
ASROC anti-submarine rocket
ASTOR airborne stand-off radar
ASTOVL advanced short take-off and vertical landing
ASTROS II artillery saturation rocket system
ASTT anti-submarine torpedo tube
ASW anti-submarine warfare
ASuW anti-surface warfare
AT tug/anti-tank
ATACMS army tactical missile system
ATBM anti-tactical ballistic missile
ATF tug, ocean going

ATGW anti-tank guided weapon
ATK attack/ground attack
ATP advanced targeting pod
ATTC all terrain tracked carrier
AV armoured vehicle
AVB aviation logistic support ship
avn aviation
AWACS airborne warning and control system
AWT water tanker
AX training craft
AXL training craft (light)
AXS training craft (sail)
BA budget authority (US)
Bbr bomber
BCT brigade combat team
bde brigade
bdgt budget
BfSB battlefield surveillance brigade
BG battle group
BMD ballistic missile defence
BMEWS ballistic missile early warning system
bn battalion/billion
BSB brigade support battalion
BSTB brigade special troops battalion
bty battery
C2 command and control
CAB combat aviation brigade
CALCM conventional air-launched cruise missile
CAS close air support
casevac casualty evacuation
cav cavalry
cbt combat
CBU cluster bomb unit
CBRNE chemical, biological, radiological, nuclear, explosive
CCS command and control systems
cdo commando
CET combat engineer tractor
CFE Conventional Armed Forces in Europe
C/G/GH/GN/L cruiser/guided missile/ guided missile, helicopter/guided missile, nuclear powered/light
cgo cargo (freight) aircraft
CISR Combat ISR
CIMIC civil–military cooperation
CIWS close-in weapons system
CLOS command-to-line-of-sight

COIN counter insurgency
comb combined/combination
comd command
COMINT communications intelligence
comms communications
CPV crew protected vehicle
CPX command post exercise
CS combat support
CSAR combat search and rescue
C-RAM counter rocket, artillery and mortar
CT counter terrorism
CTOL conventional take off and landing
CV/H/L/N/S aircraft carrier/helicopter/light/nuclear powered/VSTOL
CW chemical warfare/weapons
DD/G/H/M destroyer/with AShM/with hangar/with SAM
DDS dry dock shelter
def defence
demob demobilised
det detachment
DISTEX disaster training exercise
div division
dom domestic
DSCS defense satellite communications system
ECM electronic countermeasures
ECR electronic combat and reconnaissance
EELV evolved expendable launch vehicle
ELINT electronic intelligence
elm element/s
engr engineer
EOD explosive ordnance disposal
eqpt equipment
ESG expeditionary strike group
ESM electronic support measures
est estimate(d)
EW electronic warfare
EWSP electronic warfare self protection
excl excludes/excluding
exp expenditure
FAC forward air control
fd field
FF/G/H/M frigate/with AShM/with hangar/with SAM
FGA fighter ground attack
FLD full-load displacement
flt flight
FMA Foreign Military Assistance
FMTV family of medium transport vehicles
FROG free rocket over ground
FS/G/H/M corvette/with AShM/with hangar/with SAM
FSSG force service support group
FSTA future strategic tanker aircraft
Ftr fighter
FTX field training exercise
FW fixed-wing
FY fiscal year
GA group army

GBAD ground-based air defences
GBU guided bomb unit
gd guard
GDP gross domestic product
GEODSS ground-based electro-optical deep space surveillance system
GMLS guided missile launch system
GMLRS guided multiple-launch rocket system
GNP gross national product
gp group
GPS global positioning system
GW guided weapon
HARM high-speed anti-radiation missile
HBCT heavy brigade combat team
hel helicopter
HIMARS high-mobility artillery rocket system
HMMWV high-mobility multi-purpose wheeled vehicle
HMTV high-mobility tactical vehicle
HOT high-subsonic optically teleguided
how howitzer
HQ headquarters
HUMINT human intelligence
HVM high-velocity missile
HWT heavyweight torpedo
hy heavy
IBCT infantry brigade combat team
IBU inshore boat unit
ICBM inter-continental ballistic missile
IFV infantry fighting vehicle
IMET international military education and training
IMINT imagery intelligence
imp improved
IMV infantry mobility vehicle
incl includes/including
indep independent
inf infantry
INS inertial navigation system
IR infra-red
IR AAM infra-red air-to-air missile
IIR imaging infra-red
IRBM intermediate-range ballistic missile
IRLS infra-red line scan
ISD in-service date
ISR intelligence, surveillance and reconnaissance
ISTAR intelligence, surveillance, target acquisition and reconnaissance
JDAM joint direct attack munition
JSF Joint Strike Fighter
JSTARS joint surveillance target attack radar system
LACV light armoured combat vehicle
LACM land-attack cruise missile
LAMPS light airborne multi-purpose system
LANTIRN low-altitude navigation and targeting infra-red system night
LAV light armoured vehicle

LAW light anti-tank weapon
LC/A/AC/D/H/M/PA/PL/T/U/VP landing craft/assault/air cushion/dock/heavy/medium/personnel air cushion/personnel large/tank/utility/vehicles and personnel
LCC amphibious command ship
LFV light forces vehicles
LGB laser-guided bomb
LHA landing ship assault
LHD amphibious assault ship
LIFT lead-in ftr trainer
LKA amphibious cargo ship
lnchr launcher
log logistic
LORADS long range radar display system
LP/D/H landing platform/dock/helicopter
LPV lifespan patrol vessel
LRAR long range artillery rocket
LRSA long-range strike/attack
LS/D/L/LH/M/T landing ship/dock/logistic/logistic helicopter/medium/tank
Lt light
LWT lightweight torpedo
MAMBA mobile artillery monitoring battlefield radar
MANPAD man portable air-defence
MANPAT man portable anti-tank
MARDIV marine division
MAW marine aviation wing
MBT main battle tank
MC/C/I/O mine countermeasure coastal/inshore/ocean
MCD mine countermeasure diving support
MCLOS manual CLOS
MCM mine countermeasures
MCMV mine countermeasures vessel
MD military district
MDT mine diving tender
MEADS medium extended air defence system
MEB marine expeditionary brigade
mech mechanised
med medium
MEF marine expeditionary force
MEU marine expeditionary unit
MFO multinational force and observers
MGA machine gun artillery
MH/C/D/I/O mine hunter/coastal/drone/inshore/ocean
MI military intelligence
mil military
MIRV multiple independently targetable re-entry vehicle
MIUW mobile inshore undersea warfare
mk mark (model number)
ML minelayer
MLRS multiple-launch rocket system
MLU mid-life update
MLV medium launch vehicle

mne marine

mob mobilisation/mobile

mod modified/modification

mor mortar

mot motorised/motor

MP maritime patrol

MPA maritime patrol aircraft

MPS marine prepositioning squadron

MR maritime reconnaissance/motor rifle

MRAP mine-resistant ambush-protected

MRAAM medium-range air-to-air missile

MRBM medium-range ballistic missile

MRL multiple rocket launcher

MRTT multi-role tanker transport

MS/A/C/D/I/O/R mine sweeper/auxiliary/coastal/drone/inshore/ocean

msl missile

MSTAR man-portable surveillance and target acquisition radar

Mtn mountain

NAEW NATO Airborne Early Warning & Control Force

n.a. not applicable

n.k. not known

NBC nuclear biological chemical

NCO non-commissioned officer

nm nautical mile

nuc nuclear

O & M operations and maintenance

obs observation/observer

OCU operational conversion unit

op/ops operational/operations

OPFOR opposition training force

org organised/organisation

OTH/-B over-the-horizon/backscatter (radar)

OTHR/T over-the-horizon radar/targeting

PAAMS principal anti-air missile system

PAC *Patriot* advanced capability

para paratroop/parachute

PAX passenger/passenger transport aircraft

PB/C/F/I/R patrol boat/coastal/fast/inshore/riverine

PC/C/F/G/H/I/M/O/R/T patrol craft/coastal with AShM/fast/guided missile/with hangar/inshore/with CIWS missile or SAM/offshore/riverine/torpedo

PDMS point defence missile system

pdr pounder

pers personnel

PG/G/GF/H patrol gunboat/guided missile/fast attack craft/hydrofoil

PGM precision-guided munitions

PH/G/M/T patrol hydrofoil/with AShM/missile/torpedo

PKO peacekeeping operations

PPP purchasing-power parity

PR photo-reconnaissance

prepo pre-positioned

PSO/H offshore patrol vessel over 1,500 tonnes/with hangar

PTRL/SURV patrol/surveillance

qd quadrillion

R&D research and development

RAM rolling airframe missile

RAS replenishment at sea

RCL ramped craft logistic

RCWS remote controlled weapon station

RCT regimental combat team

recce reconnaissance

RF response force

regt regiment

RIB rigid inflatable boat

RL rocket launcher

ro-ro roll-on, roll-off

RPV remotely piloted vehicle

RRC/F rapid-reaction corps/force

RSTA reconnaissance, surveillance and target acquisition

RV re-entry vehicle

SACLOS semi-automatic CLOS

SAM surface-to-air missile

SAR search and rescue

SARH semi-active radar homing

sat satellite

SBCT Stryker brigade combat team

SDV swimmer delivery vehicles

SEAD suppression of enemy air defence

SEWS satellite early warning station

SF special forces

SHORAD short-range air defence

SIGINT signals intelligence

SLAM stand-off land-attack missile

SLBM submarine-launched ballistic missile

SLCM submarine-launched cruise missile

SLEP service life extension programme

SMASHEX submarine search, escape and rescue exercise

SMAW shoulder-launched multi-purpose assault weapon

SOC special operations capable

SP self propelled

Spec Op special operations

SPAAGM Self-propelled anti-aircraft gun and missile system

spt support

sqn squadron

SRAM short-range attack missile

SRBM short-range ballistic missile

SS diesel-electric submarine

SSAN submersible auxiliary support vessel (nuclear)

SSBN nuclear-powered ballistic-missile submarine

SSC coastal submarine

SSG guided missile submarine

SSGN nuclear-powered guided missile submarine

SSK attack submarine with ASW capability(hunter-killer)SSM surface-to-surface missile

SSN attack submarine nuclear powered

SSP attack submarine with air-independent propulsion

SSW midget submarine

START Strategic Arms Reduction Talks/Treaty

StF stabilisation force

STO(V)L short take-off and (vertical) landing

str strength

SUGW surface-to-underwater GW

SURV surveillance

SUT surface and underwater target

sy security

t tonnes

tac tactical

temp temporary

THAAD theatre high altitude area defence

tk tank

tkr tanker

TLAM tactical land-attack missile

TLE treaty-limited equipment (CFE)

TMD theatre missile defence

torp torpedo

TOW tube launched optically wire guided

tpt transport

tr trillion

trg training

TRV torpedo recovery vehicle

TT torpedo tube

UAV unmanned aerial vehicle

UCAV unmanned combat aerial vehicle

URG under-way replenishment group

USGW underwater to surface guided weapon

utl utility

UUV unmanned undersea vehicle

V(/S)TOL vertical(/short) take-off and landing

veh vehicle

VLS vertical launch system

VSHORAD very short range air defence

VSRAD very short range air defence

wg wing

WLIC Inland construction tenders

WMD weapon(s) of mass destruction

WTGB US Coast Guard Icebreaker tugs

YAC royal yacht

YAG yard craft, miscellaneous

YDG degaussing

YDT diving tender

YFB ferry boat

YFL launch

YFRT range support tenders

YTB harbour tug

YTL light harbour tug

YTM medium harbour tug

YPT torpedo recovery vessel

YTR firefighting vessel

Table 39 **General Principles of Naval Abbreviations**

Base designation	
A	Auxiliaries
B	Battleship (now redundant)
C	Cruiser
CV	Aircraft carrier
DD	Destroyer
FF	Frigate
FS	Corvette
L	Amphibious vessels (Landing)
M	Mine warfare craft
P	Patrol craft
SS	Submarine
Y	Yard craft (miscellaneous or harbour vessels)

Prefix	
T-	Military Sealift Command vessel
W	US Coast Guard vessel

Suffix	
A	Attack; Assault; Auxiliary
B	Ballistic missile; Boat; Breaker
C	Command/Control; Craft; Coastal
CM	Countermeasures
D	Destroyer; Dock; Drone
DG	Degaussing
E	Escort; ammunition
F	Fast (greater than 35 kts); Fleet; Force (command)
G	Guided missile; Gun; General
H	Helicopter hangar; Hospital; Hydrofoil; Hydrographic
I	Inshore; Intelligence
K	Cargo; Attack (Killer)
L	Light; Layer; Large; Logistics
M	Missile tracking; Mechanised; Medium
N	Nuclear-powered
O	Oil; Offshore; Oceanographic; Ocean
P	Personnel
R	Repair; Replenishment; Ro-Ro; Riverine; Rescue
S	Surveying; Salvage; Submarine/submersible; Ship; Small; Sweeper; Stores
T	Tug; Transport; Tank; Torpedo
U	Utility
V	Fixed-wing aircraft; Vehicle
W	Water; Midget (Swimmer)

Table 40 **Index of Country/Territory Abbreviations**

AFG	Afghanistan	
ALB	Albania	
ALG	Algeria	
ANG	Angola	
ARG	Argentina	
ARM	Armenia	
ATG	Antigua and Barbuda	
AUS	Australia	
AUT	Austria	
AZE	Azerbaijan	
BDI	Burundi	
BEL	Belgium	
BEN	Benin	
BFA	Burkina Faso	
BGD	Bangladesh	
BHR	Bahrain	
BHS	Bahamas	
BIH	Bosnia–Herzegovina	
BIOT	British Indian Ocean Territory	
BLG	Bulgaria	
BLR	Belarus	
BLZ	Belize	
BOL	Bolivia	
BRB	Barbados	
BRN	Brunei	
BRZ	Brazil	
BWA	Botswana	
CAM	Cambodia	
CAN	Canada	
CAR	Central African Republic	
CHA	Chad	
CHE	Switzerland	
CHL	Chile	
CIV	Côte d'Ivoire	
CMR	Cameroon	
COG	Congo	
COL	Colombia	
CPV	Cape Verde	
CRI	Costa Rica	
CRO	Croatia	
CUB	Cuba	
CYP	Cyprus	
CZE	Czech Republic	
DJB	Djibouti	
DNK	Denmark	
DOM	Dominican Republic	
DPRK	Korea, Democratic People's Republic of	
DRC	Democratic Republic of the Congo	
ECU	Ecuador	
EGY	Egypt	
ERI	Eritrea	
ESP	Spain	
EST	Estonia	
ETH	Ethiopia	
FIN	Finland	
FLK	Falkland Islands	
FJI	Fiji	
FRA	France	
FYROM	Macedonia, Former Yugoslav Republic	
GAB	Gabon	
GAM	Gambia	
GEO	Georgia	
GER	Germany	
GF	French Guiana	
GHA	Ghana	
GIB	Gibraltar	
GNB	Guinea Bissau	
GRC	Greece	
GRL	Greenland	
GUA	Guatemala	
GUI	Guinea	
GUY	Guyana	
HND	Honduras	
HTI	Haiti	
HUN	Hungary	
ISL	Iceland	
ISR	Israel	
IDN	Indonesia	
IND	India	
IRL	Ireland	
IRN	Iran	
IRQ	Iraq	
ITA	Italy	
JAM	Jamaica	
JOR	Jordan	
JPN	Japan	
KAZ	Kazakhstan	
KEN	Kenya	
KGZ	Kyrgyzstan	
KWT	Kuwait	
LAO	Laos	
LBN	Lebanon	
LBR	Liberia	
LBY	Libya	
LKA	Sri Lanka	
LSO	Lesotho	
LTU	Lithuania	
LUX	Luxembourg	
LVA	Latvia	
MDA	Moldova	
MDG	Madagascar	
MEX	Mexico	
MHL	Marshall Islands	
MLI	Mali	
MLT	Malta	
MMR	Myanmar	
MNE	Montenegro	
MNG	Mongolia	
MOR	Morocco	
MOZ	Mozambique	
MRT	Mauritania	
MUS	Mauritius	
MWI	Malawi	
MYS	Malaysia	
NAM	Namibia	
NCL	New Caledonia	
NER	Niger	
NGA	Nigeria	
NIC	Nicaragua	
NLD	Netherlands	
NOR	Norway	
NPL	Nepal	
NZL	New Zealand	
OMN	Oman	
PT	Palestinian Territories	
PAN	Panama	
PAK	Pakistan	
PER	Peru	
PHL	Philippines	
POL	Poland	
PNG	Papua New Guinea	
PRC	China, People's Republic of	
PRT	Portugal	
PRY	Paraguay	
PYF	French Polynesia	
QTR	Qatar	
ROC	Taiwan (Republic of China)	
ROK	Korea, Republic of	
ROM	Romania	
RSA	South Africa	
RUS	Russia	
RWA	Rwanda	
SAU	Saudi Arabia	
SDN	Sudan	
SEN	Senegal	
SGP	Singapore	
SLB	Solomon Islands	
SLE	Sierra Leone	
SLV	El Salvador	
SOM	Somali Republic	
SRB	Serbia	
STP	São Tomé and Principe	
SUR	Suriname	
SVK	Slovakia	
SVN	Slovenia	
SWE	Sweden	
SYC	Seychelles	
SYR	Syria	
TGO	Togo	
THA	Thailand	
TJK	Tajikistan	
TLS	Timor Leste	
TTO	Trinidad and Tobago	
TKM	Turkmenistan	
TUN	Tunisia	
TUR	Turkey	
TZA	Tanzania	
UAE	United Arab Emirates	
UGA	Uganda	
UK	United Kingdom	
UKR	Ukraine	
URY	Uruguay	
US	United States	
UZB	Uzbekistan	
VEN	Venezuela	
VNM	Vietnam	
YEM	Yemen	
ZMB	Zambia	
ZWE	Zimbabwe	

Reference

Table 41 Index of Countries and Territories